MODERN INTELLECTUAL PROPERTY LAW

Second Edition

Catherine Colston, LLB, LLM, Lecturer in IT Law
Law School University of Strathclyde
Glasgow

Kirsty Middleton, LLB, LLM, Solicitor
Shanghai, China

Cavendish
Publishing
Limited

London • Sydney • Portland, Oregon

Second edition first published in Great Britain 2005 by
Cavendish Publishing Limited, The Glass House,
Wharton Street, London WC1X 9PX, United Kingdom
Telephone: + 44 (0)20 7278 8000   Facsimile: + 44 (0)20 7278 8080
Email: info@cavendishpublishing.com
Website: www.cavendishpublishing.com

Published in the United States by Cavendish Publishing
c/o International Specialized Book Services,
5824 NE Hassalo Street, Portland,
Oregon 97213-3644, USA

Published in Australia by Cavendish Publishing (Australia) Pty Ltd
45 Beach Street, Coogee, NSW 2034, Australia
Telephone: + 61 (2)9664 0909   Facsimile: + 61 (2)9664 5420
Email: info@cavendishpublishing.com.au
Website: www.cavendishpublishing.com.au

C111072951	
Bertrams	11.03.06
346.41048COL	£35.95
	G050270

Library of Congress Cataloguing in Publication Data
Data available

ISBN-10: 1-85941-816-3
ISBN-13: 978-1-859-41816-1

1 3 5 7 9 10 8 6 4 2

Printed and bound in Great Britain
by Antony Rowe Ltd,. Chippenham, Wiltshire

PREFACE

In the five years since the first edition of this book, the law of intellectual property has leapt forward, reflected in the extensive new material included here. Major decisions from the House of Lords and European Court of Justice have both amended and clarified the law. Important decisions in 2004 alone include those of the House in *Kirin-Amgen Inc v Hoechst Marion Roussel Ltd* and *Campbell v MGN Ltd*, and of the ECJ in *British Horseracing Board Ltd v William Hill Organisation*. Legislative action includes implementation of the Information Society Directive, and amendments to patent law in the Patents Act 2004.

Nor is this progress likely to slacken. New directives are proposed, particularly the controversial Computer-implemented Inventions Directive, while technological development rampages on. Biotechnological inventions continue to fuel both ethical and legal debate, whilst developments in information technology stretch copyright and patent principles to breaking point. The Open Source Movement remains locked in battle with intellectual property right owners, as do the providers of peer to peer file sharers and the entertainment industry. Nanotechnology threatens to introduce intellectual property into the realm of the human body. The result is an area of law that remains stimulating, challenging, and exciting in equal degree.

In presenting the substance of this law we have aimed at a thoughtful, and thought-provoking, work. Heartfelt thanks are due the many people who have helped in preparation of this edition. Needless to say, mistakes which remain are all our own doing. Amanda Russell, Patricia Kay, Claire Lovat and Natalie Amer provided invaluable assistance in the research, while Konstaninos Komaitis continued to stretch my understanding of domain name regulation to its utmost. Gareth Ryan and the Law School Library at Strathclyde never failed to unearth what was asked for, and always with great promptitude. Colleagues Ian Lloyd and Jeremy Warner lent many a willing ear. Finally, without the support of Dorothy, Gay, Rowena, and my family – Rob, Bee, Elli and Andy Mac and our grandchild to be – to restore a sense of proportion when it was needed, this book would never have been finished. It remains dedicated to my parents, the GGs, who have encouraged me all the way.

Catherine Colston
Glasgow
December 2004

The impact of the competition laws of the UK, the EC and, indeed, of EU law generally on intellectual property rights has become considerably more apparent in recent years. This is perhaps best exemplified by the Commission's recent case against Microsoft. At the same time, the interaction between such inherently complex areas as competition law, EU law and intellectual property rights inevitably leads to less, not more, simplicity. In negotiating this web I have endeavoured to make the material as accessible as possible for those with little or no knowledge of competition or EU law, although in doing so I may have occasionally oversimplified matters. Students would undoubtedly benefit from a more detailed consideration of specialised texts such as Whish, R, *Competition Law* (5th edn, London: Butterworths, 2003) or Middleton, Rodger and MacCulloch, *Cases and Materials, UK and EC Competition Law* (1st edn, Oxford: OUP, 2003).

Despite the addition of my name to the second edition, I consider this to be Catherine's text and I am honoured to have been involved, however small my contribution. Given my relocation to Shanghai, China in March 2004 on research leave and subsequent pregnancy, the completion of my material presented me with certain difficulties which I hope are not reflected in the final text. The submission of the manuscript in fact coincided with the birth of my daughter in Hong Kong at the end of October 2004 and I am indebted to Catherine for her patience in the weeks that followed. Sincere thanks must also go to my colleagues in the Law School for allowing me the opportunity to study in China and for equal amounts of forbearance and encouragement during my extended absence. I would like to dedicate my contribution to my family, Patric, Riley and Tess.

Kirsty Middleton, Shanghai, China
December 2004

CONTENTS

TABLE OF CASES

TABLE OF STATUTES

TABLE OF STATUTORY INSTRUMENTS

TABLE OF EU LEGISLATION

Directives

Regulations

Treaties and Conventions

TABLE OF INTERNATIONAL LEGISLATION

USEFUL WEBSITES

	http://
Chartered Institute of Patent Agents	www.cipa.org.uk
Community Plant Variety Office	www.cpvo.eu.int
Community Trade Mark/Design Office	www.ohim.eu.int
Copyright Licensing Agency	www.cla.co.uk
Department of Trade and Industry	www.dti.gov.uk
European Commission	www.europa.eu.int/comm
European Court of Justice	www.curia.eu.int
European Free Trade Association	www.efta.int
European Patent Office	www.epo.org
European Union	www.europa.eu.int
Hague Conference on Private International Law	www.hcch.net
HM Stationery Office	www.opsi.gov.uk
ICANN	www.icann.org
IFPI	www.ifpi.org
Institute of Trade Mark Attorneys	www.itma.org.uk
Nominet (Domain Name Registration)	www.nominet.org.uk
Office of Fair Trading	www.oft.gov.uk
Office of the Information Commissioner	www.informationcommissioner.gov.uk
Society for Computers and Law	www.scl.org
UDRP	www.icann.org/udrp
UK Government – Intellectual Property Site	www.intellectual-property.gov.uk
UK Patent Office	www.patent.gov.uk
UK Plant Varieties Office	www.defra.gov.uk/planth/pvs
US Patent Office	www.uspto.gov
World Intellectual Property Organisation	www.wipo.org
World Trade Organisation	www.wto.org

TABLE OF ABBREVIATIONS

ACPA	US Anticybersquatting Consumer Act 1999
BC	Berne Convention for the Potection of Literary and Artistic Works 1886
CA 1956	Copyright Act 1956
CDPA 1988	Copyright, Designs and Patents Act 1988
CLA	Copyright Licensing Agency
CLIP	Common Law Institute of Intellectual Property
Columbia L Rev	Columbia Law Review
CPC	Community Patent Convention 1975
CRRR	Copyright and Related Rights Regulations 2003
Denning LJ	Denning Law Journal
DMCA	Digital Millenium Copyright Act 1998
DNS	Domain Name System
EC	European Community Treaty
ECJ	European Court of Justice
EEA	European Economic Area
EIPR	European Intellectual Property Review
EPC	European Patent Convention 1973
EPO	European Patent Office
EPOR	European Patent Office Reports
FACT	Federation Against Copyright Theft
FAST	Federation Against Software Theft
FSR	Fleet Street Reports
GATT	General Agreement on Trade and Tariffs
GPL	General Public Licence
Harvard L Rev	Harvard Law Review
IFFRO	International Federation of Reproduction Rights Organisation
IIC	International Review of Industrial Property and Copyright Law
IPI	Intellectual Property Institute
IPQ	Intellectual Property Quarterly
JBL	Journal of Business Law
J Law and Econ	Journal of Law and Economics
JSPTL	Journal of the Society of Public Teachers of Law
LQR	Law Quarterly Review
LS	Legal Studies
MCPS	Mechanical Copyright Protection Society
MLR	Modern Law Review
NLA	Newspaper Licensing Agency
OHIM	Community Trade Mark Office
PA 1977	Patents Act 1977
PA 2004	Patents Act 2004
PCT	Patent Co-operation Treaty 1970
PDO	Protected Designation of Origin
PGI	Protected Geographical Indication

PIPC   Paris Industrial Property Convention 1883
PLR   Public Lending Right
PLT   World Patent Law Treaty 2000
POCA   Proceeds of Crime Act 2002
PRS   The Performing Rights Society
PRT   Performing Rights Tribunal
PVA 1997   Plant Varieties Act 1997
PVR   Plant Variety Right
RDA 1949   Registered Designs Act 1949
RPC   Reports of Patent Cases
SPC   Supplementary Protection Certificate
TLD   Top Level Domain
TMA 1938   Trade Marks Act 1938
TMA 1994   Trade Marks Act 1994
TRIPS Agreement   Trade Related Aspects of Intellectual Property Agreement
UCC   Universal Copyright Convention 1952
UPOV Convention   Convention for the Protection of New Varieties of Plants 1961
USPTO   United States Patent and Trademark Office
WCT   World Copyright Treaty
WIPO   World Intellectual Property Organisation
WPPT   World Performers and Phonograms Treaty 1996
WTO   World Trade Organisation

CHAPTER 1

INTRODUCTION

The enduring fascination for the student of intellectual property law is that it has something for everyone: enough to intrigue philosopher, student of ethics, scientist, politician, artist, entertainer, economist and businessman. Intellectual property law's influence extends to every aspect of human life. The markings on a can of COCA-COLA, the rights in the books, music, pictures, drama, films and electronic information sources we all use, even the shape of our pen, architecture and the science behind the latest attempt on space exploration all form its subject matter: extending from science to art.

Intellectual property is all about the results of human creativity. Its subject matter is formed from new ideas generated by man. New ideas may be applied in as many ways as the human mind can conceive. Their application to human needs and desires can be of considerable benefit to mankind. New ideas can be embodied in familiar things such as books, music and art, in technical machinery and processes, in designs for household objects and for commercial ventures, and in all other sources of information. The list is infinite, as is the potential for discovery of new means of expression. Once applied to human needs, the value of ideas ranges from the industrial and commercial to the world of literature, art and design, contributing to technological, economic, social and cultural progress. Protecting the development and application of new ideas aids realisation of the benefits which can be derived from them.

Intellectual property law is the means used to provide this protection. It comprises a discrete body of rights (whether statutory, tortious or equitable) which are applied to the many and varied forms in which the human intellect expresses itself. The common feature that lies behind each of the intellectual property rights is that they allow right owners to stop others taking their creations. This preserves the integrity of, and reserves the exploitation and presentation of, those creations for the right owners.

Intellectual property law has a long history. The Romans used marks on pottery to denote its maker and a Venetian law of 1474 established 10-year privileges to those inventing new machines, for example. The industrial and transport revolutions, which saw an explosion in new ideas and new means with which to spread their benefits, gave the law increased significance. The commercial and information age has only served to enhance the importance of intellectual property law.

Broadly, intellectual property law can be divided into three parts. The first part, protection for industrial property, encompasses patents for inventions and protection for confidential information (trade secrets). The distinctive characteristic of this protection is that the very concept or idea underlying the invention or information is legally 'fenced', preventing others from using it. Consequently, this part of intellectual property might be regarded as encompassing creation. Secondly, there is protection for form and appearance, through copyright, design and moral rights. Here the author's idea or concept remains in a public domain; it is only the form in which it is encapsulated that is protected. This is protection for expression. Thirdly, the law includes protection for reputation, through the tort of passing off and trade mark registration. This third might be regarded as protection for image. It provides a fascinating area of study as modern concerns for image, both personal and commercial, push the boundaries of intellectual property ever wider.

In addition, common themes relating to the nature of, and justification for, intellectual property rights, as well as the enforcement of the rights, require examination. First, it is necessary to consider what comprises the subject matter of intellectual property. Secondly, it is necessary to consider the way in which the law achieves its aims with respect to this subject matter and why it should do so.

1.1   PROTECTION FOR IDEAS

It is helpful to begin a study of this branch of law by contemplating the development of an idea, from its genesis to production of a desirable commodity. Most importantly, it is necessary to ask what interests such an enterprise will create, what risks it might engender and whom the outcome will concern.

The conception and development of a new idea may require the expenditure of considerable time, effort and money, regardless of whether it is either a solution to a technical problem, or aesthetic in nature. Even if the idea was intended purely for personal use, that expenditure may need recompense. The creator of a work of art, in the sense of literature, drama, music or art, also has an interest in the reputation engendered by the work and in the integrity of its performance or exhibition. Exploiting an idea commercially, as a product, process, or service, or presenting a work to the public, can secure such recompense, reputation and possibly profit. However, if success is uncertain, embarking on exploitation may engender financial risk. The creator is also prey to the risk of being copied if the idea is sold, displayed or used in circumstances where others can see it. Copying would undermine the reputation, recompense and profit it is hoped will be gained by commercial exploitation or presentation. It might also undermine the creator's commercial or artistic reputation if the copy imitates his trade marks or signs, or is of inferior quality. However, the idea may well be one to which the public should have access, perhaps where it is a revolutionary educational, technical or medical advance, or a work of art.

The creator of an idea, and the manufacturer of its embodiment, if different persons, have an interest in gaining reward for their efforts and expenditure and in making a profit from the enterprise. This is only possible if there is protection against the risk of imitation. It is at this point that the law can step in to provide that protection in some form. However, protection restricts the activities of those with an interest in access to, and use of, the idea's embodiment, which must be balanced against the interests of both creator and manufacturer.

1.2   MEANS FOR PROTECTING IDEAS

Accepting, for the moment, that some measure of protection is desirable, it remains to consider the ways in which this may be done. Potentially, the law could intervene at one or more of several points in the progress from initial idea to product on the market, or work in the public eye, which is where the danger of imitation lies. Protection can be given to the idea itself, as an idea, or by granting rights over the product or work embodying the idea. Subsequently, the law could intervene at the point where the product reaches the market, or when the work reaches the public domain, by protecting the reputation with which it is marketed (by means of advertising themes, names, logos, slogans and the like). Alternatively, protection could be delayed until competition which is unfair takes place.

1.2.1   Secrecy

Keeping a new idea secret is the most complete form of protection possible, provided that the secrecy can be maintained after commercial production and marketing. Some notable products are protected in this way, such as the recipe for the children's toy PLASTICINE. Sometimes, physical protection is possible, through anti-copying techniques applied to electronic products, for example. It may be possible to preserve the secrecy of a process even after it is put into use. However, the disadvantage of secrecy is that disassembly which uncovers underlying design and engineering features of a product released onto the market will reveal its secrets. Moreover, physical protection is always prey to the danger that the means for avoiding it will quickly be discovered. Where secrecy can be maintained, however, there is statutory support for anti-copying measures adopted to protect copyright works in ss 296, 296ZA and 296ZB of the Copyright, Designs and Patents Act 1988. The action for breach of confidence supports secrecy where this is the chosen method of protection.

1.2.2   Exclusive rights

To protect all ideas would be to remove far too much of the raw material of industrial, commercial, educational and cultural development from the public domain. Very broadly, the model adopted has been one of exclusive proprietary rights, with one exception – the action for breach of confidence. The consequence of this is that intellectual property can be dealt with as other property: it can be assigned, licensed, mortgaged and bequeathed. In providing any protection at all for a creator of an idea, delicate balances must be drawn between the legitimate interests of creator, entrepreneur, competitor, consumer and the public. Intellectual property right owners have a natural right to their creations and an interest in a just reward. The public also has an interest in access to, and use of, the intellectual property. Consumers have an interest in the preservation of fair competition.

Beyond this, it is difficult to generalise about the intellectual property rights, as intellectual property law actually comprises a bundle of diverse rights. Each is of differing scope as the correct balance between competing interests in different types of subject matter is sought. Drawing such balances has traditionally been seen as a question for the legislature, often after lobbying from, and consultation with, interest groups, such as the Federation Against Software Theft. Consequently, most intellectual property law is statutory and the result of political and economic history.

A brief description of the varied rights follows.

Patents

A patent is a monopoly which is granted for an invention after application to, and examination for patentability by, the Patent Office and lasts for a maximum of 20 years. To be patentable, an invention must be new, show an inventive step, be industrially applicable and not fall into one of the excluded categories of invention. The patent even protects its owner against an independent creator of the same invention who makes, keeps or uses the invention.

Copyright

Copyright subsists automatically on the creation of a work; no application is needed, nor do any formalities apply. Copyright works comprise original literary, dramatic, musical and artistic works: sound recordings, films, broadcasts and the typographical layout of published editions. Additionally, a work must qualify for protection in the UK. It is a right against copying, as its name suggests; the infringer must have started from the copyright owner's work in some way, although the copying need not be direct. Copyright confers the exclusive right to reproduce the work, issue copies to the public (including a right to rental for some works), perform the work in public, communicate it or adapt it. It is infringed when one of these acts is done without permission. It is a long lasting right, lasting in the case of the original works for the life of the author plus 70 years.

Moral rights

Three moral rights conferred on the author of the original copyright works or the director of a film were introduced into the UK in 1989. The moral rights protect the integrity of a work against unsuitable treatment by others. They are: the right to be named as author; the right to object to derogatory treatment of the work; and the right against false attribution. The commissioner of photographs, or of a film, made for private and domestic purposes, also has the right to privacy for the photographs or film. The rights apply provided copyright subsists in the work.

Design rights

Design rights protect designs applied to products. There are several potential ways in which a design may secure protection. The first is by copyright if the product itself can be considered to be an artistic work. Secondly, in the UK new designs may be registered after application. Such registered design rights last for a maximum of 25 years. In addition Community design protection, both registered and unregistered, protects designs throughout the EU. Finally, UK unregistered design right protects three-dimensional aspects of shape and configuration applied to articles or parts of articles, provided that the design is original and not commonplace. It arises automatically when the design is recorded. This right will extend to purely functional designs and lasts for a maximum of 15 years.

Trade marks

Trade and service marks are protected by registration as trade marks, nationally and within the European Community. Registration confers a monopoly over use of a trade mark for as long as registration is maintained. Trade marks fall within the sphere of intellectual property because the marketing of new creations is often supported by the development and maintenance of a commercial reputation.

Common law protection

Although most intellectual property rights are statutory, the common law has developed two forms of protection: the tort[1] of passing off and the equitable remedy for breach of confidence.

The tort of passing off protects symbols denoting a trader's commercial reputation. It creates a property right in the trader's goodwill, preventing any misrepresentation by another trader which is likely to cause damage. It stands as an alternative, or adjunct to, trade mark registration.

Breach of confidence protects information of virtually any character (including ideas) which is confidential, not just industrial and commercial trade secrets. This protection can be maintained as long as secrecy can be preserved, but only applies to those owing an obligation of confidence to the owner of the information. Any use or disclosure of the information constitutes a breach. Confidence provides an important adjunct to the statutory intellectual property rights, protecting even before a substantive product, process, work or design has come into being. However, once the information is sufficiently disseminated to reach the public domain, no further protection is possible against those legitimately acquiring it from the public domain. This is so even where the release of the information was in breach of obligation.

Other protection

In addition, specific statutory provision has been made for certain types of product. Protection exists for plant and seed varieties. The Plant Varieties Act 1997 (which developed the concepts introduced by the Plant Varieties and Seeds Act 1964) creates a Plant Variety right for the UK. The Council Regulation on Community Plant Variety Rights (2100/94/EEC) creates a unitary Community Plant variety right for the European Union.

Semi-conductor chips were first protected by the US in 1984, which required reciprocal rights for their nationals in other countries before extending this protection to nationals of other States. Following the Directive on Semi-Conductor Topographies (87/54/EEC), the Semi-Conductor Products (Protection of Topography) Regulations 1987 introduced protection for semi-conductor chips in the UK. These were replaced by the Design Right (Semi-Conductor Topographies) Regulations 1989, which came into force on 1 August 1989. They treat the design of semi-conductor chips as suitable for protection by the unregistered design right.

Performers also have rights over their performances, to prevent unauthorised ('bootleg') recordings being made. These are now set out in Part II of the Copyright, Designs and Patents Act 1988. They were amended by the Copyright and Related Rights Regulations 1996, which implement the Rental Right Directive[2] and the Copyright and Related Rights Regulations 2003, implementing the Information Society Directive[3] and World Performances and Phonograms Treaty. This gives performers

---

1   Delict in Scotland.
2   Council Directive on Rental Right and Lending Right and on Certain Related Rights (92/100/EEC).
3   Directive 2001/29/EC of the European Parliament and of the Council on the Harmonisation of Certain Aspects of Copyright and Related Rights in the Information Society [2001] OJ L1767/10.

and their exclusive recording companies exclusive property rights over their performances as well as non-transferable non-property rights.

At this point, only a few generalisations can be made about the characteristics of these rights. First, those rights which require application and grant, or registration, confer monopolistic power, but, where the right arises automatically on the creation of the protected entity, protection is only exclusive against those copying from the right owner's work. Secondly, where a monopoly is to be granted, the standard of qualification for protection is one of 'novelty', a term of art from patent law, meaning new to the public. Where the right arises automatically, the required standard is one of 'originality'. This is a term of art from copyright law, meaning only that the work has not been copied. It may not be new, having been created before, independently.

1.2.3   Checks and balances on exclusive rights

Intellectual property law can achieve a balance between the various interests invested in a piece of intellectual property in a variety of ways. The balances differ from one type of right to another, but the methods adopted can be introduced in general terms. Licences, both compulsory and of right, as well as those granted voluntarily by the right owner, can enable access to the subject matter of an intellectual property right. Intellectual property rights can be limited in their duration. A variety of specific and general defences may be provided to claims of infringement in order to cater for the varying needs of different users. The actual conditions imposed before the right is secured at all also effectively protect the interests of the public, competitors and users. Examples include the requirements of novelty and inventive step for a patent, or of originality for some copyright works. Competition law, both domestic and that of the EU, also provides checks on the power conferred by intellectual property rights.

1.3   SOURCES OF INTELLECTUAL PROPERTY LAW

The sources of the UK's intellectual property law are both national and international. The UK is a member of several important treaties and conventions which dictate procedural and substantive matters. The Trade Related Aspects of Intellectual Property Rights Agreement 1994 (TRIPS) creates another vital layer to the strata of international intellectual property materials. It was established by the World Trade Organisation (WTO) in 1995 as a result of the Uruguay Round of Multilateral Trade Negotiations.

1.3.1   National sources

Most UK intellectual property law is statutory, although not all the statutory rights require registration. The following table indicates the governing statutes:

Patents	Patents Act 1977 (as amended)
Copyright	Copyright, Designs and Patents Act 1988 (as amended)
Unregistered design right	Copyright, Designs and Patents Act 1988
Registered design right	Registered Designs Act 1949 (as amended)
Performing rights	Copyright, Designs and Patents Act 1988 (as amended)
Trade marks	Trade Marks Act 1994

A question that arises with respect to the national legislation is one of interpretation. Normal principles for the interpretation of statutes apply to intellectual property statutes. However, in many cases, the UK legislation either incorporates foreign drafted conventions and treaties, as well as Regulations and Directives originating from the EU, by reference, or by re-enacting their wording. Accordingly, courts must take into account the provenance of legislation. Foreign texts are often drafted with the civilian method of making wide statements of general principle, frequently of unspecified scope. Where a UK court decides that a meaning is ambiguous, it can pay regard to the foreign text and to decisions of foreign courts, expert writings on the texts and *travaux préparatoires* (*Fothergill v Monarch Airlines* (1980)). The line has been drawn at unpublished European Council minutes in *Wagamama Ltd v City Centre Restaurants* (1995).

Both the tort of passing off and the equitable remedy of breach of confidence are common law remedies and case law provides the source for these remedies.

1.3.2 International sources

External influences on domestic intellectual property law stem from the fact that trade (which turns the realisation of an idea into reward and profit) is no longer confined to local, or even national, markets. Nor are piracy (unauthorised copying on a commercial scale) and counterfeiting (copying both of trade marks and product) confined to domestic markets. This has led to international co-operation, at both international and regional level over procedural and substantive law and to the growth of international organisations whose concern is intellectual property. At first, countries reached bilateral agreements, providing for reciprocity of treatment for each other's nationals. These were subsequently 'collectivised' to include many members, but with similar objectives and principles. At the same time, organisations were created by agreement to administer these treaties and agreements. The most notable is the World Intellectual Property Organisation (WIPO), based in Geneva. Four main principles stem from these accords: reciprocity; priority; national treatment; and independent treatment. In addition, a fifth principle has been introduced by the TRIPS Agreement 1994, that of 'most favoured nation treatment'.

Reciprocity

In some cases, conventions allow for reciprocity as an exception to the rule of national treatment. Then, parallel protection in one Member State is only provided to a national of another Member State to the extent that equivalent protection is available in that Member State for the nationals of the first State.

Priority

In some spheres of intellectual property, being able to apply for protection as early as possible is significant, as is the ability to seek protection in several countries. The principle of priority enables an intellectual property right owner to make as early an application as possible. At the same time, expensive decisions as to multiple applications may be deferred along with the costs, particularly of translation, that these will incur. This is achieved by giving a 'priority date' to the first application in one State.

This date is applied to subsequently completed multiple applications in other States, if filed within a prescribed period. The Paris Convention (see 1.3.3 below) lays down a priority period of 12 months for patent applications and six months for trade mark applications.

National treatment

This means that nationals of one Member State to an agreement shall receive the same treatment, with respect to intellectual property rights and remedies in that State, as nationals in any other Member State, whatever the level of protection provided by the first State. It is a feature of the Paris Convention, the Berne Convention, the Universal Copyright Convention and the TRIPS Agreement 1994.

Independence of rights

This principle ensures that an intellectual property right legitimately acquired in one State will not automatically be affected by decisions (such as forfeiture, or expiry of the right) regarding that right which have been taken in other Member States. This includes the country of origin of the right.

Most favoured nation treatment

This is a new element for intellectual property law, although well known in the multilateral trade sphere. Any advantage, privilege, favour or immunity granted to nationals of any country (not just a member of the WTO) must be accorded to all nationals of all the WTO Member States.

1.3.3 Treaties and Conventions

Although intellectual property rights are national, introduced by States for domestic purposes and usually territorial in their ambit, the shape of national rights is much affected by multilateral obligations. Two distinctions can be made between these agreements. First, there are those that dictate, at least to a minimum standard, the content of substantive national law and those that set out combined procedures for multiple applications for protection in more than one State. Secondly, a distinction can be drawn between those agreements of international scope and those of regional significance. One perceived weakness of the Conventions is the lack of redress against Member States which do not comply. The States party to the Conventions administered by WIPO can refer disputes to the International Court of Justice. This involved process has not yet been invoked, despite allegations of non-compliance having been made. An outline of the main Conventions and Treaties affecting UK intellectual property law follows.

Paris Industrial Property Convention 1883 (Stockholm Revision 1967)

This has not had the same impact as the Berne Convention in the UK, but provides for reciprocity of treatment of nationals and, most importantly, establishes the priority principle. The Paris Convention addresses patents, industrial design rights, trade marks, well known marks, names and unfair competition.

Berne Convention 1886

This established protection for literary, dramatic, musical and artistic works, but not for similar works, such as sound recordings, films and broadcasts. These 'neighbouring' and related rights are partially affected by the Rome Convention for the Protection of Performers, Phonograms and Broadcasting Organisations 1961. The UK Copyright Acts of 1911, 1956 and 1988 reflect the revisions which were made to the Berne Convention in 1908 in Berlin, in 1948 in Brussels and in 1971 in Paris. The Berne Convention provides a principle of independent protection. There is no requirement of reciprocal rights in the other Member States before a national of a Berne Convention Member State can secure protection in another Member State. Qualification for copyright is provided to be by personal connection of the author to any Member State, or by publication of the work in a Member State. It is the Berne Convention which dictates both that copyright protection arises automatically on the creation of a work and that the minimum period of protection should be life of the author plus 50 years. It is administered by WIPO in Geneva, an organisation of the United Nations.

Universal Copyright Convention 1952

This Convention also affects copyright and was designed to include countries with systems of registration for copyright works and shorter copyright periods. This applied especially to the US and the then USSR (although both are now Member States of Berne). The Universal Copyright Convention provides that copyright notices should be put on works showing the copyright owner's name and date; this also applies for national treatment. It is administered by UNESCO in Paris.

Patent Co-operation Treaty 1970

This Treaty provides the great advantage of a centralised start to the process of applying for a patent. One application can be made for patents in any designated Member State. While the application is subsequently transmitted to national patent offices for the actual granting (or refusal) of a patent, the system reduces patenting costs, administrative burdens and translation costs. The first application provides the important priority date and enables the applicant to defer the decision about the State or States within which he or she will seek protection. It is administered by WIPO.

European Patent Convention 1973

This Convention is of vital significance to the UK and led to the enactment of the Patents Act 1977. A central application for a European patent is made to and granted by, the European Patent Office in Munich. Once granted, the patent is treated as a national patent for the purposes of revocation and infringement. It is very popular, with increasing numbers being granted and a corresponding decline in the number of national applications to the Patent Office. It runs in parallel with the UK patent system.

Madrid Agreement 1891

This agreement established a system of deposit for trade marks registered nationally with WIPO. Deposit leads to protection in other designated Member States after 12 months, if no objection was made in those States. The system had the major disadvantage that a central attack on the validity of a trade mark's registration in one State led to the revocation of the mark in every State designated for protection. This was so even though the mark might be unobjectionable in those other States. In addition, those States which had a detailed system of examination of validity before the registration of a mark were not given sufficient time by the 12-month period to examine the mark. The UK was not a member; nor were other important trading States. In 1989, the Madrid Protocol was signed. This allows countries which have strict examination systems a longer period (18 months) to object. The Trade Marks Act 1994 enabled the UK to ratify the Protocol, entering the system on 1 April 1996.

TRIPS Agreement 1994

The TRIPS Agreement 1994 establishes a minimum level of harmonised intellectual property law to be adopted by all members of the World Trade Organisation. Least developed countries have been given an extended period in which to make the necessary changes. The Agreement operates on a foundation of two of the existing Conventions by embodying the substantive provisions of the Paris and Berne Conventions, as well as adding new provisions. In particular, Part III of the Agreement sets out provisions with regard to enforcement of intellectual property rights for which there was no multilateral precedent. The TRIPS Agreement is administered by the WTO and has enormous added significance because it is backed by the WTO's dispute settlement procedures against recalcitrant Member States. This will enable governments to assist industries by acting where other States are guilty of a breach. In 1997, the first adjudication under the dispute resolution procedure reached a rapid conclusion. This indicated the willingness of the WTO to take action and the promptness with which it can act. After complaint by the US, India was requested to bring its transitional arrangements for patent protection for pharmaceutical and agricultural chemical products into line with Article 70 of the TRIPS Agreement 1994. Sanctions may include the withdrawal of WTO advantages, including removal of concessions in the same area of trade, or the imposition of quotas and restrictions on a State's exports.

WIPO Treaties

The Convention establishing WIPO gives it the objectives of promoting protection of intellectual property throughout the world through co-operation and collaboration with any other international organisation, and to ensure administrative co-operation among the Unions. WIPO has been instrumental in initiating and promulgating new global measures harmonising intellectual property rights, as well as administering those adopted when bilateral treaties became multilateral in scope. WIPO treaties affect both procedural and substantive law, and further measures are proposed. Procedural treaties include the World Patent Treaty 2000 (WPT), which harmonises patent office practices, and the World Trademark Law Treaty 1994 (TLT), which relates to procedures for application and renewals. Substantive agreements include the World

Copyright Treaty (WCT) and the World Performers and Phonograms Treaty (WPPT), designed to accommodate the digital age and electronic works. Proposed measures include a World Database Treaty and a treaty harmonising substantive patent law. A World Patent has been tentatively mooted.

Other agreements

There is a plethora of other agreements. Those which affect the UK include the Strasbourg Convention on the International Classification of Patents 1971, the Nice Agreement Concerning the International Classification of Goods and Services for the Purposes of the Registration of Marks 1861 (last revised 1977), the Vienna Agreement Establishing an International Classification of the Figurative Elements of Marks 1985, the Hague Agreement Concerning the Deposit of Industrial Designs 1925 and the Locarno Agreement Establishing an International Classification for Industrial Designs 1970.

1.3.4 The territoriality of intellectual property rights

The UK's intellectual property rights are territorial: they apply only in the UK. Even the European patent is treated as a domestic patent after the centralised examination and decision whether to grant have been completed. Territoriality means that the right in each country is determined by the law of that country and is only effective within that jurisdiction and can only be asserted in that country's courts. It is for this reason that reciprocal rights for other nationals have been recognised through the Conventions and reciprocal scope of protection is determined by some of the Conventions. It is the principle of national treatment that largely achieves this reciprocity for other nationals.

1.4 INTELLECTUAL PROPERTY RIGHTS, FREE MOVEMENT AND COMPETITION

There is an inevitable tension between the creation of exclusive and monopolistic property rights, and the objectives of competition law, which seeks to guard against the natural tendency of competitive market towards monopolisation by the most successful competitor. This is reflected both in national and European law. Competition law provides one significant limit to the extent of market power an intellectual property right can bestow.

1.4.1 Introduction to the internal market

In particular, there is a contradiction between the objectives of the European Community (EC) (the Community), as defined and expanded in Articles 2 and 3 of the EC Treaty, and national intellectual property law. The EC aims at the establishment of a common market, and economic and monetary union. This is to be done, in part, by removing obstacles to the free movement of goods and services, and by a system ensuring that competition in the market is not distorted.[4] The EC is founded on the

---

4   Article 3(g) of the EC Treaty.

philosophy that a free market is the most efficient by keeping prices down, meeting consumer demand and inducing the production of new goods. The notion of competition is self-destructive, in that it tends, eventually, towards the achievement of monopoly by the most competitive enterprise.

Consequently, EC competition law artificially maintains competition at the expense of monopoly. Intellectual property rights, on the other hand, confer either exclusive (copyright and unregistered design right, for example) or monopolistic (patents and registered designs, for example) property rights. These give right owners power to govern markets by preventing competition. Although these rights are designed to promote national industrial and technical development and economic progress (see Chapter 2), this is achieved at the expense of temporary market exclusivity.

Intellectual property rights are also territorial in nature (see 1.3.4 above), allowing right owners to intervene in trade in their products and services across national borders by third party importers. Furthermore, national measures, which reserve to the owner an exclusive right to the exploitation of a product or process, may directly or indirectly, impede the importation of a product or service enjoying identical or similar rights in another Member State. Not only is this clearly anti-competitive, and therefore within the ambit of EC competition law, it may also provoke the application of the free movement of goods provisions as an impediment to trade within the Community (see below).

Thus, intellectual property rights can be used to interrupt competition, and in the EC, the free movement of goods. Intellectual property rights are primarily intended to protect the right owner from competition coming from infringing copies made by another individual or undertaking. Because they are territorial, intellectual property rights can be used to create barriers to trade across borders in goods emanating from the same undertaking or associated undertakings. They may do so by preventing any import of those goods from one Member State into another. This will be the case where the intellectual property owner's rights have not come to an end (not having been exhausted) once the goods have been legitimately released onto the market. If the right does not allow any further control over protected goods once they have been released onto the market (for example, by resale or export), the right is said to be exhausted. Even where national law does provide for such a limit to an intellectual property right, the resulting exhaustion often relates only to the territory in which the right was conferred. The right owner with national protection may still exercise the right to prevent imports of goods released only onto another market. Individuals known as parallel importers may purchase goods released onto the market by their right owner in one Member State, where the price may be low, and import them into another Member State, where the price of that producer's goods is higher. An intellectual property right can provide a barrier to such imports. However, one way in which uniformity within the common market can be achieved is to allow parallel importation in order to smooth out price differentials. Community institutions, including the European Court of Justice (European Court), have supported the activities of the parallel importer.

An obvious solution to the resulting tension would have been either the creation of Community-wide intellectual property rights or a unified intellectual property law embodying a Community-wide concept of exhaustion in each Member State. Although there has been some modest success, significant disparities remain at the Member State level regarding the existence and exercise of intellectual property rights. While moves have been made in both these directions, attempts at resolution of the tensions created by differing national laws have also been made both by the European Court (in *SA CNL-Sucal v Hag GD* (1991)) and the European Commission (the Commission) through a series of block exemptions (see Chapter 3). In fact, the tension may be more apparent than real. The attitude of the Commission and the jurisprudence of the European Court were initially founded on an impression of intellectual property laws as being anti-competitive, as, in the short term, they are. Nevertheless, the underlying purpose behind the exclusivity conferred by intellectual property rights is to promote competition in the long term by stimulating the development and production of new goods.

Latterly, relations between competition and intellectual property law have improved dramatically, particularly in the US,[5] with regulators as keen to encourage innovation and research and development as intellectual property owners. In the Community, the Commission and the European Court have demonstrated a shift in approach to patent licensing evidenced by the withdrawal of the 1962 Announcement on Patent Licensing Agreements (the Christmas Message) (see Chapter 3), by the difference of outcome in *RTE and ITP v EC Commission (Magill)* (1995)[6] and *Volvo v Veng* (1988)[7] and by the move away from the common origin doctrine in *SA Cnl-Sucal v Hag GD*.[8] Finding a balance between maintaining competitive markets, on the one hand, and sufficient protection for intellectual property owners on the other, nevertheless remains a key concern for regulators across the globe.

In the UK, domestic intellectual property law is influenced by membership of the EU in two ways: first, both in the harmonisation of the substantive scope of Members States rights themselves and in the provision of Community-wide rights (see 1.8); and, secondly, in the effects on the exercise of domestic intellectual property rights of Community policies relating to the free movement of goods and competition policy. These are discussed below.

1.4.2 Free movement of goods and the internal market

The relevant provisions of the EC Treaty

The EC Treaty is remarkably silent on the issue of intellectual property, although the general principle concerning property rights can be found in Article 295:

> This treaty shall in no way prejudice the rules in Member States governing the system of property ownership.

Although the Treaty recognises the existence and ownership of intellectual property rights under national law, this collides with the principle of free movement of goods. The basic principle of free movement is articulated in Article 28 which states:

> Quantitative restrictions on imports and all measures having equivalent effect shall, without prejudice to the following provisions, be prohibited between Member States.

The EC Treaty therefore limits the exploitation and enjoyment of intellectual property rights by preventing owners of such rights in Member States from using them in a way

---

5   Competition is referred to as antitrust in the US.
6   See also Chapter 3.
7   See also Chapter 3.
8   See also Chapter 17.

that hinders the free movement of goods and services within the Community. There are a number of points to note.

First, the free movement rules are addressed to the 'Member States', which embraces the legislative, judicial and administrative authorities responsible for implementation and enforcement of national intellectual property rights. Secondly, Article 28 prohibits quantitative restrictions, essentially quotas, the extreme being a nil quota (banning all imports of a product). Other examples include national legislative or administrative practices relating to labelling and packaging of goods, certificates of origin and public and consumer health requirements. Arguably these measures pose far greater hindrance to the single market project than pecuniary practices. Thirdly, Article 28 also prohibits 'any measure having equivalent effect upon imports' (a number of which arise as a direct consequence of the protection of industrial and commercial property), and Article 29 prohibits the same in respect of exports. If an intellectual property right owner can prevent imports, that right is a measure having an effect equivalent to a quantitative restriction. The European Court has been predominantly concerned with Article 28 and the expression 'measures having equivalent effect to a quantitative restriction'. Not surprisingly, the Court has expansively interpreted this phrase, as exemplified by the formula established in the seminal *Dassonville* case and developed in *Cassis de Dijon*:[9]

> [a]ll trading rules enacted by Member States which are capable of hindering, directly or indirectly, actually or potentially, intra-Community trade.[10]

The European Court has developed an impressive body of case law since these landmark decisions and this has had an important influence on intellectual property law. The *Dassonville* formula has meant that a great number of legislative and administrative practices have been struck down on the basis that they directly discriminate against imported goods or do so indirectly by imposing the same health tests on imported goods as is the case for domestically produced goods but subject imported goods to tougher controls or conditions.

Strictly speaking, intellectual property rights are not 'goods' for the purposes of Article 28. Nonetheless, the European Court has decreed that, provided the *effect* is to hinder the free movement of goods, the *exercise* of the intellectual property right may fall within the ambit of the *Dassonville* formula. Article 30, which provides for strictly defined exceptions to the free movement principle, contains an explicit reference to property rights and it would seem anomalous if the exercise of an intellectual property right did not fall within Article 28.

Accordingly, the prohibition contained in Article 28 is not absolute and Article 30 provides that:

> The provisions of Articles 28 and 29 shall not preclude prohibitions or restrictions on imports, exports or goods in transit justified on grounds of public morality, public policy or public security; the protection of health and life of humans, animals or plants; the protection of national treasures possessing artistic, historic or archaeological value; or the protection of industrial or commercial property. Such

---

9   *Rewe-Zentral AG v Bundesmonopolverwaltung für Branntwein* (1979).
10 Case 8/74 *Procureur du Roi v Dassonville, SA ETS Fourcroyand SA Breuval et Cie* [1974] ECR 837, [1974] 2 CMLR 436 at 852.

prohibition or restrictions shall not, however, constitute a means of arbitrary discrimination or a disguised restriction on trade between Member States.

The phrase 'industrial and commercial property' has been taken to include all the main forms of intellectual property right, including design rights.[11] Community law therefore permits certain restrictions on free movement to protect national intellectual property rights. However, Article 30 will not avail the right owner if the prohibition produces an arbitrary discrimination or disguised restriction on trade.[12] The prohibition is on restrictions between Member States – intellectual property rights can still be used against imports emanating from outside the European Economic Area.[13] As is the case with any derogation from the free movement principle, the European Court interprets Article 30 restrictively.

It is also important to note that intellectual property rights may also affect the free movement of services. Article 49 sets out the basic provision on services:

> Within the framework of the provisions set out below, restrictions on freedom to provide services within the Community shall be prohibited in respect of nationals of Member States who are established in a State of the Community other than that of the person for whom the services are intended.

Although there is no express derogation from Article 49, the European Court held in Coditel[14] that restrictions on the movement of services may be justified by the need to protect property rights in the same way as they may be justified under Article 30 in respect of the free movement of goods. The exact scope of the free movement provisions has been considered by the European Court in a number of cases.

Principles applied by the European Court of Justice

In applying the free movement of goods provisions to exercises of intellectual property rights, the European Court has utilised three principles:

(a) a distinction, albeit questionable, is drawn between the *existence*, and the *exercise*, of a right (*Consten and Grundig v Commission* (1966); *Deutsche Grammophon v Metro-SB-Grossmärkte* (1971)). The existence of a right remains protected by Article 295 of the EC Treaty, which preserves property rights. However, the mere exercise of a right is subject to the other Treaty provisions. Article 30 of the EC Treaty is said only to apply to the existence of the right, and not its exercise, which is, consequently, subject to Article 28 of the EC Treaty; (see below)

(b) this distinction has necessitated the definition of the subject matter of each right in order to draw the line between its existence and its exercise (*Deutsche*

---

11 *Merck & Co Inc v Stephar BV* (1981); *Industrie Diensten Groep BV v JA Beele Handelmaatschappij BV* (1982).

12 *EMI Electrola GmbH v Patricia Im- und Export Verwaltungsgesellschaft mbH and Others* (1989).

13 *EMI Records v CBS United Kingdom Ltd* (1976); *EMI Records v CBS Grammofon A/S* (1976); *EMI Records v CBS Schallplatten GmbH* (1976).

14 *Coditel SA v Ciné Vog Films SA (No 1)*; *Coditel SA v Ciné Vog Films SA (No 2)*.

Grammophon v Metro-SB-Grossmärkte (1971); *Centrafarm v Sterling Drug Inc* (1974); *Centrafarm v Winthrop BV* (1974)). The European Court has tended to regard the essence of the right as one of reward for the right owner;

(c) in turn, this has led to the line between the end of the existence and the beginning of the exercise of a right being drawn according to the doctrine of Community-wide exhaustion: all rights ceasing after the first release of legitimate goods, by the right owner or with his consent, onto the market, in any Member State. In other words, the right is to be rewarded once, when the goods are released onto the Community market, and not again whenever those goods cross national borders.

It cannot really be said that a right exists if it cannot be effectively exercised. Consequently, the existence of a right is really only the sum total of the ways in which it may be exercised. The principles adopted by the European Court represent a policy choice, preferring Community policy over national rights. This is done by distinguishing between exercises of national intellectual property rights, which it is felt can be justified and those which it is felt cannot. The underlying policy is clear: to facilitate competition from goods connected with the right owner, but to allow the right to be used against illegitimate independent competitors.

However, the use of such uncertain criteria has allowed the European Court to amend its policy as the advantages of intellectual property rights, and the potentially depressing effect of the Court's policy on innovation, have become clear. Where a right has no protection in a country from which goods are exported, the European Court's policy prevents a right owner from benefiting from the enhanced value that their right provides in the country of import (as imports will have the effect of reducing the price there to the non-protected one). This may deter a right owner from marketing in the country of export at all and deprive the public there of the goods. This was the situation which arose in *Merck v Stephar* (1981). Merck was not able to use its Dutch patent to keep out imports coming from Italy, where no patent was available for drugs at the time. This prevented Merck from making a monopoly profit in Italy, or stopping free riding by competitors. Such arguments were raised by Advocate General Roemer in *Parke, Davis and Co v Probel* (1968), but not mentioned by the Court.

The existence/exercise distinction

The existence/exercise dichotomy has been applied and parallel imports sanctioned despite the existence of an intellectual property right in the case of patents (*Centrafarm v Sterling Drug Inc* (1974)); (*Merck v Stephar* (1981)); copyright (*Deutsche Grammophon v Metro-SB-Grossmärkte* (1971)) and trade marks (*Centrafarm v Winthrop BV* (1974); *Van Zuylen v Hag* (1974)). Article 28 of the EC Treaty has also been invoked where the right being relied on is one at the periphery of intellectual property, such as breach of confidence, passing off or unfair competition: *Dansk Supermarked v Imerco* (1981); *Industrie Diensten Groep v Beele* (1982); *Pall Corp v Dahlhausen* (1990). These latter cases adopt the principle that, where there are no common rules within the EU, obstacles to the movement of goods which result from national differences in rights must be accepted. This applies to the extent that they do not discriminate between goods from different Member States and can be justified as necessary to comply with mandatory conditions to secure consumer protection and fairness in transactions. This principle was established in the seminal *Cassis de Dijon* case.[15] German law prohibited the sale of fruit liqueurs with less than 32% wine–spirit content. A trader attempted to prevent the import into Germany of a French liqueur with a lower alcohol content. The principle was laid down by the European Court, although, in this case, the German rule preventing imports was not necessary, as prejudice to consumers could be prevented by less restrictive means, for example, by accurate labelling.

The subject matter of rights

Defining the essential subject matter of each right gives the European Court a tool with the flexibility to take into account the purposes of intellectual property rights. The purposes are to be balanced against the distortion to trade threatened by their exercise. However, the European Court has not formulated a theoretical basis for defining the subject matter of rights. A more sympathetic approach seems to have been taken where rental, broadcasting and performance rights, which are not exhausted in the same way, have been challenged (*Coditel v Ciné Vog (No 1)* (1980) (substance of performance right of a film held to include the size of reward secured by repeated performance); and *Warner Bros v Christiansen* (1988) (non-discriminatory rental right allowed to be exercised against imports)). This flexibility has allowed the European Court to redefine the nature of rights as a more sympathetic attitude to the purposes of intellectual property rights has developed: *SA CNL-Sucal v Hag GD* (1990) (common origin doctrine abandoned and replaced by normal principles of exhaustion with relation to trade marks); *Allen and Hanbury v Generics (UK)* (1988) (the substance of a patent said to be to secure a fair reward, rather than an exclusive right to use and exploit an invention for the first time).

The European Court has determined that, where rights differ between the relevant Member States, it is for the national law to determine the scope and conditions of the right, unless there is a harmonisation Directive or the right has been replaced by a Community right: *Keurkoop v Nancy Kean Gifts* (1982) (design law); *Volvo AB v Erik Veng*[16] (registered designs).

The concept of exhaustion

As the principles of both the existence/exercise distinction and the specific subject matter of a right can be criticised, it is on this principle that the European Court's decisions really hang. Attitudes in the Court have also relaxed in relation to the concept of exhaustion. The intellectual property right is held to be exhausted once goods have been released onto the market in any one Member State by the right owner or with his consent. This replaces any concept of national exhaustion embodied in national intellectual property laws with Community-wide exhaustion. Nevertheless, in the case of trade marks, at first, a different approach was adopted if the marks at issue had had a common origin. In *Van Zuylen v Hag AG* (1974), the HAG trade mark had been held by one owner in Germany and Belgium, but passed into entirely separate hands in Belgium after the Second World War. The European Court held that the

---

15   *Rewe-Zentral AG v Bundesmonopolverwaltung für Branntwein* (1979).
16   See also Chapter 3.

German mark owner was entitled to market products in Belgium, with the same mark, through parallel imports or directly, as the marks had a common origin. This effectively ignored the purpose of the mark to indicate the source of goods to the consumer, who would be unable to distinguish between the German and Belgian products. This decision was, in an unprecedented move by the Court, reversed in *SA CNL-Sucal v HAG GF (HAG II)* (1990) (the reverse situation was at issue: whether the German company could prevent imports from Belgium).

If Article 28 of the EC Treaty is to apply, the intellectual property right owner must be shown to have consented in some way to the marketing in the country of export from which the parallel importer makes his purchase. No exhaustion of rights was found in *Keurkoop v Nancy Kean Gifts* (1982), as there was no consent by the proprietor of the right or by a person legally or economically dependent on him. It had been feared that the imposition of a compulsory licence under national law would constitute a notional form of consent to marketing in the country of export. As the European Court's attitude towards intellectual property softened, a more realistic view of consent was adopted in *Musik Vertrieb Membran v GEMA* (1981); *EMI Electrola v Patricia* (1989); and *Pharmon v Hoechst* (1985).

1.5   COMPETITION POLICY OF THE EC AND UK

It is not only the existence and enforcement of intellectual property rights, but also the ways in which they may be dealt with (particularly licensing), which collide with the free market competition philosophy of the EC and the laws of the Member States. The EC's competition policy, which is administered by the Commission and, in the UK, the new competition regime administered by the Office of Fair Trading (OFT) and the Competition Commission, has been touched upon but needs to be considered in more detail. Competition policy governs both the agreements that may be made with intellectual property rights and the ways in which the monopolistic power that an intellectual property right may bring can be exercised.

1.5.1   The relevant provisions of the EC Treaty

The relevant provisions of the EC Treaty concerning competition are those contained in Articles 81 and 82. Article 81 prohibits restrictive agreements between two or more independent entities, whether *horizontal* (between parties operating at the same level of the economy) or *vertical* (between parties operating at different levels). Article 82 applies to the abusive activities of one undertaking occupying a dominant position on a market.

1.5.2   Article 81 and anti-competitive agreements

The Community institutions have applied Article 81 to prohibit arrangements that adversely affect competition and hinder the development of the single market programme. The European Court in particular pursues a method of teleological interpretation, construing Treaty provisions and Community legislation in accordance with the Treaty's broad aims and objectives set out in Articles 2 and 3.

Article 81 provides:

(1) The following shall be prohibited as incompatible with the common market: all agreements between undertakings, decisions by associations of undertakings and concerted practices which may affect trade between Member States and which have as their object or effect the prevention, restriction or distortion of competition within the common market, and in particular those which:

    (a) directly or indirectly fix purchase or selling prices or any other trading conditions;

    (b) limit or control production, markets, technical development, or investment;

    (c) share markets or sources of supply;

    (d) apply dissimilar conditions to equivalent transactions with other trading parties, thereby placing them at a competitive disadvantage;

    (e) make the conclusion of contracts subject to acceptance by the other parties of supplementary obligations which, by their nature or according to commercial usage, have no connection with the subject of such contracts.

(2) Any agreements or decisions prohibited pursuant to this Article shall be automatically void.

(3) The provisions of paragraph 1 may, however, be declared inapplicable in the cases of:

    – any agreement or category of agreements between undertakings;

    – any decision or category of decisions by associations of undertakings;

    – any concerted practice or category of concerted practices,

which contributes to improving the production or distribution of goods or to promoting technical or economic progress, while allowing consumers a fair share of the resulting benefit, and which does not:

    (a) impose on the undertakings concerned restrictions which are not indispensable to the attainment of these objectives;

    (b) afford such undertakings the possibility of eliminating competition in respect of a substantial part of the products in question.

The EC Treaty does not provide any definitions of the key terms and reference must be made to the jurisprudence of the European Court. For example, the Court has interpreted the term 'undertaking' in the broadest sense to include 'every entity engaged in an economic activity regardless of the legal status of the entity and the way in which it is financed'.[17]

Any arrangement between independent 'undertakings' found to infringe the prohibition contained in Article 81(1) will be rendered automatically void by Article 81(2). The European Court has stated, however, that the sanction of nullity will only affect the provisions in the agreements that infringe Article 81(1). Provided the offending clauses can be severed from the main body of the agreement, the parties may implement the contract, although one which may differ significantly from that

---

17 *Klaus Höfner and Fritz Elser v Macrotron GmbH* (1991).

which was originally concluded. The Commission also has the power to impose fines of up to 10% of an undertaking's turnover in the preceding year of business.

Article 81(3) also allows the Commission to exempt agreements, decisions or concerted practices which meet certain criteria; for example, the agreement may be justified as contributing to improving the production or distribution of goods or to promoting technical or economic progress, while allowing consumers a fair share of the resulting benefit. Exemptions can be granted *individually* (individual exemptions) or to *categories of agreements* (block exemptions). An agreement which infringes Article 81(1) must be notified to the Commission before it can qualify for an exemption and must comply with the criteria specified in Article 81(3). The notification procedure has not worked efficiently over the years and the sheer volume of agreements notified to the Commission has resulted in administrative overload with applications for exemption often taking two to three years to resolve. The Commission adopted a series of measures designed to ease the backlog, including the publication of a number of block exemptions. In this context, the most relevant block exemption regulations are those in relation to technology transfer agreements,[18] R&D agreements[19] and vertical agreements,[20] and these are discussed in the relevant chapters. Continued difficulties with the individual exemption procedure prompted a comprehensive review in 2000 of the enforcement rules implementing Articles 81 and 82.[21] On 1 May 2004, a new regulation came into force, 1/2003[22] replacing Regulation 17/62.[23] Regulation 1/2003 abolishes the procedure for obtaining an individual exemption through a system of prior notification and replaces it with a directly applicable system, which allows national courts and national competition authorities to apply and enforce Article 81 in its entirety, including the four criteria articulated in Article 81(3). The Commission may continue to publish block exemptions and these will provide undertakings and national courts with important guidance when assessing the compatibility of an arrangement with the competition rules. Undertakings now face a significant burden in having to ensure compatibility with Article 81 without the possibility of obtaining clarification from the Commission.

Article 81 applies to agreements between two or more undertakings. The term agreement has been construed in the widest possible sense by the Community institutions and includes, for example, non-binding agreements (so-called gentlemen's agreements) and verbal arrangements. It may also apply to unilateral conduct; for example, where one party refuses to supply another with its products, in circumstances where there have been previous contractual relations between the parties.[24] Article 81 also applies to concerted practices. The concept of concerted

---

18 Commission Regulation 772/2004 on the application of Article 81(3) to technology transfer agreements ([2004] OJ L123).

19 Commission Regulation 2659/2000 on the application of Article 81(3) to categories of research and development agreement ([2000] OJ L304).

20 Commission Regulation 2790/99 on the application of Article 81(3) to categories of vertical agreements and concerted practices ([1999] OJ L336).

21 White Paper on Modernisation of the Rules Implementing Articles 81 and 82 of the EC Treaty (*formerly Articles 85 and 86*) ([1999] OJ C 132).

22 Council Regulation 1/2003 on the implementation of the rules on competition laid down in Articles 81 and 82 of the Treaty ([2003] OJ L001).

23 Council Regulation 17/62 implementing Articles 85 and 86 of the Treaty ([1962] OJ P013).

24 *Ford-Werke AG and Ford of Europe Inc v EC Commission* (1985).

practice was inserted into the EC Treaty to catch collusion between parties in a market in the absence of a formal agreement. Concerted practices can be particularly damaging to competition and are much harder to prove because there is often very little evidence. In *ICI v Commission* (2002) the Commission decided on the basis of uniform price increases introduced by a number of leading producers of aniline dyes that the parties had engaged in a concerted practice to fix prices.

Article 81 will not apply unless the agreement, decision or concerted practice *affects trade between the Member States*. The Community competition authorities have interpreted this requirement broadly in an attempt to ensure that Community law applies; where there is no effect on trade, national law will apply.[25] The arrangement must also have as its *object or effect* the prevention, restriction or distortion of competition within the common market and must do so to an *appreciable* extent (the *de minimis* principle). The 'object or effect' requirement has caused considerable difficulties for the Community institutions. It seems that where the object of an agreement is to restrict competition, for example, a price-fixing arrangement, there will be no need to examine the effects. It is only in circumstances where the agreement is clearly not intended to restrict competition, for example, a standard licensing agreement, that economic analysis of its effects on the particular market will be necessary.[26] Moreover, the development of the *de minimis* principle in Community competition law means that competition and/or intra-Community trade must be affected to an appreciable extent. Where competition in a market is not harmed to a sufficient degree Article 81(1) will not apply, even where the arrangement contains anti-competitive restrictions such as price fixing.[27] Given the importance of this principle to the business community, the Commission published a Notice on Agreements of Minor Importance in 1986 (since updated most recently in 2001) which sets out market share thresholds below which an agreement will be regarded as *de minimis*.[28]

The 2001 notice raises the *de minimis* thresholds to 10% market share for agreements between competitors and to 15% for agreements between non-competitors, whereas the previous notice had fixed the thresholds at respectively 5% and 10% market share. Generally, if a company does not have a minimum level of market power one would not expect concerns in relation to competition. This is taken into account by the new thresholds; however, they simultaneously remain low enough to be applicable whatever the overall market structure looks like. The 2001 notice specified for the first time a market share threshold for networks of agreements producing a cumulative anti-competitive effect. The previous *de minimis* notice meant that firms operating in sectors such as beer and petrol could not usually benefit from the *de minimis* notice. However, the 2001 version introduced a special *de minimis* market share threshold of 5% for markets where there are parallel networks of similar agreements.

---

25 *Société Technique Minière (LTM) v Maschinenbau Ulm GmbH (MBU)* (1966).
26 *Ibid.*
27 The principle was introduced in *Völk v Vervaecke* (1969).
28 Commission Notice on agreements of minor importance which do not appreciably restrict competition under Article 81(1) of the Treaty establishing the European Community ([2001] OJ C368/13). This notice replaces the notice on agreements of minor importance published in [1997] OJ C372).

Potentially, Article 295 excludes from the application of the Treaty any matter related to intellectual property rights (see above). However, the exact scope of the provision has not been defined and the Commission and the European Court have applied Article 81(1) to a wide range of agreements concerning intellectual property rights. For example, the decision of the Court in *Consten and Grundig* (1966) confirmed that agreements concerning intellectual property rights are subject to the prohibition in Article 81(1). The Court made it clear that interference with intellectual property rights can be justified on the basis that it 'does not affect the grant of those rights but only limits their exercise to the extent necessary to give effect to the prohibition under (Article 81)'.

1.5.3   Article 82 and abuse of a dominant position

Some companies occupy such a strong position in a market that they are able to act without any regard for their competitors or indeed their customers. If such a situation exists, competition in a market may eventually be eliminated. Thus, Article 82 of the EC Treaty prohibits undertakings from using their market strength in an abusive manner.

The full text of Article 82 provides:

Any abuse by one or more undertakings of a dominant position within the common market or in a substantial part of it shall be prohibited as incompatible with the common market insofar as it may affect trade between Member States.

Such abuse may, in particular, consist in:

(a)   directly or indirectly imposing unfair purchase or selling prices or other unfair trading conditions;

(b)   limiting production, markets or technical development to the prejudice of consumers;

(c)   applying dissimilar conditions to equivalent transactions with other trading parties, thereby placing them at a competitive disadvantage;

(d)   making the conclusion of contracts subject to acceptance by the other parties of supplementary obligations which, by their nature or according to commercial usage, have no connection with the subject of such contracts.

Sub-paragraphs (a) to (d) merely provide examples of abuses, and this list is not exhaustive.

Article 82 therefore prohibits the abuse of a dominant position where it affects trade between Member States. There are a number of points to note: first, dominance *per se* is not prohibited, only abuse of a dominant position. Secondly, unlike Article 81, which applies to collusion in a market, Article 82 applies to the activities of only one undertaking.[29] Finally, there is no parallel to Article 81(3) but any objective justification for the activity would render it non-abusive.

---

29   It used to be the case that Article 82 could not apply to independent undertakings (oligopolies). However, in *Italian Flat Glass* the Court of First Instance held that Article 82 could apply to the conduct of two or more independent economic entities which were 'united by such economic links that, by virtue of that fact, together they hold a dominant position'. This is known as 'collective', 'joint' or 'oligopolistic' dominance. See also Joined Cases C–395/96 and C–396/96 *Compagnie Maritime Belge Transports SA and Others v EC Commission*.

The main elements of Article 82, for example, 'dominance' and 'abuse' are not defined in the EC Treaty and reference must be made to the jurisprudence of the European Court.

The relevant market

Dominance does not exist in a vacuum and must be assessed in relation to a market. There are three relevant markets that are assessed; the relevant product market, the relevant geographical market and the temporal market. Although all three markets must be defined, the relevant product market is generally regarded as the most important and the most complex. The Commission, in its Notice on the Definition of the Relevant Market ,suggests that the relevant product market is one in which products are substantially interchangeable.[30]

Dominance

Having established the relevant markets it is necessary to establish whether the parties concerned are dominant within that market. The Commission has suggested that:

> Undertakings are in a dominant position when they have the power to behave independently without taking into account, to any substantial extent, their competitors, purchasers and suppliers. Such is the case where an undertaking's market share, either in itself or when combined with its know-how, access to raw materials, capital or other major advantage such as trade-mark ownership, enables it to determine the prices or to control the production or distribution of a significant part of the relevant goods.[31]

The Court takes into account significant factors such as market share, the length of time the undertaking has enjoyed its position of strength, financial and technological resources, access to raw materials and generally the behaviour of the undertaking.

Abuse

Abuse of a dominant position is prohibited by Article 82, not dominance *per se*. There are two types of abuses, exploitative abuses and anti-competitive abuses, although various kinds of behaviour can fall into both categories. Exploitative abuses occur when an undertaking uses its dominant position to gain an unfair competitive advantage over its trading partners by imposing oppressive or unfair conditions. Examples of these types of abuses include charging unfair prices, imposing unfair trading conditions and discriminatory treatment.[32] Anti-competitive abuses occur where a dominant undertaking uses its position of strength to undermine or eliminate existing competitors. Examples of anti-competitive abuse include tying-in practices, predatory pricing (reducing prices below cost), and refusals to supply (see Chapter 3).

Breach of Article 82 may result in an investigation by the Commission. Where the Commission finds that Article 82 has been infringed, the Commission can issue a

---

30   Notice on the Definition of the Relevant Market [1997] OJ C372.
31   *Re Continental Can Co* [1972] CMLR D11, para 3.
32   *United Brands Company and United Brands Continentaal BV v Commission of the European Communities* (1978).

decision ordering the undertaking to end the abusive conduct (a 'cease and desist' order). The Commission may also impose a heavy fine on the undertaking of up to 10% of its turnover in the preceding year of business. Some of the world's largest companies have been fined significant amounts of money, the largest and most recent being the fine imposed on Microsoft which amounted to $604 million.[33]

As previously noted, the European Court has drawn an important distinction between the *existence* of intellectual property rights and their *exercise*. According to the Court, ownership of an intellectual property right does not, as a basic principle, create a dominant position.[34] In other words, the mere existence of an intellectual property right cannot, as a general rule, infringe Article 82 (or indeed Article 81). However, in *Parke, Davis & Co v Probel* (1968) the Court held that an 'improper exploitation' of patent rights in the context of agreements, decisions of undertakings or concerted practices or by firms in a dominant position could breach Community competition law.

The main area of controversy concerning Article 82 and intellectual property rights is whether it is an abuse for an undertaking in a dominant position to refuse others access to its property rights. This issue is closely linked with the essential facilities doctrine in Community competition law and is discussed in detail in Chapter 3. The general principle is that a refusal to license an intellectual property right does not amount to an abuse of a dominant position unless there are 'exceptional circumstances'.[35]

1.5.4   Relationship between Articles 28–30 and Articles 81 and 82

There is considerable overlap between the Community's competition rules and the exercise of intellectual property rights embodied in Articles 28–30, and this is increasingly reflected in the European Court's jurisprudence. In *Sirena v Eda* (1971) the Court held that 'Article 30, although it appears in the Chapter of the Treaty dealing with quantitative restrictions on trade between Member States, is based on a principle equally applicable to the question of competition'.[36] However, the Court made clear in another important case, *RTE v Commission (Magill)* (1991), that 'the exercise of an intellectual property right in a manner which affects competition will not fall foul of Articles 81 and 82 provided it falls within the specific subject matter of the right'.[37] Thus, if the exercise of an intellectual property right does not fall within the specific subject matter of the right, it will be caught by Article 28 and may also be caught by Articles 81 and 82. These issues are considered in more detail in Chapter 3.

---

33   Commission decision, 24 March 2004, Case COMP/C-3/37.792. See also Chapter 3.
34   Case 238/87 *Volvo AB v Erik Veng (UK) Limited* [1988] ECR 6211, [1989] 4 CMLR 122 at para 46 and see Chapter 3.
35   Recent Community case law on this issue however has lacked clarity. See generally Chapter 3.
36   At 81.
37   At 518–19.

1.6   OTHER IMPACTS OF EU LAW ON NATIONAL INTELLECTUAL PROPERTY LAWS

Article 12 of the EC Treaty prohibits discrimination on the grounds of nationality. This affected the German provision of performers' rights. The right applied to German performers wherever a performance took place, but to other nationals only if the performance occurred in a Rome Convention country. The effect was to discriminate against the British singer, Phil Collins, who was unprotected for a performance which took place in the US (not a member of the Rome Convention) when 'bootleg' copies of the performance were sold in Germany. In *Phil Collins v IMRAT Handelsgesellschaft GmbH* (1993), the European Court ruled that the national provision was inconsistent with Article 12 of the EC Treaty. The Community obligation overrode national law drafted to comply with Convention obligations. It was applied to national intellectual property law without any relation to the policies on free movement of goods and services.

1.7   UK COMPETITION LAW

Recent changes to UK competition law have necessitated greater awareness of the application of competition rules to intellectual property rights in a domestic context. The Competition Act 1998 (CA 1998), the main provisions of which came into force on 1 March 2000, is a radical departure from the previous regime. This was principally embodied in the unintelligible, out of date and virtually unenforceable Restrictive Trade Practices legislation of 1976 and 1977, the Resale Prices Act 1976 (collectively referred to as the 'RTP' legislation) and the Competition Act 1980. The CA 1998 repealed the RTP legislation and large sections of the Competition Act 1980, and replaced it with a radically new regime to tackle anti-competitive agreements and abusive conduct based on the Community tradition of competition law.[38] The CA 1998 bestows the competition authorities, the OFT, Competition Commission and sectoral regulators with considerable powers of investigation and enforcement.[39] The Competition Appeal Tribunal (the CAT) hears appeals against decisions of the OFT and sector regulators under the CA 1998. The powers of enforcement bestowed on the UK competition authorities also draw from Community tradition. The Director General of Fair Trading (the Director) may grant an exemption (individual exemption) to a prohibited agreement or concerted practice following a request (application) by any party to it. The grounds for exemption mirror the criteria set out in Article 81(3). The Director and, by implication, the staff of the Office of Fair Trading, have substantially increased powers to police the Act, broadly similar to their counterparts at the European Commission.

---

38 See generally Wilks, S, 'The Prolonged Reform of UK Competition Policy' in *Comparative Competition Policy* Doern and Wilks S (eds) (Oxford: Clarendon, 1996); Whish, R, 'The Competition Act 1998 and the Prior Debate on Reform', in Rodger, B and MacCulloch, A (eds), *The Competition Act: A New Era for UK Competition Law* (Oxford: Hart Publishing, 2000).

39 For more detail, see OFT Guideline 404 on Powers of Investigation and Guideline 407 on Enforcement, both available at www.oft.gov.uk.

Besides modernising a drastically out of date domestic framework, the principal aim of the CA 1998 was to harmonise domestic competition law with Community law, namely Articles 81 and 82 of the EC Treaty, thereby reducing the regulatory burden on British business in having to comply with two quite distinct competition regimes. Harmonisation is achieved through s 60 of the Act, the so-called 'Euro-clause,' which requires consistency with Community law, with the added proviso, 'having regard to any relevant differences'.[40] The obligation on the British judiciary to follow Community case law where possible has already led to greater convergence between UK competition law and the EC Treaty rules, with obvious consequences for intellectual property law. Previously, under the RTP legislation, intellectual property agreements were considered similar to property agreements such as leases and generally regarded as having a benign effect on competition. The compatibility of intellectual property agreements with the Chapter I and II prohibitions of the CA 1998 must now be considered in the context of Community law. The wisdom in this approach is explained by the Department of Trade and Industry in a consultation document:

> Our present view on intellectual property rights under a prohibition-based approach is that the boundaries of what is acceptable and what is anti-competitive is best established directly from European jurisprudence. Different treatment for intellectual property rights under the Competition Act regime and European regime seems neither necessary nor desirable and is likely to increase the burden on business of compliance. To the extent to which they are covered by the [proposed] EC block exemption (or would be if there were an effect on trade) they will be parallel exempt under the Act; the same applies to agreements covered by the technology transfer block exemption.[41]

Thus, intellectual property agreements will benefit from parallel exemption under s 10 of the CA 1998. However, much of Community competition law is motivated by single market considerations and, since this is not a concern of UK competition law, Community case law on the application of Article 81 to licences of intellectual property rights may not be relevant in a domestic context. The application of UK competition law to the ownership and enjoyment of intellectual property licences may therefore diverge from Community decisional practice to a certain extent, certainly with regard to territorial restrictions. Although there is now a substantial corpus of case law on the interpretation and application of the CA 1998, it is possibly too early to determine whether this will prove the case.[42]

Given the complexity of the CA 1998, the OFT is obliged to publish general information and advice as to how it will apply the law in practice. In the past few years, the OFT has published a number of Guidelines on the application of the CA 1998, the most recent being a draft Guideline on the application of the Competition Act to intellectual property rights.[43] The draft has been broadly welcomed by the legal profession and business community, although clarification of many issues has been

---

40 For a more detailed discussion of s 60 see Middleton, K, 'The Euro-clause', in *UK Competition Law: A New Era*, (Oxford: Hart Publishing, 2000) Ch 2.
41 Competition Act 1998, Exclusion of Vertical Agreements, Consultation on draft Order, para 22.
42 Rodger, B, 'Early Steps to a Mature Competition Law System', [2002] ECLR 23(2) 52.
43 OFT 418 and see Chapter 3.

encouraged.[44] Recent statements from the OFT have indicated that it is aware of the European Commission's review of the Technology Transfer Block Exemption Regulation and the anticipated shift in Commission policy with regard to licensing of IPRs generally. The recent Community review process will inevitably have had some effect on the final outcome of the draft guidelines and the OFT intends to publish revised Guidelines.

1.7.1 The Chapter I prohibition

Chapter I of the Act applies to agreements that have as their object or effect the prevention, restriction or distortion of competition. Section 2 of the Act provides:

2. – (1) Subject to [excluded agreements] agreements between undertakings, decisions by associations of undertakings or concerted practices which –

   (a) may affect trade within the United Kingdom, and

   (b) have as their object or effect the prevention, restriction or distortion of competition within the United Kingdom,

   are prohibited unless they are exempt in accordance with the provisions of this Part.

   (2) Subsection (1) applies, in particular, to agreements, decisions or practices which –

   (a) directly or indirectly fix purchase or selling prices or any other trading conditions;

   (b) limit or control production, markets, technical development or investment;

   (c) share markets or sources of supply;

   (d) apply dissimilar conditions to equivalent transactions with other trading parties, thereby placing them at a competitive disadvantage;

   (e) make the conclusion of contracts subject to acceptance by the other parties of supplementary obligations which, by their nature or according to commercial usage, have no connection with subjects of such contracts.

   (3) Subsection (1) applies only if the agreement, decision or practice is, or is intended to be, implemented in the United Kingdom.

   (4) Any agreement or decision which is prohibited by subsection (1) is void.

   …..

   (8) The prohibition imposed by subsection (1) is referred to in this Act as 'the Chapter I prohibition'.

Readers will note the similarity between Chapter I and Article 81 (see above). This is intentional and alignment with Community law is of course further secured by s 60. Various points are also worth noting. The Chapter I prohibition generally does not apply where the parties' market share is below 25%, although this rule does not apply to price fixing and market sharing practices. Thus, restrictions imposed on a licensee's minimum prices or the fixing of prices may amount to an infringement.

---

44 See comments by the Joint Working Party of the Bars and Law Societies of the UK. Response to Consultation on OFT draft CA 98 draft Guideline 418 on Intellectual Property Rights.

1.7.2   The Chapter II prohibition

Chapter II of the Act introduces an abuse of a dominant position provision in s 18.
Section 18 provides:

18. – (1) Subject to [excluded cases], any conduct on the part of one of more
undertakings which amounts to the abuse of a dominant position in a market is
prohibited if it may affect trade within the United Kingdom.

(2) Conduct may, in particular, constitute such abuse if it consists in –

(a) directly or indirectly imposing unfair purchase or selling prices or other
unfair trading conditions;

(b) limiting production, markets or technical development to the prejudice of
consumers;

(c) applying dissimilar conditions to equivalent transactions with other trading
parties, thereby placing them at a competitive disadvantage;

(d) making the conclusion of contracts subject to acceptance by the other parties
of supplementary obligations which, by their nature of according to
commercial usage, have no connection with the subject of the contracts.

......

(4) The prohibition imposed by subsection (1) is referred to in this Act as 'the
Chapter II prohibition'.

Unlike Chapter I, there is no possibility of an exemption from the Chapter II
prohibition. Section 60 will, however, incorporate the European Court's objective
justification test.[45]

1.7.3   The Enterprise Act 2002

A relatively recent addition to the UK competition regime is the Enterprise Act 2002 (EA
2002).[46] Unlike the CA 1998, which borrows heavily from the Community competition
tradition, the EA 2002 Act leans towards the US example of antitrust, and introduces, for
the first time in UK competition law, a criminal offence for cartel activity. The EA 2002
significantly strengthens the competition regime through a raft of measures, new
arrangements for market investigations, a new merger regime and disqualification for
directors for up to 15 years for an infringement of UK or EC competition law.[47]
Intellectual property owners are unlikely to be particularly affected by the EA 2002 and
only then if there is involvement in an illegal cartel.

1.8   HARMONISATION DIRECTIVES AND COMMUNITY-WIDE
RIGHTS

The conflicting aims of competition law and intellectual property may also be resolved
either through harmonisation of intellectual property rights to include Community-
wide exhaustion, or the creation of unitary Community-wide rights.

---

45 The Competition Act 1998 entered into force on 1 March 2000.
46 Entered into force on 7 November 2002.
47 See generally, Middleton, K, 'Americanisation of UK Competition Law' [2003] SLPQ 38(1) 27.

The differences in national intellectual property laws which provide potential barriers to trade between Member States have become the subject of harmonisation measures under Article 95 of the EC Treaty. Copyright, design, trade marks and protection for databases, computer programs and semi-conductor chips have all been the subject of such harmonisation, at least in part.

1.8.1 Regulations

The other solution to national differences in substantive intellectual property law is the provision of unitary Community-wide rights. In 1975, the Community Patent Convention was signed in Luxembourg. It was intended to create a unitary patent covering the Union, granted through an application to the European Patent Office designating any one Member State. The Community Patent Convention is, however, not yet in force. In July 1998, the Council and Commission issued a Green Paper for consultation with a view to reviving the community patent proposal. The costs of translation and provision of a common court remained major stumbling blocks and the initiative has not yet succeeded. In contrast, a Community trade mark came into being on 1 April 1996, with the implementation of the Council Regulation on the Community Trade Mark (40/94/EEC). Application is made to the Office for the Harmonisation of the Internal Market (OHIM) in Alicante, Spain. The resulting Community trade mark is a unitary one, enforceable throughout the EU. The Community design right came into force on 6 March 2002 and is also administered by the OHIM.

Further Reading

Anderman, S, *EC Competition Law and Intellectual Property Rights: The Regulation of Innovation* (Oxford: OUP, 1998)

Blakeney, M, *Legal Aspects of the Transfer of Technology to Developing Countries* (Oxford: ESC, 1989)

Booy, A, 'A Half-way House for Unfair Competition in the UK – a Practitioner's Plea' [1991] EIPR 439

Cornish, W, 'Genevan Bootstraps' [1997] EIPR 336

Cornish, W, and Llewellyn, D, *Intellectual Property: Patents, Copyright, Trade Marks and Allied Rights* (5th edn, London: Sweet & Maxwell, 2003)

Furse, M, *Competition Law of the EC and UK* (4th edn, New York: OUP, 2004)

Gervais, D, *The TRIPS Agreement: Drafting History and Analysis* (2nd edn, London: Sweet & Maxwell, 2003)

Gielen, C, 'WIPO and Unfair Competition' [1997] EIPR 78

Govaere, I, *The Use and Abuse of Intellectual Property Rights in EC Law* (London: Sweet & Maxwell, 1996)

Jones, A and Sufrin, B, *EC Competition Law – Texts, Cases & Materials* (Oxford: OUP, 2000)

Kamperman Sanders, A, *Unjust Environment: The New Paradigm for Unfair Competition Law?* (London: IPI, 1996)

Kamperman Sanders, A, *Unfair Competition Law* (Oxford: OUP, 1997)

Lahore, J, 'The Herschel Smith Lecture 1992 – Intellectual Property Rights and Unfair Copying: Old Concepts, New Ideas' [1992] EIPR 428

Kitchin, D, Llewellyn, D, Mellor, J, Meade, R and Moody-Stuart, T (eds), *Kerly's Law of Trade Marks and Trade Names* (13th edn, London: Sweet & Maxwell, 2001)

Laddie, H, Prescott, P, Vitoria, M and Speck, A (eds), *The Modern Law of Copyright and Designs,* (3rd edn, London: Butterworths, 2000)

Middleton, K, Rodger, B and MacCulloch, A, *Cases and Materials on Competition Law* (Oxford: OUP, 2002)

Pendleton, M, 'Intellectual Property, Information-based Society and a New International Economic Order – the Policy Options?' [1985] EIPR 31

Sherman, B and Bently, L, *The Making of Modern Intellectual Property Law* (Cambridge: CUP, 1999)

Tritton, G, *Intellectual Property in Europe,* (2nd edn, London: Sweet & Maxwell, 2002)

Vaver, D, 'Intellectual Property: The State of the Art' (2000) 116 LQR 621

Whish, R, *Competition Law* (5th edn, London: Butterworths, 2003)

CHAPTER 2

JUSTIFICATION

Information forms the raw material of progress and is the new form of wealth. Ideas in the form of information and knowledge are the substance matter of intellectual property. Intellectual property protects ideas by creating fences around them in the form of exclusive rights. These rights restrict the flow of those ideas, creating an artificial scarcity. However, information is dynamic in the sense that it continually develops as it is put to use. It is also cumulative in that new ideas stem from those already placed in the public domain, which can be regarded as a common resource for developing ideas and information. Importantly, this dynamism is dependent on access to ideas and unrestricted communication of them.

Property rights traditionally are applied to materials restricted by their very nature – said to be 'rivalrous'. For example, if I consume an apple I deprive others of a share in that apple. If that apple was taken from the village orchard I have deprived the community of a common resource. Consequently, where a resource is shared, private property rights have emerged to avoid the pursuit of one person's self-interest by one depleting the common resource. For example, if a village held common grazing land for its stock each family would increase its wealth by increasing its stock on that land. However, over grazing would eventually deplete the supply for all. However, if the common resource is parcelled into private holdings, each family has an incentive not to over-graze its share and thus the land itself is protected for use by future generations.

However in general, ideas, which are abstract, differ by their very nature. They are non-rivalrous – so that if I have an idea I may communicate to others it without depriving myself. In addition, those others may also make use of the idea without depriving me. If I describe a method for apportioning an apple between several friends to you, you may divide your apple in the same way without preventing me from doing so with my apple. Consequently, non-rivalrous ideas may be regarded as a public good, part of the public domain and available to all: a shared resource incompatible with private ownership, such as air or (at least in some parts of the world) water.

If, in addition, all ideas are drawn from and develop those that have gone before – the intellectual 'commons' – it can even be argued that the more widely ideas are shared the more people will benefit from them.[1] Because abstract ideas are potentially available to all, intellectual property rights have the capacity to interfere with the activities of others to a much greater extent[2] than is the case for other items of property. They form the basic subject matter needed for social, cultural and economic development and can be regarded as a form of capital. Therefore, creating artificial exclusivity through intellectual property protection, and depleting the commons needs to be justified.[3]

---

1   McFarland, M, 'Intellectual Property, Information, and the Common Good' (1999) BC Intell Prop & Tech F 060503.
2   An extent that may be global rather than local or territorial.
3   Hettinger, E, 'Justifying Intellectual Property' (1989) 18 Philosophy and Public Affairs 31; Paine, L, 'Trade Secrets and the Justification of Intellectual Property: A Comment on Hettinger' (1991) 20 Philosophy and Public Affairs 247.

This must be done in the face of past and continuing criticism of intellectual property rights. In addition, the justifications given for granting exclusive rights also provide an important framework for critical evaluation of the effectiveness of intellectual property rights as we know them. The success of the substantive law can only be assessed in the light of the objectives that law was designed to achieve. In the words of the Commission on Intellectual Property Rights:[4]

> The conferring of IP rights is an instrument of public policy, which should be designed so that the benefit to society (for instance through the invention of a new drug or technology) outweighs the cost to society (for instance, the higher cost of a drug and the costs of administering the IP system).

Meanwhile, technological development continues to challenge the established rights and gives rise to demands for enhanced or new protection, illustrated, for example, by the music industry's response to file sharing technology, by moves towards patents for computer software and by biotechnological inventions. The burgeoning growth of intellectual property as technology develops and rights are expanded and increased means that the justifications for intellectual property remain a subject for debate for politicians,[5] economists,[6] scientists[7] and lawyers,[8] even judges[9]. This is particularly so where rights have been created or existing ones expanded to cater for new technology. The *sui generis* database right and new legal protection for digital rights management of copyright works have both been argued to depart from the traditional copyright balance between protection and access,[10] thus depleting the public domain or common stock from which new ideas develop. The global reach and easy access to information provided by the internet has led to arguments that its resources are a common good and should be freely available to all,[11] while the open source movement (see 11.11.2) and advocates of copyleft[12] seek to implement sharing of a common resource.

2.1 THE NATURE OF EXCLUSIVE RIGHTS

Opposition has come from several directions: economists, free traders, developing countries and socialist States. It is worth, first, considering the nature of the rights that have given rise to these objections. Intellectual property rights have been described as exclusive; indeed, they are forms of monopoly.

---

4   *Integrating Intellectual Property Rights and Development Policy*, Report of the Commission on Intellectual Property Rights, London, September 2002.
5   May, C, 'Why IPR are a Global Political Issue' [2003] EIPR 1; *Integrating Intellectual Property Rights and Development Policy*, Report of the Commission on Intellectual Property Rights, London, 2002.
6   Towse, R, 'Assessing the Economic Effects of Copyright and its Reform'; 'Copyright as an Economic Incentive', *Innovation, Incentive and Reward*, Hume Papers on Public Policy, Vol 5, No 3, p 32.
7   *Keeping Science Open*, Report of the Royal Society, 2003: www.royalsoc.ac.uk.
8   Lessig, L, *The Future of Ideas* (New York: Random House, 2001); Boyle, J, *Shamans, Software and Spleens* (Cambridge, Mass: Harvard University Press, 1996).
9   Jacob, R, 'The Herschel Smith Lecture' [1993] EIPR 312; Laddie, H, 'Copyright: Over-strength, Over-regulated, Over-rated?' [1996] EIPR 253.
10   Colston, C, 'Challenges to Information Retrieval – a Global Solution? [2002] IJLIT 294.
11   Perry Barlow, J,'The Economy of Ideas' (1994) Wired, Issue 2.03.
12   See, for example, the Creative Commons: http://creativecommons.org; Stokes, A, 'Authorship, Collaboration and Copyright: A View from the UK' [2002] Ent LR 121.

Some are monopolies. A patent confers an absolute monopoly over the use, manufacture and sale of an invention, although it is limited to a maximum of 20 years. The trade mark, too, is a monopoly over a mark. Other traders may not use a mark for the same, similar, or even dissimilar goods or services in certain circumstances. The right lasts for as long as the registration is maintained. Secrecy, protected through breach of confidence, continues to protect provided that confidentiality can be maintained, lasting as long as the information from other sources is kept out of the public domain. This is because secrecy obtains only against those owing a duty of confidence to the owner of the secret and not against the public at large.

A qualified monopoly is one which allows some imitation by 'reverse engineering', such as the protection for semi-conductor chips and for plant and seed varieties, but otherwise confers a monopoly.

Nor does copyright confer an outright monopoly, because the same work produced independently will also be protected and may compete with the first work without infringing the first work's copyright. However, this has not precluded copyright owners from monopolistic behaviour. Obvious examples include the publication of hardback editions of books before paperback versions and the release of films in the cinema before the video becomes available. Copyright could be regarded as a 'relative monopoly'.

The mere fact of having an intellectual property right will not automatically confer a monopoly on its owner. This will depend on the availability of alternative products on the market and the success of the idea. However, an intellectual property right does give the potential for monopolistic power. Having control over the provision of a product enables monopolistic producers to control the market in several ways. The price at which the goods are sold may be maximised as consumers have no alternative source. Producers also control the quantities of the product released onto the market and, therefore, can do so in the quantities, and at the price, which secures the highest price the market will stand. In addition, a monopolistic producer controls the supply and distribution of the goods, any after sales service and repair and over investment in further research and development.

This power creates a clear conflict between a consumer's interest in access to commodities at the lowest cost, and a manufacturer's interest in securing the maximum profit. Where there is no competition, the manufacturer's reward can be significant, as is illustrated by the patent case of *Improver Corp v Remington Consumer Products* (1990). After two years of marketing, the patentee had made 5.8 million units of the product (a depilator) and had a gross retail turnover in excess of US$340 million.

However, it should not be forgotten that the protection conferred by exclusive rights is constrained by a number of limitations designed to allow for the conflicting interests of users, consumers and competitors.

2.1.1 Economic objections to monopoly power

The economic arguments conflict. Against monopolistic behaviour, it is argued that the consumer is forced to buy an alternative which is inferior to a monopolist's overpriced product. This means:

(a) that too little of available resources reach the market;

(b) that a monopolist's wealth is created at the consumer's expense;

(c) that a monopolist controls the market with respect to quality, service and repair, further development and supply, removing any incentives for improvement;

(d) that a monopoly removes any incentive to keep production costs down.

However, it can also be argued in favour of monopolies that a single source of supply can be the most efficient. Further, it can be argued that it can be controlled by public accountability and that it may only be a manufacturer with monopoly profits who can afford the high cost of continued research and development.[13]

Monopoly power also conflicts with a preference for a free market economy, although Beier[14] has argued that the conflict is more apparent than real. This is because the long-term aim of granting intellectual property rights is to stimulate innovation and production and, thereby, competition. The actual rewards gained are dictated by market forces and the intellectual property right allows dissemination of the underlying idea to competitors once the right has expired.

However, intellectual property rights do not confer monopolies outright. Subsistence of each of the rights is carefully structured by the criteria for grant or subsistence, and the nature of the right then conferred. The rights are also limited in duration: compulsory licences are available for patents and competition law provides a balancing factor, as does accountability to the Copyright Tribunal. Additionally, alternative products are often available on the market. It is adjustments such as these that seek to provide both the objectives that intellectual property rights are designed to achieve and answer the arguments of intellectual property's critics. The balances needed are delicate and often specific to the nature of the particular type of creation.

McFarland[15] argues that the rights of ownership and control bestowed by intellectual property can be balanced against the common good by resort to natural law theory going back to Aristotle. In the *Nicomachean Ethics* Aristotle suggested that the good of anything lay in its nature by fulfilling its purpose. McFarland then argues that the nature of the subject matter of intellectual property is information and that the purpose of information is to be communicated. Not only that, it is dynamic and cumulative:

> [b]ecause it is the product of human thought and not itself corporeal, information is constantly changing, growing, combining, and creating offshoots. An intellectual work never springs pure and original from a single human mind. There are always influences.

If natural law recognises both the individual right and the common good, a conceptual basis can be found for achieving a balanced application of intellectual property protection. The rights themselves are crafted to preserve a public domain, through limits to their duration, qualifying criteria that must be met before protection is gained, and exceptions to infringement. However, it is the case that the emphasis appears to have shifted from circumscribed rights granted in specific circumstances in order to

---

13 The pharmaceutical industry relies heavily on patents as the mechanism for protecting the vast investment required in developing a new drug, which, once marketed, can be copied easily and cheaply without any development cost (see 2.4.3 below).

14 Beier, F-K, 'Patent Protection and the Free Market Economy' (1992) 23 IIC 159.

15 McFarland, M, 'Intellectual Property, Information, and the Common Good' (1999) BC Intell Prop & Tech F 060503.

serve the public good,[16] to emphasis on private reward,[17] eroding the 'limiting factors' substantially.[18]

Further balances may be necessary, for not only do intellectual property rights confer monopolistic potential on particular owners, they also enable collaboration between several intellectual property right owners in order to increase the market power available to them. This can be seen in patent licensing pools, for example, or divisions of markets on a regional or international basis and the activities of copyright collective agencies. One motivation for such associations may be to enable individual owners to enforce their rights effectively, but the effect is also one of increased market power. 'Antitrust' measures have been taken both by the US and by the EU to combat such accretions of power (see 1.5 above). The jurisdiction over collective licensing imposed by the Copyright, Designs and Patents Act 1988 and the creation of the Copyright Tribunal (successor to the Performing Rights Tribunal) is another manifestation of the need to answer criticisms of the anti-competitive tendencies conferred by intellectual property rights. At this point it should not be forgotten that competition law in general provides a balance to the market power that can be exerted by intellectual property right owners.

2.1.2   Objections from developing countries

A developing economy depends on acquiring technology and information from the developed world. Intellectual property protection can hinder or prevent such access, or price it at unattainable levels. In addition, developing countries have complained that large multinational enterprises import products (protected by national intellectual property rights) rather than producing them locally, hindering any technology transfer that would be attained by local production. However, the developing country finds itself in an unenviable quandary, for without protection international firms would not market in the developing country at all. In addition, strong intellectual property laws can attract important inward investment from rich multinational enterprises. In addition, as local technology develops, local entrepreneurs themselves become in need of such protective rights.

This dilemma has led to arguments from developing countries that they should receive special treatment when the international Conventions and Treaties are revised. In the past they have suggested compulsory licences for local working, local translation rights, curbs on royalties and scrutiny of licences. However, the developed world's perception of activity in the developing world has been one of large-scale piracy and counterfeiting. This has not disposed the developed world States towards a tolerant stance to the developing economies. The same applied to countries with intellectual property protection, but which had inadequate facilities for, or a lack of disposition towards, enforcement of those rights. The Uruguay Round of GATT talks tackled the issue and the resulting TRIPS Agreement 1994 establishes a required minimum content of intellectual property law for all World Trade Organisation (WTO)

---

16   Both the Statute of Anne 1710 and the Statute of Monopolies 1623 make interesting reading in this context.

17   May, C, 'Why IPRs are a Global Political Issue' [2003] EIPR 1. The Information Society Directive and the US Digital Millennium Copyright Act 1998 illustrate the point.

18   See the criticisms made of the exclusive list of optional exceptions to infringement in the Information Society Directive, for example.

Member States. Concession for the developing countries, along with those 'in the process of transformation from a centrally planned into a market, free enterprise economy' was confined to extra time having been given for implementation.[19]

Subsequently, the old controversies have resurfaced, centring around protection for foreign companies profiting from indigenous raw materials and traditional knowledge as well as the use of folklore in musical and artistic works. Access to vital health care products at affordable prices has also engendered considerable debate. The Doha Agreement 2001 accordingly allows for interpretation of the TRIPS Agreement by Member States in a manner which allows them to provide for public health and to promote access to medicines for all (see 3.8.1 below). This includes granting compulsory licences, deciding what amounts to a national emergency and what constitutes exhaustion of a right.[20] Notably, however, the Doha Agreement also recognises that intellectual property rights play an important role in the development of new medicines.[21] WIPO[22] now provides a forum for debate, having created the Intergovernmental Committee on Genetic Resources, Traditional Knowledge and Folklore in 2000. In the UK the Department for International Development also commissioned a report[23] on intellectual property and development which questions the provision of strong IPR in developing economies.[24]

May[25] suggests that the concessions made in the Doha Agreement have emphasised the social costs involved in exclusive rights in the global politics behind international intellectual property agreements which could lead to further concessions by way of compulsory licensing. While in Doha the presumption is towards the supremacy of private rights unless wholly unacceptable social costs such as the AIDS pandemic exist, in the future there is scope for the presumption to be a need for significant social benefit before private rights prevail in the developing world. Increased awareness of the effects of intellectual property protection in developing countries, which the UK Commission's report is designed to achieve, could assist increasing political pressure from developing countries for international concessions. While Rott[26] questions whether Doha has done any more than reasserting what was in the TRIPS Agreement, he recognises that it may still represent a political success in securing discussion of differing social needs and technical development.

---

19 Articles 65 and 66 of the TRIPS Agreement.

20 The European Commission published a proposal for a Regulation on Compulsory Licensing of Patents Relating to the Manufacture of Pharmaceutical Products for Export to Countries with Public health problems in November 2004, COM (2004) 737.

21 For another view see Heath, C and Weidlich, S, 'Intellectual Property: Suitable for Protecting Traditional Medicine?' [2003] IPQ 67.

22 WIPO Activities and Services, Traditional Knowledge and Cultural Expressions: www.wipo.int/tk/en/index.html.

23 *Integrating Intellectual Property Rights and Development Policy*, Report of the Commission on Intellectual Property Rights, London, September 2002. Stephen Crespi makes trenchant criticism of the Report and the assumptions on which it is founded: 'IPRs under Siege: First Impressions of the Report of the Commission on Intellectual Property Rights' [2003] EIPR 242.

24 Although Crespi provides an acute review of the report in defence of the role of intellectual property rights; Crespi, S, 'IPRs Under Siege: First Impressions of the Report of the Commission on Intellectual Property Rights' [2003] EIPR 242, for a different view, see Burkitt, D, 'Copyrighting Culture – The History and Cultural Specificity of the Western Model of Copyright' [2001] IPQ 146.

25 May, C, 'Why IPRs are a Global Political Issue' [2003] EIPR 1.

26 Rott, P, 'The Doha Declaration – Good News for Public Health?' [2003] IPQ 284.

Nor is the debate confined to the balance of protection and access between the developed and developing world. Recent technological development, particularly in relation to biotechnology and information technology, has also raised considerable debate in the developed world. Van Caenegem[27] challenges the underlying ethos of intellectual property that progress is promoted. He suggests that as the results of progress are often unequally distributed and purchased at the expense of social, environmental and cultural cost, opponents of intellectual property rights may increasingly assert these costs rather than presuming benefits from private protection.

2.2   AN ALTERNATIVE APPROACH: UNFAIR COMPETITION

Adopting a general principle penalising competition in the market place which is unfair could provide an alternative approach to guarding the interests at stake when a new idea is developed. This would have the advantage of avoiding situations deserving of protection falling into the 'gaps' which lie between the specifically defined intellectual property rights. Forms of unfair practice which lie outside the realm of intellectual property, but which are analogous to it, such as slavish imitation of a product for which the patent has expired, would also be prevented. Additionally, many intellectual property rights are granted for creations which are never exploited, suggesting that exclusive rights can be an inefficient means of protection. Only penalising uses which amount to unfair competition would also meet the objection that information is non-rivalrous and should be freely available to concurrent use. Hettinger's[28] criticism of the justifications given for granting property rights over 'intellectual' subject matter concludes that new means of stimulating the production of ideas should be found.

A principle of unfair competition could operate in one of three ways:

(i)   either by obviating the need for intellectual property rights at all;

(ii)   by acting as a failsafe to avoid the *lacunae* between rights;

(iii) or, alternatively, by providing a principle for judicial creation of new relief in specific instances.

That unfair competition is often the harm sought to be remedied will be seen in the case law, even where one of the statutory rights is at issue. Examples include the 'springboard doctrine' related to the action for breach of confidence (see 7.6.4 below), the development of the tort of passing off and the interpretation given to the copyright term 'original' by the courts. In addition, statutory trade mark law has recently introduced the concept of 'dilution' (a form of unfair competition outside traditional trade mark boundaries) to trade mark law. The courts in the UK have, however, been reluctant to develop any general principle of unfair competition.

2.2.1 Unfair competition elsewhere

By contrast, the common law developed a concept of misappropriation of value for the US in *International News Service v Associated Press* (1918). The plaintiff printed news of

---

27   Van Caenegem, W, 'Intellectual Property Law and the Idea of Progress' [2003] IPQ 237.
28   Hettinger, E, 'Justifying Intellectual Property' (1989) 18 Philosophy and Public Affairs 31.

the First World War in newspapers on the East Coast of the US. Its competitors, who had been refused reporting rights by the French Government, used the plaintiff's papers as source material. This it telegraphed to the West Coast in time to report there, in competition with the plaintiff, as a result of the time difference between the east and west coasts of North America. The plaintiff claimed property rights in its news. Pitney J cited the exchange value that news has to the misappropriator, and held that the activities of the defendant were an unauthorised interference with Associated Press's business. The rest of the court restricted itself to more orthodox principles. Holmes J held that there was an implied misrepresentation that the news came from the defendant; Brandeis J insisted that legislation was required to fashion new rights. Subsequently the doctrine has been considerably narrowed in *National Basketball Association v Motorola Inc* (1997), applying it only to 'time-sensitive' data.

In other common law jurisdictions, this reluctance to pre-empt the legislature has prevailed: *Victoria Park Racing and Recreation Grounds Co Ltd v Taylor* (1937); *Moorgate Tobacco v Philip Morris* (1985). It stems, in part, from judicial unwillingness to enter into political and commercial judgments.

In Europe, by contrast, judges have developed wide principles of unfair competition from civil codes. These now govern many unfair business practices, such as comparative advertising, seller's enticements and slavish copying.

2.2.2   Development in the UK

Harmonisation of many aspects of intellectual property law by the EU may lead the UK courts and legislation towards the European approach. It has already done so in the Trade Marks Act 1994 with respect to the remedy against dilution of a trade mark by use on dissimilar goods or services.

It can also be argued that Article 10*bis* of the Paris Convention requires the UK to adopt a principle of unfair competition, which it defines as 'any act of competition contrary to honest practices in industrial or commercial matters.'[29] Article 2 of the TRIPS Agreement 1994 also makes this binding on WTO Member States. However, it should be noted that unfair competition as laid down in the Paris Convention is restricted to acts which mislead customers and does not extend to wider concepts of misappropriation:

  (3)   The following in particular shall be prohibited:
       (i)   All acts of such a nature as to create confusion by any means whatever with the establishment, the goods, or the industrial or commercial activities, of a competitor;
      (ii) false allegations in the course of trade of such a nature as to discredit the establishment, the goods, or the industrial or commercial activities, of a competitor;
     (iii) indications or allegations the use of which in the course of trade is liable to mislead the public as to the nature, the manufacturing process, the characteristics, the suitability for their purpose, or the quantity of the goods.

Nevertheless, it has been claimed that the UK already provides *de facto* protection against unfair competition through the specific intellectual property rights. However,

---

29   Article 10*bis*(2), Paris Convention.

this claim has been made despite the need to expand these rights to accommodate new subject matter over the years (for example, computer programs), provide new remedies (dilution of trade marks), or to create wholly new rights (semi-conductor chips). Lahore[30] suggests that the possible consequence of such expansion and accretion of rights is to blur traditional boundaries of intellectual property and to erode the policy justifications which dictate the specific limits to each right. This is apparent in the Australian case law on passing off. Liability has been extended to misappropriation of a reputation without any misrepresentation having been made, or any commercial activity on the part of the complainant, effectively conferring a monopoly before any merchandising by the plaintiff has taken place: *Hogan v Koala Dundee* (1988).

Professor Michael Pendleton[31] has proposed a new approach which avoids the dangers of unjustifiable monopolies by replacing existing intellectual property law with one 'all embracing law of valuable commercial information', infringed when a rival has unjustly benefited from the labour, skill and effort invested by a claimant. This would appear to replace the specific rights with a wide and subjective economic and commercial discretion, one going further than the discretion already rejected by the common law judges in the UK and Australia. Intellectual property judges do not ignore such issues – Lord Hoffmann quoted Merges and Nelson[32] in *Biogen Inc v Medeva plc* (1997). However, they have considered them within the carefully delineated boundaries of the substantive law, which, in most cases, have been determined by the legislature. Cornish[33] makes trenchant criticism of too carefree an adoption of wide-ranging unfair competition emphasising the potential dangers as such a remedy:

> can all too easily become a weapon by which first entrants on to successful markets can engage in legalistic bullying of those who would subsequently seek to compete with them.

The WIPO Model Law on Protection Against Unfair Competition 1996 does suggest much more extensive protection, however.

A further suggestion is that of Dr Kamperman Sanders.[34] He proposes that the principle of unjust enrichment provides an attractive model for unfair competition law. It has the advantage, he says, of only providing relief where a competitive 'nexus' lies between commercial rivals. This avoids the difficulties of a proprietary approach by only providing a remedy when a rival is unjustly enriched, allowing free competition otherwise. In addition, the restriction is imposed on the method of competition, rather than being based on particular subject matter (which may be overtaken by rapidly developing technology). The unauthorised extraction right introduced by the Database Directive,[35] implemented in the UK by the Copyright and Rights in Database Regulations 1997, moves in this direction. The focus is on the nature of the use being

30 Lahore, J, 'Intellectual Property Rights and Unfair Copying' [1992] EIPR 428.
31 Pendleton, M, 'Intellectual Property, Information Based Society and a New International Economic Order - the Policy Options?' [1985] EIPR 31.
32 Merges and Nelson, 'On the Complex Economics of Patent Scope' (1990) 90 Columbia L Rev 839.
33 Cornish, W, 'Genevan Bootstraps' [1997] EIPR 336.
34 Kamperman Sanders, A, Unfair Competition: A New Approach (London: Intellectual Property Institute, 1996)
35 European Parliament and Council Directive on the Legal Protection of Databases (96/9/EEC).

made of a database, rather than the category of material to be protected (which is not worthy of copyright in its own right). This protection is earned by the substantial investment made in obtaining, verifying, or presenting the contents of the database. What is clear is that the future development of intellectual property law will remain a topic of fascination and interest.

2.3   JUSTIFICATIONS

Several arguments have been made to explain granting exclusive rights. Gathering the evidence to ascertain whether they do in fact achieve the objectives identified has been problematic. It is necessary to look at patents, copyright and trade marks separately, but a few general points can be made first. Both public and private justifications for granting intellectual property rights can be made.

An economy's growth, the creation of employment, social, technical, commercial and cultural progress,[36] all depend, to some extent, on the genesis, and then the exploitation, of new ideas, techniques, products and processes. Protecting the creation and development of ideas lies at the heart of intellectual property. The purpose of doing so is to stimulate and increase the production, development and dissemination of the ideas necessary for progress. This can be achieved by preventing the value of an idea being misappropriated by others. For ideas also differ in nature from material property in that they are more vulnerable to imitation. Intellectual property rights protect the results created when ideas are usefully exploited in products. Without any protection at all ideas are subject to being 'stolen' by competitors as soon as a product becomes publicly available. While such imitation might well be flattering, to lose all (or virtually all) one's market advantage to copyists could render exploitation so fruitless as to be abandoned, depriving the public of the innovation in the first place.

2.3.1   Public justifications

Economists argue that new ideas will be stimulated if:

(a) creators are rewarded for the effort and expenditure of creation;

(b) the investment needed to develop an idea for a commercially viable proposition is protected from unfair competition, including inward investment from other countries. The growth of the German chemical and dyeing industries has been attributed to strong intellectual property protection allowing outside companies the security needed to develop in another jurisdiction. This remains an important incentive for developing countries to adopt suitable intellectual property regimes;

(c) dissemination of the new idea is enhanced if its exploitation does not lay it open to immediate imitation, thus ensuring public access to new knowledge and ideas, whereas, without protection, the natural alternative would be to turn to secrecy and thus deprive the public of the idea.

However, economists differ in their views. While some advocate the need for protection to increase production and are willing to see the rights expand and

---

36   Van Caenegem, W, 'Intellectual Property Law and the Idea of Progress' [2003] IPQ 237.

proliferate, others are more circumspect and, like Drahos, suggest that the rights need to be balanced against other needs[37] and circumscribed accordingly.

2.3.2 Private justification

It has also been argued that creators, whether authors, inventors or designers, have a natural right to the results of their labours. This is founded on Locke's theories, stated in *The Second Treatise on Government*, that everyone has a property right in the labour of his own body and that the appropriation of an unowned object arises out of the application of human labour to that object. To this is added the condition that there must remain objects of similar quality in sufficient quantity to supply others. Hughes[38] concludes that intellectual property can be justified, although only in part, by Locke's theory.

However, this theory rests upon the assumption that no one owns an idea before its appropriation. Michael Pendleton[39] has argued that all ideas lie within the public domain in the sense that they are owned by the public and should not be available for individual appropriation. His view is that all invention can be seen as a (new) combining of known units of information.

Hughes's other justification relies on the personality theory propounded by Hegel. This regards a creation as an extension of its creator's individuality or person, belonging to that creator as part of his or her selfhood. Such a concept can in part be seen in the copyleft movement.

Both theories concentrate on the creator's private interest, when it can also be argued that creators have a social role. Any private justification for intellectual property rights must take into account the public interest in fair access to, and use of, an idea.

2.3.3 The future

No one criticism, nor any one justification can settle the controversy. Nor, with the growing 'technology of imitation',[40] as well as socially and ethically challenging developments in biotechnology, are the arguments likely to abate. As the technological, political and social environment in which intellectual property rights operate changes so too will the arguments continue. Philosophy, economics, social science, politics and morality must all play a part in the debate. If there is any consensus, it lies in the avowed aim of intellectual property rights to stimulate the creation of new 'products'. It is unlikely then, given the degree of global harmonisation achieved by TRIPS, that intellectual property rights will be removed. However, Drahos[41] shows how the

---

37 Such as freedom of expression or competition.
38 Hughes, J, 'The Philosophy of Intellectual Property' (1988) Geo LJ 287.
39 Pendleton, M, 'Intellectual Property, Information Based Society and a New International Economic Order: The Policy Options?' [1985] EIPR 31.
40 Cornish, W, and Llewelyn, D, *Intellectual Property: Patents, Copyright, Trade Marks and Allied Rights* (London: Sweet & Maxwell, 2003) p34. Developments in computing and telecommunications have arguably created a vast copying machine.
41 Drahos, P, 'The Universality of Intellectual Property Rights: Origins and Development': www.wipo.org.

continued negotiation of multilateral treaties[42] after TRIPS has been subject to organised resistance to proposed new or strengthened rights. This is likely to continue from groups as diverse as educational institutions, consumer groups, scientific bodies, library associations, representatives for indigenous peoples, environmental groups, internet service providers and software developers.

Consequently, any practical assessment of the justification for intellectual property rights should lie in measuring their impact. Both recent EU Directives and the Digital Millenium Copyright Act (DMCA) contain provision for regular review of their effects. A further step would be to develop criteria for this process and the factors to be considered. Drahos[43] argues for 'a philosophic attitude of instrumentalism'. This would replace rights in intellectual property with 'privilege-bearing duties' and accommodate the 'negative liberty'[44] of individuals not to be interfered with. Consequently the effects of intellectual property rights in social life and democratic culture need to be empirically determined.[45] At this point, the cost-benefit analyses of the economists can have a role to play in determining these effects. Andersen's extensive analysis[46] also concludes that because intellectual property rights provide a framework in which individuals and organisations interact and in which both commercial and technological directions are shaped,[47] both the justifications and social and economic effects must be addressed at the political level. Currently the empirical social and economic effects have not been widely studied.

However, other values may require consideration[48] before conclusions may be drawn and privilege-bearing duties defined. Drahos has also explored the relationship of intellectual property rights and human rights.[49] Since 1948 the Universal Declaration of Human Rights has recognised the natural right of ownership in both the moral and material interests which an author has in his or her scientific, literary or artistic creations.[50] It also recognises the need for balance. Article 27(1) states:

> Everyone has the right freely to participate in the cultural life of the community, to enjoy the arts and to share in scientific advancement and its benefits.

While a right of property is also recognised,[51] it is generally considered that most forms of property do not constitute a fundamental human right. However, in an age

---

42 Such as the WCT and WPPT. A World Patent Treaty, and World Database Treaty are under consideration.

43 Drahos, P, *A Philosophy of Intellectual Property* (Aldershot: Ashgate, 1996).

44 These negative liberties could equally be represented by positive human rights, and we are now seeing the 'intrusion' of the rights of privacy and freedom of expression into intellectual property law.

45 An example can be seen in the WIPO/UNEP study 'The Role of Intellectual Property in Evolving Benefit-Sharing Frameworks for Genetic and Biological Resources and Associated Knowledge Systems' by Professor Anil Gupta www.wipo.org/tk/en/publications/769e_unep_tk.pdf.

46 Andersen, B, 'The Rationales for Intellectual Property Rights in the Electronic Age', in Jones, D, *New Economy Handbook* (San Diego: Academic Press, 2003).

47 Microsoft providing a good example.

48 The debate over human cloning, potentially subject matter for patenting, being a topical case in point.

49 Drahos, P, 'The Universality of Intellectual Property Rights: Origins and Development': www.wipo.org.

50 Article 27(2) of the Universal Declaration of Human Rights 1948.

51 Article 17(1) of the Universal Declaration of Human Rights 1948.

when information is a capital resource, human rights such as that to freedom of expression also come into play and a conflict with intellectual property rights is immediately apparent. Less conspicuous, but increasingly of concern, is the invasion of personal rights of privacy by methods of preserving technological protection over digital works.[52] Further tensions arise as rights to development and cultural knowledge and biological resources are asserted. Consequently, Drahos calls for dialogue between the intellectual property community and that of human rights. However, with information becoming the fundament of international trade, global markets and national economies, it would seem that this is a dialogue that should extend to the trade and competition communities as well. Only then can the policies needed to adjust intellectual property rights or create new ones be properly developed.

2.4   JUSTIFICATIONS FOR PATENTS

In 1963, Machlup identified four justifications for the grant of patents: the natural law thesis, the reward-by-monopoly thesis, the monopoly-profit thesis, and the exchange-for-secrets thesis. He concluded that neither the empirical evidence nor the theoretical justifications either confirm or refute the theory that the patent system promotes technological progress or economic productivity. It is worth considering each argument in turn.

2.4.1   A natural right

It can be queried why any right should extend to the original idea or object rather than covering only the value added by that labour and skill. In addition, if a natural right can be claimed, it would be expected to be of unlimited duration, analogous to property in land. Nor is any private right of property being recognised for independent inventors of the same invention, or the first to invent, but only the first to file an application for a patent. However, the Employee Inventor Code in the Patents Act 1977 (see 3.5 below) may represent a residual feeling that an inventor has a private right.

2.4.2   Reward by monopoly

Since the Middle Ages and the systems of privileges, such as Royal Charters and the Guild system, inventors have been rewarded for their contribution to the community. However, the motivation has been largely one of securing the community benefit, rather than appreciation for the inventor. Any reward justification can be queried when the patent is granted only to the 'first to file'. Other inventors, such as the first to invent and independent inventors, go unrewarded, at least by a patent. In fact, if reward were the sole objective of the patent, a system more akin to copyright would give a reward like property because copyright has a much longer duration. As we have seen, Pendleton[53] has argued against appropriation and reward. However, his argument ignores the fact that a patent is not available purely for information. It is

---

52 Cornish, W, *Intellectual Property: Omnipresent, Distracting, Irrelevant?* (Oxford: OUP, 2004) 61.
53 Pendleton, M, 'Intellectual Property, Information Based Society and a New International Economic Order – the Policy Options?' [1985] EIPR 31.

only for a new way of putting that information to good use (a patent cannot be given for a discovery, only its application in a product or process). A reward for that effort can be justified.

2.4.3 Monopoly profit incentive

The justification proffered – that the grant of a patent will stimulate innovation by securing investment in both seeking and exploiting new ideas – needs careful consideration. This justification can be examined in two stages: first, by asking whether a patent does stimulate invention; and, secondly, whether it also helps to stimulate innovation by securing the successful exploitation of that invention.

Stimulation of invention?

Australian research[54] suggests that it is the existence of a problem needing to be solved which stimulates invention. If so, a better incentive might be provision of education in the prior art and its problems, rather than a patent, which is expensive and difficult to obtain. An academic inventor may be motivated as much by considerations of publication and recognition as profit. There is also an argument that much would be invented anyway.[55] This may have been accurate in the days when the bulk of invention consisted of improvements to mechanical inventions. However, in some sectors of industry today, such as pharmaceuticals, there is extensive research and development on which millions of pounds are expended. In 1992, the Association for the British Pharmaceutical Industry suggested that the cost of unearthing a major innovative medicine escalated from £50 million in 1985 to £125 million in 1990, increasing to £350 million by 2003 and taking 10 to 12 years to develop.

Many inventors are employed and are motivated by their employment and the problem, rather than the promise of profit or reward. This does not necessarily negate the patent as a stimulus to invention. An employer employs an inventor in order to profit and the stimulus is not diminished by being indirect. The salary an employer is able to pay will reflect the profits secured through patent protection. However, an additional incentive is needed for any additional invention an employee may make, outside the sphere of employment, thus encouraging that employee to disclose the invention. In any case, the Patents Act 1977 Employee Code is aimed at enhancing the reward and incentive factor directly for the employee, although the results have been disappointing to date.

A more effective incentive to invent may lie in a different type of protection, such as the longer duration of copyright or even State support of research.

Stimulation of innovation?

No new idea is of any value until it has been exploited. It is at this stage that an inventor may need the most support in order to find the funding to develop the idea to

---

54 Discussed by MacDonald, S, 'Australia – the Patent System and the Inventor' [1983] EIPR 154.

55 Particularly in the face of the considerable ignorance of the patent system, highlighted in the White Paper, *Intellectual Property and Innovation*, Cmnd 9712, 1986.

the point of commercial viability. If the patent succeeds in securing exploitation, its grant may well be justified. However, many patents are never exploited at all and, therefore, it has been argued that a better system might be to grant protection only when the developed invention reaches the market, and to limit that protection by a monetary, and not a temporal, limit. The complexities of such a suggestion lie:

(a) in quantifying sufficient marketing to qualify for protection;

(b) in the difficulty for a small inventor in reaching the market at all, if funding must be sought without the guarantee of protection for the idea. This leaves the inventor prey to imitation, and the investor prey to losing the investment through imitation;

(c) in that it would frustrate the important informational role of the patent.

Kingston and Kronz have proposed a market-stimulation model, although in slightly varying forms.

Kronz[56] postulates that a patent secures protection for inventions, but does not stimulate innovation, which is governed by independent factors. He states the chief benefit of the patent as being the information which it makes public, but suggests in its stead an 'innovation patent'. This would actively assist in the transfer of technology. He regards the patent as outdated, now that the flow of ideas outstrips the possibility of implementation, which is what leads to patents being granted for unexploited inventions.

Kingston[57] agrees that the existing patent system does not deliver the economic benefits its theory promises, only protecting innovation indirectly. He suggests further adjustments to the patent system to provide effective protection for information and to aid innovation.[58]

One advantage of these suggestions is the requirement for the disclosure of know-how; otherwise, general principles of unfair competition might be seen as an equally viable alternative to the patent. No change now seems likely in the face of Article 27 of the TRIPS Agreement, which sets out the requirement for patent protection. However, the points made by Kingston and Kronz continue to cast doubt upon the effectiveness of the patent to stimulate innovation.

Any incentive effect the patent has is also dependent on factors such as the level of consumer demand, marketing techniques and the availability of alternatives. Such an incentive cannot be achieved by legal means alone. The most telling force in the argument for the patent as an incentive to innovation must be its ability to stimulate a manufacturer to take a risk in exploiting the invention, by assuring at least a head start in the market. It also enables the inventor to negotiate with manufacturers, secure in the knowledge that the idea cannot be appropriated.

Another counter-argument to the stimulus to innovation justification is the long time lag that often lies between the granting of the patent and the exploitation of the invention. This may result from the difficulties of investing in development and the time that takes, together with the cost and organisational difficulties of distribution and often a resistance to the new idea. However, it is the most innovative industries

---

56   Kronz, H, 'Patent Protection for Innovations: a Model' [1983] EIPR 178, 206.
57   Kingston, W, 'Innovation Patents and Warrants', in Phillips, J (ed), *Patents in Perspective*, (London: ESC, 1985); and 'An "Investment Patent"' [1981] EIPR 131, 207.
58   Kingston, W, 'Patent Protection for Modern Technologies' [1997] IPQ 350.

(such as medicines and computer software) that have aggressively sought and used patents. The patent does have a role to play in securing the jump from invention to exploitation. It protects against competition at a very vulnerable stage and provides necessary support for making a risky investment by giving the inventor a saleable commodity. However, the force of this criticism can be seen in the fact that it takes 10 to 12 years from discovering a useful product in the pharmaceuticals field to obtaining the necessary licence to market it.

In order to act as a stimulus, the patent must not be open to avoidance by competitors. Often, the publication of a patent application and/or marketing of the invention may attract competitors' attention. They may be able to 'invent round' the patent (make an equivalent without encroaching on the patent's claims to the point of infringement). Therefore, to be an effective stimulus, the patent granted must not be open to easy challenge and the rights given must be of clear scope. This is only possible if the examination by the Patent Office of the requirements for validity (novelty and inventive step – see Chapter 5) is exhaustive. Then, a competitor cannot easily challenge the patent for validity and, thereby, undermine the advantages of seeking such a right. The need for inventive step has been criticised because it is a difficult and subjective evaluation. It makes a patent easily open to challenge, creating uncertainty about the value of the right which, in turn, devalues its incentive effect.

Whether the patent system has operated as an effective incentive is hard to assess. The 1971 Report on Intellectual and Industrial Property by the Economic Council of Canada suggested that there is no quantifiable benefit compared with systems with no equivalent protection. Machlup[59] suggests the same. That there are other vital factors in providing such stimulation is unarguable – for example, market lead time, marketing skills, demand for the invention and the product's reliability. Market lead time might actually be eroded by the grant of a patent by alerting potential competitors! The European Commission is commissioning an economic study[60] of the effects of patents in the EU market, which may yield more conclusive evidence.

Japan was a developing country after 1945. In 25 years, she became one of the world's major industrial nations and did so by enacting a strong patent law and then vigorously enforcing it. This created a flow of technology into Japan under licence agreements, joint ventures and technology transfer agreements. These had to be paid for in royalties but proved to be of considerable benefit to Japan.[61] Beier[62] provides a further defence of the incentive effect of the patent.

A study undertaken by Dr Raymond in 1996[63] suggests an important role for patents in the UK economy.

When considered in its entirety, the evidence would clearly suggest that research and patent activity have become much more important to (at least some) industries. The industries which are the most patent intensive appear to be those prospering most

59 Machlup, F, *An Economic Review of the Patent System*, 1959, Washington: US Senate Committee on the Judiciary, Subcommittee on Patents, Trademarks and Copyrights, Study No 15.
60 'Brussels: study on evaluating the knowledge economy (what are patents actually worth?) the value of patents for today's economy and society' 2004/S 125–105318.
61 Braun, F, 'The Economic Role of Industrial Property' [1979] EIPR 265.
62 Beier, F-K, 'The Significance of the Patent System for Technical, Economic and Social Progress' (1980) 11 IIC 570, 581.
63 Raymond, C, *The Economic Importance of Patents* (London: IPI, 1996).

in the face of economic changes away from traditional manufacturing and towards the service sector(s).

2.4.4 Exchange for secrets

Application for a patent compels disclosure of the idea to the community at an early stage, before the decision whether to grant one is taken. The patent can be seen as a bargain with the public as represented by the State: protection given in return for information. In addition, the information which results is both technical and commercial information which might otherwise remain secret, protected as confidential information. It is worthy of note that the (then) USSR introduced a system for the dissemination of information, when no patent system existed, because of the importance of access to such information.

The secret of many inventions will be revealed on sale. For others, secrecy does not present a viable form of alternative protection. However, publication 18 months after a patent application is made reveals the information contained within it earlier than it would otherwise reach the public domain. There are approximately 30 million patents in the Patent Office and 80% are not available elsewhere; 85% are freely usable because they have lapsed or expired. Publication also reinforces the incentive to innovate by encouraging other manufacturers to seek licences.

There are criticisms of the patent as the best way to provide information. Difficulties of classification, of language, of duplication and of searching do exist because there is no consistency across the different national systems, nor do many libraries stock Patent Office materials. The patent does not give access to additional know-how which may be vital to the actual use of the invention. Eisenschitz[64] agrees that the patent in its current form does not provide information in the best manner and argues that one granted more quickly would bring information into the public domain more rapidly. Patent specifications do need skilled interpretation. She proposes protecting research and development programmes to encourage early availability of information. However, Oppenheim[65] has pointed out that the patent provides the relevant information more quickly than other sources, such as technical and research literature, and in a greater quantity. It has the added benefit of including commercial as well as technological information.

Historically, the informational role has been the patent's strongest justification, overcoming the free traders' opposition by the 1870s. This was pointed out by Beier and Strauss.[66] Development rides on the supply of information, patent information is self-updating and avoids duplication of effort and economic waste.

2.4.5 Conclusion

On the positive side, the patent can be said to lead to better goods and protection is only temporary. This allows competition, which provides consumer choice, better

---

64 Eisenschitz, T, 'The Value of Patent Information', in Phillips, J (ed), *Patents in Perspective* (London: ESC, 1985).

65 Oppenheim, C, 'Information Aspects of Patents', in Phillips, J (ed), *Patents in Perspective* (London: ESC, 1985).

66 Beier, F-K and Strauss, J, 'The Patent System and its Informational Function – Yesterday and Today' (1977) 8 IIC 38.

standards of living and employment. Set against these advantages must be the dangers of monopolies – higher price margins, maximum profits, a temporary ban on the use of available information, a lack of direct competition and enhanced market power. With cross-licensing and patent pools, this can lead to concentration. However, when balanced by compulsory licences and competition policy, the advantages seem to outweigh the disadvantages.

There appears to be no compelling alternative. Market lead allows the manufacturer to limit production, as competition at much lower costs will quickly follow. Secrecy brings the disadvantage of restrictions on the labour market, as employees are fettered by restrictive covenants from competing against their former employer. State incentives and reward do not appear an effective suggestion because history shows that governments have not been good at encouraging innovation and, in any event, would lag behind demand. Innovation protection either for marketable ideas, or marketed products, would lead to great problems of definition.

2.5 JUSTIFICATIONS FOR COPYRIGHT

Copyright encompasses an enormous economic and cultural field, extending to the raw material of the arts, education, information, entertainment, broadcasting and the media and the design world. Although the copyright right is a relative, rather than an absolute, monopoly, monopolistic behaviour is possible. This is particularly so where a number of works come under one individual's or organisation's control. In both cases monopolistic behaviour is possible because demand is very likely to be large, but volatile, in the fluctuating market in which we live. Any monopoly power is subject to limits, including:

(a) the freedom of independent creators, as opposed to those who copy, to exploit their own ideas;

(b) the fact that protection only extends to the expression of the idea and not the idea itself;

(c) the duration of the right, albeit that it is a long one; and

(d) provision for fair dealing (see 11.2 below), other 'permitted acts' (see 11.1 below) and compulsory licences.

2.5.1 Authors' rights and neighbouring rights

One important distinction should be made in relation to the differing types of work which fall within the copyright umbrella. Works may be divided into two classes: first, the 'authors' rights' – literary, dramatic, musical and artistic works, which fall within the ambit of the Berne Convention; and, secondly, 'neighbouring' or 'related' rights – such as sound recordings and broadcasts, which can be described as the 'carriers' of the authors' rights. The justifications for each class of copyright work differ. In fact, the diversity of copyright works means that no one justification is likely to apply across the board to all works. Moral justifications are appropriate to authors' rights, to protect the creativity of the author. However, economic justifications are more appropriate to the entrepreneurial neighbouring rights. Where moral arguments are applied to neighbouring rights and vice versa, doubts arise.

2.5.2 The origins of UK copyright law

In the UK, the demand for protection came from the publishers (the Stationers) after the development of the printing industry made large scale copying viable. The demand was an economic one, to stimulate and protect investment in publication. The copyist can, of course, compete without a publisher's start up costs and avoids paying the author a royalty. This demand was first expressed in the trade customs of the Stationers, which were given royal support with a Charter and achieved statutory form with the Copyright Act 1709. Further development saw the right extended piecemeal to new forms of work. The difficulties of justifying copyright are illustrated by the Copyright Act 1842. Serjeant Talfourd unsuccessfully sought an extension of the term of copyright from the existing 28 years to the life of the author plus 60 years to reward authors for their creative effort. Opposition based on fears of monopoly, and of restriction on the dissemination of knowledge caused by raised prices, prevented the change. In 1841, TB Macaulay declared copyright a 'tax upon readers for the purpose of giving a bounty to authors'. A compromise of the duration of the author's life plus seven years, or 42 years in total, whichever was the longer, was adopted. Respect for the author's creativity lay behind the European systems of copyright, whereas economic considerations underpinned UK copyright law. The Berne Convention, and harmonisation induced by the EU, have led to a convergence of philosophies, with accompanying adjustments to the scope of the substantive law.

2.5.3 Author and entrepreneur

The fact that both author and entrepreneur are protected in parallel is one factor that has led to conflict between those seeking long-term protection for the author's moral interest in his creation and those fearing the monopoly potential thereby created. Plant[67] points out that it is not necessary to protect the publisher in tandem with the author, whose interests will be different. Where a work proves to have a long lasting popularity, doing so tends to confer a bonus on publishers because they will calculate their returns over a relatively short period. While it is argued that this enables publishers to take risks with other unpopular works, it leaves the choice of work to the publisher. A government subsidy, as a modern form of patronage, originally the support given to authors, might be a better way of securing publication of deserving works. Here, the arguments may differ from those relating to patents (where government subsidies have not been seen to be an attractive alternative), as the publisher is likely to cater to the remarkably low levels of public taste!

Nor is it clear whether the relatively long period of copyright acts as an incentive to the author. While due respect can be given to the desire to acknowledge aesthetic creativity, there is still an argument for separating the protection of author and entrepreneur. Plant's proposal was to reduce the period for publishers and to give authors a statutory royalty thereafter from any publisher choosing to exploit the work. This would secure the benefits of competition, without denying authors their due reward.

---

67   Plant, A, *The New Commerce in Ideas and Intellectual Property* (London: Athlone, 1953).

2.5.4 Justifications

In a seminal article, Breyer[68] identified both moral and economic arguments made for copyright. These bear a strong resemblance to those made for patents:

(a) a natural right to property in one's work, allowing authors to control the use of, and treatment given to, their work;

(b) to reward for investment in creation and publication;

(c) to stimulate creativity which is socially, as well as personally, beneficial;

(d) to disseminate ideas in the public interest.

Copyright works are often expensive to create. However, it is argued, the low cost of copying them (consider a cassette tape recording of popular music, for example) necessitates protection to secure creation. However, it is important not to over-protect, by making protection last for too long, or by limiting the use others may make of the work, because the end result would then have a disincentive effect. Difficult balances must be struck between the private moral and economic interests of authors and the public interest in participating in culture and scientific advancement. This is set out in Article 27 of the Declaration of Human Rights 1948.

Breyer also concludes that one can only be ambivalent on the question of whether the (then) current US copyright law (which he reviewed in 1970) was justified. However, it must be noted that his concern was not with all the different types of copyright work. Breyer points out that a law of copyright is merely one way of securing book revenues which are high enough to secure adequate protection and prices low enough not to interfere with widespread dissemination of the contents. Alternatives lie in contract (as he points out, monks and scholars in the Middle Ages wrote and were paid for their writings without copyright), subsidies and market lead time. In the 19th century, before copyright extended to British authors in the US, American publishers sold British works and paid royalties voluntarily. However, the complaints of Charles Dickens about the activities of American publishers should be set against this and the fact that, in modern conditions, copying is ever easier, cheaper and quicker, eroding any benefits from market lead time. Additionally, demand is volatile, so that the incentive to produce works in the absence of protection is decreased and publishers and others are less inclined to contract for, or subsidise, works of uncertain profit.

Breyer concludes that the case for copyright in books as a whole is weak. Abolition would not produce a large or harmful decline in production. It would benefit readers by producing lower prices, eliminate the need to incur permission costs in copying and increase the circulation of the vast majority of books that would continue to be produced. The work of Landes and Posner[69] reaches different conclusions with respect to US copyright law because of the much reduced cost of making copies today, the greater emphasis on freedom of expression and the decline of alternative institutions for realising the benefits of works. They also point out that without copyright publishers would have no incentive to advertise works before publication (due to the need to enhance any market lead). They add that the emphasis would be on the

---

68   Breyer, S, 'The Uneasy Case for Copyright: a Study of Copyright in Books, Photocopies and Computer Programs' (1970) 84 Harvard L Rev 282.

69   Landes, W, and Posner, R, 'An Economic Analysis of Copyright Law' (1989) 18 JLS 325.

production of works of very short demand in order to realise the gains of being first on the market. A lack of copyright might also, they suggest, cause a growth in private circulation of works to minimise the risks of copying.

For another very different view of the economic importance of copyright, see Cohen Jehoram's study.[70] This compares the results of surveys undertaken in several countries, including the US and the UK. They show that the industries which produce and distribute material protected by copyright law contribute significantly and increasingly to their domestic economies. This presupposes, however, that copyright law has enhanced the activities of those industries by providing appropriate protection. In the UK the Regulatory Impact Assessment[71] of the Copyright and Related Rights Regulations 2003 cite estimates of a 5% contribution to the gross domestic product (GDP) by copyright-based industries, and over 6% if industries with some copyright dependence are included. The European Commission's estimate for the EU-wide copyright market ranges between 5% and 7% of GDP.

2.5.5   Copyright in the future

The chief difficulty in relation to copyright is to achieve the correct balance between providing a stimulus to production by means of protection, and allowing for dissemination of products in order to secure the social benefits of (non-rivalrous) information being distributed. The arguments have become acute in relation to digitally stored works. Both van Den Bergh[72] and Towse[73] express doubts as to the economic efficiency of continued expansion of copyright protection. Van Den Bergh points out that one solution is a 'liability rule' rather than one based in property – assuring creators fair remuneration without denying all public access:

> If online dissemination is to replace current distribution channels such as books, television and radio, all information may become subject to licence restrictions through contractual agreements. In that case intervention may be needed to secure access to information. It cannot be excluded that the copyright law of the next century will be very different from current principles. Copyright law of the 20th century was designed to solve the problem of free-riding in a context in which no contracting was possible. On-line dissemination allows the replacement of copyright law by a contractual regime. Defining the boundaries of freedom to contract to safeguard access to information may become the primary goal of the copyright law of the 21st century.

2.6   TRADE MARKS

Trade mark justifications differ,[74] because a trade mark serves a contrasting function from the other intellectual property rights. A trade mark is a sign which is attached to a commodity, rather than a legal device for stimulating the production of the commodity

---

70   Cohen Jehoram, H, 'Critical Reflections on the Economic Importance of Copyright' (1989) 20 IIC 485.

71   Regulatory Impact Assessment: www.patent.gov.uk.

72   Van Den Bergh, R, 'The Role and Justification of Copyright: A "Law and Economics" Approach' [1998] IPQ 17.

73   Towse, R, 'Assessing the Economic Effects of Copyright and its Reform': www.oiprc.ox.ac.uk.

74   Although Maniatis also regards trade marks as justifiable property rights: Maniatis, S, 'Trade Mark Rights – a Justification Based on Property' [2002] IPQ 121.

in the first place. The purpose of attaching such a sign is to facilitate and enhance marketing of the commodity. It indicates to consumers the source and reputation of the affixer of the mark and provides an important advertising and sales tool. That trade marks are seen commercially as an essential instrument of trade can be inferred from the large numbers that have been registered: in 2002, a total of 17,656 UK applications were granted.

Trade marks are seen as an important part of intellectual property law's role because they operate as an adjunct to the other intellectual property rights. This enables exploitation of products, processes, designs and works. Trade marks also play a role in the traditional function of intellectual property rights as they continue to act as a stimulus to innovation. Marks act cumulatively to other intellectual property protection, continuing the protection necessary for innovation after other intellectual property rights have expired.

Although trade marks confer a monopoly in the mark, they do not prevent competition in a particular type of product. Competitors are free, other intellectual property rights permitting, to market the same product and are only prevented from using the same or a similar mark to identify their products.

The arguments proffered for conferring monopoly rights to a sign can be divided into private and public justifications.

2.6.1 Private justifications

It is claimed that there is a natural right to protect a commercial reputation, although an individual's private reputation is not protected by proprietary rights, but by remedies for defamation. Commercial reputation is, however, an integral part of a business, and a business is 'owned' by its proprietor. In addition, an individual does not always have an identifiable indication of reputation, whereas trade mark rights are only granted to 'signs capable of graphic representation', making proprietary rights appropriate.

2.6.2 Justifications in the public interest

The public justifications are twofold. The trade mark is seen as a form of consumer protection and as an aid to market competition.

Consumer protection

By indicating the source of goods and services, a trade mark enables consumers to choose between competing products. It is assumed that, in a competitive economy, consumers benefit from choice. A mark also enables an element of choice where a full inspection of, or information about, a product is not possible.

Protecting information about the origin of goods or services is also an indirect way of providing information about the quality of those goods or services. It enables buyers to relate to previous experience, to advertising, recommendation and other knowledge of the mark. In other words, a mark forces accountability for the product on the proprietor of the mark. It also provides an incentive to provide that quality to the manufacturer. In developing countries, experience has shown that unmarked goods, although cheaper, are shunned in the face of doubts about standards. The more expensive, but marked goods are sought out.

In effect, the mark operates as a form of consumer protection. However, enforcement is left to the mark owner and consumers have no redress in trade mark law if misled by infringing marks. Some redress lies in consumer protection legislation, however, that is not enforceable by consumers either. This has led to the suggestion from Kamperman Sanders and Maniatis[75] that consumers should be able to participate in their own protection.

An aid to competition

In addition to consumer protection, the mark may encourage competition by allowing competing products to remain identifiable on the market. The mark also facilitates increased competition by enabling mass marketing (such as supermarkets) without loss of identity, thus saving on marketing costs. Both the mark itself and mass marketing save consumers' time. Additionally, marks facilitate the creation of foreign markets. The registration of trade marks, and the law of passing off, also serve to police competition where unfair practices have been adopted by rival traders.

2.6.3 Criticisms of trade mark protection

Because marks can confer enormous market power (consider, for example, the COCA-COLA marks), criticisms have been made. Controls exist within trade mark law itself: no other trader must be unfairly hindered and the Trade Marks Act 1994 allows prior use by another to continue, as well as use of an individual's own name, and by restricting registration of marks that any other trader could legitimately have an interest in using.

Criticisms have focused around the enormous market power and expenditure incurred in advertising centred on marks. Although much advertising might be considered as wasteful, trade marks are not the cause of such advertising, merely its tool; in fact, the trade mark itself facilitates succinct advertising. The same can be said of the often exaggerated claims, and the questionable taste, of some advertising.

Other marketing techniques centred on the use of marks have also given rise to criticism. The practice of brand proliferation (marketing of the same product under a variety of names) is said to deceive the consumer and to inhibit the entry of new competitors into the market. Other undesirable practices (such as reducing the quantity in a container once reputation has been established) which deceive the consumer are subject to laws against false and misleading trade descriptions. Redress through removal of protection for the mark might only compound consumers' confusion.

Landes and Posner[76] consider the arguments that trade marks 'promote monopoly' and 'bamboozle the public', as well as leading to higher prices and sterile competition. They find that this has been, in their view rightly, rejected by economists.

---

75 Kamperman Sanders, A and Maniatis, S, 'A Consumer Trade Mark: Protection Based on Origin and Quality' [1993] EIPR 406.
76 Landes, W and Posner, R, 'The Economics of Trade Mark Law' (1987) 30 J Law and Econ 265.

A study[77] undertaken by Dr D Higgins and Dr T James for the Intellectual Property Institute concludes that 'the level of trade marking activity relative to that gross value added for the 20-year period we have considered undoubtedly points to the importance of trade marks to the UK economy', and that 'there has been a general rise in the level of trade marking activity in the UK economy over the period 1973–92'.

Further Reading

Andersen, B, 'The Rationales for Intellectual Property Rights in the Electronic Age', in Jones, D, *New Economy Handbook* (San Diego: Elsevier Academic Press, 2003)

Beier, F-K, and Strauss, J, 'The Patent System and its Information Function – Yesterday and Today' (1977) 8 IIC 387

Beier, F-K, 'The Significance of the Patent System for Technical, Economic and Social Progress' (1980) 11 IIC 570

Beier, F-K, 'Patent Protection and the Free Market Economy' (1992) 23 IIC 159

Bently, L and Sherman, B, *The Making of Modern Intellectual Property Law: The British Experience, 1790–1911* (Cambridge: CUP, 1999)

Boyle, J, *Shamans, Software, and Spleens*, (Cambridge, Mass: Harvard University Press, 1996)

Braun, F, 'The Economic Role of Industrial Property', [1979] EIPR 265

Breyer, S, 'The Uneasy Case for Copyright: A Study of Copyright in Books, Photocopies and Computer Programs' (1970) 84 Harvard L Rev 282

Burkitt, D, 'Copyrighting Culture – The History and Cultural Specificity of the Western Model of Copyright' [2001] IPQ 146

Cohen Jehoram, H, 'Critical Reflections on the Economic Importance of Copyright' (1989) 20 IIC 485

Cornish, W, *Intellectual Property: Omnipresent, Distracting, Irrelevant?* (Oxford: OUP, 2004)

Drahos, P, *A Philosophy of Intellectual Property* (Aldershot: Ashgate, 1996)

Drahos, P, 'The Universality of Intellectual Property Rights: Origins and Development' WIPO Panel Discussion Paper, 9 November 1998: www.wipo.org/tk/en/activities/ 1998/humanrights/papers/word/drahos.doc

Drahos, P with Braithwaite, J, *Information Feudalism: Who Owns the Knowledge Economy?* (London: Earthscan, 2002)

Eisenschitz, T, 'The Value of Patent Information', in Phillips, J (ed), *Patents in Perspective* (London: ESC, 1985)

Fisher, W, 'Theories of Intellectual Property', in Maurer, S, *New Essays in the Legal and Political Theory of Property* (Cambridge: CUP, 2001)

Hettinger, E, 'Justifying Intellectual Property', (1989) 18 Philosophy and Public Affairs 31

Higgins, DM and James, TJ, *The Economic Importance of Trade Marks in the UK 1973-1992: A Preliminary Investigation* (London: IPI, 1996)

Hughes, J, 'The Philosophy of Intellectual Property' (1988) 77 Georgetown LJ 287

Kamperman Sanders, A, 'Unfair Competition law – Some Economic Considerations', in Sterling, A, (ed), *Intellectual Property and Market Freedom* (London: Sweet & Maxwell, 1997)

Kamperman Sanders, A, and Maniatis, S, 'A Consumer Trade Mark: Protection Based on Origin and Quality' [1993] EIPR 406

---

77   Higgins, DM and James, TJ, *The Economic Importance of Trade Marks in the UK (1973–1992): A Preliminary Investigation* (London: IPI, 1996).

Kingston, W, 'An "Investment Patent"' [1981] EIPR 131

Kingston, W, 'Innovation Patent and Warrants', in Phillips, J (ed), *Patents in Perspective* (London: ESC, 1985)

Kingston, W, 'Patent Protection for Modern Technologies' [1997] IPQ 350

Kronz, H, 'Patent Protection for Innovations: A Model' [1983] EIPR 178

Landes, W, and Posner, R, 'The Economics of Trademark Law' (1987) 30 J Law and Econ 265

Landes, W, and Posner, R, 'An Economic Analysis of Copyright Law' (1989) 18 JLS 325

Landes, W, and Posner, R, *The Economic Structure of Intellectual Property Law* (Cambridge, Mass: Harvard UP, 2003)

MacCormick, N, 'On the Very Idea of Intellectual Property: An Essay according to the Institutionalist Theory of Law' [2002] IPQ 227

Maniatis, S, 'Competition and the Economics of Trade Marks', in Sterling, A, (ed), *Intellectual Property and Market Freedom* (London: Sweet & Maxwell, 1997)

Maniatis, S, 'Trade Mark Rights – A Justification Based on Property' [2002] IPQ 121

Martin, B, 'Against Intellectual Property', Chapter 3, *Information Liberation*, (London: Freedom Press, 1998)

Merges, R, and Nelson, R, 'On the Complex Economics of Patent Scope' (1990) 90 Columbia L Rev 839

Oppenheim, C, 'Information Aspects of Patents', in Phillips, J (ed), *Patents in Perspective* (London: ESC, 1985)

Price, T, *The Economic Importance of Copyright* (London: CLIP, 1993)

Raymond, C, *The Economic Importance of Patents* (London: IPI, 1996)

Schechter, F, 'The Rational Basis of Trademark Protection' (1927) 40 Harvard L Rev 813

Seville, C, 'Talfourd and His Contemporaries: The Making of the Copyright Act 1842', in Firth, A (ed), *The Prehistory and Development of Intellectual Property Systems* (London: Sweet & Maxwell, 1997)

Spector, H, 'An Outline of a Theory Justifying Intellectual and Industrial Property Rights' [1989] EIPR 270

Van Den Bergh, R, 'The Role and Justification of Copyright: A "Law and Economics" Approach' [1998] IPQ 17

Van Caenegem, W, 'Intellectual Property Law and the Idea of Progress' [2003] IPQ 237

CHAPTER 3

THE PATENT

Patents are granted for inventions – applications of an inventor's discovery of a solution to a practical problem, which can be put to practical use. A patent is the strongest intellectual property right. It represents a bargain forged between inventor and the public, through the agency of the State. Patentees are given an absolute right to make, use and exploit their invention for 20 years, but only in return for disclosing and describing it in clear terms. This disclosure is published even before the patent is granted and can be used by others to make further developments from the invention disclosed. Even those who independently conceive the same invention are constrained during the life of a patent. Patents are granted only after examination of an application to a national or regional patent office.

Patents can be considered to be strong rights in two ways. First, they confer extensive market power, particularly in the absence of a substitute. Secondly, the strict examination made of applications should ensure the patent can resist subsequent challenges to its validity. Because of the monopoly power being conferred, strict conditions must be met before a patent can be granted. An invention must fall within the category of inventions which are (potentially) patentable, be new, show an inventive step, be industrially applicable and be disclosed with sufficient clarity. An application is carefully examined for these criteria before the decision to grant a patent is made.

3.1   THE DEVELOPMENT OF PATENTS

The UK has the longest continuous patent tradition. Patents stemmed from the Royal Prerogative whereby the monarch granted traders and their guilds exclusive privileges by Letters Patent.[1] These were open letters, marked with the King's Great Seal, and first granted as much to encourage the introduction of industries new to the UK as to encourage invention. Henry VI is thought to have granted the earliest patent to John of Utynam in 1449. It gave a 20-year monopoly over a method of making stained glass, not previously known in England. Elizabeth I granted around 50 patents, although some requests were refused. Reaction to abuses of the prerogative[2] grew. In *Darcy v Allen* (1602) a monopoly over playing cards was held to be contrary to the common law; and in 1610 James I revoked all previous patents, declaring monopolies to be 'contrary to our laws'. However, exception was made for 'projects of new invention so they be not contrary to the law, nor mischievous to the State'. Thus, the public interest was introduced at an early stage as a limiting factor to grant.

---

1   A policy which became regular in the reign of Elizabeth I.
2   Grants of monopoly power were being used to reward those who had done favours for the Crown, and to raise money, rather than to introduce new industry. Some were even granted to staple products.

3.1.1 Establishing the UK patent system

The first UK patent statute was the Statute of Monopolies 1623,[3] which revoked all other monopolies and privileges. Patents for 'any manner of new manufacture' were allowed as an exceptional case. However, they were not to be granted if they contributed to 'raising of prices of commodities at home, or hurt of trade, or [were] generally inconvenient'. Grant was for 14 years to 'the true and first inventor' of manufactures that at the time of grant others 'shall not use'. Patents were retained in this ban on monopolies as a tool to stimulate innovation, either through importation or domestic invention, by reducing competition.

Subsequently the process of application and registration developed. The Law Officers of the Crown established that a description must be provided of the invention. This became known as a specification.[4] In 1785 Arkwright's patent for the Spinning Mule was revoked after 10 years for lack of an adequate specification. The case of *Nobel's Explosive Company Ltd v Anderson* (1894) established that the claims within a specification limited the extent of protection given by a patent. At the same time the courts developed important principles, and litigation concerning Watt's steam engine in 1796 allowed developments in known machines to be patented – provided a useful application could be shown for them.

The system became increasingly protracted, expensive and bureaucratic, however, and was criticised by Dickens in *A Poor Man's Tale of a Patent*.[5] The Patent Office was set up by the Patent Law Amendment Act 1852. Limited examination, and a requirement for claims in the specification was introduced in 1883,[6] but examination for novelty[7] and grounds for invalidity were established by the Patents Act 1907. Subsequent Acts codified the law but made no significant changes until the requirement of inventive step was added by the Patents Act (PA) 1977. This remains the foundation of UK patent law today and effected a number of revolutionary changes in the law, following international developments.

3.1.2 International developments

The patent was employed, in part, to attract the introduction of foreign industry into Britain. Consequently, applications from foreign nationals were allowed. In addition, in 1883 compulsory licensing provisions were introduced to secure the benefit of foreign patents. The Paris Industrial Property Convention (PIPC) 1883[8] was designed to facilitate easier access to national systems and guaranteed nationals of Member States the same treatment as nationals of the State in which a patent was sought. It also introduced the system of priority for applications begun in one Member State.

---

3   Statute of Monopolies 1623, 21 Jac 1, c3.
4   Puckle's 1718 patent for a machine gun was one of the first to be required to provide a 'specification'.
5   www.classicbookshelf.com.
6   Patents, Designs and Trade Marks Act 1883.
7   After the Fry Committee established that 40% of patents were granted for inventions already described in specifications. The examination was confined to searching UK specifications in the previous 50 years. Examination for novelty began in 1836 in the US.
8   Revised in 1900, 1911, 1925, 1934, 1958 and 1967 (Stockholm).

The Patent Co-operation Treaty (PCT) 1970[9] made further progress towards streamlining patenting procedures, and diminished the considerable duplication of effort and expense of making multiple national applications (with their attendant examination of the prior art). It makes no provision for harmonisation of substantive patent law, but allows one application to be filed for all States in which protection is desired. It is administered by WIPO in Geneva. The application is checked for formal requirements and published 18 months after filing. An international search is done by one of the designated international search authorities.[10] Thereafter, applicants designate those States where they desire a patent, and the application is remitted to these national offices. National examiners determine grant on national criteria. A second Chapter of the PCT also allows for an International Preliminary Examination, which is of use to Member States that do not have an examining infrastructure. The PCT therefore allows applicants to initiate the process of obtaining international protection with one application, and to delay their final decision as to which countries in which to proceed for up to 30 months after the filing date, along with the fees and translation costs entailed. However, it does not give international protection; only a portfolio of national patents. Reforms[11] which came into force on 1 January 2004 have simplified and streamlined the process.

3.1.3 The European patent

The European[12] Patent Convention (EPC) 1973[13] advanced the concept of a single application leading to extended protection in a European Patent, and established the regional European Patent Office[14] (EPO). However, it also harmonised substantive criteria relating to patentability and validity. Both searches and grant are determined centrally in the EPO. The patent may then be opposed centrally in the EPO within nine months of grant. However, once granted, the European patent effectively becomes a bundle of national patents, enforced domestically in Member States. Further challenges to validity, and infringement proceedings, must be undertaken in national courts. EPO proceedings were much criticised for being very slow.

The EPC was revised in 2000, although some unresolved issues remain. Substantive changes relate to the method of construing specifications by adopting a doctrine of 'equivalents', and the 'morality' and medical treatment exceptions to patentability. However, changes relating to the patentability of software, and biotechnological inventions, were delayed. Procedural changes aimed at streamlining the grant process were made, and measures adopted to enable the EPC to follow EU

---

9   It came into force in 1978.

10 Primarily, the US, Australian, Russian, Japanese or European Patent Offices.

11 Implemented by the Regulatory Reform (Patents) Order 2004, SI 2357/2004 and the Patents (Amendment) Rules 2004, SI 2358/2004, which came into force on 1 January 2005.

12 The EPC is not coextensive with the EU, nor part of it.

13 It came into force on 1 June 1978. Membership currently comprises Austria, Belgium, Bulgaria, Cyprus, the Czech Republic, Denmark, Estonia, Finland, France, Germany, Greece, Hungary, Ireland, Italy, Latvia, Lithuania, Liechtenstein, Luxembourg, Monaco, the Netherlands, Poland, Portugal, Romania, the Slovak Republic, Slovenia, Spain, Sweden, Switzerland, Turkey and the UK.

14 The EPO is in Munich. It comprises an Examining Division, Technical and Legal Boards of Appeal, and an Enlarged Board of Appeal. It operates in three official languages, English, German and French.

changes. The Act requires ratification[15] and is not yet in force. In the UK the Patents Act 2004 includes provisions to allow ratification.

Although the EPC is entirely separate from the EU, there is considerable overlap in the membership of both institutions, and a number of EU directives have been addressed to patents, including the Biotechnology Directive[16] and the proposed Computer-implemented Inventions Directive.[17] The former raised the question of resolving any conflict in national courts between EU measures and the EPC. However, the Administrative Council of the EPC adopted the Biotechnology Directive into the EPC Implementing Regulations, and provided that the Directive should be used as an aid to interpreting the EPC.

3.1.4 A Community patent

As yet, there is no unitary patent either on a regional or international basis. The Community Patent Convention (CPC) 1975 did propose a single Community Patent but it was not ratified by sufficient Member States to come into force. Both the question of operative languages and the proposed system of litigation proved insurmountable stumbling blocks. Any duplication in the number of translations of the patent documents served to undermine any advantages in savings in administrative burdens and costs. The Convention was revised in 1989 but suffered a similar fate.

Considerable differences exist between the cost of obtaining a European and an American or Japanese patent, and one major factor is the cost of translation. Another disadvantage lies in the burden and expense of litigating in separate national jurisdictions to enforce the patent. These factors have been considered to put European innovation at a disadvantage. In 2000 the European Commission revived proposals for a Community Patent.[18] Implementation is to be by way of Regulation, replacing the CPC, which would have direct effect within Member States. Subsequent progress of the proposal has been fraught with dispute over languages and jurisdiction of the proposed Community Patent Court and no agreement has been reached.[19]

3.1.5 Further developments

The TRIPS Agreement 1994 introduced a measure of harmonisation of substantive rules and enforcement procedures on a wider, global basis. Largely based on the EPC, it had little impact on UK law, other than imposing limits on compulsory licences. It provides for patentable subject matter, disclosure, the patent term and the scope of rights acquired. The agreement is currently being reviewed.

---

15 Article 6 of the EPC Revision Act provides that it will come into force three months after ratification by all Member States, or two years after ratification by the 15th member.

16 Directive 98/44/EC of the European Parliament and Council on the Legal Protection of Biotechnological Inventions, [1998] OJ L213/13.

17 Directive of the European Parliament and Council on the Patentability of Computer-implemented Inventions, COM (2002) 92 final, 2002/0047 (COD).

18 Proposal for a Council Regulation on a Community Patent, COM (2000) 412 final, 2000/0177 (CNS).

19 Progress of the proposal can be followed at http://europa.eu.int/comm/internal_market/en/indprop/patent.

WIPO initiatives are also advancing world harmonisation and international protection, both in relation to procedure and substantive provisions. The World Patent Law Treaty[20] (PLT) 2000 standardised procedure worldwide.[21] It streamlines and harmonises formal requirements in patent offices for filing applications, maintenance of patents, and other requirements. It should reduce the cost of patenting as national offices share results of searches and examination. Electronic filing of applications is proposed.[22] Further substantive harmonisation in another Treaty is under discussion, although national differences towards periods of grace, and grant to the first-to-file or first-to-invent have proved to be stumbling blocks. A world patent has been mooted, but is some way off.

Developing countries have increasingly voiced concerns both over the preservation and use of their traditional knowledge and natural resources by multinational concerns. Environmental concerns are also having an impact on patent practice and law. The neem tree, for instance, indigenous to India, and traditionally long used to produce medicinal products, insecticides and contraceptives, has nevertheless been the subject of more than 70 Western and Japanese patents.[23] Patents also cover maize, potato, rice, wheat, sorghum, cassava, millet, soybean, tea, coffee, cotton, pepper, cauliflower, turmeric, peas, melons and cabbages.

The Rio Convention on Biological Diversity[24] represents a change of approach. Its objectives are the conservation of biological diversity, the sustainable use of its components and the fair and equitable sharing of the benefits arising from use of genetic resources. It may increasingly affect the development of patent law. In 2000 the EPO revoked a patent[25] held by an American multinational company, WR Grace Corp, and the US Department of Agriculture on a method of producing oil from neem tree seeds for an anti-fungal product after it was shown to be invalid. The process of revocation is expensive and slow, however. Negotiations for the reform of the TRIPS Agreement propose at least a sharing of benefits for countries of origin of patented life forms, although prospects for agreement may be slim.

3.1.6 Second-tier protection

Many European States provide further intellectual property rights for inventions which do not reach the rigorous criteria for patents, but are nevertheless worthy of protection, known variously as utility models, petty patents, or registered inventions. There is no direct UK equivalent requiring registration.[26] In 1997 the EU Commission proposed harmonisation of these regimes[27] and, if eventually adopted, a new right

---

20 Adopted 1 June 2000. It will come into force when ratified by 10 States: www.wipo.int.
21 The Regulatory Reform (Patents) Order 2004 (SI 2357/2004) and the Patents Act 2004 make the necessary changes to the PA 1977.
22 Phillips Electronics became the first company to file a PCT application electronically on 25 August 2003: www.wipo.int.
23 Dubbed by some as 'biopiracy'.
24 Convention on Biological Diversity 1992, which has 188 parties, signed by 168. It was ratified by the UK in June 1994.
25 EP number 436257.
26 Although unregistered design protection provides an alternative.
27 Proposal for a European Parliament and Council Directive Approximating the Legal Arrangements for the Protection of Inventions by Utility Model, 1997. The proposal was amended in 1999, COM (1999) 309 final/2, 97/0356 (COD).

will be required in the UK. The original proposal recommended a 10-year term for products and process, but excluded biological, chemical, or pharmaceutical inventions and computer programs. Examination on application would be restricted to formalities. The proposal included a Community Utility Model. Consultations on this have not yielded a favourable response.[28]

3.2   PATENT TERMINOLOGY

Patent law has a terminology of its own. The following is a brief guide to terms of art, which will appear at various points in the text. Early explanation may make what follows more understandable.

(a) Novel, novelty – an invention must be new to be patentable. Determining whether this is the case involves comparing the invention as it is claimed in the patent application with the state of the art (see (d), below). If the invention is new, it is said to be novel; 'novelty' is used to indicate reference to an invention's 'newness'. An invention that has been revealed in the prior art and so is not new, is said to have been 'anticipated'.

(b) Obvious, obviousness, non-obvious – an invention must also show inventive step. If it does not, it is said to be 'obvious'; if it does, it is 'non-obvious'. Determining the presence of inventive step requires comparing the invention claimed with the state of the art in order to decide whether the advance made by the inventor was an obvious one or was inventive.

(c) Hypothetical technician skilled in the art – to make the comparisons required for novelty and non-obviousness, the prior art is interpreted through the eyes of a hypothetical person, someone acquainted with the technology concerned, and skilled to a moderate, but not inventive, level. The same individual is brought into play to test whether the documents revealing the invention for publication are sufficiently clear. Confusingly, the technician appears to have reached different levels of expertise, depending on whether the enquiry relates to novelty, non-obviousness or disclosure.

(d) Art, state of the art, prior art – the area of technology into which an invention falls is known as the 'art'. The 'state of the art' is what is known about that area at any given point in time. 'Prior art' is the art known at or before the date at which the art and the invention are being compared.

(e) Specification – this is a vital component of a patent application in which the invention is described and defined. It is the source of all the information about the invention that reaches the public domain as a condition of awarding a patent.

(f) Description, drawings, claim(s) – these are all constituents of the specification. The claims are also vital, because they determine the boundaries of protection given to an invention.

(g) Sufficiency of disclosure – inventions are protected, in part at least, in order to secure public dissemination of information about them. The function of the

---

28   *Summary Report of replies to the Questionnaire on the Impact of the Community Utility Model with a View to Updating the Green Paper on the Protection by the Utility Model in the Internal Market,* (SEC (2001) 1307), 1 March 2002.

patent would be frustrated if the quality of information provided was insufficiently clear for the invention to be performed by those with ordinary technical skills and knowledge of the state of the art. The disclosure made by the specification and claims is said to be insufficient if it does not meet the standard laid down – capable of being understood and performed by a hypothetical technician.

3.3   PATENTS ACT 1977

The PA 1977 governs UK patent law. However, domestic law cannot be regarded in isolation. Membership of the European Patent Convention (EPC) dictates much of the substantive law, as does the TRIPS Agreement. The UK's membership of the EPC requires that domestic courts give heed to decisions of the EPO and its Boards of Appeal. Regard will also have to be paid to decisions of the community court that will be established to adjudicate on issues relating to community patents, if the Community Patent is adopted.

The PA 1977 made considerable changes to domestic patent law and came into force on 1 June 1978. Worldwide novelty was introduced for the first time, requiring an invention to be compared with all previous technical knowledge to be found anywhere in the world. Examination for inventive step, a sufficient advance beyond previous development, was introduced. New definitions of patentability were adopted, in the process abandoning the definition of invention as 'any manner of new manufacture' which had been at the base of patent law since the Statute of Monopolies 1624. A system of revocation after grant replaced the pre-grant system of opposition to the grant of a patent and strong examination before grant by the Patent Office was introduced. Another innovation was the creation of the Patents Court in the High Court, with two specialist judges. The Copyright, Designs and Patents Act (CDPA) 1988 added a Patents County Court.

There were three main reasons for radical change. The recommendations of the Banks Committee (1970) relating to domestic law required implementation. So did government proposals concerning inventions made by employed inventors. However, the main impetus lay in the need to ratify international obligations under the EPC, CPC and PCT.

The EPC Act 2000 required revision of the PA 1977. Other reforms have also been suggested. The Patents Act 2004[29] passed after Patent Office consultation[30] makes changes which will be discussed within in their context in the succeeding chapters.

3.3.1 Provision for Convention conformity

The PA 1977 ties interpretation of domestic law to decisions taken elsewhere and this is reflected in two important provisions. Section 130(7) of the PA 1977 lays down that key sections of the Act (relating to patentability of inventions, disclosure, infringement, revocation and validity) 'are so framed as to have, as nearly as practicable, the same

---

29 Which received royal assent on 22 July 29.
30 Lambert, J, 'The Proposed Patents Act 1977 (Amendment) Bill' [2003] EIPR 556.

effects in the UK as the corresponding provisions' of the EPC, CPC[31] and PCT have in the territories to which they apply. Different techniques of drafting are employed on the Continent. There, legislation is composed of statements of general principle, and processes of interpretation in the courts of other Member States vary, because their reasoning is inductive rather than deductive. This requires UK judges to marry familiar with unfamiliar techniques when applying the PA 1977. The Conventions' language has not been directly incorporated into the PA 1977, adding to judicial headaches. Section 91 of the PA 1977 does allow for judicial notice of the Conventions, bulletins, journals, gazettes and decisions by Convention courts.

The courts therefore use *travaux préparatoires* (documents used in the production of the final text) and the Conventions as an aid to interpretation. In *Smith Kline and French Laboratories v Harbottle* (1980), convention terminology, 'stocking', prevailed (see 6.2.1 below). The judges are alive to the need for a common approach and to the dangers of different conclusions being reached in relation to patents for the same invention in different jurisdictions. In *B and R Relays' Application* (1985), Whitford J said:

> ... it is of the greatest importance ... we should take note of the decisions of the EPO and that ... an attempt should be made to give the same meaning to relevant provisions, whichever jurisdiction is being invoked.

National intellectual property judges meet biennially to exchange views and consider common problems. Nevertheless, in two recent House of Lords judgments relating to patents, the House has paid lip service to judicial comity, but has not felt bound to follow the European approach. In both *Merrell Dow v HN Norton* (1996) and *Biogen Inc v Medeva* (1997), the patent was revoked in the UK, but not by the EPO. Concern at the divergence of national decisions, among other things, led to proposals[32] that a common court be introduced for the EPC, while Jacob J suggested[33] that the EPO Board of Appeal be staffed by national judges.

3.4 APPLICATION FOR A PATENT

Familiarity with the procedures and documents involved in a patent application aids an understanding of substantive patent law. Important dates for the purposes of the comparisons dictated by the need for novelty and inventive step are secured during the process to grant. The documents so important to considerations of infringement are also products of the application process.

The process of applying for patent protection for an invention is lengthy and complex, involving a number of choices. It is usual to engage a patent agent for expert assistance, particularly with the drafting of specification and claims. Anyone may act as an agent, but only those who register may describe themselves as patent attorneys or patent agents: s 276 of the CDPA 1988. Purely domestic protection is likely to be insufficient for inventors in an era of global markets. Accordingly, a potential patentee

---

31 Reference to the redundant CPC was removed by the Patents Act 2004. The effect of the CPC is confined to the interpretation of those provisions of the PA 1977 which correspond to the CPC by virtue of s 130(7) of the PA 1977.

32 By Judge Willens of The Netherlands 'The EPC: The Emperor's Phantom Clothes?' [1998] IPQ 1.

33 Jacob, R, 'The Enlarged Board of Appeal of the EPO: A Proposal' [1997] EIPR 5.

must decide where protection is to be sought and which 'route' is to be followed to secure patents in the jurisdictions opted for.

3.4.1 Routes to grant

There is no one international patent, nor is the unified Community Patent yet in place, so that the patents which are sought are necessarily national ones (even the European patent, once granted, comprises a bundle of national patents). However, both the EPC and PCT have simplified the processes of application where multiple patents are required. There are three alternatives. First, application may be made to individual national patent offices if an inventor so wishes.

Secondly, a harmonised European route may be adopted through the EPO for applications for a European patent. The EPC provides for one application to be made to the EPO, designating the States in which protection is desired. The process of application and the decision as to grant are centralised within the EPO; a European patent is granted if the application is successful. However, once the process of grant has been completed, for the purposes of infringement, transfer and revocation, the European patent is treated as though it were a bundle of domestic patents from the States designated. The process is, then, an alternative to a series of domestic applications in those States. The decision whether to grant is taken centrally for all jurisdictions, whereas individual domestic applications might succeed in some States and fail in others. The one significant difference lies in the availability of attack by opposition for nine months after grant for a European patent (see 6.4.3 below). By contrast, a Community Patent would, if introduced, be granted, transferred or revoked for the whole of the EU at once.

Thirdly, the final option is international in scope. The PCT established a centralised system of application for its Member States. Initial searches are centralised, before the transferral of the applications and search results to designated national patent offices. The result is also a bundle of national patents, with the decision to grant being taken in national offices. The advantage lies in the reduction in search fees and translation costs. The PCT is administered by WIPO in Geneva.

Both EPC and PCT applications can be made through the UK Patent Office. Where the applicant is a British resident, this must be the case in order to allow a 'security check' to be made before the application is transmitted to the EPO or WIPO.[34]

3.4.2 Priority

Article 4 of the PIPC establishes a system of priority. The date at which a patent application is made has considerable significance. It is from this date that the eventual duration of the patent is measured. More importantly, it is the point from which an application is examined for novelty and inventive step. To establish whether an invention satisfies the requisite conditions (that it is new and has inventive step), it is compared to the prior art. This comparison is made at the date of application. Therefore, having as early an application date as is feasible will aid the application's success, by avoiding the danger of a rival simultaneously discovering and applying for the same invention. However, an applicant also has a reason for delaying the

---

34 Section 23 of the PA 1977.

application as long as possible, and is therefore pulled in two directions at once. If the invention is described in the specification, and the claims drafted, before its full ramifications have been understood and its commercial potential assessed, the danger is that the claims will be too narrow. This makes it too easy for a competitor to 'invent round' the patent eventually granted, by finding another, unclaimed, way to achieve the same effect. The applicant may also want time to decide which markets to enter, and so to defer decisions as to where patents are needed for as long as possible, avoiding the expense of superfluous multiple applications.

The priority system provides a compromise. It gives an applicant a period of grace in which to make such decisions about multiple applications without losing the all-important early filing date. This is achieved by giving the filing date of the first application in any one signatory State to subsequent applications made elsewhere within the period of priority, provided that they are in conformity with national requirements for applications. Without provision for priority the first application would anticipate the later ones by becoming part of the state of the art.

The period of priority laid down for patents is 12 months. It is embodied in s 5 of the PA 1977. The PA 1977 also allows an applicant to initiate an application without submitting the full documentation required, in order to secure a priority date, provided the application is completed within 12 months.[35]

3.4.3 Priority and enabling disclosures

Because the time lapse allowed by the priority system enables further investigation, and a fuller appreciation of, the invention, the final application may contain a fuller description of the invention and include new information. This has raised the question whether it should be able to claim the priority date derived from the earlier one. It was raised in the House of Lords in *Asahi Kasei Kogyo KK's Application* (1991).

The invention claimed was a protein (human tissue necrosis factor (HTNF)) produced by techniques of genetic engineering. The patent was granted. However, its novelty was challenged because a European patent revealed the same protein. This European patent had a filing date later than Asahi's. Therefore, it could not destroy the necessary novelty of Asahi's invention unless it could claim the earlier priority date of a Japanese application. There was no issue as to the system of priority. The issue was whether the Japanese priority date could be applied to the European patent. The Japanese application only revealed the genetic structure of HTNF, without showing how it could be made. The issue therefore was how much information must be contained in the priority application in order to 'support'[36] a later filing. There were two conflicting lines of authority. The House of Lords held that the priority document must be an 'enabling disclosure' in order to confer the priority date on the later application.

The concept of an enabling disclosure is one that occurs at three stages of patent law – priority, novelty and disclosure – and will be elaborated further below at 5.1.3. The Japanese application was not an enabling one because it did not reveal a method of making HTNF. Nor could the method be discovered in the prior art by a hypothetical technician skilled in the art. Therefore, the European patent had a date

---

35   *Ibid*, s 5.
36   As required by s 5 of the PA 1977.

later than Asahi's. It could not be used for the purpose of determining whether Asahi's invention was new. The validity of the invention was upheld.

The House of Lords read s 5 of the PA 1977 in conjunction with s 14 of the PA 1977. Section 5 of the PA 1977 provides that an application may claim the priority date of an earlier application if it is 'supported by matter disclosed in the earlier relevant application'. The Act does not define the word 'support', but it is included in s 14 of the PA 1977. This section sets out the contents of an application and lays down how clear the description of the invention must be. The claims must be 'supported' by the description. The specification, of which the claims and description form part, must 'disclose the invention in a manner which is clear enough and complete enough for the invention to be performed by a person skilled in the art' (a hypothetical technician). Accordingly, the House of Lords held that the earlier application must enable the technician to make the invention.

This is not a necessary reading of the statute and it is one that frustrates part of the purpose of the system of priority. The ability to make the invention from the specification and the fact that the description must support the claims are two separate conditions. The specification must enable the invention to be made, in order to achieve the information function of the patent. The claims, only part of the composite that is the specification, serve a different purpose. They define the exact limits of the monopoly granted to the patentee and must not, of course, include more than the inventor has realised. However, if the specification's purpose can be achieved by completed application, it is not necessary to require fulfilment of that purpose at the stage of early application. However, the House of Lords upheld its interpretation of s 5 of the PA 1977 in *Biogen v Medeva* (1997).

3.4.4 Application for a UK patent

This is a process involving five steps: application; publication; preliminary examination; substantive examination; and grant. Applicants may withdraw at any stage and fees are paid at each stage, so that withdrawal does not incur loss of fees.

Application

Any national of a signatory of the PIPC, or anyone, in the case of the PA 1977 and the EPC, may apply for a patent. Joint applications may be made.[37] *Prima facie*, grant is to the inventor and it is presumed that the applicant is the inventor.[38] If the patent is granted to another, the inventor has a right to be named in any published application and in the patent.[39] If an application is made by the wrong recipient, this may be challenged either before or after grant.[40] Applications may be amended during their progress through the Patent Office.[41]

A full application requires a request for grant of a patent, a specification which includes a description of the invention, any drawings and claims and an abstract of the

---

37 Section 10 of the PA 1977.
38 *Ibid*, s 7.
39 *Ibid*, s 13.
40 *Ibid*, ss 8, 37.
41 *Ibid*, s 19.

invention.[42] The appropriate fees must be paid (current fees, recently reduced to help small businesses, can be found on the Patent Office's website). Initially, only the request and a description need to be filed (and also one claim if the application is through the PCT route), provided that the full requirements are met within the priority period of 12 months.

Publication

Once the completed application has been filed, it is published, usually about 18 months from the first filing.[43] This does not prejudice the applicant. Though the information is now available to all and before any patent has been granted, if the application is successful, the patent will be dated from the filing/priority date. Any infringements that take place in the interval between publication and grant may be sued for, although not until the patent has been granted.[44]

Preliminary examination

This is an examination to ensure that all the requisite formalities have been complied with and included a limited search of the written prior art.[45]

Substantive examination and search

It is at this stage that the application is subjected to examination for patentability, novelty, inventive step and sufficiency of disclosure,[46] the Patent Office reports the result of its searches to the applicant, who may amend the application in response. Outsiders may make observations.[47] This stage must be completed within four and a half years of the filing date.[48]

Grant

If the application satisfies the searches, the patent will be granted. The applicant is notified, a certificate is issued and publication of the decision is made.[49] The patent takes effect from the date of this publication, but is backdated to the filing date, and continues in force for 20 years.[50] The initial grant is for four years and the patent must be renewed annually from the fifth year, on an ascending scale of fees. Those patents which are not renewed lapse. The patent term may be extended for patented pharmaceuticals by a Supplementary Protection Certificate (SPC). Pharmaceuticals must undergo extensive testing by government bodies before being released onto the

42 *Ibid*, s 14.
43 *Ibid*, s 16.
44 *Ibid*, s 25.
45 *Ibid*, s 17.
46 *Ibid*, s 18.
47 *Ibid*, s 21.
48 *Ibid*, s 20.
49 *Ibid*, ss 18(4), 24.
50 *Ibid*, s 25.

market and this testing takes place during the patent term. Consequently, the EU[51] introduced SPCs to compensate patentees prejudiced by approval processes. The length of a SPC is dependent on the interval between patent filing date and the receipt of authorisation.

Re-examination

By inserting s 74A into the PA 1977, the Patents Act 2004 allows for re-examination of the validity of a patent in the Patent Office after its grant at the request of any party. This is based on a new case being made – such as the emergence of a new piece of prior art. This procedure would allow examination of validity without resort to litigation either before the Comptroller of Patents or in the courts. The decision is non-binding in order to achieve a rapid and relatively inexpensive assessment of validity. It should encourage settlement of claims and reduce litigation but would not result in revocation of the patent.

3.4.5 Specification and claims

It is important to understand the structure of a specification. This is not just for the purposes of applying for a patent, but also because both the specification and its constituents play an important role in issues of infringement and validity.

The specification

Every patent application must have 'a specification containing a description of the invention, a claim or claims and any drawing referred to in the description or any claim'.[52] In addition, the specification must 'disclose the invention in a manner which is clear enough and complete enough for the invention to be performed by a person skilled in the art'.[53] If the disclosure is not clear and complete enough, this is a ground for revoking the patent, as well as a reason for refusing to grant.

The claims

The claims do precisely what their name suggests. They define the inventions that patentees claim to be exclusively their own.[54] They are required to be clear and concise and supported by the description.[55] There are three types of invention which clearly may be claimed – products, processes and products obtained by a particular process. The PA 1977 provides no definition of the nature of an invention. However, s 60 of the PA 1977 implies three types of invention by providing this threefold categorisation of

---

51   Council Regulation (EEC) 1768/2 Concerning the Creation of a Supplementary Protection Certificate for Medicinal Products, [1992] OJ L182/1. Regulation (EC) 1610/96 of the European Parliament and Council Concerning the Creation of a Supplementary Protection Certificate for Plant Protection Products, [1996] OJ L198/30.

52   Section 14(2)(b) of the PA 1977.

53   *Ibid*, s 14(3).

54   *Ibid*, s 14(5)(a).

55   *Ibid*, s 14(5)(b)(c).

infringing acts: where the invention is a product; or where it is a process; or, where the invention is a process, a product has been directly obtained by means of that process. The EPO has indicated a willingness to accept other types of claim (see 4.10.6 below).

The type of invention claimed is significant because the scope of protection varies. A product patent monopolises the product or substance for any purpose and any manner of using it. This is a broad monopoly. A process or method patent, by contrast, is a narrow monopoly because it is only that process or manner of use that is protected. Where a product or substance is already within the state of art, however, a process claim used to allow some protection for a mode of using it. A product by process claim monopolised the product only when obtained by using the specified process. However, in *Kirin Amgen Inc v Hoechst Marion Roussel Ltd* (2004), the House of Lords held that such a claim would be anticipated if the product were already known (see 5.1.5 below).

Drafting patent claims presents a patentee with a dilemma. In order to avoid encroaching on the prior art (and succumbing to a lack of novelty), the aim is to draft the claims as narrowly as possible. However, to achieve the maximum protection from the patent, the aim is to draft the claims as widely as possible. It is therefore a specialised process best left to a patent agent.

3.5 OWNERSHIP OF THE PATENT

The PA 1977 confers the right to ownership of a patent on the inventor or co-inventor. However, if an invention is made during the course of employment, the employer has the right to the patent. In addition, if foreign law applies, some other person may be entitled to the patent.[56] Once a patent has been granted, it may be transferred to another owner by assignment, bankruptcy or bequest.

3.5.1 Employee inventions

In practice, a high proportion of inventions are made by employees (more than 80%). The stimulus of patent reward may well be no less effective where it operates indirectly, through an employer. It will be in an employer's interests to institute research, provide the necessary facilities and resources and exploit the results, motivating and rewarding employees through the provision of a problem, the means of finding a solution and appropriate remuneration. However, it can be argued that an even more direct incentive, which links employees' rewards to the profits made by the patented inventions themselves, might be even more productive. Employees may also invent outside the sphere of their employment. It may be asked whether the patent system acts as an incentive to employees to disclose those inventions. The issue becomes one of determining the most appropriate proprietor of the patent.

After 1955, the common law took a harsh view of ownership of patents emanating from inventions made by employees. In *Patchett v Sterling* (1955), the House of Lords decided that contracts of employment contained an implied term that an employee's invention was held on trust for the employer, who could decide whether to seek a

---

56 *Ibid*, s 7.

patent. This implication could be replaced by clear agreement, however. The employee concerned headed his employer's development and design department. However, in *Worthington Pumping Engine Co v Moore* (1903), an employee not employed to invent found himself similarly fettered. This was seen as a disincentive to employees inventing outside their sphere of employment, particularly where the employer decided not to seek a patent for the invention, or in situations where a patent proved unusually lucrative for employers.

3.5.2 Section 39 of the Patents Act 1977

For the first time, the PA 1977 laid down a statutory code determining ownership and also instigated a system of compensation for employees. Clear statutory delineation of ownership could have been expected to provide certainty and the compensation scheme an additional stimulus to invention. However, it is not clear that either provision has proved a success. It is possible to regard s 39 of the PA 1977 as a statutory codification of the common law position. In *Harris's Patent* (1985), Falconer J considered this argument and held that s 39 of the PA 1977 alone governed patent ownership as between employer and employee. He was only prepared to accept guidance from earlier case law on the way in which courts had assessed the duties of employees and considered circumstances relating to employment relevant.

Employee

Section 39 of the PA 1977 draws a distinction between inventions made by an employee, any patent for which is to be taken to belong to the employer and those where the employee retains ownership of any patent. Both 'employee' and 'employer' are defined in s 130(1) of the PA 1977. Where any issue arises as to ownership of a patent, the first consideration must be whether the inventor was employed, rather than working as a consultant or an independent contractor or anyone else engaged for a specific task.

3.5.3 Employer ownership

An employer is treated as owner of a patent for an employee's invention in two situations in s 39: the first is where the employee could be loosely dubbed one 'employed to invent'; the second is where the employee was not expected to invent, but did occupy a responsible position. It is easier to subdivide the first category than to follow the statutory format, which produces three situations in which the employer is awarded any patent:

(a) an invention was made in the course of the employee's normal duties;

(b) an invention was made in the course of duties falling outside the employee's normal duties, but specifically assigned to him.

In both (a) and (b), an additional criterion is added, namely, that the circumstances were such that an invention might reasonably be expected to result from the execution of the employee's duties:

(c) an invention was made in the course of the employee's duties and, at the time of making the invention, the employee had a special obligation to further the interests of the employer's undertaking because of the nature of his duties and the particular responsibilities arising from them.

In the course of the employee's duties

In all three categories, one consideration is common: that the invention be made in the course of the employee's duties. Because s 39(1) of the PA 1977 only applies to 'employees', 'in the course of the employee's duties' must mean more than that the inventor was employed (and not an independent contractor) at the time of making the invention. The inventor, at the time of invention, is required to be performing tasks, the nature of which are dictated by the employment and not being undertaken on the employee's or any other's behalf. The nature of duties required by employment is a matter for the contract of employment. However, the contractual duties are commonly varied by actual practice, making it difficult to determine the precise nature of an employee's duties at any given moment.

The circumstances

In the two cases of the employee 'employed to invent', another condition must be taken into account: that an invention might be expected to result. The PA 1977 gives no guidance as to what circumstances might be relevant; presumably the actual terms of employment will have been considered in determining that the invention was made in the course of the employee's duties. The 'circumstances' relate to the manner in which those duties have been performed; for example, the time and place at which they were executed, who requested them, who provided the facilities and resources and who had the authority to request alterations. The court is free to take all circumstances it considers relevant into account.

An invention expected

'An invention' must be reasonably expected to result from the employee's performance of his duties. Two interpretations are possible. Either a distinction must be drawn between an expectation that no invention result at all, and an expectation that an invention of any nature at all may result. Or a distinction must be drawn between an expectation of an invention of a type to be expected from that particular employee, as opposed to an invention that would not. No guidance is given as to by whose standards the expectation must be reasonable. It could be the reasonable employee, employer, outsider, or inventor.

Case law should resolve some of these difficulties. The first case to involve s 39(1) of the PA 1977 was *Harris's Patent* (1985). Falconer J considered that the circumstances to be taken into account were those in which the invention was made. He also considered that the provision that an invention be expected to result referred to an invention which contributed to achieving the aim at which the employee's efforts were directed in carrying out his duties. Harris was awarded the patent for his invention. He was employed as the manager of the valve division of a company which made Wey valves (used in chutes and ducts carrying coal dust) under licence from a Swiss company. He invented an improved valve. The judge found that his normal duties were confined to selling valves and dealing with customers' commercial difficulties;

technical difficulties were referred straight to the Swiss company. The employer did not engage in research and an earlier suggestion by Harris for an improvement to the valves had been ignored. Accordingly, Harris's normal duties were not such that an invention might be expected to result. In *Patchett v Sterling* (1955), by contrast, Patchett was 'employed to invent' as part of his normal duties. He was a production engineer in the defendant's armament company, which converted to making domestic appliances in 1945, and was leader of the design and development department.

Because of the varied nature of employment, most cases will have to be decisions on their own particular facts, as should be the case if justice is to be done to individual employees. Take, for example, the position of a university lecturer, employed to teach, but expected to research, doing both in the employer's time and lecturer's own time. In *Greater Glasgow Health Board's Application* (1996), Jacob J took into account the evidence of the employee's head of department as to the employee's duties, and not just his job description, as well as the fact that the invention was made in the doctor employee's own time. He also stressed that the circumstances in which an invention must be expected to result were the particular ones surrounding the making of the invention and not merely the general circumstances of employment. In this case, it was very relevant that the employee was working at home for examinations.

A special obligation

An example from the pre-1977 case law of an invention falling into the third category of employer owned inventions is *Worthington Pumping Engine Co v Moore* (1903). The American plaintiff company employed Moore as its general manager in Europe, at a high salary. He developed two improvements to the company's pumps. Byrne J regarded the considerable measure of trust reposed in Moore by his employers as indicating that the latter were the appropriate patent owners. It is significant that Byrne J adverted to the fact that the invention competed with the employer's business. In fact, employees in this position are subject to triple prejudice: being open to dismissal for the breach of their obligation of good faith (an obligation implied into every contract of employment) (as Moore was), liable for any breaches of confidence in their competitive endeavour, and loss of the patent right. In the US, the employer does not gain outright ownership of the patent, but a 'shop right' in it, which reverts to the employee should the employer not wish to exercise the right.

In *British Syphon Co v Homewood* (1956), the employee was the chief technician of the employer company. Again, it was the impossibility of reconciling the duty of good faith imposed on an employee of such status with the competitive nature of the invention made by the employee that troubled Roxburgh J. The patent was awarded to the employer. In cases where the employee's invention has had non-competitive uses, the courts have had less difficulty in allowing the employee to retain the patent: *Re Selz's Application* (1953). This may be reflected in the wording of s 39(1)(b) of the PA 1977: '... a special obligation to further the interests of the employer's undertaking.' The emphasis in both these cases lay more on the employee's status than actual duties. This was also the approach taken by the Patent Office in *Staeng's Patent* (1996) to s 39(1)(b) of the PA 1977. The employee was a senior executive at group level, involved in a profit bonus scheme and reported direct to the managing director, operating to all intents and purposes at a 'director level'.

3.5.4 Employee ownership

Section 39(2) of the PA 1977 awards any invention not falling within s 39(1) of the PA 1977 to the employee.

3.5.5 Ownership agreements between employee and employer

Unlike copyright, employer and employee are not completely free to make their own arrangements before the invention is made. They may not contract out of s 39 of the PA 1977 where to do so would 'diminish the employee's rights in inventions of any description made by him' after the agreement. Any agreement that does so is unenforceable to that extent.[57]

Free bargaining is possible after the invention is made, although the employer may well govern the market, reducing the employee's bargaining power.

3.6　THE COMPENSATION SCHEME

This scheme aids both the reward and disclosure functions of a patent. It may represent a nod towards a natural right to property in one's labour (although to do so entirely would require automatic award of a patent to its inventor). Other jurisdictions have long administered analogous schemes, as in Germany, Sweden and Japan, for example. The scheme confers a discretion on the comptroller or court to award employees compensation for patented inventions made by them where it is just to do so, and on application by the employee.[58]

The compensation is to be paid by the employer, which immediately serves as a limitation to the usefulness of the scheme. Many employees may be very unwilling to disturb their relationship with their employer by making demands for compensation through official channels.

The conditions for making such an award, and the guidelines for determining the amount of compensation, differ according to whether the patent for the invention is owned by the employer or by the employee.

3.6.1 Employer's patent

Before amendment by the PA 2004, the PA 1977 provided that where the patent belongs to an employer, three conditions applied before an award of compensation could be made to an employee:

(a) a patent must have been granted;

(b) it must have been of outstanding benefit to the employer, having regard, among other things, to the size and nature of the employer's undertaking; and

(c) it appeared that it was just to make an award.

57　*Ibid*, s 42.
58　*Ibid*, s 40.

A patent

This meant that, if the employer chose not to apply for a patent, but relied instead on obligations of confidence, or another intellectual property right, the compensation scheme could be bypassed unless s 43(4) of the PA 1977 allowed for similar compensation despite the reliance on alternative protection. Even if the employer did patent the invention, the inventor was dependent on the efforts the employer made to exploit it, because it was the benefit realised, and not potential benefit, that was taken into account. In *British Steel's Patent* (1992), the employee argued unsuccessfully both that the benefit would have been greater had the employer exploited it more effectively and that its value was what an outside inventor would have had to have been paid for it.

Under the unamended law, the benefit had to come from the patent. In *Memco-Med Ltd's Application* (1992), Aldous J said:

> The benefit from the patent may be readily recognisable where the patent is licensed and royalties are paid. However, the task of the court will be more difficult in cases where an employer exploits the patent by manufacturing articles in accordance with the invention of the patent. In such cases, the court will need to differentiate between the benefit from using the inventive advance and that from the patent. It is also possible to imagine a case where the patent is not licensed and the invention is never put into practice, but the patent is of great benefit to the patentee to prevent activities which would compete with those carried on by the patentee.

It was found that the sales made by the employer in this case could be attributed to factors other than the patent: price, quality and the employer's relationship with the customer. The benefit must also accrue to the employer, and if the patent is assigned to another an employed inventor cannot claim compensation.

In response to the Consultation Document, the PA 2004 amends s 40(1) and s 41(1) of the PA 1977. Although the invention must have been patented (so that no compensation lies for an invention protected by trade secret), the benefit flows from the patented invention and not the patent alone. However, it does not extend the obligation to compensate to assignees of the patent.

Outstanding benefit

The requirement that the benefit to the employer must be outstanding has been criticised. 'Benefit' is defined as benefit in money or money's worth by s 43(7) of the PA 1977. It is not clear whether this would include the benefit of enhanced reputation. The only guidance as to the means of measuring whether a benefit is outstanding is that it must be measured in proportion to the size and nature of the employer's undertaking. This has the potential to lead to absurd results. An inventor employed by a small company may make an invention which produces a given profit. That profit may represent a high proportion of the small company's turnover, but exactly the same invention would represent only a small proportion of a large company's turnover. The effort expended by the inventor is the same.

It is for this reason that the applications in *GEC Avionics Ltd's Patent* (1992) and *British Steel's Patent* (1992) failed. Sales of the invention by GEC amounted to US$72 million, a profit of US$10 million, but were held not to amount to an outstanding benefit to a major international firm making multimillion dollar transactions. The proven benefit of the invention to British Steel represented only one hundredth of its turnover and eight hundredths of its profit. However, the payment of an award is far less likely to place a strain on a large company than a small one. In *British Steel's Patent* (1992), the invention had been of great benefit in one particular plant, although minuscule in relation to British Steel as a whole. The Patent Office hearing officer felt constrained to make his decision on the evidence submitted of the undertaking's size and nature, which was of British Steel as a whole. He did not 'rule out the possibility that in appropriate circumstances, and when supported by evidence to justify such an interpretation, the proper "undertaking" to be considered might be constituted by a particular sector or site of the employer's total organisation'.

The word 'outstanding' is a superlative and the courts have felt constrained to interpret it restrictively. Aldous J was not prepared to attempt a definition in *Memco-Med Ltd's Application* (1992):

> The word 'outstanding' denotes something special and requires the benefit to be more than substantial or good. I believe that it is unwise to try to redefine the word 'outstanding'. Courts will recognise an outstanding benefit when it occurs.

The fact that the employee has been rewarded through salary, and in other ways, will also be taken into account: *GEC Avionics Ltd's Patent* (1992); and *British Steel's Patent* (1992). In the latter the employee had received an *ex gratia* payment of £10,000 and had been honoured with the award of an MBE.

No change was made by the PA 2004, as respondents to the Consultation Document favoured retaining a high threshold of a significant and real, not potential, benefit.

An award is just

If the third stage is reached (determining whether it is just than an employee should be compensated), s 41 of the PA 1977 sets out the objective of compensation: the employee is to receive a fair share, in all the circumstances, of the employer's benefit from the patent. Factors to be taken into account in assessing a fair share are set out in s 41(4) of the PA 1977. To take account of these factors before it has been decided that compensation is just would prejudice such a conclusion and are more appropriate as a balancing factor at the later stage of quantifying an award. However, the factors in s 41(4)(a) of the PA 1977 were precisely those that weighed against the employee in *GEC Avionics Ltd's Patent* (1992) and in *British Steel's Patent* (1992) at the initial stage of deciding whether an award should be made at all. Other matters that are relevant may also be taken into account, such as the extent to which the employer has advanced over the competition.

3.6.2 Employee's patent

Where the patent is an employee's, s 40(2) of the PA 1977 provides that he may seek compensation if:

(a) he has assigned the patent to the employer, or granted the employer an exclusive licence;

(b) the benefit derived from the transfer is inadequate in relation to the benefit derived by the employer from the patent; and

(c) it is just that the employee should be awarded compensation.

Once again, the benefit to the employer must be derived from the patent and not from commercial or other factors. Employers can also frustrate any award of compensation by refusing to take a licence or assignment in circumstances where they are the only likely exploiter of the invention.

Where compensation is just, the aim is to give the employee a fair share of the benefit, taking into account the factors listed by s 41(5) of the PA 1977, including contributions made by the employer and others to the making of the invention. Other relevant factors may be considered, such as the employee's loyalty in using the employer to exploit the invention, or the benefits that might have been gained by exploiting elsewhere.

3.6.3 Criticisms of the scheme

The code of ownership and the compensation scheme have been said to be unnecessarily complex and there is little evidence of employees' success in securing awards. At the time of issuing the Consultation Document on the PA(A) Bill[59] there had been no successful actions under s 40. It was suggested either that employers had opted to settle claims rather than face litigation, or that the policy objective of a fair balance was not being achieved. It was this part of the Consultation that evoked the greatest response. However, the majority favoured the status quo. Commercial respondents emphasised the existence of in-house arrangements to reward employee contributions. There are six points worthy of note.

First, the scheme requires a heavy burden of record keeping, not just because of the emphasis on the contractual and actual duties of the employee, but also the relevance of the resources used, the input of others and other pertinent circumstances. Keeping a detailed research history will be essential. This may add to the expenses of employers' administration, but is a more serious handicap for employees, who may not have kept, or may not have access to, such records. Nor does reliance on contractual duties provide certainty, because job descriptions are notoriously ephemeral and fluctuate.[60]

Secondly, to focus on the benefit conferred by the patent, and not the invention, makes any award of compensation problematic unless the patent is licensed to others and income is generated from it by way of royalties. A patent is primarily a right to prevent others manufacturing and, where a patentee has no competitors, no benefit is obtained from the patent itself, although profits may be generated from sales and marketing.

Thirdly, the employee employed to invent is at the employer's mercy if no patent is sought. A better system might be to give the employee the right to the return of the invention after a defined period, as is the case in Germany; or only ever to confer a 'shop right' on the employer, as in the US.

Fourthly, there is no right to compensation until the benefit has been incurred. This may involve a considerable time lapse between invention and compensation, reducing

---

59 Consultation Paper on the Proposed Patents Act (Amendment) Bill, IPPD, Patent Office and DTI, November 2002.
60 Pointed out by Bercusson, B, 'The Contract of Employment – The Patents Act 1977' [1980] EIPR 257.

any incentive effect the scheme is intended to have. It is not clear whether an employee who has left the employer under whom the invention was made may make a claim against the former employer.

Fifthly, the fact that the onus is on the employee to make a claim may discourage employees who are still on good terms with their employers from provoking a potential dispute with their employers. The costs of such claims may also prove a deterrent.

Sixthly, the discretion given to the court is a wide one and centres on considerations normally left to specialist tribunals – commercial factors of profit, competition and market share, as well as employment factors.

3.6.4 Alternatives

There are alternatives. The Green Paper[61] approved the German system, the most generous and detailed of the European systems. There, compensation is calculated according to a scale and the system is State run and well used. Importantly, it is automatic and contains a 'right back' to the invention for the employee. The employee has a duty to disclose inventions to the employer, but is then compensated in proportion to the economic value of the invention, irrespective of whether or not it is exploited. This provides both an incentive to invent and to disclose the invention. However, whether the employee would have the resources to exploit an invention not taken up by the employer is doubtful. The right to compensation could prove a source of friction between employer and employee. In 1986, the Government argued in the White Paper[62] that the scheme is a source of unnecessary and circuitous research, a source of burdensome bureaucracy, expensive to administer and results in large numbers of patents. The White Paper stated that the government of the time was still studying the situation. The Response to the Consultation on the PA(A) Bill was clearly against such compensation schemes. It was even reported that the German scheme had a detrimental effect on investment in innovative industries. No change was made by the PA 2004.

Other proposals have been made. Phillips proposed[63] a scale of automatic compensation funded from patent renewal fees. This removes the potential for friction between employer and employee and exercises of discretion by the Patent Office or court. However, the contemplated awards would have been low and subsidised by industry in general.

Employees' greatest hope may lie in the hope that the existence of a statutory scheme might encourage voluntary awards by employers, or that the provision in s 40(3) of the PA 1977 for collective agreement to replace the statutory formula for compensation induces unions to negotiate on their behalf. This could well encompass agreements negotiated by a research team. No change was made by the PA 2004.

---

61   *Intellectual Property Rights and Innovation*, Cmnd 9117, 1983.
62   *Intellectual Property and Innovation*, Cmnd 9712, 1986.
63   Phillips, J, 'Rewarding the Employee-inventor' [1995] EIPR 275.

3.7   THE PROPRIETARY RIGHT

A patent, and an application for a patent, confer a proprietary right, a personal property right.[64] Both a patent and an application may be assigned, mortgaged or licensed. Both assignments, and mortgages, of applications, patents, or rights in patents (for example licences) are void unless they are in writing and signed by the parties.[65]

This distinguishes the position of assignees from that of licensees. Licences may be created informally, however unwise this might be in practical terms. An assignee steps into the shoes of the patentee, whereas a licensee merely acquires a right not to be sued by the patentee. The proprietor of a patent, an assignee or an exclusive licensee may bring proceedings in relation to infringement.[66]

The Comptroller of Patents maintains a register of transfers of property in patents and patent applications.[67] Registration only gives *prima facie* evidence of the items registered, and there is no obligation to register. However, failure to do so has two consequences: registration confers priority of rights which defeat earlier unregistered dealings,[68] and the proprietor or exclusive licensee will not be awarded damages or an account of profits for infringement unless the transfer is registered within six months.[69]

3.7.1   Duration of patents

A patent is treated as taking effect on the date at which its grant is published by the Patent Office. It continues in force until the end of the 20-year period beginning from the date of filing (or an earlier priority date to which it is entitled).[70] Proceedings may only be taken from the date on which notice of grant is published, but damages may be secured from the date of early publication.

3.8   PATENT LICENCES

Prima facie, parties are free to make any bargain that they wish and have the bargaining power to secure. Patent rights may be divided temporally, geographically, by activity, or in any other way desired.

Patents can, however, be employed in anti-competitive ways, quite apart from the initial monopoly that a patent confers. Patentees could refuse to produce at all, patents may be 'pooled' by their owners to secure supra-market power, or licence terms may be used to restrict intra-product competition (between the patentee and his licensees). A balance can be drawn between justifiable exercise of the monopoly and licence terms chosen as the best way of exploiting the invention, and unjustifiable practices. It is at

---

64   Section 30 of the PA 1977.
65   *Ibid*, s 30(6).
66   *Ibid*, ss 61, 30(7).
67   *Ibid*, s 32.
68   *Ibid*, s 33.
69   *Ibid*, s 68.
70   *Ibid*, s 25.

this point that the patent right abuts competition law, both domestic competition law and that of the EU.

3.8.1 Compulsory licences

If compulsory licences are to be imposed on a patentee, a compromise with the nature of the patent as a monopoly is being drawn. This is important in relation to the justifications that are made for granting patents, helping to counteract some of the objections to monopoly power. Compulsory licences are unusual in relation to property rights. A compulsory licence forces a patentee to face competition and competition at a royalty determined by an outside arbiter. Compulsory licences were at the heart of battles between developed and developing countries over conventions on intellectual property rights. The developing countries sought to secure working of the patent in their own territory (so that local manufacturers could learn all the important lessons from Western technology) and to secure favourable treatment for home inventors. It is worth noting that in the same vein the Statute of Monopolies 1624 did not require that an invention be new, only new to the UK, because the prime objective was to secure technology transfer from technologically advanced European countries.

Section 48 of the PA 1977 provides for the grant of compulsory licences after three years in a number of situations. Anyone may apply for a compulsory licence. The Comptroller General may grant the licences as he thinks fit, but s 50 of the PA 1977 sets out the policy to be followed in doing so. Compulsory licensing is also constrained by the TRIPS Agreement. Article 31 lays down a series of conditions to be observed where a compulsory licence is being considered. The PA 1977 has been amended to take account of TRIPS, and s 48A of the PA 1977 lays down the relevant conditions where an application is made against a patentee from a WTO State. It is these conditions that will apply in the majority of cases.

The grounds for a compulsory licence are threefold:

(a) that demand in the UK for the patented product is not being met on reasonable terms;

(b) that licensing restrictions are preventing or hindering exploitation of another patented invention which is technically an advance or of considerable economic significance;

(c) that either the manufacture, use or disposal of unpatented materials, or commercial or industrial activities in the UK are unfairly prejudiced by conditions imposed on licensing a patent, or on disposal or use of a patented product or process.

A patentee is not able to expect monopoly profits from a compulsory licence. In practice, compulsory licences are not often granted; their value lies more in the threat of an application in negotiations for a voluntary licence.

There is some ambivalence in attitudes to compulsory licences. South African legislation designed to gain affordable access to patented drugs (particularly HIV related treatments) caused a furore among multinational patentees,[71] although

---

71   May, C, 'Why IPRs are a Global Issue' [2003] EIPR 1.

threatened litigation was eventually dropped. However, the US Government was very quick to secure access to anti-anthrax drugs in the wake of terrorism threats. In 2003 the WTO announced that Member States had broken the deadlock over intellectual property and public health. The Doha Agreement,[72] which waives developing countries' obligations under Article 31(f) and (h) of TRIPS, is to be implemented. This will allow countries without the facilities to make pharmaceuticals domestically to import generic drugs made under compulsory licences. Article 31(f) states that products made under compulsory licence must be predominantly for domestic markets alone. Now these may be exported. While all WTO members are entitled to employ this concession, 23 developed countries have agreed voluntarily to refrain from importing such drugs. Other States will only do so in emergency situations. The UK will be required to change patent and other medical regulatory and licensing procedures.[73] In November 2004 the European Commission published a proposal for a Regulation on compulsory licensing.[74]

3.8.2 Licences of right

A patentee may apply at any time to have the patent endorsed 'licence of right', whereupon patent renewal fees are halved.[75] The result is notification to the public that a licence is available to all comers, which will assist the patentee who has not been able to exploit the invention unaided. If the patentee and applicant cannot agree terms, the Comptroller General will settle them.

3.8.3 Crown use

Sections 55–59 of the PA 1977 confer sweeping powers on the government to ignore a patentee's rights. These are not limited to circumstances of war or emergency and include drug supply to the National Health Service. Compensation (as agreed by the parties, or settled by the court) is paid.

3.9 PATENTS AND UK COMPETITION LAW

The principal aim of the Competition Act (CA) 1998 was to harmonise domestic competition law with Community law, namely Articles 81 and 82, and s 60 of the Act, the so-called 'Euro-clause,' requires consistency with Community law, 'having regard to any relevant differences' (see 1.7 above). Community competition law is motivated by single market considerations which are not a concern of UK competition law and hence Community case law on the application of Article 81 to licences of intellectual property rights may not be relevant in a domestic context. The application of UK competition law to the ownership and enjoyment of intellectual property licences will

---

72 Para 6, Doha Declaration, 2001. The declaration resulted from the Fourth Ministerial Conference of the WTO in Doha, Qatar, November 2001.

73 TRIPS and Essential Medicines: www.patent.gov.uk.

74 Proposal for a Regulation of the European Parliament and of the Council on compulsory licensing of patents relating to the manufacture of pharmaceutical products for export to countries with public health problems, COM (2004) 737.

75 Section 46 of the PA 1977.

therefore diverge from Community decisional practice, certainly with regard to territorial restrictions.

3.9.1   Chapter I prohibition and licences

Section 2 of the CA 1998 (Chapter I prohibition) applies to agreements that have as their object or effect the prevention, restriction or distortion of competition. Section 2 also requires that the agreement 'may affect trade within the United Kingdom'. There is no specific requirement that this effect must be 'appreciable' or 'substantial' but the OFT generally takes the view that the Chapter I prohibition will not apply where the parties' combined market share is below 25%, although this rule does not apply to price fixing and market sharing practices. Thus, restrictions imposed on a licensee's minimum prices or the fixing of prices may amount to an infringement.

Section 50 of the CA 1998 makes provision for the exclusion or exemption of vertical agreements from the Chapter I prohibition. The exclusion was achieved by the Competition Act 1998 (Land and Vertical Agreements Exclusion) Order.[76] However, on 1 May 2004, the Competition Act 1998 (Land Agreements Exclusion and Revocation) Order 2004[77] came into force, revoking the 2000 Order. The main difference between the two Orders is that the 2004 Order does not exclude vertical agreements from the Chapter I prohibition except to the extent that a vertical agreement is a land agreement. Intellectual property licences will continue to benefit from parallel exemption by virtue of the combination of s 10 of the CA 1998 with the new technology transfer agreement block exemption (see 3.16 below). Vertical agreements are not excluded from the Chapter II prohibition.

The OFT has published a number of Guidelines on the application of the CA 1998 over the past few years, the most recent being a draft Guideline on the application of the Act to intellectual property rights.[78] At the time of writing this is in the process of consultation and revision. The draft Guideline sets out the manner in which the Director General expects the CA 1998 to operate in terms of intellectual property matters. Section 2 details the Chapter I prohibition (see above) and a comprehensive list of agreements, identical to Article 81 of the EC Treaty, can be found in s 2.2. The remainder of the section provides a framework for determining whether an agreement infringes the Chapter I prohibition, and also sets out the three categories of exemption. The final section of the draft advises that s 70 of the CA 1998 repeals ss 44 and 45 of the Patents Act 1977 since the aforementioned prohibitions provide sufficient protection against anti-competitive restrictions. Responses to the draft Guideline so far have been broadly positive.

3.9.2   Dominance and Chapter II

The OFT has made it clear that the conduct of a dominant undertaking will not escape the Chapter II prohibition simply on the basis that its market power arises from the

---

76 The Competition Act 1998 (Land and Vertical Agreements Exclusion) Order 2000 (SI 2000/310).
77 www.legislation.hmso.gov.uk/si/si2004/20041260.htm.
78 OFT 418.

ownership of intellectual property rights. Thus, the Chapter II prohibition of the CA 1998 may apply to abusive behaviour in relation to intellectual property rights and Community Court judgments and Commission decisional practice would be relevant under s 60 of the Act. The market investigation provisions of the Enterprise Act 2002 may also be relevant where features of a market are anti-competitive as a result of intellectual property rights.[79] Merely holding a dominant position does not constitute an abuse and s 3.5 refers to the criteria for determining whether an abuse exists, although this is not an exhaustive list and the guidelines point out that the real test is whether the dominant undertaking is using its dominant position in a manner that is abusive. Again, there are a number of exclusions to which the Chapter II prohibition will not apply.

3.10 PATENTS AND THE COMMUNITY COMPETITION RULES

3.10.1 Patents and the EC Treaty

The doctrine of exhaustion of rights applies to patents in the same way as it does to trade marks and copyright. The ECJ referred to the doctrine in *Consten and Grundig* (1966) and it has since been applied on many occasions (see Chapter 1). Essentially, the owner of an intellectual property right who consents to the marketing of his goods or articles in one Member State cannot use that right to prevent the importation of the goods in another Member State or their subsequent sale. The right is said to be exhausted by the initial consent to marketing. Article 28 of the EC Treaty and the exercise of a patent right often arises in cases concerning parallel imports. In *Centrafarm BV v Sterling Drug* (1974) Centrafarm purchased a drug called Negram in the UK where prices were controlled by a government regulation and exported large quantities to the Netherlands where prices were generally higher. The owner of the patent for the drug in both countries, Sterling Drug, sought to prevent Centrafarm from selling the product at a lower price in the Netherlands. The Court was asked to consider the compatibility of Sterling Drug's rights with Articles 28 and 30 of the EC Treaty. The Court confirmed that Article 30 only permitted derogations from Article 28 where this was necessary to protect the 'specific subject-matter' of a property right. The Court stated that the specific subject-matter of a patent was:

> ...the exclusive right to use an invention with a view to manufacturing industrial products and putting them into circulation for the first time, either directly or by the grant of licences to third parties, as well as the right to oppose infringements.

The Court concluded that a derogation from the free movement of goods provisions was not justified 'where the product has been put onto the market in a legal manner, by the patentee itself or with its consent, in the Member State from which it has been imported, in particular in the case of a proprietor of parallel patents'. Thus, Sterling Drug could not rely on its Dutch patent because it had consented to marketing the drug in the UK through its licensee, the subsidiary company. A different outcome was achieved in *Parke, Davis & Co v Probel* (1968). Here the Court decided the doctrine of exhaustion did not apply and the patentee could prevent parallel imports from a territory because the goods were marketed by a third party without its consent.

---

79   Chapter 1, Part 4, Enterprise Act 2002, ss 131–33.

Conversely, if the goods were put into circulation with the consent of the patentee all rights will have been exhausted and it would not be possible to prevent parallel imports. This is the case even where the patentee had no opportunity to earn profit from a patent monopoly in the Member State where it had no patent protection.[80]

3.11 THE APPLICATION OF ARTICLE 81(1) TO LICENCES OF INTELLECTUAL PROPERTY RIGHTS

The Community's competition policy affects not only attempts to prevent parallel importing, which cannot be justified, but also direct national licensing. The mere existence of an intellectual property right does not offend competition policy as a licence must be given or concerted practice established or an anti-competitive element added to use of the right for questions to arise. Exclusive licences of intellectual property rights must be examined to determine, first, whether they affect competition and, secondly, whether the effect on competition can be justified under Article 81(3) or regarded as non-abusive in terms of the ECJ's objective justification test under Article 82. It is at this stage that the purpose of intellectual property should be remembered, namely to promote trade and innovation and, thereby, competition in goods which, without the right, might never be produced at all by an *ex-ante* approach. The right only appears as a barrier to competition if looked at after the decision to award it at all has been made by an *ex-post* approach. Often, the only viable method of exploiting a right is through licensing. This is pro-competitive because it facilitates exploitation of the product and ensures that there is more than one supplier. Excessive controls over licensing are, therefore, potentially counterproductive, both generally in relation to the long term goals of intellectual property and more specifically in relation to the effect of particular licences. Any analysis of an intellectual property licence should concentrate on the effect of the licence in the particular market where intellectual property protection exists. A right owner may grant exclusive or sole licences of all or part of the right in order to maximise production outside his own expertise. Such licences may restrict competition in other ways (vertical agreements). There are a number of types of clause which can be considered to be anti-competitive, such as tie-ins which require the licensee to acquire goods only from the patentee, non-competition clauses which prevent a licensee handling competing goods, tie-ups which outlive the term of the right, minimum quantities clauses, no challenge clauses which prohibit the licensee challenging the validity of the right, geographical limits or clauses for the grant-back of know-how.

In the past, the ECJ and the Commission have tended to combine the two approaches and give way to a general antipathy to the anti-competitive nature of intellectual property (see, for example *Raymond/Nagoya* (1972); *Davidson Rubber* (1972); and the now withdrawn Announcement on Patent Licensing Agreements 1962). It is interesting to draw comparisons with the US intellectual property guidelines adopted by the US antitrust enforcement agencies as discussed by the authors of the following note:

---

80   *Merck & Co Inc v Stephar BV* (1981) and the contrasting case *Merck v Primecrown* (1996)

The EC Block Exemption and the USIP Guidelines reflect their very different jurisprudential ancestry. In the EC, the strict construction of the complementary roles of Article [81(1)] and Article [81(3)], coupled with a virtual anathema for provisions which restrict free movement of trade between Member States has resulted in much less balancing of such purpose and effect factors than in the United States. In contrast, the USIP Guidelines place great emphasis on the factual context in which the licensing operates, that is, its purpose and effect.[81]

3.12   THE APPLICATION OF ARTICLE 81 TO LICENCES

3.12.1 The Commission's approach

The Commission has applied Article 81 of the EC Treaty to both horizontal and vertical intellectual property agreements. Individual agreements may be notified for exemption, but this is a lengthy process and provides considerable uncertainty for the parties. In addition, the approach of the Commission to intellectual property licences has fluctuated over the years. This can be seen in the withdrawal of the Commission's Notice on Patent Licensing Agreements.[82] In the early 1960s, the Commission had indicated that some limiting terms in non-exclusive licences would not fall within Article 81 of the EC Treaty and this view was articulated in the so-called 'Christmas Notice'. However, towards the 1970s, the Commission took a tougher stance following the seminal judgment of the ECJ in *Consten and Grundig v Commission* (1966).

3.12.2 *Consten and Grundig v Commission*

Grundig, a German manufacturer of electrical goods, appointed the French company, Consten, as its exclusive distributor in France. Of particular relevance to the Commission was the assignment by Grundig of the GINT trademark to Consten in order to support exclusivity. This enabled Consten to prevent parallel imports from other Member States. A parallel importer began importing Grundig's products into France from elsewhere in the EC and Consten sued for unfair competition and trade mark infringement. Meanwhile, in an Article 81 proceeding, the Commission decided that the exclusive distribution agreement between Consten and Grundig was void under Article 81(2) and refused to grant an exemption under Article 81(3). In broad terms, the ECJ agreed with the Commission's decision that vertical agreements infringed Article 81(1). The ECJ held that the assignment went beyond the mere grant of exclusive distribution rights as it conferred absolute territorial protection on the distributor, enabling it to prevent parallel imports in the Community. This was distortive of competition and any efficiency gains in the distribution of Grundig's products could not be justified under the grounds for exemption articulated in Article 81(3.) After a number of other equally severe decisions in the 1970s (*Raymond/Nagoya* (1972); *Davidson Rubber* (1972); *Kabelmetal/Luchaire* (1975); *AOIP/Beyrard* (1976)), which radically departed from the 1962 'Christmas Notice', the Commission came under intense pressure to revise its policy towards patent licences. The Commission's policy that subject to a *de minimis* threshold, the granting of an exclusive territory would

---

81   Togt, HW and Gotts, IK, 'A Tale of Two Continents: European Technology Transfer Block Exemption Takes Different Approach From US Counterpart Guidelines' [1996] 6 ECLR 327.

82   [1962] OJ 2922, withdrawn in 1984; [1984] OJ C220/14.

infringe Article 81(1) and required exemption under Article 81(3) raised the possibility that an application for exemption would be rejected in every case. Over time, however, the block exemptions were formulated and these contained a softening of the Commission's approach (see 3.13 below).

3.12.3 The European Court's view

In the first case to come before the Court, *Nungesser v Commission* (1981), better known as the *'Maize Seeds'* case, the central issue for the Court was whether an exclusive licence of plant breeders' rights in itself infringed Article 81(1). A French institute, INRA, had developed certain varieties of maize seeds for which it held plant breeders' rights in France and Germany. Following a number of agreements, the German rights were partly assigned and licensed to Mr Eisele and his company, Nungesser, in return for absolute territorial protection in respect of the production and sale of the seeds in Germany. The Commission condemned the agreement under Article 81(1) in line with its decision on territorial exclusivity in *Consten and Grundig*. By contrast, the Court sought to distinguish between an 'open exclusive licence' which it defined as an agreement:

> ... whereby the owner merely undertakes not to grant other licences in respect of the same territory and not to compete himself with the licensee in that territory ...

and an exclusive licence which confers absolute territorial protection so that there is no competition from other parties.

The Court decided that the open exclusive licence could be justified in commercial terms. At paragraph 56 the Court specifically referred to the considerable investment required by the licensee and the inevitable risk of developing and marketing new technology. The Court noted that a licensee might be deterred from innovation if it could not be protected in some way from competition from other licensees in its territory. Such a result, the Court noted, 'would be damaging to the dissemination of a new technology and would prejudice competition in the Community between the new product and similar existing products'.

Thus the Court concluded that:

> ...the grant of an open exclusive licence, that is to say, a licence which does not affect the position of third parties such as parallel importers and licensees for other territories, is not in itself incompatible with Article 81(1) of the Treaty.

This is the so-called rule of reason approach formulated by the Court in previous judgments concerning Article 81.[83] Like the Commission, the Court would not countenance absolute territorial protection and said this would be automatically caught by Article 81(1) and would not qualify for an exemption under Article 81(3).

The Court's distinction in this decision between 'open' and 'exclusive' licences was not well received by the Commission and in the years following the case the Commission adopted a narrow approach to the *Maize Seeds* doctrine. This is exemplified in the case of *Metropole Television SA (M6)* (2001), which concerned a Eurovision broadcasting agreement. The applicants argued that a rule of reason existed in Community competition law and had been confirmed by the Court in a

---

83 *Société Technique Minière v Maschinenbau Ulm* (1966).

number of cases, including *Nungesser*. They submitted that the application of this rule would have shown that Article 81(1) did not apply to both the exclusivity clause and to the clause relating to special-interest channels, which were at issue.

The Commission acknowledged that various judgments of the Community courts had indeed interpreted the prohibition laid down in Article 81(1) of the Treaty in a flexible manner but noted that:

> Those judgments cannot, however, be interpreted as establishing the existence of a rule of reason in Community competition law. They are, rather, part of a broader trend in the case law according to which it is not necessary to hold, wholly abstractly and without drawing any distinction, that any agreement restricting the freedom of action of one or more of the parties is necessarily caught by the prohibition laid down in Article 81(1) of the Treaty.[84]

3.13   BLOCK EXEMPTION REGULATIONS

A need for clarification of the Community position led to the publication of Block Exemption Regulations on patent licences and know-how licensing agreements in 1984.[85] Block exemption regulations automatically exempt certain types of agreements from the scope of Article 81(1), obviating the need for individual examination of the anti-and pro-competitive effects of a restrictive agreement. The publication of these regulations was welcomed by the business community and led to a significant reduction in the number of notifications for individual exemption. However, several patent licences did not fall within the general framework and continued to be assessed on an individual basis. In *Windsurfing International v Commission* (1986), the ECJ found a number of provisions of a licensing agreement to be 'ancillary restrictions' beyond the specific subject matter of the right and in the absence of a block exemption, prohibited by Article 81(1). This was the first case to come before the Community competition authorities following the block exemption regulation coming into force and the Court's decision provided important guidance on the assessment of individual patent licences.

The block exemption regulations of the 1980s were eventually replaced by a unified Commission Regulation on the application of Article 81(3) of the Treaty to certain categories of technology transfer agreements in 1996.[86] Regulation 240/96 was adopted on 31 January 1996 and it was intended to apply until 31 March 2006.[87] The Technology Transfer Block Exemption regulation (TTBE) represented a more permissive approach on the part of the Commission to patent licensing agreements, allowing parties greater freedom. The Commission initiated a review of the regulation in 2001 with a view to introducing a new block exemption before the intended expiry date. The Evaluation Report on the Transfer of Technology Block Exemption Regulation No 240/96 published in January 2002 criticised the old Regulation for its 'straitjacketing' effect, which the Commission concluded impeded efficient

---

84 Cases T–185, 216, 299, and 300/00 *Metropole Television SA (M6) and Others v Commission* [2001] ECR II–3805, para 76.
85 Reg 2349/84, [1984] OJ L219/15 and Reg 556/89, [1989] OJ L61/1.
86 Reg 240/96, [1996] OJ L31/2. On the nature of block exemptions generally, see Whish, R, *Competition Law* (5th edn, London: Butterworths, 2003), Chapter 4.
87 On technology transfer agreements, see Korah, V, *Technology Transfer and the EC Competition Rules* (Oxford: OUP, 1997).

transactions and discouraged innovation. On 1 October 2003, the Commission published a draft TTBER, together with draft Guidelines.[88]

The old regulatory framework merits a brief discussion.

3.14 BLOCK EXEMPTION REGULATION 240/96

Recital 5 provides that the Regulation applies to national patents, Community patents and to European patents. The term 'patent' applies to pure or mixed patent licensing or know-how licensing agreements, including those addressing utility models, topographies, and semi-conductors, and plant breeders' rights between two parties. The Regulation also applies to patent applications and to licences that are automatically prolonged by the inclusion of new improvements.[89] By virtue of Article 6, sub-licences are also included and assignments where the risk remains with the assignor.[90]

Article 1(1) provides:

> Pursuant to Article 81(3) of the Treaty and subject to the conditions set out below, it is hereby declared that Article 81(1) of the Treaty shall not apply to pure patent licensing or know-how licensing agreements and to mixed know-how and patent licensing agreements, including those agreements containing ancillary provisions relating to trade marks or intellectual property rights other than patents, to which only two undertakings are party and which include one more of the following obligations.

The Commission's Evaluation Report concluded that the TTBE is too narrow in scope, applying only to patents and know-how and excluding other intellectual property rights, unless those rights are deemed ancillary to the patent or know-how licence. Further, the TTBE is limited to agreements between not more than two undertakings. Licences between parent and subsidiary are regarded as a single corporate entity and do not need an exemption since there is no agreement between independent undertakings.[91]

3.14.1 The white list

Article 2 (the so-called 'white list') provides a list of provisions of a standard licensing agreement 'which are generally not restrictive of competition' in terms of Article 81 of the EC Treaty, but which are exempted in any case if they are found to be restrictive to provide legal certainty. The Commission may withdraw the benefit of the block exemption if the criteria articulated in Article 81(3) are not met. The Commission introduced a single 'umbrella' Block Exemption Regulation for Vertical Agreements 2790/99 on 1 June 2000 which signals an end to the 'white list' approach for many vertical agreements (BER 2790/99). Changes have also been made to the opposition procedure (see below).

---

88 See the draft Guidelines on the Application of Article 81 of the EC Treaty to Technology Transfer Agreements (the 'draft Guidelines') [2003] OJ C235/17 para 5.

89 Regulation 240/96, Article 8(3).

90 Regulation 240/96, Article 6(1); see recital 9.

91 *Viho v Commission* (1995).

3.14.2 The black list

Conversely, Article 3 (the so-called 'black list') sets out an exhaustive list of provisions (shorter than the regulations of the 1980s) which will not be exempted and are prohibited; for example, limitations on research and development, production or distribution, price, quantity and some export and post termination restraints. The inclusion of a 'black-clause' brings the entire agreement outside the scope of the block exemption. An obligation not to divulge know-how after an agreement has expired or one not to grant sub-licences or assign the licence will be allowed, but not restrictions on the determination of prices or discounts. Agreements which do not fall within the block exemption may be notified to the Commission for individual exemption. The Commission's Evaluation Report was particularly critical of the TTBE's blacklist approach for excluding certain restrictive clauses from the block exemption without valid economic justification. For instance, the TTBE generally blacklisted tying clauses, which are now considered to enhance efficiency provided they are imposed by non-dominant firms. The black list approach has been abolished by the new TTBER, bringing greater flexibility to the assessment of the competitive effects of technology licensing agreements (see below).

3.14.3 The opposition procedure

In some of the earlier Commission Regulations it was thought that provisions that restrict competition, which are neither exempted nor expressly excluded could not benefit from the application of the block exemption. These are so-called 'greylisted' clauses, the effects of which have to be examined on a case-by-case basis. For agreements contained these types of clauses, the Commission introduced an opposition procedure. All Commission regulations published after the TTBE in 1996 contained an opposition procedure. Article 4 of the TTBE provides that parties may notify the licensing agreement to the Commission for an individual assessment if the agreement contains restrictions that do not fall within Articles 1–3. The Commission has four months from notification in which to object or accept the clause.

However, the opposition procedure in Community block exemption regulations has been abolished following the entry into force of the Modernisation Regulation 1/2003 on 1 May 2004[92] (see below).

3.14.4 Exclusions

Article 5 of the old TTBE provides that the Regulation does not apply to technology pools; joint ventures between competitors or agreements between competitors involving reciprocal rights, or sales licences. The most important exclusion is for licences that include intellectual property rights other than patents, such as trade marks, copyright, design rights or software, unless the rights or software are ancillary to the technology licence.[93] Provided that the overriding purpose of the licence is the licensing of patents or unpatented know-how, or a combination thereof, the inclusion

---

92 Council Regulation No 1/2003 on the implementation of the rules on competition laid down in Articles 81 and 82 of the Treaty.
93 See Korah, V, *Technology Transfer and the EC Competition Rules* (Oxford: OUP, 1997).

within the licence of other rights such as trade marks will not prevent the granting of exemption provided that these other rights are ancillary.[94] For example, in *Moosehead/Whitbread* (1990), a trade mark licence did not fall within the ambit of the then Know-How Regulation 556/89 because the trade mark in question was vital to the commercial viability of the transaction and was not therefore ancillary. The Commission in this case, however, was prepared to grant an individual exemption in respect of a number of restrictive clauses.

Ancillary provisions relating to intellectual property rights may also benefit from the Commission's single umbrella Block Exemption for Vertical Agreements, Regulation 2790/99 (see below).[95]

3.15 REVIEW OF THE TECHNOLOGY TRANSFER REGULATION

As previously noted, the TTBE was criticised for its formalistic and inflexible approach with exemption dependent on a large number of complex formal requirements found in the 'white', 'grey' and 'black' lists. The TTBE was also narrow in scope since it only covered certain types of exclusive licensing agreements. Moreover, with the focus mostly on intra-brand competition and market integration, the TTBE attracted criticism for its 'straitjacket' effect, limiting the ability of companies to enter into effective agreements. For instance, territorial restrictions in know-how licences between non-competitors were subject to time constraints lasting no longer than 10 years from the date the first licensee placed the licensed product on the market. The publication in 1999 of Block Exemption Regulation (BER) 2790/99, reflecting a more flexible, economic and effects-based approach to vertical agreements, prompted the Commission to investigate the appropriateness of alignment of the TTBE with the new block exemption Regulation and other policy developments.[96] BER 2790/99,[97] introduced for the first time, market share thresholds, eliminated lists of white and grey clauses and the opposition procedure, and formulated detailed Guidelines.[98] Article 1(3) of BER 2790/99 provides:

> This Regulation applies to provisions contained in vertical agreements concerning the assignment or use of intellectual property rights for the purpose of using or reselling the goods or services supplied, on condition that these provisions do not constitute the primary object of, but are directly necessary for the implementation of such agreements and do not contain restrictions or competition having the same object or effect as vertical restraints not exempted under the present Regulation.

Thus, assignments or licences of intellectual property rights, which are ancillary to vertical agreements, for example, distribution agreements, may be block exempted subject to the specific rules set out in the Regulation. Other Commission regulations introduced as part of its reform programme concerning intellectual property issues included Regulation 2658/2000, which applies to specialisation agreements and

---

94 Article 5(1)(4).
95 Commission Regulation 2790/99 for Vertical Agreements [1999] OJ L336.
96 Article 12 of the Regulation obliged the Commission to carry out regular reviews of the application of the Regulation.
97 Entered into force 1 June 2000.
98 Guidelines on Vertical Restraints [2000] OJ 291.

Regulation 2659/2000, which sets out new rules concerning the development and joint exploitation of intellectual property rights resulting from R&D agreements.[99]

Reassessment of the TTBE must therefore be viewed in the wider context of reform of Community competition law. The new Modernisation Regulation, Regulation 1/2003 on the Implementation of Article 81 and 82, introduces radical reform to the mechanics of Article 81(3), and Regulation 17/62 in particular.[100] The *ex-ante* notification procedure has been abandoned and the Commission's monopoly on the application of Article 81(3) abolished. National courts and national competition authorities (NCAs) now share this competence with the Commission. Since there is now no need to notify the Commission, the opposition procedure in many Community block exemption regulations has been widely abolished.

All these developments prompted an indepth review of the Commission's approach to IPR issues and the TTBE in particular.[101] On 1 October 2003, after a lengthy review process, the Commission published a draft regulation to replace 240/96. The draft text sought to establish a more flexible regime applying not only to patents and know-how but also to software copyright licensing. It also sought to make a clear difference between licensing between competitors and non-competitors (see below). The new TTBE came into force on 1 May 2004 to coincide with the Modernisation Regulation, 1/2003. The new regime will have a dramatic impact on technology licensing for companies operating in the EU. The TTBE will reduce the regulatory burden on companies although the degree of economic analysis now required introduces great complexity and more legal uncertainty. The Commission has followed the precedent set by BER 2790/99 and introduced detailed Guidelines accompanying the new TTBE. The Guidelines will play a key role in interpreting the TTBE.

3.16 THE NEW TECHNOLOGY TRANSFER BLOCK EXEMPTION 772/2004

The key elements of the new framework are as follows.

3.16.1 Scope

The TTBE 240/96 exempted technology licensing agreements from Article 81(1) under Article 81(3) if there were demonstrable positive effects which outweighed the negative effects. However, TTBE 240/96 only extended to know-how and patent licences, or agreements involving a mixture of the two. Copyright, design rights and trade marks were not covered unless ancillary to an exempted patent and/or know-how licence. IPRs are rarely licensed as a single element and are often bundled

---

99 Regulation 2658/2000 for specialisation agreements, and Regulation 2659/2000 for R&D agreements (both [2000] OJ L304).

100 Regulation 17 provides the Commission with the tools to enforce the Community competition rules.

101 For an insight into some of the competition policy issues concerning technology transfer agreements in the context of reform see Peeperkorn, L, 'IP Licences and Competition Rules: Striking the Right Balance' (2003) 26(4) World Comp 527.

together. Copyright, for example, is often licensed together with patent or know-how rights. While some copyright agreements are covered by regulations such as BER 2790/99 (which covers agreements that state that the reseller of hard copies of software supplied purely for resale does not acquire a licence to any rights in the software), many other arrangements (for example, distribution licences, whereby the distributor duplicates software and provides a physical medium on which a program is stored) did not benefit from 240/96. Bowing to pressure from the software industry, the Commission has extended the scope of TTBE 772/2004 to include software copyright licences (either stand-alone or incorporated with patents and/or know-how). Although the Commission indicated in its Evaluation Report of 240/96 that it would extend block exemption status to other types of IP right (including non-software related copyright licences), TTBE 772/2004 does not adopt this approach. Thus, a number of copyright and database-related agreements will not benefit from the legal certainty provided by the new TTBE; for example, those that relate to merchandising, broadcasting, satellite distribution rights and phonographic production. Non-software copyright agreements clearly present different issues for the Commission than those related to software. The Commission has argued in its defence that some of these other agreements (i) have less impact on competition, or (ii) do not raise the same exhaustion issues.

The TTBE 772/2004 applies only to agreements that have as their primary object a transfer of technology, as opposed to the purchase of goods and services. Unless the licence is for the purpose of manufacturing goods, it is not a technology transfer. Where agreements contain provisions that relate to the purchase and sale of products, the TTBE will apply to the extent that those provisions do not constitute the primary object of the agreement and are directly related to the application of the licensed technology. While the licensing of copyright for the purpose of reproduction and distribution of a protected work will not be directly covered by the TTBE, the accompanying guidelines make it clear that the Commission considers such an agreement to be similar to a technology licence and within the ambit of the new TTBE.

The TTBE will apply only to agreements between two parties (as the current regime does). Agreements between more than two parties or patent pools will not be exempt.

3.16.2 Competitors vs non-competitors

The new regime makes the important distinction between agreements concluded between 'competitors' (horizontal licences) and agreements concluded between non-competitors (vertical licences), the test being whether the parties to an agreement would have been actual or potential competitors in the absence of the agreement. The Commission's guidelines provide additional assistance at paragraphs 26–32. If the parties are both active in the same product or technology market, the parties will be deemed to be competitors.[102] If, without the agreement, the parties would not have been actual or potential competitors in any relevant market, the parties will be deemed to be non-competitors.[103] The Guidelines indicate that if the parties own technology that is either in a one-way blocking position (ie, the technology cannot be exploited without infringing on another technology) or in a two-way blocking position (ie, neither technology can be exploited without infringing on the technology of the other),

---

102 Paragraph 28, TTBE Guidelines.
103 *Ibid*, para 27.

the Commission will treat the licensor and the licensee as non-competitors.[104] In the case of a 'sweeping breakthrough', where the parties to the agreement may compete in the product market but are unlikely to do so in the future because the new product will replace existing products, the Commission will consider the parties, in most instances, to be non-competitors. However, where the licensed technology replaces the licensee's technology by rendering it obsolete or uncompetitive at the time of the conclusion of the agreement, the parties will be considered to be competitors.[105] Licences between competitors will be therefore be subject to stricter controls than licences between non-competitors.

Sometimes a licensor and licensee can become competitors after an agreement has been concluded. For instance, this may occur if the licensee develops its own technology and begins to license it, or produces its own technology in competition with the licensor. If the TTBE's distinction between competitors and non-competitors is applied then there would be a change to the list of blacklisted provisions (see below) applicable to the agreement. In these circumstances it is expected that the Commission will apply an *ex-ante* approach. Where the parties to an agreement become competitors subsequent to the conclusion of the agreement, the blacklisted restrictions applicable to non-competitors would continue to apply to the agreement, even though the position of the parties has changed.

3.16.3 Market share thresholds

In a radical departure from the old TTBE, TTBE 772/2004 introduces market share thresholds. Advisers must now carry out an economic analysis of the relevant market to determine the market share of the parties to an agreement. Although this approach is consistent with other block exemption regulations, for example BER 2790/99, the definition of the relevant market is notoriously difficult[106] and the introduction of market shares generally to Community block exemption regulations has been controversial.[107] Calculating market shares is a complex exercise, particularly where a market is innovative, and advisers will need to assess both the relevant technology and product markets carefully (see below). Agreements between competitors will be automatically exempt under the new TTBE where the *combined* market share of the parties does not exceed 20%. Where the parties are non-competitors, an agreement may benefit from block exemption where the market share of each party does not exceed 30%. If the market share thresholds are exceeded the agreement cannot benefit from block exemption status and the agreement must be carefully reviewed to determine whether it is non-restrictive or can benefit from an individual assessment under Article 81(3).

The 'relevant technology market' is defined as comprising the licensed technology as well as any substitute technology.[108] The Commission will calculate the licensor's market share on the basis of all sales by the licensor, the licensee and other licensees of

---

104 *Ibid*, para 25.

105 *Ibid*, para 26.

106 The Commission has published Guidance on this issue see, eg, Commission Notice on Market Definition of 9 December [1997] OJ 1997 C372.

107 Nazerali, J and Cowan, D, 'Reforming EU Distribution Rules – Has the Commission Found Vertical Reality?' [1999] 20 ECLR 159.

108 Article 1(1)(j)(i).

product (Article 3(3)). Technology market share would then be calculated on the basis of sales of products incorporating the relevant technology on downstream product markets.[109] The 'relevant product market' is defined as the market for final and intermediate products incorporating the licensed technology as well as potential competing substitutes in Article 1(1)(j)(ii). Market share will be calculated on the basis of sales value data available for the preceding calendar year. Estimates will be used if no data is available. In cases where new technology is created, it is anticipated that the Commission will calculate a market share of 100% and block exemption status will not apply.

Market shares can of course fluctuate and market share analysis will be an ongoing exercise. If the TTBE thresholds are exceeded for a period of more than two years, the benefit is lost and the exemption is withdrawn. Where this is the case, the parties would need to review the agreement to see whether it may benefit from an individual exemption under Article 81(3).

Given the complexities involved and the level of economic analysis required, the extension of market share thresholds to technology transfer agreements has been controversial. Some have questioned whether the introduction of market share thresholds is necessary since Article 82 of the EC Treaty will always prevail over a block exemption regulation.[110] One of the main objectives of the TTBE reform was to enhance legal certainty and it is arguable that the introduction of market share analysis has compromised that goal.[111]

Advisers must ensure that the parties closely monitor the relevant market shares even after an agreement is signed and the restrictive nature of the agreement may need to be reassessed at a future date. National courts must also carry out difficult economic assessments, adding to the general climate of legal uncertainty.

3.16.4 Blacklisted provisions

TTBE 772/2004 abolishes the inflexible system of blacklists, white lists and grey lists and replaces it with a more streamlined system incorporating only blacklisted provisions. The TTBE introduces two lists of blacklisted or 'hardcore' provisions – one for competitors and one for non-competitors.[112] The inclusion of any blacklisted provision will render TTBE 772/2004 inapplicable to the entire agreement (as was the case under TTBE 240/96). The blacklisted provisions relate to various restrictive provisions, such as price determination; allocation of markets and territories; and restrictions on active and passive sales. It will be considered at all times anti-competitive to restrict the ability of a licensor or licensee to conduct research and development activities, unless such restriction is essential to prevent the disclosure of know-how to third parties. Certain other obligations, articulated in Article 5, are called 'conditions' and will be grey listed, meaning they are neither blacklisted nor block exempted. These conditions must be individually assessed in terms of their pro -and anti-competitive effects. If the Commission finds that the condition infringes Article 81

---

109 Article 3(3).
110 See *Tetra Pak v Commission* (1990).
111 See Dolmans, M and Piiloa, A, 'The Proposed New Technology Transfer Block Exemption: Is Europe Really Better Off than with the Current Regulation?' (2003) 26(4) World Comp 541.
112 Article 4, 'hard core restrictions'.

it may be severed from the main body of the agreement.[113] Conditions will be particularly relevant when assessing software copyright licensing under the new regulation.

The new approach brings about greater flexibility and will encourage companies to devise their licensing agreements to meet genuine commercial needs rather than the rigid blacklist provisions of the old regime.

3.16.5 Grant back clause

Most licence agreements incorporate a grant back clause which requires the licensee to assign, or at least license, any improvements it may make to the licensed technology during the term of the agreement. The new TTBE will exempt an exclusive licence to improvements that cannot be separated from the licensed technology, ie, *non-severable* improvements.[114] An exclusive grant-back licence to *severable* improvements however will require individual examination. An obligation on the licensee to assign to the licensor the rights to any improvements made to the licensed technology will also require an individual examination.

3.16.6 No challenge clause

Another common feature of licensing agreements is a clause which restricts the ability of the licensee to challenge the licensed technology. An obligation on the licensee not to challenge the validity or secrecy of the intellectual property rights of the licensor are not automatically exempt but examined individually to establish whether such an obligation is in breach of Article 81(1). If the licensed agreement contains invalid rights, it would be anti-competitive to prevent a licensee from challenging such rights. The new TTBE recognises the right established by the old TTBE whereby the licensor may terminate the agreement if the licensee challenges the validity of the intellectual property right.

3.16.7 Non-compete restriction

TTBE 772/2004 permits the inclusion of non-compete restrictions in technology licence agreements. Restrictions on the licensor or the licensee to conduct research and development activities, or restrictions on the licensee to exploit its own technology, are not however, acceptable. Although the new TTBE is more permissive than TTBE 240/96 in this regard, advisers will still need carefully to review non-compete provisions to ensure that they do not infringe Article 81(1). Where the imposition of non-compete restrictions results in foreclosure of the market because, for example, of the nature of the technology and of the activities of the licensor, such provisions are likely to be deemed anti-competitive.

---

113 The severability rule applies only to restrictions contained in Article 5. Blacklisted provisions contained in Article 4 are not severable and the inclusion of one or more of these clauses in the agreement renders the block exemption inapplicable.

114 TTBE Guidelines, fn 88.

3.16.8 Tying

The new TTBE does not contain any restrictions on tying obligations (ie, when the licensor makes the licensing of its technology conditional on the licensee taking a licence for other technology or purchasing a product) in contrast to the position under TTBE 240/96, which prohibited tying obligations.

3.16.9 Transitional period

TTBE 772/2004 makes provision for a transitional period. Licensing agreements that come into force before 30 April 2004 and which are currently exempt under TTBE 240/96 will have provisional validity until 31 October 2005. After that date advisers will need to ensure that all agreements, regardless of whether they are compatible with TTBE 240/96, comply with the new regime, noting in particular the new market share thresholds.

3.17 INDIVIDUAL ASSESSMENT UNDER ARTICLE 81(3)

Licensing agreements which did not fall within the ambit of TTBE 240/96 and which contained provisions which were not ancillary to an agreement covered by that Regulation or by BER 2790/99 benefited from an individual exemption provided the four cumulative conditions articulated in Article 81(3) were met. A number of individual exemptions have been granted over the years in respect of licences of intellectual property rights.[115] However, new Regulation 1/2003, which entered into force on 1 May 2004, abolishes the system of notification for individual exemption rendering Article 81(3) directly applicable by national competition authorities and the national courts. Companies are no longer required to notify the Commission under Article 81(3) and must assess the validity of their intellectual property licences for themselves. As far as intellectual property licences are concerned, legal advisers will need to follow closely the terms of the new TTBE to get a sense of what provisions might be acceptable.

3.18 COPYRIGHT LICENCES AND THE NEW TTBE

Although the Commission considered extending block exemption status to include other types of intellectual property rights such as trademark and non-software copyright licensing, the new TTBE does not cover other types of property rights. Consequently, there is no specific block exemption regulation for copyright licences.

However, software copyright licenses may benefit from the new TTBE and BER 2790/99 provided they are 'ancillary' to a licence of a patent and/or know-how.

---

115 For example, in *Moosehead/Whitbread* a trademark licence was individually exempt [1990] OJ L100/32.

3.19   TRADE MARK LICENCES AND THE NEW TTBE[116]

Trade mark licences often form an important part of a franchise or distribution agreement. Where the licence is not the primary object of the agreement and is ancillary, the trade mark licence may benefit from BER 2790/99 (see above). The new TTBE does not apply to trademarks even though exclusive trade market licenses may infringe Article 81(1). Nevertheless, the Commission's principal decisions on trade mark licences, *Campari* (2002), and *Moosehead/Whitbread* (1990), demonstrate that it regards trade mark licences as broadly similar to patent and know-how licences and thus the new TTBE will be a very useful reference point for advisers when drawing up a trade mark licence.

In *Moosehead/Whitbread*, an English brewer (Whitbread) was granted the exclusive right in the UK to brew and sell Canadian Moosehead beer. The Commission held that the agreement was primarily a trade mark licence and that the know-how was really secondary to the trademark. This meant that the know-how licensing block exemption was not applicable since trade mark licensing is not within the scope of a technology transfer agreement as defined in Community regulations. The Commission decided that the exclusive grant of the trade mark rights was within the ambit of Article 81(1) but granted an individual exemption on the basis that the agreement would be enhancing competition between brands.

The Commission held that the grant of exclusive trade mark rights, the prohibition on the licensee making active sales outside the territory, and the obligation on the licensee not to produce or promote within the territory any other beer identified as a Canadian beer, all infringed Article 81(1) since its aim was to restrict competition within the Community. The obligation on Whitbread to maintain a quality standard did not fall within Article 81(1), nor did the obligations to follow specific instructions in relation to use of the know-how, and to maintain confidentiality in this respect. The Commission also held that the obligation to buy special yeast only from Moosehead or a third party designated by Moosehead did not infringe Article 81(1).

The Commission advised that clauses that restricted challenges may constitute a restriction on competition within the meaning of Article 81(1), because they assist the perpetuation of a trade mark that constitutes an unfair obstacle to entry into a market. The Commission concluded that the clause preventing Whitbread from challenging the validity of the trade mark did not significantly restrict competition and that the Moosehead trade mark would not therefore prevent other companies hoping to enter the UK beer market. Having concluded that certain provisions of the Moosehead trade mark licence infringed Article 81(1), the Commission granted an exemption under Article 81(3).[117]

---

116 For discussion of trade marks generally in EC law, see Chapter 1.

117 For a more detailed discussion see Parr, N, 'Avoiding Antitrust Pitfalls in Drafting and Enforcing Intellectual Property Agreements in the European Union' [1997] EIPR 43.

3.20 LICENSING AND OTHER HORIZONTAL INTELLECTUAL PROPERTY AGREEMENTS

3.20.1 Pooling agreements

Certain horizontal agreements relating to intellectual property rights may infringe Article 81. Intellectual property right owners in different Member States, with rights for similar products, can share exploitation of their intellectual property right by cross-licensing those rights. Where rights are complementary in the stages of production of a product, they can be pooled to monopolise the whole production of the product (horizontal agreements) and, thus, divide the market between right owners. Such agreements may achieve supra-competitive profits and keep new entrants out of a market, but they may also be essential to continued research and development or may constitute a reasonable response to the superior bargaining power of a third party (for example, copyright collective societies allow viable exploitation and enforcement of copyright for individual owners in the face of the bargaining power of media users and mass infringers). A careful balance between restrictions harmful to the public interest and those which are beneficial is needed.

The Commission has, for instance, prohibited a patent pooling scheme whereby companies in a particular industry pool their patents and agree not to grant licences to third parties. Quotas and prices might also be fixed and entry to the market prohibited for third parties.[118] Occasionally an exemption or comfort letter has been granted by the Commission where pooling of patents and know-how contributes to technical or economic progress in the market.

Sometimes collecting societies enter into reciprocal agreements and these may be caught by Article 81. In *IFPI 'Simulcasting'* (2003) the Commission concluded that the collecting societies had jointly fixed a simulcasting royalty fee and this infringed Article 81(1). The collecting society acted on behalf of various record companies whereby a 'one-stop' licence could be granted to media broadcasters with the intention of simulcasting radio and TV programmes and also by the internet. Although the Commission objected to the territorial restrictions that would have restricted competition between national collecting societies, the Commission decided that the requirements of Article 81(3) were met because the agreement created a new licence, giving consumers much wider access to programmes via the internet.

Pooling agreements may be legitimate as a necessary response to superior bargaining power. A great many collecting societies exist for instance to which individual artists assign their copyrights. The collective society has far greater bargaining power and will negotiate royalties on an individual's behalf with the media. In these circumstances, Article 82 may apply to prevent the society abusing their position of strength (see below).

3.20.2 Trade mark delimitation agreements

Sometimes owners of trade marks will accept restrictions on the exercise and use of those rights if a dispute arises with another party. These settlement agreements, however, may fall foul of Article 81(1). The ECJ has ruled that trade mark delimitation agreements are, in principle, legitimate, provided there is a genuine dispute between

---

118 *Video Cassette Recorders Agreements* [1978] OJ L47/42, [1978] 2 CMLR 160.

the parties and that the agreement is no more restrictive than is necessary to resolve the issue of contention and confusion. The Commission tends to regard agreements where the parties agree not to use specific trade marks in certain Member States as a form of market-sharing arrangement.[119] Nevertheless, the attitude of the Commission with regard to trade mark delimitation agreement that allow free movement of products between Member States is one of approval.[120]

3.21   ARTICLE 82 OF THE EC TREATY AND LICENCE AGREEMENTS

Mere possession of an intellectual property right might confer a dominant position, but dominance *per se* is not contrary to the EC Treaty, only an *abuse* of a dominant position (see Chapter 1). In *Parke, Davis & Co v Probel* (1968) the European Court held that ownership of a patent is not an abuse in itself, although 'the utilisation of the patent could degenerate into an improper exploitation of the protection'.[121] Thus, before Article 82 applies there must be a dominant position, an improper exercise of that position and the possibility that trade between Member States might be affected. An analysis under Article 81 of the EC Treaty does not affect the application of Article 82. Accordingly, a licence justified under Article 81(3) of the EC Treaty may still fall to be considered as abusive of a dominant position. In *Tetra-Pak Rausing SA v Commission* (1990) the Commission controversially decided that Tetra-Pak had abused its dominant position in the market for cartons and machines for packaging milk following the acquisition of another company, Liquipak, and an exclusive licence held by Liquipak relating to a new method of sterilisation of cartons suitable for long-life milk. Tetra-Pak had an almost monopolistic position in the market for the supply of machines for sterilising and filling drinks cartons (91% of the market). The Commission objected to the exclusive nature of the licence when Tetra-Pak was already in such a dominant position. It was held that the mere acquisition of the right could constitute an abuse in the exceptional factual background. The dominance of Tetra-Pak's position meant that acquiring the licence effectively prevented any other competitor entering the market. Tetra-Pak was fined 75 million ECUs (European Currency Units) for abuse of a dominant position. The Court of First Instance upheld the Commission's decision despite the fact that the exclusive licence was compatible with TTBE 240/96. In a subsequent case, *Eurofix-Bauco v Hilti* (1994), the Court decided that the undertaking concerned had abused its dominant position by demanding excessive royalties from third parties for the grant of licences of right.

3.21.1 Compulsory licences

The decisions in *Tetra-Pak* and *Hilti* involved a straightforward application of Article 82. Three far more revealing judgments concerning Article 82 dominance are those in *Renault* (1988), *Volvo v Veng* (1988) and the controversial *Magill TV Guide* cases (1995).[122] All three cases concerned the issue of compulsory licences.

119 See, for example, *Re Toltecs and Dorcet Trade Mark* (1983).
120 See, for example, *Re Persil Trade Mark* (1978).
121 Paragraph 4.
122 Case C241/91, *Radio Telefis Eireann v Commission* [1995] ECR I–743, [1995] 4 CMLR 718 affirming [1991] ECR II–485, [1991] 4 CMLR 586.

An intellectual property right confers the ability on its owner to decide whether to grant licences to others. The question has arisen under Article 82 whether the owner of an intellectual property right can be forced to grant a licence of that right to a third party. This issue arose in the cases on spare parts for cars, *Renault* and *Volvo Veng*. In *Volvo*, a third party had imported spare motorcar parts (consignments of front wings of Volvo cars) into the UK. Volvo, the car manufacturer, owned the UK registered industrial design for the spare parts and commenced proceedings in the English courts for infringement of its design right. Veng claimed that a refusal to grant a licence to import and supply the spare parts was an abuse of Volvo's dominant position under Article 82. The European Court held that it was for national law to determine the scope of intellectual property rights and that it was for a design right owner to decide on granting of licences. The Court stated that:

> ... the right of the proprietor of a protected design to prevent third parties from manufacturing and selling or importing, without its consent, products incorporating the design constitutes the very subject-matter of its exclusive rights. It follows that an obligation imposed upon the proprietor of a protected design to grant to third parties, even in return for a reasonable royalty, a licence for the supply of products incorporating the design would lead to the proprietor thereof being deprived of the substance of its exclusive right, and that refusal to grant such a licence cannot in itself constitute an abuse of a dominant position.[123]

Volvo was able to continue as sole supplier of Volvo spare parts. Clearly, the key phrase in the Court's judgment is *in itself* because the Court added that the *exercise* of the exclusive right may infringe Article 82 for example, an arbitrary refusal to supply spare parts to independent repairers, to fix prices at an unfair level or refuse to supply when the model of car was still in circulation.

A contrary position was adopted in *RTE and ITP v EC Commission* in 1995, commonly known as the *Magill TV Guide* cases. Three television companies each published weekly guides which contained details of their own programme schedules for which copyright protection was available under UK and Irish law then in force. An Irish company, Magill, began publishing its own weekly guide in response to consumer demand containing schedules for all three services. No publication at the time contained the details of all three companies' programmes for a week in advance in contrast to the position in other countries on the continent where a single publication for was widely available. RTE, BBC and ITP sought a restraining order from the Irish High Court for breach of copyright and were successful. Without the licence, Magill was forced to cease publication. A complaint was subsequently lodged at the Commission under Regulation 17/62 and an investigation commenced. The Commission found that RTE, BBC and ITP had abused their dominant positions in the relevant markets (their own TV listings) by refusing to provide Magill access to the TV information. On appeal to the Court of First Instance the Court agreed on the following grounds:

> [Each] applicant, by reserving the exclusive right to publish its weekly television programme listings, was preventing the emergence on the market of a new product, namely a general television magazine likely to compete with its own magazine, the [RTE/Guide/Radio Times/TV Times]. The applicant was thus using its copyright in

---

123 At 6235.

the programme listings which it produced as part of its broadcasting activity in order to secure a monopoly in the derivative market of weekly television guides ...

Conduct of that type – characterised by preventing the production and marketing of a new product, for which there is potential consumer demand, on the ancillary market of television magazines and thereby excluding all competition from that market solely in order to secure the applicant's monopoly – clearly goes beyond what is necessary to fulfil the essential function of the copyright as permitted in Community law.[124]

Essentially, the European Court initiated compulsory licensing under Article 82 and found that a refusal to make television listings available to third parties for publication constituted an abuse of a dominant position. The Court added that the refusal could not be objectively justified. Effectively, this forced a compulsory licence on the copyright owner and introduced for the first time the 'essential facilities' doctrine to intellectual property rights (see below). However, the circumstances in *Magill* were said to be 'exceptional':

(1) there was no substitute for a composite weekly television guide for which there was a specific, constant and regular potential demand on the part of consumers;

(2) the refusal to supply prevented the appearance of a new product for which there was a potential consumer demand;

(3) there was no justification for such refusal; and

(4) the broadcasters were reserving to themselves, the secondary market of weekly television guides by excluding all competition on the market.

The judgment attracted much controversy.[125] For instance, it was not clear whether the list of 'exceptional circumstances' are cumulative. Moreover, the case did not clearly establish when such a power to force licensing might be employed, the concern being that the precedent might be applied to intellectual property rights acquired by investment and innovation; for example patents, in contrast to TV listings. The situation was one in which many Member States would not accord copyright to the factual information at issue at all and was ancillary to the separate controls exercised over broadcasting.

3.21.2 Essential facilities and intellectual property licensing

Article 82 and the essential facilities doctrine is an enormously complex issue.[126] It was introduced into EC competition law following the decision of the ECJ in *Commercial Solvents* (1974), although the Court did not actually use the term 'essential facilities'. The doctrine has its origins in US antitrust and was first considered in *United States v Terminal Railroad Association of St Louis* (1912).

The key issue is whether the owner of an essential facility can be required under Article 82 to grant competitors access to that facility in order to provide complementary or ancillary services in another market. In a series of cases, the Community Courts have found that refusal to allow access to an essential facility constitutes an abuse of a dominant position. Although originally intended to describe

---

124 Paragraph 73.
125 Pathak, A, 'Vertical Restraints in EEC Competition Law' [1988] 2 LIEI 15.
126 On essential facilities and competition law generally, see Whish, R, *Competition Law* (5th edn, London: Butterworths, 2003), Chapter 17.

a physical infrastructure such as a port or airport, the doctrine has gradually expanded over the years to encompass intellectual property rights (*Magill* (1995)) or spare parts (*Hugin* (1979)). Community case law has not satisfactorily resolved the issue of compulsory licensing and essential facilities, although the Advocate General in *Oscar Bronner v Mediaprint* (1998) attempted to clarify the scope of the doctrine (see below).

The essential facilities doctrine is particularly relevant in industries such as telecommunications, energy and transport where involvement of the state has tended to create a monopoly. The Commission has adopted a policy over the years of liberalisation and de-monopolisation of these sectors with varying degrees of success. The use of the essential facility doctrine in these sectors has been relatively uncontroversial. Concern has arisen, however, in the private sphere as to the appropriateness of intervention and companies have expressed concern over the need to protect their investment and prevent competitors from taking a free ride. If companies are discouraged from making an investment because of free rider concerns, granting access under Article 82 to the essential facilities of a dominant undertaking although appearing to be pro-competitive, might in fact turn out to be anti-competitive in the long run.[127] Compelling dominant firms to grant access to an essential facility often entails significant economic disadvantages. For instance, the incentive to innovate and invest is greatly reduced if others can enjoy a 'free ride'. The incentive to develop a second source is also reduced and assessing compensation in return for granting access is notoriously difficult. Certainly, the *Magill* judgment raised fears that the holder of an intellectual property licence might be compelled to grant a licence to rivals. Subsequent essential facilities cases, however, suggested that the decision in *Magill* was exceptional and assuaged concerns that the precedent established might apply to intellectual property rights acquired by innovation and investment. The European Court's judgment in *Oscar Bronner v Mediaprint* (1998) and the Court of First Instance's decisions in *Tierce Ladbroke v Commission* (1997) and *European Night Services v Commission* (1998) confirmed a narrow interpretation of the essential facilities doctrine established in *Magill*. However, recent Commission cases against Microsoft and IMS Health have introduced unwelcome confusion to this issue once again (see below).

Oscar Bronner

Although *Oscar Bronner* was not an intellectual property case, the European Court, and the Advocate General in particular, clarified the main features of the doctrine in an attempt to limit its application. In this sense, the case forms part of a single strand of case law alongside *Magill* and ought to be considered in this context.[128] A large Austrian newspaper group, Mediaprint, refused to include the smaller publisher's newspaper in its national home-delivery service. *Oscar Bronner* brought an action under national competition legislation and the case was referred to the European Court to determine whether the refusal might constitute an abuse of a dominant position under Article 82.

The Court described *Magill* as an exceptional case and stated that for there to be an abuse the refusal would have to be: (1) likely to eliminate all competition in the

---

127 See Whish. Whish, R, *Competition Law*, (5th edn, London: Butterworths, 2003), Chapter 17.
128 The Court in fact relied upon its earlier decisions in *Renault*, *Volvo*, *Magill* and *Ladbroke* to resolve the *Bronner* case.

downstream market by the person refused; (2) incapable of objective justification; and (3) indispensable to business in that downstream market, in that there would be no actual or potential substitute in existence for it. The Court proceeded to distinguish *Magill* and stated that these conditions were not met in *Oscar Bronner*, as newspapers are often distributed by post or through shops and kiosks. The Court also stated that in order to demonstrate that the home-delivery scheme was indispensable, it was not enough to argue that it was not economically viable to set up another scheme by reason of small circulation. Instead, the complainant must demonstrate that it was 'not economically viable to create a second home-delivery scheme for the distribution of daily newspapers with a circulation comparable to that of the daily newspapers distributed by the existing scheme'.[129] Referring to the exceptional circumstances of *Magill*, the Court stated that the information required by *Magill* was indispensable to the publication of a comprehensive listings guide; there was clear consumer demand for the new product, there were no objective justifications for the refusal to supply and the refusal would eliminate all competition in the secondary market for TV guides. The Court's decision in *Oscar Bronner* confirmed the general proposition that a refusal to supply intellectual property rights will *not* amount to abuse under Article 82, restating the law established in *Renault* and *Volvo* and narrowing the application of *Magill*.[130]

IMS Health and Microsoft

Despite the limits placed on the essential facilities doctrine in *Oscar Bronner*, the Commission has adopted two decisions in recent years, which in many respects have revived the *Magill* precedent, *IMS Health* and *Microsoft*.

In *NDC Health/IMS Health: (Interim Measures)* the Commission granted interim measures (for the first time since 1995) against IMS Health, the world leader in data collection on pharmaceutical sales and prescriptions, as a result of its refusal to grant a licence to competitors to enable them to have access to its copyright format for processing regulation sales data, the so-called '1860 brick structure'. The 1860 brick structure divides Germany into 1860 geographical areas, and then collects information on sales and prescriptions of pharmaceutical products for each area. The Commission concluded that IMS's brick structure had become a *de facto* industry standard and that the pharmaceutical companies were dependent upon receiving sales data in this format. Two competitors, NDC and AzyX, had tried to enter the market but without access to the favoured 1860 brick structure, data delivery of these companies could not be presented in the same format as the 1860 structure and thus was not marketable. The Commission ruled that IMS's refusal to license its 1860 brick structure was an abuse of its dominant position in the German market and ordered IMS to license its intellectual property rights to third parties so they could access the market. The Commission stated that the four factors the Court had said amounted to 'exceptional circumstances' in *Magill* were not cumulative. Distinguishing *IMS* from *Magill*, the Commission noted that IMS was not actually preventing the emergence of a new product. Adopting an interim order requiring a licence, the Commission ruled that it

---

129 Paras 45–46.
130 For a more detailed discussion than space permits here see Derclaye, E, 'Abuses of Dominant Position and Intellectual Property Rights: A Suggestion to Reconcile the Community Courts (2003) 26(4) Case Law' World Comp 685.

need not establish a definitive infringement of Article 82 and that a *prima facie* case would suffice. The Commission stated at paragraph 90: ' ... [that] there is good reason to suppose that unless NDC is granted a licence to the 1860 brick structure its German operation will go out of business and that there will be intolerable damage to the public interest.'

In an unusual step, and using powers untouched in almost 20 years, the President of the Court of First Instance suspended the Commission's decision by order, pending a full submission from the Commission.[131] At a subsequent hearing of the application for suspension, the President made a further order continuing the suspension of the interim measures until the full appeal was heard.[132] The President considered that there was a serious doubt as to whether there was a duty to license when the holder of an intellectual property right was itself offering a similar product as the complainant requesting a licence. He went on to say: 'The Commission's provisional conclusion that the prevention of the emergence of a new product or service for which there is a potential consumer demand is not an indispensable part of the notion of 'exceptional circumstances' developed by the European Court in *Magill* constitutes, at first sight, an extensive interpretation of that notion ...'[133] The President added that the requirements in *Magill* may, in fact, be cumulative. Moreover, the seriousness of the issue merited a final decision on the merits and could not be decided by an interim measure. The decision of the Court of First Instance was appealed to the European Court by NDC and rejected.[134] However, this left unaffected the Article 234 reference from the German court. The European Court issued its judgment on the preliminary reference on 29 April 2004.

The Court's judgment highlights significant disparities in Community decision-making. Certainly, the Commission's surprising and controversial decision goes much further than *Magill* in several respects. First, the decision seems to suggest that the 'exceptional circumstances' which justify a compulsory licence is customer preference. If sufficiently strong, these preferences can convert a competitive advantage into an essential facility, which the dominant owner must share with competitors. Secondly, the Commission's decision establishes the principle that it is sufficient if the proposed licensees intend to offer substantially the same product or service as the owner of the intellectual property right. This extends *Magill* in that the proposed licensee does not need to offer a new kind of product or service for which there is an unsatisfied demand; a *similar* product will suffice. Finally, the interim decision ordering a compulsory licence suggests that the Commission regards the primary purpose of Article 82 as being to protect competitors. The European Court's decision to reject the appeal by NDC against the suspension order in 2002 was therefore welcomed and reinforces the Court's views expressed in a number of essential facilities cases post-*Magill* that the primary purpose of Article 82 is to safeguard the interest of consumers and *not* the interests of competitors.[135] Moreover, the Court's judgment clarifies the list of conditions that have to be fulfilled to constitute a refusal to license a copyright as an

---

131 Case T–184/01 R, *IMS Health*, Order of 10 August 2001 (First Order).

132 Case T–184/01 R, *IMS Health*, Order of 26 October 2001 (Second Order).

133 Second Order, para 106.

134 Simultaneously, the German national courts referred to the Court of Justice under Article 234 a number of questions intended to resolve the conflict between the judgments of the German courts and the decision adopted by the Commission.

135 See, eg, *European Night Services* and *Tierce Ladbroke*.

abuse. For instance, there must be a 'new product' involved and there must be an exclusion of competition from a secondary market arising from the 'indispensability' of the protected input.[136]

The European Court's judgment in *IMS* is likely to have increased resonance following the Commission's recent decision to impose record fines on the US software giant, Microsoft, effectively compelling Microsoft to license its software to competitors. The Commission's decision suggests that it considers the *Magill* case is no longer the exception to the rule.

Microsoft

In March 2004, the Commission imposed a record €517.2 million ($604 million) fine on Microsoft[137] for abusing its dominant position in the European market. Following a five-year investigation, the Commission found that the US software giant had violated the competition rules by deliberately restricting the interoperability of its Windows software with competing computer applications. Microsoft's operating systems run on more than 95% of the world's personal computers, a situation which the Commission described as a 'near monopoly'. This is the first case in Community competition law where a software company of such magnitude has been condemned for anti-competitive behaviour, since cases involving IBM and Digital in the 1980s and 1990s respectively were settled via undertakings without prejudice to the rights of the parties. In addition to the record fine, the Commission gave Microsoft three months to present PC manufacturers with a stripped-down version of its Windows operating system that excludes the Windows Media Player. The Commission said that Microsoft must release information that may be protected by intellectual property laws to its competitors.

The Commission was concerned that Microsoft's business model of strengthening its near monopoly in computer operating systems by tying in peripherals such as Windows Media Player, would deter innovation and ultimately suppress consumer choice, as potential competitors would be unable to compete. Without the ruling, Microsoft could have achieved dominance in other markets. The Commission noted that the company had future plans to introduce additional functionalities such as virus protection and search engine capabilities. Although the Commission's ruling will still allow Microsoft to retain the right to offer the option of its operating system including Windows Media Player, the company has been forbidden from making the latter package more attractive to PC manufacturers, for example by way of discounts or incentives. The ruling that tying Windows Media Player with Windows operating system constitutes an abuse is not in fact a deviation from Community law precedent. The Commission has taken a more lenient view of the tying prohibitions contained in Article 82 than many recent Community court decisions.[138]

---

136 See Sufrin, B, 'The IMS Case' (2004) Comp Law 18–30.
137 Commission decision, 24 March 2004, Case COMP/C–3/37.792, *Microsoft United States v Microsoft Corporation*, No 00–5212, Judgment of 28 June 2001, United States Court of Appeals for the District of Columbia, ecfp.cadc.uscourts.gov/MS-Docs/1720/0.pdf.
   available at http://europa.eu.int/comm/competition/antitrust/cases/decisions/37792/en.pdf.
138 Case T219/99, *British Airways plc v Commission* [2004] 4 CMLR 19, Case T–203/01 *Michelin v Commission* ([2001] OJ C331).

The Commission also ordered Microsoft to disclose within 120 days complete and accurate interface documentation to its competitors allowing them to develop competing products, as previously Microsoft had refused to supply rivals with the necessary interoperability specifications thus preventing them from developing interoperable workgroup server operating system products. The disclosures would need to be updated with every new Microsoft release. If any such information was protected by intellectual property rights, the Commission said that Microsoft 'would be entitled to reasonable remuneration'. The decision does not, however, specify what constitutes 'reasonable remuneration', again demonstrating the problems of compulsory licensing in the private sphere. According to the Commission, the disclosures, which will not include the Windows source code, were necessary because the 'illegal behaviour is still going on' and disclosure was the only solution to restore the conditions of fair competition. The Commission appears to follow its decision in *IMS* and suggests once again that the 'exceptional circumstances', which justify a compulsory licence, is customer preference. As was the case in *IMS*, where these preferences are sufficiently strong, they may convert a competitive advantage into an essential facility, which the dominant owner must share with competitors. Moreover, the Commission's decision reaffirms the principle it established in *IMS* that it is sufficient if the proposed licensees intend to offer substantially the same product or service as the owner of the intellectual property right.

Microsoft has appealed the ruling and asked for the Commission's decision of 24 March to be annulled or, alternatively, that the fine imposed be reduced substantially.[139] The principles established in the Court's judgment in *IMS* are therefore likely to be applied in the final appeal.

The *IMS* and *Microsoft* cases do not contain any radical new interpretation or application of Article 82 of the EC Treaty and consequently Chapter II of the Competition Act 1998. However, it is suggested that 'they do illustrate differences – sometimes subtle, sometimes obvious – between the European Union and the United States to balancing the interests of IP right holders with that of stimulating competition where a proprietary technology has become the *de facto* industry standard'.[140] Unfortunately, the cases also demonstrate a lack of clarity in Community decision-making, rendering compulsory licences and essential facilities a key area of concern for intellectual property owners.[141]

3.21.3 Copyright collecting societies

Copyright collecting societies, in particular, have been the subject of investigation under Article 82 of the EC Treaty. Although the *existence* of collecting societies, designed to ensure that individual artists receive appropriate remuneration for their work, is not objectionable under the EC Treaty, certain activities may fall foul of

---

139 The Court has assigned the case number T-201/04. Although a final decision is unlikely for several years, Microsoft has expressed a desire to reopen settlement talks with the Commission as the case progresses.

140 Volcker, SB, 'Competition Law and IP – The Implications of Microsoft and IMS Health: Interesting Times for Dominant Intellectual Property Holders in Europe'(2004) 17(14) CLI.

141 For recent US case law on this issue see *Intergraph Corporation v Intel Corporation* (1998) and the decision of the Federal Court, *Intergraph Corporation v Intel Corporation* (1999).

Article 82. For example, discrimination against individuals from other Member States has been considered to be potentially abusive (*Re GEMA (No 1)*) (1971), as have clauses that restrict an author from acting unilaterally, provisions which are unreasonable with respect to use by the media or any attempt to extend protection to non-copyright works. Recently, the Commission warned 16 copyright collecting societies which collected royalties on behalf of musicians that they may be infringing Community competition rules. The Commission objected to the cross-licensing arrangement (the so-called 'Santiago agreement') that the societies had between each other, which the Commission stated caused an 'effective lock-up of national territories, which extended to the internet the national monopolies the societies have held in the off-line world'. The Commission made it clear that there should be competition between collecting societies to the benefit of companies that offer music on the internet and to consumers that listen to it.[142]

Further Reading

Bercusson, B, 'The Contract of Employment and Contracting Out – The Patents Act 1977' [1980] EIPR 257

Brinkhof, J, 'The Desirability, Necessity and Feasibility of Co-operation Between Courts in the Field of European Patent Law' [1997] EIPR 226

Chandler, P, 'Employee's Inventions: Inventorship and Ownership' [1997] EIPR 262

Derclaye, E, 'Abuses of Dominant Position and Intellectual Property Rights: A Suggestion to Reconcile the Community Courts Case Law' (2003) 26(4) World Comp 685

Dolmans, M and Piiloa, A, 'The Proposed New Technology Transfer Block Exemption: Is Europe Really Better Off than with the Current Regulation?' (2003) 26(4) World Comp 541)

Gagliardi, AF, 'Territorial Restraints in Pure Trade Mark Licence Agreements: An Unsettled Issue' 19(12) [1997] EIPR 723

Garzaniti, L, 'Recent Developments in the European Commission's Practice in the Communications Sector: Part 2' [2004] 25(4) ECLR 234

Harrington, J, 'Access to Intellectual Property in the Light of Convergence: Should New Rules Apply?' [2001] 12(5) Ent LR 133

Hoolahan, M, 'Employees' Inventions – The Practical Implications – Ownership and Compensation – The UK Patents Act 1977' [1979] EIPR 140

Jacob, R, 'The Enlarged Board of Appeal of the EPO: A Proposal' [1997] EIPR 224

Karet, I, 'Analysis: English Courts and the EPO: What Next?' [1997] IPQ 244

Moore, M, 'A General Period of Grace in a First-to-file World: Key Issues' [2002] IPQ 75

McCurdy, GVS, 'Intellectual Property and Competition: Does the Essential Facilities Doctrine Shed Any New Light?' [2003] 25(10) EIPR 472

Nazerali, J and Cowan, D, 'Reforming EU Distribution Rules – Has the Commission Found Vertical Reality?' [1999] 20 ECLR 159

Peeperkorn, L, 'IP Licences and Competition Rules: Striking the Right Balance' (2003) 26(4) World Comp 527

Phillips, J, 'Employees' Inventions: the Green Paper Proposal', in Phillips, J (ed), *Patents in Perspective* (Oxford: ESC, 1985)

---

142 Reuters News Article, 3 May 2004. Link to Commission press release: http://europa.eu.int/rapid/pressReleaseAction.do?reference=IP/04/586&format=HTML&aged=0&language=EN &guiLanguage=en.

Phillips, J, 'Rewarding the Employee-inventor' [1985] EIPR 275

Phillips, J and Hoolahan, M, *Employees' Inventions in the United Kingdom* (Oxford: ESC, 1982)

Ratcliff, J, 'Major Events and Policy Issues in EC Competition Law' 2002–03: Part 1, [2004] 5(2) ICCLR 19 and Part 2 [2004] 15(3) ICCLR 55

Reid, B, 'Employee Inventions under the Patents Act 1977' [1979] JBL 350

Stothers, C, 'The End of Exclusivity?: Abuse of Intellectual Property Rights in the EU *IMS Health* case' (Commission Interim Measures, Suspended by Order of the President of the Court of First Instance)' [2002] EIPR 86

Vollebregt, E, 'The New Technology Transfer Block Exemption: From Straitjacket to Moving Targets' [2004] 10(6) CTLR 123

Wielsch, D, 'Competition Policy for Information Platform Technology' [2004] 25(2) ECLR 95

Willens, J, 'The EPC: The Emperor's Phantom Clothes? A Blueprint Instead of a Green Paper' [1998] IPQ 1

CHAPTER 4

PATENTABLE SUBJECT MATTER

Patents are granted for inventions, but only those inventions satisfying the statutory criteria for patentability. Section 1(1) of the Patents Act (PA) 1977 sets out four conditions that must be satisfied before an invention can be said to be patentable:

(a) that the invention is new;

(b) that it involves an inventive step;

(c) that it is capable of industrial application; and

(d) that it does not fall into one of the categories of excluded invention in s 1(2) and (3) of the PA 1977.

These criteria reflect Article 52 of the European Patent Convention 1973 (EPC) and decisions of the European Patent Office (EPO) are relevant to interpretation of the PA 1977. Judicial notice is to be taken of the EPC, CPC and PCT, any bulletin, journal or gazette published under the relevant conventions and the relevant decisions and opinions of relevant convention courts: s 91 of the PA 1977. The EPO publishes Guidelines to the EPC[1] for its examiners, which can also provide a useful reference point.

The long title of the PA 1977 provides that the Act establishes a new law of patents. Although the PA 1977 was, in part, enacted to give effect to the UK's obligations under the EPC, the agreement reached as to substantive criteria in the EPC largely reflected UK law. This raises the question of how far UK case law decided under the PA 1949 can still be relied on as precedent. In *Unilever (Davis's) Application* (1983), Falconer J referred to the new law of the PA 1977, whilst Bailey J thought no change had been indicated on the issue at hand and followed earlier case law. The earlier case law is at least of persuasive precedent.

Subsequently, the Patents Regulations 2000,[2] implementing the Biotechnology Directive[3] and Article 27 of the TRIPS Agreement, have amended the PA 1977. Further changes were made to implement the EPC Act 2000 in the Patents Act 2004.

4.1 INVENTIONS

Although four conditions for patentability are clearly set out, the wording of s 1(1) of the PA 1977 is capable of two interpretations. These are that either any creation which satisfies these four criteria will be a patentable invention, or that the creation for which an application is made must also surmount an initial hurdle of being describable as an 'invention', as well as satisfying the four conditions laid down.

The Act does not define the word 'invention', although certain potential inventions are excluded by s 1(2) of the PA 1977 as, among other things, not being 'inventions'. The first part of the section – 'a patent may be granted only for an invention in respect

---

1 Guidelines for Examination in the EPO: http://www.european-patent-office.org/legal/gui_lines.

2 SI 2000/2037.

3 Directive 98/44/EC of the European Parliament and Council on the Legal Protection of Biotechnological Inventions [1998] OJ L289/28.

of which the following conditions are satisfied ...' – suggests the first interpretation, that there is no additional step to be met. However, the concluding line – 'and references in this Act to a patentable invention shall be construed accordingly' – suggests the second, that there must be an 'invention'.

4.1.1 Judicial *dicta*

There is some judicial disagreement as to the correct test. Mustill LJ (as he then was), in *Genentech Inc's Patent* (1989), favoured the view that there must be an 'invention'. In that case, the description of the hitherto unknown genetic construction of a known, naturally occurring substance (a human protein, t-PA) did not accord with Mustill LJ's view of invention as being the creation of a product, or a process for the production of a product. He would have been willing to regard a process for synthesising the substance as an invention.

The issue was raised again in *Biogen Inc v Medeva plc* (1997). The claims again related to a synthetic molecule of a naturally occurring virus, hepatitis B, which enabled the construction of diagnostic kits for its detection. In the Court of Appeal, Hobhouse LJ applied Mustill LJ's test and held that choosing a method of research (the source of the patentee's breakthrough in finding a cure for the hepatitis B virus) did not constitute invention. However, the same reason was given for denying any inventive step. As in *Genentech* (1989), the extra step was proving superfluous. In the House of Lords, in *Biogen Inc v Medeva plc* (1997), Lord Mustill remained unrepentant, albeit *obiter*, as he held that *Biogen* (1997) did not raise the issue. He stated that there might be cases where a conceptual analysis of the nature of an invention might be necessary, as *Genentech* (1989) had been. Lord Hoffmann, who gave the leading judgment, however, denied the need for any such hurdle of patentability. Nevertheless, in *Kirin-Amgen Inc v Hoechst Marion Roussel Ltd* (2004) Lord Hoffmann stated that an invention is 'a practical product or process, not information about the natural world'.[4]

4.1.2 The concept of invention

Arguably, any product of man's efforts which is new, useful, inventive and not excluded on grounds of policy should be deserving of the patent incentive. To add this extra step in determining patentability may be thought unnecessary and undesirable. Mustill LJ's real objection lay in awarding a patent to the stage of discovery which often precedes the addition of something new, inventive and useful to mankind's technical armoury. Section 1(2)(a) of the PA 1977 already excludes mere discoveries from patentability. Many felt that the patent in *Genentech* (1989) was wrongly revoked, denying the reward needed after years of expensive research which had given rise to an undoubtedly needed outcome: a synthetic t-PA protein in sufficient quantities to be useful.

To adopt Mustill LJ's approach prevents a patent ever being awarded to a naturally occurring substance, yet the exclusions in s 1(2) of the PA 1977 come with the proviso that only the excluded thing 'as such' will be denied a patent. If sufficient human

---

4   Para 77.

technical input can be determined in the claims, a patent may still be forthcoming. The EPO looks for a sufficient level of human technical intervention when deciding on the patentability of natural substances, the patent reward and incentive being of the human intervention. In *Stern-heimer/Harmonic Variations* (1989), the EPO applied Article 52 of the EPC, the equivalent provision to s 1 of the PA 1977, and stated that the exclusions related to inventions which did not use 'technical methods to produce a concrete technical effect'.

This approach is now applied in Schedule A2 to the amended PA 1977. Paragraphs 2 and 5 assert that biological material, or an element from the human body,[5] isolated from their environment or produced by a technical process may be the subject of an invention even if previously occurring in nature.

There are three good reasons for rejecting a hurdle of 'invention'. First, technological advance would quickly outstrip any definition and become a straitjacket to inventors. Secondly, the conditions set out in s 1(1) of the PA 1977 are sufficient to prevent patenting the undesirable (as they were in both *Biogen Inc v Medeva plc* (1997) and *Genentech Inc's Patent* (1989)). Thirdly, arriving at any definition would be virtually impossible – even the parties to the EPC were unable to agree on one, as Lord Hoffmann points out in *Biogen* (1997).

However, Thurston[6] takes the view that effort alone should not be deserving of a patent. Invention implies making, originating or creating something useful from a discovery. There is a basic distinction between an idea and the useful application of that idea to human needs, which lies at the heart of patentability. However, the conditions of s 1(1) of the PA 1977 seem sufficient to secure this distinction. The real issue must be whether the inventor has contributed something new and useful and non-obvious to the technical world: *Re NRDC* (1961). If so, a patent is warranted. Nevertheless, recent expansions at the boundaries of patentability, particularly in the sphere of computer software and biotechnological inventions have proved controversial. Retaining judicial discretion to reject a patent for an advance in technology on the ground that it is not an invention may provide a needed check.

Technical

EPO decisions on the 'as such' proviso, the Biotechnology Directive and proposed Computer-implemented Inventions Directive rest distinctions between the patentable and unpatentable on their technical contribution to the state of the art.

It was proposed in the Patents Act 1977 (Amendment) Bill to incorporate EPC 2000's addition to Article 52(1) of the EPC:

> European patents shall be granted for any inventions, *in all fields of technology*, provided that they are new, involve an inventive step and are susceptible of industrial application.

This explicitly ties the concept of invention to the nature of technology, so that it can be said that the 'invention' hurdle has been replaced by a test of technical contribution. Effectively there is a test of invention (and not just inventiveness), but it has been redefined as one of technicality. Continuing investigation must lie in attempting to

---

5   Including a sequence or partial sequence of a gene.
6   Thurston, J, 'The Commercial and Legal Impact of the Court of Appeal's Decision in *Genentech v Wellcome*' [1989] EIPR 66.

define the limits of technology. The word 'technical' is derived from the Greek *technikos*, meaning skill or art, and defined as having special, usually practical, knowledge of a mechanical or scientific subject. Dictionary definitions of 'technology' refer to applied science, or a technical method of achieving a practical purpose, or the means employed to provide objects necessary for human sustenance or comfort. 'Technological' is defined as resulting from improvement in technical processes that increase productivity of machines, and eliminate manual operations or operations done by older machines.

Emphasis is turning to the 'contribution' made by an invention, rather than the nature of its substance matter. As lines become increasingly difficult to draw the focus must turn to these criteria. However, this can be seen as a reformulation in current terminology of the test in the Australian case *Re NRDC* (1961): that an inventor has contributed something new and useful and non-obvious to the technical world.

Whether such an interpretation will be adopted by UK courts remains uncertain, however, as the Patents Act 2004 did not make the suggested change. This may well represent recognition that UK law already incorporates this approach.

4.1.3 Valid patents for inventions

The subject matter of a patent is an invention, one which falls within the category of patentable inventions, which is the subject of this chapter. Once patentable subject matter has been established the further criteria of novelty, inventive step and industrial applicability must also be satisfied. These form the subject of Chapter 5. Finally, before a patent can be granted all correct procedures for an application, including permissible amendments must be complied with; and the disclosure made in the specification (including the claims) must satisfy s 14 of the PA 1977.

4.2   EXCLUDED CATEGORIES

By virtue of s 1(1)(d)[7] of the PA 1977, some categories of invention are excluded from patentability by s 1(2) and (3), and s 4A of the PA 1977. Section 76A and Schedule A2 make specific provision for biotechnological inventions, including some further exclusions. The exclusions falling within s 1(2) of the PA 1977 are stated not to be inventions, 'among other things'.

Excluded subject matter includes:

(a) discoveries, scientific theories and mathematical methods;

(b) literary, dramatic, musical or artistic works, or any other aesthetic creation whatsoever;

(c) schemes, rules or methods for performing a mental act, playing a game or doing business or programs for a computer;

(d) presentations of information;

(e) inventions the commercial exploitation of which would be contrary to public policy or morality;

---

7   Amended by the Patents Act 2004 to include the new s 4A of the PA 1977.

(f) varieties of animal or plant, not being the product of a microbiological process;

(g) essentially biological processes for the production of plants or animals, not being microbiological processes or the products of such processes; and

(h) other biotechnological inventions related to humans or animals.

The excluded categories of s 1(2) of the PA 1977 reflect the position reached under the PA 1949 in creating *ad hoc* exceptions to patentability. Broadly, the s 1(2) exclusions represent the rejection of purely intellectual and aesthetic creations from patentability, while s 1(3) of the PA 1977 refuses a patent for moral and ethical considerations. There is no clear underlying principle behind these exclusions and each must be examined in turn. It is worth noting that s 1(2) of the PA 1977 is not necessarily a complete list of 'things' that are not inventions: s 1(5) of the Act contemplates variation of the sub-section by the Secretary of State. Some support for Lord Mustill's interpretation of s 1(1) of the PA 1977 can be drawn from this provision.

4.2.1 The proviso to s 1(2) of the PA 1977

The categories of excluded subject matter from s 1(2) is subject to the concluding proviso:

> ... but the foregoing provision shall prevent anything from being treated as an invention for the purposes of this Act only to the extent that a patent or an application for a patent relates to that thing as such.

This presupposes that a distinction must be drawn between the excluded thing claimed on its own, and a claim that includes the excluded thing, but only as a component of the totality of the invention being claimed. Only the first is automatically refused a patent.

Under the earlier law, a distinction was drawn between a claim for an idea (which was not patentable) and a claim for an application of an idea (which was). This was explained by Buckley LJ in *Hickton's Patent v Patents and Machine Improvements* (1909):

> Every invention ... must ... either suggest a new way of making something ... or it may mean the way of producing a new article altogether; but I think you are losing the grasp of the substance and seizing the shadow when you say that the invention is the manufacture as distinguished from the idea. It is much more true to say that the patent is for the idea ... but the invention consists in thinking or conceiving something and suggesting a way of doing it.

The line was then drawn between an idea, however innovative, on its own and a useful way of employing the idea – the idea being embodied in an application. The case of *Otto v Linford* (1882) provides a practical illustration. A new method of introducing air into a car engine was discovered. The patent was held to be valid because it was not for the discovery of the role of air in the engine, but for the machine embodying the discovered usefulness of air that was claimed.

Under the PA 1977, it is case law relating to computer programs and discoveries that has determined how the 'as such' proviso is to be applied. As the proviso applies to each of the constituents of the paragraphs of s 1(2) of the PA 1977, the same test should apply to each excluded 'thing'.

4.3   COMPUTER PROGRAMS

The exclusion is of computer programs; computer hardware is a proper subject for patentability (provided the other conditions of patentability are satisfied). In addition, the exclusion is only of a computer program 'as such'. There are several methods by which a claim to a computer program *per se* and a claim to an invention incorporating a computer program could be distinguished. The courts moved through several steps in determining the appropriate test, which was laid down by the EPO in *Vicom* (1987).

4.3.1   Formal approaches

'Computer program' is not defined, nor is it a question of the form of claims used in the specification. This approach was adopted under the PA 1949, with the result that a patentee was often sent away to reword the claims before establishing the validity of the invention. Claims to a 'computer as programmed' were patentable, as the claim was not regarded as being directed to the program, but to the computer, however conventional. Claims to a 'means of controlling a computer' were unpatentable, the claims being directed at the controlling program. The test is not quite as absurd as it appears. There is a difference between the two ways of claiming which goes some way to justifying this method of drawing the necessary distinction. The claims determine the extent of monopoly conferred by a patent. To protect a 'computer as programmed' confers only a monopoly on that particular way of using a computer to achieve the intended result, whereas the 'means of controlling a computer' would confer a monopoly on any purpose for use of the computer program on any computer. However, the fact that claims could be redrafted into an acceptable form showed the formalistic nature of the test. In *Burrough's Patent* (1974), it was rejected by Graham J as a means of distinguishing between idea and application under the PA 1949.

4.3.2   Location of novelty

The 'location of novelty' test was a relatively simple and certain method of distinguishing the patentable from the unpatentable and one which gave clear results. Given that the essence of an invention is the contribution of something new to technology, the test involved identifying what was new in the invention claimed. If that component of the invention as a whole fell within an excluded category, the claim was treated as a claim to an excluded invention as such (an idea). If novelty lay in an element not within the exclusions, the excluded feature was regarded as having been applied and patentable. Sir John Simon explained this approach in *Ward's Application* (1912):

> ... you may rightly patent that which, when the invention is applied, produces an article of manufacture, the novelty of which consists in the manufacture; on the other hand you cannot, of course, patent an idea, or scheme, or a mere method.

The first version of the EPO Guidelines adopted this approach to the proviso. However, a third approach was adopted in *IBM's Patent* (1980), when a patent for an automated data handling system which established prices in an auction market was upheld. The novelty lay in the program (any conventional computer could be used to run it), but Whitford J regarded the computer as having acquired novel characteristics when programmed – he 'transferred' the program's novelty to the computer as a whole. There is an artificiality in the location of novelty test when applied to programs, for it is the overall function the program performs which is the real subject of programming advances.

4.3.3 The whole contents approach

When the PA 1977 proviso came to be applied, it remained to be seen whether, or which, of these existing tests might be employed. The location of novelty test was rejected by the Court of Appeal in *Merrill Lynch* (1989). The claim was to a data processing system implementing an automated trading market for securities, which could be used on any conventional computer apparatus. At first instance, Falconer J rejected the application, as had the Patent Office, using the location of novelty test. The Court of Appeal had already rejected location of novelty as an appropriate test in *Genentech Inc's Patent* (1989), albeit in a case concerning the patentability of a discovery. In *Merrill Lynch* (1989) the Court of Appeal reversed Falconer J's decision, following the approach laid down by the EPO in relation to a mathematical method and computer program in *Vicom* (1987).

4.3.4 *Vicom*

In *Vicom* the claims related to a computerised process for digitally enhancing images which employed a particular mathematical method. Considering whether the claims were confined to mathematical methods and computer programs as such, the Technical Board of Appeal said:

> There can be little doubt that any processing operation on an electric signal can be described in mathematical terms ... A basic difference between a mathematical method and a technical process can be seen, however, in the fact that a mathematical method or a mathematical algorithm is carried out on numbers (whatever these numbers may represent) and provides a result also in numerical form, the mathematical method or algorithm being only an abstract concept prescribing how to operate on the numbers. No direct technical result is produced by the method as such. In contrast thereto, if a mathematical method is used in a technical process, that process is carried out on a physical entity (which may be a material object, but, equally, an image stored as an electric signal) by some technical means implementing the method and provides as its result a certain change in that entity. The technical means might include a computer comprising suitable hardware or an appropriately programmed general purpose computer.

Thus, *Vicom* (1987) established a new method for making the distinction. The claims are read as a whole and the purpose or function of the invention ascertained. The decisive factor is to consider what 'technical contribution' the invention, as thus defined by its function or result, makes to the known art. If the contribution is not technical, but aesthetic or intellectual, for example, the patent will be refused. The new test was reflected in a revised version of the EPO Guidelines in 1985. The Director of Legal Affairs of the EPO explained the new version thus:

(a) the 'as such' proviso was the old distinction between idea and application of idea;

(b) this distinction was not to be drawn by a 'location of novelty' test;

(c) there would be a patentable invention if a technical effect, or technical result, could be found in the claims;

(d) once an application of the unpatentable subject matter had been found to constitute a technical result, then the requisite novelty and inventive step could be located anywhere within the composite of idea plus application plus result;

(e) the distinction was not one between hardware and software.

Fujitsu Ltd's Application (1997) confirms that it is not the form, but the substance of the claims that is considered. The applicants argued that the claims were directed to a method of manufacturing and to apparatus and could not, therefore, relate to a computer program as such. Aldous LJ said that there was only one invention (however it may be designated) and described it as a system for modelling synthetic combined crystal structures. To describe it in any other way did not alter its substance as a computer program.

4.3.5 Technical effect

Consequently, subsequent case law has sought to establish what constitutes a technical effect or technical result. In the UK, the Court of Appeal upheld refusal of a patent to the claim for a computerised method and apparatus for modelling synthetic crystal structures for chemicals in *Fujitsu Ltd's Application* (1997). The applicants had argued that the claims were not to a computer program as such, but to a method for processing images of real objects, akin to the invention in *Vicom* (1987). However, the Court of Appeal distinguished *Vicom* (1987): there the technical contribution lay in the enhanced technical quality of the picture produced. The Fujitsu process merely automated a known process, previously carried out manually, by constructing models; and, though crystal structures lie within the technical field, the end result of the process was an intellectual process of substituting part of one crystal with part taken from another. However, Aldous LJ found difficulty in distinguishing *Vicom* (1987). The applicants' final argument was that the technical effect provided by the system lay in the creation of a new tool which saved considerable labour and error. This also failed to convince Aldous LJ, as the only advance on the manual method was that the structure was produced more quickly. Avoidance of labour was the normal effect of computerisation, he said, and was not technical. Because the boundary line between technical effect and excluded matter was not clear, he concluded that each case had to be decided on its own facts.

Two cases from the EPO illustrate the distinction that is being drawn. In *IBM/Computer Related Invention* (1990), the claims related to a program which facilitated self-diagnosis of faults within a computer and resulted in a screen display. This secured a patent. The screen display was treated as a specific solution to a technical problem. In contrast, in *IBM/Document Abstracting and Retrieving* (1990), no patent was secured for a program which contained a method of storing and retrieving documents. The end result of its operation was merely a presentation of information.

Amid continuing judicial uncertainty the Patent Office have stated that:

> Software should not be patentable when there is no technological innovation, and technological innovations should not cease to be patentable merely because the innovation lies in software.[8]

In addition, they state, 'there is a need for the law to express this more clearly'.

---

8 'Software Patents': www.patent.gov.uk.

Product claims

At first, mere embodiment of a program in physical form, or loaded into a conventional computer, did not suffice: *Re Gale* (1991). Gale discovered a quicker method for the calculation of square roots, potentially applicable in all computers and calculators. The program itself was not patentable, but Gale claimed the method as embodied on read only memory (ROM), so that it became a dedicated part of any apparatus in which it was incorporated. This was refused by the Court of Appeal as lacking any technical result.

Methods of doing business

The UK courts refused whole claims if they amounted to one of the other excluded categories, and the Patent Office continue to state that 'ways of doing business should remain unpatentable'.[9] In *Merrill Lynch* (1989) the result of the computer plus program was a method of doing business, albeit an automated one, which is in itself an excluded category of invention. The patent was refused. However, it can be argued that 'technicality' and the excluded categories should not be co-extensive, and that a business method with technical effect should be patentable in the same way as a computer program with technical effect. The decision in *Kirin-Amgen Inc v Roche Diagnostics* (2001) discussed below suggests that this is so.

Methods for performing mental acts

Many of the functions performed by software are calculations, which fall within the category of mental acts. In *Wang's Application* (1991) claims to an expert system were refused as a scheme for doing a mental act, the purpose of the program being judged objectively. Other claims to a computer shell system also failed because the computer and program remained separate and did not combine to create a new machine.

At first instance the mental acts exclusion was also held to apply to the method in *Fujitsu Ltd's Application* (1997). The Court of Appeal declined to give a detailed consideration to this issue, but Aldous LJ stated that the concept should be widely construed, and not confined to acts actually carried out mentally. He concluded that methods of performing mental acts (methods of the type performed mentally) are unpatentable 'unless some concept of technical contribution is present'. This *dictum* appears to contradict the *Merrill Lynch* approach that once the contribution was found to fall within an excluded category no further examination of technical contribution applied.

In *Kirin-Amgen Inc v Roche Diagnostics* (2001)[10] Neuberger J considered the exclusion of discoveries as such, and applied Aldous LJ's dictum that discoveries or ideas which have a technical aspect or make a technical contribution are patentable. Subsequently a Patent Office Practice Note[11] accepted that prior practice, which had read *Fujitsu* along with the earlier *Merrill Lynch*, must change. Therefore, inventions

---

9   'Software Patents': www.patent.gov.uk.
10   The decision has been overruled by the Court of Appeal, and the House of Lords in *Kirin-Amgen Inc v Hoechst Marion Roussel Ltd* (2004), but not on this point.
11   'Patents Act 1977: Interpreting Section 1(2)': www.patent.gov.uk.

involving a mental act or business method which can be shown to involve a technical contribution will be accepted.

4.3.6 Wider patentability

Despite the exclusion for computer programs, the EPO had granted some 20,000 patents[12] for computer-implemented inventions by 2002. However, even wider patentability for computer programs was available in the two big markets of Japan and the US. In the US there was no requirement for the invention's effect to be technical, provided that a new and 'useful, concrete and tangible' result was achieved.[13] The result was to extend patentability to programs embodied on a physical carrier,[14] and to business methods. In *State Street Bank & Trust Co v Signatures Financial Group* (1998) a patent was granted for 'hub and spoke' software which managed a computerised system administering mutual funds. It allowed small mutual fund operators to pool their resources in a combined investment portfolio in order to secure efficiencies of scale. In *AT & T Corp v Excel Communications* (1999) a patent for software for remote telephone billing was upheld despite the fact that no physical transformation of the data was achieved. However, despite the many software and business method patents granted it is likely that the majority would prove invalid if challenged for obviousness, as was the case in the Amazon 'One-Click' patent: *Amazon.com v Barnesandnoble.com* (2001).

The European approach was perceived to put the software industry at a considerable disadvantage. Pressure for fuller patent protection grew. This pressure and the difficulties of maintaining a distinction based on 'technical effect', which the courts have such difficulty in defining and applying, did not seem to bode well for the continued application of the exclusion. In *In re IBM's European Patent Application No 96 (305 851.6)* the EPO appeared to presage a more relaxed approach to the patentability of computer programs. They allowed claims to 'computer program products', reversing the ban on programs claimed on a carrier. The program arranged displays in windows on a computer screen so that the material the user was viewing was not obscured. The claims were not just to a computer so programmed, but to a product which held the program on any medium, and which had a potential technical effect. Little seemed to remain of the computer program exclusion in the EPO and the UK Patent Office issued a Patent Practice Notice[15] saying that they would follow EPO practice. However, this notice also pointed out that running a program so claimed still required to have a technical effect beyond that of normal running in a computer. The change related only to the nature of the claims.

Business method claims also seemed to receive favourable treatment in the EPO following the decisions in *Petterson, Sohei* and *Pension Benefits System*. In *Petterson* (1995) a system determining customer queuing was held to be patentable, because the problem solved by the system related to the interaction of several components, and this was a technical, if ephemeral, problem. In *Sohei* (1995) a system of financial and inventory management was held to be patentable because technical considerations had

---

12 Many of which were held by non-European companies.
13 *Re Alappat* 1994).
14 *Re Iwahashi* 1989).
15 'Claims to Programs for Computers': www.patent.gov.uk.

been applied and technical problems solved although the result was a method of doing business. In the *Pension Benefits System* (2000) case, 'apparatus' claims to software operating a pension scheme by calculating amounts due on standard factors were not disallowed on the basis of the exclusion, although claims to the methods of making the calculations were rejected as computer programs as such. In the apparatus claims the mere presence of a computer served to provide a technical element although the computer did not contribute to the system and merely implemented it. However, no inventive step could be shown.

In Australia the Advisory Council on Intellectual Property has recommended no change to the law,[16] which does not bar patents for business methods, staying in line with Japan, the US and New Zealand, and adding to the pressure for change in Europe. It concludes that there is little evidence to suggest that business method patents either stimulate or inhibit innovation (in Australia), but calls for IP Australia[17] to maintain records of the number of business system patents and their significance, and to report annually until 2009.

4.3.7 Computer-implemented Inventions Directive

The resulting uncertainty led to a proposal to remove the exclusion of computer programs at the Diplomatic Conference on the EPC in 2000. At the same time the EU Commission issued a proposal for a directive[18] harmonising the law relating to computer-implemented inventions. Both the Commission and the UK Patent Office consulted extensively on the question. Consequently, although the EU is not a member of the EPC, the Conference decided to await the result of the proposed directive.

Regarding the current situation as unclear and uncertain, the aim was to promote clarity of interpretation for software patentability. Clarity can only be achieved by three means. These are either by excluding any patentability at all for all computer program inventions, by providing clear and workable definitions of the key concept of technical contribution or by abandoning the exclusion altogether and relying on the requirements of novelty, inventive step and industrial application to exclude undesirable patents. The Commission rejected removing the exclusion as it would allow patents for computer-implemented business methods, and it was too early to judge the effects of the US experience.[19] Broadly, the draft confirmed EPO practice, but did not extend patentability to business methods. It also proposed ending patentability for computer product claims. The draft does not achieve its aim of clarity, both by continuing to rely on the nebulous criterion of 'technicality', and by confusing the enquiry into patentability of an invention's subject matter with its validity in terms of novelty and inventive step. These latter questions have always been regarded as two separate and distinct enquiries by the EPO.

---

16 *Report on Patenting of Business Systems*, 25 February 2004: www.acip.gov.au.
17 The patent granting body in Australia.
18 Directive of the European Parliament and Council on the Patentability of Computer-implemented Inventions COM (2002) 92 final 2002/0047 (COD).
19 This changed considerably in 2003 with the appointment of a new Commissioner of Patents. Despite a finding of infringement and award of $521million against Microsoft in *Eolas v Microsoft* (2003), the USPTO is to re-examine the validity of the Eolas patent for browser software.

The draft provided that computer-implemented inventions are those whose performance involves the use of a computer, network, or other programmable apparatus.[20] However, the definition goes on to provide that the invention must have one or more *prima facie* novel feature realised wholly or in part by a program. It further provides that computer-implemented inventions belong to a field of technology.[21] They are to be patentable to the extent that they are new, involve an inventive step and are susceptible of industrial application. Having an invention step means that the invention must make a 'technical contribution'.[22] A technical contribution is one in a technical field which is not obvious to a person skilled in the art.[23] Given the difficulties in defining the difference between technical and non-technical contributions this proposal seems to add little to existing case law.

The proposal suffered considerable amendment in the European Parliament and in November 2003 the Council decided to delay any adoption of it. In September 2004 the Council of Ministers refused to accept the Common Position adopted by the Commission in May, and referred the draft to COREPER[24] for further discussion. A directive would, in any case, have little harmonising effect unless the EPO voluntarily followed its provisions. The Patents Act 2004 made no change to the computer program exclusion, in the light of the unresolved position on the proposed directive.

4.4   DISCOVERIES AND MATHEMATICAL METHODS

Discoveries, as such, are an excluded category, and must be distinguished from inventions. A discovery is the exposure of an existing phenomenon, illustrated by Lindley LJ in *Lane-Fox v Kensington and Knightsbridge Electrical Lighting Co* (1892), thus: '... when Volta discovered the effect of the electric current from a battery on a frog's leg, he made a great discovery, but no patentable invention.' Invention can be regarded as the subsequent putting of the discovery to specific practical use, as explained by Buckley J in *Reynolds v Herbert Smith* (1913):

> Discovery adds to the amount of human knowledge, but it does so only by lifting a veil and disclosing something which before had been unseen or dully seen. Invention also adds to human knowledge, but not merely by disclosing. Invention necessarily involves also the suggestion of an act to be done and it must be an act which results in a new product, or a new result, or a new process, or a new combination for producing an old product or an old result.

Allowing a patent for a bare discovery would monopolise every application subsequently found for it within the duration of the patent. This would have the effect of deterring further research, inhibit competition and deprive the public of a truth that had always existed, only waiting to be uncovered.

The consequence of the exclusion is that a discovery of a new chemical substance without any revealed use goes unrewarded by a patent, despite the high costs of research. In addition, if the discoverer resorts to secrecy as a result, the public is denied

---

20   Article 2(a).
21   Article 3.
22   Article 4.
23   Article 2(b)
24   The committee for EU permanent representative offices.

access to the new information, while further research by others is inhibited. However, if a product patent for the substance were to be granted to the substance when one use for it were revealed, the patent would equally deter further research into new uses. Accordingly, a patent is granted only for the use that has been invented for the discovered substance, thus achieving an incentive and reward for the provision of new and inventive uses and leaving an incentive for more investigation into further uses.

However, pure research is not encouraged by the patent, because of the unwarranted extent of the monopoly that would result. This can deny the investment that is needed for innovation. It also poses particular difficulties in industries where the substances, their uses and their processes of manufacture are known and it is the discovery of information about those substances that is the focus of research. This is true of the burgeoning biotechnological industry. With the discovery of the DNA construction of known substances, those substances may be synthesised in useful quantities and applied to important applications. However, patents for the information are unlikely.

4.4.1 Discoveries as such

The exclusion of a discovery as such reflects the distinction between discovery and application. It is expressed in the EPO Guidelines as a refusal for the purely abstract, whereas a device, substance or method embodying a discovery may be patentable. So, a claim to a method for using a known substance as a selective herbicide was allowed a patent in *Re NRDC* (1961), as the discovery had been embodied in a new and useful effect.

The distinction is drawn in the same way as for computer programs, following *Genentech Inc's Patent* (1989). The claims are read as a whole and if, as a matter of substance, not form, they reveal a technical effect, they are not treated as claims to a discovery as such. Then, the requisite novelty and inventive step may be located within any component of those claims and may, therefore, lie in the discovery, the application being obvious once the discovery has been made. The Court of Appeal, in *Chiron v Murex Diagnostics* (1996), confirmed that the application of a discovery need be neither novel nor inventive once the discovery has been made. The novelty of the discovery may be 'transferred' to the invention as a whole.

In *Genentech Inc's Patent* (1989), the patentee discovered the DNA sequence of the human protein t-PA. It was known to have important medical uses against blood clots in the treatment of thrombosis, but was not available naturally in medically useful quantities. The discovery of the DNA structure enabled t-PA's synthesis. In the event, the patent was revoked for lack of inventive step, but both Purchas and Mustill LJJ held that some or all of the claims were to discoveries as such. Purchas LJ held that the claims to t-PA amounted to no more than claims to discoveries 'as such', as the claims covered any method of production of the plasmids.

4.4.2 Patentable discoveries

However, Purchas LJ held that claims limited to the plasmids in which the t-PA encoding gene was incorporated would not be claims to the discovery as such and would be valid. These would be of no value to the patentee because competitors in possession of the DNA sequence would be able to find other unclaimed methods for production of the plasmid. However, he held the failure to claim the method used invalidated the claims. He said:

> The authorities seem to support the proposition that where the discovery is of a new substance, a patent can be claimed for that substance 'however made' and will be valid as long as the specification discloses one method of manufacture, even if that method be not the most favoured one. This proposition does not apply, however, where, as in the case of t-PA, the discovery is merely part of the process by which a product already known to exist and with properties already described can be manufactured. In the latter case, the discovery can only form the basis of an invention limited to the method of producing the known artefact, that is, a process patent.

This may be to confuse the requirement of an enabling disclosure of an invention with the exclusion of a discovery as such. The difficulty that this poses to inventors of such products is that the processes are likely to be known and obvious. The selection patent (see 5.1.6) remedies the analogous difficulty faced by discoverers of new advantages in selections from known classes of substances. It carves out an area of monopoly commensurate with the patentee's contribution, leaving the prior art in the public domain, but rewarding where research has produced unknown and useful results. However, Dillon LJ held that only two of Genentech's claims related to discoveries as such.

Two discoveries lay behind the claims in *Chiron v Murex Diagnostics* (1996). The patentees discovered that the hepatitis C infection provokes a detectable antibody response, and its causal agent and the genetic DNA sequence of an isolate of the virus. These were embodied in claims limited to diagnostic kits, methods of testing, vaccines and cell cultures, and were held not to be discoveries 'as such'.

4.4.3 Technical contribution

In *Kirin-Amgen Inc v Roche Diagnostics* (2001),[25] Neuberger J applied the technical contribution test, following *Fujitsu* (1997). Amgen was proprietor of a patent for a naturally occurring hormone EPO which could be used to treat anaemia. Sufficient quantities of the natural substance could not be secured for effective treatment of patients. The patentee cloned the DNA of the hormone, enabling production of the synthetic substance. The patent revealed the DNA sequence of human EPO and the amino acid sequence for the human EPO protein for the first time. Amgen's competitors also produced a synthetic EPO, but by different routes, and sought revocation of the patent. While it was clear that the discovery of the DNA sequence lay at the root of the invention claimed, Neuberger J held that it made a technical contribution in teaching biotechnologists to express EPO in cells by routine methods. It did not entitle protection for any particular technique. He distinguished *Genentech Inc's Patent* (1989), which also related to discovered DNA sequences, by applying the correct principles to the facts before him and establishing a technical effect. Purchas and Dillon LJJ, by contrast, had not found a technical contribution in the t-PA patent.

---

25 Overruled on a different point by the Court of Appeal, and the House of Lords in *Kirin-Amgen Inc v Hoechst Marion Roussel Ltd* (2004).

Natural substances and technical contribution

Discovering a natural substance remains discovery as such; however, the process of doing so may be patentable. If the natural substance is isolated and can be defined by its structure or the technical process by which it is made it may be patentable. This is explicitly provided by the Biotechnology Directive and paragraphs 2 and 5 of Schedule A2 to the PA 1977:

2. Biological material which is isolated from its natural environment or produced by means of a technical process may be the subject of an invention even if it previously occurred in nature.

5. An element isolated from the human body or otherwise produced by means of a technical process, including the sequence or partial sequence of a gene, may constitute a patentable invention, even if the structure of that element is identical to that of a natural element.

Where natural substances are involved, it is the presence of human intervention in producing the substance, or the process of doing so, which constitutes the 'technical' element.

However, where substances relate to the human genetic structure the issue remains controversial. Despite the inclusiveness of paragraphs 2 and 5, paragraph 3(a) of the Schedule also prevents patents for the human body at its various stages of formation and development, and for the 'simple' discovery of one of its elements, including the sequence or partial sequence of a gene. However, the sequence or partial sequence of a gene remains the same in paragraphs 5 and 3(a). Any patentability must rest in the process of isolation or other technical process.

The purpose of excluding discoveries from patentable subject matter is, at least in part, to prevent monopolisation of pure research and to stimulate its application to concrete uses. It becomes a matter of the requirement for industrial application for an invention (see 5.3). The USPTO requires that 'specific, substantial and credible' utility must be claimed for such inventions. The Patent Office Guidelines[26] adopt a similar approach, in the absence of any judicial or EPO authority.

4.4.4 Mathematical methods

Mathematical methods are treated in the same way as discoveries: *Vicom* (1987).

4.5 SCHEMES, RULES AND METHODS

Again, the 'as such' proviso applies to the exclusion in s 1(2)(c) of the PA 1977 and will be determined according to *Vicom* (1987) and *Genentech Inc's Patent* (1989). Earlier case law that relied on the location of novelty test can no longer be applied.

It is only schemes, rules and methods for certain purposes that are excluded: performing a mental act, playing a game or doing business. Examples given by the EPO Guidelines include schemes for learning a language, solving a crossword, rules

---

26 Paras 33–35 of the 'Examination Guidelines for Patent Applications relating to Biotechnological Inventions in the UK Patent Office': (September 2002) www.patent.gov.uk.

for a card game or a scheme of office management, unless they involve a novel apparatus, in which case the invention would fall within the proviso.

4.5.1 Schemes, rules and methods as such

Examples from earlier case law that would probably remain unpatentable as schemes for the performance of a mental act include *W's Application* (1914) and *Hiller's Application* (1969). In the former, an arrangement for navigation buoys was held unpatentable because the claim was merely for a system of arranging known objects. In the latter, the claims related to a plan for arranging underground cables. It was claimed in the form of an underground installation for the distribution of utilities, the improvement (novelty) characterised by a specified layout. The court looked at the substance of the claims and a patent was refused. In *Raytheon's Application* (1993), a system for improving ship recognition by creating a digital record was held unpatentable as a system for performing a mental act under the PA 1977.

Where a scheme is excluded, alternative protection may be found in confidence, copyright and contract.

4.5.2 Patentable schemes, rules and methods

It has been suggested, however, that the claims in *Rolls Royce's Application* (1963), which were refused because they did not result in a 'vendible product' as required by the PA 1949, might have been successful under the PA 1977. The applicant claimed a method for operating a known aircraft engine in such a way as to reduce noise emissions. This is a method for performing a physical, rather than a mental act.

The case of *Lux Traffic Controls Ltd v Pike Signals Ltd* (1993) illustrates a scheme that was not excluded because it related to a technical effect. The patentee made traffic light control systems. It had been granted a patent for a moving vehicle detector for each unit of a set of lights and a common controller. The defendant, whom it sued for infringement, argued that the patent was invalid, *inter alia*, as not being an invention. Aldous J held the patent was valid. He said:

> There can be no doubt that devices that regulate traffic flow can have a technical contribution and are patentable. For example, a claim to a process of regulating traffic using lights with a detector which used sound waves would undoubtedly be patentable. It would be patentable because of the technical contribution provided by a detector which used sound waves.

This 'minimum green extension' patent does include, as part of its invention, a technical contribution. The inventors realised that a different controller was needed to deal with the problem of stalled cars and red runners. They appreciated that a detector which registered movement could equally be used to detect absence of movement. Thus, they rearranged the electrical connections so that the controller provided an extended green period if no detection was made during the minimum green period. The idea of regulating traffic was incorporated into the controller, thereby producing a novel technical machine which operated if no detection was made.

4.5.3 Methods for performing mental acts

In *Fujitsu Ltd's Application* (1997), the Court of Appeal considered, *obiter*, the interpretation of the word 'for' in the phrase 'method for performing a mental act'. The applicants had argued that s 1(2)(c) of the PA 1977 should be interpreted subjectively to mean that the exclusion only covered methods which were intended to be, and capable of being, carried out by the human mind and not to include all the acts which, objectively, the human mind could do. The specific method used by the Fujitsu invention was not one that was actually carried out by the human mind.

Aldous LJ cited both *Vicom* (1987) and *Petterson* (1996), in which claims to methods with technical results were upheld without any consideration of the way in which the human mind worked. He held that there were three reasons to reject Fujitsu's construction. First, a decision as to the patentability of an invention should be capable of being made without needing evidence as to how the human mind actually works. Secondly, to do so, in effect, introduced questions of the novelty of the method, which should remain an issue separate to the issue of patentability (*Vicom* (1987)). Thirdly, the words used in the PA 1977 suggest any mental act, whether done previously or not.

As a matter of substance, a claim to a method remains excluded, whether a computer is used to perform the method or not and whether the claim is worded as a method of using a computer or to a method *per se*, if the result is the product of a mental act, however it is actually performed in practice.

4.5.4 Methods of doing business

Despite US practice, methods of doing business as such remain excluded subject matter (see 4.3.6 above). A Patent Office Practice Note[27] observes that the practice is to issue reports under s 17(5)(b) of the PA 1977 that a search would not serve any useful purpose where the applications have no prospect of maturing into patents. Nor does the proposed Computer-implemented Directive posit any change.

In the UK, following the application of *Fujitsu* (1997) in *Kirin-Amgen* (2001), a method of doing business which could be shown to make a technical contribution should be patentable. The EPO so held in *Petterson* (1995). Although the queuing system was to be used in a commercial context (and the patent was rejected in Sweden), the apparatus claimed was held to be technical and the contribution made in the way its components were organised. This was a solution to a technical and not a business problem. However, mere computerisation of methods is unlikely to constitute a technical effect over and above the mere use of a computer, in the same way that it did not suffice in *Fujitsu* (1997).

However, EPO case law is less resistant. The technical contribution of such claims does lie in a method's computerised application, so that the issue largely becomes one of the patentability of computer programs (see 4.3 above). In *Sohei* (1996) the EPO stated, *obiter*, that 'business' should be narrowly interpreted:

> ... the plural types of management to be performed may include, for instance, 'personnel' and 'construction' managements. While personnel management, as an administration kind of management, would seem to be of similarly abstract character

---

27 'Handling Patent Applications for Excluded Subject Matter': www.patent.gov.uk.

as the afore mentioned inventory management, construction management dealing with works to be done, and having been done, by workers on construction sites could more realistically seem to be comparable with management of manufacturing processes. It would appear debatable whether management of such technical processes would still fall under 'doing business' in the sense of Article 52(2)(c) EPC.

The claims related to a computerised multiple type of financial and inventory management system. They were in very general terms and therefore were not confined to non-technical fields. The technical element lay in the synthesising of different management operations so that the field of management was not material.

The decision in *Pensions Benefits System* (2000) moved a stage further and may yet prove significant. Although the application for a patent did not succeed, the case suggests that the issue is one of inventive step. On the facts the use of a computer did not surmount the obviousness hurdle, but the Technical Board of Appeal opened the way for decisions to be made on each case's facts. It said:

> In the board's view a computer system suitably programmed for use in a particular field, even if that is the field of business and economy, has the character of a concrete apparatus in the sense of a physical entity, man-made for a utilitarian purpose …

It rejected the EPO Guidelines' approach to the exclusion which suggested that examiners identify the technical contribution to the art in the invention as a whole. This, it said, was to confuse the examination for patentable subject matter with that of inventive step. Accordingly the claims survived the subject matter barrier, but were rejected on the latter. An inventive method would then have been patentable.

4.6 PRESENTATIONS OF INFORMATION

Mere presentations of information are excluded, but if a technical contribution can be found, the invention will fall within the proviso. An illustration may be found in *Pitman's Application* (1969). A claim was made to a layout of words on a printed page, which conveyed visually to the reader the correct way of pronouncing the words. This achieved a patent because the printed sheets were designed to be used in a reading machine (a technical device in modern terminology) and had a mechanical purpose.

In *Philips Electronics NV* (2000) the EPO distinguished between information in a form designed for human recognition (cognitive content) and where the essence is the content of the information, and data in machine-readable representation (functional data). The latter would involve interaction between devices and have no human meaning. The Technical Board of Appeal used the example of a television signal to illustrate the distinction. Loss of cognitive content would be akin to '"snow" on a television screen' and have no technical effect on the working of the system. Loss of functional data, on the other hand, would bring the system to a halt.

4.7 AESTHETIC CREATIONS

This exclusion is illustrated by the case of *Fuji/Coloured Disc Jacket* (1990). The EPO refused a patent for a colour for a compact disc jacket. Alternative protection lies in copyright and design rights. A process for producing an aesthetic product, provided it was novel and non-obvious, would be patentable.

4.8   EXCLUSIONS ON THE GROUND OF MORALITY AND PUBLIC POLICY

Inventions are also excluded on the grounds of public policy and morality. Section 1(3)[28] of the PA 1977 refuses a patent to an invention:

> ... the commercial exploitation of which would be contrary to public policy or morality.

The wording of the exclusion was amended to reflect that of the EPC and Article 6 of the Biotechnology Directive. It is not only behaviour objectionable in law that falls within this standard.[29] Article 27(2) of the TRIPS Agreement states the exclusion in positive terms and provides reasons for it:

> Members may exclude from patentability inventions, the prevention within their territory of the commercial exploitation of which is necessary to protect *ordre public* or morality, including to protect human, animal or plant life or health or to avoid serious prejudice to the environment, provided that such exclusion is not made merely because the exploitation is prohibited by their law.

Examples from UK case law are difficult to pinpoint, suggesting that the domestic equivalent in the PA 1949 was regarded only as a rare 'fail safe' provision. It has been suggested that *Palmer's Application* (1970) might illustrate the type of invention that would fall within the exclusion. There, a patent was granted for an injection used as a defence against attack, which was non-lethal, but painful and a chemical irritant.

One point worth remembering is that refusing a patent will not completely prevent such inventions being made, nor research being pursued, where it is seen to have other merits. Nor will refusal of a patent avoid any potential risks if the research is pursued. In many instances, a potentially objectionable invention is likely to have both positive and detrimental aspects, making any decision an exercise in ethical delicacy. However, it should not be thought that refusal or grant of a patent is the only official avenue for regulation of research. Health, safety, medical, environmental and ethical bodies charged with a regulatory role exist, such as the Human Fertilisation and Embryology Authority and Human Genetics Commission.

Some guidance may be found in the EPO Guidelines. The equivalent phrase used in the EPC is '*ordre public*'. The French concept of *ordre public* approximates to public policy, rather than public safety. The Guidelines state that such circumstances are expected to be rare and extreme, giving as examples inventions which are likely to induce riot, public disorder or to lead to criminal or other offensive behaviour. The test is whether the general public would regard the invention as so abhorrent that the grant of patent rights would be inconceivable. If this is applied to the PA 1977, the relevant public would presumably be that of the UK. For the EPO, difficulties in applying a standard to the general public of much of Europe can be foreseen, because wide cultural and social differences may be encountered. There may be potential for

---

28   Amended by the Patent Regulations 2000.
29   Section 1(4) of the PA 1977.

differences to emerge as national patent offices in differing EPC States reach different conclusions on an invention. However, if circumstances falling within the exclusion are expected to be rare and extreme, consensus is possible despite national differences.

4.8.1 Morality and biotechnology

Recent developments in biotechnology, and enhanced attention to environmental concerns, have given the 'morality' exclusion significantly increased importance. With the advent of applications for patents for animal and plant life forms, opposition has been focused, in part, under this ground of exclusion. It is at this point that scientific, medical, ethical, social, moral and philosophical considerations coincide. Concerns centre on applications relating to animals, gene therapy, isolation of genes to produce medical substances, human tissue, plants and micro-organisms. Biotechnology companies rely heavily on patents to support their resource-intensive research. In the first 20 years of operation of the EPO, some 320,000 patents were granted, about 12,500 of which related to biotechnology in general and 2,400 involved genetic engineering. The OECD has found that biotechnology inventions were the fastest growing area of patent applications between 1991 and 1998.[30]

The case of *Plant Genetic Systems/Glutamine Synthetic Inhibitors* (1995) made clear that there was no general objection to biotechnology or genetic engineering. Whether a moral evaluation was a proper concern for patent offices was a matter of considerable debate.[31] However, considerable opposition mounted to patent applications in this field, resulting in the Biotechnology Directive. This had a very troubled and protracted[32] genesis, and was faced with an action for annulment in the ECJ,[33] brought by the Government of the Netherlands. Upheld by the ECJ, it has not been implemented by a majority of Member States. In July 2003 the Commission referred eight countries to the ECJ for this failure.

Three situations illustrate the issues: genetically engineered animals, genetically modified plants and genetic engineering of human DNA.

4.8.2 Genetically engineered animals

The concerns first became apparent in *Harvard/Onco-mouse* (1990). An application was made for a patent for a genetically engineered mouse, or other non-human mammal, which had an increased susceptibility to cancer. The mice were to be used in cancer research. The patent had been granted in the US. In the EPO, it was first refused. After

---

30 OECD Science, Technology and Industry Scoreboard, 2003, A.6.1: www.oecd.org.
31 The traditional view, as represented by E Armitage and I Davies (in *Patents and Morality in Perspective* (London: Common Law Institute of Intellectual Property, 1994)) was that the Patent Office was not equipped to undertake the necessary investigation. To do so would involve the patent process in unwarranted uncertainty, delays and costs. Consequently, they argued that intervention on moral grounds should be made only in the clearest of cases. The opposite view was put by D Beyleveld and R Brownsword (in *Mice, Morality and Patents* (London: Common Law Institute of Intellectual Property, 1993)). They took the view that both the EPC and the PA 1977 forced the issue on to the patent offices concerned, and that there was a standard to be applied in the common cultural morality which underlies the European Convention on Human Rights (ECHR). This standard is rights based, and not utilitarian in approach.
32 It was finally adopted on 6 July 1998 ,10 years after its proposal.
33 *Netherlands v European Parliament* (2001).

an appeal the Board of Appeal sent the application back to the Examining Division. They provided instructions on the application of the provisions at issue including Article 53(a) of the EPC and the patent was eventually granted. The Board of Appeal set out the approach to be taken. The 'moral' issue was one that must be taken on by the EPO, as required by Article 53(a) of the EPC, because there was suffering to the animals involved and potential risks to the environment if the animals were ever released. This was to be done by a 'careful weighing up' of the suffering and risks, on the one hand, and the invention's usefulness to mankind on the other.

Applying this, the Examining Division stated, first, that if certain types of technology should be used under limited conditions it was for the legislator to impose those conditions. They pointed out that a patent is not a positive right to use an invention, only a right to prevent others from doing so for a limited time, so that refusal could not provide the requisite control. Secondly, Article 52 of the EPC laid down general principles for patentability; the exclusions to it should be construed narrowly because the Article only denies a patent if the conditions set out are not satisfied. Thirdly, the EPO set itself to make a utilitarian evaluation of the merits of the invention, as opposed to its demerits, including moral objections. Moral objections could, they said, be outweighed by benefits to mankind. The suffering involved did not render the invention immoral because of the clear benefits to be gained from cancer research. Fewer mice were required if an onco-mouse was used, and there was no alternative to animal testing. The risks to the environment were small in carefully controlled laboratory conditions. Finally, they stated that biotechnological inventions and inventions relating to genetic engineering were not, in general, excluded from patentability. Each case must be decided on its merits. Opposition proceedings were begun after grant by ecological and animal welfare organisations, as well as over 1,000 individuals, but did not succeed.

4.8.3 Genetically modified plants

The EPO again considered the approach to be taken to 'moral' objections, in particular the relevance of environmental concerns, in *Plant Genetic Systems/Glutamine Synthetic Inhibitors* (1995). A patent was granted for plant cells, plants and seeds. They were genetically engineered to make them resistant to a class of herbicides so that they would be selectively protected against weeds and fungal diseases. Greenpeace opposed the patent. The Technical Board of Appeal found that there was no case to answer on the morality issue. Of *ordre public*, the board said:

> It is generally accepted that the concept of *'ordre public'* covers the protection of public security and the physical integrity of individuals as part of society. This concept encompasses, also, the protection of the environment. Accordingly, under EPC, Art 53(a), inventions the exploitation of which is likely to breach public peace or social order (for example, through acts of terrorism) or seriously prejudice the environment are to be excluded from patentability as being contrary to *ordre public*.

In addition, of morality:

> The concept of morality is related to the belief that some behaviour is right and acceptable, whereas other behaviour is wrong; this belief is founded on the totality of the accepted norms which are deeply rooted in a particular culture. For the purposes of the European Patent Convention, the culture in question is the culture inherent in European civilisation and society and civilisation.

The board held that the EPC contained no bar to patenting living matter as such and, therefore, the issue under the morality and *ordre public* exclusion was whether this particular invention was to be excluded. Had it been established that genetic engineering techniques had been misused, or put to destructive use, the objection on the grounds of *ordre public* would have been sustained. On the particular objections made, the Technical Board of Appeal was unable to carry out an *Onco-mouse* style 'balancing exercise' as there was no satisfactory evidence of any real risks, but said that this method was not the only way of assessing patentability under Article 53(a) of the EPC. Survey evidence of public attitudes in Sweden and Switzerland was rejected as not being related to specific risks posed by the invention at issue, nor necessarily representative of norms of European culture. The Technical Board of Appeal has not provided any guidance on ascertaining public opinion, or a common cultural standard; nor how 'abhorrent' an invention must be in order to be excluded from a patent.[34]

4.8.4   Genetic engineering and human DNA

A patent was granted for a human protein, H2-relaxin, genetically engineered from a pregnant woman's DNA. She had given her consent to the process. To repeat the invention further human tissue would have to be used. The patent was opposed in *Howard Florey/Relaxin* (1994). The opponents argued that patenting human genes was immoral, and that it was an offence to human dignity to use the condition of pregnancy for a technical process aimed at profit. It also, they said, infringed an individual's right to self-determination as it involved the 'dismemberment' of women and their piecemeal sale to commercial enterprises. The Opposition Division said that had these arguments been made out the patent would have been abhorrent to the majority of the public, the test supplied by the EPO Guidelines. However, first, there was nothing immoral in a patent for the product of the process for isolating the gene from human tissue, a process much in use to supply life-saving substances unobtainable elsewhere, and welcomed by the public. Secondly, the slavery and dismemberment allegations were based on a fundamental misunderstanding of the nature of a patent – which conferred no rights to individual human beings, nor was any dismemberment involved in obtaining the unicellular host. Thirdly, no patent on 'life' was obtained: 'the patenting of a single human gene had nothing to do with the patenting of human life'. Finally, they gave very short shrift to general concerns over the morality of patenting genes and genetic engineering.

4.8.5   The Biotechnology Directive

The Directive defines areas of invention where patents are to be regarded as objectionable,[35] and largely embodies the jurisprudence of the EPO. This was enacted by the addition of s 76A of and Schedule A2 to the PA 1977 (see 4.9 below). Consequently patents may not be granted for:

*   the human body, at the various stages of its formation and development;

---

34   Pointed out in Llewellyn, M, 'Article 53 Revisited' [1995] EIPR 506.
35   Curly, D, and Sharples, A, 'Patenting Biotechnology in Europe: The Ethical Debate Moves On' [2002] EIPR 565.

- the discovery of one of its elements, including the sequence or partial sequence of a gene;
- processes for cloning human beings;
- processes for modifying the germ line genetic identity of human beings;
- use of human embryos for industrial or commercial purposes;[36]
- processes for modifying the genetic identity of animals which are likely to cause them suffering without any substantial medical benefit to man or animal;
- animals resulting from such processes.

The Government of the Netherlands, supported by Italy and Norway, challenged the Directive in the ECJ. Opposed to genetic manipulation of plants and animals and claiming that no living material should be patented, they argued that the concepts of *ordre public* and morality were not sufficiently clear. They also argued that their application in Member States was bound to be inconsistent because recital 39 referred to the application of national ethical and moral principles. The ECJ refuted the challenge, holding that both *ordre public* and morality were clear concepts in international jurisprudence and that the Directive provided appropriate guidance in Article 6, so that Member States' discretion was restricted. Articles 5 and 6 were also held to contain sufficient safeguards for the fundamental human right to human dignity and integrity; particularly as the Directive did not preclude Member States imposing legal limitation of research into or the exploitation of patentable products. The restriction of patentability for biological elements to those combined with a technical process and specific practical application was sufficient protection for human rights, coupled with the ban on human cloning, use of embryos, and processes for modifying genetic identity. Nevertheless, by September 2004 Belgium,[37] Luxembourg[38] and France[39] had been convicted by the ECJ for not implementing the controversial directive, and proceedings also commenced against Italy.

This decision did not stem the controversy, however, which is likely to continue to rage with new technological advances. Stem cell research is one such area,[40] and already the subject of Patent Office guidance and the Commission's first annual report on the Directive.[41] The fact that patents can be abused, or be granted to cover basic research material, fuels the debate, as the opposition launched in 2002 to the patents held by Myriad Genetics for diagnostic test for breast cancer show (see 4.9.4 below). The European Parliament, scene of the rejection of the first attempt at the Directive, has also adopted a resolution opposing these patents.

In addition, the Supreme Court of Canada ruled in *Harvard College v Canada (Commissioner of Patents)* (2002) that the Onco-mouse is not patentable, despite the many patents for it then held in the US, Japan, Australia and European States. The majority, in a 5:4 split decision, held that patenting of higher life forms was a matter for

---

36 Further clarification as to patents for advances in stem cell technology was given by the Patent Office in Practice Notice 'Inventions Involving Human Embryonic Stem Cells' in April 2003. See also www.patent.gov.uk.
37 Case C–454/03 *European Commission v Belgium*.
38 Case C–450/03 *European Commission v Luxembourg*.
39 Case C–448/03 *European Commission v France*.
40 Laurie, G, 'Patenting Stem Cells of Human Origin' [2004] EIPR 59.
41 'Development and Implications of Patent Law in the Field of Biotechnology and Genetic Engineering', COM (2002) 545 final.

Parliament and not the courts. Subsequently, the Technical Board of Appeal has further restricted the European patent[42] to 'transgenic mice'.

4.8.6 The future

The issue is not one of public policy and morality alone, but of the extent and means of exploitation of patents that are granted. The ethical debate centres on establishing whether patent offices are appropriate for raising such objections, and what criteria should be used. It should not be forgotten that award or refusal of a patent is only one element of a complete structure of medical, environmental and ethical regulation, and that issues of patentability only arise after research has been done and an invention achieved. A full consideration of biological and biotechnological inventions must include the extent of claims allowed, and defences to infringement aimed at allowing continued research by others, as well as the possibility of compulsory licensing to secure continued research. Nor can the concerns of the developing world over access to agricultural resources, and use of indigenous resources, be ignored. The full answer must encompass all political, legal, ethical, environmental, medical and social considerations. This must surely be beyond the remit of a patent office. Nevertheless, patents are granted by a state to facilitate commercial profit as well as stimulate innovation and, as such, moral, social and ethical issues cannot be ignored in decisions whether to grant protection. As yet, the EPO has shown little comprehension of the philosophical and ethical questions raised, while opponents have failed to supply convincing evidence of their concerns. Until this failure of communication and state of mutual misunderstanding is overcome, controversy must continue.

Future development must lie in co-ordinated action. The Commission is required to report annually by the Biotechnology Directive[43] and has established an Expert Group on scientific, legal and economic aspects of biotechnological inventions. The Directive[44] established a separate European Group on Ethics (EGE). At present its guidance is given in general terms and is not related to specific inventions. This latter group could play a more fundamental part in oppositions to patents for inventions on moral grounds if its[45] role were to become a compulsory part of the patent application process for biotechnological inventions – in the same way that clinical trials must be considered ethically acceptable before being given approval.[46]

---

42 Patent Number EP 0 169 672. 'Technical Board of Appeal Restricts "Oncomouse" Patent', EPO Press Release, 6 July 2004: www.european-patent-office.org.
43 Article 16c of the Biotechnology Directive.
44 Article 7 of the Biotechnology Directive.
45 Or an equivalent body created for the purpose. The EGE itself has made this recommendation, *Ethical Aspects of Patenting Inventions Involving Human Stem Cells*, Opinion No 16, 7 May 2002. http://europa.eu.int/comm/european_group_ethics/docs/avis16-en.pdf.
46 Directive 2001/20/EC Relating to the Implementation of Clinical Practice in the Conduct of Clinical Trials on Medicinal Products for Human Use; Sampson, T, 'Achieving Ethically Acceptable Biotechnology Patents: A Lesson from the Clinical Trials Directive?' [2003] EIPR 419.

4.9   BIOLOGICAL INVENTIONS

Biology relates to the naturally occurring living matter of which the human, animal and plant world consists. As such it might be regarded as falling outside the sphere of technology; however, medicine,[47] agriculture and horticulture have long been regarded as a field of technology in which the incentive of patents has an important role. The PA 1977 provisions relating to biological and biotechnological inventions were amended by implementation of the Biotechnology Directive, and are now subject to s 76A and Schedule A2.[48] Biotechnological inventions are defined as products or processes containing 'biological material', which is material 'containing genetic information and capable of being reproduced in a biological system'.[49]

The fact that an invention consists of a product consisting of or containing biological material or a process by which such material is produced, processed or used does not of itself render the invention unpatentable: paragraph 1 of Schedule A2 to the PA 1977. It could still be argued that biological material is not novel or that its identification is a discovery, as it has always existed in nature, but paragraph 2 of Schedule A2 distinguishes between naturally occurring material and that which has either been isolated from its natural environment, or produced by means of a technical process. These latter may be patentable even if previously existing in nature. The distinction is equivalent to that of s 1(2)'s 'as such' proviso – looked at as a whole the element of human intervention provides a 'technical contribution', and the novelty of that contribution may be 'transferred' to the invention.

A further element of patents in this sphere lies in the ability of biological material to reproduce. Paragraphs 7 and 8 of Schedule A2 provide that the patent will extend to material derived from the patented material through propagation or multiplication in an identical or divergent form if it posses the same characteristics. Similarly, a patent for a process for producing biological material extends to material directly obtained from the process or from that material through propagation or multiplication in an identical or divergent form if it posses the same characteristics.

However, there are limits additional to those of novelty, inventive step and industrial application. Paragraph 3(f) makes specific provision for varieties of plants or animals and biological process for their production. It divides into three sections. The first two contain exclusions: the first relates to plant and animal varieties; the second to biological processes for the production of plants and animals. The third section is an exception to the two preceding exclusions, and therefore provides an assertion of patentability for inventions that might otherwise have been caught by the two preceding exclusions – microbiological processes and the products of such processes. This is because there is no clearly defined division between the biological and microbiological. Article 53 of the EPC (now embodied in paragraph 3(f)) was drafted in the 1970s to reflect the Strasbourg Convention 1963, which unified points of patent law relating to biology. That, however, was written at a time when biotechnology was in its infancy. Biotechnology is now at the forefront of medical, veterinary, agricultural, nutritional and horticultural research.

Further exclusions are listed in paragraph 3, based on moral objections (see 4.8.5).

---

47   Subject to s 4(2) of the PA 1977.
48   Inserted by the Patent Regulations 2000, SI 2000/2037.
49   Section 130 of the PA 1977.

4.9.1 Animal varieties

Originally, it was thought that the exclusion related to animals in general. It is the developments in biotechnology which have challenged this interpretation. The case of *Harvard/Onco-mouse* (1990) showed that the exclusion is confined to 'varieties' of animal alone. The EPO applied the taxonomy (classification) of animals which subdivides a species into subspecies and varieties. Varieties constitute the lowest subdivision. Although the invention was to be applied to mice, any non-human mammal (a genus) was claimed. As this did not confine the claims to a variety, the patent was granted.

The Biotechnology Directive and Implementing Regulations for the EPC Act 2000 confirm this approach. Inventions which involve animals may be patented provided that they are not claims to animal varieties. Paragraph 4 of Schedule A2 of the PA 1977 states:

> Inventions which concern plants and animals may be patentable if the technical feasibility of the invention is not confined to a particular plant or animal variety.

4.9.2 Plant varieties

Patents shall not be granted for plant varieties. This exclusion was included to preserve a division between patents and the protection for plant and seed varieties provided by the Plant Varieties and Seeds Acts (PVSA) 1964 and 1983, and the Plant Varieties Act 1997 (PVA) as well as Community Plant Variety Rights (PVRs).[50] The PVSA grants proprietary rights to breeders or discoverers of distinctive, uniform, stable plant varieties for up to 30 years. These rights envisaged the production of new varieties by standard biological techniques such as grafting, hybridisation and cross-pollination. Grant of a PVR involved testing to ascertain that a new variety was distinctive in its characteristics (such as shape, size and colour) and was homogenous and stable, according to an established procedure.

Lubrizol (1990) and Ciba-Geigy (1984)

Following its view that exclusions are to be narrowly interpreted,[51] the EPO first gave 'plant varieties' a narrow meaning, showing a willingness to grant patents. The exclusion did not relate to plants in general, but only to 'varieties'. These were excluded because of the alternative protection available. The definition of 'variety' in the Convention for the Protection of New Varieties of Plants 1961 (UPOV Convention) was adopted:

> ... a multiplicity of plants which are largely the same in their characteristics (that is, 'homogeneity') and remain the same within specific tolerances after every propagation or every propagation cycle (that is, 'stability').

Accordingly, in *Ciba-Geigy/Propagating Material* (1984), a patent was granted over propagating material (seeds) treated with an oxime derivative because the claim was

---

50 Established by Council Regulation 2100/94/EC on Community Plant Variety Rights [1994] OJ L227/1.

51 Which is not based on a necessary interpretation of the EPC.

to a chemical seed coating which made seeds more resistant to agricultural chemicals. It was not to a plant variety, nor a claim in the sphere of plant breeding. In addition, in *Lubrizol/Hybrid Plants* (1990), a patent was granted to hybrid seeds and plants. They were not a 'variety' because succeeding generations of the plants were not stable in the new characteristics and the invention relied on going back repeatedly to the parent plants for further propagation by cloning.

This generous approach to patentability was not without its critics. Objections were made on three grounds: that living matter should never be patented; that genetic resources are part of mankind's common heritage and should not be monopolised; and that the result was developing countries' increasing agricultural dependence on large multinational enterprises. These were met by the refutations that patents are granted for living matter in other spheres; the conditions of novelty and inventive step secure the common heritage; and the grant of patents stimulates the development which is the basis of technology transfer to the developing world.[52] Europe's ability to compete with Japan and the US was also used to justify the grant, as plant patents were available in those countries.

Plant Genetic Systems (1995)

Subsequent EPO case law cast some doubt over plant patents. In *Plant Genetic Systems/Glutamine Synthetic Inhibitors* (1995), Plant Genetic Systems claimed plants generically and not the starting materials, as had been the case in *Ciba-Geigy/Propagating Material* (1984) and *Lubrizol/Hybrid Plants* (1990). The plants had been genetically engineered to be resistant to specific weedkillers. The claims included plants bred from those with the transmitted characteristic. The EPO Board of Appeal found that the characteristic was stable and that the succeeding generations would constitute a variety. The claims were not patentable because they 'embraced' a variety, which would be produced when the plants reproduced. They adopted the interpretation of 'variety' as the lowest sub-grouping within a species from the *Harvard/Onco-mouse* (1990) case. The result was that, as nearly all genetically engineered plants will be stable in succeeding generations, patent protection would not be available.[53] In addition, as the process by which the plants were propagated was not wholly microbiological, the plants did not fall within the inclusionary third section of Article 53(b) of the EPC. In the face of the resulting controversy, the President of the EPO referred a question to the Enlarged Board of Appeal to resolve the anomaly. However, any conflict was denied.

Novartis (1999)

Finally, the *Novartis/Transgenic Plant* (1999) decision by the Enlarged Board of Appeal attempted to lay down clear guidelines after the Technical Board of Appeal upheld refusal of a patent for plants genetically engineered to be resistant to pathogens. It was held that, provided particular plant varieties were not specifically claimed, the claims might be patented even though they might embrace plant varieties, effectively

---

52   Moufang, F, 'Plant Protection' [1992] IIC 328.
53   The decision was much criticised: Schrell, A, 'Are Plants (Still) Patentable?' [1996] EIPR 242; Roberts, T, 'Patenting Plants Around the World' [1996] EIPR 531.

overturning the *Plant Genetic Systems/Glutamine Synthetic Inhibitors* (1995) decision. The board referred to the intention in the EPC to separate plant variety protection and patents. Therefore, if no PVR could be granted because a variety was not specified, there was no objection on this ground to the grant of a patent. A plant variety produced by a microbiological process remains unpatentable if the claim is to a plant variety.

The Biotechnology Directive and EPC Act 2000

The Biotechnology Directive also clarified the issue for Member States of the EU, for both plant and animal varieties. Only inventions consisting of individual varieties are excluded, an invention comprising a range of varieties is patentable.

Paragraph 11 of Schedule A2 now defines plant variety as:

... a plant grouping within a single botanical taxon of the lowest known rank, which grouping can be:

(a) defined by the expression of the characteristics that results from a given genotype or combination of genotypes; and

(b) distinguished from any other plant grouping by the expression of at least one of the said characteristics; and

(c) considered as a unit with regard to its suitability for being propagated unchanged.

The Implementing Regulations of the EPC 2000 provide that this definition (taken from the Community PVR Regulation) should also be applied to the EPC.

'Biopiracy'

There remains considerable resistance to such patents in developing countries, which view protection for genetically modified indigenous crops as 'biopiracy' of their heritage. An American patent[54] for Basmati rice caused an outcry though its protective power does not extend beyond the US and 13 of the 16 claims were revoked on re-examination. Similar opposition was voiced by the Thai Government when it was discovered that the University of Florida was using genetic data from Jasmine rice, vital to Thailand's export economy, to produce a variety that would grow in the US. Access to, and compensation for, indigenous resources and knowledge are an important part of the renegotiation of the TRIPS Agreement. This must be combined with public resistance to genetically modified plants in general. Both concerns may have to be balanced against the need for greater yields to feed growing populations.[55]

4.9.3 Essentially biological processes

The second section of paragraph 3(f) of Schedule A2 excludes some process claims from patentability:

---

54 Although termed a patent the rights concerned the results of traditional plant breeding which would not have secured a patent in Europe: Patents for Biotechnological Inventions: FAQ, Patent Office: www.patent.gov.uk.

55 Shillito, M, Smith, J and Morgan, G, 'Patenting Genetically Engineered Plants' [2002] EIPR 333.

... any essentially biological process for the production of animals or plants

but does not relate to product claims.

Processes 'for' the production of animals or plants

It should first be noted that a biological process that is not 'for' the production of an animal or plant is not excluded on this ground. Biological processes for, for example, methods of controlling the growth of weeds among crops by the application of chemicals or for controlling pest infestation among crops by applying chemicals remain potentially patentable (provided they are novel, non-obvious and industrially applicable). Biological processes that might be caught by this exclusion include, for example, methods of pruning trees to control fungal disease (*Lenard's Application* (1954)), or a method of selective cultivation to produce seeds with a high oil content (*Rau Gesellschaft's Application* (1935)) or even a method of tenderising meat by injecting enzymes before slaughter (*R v PAT ex p Swift* (1962)).

Essentially biological

It is only 'essentially' biological processes that are excluded. The phrase does not represent a distinction between processes occurring naturally and those which involve any element of human intervention. In *Lubrizol/Hybrid Plants* (1990), the EPO described entirely natural processes with no human intervention as 'purely' biological. Determining whether a process that involves human intervention is essentially biological involves a consideration of the effect of man's intervention into the biological process. It is not a measure of the quantity or quality of that intervention, merely its effect. If, despite the intervention, the process could occur naturally, the EPO considered it to be essentially biological.

An essentially biological process is, therefore, one not capable of occurring in nature of its own accord through the right combination of circumstances. In *Lubrizol/Hybrid Plants* (1990), the multistep process was biological in all its steps, but these occurred in an unusual order and were a modification of biologists' and breeders' techniques. So, too, in the *Harvard/Onco-mouse* (1990) case, where the process involved microbiological steps (inserting the oncogene into a vector and micro-injecting at an early embryonic stage). Nor were subsequent generations of the mice caught, because, though reproduction occurred naturally, the result was a product, albeit a 'product by process' claim.[56] If the product is not a 'variety', this interpretation enables circumvention of the prohibition on essentially biological processes by making a product claim.

Plant Genetic Systems/Glutamine Synthetic Inhibitors (1995) also considered this exclusion. The EPO held that if the invention was the result of a technical step essential to its production, which would not occur without human intervention and that step was decisive to the product, then the process could not be considered essentially biological. However, in the circumstances of the case, the technical steps involved in altering the genetic structure of the plants related only to the first generation of altered

---

56 The House of Lords disapproved such claims in *Kirin Amgen Inc v Hoechst Marion Roussel Ltd* (2004) (see 5.1.5).

plants; subsequent generations were bred in the usual way. The claims related also to succeeding generations and, therefore, involved an essentially biological process.

The Biotechnology Directive and EPC Act 2000

However, the Directive and paragraph 11 of Schedule A2 now defines 'essentially biological process' as a process for the production of animals and plants which consists *entirely* of natural phenomena such as crossing and selection. This might be interpreted as reverting to exclusion only of 'purely' biological processes. The *Novartis/Transgenic Plant* (1999) decision of the Enlarged Board of Appeal suggests that this might be adopted in the EPO. The Enlarged Board of Appeal referred to the three potential meanings to 'essentially biological' given by the Technical Board of Appeal. On the first, a process containing any one biological step would be excluded. The second adopted the *Lubrizol* approach. By the third, any one step of human intervention in the process would prevent it from being essentially biological. The Technical Board of Appeal regarded this as representing the Directive's approach. The Enlarged Board of Appeal did not decide the point so that the question remains open.

4.9.4 Microbiological processes

The prohibitions of paragraph 3(f), Schedule A2 to the PA 1977 can be overcome if the claims fit into the third section: 'a microbiological process or other technical process or the product of such a process', as was confirmed by the Technical Board of Appeal in *Harvard/Onco-mouse* (1990):

> EPC, Article 53(b), first half-sentence, is an exception to the general principle of patentability contained in EPC, Article 52(1). The second half-sentence is an exception to this exception, ensuring that the patentability bar does not cover microbiological processes or the products thereof. In other words, the general principle of patentability under EPC, Article 52(1) is restored for inventions involving microbiological processes and the products of such processes. Consequently, patents are grantable for animals produced by a microbiological process.

If this is interpreted widely it has the potential to limit inventions that would be excluded as varieties (see 4.9.1, 4.9.2) or biological processes (see 4.9.3) very considerably. Article 4(3) of the Directive states that the exclusion for essentially biological processes shall be without prejudice to microbiological and technical processes and their products.

However, in *Novartis/Transgenic Plant* (1999) the Enlarged Board of Appeal overruled the finding in *Plant Genetic Systems/Glutamine Synthetic Inhibitors* (1995) that production of a plant variety by a microbiological process overrode the exclusion. The board held that the exclusion continued to apply whatever the means by which a variety was produced. The preamble to the Biotechnology Directive[57] states that:

> … if an invention consists only in genetically modifying a particular plant variety, and if a new plant variety is bred, it will still be excluded from patentability even if the genetic modification is the result not of an essentially biological process but of a biotechnological process.

---

57 Recital 32, Biotechnology Directive.

This must be read in conjunction with Article 4, which also provides that inventions concerning plants and animals shall be patentable if their technical feasibility is not confined to the variety.[58]

Microbiological

Micro-organisms are small independent units of matter invisible to the naked eye such as bacteria, yeasts, viruses and plasmids. In *Plant Genetic Systems/Glutamine Synthetic Inhibitors* (1995), plant cells were not considered to constitute varieties, but to be microbiological products. Microbiological processes involve such organisms, such as bacterial fermentation processes used in brewing and baking. In *Plant Genetic Systems* they were described as processes in which micro-organisms or parts of micro-organisms were used to make or modify products, or processes which produced new micro-organisms for specific purposes. Paragraph 11 of Schedule A2 defines a microbiological process as one involving or performed upon or resulting in microbiological material.

Products and processes in this sphere have long been the subject of patents, although they involve living matter. In *Commercial Solvents Corp v Synthetic Products* (1926), a patent was granted to a process for the production of butyl alcohol and acetone from maize and other grain starch by bacterial fermentation. Claims relating to plasmids were upheld in *Genentech Inc's Patent* (1989) and in *Genentech (Human Growth Hormone)* (1989).

The ethical issues were early raised in the US in *Diamond v Chakrabarty* (1980). The court did not regard the fact that living matter was involved a bar to patentability and said that, where unforeseen technological developments arose, it was for the legislature to lay down the appropriate policy. The court felt that refusing a patent would not prevent any risks involved in the invention and that Congress was the correct forum for issues where risks had to be weighed against potential benefits. However, the expansive *dictum* that Congress had intended patentability to 'include anything under the sun that is made by man' was not found to extend as far as higher life forms by the Canadian Supreme Court in *Harvard College v Canada (Commissioner of Patents)* (2002).

The provision originally distinguished between the biological and the microbiological, a distinction that did not really exist. It was removed by the Biotechnology Directive so that microbiological and other technical processes are included.

Multistep processes

The EPO considered the inclusion of patentability for the microbiological in *Plant Genetic Systems/Glutamine Synthetic Inhibitors* (1995), where the process used had involved both biological and microbiological steps. The process was held not to fall within the inclusionary third section of Article 53(b) of the EPC. A multistep process had to satisfy the test of not being essentially biological before it was patentable. Nor would the products of such a mixed multi-step process be treated as the products of a microbiological process. The transformation of plant cells by recombinant DNA was

---

58   Para 4, Schedule A2, PA 1977.

microbiological, but the subsequent steps of regeneration and transformation were not, and were significant in achieving the end result.

However, Article 4(3) of the Biotechnology Directive states that the exclusions for varieties and biological processes 'shall be without prejudice to the patentability of inventions which concern a microbiological *or other technical process* or a product obtained by means of such a process'.[59] The addition of 'technical processes' suggests that processes of genetic engineering would now be patentable as falling within the inclusion, provided that they do not result in a variety.

Gene sequences

While the human body, including the sequence or partial sequence of a gene, cannot be patented,[60] elements from the human body including gene sequences or partial sequences are patentable. However, only if they have been isolated from the body or produced by a technical process, and provided that the application discloses an industrial application for the invention.[61]

The French Government regarded this compromise as unacceptable, and included a ban on all gene sequences when implementing the Directive. Stem cell research and therapeutic cloning has been criticised as unethical, although it has the potential to provide cures for diseases such as Alzheimer's and Parkinson's. Stem cells have the capacity to change into any cell type of a given organism, thus offering the possibility of developing new methods of repairing or replacing tissues or cells. In opposition proceedings in 2002, the EPO limited the patent[62] held by Edinburgh University for altering cells of mammals to generate transgenic animals.[63] The patent related to a method of genetic engineering for isolating stem cells, including embryonic cells, in cell cultures. It referred to all animals and so originally extended to human cells.

The European Group on Ethics (EGE) urges[64] compulsory licensing to allow for research where access to diagnostic measures and treatment is blocked by misuse of patent rights. Opposition in the EPO to the patents held by Myriad Genetics on the BRCA 1 and BRCA2 genes and diagnostic tests for breast cancer illustrates the perceived misuses.[65] The Opposition Division[66] revoked one BRCA1 patent[67] in May 2004, although the decision is likely to be appealed to a Technical Board of Appeal. Two further Myriad BRCA patents are to be challenged (not yet published). In January 2005, the EPO announced that the Opposition Division had upheld one BRCAI patent, but in amended form. Notably, the proprietor of the UK patent covering BRCA2, Cancer Research Campaign Technology, grants free licences for gene testing to the NHS. The EGE regard only human stem cell lines that have been modified by an inventive technical process and giving rise to a specific industrial application as patentable. Stem cells that have been isolated but not modified should not be

---

59   And incorporated in para 3(f), Schedule A2, PA 1977.
60   Para 3(a), Schedule A2, PA 1977.
61   Paras 2, 5 and 6 of Schedule A2.
62   European Patent No EP 0695351.
63   Granted to Dolly the Sheep's creators.
64   The Ethical Aspects of Human Stem Cell Research and Use, Opinion No 15, 14 November 2000, http://europa.eu.int/comm/european_group_ethics.index_en.htm
65   Rimmer, M, 'Myriad Genetics: Patent Law and Genetic Testing' [2003] EIPR 20.
66   When published the decision may be found at www.epoline.org.
67   Patent No EP 0 699 754.

patentable. It also called for caution over the use of cloning techniques to obtain human embryonic stem cells for therapeutic purposes. It suggests creating an EU Registry of unmodified human stem cell lines.

A different suggestion would confine any patents to new medicinal products, vaccines and genetic tests developed from discoveries relating to DNA. The distinction lies in the type of claims. Product claims to DNA have the potential to block research by others and to monopolise raw research data, while use claims to the end results would reward and protect only the specific end result produced.[68]

4.10 MEDICAL INVENTIONS

One sphere in which the patent incentive is seen to be inappropriate, at least in part, is the medical field. Some areas of medical invention were removed from patentability, by being treated as not capable of industrial application rather than as an excluded category. However, the effect of section 4(2) of the PA 1977 was to create a further category of excluded subject matter for patents.

The EPC Act 2000 amends the EPC to incorporate the exclusion of medical methods in Article 53, on the basis that it is in substance one based on policy grounds rather than industrial applicability. This is also thought to reflect the TRIPS Agreement 1994. Consequently, the Patents Act 2004 recasts this exclusion as part of s 1 of the PA 1977,[69] and by replacing s 4(2) and (3) with s 4A of the PA 1977. No change in practice is expected to result. The amendment to s 1 of the PA 1977 also means that a patent may be revoked on the grounds of this exclusion under s 72(1)(a) of the PA 1977 (see 6.4.2), as it forms part of the definition of patentability.

Section 4A(1) states:

A patent shall not be granted for the invention of –

(a)   a method of treatment of the human or animal body by surgery or therapy, or

(b)   a method of diagnosis practised on the human or animal body.

4.10.1 Public policy

This exclusion reflects public policy by leaving methods of treatment unfettered so that they can be disseminated freely, allowing doctors freedom to adopt the methods they choose (*Schering and Wyeth's Application* (1985)):

... the use in practice by practitioners of such methods of medical treatment in treating patients should not be subjected to possible restraint or restriction by reason of any patent monopoly ...

Phillips,[70] however, queries whether to grant patents, balanced by compulsory licences, might not stimulate further medical research and provide appropriate rewards where funding is difficult to obtain. Amendment of the PA 1977 to include second and subsequent medical uses, as well as narrow interpretation of surgery,

---

68   Jacobs, P and Van Overwalle, G, 'Gene Patents: A Different Approach' [2001] EIPR 505; Schertenleib, D, 'The Patentability and Protection of DNA-based Inventions in the EPO and EU' [2003] EIPR 125.

69   Para 2, Schedule 2 to the Patents Act 2004.

70   Phillips, J and Firth, A, *Introduction to Intellectual Property Law* (London: Butterworths, 2001).

therapy or diagnosis on the body, may lead to renewed consideration of compulsory licensing if patents in the medical sphere are perceived to restrict the activities of practitioners unduly.

The policy arguments were canvassed in the New Zealand case *of Wellcome Foundation* (1983). The New Zealand Court of Appeal refused a patent for a new medical use of a known compound. Cooke J accepted that there were humanitarian and economic arguments for medical advances to be encouraged and rewarded, but said that the medical issue was too wide for the court, and any extension to patentability should be left to the legislature. (Note that similar arguments were made in *Diamond v Chakrabarty* and *Harvard/Onco-mouse* (1990), but the decision was to grant the patent, leaving the issue to be fought out elsewhere, in the legislatures and Congress.)

Cripps[71] argues that denial of a patent for a process is unlikely to hinder research and development. A process patent has less of an incentive effect, as the process is published early in the application, enabling others to achieve the same result by different means, and can be adequately protected by secrecy. There is a countervailing argument that, without protection, secrecy might be resorted to and the benefits of disclosure under the patent system lost. Both Israel and Australia have abandoned the medical methods exclusion.

4.10.2 Method of treatment

Distinguishing a method of treatment from a claim for a substance to be used in a method, particularly one claimed in the 'Swiss' form (see 4.10.6), was considered by the Court of Appeal in *Bristol-Myers Squibb Co v Baker Norton Pharmaceuticals Inc* (2000). A patent was granted to the claimants for use of the drug Taxol in the manufacture of a medicament to treat cancer. The claimants had participated in trials of the drug and the patent was the result of their finding that infusion over three hours was safe. They alleged its infringement by clinical trials conducted by the defendants on its use to treat ovarian cancer. At first instance Jacob J held the patent to be invalid. On appeal the claims were also held to constitute a method of treatment, and not use of a substance in a method of creating a medicament.

In the Court of Appeal Aldous LJ held that a Swiss claim is a matter of form and therefore relates to an invention that substantively is indistinguishable from a method of treatment. Therefore, he said, any distinction between patentable subject matter and excluded methods of treatment lay in the legislative purpose behind the exclusion. Section 4(2) of the (unamended) PA 1977 does not preclude patentability of substances used in treatment (see 4.10.5), so that some restrictions are placed on medical practitioners by patents. The section therefore had the limited purpose of ensuring that patentees should not be able to restrict practitioners' actual use of methods of treatment when treating patients. It was notable that the alleged infringement was incurred during clinical trials of treatment – amounting to treatment of humans by therapy. The result was the need to draw a fine line between a method of treatment and what was available to be used in treatment. The patentee had discovered that changing treatment from a 24-hour to three-hour infusion was effective. This was held to be a discovery of a change in the method of treatment with Taxol. It was an

---

71   Cripps, Y, 'Refusal of Patents for Medical Treatment Methods' [1983] EIPR 173.

unsuccessful attempt to monopolise a new method of treatment under the guise of a Swiss claim because the claims provided a step-by-step direction to treatment. Doctors determined the pre-medication and amount of Taxol, and supervised their administration. The actual medicament suitable for treatment was produced in the patient directly under the supervision of a medical team. It was not part of a method of manufacture and was therefore an excluded invention. The changes wrought to s 4 by the Patents Act 2004 should not alter this result for the future, as the same substance was being used for the same specific use, merely in a different way.

This reasoning was followed in *Istituto Gentili SpA v Teva Pharmaceutical Industries Ltd* (2003). However, the patentee in that case reserved the right to challenge *Bristol-Myers Squibb*.

4.10.3 Treatment

Treatment was defined as any non-insignificant intentional physical or psychic intervention performed directly or indirectly by one human being on another using means of medical science in *Shell/Blood Flow* (1993). It is treatment of a living human or animal body. Consequently, as the experimental method at issue in the case involved the 'sacrifice' of the animal 'treated' it did not fall within the exclusion.

The use of 'therapy' also raised the question whether both preventative and curative treatments are included in the exclusion. *Unilever (Davis's) Application* (1983) laid down that both preventative and curative treatments fell within the meaning of 'therapy'. The claims related to a method of immunising poultry by additives to feed, a preventative treatment. The claims were refused under s 4(2) of the PA 1977 as Falconer J held that 'therapy' had two dictionary meanings, preventative and curative, which the PA 1977 was intended to include.

4.10.4 Surgery, therapy or diagnosis

The exclusion is for methods of treatment by 'surgery or therapy or of diagnosis'. The PA 1977 and the EPC did not follow the previous law, which distinguished between methods of treatment of 'disease' and other, patentable, methods. For example, a method of contraception was allowed in *Schering's Application* (1971), as contraception did not amount to the treatment of disease; and a method of treatment for lice infestation, in *Stafford-Miller's Application* (1984), was regarded as an insecticide rather than treatment of disease. Cosmetic treatments were also patented: in *Joos v Commissioner of Patents* (1973) (an Australian case), a process for strengthening hair and nails was allowed, as it was of commercial significance and applied to healthy hair and nails. The commercial significance of the invention was also an important factor in *Schering's Application* (1971). By contrast, a method of abortion was refused a patent in *Upjohn's Application* (1976).

The EPO requires that the purpose of the method is surgery, diagnosis or therapy: (*R v Cygnus/Diagnostic Method* (2002)).

Surgery

In *Shell/Blood Flow* (1993) the EPO quoted one definition of surgery as 'medicine concerned with the healing of disease, accidental injury or bodily defects by operating on the living body – including both conservative (non-invasive) procedures such as repositioning, and the far more numerous operative (invasive) procedures using instruments'.

The method at stake involved injecting labelled microspheres into the left atrium of an animal and inserting a femoral artery catheter. The EPO held that surgical treatment is not confined to treatment having a curative purpose and was found to be surgical. It was not excluded, however, because the animal did not survive – slaughter of animals did not constitute surgical treatment.

Therapy

The question was raised whether 'therapy' is confined to diseases or includes other treatments. 'Therapy' was defined by the EPO in *Salminen-Pigs III* (1989). The claims were for a method and apparatus for preventing a sow from suffocating her piglets within the confines of a brooding pen. A sensor detected when the sow stood up and blew hot air underneath her to discourage the piglets from going to her until she settled again. Therapy was defined to include:

> ... any non-surgical treatment which is designed to cure, alleviate, remove or lessen the symptoms of, or prevent or reduce the possibility of contracting any malfunction of the animal body ...

and

> ... the treatment of a disease in general or to a curative treatment in the narrow sense as well as the alleviation of symptoms of pain and suffering.

The claims were allowed as they were designed to prevent accidents, not to treat the piglets, and because the method was not 'on' the animal body.

Diagnosis

Interim steps amounting to collection of data are not excluded as methods of diagnosis (*Bruker/Non-invasive Measurement* (1988)). However, it was held in *R v Cygnus/Diagnostic Method* (2002) that excluded diagnostic methods are not limited to those including all the steps necessary to reach a diagnosis. The method at issue was one of sampling blood by applying an electrical current to establish symptoms. The EPO held that fact that the data collected by the sampling of blood required mental steps of interpretation did not prevent it falling within the exclusion. The EPO held that the earlier narrow interpretation of diagnosis in *Bruker* restricting it to methods whose results made it possible to decide on a particular course of medical treatment and which contained *all* the necessary steps went against the spirit of the exclusion and its underlying purpose, rooted in policy. Such an interpretation was also found to be consistent with the treatment of methods of therapy and surgery – where one step falling within the area of exclusion is sufficient to prevent a patent being granted.

It was also held to be immaterial that the method could be performed by patients themselves, or that its execution did not have any significant impact on the body or involve a serious health risk:

...what is decisive is the fact that all method claims on file comprise the step of taking of a body sample for the purpose of diagnosis and that such a step is to be regarded as an essential activity pertaining to diagnosis and practised on the living body.

4.10.5 Product claims

The exclusion is for methods of treatment. Medical product claims are not unpatentable. A product claim can be made in one of two ways, either for a device to be used in medical treatment, or for a substance or composition.

Device claims

Medical hardware is patentable provided it meets the usual criteria of novelty, inventive step and industrial applicability: *Siemens/Flow Measurement* (1989). The applicant sought a patent for a method of measuring the flow of small quantities of liquid through a tube. This was achieved by injecting a bubble into the liquid and then measuring its rate of progression between two points in the tube. This method could be applied in particular in a device planted in the human or animal body for the administration of a drug such as insulin. The Technical Board of Appeal allowed the claims:

> In the board's opinion, the introduction of a drug into the human body by means of a device for controlled drug administration that has already been implanted is clearly unconnected with either a surgical or a diagnostic method ... The check on the operation of the device therefore requires no medical knowledge whatsoever as regards the behaviour of the body into which the device is introduced ... The operating parameters measured according to the method claimed allow the doctor complete liberty to plan the operating timetable of the pump - and thus the drug intake required for treatment - with medical discretion.

Substance claims

The PA 1977 does not exclude substances designed for medical use from patentability (again provided that the other criteria of patentability are satisfied). Section 4A(2) provides:

> (2)   Sub section (1) above does not apply to an invention consisting of a substance or composition for use in any such method.

The pharmaceutical industry is one of the prime users of the patent system, protecting the very expensive development of new drugs.

Medical uses for known substances

In fact, the PA 1977 allows an inroad to the normal principles of novelty in relation to such substances. The patent incentive has been of vital importance in the pharmaceutical field where new substances have been found. There is logic in extending that incentive to research and development with known substances in the medical field where new uses can be found, and the special concession with regard to novelty was the result of lobbying by the drug industry. The effect is to allow a patent over a substance even though the substance is already known.

Under the old law, section 2(6) of the PA 1977 provided that in the case of an invention consisting of a substance or composition for use in a method of treatment, the fact that the substance or composition formed part of the state of the art would not prevent it from being taken to be new. However, this was only the case if the use of the substance or composition in *any* such method did not form part of the state of the art.

This only extended to the discovery of the first medical use for that substance. Once one medical use was uncovered the substance fell into the state of the art. This was made clear by *Sopharma's Application* (1983). A substance was already known as an anti-inflammation agent, then it was discovered to have a use in the treatment of cancer. The patent was refused. The 'any' in the last line of s 2(6) of the PA 1977 was interpreted to refer not to the newly discovered use (cancer treatment), but to use in any method of treatment at all falling within s 4(2) of the PA 1977. This was held to be consistent with s 130(7) of the PA 1977 and EPO case law. In addition, it was consonant with a policy of leaving the medical profession as unfettered as possible, while stimulating research.

Reform

However, there remains considerable merit in encouraging and rewarding second and subsequent medical uses of known substances and at first the courts allowed adoption of Swiss claims (4.10.6 below) to extend patentability to second medical uses. Further reform came with the EPC Act 200 and Patents Act 2004,[72] extending this inroad into normal principles of novelty to newly uncovered second and subsequent medical uses. It should no longer be necessary to resort to the form of a Swiss claim.

Section 4A(3) and (4) states:

(3)   In the case of an invention consisting of a substance or composition for use in any such method, the fact that the substance or composition forms part of the state of the art shall not prevent the invention from being taken to be new if the use of the substance or composition in any such method does not form part of the state of the art.

(4)   In the case of an invention consisting of a substance or composition for a specific use in any such method, the fact that the substance or composition forms part of the state of the art shall not prevent the invention from being taken to be new if that specific use does not form part of the state of the art.

The Explanatory Notes to Patents Act 2004 state that the new sub-sections enable patents for second and subsequent uses of a substance in a method of treatment to be claimed directly in the form 'substance X for use in treatment of disease Y'. The new use will be novel if that specific use was not previously known as part of the state of the art. Swiss claims may be used but the direct form may also be used. The direct claim is to the substance, whereas a Swiss claim is to use of the substance, with the differences of scope in protection that substance and method claims bring.

In the Patent Office consultation on the Bill some academic concern was expressed that to do so would result in wider patentability than had been achieved through the Swiss claim and that, as such uses are often the result of clinical trials, patents would be difficult to justify. The response of the Patent Office, constrained by the need to

---

72   Para 2, Schedule 2, PA 2004 removes s 2(6) from the PA 1977.

implement the reforms to the EPC, is to emphasise that the new medical use must be new and inventive.

4.10.6 Alternative types of claim

Where doubts arise as to the patentability of an invention involving a method of treatment, claims may be made in an alternative form to secure patent protection. These include making a 'Swiss' claim, or a 'pack' claim.

Swiss claims

In the case of *Eisai* (1987), the EPO accepted a form of claim developed in the Swiss Patent Office, an unusual inroad into the principle that the nature of a claim is a matter of substance and not form. The Swiss claim extends to second medical uses of known substances. The substance must be claimed in the form:

... use of substance A in preparation of a medicament for the treatment of B.

It is a claim to a method for making a substance, but limited to the substance being made for the new use from whence the novelty derives. It was accepted in the EPO Guidelines and by the EPO, although the effect is to confer a patent for a method of treatment, linguistically claimed as a substance claim. It was applied in the UK in *Schering* and *Wyeth's Application* (1985), with reluctance, by Whitford and Falconer JJ. They pointed out that the claim is open to the argument that novelty is lacking if the new medicament is not itself new.

The Swiss claim was the forerunner to another means of claiming new uses found for known substances (see 5.1.6) and is an extension of the transfer of novelty approach adopted after *Vicom* (1987) and *Genentech Inc's Patent* (1989). This approach allows transfer of the novelty to be found in an objectionable component of claims to their patentable component by reading the claims as a whole. The ability to do so can be seen to lie at the root of subsequent developments that may be leading the EPO into uncharted and difficult waters.

Eisai (1987) was considered twice in the UK in 1996, and its application was restricted to tried and tested second medical uses, not speculative ones. This was done on the ground that to be patentable, disclosure must be sufficient (see 5.4). In *Hoerrmann's Application* (1996), the claims were correctly made in the Swiss form when a new medical use for a known substance was found. However, the patent was refused on the ground that under a Swiss claim, the new treatment must be supported by the specification under s 14(5)(c) of the PA 1977. As no evidence that the treatments worked was given (the applicant argued that he needed a patent before he could undertake the expense of extensive clinical testing), the claims were not supported by the description. This was followed in *Consultants Suppliers Ltd's Application* (1996). The reason given was that to do otherwise 'would leave the path open for speculative patenting of ranges of new potential, but untried uses for known medicaments'. In this case, some testing had been done, but did not give clear evidence that the treatment had been sufficiently tried and tested.

However, the Court of Appeal urged consonance with the EPO in *Bristol-Myers Squibb Co v Baker Norton Pharmaceuticals Inc* (2000). Consequently, novelty in a Swiss claim is to be found in the new use and not the substance. Both the *Merrell Dow* and

Mobil Oil cases on novelty of new uses for known substances (see 5.1.6) were considered, but held to rest on different grounds, leaving *Eisai* unqualified to be applied to second medical use claims.

While reform of the PA 1977 may render Swiss claims unnecessary, many patents claimed in this form remain and may still form the basis of infringement or revocation proceedings.

Pack claims

A pack claim may be used to overcome any objection to patentability,[73] but its successful use has been in relation to methods of treatment. The claim is directed to the package in which the invention is contained. If there is a link between the working of the invention and the pack, this device may confer appropriate patent protection. In *Organon's Laboratory* (1970), the claim was directed to a card containing the monthly contraceptive pill, which was so designed that it dictated the correct sequence for taking the pill. The actual invention was the new method of taking and dosage of the pill. As the card itself was novel and non-obvious, the claim succeeded.

However, this must be contrasted with *Ciba-Geigy (Duerr's) Application* (1977), where a similar claim did not succeed in securing a patent. A new use, as a selective weedkiller, was discovered for a known substance. It was doubtful whether a process claim would be successful, so the claims were directed to the chemical and its container and instructions for use. The container was held not to be a patentable invention, as, in itself, it was conventional (unlike the *Organon* blister pack). The information the container bore could not confer novelty nor inventive step when there was no interaction between the container, its contents and the instructions. There is a distinction between reading composite claims, such as those in *Vicom* (1987), where program and computer were interrelated in the achievement of the new result and piecemeal claims to individual and unrelated components such as those of *Ciba-Geigy (Duerr's) Application* (1977).

Further Reading

Armitage, E and Davies, I, *Patents and Morality in Perspective* (London: CLIP, 1994)

Beyleveld, D and Brownsword, R, *Mice, Morality and Patents* (London: CLIP, 1993)

Booton, D and Mole, P, 'The Action Freezes? The Draft Directive on the Patentability of Computer-implemented Inventions' [2002] IPQ 289

Brownsword, R and Cornish, W, *Law and Human Genetics: Regulating a Revolution* (Oxford: Hart Publishing, 1998)

Carbone, J, 'Ethics, Patents and the Sustainability of the Biotech Business Model' [2003] International Review of Law, Computers and Technology 203

Cripps, Y, 'Refusal of Patents for Medical Treatment Methods' [1983] EIPR 173

Cornish, W, *Intellectual Property: Omnipresent, Distracting, Irrelevant?* (Oxford: OUP, 2004)

Curly, D and Sharples, A, 'Patenting Biotechnology in Europe: The Ethical Debate Moves On' [2002] EIPR 565

---

73 That the invention falls into an excluded category is a second medical use or a method of treatment, for example.

Davies, S, 'Computer Program Claims' [1998] EIPR 429

Ford, R, 'The Morality of Biotech Patents: Differing Legal Obligations in Europe?' [1997] EIPR 315

Koo, D, 'Patent and Copyright Protection of Computer Programs' [2002] IPQ 172

Laurie, G, 'Biotechnology: Facing the Problems of Patent Law', chapter in *Innovation, Incentive and Reward: Intellectual Property Law and Policy* (1997) Edinburgh UP, Vol 5(3) 45

Laurie, G, 'Patenting Stem Cells of Human Origin' [2004] EIPR 59

Llewellyn, M, 'Article 53 Revisited' [1995] EIPR 506

Moufang, R, 'Plant Protection' [1992] IIC 328

Newman, J, 'The Patentability of Computer-Related Inventions in Europe' [1997] EIPR 701

Nott, R, '"You did it!": The European Biotechnology Directive at Last' [1998] EIPR 347

Nuffield Council on Bioethics Discussion Paper, 'The Ethics of Patenting DNA' 2002 www.nuffieldbioethics.org

Ricketson, S, 'Business Method Patents – A Matter of Convenience?' [2003] IPQ 97

Roberts, T, 'Patenting Plants around the World' [1996] EIPR 531

Sampson, T, 'Achieving Ethically Acceptable Biotechnology Patents: A Lesson from the Clinical Trials Directive?' [2003] EIPR 419

Schertenlieb, D, 'The Patentability and Protection of DNA-based Inventions in the EPO and the EU' [2003] EIPR 125

Schrell, A, 'Are Plants (Still) Patentable?' [1996] EIPR 242

Sherman, B, 'Regulating Access and Use of Genetic Resources: Intellectual Property Law and Biodiversity' [2003] EIPR 301

Sherman, B and Bently, L, 'The Question of Patenting Life', in Bently, B and Maniatis, S (eds), *Intellectual Property and Ethics*, Vol 4: Perspectives on Intellectual Property (London: Sweet & Maxwell, 1998)

Sherman, B, 'Patentability of Computer-related Inventions in the UK and EPO' [1991] EIPR 85

Sterckx, S (ed), *Biotechnology, Patents and Morality* (Aldershot: Ashgate, 1997)

Thurston, J, 'The Commercial and Legal Impact of the Court of Appeal's Decision in *Genentech v Wellcome*' [1989] EIPR 66

Warren, A, 'A Mouse in Sheep's Clothing: the Challenge to the Patent Morality Criterion posed by "Dolly"' [1998] EIPR 445

Wegner, H, 'The *Chakrabarty* Decision Patenting Products of Genetic Engineering' [1980] EIPR 304

CHAPTER 5

PATENTABLE INVENTIONS

Once it has been established that an invention consists of patentable subject matter, before a patent may be granted it must also be determined whether that invention is new, has inventive step, is industrially applicable and has been sufficiently disclosed in the application. If a patent has been granted in breach of any of these criteria it may subsequently be revoked (see 6.4.2).

5.1 NOVELTY

Section 1(1)(a) of the Patents Act PA (1977) provides that an invention must be new. It is worth considering first why this should be so.

5.1.1 The right to work

To allow a monopoly over something potentially already within the public domain, available for public use and within the public's knowledge, would deprive the public of material to which it already had access and render illegal that which it had hitherto been entitled to do. Such a monopoly would not coincide with the policy objectives of the patent system (to encourage fresh industry without preventing free competition within existing industry) and would clearly be objectionable, as explained by Judge Rich:[1]

> ... the good monopoly is one which serves to give the public, through its incentive, something which it has not had before and would not be likely to get without the incentive - at least not so soon. The bad monopoly is one which takes from the public that which it already has or could readily have without the added incentive of the patent right.

This is known as the 'right to work' principle. The simple way of ensuring that the grant of a patent does not encroach on this principle is to require that a patentable invention be new to the public and not already either expressly or inherently within its grasp. An invention is inherently available to the public where the invention has been achieved, but not understood, an example being the discovery of a new effect of a known substance. Any use of the substance will have achieved the effect, although its user will not have appreciated it.

An effective way of securing the right to work is to test the invention which is the subject of a patent application by comparing the invention and the prior art and asking whether the invention would 'infringe' the prior art – a test of 'reverse infringement'. For the purpose of infringement, it is not necessary that defendants should have realised that their actions infringed. If a reverse infringement test is not used the right to work principle is jeopardised.

---

1   (1978) 60(5) JPOS 271, 288.

5.1.2   Testing novelty

Section 2 of the PA 1977 elaborates s 1(1)(a) of the PA 1977. An invention that forms part of the 'state of the art'[2] is not new.

To decide whether an invention is new is a three-step process:

(a) finding the state of the art;

(b) interpreting (construing) the specification to establish the boundaries of the invention being claimed;

(c) comparing the invention as claimed to the prior art on the priority date of the invention.

If the invention has been disclosed before its priority date, it is not new: it has been 'anticipated'. The investigation into an invention's novelty is made for an application before any grant of a patent. It may also be made after a patent has been granted if the validity of that patent is challenged, or its revocation sought. For this reason, s 2 of the PA 1977 refers both to applications and to patents.

5.1.3   The state of the art

The constituents of the state of the art are set out in s 2(2), (3), and (4) of the PA 1977.

Matter

All 'matter' made available to the public before the invention's priority date must be taken into account. 'All matter' is interpreted literally, and the Patent Office will cite any source of information it unearths about the invention; the comic *The Beano* was once cited! Under the PA 1977, the nature and manner of disclosure is irrelevant: it can be by a 'product, a process, information about either, or anything else', or 'by written or oral description, by use or in any other way'.[3] To anticipate the prior art must be found in a single disclosure. Several disclosures may not be 'mosaiced' as they can when obviousness is at issue (see 5.2.3).

Prior specifications under s 2(3)

The main source of prior information will lie in earlier applications and patent specifications. This will include all specifications published on, or after, the priority date of the invention being tested. Because an application is not published for 18 months after its priority date, there is a danger, if consideration of prior specifications is confined to those already published, that a patent could be granted twice for the same invention. This is because the same invention might be revealed in an application with an earlier date to the one at issue, but which has not yet been published.

Section 2(3) of the PA 1977 prevents this double patenting. It brings applications and patents with a priority date before the priority date of the invention at issue within the state of the art, although they are not published until after that date, provided that the eventual publication also contains the relevant information.

2   The state of the art is often referred to as the prior art.
3   Section 2(2) of the PA 77.

The prior art under both s 2(2) and s 2(3) must be 'enabling': *Synthon BV v Smithkline Beecham plc* (2002). The claimant sought revocation of a patent. Evidence of experiments was admitted which showed that following the teaching of the anticipating application did inevitably result in the patented substance. It was held that anticipation from a disclosure under s 2(3) of the PA 1977 did not have to be on the face of the document alone and could comprise such experiments. To the extent that a prior disclosure is not enabling, double patenting is not entirely avoided.

Absolute novelty

The standard adopted by the PA 1977 and the EPC is one of absolute novelty: there is no temporal or geographical restriction on the prior art. It includes matter available anywhere in the world, at any time. Previously, the prior art was restricted to matter available in the UK and within the 50 years preceding the priority date. This was domestic novelty and allowed the rediscovery of an idea first revealed before its time.

It may be that some anticipating material is so remote that it might not be considered to fall within the state of the art. There is precedent from the US for such an approach. In *Badowski v US* (1958), a Russian diplomatic document was discounted as being so remote as to be effectively unavailable. In the EPO Guidelines, it is provided that the PCT applications through WIPO which are in Japanese or Russian are included within the art only if the relevant fees have been paid and translations in English, German or French have been submitted, such is the difficulty of those languages.

Excepted disclosures

Section 2(4) of the PA 1977 lays down two limited exceptions to the absolute nature of the 'matter' considered. It removes from the art:

- disclosures made in breach of confidence within the six months before the invention's filing[4] date, and
- disclosures made by the inventor displaying the invention at an international exhibition.

International exhibitions are narrowly defined by s 130(1) of the PA 1977.

No distinction is made between disclosures emanating from others and those coming from the applicant or patentee himself. Both the PA 1977 and the EPC confer a patent on the 'first to file', and not necessarily on the first to invent: *Catnic Components v Evans* (1983).

Grace periods

The fact that no distinction is made between disclosures made by the inventor and those made by third parties is seen to prejudice academic inventors in particular, as they are subject also to considerable pressure to publish their results. An example of such prejudice can be seen in *Bristol-Myers Squibb Co v Baker Norton Pharmaceuticals Inc*

---

4   It is the filing date, and not the priority date of the full application: *University Patents Inc/Six Month Period* (2000), G3/98 [2001] OJ EPO 62.

(2000). A lecture given by the director of Bristol-Myers' research and development anticipated one claim in the Taxol patent (see 4.10.2). In fact, the number of inventions so prejudiced is relatively low.[5]

Some protection against an inventor's own disclosures is available. The priority period (see 3.4.2) allows for lodging applications early (so disclosure may be made by the inventor at a relatively early stage), thus providing 12 months in which to develop the invention and test its market before the application is completed. In addition, disclosures may also be protected by obligations of confidence, although this can be cumbersome.

Other patent systems differ, and also provide a period of grace for an inventor's disclosures before any application is made. In the US disclosures made within the year preceding the filing of an application are discounted from the prior art; in Japan the period of grace for an inventor is six months. An invention may be made and sold without prejudicing a patent application if made within 12 months of the first disclosure. The advantage for an inventor would be to allow market testing before making a final commitment to patent protection. However, such a disclosure would still prejudice the invention's novelty in jurisdictions without a grace period. It would also increase the period of uncertainty for competitors, who would not be able to establish which of their rivals' products were subject to patent protection, as the priority period based on the PIPC would remain. It would also be a more complex task to decide which publications would work against a patent.

The UK Patent Office consulted on the question of introducing a grace period in 2002. The majority of responses did not favour any change. An important factor in this was the right of third parties to information. Nor did the academic community appear to favour any change and no change has been included in the Patents Act 2004.

Public

Patent law takes a strict view of the public domain (which may be contrasted with the law of breach of confidence (see Chapter 7). The 'public' constitutes any one or more individuals unfettered by any obligation in law or equity to maintain confidence. This was established in *Humpherson v Syer* (1877). A patentee asked one man to make the device for preventing waste water; this anticipated the invention as disclosure to one person, without obligations of confidence, constituted disclosure to the public.

Thus, it is essential that an inventor takes great care not to reveal the invention, unless under strict conditions of confidentiality, until an application has been filed. The action for breach of confidence provides important support for the inventor at this point. Any confidence must be real and not nominal. Mere membership of a common organisation will not import any confidence. In *Monsanto's Application* (1971), a bulletin was given to company salesmen and over 1,000 copies sent to the British Baking Industry's Research Association. This was not confidential, as no fetter was placed on the salesmen with respect to the information and it had been given for the purposes of dissemination. So too, in *Dalrymple's Application* (1957), a research bulletin circulated in the trade under notional obligations of confidence was held to form part of the state of the art.

---

5   UK Consultation on Patents Grace Periods www: patents.gov.uk.

Available

The prior art must be 'available' to the public. This raises two issues. The first relates to the clarity of the potentially anticipating information. The second concerns the appreciation of it that the public actually has.

The courts have taken a strict line on the first issue, the anticipating art must reveal the invention now being claimed both clearly and precisely: in the phraseology of *General Tire v Firestone* (1972), it must 'plant a flag' at the inventor's precise destination. In *Fomento Industrial v Mentmore Manufacturing* (1956), the invention was a nib for an early ballpoint pen. There had been prior publication of the innovation introduced to the nib; however, this was held not to anticipate the invention because following the instructions of the prior publication did not inevitably result in the innovation now claimed.

On the second issue, the use of the word 'available' in the EPC and the PA 1977 has been interpreted to imply some real prior access to the invention in terms of either the public's understanding or use of it from the prior art. This represents a significant departure from the position under the PA 1949 and, arguably, an encroachment on the right to work principle. Under the old law, in *General Tire v Firestone* (1972), the Court of Appeal held that the prior art need only reveal 'a clear description of, or clear instructions to do or make, something that would infringe the patentee's claim'. This was taken to mean that the public need not appreciate or understand the invention now being claimed if the description or instructions for it could be discerned in the prior art. Consequently, both inherent and secret disclosures of the invention in the prior art anticipated despite the fact that their teaching was not understood to reveal the invention claimed.

Secret use

In *Bristol-Myers Co (Johnson's) Application* (1975) the House of Lords considered prior secret use of ampicillin. Bristol-Myers had a patent for ampicillin, an antibiotic. Before its priority date Beecham made small quantities of it without knowing about the invention or its advantages. The House of Lords applied both the right to work and reverse infringement principles and held that secret prior use anticipated.

Inherent disclosures

Molins Machine Co v Industrial Machinery Ltd (1938) illustrates the old law relating to inherent disclosures. In this case, it was argued that a patent for a method of making cigarettes that improved the distribution of tobacco in them had been anticipated. The invention gave the tobacco a 'forward push'. An earlier machine, the Bonsack patent, revealed a similar movement, although moving at a slower speed. The purpose for the movement there was entirely different, although it would have had a similar effect to the movement for which the patent was now being claimed. This new purpose had not previously been appreciated as resulting from the motion claimed. Lord Greene MR said:

> It is said ... that Bonsack cannot be an anticipation because it does not appear and ought not to be assumed that, in giving directions for the inclination of the trough, he was envisaging the same problem as that with which the present inventor was

concerned; and that if the problems were not the same, the validity of the present claim is not affected by the fact that this particular element is to be found inserted for no apparent purpose in Bonsack's machine ... Bonsack's instruction is to make a machine of a particular kind ... The inclination which he gives to his trough is a physical fact necessarily present in each machine made in accordance with his specification and is as much a part of the true nature of that machine as any other element in it.

So the 'forward push' had been anticipated, although its effect had not been realised because the effect would have still have been achieved by using the Bonsack machine. The Court of Appeal allowed an amendment to the specification that restricted it to faster machines, avoiding the anticipating information. Similarly, in *Fomento Industrial v Mentmore Manufacturing* (1956), a few samples of the nib had been given away as samples, although the advantage of the new nib had not been appreciated. This anticipated the invention.

So far, these cases represent the high water mark of the right to work principle. Before 1977, patent law concentrated on prior use as the principal means of anticipation because the prime function of a patent was seen as introducing new industry to the UK. The emphasis under the new law of the EPC and PA 1977, however, is on the information contained in a patent and whether it has been contained in the prior disclosure. The information function has been stressed by the provision for disclosure in s 14 of the PA 1977. It is a logical corollary that only if the new information or idea disclosed by an inventor has been revealed in the prior art should the invention be anticipated. Otherwise, the substance of invention (information) has not been made available to the public. The EPO has stated that the essence of a patent is the information that it contains.

Enabling disclosure

The requirement that the invention be made available to the public before its priority date for it to have been anticipated has been interpreted to mean that an 'enabling disclosure' be made by the prior art. An unappreciated or inherent disclosure, such as that in *Fomento Industrial v Mentmore Manufacturing* (1956) or *Molins Machine Co v Industrial Machinery Ltd* (1938), is not enabling. Falconer J explained the changes made by the new law in *Quantel v Spaceward* (1990) and *Pall Corpn v Commercial Hydraulics* (1990).

In *Pall Corpn v Commercial Hydraulics* (1990), the invention related to hydrophilic filters. The inventor had supplied a customer with experimental sample filters, containing the new membrane, for testing. The filters were contained in cartridges so that the inventive membrane could not be examined, although there had been a public demonstration of their use. Falconer J held that an enabling disclosure is:

> ... one sufficient in the case of a claim to a chemical compound to enable those skilled in the art to make the compound claimed, was required to make the claimed invention available to the public and so to anticipate it.

The disclosure had not been enabling. Neither use of the cartridges nor attendance at the demonstration would enable the public to recreate the invention. Falconer J had earlier applied the same principle to a disclosure by publication of a biochemical compound in *Genentech (Human Growth Hormone)* (1989).

The House of Lords confirmed that an enabling disclosure is required to anticipate in a case relating to a chemical compound: *Asahi Kasei Kogyo KK's Application* (1991). This was seen to be in accord with the EPO decisions of *ICI plc's (Herbicides) Application* (1986) and *Collaborative Research Inc (Preprorennin) Application* (1990).

Derogation from the 'right to work' and reverse infringement principles

The 'right to work' principle protects the public by preventing the grant of a patent monopoly over any activity in which it has freely participated. This was achieved by adopting a test of anticipation that required the invention to have been revealed, but not necessarily with all its advantages having been fully appreciated, and then deciding whether that anticipation would 'infringe' the invention. The new 'enabling disclosure' test of anticipation encroaches on the right to work, as use of an invention without explanation will not anticipate. Continuing to do acts which the public had been free to do previously will infringe the new patent. The defence to infringement provided by s 64 of the PA 1977 secures some protection for the right to work, but is of limited application (see 6.3.3). To require an enabling disclosure also encroaches on the 'reverse infringement' test of anticipation as infringers are not required to appreciate the consequences of their activities. However, prior art that does not 'teach' these consequences no longer anticipates.

The new situation has not always been welcomed.[6] Nor is the interpretation of 'available to the public' as an 'enabling disclosure' inevitable. The reference to enabling disclosures in the EPO Guidelines refers to chemical compounds alone. There is good reason to apply special considerations to chemicals. It is possible to speculate on the creation of large numbers of new compounds purely by manipulation of chemical formulae, without showing any practical way to make these compounds. In these circumstances, there is no real anticipation in a mere paper formula.

Merrell Dow Pharmaceuticals v HN Norton

The House of Lords reconsidered the question in *Merrell Dow Pharmaceuticals v HN Norton* (1996). Their lordships accepted Falconer J's approach to anticipation by a prior *use* of an invention, as applied in *Pall Corpn v Commercial Hydraulics* (1990). However, they distinguished prior art contained in a *publication*, an earlier patent specification. The House of Lords considered the single issue of novelty, in a judgment that repays careful reading.

Merrell Dow discovered and patented a new anti-histamine drug, called 'terfenadine', for use in allergies and hay fever. Terfenadine had the advantage of being free of drowsiness as a side effect. The patent expired in 1992, and other drug manufacturers began to make terfenadine. Research subsequent to the grant of the terfenadine patent showed why it was effective. In use, the drug is metabolised in the liver and Merrell Dow were the first to identify the composition of the acid metabolite formed in the liver. It patented the metabolite and this patent was granted in 1980. Taking the drug inevitably resulted in the formation of the acid metabolite within the user. Thus, Merrell Dow claimed that to make and sell terfenadine infringed this

6   White, A, 'The Novelty – Destroying Disclosure: Some Recent Decisions' [1990] EIPR 315.

second patent (the metabolite patent) under s 60(2) of the PA 1977 (see 6.2.2), by knowingly supplying the means for putting the invention (the metabolite) into effect.

It is worth examining the consequences of Merrell Dow's arguments. If its claim were to succeed, the effect would be to extend protection for terfenadine for a further eight years, to the year 2000. This would endorse a second monopoly, albeit indirectly, for the drug. In this particular case, Merrell Dow owned both patents. However, independent researchers could have discovered the metabolite and that patent granted to them. Two manufacturers would then effectively have patents protecting the same product. The facts of the case squarely raised the issue of the right to work. Lord Hoffmann said:

> A patent is granted for a new invention. However,, in 1980, there was nothing new about terfenadine. Full information about its chemical composition and method of use had been published in its patent specification in 1972. Participants in clinical trials had actually been taking the drug. Making and using terfenadine was, therefore, part of the state of the art. What did the acid metabolite patent teach the person who was using terfenadine? It gave him some information about how the product worked in terms of chemical reactions within the body. However, it did not enable him to do anything which he had not been doing before ... Why, therefore, should the later patent confer a right to stop people from doing what they had done before?

For Merrell Dow it was argued that the PA 1977 introduced new law; that the test for novelty had changed (as it was required that information about the invention be found in the prior art for there to be anticipation); and that s 64 of the PA 1977 showed that Parliament had intended the change by providing protection for the prior user. However, the House of Lords found the metabolite patent to have been anticipated and upheld the decision of Aldous J and the Court of Appeal to strike out the action.

First, the House of Lords distinguished between anticipation by a prior use of the invention; and anticipation by disclosure: in this case, the publication in the first terfenadine patent specification.

Secondly, their lordships held that there had been no anticipation by use – the use being the actual taking of terfenadine by volunteers in clinical trials of the drug before the priority date of the metabolite patent, but without the opportunity to study the composition of the drug. The House of Lords confirmed that the law had changed in relation to 'inherent' use. The use must have formed the acid metabolite, but this was unappreciated until the later research. This was because Article 54 of the EPC, as reproduced in s 2(2) of the PA 1977, requires that the invention must have been made public. They said 'an invention is a piece of information', so that: 'The use of a product makes the invention part of the state of the art only so far as that use makes available the necessary information.' Therefore, there was no enabling disclosure in the prior use. The House acknowledged that this introduced a 'substantial qualification' to the right to work principle and the reverse infringement test of novelty. Consequently, had there been no anticipating publication, users of terfenadine could have been stopped from doing what they had already done.

Thirdly, the House of Lords held that there had been anticipation by disclosure in the terfenadine patent. This specification did not mention the metabolite in terms. However, applying the same principle that it is the invention which must be new, the House of Lords said that the invention would be anticipated if information disclosed in the state of the art enabled the public to know the product under 'a description sufficient to work the invention'. The description need not be chemical for 'if the recipe which inevitably produces the substance is part of the state of the art, so is the substance as made by that recipe'. The anticipating use was distinguished because it conveyed no information enabling the metabolite to be made. By contrast, the prior specification did communicate information which inevitably resulted in the formation of the metabolite and so did amount to an enabling disclosure in the prior art. However, it is only use that does not enable the user to discover the new substance which fails to anticipate. *Merrell Dow* was distinguished in *Evans Medical Ltd's Patent* (1998) where the anticipating vaccine was open for users to analyse.

Fourthly, the House of Lords distinguished the EPO case of *Mobil/Friction Reducing Additive* (1990) (see 5.1.6). Where the invention is a use for a product claimed as a product and not as a use (*Mobil*) claim, anticipation is only enabling if the use is revealed, and not just the product.

The House of Lords' decision in *Merrell Dow Pharmaceuticals v HN Norton* (1996) goes some way to avoiding the worst effects of the enabling disclosure approach, where the prior art includes 'anticipation by disclosure'. It reconciles the *General Tire v Firestone* (1972) test of anticipating prior art of clear instructions to make or a clear description with s 2(2) of the PA 1977.

However, there remain hazards in the House of Lords' decision that inherent prior use does not anticipate. It enables an inventor to keep an invention secret and enjoy a *de facto* monopoly, applying for a patent only when it appears that the secret is in jeopardy and, so, extending that *de facto* monopoly at precisely the point when it would otherwise have come to an end.[7] The doctrine of non-informing public use would prevent this in the US. The House of Lords' decision as to anticipation by disclosure also poses the hazard to patentees that a first application may act as a domino, knocking out patents for subsequent research.[8] Note that Lord Hoffmann did state that there would have been no challenge to the novelty of a claim to the synthesisation of the acid metabolite or to the product in isolation; the only respect in which it was not new was in relation to its manufacture by the ingestion of terfenadine in the human body.

The area in which the judgment in *Merrell Dow Pharmaceuticals v HN Norton* (1996) may prove most significant is in relation to *Mobil/Friction Reducing Additive* (1990).

5.1.4 Construing the claims

The second stage of determining whether an invention is new is to establish both the boundaries of the invention being claimed and those of the prior art, so that they may be compared. The same process must be utilised when considering issues of infringement, and will be considered at 6.1.

Inhale Therapeutic Systems Inc v Quadrant Healthcare plc (2002) illustrates the significance of defining an invention by construing the claims when a patent's novelty is challenged. The claims related to stabilising biologically active material by incorporating the unstable material in a glass formed from a water-soluble or water-swellable substance in order to store it at room temperature. The claims referred to 'storage stable' compositions, and to the material being 'dissolved' in an amorphous

---

7   Lim, HG, 'Made Available to the Public – the Final Saga?' [1996] JBL 286.
8   Karet, I, 'A Question of Epistemology' [1996] EIPR 97.

carrier substance. Laddie J held that the patentee had expressly limited the claims to material that was dissolved and did not extend to material that was dispersed.

5.1.5 Comparing invention and prior art

Just as testing novelty is a three-step process, so the third of those steps, making the comparison between the state of the art and the claimed invention, is also a three-part process. First, the prior art must be discovered; next the prior art must be interpreted through the eyes of the hypothetical technician; finally, the comparison is made.

A claim is anticipated in one of two ways:

- A patentee's claim will have been shown to lack necessary novelty and will have been anticipated if a prior inventor's publication contains a clear enabling description of the invention claimed.
- If the art provides clear instructions to do or make something by which the invention would inevitably be achieved if carried out after the grant of the patentee's patent it is equally anticipated.

Anticipation by description

In *Inhale Therapeutic Systems Inc v Quadrant Healthcare plc* (2002) Laddie J said:

> First, if the prior art describes something falling within its scope then, assuming that the description is enabling, the claim is anticipated. In such a case it is not necessary to carry out any experiments, or give evidence of what would have happened if the prior art were put into practice, because it already describes what it achieves ...

He went on to point out that expert evidence might be required to explain technical language in the prior art, which might differ from that in the patent. A patentee could then avoid the prior art by amending his claims, or by demonstrating that the prior art was not enabling. This proof would be secured either by expert evidence or by performing experiments.

Anticipation by process

Laddie J continued:

> The second way of proving anticipation is by showing that the inevitable result of carrying out what is described in the prior art would be a product or process falling within the scope of the claim.

A disclosure capable of being carried out in a manner that does not fall within the claims will not anticipate (though it may still point to obviousness). Patentees may challenge experiments designed to show that the claims do fall within the prior art in two ways. They can suggest that the instructions in the art were not followed exactly so that they do not inevitably result in the invention, or by show that other ways of carrying them out do not result in the invention.

'Inevitably' does not require a 100% success rate. In *Kirin-Amgen Inc v Roche Diagnostics* (2002) Neuberger J said that if an experiment reliably produces a particular result on more than 99% of the occasions on which it is conducted it inevitably leads to the result, as the law of patents is ultimately concerned with practicality.

Guidance from the House of Lords

In *Synthon v SmithKline Beecham* (2003) the prior art lay in Synthon's unpublished patent application. It revealed the product claimed by SmithKline Beecham only as one example in a wide range of compounds. Experiments performed as part of the case showed that the example was not repeatable to provide the form claimed by the defendants. At first instance, Jacob J held the patent to be invalid as both documents revealed the substance at the same level of generality. The Court of Appeal reversed this finding, and applied the enabling disclosure test strictly. As Synthon's application did not provide 'clear and unmistakable directions' to the defendant's substance it was not anticipated. It is expected that this decision will be appealed and may provide clear guidance.

Product by process claims

In a significant departure from UK practice under the PA 1949, in *Kirin Amgen Inc v Hoechst Marion Roussel Ltd* (2004) the House of Lords brought to an end the practice of treating a product as new if it was made by a different process to the same product already within the state of the art – the 'product by process' claim. They did so to bring UK practice in line with that of the EPO,[9] pointing out that s 60(1)(c) of the PA 1977 allowed a patentee to rely on a process claim when confronted with a product made by that process. The patent related to EPO, a product already made by a different process and the claim was revoked by the House for lack of novelty.

Interpreting the prior art

First, the art at the invention's priority date must be interpreted. In *General Tire v Firestone* (1972), the Court of Appeal said that 'the earlier publication must, for this purpose, be interpreted as at the date of its publication, having regard to the relevant surrounding circumstances then existing'. It is not permissible to combine different pieces of prior material in order to anticipate by collocation; this is known as 'mosaicing'. The prior disclosure must anticipate without addition from another source.

Through the eyes of a hypothetical skilled technician

Secondly, the mantle of a technician skilled in the art must be taken on, as the comparison is made objectively through this hypothetical individual's eyes. In the words of Sachs LJ in *General Tire v Firestone* (1972):

> The earlier publication and the patentee's claim must each be construed as they would be at the respective relevant dates by a reader skilled in the art to which they relate, having regard to the state of knowledge in such art at the relevant date. The construction of these documents is a function of the court, being a matter of law, but, since documents of this nature are almost certain to contain technical material, the court must, by evidence, be put in the position of a person of the kind to whom the

9   *International Flavours & Fragrances Inc* [1984] OJ EPO 309. The EPO only accept a product by process claim where a product is new but cannot be distinguished from the prior art by any other form of description in chemical or physical terms.

document is addressed, that is to say, a person skilled in the relevant art at the relevant date. If the art is one having a highly developed technology, the notional skilled reader to whom the document is addressed may not be a single person but a team, whose combined skills would normally be employed in that art in interpreting and carrying into effect instructions such as those which are contained in the document to be construed.

The comparison

Thirdly, the comparison is made. This is a question of fact. The process was explained by the Court of Appeal in *General Tire v Firestone* (1972) thus:

> To anticipate the patentee's claim, the prior publication must contain clear and unmistakeable directions to do what the patentee claims to have invented … A signpost, however clear, upon the road to the patentee's invention will not suffice. The prior inventor must be clearly shown to have planted his flag at the precise destination before the patentee …

Vulnerability of patents

The requirement for novelty has been criticised as counterproductive: it is a difficult judgment; the patent is open to challenge on these grounds throughout its life; and challenges are expensive and time consuming. Advocates of an innovation warrant or innovation patent (see 2.4.3) argue that the real issue is whether a viable innovation is the result of the patentee's activities. It need only be new in the sense that the innovation is not already on the market, as technology can be rediscovered and patents go unexploited, making second patents a desirable proposition. The lengths that competitors will go to to protect their products by challenging a patent's novelty are well illustrated by *Windsurfing International v Tabur Marine* (1985). There, evidence of the holiday activities of a child on Hayling Island was sufficient to anticipate a patent for a windsurfer.

5.1.6 New uses of a known thing

The case of *Molins Machine Co v Industrial Machinery Ltd* (1938) illustrates the difficulties encountered by an inventor discovering a new advantage in a process, or a new use for a known substance. However, just as the exclusions for patentability of certain categories of invention may be avoided by adopting a different form of claim, so too difficulties posed to an invention by the presence of prior art may sometimes be avoided. Three types of invention are apparently envisaged by s 60 of the PA 1977 – products (substances), processes (methods) and products obtained by a specified process (product by process).[10] Where a new use for a known substance is discovered, a patent may still be achieved by making a different type of claim. It may be that claims of a type not itemised by s 60 of the PA 1977 may also be accepted by the Patent Office and the courts. This is not 'cheating'. The distinction between these differing types of claim lies in the extent of the resulting monopoly. If the monopoly can be

---

10   Now subject to the decision of the House of Lords in *Kirin Amgen Inc v Hoechst Marion Roussel Ltd* (2004) (see 5.1.5).

restricted to the new discovery made by the inventor, there is nothing objectionable in granting a patent.

Five alternatives, two of which have already been considered, present themselves:

(1) a pack claim (see 4.10.6 above);

(2) a Swiss Claim (see 4.10.6 above);

(3) a method claim.

If a new use is discovered for a known substance a substance claim would fail for lack of novelty. However, a method claim will restrict the monopoly to the new use. However, such a claim will be of limited value, if the method of achieving the new use does not differ from the prior art: *Shell's Patent* (1960). The patentee claimed a particular mixture as a fuel, but the anticipating document (an unexploited patent) described the same mixture, though for different reasons. The application could not succeed merely by an adding a statement of the new advantage.

(4) A selection patent

Selection patents were developed by the courts (the phrase does not appear in the PA 1977) for the chemical industry, although not confined to chemicals. Many chemical substances are theoretically known and inventive activity lies in discovering new uses for known substances, rather than discovering new substances or finding better processes for making known substances. Thus commercially desirable development was falling outside the ambit of the patent incentive. Substance (product) claims for classes of chemicals have been permitted since 1949 in the UK, and now are allowed under the EPC. Classes of chemicals may be very large indeed, although in practice only a few examples from the class will have been tested for use.

Accepting a claim to a class of substances raised the issue of how wide a monopoly should result. Restricting a patentee to the few examples from the class actually tested would allow competitors a free ride using the nearest alternatives from the class. However, to allow a monopoly for the whole class would be very wide protection indeed. In *Olin Mathieson Chemical v Biorex Laboratories* (1970), a patent was allowed for the whole class – provided that it could not be shown that some members of the class did not have the advantage (use) claimed.

In turn, the next problem to be resolved was that of further uses being discovered for other members of a class already claimed. The result was the selection patent. This allows a fair bite at the patent cherry for the second inventor. The first patentee is awarded a patent for the whole class of substances, so the second inventor may well have to pay royalties during the life of that patent. The second patentee is granted a patent for a selection of substances from the class, to protect the newly discovered use. The progenitor of the selection patent is the case of *IG Farbenindustrie's Patents* (1930). In that case, Maugham J justified the new device because: 'There is no short cut to knowledge of this kind. A laborious and systematic investigation of a long series of combinations becomes necessary.'

The purpose of the selection patent was the same as the *Mobil/Friction Reducing Additive* (1990) new use claim: to reward and stimulate the discovery of new uses for known substances. Where the selection patent differs, however, is in the re-monopolisation of the prior art which *Mobil/Friction Reducing Additive* (1990) allows. If a selection patent is restricted to selected examples from the class previously claimed which were not previously tested and used, there is no re-monopolisation in practice.

Users of the class for the first patented use will not infringe the second, neither will users of the selection for the new use infringe the first patent (if it is still in force).

IG Farbenindustrie's Patents (1930) set out three conditions to be satisfied for the grant of a selection patent:

(a) the new advantage must be claimed as a *quid pro quo* to grant;

(b) all the examples in the selected group must show the new advantage; and

(c) only those selected from the class must have it.

When applied in *Shell's Patent* (1960), little attention was paid to the second and third conditions. A selection patent was granted for the fuel mixture, with a disclaimer for the old use.

The selection patent is, therefore, clearly founded on the discovery of the new use. It can be seen as a forerunner of the *Vicom* (1987) method of treating a use as an integral technical feature of the invention being claimed, provided that it can be clothed in a product claim, the novelty being derived from the use, not the product. A selection patent will be tested for novelty and inventive step in the normal way, but these may be found in the use: *Beecham Group's (Amoxycillin) Application* (1980).

However, the House of Lords' decision in *EI Du Pont's (Witsiepe) Application* (1982) appears to have widened the selection patent device. The House of Lords allowed the patent without restricting the claims to the new advantage, so that the patentee did gain a second monopoly over the substance. This decision was reached before the 'enabling disclosure' approach to novelty under the EPC and the PA 1977, and may foreshadow that change, but it was roundly criticised for giving the effect of re-monopolisation of the polymer despite the expiry of the first patent.[11] Jeffs argues that selection patents should be limited to a selection which does not include any examples from the prior publication, and this is the position adopted by the EPO: *Bayer (Baarz's – Carbonless Copying Paper) Application* (1982). However, Armitage and Ellis counter this by arguing that to restrain the patent to the discovered use is a disincentive to original research into substances, depriving the inventor of royalties from subsequent research.[12]

(5) A use claim

In *Mobil/Friction Reducing Additive* (1990), the EPO accepted a new type of claim, in circumstances which fall outside those of a selection patent, provided that the claims are correctly drafted – a claim to a use for a substance. Both substance and its method of use may be known, it is the result or effect achieved that forms the invention.

Mobil had attempted to patent a substance for use as an additive in lubricating oil because it reduced friction. This was opposed by a rival because the substance was known and already used as an additive for inhibiting rust. Clearly a product claim could not succeed as the substance was not new. Mobil sought to amend the application to claim the new use for the substance. The question whether this could be done was referred to the Enlarged Board of Appeal. The board accepted that, while

---

11 Jeffs, J, 'Selection Patents' [1988] EIPR 291; Reid, B, 'Du Pont and ICI – Chemical Anticipation and Prior Patent Specifications' [1982] EIPR 118.
12 Armitage, R and Ellis, D, 'Chemical Patents in Europe' [1990] EIPR 119.

using an old substance in a new way might be novel, to use an old substance in an old way would not, even if the reason for doing so was new – the only difference would lie in the mind of the user. However, the board continued by saying that the new effect might be regarded as a functional technical feature of the invention and not merely a motive of the user and, if new, could constitute a patentable invention. This would be the case, even though the technical effect may have inherently taken place in the course of carrying out the previous method of use of the substance.

This case represents an extension of the reasoning of *Vicom* (1987), combined with that of the enabling disclosure approach (endorsed by the Enlarged Board of Appeal in *Vicom* (1987)) to novelty. It is only by defining the new use as a 'technical effect' (that is, as an 'invention'), reading the claims as a composite whole and transferring the novelty of use to the technical effect, that patentability can be achieved. In addition, the use is only novel because its inherent, but unappreciated, part in the prior art is discounted by looking for enabling information of that use in the state of the art. It is not a wholly unjustifiable approach, if giving a patent to a new use stimulates a search for appreciating new and useful advantages. However, two considerable difficulties are caused by a 'new use' claim.

First, there is the prejudice to those already using the substance, particularly if any patent protection it may have had has expired, as monopoly prices can be charged for the new use. In addition, anyone using the substance for the old use will inevitably also achieve the new use, raising questions of infringement (see Chapter 6). Although s 64 of the PA 1977 provides as defence, it is of limited application (see 6.3.3).

Secondly, as the House of Lords discussed in *Merrell Dow Pharmaceuticals v HN Norton* (1996), determining infringement will pose problems. If the patent monopoly is confined to the use made of the substance, an element of *mens rea* must be introduced to infringement which will be very difficult to ascertain and prove, for only those using the substance with the intention of achieving the new use will infringe. In the UK, liability for infringement has always been absolute. *Mobil/Friction Reducing Additive* (1990) was distinguished on its facts in *Merrell Dow Pharmaceuticals v HN Norton* (1996): in *Merrell Dow*, the second patent concerned a new substance for an old use, rather than a new use for an old substance. However, to apply the House of Lords' test of novelty to the *Mobil/Friction Reducing Additive* facts gives the result that there was sufficient information in the prior art to enable working of the new use,[13] (although without the knowledge that was the case, in the same way as the metabolite had been revealed in the terfenadine patent). This suggests that the cases are not distinguishable in substance.

Consequently, *Mobil/Friction Reducing Additive* (1990), approved by the House of Lords, will allow re-monopolisation of the state of the art. The real culprit in reaching this point is the dual willingness of the EPO to define an invention as a 'technical effect', departing from the product, process, product by process[14] classification of inventions; and to regard an invention as a piece of information, thus turning the test of novelty into one of communication of that information, rather than finding the invention in the prior art.

---

13 As discussed by Christopher Floyd in 'Novelty under the Patents Act 1977: the State of the Art after Merrell Dow' [1996] EIPR 480.
14 But see *Kirin Amgen Inc v Hoechst Marion Roussel Ltd* (2004) (see 5.1.5).

Some mitigation of these effects may be provided by the EPO's holding that there must be a new (and non-obvious) purpose, and not merely new information about a known use. In *Robertet/Deodorant Compositions* (1999) the Board of Appeal stated that a newly discovered technical effect does not confer novelty on a claim to use of a known substance if it already underlies the known use of the known substance. The board pointed out that in *Mobil/Friction Reducing Additive* (1990) the newly discovered friction-reducing effect of the known substance was an entirely different effect (or use) to that of inhibiting rust for which it had been previously used. This should be distinguished from the situation where a known substance for a known purpose was found to have a newly discovered technical effect. The patentee claimed known aromatic esters for known use as active ingredients in deodorants, but discovered that they inhibited esterase-producing micro-organisms. While this amounted to a new piece of knowledge or explanation about the known use, it did not amount to a new use for the known substance. Describing it as a technical effect might also be challenged, as divorced from the deodorant, the information amounted to a discovery rather than an application of that discovery. Like the House of Lords in *Merrell Dow*, the EPO is refusing to countenance protection for mere information.

5.2 INVENTIVE STEP

Section 1(1)(b) of the PA 1977 requires that an invention involve an inventive step to be patentable. This condition also serves the purpose of preserving what lies within the public domain, by refusing to patent whatever can be discovered by routine investigation and development. This is not to say that patents are not granted for developments, but the step forward must be more than could be routinely made.

It is an evaluation, a question of fact, which renders any application or patent vulnerable. The challenge of invalidity and revocation can be made, not only during the process of grant, but at any time throughout the patent's life. This vulnerability is well illustrated both by *Genentech Inc's Patent* (1989) and *Biogen Inc v Medeva plc* (1997).

Guidance as to the meaning of 'inventive step' is laid out in s 3 of the PA 1977: an invention involves inventive step if it is not obvious to a person skilled in the art. Lack of inventive step is known as 'obviousness'. Once again, comparison must be made between the invention and the state of the art, through the eyes of a hypothetical skilled technician and a judgment reached as to whether the invention shows a sufficiently innovative step forward from the art. It is a particularly difficult judgment to make because the issue often arises long after the making of the invention and must, therefore, effectively be performed with hindsight, ignoring all developments since the invention's priority date.

Because it is an evaluation of fact appellate courts are reluctant to overturn trial judges findings unless they err in principle: *Biogen Inc v Medeva plc* (1997) and *Dyson Ltd v Hoover Ltd* (2001).

The burden of proof lies on the person making the allegation of obviousness: *Mölnlycke v Procter & Gamble (No 5)* (1994).

5.2.1 The invention

A preliminary step lies in establishing what the invention to which the test must be applied is, as was made clear by the House of Lords in *Sabaf v MFI Furniture Centres* (2004).

In the *Sabaf* case the House of Lords both upheld the *Windsurfing* approach to inventive step, and reconciled it with the EPO approach. The patent at issue related to gas burners for kitchen hobs. Sabaf alleged that the defendants had imported burners which infringed its patent, the defendants alleging that the patent was invalid for obviousness. At first instance Laddie J held that the patent was obvious by applying pre-1977 case law on collocations – combinations of obvious elements to create an invention[15] – stating that this test was difficult to reconcile with the structured approach of *Windsurfing*. The Court of Appeal disapproved of this side-stepping of the *Windsurfing* test, and overturned the decision on validity. However, the House of Lords reinstated the first instance finding of invalidity by explaining Laddie J's approach. When considering the 'law of collocation' he was, said Lord Hoffmann, first deciding what constituted the invention, to which the s 3 test must be applied. The EPO Guidelines take the same approach:

> 9.5 COMBINATION V JUXTAPOSITION OR AGGREGATION
>
> The invention claimed must normally be considered as whole. When a claim consists of a 'combination' of features', it is not correct to argue that the separate features of the combination taken by themselves are known or obvious and that 'therefore' the whole subject-matter claimed is obvious. However, where the claim is merely an 'aggregation or juxtaposition of features' and not a true combination, it is enough to show that the individual features are obvious to prove that the aggregation of features does not involve an inventive step. A set of technical features is regarded as a combination of features if the functional interaction between the features achieves a combined technical effect which is different from, eg greater than, the sum of the technical effects of the individual features. In other words, the interactions of the individual features must produce a synergistic effect. If no such synergistic effect exists, there is no more than a mere aggregation of features ...

Having decided that the two elements of the gas burners had no effect on each other, Laddie J considered each individually for inventive step. As each was obvious the patent was invalid. Lord Hoffmann said:

> I quite agree that there is no law of collocation in the sense of a qualification of, or gloss upon, or exception to, the test for obviousness stated in section 3 of the Act. However, before you can apply section 3 and ask whether the invention involves an inventive step, you first have to decide what the invention is. In particular, you have to decide whether you are dealing with one invention or two or more inventions. Two inventions do not become one invention because they are included in the same hardware.

---

15 *British Celanese Ltd v Courtaulds Ltd* (1935) 52 RPC 171. '...a mere placing side by side of old integers so that each performs its own proper function independently of any of the others is not patentable combination ...'. Cited by the HL at para 17.

5.2.2 Determining obviousness

Once the invention has been identified, in the UK a four-step evaluation as set out by the Court of Appeal in *Windsurfing International v Tabur Marine* (1985) is often followed. However, the EPO adopts a different approach; nor has the *Windsurfing* test invariably been adopted by UK courts.

The EPO

The EPO sought to harmonise approaches from Member States by adopting a 'problem-solution' approach to obviousness. Many inventions are made in the process of attempting to solve problems, and the inventive step is deemed to be the step taken from a technical problem to be found in the prior art to the solution adopted by the inventor. The question the EPO asks is whether the solution provided by the invention would have been obvious to a hypothetical technician skilled in the art at the invention's priority date.

The Windsurfing Test

The Court of Appeal adopted a four-step test:

> The first is to identify the inventive concept embodied in the patent in suit. Thereafter, the court has to assume the mantle of the normally skilled but unimaginative addressee in the art at the priority date and to impute to him what was, at that date, common general knowledge in the art in question. The third step is to identify what, if any, differences exist between the matter cited as being 'known or used' and the alleged invention. Finally, the court has to ask itself whether, viewed without any knowledge of the alleged invention, those differences constitute steps which would have been obvious to the skilled man or whether they require any degree of invention.

This was decided under the PA 1949, but affirmed in relation to the PA 1977 by the Court of Appeal in *Mölnlycke v Procter and Gamble* (1994) and by the House of Lords in *Biogen Inc v Medeva plc* (1997). It is seen as providing a structured format for making finding of facts: as to what was included in the state of the art at the priority date; and whether, having regard to the state of the art, the alleged inventive step would have been obvious to a person skilled in the art.

However, in *Hewlett Packard v Waters Corp* (2001) Pumfrey J found the *Windsurfing* test to be inapt where the ambiguities and obscurities of the disclosure in the prior art made it difficult to assess the step represented by the invention. He substituted it by asking whether the hypothetical technician would resolve these in such a way as to produce something falling within the claims without exercising 'inventive ingenuity'. The Court of Appeal[16] did not follow this after the parties agreed that *Windsurfing* was the right approach to take, but did uphold the first instance finding that the patent was not obvious.

In *Instance v Denny Bros Printing Ltd* (2001) the Court of Appeal held that, although *Windsurfing's* structured approach was useful, it was not essential. Provided that a judge adopted the mantle of a skilled person and asked the correct question he could proceed straight to the question whether the invention was obvious. The danger of doing so, however, was said to be that the judgment might be made with hindsight.

---

16 *Hewlett Packard v Waters Corp* (2002).

5.2.3 The state of the art

The prior art is not co-extensive with that used for novelty. It will include all that falls within s 2(2) of the PA 1977, but excludes patent specifications not published at the invention's priority date (though bearing a priority date before the one at issue).[17]

It will also include common general knowledge of the art at the relevant priority date, as stated in *Windsurfing International v Tabur Marine* (1985), and all relevant literature whatever its source or language. This material must be read carefully: *John Manville's Patent* (1967).

For inventive step documents may be 'mosaiced' together, although the EPO Guidelines provide that this may only be done if it would be obvious to do so: *Mobey Chemical's Application* (1982). The applicant claimed a process for producing MBP, which was liquid and stable in storage, by heating the substance in the presence of a catalyst to a temperature of 180–360°C and then quenching it to 100°C or less. This was said to be an improvement over the prior art, in which quenching was not used and the catalyst removed by using a poison, with undesirable side effects. The EPO said:

> In summary, it is clear that, given the problem to be solved, neither the methods of the prior art individually, nor their respective combination with the generally available specialist knowledge, would make the solution according to the invention with the advantageous effects achieved foreseeable. While it is inadmissible to combine unrelated or conflicting documents in order to deny inventive step, it is indeed permissible to consider various documents together mosaically in order to prove a prejudice or a general trend pointing away from the invention. The idea of departing from the catalyst poison regarded as indispensable, in conjunction with the teaching that the catalysts decompose at higher temperature, represents a valuable simplification of the state of the art which could not have been found without an inventive step.

If the documents may only be combined to point to a trend away from the invention where it is obvious to do so, it does raise the question why this has not been done before.

5.2.4 The hypothetical technician

To make the assessment in this way avoids a subjective judgment by inventor, judge or patent office; however, the subjective element cannot be entirely dismissed. It lies in the choice of the relevant art, the degree of appreciation of the information attributed to the hypothetical individual and the supreme difficulty that the assessment is always made with hindsight.

The nature of the 'person skilled in the art' was described by Lord Reid in *Technograph Printed Circuits v Mills and Rockley (Electronics) Ltd* (1972):

> It is not disputed that the hypothetical addressee is a skilled technician who is well acquainted with workshop technique and has carefully read the relevant literature. He is supposed to have an unlimited capacity to assimilate the contents of, it may be, scores of specifications, but to be incapable of a scintilla of invention.

---

17 Section 3 of the PA 1977.

An omniscient artisan

Some documents may be very obscure. Before the PA 1977, there was judicial disagreement, *obiter*, in *Technograph Printed Circuits v Mills* and *Rockley (Electronics) Ltd* (1972) as to the level of knowledge to be attributed to this 'person'. Lord Diplock favoured an 'omniscient artisan' – taken to have found and read everything, whereas Lord Reid favoured a 'diligent searcher' – described in *General Tire v Firestone* (1972) as knowing 'what research groups employed by large scale concerns ought to know'. A compromise was postulated by Whitford J in *ICI (Pointer's) Application* (1977): an omniscient artisan, who would attach different significances to differing sources.

The PA 1977 adopts the omniscient artisan, or a team of artisans. An invention may straddle several different areas of expertise within a particular art, particularly if the scope of its claims is wide. The team is attributed with the common general knowledge from both areas of expertise, rather than that which is common to each member (dubbed the 'smallest common denominator' approach). The court did not consider that to be unfair to the patentee in *Inhale Therapeutic Systems Ltd v Quadrant Healthcare plc* (2002); it was merely a reflection of the width of the claims.

Appreciation of the art

Although omniscient, the 'artisan' will attach different weighting to different documents. The EPO Guidelines suggest asking a series of questions in order to determine the requisite knowledge:

(a) whether the hypothetical technician would regard the documents as a useful starting point;

(b) how much similarity there is between the field of disclosure and the inventor's research;

(c) how obscure or clear the particular art is;

(d) whether the technician would have believed the document's teaching.

This approach follows previous practice with respect to the weighting of documents. At first instance in *Inhale Therapeutic Systems Ltd v Quadrant Healthcare plc* (2002), Laddie J stated that the technician would not find all items of the prior art equally interesting:

> It is no answer to say that in real life the prior art would never have come to the attention of a worker in the field, for example because it was tucked away on the top shelf of a public library or because it was in a language which nobody in the art knew. The notional skilled person is assumed to have read and understood the contents of the prior art. However, that does not mean that all prior art will be considered equally interesting.

This was approved by the Court of Appeal in *Amersham Pharmacia Biotech v Amicon Ltd* (2001).

The question that is then asked is whether the hypothetical person skilled in the art would have thought the step between the prior art and the invention was obvious, and not whether it would have been commercially viable. Nevertheless, the court must adopt the 'mindset' of the relevant hypothetical individual. In *Dyson Ltd v Hoover Ltd*

(2002) Sedley LJ stated that perceived limits of practicability were a relevant mindset, and that it would be affected by considerations of need, including commercial potential. Secondary evidence in that case showed that the industry would not have considered a 'bagless' vacuum cleaner at the time. As it was put in *Asahi Medical Co Ltd v Macopharma (UK) Ltd* (2002) '[t]hat mantle will include the prejudices, preferences and attitudes that such persons had at the priority date'.

A higher standard?

Genentech Inc's Patent (1989) appears to have revised the standard of skill attributed to the hypothetical 'person'. The equivalent individual in German patent law is far from being a technician, being allowed some measure of creativity. In *Genentech Inc's Patent* (1989), Purchas LJ noted that the traditional model of a workshop technician, well read, but determinedly uninventive, was totally unrealistic in the field at issue - biotechnology:

> ... the artisan has receded into the role of the laboratory assistant and the others have become segregated into groups of highly qualified specialists in their own spheres all of whom must possess a degree of inventiveness.

It was recognised, in that case, that all researchers in the field were at a doctorate level and that the hypothetical 'person' must be attributed with some inventive ability. Such an apparent raising of the standard of skill for assessing inventive step only adds to the difficulties of securing patents in the biotechnological field. *Genentech Inc's Patent* (1989) also establishes that, where research in a field is carried out by teams of researchers, the hypothetical 'person' would actually constitute such a team – and would be a team equipped with the best equipment and materials.

5.2.5 The relevant field

When novelty is at issue, the state of the art includes all material that can be unearthed. However, for inventive step, it is obviousness within the field of research in which the invention lies that must be determined. Some of the information that exists, however relevant to the invention, may lie outside this field and be discounted from the skilled technician's attributed knowledge. This is illustrated by *ICI (Pointer's) Application* (1977). The patent being challenged lay in the field of electrical insulation. Two brochures revealed a different use for the same substance in different fields: those of the manufacture of inks and of PVC. The patent was held to be valid (non-obvious) because the brochures were so unrelated to the problem being solved by the patentee.

5.2.6 Making the comparison

Once the state of the art has been established and the mantle of an appropriate hypothetical 'person' adopted, the question that is asked is whether that individual (or team) would think that the step identified as being inventive is obvious in the light of the prior art.

'Obvious'

'Obvious' has been given its normal dictionary meaning of 'very plain' (*General Tire v Firestone* (1972)) or 'worth a try' (*John Manville's Patent* (1967)). The EPO Guidelines define an obvious development as one not going beyond normal technical progress, or one following logically or plainly from the prior art with no exercise of skill or ingenuity. However, the Court of Appeal discouraged attempts to adopt paraphrases of the test in *Mölnlycke v Procter & Gamble (No 5)* (1994).

A lucky or accidental invention is not necessarily obvious merely because it was not deliberately achieved. It is the advance from what has gone before, and not the manner with which the progress was made, that is important. A small and simple step may nonetheless be inventive: *Haberman v Jackel International Ltd* (1999).

Isolating the inventive step

The first step laid down in *Windsurfing International v Tabur Marine* (1985) is to identify the inventive step in the invention claimed. This step can be vital to the eventual outcome. The House of Lords, in *Biogen Inc v Medeva plc* (1997), said that Aldous J had identified too general an inventive step. Their lordships narrowed it down to the specific choice of method adopted for achieving the desired goal by trying to express unsequenced eukaryotic DNA in a prokaryotic host.

In the same case, Lord Hoffmann attempted to define the nature of an inventive step:

> Whenever anything inventive is done for the first time, it is the result of the addition of a new idea to the existing stock of knowledge. Sometimes, it is the idea of using established techniques to do something which no one had previously thought of doing. In that case, the inventive idea will be doing the new thing. Sometimes, it is finding a way of doing something which people had wanted to do but could not think how. The inventive idea would be the way of achieving the goal. In yet other cases, many people may have a general idea of how they might achieve a goal but not know how to solve a particular problem which stands in their way. If someone devises a way of solving the problem, his inventive step will be that solution, but not the goal itself or the general method of achieving it.

While clear guidance from the House of Lords as to the nature of the inventive step identified from the specification so as to determine non-obviousness is to be welcomed, the importance of the first step from *Windsurfing International v Tabur Marine* (1985) was made clear by the case itself. If this 'definition' were to become a straitjacket, as technology advances, it would be counterproductive. To have flexibility in determining the inventive step allows courts to adjust the monopoly the patentee gets for achieving an obviously desirable goal in order to facilitate continued research and competition, as Merges and Nelson[18] suggest. Biotechnology companies have been criticised for making broad patent claims securing wide monopolies. To have discretion in identifying the inventive step allows a court to effect a nice balance between monopoly and competition so as to forward the aims of the patent system without restricting competition unduly. If Lord Hoffmann's third category of inventive

18   Merges, R and Nelson, R, 'On the Complex Economics of Patent Scope' (1990) 90 Columbia L Rev 839.

step accommodates the inventiveness of finding new advantages in known substances this guidance from the House of Lords may not prove over-restrictive.

Evidence

In *Mölnlycke v Procter & Gamble (No 5)* (1994) the Court of Appeal stated that courts would almost invariably require expert evidence to make their findings. They also distinguished between primary and secondary evidence. Primary evidence is that of expert witnesses giving their opinion as to whether the step would have been obvious to a skilled technician. Any other evidence, such as the commercial success of the invention, is secondary to it.

Making the comparison

There are no formal rules for making the assessment of inventiveness, but the courts have adopted a number of rules of thumb:

(a) Close proximity between the invention and the prior art suggests obviousness. In *Williams v Nye* (1890), a sausage-mincing-and-filling machine was an obvious combination of known techniques. However, a 'cunning juxtaposition of ideas' may not be obvious if a new and surprising result is achieved. This was the case in *Hickman vAndrews* (1983), where the combination of a workbench, saw horse and vice, using a frame from the fishing industry, was sufficiently inventive. This should now be seen as an application of the preliminary step established in *Sabaf v MFI Furniture Centres* (2004).

(b) If the invention is a commercial success, it is likely not to be obvious, the implication being that, if there was such a need for the invention and it was obvious how to satisfy the need, someone would have done it before. This is illustrated by *Hickman v Andrews* (1983) and *Rotocrop v Genbourne* (1982). However, the courts are careful to ensure that it is the invention and not commercial and marketing factors which are responsible for the success. Commercial success may also throw light on the thinking in an industry as a whole, as evidence from expert witnesses might have greater insight than that of the hypothetical technician: *Haberman v Jackel International Ltd* (1999).

(c) If the inventor was seeking a solution to a problem and the resulting invention is no more than an idea that would have been 'worth a try', it is likely to be obvious: *John Manville's Patent* (1967) and *Parks-Cramer Co v Thornton* (1966). What would be worth a try in any given case depends on the circumstances, which may include the expectation of a good result. Each case must be decided on its own facts: *Lilly Icos Ltd v Pfizer Ltd* (2002). However, if the result is unexpectedly successful, there may be an inventive step: *Beecham Group's (Amoxycillin) Application* (1980).

(d) The result of applying an 'obvious to try' test to genetic engineering has had the result of denying patents to the application of known techniques to different types of subject matter with known objectives in mind. Such research is risky, expensive and often laborious but it has been deemed obvious to do so, the decision is merely a commercial one as to taking the risk: *Genentech Inc's Patent* (1989). However, in *Biogen Inc v Medeva plc* (1997) Lord Hoffmann did suggest it could be inventive to do so where a technician would regard it as obvious but an expert would consider it to be so fraught with difficulties as to be not worth trying.

5.3 INDUSTRIAL APPLICATION

An invention must also be 'capable of industrial application'.[19] In the EPC this provision is primarily aimed at defining the types of subject matter that may be patented, complementing the need for the technical effect required to surmount objections to one of the excluded categories. The Biotechnology Directive[20] added the statement that inventions concerning biological matter or process may be patentable.

5.3.1 Industry

Section 4(1) of the PA 1977 provides that an invention shall be taken to be capable of industrial application if 'it can be made or used in any kind of industry, including agriculture'. The EPO Guidelines interpret 'industry' widely, to include anything of a 'technical' character within the useful or practical arts.

5.3.2 Useless inventions

However, the requirement for industrial application may also bar an invention with no identified use. This was done in *Chiron Corpn v Murex Diagnostics* (1996) to revoke claims to a number of polypeptides 'which were useless for any known purpose':

> We accept that the polypeptides claimed in the second part of claim 11 can be made, for, as will become apparent from the section of our judgment dealing with insufficiency, it is a routine task to see whether one polynucleotide will hybridise with another. However, the sections require that the invention can be made or used 'in any kind of industry' so as to be 'capable' or 'susceptible of industrial application'. The connotation is that of trade or manufacture in its widest sense and whether or not for profit. However, industry does not exist in that sense to make or use that which is useless for any known purpose.

> On this point, we prefer the submissions for the appellants. We think that they more accurately reflect the true meaning of ss 1(1)(c) and 4 and the manifest intention of the PA 1977 and the EPC that monopoly rights should be confined to that which has some useful purpose.

Paragraph 6 of Schedule A2 to the PA 1977 makes this requirement explicit where sequences or partial gene sequences are claimed. There can be no patent protection for the information gained from mapping the human genome until useful applications are found.

The lack of success of the biotechnology companies in the courts before the Biotechnology Directive led to arguments that the standards of patentability were too high for a new science. In *Chiron* the Court of Appeal also heard, but rejected,

---

19 Section 1(1)(c) of the PA 1977.
20 Article 3(1), Biotechnology Directive, implemented in paragraph 1 of Schedule A2 of the PA 1977.

arguments that a less onerous test of disclosure should be applied to inventions which were 'akin to principle' or for 'something fundamentally new'.

5.4 DISCLOSURE

Adequate disclosure is a condition of grant.[21] It is also a ground of challenge to a patent's validity and for revocation.[22] This is determined by the adequacy of the disclosure made of the invention in the specification and claims. It does not relate to the invention itself but is nevertheless an important part of granting a monopoly and not a formality of procedure. Because a patent is an important source of technical information, it is a condition of validity and grant that the information is supplied in a form that the relevant technical public can understand and apply.

5.4.1 The specification

A specification must:

> ... disclose the invention in a manner which is clear enough and complete enough for the invention to be performed by a person skilled in the art.[23]

The sufficiency of a specification is a question of fact for the court.

A relatively high standard of clarity is required, as the disclosure must be capable of being understood not only by an expert, or research team, but an ordinary technician.

It is quite possible for developments subsequent to the priority date of a patent specification to enable gaps and errors in a specification to be made good. An important question is, therefore, the date at which a specification must be sufficient. This was also at issue in *Biogen Inc v Medeva plc* (1997). The House of Lords decided that the right date was not the date of publication of the application, but the filing/priority date of the application.

The person skilled in the art

The hypothetical technician is employed at three stages of the patentability of inventions. The state of the art is interpreted through his eyes for novelty (see 5.1.5); the judgment as to inventive step is undertaken through these hypothetical eyes (see 5.2.4); and he is brought into aid for the disclosure in the specification. However, it appears that the hypothetical technician is attributed with differing characteristics in each of these three roles. For the purposes of s 14(3) of the PA 1977, the technician does not have the inventive potential of *Genentech Inc's Patent* (1989), but is an ordinary workshop technician, one of the 'mechanical men of common understanding' (*per* Buller J, in *R v Arkwright* (1785)).

---

21 Section 14 (3), (5) of the PA 1977.
22 *Ibid*, ss 72(1)(c), 74(1).
23 *Ibid*, s 14(3).

Degree of clarity

The specification is not required to spell out every detail if the normal skills of the hypothetical technician would enable these to be inferred. In *No Fume v Pitchford* (1935), Romer LJ explained:

> Specifications very frequently contain mistakes; they also have omissions. However, if a man skilled in the art can easily rectify the mistakes and can readily supply the omissions, the patent will not be held to be invalid. The test to be applied for the purpose of ascertaining whether a man skilled in the art can readily correct the mistakes or readily supply the omissions, has been stated to be this: can he rectify the mistakes and supply the omissions without the exercise of any inventive faculty? If he can, then the description of the specification is sufficient. If he cannot, the patent will be void for insufficiency.

Consequently, a specification for a smokeless ashtray was held to be sufficient though the relative proportions of the elements involved were not specified, because the technician could readily discover these by trial and error.

In *Badische Anilin v Usines de Rhône* (1898), by comparison, the patent was insufficient. There, the specification did not specify that components must be heated in an iron autoclave. In fact, the process did not work in better quality enamel lined autoclaves, because the iron absorbed the hydrochloric acid produced by the process. The omission was unintentional – the patentee had not realised the role of the iron in the process, and had only used iron autoclaves.

As not every detail is required to be laid out in the specification, an applicant or patentee may retain teaching on the best method of achieving the invention. This forces licensees also to seek and pay for know-how licences. The patent, therefore, only alerts the public to the source of the necessary supplementary information.

Enabling the invention to be performed

Criticisms were made, in particular, of claims by biotechnology companies which were felt to be too broad. Broad claims inhibit further development of an invention and confer too much monopoly power. Such claims were made, however, because, in such research the substance is often already known, as is its use and the methods of manufacturing and of using it. Narrower claims would, therefore, be caught by the requirements of novelty and inventive step. However, the research is very costly and the results highly beneficial and, without the incentive of a patent, such research might be deterred, however humanitarian the objectives.

It is clear, albeit *obiter*, from *Biogen Inc v Medeva plc* (1997) that the disclosure made in the specification must be enabling in order to be sufficient. Lord Hoffmann also held that the specification must enable the invention to be performed to the full extent of the monopoly claimed. Broad claims that go beyond what the inventor has demonstrated will not be sustained. He reaffirmed this in *Kirin Amgen Inc v Hoechst Marion Roussel Ltd* (2004).

The invention claimed

The nature of a claim makes a difference to the question whether claims are supported by the description, depending on whether the claims disclose a principle of general application, or discrete products or processes. If the former, the claims may be in general terms, but, if the latter, the patentee must enable the invention to be performed in each case. Lord Hoffmann said:

> Thus, if the patentee has hit upon a new product which has a beneficial effect, but cannot demonstrate that there is a common principle by which that effect will be shared by other products of the same class, he will be entitled to a patent for the product, but not for the class, even though some may subsequently turn out to have the same beneficial effect ... On the other hand, if he has disclosed a beneficial property which is common to the class, he will be entitled to a patent for all products of that class (assuming them to be new), even though he has not himself made more than one or two of them.

This can be illustrated where the claims relate to a range of products such as a biological substance, based on a number of examples having been made. The specification must 'enable' making all the products and the monopoly will not extend to products that have not been shown how to be made. Consequently, as the specification did not disclose methods for making the HBV antigens other than the one used, it was insufficient to sustain claims to every recombinant DNA method for making them. However, if the specification discloses a general principle on which the range of products can be made it will be a sufficient disclosure even though only a number of examples have been made.

In *Kirin Amgen Inc v Hoechst Marion Roussel Ltd* (2004) Lord Hoffmann returned to this aspect of sufficiency, stressing that 'whether the specification is sufficient or not is highly sensitive to the nature of the invention'. Consequently, the first step for the court is to identify the invention and decide what it claims to enable the skilled technician to do. Then the question can be asked whether the specification enables him to perform it. That this is an essential element in determining sufficiency of disclosure may be illustrated by the fate of the Amgen patent. At first instance claim 19 was revoked for insufficiency, but claim 26 upheld. In the Court of Appeal both claims were held to be valid, while the House of Lords revoked claim 19 for insufficiency, and claim 26 for lack of novelty.

Lord Hoffmann, *obiter*, explained a principle of general application to mean no more than an element of a claim stated in general terms. This would be sufficiently disclosed if the invention could reasonably be expected to work with anything falling within the general term.

In the specific case where a micro-organism which is part of claims to a microbiological product or process cannot be described and is not available to the public a sample is required to be deposited in a recognised culture collection[24] at the filing date.[25]

5.4.2   The claims

Claims must 'be clear and concise' and be 'supported' by the description.[26]

---

24   Most are operated under the Budapest Treaty on the International Recognition of the Deposit of Micro-organisms for the Purposes of Patent Procedure 1977.
25   Section 125A of the PA 1977.
26   *Ibid*, s 14(5).

Clear and concise

Under the PA 1949, these provisions were regarded as disciplinary in preserving clear claims, so that clear and accurate decisions could be made on issues of validity. Lord Loreburn objected to attempts to 'puzzle a student and frighten men of business into taking out a licence' (*Natural Colour Kinematograph v Bioschemes* (1915)) by using difficult language, although genuine difficulties of description would not be so penalised.

General words can be used. 'Large' used with respect to electric filaments was upheld in British *Thomson-Houston v Corona* (1922), as it was to be read in the light of knowledge about filaments in use and would be clear to the informed worker. In addition, the court will look for a meaning: *Henricksen v Tallon* (1965). The patent related to ball point pens. The claims did not specify what bore of tube should be used for the ink reservoirs, but the claims were upheld as valid. Two interpretations were possible, but the House of Lords said:

> It is a general principle of construction that, where there is a choice between two meanings, one should, if possible, reject that meaning which leads to an absurd result. One must construe this claim with the knowledge that the skilled addressee would know that it would be absurd to claim that any kind of liquid plug could be effective in a jumbo tube.

Too stringent an application of the rule would make it easy for the competitor to 'invent round' the patent.

Imprecision caused by the art itself is not penalised. In *Inhale Therapeutic Systems Inc v Quadrant Healthcare plc* (2002) it was held that all those versed in the art knew what a glass transition temperature was. The fact that it was an imprecise figure and difficult to measure did not detract from the fact that it was a well-understood and defining characteristic of glass. Therefore, imprecision in the claim was not the patentee's fault but a reflection of the technology concerned.

Supported by the description

Claims are not 'supported' by the specification if the description therein does not enable making the invention claimed. Applicants must take care not to claim more than their actual activities have established to be possible. This has become the crux of challenges to sufficiency since *Biogen Inc v Medeva plc* (1997).

If the invention includes an advantage claimed for a selected class of products to secure a certain result the patent will be insufficient if the specification does not also describe that advantage; and all the compounds monopolised must have the advantage: *Pharmacia Corp v Merck & Co* (2001).

Enforcement

In *Genentech Inc's Patent* (1989), the Court of Appeal uncovered an apparent gap in the PA 1977. The condition as to sufficiency of disclosure in a specification laid down by s 14(3) of the PA 1977 is mirrored in the provisions for revocation of a patent in s 72(1)(c) of the PA 1977. However, there is no apparent reflection of s 14(5) of the PA 1977, with respect to the claims, in s 72(1) of the PA 1977. The real objection to Genentech's claims was their width, because they were unsupported by the description in the specification, but this apparent legislative lapse prevented revocation on this ground, unlike the PA 1949. This appeared to have the result, as the Court of Appeal acknowledged, that, once a patent with invalid claims had been granted, there was no possibility of revocation.

The House of Lords faced the *Genentech* conundrum again in *Biogen Inc v Medeva plc* (1997) and provided a solution. Their lordships held that a specification could not be sufficient if it did not provide an enabling disclosure of the invention (see 3.4.3) and that a specification could not be enabling if the claims were not supported by the description in the specification. The House of Lords had interpreted the need for 'support' in s 5(2)(a) of the PA 1977 as requiring an enabling disclosure. Therefore, claims which did not satisfy s 14(5) of the PA 1977 rendered the specification non-enabling and insufficient, revocable under s 72(1)(c) of the PA 1977.

In *Kirin-Amgen Inc v Transkaryotic Therapies Inc* (2002) claim 19 was challenged as being unclear, and the Court of Appeal applied this approach. Clarity, conciseness and support in the claims were, they said, matters for the Patent Office and not grounds of revocation. When considering an attack on disclosure the test was restricted to whether the specification enabled the width of the claims. Lack of clarity and support were not likely to be relevant to that test. However, they also pointed out that claims that were not clear could not be infringed.

Further Reading

Armitage, E and Ellis, G, 'Chemical Patents in Europe' [1990] EIPR 119

Cole, P, 'Inventive Step: Meaning of the EPO Problem and Solution Approach and Implications for the United Kingdom' [1998] EIPR 214

Doble, R, 'Novelty under the EPC and the Patents Act' [1996] EIPR 511

Jeffs, J, 'Selection Patents' [1988] EIPR 291

Karet, I, 'A Question of Epistemology' [1996] EIPR 97

Karet, I, 'Over-broad Patent Claims: an Inventive Step by the EPO' [1996] EIPR 561

Llewellyn, M, 'Article 53 Revisited' [1995] EIPR 506

Lim, HG, 'Made Available to the Public - the Final Saga?', [1996] JBL 286

McInerney, A, 'Biotechnology: *Biogen v Medeva* in the House of Lords' [1998] EIPR 14

Paterson, G, 'The Patentability of Further Uses of a Known Product under the European Patent Convention' [1991] EIPR 16

Reid, B, 'Du Pont and ICI – Chemical Anticipation and Prior Patent Specifications' [1982] EIPR 118

Roberts, T, 'Broad Claims for Biotechnological Inventions' [1994] EIPR 371

Sheraton, H and Sharples, A, 'The Court of Appeal Puts *Biogen* Insufficiency Back where it Belongs' [2002] EIPR 596

White, A, 'The Novelty–Destroying Disclosure: Some Recent Decisions' [1990] EIPR 315

CHAPTER 6

INFRINGEMENT, VALIDITY AND REVOCATION

Once a patent has been granted, a patentee owns a piece of property. This can both be exploited, and protected from trespass by the unauthorised. This trespass is termed 'infringement'. For infringement to be determined, the boundaries of the patentee's property must be marked out. This is done both by the claims, which define the invention, and by the infringing acts which are defined in s 60 of the Patents Act (PA) 1977.

Consequently, when allegations of infringement arise, there are two issues which must be resolved:

(a) whether alleged infringer's activities fall within the boundaries of the patentee's claim or claims. This is a matter of construing the claims and specification to determine their extent;

(b) whether the acts committed by the infringer fall within the prohibited territory defined in s 60 of the PA 1977.

If infringement is established it remains to see whether the defendant may rely on one of the common law or statutory defences.

Finally, a patent may have its validity challenged during infringement proceedings, or be revoked.

6.1   CONSTRUCTION OF CLAIMS

Construing a patent is a matter of interpreting the specification, and particularly the claims within it. The claims act as a map of the patentee's territory.[1] It is, therefore, largely a linguistically drawn map and must be interpreted accordingly. The claims form a part of the specification, which also includes a description, and may include drawings.[2] These may also be used in the process of interpretation, as s 125(1) provides. The claims and specification are construed in the same way for questions of anticipation, and infringement.

The process of interpretation is usually necessary because the scope of an invention is rarely crystal clear from the specification, nor is the defendant's version often a carbon copy of the patentee's invention. However, interpreting, or construing, the claims is one of the most difficult issues in patent law. The process has recently been complicated by the existence of different traditions for performing this function in the Member States to the EPC, despite the necessity for interpreting the PA 1977 in conformity with the EPC.[3] Amendment of the Protocol to Article 69 of the EPC will also introduce a doctrine of 'equivalents' into UK law.

---

1   Section 125(1) of the PA 1977.
2   *Ibid*, s 14(2)(b).
3   *Ibid*, s 130(7).

6.1.1 'Flagpost' claiming

The traditional approach to construction by UK courts was to treat the claims as a flagpost to the invention. Only what was claimed could be protected. The House of Lords set out the importance of the claims' role in the specification to the process of interpretation in *Electrical and Musical Industries Ltd v Lissen* (1939). Reading the claims as they would be by a technician skilled in the art, Lord Russell said:

> The Court of Appeal have stated that in their opinion no special rules are applicable to the construction of a specification, that it must be read as a whole and in the light of surrounding circumstances; that it may be gathered from the specification that particular words bear an unusual meaning; and that, if possible, a specification should be construed so as not to lead to a foolish result, or one which the patentee could not have contemplated. They further point out that the claims have a particular function to discharge. With every word of this I agree; but I desire to add something further in regard to the claim in a specification.

The function of the claims is to define clearly and with precision the monopoly claimed, so that others may know the exact boundaries of the area within which they will be trespassers. The primary object is to limit and not to extend the monopoly. What is not claimed is disclaimed. The claims must undoubtedly be read as part of the entire document, and not as a separate document; but the forbidden field must be found in the language of the claims and not elsewhere.[4]

> A claim is a portion of the specification which fulfils a separate and distinct function. It, and it alone, defines the monopoly; and the patentee is under a statutory obligation to state in the claims clearly and distinctly what is the invention he desires to protect ... If the patentee has done this in a claim the language of which is plain and unambiguous, it is not open to your Lordships to restrict or expand or qualify its scope by reference to the body of the specification.

6.1.2 Non-literal infringement and the 'pith and marrow' doctrine

Lord Russell's final *dictum* appeared to suggest that claims should be interpreted literally. However, the UK courts have always made some allowances for 'non-literal' infringements. The claims would be read according to *Electrical and Musical Industries Ltd v Lissen* (1939), and the 'essential integers' of the invention identified. Then, the so called 'pith and marrow' doctrine was applied. The defendant's infringement would fall within the claims even if it contained additional elements, or a best selection from the claims, but would not do so if an 'essential integer' of the patentee's claims had been left out (*Clark v Adie* (1877)). This prevented 'colourable evasions' of a patent escaping infringement. It was not a different method of interpretation for giving a sympathetic construction of unclear claims, but an application of the approach subsequently explained in *Electrical and Musical Industries Ltd v Lissen* (1939).

Whether an element in the claims constituted an essential integer was determined by the express wording of the claims as understood through the eyes of a skilled technician. It was not the function that that element performed within the invention that rendered an integer essential or inessential. The results could sometimes be harsh.

---

4   The same applies today, governed by s 125(1) of the PA 1977.

This is illustrated by the House of Lords' decision in *Van der Lely v Bamfords* (1963). The patentee claimed a mechanised hayrake. One feature of the hayrake (found to have been anticipated) was that it could also be turned to use as a swathe turner. This was done by moving some of the wheels, arranged in a line longitudinally behind the machine, laterally to lie side by side with the remaining wheels. The claims stated that the 'hindmost' wheels be moved forwards. The defendant's hayrake served the same dual function, but the foremost wheels were moved backwards. The House of Lords held that it did not infringe. The patentee had rendered the movement of the hindmost wheels essential by the wording adopted in the claims.

The House of Lords reached a similar decision was reached in *Rodi and Weinberger v Showell* (1969). The patent related to an expanding watch strap. Each link was connected to its neighbours by 'U-shaped connecting bows'. The top and bottom of each link was joined to its neighbour by a separate connector. The defendant's straps replaced the U-shaped bows lying along the top and bottom of the strap with C-shaped connectors which joined the links at top and bottom by running inside the link. This made no difference to the way the strap worked. The majority of the Lords (Lords Upjohn, Morris and Hodson) held that U-shaped connectors were an essential integer of the invention. However, Lords Reid and Pearce dissented.

The difference represented a difference of policy. The majority emphasised the patentee's statutory duty to be clear, the minority were concerned that too strict an approach deprived the patent of any practical effect. It was these decisions, and a similar one in *Henricksen v Tallon* (1965), in the 1960s which alarmed the Europeans as to the British approach to construing claims. In fact, they were all decisions relating to simple mechanical inventions.

In more complex areas, the House of Lords proved more accommodating. In *Beecham v Bristol Laboratories* (1978), the defendant imported a semi-synthetic penicillin called 'hetacillin'. The plaintiff held four patents to a new class of these semi-synthetic penicillins and methods for their manufacture. One was known as 'ampicillin', a valuable antibiotic. Hetacillin was merely a masked version of ampicillin and converted itself into Ampicillin when placed in water. Importing hetacillin was held to infringe the patent. The House of Lords was not prepared to confine the pith and marrow doctrine to mechanical inventions, or to inventions comprising a new combination of elements, and so applied it to a new product. Lord Diplock said that: 'The substitution for the postulated amino group of the variant incorporated in hetacillin is evanescent and reversible and, for all practical purposes of use, can be regarded as the equivalent of the amino group in ampicillin.' This appears to be taking a much more functional approach to the variant adopted by the defendant. They had argued that the claims expressly claimed the presence in ampicillin of an amino group in the alpha position, a feature absent in hetacillin.

The American approach is to apply a 'doctrine of equivalents', which protects the patentee beyond a literal interpretation of the claims to include equivalent features which serve the same purpose or function. The Germans applied a doctrine of obvious equivalents, allowing a competitor only to adopt non-obvious equivalent integers from the claims. In both cases, patent protection extends to functional equivalents, whereas the pith and marrow doctrine concentrated on equivalents to the claimed integers as a matter of the terminology used.

6.1.3   Purposive construction

The question was raised again before the House of Lords in *Catnic Components Ltd v Hill and Smith* (1982). This was a decision relating to a patent granted under the PA 1949. The plaintiff had been granted a patent for galvanised steel lintels for doors and windows, to be used in cavity walls. The lintel was a breakthrough in the industry and a huge commercial success. The claims read:

> A lintel for use over apertures in cavity walls having an inner and outer skin comprising a first horizontal plate or part adapted to support a course or a plurality of superimposed units forming part of the inner skin and a second horizontal plate or part substantially parallel to the first and spaced therefrom in a downward vertical direction and adapted to span the cavity in the cavity wall and be supported at least at each end thereof upon courses forming parts of the outer and inner skins respectively of the cavity wall adjacent an aperture, and a first rigid inclined support member extending downwardly and forwardly from or near the front edge adjacent the cavity of the first horizontal plate or part and joining with the second plate or part at an intermediate position which lies between the front and rear edge of the second plate or part and adapted to extend across the cavity, and a *second rigid support member extending vertically from or from near the rear edge of the first horizontal plate or part to join with the second plate or part adjacent its rear edge.* [Emphasis added]

The defendant introduced a variation into his lintel so that the second support member was inclined at six degrees to the vertical for a lintel three bricks high, and eight degrees from the vertical for a lintel two bricks high. Lord Diplock adopted a 'purposive construction', rather than a purely literal one; the question to be asked was, he said:

> ... whether persons with practical knowledge and experience of the kind of work in which the invention was intended to be used would understand that strict compliance with a particular descriptive word or phrase appearing in a claim was intended by the patentee to be an essential requirement of the invention, so that any variant would fall outside the monopoly claimed, even though it would have no material effect upon the way the invention worked.

The word 'vertical' to a builder would not imply a literal interpretation, in order to achieve the strength intended, and the defendant's lintels were infringing.

It is important to understand what 'purposive' means in the 'Diplock Question'. Purposive construction of a statute allows a court to interpret a word in it in the light of the function it was intended to serve. This could be applied to mean that the court must determine whether the function of the integer claimed was being achieved by the defendant, as did the minority in *Rodi and Weinberger v Showell* (1969). There are hints of this in Lord Diplock's speech, as he interprets 'vertical' within the context of a specification for a box girder to 'enable it in actual use to perform satisfactorily all the functions it could perform as if it were precisely vertical'. Lord Diplock also provides a second explanation: '... putting the same thing in another way, it would be obvious to him that the patentee did not intend to make exact verticality ... an essential feature of the invention claimed.' This is to apply a *linguistic* purposiveness – looking at the word or phrase in the light of the understanding of the technician skilled in the art, and concentrating on the essentiality of the language chosen by the patentee to achieving the function of that integer as part of the invention. Linguistic essentiality is the foundation of the majority decisions in *Van der Lely v Bamfords* (1963) and *Rodi and Weinberger v Showell* (1969).

6.1.4   Article 69 of the EPC and the Protocol

In Europe, the 'flagpost' approach was not adopted; instead, the claims were treated as a 'signpost' to an invention's boundaries. It was left to courts to decide where those boundaries lay, and whether a 'non-literal' infringement lay within them. The British approach had the advantage of certainty for competitors, who could read and interpret specifications with some confidence as to the territory being marked out. It had the disadvantage for the patentee that language in the claims which was too limiting made inventing round the invention all too easy, particularly as technology advanced and alternatives become apparent. The European approach was seen as providing fair protection for patentees, who may not have foreseen simple equivalents which could be substituted for integers within the claims. However, it also left competitors with fine judgments to make in order to avoid infringement, and at risk of serious consequences if they guessed incorrectly. An attempt to reconcile these differences of approach was made by the Protocol to Article 69 of the EPC.

Following the formulation of the Diplock Question, the governing provisions became s 125 of the PA 1977, taken from Article 69 of the EPC and the Protocol to Article 69. The Protocol represented an attempt by Europe to reconcile what was seen as the strict British approach with the signpost approach of other Member States. It states:

> Article 69 should not be interpreted in the sense that the extent of protection conferred by a European patent is to be understood as that defined by the strict, literal meaning of the wording used in the claims, the description and drawings being employed only for the purpose of resolving an ambiguity found in the claims. Neither should it be interpreted in the sense that the claims serve only as a guideline and that the actual protection conferred may extend to what, from a consideration of the description and drawings by a person skilled in the art, the patentee has contemplated. On the contrary, it is to be interpreted as defining a position between these extremes which combines a fair protection for the patentee with a reasonable degree of certainty for third parties.

As a statement of objectives, it is admirable, but in terms of guidance to courts as to a method for interpreting claims as they appear in patent specifications, it leaves much to be desired. It is from this base that construction of claims under the PA 1977 must begin.

6.1.5   The *Improver* questions

Hoffmann J (as he then was) reformulated the Diplock Question in *Improver Corp v Remington Consumer Products Ltd* (1989). The plaintiff had been granted a European patent for a depilatory (hair removing) device, marketed as the 'Epilady'. It consisted of an electric motor contained in a hand held housing, to which was attached a helical steel spring in a looped shape. It was a substantial commercial success. The defendant produced the 'Smooth and Silky', replacing the helical spring with a looped cylindrical rod of elastomerised synthetic rubber. The rubber rod was functionally equivalent to the helical spring. The plaintiff claimed a 'helical spring'. The plaintiff's specification also contained an 'equivalents clause', by which the draftsman hoped to claim any equivalent to the spring that could be used.

Hoffmann J considered himself bound by earlier Court of Appeal authority to apply a purposive construction of the plaintiff's claims. He held that the patent had not been infringed by the use of a rubber rod. Although the rubber rod was a functional equivalent to the helical spring, the word 'spring' had been expressly claimed and no wide generic construction could be given to this word to include 'slitty bendy rubber rod'. He also held that the equivalents clause could not mean any more than that the language of the claims would be interpreted in accordance with s 125 of the PA 1977 and the Protocol to Art 69 of the EPC. He distinguished *Catnic Components Ltd v Hill and Smith* (1982), where the word 'vertical' was capable of bearing a meaning to include slightly off the vertical within a building trade context. This was not, however, true of 'spring' and 'rubber rod', no matter what the context.

In the course of his judgment, Hoffmann J recast the Diplock Question as a series of three questions; these have subsequently met the approval of patent practitioners, because they give a structured and methodical approach to claim construction, resulting in predictable and accurate decisions. The three questions are:

(1) Does the variant have a material effect upon the way the invention works? If yes, the variant is outside the claim. If no –

(2) Would this (that is, that the variant had no material effect) have been obvious at the date of publication of the patent to a reader skilled in the art? If no, the variant is outside the claim. If yes –

(3) Would the reader skilled in the art nevertheless have understood from the language of the claim that the patentee intended that strict compliance with the primary meaning was an essential requirement of the invention? If yes, the variant is outside the claim.

The first two questions are questions of fact that enable the third to be asked. The first is uncontroversial, as is the requirement that the claims be read through the eyes of a worker in the field, and not just given their strict scientific meaning. Clearly, any non-functional equivalent and a non-obvious functional variant fall outside the claims because they represent an inventive advance on the claims.

However, if the variant is functionally equivalent and obvious, then the third, linguistic, question needed to be asked: whether the variant fell within the language used by the patentee in the claims. This put a heavy burden of precision and foresight on the patentee to choose clear, but accommodating, language. The third question appears to limit the patent's protection to variants foreseen by the patentee alone. It has been argued that this denies fair protection to patentees.[5]

6.1.6 The Protocol question

The *Improver Corp v Remington Consumer Products Ltd* (1989) case gave rise to concern because the patent was held to have been infringed in Germany and Holland, where there was not the same heavy reliance on the patentee's actual wording in the claims. However, after a brief flirtation with a German approach to construction by the Court of Appeal in *PLG Research Ltd v Ardon International* (1995), the courts have continued to apply the *Improver* questions.[6]

---

5 Turner, J, 'Purposive Construction' [2001] EIPR 118.

6 Neither Aldous J (as he then was) nor Jacob J followed *PLG Research Ltd v Ardon International* (1995) in *Assidoman Multipack Ltd v The Mead Corp* (1995) and *Beloit Technologies Inc v Valmet Paper Machinery* (1995). It was reconsidered by the Court of Appeal in *Kastner v Rizla* (1995), in a decision given by Aldous LJ.

In *Kastner v Rizla* (1995) the patent related to a process for cutting and stacking cigarette papers. The claim related to the separate steps involved in the process. The defendant's process was substantially similar, but had two differences. The knife used for cutting the interleaved paper was a crescent shaped rotary blade, as opposed to the plaintiff's knife, which moved towards and away from the moving strips of paper. In addition, the respective 'pushers' (which moved the separated stacks of papers after cutting by the knives) moved in different ways to match the knives along with which they operated. Aldous LJ applied the three Hoffmann questions.

However, the decision was controversial on a different ground. The issue was not one of the meaning of a word or phrase, as it had been in *Catnic Components Ltd v Hill and Smith* (1982) and *Improver Corp v Remington Consumer Products Ltd* (1989), but of the separate mechanical components of a process. Additionally, Aldous LJ differed from the trial judge by taking a very general view of the nature of the invention before asking whether the equivalent features adopted by the defendant's process fell within the plaintiff's claims. However, the plaintiff had claimed very specific means of achieving each stage of the process. The decision came close to extending patent protection to any functional equivalent, and was been criticised[7] for doing so.

It is the third *Improver* question which is controversial. In *Wheatley v Drillsafe Ltd* (2001) both Aldous and Mance LJ regarded the *Improver* questions as representing a Protocol approach, and providing the court with a useful aid to construction.[8] However, they differed in their application of the third question to the facts of the case. Aldous LJ stated that it was reasonable to infer that patentees intended to include all immaterial variants in their claims, unless it was clear that they were not intended to be covered either because of the words chosen, or because they would have materially affected the invention's working. This can be regarded as a shift from strict to liberal construction of claims.[9]

However, the courts did not find it easy to apply the *Improver* questions in all cases, in particular in relation to chemical and biochemical inventions.[10] In *Pharmacia Corp v Merck & Co Inc* (2001) Aldous LJ preferred to seek the Protocol's middle way by asking what the effect on the patentee and the public would be of reading the claims to cover the defendant's variant. The Court of Appeal also followed this approach in *Kirin-Amgen Inc v Transkaryotic Therapies Inc* (2002), by checking the conclusions reached from applying the Protocol questions. In *Wheatley v Drillsafe* Mance LJ would have been content to apply a 'unitary' approach to construction.

It was thought that the 'Protocol questions' might give way to a direct application of the Protocol's balance of fairness to patentees with reasonable certainty for third parties. Thomson and Kempton suggested that such a 'holistic' (or 'unitary') approach may lead to courts increasingly looking for the true 'contribution to the art' made by an invention and deserving of monopoly protection.

---

7   Oliver, P, '*Kastner v Rizla*: Too Far, Too Fast' [1996] EIPR 28.
8   And followed by the Outer House, Court of Session in *ITP SA v Coflexip Stena Offshore Ltd* 2003.
9   Turner, J, 'Purposive Construction' [2001] EIPR 118.
10 Thomson, G, and Kempton, L, 'Construction Issues in Pharmaceutical and Biotech Cases' [2002] EIPR 591.

In *Amersham Pharmacia Biotech v Amicon Ltd* (2001) Aldous LJ stated that he did not think that the (unamended) Protocol introduced a doctrine of infringement by equivalent effect.

Other Member States of the EPC approach non-literal infringement with a variety of tests. One commentator gave approval to the *Improver* questions in this diversity of approach, provided that further tests are established.[11] These are, first, to define how to establish whether a variant has a material effect on the invention's working, secondly how to evaluate whether this would have been obvious and, thirdly, how to evaluate the patentee's intention.

6.1.7   *Kirin Amgen v Hoechst Marion Roussel*

Subsequently detailed new guidance has come from the House of Lords in *Kirin-Amgen Inc v Hoechst Marion Roussel Ltd* (2004). Lord Hoffmann clearly traces the history of UK law on construction of claims, though he himself notes that as a result 'patent lawyers may feel cast adrift on a sea of interpretative uncertainty'. The patent related to the hormone EPO, artificially made by the patentee. The defendants imported the same substance, made by a different process. The question for the court rested on whether the differently made EPO fell within the patent's claims. In the leading judgment, Lord Hoffmann reaffirmed the primacy of Article 69 and the Protocol in any question of construction, relegating the *Catnic* and *Improver* questions to secondary importance as occasional guidelines:

(1) The Protocol

Article 69 adopts the former UK principle: the claims determine the extent of monopoly a patent gives. In its first sentence the Protocol rejects what were understood to be the UK rules of construction. The second sentence prevents going beyond the claims to ascertain from the specification as a whole what the patentee intended. The third sentence does not, however, provide a principle of construction for claims, but a principle for construing Article 69.

(2) Rules of Construction

It is purposive construction of the claims which is required – the meaning that the notional addressee of the patent specification would reasonably understand the author to have intended to convey:

> Purposive construction does not mean that one is extending or going beyond the definition of the technical matter for which the patentee seeks protection in the claims. The question is always what the person skilled in the art would have understood the patentee to be using the language of the claim to mean.

Lord Hoffmann noted the care with which the language in a specification would be chosen with skilled advice from a patent agent. However, he pointed out that it also must be recognised that patentees are necessarily describing something new and for which there may be no generally accepted definition. In some cases it might be obvious to the addressee that the patentee may have departed from conventional use of language or have included an element not intended to be essential. However, he said, 'one would not expect that to happen very often'.

---

11   Franzosi, M, 'Equivalence in Europe' [2003] EIPR 237.

Furthermore, the skilled addressee does not have access to the patent office file[12] and it may be that some otherwise inexplicable restriction within the claims may relate to the need to avoid prior art, or arguments over enablement with the examiner.

(3) *Catnic* and the Protocol

The House approved Aldous J's explanation of the accord between *Catnic* and the Protocol, which, in its third sentence, provides the object at which construction aims, but not a principle to be applied:

> How is this to be achieved? The claims must be construed in a way which attempts, so far as is possible in an imperfect world, not to disappoint the reasonable expectations of either side. What principle of interpretation would give fair protection to the patentee? Surely, a principle which would give him the full extent of the monopoly which the person skilled in the art would think he was intending to claim. In addition, what principle would provide a reasonable degree of protection for third parties? Surely again, a principle which would not give the patentee more than the full extent of the monopoly which the person skilled in the art would think he was intending to claim. Indeed, any other principle would also be unfair to the patentee, because it would unreasonably expose the patent to claims of invalidity on grounds of anticipation or insufficiency.

(4) Equivalents as a guide to construction

Both the *Catnic* and *Improver* questions[13] were designed to deal with a defendant's use of an equivalent to an element claimed by a patentee. As Lord Hoffmann emphasised, the amendment to the Protocol by EPC 2000[14] (see 6.1.8) requires consideration of equivalence to be taken into account, although it cannot extend protection beyond the claims. However he also emphasised the need to distinguish between the principle of purposive construction ('the bedrock of patent construction'), and the guidelines the questions provide for giving effect to the principle. These may prove of limited application, particularly in cases involving 'high' technology, rather than figures, measurements or a word or phrase. On the facts of the case the second *Improver* question was of limited use when the equivalent process used by the defendants was unknown at the time of the patent claims. The question whether it would have been obvious to the skilled technician that it would work in the same way as the invention was impossible to answer.

6.1.8   Amended Protocol to Article 69 EPC

The Protocol to Article 69 was amended by the EPC Diplomatic Conference of 2000 to include a doctrine of equivalents. The limits of the claims will no longer be determined solely by their linguistic effect, and equivalents with a similar functional effect will fall within infringement. The new article added to the Protocol states:

---

12   The courts in the UK, the Netherlands and Germany actively discourage litigants from use of the Patent Office file in aid of construction: para 35.

13   Or, as dubbed in *Wheatley v Drillsafe*, the 'Protocol' Questions.

14   Not yet in force.

Article 2: Equivalents

For the purpose of determining the extent of protection conferred by a European patent, due account shall be taken of any element which is equivalent to an element specified in the claims.

As s 125(3) of the PA 1977 requires the Protocol 'for the time being in force' to be applied by UK courts no change is necessary to the PA 1977 to give effect to the change. However, the new doctrine must be applied once it comes into effect.[15]

It is not yet clear how it will be applied, although it appears to take a more patentee-friendly approach to non-literal infringements. The change originally proposed stated explicitly that functional equivalents were intended to be covered[16]. The German approach has been to extend a patent's monopoly to non-obvious functional equivalents, tantamount to asking only the first two *Improver* questions.

However, the version adopted only requires that 'account be taken' of equivalent elements. Lord Hoffmann's approach in *Kirin-Amgen Inc v Hoechst Marion Roussel Ltd* (2004) suggests that equivalents will form part of the background to the facts known to the addressee of the claims and affect what he would understand from their language. However, equivalence cannot, he said, 'extend protection outside the claims'.

Not a doctrine of equivalents

A further proposed addition to cater for so-called 'file wrapper estoppel' was not adopted. This, as well as the doctrine of equivalents, has been the cause of a great deal of litigation in the US. The US doctrine of equivalents allows a product or process to infringe a patent if it performs substantially the same function in substantially the same way to obtain substantially the same result as the invention. This broad protection allowed patentees to license their invention and curb competition. In 2000 the US Court of Appeals for the Federal Circuit[17] (CAFC) imposed limits on the doctrine in *Festo Corp v SMC Corp* (2000). They did so to protect the proper functioning of the patent system by taking the history of the patent's application process into account – file wrapper (or prosecution history) estoppel. A patentee could not use the doctrine of equivalents to allege infringement for an equivalent discarded in the process of amendment during their application. The Supreme Court overturned this 'absolute' bar to equivalents in 2001, but did restrict the doctrine so that a patentee could only rely on it in one of three circumstances (the 'flexible' bar).

When the case was remitted to the CAFC it held in 2003 that only one of these three circumstances should apply. Consequently, just as the EPC moves tentatively towards a doctrine of equivalent effect, that applied in the US has been restricted by a doctrine of prosecution history estoppel in the interests of certainty for third parties. Holders of a US patent may rely on the doctrine of equivalents where the claims were amended during grant only if they can show that the variant was unforeseeable at the

---

15 It comes into force two years after ratification by at least 15 Member States. This was not expected to be before 2005.

16 It said: '[a] means shall generally be considered as being equivalent if it is obvious to a person skilled in the art that using such means achieves substantially the same result as that achieved through the means specified in the claim.'

17 The specialist patent court in the US.

time of amendment. A similar restriction for variants intentionally excluded from the application is applied to the Japanese doctrine of equivalents.[18]

Any doctrine of equivalents in the UK was rejected in *Kirin-Amgen Inc v Hoechst Marion Roussel Ltd* (2004).

6.1.9   Summary

Construing patent claims remains a difficult task in practice. However, it is clear that:

- claims must not be given a strict and literal interpretation, nor merely be regarded as a guideline to the scope of monopoly;[19]

- they must be given a purposive construction as read objectively through the eyes of a person skilled in the art having regard to the whole specification;

- an integer cannot be struck from the claims merely because it does not make any difference to the inventive concept as the patentee may have inserted it for a reason;[20]

- if the patentee would be understood to have intended a literal interpretation claims will be given their literal meaning;

- it is open to patentees to provide definitions in the specification and these will be taken into account;[21]

- if variants were intended, the *Improver* questions may be applied to determine the extent of variant covered;

- where the *Improver* questions are inapt a unitary Protocol question will be applied;

- in the future variants of an equivalent effect will also fall within the skilled technician's understanding of the patentee's intention.

6.2   INFRINGING ACTS

Once it has been determined that a defendant's product or process falls within a patentee's claims, it remains to establish whether the defendant's activities with that product or process are activities which will infringe the patent.

The proprietor of the patent (or an exclusive licensee) may bring civil proceedings where infringement is alleged, seeking an injunction (interdict), an order for delivery up, damages, an account of profits or a declaration that the patent is valid and has been infringed.[22] Damages and account of profits may not be awarded in respect of the

---

18 Kim, L, 'A Comparative Analysis of the Japanese Supreme Court Decision on Doctrine of Equivalents' [2002] IPQ 18.

19 And this remains the case even where they are unambiguous: *American Home Products v Novartis* (2001) and *Pharmacia Corp v Merck & Co Inc* (2001); although at first instance in *Pharmacia* Pumfrey J concluded that an uambiguous term must be given its literal meaning. The same was applied to a numerical range at first instance in *Auchincloss v Agricultural and Veterinary Supplies* (1997).

20 Hoffmann LJ in *Société Technique de Pulversatur STEP v Emson Europe Ltd* (1993), affirmed by Aldous LJ in *Amersham Pharmacia Biotech v Amicon Ltd* (2001).

21 *Kirin-Amgen Inc v Transkaryotic Therapies Inc* (2002).

22 Section 61(1) of the PA 1977.

same infringement.[23] Proceedings may be brought in the Patents Court, the Court of Session,[24] the Patents County Court or before the Comptroller of Patents. The Patents Act 2004 makes provision for non-binding assessments of infringement to be given by the Patent Office, on the lines of re-examination for validity after grant (see 6.5).

Patent infringement is a statutory tort (delict). Consequently a patentee may also proceed against those who do not fall within the statutory acts, but may be regarded as joint tortfeasors. There is also tortious liability for conspiracy or for inducement to wrongdoing.

A patentee suspecting infringement must remember the remedy against groundless threats provided by s 70 of the PA 1977 before issuing warnings to the potential infringers (see 19.10).

Intellectual property infringements can be divided into acts of primary, secondary and contributory infringement. In the PA 1977, primary and secondary acts of infringement are treated together. Primary infringement relates to direct infringement by making or using the patented invention. Secondary infringement relates to commercial dealings with infringing products or processes, which may have been made by another. Contributory infringement relates to the supplying of the means to another in order to enable that other to infringe.

6.2.1 Primary and secondary infringement

The infringing acts are set out in s 60 of the PA 1977. This is derived from the Community Patent Convention, which may be used as an aid to interpretation: *Menashe Business Mercantile Ltd v William Hill* (2002). Interpretation is purposive or teleological and includes other language versions of the Convention, as well as *travaux préparatoires*.

Infringement must take place while the patent is in force, in the UK, and without the patentee's consent. The infringing acts according to the type of claims in the patent. An act will infringe:

(a) where the invention is a product: to make, dispose of, offer to dispose of, use, import or to keep the product, whether for disposal or otherwise. This includes doing the appropriate in relation to a kit of parts which together make up the patented product;[25]

(b) where the invention is a process: to use the process or offer it for use in the UK, where the infringer knows, or it would be obvious to a reasonable person in the circumstances, that its use there without the consent of the proprietor would be an infringement of the patent;

(c) where the invention is a process: to dispose of, offer to dispose of, use or import any product obtained directly by means of that process, or to keep any such product, whether for disposal or otherwise.

---

23 *Ibid*, s 61(2).
24 *Ibid*, s 98.
25 *Rotocrop v Genbourne* (1982).

It is important to note the differences of each sub-section of s 60(1) of the PA 1977. There is no requirement of knowledge where a product patent is at stake, or a product has been directly obtained through use of a patented process; liability is absolute. However, knowledge is required if the invention is a process. Where a process patent is at issue, both the infringing offer, and the subsequent use made by the purchaser, must be in the UK. Section 100 of the PA 1977 provides a presumption that, where a patented invention is a process for obtaining a new product, production of that product by another without authority shall be taken to be by means of the process.

Section 60(1) of the PA 1977 includes all the usual commercial activities of the infringer, but has presented some difficulties of interpretation.

'Keeps'

In *Smith Kline and French v Harbottle* (1980), the word 'keeps' was in issue because the equivalent provision in the CPC uses the word 'stocks'. The plaintiff held a patent in the UK for a drug. The defendant ordered the drug from Italy, to be imported into the UK, intending to re-export it. British Airways carried the offending drug to the UK and stored it in their bonded warehouse at Heathrow Airport. The plaintiff alleged that British Airways was keeping the drug in the UK. The plaintiff argued that the choice of a different word in the PA 1977 implied that a wider infringement had been intended. Oliver J held that the otherwise close similarity of the PA 1977 to the CPC provisions indicated that the draftsman had 'keeping in stock' in mind, and applied s 130(7) of the PA 1977, requiring harmony of interpretation between the EPC, CPC and PA 1977. In addition, the dictionary definition of 'keep' included 'stock'.

'Dispose'

The PA 1949 used the term 'sale', which raised the question of the meaning of 'dispose' and 'disposal' in the PA 1977. Disposal will include a transfer of physical possession in the course of trade, but doubts arise as to whether this would extend to a gift, lease or exchange. It was held, *obiter*, that 'dispose' included sale and lease in *Kalman v PCL Packaging* (1982), but that delivery in the UK when property and possession had already passed did not infringe. The infringing act must take place in the UK, so that if a chain of disposal (offer, acceptance, shipment, delivery, for example) begins abroad, it is only those steps which take place within the jurisdiction which will infringe: *Badische Anilin v Johnson* (1897). An order for an infringing dye was made from the UK, and a forwarding agent transported the dye from Switzerland to London. The defendant was held liable because, although sale and delivery took place in Switzerland, the offer was made in the UK.

'Import'

Where an infringing product has been imported, the purposes for which it is resold are of no avail to the importer where the resale is made as a matter of commerce and profit. In *Hoffmann-La Roche v Harris Pharmaceuticals* (1977), an infringing drug, Diazepam, was imported by the defendant, and resold to three purchasers: to one for experimental purposes;[26] to compulsory licensees; and exported direct to a foreign customer. Whitford J held that, though the rights of a mere carrier must be protected, possession 'with the intention of using the articles for trade purposes and for the securing of a profit' amounted to infringement.

In *Sabaf v MFI Furniture Centres* (2004) MF imported gas burners for kitchen hobs into the UK from its Italian manufacturer, Meneghetti. It was the Italian company who arranged the transport for the infringing products to the UK, and Sabaf alleged that it had 'imported' the goods into the UK. The House of Lords were quick, *obiter*, to dismiss this suggestion. Lord Hoffmann acknowledged that the act of arranging the transport (for which MFI paid) 'may or may not have been sufficient to amount to participation in the act of importation so as to make [Meneghetti] jointly liable as a secondary party'. However, no joint liability was advanced, and they could not be regarded as the primary importers.

'Uses'

Use does not include mere possession: *British United Shoe Manufacturers v Collier* (1910). The defendant held a patented sole making machine, but had not used it. This did not infringe.

'Makes'

Making does not include repair; in fact, the owner of a patented product or process has a residual right to repair his property: *United Wire Ltd v Screen Repair Services (Scotland) Ltd* (2001).

In the past the right to repair has been based on an implied licence: *Solar Thomson v Barton* (1977). The plaintiff licensed a patented pulley and repaired the pulleys without infringing the patent. It was held that the implied licence included repair, but did not extend to making a new product. In *United Wire Ltd v Screen Repair Services (Scotland) Ltd* (2001) the House of Lords held that if infringement by making a patent product was alleged neither implied licence nor exhaustion of rights had a part to play. If the purchaser's ability to repair were to be based on an implied licence it might be expressly excluded or subjected to conditions. Rather, repair of a patented product was an act which did not amount to making, a residual right which did not fall within the sphere of patent protection. Repair and making were regarded as concepts which did not overlap. Deciding whether a particular act amounted to making or to repair was a question of fact. It is therefore important that the invention is correctly identified from the claims before the distinction between making and repair can be determined. The patent related to improved screens used in vibratory sifting or filtering machines. The mesh screens had a relatively short life and the defendants provided replacements by renewing the original frames. Lord Hoffmann held that the patented screens were a combination of the frame and screen meshes pre-tensioned by attachment with adhesive as detailed in the patent. To renew the whole therefore might have prolonged the life of the frames, but constituted making of the screens as claimed. The defendants therefore infringed the patent.

---

26   Acts which in themselves would not infringe: s 60(5)(b) of the PA 1977.

However, modifying a product does not constitute repair: *Dellareed v Delkin* (1988). The defendant described its treatment of the patented fishing reels as a 'complete rebuild'. This was held to go beyond merely prolonging the life of the product.

'Directly'

Section 60(1)(c) of the PA 1977 may have restricted the earlier position with respect to products obtained from a patented process, by precluding infringement where the patented process is only employed at an initial or intermediate stage of the production of the product. Previously, if earlier steps in the process of producing a product were sufficiently significant to the process as a whole, infringement might be found. This was known as the 'Saccharin doctrine' after *Saccharin Corp v Anglo-Continental Chemical Works* (1900). Now, the product must be obtained 'directly' by use of the process. The change could be of some significance in a multi-step chemical process if an alternative final step can be found.

The sub-section was tested in *Pioneer Electronics Capital Inc v Warner Music Manufacturing* (1997). The plaintiff held patents relating to steps taken within the process of manufacturing compact discs. The defendant manufactured discs in Germany and sold them in the UK. It was agreed that the defendant had used the patented steps, but it argued that the resulting compact discs had not been obtained directly by means of the processes. There are many steps involved in the manufacture of a compact disc. In this case, a metallic film was evaporated on to the recording layer of a master recording (known as a 'father'). This was then used to make a number of positive impressions of the recording layer ('mothers'), each of which was used to produce a number of negative impressions ('sons'). The sons were then used in a pressing process to mass-produce the compact discs. The step used by the defendant was the one involved in the production of the father.

The Court of Appeal upheld the striking out of the infringement claim by Aldous J. They held that s 60(1)(c) of the PA 1977 had altered the previous law and adopted a 'loss of identity' test for determining whether a product remained a direct product of a process. This stemmed from European law. It was found that 'directly' was derived from the EPC, and in turn from German law, where the equivalent word used was *'unmittelbar'*, and that this meant that German authorities could and should be taken into account. These authorities were consistent in requiring that a product obtained directly from a process was the product with which the process ended. It did not cease to be directly obtained if subjected to further processing, provided that processing did not cause it to lose its identity. Identity was to be determined by the product's 'essential characteristics'. The same 'loss of identity' test could be found in other European jurisdictions and could be taken to represent the European law. The court held that the finished compact disc sold to the consumer was not the direct product of the process. It was not an identical copy of the master, which differed in material, and had been subjected to three further processes. The master was incapable of performing the same function as the compact disc (it could not be played in a compact disc player). Each stage in the full process produced a new product which was necessary to the creation of the final compact disc. The Court of Appeal concluded that the 'loss of identity' test was one of fact and degree, to be determined on the facts of each case; but, on the evidence given, the result was clear in this case and the action could be struck out.

Biological inventions

The Biotechnology Directive provides that a patent for biological material possessing specific characteristics extends to any material obtained from it through propagation or multiplication in an identical or divergent form and possessing those characteristics.[27]

Similar provision is made for patent protection for a product containing genetic information to extend to all material in which the product is incorporated (subject to the exclusion for protection for the human body) and in which the genetic information is contained and performs its function.[28] This would apply to the offspring of the Onco-mouse, for example.

Finally, the same provision is made for process containing biological material with specific characteristics to be produced. Both biological material derived directly from the process, and further material derived from that derivative material, through propagation or multiplication, and in an identical or divergent form possessing the same characteristics falls within the patent protection.[29]

The farmers' exception[30] allows farmers to use seed from crops they have grown from patented material, or to breed animals from patented material, despite the patent. The patented material must have been sold to the farmer for 'agricultural use'. Schedule A1 of the PA 1977 sets out the plant species to which the seeds exception applies.

6.2.2 Contributory infringement

A person supplying, or offering to supply, anyone unauthorised to use an invention with any of the means relating to an essential element of it in the UK in order to put the invention into effect, will infringe a patent, provided it is in force, and the patentee has not consented. However, this will be so only when the person knows, or it would be obvious to a reasonable person in the circumstances, that those means are suitable for putting, or are intended to put, the invention into effect in the UK.[31]

Both the supply, and the putting into effect of the invention by the person supplied must take place in the UK; if the infringement takes place in another jurisdiction, it is in that jurisdiction that proceedings must be brought. This was made clear in *Kalman v PCL Packaging* (1982), where the supply of the filters took place in the US.

The courts have been careful not to allow infringement to be avoided altogether by this provision. In *Menashe Business Mercantile Ltd v William Hill* (2002) the claimants were proprietors of a patent for a computerised gaming system. The system incorporated a host computer connected to users' own terminals, and software for the terminals. The defendants supplied a gaming system to customers in the UK by supplying a program that effectively turned the customers' computers into a terminal in its system. It placed its host computer outside the jurisdiction. At first instance Jacob

---

27 Para 7, Schedule A2, PA 1977.
28 *Ibid*, para 9, Schedule A2.
29 *Ibid*, para 8, Schedule A2.
30 Article 11, Biotechnology Directive; s 60(5)(g), (h), PA 1977; Schedule A1, PA 1977.
31 Section 60(2) of the PA 1977.

J held that the defendants infringed because s 60(2) merely required 'an effect' within the UK. The Court of Appeal upheld the result but disagreed on his reasoning. Merely to require an effect could extend to economic, physical or even emotional effects. Instead, the Court held that s 60(2) required the invention to be used in the UK as a result of the means supplied. However, the fact that the host computer was not in the UK was immaterial as performing the invention required customers to access the host from the UK, and they used the gaming system as though it were in the UK.

Neither the Act, nor the case law, elaborates on the 'reasonable person' for s 60(1)(b) and 60(2) of the PA 1977. The level of knowledge of patent law that should be attributed to the reasonable person, whether that of the ordinary man in the street, or the ordinary commercial man or the ordinary dealer in that product, remains to be clarified by the courts. Questions of interpretation also arise with respect to 'means', 'suitable' and, in particular, 'essential'; does 'means' include know-how? Doubts also arise if only one of the uses (among many) of the thing supplied infringes the patent.

If the thing supplied must relate to an essential element of the invention, a further query is whether it is essentiality to that element's function, or essentiality determined by the language with which that element has been claimed, which is required. The same inquiry must be made in construing the claims (see 5.1.4).

Section 60(3) of the PA 1977 provides that contributory infringement does not apply to staple commercial products, unless the offer is an inducement to infringement.

6.2.3   New use claims

Claims to second medical uses of known substances, or *Mobil Oil* claims have yet to reach the UK courts. The distinctive feature of these claims is that the substance must be used for the appointed purpose if its use is to fall within the technical effect for which the patent was granted. This raises an enquiry into the reasons for a defendant's use of the substance which were not formerly part of patent law. The House of Lords expressed doubts as to this in *Merrell Dow Pharmaceuticals v HN Norton* (1996). However, to apply strict liability would prejudice a defendant using the substance for an 'old' purpose in the public domain.

6.3   DEFENCES

A defendant has a number of ways in which to defend against an action of infringement.

6.3.1   Putting the validity of the patent in issue

It is provided in s 74(1)(a) of the PA 1977 that the validity of a patent may be put in issue by way of defence in proceedings for infringement. The grounds upon which this may be done are set out in s 74(3), and are the same grounds on which revocation of a patent may be sought (see 6.4.2). To sue for infringement is to risk provoking such a challenge to a patent.

6.3.2   Section 60(5) of the PA 1977

Section 60(5) of the PA 1977 lists otherwise infringing acts for which a defence is provided. These were added to by the Biotechnology Directive to include the farmer's exemption.[32]

Acts done privately and for purposes which are not commercial

It will not infringe to do acts that are both private and done for non-commercial purposes.[33] Consequently, acts by non-commercial organisations such as universities are unlikely to be private.

Acts done for experimental purposes relating to the subject matter of the invention

Again this exception requires two elements: that the act is experimental and that its purpose relates to the subject matter of the invention.[34] No express limitation to non-commercial acts has been drawn, and it is an exception whose scope has widened to embrace commercial acts in some European jurisdictions in recent years. However, in *Inhale Therapeutic Systems Inc v Quadrant Healthcare plc* (2001) Laddie J refused to regard exploitation of products intended to sell the technology to third parties as experimental. As he had already found the patent invalid and the defence was given little consideration, it is unlikely that this was intended to mean that all commercial experiments fall outside the defence. It does suggest that acts entirely directed to commercial development rather than the attributes of the invention are not 'experiments'.

Most of the European case law relating to this exception falls into the area of pharmaceutical patents. Field trials intended to widen commercial markets do not relate to the subject matter of the invention. In *Monsanto v Stauffer* (1985), the defendant sought to vary an interlocutory injunction preventing them from using the allegedly infringing product TOUCHDOWN, a herbicide, in order to allow field trials and experiments on the product. It had already carried out some field trials in the UK and obtained limited clearance under the relevant non-statutory scheme (PSPS) for use on stubbles and non-crop areas. Now it wished to carry out renewed trials in order to secure further pre-harvest PSPS clearances. It argued that it was entitled to such trials under s 60(5)(b) of the PA 1977. The sub-section was held not to extend to such trials, which were intended to widen the commercial market for the product. It was held that s 60(5)(b) of the PA 1977 limits experimental purposes to those relating to the subject matter of the invention. Falconer J said:

> As a matter of language, that limitation seems to me to restrict the paragraph to experiments directed to the patented invention as such, experiments such as testing whether a patented product can be made, or a patented article made to work, as described in the patent specification, or experiments to see whether the patented invention can be improved or testing the effect of a modification in some particular to see whether it is an improvement or not. However, the limitation would, it seems to

---

32   *Ibid*, s 60(5)(g), (h).
33   *Ibid*, s 60(5)(a).
34   *Ibid*, s 60(5)(b).

me, as a matter of language, exclude from the exemption of the paragraph use of a patented article or process in experiments to test or evaluate some other product or process û the purpose of any such experiments would not relate to the subject matter of the patented invention.

Again, it seems to me that the limitation would exclude tests or trials having as their purpose achieving or extending the commercial acceptance of some commercial embodiment of the patented invention û such tests or trials would not, it seems to me, as a matter of language, be for purposes related to the subject matter of the patented invention.

Determining what the subject matter of the invention is is a matter of interpretation of the whole specification, and not just the claims: *Auchincloss v Agricultural and Veterinary Supplies* (1997).

German case law[35] extends the exception to experiments on a patented substance for further medical uses (including clinical trials) where the patentee had refused to grant a licence. This extended to trials aimed at gaining approval for a pharmaceutical identical in composition to the patented drug. However, trials not justified for the purpose of the experiments or conducted to interfere with the patentee's marketing were not within the defence. Despite criticism from drugs companies the German Supreme Court affirmed the decision.[36]

6.3.3 Prior use

The principle of the 'right to work' was explored in relation to novelty (see 5.1.1). With the advent of novelty being tested by the absence of an enabling disclosure of the invention in the prior art, it has been argued that this principle has been abandoned, subject only to the protection conferred by s 64 of the PA 1977.

This section purports to enable acts prepared for, or begun, before the priority date of an invention, to be continued, despite the fact that they would infringe a patent subsequently granted. However, the wording of the section is such that the protection it gives is of limited application. It is only acts done in the UK in good faith, or effective and serious preparations made in good faith, which fall within s 64 of the PA 1977. The section will not enable the prior user to license others to do those acts, nor will it extend to an individual who begins the acts or preparations after the invention's priority date, but before publication of the patent.

A final limitation was revealed by the case of *Helitune v Stewart Hughes* (1991). The patent related to a method of detecting the degree of unbalance in helicopter rotor blades by directing light or other radiation at the blades and measuring the reflected signals (an active system). The defendant pleaded s 64 of the PA 1977 in defence to allegations of infringement. The infringing act which the defendant wished to continue was to sell an active tracker. However, at the patent's priority date, all that the defendant had done was to produce a prototype with a view to further development. It had not sold a tracking device and, in fact, was concentrating its efforts on developing a passive system in which the rotors' interruptions of ambient light were measured. In these circumstances, it was held that the defendant had not reached the

---

35 *Klinische Versuche (Clinical Trials) I* [1997] RPC 623; *Klinische Versuche (Clinical Trials) II* [1998] RPC 423.
36 German Constitutional Court, 10 May 2000.

stage of effective and serious preparations to sell an active tracker and could not rely on the 'statutory licence' provided by s 64 of the PA 1977.

6.3.4 Exhaustion

In UK law, no doctrine of exhaustion applied to patents; a patentee was able to place further restrictions on sale or use, as a condition of selling of patented goods or a patented process: *Betts v Willmott* (1871). Now this is subject to the European Community Treaty's policies of competition and free movement of goods (see 3.10) in relation to exports within the EU and European Economic Area (EEA). If the Community Patent Regulation comes into effect, it will introduce a doctrine of exhaustion which also relates to national patents and will provide that, once the patented goods have been put on to the EU and EEA market, the patent rights can no longer be applied to them.

The Biotechnology Directive added specific exhaustion for biological material. Patent protection does not extend to material obtained from the propagation or multiplication of biological material placed on the market by patentee (or with his consent) – if that replication is a necessary result of the reason for which the material was marketed.[37] Consequently, a farmer may sell a crop grown from patented seed, but may not sell the crop's seed for sowing to other farmers.

6.3.5 The 'Gillette defence'

The Gillette defence is not another ground of defence, but a shortcut to proving that a patent has not been infringed. It derives from the case of *Gillette Safety Razor v Anglo-American Trading* (1913). If a defendant raises as a defence the argument that the patented invention is novel and/or obvious, the court must make a comparison of three 'versions' of the invention. The first is that revealed in the prior art; the second is the patented invention as claimed; and the third is the defendant's version which is alleged to be infringing the patent. The laborious method for dealing with a claim of infringement and the defence that the invention is not patentable, would be to compare the patented invention with the defendant's, to determine whether it fell within the claims. Then the court must compare the patented invention with the prior art to determine whether the patent is valid or not. This makes for extended, time consuming and expensive proceedings.

However, the double comparison can be avoided by merely comparing the defendant's version of the invention with the prior art. If the defendant's invention falls within the prior art, it is obvious or anticipated. In that case, if the defendant's invention is the same as the patentee's, the patent cannot be valid; but if the patent is valid, then the defendant's invention cannot fall within the claims. Either way, if the defendant's invention is found to fall within the prior art, the claimant cannot win; the patent is either invalid or has not been infringed. This illustrates the drafting dilemma of a patentee (see 3.4) and the importance of seeking professional help in doing so.

---

37 Paragraph 10, Schedule A2 PA 1977.

6.4   REVOCATION AND OPPOSITION

Not only may a potential infringer retaliate by challenging the validity of a patent in infringement proceedings (see 6.3.1), but the validity of a patent may be challenged in three other ways: third party observations during the application process; revocation; and opposition of a European patent.

6.4.1   Third party observations

After publication of a patent application, but before any patent has been granted, any other person may make written observations to the comptroller on the question of whether the invention is a patentable invention, stating reasons.[38] This allows competitors and other interested parties to participate in the granting process. The comptroller shall consider the observations in accordance with the relevant rules.

6.4.2   Revocation

Any person may apply to the comptroller or the court, after the patent has been granted, for an order revoking the patent, at any time during the life of the patent.[39] Proceedings in the Patent Office are largely documentary and provide an alternative to expensive court proceedings. In *Oystertec plc v Edward Evans Barker* (2002) it was confirmed that even a firm of patent agents acting for an undisclosed principal may apply. No interest in the revocation is required,[40] and the motives of the person applying were held to be irrelevant.

The only grounds on which a UK patent may be revoked are:

(a) that the invention is not a patentable invention;

(b) that the patent was granted to a person who was not entitled to be granted that patent;

(c) that the specification of the patent does not disclose the invention clearly enough and completely enough for it to be performed by a person skilled in the art;

(d) that the matter disclosed in the specification of the patent extends beyond that disclosed in the application for the patent, as filed; and/or

(e) that the protection conferred by the patent has been extended by an amendment which should not have been allowed.

6.4.3   EPO opposition

The European patent differs from a domestic UK patent in that it can be revoked centrally by the EPO for all the countries for which it was granted, but only in the first nine months after grant, as a result of opposition by interested parties.[41]

It is set out in Art 100 of the EPC that opposition may be made on three grounds:

---

38   *Ibid*, s 21.
39   *Ibid*, s 72(1).
40   A significant change from the PA 1949.
41   Article 99 of the EPC.

(a) that the subject matter of the European patent is not patentable within the criteria of Arts 52–57;

(b) that the European patent does not disclose the invention in a manner sufficiently clear and complete for it to be carried out by a person skilled in the art; and/or

(c) that the subject matter of the European patent extends beyond the content of the application as filed.

Opposing a patent has proved to be a long, protracted process in the EPO.

6.5   NON-BINDING OPINIONS AS TO VALIDITY BY THE PATENT OFFICE

Patent litigation is expensive, slow and time consuming, providing a real deterrent to small enterprises, as is recognised in the remedy against threats (see 19.10). Consequently, the Patents Act 2004 inserts s 74A into the PA 1977. This allows a patentee, or any other person, to seek an informal opinion from the Comptroller as to whether any act infringes a patent, or whether a patent is invalid under s 1(1)(a) or (b)[42] of the PA 1977. The Comptroller must issue an opinion[43] if requested to do so, but has a discretion to refuse to do either in prescribed circumstances, or if he considers it 'inappropriate in the circumstances' to do so. Further provision relating to circumstances in which an opinion may not be given, and for review of opinions is to be made by Rules.[44] This procedure will allow for quick and relatively inexpensive resolution of questions of validity before full-scale litigation, enabling settlement of disputes, while continuing to allow parties to seek resolution in the courts. It stands in addition to revocation proceedings and post-grant amendment of a patent.

It is clear that s 74A of the PA 2004 is to be supplemented by detailed secondary legislation. In particular, the responses to the Patent Office Consultation suggest that reassessment of a patent's validity should not be made unless new prior art comes to light after grant. Re-examination of the prior art considered pre-grant could seriously undermine confidence in the Patent Office's granting procedures.[45] It is expected that both the application for an assessment, and its result, should be made public, but that an opinion of invalidity should not result in revocation of the patent at issue.[46]

Further Reading

Davies, I and Cohen, S, 'Section 64 of the UK Patents Act 1977: Right to Continue Use Begun before Priority Date' [1994] EIPR 239

Franzosi, M, 'Equivalence in Europe' [2003] EIPR 237

---

42   Novelty and inventive step.
43   Opinions will be prepared by patent examiners.
44   Section 74B of the PA 2004.
45   Para 168, 'Consultation on the proposed Patents Act (Amendment) Bill: Summary of responses and the Government's conclusions': www.patent.gov.uk.
46   Paras 174–76, 'Consultation on the proposed Patents Act (Amendment) Bill: Summary of responses and the Government's conclusions': www.patent.gov.uk.

Gilat, D, *Experimental Use and Patents*, 11C Studies, Vol 16, 1995, Munich: Max Planck Institute

Hurdle, H, 'What is the Direct Product of a Patented Process?' [1997] EIPR 322

Jacob, R, 'The Herschel Smith Lecture 1993' [1993] EIPR 312

Karet, I and Watson, K, 'Questions about Patent Construction' [1998] EIPR 192

Oliver, P, '*Kastner v Rizla*: Too Far, Too Fast' [1996] EIPR 28

Sherman, B, 'Patent Claim Interpretation: the Impact of the Protocol on Interpretation' (1991) 54 MLR 499

Thomson, G, and Kempton, L, 'Construction Issues in Pharmaceutical and Biotech Cases' [2002] EIPR 591

White, A, 'The Structure and Function of Patent Claims' [1993] EIPR 243

CHAPTER 7

BREACH OF CONFIDENCE

When information is imparted to another in confidential circumstances, and is either used or disclosed without authority, breach of confidence provides a remedy. The action applies to any type of information, whether commercial, private or governmental. In the intellectual property field, the action stands as an alternative, or an adjunct, to statutory design, copyright or patent protection. Confidence has the advantage of not needing any formalities of application or registration, or the payment of fees. It also has the advantage that it can be implied from the circumstances in which information is divulged between the parties to an action. However, the obligation to preserve confidence is dependent on there being a relationship between those parties and, once the information has been disclosed to the public, there can be no effective further secrecy.

7.1   THE JURIDICAL BASIS OF THE ACTION

Determining the legal jurisdiction for conferring such a remedy is difficult. The modern origins of the action can be traced to *Prince Albert v Strange* (1849); so too can the obscurity that still clouds its juridical basis. Lord Cottenham based the action on 'breach of trust, confidence or contract'. Two years later, Turner VC referred to the doubts surrounding the courts' jurisdiction in *Morison v Moat* (1851). He said:

> In some cases, it [the jurisdiction of the court] has been referred to property, in others to contract, and in others, again, it has been treated as founded upon trust or confidence, meaning, as I conceive, that the court fastens the obligation on the conscience of the party, and enforces it against him in the same manner as it enforces against a party to whom a benefit is given the obligation of performing a promise on the faith of which the benefit has been conferred; but, upon whatever grounds the jurisdiction is founded, the authorities leave no doubt as to the exercise of it.

Modern development of the action sprang from a growing appreciation after the Second World War of the value of technical information. Then, in *Saltman Engineering Co Ltd v Campbell Engineering Co Ltd* (1948), the Court of Appeal dismissed any need for a contractual nexus between the parties in order to found the necessary relationship of confidence. The remedy most often sought for threatened breaches of confidence was an injunction (an equitable remedy). The fundamental basis of the action is also a relationship giving rise to an obligation in conscience to maintain confidence. Consequently, *dicta* in modern cases suggest that the courts now consider breach of confidence to rest on an equitable jurisdiction founded on 'good faith'. In *Seager v Copydex Ltd* (1967) Lord Denning MR said that: 'The law on this subject 'depends on the broad principle of equity that he who has received information in confidence shall not take unfair advantage of it'.

More recently, the Court of Appeal, in *R v Department of Health, ex parte Source Informatics Ltd* (1999), emphasised that this basis in equity constitutes an obligation of conscience arising from the circumstances of communication, only breached by an abuse or 'unconscientious use' of the protected information. Simon Brown LJ stated that 'the touchstone by which to judge the scope of his duty and whether or not it has been fulfilled or breached is [the confider's] own conscience'. This appears to amount to a subjective test of the extent of the duty to maintain secrecy, if not of the existence of an obligation in the first place. If so, it may prove a very difficult test to apply.

Professor Jones concluded that confidence is an equitable obligation based on good faith.[1] However, North argued[2] that to recognise a tortious liability for breaches of confidence would have the advantage of importing a right to damages and the accepted parameters of a remedy in tort. The Law Commission recommended the enactment of a statutory duty.[3]

The remedy could also be based on a proprietary right in information. Traditionally, information has not been treated as property by the criminal law in either England: *Oxford v Moss* (1979) or Scotland: *Grant v Allen* (1988). However, Libling argues that there could be a proprietary right to the commercial exploitation of an intangible distinct from ownership in the entity itself.[4] In the sphere of intellectual property information has a clear economic value, and recent proposals of the Law Commission recommend that unauthorised use or disclosure of confidential information should be a crime (see 7.10.2). It remains to be seen whether this value could be regarded as sufficient to confer the nature of property on information. This would be clearly demonstrated if the courts were to hold that an innocent recipient, unaware of the confidentiality of the information at the time of its use or disclosure, is bound by an obligation of confidence. In particular, it is possible that information might be regarded only as a form of 'intellectual' property, not carrying all the attributes of property in general. Further indication that confidential information has proprietary characteristics can be seen in a move away from requiring a relationship of confidence between the parties in an action. In *Venables and Thompson v News Group Newspapers Ltd* (2001) the court focused on the nature of the information in order to establish an obligation of confidence, rather than the relationship of the parties. This, too, might indicate a property basis to protection for confidential information. It was, however, a wholly exceptional case.

In Scotland, protection for confidential information does not lie on a juridical basis of common law and equity. However, since the case of *Saltman Engineering Co Ltd v Campbell Engineering Co Ltd* (1948) the same principles have been adhered to. Although the action is still developing, the report of the Scottish Law Commission[5] and the draft bill it contains did much to clarify the remedy. More recently, the leading case of *Lord Advocate v Scotsman Publications Ltd* (1988), affirmed by the House of Lords in 1989, set out the relevant principles, in part following English authorities, and established the action for Scotland. The Law Lords, constituted as an English House but sitting as a Scottish one, contained four of the Lords Ordinary who disposed of the *Spycatcher Case*. Lord Keith stated:

> While the juridical basis may differ to some extent in the two jurisdictions, the substance of the law in both of them is the same.

1　Jones, G, 'Restitution of Benefits Obtained in Breach of Another's Confidence' (1970) 86 LQR 463.
2　North, P, 'Breach of Confidence: is there a New Tort?' [1972] JSPTL 149.
3　*Breach of Confidence* Cmnd 8388 (1981).
4　Libling, D, 'The Concept of Property: Property in Intangibles' (1978) 94 LQR 103.
5　*Breach of Confidence*, Scot Law Com No 90, Cmnd 9385 (1984).

Although the existence of the remedy can no longer be disputed, the obscurity of its origins have led to uncertainty at the fringes of the action; a clear foundation in tort, contract, property or equity would provide clear answers to new combinations of circumstances. The uncertain nature of the juridical base for the action provides courts with the flexibility to take advantage of the indefinite boundaries of the action. The positive effect of this is to allow judicial development, or just interpretation, of the action to accommodate new situations; the negative effect is the uncertainty that must accompany any legal advice in those situations.

Consequently, the action has developed on a case by case basis, leaving unanswered questions, first, as to the extent of liability of third party recipients of confidential information, secondly, whether any obligation arises where unsolicited confidential information is received, or is taken, by the defendant and, thirdly, where the defendant is innocent of fault.

7.2 DEVELOPMENT OF THE ACTION

This ability to evolve also has the advantage that the action can respond to changing social conditions, and to the perceived needs of legal policy. This function was articulated by Keene LJ in *Earl Spencer and Countess Spencer v The United Kingdom* (1998):

> ... breach of confidence is a developing area of the law, the boundaries of which are not immutable but may change to reflect changes in society, technology and business practice.

The driving factor behind the most recent developments was the coming into force of the Human Rights Act 1998 (HRA 1998). The rights to privacy and freedom of expression established by the European Convention of Human Rights (ECHR) have been 'absorbed into the long-established action for breach of confidence (*per* Lord Woolf CJ in *A v B & C* (2002)). Adopting these two rights – which pull in opposite directions, privacy providing an additional source of protection to private information, while freedom of expression restricts the area in which remedies lie for breaches of confidence – has created a tension requiring the courts to hold the balance between them. Doing so has required adjustments to the balance between the interest in confidentiality and that of the public interest previously established by the courts (see 7.13).

Additionally, these changes have the potential to redound on other aspects of the action, notably the nature of confidential information as property, and the existence of confidentiality where no relationship exists between confider and confidant, as well as to the scope of appropriate remedies.

7.3 THE CONDITIONS FOR A REMEDY

Despite the confusions concerning the origins and juridical nature of the action for breach of confidence, Megarry J laid a clear three-sided structure of necessary conditions for the action in *Coco v AN Clark (Engineers) Ltd* (1969). He said:

> Where there is information that is confidential, an obligation to maintain that
> confidence has come into being, and the information has been used or disclosed
> without authority, an action for breach of confidence will lie.

Consequently, the subject matter of the action lies in the existence of information
which is confidential. No liability can arise until an obligation or duty to maintain
confidence has arisen and there is no breach of the duty without an unauthorised
disclosure or use of the information.

Although *Lord Advocate v Scotsman Publications Ltd* (1989) gives authority for an
obligation in Scots law, the House of Lords did not define when such an obligation
should arise. Their lordships' recognition of English authority, however, justifies
relying on Megarry J's *dictum*. Consequently, we can examine the substance of the
principles governing the action in three main sections:

- confidential information (7.4 and 7.5);
- obligation of confidence (7.7);
- breach of the obligation (7.11).

However, Megarry J himself was careful to point out that the authorities from which
he derived these conditions did not lay down clear tests for establishing the
confidentiality of information, nor for the creation of the necessary obligation, or
whether the breach need be detrimental to the claimant in order for him to secure a
remedy. Given that the common law has the capacity to develop by analogy as new
circumstances arise, the boundaries of breach of confidence remain blurred and open
to interpretation by subsequent courts.

7.4   INFORMATION

The subject matter of the action as set out in *Coco v AN Clark (Engineers) Ltd* (1969) is
information which is confidential. This makes it necessary to establish, first, the type of
information that may be protected and, secondly, how to test its confidentiality. In
Saltman Engineering Co Ltd v Campbell Engineering Co Ltd (1948), Lord Greene MR
described this subject matter as information which was not common knowledge and
which 'must have the necessary quality of confidence about it'.

'Information' carries its general meaning. There is apparently no restriction on the
content or form of protectable information: whether industrial (*Saltman Engineering Co
Ltd v Campbell Engineering Co Ltd* (1948); *Coco v AN Clark (Engineers) Ltd* (1969));
commercial (*Faccenda Chicken v Fowler* (1986); *Roger Bullivant Ltd v Ellis* (1987));
personal (*Duchess of Argyll v Duke of Argyll* (1967); *Stevens v Avery* (1988)); political
(*Fraser v Evans* (1969); *Attorney General v Jonathan Cape Ltd* (1976)); or literary or artistic
(*Attorney General v Guardian Newspapers (No 2)* (1988); *Prince Albert v Strange* (1849)).

This does not mean that all possible pieces of information receive protection. 'Tittle
tattle' may not be protected as confidential information. At first instance, Goulding J,
in *Faccenda Chicken v Fowler* (1986), separated confidential information into three
categories:

> First, there is information which, because of its trivial character or its easy accessibility
> from public sources of information, cannot be regarded by reasonable persons or by
> the law as confidential at all ...

the first of which, he said, was unprotectable trivia or 'tittle tattle'. There is justification for this view. Megarry J said, *obiter*, in *Coco v AN Clark (Engineers) Ltd* (1969): 'I doubt whether equity would intervene unless the circumstances are of sufficient gravity – equity ought not to be invoked merely to protect trivial tittle tattle, however confidential.'

However, this should not be understood to mean that salacious gossip or personal secrets will always go unprotected. In *Stevens v Avery* (1988), a case concerning wholesale revelations of an individual's lesbian conduct, Sir Nicolas Browne-Wilkinson VC accepted the principle that a court of equity will not enforce copyright relating to matters with a grossly immoral tendency, and presumed that the same would apply to confidential information. In the absence of any generally accepted moral code in 1988 and, in the face of a claim that the information should not be protected being made by the very party who had published it in a major national Sunday newspaper, he declined to dismiss this particular information as immoral. Moreover, he doubted whether it could properly be described as 'tittle tattle'.

A question does arise from these two cases whether it is the content of the information (as is relevant in copyright law where works are immoral – see 9.5), or the nature of the harm, that causes the court to refuse a remedy. If it is the nature of the harm Megarry J's *dictum* is not inconsistent with *Stevens v Avery* (1988). Sir Nicolas Browne-Wilkinson VC suggested that it is not the classification of the information which is significant (although Megarry J's *dictum* did appear in the portion of his judgment in *Coco v AN Clark* (1969) dealing with confidential information), but that Megarry J was considering whether equity, in its discretion, would be prepared to give a remedy, and concluded that it would not be prepared to do so for a trivial breach.

As well as refusing protection in these circumstances, the courts have distinguished between different types of information. The effect is to shape the extent of protection for particular classes of information. Whether the differences of result rest on the nature of the information, or on the extent of the breach, the category of information at issue may be significant to the outcome of a particular case.

7.4.1 Classifying classes of information

Quoting Gurry,[6] the Court of Appeal suggested in *R v Department of Health ex p Source Informatics Ltd* (1999) that information can be broadly categorised into four main classes: trade secrets, personal confidences, Government information, and artistic and literary confidences. In doing this the Court was following Gurry's suggestion that there is a correlation between personal confidences (such as the patient prescriptions at issue) and the protection of privacy. The reason for doing so was to determine the appropriate extent of protection for the information concerned in the case, thus linking the extent of the obligation owed by a confidant to the nature of the information being protected.

---

6   Gurry, F, *Breach of Confidence* (Oxford: Clarendon Press, 1984).

7.4.2 The relation between the nature of information and the extent of the obligation owed

Source Informatics Ltd (1999) related to sales of anonymised patient and prescription details to Source Informatics by pharmacists. From these Source created a database of doctors' prescribing habits. Pharmaceutical companies used this to target marketing of their products. For policy reasons related to the cost to the NHS of drugs, the Department of Health opposed this practice. It argued that selling the data amounted to a breach of the duty of confidentiality pharmacists owed to patients. Despite detailed argument, the Court of Appeal held that broad principles of equity were involved and should be resolved on a similarly broad basis. Simon Brown LJ pointed out that while *Coco v AN Clark (Engineers) Ltd* (1969) provided a test for imposing of an obligation of confidence, the scope, or extent, of that obligation was not defined. He suggested that the scope of obligation differs in different circumstances. In support of this conclusion he cited the treatment of disclosures made for limited purposes in *Smith Kline & French Laboratories v Department of Community Services and Health* (1991) (see 7.5.5), the springboard doctrine (see 7.6.4), and breaches being found where only a material part of the confidential information imparted (and not the whole) had been divulged: *Amber Size and Chemical Co Ltd v Menzel* (1913).

He concluded that the scope of any obligation must be determined by the effect of the receipt of confidential information on the confidant's conscience. Accordingly, he held, the relevant test of this scope lay in the question 'What interest, one must ask, is the law here concerned to protect?' The answer to this question lay in the nature of the information. He suggested that where government information was concerned, as in the *Spycatcher* case, the question whether the information had reached the public domain might be conclusive, but that this may not be so if trade secrets were at issue. As the information at issue related to personal confidences the law's concern was to protect personal privacy. Finding that the pharmacists' consciences ought not reasonably to be troubled by Sources' scheme there was no breach.

This case may confirm the trend begun in *Faccenda Chicken v Fowler* (1986) of treating different classes of information differently. Doing so may lead to separate principles developing where the justifications for protecting particular categories of confidence differ; a consequence Simon Brown LJ explicitly accepted.

Goulding J's second and third categories in *Faccenda Chicken v Fowler* (1986) distinguished 'confidential information' from 'trade secrets' specifically within the context of employment, and are best discussed at 7.8.2. The result is to differentiate between protection bestowed on information imparted during employment according to whether the employment was continuing or had been terminated at the time of breach.

7.4.3 The form of information

Just as the existence (as opposed to the scope) of protection is not dependent on the content of information, equally there is no restriction on the form in which the information is embodied. It is necessary, however, that the information, whatever its form, be identified when proceedings are brought: (*Ocular Sciences Ltd v Aspect Vision Care Ltd* (1997); *CMI-Centers v Phytopharm* (1999)). This is to ensure both that any injunction granted can be enforced with sufficient certainty and that defendants can know the case they have to answer.

Information in the form of artistic works and photographs has been held to be confidential (*Douglas v Hello! Ltd* (2000) and (2003)), as have devices (*Saltman Engineering Co Ltd v Campbell Engineering Co Ltd* (1948)). Confidential information can also include matter which has been observed by a defendant. Nor is there any necessary requirement that confidential information be recorded, and it may be oral (*Seager v Copydex (No 1)* (1967). In *Printers and Finishers v Holloway (No 2)* (1965), the manager of the plaintiff's printing plant showed members of a rival concern around the factory despite instructions to keep the processes there secret. Cross J held that an injunction could be granted where the information had been carried away in the defendant's memory.

7.4.4 Ideas as information

In particular, ideas can be the subject matter of protection. By contrast, copyright protects form, or expression (the particular way in which an idea had been recorded in a work), but not the underlying ideas. Users of a copyright work may employ these elements unhindered by the copyright protection. No such restriction applies to breach of confidence. Where a limit is drawn, it is not in the form of the information, but in its particularity. In *Fraser v Thames Television Ltd* (1983), the plaintiff had communicated an idea for a programme based on the activities of a rock group to the defendant. The defendant eventually made the programme without authority. In an action for breach of confidence, it was argued for the defendant that a literary or dramatic idea could not be protected unless fully developed in the form of a synopsis and recorded, by analogy with copyright law. Hirst J held that confidential information included orally communicated information and that ideas were capable of protection. He also held, however, that ideas must be sufficiently developed, have some element of originality not already in the public domain, be of potential commercial attractiveness and be capable of being realised.

The extent to which the information must have 'originality' may be assessed from *De Maudsley v Palumbo* (1996), where *Fraser v Thames Television* (1983) was distinguished. The plaintiff's action for breach of confidence was based on an idea for a nightclub which was alleged to have five features:

(a) that the club would operate all night, legally;

(b) be big, with novel decor in a 'high tech industrial' warehouse style;

(c) incorporate separate spaces for dancing, resting and socialising, with a 'VIP lounge';

(d) the dance area would have excellent sound, light and atmosphere which did not penetrate into the surrounding elements;

(e) top disc jockeys worldwide would appear.

Knox J was not prepared to treat such an idea as protectable. Although some elements of the features enumerated were novel, all were too vague and general to constitute confidential information. He identified three points from Hirst J's judgment in *Fraser v Thames Television* (1983):

(a)   It is not essential for confidential information to be in writing or other permanent
       form.

(b)   It is essential for the information to 'have at least some attractiveness to an end
       user and be capable of being realised as an actuality', in the sense of a finished
       product in the relevant medium.

This does not preclude simple confidential information: '... vagueness and simplicity
are not the same.'

(c)   A trade or industry practice of treating an idea as confidential information was a
       significant part of the result in *Fraser v Thames Television Ltd* (1983).

Information, therefore, needs to be defined with some precision before protection may
be conferred, but a distinction can be drawn between information with nebulous
boundaries, and information which is merely simple. The need for clarity was
explained by Mummery LJ in *Inline Logistics Ltd v UCI Logistics Ltd* (2001):

> ... in confidential information cases it is important to identify with some precision the
> information claimed to be confidential and to have been used without the necessary
> permission. Confidential information is intangible. In some cases it may not have even
> taken any material or permanent form. It may consist, for example, of an oral
> communication. Confidentiality may exist in individual items of information. It may
> exist in a drawing or a document as a whole or it may take a more limited form as ... a
> particular combination of ideas, concepts or features which have been embodied
> within a drawing. The definition of the information in every case must be reasonably
> specific for the purposes not only of determining whether it is confidential but also
> whether it has been communicated and whether what has been communicated as
> confidential has been the subject of unauthorised use.

Practice in the industry concerned may be taken into account in deciding whether
sufficient clarity or detail has been achieved and Hirst J regarded as a significant factor
in his conclusion that it was normal practice within the entertainment industry to
regard general ideas for new programmes as protected.

7.4.5   A qualitative standard for protection developing

It is possible, at least where trade secrets are concerned, that the courts are beginning
to impose qualitative standards on information before it can be protected, as pointed
out by Bently and Sherman. Terminology more familiar in the patent and copyright
sphere has been used, albeit *obiter*. In *De Maudsley v Palumbo* (1996) Knox J refers to
novelty in conjunction with the nightclub idea, while in *Coulthard v Disco Mix Club Ltd*
(1999) Judge Jules Sher QC referred to the sound mixing techniques at issue as being
'pretty obvious' and unlikely to be confidential. This might serve to protect the
recipients of unsolicited and general confidential ideas from being overly constrained
in going on to develop the idea into concrete form. However, any such development
has the potential to leave such recipients with little guidance as to their obligations
until a body of case law has developed. In both cases the *dicta* can be better explained
as reference to such ideas already lying in the public domain and therefore failing the
test of confidentiality. If a test of 'obviousness' (see 5.2) were to be applied, on the other
hand, it might be asked whether the reasonable man in the shoes of the recipient
would regard the idea as obvious.

7.5   CONFIDENTIALITY OF INFORMATION

The second criterion to be satisfied before information can be protected is that it is confidential. In Lord Greene MR's view, information had the necessary quality of confidence where it was not 'something which is public property and public knowledge'. This suggests that where the public has access to the information it cannot be regarded as confidential. This includes publication outside the United Kingdom: *Attorney General v Guardian Newspapers Ltd (No 2)* (1988). However, the concept of publicity being applied is relative, rather than absolute. Where information is related to an invention, the law takes a notional view of the public's access to the invention (see 5.1.3), whereas, for confidence, a realistic attitude is adopted to the public availability of the information. Confidentiality, therefore, may be relative. There are three ways in which this is apparent – the numbers of the public having access to the information, the treatment of what might be termed 'composite information', and the treatment of information communicated for limited purposes.

7.5.1   The degree of disclosure to the public

Where the information sought to be treated as confidential has been revealed to a number of people, but in a limited manner, confidentiality can survive. As put by Cross J in *Franchi v Franchi* (1967), 'it must be a matter of degree, depending on the particular case, but if relative secrecy remains, the plaintiff can still succeed'. If, relative to the public at large, the matter is not widely known, it may remain protected. It is a matter of having regard to all the circumstances of the case.

In *Dunford and Elliott v Johnson and Firth Brown* (1978), the plaintiff company was attempting to raise money by a rights issue to shareholders. The company's institutional shareholders, who held 43% of the shares, were shown a confidential report on the company's prospects under an obligation of confidence. These shareholders approached the defendant and another company in an attempt to secure further funding, doing so without consulting the plaintiff. Representatives of the defendant and the company were allowed to study the report. The defendant made a takeover bid for the plaintiff, which sought an injunction restraining the use of the confidential information in the report. Having referred to use of the information by the plaintiff's own directors in buying shares when the share price was at a very low point, Lord Denning MR said:

> The widespread use of the information drives a hole into the blanket of confidence; especially when that information is being used – or, shall I say, misused – for the benefit of some potential shareholders, and not for the benefit of the others. So much so that it would not be reasonable that the stipulation for confidence should be enforced.

In fact, Lord Denning added a fourth condition to Megarry J's three in *Coco v AN Clark (Engineers) Ltd* (1969): that the stipulation for confidence be reasonable. This has not been generally adopted by the courts because the relative nature of confidentiality achieves the same result. Whatever the stipulations for confidence made by Dunford and Elliott, the dissemination of the report was too wide for any real secrecy to remain.

Conversely, in *Schering Chemicals Ltd v Falkman Ltd* (1982), the fact that the information sought to be protected had been previously available in the press was not enough to destroy its confidentiality when the story was revived by the defendant. The plaintiff had manufactured and sold a drug, Primodos, used as a pregnancy test. This was withdrawn in 1978, after concerns that it was related to abnormalities in new-born babies. There was much media coverage of the story and, in 1979, the defendant company was employed by the plaintiff to train executives in presenting the company's view. To this end, information was given to the defendant in confidence. Later, one of the defendant's employees made a film for television about the drug, using information given by the plaintiff for the training. It was claimed that all of this information could have been obtained from public sources. The plaintiff sought an injunction against broadcast of the film, and the grant of this injunction by McNeill J was upheld by the Court of Appeal. The majority held that, where information was communicated in a commercial context in confidence and that information had a material connection with the commercial interests of its communicator, a fiduciary duty to observe the confidence arose in the recipient, whether or not the information was available from other sources.

7.5.2   Factors in determining the degree of dissemination

It is the degree of dissemination to the public which is material. The court will take all relevant circumstances into consideration. Thus, for example, the degree of publication within the area of business in which publication took place was a factor in *Dunford and Elliott v Johnson and Firth Brown* (1978), where the court took the City Code on Takeovers and Mergers into account. Where the publication took place may, however, be a factor that is losing its significance. In *Franchi v Franchi* (1967) the information had been published in a patent specification in Belgium, and the court had to decide whether any relative confidentiality remained in the UK. On the facts it was found to be public in the UK, because patent agents search patent information internationally. Once publication takes place over the internet it is likely to be regarded as available to the public in the United Kingdom. In the *Spycatcher Case*, Sir Nicolas Browne-Wilkinson VC stated:

> The truth of the matter is that in the contemporary world of electronics and jumbo jets news anywhere is news everywhere. However, whilst the news is international, the jurisdiction of this court is strictly territorial. Once the news is out by publication in the United States and the importation of the book into the country, the law could, I think, be justifiably accused of being an ass and brought into disrepute if it closed its eyes to that reality and sought by injunction to prevent the press or anyone else from repeating information which is now freely available to all.

Another factor which has proved to be material is the extent of harm likely from the further publication. This may lie behind the decision in *Schering Chemicals Ltd v Falkman Ltd* (1982) and clearly was regarded as relevant in *Spycatcher*. As publication in England was seen as unable to cause any further harm to the Government, there was no public interest in preserving confidentiality.

7.5.3   Disguised publication

Although a measure of publication may not destroy confidence, publication to all, but in a form which only those with specific skills can interpret it does destroy confidentiality. It might be thought that protecting one's information in a sealed container might be a means of preserving confidentiality whilst also allowing public use of that information.

To do so would, however, extend protection to information falling outside the accepted categories of intellectual property subject matter. It appears that it is this consideration which underlies Jacob J's decision in *Mars UK Ltd v Teknowledge Ltd's Application* (1999). He held that the information contained within an encrypted semi-conductor chip did not constitute confidential information. As he pointed out, 'anyone can acquire the skills' necessary to decrypt the information. That is not, however, to mean that anyone 'stealing' the unencrypted information would not be bound by confidence, as the information in its plain text form had not been published.

This should be contrasted with the situation where the information has been made available to the public in a form in which it may be 'reverse engineered'. In *Saltman Engineering Co Ltd v Campbell Engineering Co Ltd* (1948) the defendant had been engaged on the plaintiff's behalf to make leather punches from the plaintiff's copyright drawings for the tool. These drawings were given to the defendant in circumstances implying confidence. Later, the defendant made a punch. The Court of Appeal held that it was an unjustified shortcut to use the drawings for the defendant's own purposes, even though a competent draftsman could have replicated the drawings after studying one of the plaintiff's punches, which were freely available on the market. It could be argued that this case is an early application of the springboard doctrine (see 7.6.4), as the defendants presumably gained an advantage over the reverse engineer, who would have had to undertake the process of dismantling the punches and recreating the drawings.

The decision in *Mars UK Ltd v Teknowledge Ltd's Application* (1999) can be criticized, however, as in another context the quite literal 'fencing' of confidential information in the Australian case *Franklin v Giddins* (1978) was sufficient to impose confidentiality.

7.5.4 Composite information

The second situation which displays the relative nature of confidence is that of 'composite information'. In *Coco v AN Clark (Engineers) Ltd* (1969), Megarry J said:

> Something that has been constructed solely from materials in the public domain may possess the necessary quality of confidence: for something new and confidential may have been brought into being by the application of the skill and ingenuity of the human being. Novelty depends on the thing itself, and not upon the quality of its component parts.

However, the mere act of compiling publicly available information will not confer confidentiality. In *Ocular Sciences Ltd v Aspect Vision Care Ltd* (1997) confidentiality was claimed in the complete set of specifications for the claimants' contact lenses which had been marketed for some time. To have compiled all these dimensions would undoubtedly have taken time and effort. Laddie J specified, however, that 'there must be some product of the skill of the human brain' beyond the expenditure of time and effort. He emphasised the importance of Megarry J's *dictum* that something new and confidential *may* have been brought into being. Consequently, a mechanical collection of data in the public domain, however large the list, could not constitute confidential information without the use of relevant skill.

Even where such compiled information is confidential, the extent of protection may be restricted. In *Inline Logistics Ltd v UCI Logistics Ltd* (2001) the defendants operated warehouses and wished to develop a particular warehouse to the specific requirements of a customer. When the customer issued an invitation to tender the appellants, who provided design and construction services, supplied designs to the defendants. However, the relationship broke down and the design work was completed without the appellants, and a new design drawing prepared. The appellants contended that design features from their drawing had been used in the final design and that their drawing constituted confidential information. Mummery LJ held that it was clear law that 'a particular combination of individual design features – themselves not confidential because they are common knowledge, obvious or commonplace – may be protected as confidential information'. However, he found that, on the facts of this 'borderline' case, only a very limited extent of confidentiality resulted, being restricted to the particular form in which the design features had been combined.

This raises the possibility of so-called 'thin' protection, protection which is proportional to the degree of confidentiality of the information. The majority held that the just-confidential information had not been used as the particular combination of features which merited confidentiality had not been replicated in the eventual design, although there were similarities. Protection was to be confined to the particular combination where composite information was at issue.

7.5.5 Disclosure for limited purposes

A third way in which confidence can be regarded as relative to the circumstances relates to information disclosed for limited purposes. Should the recipient make use of the information for purposes other than those intended when the information was communicated, this may amount to a breach of confidence. This was the situation in *Schering Chemicals Ltd v Falkman Ltd* (1982) and *Saltman Engineering Co Ltd v Campbell Engineering Co Ltd* (1948).

A similar result can be seen in *Interfirm Comparison (Australia) Pty Ltd v Law Society of New South Wales* (1977). Interfirm compared factors such as costs, productivity, and profitability between companies within the same business or profession. The defendants approached the company for data and were sent a proposal with a questionnaire. The defendants did not use the questionnaire, rejecting its suitability for their purposes, and designed their own in collaboration with the University of New South Wales. In doing so they photocopied the defendant's questionnaire and sent a copy to the university. This was an oversight and there was no evidence that it had been used. The claimants alleged that this constituted a breach of confidence because the questionnaire had been sent only to enable the Law Society to decide whether to use their services. It was argued on the Law Society's behalf that a good deal of the information embodied in the questionnaire was well-known and could not be confidential. Bowen J held that:

> ... having regard to the amount of skill, judgment and labour involved in the preparation of the proposal and the 1972 questionnaire, and to the limited purpose of the negotiation between the plaintiff and defendant in furtherance of which the material was supplied, both documents were confidential, in the sense that they could be used by the Law Society only for the purpose for which they had been given it, that is to say, for the purpose of considering and deciding whether it would engage the services of the plaintiff for its own survey and interfirm comparison; they could not, without the plaintiff's assent, be used for other unrelated purposes – for example , for the purpose of publishing a book of precedents or writing an article in the Law Society's Journal.

This would appear to remain the case whether the purpose for which the information has been communicated has been expressly or impliedly defined.

7.5.6 An objective or subjective test?

The test to be applied in determining whether information is confidential is to ask whether it has become public property and public knowledge. It remains to be seen whether this is a subjective test of the information owner's intention, or an objective test of the reasonable man's appreciation of the status of the information. Megarry J stated his first condition in objective terms in *Coco v AN Clark (Engineers) Ltd* (1969). Later, however, he added a subjective element to the test in *Thomas Marshall (Exports) v Guinle* (1979). He said:

> First, I think that the information must be information the release of which the owner believes would be injurious to him or of advantage to his rivals or others. Second, I think the owner must believe that the information is confidential or secret, that is, that it is not already in the public domain. It may be that some or all of his rivals already have the information: but, as long as the owner believes it to be confidential, I think he is entitled to try and protect it.

This is a test of the claimant's subjective belief. However, Megarry J went on to add two further conditions to his test:

> Third, I think that the owner's belief under the two previous heads must be reasonable. Fourth, I think that the information must be judged in the light of the usage and practices of the particular industry or trade concerned.

The objective element of the test is embodied in these two conditions; but it remains possible under these conditions for a claimant to have a mistaken, but entirely reasonable belief, that the secret is confidential, when, on a fully objective test, a reasonable man would not do so. Carnwath J points out in *Lancashire Fires Ltd v SA Lyons and Co Ltd* (1996) that *Thomas Marshall (Exports) v Guinle* (1979) was specifically concerned with the construction of a particular provision in the Guinle's contract of employment with Thomas Marshall (Exports).

The first advantage of an objective test is that it can prevent over zealous attempts to protect the unprotectable. The British Government's attempts to prevent the publication of *Spycatcher*, when the book was freely available in Australia and the US, is a case in point: *Attorney General v Guardian Newspapers Ltd (No 2)* (1988). Secondly, an objective test allows the defendant to predict, or be advised, with some degree of accuracy, how far information received from another may be utilised. In *Lancashire Fires Ltd v SA Lyons and Co Ltd* (1996), the Court of Appeal followed an objective test of confidentiality. The plaintiff's belief was treated as a relevant consideration, but could not be decisive.

7.6 RESIDUAL CONFIDENTIALITY IN PUBLISHED INFORMATION

It might be thought that any confidence would automatically be destroyed where information is published to an extent beyond that in which any relative confidentiality might remain. However, it is necessary to examine the circumstances in which publications of information are treated as having reached the public domain, contrary to what we might have expected. There are three situations which require examination: publication of the information by its owner; publication by the defendant; and publication by a third party. In addition, it is necessary to examine the 'springboard' doctrine which continues to provide a measure of protection after confidential information reaches the public domain.

7.6.1   Publication by the owner

Where information is published by its owner, the confidentiality, as one would expect, is destroyed. Thus, in *Mustad v Allcock and Dosen* (1928), the House of Lords held that the fact of the plaintiff's patent application, after disclosure by the defendant, prevented any grant of an injunction. Lord Buckmaster said: 'The secret, as a secret, had ceased to exist.'

7.6.2   Publication by the confidant

Publication by the defendant should have the same result: if the information has been too widely distributed for any confidentiality to remain on any objective view. The initial publication by the defendant will be a breach of any confidential obligation owed to the claimant. However, no future protection should lie for the information. This was the view, *obiter*, of Lord Goff in *Attorney General v Guardian Newspapers Ltd (No 2)* (1988).

However, to allow the defendant free further use of the information might appear to sanction the initial breach, or at least enable a cynical defendant to calculate that further use might make the initial breach worth paying for in damages in view of the ultimate profits to be made. Conversely, to restrain the defendant once other competitors become able to make free use of the (now published) information, would prejudice the defendant.

The Court of Appeal, in *Speed Seal Products v Paddington* (1986), refused to strike out a claim in these circumstances, holding that breach of confidence was arguable, citing *Cranleigh Precision Engineering v Bryant* (1964). Either this reinforces the relative nature of confidentiality or substitutes breach of confidence for a remedy against unfair competition. To adhere to Megarry J's three conditions in *Coco v AN Clark (Engineers) Ltd* (1969) would confine the test of confidentiality of information to the extent to which it has been disclosed to the public, and not to take into account the individual responsible for that disclosure. Although continuing confidentiality was considered arguable in *Speed Seal Products v Paddington* (1986), it was doubted whether any injunction could be obtained to restrain further breaches, leaving only a remedy in damages.

Rather than arguing that the information was confidential despite its publication, a better explanation for the continued protection in *Speed Seal Products v Paddington* (1986) would lie in the 'springboard doctrine'. The springboard doctrine continues to protect information released into the public domain against those who obtained the information in confidence where an advantage is still gained compared with those who secure the information from the public domain.

7.6.3 Publication by a third party

The third situation to be considered is that where information is published by a third party. To take a strict *Coco v AN Clark (Engineers) Ltd* (1969) approach, again, the information should no longer be capable of being treated as confidential. However, in the case of *Cranleigh Precision Engineering v Bryant* (1964), *Mustad v Allcock and Dosen* (1928) was distinguished. Bryant acted as Managing Director for the plaintiff, which manufactured swimming pools to Bryant's design. While so employed, Bryant discovered the existence of the 'Bischoff' patent, which covered features of his design. Accordingly, the plaintiff needed a licence. However, the defendant did not inform the plaintiff of this, but instead left its employ and set up a rival business, in the process purchasing the Bischoff patent. Cranleigh sought to restrain use of confidential information by an injunction. Roskill J distinguished *Mustad v Allcock and Dosen* (1928) because in that case the publication had been by the employer (the plaintiff), and went on to grant the injunction. This could be taken to suggest that, in these circumstances, the information remained confidential despite its publication in the patent.

However, this case can be interpreted in one of two ways: either that the information was still confidential; or that Bryant's breach was that he did not disclose the existence of the patent to his then employer which, as an employee, he had a duty to do. In addition, Roskill J said:

> Mustad's case was, as I have said, a case where the employer made the publication in question. In the present case, Bryant, as possessor of what I have held to be the plaintiff's confidential information, is seeking to free himself from his obligation of confidence, not because of what the plaintiffs have published, for they have published nothing, but because of what Bischoff published – a publication of which Bryant only became aware because of his contractual and confidential relationship with the plaintiffs.

The latter interpretation has the advantage of reconciling the *Coco v AN Clark (Engineers) Ltd* (1969) and *Saltman Engineering Co Ltd v Campbell Engineering Co Ltd* (1948) test of confidentiality of information with the injunction imposed on Bryant. Interestingly, it was the case of *Terrapin Ltd v Builders' Supply Co (Hayes) Ltd* (1960) which led Roskill J to his conclusion. In addition, *Terrapin Ltd v Builders' Supply Co (Hayes) Ltd* (1960) is the progenitor of the springboard doctrine. If *Cranleigh Precision Engineering v Bryant* (1964) can be explained in these terms, the decision in *Speed Seal Products v Paddington* (1986) can equally be interpreted as a 'springboard breach' by the former employee.

7.6.4 The springboard doctrine

Where the information has been published, protection can still be obtained through the springboard doctrine. At this point, the action for breach of confidence, while maintaining its origins in a breach of trust, departs from its boundaries within the confidential. It does so for the purpose of remedying acts of unfair competition by those abusing a formerly confidential relationship. In the process, information which is at least partially in the public domain receives protection.

The origins of the doctrine can be traced to *Terrapin Ltd v Builders' Supply Co (Hayes) Ltd* (1960). Roxburgh J said:

> As I understand it, the essence of this branch of the law, whatever the origin of it may be, is that a person who has obtained information in confidence is not allowed to use it as a springboard for activities detrimental to the person who made the confidential communication, and springboard it remains, even when all the features have been published or can be ascertained by actual inspection by any member of the public.

In Scotland the doctrine has also been applied by the Outer House in *Levin v Farmers' Supply Association of Scotland* (1973).

The 'springboard' that the defendant would otherwise have is a head start over other users who have obtained the information from the public source. The doctrine was applied in *Coco v AN Clark (Engineers) Ltd* (1969) and *Seager v Copydex (No 1)* (1967). In *Seager v Copydex (No 1)* (1967), Lord Denning MR held that there had been a breach of confidence. The plaintiff had invented and patented a carpet grip, and discussed with the defendant the possibility of Copydex marketing his invention. During these discussions, the plaintiff disclosed in confidence an idea for another grip and its characteristics. The negotiations came to nothing, but later the defendant produced a grip very like the alternative which Seager had disclosed, even, he said, using the name, 'Invisigrip', which he had suggested. Although much of the information divulged was public – the first grip was patented – Lord Denning found that some of the information was not public and, in the case of such 'mixed' information, the defendant should 'take special care to use only the material which is in the public domain ... He should not get a start over others by using the information which he received in confidence'.

However, if the springboard were to be eternal, the defendant would continue to be penalised long after legitimate competitors had entered the market. There is an inconsistency between the doctrine that information which is in the public domain cannot be confidential and the springboard doctrine. This raises the question of how long the springboard lasts. Lord Denning faced this question in *Potters-Ballotini v Weston-Baker* (1977). The defendants were former employees of the plaintiff, who, while working out their notice, had formed a rival company along with an employee of the firm which had installed the plaintiff's furnace. This meant that they were ready for production almost before the plaintiff became aware of their activities. Lord Denning said:

> Although a man must not use such information as a springboard to get a start over others, nevertheless that springboard does not last for ever. If he does use it, a time may come when so much has happened that he can no longer be restrained.

Covenants in the employees' contracts of employment prevented the use of confidential information after the end of the employment for a year. The case was heard by the Court of Appeal shortly before the end of that year. In those circumstances, Lord Denning refused to grant an injunction. It would seem that the springboard lasts until other competitors, obtaining the information from the public domain, would be in a position to compete with the claimant.

A further question hangs over the springboard doctrine: that of the appropriate remedy, given the public element to the information involved. In *Coco v AN Clark (Engineers) Ltd* (1969), Megarry J expressed his doubts as to what was to be expected of the conscientious holder of springboard information. Taking a hypothetical example of a recipient of partly public, partly private information to which had been added the recipient's own ideas, after the parties have parted company without any agreement, he said:

How is a conscientious recipient of [the] ideas to comply with the requirements that equity lays upon him? ... Communication thus imposes upon him a unique disability. He alone of all men must for an uncertain time abjure this field of endeavour, however great his interest ... The relevance of the point, I think, is this. If the duty is a duty not to use the information without consent, then it may be the proper subject of an injunction restraining its use, even if there is an offer to pay a reasonable sum for that use. If, on the other hand, the duty is merely a duty not to use the information without paying a reasonable sum for it, then no such injunction should be granted ... However, I do feel considerable hesitation in expressing a doctrine of equity in terms that include a duty which law abiding citizens cannot reasonably be expected to perform. In other words, the essence of the duty seems more likely to be that of not using without paying, rather than of not using at all.

This was also the view of Lord Denning MR in *Seager v Copydex (No 1)* (1967). In a subsequent case, however, an injunction was granted: *Roger Bullivant v Ellis* (1987). The injunction was granted to last the length of the springboard advantage, again using the defendant's contract of employment as a guide to that period of advantage. The injunction was carefully worded on appeal to allow the defendant to continue his business, while restraining use of confidential information:

The present case is one where the date upon which it is clear that the advantage gained by the springboard will cease cannot precisely be fixed. On a view wholly favourable to the defendants it might be said that the period expired when Mr Ellis had drawn up his own car index as mentioned in paragraph 16 of his second affidavit. However he had no means of knowing whether it was as complete as the plaintiff's card index and I am certainly not prepared to assume that it was. On the other hand, the plaintiffs' business is not one in which there is a vast number of competitors and I think that it would be right to assume that if Mr Ellis had acted lawfully and gained his customers either by approaching those whom he knew without using the card index, or as a result of general circulars and advertisements in the trade press, it would not have been a very long period of time before it would have been well-known in the trade that he and the other defendants were in business on their own account. There is also the significant feature that under clause 14 of the standard contract the plaintiffs would have been unable to achieve a period of restraint longer than one year after the termination of Mr Ellis's employment. That period expired on 20th February 1986. That is a clear indication of the period which the plaintiffs themselves regarded as reasonable for the purposes of clause 14. It is difficult to see how they can reasonably expect, or how the law can reasonably allow, a longer period in regard to an injunction whose effect is very much the same.

In circumstances where claimant and defendant remain the only two competitors using the confidential information, as in *Speed Seal Products v Paddington* (1986), an injunction would appear to be justified in order to prevent the defendant benefiting from the breach.

7.7   THE OBLIGATION OF CONFIDENCE

The action for breach of confidence protects the transfer, or flow, of information. Without such protection, the temptation for the information's 'owner' would be to keep the information secret, thereby depriving the public of its usefulness. No duty to maintain the confidentiality of a piece of information which is to be transferred can come into being unless an obligation to do so arises between the person confiding the information and the recipient of that information.

In *Coco v AN Clark (Engineers) Ltd* (1969), Megarry J stated the need for an obligation thus:

> The second requirement is that the information must have been communicated in circumstances importing an obligation of confidence. However secret and confidential the information, there can be no binding obligation of confidence if that information is blurted out in public or is communicated in other circumstances which negative any duty of holding it confidential ... It seems to me that, if the circumstances are such that any reasonable man standing in the shoes of the recipient of the information would have realised that upon reasonable grounds the information was being given to him in confidence, then this should suffice to impose upon him the equitable obligation of confidence.

It is the circumstances in which information is imparted that create such an obligation, including the nature of the relationship between 'confider' and 'confidant'. Necessary conditions appear then to be, at least, both the privacy of the circumstances of communication and the fact of a transferring of information, such that the recipient is aware of its confidentiality.

Information may be imparted directly or indirectly. However, information can also be transferred by being 'taken' from its owner by the recipient. This raises the question of whether any obligation can arise in these circumstances. It is not clear whether it is essential that the communication must be from owner to recipient, rather than a taking by recipient from owner. Any answer must depend on the source of the obligation, whether it is the good faith of the parties concerned, as might be expected from an equitable remedy, or the type of relationship concerned or, perhaps, merely the recipient's knowledge that the information is confidential. We shall examine each of these circumstances, direct, indirect and 'stolen' impartations of information, in turn.

If liability is based on an obligation, the action for breach of confidence is not conferring a proprietary right in information, in contrast to the property right in goodwill conferred by the common law tort of passing off (see 14.4). Owners of land have a remedy against unauthorised invasions of their property regardless of any relationship with the invader. Although Megarry J refers to the 'owner' of confidential information in *Coco v AN Clark (Engineers) Ltd* (1969), this is not ownership in the true sense.

7.8   THE DIRECT RECIPIENT – EXPRESS OBLIGATIONS

Where the information is transferred by owner to recipient, an obligation may be created expressly, or it may be inferred from the circumstances. An obligation can even be imposed after the communication of the protectable information if it remains unpublished and the confidant is notified: *Surface Technology plc v Young* (2001).

Express obligations of confidence are often created by contract. This has the advantage of providing the parties with the opportunity to define the information which to be protected precisely, as well as the uses the recipient may make of it. Such a contractual obligation will also act as a warning to the recipient against any potential breach. Contractual agreements may also determine the boundaries of the obligation being imposed. It would be prudent to provide that the obligation should not arise if the information was known to the recipient prior to the disclosure, and that it should cease if the information falls into the public domain otherwise than by the recipient's breach, or if it were to be acquired by him from a third party who was not bound by obligations of confidence to the discloser. Both the restraint of trade doctrine (see 7.8.5) and the public interest defence (see 7.13) will impose limits on express contractual obligations. Nor will a contract prevent any applicable equitable obligations additionally being imposed: *Saltman Engineering Co Ltd v Campbell Engineering Co Ltd* (1948).

Contracts can also negate any obligation, in circumstances where it might otherwise arise. In *Fraser v Evans* (1969), the plaintiff was commissioned to write a report for the Greek military government. The contract expressly imposed a duty of confidentiality on the plaintiff, but provided for no reciprocal confidentiality on the other party. Restrictive covenants against competition with the employer, which may include prohibition against the disclosure or use of confidential information, by an employee on leaving employment, are common in contracts of employment, although subject to the contractual doctrine of contracts in restraint of trade. Express obligations can also be laid down in letters. However, an express obligation need not be written; it may be informal.

7.8.1 The direct recipient – implied obligations

Implied obligations arise if the circumstances of communication warrant such an implication, based on the understanding of a reasonable man as envisaged in Megarry J's test of obligation in *Coco v AN Clark (Engineers) Ltd* (1969).

This appears to be an objective test of acceptance of obligation, based on knowledge of the relevant circumstances. However, if the action for breach of confidence is based on good faith, a subjective test of acceptance of obligation might have been expected. Jacob J queried the objective test in *Carflow Products (UK) Ltd v Linwood Securities (Birmingham) Ltd* (1996) because 'equity looks at the conscience of the individual', and preferred the subjective view. The plaintiff had showed a prototype for a car steering lock to a company buyer without any express obligations of confidence, knowing that the buyers were apt to leave samples in their offices on view to all comers. On the facts, Jacob J held that no obligation of confidence arose, whether an objective or a subjective test were to be applied. It may be that, in most cases, the result of either test would be the same, particularly if the appropriate objective test is of the reasonable individual invested with any special characteristics of the parties. The difficulty posed by a subjective test lies in showing evidence of the parties' intentions. As Jacob J himself used an objective test in *Mars UK Ltd v Teknowledge Ltd* (1999) it is not clear which is the correct test to apply. This case also appears to suggest that it is both the circumstances of communication and the relationship of confidant and confider which must be taken in to account in determining the existence of an implied obligation of confidence, so that mere knowledge of the information's secrecy is insufficient.

All the circumstances of communication are taken into account in determining whether an obligation arises. The relationship of the parties is relevant, because some relationships are recognised as inherently giving rise to a duty to maintain confidentiality. This is so for fiduciary relationships, such as that of partner to partner, trustee to beneficiary, agent to principal; it is also so for other common relationships, such as marriage (as in *Duchess of Argyll v Duke of Argyll* (1967)), employment and commercial negotiations. In the *Argyll* case Ungoed-Thomas J recognised that the list of confidential relationships is not closed.

The circumstances in which negotiations take place may be significant, as in *Coco v AN Clark (Engineers) Ltd* (1969) itself; Megarry J said:

In particular, where information of commercial or industrial value is given on a business like basis and with some avowed common object in mind, such as a joint venture or the manufacture of articles by one party for the other, I would regard the recipient as carrying a heavy burden if he seeks to repel a contention that he was bound by an obligation of confidence: see the *Saltman* case at 216.

Jacob J distinguished this case in *Carflow Products (UK) Ltd v Linwood Securities (Birmingham) Ltd* (1996), on the basis that another significant circumstance to be taken into account was the reasonable man's knowledge that the law provided alternative means of protecting a prototype through design law. It would seem that Jacob J was taking the understanding of the reasonable designer, rather than the reasonable man in the street, who may know little or nothing of intellectual property or, more specifically, design protection. The relationship between the plaintiff and the buyer to whom the prototype had been shown also differed from that between the parties in *Coco v AN Clark (Engineers) Ltd* (1969) in that it was a one-off meeting between designer and buyer, whereas the plaintiff and the defendant had built up a relationship over several months of (eventually fruitless) negotiations in *Coco v AN Clark (Engineers) Ltd* (1969).

The test of implied obligation propounded by Megarry J has the potential to cause difficulties to companies which are sent unsolicited information. To use the information could be regarded as acceptance of obligation, if the circumstances otherwise were sufficient to suggest that the information had been sent in confidence. However, the recipient may have already been in possession of the information, or may receive it later, from another source, and possibly at a lower price. In fact, an unscrupulous communicant could 'plant' information on an unwilling recipient, purely in order to prevent that recipient making use of the information in order to preserve a competitive advantage. In addition, the dangers to the unwilling recipient could be exaggerated by the finding in *Seager v Copydex Ltd (No 1)* (1967) that unconscious use was a breach.

The problem of unsolicited information being received was considered by the Law Commission.[7] Evidence to the Law Commission showed that some companies were taking elaborate precautions to ensure that no obligation arose in such circumstances. It recommended that an obligation should only come into existence if there had been an express representation of confidence, or if one could be inferred from the relationship or conduct of the parties. Given that the statutory tort of breach of confidence recommended by the Law Commission has not been enacted, it remains prudent to take precautions, such as adopting 'clean room' tactics for the opening of mail, by individuals kept entirely separate from design teams or by requiring the sender to sign a document repudiating any obligation of confidence.

7.8.2 The direct obligation – employees

The employment relationship may carry both express and implied obligations. However, the interests of employer and employee may conflict. As well as the employer's private interest in maintaining confidentiality, there is a public interest in the freedom of movement of labour, and of competition. One obvious way of reconciling these conflicts of interest is to distinguish between the serving employee and an ex-employee, as the balance of interests shift when employment ends. An

---

7   *Breach of Confidence*, Cmnd 8388 (1981).

employee may have express obligations of fidelity, and confidentiality, to the employer. Such obligations will also be implied into the contract of employment.

The principles to be employed in relation to an employee were set out by Neill LJ in *Faccenda Chicken v Fowler* (1986):

(1)   Where the parties are, or have been, linked by a contract of employment, the obligations of the employee are to be determined by the contract between him and his employer (see *Vokes v Heather* (1979)).

(2)   In the absence of any express term, the obligations of the employee in respect of the use and disclosure of information are the subject of implied terms.

(3)   While the employee remains in the employment of the employer, the obligations are included in the implied term which imposes a duty of good faith or fidelity on the employee. For the purpose of the present appeal, it is not necessary to consider the precise limits of this implied term, but it may be noted:

(a)   that the extent of the duty of good faith will vary according to the nature of the contract (see *Vokes v Heather* (1979)); that the duty of good faith will be broken if an employee makes or copies a list of the customers of the employer for use after his employment ends or deliberately memorises such a list, even though, except in special circumstances, there is no general restriction on an ex-employee canvassing or doing business with customers of his former employer (see *Robb v Green* (1895) and *Wessex Dairies Ltd v Smith* (1935)).

The duty of fidelity involves the protection of trade or commercial secrets, but also involves a duty not to compete with the employer: *Hivac Ltd v Park Royal Scientific Instruments Ltd* (1946). This does not preclude the taking of preliminary steps for starting a competitive business, but the dividing line between legitimate preparation and actual competitive activity is crossed if an employee's activity creates a conflict of interest between the employee's own interests and his duties as an employee: *Lancashire Fires Ltd v SA Lyons and Company Ltd* (1996).

The duty of confidentiality extends to both information expressly indicated to be confidential to the employee or that satisfying the general test of confidentiality (see 7.5).

7.8.3   The direct recipient – ex-employees

An ex-employee is differently constrained. He may be restrained in one of two ways: either by an express restrictive covenant contained in his contract of employment, or by a continuing duty of confidence which outlasts the employment relationship. These restraints differ in their scope, related to the second two categories of information identified at first instance by Goulding J in *Faccenda Chicken v Fowler* (1986). ('Tittle tattle' was discussed at 7.4.) The second category ('type 2 information') may be protected by a restrictive covenant, but falls outside the continuing implied post-employment duty of confidence:

Information which the servant must treat as confidential (either because he is expressly told it is confidential, or because from its character it obviously is so) but which once learned necessarily remains in the servant's head and becomes part of his own skill and knowledge applied in the course of his master's business. So long as the employment continues, he cannot otherwise use or disclose such information without infidelity and therefore breach of contract. However, when he is no longer in the same service, the law allows him to use his full skill and knowledge for his own benefit in competition with his former master; ... If an employer wants to protect information of this kind, he can do so by an express stipulation restraining the servant from competing with him (within reasonable limits of time and space) after the termination of his employment.

This allows the departing employee to make use of skills and knowledge gained during employment, allowing free movement of labour and transfer of skills. The third category ('type 3 information') remains subject, however, to both the implied duty of confidence and any express restrictive covenant, despite the end of the employment, and comprises:

Specific trade secrets so confidential that, even though they may necessarily have been learned by heart, and even though the servant may have left the service, they cannot be lawfully used for anyone's benefit but the master's. An example is the secret process which was the subject matter of *Amber Sise and Chemical Company Ltd v Menzel* (1913).

This is information so sensitive to the employer that his private interest in protection outweighs the need for freedom of movement of labour, and use of which by a competitor would amount to unfair competition.

7.8.4 Continued confidence

The courts have been challenged, however, by the need to draw this distinction between skills and knowledge acquired during employment, which an employee must be free to continue to use, and specific information which may remain protected on the former employer's behalf posed by type 3 information. That the information remaining protected after the employment ends is more restricted than that protected during it is clear from *Printers and Finishers v Holloway* (1965) and *Faccenda Chicken v Fowler* (1986):

The implied term which imposes an obligation on the employee as to his conduct after the determination of the employment is more restricted in its scope than that which imposes a general duty of good faith. It is clear that the obligation not to use or disclose information may cover secret processes of manufacture such as chemical formulae (see *Amber Sise and Chemical Co Ltd v Menzel* (1913)), or designs or special methods of construction (see *Reid and Sigrist Ltd v Moss and Mechanism Ltd* (1932)), and other information which is of a sufficiently high degree of confidentiality as to amount to a trade secret.

The obligation does not extend, however, to cover all information which is given to or acquired by the employee while in his employment and, in particular, may not cover information which is only 'confidential' in the sense that an unauthorised disclosure of such information to a third party while the employment subsisted would be a clear breach of the duty of good faith.

In the absence of a line expressly drawn by the contact of employment, two approaches to distinguish information protected during employment, and that remaining to be within protection when the employment ends, have offered themselves as an appropriate test. The court can either define which particular types of information which could be obtained by an employee during employment fall into the more restricted post-employment category of confidential information; or it can lay down a general test of discretion to use according to the circumstances.

Earlier cases adopt the second of these approaches, distinguishing between information which is 'separable' from the ex-employee's knowledge and skill, and that which has merged with those skills gained during the employment. This allows the court to take into account the position held by the employee, the efforts to preserve secrecy made by the employer, and other relevant circumstances. In *Printers and Finishers v Holloway* (1965), Cross J adopted a reasonable man test so that if 'a man of ordinary honesty and intelligence would recognise [information] to be the property of his old employer' the information would remain confidential. Any other information could continue to be protected by a restrictive covenant in the contract of employment. In *Potters-Ballotini v Weston-Baker* (1977), the Court of Appeal equated the judgment to be made with the test applied to the legitimacy of restrictive covenants; protection reasonably necessary to protect the employer against unfair competition.

The Court of Appeal apparently adopted the first approach in *Faccenda Chicken v Fowler* (1986), stating that post-employment confidentiality was restricted to 'trade secrets'. In *Printers and Finishers v Holloway* (1965), two areas of protection regarded as legitimate for the employer were trade secrets (in the sense of secret process or formulae) and commercial information relating to the employer's goodwill with customers. However, the phrase 'trade secret' had not been understood in any more defined sense than as information to be found in the employment and industrial context. However, in *Faccenda Chicken v Fowler* (1986), Neill LJ explained the category of 'trade secret' in terms that appeared to equate it with the patentable, saying:

(5) In order to determine whether any particular item of information falls within the implied term so as to prevent its use or disclosure by an employee after his employment has ceased, it is necessary to consider all the circumstances of the case. We are satisfied that the following matters are among those to which attention must be paid.

 (a) The nature of the employment. Thus, employment in a capacity where 'confidential' material is habitually handled may impose a high obligation of confidentiality because the employee can be expected to realise its sensitive nature to a greater extent than if he were employed in a capacity where such material reaches him only occasionally or incidentally.

 (b) The nature of the information itself. In our judgment, the information will only be protected if it can be properly be classed as a trade secret or as material which, while not properly to be described as a trade secret, is in all the circumstances of such a highly confidential nature as to require the same protection as a trade secret *eo nomine*. The restrictive covenant cases demonstrate that a covenant will not be upheld on the basis of the status of the information which might be disclosed by the former employee if he is not restrained unless it can be regarded as a trade secret or the equivalent of a trade secret: see, for example, *Herbert Morris Ltd v Saxelby* (1916) *per* Lord Parker and *Littlewoods Organisation Ltd v Harris* (1978) *per* Megaw LJ.

 It is clearly impossible to provide a list of matters which will qualify as trade secrets or their equivalent. Secret processes of manufacture provide obvious examples, but innumerable other pieces of information are capable of being trade secrets, though the secrecy of some information may only be short lived. In addition, the fact that the circulation of certain information is restricted to a limited number of individuals may throw light on the status of the information and its degree of confidentiality.

 (c) Whether the employer impressed on the employee the confidentiality of the information. Thus, though an employer cannot prevent the use or disclosure merely by telling the employee that certain information is confidential, the attitude of the employer towards the information provides evidence which may assist in determining whether or not the information can properly be regarded as a trade secret. It is to be observed that, in *E Worsley and Co Ltd v Cooper* (1939), Morton J attached significance to the fact that no warning had been given to the defendant that the 'source from which the paper came was to be treated as confidential'.

(d) Whether the relevant information can be easily isolated from other information which the employee is free to use or disclose. In *Printers and Finishers v Holloway* (1964), Cross J considered the protection which might be afforded to information which had been memorised by an ex-employee.

For our part, we would not regard the separability of the information in question as being conclusive, but the fact that the alleged 'confidential' information is part of a package and that the remainder of the package is not confidential is likely to throw light on whether the information in question is really a trade secret.

Staughton LJ emphasised in *Lansing Linde Ltd v Kerr* (1991) that information might be protected on this basis, although it may not 'ordinarily be called a trade secret'. Both *Faccenda Chicken* and *Lansing Linde* were followed in Scotland in *TSB Bank plc v Connell* (1997). *Faccenda Chicken v Fowler* (1986) may be criticised if protectable confidential information is confined to 'secret processes of manufacture' and their equivalent. Nor does the judgment meet the criticism that the separability test is not conducive to certainty, being dependent on a detailed assessment of all the circumstances, as the Court of Appeal itself admits the impossibility of listing all information capable of being regarded as a trade secret.

That the decision is one dependent on the facts can be seen in *Poly Lina Ltd v Finch* (1995), where *Faccenda Chicken v Fowler* (1986) was distinguished, on its facts, and the commercial information used by the defendants held to be 'trade secrets *eo nomine*'. To confirm this conclusion, Judge Phelan applied the reasonable man separability test from *Printers and Finishers v Holloway* (1964). In the event, the question that a court must ask was expounded by Sir Thomas Bingham MR in *Lancashire Fires Ltd v SA Lyons and Co Ltd* (1996) as being 'whether an ex-employee has illegitimately used the confidential information which forms part of the stock in trade of his former employer, or whether he has simply used his own professional expertise, gained in whole or in part during his former employment'. This can be said to combine the requirements of *Faccenda Chicken v Fowler* (1986) and *Printers and Finishers v Holloway* (1964).

One very relevant circumstance will be the express efforts made by an employer to emphasise the confidentiality of defined pieces of information. At first instance, in the *Lancashire Fires Ltd* case, Carnwath J had held that the information taken was not protected because the employer had not 'defined expressly those parts of his operations which he regard[ed] as entitled to protection, and instructed his employees accordingly'. The Court of Appeal took a more realistic view of the employers' need to define confidentiality expressly, holding that 'it would be unrealistic to expect a small and informal organisation to adopt the same business disciplines as a larger and more bureaucratic concern'. This will not apply, however, where a claim to confidential information is inflated and the employers might have protected themselves by covenant or other intellectual property protection; particularly where a junior employee is concerned: *AT Poeton (Gloucester Plating) Ltd v Horton* (2000). Other relevant factors, at least within the context of a restrictive covenant, include the extent of use of the information in the public domain and the damage likely to caused by its use and disclosure in competition with the employer: *FSS Travel v Johnson* (1997).

7.8.5 Restrictive covenants

In *Faccenda Chicken v Fowler* (1986) the Court of Appeal added a gloss to type 2 information. This may be criticised as a misunderstanding the field of operation of the restrictive covenant. Neill LJ suggested that a covenant is restricted to trade secret, type 3 information. However, if this were so, the ambit of the express obligation after employment through the restrictive covenant and the implied post-employment obligation, would be co-extensive. That this was not the case was observed by Scott J in *Balston v Headline Filters* (1987). In addition, Sir Thomas Bingham MR suggested *obiter* in *Lancashire Fires Ltd v SA Lyons and Co Ltd* (1996) that Goulding J's second category was consonant with Cross J's decision in *Printers and Finishers v Holloway* (1965), contrary to Neill LJ's view.

The point arose again in *FSS Travel v Johnson* (1997). Here the Court of Appeal may have provided the means of reconciling the two approaches to distinguishing unprotectable skill and knowledge from continuing trade secrets falling within the third category. They did so by providing that the covenant must only extend to trade secrets, but then applying a wide interpretation of the nature of a trade secret, following *Lansing Linde v Kerr* (1991). The *Faccenda* case is not cited in the judgment, and the *Printers and Finishers v Holloway* (1965) separability test was employed to determine the validity of the restrictive covenant at issue. However, there appears a clear, if implicit, reference to Neill LJ's judgment in the factors cited as relevant to this test.

7.9 THE INDIRECT RECIPIENT

Information may be imparted by the owner of confidential information, in circumstances importing an inference of confidentiality, which subsequently is further communicated to a third party: an indirect impartation from owner to recipient. Can an indirect recipient be subject to obligations of confidence? They may be subject to any breaches of copyright or passing off involved, but it might be expected that no obligation would arise where no direct relationship between owner and recipient is created by the communication of the information. If an obligation is found, this is significant in an analysis of the juridical basis of the action for breach of confidence.

An indirect recipient was found liable for breach of confidence both in *Prince Albert v Strange* (1849) and *Morison v Moat* (1851). In the latter case, a partner's son used a secret formula employed by the two partners. The secret had been transferred from one partner to the other on the condition that it would never be revealed to anyone, but was divulged to the partner recipient's son. It was held that the plaintiff had a right of action against the defendant because the secret had been divulged in breach both of contract and of faith.

To be a breach there must be a chain of impartation of the information from the original owner to the final recipient. However, to find an obligation in such circumstances suggests that it is not so much the act of imparting information in suitably confidential circumstances as the eventual recipient's knowledge that the information was confidential which is the source of the duty. Had the final recipient received the information from another source, either the information would be in the public domain, or the obligation be owed to another.

7.9.1 Good faith or property?

Liability based on knowledge of confidentiality, that knowledge being tested objectively, is consistent with an action founded on good faith. Lord Goff's *dictum* in *Attorney General v Guardian Newspapers (No 2)* (1992) focuses on the recipient's knowledge:

> I start with the broad principle [...] that a duty of confidence arises when confidential information comes to the knowledge of a person (the confidant) in circumstances where he has notice, or is held to have agreed, that the information is confidential, with the effect that it would be just in all the circumstances that he should be precluded from disclosing the information to others ...

He did, however, also state that he did not intend this principle 'to be definitive'. Certainly in Scotland the House of Lords based liability on the confidant's knowledge that information was received in confidence, in *Lord Advocate v Scotsman Publications Ltd* (1989).

If this is the case, a distinction should be made between an innocent breach, and the situation where the third party acts deliberately or negligently in breaching the confidence of which he or she is aware. To restrain an innocent breach would be to give a property right in the confidential information. It has been argued that *Seager v Copydex (No 1)* (1967) did do so (see 7.6.4). Liability has been imposed on third party recipients who were unaware of the confidentiality at the time the information was received, but only from the time at which that recipient became aware of the confidentiality. This tends to confirm that the obligation is an equitable one. Thus, in *Printers and Finishers Ltd v Holloway* (1965), an injunction was granted against the third party employers of the direct recipient of the confidential information, their employee, who had been shown around the plaintiff's plant. In *Stevenson Jordan and Harrison v MacDonald Evans* (1951), the defendant contracted with an employee of the plaintiff for a book written by that employee. One issue centred on the liability of the third party publishers. When the contract was made, the publishers were unaware that the book contained confidential information. Lloyd-Jacob J held that the wrong to be restrained was not the entry into the contract of publication, but the act of publishing, and that an innocent mind at the time of the contract could not overcome the consequences of full knowledge at or before the time of the publishing.

7.9.2 Potential limits to an indirect recipient's liability

In *Morison v Moat* (1851), Turner VC doubted whether any obligation would have been owed by a third party purchaser for value of the secret without notice of any obligation affecting it. However, as a mere volunteer, the defendant was liable. Such a defence would be consistent with the equitable nature of the action for breach of confidence. Professor Jones argued[8] that to base breach of confidence in equity would

---

8   Jones, G, 'Restitution of Benefits Obtained in Breach of Another's Confidence' (1970) 86 LQR 463.

provide a framework for resolving such questions. Equity would recognise a defence both for the *bona fide* purchaser for value without notice, and for a defendant who had irrevocably changed his position to his detriment before becoming aware of the confidence.

However, in *Stevenson Jordan and Harrison v MacDonald Evans* (1951), Lloyd-Jacob J did not recognise such a defence and the Court of Appeal left the point open.

The Supreme Court of New South Wales was not prepared to provide such a defence in *Wheatley v Bell* (1984). The plaintiff had developed a system of providing information about businesses in a defined suburban area. The system was marketed by granting franchises in each such area of a city. Bell learnt about the system as a potential franchisee in Perth, Western Australia. He exploited the idea for his own benefit in Sydney, New South Wales, marketing to franchisees in advance of the plaintiff's introduction of its scheme there. One issue for the court was whether the defendant's franchisees, who were the purchasers of the information, but did not know of its confidential nature at the time of purchase, were liable for breach of confidence. Helsham J considered whether injunctions should extend to the franchisees, but rejected the analogy to *bona fide* purchasers for value without notice. That was a device for adjusting competing claims to property rights in equity, he said, and inappropriate to breach of confidence where property rights were not at stake. Injunctions were granted against the franchisees. Liability was imposed on the indirect recipients because of their knowledge of the information's confidentiality. The position of the innocent indirect recipient remains unresolved. It could be argued that if the disclosure is to a wide circle of third party recipients that the information has reached the public domain, and that no liability could lie against the indirect recipients for that reason. On the facts, Helsham J rejected such an argument in *Wheatley v Bell* (1984).

The Law Commission considered the position of third party recipients acquiring confidential information for value in its report *Breach of Confidence*.[9] Its view was that, while this was a pertinent circumstance for the court to take into account, the court's discretion should not be fettered by a definite rule in favour of the *bona fide* purchaser for value without notice. The Commission did, however, suggest adopting a new discretionary remedy, an adjustment order. Had the suggestion been enacted, this would have enabled a court to do justice between the conflicting interests of two 'competing innocents'.

In the case of *Valeo Vision Société v Flexible Lamps* (1995) Aldous J found that an obligation arose, but distinguished between the remedies available against an indirect recipient. Valeo revealed details of a design for vehicle rear lights to a German manufacturer, which in turn disclosed them to the defendants, a competing manufacturer of lamps. Although the defendant was a *bona fide* purchaser of the drawings an obligation of confidence was held to arise. The *bona fide* purchaser for value rule was held to be too narrow where injunctive relief against further use or disclosure was being sought, and the injunction was granted. However, an action for damages would not lie where the conscience of the defendant was not affected.

---

9   *Breach of Confidence*, Cmnd 8388 (1981).

7.10   NO RELATIONSHIP

It also needs to be considered whether any obligation of confidence can arise when the defendant has improperly acquired, or 'stolen' the information from its owner. If liability is founded on a relationship created by the claimant communicating that information to the defendant, then it would be expected that no obligation would be created in such circumstances. However, indirect recipients of confidential information are liable, given that there has been a chain of communication from claimant to defendant, because of their knowledge of that information's confidential nature. In addition, the 'taker' of confidential information may well have equivalent knowledge if the circumstances of acquisition are such as to suggest to the reasonable man that the information is not intended for the public's eyes. There is also a form of communication, although in the reverse direction, as it were, by defendant from claimant, rather than from claimant to defendant. Accordingly, it is logical to impose liability for breach of confidence in such circumstances. It is also necessary. Both industrial espionage and media 'snooping' provide examples of situations where a remedy is apt. This is only exacerbated by the new technologies which allow for surreptitious access to confidential information.

Newly postulated protection for observed (private) information tested by the understanding of a 'reasonable person of ordinary sensibilities' (*A v B & B* (2002)) supports such an action. *Douglas v Hello! Ltd* (2000) was decided, in part, on the basis that the unauthorised photographs may have been taken by an intruder with whom no relationship of trust had been established and that in such circumstances the existence of a right of privacy (see 18.7) was material to the action. This case should not be interpreted to mean that no obligation would come into existence in analogous circumstances where the information at stake could not be described as personal. In the words of Lord Goff's *dictum* in the *Spycatcher* case:

> I realise that, in the vast majority of cases, in particular those concerned with trade secrets, the duty of confidence will arise from a transaction or relationship between the parties – often a contract, in which event the duty may arise by reason of either an express or implied term of that contract. It is in such cases as these that the expressions 'confider' and 'confidant' are perhaps most aptly employed. However, it is well settled that a duty of confidence may arise in equity independently of such cases; and I have expressed the circumstances in which the duty arises in broad terms, not merely to embrace those cases where a third party receives information from a person who is under a duty of confidence in respect of it, knowing that it has been disclosed by that person to him in breach of his duty of confidence, but also to include certain situations, beloved of law teachers – where an obviously confidential document is wafted by an electric fan out of a window into a crowded street, or where an obviously confidential document, such as a private diary, is dropped in a public place, and is then picked up by a passer-by. I also have in mind the situations where secrets of importance to national security come into the possession of members of the public ...

It is clear that in some circumstances a remedy has been provided against an abuser of confidential and personal information despite the absence of a relationship of confidence. However, UK case law has done so only to a limited extent leaving a gap in protection for unauthorised acquisition of secrets that any right of privacy would also leave untouched. Two notable 'gaps' in protection for confidential information have been identified: where it is overheard, or where it is stolen.

7.10.1 Information overheard

Where confidential information had been overheard by a third party when being communicated, Megarry J rejected the creation of an obligation of confidence. In *Malone v Metropolitan Police Commissioner* (1979), he held that the plaintiff could not protect information obtained by a lawful police 'tap' of his telephone. This decision can be defended to the extent that it is a decision that to communicate secrets over the telephone did not do so in circumstances which 'import an obligation of confidence' because the risks of being overheard were such that the reasonable man would not regard such communication as secure. The examples Megarry J used to illustrate his finding suggest that was what he intended. He went on to suggest that there would be just cause and excuse for such action by, or on behalf of, the police; in other words, use of the information, had there been any confidentiality, would have fallen within the public interest.

7.10.2 Unauthorised acquisition

It was unfortunate, however, that this decision stood in the way of importing an obligation where confidential information has been 'taken' without authority. Neither did it distinguish between inadvertent overhearing and deliberate eavesdropping. In *Francome v Mirror Newspapers* (1984), the Court of Appeal held that there was a serious issue to be tried, and granted an interlocutory injunction. Information was obtained by an illegal tapping of the plaintiff's telephone line and passed to the defendant. *Malone v Metropolitan Police Commissioner* (1979) was distinguished on the ground that it would be questionable whether the user of a telephone could reasonably be said to be taking the risk of being overheard by an illegal eavesdropper, rather than the ordinary 'accidents and imperfections of the telephone system itself'.

Unauthorised taking of confidential information may amount to trespass and other criminal offences. If the information is contained within an item of property, its unauthorised acquisition may amount to theft, for example. However, the appropriate remedies for these wrongs do not prevent subsequent use or disclosure of the information.

The Law Commission identified this gap in the action for breach of confidence as a 'glaring inadequacy'.[10] It proposed that an obligation of confidence should arise where information was improperly obtained in a number of specified circumstances.

In Australia, the courts found another solution to this problem, by treating confidential information as being tantamount to a piece of property. In *Franklin v Giddins* (1978), the plaintiff bred a new form of nectarine. The defendant stole a budwood cutting from the plaintiff's nectarine orchard, and developed an orchard in direct competition. Dunn J said:

> I find myself quite unable to accept that a thief who steals a trade secret, knowing it to be a trade secret, with the intention of using it in commercial competition with its owner, to the detriment of the latter, and so uses it, is less unconscionable than a traitorous servant. The thief is unconscionable because he plans to use and does use his own wrong conduct to better his position in competition with the owner, and so to

10   *Breach of Confidence*, Cmnd 8388 (1981).

place himself in a better position than that of a person who deals consensually with the owner.

He imposed a constructive trust, a proprietary remedy, on the defendant's trees and fruit, and granted an order for delivery up of the trust property. However, in Scots law and English criminal cases, confidential information has not been treated as property: *Grant v Allen* (1988), *Oxford v Moss* (1978). It was held that theft requires the misappropriation of another's property. However, to read an examination paper, although improperly obtained, did not amount to theft because there was no property in the information and the paper was not misappropriated.

In 1997, the Law Commission issued a Consultation Paper.[11] It proposed criminal sanctions for the use or disclosure of trade secrets belonging to another without that other's consent. 'Trade secret' would not take the restrictive meaning of *Faccenda Chicken v Fowler* (1986), but would comprise information not generally known whose owner had expressly or impliedly expressed a wish that it remain secret. A criminal remedy may act as a deterrent, and allow for the use of public authorities to detect and enforce the offence, although to extend the offence to the acquisition of trade secrets (as well as their use and disclosure) would go further towards preserving the secrecy of the information. However, the Law Commission has not proposed that the mere unauthorised acquisition of trade secrets should amount to an offence. The United States adopted the Economic Espionage Act in 1996. It provides monetary penalties and imprisonment if persons or companies knowingly steal or misappropriate a company's trade secrets incorporated in or related to a product made for domestic or foreign trade for economic benefit. This includes taking information from a computer.

Merely to construct a metaphorical 'fence' around information that otherwise has the 'necessary quality of confidence' in order to impose an obligation of confidentiality will not suffice: the use of encryption in *Mars UK Ltd v Teknowledge Ltd* (1999) did not do so. However, contractual and other security measures may impose confidential obligations. In an interlocutory hearing the security measures taken to protect the film set for the film 'Frankenstein' were found sufficient to raise a serious question to be tried for its producers against an unauthorised photographer in *Shelley Films v Rex Features* (1994). So, too, in *Douglas v Hello! Ltd* (2003) the security measures taken in a hotel were found to impose obligations of commercial confidence against an intruder. The House of Lords has also held 'Chinese walls' sufficient to prevent a threatened breach of confidentiality, provided they are found to be properly constructed: *Prince Bolkiah v KPMG* (1999). As there are specific provisions in relation to decompilation of computer programs in the CDPA 1988 (see 11.8) *Mars* may represent an exceptional situation, leaving room for an obligation to be constructed in different circumstances. The Law Commission specifically excluded reverse engineered information from its proposed definition of trade secrets. Where no relationship between the parties exists, it will remain a question of fact as to whether claimants have done enough to protect their confidentiality, in the absence of any general right to privacy. Contractual obligations, and the posting of notices sufficed in the *Shelley* and *Douglas* cases. However, these cases both relate to photographic images and may be confined to such circumstances if the security measures can be regarded as being analogous to a communication of the information from confider to confidant.

---

11 *Legislating the Criminal Code: Misuse of Trade Secrets*, Law Commission Consultation Paper No 150, 1997.

Article 39 of the TRIPS Agreement could lead to further change, containing a wide provision that persons who have confidential information legally within their control should be able to prevent its unauthorised disclosure, acquisition or use in a manner contrary to honest commercial practices.

The right to privacy embodied in the HRA 1998 provides the potential for further development of the action for confidence if there is to be protection for privacy when no direct nor indirect relationship exists between the parties. Jurisdiction for this could be found in the ECHR and HRA 1998, rather than any general right to confidentiality, but there appears little logic in continuing to refuse protection to information improperly obtained which is confidential, although not 'private', if such privacy is to be recognised. The courts' treatment of confidence in personal information (see 18.7) could have this effect.

7.10.3 Information as property

Bestowing information with some characteristics of property, as protection against unauthorised acquisition suggests, could lead to confidential information being regarded as falling within the ambit of the Convention right to respect for property. Consequently, an argument based on this right could succeed in preventing disclosure of such confidential information, particularly so in relation to 'know-how', which is already assigned and licensed in the nature of property.

7.11   BREACH

Megarry J's third condition for the action of breach of confidence in *Coco v AN Clark (Engineers) Ltd* (1969) requires 'an unauthorised use of the information to the detriment of the person communicating it'. Use will include disclosure of the information, but apparently not its unauthorised acquisition.

7.11.1 Establishing breach

It must first be shown that the defendant's information has come from the claimant and not been independently generated: *CMI-Centers v Phytopharm plc* (1999). Laddie J identified three ways in which a claimant can prove that a defendant has used their information:

> The first is to produce direct evidence of use, for example from an employee of the defendant who has seen the information being put into practice or by finding documents showing what the defendant has done.

> Secondly, it may be possible to prove use indirectly by demonstrating the existence of some significant fingerprint. For example the defendant's product may have dimensions, a design, composition or behaviour which is only to be found in the plaintiff's and which is consistent with the use of the information and inconsistent with use of non-contaminated sources. Similarly it may be possible to show that the defendant has gone to all the same suppliers and customers as the plaintiff and that it would be highly unlikely that the same group would have been approached had the defendant been working from uncontaminated sources.

Thirdly, it may be possible to persuade the court that the defendant could not have got to the position he has with the speed he has had he simply started from legitimate sources and worked everything out for himself. This last is particularly difficult. It depends on comparing how far the defendant has gone with an assessment of how long it would have taken him to reach that stage deploying the resources he has put into the endeavour without cutting corners. Whether the defendant's progress suggests misuse of confidential information therefore involves assessing (a) how far he has got, (b) how long it took him to get there, (c) what resources he put into the development and (d) the quality of the personnel he used for the development work.

7.11.2 The test for breach

Once the derivation of the defendant's information has been established, unauthorised use or disclosure needs to be made out. Where breach consists of use of confidential information, in general the proper test is one of use and not of similarity between claimant and defendant's work. The addition of other materials and modifications to the confidential information do not prevent a finding of use: *Inline Logistics Ltd v UCI Logistics Ltd* (2001), although they may be significant. It was also pointed out in this case that, confidence being an equitable remedy, trivial or inconsequential use will not suffice.

Megarry J's condition suggests any finding of an unauthorised use or disclosure, if to a material extent, should suffice to establish breach, based on an objective test of good faith to impose the obligation in the first place. The Court of Appeal appeared to adopt a further test of breach in *R v Department of Health ex p Source Informatics Ltd* (1999), one of unconscientious use. Simon Brown LJ asked:

> One asks, therefore, on the facts of this case: would a reasonable pharmacist's conscience be troubled by the proposed use to be made of the patients' prescriptions? Would he think that by entering Source's scheme he was breaking his customers' confidence, making unconscionable use of the information they provide?

This is objective good faith and appears to impose an unnecessary step in the determination of breach. If the obligation to preserve confidence has been expressly imposed by agreement or defined relationship (see 7.8) any breach will necessarily be unconscientious, at least in objective terms. If the obligation is implied by the reasonable man test, while a subjective good faith at the time of breach might serve to prevent a breach (see 7.8.1), any use or disclosure would surely meet this objective test.

The proposed extra hurdle derives from the Australian case of *Smith, Kline and French Laboratories v Department of Community Services and Health* (1991). This case centred, however, on the extent of any obligation to be inferred from the circumstances of disclosure when information is divulged by a confidant for limited purposes. Smith, Kline and French disclosed details of a drug to the Department in its application for permission to place the drug on the market. This information was later used by the Department in a third party's application. It was held that the scope of the Department's obligation was determined not by the subjective expectation of the pharmaceutical company in disclosing the information for one purpose alone, but by an objective test of the obligation good faith bestowed on them in the circumstances. The question then was what the Department ought to have known in relation to the disclosure. Several factors were considered relevant. These included whether the information had been disclosed gratuitously, whether past practice gave rise to an understanding as to the purpose of disclosure, the sensitivity of the information, and whether there had been any express warning as to particular disclosures or use.

Source Informatics centred on the same issue. In these circumstances of a limited obligation, delimited by how far objective good faith requires the confidant to maintain the confidence, a test of conscience may be appropriate. However, this is a matter of the scope of obligation, rather than of breach. Sedley LJ disapproved of the conscience test in *London Regional Transport v The Mayor of London* (2001).

7.11.3 Partial use of information

Questions may arise where only a part of the claimant's information has been taken. Partial use may infringe: *Amber Size and Chemical Co Ltd v Menzel* (1913). However, it may be that only 'thin' protection will be afforded to the claimant if the confidential information taken was not the subject of considerable effort. In *R v Department of Health ex p Source Informatics Ltd* (1999) the Court of Appeal approved Gurry's[12] conclusion that a confidant will remain liable for breach if he misuses only part of the confidential information disclosed to him, but only provided that this relates to a 'material part' of that information. Consequently, information that has taken little effort to generate may go unprotected, particularly if only a small proportion has been used. This was suggested in *De Maudsley v Palumbo* (1996). The defendant used only two of the five features for the proposed nightclub, information which was too 'vague' to be protected (see 7.4.4). Knox J also stated, *obiter*, that the extent of use by the defendant was insufficient to constitute unauthorised use 'because the club Ministry of Sound was, as it opened, a substantially different club principally in that it was primarily based on Paradise Garage rather than Mr de Maudsley's idea. There were very important features which formed no part of Mr de Maudsley's idea ...'.

The addition of other features to the information used should not be a conclusive factor in a finding that there was no breach following *R v Department of Health ex p Source Informatics Ltd* (1999). In *Ocular Sciences Ltd v Aspect Vision Care Ltd* (1997) the question whether the alteration of, or addition, to confidential information derived from the claimant amounted to a breach was found to be one of fact; 'a matter of degree whether the extent and importance of the use of the confidential information is such that continued exploitation of the derived matter should be viewed as continued use of the information'. Laddie J went on to suggest that any remedy in relation to the altered use on the facts of the case would not extend to injunctive relief. It may be, therefore, that altered use may also be significant to the appropriate remedy even if the changes are not sufficient to deny any breach at all.

7.11.4 Subconscious breach

There is no necessity for the breach to be either deliberate or conscious. In *Seager v Copydex (No 1)* (1967), the Court of Appeal held that the plaintiff was in breach of confidence despite acting honestly. The same was held by Harris J at first instance in the Australian case of *Talbot v General Television Corp Pty Ltd* (1981). However, this is not consistent with an action based on good faith, as the honest and innocent defendant has not broken good faith, although it is consistent with the imposition of liability

---

12 Gurry, F, *Breach of Confidence* (Oxford: Clarendon, 1984).

imposed on an indirect recipient who receives the information innocent of its confidentiality. In this latter circumstance, though, liability only lies from the time that the defendant becomes aware of the information's confidentiality. To make the entirely innocent defendant liable is to treat the information as property.

A different interpretation of *Seager v Copydex (No 1)* (1967) is that the defendants were aware of the confidential source of the information, but unaware that its use constituted a wrong. Lord Denning MR said:

> They were quite innocent of any intention to take advantage of him. They thought that, as long as they did not infringe his patent, they were exempt. In this they were in error. They were not aware of the law as to confidential information.

In addition, on appeal, in *Talbot v General Television Corp Pty Ltd* (1981), the court expressed reservations about the finding of subconscious copying, while upholding the decision. Murphy J preferred the inference from *Seager v Copydex (No 1)* (1967) that the defendant used the idea without realising the plaintiff's rights, rather than not realising that they were copying at all.

7.11.5 Detriment to the claimant

Although Megarry J stipulated that the breach should be to the detriment of the plaintiff in his three conditions, he himself did not preclude the conclusion that the detriment might be to an individual other than the plaintiff. He noted that, *prima facie*, a remedy based in equity should be founded on a detriment, but could envisage situations where the detriment might be incurred by a third party, such as a relative of the owner of the information. In *Stevens v Avery* (1988), the damage was to the reputation of the deceased subject of the information. Lord Keith considered this issue in *Attorney General v Guardian Newspapers (No 2)* (1988) and took the view that the relevance of detriment was to the remedy sought. Where damages were claimed, compensatory, damages (other than nominal damages) would be unlikely if no detriment had been suffered. If an injunction was sought, he felt that the definition of detriment ought to be wide enough to include invasions of privacy, and include accounting for any profit made by the defendant, or that no detriment should be required. Where the government was the plaintiff, the required detriment would be harm to the public interest.

7.11.6 Inducing breach of contract

Where confidential information has been communicated, but no use or disclosure made of it, the claimant may secure protection through the tort of inducing breach of contract. In *Hivac v Park Royal* (1946), five of the plaintiff company's skilled workers worked on Sundays for the defendant company. No confidential information had been disclosed or used, nor was such a breach of confidence threatened. However, the plaintiff feared that eventual use was inevitable. The employees could not be dismissed under wartime restrictions, and the plaintiff successfully sought interlocutory relief preventing the defendant procuring a breach of the employees' contracts of employment.

7.12 DEFENCES

There are a number of defences to allegations of breach of confidence: the confider may have expressly consented to the use of the information; a licence to use it may be implied; or the confidant may establish that the information was already known to him or in the public domain. In addition, however, confidentiality should not prevent publication of information of overriding public significance.

7.12.1 Licensed breach

Where confidential information is communicated within a contractual relationship it may be possible to imply a licence to use that information. In *Inline Logistics Ltd v UCI Logistics Ltd* (2001) the drawings prepared by Inline for the purposes of UCI's tender were used after their relationship had broken down. It was found that Inline knew and intended their drawings to be used in UCI's tender. Had the tender been accepted the work would have been done in accord with the drawings, and in the absence of a joint-venture this could have been an independent third party. Using the test of business efficacy the court implied a licence to use the drawings for the purpose of submitting the tender as it was unlikely that it could have been the parties common intention that Inline would be able to unilaterally object to their use and frustrate the tendering process. However, the fact that Inline had not prepared the modifications to the design required by UCI within the tender deadline, necessitating the involvement of other designers, was a significant feature of this finding.

7.13 PUBLIC INTEREST

If all information can be protected by a court, no matter what its content, there would be nothing to stop the unscrupulous preventing the use or disclosure of information that 'should' be available to the public for a variety of reasons by imposing obligations of confidence on those with access to it. The public interest therefore requires a limit to confidentiality in some circumstances. The development of the public interest as a reason for refusing to enforce confidentiality has been a long one. It is also a principle still in the course of development, having been given a new aspect by the enactment of the HRA 1998 and the application of the ECHR right to freedom of expression. It is clear that in some circumstances confidence may be breached in the 'public interest' but also that this is a concept of some fluidity, and one that may fluctuate with social change.

Where the public interest is relevant, it is necessary, first, to establish whether the information's disclosure can be regarded as being in the public interest. Then, secondly, whether the disclosure has been made to the appropriate recipient; and finally whether on balance with any other rights involved, the breach of confidence may be sanctioned. This may amount only to a refusal of a particular remedy, rather than an outright excusal of the breach.

7.13.1 Defence or lack of confidentiality?

It is not clear whether such an exception constitutes a defence to an action for breach of confidence, or whether such information is regarded as falling outside the category of information with the necessary quality of confidence. Refusing to protect information relating to an iniquity could be achieved in one of three ways: by removal from the category of information that can be protected by breach of confidence, by providing that such an obligation cannot arise, or by providing a defence to any allegation of breach. Page Wood VC's *dictum* in *Gartside v Outram* (1856) does not make clear which method is intended.

The difference lies in the burden of proof. If a defence, the obligation will lie on the defendant to make out the public interest. In *Commonwealth of Australia v Fairfax* (1980), the High Court of Australia held that the onus lay on the defendant, as did Lord Griffiths in *Attorney General v Guardian Newspapers Ltd (No 2)* (1988). However, if the information is not within the sphere of protection, the obligation will lie on the claimant to make out the lack of any public interest in the information, as is suggested by *Attorney General v Jonathan Cape* (1976). It has been suggested[13] that a willingness to regard public interest as a defence has grown with the recognition of breach of confidence as an equitably based remedy. The discretionary nature of equity enables the courts at once to recognise the existence of an obligation, while refusing to enforce it. Most recent cases have treated the public interest in the nature of a defence.

7.13.2 Information in the public interest

The first issue is to determine what information may be revealed despite its confidentiality. In *Gartside v Outram* (1856), Page Wood VC said:

> ... the true doctrine is that there is no confidence as to the disclosure of an iniquity. You cannot make me the confidant of a crime or a fraud ... such a confidence cannot exist.

'Iniquity' is not a concept well adapted to definition, and is one that appears to be based on perceptions which might fluctuate with public mores: Salmon LJ pointed out in *Initial Services Ltd v Putterill* (1967) that opinions change on matters of public policy. Subsequent case law defined 'iniquity' as information about a crime, a tort or other legal wrong; so that, in *Hubbard v Vosper* (1972), Megaw LJ held that books which indicated medical quackeries of a sort which might be dangerous if practised behind closed doors were 'so dangerous' that it was in the public interest that they be made known. Ungoed-Thomas J defined iniquity to mean 'misdeeds of a serious nature and importance to the country' in *Beloff v Pressdram* (1973).

7.13.3 'Just cause and excuse'

Lord Denning MR took a wider view. He held, in *Fraser v Evans* (1969), that wherever there was any 'just cause and excuse' for breaking confidence no confidence should lie, and said, in *Initial Services Ltd v Putterill* (1967):

> [Counsel] suggested that this exception was confined to cases where the master has been 'guilty of a crime or a fraud'. However, I do not think that it is so limited. It extends to any misconduct of such a nature that it ought to be in the public interest to be disclosed to others ... The exception should extend to crimes, frauds and misdeeds,

---

13   Cripps, Y, *The Legal Implications of Disclosure in the Public Interest: An Analysis of Prohibitions and Protections with Particular Reference to Employers and Employees* (London: Sweet & Maxwell, 1994).

both those actually committed as well as those in contemplation, provided always – and this is essential - that the disclosure is justified in the public interest. The reason is because 'no private obligations can dispense with that universal one which lies on every member of the society to discover every design which may be formed, contrary to the laws of the society, to destroy the public welfare': see *Annesley v Anglesea (Earl)* (1743).

This shifts the focus of concern from the nature of the information to the justification for revealing it to the public, and is more in line with the argument that public interest constitutes a defence. 'Just cause and excuse' for disclosure in the public interest has now received the sanction of other members of the Court of Appeal and of the House of Lords in *British Steel Corporation v Granada Television* (1981) and *Attorney General v Guardian Newspapers Ltd (No 2)* (1988).

The clearest example of a disclosure made in the public interest which would not also fall within the traditional parameters of 'iniquity' as a crime, fraud or misdeed is the case of *Woodward v Hutchins* (1977). Tom Jones, and other pop stars, sought unsuccessfully to prevent their former manager, Hutchins, revealing their discreditable antics observed during the course of his employment. It was the hypocrisy of the plaintiffs' attempt to preserve a carefully nurtured, but untrue, image that justified disclosure. With the introduction of a right of privacy, this approach is one that has become particularly significant when celebrities seek to rely on privacy while actively promoting a public persona, particularly one which is false (see 18.8.2).

7.13.4 Disclosure to the right recipient

There are limits to publication in the public interest. The second principle applied by the courts in determining whether there is an excuse for breach is that the disclosure should only extend to a proper recipient for the information. That the information is in the public interest will not necessarily permit publication to all the world through the press, if a more limited disclosure to a responsible authority able to tackle the problem is possible. Thus, in *Cork v McVicar* (1984), an injunction was varied to allow disclosures about alleged miscarriages of justice and corrupt police practices in *The Daily Express* because the press is a major exposer of corruption. Equally, disclosures in the press relating to the breathalyser were sanctioned in *Lion Laboratories Ltd v Evans* (1984); but, in *Francome v Mirror Group* (1984), disclosures of breaches of Jockey Club rules were confined to the Jockey Club and not the general press. Lord Goff said the same of breaches of public security in *Attorney General v Guardian Newspapers Ltd (No 2)* (1988), where extensive alternative controls and channels for complaint existed through the Director General of MI5, the Security Commission and the provisions of the Interception of Communications Act 1985.

7.13.5 Balancing public interest against the interest in confidentiality

The third consideration in making out an excuse for the breach is that of any other rights or interests at stake. Focusing on the justification for disclosure requires courts to balance several conflicting public interests, including the public interest in preserving confidence, and to reconcile these interests to decide whether confidence or disclosure should prevail. It was, again, Lord Denning MR who articulated this balancing function of the court, in *Initial Services Ltd v Putterill* (1967). It allows the court to take every circumstance into consideration, and seek to do justice in every case, as might be expected of an action rooted in equity. This balancing function gives the courts a discretion which was described by Lord Griffiths in *Attorney General v Guardian Newspapers Ltd (No 2)* (1988):

> This involves the judge in balancing the public interest in upholding the right to confidence, which is based on the moral principles of loyalty and fair dealing, against some other public interest that will be served by the publication of the confidential material ... Judges are used to carrying out this type of balancing exercise and I doubt if it is wise to try to formulate rules to guide the use of this discretion that will have to be exercised in widely differing and as yet unforeseen circumstances.

Examples of other public interests taken into account in breach of confidence cases include:

(i) the public interest in the freedom of the press to publish information concerning matters of real public concern in *Lion Laboratories Ltd v Evans* (1984) (inaccuracy in breathalyser readings);

(ii) the public interest in the administration of justice in *British Steel Corporation v Granada Television Ltd* (1981) (disclosure of the source of leaked secret documents);

(iii) the public interest in knowing the truth behind a public image in *Woodward v Hutchins* (1977).

These interests must now be supplemented with the right to freedom of expression embodied in Article 10 ECHR (discussed more fully at 18.8).

Despite the fears of Gummow J that this discretion is an invitation to 'judicial idiosyncrasy' as suggested in *Smith Kline and French Laboratories (Australia) Ltd v Secretary to the Department of Community Services and Health* (1990):

> ...(i) an examination of the recent English decisions shows that the so called 'public interest' defence is not so much a rule of law as an invitation to judicial idiosyncrasy by deciding each case on an ad hoc basis as to whether, on the facts overall, it is better to respect or to override the obligation of confidence, and (ii) equitable principles are best developed by reference to what conscionable behaviour demands of the defendant, not by 'balancing' and then overriding those demands by reference to matters of social or political opinion ...

in *London Regional Transport v The Mayor of London* (2001) the Court of Appeal was anxious to stress that, although the balancing exercise is a matter of discretion for the judge, it is a discretion to be exercised according to 'well-settled' principles. The same approach is required by section 12(3) HRA 1998 (see 18.8.2). At the same time, the judge disapproved the conscience test posed by the *Source Informatics* case.

In *British Steel Corporation v Granada Television Ltd* (1981), Lord Wilberforce pointed out that a public interest in the truth must not be confused with what the public is interested in knowing. In addition, where the public interest can be served without a breach of confidence, the confidence will prevail. In *Schering Chemicals v Falkman* (1982), the majority of the Court of Appeal affirmed the injunction granted at first instance because an injunction would not interfere with the freedom of the press to inform the public by obtaining the necessary information about the Primodos drug from a public source.

7.14 REMEDIES

The usual intellectual property remedies apply also to an action for breach of confidence. Equity has no difficulty providing the equitable remedies of injunction, account of profits, and an order for delivery up. An interdict may be granted in Scotland. A further suggestion has been the imposition of a constructive trust, based on a proprietary interest in confidential information.

7.14.1 Account of profits

Where the confidential obligation is equitable, rather than contractual, an account may be ordered, based on the principle that no one should profit from his wrongdoing: *Spycatcher* (1990). In *Peter Pan Manufacturing v Corsets Silhouette* (1963) Pennycuick J awarded the plaintiff the whole of the defendant's profit on the product, made using confidential information belonging to the plaintiff. The defendant had argued, unsuccessfully, that only the profit attributable to the confidential information should be awarded.

There were unusual circumstances in *Attorney General v Blake* (2000) which extended account to a breach of a contractual obligation of confidence. Blake is a convicted double-agent, living in Moscow. He wrote a book for which he was to be paid a substantial amount by the publisher. This was in breach of his obligations as a former member of the Secret Intelligence Service under the Official Secrets Act 1989. The House of Lords held that an injunction could not be granted, but that in such an exceptional case, where the normal remedies are inadequate, and if justice demanded, the court could exercise its discretion to require the defendant to account for the benefits received from the breach. This was so even though the information was no longer confidential and there was no public interest in restraining publication.

7.14.2 Injunction

An injunction, particularly an interlocutory injunction, is attractive to a claimant anxious to prevent threatened disclosure of confidential information, as the only means of preserving the value of the information. The jurisdiction to grant injunctions in support of equitable rights, including confidence, was discussed in *Venables and Thompson v News Group Newspapers Ltd* (2001), and is one which may extend to new categories of injunction where justice demands, limited only by statutory restrictions.

However, there are three factors that may affect the grant of an injunction. These are where disclosure has taken place and the information published ('springboard' disclosures), disclosures where the public interest is concerned and the Human Rights Act 1998.

In the first instance, doubts were expressed about the appropriateness of an injunction in 'springboard' breaches of confidence in *Coco v AN Clark (Engineers) Ltd* (1969), as we have seen (see 7.6.4). Only damages were awarded in *Seager v Copydex (No 1)* (1967), but an injunction, although of limited duration, was discussed in *Roger Bullivant Ltd v Ellis* (1987). In *Attorney General v Guardian* (1990) Lord Goff took the view (*obiter*) that once information is published an injunction cannot be awarded, and this was applied in *Ocular Sciences Ltd v Aspect Vision Care Ltd* (1997).

Secondly, pleading public interest may have a bearing on the remedy available for a breach. Where disclosure in the public interest is pleaded, an injunction may be refused. In defamation, an injunction will not be granted where the defendant pleads justification; in copyright, a defence of public interest may amount only to a refusal of an injunction (rather than a defence to any infringement at all). In *Woodward v Hutchins* (1977), the interlocutory injunction against publication granted at first instance was discharged by the Court of Appeal for the breach of confidence. The plaintiffs had issued a writ for libel against the defendant, and the defendant proposed to plead justification. In these circumstances, an injunction for breach of confidence would have frustrated the principle applied in cases of defamation. However, no general principle was established for other cases of disclosure in the public interest, or breach of confidence generally.

Thirdly, courts, being public authorities must act compatibly with the ECHR (s 6 of the HRA 1998). Accordingly, any injunction against a threatened breach confidence must be balanced against the right to freedom of expression (see 18.8). In interlocutory proceedings, s 12(3) of the HRA 1998 further provides that in such circumstances 'no such relief is to be granted so as to restrain publication before trial unless the court is satisfied that the applicant is likely to establish that publication should not be allowed'. Consequently, the court must consider the merits of the case. This is because the balance of convenience test (see 19.9.1) is likely to favour restraint in order to preserve the confidence until the trial. Hence the Court of Appeal refused an injunction in *Douglas v Hello!* (2000). Keene LJ stated that the test was on of the case's merits. The merits include both the risk of breach, the nature of that risk, and the consequences of the breach. It remains discretionary for the court but one where these factors must be considered:

> ... the court has to look ahead to the ultimate stage and to be satisfied that the scales are likely to come down in the applicant's favour ... it is merely requiring the court to apply its mind to how one right is to be balanced, on the merits against another right, without building in additional weight on one side. In a situation ... where the non-Article 10 right is of fundamental importance to the individual, such as the Article 2 right to life, the merits will include not merely the evidence about how great is the risk of that right being breached, but also a consideration of the gravity of the consequences for an applicant if the risk materialises. The nature of the risk is part of the merits, just as it would be at trial when the balance had to be struck. That is as relevant at the interlocutory stage as it would be at trial ...

> Certainly section 12(3) is making prior restraint (ie before trial) more difficult in cases where the right to freedom of expression is engaged than where it is not ...

Consequently, the test to be applied at this stage is whether this court is satisfied that the applicant is likely to establish at trial that publication should not be allowed. Even then, the court retains a discretion. 'Likely' was stated to bear the natural and obvious meaning of 'more probable than not' in *Cream Holdings Ltd v Banerjee* (2003).

If an interlocutory injunction is refused, it may be that a final injunction will also be refused at trial and damages awarded, as the information has already been disclosed: *Campbell v Frisbee* (2002), *A v B & C* (2002). However, in *Douglas v Hello!* (2003) an injunction (or undertaking in lieu) was ordered against future publication, the confidence outweighing any freedom of expression, given the breach of the PCC Code by the surreptitious taking of the photographs. This was done on the basis that, although publication had already taken place, it did not mean that confidentiality had been irrevocably lost. The court held that the unauthorised photographs would quickly be forgotten once the authorised publication by OK! Magazine had taken place.

7.14.3 Damages

Damages can be awarded where the breach of confidence is also a breach of contract or tort on normal common law principles. Where the action is based purely in equity, in England damages can be awarded in lieu of, or in addition to, an injunction (s 50 of the Supreme Court Act 1981). Damages were awarded for harm already incurred; in addition, an injunction was granted to prevent future breaches in *Peter Pan Manufacturing v Corsets Silhouette* (1963). It is doubtful if damages could be awarded if the only possible breach has occurred, for then no injunction lies in lieu of which damages can be granted. The English authorities relating to equitable damages are likely not to apply in Scotland, but there will be a right to a permanent interdict where the obligation of confidence remains.

Damages will be awarded to put the claimant in the position that he would have been in had there been no breach of confidence. Guidelines for awarding damages for future injuries in lieu of an injunction were laid down in *Seager v Copydex (No 2)* (1969) (followed in *Levin v Caledonian Produce (Holdings) Ltd* (1975) in Scotland). Lord Denning MR said that, where the information could have been obtained by employing a consultant, damages should reflect a consultant's fee but, where the information was inventive and not available elsewhere, its value would be much higher. This would be estimated by the price payable for it as between a willing buyer and willing seller – a notional royalty. The result, however, said Lord Denning, would give the information to the defendant as though it had been paid for, allowing its use by the defendant and, if appropriate, the ability to apply for a patent for it. Such a result frustrates any wish retained by the claimant to continue to utilise the information.

It is possible that exemplary damages might be awarded for breach of confidence. In *Douglas v Hello!* (2003), Lindsay J held that he was content to assume that exemplary damages, or equity's equivalent, are available for breach, but that on the facts he did not award these damages.

Damages for injury to feelings may also be awarded. This has been done for copyright and was extended to confidence by Morland J in *Cornelius v De Taranto* (2001). Where the information disclosed is of a personal and private nature this may be the only damage suffered. Morland J took the view that the Convention right to privacy would be 'hollow' if the only remedy was nominal damages, no economic loss having been incurred. This case can be distinguished from *W v Edgell* (1990), where Scott J had taken a different view. In the *Douglas* (2003) case the claim for aggravated damages failed, the defendant's conduct having been found not to be flagrant or offensive enough to justify an award. This was a case, however, where the private information had been commercialised and ordinary damages[14] would constitute adequate compensation.

---

14 In the event, the damages awarded by Lindsay J for the breach of confidence were moderate. The Douglases had requested an amount of £500,000, but were awarded just £3,750 each for their distress at publication of the pictures: *Douglas v Hello!* (2004).

7.14.4 Delivery up

Delivery up or destruction of material in breach may be ordered. In *Franklin v Giddins* (1978) the court ordered delivery up of the nectarine trees generated from the stolen cuttings.

7.14.5 Constructive trust

It may be possible to secure the proprietary remedy of a constructive trust where a breach of confidence occurs within a fiduciary relationship. The House of Lords suggested, *obiter*, that a constructive trust might be a remedy in the *Spycatcher* case. The majority of the Supreme Court of Canada imposed a constructive trust on property acquired in breach of confidence in *Lac Minerals v International Corona Resources* (1990). Lac Minerals acquired a property owned by a Mrs Williams following negotiations about a proposed joint-venture with Corona. During these negotiations core drilling results showing the ore-bearing value of the land were revealed to Corona. The decision is not without its difficulties, but a majority of the court found that there was an obligation of confidence, although not a fiduciary relationship, and that the land was held on constructive trust.

English authority is equally unclear and was discussed by Laddie J in *Ocular Sciences Ltd v Aspect Vision Care Ltd* (1997). He was prepared to hold that the imposition of a constructive trust is 'part of the equitable armoury of the court', although in this case it was not appropriate. Citing the *Lac* (1990) case, where the breach meant that Lac had diverted the Williams property from Corona, he found that the same factors did not apply on the facts. Any 'contamination' of the defendant's business and assets by the breach of confidence was 'small and technically inconsequential', so that it would be wrong to impose such a trust over a minor infraction. Any imposition of a constructive trust remains, however, controversial.[15]

Further Reading

Birks, P, 'The Remedies for Abuse of Confidential Information' [1990] LLMCLQ 460

Coleman, A, *The Legal Protection of Trade Secrets* (London: Sweet & Maxwell, 1992)

Cripps, Y, *The Legal Implications of Disclosure in the Public Interest: An Analysis of Prohibitions and Protections with Particular Reference to Employers and Employees* (London: Sweet & Maxwell, 1994)

Dworkin, G and Taylor, R, *Blackstone's Guide to the Copyright, Designs and Patents Act 1988* (London: Blackstone, 1989)

Gurry, F, *Breach of Confidence* (Oxford: Clarendon, 1984)

Hull, J, 'Analysis: Stealing Secrets: A Review of the Law Commission's Consultation Paper on the Misuse of Trade Secrets' [1998] IPQ 422

Jones, G, 'Restitution of Benefits Obtained in Breach of Another's Confidence',

(1970) 86 LQR 463

Lavery, P, 'Secrecy, Springboards and the Public Domain' [1998] EIPR 93

---

15   Wu, TH, 'Confidence and the Constructive Trust' [2003] Leg Stud 135; Birks, P, 'The Remedies for Abuse of Confidential Information', [1990] LLMCLQ 460.

Law Commission, *Breach of Confidence*, 1981, Law Com No 110, Cmnd 8388, London: HMSO

Law Commission, *Legislating the Criminal Code: Misuse of Trade Secrets*, 1977, Law Com Consultation Paper No 150, London: HMSO

Libling, D, 'The Concept of Property: Property in Intangibles' (1978) 94 LQR 103

MacQueen, H, 'Copyright and the Internet', in Edwards, E and Waelde, C (eds), *Law and the Internet* (Oxford: Hart Publishing, 1997)

North, P, 'Breach of Confidence: Is There a New Tort?' [1972] JSPTL 149 Public Interest

Ricketson, S, 'Developments in the Law Relating to Breach of Confidence' [1980] EIPR 149

Steele, C and Trenton, A, 'Trade Secrets' [1998] EIPR 188

Stewart, A, 'Confidential Information and Departing Employees: the Employer's Options' [1989] EIPR 88

Wu, TH, 'Confidence and the Constructive Trust' [2003] Leg Stud 135.

CHAPTER 8

COPYRIGHT PRINCIPLES, COPYRIGHT WORKS AND RELATED RIGHTS

Copyright is a statutory property right conferred by the Copyright, Designs and Patents Act (CDPA) 1988. It subsists in a work, conferring exclusive rights on copyright owners for a sustained period. This period varies according to the type of work. Copyright allows its owner to exploit ideas once they have been expressed and recorded in a work, and provides the means for allocating the risks of doing so. Works are created by authors, but copyright only subsists in the UK if connection with the UK qualifies the work for protection. Copyright in a work may be exploited according to the acts permitted, by place of exploitation or for specific periods of time. It may be licensed or assigned.

Although statutory, copyright differs from patents, registered designs or trade marks because it arises automatically once a work has been created and recorded. It also differs in that the interests of three main groups (rather than two – creator and user) must be reconciled in creating a copyright regime: authors, publishers, and users.

Copyright subsists without any formality; there is no application, examination or registration, nor any fees. For competitors this also means that there is no register to consult to ascertain other's rights in a work. Although copyright notices[1] are common, there is no requirement for them to be placed on a work unless protection is sought in a Member State of the Universal Copyright Convention. Such notices do, however, have evidential value.[2]

8.1 THE DEVELOPMENT OF COPYRIGHT

There has been concern for recognition of authorship of written works since the time of Ancient Greece and the Roman Empire, and the word 'plagiarist' is derived from the Latin word *plagiarus* for kidnapper. However, much of the development of copyright law is related to the ability to copy the results of others' efforts unfairly. A third element lies in a public interest in having access to works for cultural, educational, and scientific progress. These strands are not necessarily mutually exclusive. Establishing how these principles shape specific rules of copyright law is necessary to any evaluation of those rules, and to consideration of how they should meet new technologies.

8.1.1 From trade custom to statute

In Britain opportunities for copying were limited before the development of Caxton's printing press in 1478; works were largely religious, laboriously hand written and illustrated by monks, and the majority of the population illiterate. Once copying became viable and a market developed, stationers (publishers) exploited books by purchasing manuscripts from authors. Their guild structure and trade customs, with

---

1   © Cavendish 2005, for example.
2   Sections 104–06 of the CDPA 1988.

the backing of the royal prerogative, provided exclusive rights, thereby protecting against piracy. The Stationers' Company received a Royal Charter in 1556. Thus, it regulated the printing trade, establishing a register for lawfully printed books, and was entitled to use powers of search and seizure. The right of Company members to print its books in perpetuity became known as 'copy-right'. Consequently, exploitation, piracy, and enforcement of exclusive rights as a means of protection, developed from trade customs rather than through the needs of authors. Parliament finally revoked the Charter in 1694 after a troubled history in a changing political climate, and amid fears of abuse of their monopoly by the Stationers.

This left the Stationers prey to a period of flourishing piracy (or competition)[3] until their demands for protection were met in the first copyright statute, the Statute of Anne 1709.[4] It had some notable features of relevance today: its purpose was 'the encouragement of learned men to compose and write useful books'. It also graphically described the effects of producing books without their authors' consent 'to their very great detriment, and too often to the ruin of them and their families'. The Act gave authors sole right of printing, rather than the Stationers, for a term of 14 years, provided that the title had been registered in the Stationers' Company Register. However, 'authors' included their assigns (the publishers). A further 14 years of protection was granted if the author was still living at the end of the first term. Any unauthorised publication was subjected to forfeit of the books and a fine of one penny per sheet (a considerable sum in those days). Abuse of the monopoly by 'high and unreasonable' prices was subjected to the 'full power and authority' of religious, legal, academic and administrative authorities to adjust them to that 'which shall seem just and reasonable', on the complaint of any person. Thus, considerable restriction was imposed on the perpetual right formerly enjoyed by the Stationers. However, although granted to authors, it remained largely protection for entrepreneurs.

8.1.2 Statutory developments

At first the Act was seen as supplementing an author's perpetual common law copyright during the stage at which unfair competition would be at its most damaging and in *Millar v Taylor* (1769) the King's Bench agreed. However, in *Donaldson v Beckett* (1774) the House of Lords held that, although authors did potentially have perpetual common law rights for unpublished works,[5] these came to an end once a work was published and the Act alone governed.[6]

Subsequently, a process of accretion by statute added different types of work to the copyright fold, so that engravings, textiles, sculptures, and the fine arts secured

---

3   It has been argued that it was 'parallel imports' from Scotland that the Stationers feared after the Act of Union in 1701 that led to the Statute of Anne. Prescott, P, 'The Origins of Copyright: A Debunking View' [1989] EIPR 453.

4   8 Anne, c 19. Enacted in 1709, it came into force on 10 April 1710.

5   Abolished by the Copyright Act 1911.

6   Ronan Deazley argues that the Court did not recognise any common law copy-right at all, even for unpublished works, and that instead the case recognises the underlying social interest in copyright works rather than the commercial interests of authors. His argument does call into question the principle of protecting authors relied on by Lord Bingham in *Designers Guild v Russell Williams (Textiles) Ltd* (2001). Deazley, R, 'Re-reading Donaldson (1774) in the Twenty-First Century and Why it Matters' [2003] EIPR 271.

protection. Some protection for performers came with the addition of dramatic and musical works. Later sound recordings, broadcasts, typographical arrangement and films were added. Changes were also made to the term of protection, although it was only international pressure which saw its extension to long periods after an author's death.

Collective licensing of works by organisations representing copyright owners was a further development, with the addition of control over such potentially monopolistic exercises of the exclusive right. The Performing Right Society (PRS) and Phonographic Performance Limited (PPL) illustrated the value of joint action but also the dangers. The latter, for example, controlled licences so as to preserve employment for live musicians. The Copyright Act 1956 (CA 1956) created the Performing Right Tribunal, giving it jurisdiction over collective licences.

Technological development led to the Copyright, Designs and Patents Act (CDPA) 1988, which remains the governing copyright statute, albeit in much amended form.

Therefore, UK copyright law is founded on exclusive rights which are wholly statutory and require legislative amendment for recognition of any changes. The rights are granted to authors; however, it was pressure from publishers to preserve their economic interests which brought them about. As new works have been added, entrepreneurs have received protection without discrimination between 'authors" and 'neighbouring' rights. These rights are founded in concepts of property rather than rights to remuneration, yet are subject to defined limits of duration. Nor can the legal right be divorced from its technological framework, which may have an increasingly important role to play as the law continues to develop.

8.1.3 Civil law

In civil law copyright was rooted in *droit d'auteur* (most particularly in France); based on recognition of authors' creativity and a natural right in its expression. However, there are parallels with the development of UK copyright. In 18th century France pre-Revolution copyright was a tool for controlling the dissemination of literature, and a guild system of trade agreements. However, it was justified on a philosophical rather than an economic basis: Diderot stated ideas to be the highest form of property because of their association with the person creating them.[7] He argued for a perpetual property right passing to an author's heirs. Thus, emphasis was on authors' moral rights, rather than their economic interests. Countervailing arguments were propounded by Condorcet, who stated ideas to exist in nature, belonging to all and available for the common good.[8] In 1789 the French Revolution led to declarations of freedom for the press. In turn this led to piracy of old and new works on such a scale that publication of them virtually ceased. In 1793 the Declaration of the Rights of Genius granted an author and his heirs or assignees publication rights for the author's life plus 10 years. French copyright law only reverted to an author-centred status with the creation of the *droit moral* when in 19th century Europe the need to protect authors'

---

7   Diderot, D, 'Lettre Historique et Politique Addressée à un Magistrat sur le Commerce de la Librairie', cited in Hesse, C, *Publishing and Cultural Politics in Revolutionary Paris 1789–1810* (Berkeley: University of California Press, 1991) 98.

8   See Caritat, M-J-A, Marquis de Condorcet, *Fragments sur la liberté de la presse* (1776), in Arago, M-F (ed), *Oeuvres de Condorcet* (Paris: Didot, 1847) Vol ll: 253–314. Condorcet, 'Fragments sur la Liberté de la Presse'.

artistic integrity in their relations to entrepreneurs was strongly argued and moral rights enacted.

8.1.4 International measures

Exploitation of copyright was never purely domestic (Henry VIII banned the importation of books into England). Because the UK was an exporter of copyright works there was an interest in securing protection for authors elsewhere. Further development came both with international co-operation, and dissent.

The multinational Berne Copyright Convention 1886 (and its later revisions)[9] brought greater uniformity of protection with civil countries (but not harmonisation; it accepts differences in national regimes). The Convention applies to literary, musical, dramatic, artistic works, films, and audio-visual works. It establishes the principle of national treatment for the works of those from Member States, based on the country of origin of a work. The minimum term of protection was harmonised at life of the author plus 50 years, as was the requirement for protection without any formalities, ending the role of the register at Stationers' Hall in UK copyright.

However, protest came from developing countries, which argued for easier access to works. The Berne Convention was amended: to allow national translations, and publication for the purpose of teaching, scholarship or research after three years from first publication, and, secondly, to license national publication within a set period after first publication if the copyright owner did not publish. These measures were reflected in the Copyright Acts of 1911 and 1956.

The US was not brought into the international fold until the Universal Copyright Convention (UCC) 1952.[10] It also guaranteed national protection, but on less stringent terms.

The Rome Convention 1961 added protection against piracy of performances, and further measures enabled co-operation in relation to broadcasting. It provides for national treatment for rights given to performers, record producers and broadcasters.

The Trade Related Aspects of Intellectual Property (TRIPS) Agreement 1994 embodies the first 21 Articles of the Berne Convention, but also incorporates the American statutory exclusion of protection for ideas, so giving international impetus to a means for balancing conflicts of protection against access to works. The Berne 'three steps test', which limits exceptions to the right of reproduction, is also incorporated; thus providing a significant principle on which any derogations to copyright must be based. TRIPS does not incorporate the Rome Convention in the same way, but sets out requirements for an exclusive right for fixation of performances (lasting 50 years from performance), reproduction of phonograms (lasting 50 years from fixation), and broadcasts (lasting 20 years from broadcasting).

8.1.5 EU harmonisation

Membership of the EU added a new dimension, with measures aimed at harmonising aspects of the wider copyright environment. Differences between *droit d'auteur* and

---

9   The Berlin Act 1908, Brussels Revision 1948, Stockholm Protocol 1967, and Paris Act 1971.
10   The US became a member of the Berne Convention on 1 March 1989.

common law entrepreneurial copyright have been further reconciled. The necessity for doing so stemmed from developing technologies (from the tape recorder to photocopying and personal computers). These enabled both widespread home copying and commercial piracy, as well as creating new demands for protection for 'electronic' works. Conflicts in relation to broadcasting across borders also required resolution. The result has been a number of directives creating piecemeal harmonisation:

- Directive on Semi-conductor Topographies;[11]
- Directive on Computer Programs;[12]
- Directive on Rental, Lending and Neighbouring Rights;[13]
- Directive on Satellite Broadcasting and Cable Retransmission;[14]
- Directive on Copyright Duration;[15]
- Directive on the Legal Protection of Databases;[16]
- Directive on Conditional Access Services;[17]
- Directive on Copyright and Related Rights in the Information Society;[18]
- Directive on Resale Rights in Works of Art.[19]

Currently, the European copyright regime is under review. The European Commission launched a consultation in July 2004, based on a Working Paper.[20] This assesses whether there are inconsistencies in the directives, particularly ones which might hamper the balance of rights between right owners and users of copyright works. It is thought that some small adjustments are needed.

8.1.6 A world regime

Modern developments in methods of storage and transmission are having a profound effect on copyright law. The rapid growth of digital technology provides new markets, but also allows easy copying on a wide scale. These copies are of high quality and have

---

11 Council Directive 87/54/EEC on the Legal Protection of Semiconductor Products, [1987] OJ L24/36.
12 Council Directive 91/250/EEC on the Legal Protection of Computer Programs, [1991] OJ L122/42.
13 Council Directive 92/100/EEC on Rental Right and Lending Right and on Certain Rights Related to Copyright, [1992] OJ L346/61.
14 Council Directive 93/83/EEC on the Co-ordination of Certain Rules Concerning Copyright and Rights Related to Copyright applicable to Satellite Broadcasting and Cable Retransmission, [1993] OJ L248/15.
15 Council Directive 93/98/EEC Harmonising the Term of Protection of Copyright and Certain Related Rights, [1993] OJ L290/9.
16 Council and Parliament Directive 96/9/EC on the Legal Protection of Databases, [1996] OJ L028/11.
17 Directive 98/84/EC on the Legal Protection of Conditional Access Services, [1998] OJ L320/54.
18 Directive 2001/29/EC of the European Parliament and of the Council on the Harmonisation of Certain Aspects of Copyright and Related Rights in the Information Society [2001] OJ L1767/10.
19 Directive 2001/84/EC of the European Parliament and of the Council on the Resale Right for the Benefit of the Author of an Original Work of Art, 2001/84, [2001] OJ L272/32.
20 Commission Staff Working Paper on the Review of the EC Legal Framework in the Field of Copyright and Related Rights, SEC (2004) 995.

meant a perceived explosion (or fear) of the activities of copyright pirates, file-sharers and bootleggers (those who make unauthorised copies of copyright works or performances). The so-called 'global information society', in which information is of increasing value and wide availability, also poses increasing challenges to copyright. The internet allows worldwide dissemination of works, which may have been uploaded without authority. However, resulting infringement, although very widespread, is often almost impossible to detect. Even where it is identified, enforcement of rights remains subject to questions of jurisdiction and cross-border enforcement.

Accordingly, authors argue strongly for enhanced protection for their works, without which the incentive to produce might be entirely removed. At the same time, a fourth member has been added to the 'copyright triangle' of author, entrepreneur, and user; that of the Internet Service Provider (ISP). Several prominent studies[21] preceded new legislative initiatives.

The final step in international provision for copyright has been promulgation of two world treaties by WIPO – the World Copyright Treaty (WCT) 1996, and the World Performance and Phonograms Treaty (WPPT) 1996. The WCT caters for digital technology by confirming rights of reproduction and communication in the new medium, despite the fact that works may be accessed by the public individually and at a time chosen by them. Technological protection for digitally stored and transmitted works is also given legal backing. The WPPT gives performers and producers of sound recordings, reproduction, distribution and rental rights, as well as a right to equitable remuneration for broadcasting and communication to the public. Performers are given protection against bootlegging of extempore performances, and a degree of moral rights. Legal protection for technological protection measures is incorporated. A World Database Treaty and a World Broadcasting Treaty are also proposed. The latter is intended to provide protection for web-casters over digital networks, updating the Rome Convention.[22] It is designed to prevent 'signal piracy' of broadcast[23] programmes by giving property rights[24] to transmitters, even, perhaps, over works already in the public domain.

Attempts in the WCT to impose liability on all the providers of intermediate steps involved in transmission over the internet by virtue of an all-encompassing right of reproduction did not succeed.[25] At the same time debate has escalated over questions of access to works, while new models of copyright have emerged in the open source movement. In particular, technological protection is perceived to give right owners greater protection than did 'traditional' copyright, and to restrict free access for particular classes of user (such as those involved in libraries, education and research). Now that all access to electronic works may be controlled, the problem of enforcing

---

21 Intellectual Property and the National Information Infrastructure, National Information Infrastructure Task Force, 1995; Copyright and Related Rights in the Information Society; Copyright and Related Rights in the Information Society (COM (95) 382 final); The Challenge of the Information Highway, Final Report of the Information Highway Advisory Council, Canada, 1995.
22 The Rome Convention on the Protection of Performers, Producers and Phonograms and Broadcasting Organisations, 1961.
23 By television, radio and satellite.
24 Extending for up to 50 years. The Rome Convention protection is for 20 years.
25 The Directive on Electronic Commerce grants ISPs exemptions from liability, 2000/71 [2000] OJ L1178/1.

copyright is removed, and so the practical need to accede to some 'fair' uses such as fair dealing (or fair use in the US) no longer remains. This is perceived to jeopardise the public interest in access to works on which copyright law is founded leading to arguments that the public interest lies in allowing free and unfettered access to works, as well as private copying in some cases. Similar concerns have been expressed in relation to the Broadcasting Treaty, if protection extends to preventing retransmission of webcasts of public domain content, or even covers webpages of out-of-copyright material. As copyright law struggles to cope with increasingly rapid technological change, fundamental principles which have underlain its development from the start cannot be ignored.

Further global harmonisation could follow, spurred by global delivery of works via the internet, and the difficulties posed by cross-border disputes.[26] However, the differing needs of developing countries must not be forgotten in such a process.[27]

8.2   BASIC PRINCIPLES

Copyright subsists in certain descriptions of work.[28] Before describing these works, certain basic principles, which are not always embodied in the statute, need explanation. These principles apply to the works described in 8.3.

8.2.1   A work

There is no statutory definition of 'work', but case law suggests that its author must have been expended a minimum level of effort. A similar principle is attached to the requirement of originality (see 8.4) and the same conclusion is often reached: either that there is nothing substantive enough to be protected as a work, or that it is not 'original'.

Copyright protection has been refused to works which are very trivial or very small (in terms of creative effort). In *Sinanide v La Maison Kosmeo* (1928) the advertising slogan 'Beauty is a social necessity, not a luxury' was held to be too slight a work to found allegations of infringement by the rival slogan 'A youthful appearance is a social necessity'.

A court may also apply the maxim *de minimis non curat lex*. A single word was refused copyright protection in the controversial case of *Exxon v Exxon Insurance* (1982). The plaintiffs incurred considerable cost in having the name EXXON invented for their business. It was held not to constitute an 'original literary work' (although it was, if each element of the phrase be taken separately, original and literary) because it conveyed no information, provided no instruction and gave no pleasure. The statutory phrase must be read as a composite entity: original–literary–work. Additionally, the court noted that there was other protection for names. The policy behind this decision is clear. Copyright would have conferred a long-term monopoly over the name for all uses, whereas trade mark registration is made within classes of goods and services (see 15.2.1) and passing off is otherwise confined (see Chapter 14). However, the word did provide information, and dual protection of artistic works as trade marks is

---

26   Fitzpatrick, S, 'Prospects of Further Copyright Harmonisation?' [2003] EIPR 215.
27   Final Report, Commission on Intellectual Property Rights: www.iprcommission.org.
28   Section 1(1) of the CDPA 1988.

countenanced. The case must also be distinguished from *Express Newspapers v Liverpool Daily Post* (1985). Here, a simple grid containing randomly selected numbers and letters constructed for a newspaper game was held to have the sole purpose of conveying information. It was also held that 'skill, labour and judgment' had been exercised in its production (see 8.4.2).

Titles and names have been refused copyright. In *Francis Day and Hunter v Twentieth Century Fox* (1940), no protection was given to the name of the song 'The Man Who Broke the Bank at Monte Carlo'; nor to the WOMBLES name in *Wombles v Wombles Skips* (1975), or the KOJAK name in *Tavener Rutledge v Trexpalm* (1977). Material that is trite and obvious has fallen at the same hurdle, so that, in *Cramp v Smythson* (1944), there was held to be no copyright in the tables included in the plaintiff's Liteblue Diary 1933 where no skill or judgment had been exercised in their compilation.

Logos and devices have not fared so badly and in *IPC Magazines Ltd v MGN Ltd* (1998) the 'Woman' masthead was regarded as, at least arguably, a copyright work.

8.2.2 Fixation of a work

It is a statutory requirement that literary, dramatic and musical works must have been recorded (or fixed) in a tangible form before copyright can subsist: s 3(2) of the CDPA 1988. This ensures that there is an entity capable of being regarded substantively as a work in situations where creation without producing anything external is possible, as, for example, in the composition of music, or a poem or improvised dramatic action. The other copyright works (films, videos, sound recordings, broadcasts) necessarily have tangible form. In a case where there might have been doubt in relation to an artistic work, the requirement that there be a work was applied. In *Merchandising Corp of America v Harpbond* (1983), it was held that facial make-up used by the pop star Adam Ant was not a painting because 'a painting is not an idea: it is an object; and paint without a [permanent] surface is not a painting'. This decision and the requirement of fixation are a reflection of the principle that copyright does not protect ideas, but the expression of ideas (see 8.2.3).

In writing or otherwise

The work must be recorded 'in writing or otherwise'. Writing is defined in s 178 of the CDPA 1988. It includes any form of notation or code, whether by hand or otherwise, regardless of the medium in or on which the recording is made. This was amended in 1988 to accommodate new technologies, so that a work is recorded as soon as it is stored on a computer; it does not have to be printed out. Notation and code will include, for example, the symbols used for the choreography of a ballet. The amended definition also allows for the creation of a greater number of works than was previously the case. Previously, it was not clear that a literary work could be fixed by tape recording, for example, but the new definition encompasses tape or video recording as fixation for a literary, dramatic or musical work. If the person making such a recording also secures a copyright right in the recording, as opposed to the underlying work, the recording of one work may generate multiple copyrights (see 8.4.5).

Improvised works

If, as now seems to be the case, a literary, dramatic, or musical work may be fixed by recording it (for example, as a sound recording, film or broadcast), it is possible for a very ephemeral work to be recorded and for copyright to arise. This would be the case even for a mere improvised performance of dance, poetry or music, for example. Copyright would arise despite the fact that the performer may not otherwise have been able to repeat the work. This will be so unless the requirement that there be a 'work' serves to exclude an extempore performance. That this may be so is suggested by s 180(2) of the CDPA 1988, which contemplates that a performance may be made without there being an underlying work to perform. Two early cases relating to dramatic works lead to a similar conclusion. The issue to be decided was whether characters, acting style and scenic effects could be protected as copyright dramatic works before the CA 1956 introduced the requirement of recording in writing. It was held that they could not because they were not capable of being printed: *Tate v Fulbrook* (1908); *Tate v Thomas* (1921). The implication is that an extempore performance can only constitute a work to the extent that it is capable of being recorded in writing. Dworkin and Taylor[29] state that a 'work is a distinct thing from the performance of it and also from the recording of that performance, but if the recording is the only evidence of the existence of the work, these latter two are likely to become confused'. In other words, the mere fact that a performance is possible does not imply the necessary presence of a work.

Similarly, in *Creation Records Ltd v News Group Newspapers Ltd* (1997), arranging everyday objects photographed for an Oasis album cover, albeit in an unusual setting, was held to be too ephemeral to be an artistic work of collage, even though a picture had been taken.

8.2.3 The idea–expression dichotomy

The tenet 'there is no copyright in an idea; copyright only subsists in its expression' is another fundamental copyright principle not expressed in the CDPA 1988. This can be illustrated by imagining a piece of narrative writing. The story-line originates in the author's idea; it is the particular words used which are the expression the author has adopted. Anyone may write a story generally along the same lines, but he or she must not adopt the first author's particular choice of words. Consequently, a work needs to be fixed before copyright subsists because it must have a particular form of expression.

The principle can be traced to the US decision in *Baker v Selden* (1879). It was held that no copyright could subsist in the system of accounting described in Selden's book, which remained free for anyone to use.[30] It was expressed in the UK by Petersen J in *University of London Press v University Tutorial Press* (1916). *Walter v Lane* (1900) can be explained on this basis (see 8.4.5). Lord Rosebery's speech constituted the idea, but it was the *Times* reporter who gave it particularity of expression. It also forms part of the TRIPS Agreement 1994, which states that copyright shall 'extend to expressions and not to ideas'.

---

29 Dworkin, G and Taylor, R, *Blackstone's Guide to the Copyright, Designs and Patents Act 1988* (London: Blackstone, 1989).

30 This principle is now embodied in s 102(a) of the US Copyright Act 1976.

The House of Lords confirmed the application of the rule in *LB Plastics v Swish* (1979). The plaintiff made 'knock down' furniture with drawers, for which there were copyright drawings. The defendant copied the drawers, rather than the drawings, although it had had access to them. The defendant argued that it had merely used the plaintiff's idea and the similarity of its own drawers stemmed from the need to make them compatible with the plaintiff's furniture. It was held that, although there is no copyright in an idea, on the facts, the defendant had copied details of expression. Lord Wilberforce said:

> There can be no copyright in a mere idea, so if all that the respondents had done was to take from the appellants the idea of external latching, or the 'unhanding' of components, or any other idea implicit in their work, the appellants could not complain.

However, the line between idea and expression can be a very fine one, giving courts leeway in determining where the boundaries of copyright protection lie, so that, to an extent, the rule makes up for the lack of any general principle of unfair competition.

Process of abstraction

Drawing the line involves a process of abstraction, as described in relation to a play in the American case of *Nichols v Universal Pictures Corp* (1930):

> Upon any work ... a great number of patterns of increasing generality will fit equally well, as more and more of the incident is left out. The last may perhaps be no more than the most general statement of what the play is about, and at times might consist only of its title; but there is a point in this series of abstractions where they are no longer protected, since otherwise the playwright could prevent the use of his 'ideas', to which, apart from their expression, his property is never extended.

However, no one layer of abstraction clearly represents a distinction between an idea and its specific expression. This was illustrated in *Plix Products v Winstone* (1986), in which it was found necessary to distinguish between two sorts of 'ideas': the 'general idea or basic concept of the work', and the idea formed of how to express this basic concept in concrete form. This was, however, said to be 'an ill defined boundary'. In addition, the complexity of the general concept will influence how the distinction is drawn. Pritchard J said:

> The way the author treats the subject, the forms he uses to express the basic concept, may range from the crude and simplistic to the ornate, complicated – and involving the collation and application of a great number of constructive ideas.

> It is in this area that the author expends the skill and industry which (even though they may be slight) give the work its originality and entitle him to copyright ... So he who seeks to make a product of the same description as that in which another owns copyright must tread with care. If he copies the details which properly belong to the expression and not the basic concept, he will infringe the copyright. That is why, when the basic idea is expressed in a crude or simplistic form, the potential plagiarist or business competition can, without offending, come very close to an exact reproduction of the copyright work. However, where the expression is ornate, complex or detailed, then he must keep his distance: the only product he can then make without infringing may bear little resemblance to the copyright work.

Expression equated to originality

The rule's main significance lies in determining infringement when the defendant's copy is not literal, so that the extent to which the copyright owner's 'skill, labour and judgment' have been taken must be assessed. In *Designers Guild Ltd v Russell Williams Ltd* (2001), the House of Lords stated that the principle should be 'handled with care'. The distinction between idea and expression plainly meant more than just that a work required expressing as a work. Lord Hoffmann gave it two distinct interpretations:

> The first is that a copyright work may express certain ideas which are not protected because they have no connection with the literary, dramatic, musical or artistic nature of the work ... for example, a literary work which describes a system or invention ...

> The other proposition is that certain ideas expressed by a copyright work may not be protected because, although they are ideas of a literary, dramatic, musical or artistic nature, they are not original, or so commonplace as not to form a substantial part of the work.

Consequently, the idea of combining stripes with flowers in a fabric design fell within the second proposition. This interpretation squarely equates idea/expression with originality. Nor does it distinguish between them, if 'commonplace' means the *de minimis* level of effort required to constitute a work at all, or a protectable level of 'skill, labour and judgment'. Lord Millett applied this second proposition by isolating similarities between the copyright work and its alleged copy, discounting those consisting of commonplace, unoriginal or general ideas.

The uncertainty that surrounds such key concepts (originality, substantial part, and idea/expression) makes understanding the underlying functions and justifications for copyright important, as they ultimately shape the courts' conclusions. Lord Hoffmann's interpretation should be welcomed if it restricts the idea/expression dichotomy to a rule of evidence that some similarities of a general nature cannot raise a presumption of copying, rather than a question of whether copyright subsists at all. What it does not do is clarify how to assess whether the level of originality in a feature of a work is sufficient to surmount the 'skill, labour and judgment' hurdle. It has been argued[31] that the uncertainty that underlies basic copyright principles such as originality, fixation and the idea/expression dichotomy is 'dangerous to the functioning of the law', leaving those principles lost in an 'identity crisis' with little meaning at all.

The imprecision of the rule has made its application particularly difficult and uncertain in relation to infringements of copyright computer software:[32] *Ibcos Computers Ltd v Poole* (1994); *John Richardson Computers v Flanders* (1993). Similar confusion has surrounded its application to non-literal infringement of copyright in programs in US case law.

In the US, the maxim is employed differently; rather than being significant to the determination of infringement, it has the effect of denying that any copyright subsists in a work at all. The consequence is that, if a work takes on the only form possible to express the underlying idea, idea and expression are taken to have merged, and no

---

31 Lichtman, D, 'Copyright as a Rule of Evidence' *The Berkeley Law & Economics Working Papers*: Vol 2001: No 2, Article 8; 52 Duke LJ 683 (2003).

32 Gordon, S, 'The Very Idea! Why Copyright Law is an Inappropriate Way to Protect Computer Programs' [1998] EIPR 10.

copyright subsists. A similar conclusion is reached in the UK, without denying copyright, by concluding that no infringement has taken place if only idea is copied. The results have seemed generous on some occasions: *Elanco v Mandrops* (1980); *ITV Publications v Time Out* (1984) (see 8.4.3).

That the dichotomy is not absolute can be seen in the fact that to adapt a work infringes even where a change of expression is involved, as does a change of dimension in relation to an artistic work (ss 16(1)(e) and 17(3) of the CDPA 1988). Should the distinction between idea and expression be eroded too far, more emphasis may be placed on the need for a 'work'.

8.2.4   Overlapping copyrights

A product may embody more than one copyright. Take, for example, a compact disc of popular music. Copyright will subsist in the music for the songs as musical works, and in the songs' lyrics as literary works. The disc itself will have copyright as a sound recording, and there may be copyright both in literary and artistic works making up the cover design and any written and pictorial material inserted in the case. Should the compact disc be broadcast, copyright will also arise in the broadcast. In the same way, photographs and other illustrations will constitute separate copyright works to the literary copyright in the text in an illustrated book. Separate copyrights, literary and artistic, will subsist in the text and drawings in a map or diagram.

However, in *Electronic Techniques (Anglia) Ltd v Critchley Components Ltd* (1997) Laddie J cautioned against taking overlapping rights too far. At issue were circuit diagrams for electronic components, which comprised both text and drawings. These were argued to be literary works. He pointed out that correct identification of a work determined its duration and scope of protection. While a product might contain many copyrights it was 'quite another thing to say that a *single* piece of work by an author gives rise to two or more copyrights in respect of the *same* creative effort'. He added that, while determining the dividing line between categories of work might be difficult, it did not justify giving an author protection in both categories. In difficult cases the proper category was the one most suited to the characteristics of the work at issue. Consequently, the literary element of the circuit diagrams, after elimination of anything appreciated by the eye as an artistic work, comprised no more than a list of components and arguably was too insubstantial to qualify as an original work.

Further 'overlap' is possible. Each of these copyrights is divisible, and may be licensed or assigned separately for different times, places, and activities. Thus, for example, the French, German and Spanish translation rights in a book may be dealt with separately, as may the adaptation and broadcast rights, each transaction being for a different period during the full life of the copyright.

8.3   COPYRIGHT WORKS

Copyright only subsists in the works described by s 1(1) of the CDPA 1988:

(a) original literary, dramatic, musical or artistic works;

(b) sound recordings, films, or broadcasts; and

(c) the typographical arrangement of published editions.

The first class is known as 'authors' rights' in civil law, and the second derivative or neighbouring works. Often these latter works are the means for exploiting and disseminating an underlying original work, such as an album of modern music, or a video recording of a recent film. The Berne Convention only applies to original works, films and audio-visual works, which may be regarded as the raw material of authors' creativity. The third class protects publishers, and may apply to new editions of original works which have fallen out of copyright.

8.4   ORIGINAL WORKS

Literary, dramatic, musical and artistic works must be original,[33] but 'originality' is not defined in the statute. This judicially initiated principle has two aspects: a work must emanate from its author, and the author must have exercised a modicum of 'skill, labour, and judgment' in its creation.

8.4.1 Not copied

First, to be original a work must not be a copy, but this is not a difficult standard to meet (unlike displaying 'novelty' for a patent). The leading case is *University of London Press v University Tutorial Press* (1916). Deciding whether examination questions were copyright original literary works, Petersen J said:

> The word 'original' does not in this connection mean that the work must be the expression of original or inventive thought. Copyright Acts are not concerned with the originality of ideas, but with the expression of thought ... the work must not be copied from another work – it should originate from the author.

This aspect of the requirement of originality has four consequences:

(a) no evaluation of merit need be made before a work can be protected in copyright, which would not be practical without a regime of application and examination;

(b) protection is given for authors' effort as much as creativity, which has the effect of protecting against unfair competition in some circumstances, and extends protection to the non-aesthetic (such as the newspaper game grids in *Express Newspapers v Liverpool Daily Post* (1985));

(c) it prevents indefinite extensions of copyright in a work; and

(d) overlapping of copyrights is possible where copyright sources are reworked by an author rather than merely copied.

The concept of originality applied in some European jurisdictions is a more stringent one, requiring an element of creativity on an author's part, and is incorporated into UK law in relation to database copyright. As a result of harmonisation resulting from the Database Directive, s 3A(2) of the CDPA 1988 provides that a database, unlike other literary works, including compilations, is original only if its selection or arrangement constitutes the author's own 'intellectual creation'. As a result the Directive created a new form of protection for unoriginal collections of fact (see 8.11).

---

33   Section 1(1) of the CDPA 1988.

8.4.2 'Skill, labour and judgment'

Secondly, works may be regarded as original if an element of 'skill, labour and judgment' has been expended in their creation, and this remains so even if the work has been derived from other sources. *University of London Press v University Tutorial Press* (1916) also expressed this principle as the examination papers involved 'selection, judgment and experience', but the leading case is *Ladbroke (Football) v William Hill* (1964). The House of Lords held that coupons for football pools constituted original literary works. It was accepted that the 'vast amount of skill, judgment, experience and work' employed in building up the coupon constituted an original work. This was so, although the effort and skill had not gone into the production of the literary work itself, but into the commercial selection of bets to offer, providing a remedy against unfair competition. The work was to be considered as a whole and not divided into its constituent parts. The principle applies however commonplace the sources used: *Macmillan v Cooper* (1923). This effort may be expended either in the expression of the work, or in its preparation and is sometimes termed 'sweat of the brow'.

The principle has recently received extensive consideration in common law jurisdictions. Following *Feist Publications Inc v Rural Telephone Co* (1991) protection is not so easily secured for collections of information in the US. The 'white pages' of a telephone directory were at issue. It was held that the minimal arrangement that such subscriber information needs did not reach the level required for originality. No copyright could subsist in facts alone. It was significant that as a certified public utility, Rural was required to publish directories as a condition of its monopoly. However, copyright did subsist in the 'yellow' pages. A similar result is likely for databases in the UK (unless they can still be considered original compilations).[34]

Subsequently, the Federal Court of Australia took a different view after an exhaustive review of common law authority. In *Desktop Marketing Systems v Telstra Corp* (2002) the issue was whether copyright subsisted in Telstra's White and Yellow Page directories. It was held that the expense and effort expended in producing 'whole universe' directories (completely comprehensive listings of all subscribers) was sufficient to confer originality, and therefore copyright, despite the fact that anyone attempting to collate the same information would produce a virtually identical result. While this can be regarded as 'distinguishing' *Feist* on the facts, Lindgren J emphasised that determining originality was a matter of fact and degree related to the particular type of work. If the result was to confer copyright on factual data, it was noted that no other protection for databases existed in Australia. The fact that Telstra enjoyed a monopoly, had a statutory duty to produce directories, and did so free of charge and as an incident to broader business activities did not alter this conclusion.

In the Canadian case of *CCH Canada Ltd v The Law Society of Upper Canada* (2004) the Supreme Court also reviewed the concept of originality. It appeared to set a standard mid way between the UK's skill, *labour* and judgment and the European or American requirement for an element of creativity.[35] It is significant that this judgment sought to secure a fair balance of rights between the power conveyed to authors by copyright and the public interest in the generation of and access to copyright works.

---

34 *Ibid*, s 3A(2).
35 Tumbridge, J, 'Canada Defines "Originality"and Specifies the Limits of "Fair Dealing"' [2004] EIPR 318.

The Chief Justice states that a 'sweat of the brow' approach would overprotect authors' industry, but to require an element of creativity, a nebulous enough concept at the best of times, would under-protect authors' interests. Consequently, skill and judgment were to be required: skill in the use of knowledge, aptitude or ability; judgment in the capacity for discernment or to form an opinion or evaluation by comparison of different options. Thus, case headnotes were held to be original works, as were case summaries and topical indexes. Judgments including edited reasons and headnotes also attracted copyright, as did compilations of cases (although copyright would not subsist in the component parts). It may be significant that there is no protection for typographical arrangements in Canadian copyright law.

It is difficult to resolve the uncertainty over the meaning of 'originality' by asking why originality is required. If it is a rule to ensure that there is sufficient evidence that copyright subsists in a work, as some argue,[36] it does not provide good reason to refuse the incentive of copyright for creating factual and comprehensive databases, particularly in jurisdictions where other protection is not available. A better view may be that originality rewards creations beyond obvious development and is one means of preserving public domain material, particularly factual information. In *Feist* the court stated that: '[R]aw facts may be copied at will … It is the means by which copyright advances the progress of Science and Art.' If a rule of evidence is necessary it is served by the requirement of fixation.

8.4.3 Secondary works

The work at issue in *Ladbroke's* case was a compilation, but the 'skill, labour and judgment' aspect of originality does not appear confined to compilations, or to literary works. It has also been applied to what might be termed secondary works. In *Warwick Films v Eisinger* (1969), the defendant made a film of the trials of Oscar Wilde, using two books as verbatim sources for the words of counsel, the judges and Wilde himself. The defendant argued that the books were not original works because they were taken (copied) from the trial transcripts and other sources. Plowman J held that there was copyright in both books. In the first, there had been considerable selection from the transcripts, sufficient to confer originality. In the second, although much had been copied from the first, there had also been considerable editing, the author had included his own contributions, and 'he had added material, omitted material, made verbal alterations, re-arranged material, transposed material and abbreviated material'. Each book therefore had its own copyright.

Drafts

Consequently, copyright also subsists in a series of drafts produced in the process of creating a drawing, as each draft is the work of the artist: *LA Gear Inc v Hi Tech Sports plc* (1992). In *Sweeney v MacMillan Publishers Ltd* (2001) this question was considered in relation to the many drafts James Joyce produced in creating *Ulysses*. Lloyd J held that each constituted a new and original copyright work. Only the final proof with the author's alterations was the same work as the 1922 published version. He

---

36 Lichtman, D, 'Copyright as a Rule of Evidence', *The Berkeley Law & Economics Working Papers*: Vol 2001: No 2, Article 8; 52 Duke LJ 683 (2003).

distinguished the passage from the Scots case *Black v Murray* (1870), relied on by Lord Oliver in *Interlego*,[37] as relating to a later edition of a published work rather than drafts of a work in preparation. For copyright to subsist these later editions had to impart a 'true and real value, over and above that belonging to the text'.

Whether the same could be said of a conversion of a work into digital format is questionable. Despite the different format when displayed, the work itself would be the same.

Infringing copyright secondary works

Copyright may subsist in a secondary work, even though the author has infringed copyright subsisting in the sources used for it, provided that the 'skill, labour and judgment' employed in the creation of the secondary work is sufficient to create a new work: *Redwood Music v Chappell* (1982). In *Macmillan v Cooper* (1923) the court stated that the skill, labour and judgment expended must give the new work a quality or character which the sources used did not possess, and which would differentiate the two.

The new copyright does not prevent others using the same sources, but prevents copying of the effort made in creating the secondary work. Subsequent authors must go back to the original sources. The consequences can be profound if these sources are not available to others. This was illustrated in *ITV Publications v Time Out* (1984). The defendant published television listings for BBC and ITV channels, infringing the broadcasters' copyright. No other source existed for the information, so that the broadcasters enjoyed a duopoly in their publications of programme listings. Whitford J upheld the subsistence of copyright in the compilations of programme information, rejecting the argument that they were merely information in which no copyright could subsist. It took legislation in the form of the Broadcasting Act 1990 to end this duopoly.

The consequences in *Elanco v Mandops* (1980) were also controversial, when the same reasoning was applied to a secondary work, and have led to arguments that the 'skill, labour and judgment' principle should be confined to compilations. The plaintiff had copyright in instructions for the use of a weedkiller, drawn from public sources. The defendant produced instructions for its product using the plaintiff's material. After objections from the plaintiff, the defendant recast these instructions several times. In an interlocutory application the final version was treated as arguably infringing despite these revisions because the defendants had not returned to public sources. Thus, Elanco effectively secured a monopoly over the information in its instructions despite the fact that it was in the public domain.

8.4.4   Secondary artistic works

It may be that the Privy Council decision in *Interlego v Tyco Industries* (1989) introduced a limitation for secondary works in the UK. An alternative conclusion, however, is that 'original' is to be interpreted differently for artistic works, although Lord Oliver stated that there was no distinction in principle in the case of artistic copyright. The plaintiffs attempted to establish copyright in drawings for the DUPLO children's construction

---

37   See 8.4.4 .

toy. They had been copied from design drawings, and information as to dimensions, which had been slightly changed. Lord Oliver said:

> ... in *Ladbroke (Football) Ltd v William Hill (Football) Ltd* (1964), it is stressed that the amount of skill, judgment or labour is likely to be decisive in the case of compilations. To apply that, however, as a universal test of originality in all copyright cases is not only unwarranted by the context in which the observations were made, but palpably erroneous. Take the simplest case of artistic copyright, a painting or a photograph. It takes great skill, judgment and labour to produce a good copy by painting or to produce an enlarged photograph from a positive print, but no one would reasonably contend that the copy, painting or enlargement was an 'original' artistic work in which the copier is entitled to claim copyright. Skill, labour or judgment merely in the process of copying cannot confer originality ... There must, in addition, be some element of material alteration or embellishment which suffices to make the totality of the work an original work.

Dworkin and Taylor point out that there is little difference between a skilful copy of an artistic work and the copyright conferred on a 'shorthand writer's copyright in his report of someone else's speech' (see 8.4.5 and 9.2.2). It is possible to distinguish *Ladbroke* and *Interlego*. In the latter, all the skill went into the copying of the drawings, whereas, in the former, the skill employed resulted in a new work being created. That this is the correct principle may be suggested by Goff LJ, in *Elanco v Mandrops* (1980), when he said 'the compilation cases ... all go on there being skill and labour involved in making the compilation, as distinct from skill and labour in ascertaining the information'. That the issue remains relevant is shown by *The Reject Shop v Robert Manners* (1995), in which enlarged photocopies of designs, used in the production of handmade tiles, were held to be unoriginal.

Whether sufficient 'skill, labour and judgment' has been exercised to confer originality on a work must depend on first defining the type of effort required for particular types of work. The nature of works changes with the times, particularly in the artistic world. Consequently, each case must, to an extent, depend solely on its own facts. The intentions of the creator in producing the work, however, subjective, can provide some guidance as to the type of work; it remains for courts to determine which skills are relevant.

8.4.5 Reporter's copyright

A related question is the originality of a work which is a record of another's work. Section 3(3) of the CDPA 1988 provides that it is immaterial who fixes a copyright work, nor need the work's author consent to the recording being made. Making a record of a hitherto unrecorded work may, therefore, result in the creation of two copyright works. It may confer copyright on the work's author, and confer another copyright on the recorder's record, provided that 'skill, labour and judgment' have been exercised in making the record.

In *Walter v Lane* (1900), a reporter from *The Times* recorded a speech made by Lord Rosebery. The defendant copied this record. The House of Lords held that copyright subsisted in the transcribed speech, overruling the Court of Appeal's finding that the speech must be original in the sense of containing the author's own words and ideas. Earl Halsbury LC was unconcerned about the multiplicity of copyrights that might ensue:

It is said that in the view I have suggested there would be as many copyrights as reporters. I do not see the difficulty. Each reporter is entitled to report, and each undoubtedly would have a copyright in his own published report; but where is the difficulty?

The reporter had edited the speech before publication.

Section 3(3) of the CDPA 1988 leaves open the question whether *Walter v Lane* (1900) is to be followed. In *Roberton v Lewis* (1960), it was argued that the plaintiff had copyright in the printed record he had made of a folk tune in the same way as the *Times* reporter. *Obiter*, Cross J said that this was unlikely. He distinguished *Walter v Lane* (1900) both as having been decided before the statutory requirement of originality was instituted, and on its facts. Lord Rosebery's speech had been recorded for the first time, whereas the tune must have been written down by others previously. This may represent the extent of a reporter's copyright, but *Walter v Lane* (1900) was approved in *Express Newspapers v News UK Ltd* (1990), though the record of an interview there was the first report to be made of it.

8.4.6 Independent creation

The interpretation given to 'original' has a further consequence in that, provided that the works have been created without copying, it is quite possible for copyright to subsist in two or more identical works. For example, pictures simultaneously taken by press photographers from the same vantage point and in the same lighting conditions may bear a very close resemblance; however, provided that they are taken individually, each photographer will secure copyright (the qualification provisions being satisfied (see 9.1)).

8.5 LITERARY WORKS

A literary work is any work that is written, spoken or sung, other than a dramatic or musical work: s 3(1) of the CDPA 1988. It might be tempting to read 'literary' as implying that an element of merit is required before a piece of writing can be treated as a copyright work. Case law establishes that this is not a qualitative standard, merely an indication that the work be recorded by means of letters or numbers. In *University of London Press v University Tutorial Press* (1916), Petersen J explained a literary work to be a work 'expressed in print or writing, irrespective of the question whether the quality or style is high'.

Section 3(1) of the CDPA 1988 provides examples of works included in this category:

- tables and compilations other than databases;
- computer programs;
- preparatory design material for computer programs; and
- databases.

Literary works, therefore, include the very mundane, such as tide tables, mathematical tables, examination papers, television schedules, football pools or lottery coupons and the like.

8.5.1 Databases

Copyright for databases as literary works was harmonised by the Database Directive,[38] which came into force on 1 January 1998. The Directive also introduced new protection for unoriginal databases (see 8.11).

A copyright database comprises a collection of independent works, data or other materials which are arranged in a systematic or methodical way and are individually accessible by electronic or other means.[39] It must satisfy a different standard of originality: whether by reason of the selection itself or arrangement of the contents, it must constitute the author's own intellectual creation.[40] Like copyright in an original compilation, this is protection for the effort of collation, but potentially to the civilian standard (see 8.4.1). A database not meeting this standard may have protection as a compilation, as well as under the new *sui generis* right, unless s 3(1)(a) of the CDPA 1988 is intended to render the two mutually exclusive. This is not a necessary interpretation.[41] The two may be distinguished as literary works to meet the Directive's standard of originality, and the fair dealing defence.

Protection for the database as a literary work then extends to individual entries in the database, whereas a compilation is a composite work and protection only extends to the work as a whole, or to a substantial part of it (see 10.1.3).

8.5.2 Computer programs

The Copyright (Computer Software) Act 1985 confirmed copyright for computer programs as literary works, and this was reaffirmed by the CDPA 1988. However, 'computer program' is not defined. Australian and American legislation does define program, but runs the risk of becoming outdated as technology advances. Preparatory and design material (such as flowcharts and specifications) is included as a separate sub-set of literary works. The Software Directive did not affect the principles applied to copyright software. However, it is arguable that the 'author's own intellectual creation' standard of originality should have been implemented, requiring a greater level of creativity than the traditional UK standard of 'not copied', as it has in relation to databases.

Much programming comprises rearrangement of well-known routines, and is arranged in modular fashion in suites of programs. Consequently, when questions of originality and infringement arise, it can be significant whether a program is treated as a single entity or as a compilation. Much effort may have gone into a single module, forming part of a much larger combination of programs. In *Ibcos Computers Ltd v Barclays* (1994) Jacob J identified copyright in a compilation of modules each of which performed functions that any similar system would require. In *Cantor Fitzgerald International v Tradition (UK) Ltd* (1999) Pumfrey J also likened the complex program at issue to a compilation. He warned against undiscerning applications of principles

---

38   Implemented by the Copyright and Rights in Databases Regulations 1997.
39   Section 3A of the CDPA 1988.
40   *Ibid*, s 3A(2).
41   Derclaye, E, 'Do Sections 3 and 3A of the CDPA Violate the Database Directive? A Closer Look at the Definition of a Database in the UK and its Compatibility with European Law' [2002] EIPR 466.

developed for traditional literary works to programs, which serve a different, and mechanical, function. However, just as skill can be applied to plot in a play or novel, so too the 'architecture', or structure, of a program may be protected if it represents programmers' skills. He equated the taking of a substantial part (see 10.1.3) of a program to the question whether that part would be sufficiently original for copyright to subsist at all.

8.5.3   Electronic works

Storage of the original works in electronic format does not alter their status as works. The definition of writing includes 'any form of notation or code … regardless of the method by which, or medium in or on which, it is recorded': s 178 of the CDPA 1988. The definition of 'electronic' as 'actuated by electric, magnetic, electro-magnetic, electro-chemical or electro-mechanical energy' is equally wide.[42] Sound recordings, broadcasts and films can also be stored digitally. It can be queried whether a work only temporarily stored in the RAM[43] of a computer has been 'recorded'.

Websites

Equally, works incorporated into websites retain their characteristics as copyright works in the usual way, and normal copyright principles apply to them. Webpages and websites may comprise compilations, although it may be questioned whether compilations include works other than literary works.

Collections of works available on the internet such as bulletin board services may also constitute databases. A website as a whole may constitute a copyright work as a typographical arrangement of a published edition.[44] In *Shetland Times v Wills* (1997), a Scottish case, a website was found to be a cable programme service[45] or a cable programme (see 8.9.3).

Multimedia works

Multimedia works,[46] which comprise collections of many different types of work in structured and unified format such as a CD-ROM or web resource, may be protected by database copyright, if original, or the new database right. Each work may also have its own copyright protection, and one of the main investments in creating such works is securing all the necessary copyright permissions to include them. The Database Directive excludes a compilation of music from copyright or *sui generis* database protection.

---

42   Although it is not clear whether this would extend to nanotechnology and computers.
43   Random access memory. Stored here the work will be lost if a computer is turned off.
44   As suggested by Holyoak, J and Torremans, P, *Intellectual Property Law* (London: Butterworths, 1998)
45   A category of work subsumed under the definition of broadcast after implementation of the Information Society Directive. This removes internet transmissions from broadcasts (see 8.9.3).
46   Stamatoudi, I, *Copyright and Multimedia Products* (Cambridge: Cambridge University Press, 2001).

8.6   DRAMATIC WORKS

Section 3(1) of the CDPA 1988 includes works of dance and mime as dramatic works, but provides no other definition of this type of work. The sub-section suggests that the categories of literary and dramatic work are mutually exclusive. This could be interpreted to mean that any record of words intended to be performed (such as a television script) is to be treated as a literary work, and that the category of dramatic works is confined to those elements peculiar to dramatic performance (such as stage directions or the choreography for a dance). A better view is that any literary work intended to be performed is a dramatic work. In any case, protection for literary and dramatic works is co-extensive.

It is clear from the inclusion of dance and mime that a dramatic work does not necessitate any 'literary' or verbal element. Other systems of performance, such as skating and gymnastic routines, should fall within the category of a dramatic work because systems exist for recording them.

The means of recording a dramatic work, and the dramatic work itself, must not be confused. The work must be recorded (see 8.2.2), in writing or otherwise, but it is the sequence of words or actions so recorded that constitute the dramatic work itself. The dramatic work exists apart from the recording of it: *Norowzian v Arks Ltd (No 2)* (1998).

8.6.1   Capable of being recorded

The nature of a dramatic work has yet to be fully determined. It was an issue in two earlier cases. In both, suggestions had been made to the authors of plays. The contribution had to be to a dramatic work to found a claim to joint authorship and a copyright interest. In *Tate v Thomas* (1921), suggestions as to 'such accessorial matters such as scenic effects, or stage "business" were found not to be the subject matter of copyright. However, this was only because they were too insignificant or negligible to be capable of being printed and published. Similarly, in *Wiseman v George Weidenfeld and Nicolson* (1985), Whitford J held that 'a dramatic work involves ... not only dialogue but a series of incidents – dramatic situations – which in a particular order or occurrence can form the backbone of a piece'. On the facts however, the plaintiff's suggestions had not proved sufficient to earn an interest in the copyright. Dramatic works clearly extend beyond dialogue to other stage effects, but it would appear that they must be capable of being recorded in some way.

8.6.2   Capable of being performed

The nature of a dramatic work was raised again in *Norowzian v Arks Ltd (No 2)* (1998). The claimant was a film director who produced a short length of film, *Joy*, depicting a dancer performing a routine. It was edited and cut using known and common techniques, including jump cutting, to produce a striking sequence in which the dancer apparently made movements which could not have physically been successively made. Rattee J held that the sequence shown in the film did not constitute a dramatic work because it was not capable of physical performance. He said that 'to be a dramatic work, a work must be, or capable of being, physically performed', following *Green v Broadcasting Corporation of New Zealand* (1989). He was distinguishing between the film and its content. This decision appeared to leave a gap in copyright protection for some types of work. Whether the sequence depicted in the edited version of the film could not be physically performed may be queried. Dancers acting in concert could recreate it.

The Court of Appeal, however, held that a film could simultaneously constitute a dramatic work, and a recording of a dramatic work. The statutory definition of 'dramatic work' was not comprehensive (as those for literary and musical works are) and should be given its normal meaning of 'a work of action, with or without words or music, which is capable of being performed before an audience'. A filmed sequence could fall within this, as *Joy* did. Nor did s 1(1) of the CDPA 1988 preclude an overlap between categories of work. The decision should bring some relief to the entertainment industry. Cartoons films were also stated to be dramatic works, for example. However, it is doubtful how beneficial it will be to film directors. Their contribution often lies in interpreting a screenplay, which is as much a matter of technique as action capable of being performed.[47] The Court rejected any copyright in technique, holding that the defendant had not copied a substantial part of the work. The most that could be said was that there was a similarity between the filming and editing styles and techniques used.

Three distinct elements should be identified: the choreographed dance, the edited depiction of it in the film, and the recording itself. Each is potentially a work. First, the dance, if fixed and capable of being performed, could constitute a dramatic work. Secondly, its edited depiction, which could be termed a 'cinematic work', *Joy*,[48] is now also held to comprise a dramatic work. Finally, the recorded film will bear copyright as a work of film. The Court of Appeal termed the cinematic work the 'film'; in so doing it confused the two and held that *Joy* was not a recording or fixation of a dramatic work because the editing process precluded the work of choreography being performed. It may not have been a recording of the dance as a dramatic work because that was not capable of being performed without the aid of jump cutting. However, it seems wrong to hold that the film was not a recording of the edited cinematic (dramatic) work *Joy*, which must be fixed for copyright to subsist.[49] Stamatoudi[50] argues that this work could not be performed. However, showing the film would perform the edited dance. Careful identification of all potential works is required. If this is done then the question of overlapping works (see 8.2.4) is also resolved; it was not the film but the cinematic work which fell into the 'dramatic work' category. The underlying dance in this case did not secure its own protection; had it been capable of being performed however, a second dramatic work would have existed.

Nourse LJ rejected the Berne Convention as an aid to interpretation of the CDPA 1988. However, Buxton LJ drew attention to the fact that Article 14*bis* requires protection to be given to audio-visual and 'cinematographic' works as original works. This includes protection against more than mere identical replication of the work, which is all that film copyright would provide.

---

47   Porter, H, 'A "Dramatic Work" Includes ... A Film' [2000] Ent LR 50.
48   Arnold, R, '*Joy*: A Reply' [2001] IPQ 10.
49   Section 3(2) of the CDPA 1988.
50   Stamatoudi, I, 'Joy for the Claimant: Can a Film Also be Protected as a Dramatic Work?' [2000] IPQ 117.

8.6.3 Formats

Green v Broadcasting Corporation of New Zealand (1989) revealed another gap in protection. The Privy Council refused to treat the format for a television talent contest (repeated catch phrases, the show's title, and use of a 'clapometer' to measure audience reaction) as a dramatic work for three reasons. First, Lord Bridge did not regard repeated, but unconnected, use of such features in conjunction with changing material for each show as a 'format' and, therefore, substantial enough to be regarded as a work (see 8.2.1). Secondly, he said that these features did not have sufficient certainty to found a copyright monopoly. Finally, he said:

> ... a dramatic work must have sufficient unity to be capable of performance and ... the features claimed as constituting the 'format' of a television show, being unrelated to each other except as accessories to be used in the presentation of some other dramatic or musical performance, lack that essential characteristic.

However, this leaves open the possibility of a more defined format securing protection. In *Medcalf v Mardell* (2000) the Court of Appeal upheld Lloyd J's finding of copyright in both the drafts and final versions of a written format for the television show *Big Break*. He did so, however, as literary rather than dramatic works.

8.7 MUSICAL WORKS

Section 3(1) of the CDPA 1988 defines a musical work as:

> a work consisting of music, exclusive of any words or action intended to be sung, spoken or performed with the music.

However, the elements excluded from the musical work may qualify as literary or dramatic works, with the consequence that in a song two copyrights with different owners and of different duration may arise, musical copyright in the melody, and literary copyright in the libretto.

'Music' is not defined,[51] and does not connote any need for musical merit or quality, provided that a sequence of notes or sounds are involved. Some sequences of sounds are so simple that they may be held not to constitute a work at all (see 8.2.1). However, four chords were regarded as distinctive in *Lawton v Lord David Dundas* (1985). Sounds are now registrable under the Trade Marks Act 1994, so that the alternative protection reasoning of *Exxon v Exxon Insurance* (1982) may apply to deny copyright to very short sequences of sound (see 8.2.1).

Copyright can also subsist in secondary musical works, so that transcriptions and arrangements of another's work may secure copyright for the transcriber or arranger. There is no clear guidance as to the level of 'skill, labour and judgment' required. In *Wood v Boosey* (1868), it was held that 'some judgment and taste' were required on the part of the arranger.

---

51 It has been defined in other jurisdictions, such as Canada; however, doing so may prejudice protection both for traditional music, and new forms of expression.

8.8 ARTISTIC WORKS

Section 4 of the CDPA 1988 expands the meaning of 'artistic work', which is divided into three categories:

(a) graphic works, photographs, sculpture or collage, irrespective of artistic quality;

(b) works of architecture;

(c) works of artistic craftsmanship.

No definition is given of 'art', in the same way that 'music', 'literary' and 'dramatic' are left undefined. This suggests that 'artistic' may be interpreted to mean anything depicted visually, by whatever means, in the same way that 'literary' includes anything in print or writing (see 8.5), or 'dramatic' relates to anything capable of performance. In *Interlego v Tyco Industries* (1989), Lord Oliver explained the essence of an artistic work to be its visual significance.

Artistic quality

Artistic works differ from the other original works in that it is only for the first category that artistic quality is expressly stated to be irrelevant. Yet, considerations of the merit of a work are clearly irrelevant for the other original works. Therefore, express exclusion of 'quality' raises the question whether 'quality' is being used to mean merit in relation to artistic works in the same way that merit is irrelevant to literary, dramatic and musical works. 'Quality' is capable of meaning either merit, or character and nature. It may be that the statute is expressly removing consideration of whether a s 4(1)(a) work is artistic in character, rather than how good it may or may not be (this being implied in the same way as it is for literary, dramatic and musical works).

Cases where the simplest of technical drawings have been treated as copyright artistic works (*British Northrop v Texteam Blackburn* (1974); *Solar Thomson v Barton* (1977)) suggest that the meaning implied is the lack of any requirement of merit. However, the earlier case of *Kenrick v Lawrence* (1890) suggests otherwise. It was doubted in this case whether copyright subsisted in an extremely simple drawing of a hand and pencil intended to be used on electoral forms for the illiterate. To provide copyright protection for this 'mere choice of subject' would have conferred a long-term monopoly on the only way of indicating the means of voting. Wills J suggested that 'something special in the way of artistic treatment ... might be the subject of copyright', but that 'there is nothing which in any flight of imagination can be called artistic about either the plaintiffs' or the defendants' representation'. He appeared to be looking for merit in the drawing as it was clearly visual in character. If there were to be protection, he went on to suggest, only the most exact and literal copy, such as a photograph, could infringe. This case was, however, decided under the Fine Arts Copyright Act 1862.

Under current copyright legislation, it is clear that very little is required in the way of artistry (whether of merit or in a work's nature). However, where industrial designs continue to be treated as copyright works (although infringement is constrained by s 51 of the CDPA 1988) the question assumes significance, in particular in relation to works of artistic craftsmanship. One solution to the potentially very wide monopolies that may result if questions of both artistic merit and character are to be excluded, is to adjust the extent of protection to the 'skill, labour and judgment' embodied in the work, requiring very close reproduction for very simple works.

8.8.1 Section 4(1)(a) of the CDPA 1988

Works falling within this sub-section receive further explanation and definition in s 4(2) of the CDPA 1988. Graphic works include any painting, drawing, diagram, map, chart or plan, and any engraving, etching, lithograph, woodcut or similar work. It should be noted that a diagram, drawing, map, plan or the like may include both literary and artistic works because any written matter on the drawing will be treated as a literary work: *Interlego v Tyco Industries* (1989). This distinction is more significant than that between literary and dramatic works because the extent of protection for artistic works does vary from that of literary works. In *Electronic Techniques (Anglia) Ltd v Critchley Components Ltd* (1997) only literary copyright was relied on. Laddie J refused to conflate the artistic and literary elements in circuit diagrams as a single literary work (see 8.2.4). He did not dismiss the possibility that two separate copyrights might exist in the diagrams, as in a map.

Paintings

No further definition is given to 'painting', but it would appear that a painting requires some permanency of surface, although there is no requirement of fixation for artistic works. In *Merchandising Corporation of America v Harpbond* (1983), it was held that an artiste's facial make-up did not constitute a painting for the purposes of copyright (see 8.2.2).

Photographs

'Photograph' is defined as a recording of light or other radiation on any medium on which an image is produced or from which an image may by any means be produced, and which is not part of a film. This wide definition should include X-rays, holograms and digital images, as well as new means of recording images yet to be developed.

In one respect taking photographs could be regarded as making copies, and therefore as unoriginal. This might be particularly so if a photograph was merely representational of a two-dimensional object. In the US it was held that photographs of paintings in a gallery were not original works in *The Bridgeman Art Library Ltd v Corel Group* (1998). Following *dicta* in the *Interlego* case, the case raises doubt as to the originality of photographs replicating other works of art, although it is not binding in the UK. Nor is it easy to reconcile with *Walter v Lane* (1990). The editing skills exercised by the reporter seem analogous to the photographic skills of the photographer.

Copyright in photographs of single three-dimensional objects was considered in *Antiquesportfolio.com plc v Rodney Fitch & Co* (2000). Neuberger J accepted that provided the photographer could demonstrate a small degree of time, skill and labour in producing the pictures, for example by the exercise of judgment as to angle, lighting, film speed, focus and filters, copyright should subsist whatever the subject-matter of a photograph. Even the choice of subject matter in order to illustrate a typical type of antique might be sufficient. However, a slavish copy, such as reusing a negative, re-photographing a print or recreating the effect of an earlier photograph, would not be original. The judgment recognised by Neuberger J should apply equally to photographs of two-dimensional objects, but Lord Oliver's *dicta* in the *Interlego* case that effort confined to copying could not constitute originality may remain a stumbling block.

Collage

The nature of collage, added to copyright by the CDPA 1988, was considered in *Creation Records Ltd v News Group Newspapers Ltd* (1997) (see 8.2.2). Lloyd J refused to consider that temporary arrangement of everyday objects amounted to collage because 'collage' implied as an 'essential element the sticking of two or more things together'. It did not extend to the collation of random, unrelated and unfixed elements, whether or not this was done with artistic intent. The case has important implications for some forms of modern art which make use of everyday objects.[52] Had the collage had sufficient permanence the intentions of the creator could play a significant role in determining whether the result was an artistic work.

Sculpture and engraving

Controversial use was made of copyright for sculptures and engravings in the New Zealand case of *Wham-O Manufacturing v Lincoln Industries* (1985). Techniques similar to a sculptor's may be used industrially and, if the artistic nature and/or quality of a work is irrelevant, copyright may lie, as it does for a design drawing. The plaintiffs developed and made a plastic frisbee and successfully claimed copyright infringement of preliminary drawings, wooden models for moulds and the frisbees themselves. The New Zealand legislation did not differ in any pertinent way from that of the UK. The moulds and frisbees were held to be engravings, and the wooden models were found to be sculptures. This appears to ignore any need for artistic nature in these artistic works and extends copyright protection into the design field.

In *J and S Holdings v Wright Health Group* (1988), a more restrictive approach was taken. The plaintiff claimed infringement of casts made for the production of dental impression trays. It was held that the trays did not constitute sculptures because they were not made for the purposes of sculpture, nor were they original, being copies of earlier models. *Wham-O Manufacturing v Lincoln Industries* (1985) was distinguished on the ground that the models there had been carved. In the CDPA 1988, sculpture is said to include a cast or model made for the purposes of sculpture, perhaps implying sculpture as an artistic, rather than industrial, activity. However, this was interpreted in *Breville Europe plc v Thorn EMI Domestic Appliances* (1985) as extending 'sculpture' to casts and models made for the purposes of sculpture, which should be given its dictionary meaning of:

> Art of forming representations of objects, etc or abstract designs in the round or in relief by chiselling stone, carving wood, modelling clay, casting metal, or similar processes ...

Sculptures and engravings are protected 'irrespective of artistic quality'. If this refers to the nature of a work as falling within the field of art, it will be sufficient to establish the technique used in order to determine whether an activity or work falls within this category of artistic work. If it refers to merit, then whether the work was made for

---

52   Stokes, S, *Art and Copyright* (Oxford: Hart Publishing, 2003).

reasons of art rather than industry may be relevant. Laddie J appears to suggest that this is the case in *Metix (UK) Ltd v Maughan (Plastics) Ltd* (1997). The plaintiffs unsuccessfully claimed copyright in moulds used to make industrial cartridges. He said:

> There is nothing ... which suggests that the manufacturers of these moulds considered themselves, or were considered by anybody else, to be artists when they designed the moulds or that they were concerned in any way with the shape or appearance of what they were making, save for the purpose of achieving a functional effect.

It was also held in *Metix (UK) Ltd v Maughan (Plastics) Ltd* (1997) that *J and S Holdings v Wright Health Group* (1988) should not be interpreted to suggest that an object with a transient existence could not be a work of sculpture. Laddie J cited ice sculptures as an example.

8.8.2 Works of architecture

It may be that either or both the artistic merit or artistic character of a work of architecture may be relevant. In the Copyright Act 1911, protection was given to 'architectural works of art', defined as 'any building or structure having an artistic character or design'. If artistic character must be taken into account, buildings made from the common stock of ideas may fall outside copyright protection. However, buildings will also receive indirect copyright protection by virtue of any copyright in the plans for them: *Pearce v Ove Arup Partnership Ltd* (1999).

8.8.3 Works of artistic craftsmanship

The Act does not define 'artistic craftsmanship', and the courts have had difficulty in determining which works fall into this category. It was first included in the Copyright Act 1911. Before 1911, copyright was only given to works of fine art, which represented the general understanding of the nature of art until the Arts and Crafts Movement, led by William Morris, led to items of applied and decorative art. Lord Simon describes this development in *Hensher v Restawile* (1976). Functional, but decorative items, such as jewellery, glassware, cutlery, hand made toys, leather goods, pottery and designer fashion items, should fall into this class of artistic work.

As a matter of construction, two interpretations of the phrase 'artistic craftsmanship' seem possible. Either the work must fit within a composite concept of 'artistic craft', or it must satisfy a dual test of artistry and craftsmanship. If the former, a definition is necessary; perhaps, the best definition is that supplied by Lord Simon. If the latter is adopted, it must also be determined whether artistic merit or artistic character is necessary. Other questions also present themselves: whether it is the maker's, buyer's, judge's or general public's view that is relevant, and what level of artistry and craftsmanship is required.

Artistic 'quality' must be taken into account. The House of Lords agreed that this referred to the character of a work as a work of art in *Hensher v Restawile* (1976).

Craftsmanship

In *Hensher v Restawile* (1976) the parties conceded that the prototype was a work of craftsmanship, perhaps misguidedly, because the court doubted that this was so. In

Guild v Eskandar Ltd (2001) Rimer J, following *Merlet v Mothercare plc* (1986), considered first whether the work was one of craftsmanship: one requiring a 'manifestation of pride in sound workmanship'. He held that prototypes for mass production of garments were not craftsmanship. The second question to be asked was whether it was a work of art.

A work of art

The House of Lords struggled with the phrase in *Hensher v Restawile* (1976). The appellants alleged infringement of copyright in the prototype for a very popular suite of furniture. At first instance, Graham J had found that the prototype was a work of artistic craftsmanship, but the Court of Appeal disagreed on the basis that the work did not have the requisite artistry, not in terms of merit, but in terms of character. In the House of Lords, upholding the Court of Appeal's conclusion, each of the judges adopted a different test of artistry. Lord Reid said that the work must be capable of giving pleasure, satisfaction or uplift to those looking at it, in the eyes of a substantial section of the public, and that the maker's intention was relevant, but not conclusive. Lord Morris declined to define 'artistic', but saw it falling between the visual appeal of designs and the high art of the fine arts, judged objectively, although the maker's intention could be considered, taking into account evidence of those with special capabilities for forming an opinion. Viscount Dilhorne regarded a work of craftsmanship as one that was hand made, and said that a work of art could be functional, but that mere originality of design did not constitute artistry. This, he said, was a question of fact, looking to the buyer's reasons for acquiring the work. Rejecting any test of the motives of the purchaser, Lord Simon felt that the phrase was a composite one to be construed as a whole, according to expert evidence of artist-craftsmen. Lord Kilbrandon, however, focused on the intentions of the work's maker.

The maker's intention

Faced with such lack of consensus, Walton J adopted a test of the maker's intention in *Merlet v Mothercare plc* (1986). Considering whether the prototype for a baby's rain covering constituted a work of artistic craftsmanship, he held that, although soundly made, it was unlikely to be a work of craftsmanship. The appropriate question to ask was whether the maker of the work had the conscious purpose of creating a work of art. This was to avoid the court having to make a value judgment as to the nature of the work. There are restrictions in adopting such a test, as the plaintiff discovered, for where a good idea is made up for personal use, but is subsequently seen to have commercial potential, the work will not satisfy the test. It will also be difficult to apply if the work's maker is unavailable to give evidence and will force the court to determine whether the avowed intention has, in fact, been achieved. In *Guild v Eskandar Ltd* (2001) Rimer J held that this was a primary, but not the only, consideration; and that it was a matter of evidence and not the court's own value judgment.

In *Shelley v Rex Features* (1994), it was accepted that there was a serious question to be tried in relation to copyright in the prosthetic make up used to create a Frankenstein monster for a film, either as sculpture or a work of artistic craftsmanship. The film sets were to be treated as works of artistic craftsmanship. The judge rejected the stance taken in *Merlet v Mothercare plc* (1986) that the work's appeal must be considered in isolation, and not in the context of its setting, as unduly narrow where a composition was made up of artefacts especially constructed and arranged to create a particular artistic effect. This was distinguished in *Creation Records Ltd v News Group Newspapers Ltd* (1997) in relation to the Oasis album cover photograph, but because it lacked any element of craftsmanship. In *Guild v Eskandar Ltd* (2001) Rimer J doubted whether considering the work in isolation, a garment, excluded considering it as worn by a mannequin.

The meaning of 'work of artistic craftsmanship' has received an added significance with the CDPA 1988 because s 51 of the CDPA 1988 removes some of copyright protection for design documents, but only if the object depicted is not itself an artistic work. The full term of copyright protection, rather than the shorter terms of design law, will, therefore, be available for designs for articles which can be regarded as works of artistic craftsmanship.

8.9 DERIVATIVE WORKS

Copyright for derivative works protects entrepreneurs, rather than authors' acts of creativity. While such exploitation enhances authors' reward, falling within the private justifications for copyright, it also serves the public justification of encouraging widespread dissemination of works.

No standard of originality is expressly applied to the derivative works: sound recordings, films, broadcasts, and the typographical arrangement of published works. However, copyright does not subsist in sound recordings or films to the extent that they are copies of another sound recording or film.[53] Nor does copyright subsist in a broadcast, or typographical arrangement to the extent that it infringes copyright in another broadcast, or arrangement.[54]

In the case of sound recordings and films, the result is that the recording purchased by consumers is not a copyright work, being merely a copy of the master recording. However, to do an infringing act in relation to the copy will indirectly infringe the copyright in the master recording (see 10.1.2).

The derivative works often provide the means for disseminating original works, and the underlying and derivative works must be distinguished. For example, a video of a recent film will have film copyright for the film, but also literary or dramatic copyright in the script, and musical copyright in the music.

8.9.1 Sound recordings

'Sound recording' is defined by s 5A of the CDPA 1988 as:

(a) a recording of sounds, from which the sounds may be reproduced; or

(b) a recording of the whole or any part of a literary, dramatic, or musical work, from which sounds reproducing the work or part may be reproduced, regardless of the medium on which the recording is made or the method by which the sounds are reproduced or produced.

---

53 Sections 5A(2), 5B(4) of the CDPA 1988.
54 *Ibid*, ss 6(6), 7(6)(b), 8(2).

This is wide enough to include future means of recording sound, not being tied to any method or material by which sounds may be recorded or reproduced. Consequently MP3 digital files should fall within sound recording copyright. There is no necessity for the sounds to be heard in the recording, provided that they can be reproduced. Thus, pianola rolls and the pimpled rubber rolls in musical toys are protected, as should be the chips in musical cards and the like.

There is no requirement that the literary, dramatic or musical work being recorded be original, so that copyright subsists in a recording of Shakespeare's plays or a Beethoven symphony, although their copyright has long expired. Equally, different recordings of the same work will secure their own copyright. Amendments made by the Duration of Copyright and Rights in Performances Regulations 1995 allow the sound track of a film to be treated as part of a film without prejudice to any copyright as a sound recording.[55]

8.9.2 Films

A film is 'a recording on any medium from which a moving image may by any means be produced'. This definition is wide enough to include multimedia discs, although they also incorporate written texts, and even video games. To film a previously unrecorded dramatic work will create two copyrights: in the film, and in the dramatic work: *Norowzian v Arks Ltd (No 2)* (1998). The dramatic work may in itself be based on an underlying third copyright work such as a novel or a play.

Film copyright applies to the recording and is restricted to identical copies being made: *Norowzian v Arks Ltd (No 1)* (1998); recording a video, for example. Attempts to replicate the performance depicted in a film are subject to any copyright in the dramatic work in the film (see 8.6.2).

The creative effort in making a film means that films as a whole are not really solely derivative works. This went unrecognised until the harmonisation of UK copyright law by the Copyright and Related Rights Regulations 1996, which came into force on 1 December 1996 and conferred a copyright interest on film directors as well as producers (see 9.4.3). However, this is to confuse the film and dramatic work. If *Norowzian v Arks Ltd (No 2)* (1998) is correct a director's effort will also be protected by the dramatic work.[56]

Although the essence of a film is a moving sequence of images, it was held in *Aaron Spelling v Goldberg* (1981) that to copy a still shot from a film constituted infringing copying, and this was confirmed by s 17(4) of the CDPA 1988.

8.9.3 Broadcasts

Broadcast copyright is distinct from any copyright in underlying works being broadcast (there may be none, as in sports broadcasts, for example), and forms part of the regime of control over television, radio and other broadcasting. Although transient, intangible and ephemeral, broadcasts are treated as works for the labour involved in their production and dissemination.

---

55 *Ibid*, s 5B(2), (5).
56 Rivers, T, '*Norowzian* Revisited' [2000] EIPR 389.

'Broadcast' is defined by s 6(1) of the CDPA 1988 as:

... an electronic transmission of visual images, sounds or other information which –

(a)   is transmitted for simultaneous reception by members of the public and is capable of being lawfully received by them, or

(b)   is transmitted at a time determined solely by the person making the transmission for presentation to members of the public, ...

Internet transmissions (as distinct to any underlying works) are excepted from this definition unless they are:

(a)   a transmission taking place simultaneously on the internet and by other means,

(b)   a concurrent transmission of a live event, or

(c)   a transmission of a recorded moving images or sounds forming part of a programme service offered by the person responsible for making the transmission, being a service in which programmes are transmitted at scheduled times determined by that person.

For the purposes of s 6(4), 'Wireless broadcast' and 'wireless telegraphy' are defined by s 178(1) of the CDPA 1988 as:

... the sending of electromagnetic energy over paths not provided by a material substance constructed or arranged for that purpose but does not include the transmission of microwave energy between terrestrial fixed points ...

This excludes transmission by wire or optical fibre, but includes satellite and terrestrial transmission, including teletext services and digital broadcasting. Broadcast extends to encrypted transmissions where decoding equipment has been made available to the public by or with the authority of the person making the broadcast or the person providing the contents of the transmission: s 6(2) of the CDPA 1988. Broadcast copyright extends to transmissions made from the UK or, if made by satellite, from the place of the uplink to the satellite.

Section 6(1) was amended by the Copyright and Related Rights Regulations (CRRR) 2003 implementing the Information Society Directive, replacing the separate rights to broadcast and to 'include in a cable programme service' with this wider and technologically neutral right to communicate to the public. Internet transmissions without broadcast characteristics, such as 'on request services' are excluded. These remain subject to copyright and database protection for web pages and web sites, and the right of communication in s 20 of the CDPA 1988 (see 9.6.5).

Before the Regulations came into force on 31 October 2003 a website was found to be a cable programme service or a cable programme in *Shetland Times v Wills* (1997), a Scottish case, by rejecting the argument that a website was a two way system. However, many websites are interactive, such as mail order catalogues. The case was an interim (interlocutory) hearing; however, Peter Smith J considered it correct, *obiter*, in *Sony v Easyinternetcafe Ltd* (2003).

Encrypted transmissions

A separate quasi-copyright is created by s 298 of the CDPA 1988. It relates to persons who charge for the reception of programmes included in a broadcast from the UK, or sends encrypted transmissions from the UK. They are given copyright rights and remedies against anyone who makes or deals in any apparatus or device designed or adapted to enable reception of those transmissions by anyone not entitled to do so. In *BBC Enterprises v Hi Tech Xtravision* (1990), the plaintiffs transmitted encrypted broadcasts to Europe from the UK. The defendants made unauthorised decoders. At first instance, Scott J looked for a denial of entitlement for the reception of the programmes in law, rather than contract, which had the effect of emasculating the remedy. Both the Court of Appeal and House of Lords held that the section had the dual effect of denying the legal right to receive the transmissions and providing a remedy for the transmitter. Lord Brandon adopted a purposive construction of the section to interpret 'not entitled to do so' as 'not authorised by the sender to do so'.

8.9.4 Typographical arrangements of published editions

Copyright subsists in the layout of a published edition of the whole or any part of one or more literary, dramatic, or musical works, provided that the edition is not a copy of an earlier arrangement: s 8 of the CDPA 1988. It is for this reason that, for example, photocopying the pages of republication of a work which has long been out of copyright may still amount to copyright infringement, and represents protection for publishers' expenditure in producing such editions. Infringement of a typographical edition differs from that of other works and is confined to making a facsimile copy of the work.[57]

Edition

It is clear from s 8(1) that an edition may include one or more underlying works. Even though 'substantiality' is not a quantitative test (see 10.1.3), in the case of a newspaper or other collection of works, whether each underlying work is considered to be the edition or not can make a considerable difference to the outcome if extracts are taken from it without authority. The House of Lords considered the meaning of 'edition' in *NLA Ltd v Marks & Spencer plc* (2002). Newspaper publishers assigned their typographical copyright to the Newspaper Licensing Agency (NLA), which administered the right on their behalf. The defendants subscribed to a press cuttings agency, which was licensed by the NLA. It recompiled the cuttings by compiling them, and copying the compilation widely to employees. The NLA argued that this infringed copyright in the papers' typographical copyright. In order to determine whether a 'substantial part' of the copyright in the typographical edition had been reproduced the court had to determine whether 'edition' comprised each article, or the paper as a whole. At first instance Lightman J held that 'edition' meant a version of a literary work and was coextensive with copyright in each article as a single work. The Court of Appeal did not agree and interpreted 'edition' to mean the paper as a whole, as did the House:

> The words 'or more' show that one may have a single published edition of more than one literary work and that there is no necessary congruence between the concept of an edition and the underlying works.

This was based on copyright protection being for the benefit of the publishing trade. It was the publisher's product, 'generally between covers', which was intended to be the

---

57 Section 17(5) of the CDPA 1988.

object of copyright protection, although this did not preclude some products being offered together at a single price, such as newspaper inserts. Lord Hoffmann distinguished the overlapping copyrights in a compilation (in the constituent works, and in the compilation as a whole) because there the copyrights would arise in different people and at different times. In the case of a newspaper the underlying copyright and that in the edition would arise simultaneously and all vest in the publisher. This leaves the question of whether a published book comprising chapters by one author should receive different treatment from one whose chapters are contributed by different writers.

To decide whether a substantial part had been copied, Lord Hoffmann went on to consider where the 'skill, labour and judgment' lay in a typographical edition of a newspaper. He found it to lie in the overall design (doubting whether this head of copyright had originally been intended to include newspapers at all). It was the combined effect of choice of typeface, number and width of columns, breadth of margins, relationship of headings to text, the number of articles per page and distribution of photographs and advertisements. This could not be expressed in any less than a full page.

Published

While the decision is clearly a correct one on its facts it does raise questions in relation to other types of work. Would the decision have been the same had the copies been taken from the newspapers' online versions? Design of a website, or even individual webpages, could fall within 'typographical edition'. The answer lies therefore in the definition of 'published'. Publication of a work constitutes issuing copies to the public.[58] In the case of literary, dramatic, musical or artistic works, this includes making the work available by an 'electronic retrieval system', but not therefore a published edition.[59] Communication to the public by way of the newly defined broadcast right constitutes publication of these works if it is 'by way of electronic retrieval system'.[60] The internet may be regarded as an electronic retrieval system. If so, the website or page is protected only if it falls into an 'original' category of work and is published by issuing copies to the 'public'. The stumbling block remains the fact that these copies will be individually and not collectively retrieved, for s 18 of the CDPA 1988 requires copies to be 'circulated'. In practice, therefore, protection for websites lies either in database protection, literary compilations, or individual 'original' works.

8.10 RELATED RIGHTS

Further intellectual property protection is provided for performers and their performances, and for databases not falling into copyright.

---

58 Section 175(1) of the CDPA 1988.
59 A separate category of work by virtue of s 1(1)(c) of the CDPA 1988.
60 Section 175(4) of the CDPA 1988.

8.11　UNORIGINAL DATABASES

Databases not reaching the copyright standard of originality may be protected by the new *sui generis* database right. This is a property right in a database (whether or not the database or any of its contents is a copyright work), provided that there has been substantial investment in obtaining, verifying or presenting its contents. It was introduced by the Database Directive, implemented by Part III of the Copyright and Rights in Databases Regulations 1997. To extract or reutilise all or a substantial part of the database's contents without the owner's consent will infringe this right.

8.11.1 The *sui generis* right

'Database' is defined as:

> ... a collection of independent works, data or other materials arranged in a systematic or methodical way and individually accessible by electronic or other means.

The right runs for 15 years from 1 January of the year following the date of completion of its making, or the first making public of the database within the 15-year period from its making. Substantial changes resulting in the database being regarded as a substantial new investment qualify the renewed database for its own term of protection. This allows for potentially eternal protection for a 'dynamic' database.

Recital 40 of the Directive indicates that protection is specifically for investment in deploying financial resources and/or the spending of time, effort and energy. Damage to this investment, and not merely parasitic competition, is being guarded against. This was a significant factor in the interpretation of the Directive by Laddie J and the Court of Appeal in *British Horseracing Board Ltd v William Hill Organisation* (2001). In turn, Recital 6 makes clear that the *sui generis* right is a response to the lack of harmonised unfair competition principles within the European Union and underlines the purpose of the right. In other European states, courts have refused to recognise protection for 'spin-off' databases which are not the central part of an organisation's business and investment. The issue was one that was referred to the ECJ (see below).

8.11.2 Exceptions

Lawful users' right to extract or reutilise insubstantial parts of the contents for any purpose is preserved by Article 8 of the Directive, subject to any copyright subsisting in the contents themselves. It is possible, though, that most uses could be regarded as substantial if they are of benefit to a user and Laddie J took William Hill's interest in the information they extracted into account when determining substantiality in *British Horseracing Board Ltd v William Hill Organisation* (2001).

Further access to, and use of, underlying information for specific purposes is provided for in Article 9 but only relates to 'lawful users'. This phrase is not defined in the Directive or the Regulations. Article 9 is implemented by reference to fair dealing with a substantial part for the approved purposes. No general right of private use is given for electronic databases, even though Recital 50 does not distinguish between electronic and non-electronic databases. A substantial part of a database's contents may be extracted for teaching or scientific research, provided that this is non-commercial and that the source is indicated. Scientific research relates both to the natural and human sciences. Additionally, Article 8(2) of the Directive provides that a lawful user may not:

... perform acts which conflict with normal exploitation of the database or unreasonably prejudice the legitimate interests of the maker of the database.

8.11.3 Protection for information

Just as copyright is confined to expression, the Database Directive was not intended to create any new rights in underlying data, nor to extend copyright to data, as Recitals 45 and 46 state. This implies that it was intended to preserve the traditional copyright balance of access and protection in regard to information. Protection for investment in the collation of information allows competitors to recreate that collation. The decision in *British Horseracing Board Ltd v William Hill Organisation* (2001) seemed to protect underlying information once collated in a database. Laddie J emphasised protection of investment in generating a database. He pointed out that it is jeopardised not only by taking the form of the data, but also by making use of its accuracy, and that infringement is not confined to rival database manufacturers. The decision of the ECJ, however, suggests otherwise by removing protection at all where investment is concentrated on the creation of information rather than the architecture of a database. However, where a database is protected so may be its underlying content.

The exceptions may confine access to information held in databases, particularly information whose sole source is the database, to those already licensed, possibly at a fee, and for a limited set of non-commercial purposes. If the right itself were to be widely interpreted monopoly power over information could result. Information such as that in the human genome databases, for example, seems to be a prime example of that which should not be so constrained. Initial drafts of the Directive contained proposals for compulsory licences, but these were not adopted. Much will depend on guidance given by the ECJ and its application by national courts.

It could be asked whether a form of unfair competition remedy would have been a solution better adapted to the nature of the right's subject-matter. In relation to the Directive, further development may come with the application of European Competition Law.[61] Meanwhile, WIPO has been considering a World Database Treaty providing *sui generis* protection. Economic studies on the potential effects of such protection are being studied before further debate over the draft treaty.

8.11.4 *British Horseracing Board Ltd v William Hill Organisation*

British Horseracing Board Ltd v William Hill Organisation (2001) was the first case on the *sui generis* database right in the UK. The claimant established and maintained an extensive and comprehensive computerised collection of information relating to the UK horseracing industry. It expended considerable investment in collecting, selecting and verifying data, as well as its design, and the insertion and arrangement of the data. Laddie J cited an estimated 8,000,000 new records or changes added annually, at an annual cost of £4 million, approximately 25% of the British Horseracing Board's (BHB's) yearly expenditure.

Although the defendants were licensed users, both directly and indirectly, the action related to their use of the database for a new venture – internet betting services.

---

61   Colston, C, 'Challenges to Information Retrieval: A Global Solution?' [2002] IJLIT 294.

The BHB alleged, successfully, that the defendant had infringed its database right by unlicensed use of information from the database via a sub-licence granted by Satellite Information Services Ltd. By the time the data used by William Hill was published on its internet service the information was available from other sources such as the press and teletext. Giving the Database Directive a purposive construction, Laddie J held that the information used amounted to extraction of a substantial part of the database, as well as repeated extraction of insubstantial parts, and that the *sui generis* right was not confined to the 'database-ness' of the collected information. The fact that the extraction and reutilisation was indirect, via the SIS raw data feed, did not prevent infringement. He also confirmed that the duration of protection for a database is renewed by 'substantial changes' and rejected the defendant's argument that substantial changes created a new database, so that repeated extractions from a dynamic database would not amount to repeated extraction for '*the*' database. Finally, he also rejected the defendant's argument (predicated on the argument that the underlying information must be unprotected) that to use the information after manipulation and re-presentation would not infringe, as this would continue to amount to reutilisation of the data.

The implications of the first instance judgment were significant for a number of reasons. First, the case appeared to confirm that protection lay for underlying information contained in a database and was not confined to its characteristics as a database. Secondly, that protection was shown to be potentially eternal where the database was 'dynamic', and the renewed protection extended to the earlier versions preceding the renewed updating or verification. Thirdly, copyright principles were not to be applied by analogy to the new right. In addition, finally, that use of information derived from a protected database amounted to 'extraction' from that database.

8.11.5 The Court of Appeal and reference to the ECJ

The Court of Appeal lifted the permanent injunction, nevertheless holding that there should be a reference to the ECJ on the interpretation of the Directive. It seemed unlikely that Laddie J's wide interpretation of the Directive would be overruled on appeal as the Court indicated its support for the decision. However, William Hill argued that information in the public domain could be used without the user realising its derivation from a protected database. The Court of Appeal recognised the importance of this point.

Five of the Court of Appeal's questions directly related to protection over underlying information. The Court asked whether either 'substantial part' or 'insubstantial part' of the contents of the database in Article 7(1) included information derived from the database, although not having the same arrangement and organisation as that in the database. The Court also referred to the indirect taking by William Hill in the interpretation of 'extraction' and 'reutilisation' – where it is the information rather than its source in the database that was used. Was reutilisation limited to the first making of contents taken from a database available to the public? The Court also adverted to the perceived harm to the BHB's interest in the database, particularly as the William Hill service did not reproduce all information necessary to placing a bet. It left their customers to seek additional material from other sources. In addition, while some users of the database pay for pre-race information, others have refused to do so.

The final, 11th, question indirectly asked about protection for information as it related to the potential for eternal protection of 'dynamic' databases. It queried whether substantial changes constitute new separate databases for the purposes of repeated insubstantial takings in Article 7(5).

The Court of Appeal also asked the ECJ to provide clear definitions of the nature of database protection, by asking for clarification of the investment necessary for its subsistence. It asked what constitutes 'obtaining' with particular reference to the procedure by which the BHB obtained and checked information as to race-runners given by telephone calls from trainers, a procedure directed at its function as the governing authority for British horseracing. Other references to the ECJ raised similar considerations. The Court of Appeal also asked what amounts to verification, and whether this is confined to ensuring the accuracy of information in a database from time to time. If so, this would not include the BHB's efforts to verify information before inclusion in the database. The reference in *Fixtures Marketing v OY Veikkaus Ab* directly asked the ECJ to provide guidance on the purpose of the Database Directive, and in particular whether users of information are to be restrained only from reuse for commercial purposes.

Finally, questions were directed to the interpretation of 'substantial' in Article 7.

In her Opinion,[62] Advocate General Stix-Hackl reaffirmed the intention to protect the database and not information within it, as the object was to protect investment, not information. 'Obtaining' was said not to include the generation of new data, but where the act of generation coincided with the collection and screening of data, protection would apply. However, she went on to state that the purpose for which a database was created did not affect the question whether it may be protected, so that databases created as a 'spin-off' to an enterprise's main activity were subject to the right. Verification, she said, applied to checking information within a database, and not to prior acts before information was included. 'Extraction' was interpreted to include permanent or temporary transfer of all or a substantial part of a database's contents. It only applied to direct transfers. Substantiality was a qualitative and quantitative test. 'Utilisation' related to making a substantial part available to the public, and might be indirect. Rearranging such data would continue to infringe. Finally, she decided, protection for dynamic databases resulted in new protection for the whole database on a 'rolling' basis.

8.11.6 The ECJ references

The ECJ decided both the *BHB* and *Fixtures Marketing*[63] references in November 2004. The Court took a more restricted view of the ambit of *sui generis* database protection, emphasising the Directive's purpose to protect investment in the generation of databases as storage and processing tools for information, not investment in generating the information itself.

Fixtures Marketing Ltd grants licences to exploit UK football fixture lists outside the UK. The lists were collated electronically and in printed booklets, at a cost of some £7 million annually. The defendant operated pools using data from the lists. It obtained

---

62 *BHB v William Hill Organisation* (2004).
63 *Fixtures Marketing Ltd v Svenska Spel AB, Fixtures Marketing Ltd v Oy Veikkaus Ab, Fixtures Marketing Ltd v OPAP.*

the information from the internet and newspaper sources, or from the football clubs, and was not a licensed user of the Fixtures lists.

The definition of a database

In *Fixtures Marketing Ltd v OPAP* (2004) the Court considered the definition of a database. It held that it was irrelevant whether a database contains materials created by the database maker himself, or taken from other sources; nor was the fact that a database contained sporting information significant. What was important was to interpret the definition within the context of its purpose as defined in the Directive. Accordingly, protection was designed to encourage development of systems for storing and processing information.[64] A database should therefore consist of a collection of independent materials, separable from one another without their informative value being affected. It is for this reason that a collection of audio-visual, cinematographic, literary or musical works does not fall within the definition.[65] The requirement that the database contents be systematically arranged and individually accessible then presupposes a 'fixed base' and technical[66] or other means[67] to allow retrieval of independent items. The Court expressed the view that football league fixture lists fell within this definition.

Investment in obtaining and verifying the contents

This too was give a purposive interpretation, so that it is not investment in the creation of the contents of a database that is required, but investment in resources to seek out independent materials and collect them.[68] The Court said:

> The purpose of the protection by the *sui generis* right provided for by the directive is to promote the establishment of storage and processing systems for existing information and not the creation of materials capable of being collected subsequently in a database.

Investment in verification of contents relates to resources used to ensure the reliability of information in a database, and to monitor the accuracy of materials collected when the database was created and during its operation. This must be distinguished from resources employed in verification when data is created and before subsequently being collated.

The Court was not prepared completely to exclude 'spin-off' databases from protection. However, where a database's creation is linked the database maker's principal activity of creating the data, they emphasised that only substantial investment in obtaining and verifying the data as part of creating the database, and not its creation, could be considered relevant:

> ... the collection of those data, their systematic or methodical arrangement in the database, the organisation of their individual accessibility and the verification of their

---

64   Recitals 10 and 12, Database Directive.
65   Recital 17, Database Directive.
66   Such as electronic, electromagnetic or electro-optical processes.
67   Such as an index, table of contents, or plan or method of classification.
68   Recital 39, Database Directive.

> accuracy throughout the operation of the database … require substantial investment in quantitative and/or qualitative terms …

Consequently, resources invested in selecting the horses to run in certain races, and the checks made before entering runners on the list, related to creation of data for the lists in the BHB database. However, it is likely that the BHB will challenge the ECJ's finding of fact when the case returns to the Court of Appeal. In the same vein, the ECJ held that the resources used to establish the dates, times and team pairings for football league matches could not be taken into account in the *Fixtures Marketing Ltd* references.

Extraction and reutilisation

Purposive interpretation was also applied to the acts of extraction and reutilisation and extended to acts harmful to a database maker's investment[69] in forming the database:

> … the *sui generis* right has an economic justification, which is to afford protection to the maker of the database and guarantee a return on his investment in the creation and maintenance of the database.

The acts themselves are to be widely interpreted as any act of appropriating the results of the database maker's investment[70] and making it available to the public. It is irrelevant that an unauthorised act is for the purpose of creating another database, whether in competition or not, and of the same or a different size. Nor is it relevant that the act is for a different purpose altogether, commercial or non-commercial. The ECJ also reaffirmed that unauthorised acts need not be direct as indirect taking would equally jeopardise the protected investment.

However, the prohibition against extraction and reutilisation does not extend to consulting a database if access has not been otherwise reserved. If a database maker authorises another to reutilise the contents of his database his consent to making those contents available to the public is implied, creating an alternative means of access to the information. However, if the database maker's consent only extends to consultation, it does not entitle the user to extract or reutilise the information in the whole or a substantial part of the database. Only insubstantial part may be extracted or reutilised.

The same applies even where the database maker has made his database available to the public unless one of the exceptions applies. Consequently, even though the BHB database was made available to the public, William Hill was not entitled to extract or reutilise a substantial part without authority. This it had done by transferring BHB data from one medium to another, integrating the data into its own system, and reutilising it by making it available to the public on the internet.

Substantial part

Whether a part is substantial quantitatively or qualitatively depends on the prejudice caused to the substantial investment in the database's creation by its maker.

---

69 Recitals 42 and 48, Database Directive.
70 Depriving him of the revenue which should have enabled him to redeem the cost of that investment. One assumes that the ECJ did not intend that database maker's should not profit from their investment.

Quantitative evaluation of a substantial part relates to the volume of data taken assessed in relation to the volume of the whole. Qualitative evaluation refers to the scale of investment in the obtaining, verifying and presenting of the extract's contents regardless of whether it is quantitatively significant in terms of the whole. Therefore, a 'quantitatively negligible part of the contents of a database may in fact represent, in terms of obtaining, verification or presentation, significant human, technical or financial investment'.

The intrinsic value of individual items of information themselves is not a relevant factor, as the Directive does not provide protection for the information itself.[71] Consequently, BHB's argument that, without the information which William Hill had extracted, races could not run was not a relevant consideration in deciding whether the taking was substantial. Quantitatively it was insignificant, and the investment adverted to had been expended in creation of the data, not putting it into database form. Therefore, it was not extraction and reutilisation of a substantial part in the ECJ's eyes, a finding BHB may challenge.

Repeated insubstantial taking

The ECJ emphasised that the provision against repeated insubstantial taking is intended to prevent the acts of taking a substantial part being circumvented. It is to prevent repeated and systematic taking the cumulative effect of which 'would be to seriously prejudice the investment made by the maker of the database' in the same way that taking under Article 7(1) of the Directive would. The insubstantial taking would therefore have to lead to the recreation of the whole or a substantial part of the database, whether or not the taking was intended to create a second database. The Court found that William Hill's taking was not intended to circumvent Article 7(1).

Dynamic databases

The ECJ did not address the Court of Appeal's 11th question, and this point remains moot.

8.12   RIGHTS FOR PERFORMERS IN PERFORMANCES

Many copyright works are performed and recorded. Performers may contribute a great deal to the artistic and economic value of their exploitation. They may not have sufficient individual bargaining power to secure contractual remuneration commensurate with that contribution, despite strong representation by the actors' and musicians' unions. These unions are a substitute for the property rights given to the works' authors. However, to give copyright protection to performers would create a considerable administrative burden in exploiting works, potentially even preventing it where consents cannot be secured.

---

71   Recitals 46, Database Directive.

Even so, 'bootleg'[72] recordings of live performances do much to undermine the economic rights of those with recording rights for them, in turn limiting the remuneration secured by performers. Both authorised recorders and performers have an interest in protection.

Initially, the Performers' Protection Acts[73] provided some protection by granting criminal penalties. However, no civil rights of action were granted, and attempts by the courts to construct civil liability only extended to performers and not to record companies.[74] Nor did the acts extend to all types of performances. The Rome Convention[75] allowed the approach through criminal offences to continue. Advances in recording technology and new means of distribution exacerbated the problem; in Part II the CDPA 1988 repealed the earlier Acts and created a new regime. This has subsequently been amended by implementation[76] of the Rental Directive, which added transferable property rights for performers, and the Duration Directive, which extended them. Further amendment[77] has come with the Information Society Directive, in turn implementing the WPPT.[78]

8.12.1 Rights in performances

Rights in performances, which should not be confused with copyright performing rights, have become a right related, and additional, to copyright. Performers have been granted new transferable property rights in relation to copies of performances, while the non-transferable non-property rights are preserved, and remuneration rights added.

Those with recording rights in relation to a performance are also given rights in relation to unauthorised recordings, while criminal offences are preserved.

The rights in performances last for 50 years from the end of the calendar year in which the performance takes place, or if a recording is released within that period, for 50 years from the end of the calendar year in which it is released.[79]

These rights provide effective protection against bootlegging. However, those producing and exploiting recordings of live performances must take care to secure consents from all performers involved, or risk obstacles to further use of old recordings to produce new ones. Unreasonable refusal of consent can be referred to the Copyright Tribunal.

---

72 Recordings of live performances made without consent. They do not infringe the copyright in a sound recording because the authorised recording is not reproduced; the two are made contemporaneously.
73 The Musical Performers' Protection Act 1925, and the Performers Protection Acts 1958–72.
74 *Rickless v United Artists* (1987), *RCA v Pollard* (1983).
75 The Rome Convention for the Protection of Performers, Producers of Phonograms and Broadcasting Organisations 1961.
76 The Duration of Copyright and Rights in Performances Regulations 1995, and the Copyright and Related Rights Regulations 1996.
77 The Copyright and Related Rights Regulations 2003.
78 WIPO World Performances and Phonograms Treaty 1996.
79 Section 191 of the CDPA 1988.

Performance

The rights are in qualifying performances. 'Performance 'is defined by s 180(2) of the CDPA as a live performance of dramatic works (including dance or mime), musical works, reading or recitation of literary works, and performance of a variety act or similar presentation. While including circus and comedy acts, this leaves out some possible performances, such as those of ice skaters and gymnasts. A performance may be given by a number of individuals, all of whom get separate rights, and all of whom must consent to its use. No formalities attach to the conferring of the rights; they are created by the act of performing.

Qualification

For the performers' rights the performance must be connected to the UK either by the status of a qualifying individual or take place in a qualifying country.[80] Section 206(1) provides that a qualifying country is the UK, a Member State of the EU, or one designated by order as providing reciprocal protection. A qualifying individual is a citizen or subject, or resident of a qualifying country.

For the recording right the person with the recording right must qualify. The person may be a qualifying individual or a legal person formed under UK law or that of a qualifying country, or with a place of business with substantial business activity within a qualifying country.

8.12.2 Performers' property rights

Performers are given new reproduction, distribution, rental and lending rights over copies of their qualifying performances made legitimately but improperly copied, or made improperly by a bootlegger.[81] Performers also have rights in performances distributed over the internet. Section 182CA[82] added a new right of making available by electronic transmission in such a way that members of the public may access the recording from a place and at a time individually chosen by them. Reproduction includes transient or incidental copies: s 182A(1A) of the CDPA 1988.[83] The CRRR 2003 removed the exception to the need for consent to reproduction for private and domestic recordings.

Doing these acts without their performers' consent will infringe. The temporary copies made by intermediaries during transmission over the internet will not infringe.[84]

Section 193 provides that consent may be for a specific performance, a specified description of performances, or generally, and related to past or future performances.

They are property rights[85] and may be dealt with in the same way as copyright.[86]

---

80 Section 181 of the CDPA 1988.
81 Sections 182A-C of the CDPA 1988.
82 Added by the CRRR 2003.
83 Added by the CRRR 2003.
84 R. 8(2) CRRR 2003.
85 Section 191A(1) of the CDPA 1988.
86 Section 191B of the CDPA 1988.

Infringement is remedied by damages, injunctions (interdicts), account of profits and any other remedy for infringement of intellectual property rights.[87] Injunctions may be sought against internet service providers who knowingly use their service to infringe a performer's property right (s 191JA of the CDPA 1988)[88]. Damages do not lie if the defendant did not know and did not have reason to believe that the rights subsisted in the recording.[89]

8.12.3 Performers' non-property rights

A performer has the right to consent to any recording of a live performance, broadcast, or recording of a broadcast being made of his performance. Defendants who can show that they had reasonable grounds to believe that consent had been given at the time of infringement are not liable for damages.[90] The CRRR 2003 removed the exception to the need for consent to reproduction for private and domestic recordings. This right is not transmissible except on death.[91]

'Secondary' acts of infringement are also provided for by using or dealing with illicit copies of performances made without consent[92] or showing a recording which is known or reasonably believed to have been made without consent.[93]

Consents given by the performer bind anyone acquiring rights from the performer or person with recording rights takes subject to the consent. It is therefore important that contractual warranties are secured from the transferor.

Infringements are breaches of statutory duty.[94] Provision is made for delivery up and seizure of illicit recordings.[95]

8.12.4 Rights to remuneration

If the rental right is transferred to the producer of a sound recording or film it includes a right to guaranteed equitable remuneration which may not be abrogated by contract.[96]

Performers are also given a right to equitable remuneration where a commercially published sound recording is played in public or broadcast from the owner of the copyright in the recording.[97] This does not include internet transmission.[98]

The Copyright Tribunal has jurisdiction over the remuneration to be paid.[99]

---

87 Section 191I of the CDPA 1988.
88 Added by the CRRR 2003.
89 Section 191J of the CDPA 1988.
90 Section 182 of the CDPA 1988.
91 Section 192A of the CDPA 1988.
92 Section 184 of the CDPA 1988.
93 Section 183 of the CDPA 1988.
94 Section 194 of the CDPA 1988.
95 Sections 195, 196 of the CDPA 1988.
96 Section 191G of the CDPA 1988.
97 Section 182D of the CDPA 1988.
98 R 7(2) CRRR 2003.
99 Sections 182D, 191H of the CDPA 1988.

These rights may only be assigned to a collecting society and are not properly property rights. They may be transferred other than by way of assignment.

8.12.5 Rights of those with recording rights

The copyright of those making authorised sound and other recordings of performances only extends to their own recordings and provides no protection against the illicit recordings of bootleggers. Consequently, they are given rights parallel to the performers' non-property rights.[100] These rights are given to those with exclusive recording contracts with the performer and who are qualifying persons. A person with recording rights is bound (regardless of knowledge) by any consent to an otherwise infringing act given by the performer.

8.12.6 Exceptions

The exceptions to these rights largely paralleled those to copyright and are contained in Schedule 2 of the CDPA 1988. They have been amended by the CRRR 2003 in line with amendment of the copyright permitted acts. Fair dealing with a performance or a recording of a performance for the purpose of criticism and review will not infringe if the performance or recording has been made available to the public; nor will fair dealing for reporting current events. Only private and domestic recordings of broadcasts and photographs of broadcasts will not infringe, and any dealings with them constitute illicit recordings.

The transitional provisions of the CRRR 2003 provide that acts permitted before commencement of the Regulations will continue to apply to anything done after commencement to complete an act begun before it.

8.12.7 Offences

Section 198 provides for criminal offences. A person who:
- makes for sale or hire;
- imports into the UK;
- possesses in the course of business with a view to committing any infringing act;
- infringes a performer's making available right in the course of a business;[101]
- infringes a performer's making available right otherwise than in the course of a business to such an extent as to prejudicially affect the owner of the right;[102] or
- sells, lets for hire, offers or exposes for sale or hire, or distributes

a recording which he knows, or has reason to believe, is an illicit recording commits an offence.

It is also an offence for a person to cause a recording to be played or shown in public or broadcast without consent knowing or having cause to believe that to do so

---

100 Sections 185-188 of the CDPA 1988.
101 Added by the CRRR 2003.
102 Added by the CRRR 2003.

will infringe rights in performances. Falsely representing authority to give consent without belief in the authority to do so is an offence.[103]

Orders for delivery up, search warrants, and the disposal of illicit recordings may be made.[104] Punishment is by way of fines or imprisonment depending on whether conviction is summary or on indictment.

Further Reading

Bainbridge, D, *Software Copyright Law* (London: Butterworths, 1999)

Booton, D, 'Framing Pictures: Defining Art in UK Copyright Law' [2003] IPQ 38

Campbell, K, 'Copyright on the Internet: the View from Shetland' [1997] EIPR 255

Chalton, S, 'The Copyright and Rights in Databases Regulations 1997: Some Outstanding Issues on Implementation of the Database Directive' [1998] EIPR 178

Colston, C, 'Challenges to Information Retrieval: A Global Solution?' [2002] IJLIT 294

Davidson, *The Legal Protection of Databases* (Cambridge: CUP, 2003)

Derclaye, E, 'Do Sections 3 and 3A of the CDPA Violate the Database Directive? A Closer Look at the Definition of a Database in the UK and its Compatibility with European Law' [2002] EIPR 466

Dworkin, G, 'Elanco Products – the Ideas–Expression Dichotomy' [1979] EIPR 17

Fitzpatrick, S, 'Prospects of Further Copyright Harmonisation?' [2003] EIPR 215

Garnett, K, 'Copyright in Photographs' [2000] EIPR 229

Grewal, M, 'Copyright Protection of Computer Software' [1996] EIPR 454

Hobbs, G, 'Mr Justice Whitford Upheld – *LB Plastics v Swish* – in the House of Lords' [1979] EIPR 56

Jones, J, 'Copyright History' [2001] New Zealand LJ 480

Kamina, P, 'Authorship of Films and Implementation of the Term Directive: The Dramatic Tale of Two Copyrights' [1994] EIPR 319

Laddie, H, 'Copyright: Over-strength, Over-regulated, Over-rated?' [1996] EIPR 253

Lipton, J, 'Databases as Intellectual Property: New Legal Approaches' [2003] EIPR 139

Rushton, M, 'An Economic Approach to Copyright in Works of Artistic Craftsmanship' [2003] IPQ 255

Stamatoudi, I, *Copyright and Multimedia Works* (Cambridge: CUP, 2002)

Stokes, S, *Art & Copyright* (Oxford: Hart Publishing, 2003)

Thakur, N, 'Database Protection in the European Union and the United States: the European Database Directive as an Optimum Global Model?' [2001] IPQ 100

Tumbridge, J, 'Canada Defines 'Originality' and Specifies the Limits of 'Fair Dealing'' [2004] EIPR 318

---

103 Section 201 of the CDPA 1988.
104 Sections 199, 204A, 204B of the CDPA 1988.

CHAPTER 9

THE SUBSISTENCE AND SUBSTANCE OF COPYRIGHT AND RELATED RIGHTS

Although a work fits into one of the statutory descriptions of works, it must also qualify for protection before copyright can be said to subsist. Once the subsistence of copyright has been ascertained, it remains to determine who will be the first owner of that copyright, and then how long the right will last. Ownership is established by identifying a work's author.

Copyright subsisting by virtue of the Copyright, Designs and Patents Act (CDPA) 1988 extends to the UK.[1]

9.1   QUALIFICATION

The provision for qualification implements the UK's obligation to provide copyright protection for nationals and residents of Convention Member States to the same extent as that given to UK nationals and residents.[2] The Universal Copyright Convention also requires a copyright notice, otherwise the work will fall into the public domain in States which are members only of that Convention. Protection under the Berne Convention is required to be without formality.[3] A work qualifies for copyright in the UK if it is connected to the UK, a Convention country or a country to which the CDPA 1988 has been extended by order. There are two connecting factors: the status of the work's author, and the place of its first publication or transmission.[4]

9.1.1   Author's status

Reference is made to a work's author for the purposes of qualification. The author is not necessarily the first owner of copyright (see 9.2). A work qualifies if the author is a qualifying person at the material time.[5] A qualifying person is a British citizen, or a British Dependent Territories citizen, or a British National (Overseas), or a British subject, or a British protected person, or an individual domiciled or resident in the UK or in a country to which the Act has been extended by Order, or a body incorporated under the law of the UK or country to which the Act has been extended by Order.[6]

Material time

In relation to a literary, dramatic, musical or artistic work, the material time is: for an unpublished work, the time when the work was made (or, if making is extended, a substantial part of that period); and, for a published work, the time when the work is

---

1   Section 157 of the CDPA 1988.
2   Articles 3, 5 of the Berne Convention, Article II of the Universal Copyright Convention.
3   Article 5(2) of the Berne Convention.
4   Section 153 of the CDPA 1988.
5   *Ibid*, s 154(1).
6   *Ibid*, s 154(1), (2).

first published (or if the author has died before publication, immediately before his death).

For sound recordings and films, the material time is when the work was made; for broadcasts, the time is when broadcast or transmitted; and, for typographical arrangement, when the edition was first published.[7]

A work with joint authors may qualify by any of the authors satisfying these requirements at the material time, but where some of the authors are non-qualifying it is only the qualifying author(s) who shall be taken into account for first ownership of copyright, for the right's duration, and permitted acts in relation to anonymous and pseudonymous works.[8]

9.1.2 Place of first publication

If the author does not qualify by status, qualification may be by place of first publication. A literary, dramatic, musical or artistic work, a sound recording or film and a typographical arrangement qualify if first published in the UK or a country to which to which the Act has been extended by order. A broadcast qualifies if made from the UK, or a country to which the Act has been extended by order.[9] Qualification is not denied by simultaneous publication elsewhere. Simultaneous publication is generously defined as publication elsewhere within the previous 30 days.[10]

9.1.3 Publication

It is necessary to determine what constitutes publication of a work, both for the purposes of qualification, and the duration of copyright. 'Publication' in relation to a work is defined by s 175 of the CDPA 1988 to mean issuing copies to the public, including making the work available to the public by means of an electronic retrieval system in the case of a literary, dramatic, musical or artistic work. Construction of a building publishes a work of architecture, or an artistic work incorporated in a building. No account is to be taken of any unauthorised act for the purposes of publication.

Certain acts, in relation to particular types of work, will not constitute publication. Performing a literary, dramatic or musical work, or broadcasting it is not publication. Exhibiting an artistic work, issuing copies to the public of a film including the work, broadcasting it, or issuing copies to the public of graphic works or photographs representing works of architecture, sculpture or works of artistic craftsmanship does not constitute publication.

Colourable publication

In addition, publication considered 'merely colourable and not intended to satisfy the reasonable requirements of the public' will not suffice.[11] In *Francis Day and Hunter v*

---

7   *Ibid*, s 154(4).
8   *Ibid*, s 154(3).
9   *Ibid*, ss 155, 156.
10 *Ibid*, s 155(3).
11 *Ibid*, s 175(5).

Feldman (1914), Neville J held that the words 'not intended to satisfy the reasonable requirements of the public' were, in effect, a definition of 'colourable'. In *Bodley Head v Flegon* (1972) Brightman J doubted, *obiter*, that private, clandestine circulation of typed copies of Solzhenitzen's novel *August 1914* among the USSR's intelligentsia could amount to an effort to satisfy the Russian public's reasonable requirements, when such requirements could not, at the time, be lawfully voiced or satisfied. Where public demand is small, few copies need be available to amount to publication. In *Francis Day and Hunter v Feldman* (1914), the song 'You Made Me Love You (I Didn't Want To Do it)', composed by a US citizen, was published simultaneously in New York and London. Six copies were placed for sale in the plaintiffs' London showroom. Neville J held that this constituted publication and was not colourable, because demand was insignificant. The evidence was that, should demand increase, the plaintiffs would make efforts to ensure that it was met. The test is one of the publisher's intention when copies are issued to the public. There is no requirement that any advertisement or announcement or promotion of the copies be made, provided that the publisher is prepared to supply on demand: 'Passive availability suffices, without active offering' (*per* Megarry J, in *British Northrop v Texteam Blackburn* (1974)).

Issuing copies

Copies are 'issued' by being offered, sold, hired or given to the public. They are issued at the place where the public are invited to acquire copies. In *British Northrop v Texteam Blackburn* (1974), publication rested on reproductions of the work being issued to the public in the form of machine spare parts made from unpublished drawings. The defendant argued that publication took place at the place where the spares were received by customers, but it was held that publication took place at the place where copies were put on offer to the public, and that an offer *gratis* would suffice. Otherwise, there would be as many places of publication as there were customers.

Copies

A final question in determining publication relates to the nature of the 'copies' issued. Copies in the same form as the work pose no difficulties. However, it is not clear whether copies amounting to reproduction in another material form (see 9.6.1), or adaptations of a work (see 10.1.1), would constitute copies of an unpublished original for the purposes of a copyright qualifying publication.

The CDPA 1988 is silent on the point, but some conclusions may be drawn from provisions relating to the exclusive rights of reproduction and adaptation conferred on the owner of copyright in a work by s 16(1) of the CDPA 1988 (see 10.1). Reproducing a literary, dramatic, musical or artistic work in any material form amounts to copying, as does making a three-dimensional copy of a two-dimensional artistic work, and vice versa.[12] Consequently, it might be expected that issuing reproductions of an unpublished work to the public should amount to publication. That this is so is supported by *British Northrop v Texteam Blackburn*. It could also be argued that adapting a literary, dramatic or musical work is publication, for to do an infringing act to both a reproduction or an adaptation of a work amounts to indirect infringement of

---

12   *Ibid*, s 17(2), (3).

the original work.[13] However, there is a difference in relation to adapting a work because the adaptation secures its own copyright (provided that the work also qualifies), so that it is not so easy to argue that publication of an adaptation should also qualify the adapted work for copyright. If this is correct, the consequence is that if a non-qualifying literary work is translated (an adapting act) and qualifying publication made of the translation, the translation will secure copyright in the UK, but the original work will remain unprotected, and any other translation or adaptation may be made.

9.2 AUTHORSHIP

The person making a work is its author.[14] It is authorship of a 'work' in the copyright sense that is required. Neither the mere generation of an idea nor the mere recording of a work will suffice. Authorship involves the expenditure of 'skill, labour and judgment' in expression. The author of a work will be unknown if it is not possible to establish his identity by reasonable enquiry.

9.2.1 Joint authorship

Ownership may be shared.[15] Joint ownership only arises where the individual author's contributions to a work cannot be distinguished from each other, and the authors have collaborated with each other. However, there is no need for a joint intention to create a joint work: *Beckingham v Hodgens* (2002).

Contributions leading to joint authorship must be in the nature of the work done by an author, and must amount to more than the mere suggestion of ideas (*Tate v Thomas* (1921)), or other administrative assistance. It must contribute to the skill employed in determining the way in which a work is expressed (see 8.2.3).

In *Cala Homes v Alfred McAlpine Homes* (1995) an employee of a building company gave a very detailed brief as to the design of certain buildings, and the choice of materials to be used, to a firm of technical draftsmen, but without making any record of them himself. He was held to be a joint author. However, Lightman J cast some doubt on this result in *Robin Ray v Classic FM plc* (1998), stating that the draftsmen acted 'in large part' as mere scribes (see 9.3.2). He held that a joint author must have a 'direct responsibility for what actually appears on the paper', although actual penmanship was not required as it is not necessary for a sole author.

The issue was also raised before Laddie J in *Fylde Microsystems Ltd v Key Radio Systems Ltd* (1998). The plaintiffs supplied the defendants with specialist bespoke software for mobile and portable radios. The defendants assisted in the adjustment of the software during five years of collaboration. They had set the specification for the software, reported errors, made suggestions as to the causes of some faults and provided technical information about the hardware with which the software had to work. In an infringement action, they claimed to be joint authors by virtue of this

13   *Ibid*, ss 16(3), 21(2).
14   *Ibid*, s 9(1).
15   *Ibid*, s 10.

contribution. It was held that two questions must be addressed: first, whether the alleged joint author had contributed the right kind of skill and labour; and, secondly, whether, as a matter of fact and degree, that contribution was sufficient. On the facts, although the contribution made by the defendants was extensive, technically sophisticated and saved considerable time for the plaintiffs, in relation to software it amounted to the contribution of skills analogous to proof-reading, and not the skills of authorship.

9.2.2 Original works

The creator of a literary, dramatic, musical or artistic work is its author. The person recording a work is not necessarily its author[16] (see 8.2.2). Once recorded, it is usually clear who has created a work; however, it must be remembered that a work constitutes the particular way in which its idea has been expressed (see 8.2.3), so that the provider of an idea, without more, is not the creator of a work. It is the skill and effort put into the specific means of expressing of an idea that constitutes creation of a work.

There is a distinction to be made between works made by a 'reporter' and works recorded by an amanuensis. A reporter is the creator of the work, such as the newspaper report of Lord Rosebery's speech (*Walter v Lane* (1900)). However, a work such as a letter dictated to a secretary, or the works of Bede, which were dictated to a scribe, is not authored by its scribe. The amanuensis does not supply the details of expression, but the person dictating; the amanuensis is treated as much as a tool employed by the author as a pen or typewriter would be. An interesting example is presented by the case of *Cummins v Bond* (1927), in which a spiritualist medium, and not her spirit guide, was found to be the work's creator, although she professed merely to have recorded what was dictated to her by the guide. However, the communication was said to have been made to her in an unknown language, translated by the medium into an 'archaistic' English intelligible to modern readers. It was the skill involved in such transcription that rendered the medium the work's creator.

The same applies to a 'ghosted' work. Such a work is often credited to a celebrity, who supplies the information for the work, but is written with the help of a ghost author. In *Donoghue v Allied Newspapers* (1938) it was held that because the ghost writer supplied the particular words in which a celebrity's ideas were expressed, copyright lay with the writer.

Therefore, to find the creator of a work it is necessary to identify the person whose skill, labour and judgment have been invested in the way the work has been expressed, not the person supplying only the inspiration or idea for it. However, expression involves more than the mere physical act of recording a work, and includes the supplying of concepts, the selection of data, emotion, language, arrangement and the like. Laddie J explained this in *Cala Homes v Alfred McAlpine Homes* (1995):

> ... to have regard merely to who pushed the pen is too narrow a view of authorship. What is protected by copyright in a drawing or a literary work is more than just the skill of making marks on paper or some other medium. It is both the word or lines and the skill and effort involved in creating, selecting or gathering together the detailed concepts, data or emotions which those words or lines have fixed in some tangible

---

16   *Ibid*, s 3(3).

form which is protected. It is wrong to think that only the person who carries out the mechanical act of fixation is the author. There may well be skill and expertise which is relevant.

9.2.3 Works of artistic craftsmanship

Where one craftsman makes such a work, identification of its author presents no difficulties, but doubts have been expressed where the skills of artistry and craftsmanship have been exercised by separate individuals. This was the case in relation to a designer dress in *Burke v Spicers Dress Designs* (1936), where Clauson J held that the dress's designer was the artist and that its seamstress was the craftsman, so that no copyright subsisted in the work. He doubted whether it constituted a work of artistic craftsmanship as a result. Subsequently, it was held in *Radley Gowns v Spyrou* (1975) that copyright could subsist, despite the presence of two authors. As provision is made for joint authors by the 1988 statute, this is a better result.

9.2.4 Photographs

The CDPA 1988 altered the position under the Copyright Acts 1911 and 1956, so that the creator of a photograph is treated as its author. If one individual does all that is necessary to fix an image of an unposed or naturally occurring scene, that person will be the photograph's author. The amanuensis principle (see 9.2.2) will also apply to photographs. If one person does all that is needed to direct a picture's composition and the setting of the camera, that individual will be the creator of the photograph, even if an agent actually operates the camera: *Creation Records Ltd v News Group Newspapers Ltd* (1997).

There will be more difficulty where more than one person is responsible for the composition and camera position and settings. The 'person who creates' a photograph will be determined by deciding who has contributed the 'skill, labour and judgment' in its creation. *Dicta* in *Nottage v Jackson* (1883) suggest that it is the person 'who was the most effective cause of the final result', 'who really represents or creates or gives effect to the idea or fancy or imagination'. This necessitates defining the essence of a photograph, which combines the artistry of composition, the techniques of operating the camera (for example, choice of film, aperture, shutter speed, lighting) and skills of development as well as of digital manipulation.

Joint ownership in such circumstances is possible, provided that the individuals have collaborated. In *Creation Records Ltd v News Group Newspapers Ltd* (1997) the plaintiff claimed (unsuccessfully) to be the author of a photograph taken by an independent press photographer without his consent or knowledge. The plaintiff had arranged the composition of a scene to be photographed for an Oasis album cover, which was also taken by the independent photographer from a similar vantage point. The claim was rejected on the ground that the plaintiff had had nothing to do with the taking of the defendant's photograph other than to provide its subject matter. This is not to say that setting a scene may not be an important part of the creation of a photograph, but that there must be some link between scene setting and the act of photography before the scene setter may be regarded as a creator of the photograph.

9.2.5   Computer-generated works

Copyright cannot subsist without an author. If a literary, dramatic, musical or artistic work is computer-generated, its authorship must be treated differently if no individual can be identified as the source of the 'skill, labour and judgment' embodied by the work. In such circumstances, the author is taken to be the person by whom the arrangements necessary for the creation of the work were undertaken.[17]

'Computer-generated' in relation to a work is defined as being 'generated by computer in circumstances such that there is no human author of the work'.[18] The mere use of a computer will not turn every resulting work into a computer-generated work. A computer can be used as a human tool in the same way as a pen, the artist's brush or sculptor's chisel. This was held in a case preceding the 1988 Act, *Express Newspapers v Liverpool Daily Post* (1985). A computer programmer produced a grid containing a random selection of numbers and letters for a newspaper game. The defendant argued that there could be no copyright in the grids as they had no human author, but Whitford J held that the computer had been used as a tool in the same way as a pen, and that the instructions had come from the programmer. Where the software used contributes nothing to the expression of a work, it is possible to identify a human author. This would be the case, for example, for a word-processed novel. Even if programs, such as spelling or grammar checks, have been employed, the choice of words and grammatical style is the human author's and the word processor can be regarded as a sophisticated typewriter. Such a work might be dubbed a computer-assisted work.

However, the analogy used by Whitford J is not necessarily sound. It may have been very significant that it was the programmer who operated the computer. He used undoubted skill in programming the computer to produce selections for the grids' contents that would lead to neither too many winners to be uneconomic, nor too few to discourage participation in the game (and, presumably, purchase of the newspapers). However, it was the program, and not the computer operator, in this case, which supplied the content of the resulting grids. Had someone else operated the computer, it is not clear that the result in this case would be the same (copyright given to the computer's operator) following the CDPA 1988. Although a good deal of skill would have gone into the program, it is artificial to regard a mere operator of it as the human author of the resulting selection of the grids' contents.

Computer-assisted works

Accordingly, it may be necessary to draw a distinction between computer-generated works, and those which are computer-assisted. Examples of computer-assisted works would include word-processed documents, music composed with the aid of a computer, computer aided designs, or accounts produced with the aid of a spreadsheet. In each case, the user of the program contributes to the content (expression) of the work, although the software provides its form. Examples of computer-generated works would include computer-compiled crosswords, the moves of a computer chess program, weather forecasts or the random selection of Premium

---

17   *Ibid*, s 9(3).
18   *Ibid*, s 178(1).

Bond numbers. Here, the both content and form of the work are determined by the software alone.

No human author

The 1988 Act does not specify which circumstances will be relevant to determine that there is no human author. It can be argued that there is always a human author because it is the skill of the programmer which determines the content of a computer generated work. In addition, if *Express Newspapers v Liverpool Daily Post* (1985) remains good law, there will always be a human author: the computer's operator or the software's programmer. Neither is a happy result. The operator may be in the same shoes as an amanuensis (see 9.2.2), having no contribution to make to the work. The programmer would benefit doubly from the copyright in the program itself (see 8.5.2), and copyright in every product of the use of the work; but it would often be difficult to identify who the programmer was – it could have been a team effort. Moreover, consider the consequences if the Microsoft Corporation (as the programmer's employer) were to be the author of every work produced using their software. The result is patently absurd.

Consequently, the distinction between computer-assisted and computer-generated works seems necessary to achieve a justifiable result. If so, circumstances relevant to a work being regarded as computer-generated should include the impracticality, as well as impossibility, of identifying a human author, as well as control over the work's content, and the source of the skill in producing the work. This result is in line with the treatment of authorship for the derivative works, where reward is being bestowed on the entrepreneurship which disseminates copyright works, rather than the act of creativity. This has already seen its reward in the copyright bestowed on an original work (in this case, the computer program used to generate the computer-generated work).

9.2.6 Derivative works

In relation to the derivative works, the definition of 'author' is an artificial one, which reflects the pragmatic UK approach to copyright as an economic right, rather than recognising an act of personal creativity. Recent changes in relation to films have, however, recognised the creative input of a director, so that the author of a film is both the producer and principal director.[19] The author of a sound recording is its producer,[20] of a broadcast the person making the broadcast, while the author of a typographical arrangement is the edition's publisher.[21] In the case of a broadcast relaying another broadcast by its reception and immediate retransmission, the author is the person making the initial broadcast.

---

19 As joint authors: s 10(1A) of the CDPA 1988.
20 Which devalues the contribution made by sound engineers, particularly in some forms of modern music.
21 Section 9(2) of the CDPA 1988.

9.3   OWNERSHIP OF COPYRIGHT

Initial ownership of copyright in a work is dictated by its authorship.[22] Any subsequent ownership of the copyright is a matter of contractual dealings.

There are two exceptions to this rule. The first relates to literary, dramatic, musical and artistic works or films made by employees. The second relates to Crown and parliamentary copyright and copyright of certain international organisations.[23]

9.3.1   Employed authors

An employer is the first owner of copyright in a literary, dramatic, musical or artistic work, or a film, made by an employee. The Copyright Act (CA) 1956 provided shared copyright for journalists employed on newspapers and magazines, so that employers had copyright for the purpose of exploiting the work in the course of their business, while employees retained copyright for all other purposes. Under the 1988 Act all employees are subject to the same rule, although both the Whitford Committee[24] and the Green Paper[25] had recommended that the exception for journalists be extended to all employees. The White Paper[26] rejected this move as being too uncertain. This leaves employers free to exploit works created by employees in the course of their employment, not only in the employer's business, but also for any other purpose. In the US disputes have arisen over reuse of journalists' works in electronic databases.[27] The issue becomes one of interpretation of contracts with free-lance journalists or of agreements with employers. It is open to employees to seek a different agreement, although this will be subject to the likely superiority of the employer's bargaining power.

Three conditions must be satisfied:

* that the author is employed;
* that the work is created during the course of the employment; and
* that the parties have not made any agreement to the contrary.

'Employee'

An employee is one employed 'under a contract of service or of apprenticeship'.[28] This is a matter of substance, rather than form. The courts use a test composed of multiple factors to distinguish between a contract of service and an independent commission (a contract for services). Factors such as the level of control exercised by employer over the employee's work and all other relevant circumstances, such as sick pay, holiday provision, salary, pension, tax arrangements and the level of integration of the

---

22   *Ibid*, s 11(1).
23   *Ibid*, s 11(2), (3).
24   *Copyright and Designs Law*. Cmnd 6732, 1977.
25   *Reform of the Law Relating to Copyright, Design and Performer's Protection*, Cmnd 8302.
26   *Intellectual Property and Innovation*, Cmnd 9712.
27   The Supreme Court held that authors should receive their reward for these reuses of their works: *Tasini v New York Times* (2001); *National Geographic v Greenberg* (2001) (00–10510) 11th Circuit, Court of Appeals, 22 March 2001.
28   Section 178(1) of the CDPA 1988.

employee into the employer's business are taken into account. All factors must be weighed before a conclusion is drawn, and in *Beloff v Pressdram* (1973) it was held that the plaintiff journalist was an employee, despite the independence with which she worked, because of the working arrangements which applied to her.

'In the course of employment'

A work is made in the course of employment if it is created while an employee is performing duties within his job description or other normal duties. The duties of employment commonly alter with changing circumstances, so that establishing an employee's duties at any given time is one of evidence. In *Stephenson Jordan and Harrison v MacDonald Evans* (1952), a professional engineer was employed by the plaintiffs to give on-site consultancy services to their customers. He wrote a book which contained three elements: the text of public lectures given by him to universities and professional bodies during the time in which he was employed by the plaintiffs; a section composed during the time of employment and included in manuals prepared for the plaintiffs' customers; and sections composed after he had moved to another employer. This last section was clearly not created in the course of the engineer's employment with the plaintiffs. The first two sections were created during the period of employment, but with different results in relation to the ownership of copyright. The Court of Appeal held copyright in the lectures to belong to the employee, but copyright in the section prepared for the plaintiffs' manuals to the employers. The difference lay in the activity being performed by the author when these sections were created. The material in the second section was composed as part of the services rendered to the plaintiffs' clients and was included in two copies of the resulting manual. It was written at night, but secretarial services were rendered as part of the employment and the manuscript had been sent to the plaintiffs. This was, accordingly, found to have been written during the performance of the duties of employment. On the other hand, the lectures did not constitute part of the duties required by the plaintiff employers. This was so even although the employers could ask the employee engineer to deliver lectures, had asked to see the text of any lectures to be delivered (falling short of any substantial interference with their composition or delivery), some of the typing was done in office hours by the plaintiffs' typists and expenses were paid by them.

The Court of Appeal relied in particular on what they thought to be the normal approach in relation to such lectures: one of justice and common sense. This was applied in *Noah v Shuba* (1991) in relation to the writings of an employed consultant epidemiologist. In both the *Stephenson* case and *Byrne v Statist* (1914), it was contemplated that an employee might perform duties at the request of his employer, some of which fell within, and some outside, the duties of employment. In *Byrne v Statist* (1914) a journalist employed by a newspaper was asked to make a translation for the paper in his spare time. Copyright was held to belong to him and not to the paper.

Agreement to the contrary

Employees with sufficient bargaining power are free to negotiate their own terms with employers, whereas it is not possible for independent authors to contract out of the general rule as to ownership. Any other arrangement by unemployed authors must involve assignment of copyright,[29] although copyright in a work yet to be made may also be assigned.[30]

An agreement between employer and employee, in contrast, may be implied from the circumstances: *Noah v Shuba* (1991). *Obiter*, Mummery J said that there was an implied term in Dr Noah's contract of service excluding the statutory rule relating to an employer's ownership of copyright. The employer's long standing practice was that employees should retain copyright in works written in the course of employment, and they had acquiesced in their employees' practice of assigning copyright in articles written for scientific journals. In *Robin Ray v Classic FM plc* (1998) it was stated, *obiter*, that an agreement to the contrary must satisfy two requirements. First, it must be an agreement that, notwithstanding the presence of a contract of employment, title to works created in the course of employment should not vest in the employer; and, secondly, that the agreement be a legally effective one.

9.3.2 Commissioned works

The normal rule of ownership applies when a work is commissioned from its author. The CDPA 1988 removed the old provisions relating to commissioned photographs, portraits and engravings, replacing them with the new moral right of privacy for photographs and films commissioned for private and domestic purposes.[31] A commissioner can only achieve protection through contract or by seeking an assignment of copyright, including future copyright. In the case of works commissioned for commercial purposes, the ownership of copyright is an issue of importance. There is no protection from the right of privacy, yet considerable economic damage may be incurred if a work commissioned for use in business is copied or otherwise infringed. The author may not have the resources, or may have no interest, in seeking redress.

It is important that contractual arrangements for the ownership of commissioned works are clearly drafted. In *Cyprotex Discovery Ltd v University of Sheffield* (2004) the courts struggled to give an unclear and contradictory agreement commercial sense. Although the result of the case reflects the relationship the parties envisaged, this was only achieved at the expense of 'strained construction'.

Additionally, authors of commissioned works themselves may pose a considerable threat if the work made proves to have unexpected uses (see *Robin Ray v Classic FM plc* (1998)). The author may then wish to exploit it with the commissioner's commercial rivals, or to hold the commissioner to ransom over later additions, amendments or modifications. The dangers have become apparent, in particular, in cases relating to computer software commissioned from independent consultants and the courts have sought to protect commissioners. They may do so by the implication of licences in the commissioning contract, in the same way that licences are implied in relation to architectural plans (see 10.8.1).

In *Robin Ray v Classic FM plc* (1998), Lightman J held that only a licence would be implied where it was necessary to imply some grant of rights in a contract of

---

29 Which must be signed and in writing: s 90(3) of the CDPA 1988, although see 9.3.2.
30 Section 91 of the CDPA 1988.
31 *Ibid*, s 85.

commission, and that need could be met either by the grant of a licence or an assignment of copyright. In such circumstances, the ambit of the implied licence would be the minimum necessary to secure the entitlement which the parties must have intended according to their joint contemplation at the date of the contract, and would not include subsequently appreciated profitable opportunities. The price paid under the contract would be a relevant consideration. Lightman J also stated that a term as to the assignment of copyright would only be implied if the commissioner needed not only the right to use the work, but also the right to exclude the contractor from using it and the ability to enforce the copyright against third parties.

Equitable interests in England

More controversially, however, the English courts have been willing to confer beneficial ownership in copyright on the commissioner of a work. This has been done either by the implication of a term in the contract of commission or by the creation of a trust, despite the statutory provisions relating to the formalities for assignment of copyright.[32]

In *Warner v Gestetner Ltd* (1988), the defendant commissioned drawings of cats for use in advertising from the plaintiff. Subsequently, the defendant used the drawings for purposes not contemplated by the original commission. This was an informal contract. Whitford J implied a term in the contract vesting equitable ownership in the defendant. The effect is to interfere with otherwise clear statutory rules as to first ownership of copyright, and to create an unpredictable discretion as to the location of beneficial interests in copyright. The House of Lords has also adverted to equitable interests in copyright; in *Attorney General v Guardian* (1988), it was suggested that copyright in *Spycatcher* might belong in equity to the Crown as a consequence of the author's breach of confidence.

In *Robin Ray v Classic FM plc* (1998) Lightman J stated that copyright vested in the commissioned author unless an express or implied term stated otherwise. He gave examples of circumstances in which such a term might be implied:

- if the purpose of the commission was to enable the client to sell copies free of competition;

- if the work was derived from an earlier work belonging to the client;

- if the author was engaged as part of a team with employees of the client to produce a composite or joint work and could not or was not intended to be able to exploit the work or his contribution to it.

This was applied in *Durand v Molino* (1999). The claimant artist was commissioned to produce a portrait of a family for use in its restaurant business. Pumfrey J found that the clear overriding purpose of the commission was commercial, although it also comprised portraits of the family. The minimum interest that the commissioner should have, therefore, was a perpetual exclusive licence. Finding as a fact that it was the parties' clear intention that the picture should hang in the restaurant, he held that the commissioner, the subject of the portrait, should have complete control of the work. The artist had the protection of moral rights in relation to any exploitation of the work

---

32   *Ibid*, s 90(3).

by the commissioner. As the defendant was beneficially entitled to the copyright, it should be transferred to him.

Lightman J's judgment was further applied in *Griggs v Evans* (2004). In particular, it was stated, as matter of business efficacy, that a designer[33] would rarely be free to assign his legal title to a third party. Nor was the term to be implied limited to an exclusive licence. Consequently, Griggs were entitled to an order that Evans's legal title be assigned to them. The case appears to extend beneficial ownership to all commissioned works, at least in England and Wales, and to render s 11 of the CDPA 1988 always subject to a non-statutory exception in the case of works made by independent contractors. Whether this can have been the legislators' intention must be queried, particularly in light of the differing approach to title in Scotland.

In a case relating to a computer program, copyright was found to be held on trust for its commissioner: *John Richardson v Flanders* (1993). The programmer had been an employee of the commissioner and had subsequently left, but continued to provide services as a freelance programmer. Ferris J said (emphasis added):

> However, in appropriate circumstances, it may appear that the author is to be regarded as holding the copyright on trust for the person to whom he engaged himself. Thus, in *Massine v de Basil* (1936-45), a question was raised as to the ownership of copyright in a ballet ... However, even if the plaintiff could rightly be regarded as an independent contractor, the court was of the opinion that it ought to be implied as a term of the agreement that any work done by the plaintiff would be done on the basis that the defendant who had paid for the work should be entitled to such rights as might arise from that payment, and that he should not be deprived of the benefit of it merely on the ground that the person whom he paid was an independent contractor. *It was important ... to remember that the subject of the copyright which was claimed was the ballet as a whole. The choreography was but one part of a composite whole. The defendant had paid the money under the agreement for the supplying to his ballet of a part which was necessary for its completeness* and, unless he was entitled to the copyright in that part of the ballet, he would not be getting that benefit from the contract which must have been the intention of the parties. It was a necessary implication from all the facts of the case that the right to the choreography and the libretto in those cases where the plaintiff was responsible for them should in equity be the property of the defendant and that he should be entitled to have the rights assigned to him.

This may suggest the limits of the implication of such a trust.

Scotland

It is unlikely that a similar result would be reached in Scots law. In *Sharp v Thomson* (1997) the House of Lords upheld the Lord President's analysis of Scots property law in the Inner House of the Court of Session.[34] The case did not concern intellectual property, but the possibility of a beneficial interest in property or a constructive trust was raised. A company granted a floating charge over 'the whole of [its] property'. They were the heritable proprietors over certain subjects and concluded missives for their sale. The purchasers paid and an executed disposition was delivered to them. Before this disposition could be recorded, the holder of the floating charge appointed

---

33 Provided that he had been paid: para 39, *Griggs v Evans* (2004).
34 The House of Lords overturned the decision on statutory interpretation of the floating charge legislation, and not property law.

joint receivers for the company's property. It was argued that the holders of a delivered but unrecorded disposition had a beneficial property right exceeding that of the ordinary personal right against the seller, although falling short of a real right. Lord Hope held that Scots law does not recognise a right lying between a personal and a real right. Accordingly, there was no such thing as an incomplete or imperfect real right, and only one real right of ownership can be recognised in any one thing at any one time. A trust was no exception to this principle, and a constructive trust could only be created by circumstances, not mere delivery or constructive delivery under a contract of sale. It was expressly recognised that this was different in England. The court had been urged to avoid the injustice of the result by applying equitable principles, but declined to do so.

The Scottish Law Commission issued a Discussion Paper[35] on *Sharp v Thomson* in July 2001 but neither the application of *Sharp* nor its proposed reform on the provisions for ownership of copyright was discussed.

In *Burnett's Trustee v Grainger* (2004), despite the suggestions of Lord Hobhouse, Lords Hope and Rodger denied that a trust could be created by delivery in analogous circumstances; a trust could only be expressly created. Consequently, it would appear that in Scotland the provisions of s 11 of the CDPA 1988 should prevail. Ownership of copyright in a commissioned work would pass to its author in the absence of any written and signed assignation as provided for by s 90(3) of the CDPA 1988. Section 91 should prevail if signed agreement as to the ownership of future copyright were reached between commissioner and author. Clear arrangements for the ownership of commissioned works should therefore be made at the time of commission.

9.3.3   Crown and parliamentary copyright

Section 163 of the CDPA 1988 provides that the Crown is first owner of copyright in works made by officers or servants of the Crown in the course of their duties. Special provision is also made for the duration of original works made in this way. Copyright in works made under the control of the House of Commons or House of Lords vests in the appropriate House.[36] Copyright in Bills vests in the appropriate House, the Scottish Parliament or the Northern Ireland Assembly.

9.4   DURATION OF COPYRIGHT

The 1988 Act was amended by the Duration of Copyright and Rights in Performances Regulations 1995, enacting the Duration Directive. Two changes were made. The Berne Convention dictates a minimum term of copyright for the original works of the life of the author plus 50 years; this minimum was extended to the life of the author plus 70 years. In addition, Article 7(8) of the Berne Convention allows a Member State to provide a lesser term of protection to works whose country of origin confers a lesser term than the normal period in the Member State (see 9.4.1). This was also introduced, putting pressure on such countries to introduce longer copyright terms.

---

35 Scottish Law Commission, Discussion Paper on *Sharp v Thomson*, Discussion Paper No 114, July 2001.
36 Section 165 of the CDPA 1988.

Broadly, the duration of copyright in a work is measured in a period of years after one of three triggering events. These comprise:

(1) the author's death;

(2) the year of making the work; or

(3) the year of first making the work available to the public.

The period of years is calculated from the end of the year of the triggering event. This is taken to be midnight on 31 December of the appropriate year.

9.4.1 Lesser terms of protection

In the case of an original work or a film copyright is restricted to the duration of its country of origin if it is not a State within the European Economic Area (EEA), and the author is not a national of an EEA State. In the case of the other copyright works apart from typographical editions, the duration of copyright is restricted to that of the country of origin if the work's author is not a national of an EEA State.

This applies provided that the term is not longer than the new UK term (ss 12(6), 13A(4), 13B(7), 14(3) of the CDPA 1988).

'Country of origin' is defined by s 15A of the CDPA 1988. The country of origin of works first published in a Berne Convention country will be that State. For works which are unpublished or published in a State which is not a member of the Berne Convention the country of origin will be the country of which the author is a national. Special provision is made for films, works of architecture, and artistic works incorporated into a building.

9.4.2 Original works

For works created after 1 January 1996, copyright expires 70 years from the end of the calendar year in which the author (or the last of joint authors whose identity is known) dies. If the author is unknown, copyright expires 70 years from the end of the calendar year in which the work was made, unless the work was made available to the public during that period. If so, copyright expires 70 years from the end of the year in which that takes place.[37] This rule does not apply to computer-generated works, where copyright expires 50 years from the end of the year in which the work was made: s 12(7) of the CDPA 1988. Anonymous and pseudonymous works are calculated on a period of 70 years from the end of the year in which the work was made unless the work was made available to the public during that period, in which case it is the year of publication (not of creation) which is adopted. If the identity of the author becomes known during the 70 year period, the normal rules apply. Copyright in artistic works is reduced to 25 years from the end of the year in which articles are first marketed if the work is exploited by an industrial process.[38]

---

37   *Ibid*, s 12.
38   *Ibid*, s 52.

9.4.3 Films

Film copyright has a similar term to that of the original works. It expires 70 years from the end of the year of death of the last of the relevant persons. They are the principal director, author of the screenplay, author of the dialogue or composer of music specially created for and used in the film, whose identity is known.[39] Where the identity of none of the relevant persons is known, the period is 70 years from the end of the year of making or, if the film was made available to the public during that period, 70 years from the end of the year of publication.

Making a film available to the public includes showing in public or broadcasting it, but no account will be taken of any unauthorised act. Identity is unknown if it cannot be ascertained by reasonable enquiry. The normal rules revive if the identity of one of the relevant persons becomes known during one of these 70-year periods. If there is no relevant person, copyright expires 50 years from the end of the year in which the film is made. It is only in the case of films that the term of copyright is not tied to the life of the work's author(s).

9.4.4 The other derivative works

Copyright in a sound recording expires at the end of 50 years from the end of the year in which the recording was made. If released during that period, copyright expires 50 years from the end of the year of release, or if it is made available to the public within that period, 50 years from the end of the year of making available.[40] A sound recording is released when first published, played in public, broadcast, provided that the release is authorised.[41] A similar 50-year period is applied to broadcasts, from the end of the year of broadcast.[42] The term of copyright in a repeat broadcast is the same as the original broadcast. Copyright in the typographical arrangement of a published edition expires 25 years from the end of the year in which the edition was first published.[43]

9.4.5 Revived copyright

The application of these provisions is complex, and has had the effect in some cases of reviving copyright which had expired in a work. They apply to works made after 1 January 1996 and works already made at that date, but which qualify for copyright after it. Finally, they also apply to those existing works in which copyright subsisted immediately before 1 January 1996 (unless the 1988 provisions would have resulted in a longer term than the new one). In addition, they apply to existing works in which copyright expired before 1 December 1995, but which were protected in any EEA State on 1 July 1995.

Where copyright is revived, a statutory licence is provided by reg 24 of the Duration of Copyright and Rights in Performances Regulations 1995. Acts which infringe the revived copyright are treated as licensed, subject to the payment of a

---

39   *Ibid*, s 13B.
40   Added by the CRRR 2003.
41   Section 13A of the CDPA 1988.
42   *Ibid*, s 14.
43   *Ibid*, s 15.

reasonable royalty or other agreed remuneration, or that determined by the Copyright Tribunal if agreement is not reached.

9.4.6 The length of copyright

Despite the extensions of duration, the appropriateness of the long period of copyright has been queried. One of the difficulties in setting a copyright term is the very wide range of works falling under the copyright umbrella, grouped under broad headings. The same term of protection is conferred on relatively short lived computer programs, and ephemeral fashion items, as on classic works of literature or a symphony. The term of design protection stands in contrast: from 10–25 years. Copyright duration has extended as the costs of copying have decreased, yet the copyright term is the prime way in which the incentive to create supplied by recognising an author's private interest in a work, and the provision of access to works in the public interest, is balanced. It should also be remembered that the creation of works is often a derivative process, so that later works develop from earlier works; therefore, over-protection will potentially act as a disincentive, rather than stimulus, to the production of the later works.

It has also been queried whether the copyright term for original works should be fixed to their author's life. This has been justified as providing a fair reward for authors, and publishers claim that the inflated benefits of unexpectedly long lasting popularity allows them to take risks with less popular works. It has been said that no real hardship has resulted and that an extensive term is needed to protect classical works, as well as providing a necessary incentive for the creation of works which take a long time to produce. It is also argued that suitable protection is thereby given to works that prove to be ahead of their time, only achieving importance some time after their creation. A period fixed to the author's life does also have the advantage of keeping all an author's works co-extensive.

Counter-arguments include the potentially monopolistic effects of long terms of protection, suggesting that without it prices would fall and works would fall into the public domain more quickly. In practice, the demand for many works fades long before the expiry of copyright and new technology has both increased and accelerated the means of returns to an author. It seems unlikely that many authors calculate income prospects over such long periods, making one suggested justification for the extended period of the Duration Directive, that longer life expectancy necessitated longer protection to cover succeeding generations of the author's family, questionable. In addition, duration attached to life is difficult to determine.

Alternatively, it can be argued that long copyright may justifiably protect the author, but that there is no need for coterminous protection for publishers, who rarely calculate the risks of publication over the full copyright term. The other entrepreneurial copyrights are of shorter duration than that of the original works because the entrepreneur, rather than the author, is being protected.

9.5   REFUSAL OF COPYRIGHT

In some circumstances, despite the existence of a qualifying copyright work, courts may refuse to enforce copyright in a work in the public interest because of the nature of its content. Section 171(3) of the CDPA 1988 preserves this common law principle. The immoral content of the work *Three Weeks* by Elinor Glyn led to refusal of copyright protection in *Glyn v Weston Feature Film Co* (1916). There is some confusion as to the grounds on which this is done – whether no copyright subsisted at all, or the court relied on its inherent jurisdiction to refuse to enforce it. Younger J said:

> Now it is clear law that copyright cannot exist in a work of a tendency so grossly immoral as this ...

and:

> ... to a book of such a cruelly destructive tendency, no protection will be extended by a Court of Equity.

In *Attorney General v Guardian* (1988), Lord Jauncey suggested that no copyright in *Spycatcher* should be enforceable because:

> The publication of *Spycatcher* was against the public interest and was in breach of the duty of confidence which Peter Wright owed to the Crown. His action reeked of turpitude. It is, in these circumstances, inconceivable that a UK court would afford to him or his publishers any protection in relation to any copyright which either of them may possess in the book.

Public interest

Both cases were examples of extreme immorality (judged by 1916 standards) or turpitude, but no definition of when protection would be refused was advanced. In *Hyde Park Residence Ltd v Yelland* (2000) Aldous LJ suggested that a court would refuse to enforce copyright if it would be:

(i)   immoral, scandalous or contrary to family life;

(ii)   injurious to public life, public health and safety or the administration of justice;

(iii) incites or encourages others to act in a way referred to in (ii).

The photographs at issue (see 11.2.6) did not fall within these categories. Mance LJ was not prepared to proffer a categorisation of circumstances. In *Ashdown v Telegraph Group Ltd* (2001) the Court of Appeal agreed that the public interest was not capable of precise definition. However, refusal of recognition for copyright in a work on grounds of public policy, and refusal to grant an injunction in the public interest (see 10.8.3), should be distinguished. The circumstances in which copyright cannot be enforced are likely to be more restricted than those where the public interest refuses an injunction against infringing publication, but does allow a claim for damages or an account of profits.

In *Hyde Park Residence Ltd v Yelland* (2000) Aldous LJ (but Mance LJ *contra*) also held that the ground of objection should lie within the work itself, and not extraneous circumstances such as ownership of the copyright.

9.6   THE EXCLUSIVE RIGHTS

A work may not lie as exclusively within the copyright owner's control as an invention does within a patentee's because, in creating the work, the author may have infringed another's copyright (see 8.4.3). Effectively, copyright owners gain a negative right to prevent others doing certain acts in relation to their work.

Section 16(1) of the CDPA 1988 confers exclusive rights on the copyright owner. To do one of these acts without authority in the UK infringes copyright: s 16(2) of the CDPA 1988. It should be noted that, unlike a patent, there is no redress against those who do not start with the right owner's work. Creation, even of an identical work, without recourse to the right owner's work does not infringe. The exclusive rights do not all apply to all the descriptions of copyright work, so must be carefully applied; for example, the right of adaptation only applies to literary, dramatic or musical works. Acts that may be performed in relation to a work but which fall outside the exclusive rights lie within the public domain – free for all. For example, anyone may use the method set out in a copyright recipe, read a book, or lend it to a friend, play a sound recording or view a film within the domestic circle, or use ideas expressed in a work.

The exclusive acts comprise the right to:

(1) copy the work;

(2) issue copies of the work to the public;

(3) rent or lend the work to the public;

(4) perform, show, or play the work in public;

(5) communicate the work to the public; and

(6) make an adaptation of the work, or do any of the preceding acts in relation to an adaptation.

9.6.1 Copying

Copying applies to all descriptions of copyright work.[11] The statute does not define 'copying', although certain acts of copying are specified. Section 17(6) of the CDPA 1988 provides that copying in relation to any description of work includes the making of copies which are transient and incidental to some other use of the work. This includes the copying of works by accessing the internet when they will be loaded into the user's computer's temporary memory (RAM), as well as disk to disk copying, and the intermediate copies made during passage of a work over the internet. In *Sony Computer Entertainment v Ball* (2004) Laddie J stated that copying to a computer's RAM constituted reproduction which created an infringing copy, however short its life. While a licence would be implied to enable legitimate use of a program, this may have implications for some forms of online software such as that written in the JAVA language, which does not need to be loaded onto a hard drive before it can be used.

It is implicit in s 17(2) of the CDPA 1988 that copying, in relation to any of the works, involves reproduction (although the change of form only applies to the original works). 'Reproduction' implies both that there is a connection between a work and its alleged copy and that there is more than a passing resemblance in the latter to the copyright work (see 10.1.1). Changes to the form, or dimension, of a work may also constitute reproduction. It is specifically provided that copying in relation to an artistic work includes copies in three dimensions of a two-dimensional work, and two-

---

44 *Ibid*, s 17(1).

dimensional copies of three-dimensional work.[45] In relation to a film or broadcast, copying includes making a photograph of the whole or a substantial part of any image forming part of the work.[46]

Otherwise, what amounts to copying varies according to the type of work. The broadest protection is given to the 'original' category of works. 'Thinner' protection is given to sound recordings and films. It is reproduction of the recording and not its content that infringes, so that, for example, to re-enact the scenario of a film in a play will not infringe the film copyright. It might, however, infringe copyright in the underlying dramatic work. Cover recordings of songs likewise do not infringe the sound recording copyright. It is not necessary that the copy be in exactly the same form as the protected work, so that a tape recording of a CD amounts to copying.

The thinnest protection is given to typographical arrangements of published editions. A facsimile copy is required.[47] A facsimile copy is exact. Photocopying, scanning into a computer, a fax will infringe, but not retyping the work. In *NLA Ltd v Marks & Spencer plc* (2002) the question to be asked was whether there had been copying of sufficient of the skill and labour attracting copyright protection to this category of work – the editor's typographical arrangement of a full page or an edition as a whole.

9.6.2 Issuing copies to the public

This right also applies to all descriptions of copyright work and is a right to put copies (including the original) of the work into circulation in the EEA, or to put copies not already circulated in the EEA into circulation outside the EEA, for the first time.

It does not extend to subsequent dealings with those copies, such as distribution, resale, hire, loan (subject to the rental right) or subsequent importation, which, subject to the rental right, cannot be controlled by the copyright owner.[48] Thus, the European doctrine of exhaustion of rights after the first circulation within the EU and the EEA is incorporated, allowing the copies to move free of copyright restrictions in subsequent dealings. Copies only put into circulation outside the EEA may not be imported into the EEA without authority.

9.6.3 Rental right

A rental right is reserved from the inability to control subsequent dealings with copies of a work put into circulation. It was extended by the Copyright and Related Rights Regulations 1996 to include literary, dramatic and musical works, artistic works other than a work of architecture in the form of a building, or a model for a building or a work of applied art and films and sound recordings.

The copyright owner has the exclusive right to rent or lend copies of the work to the public.[49] 'Rental' is defined as making a copy of the work available for use on

---

45 *Ibid*, s 17(3).
46 *Ibid*, s 17(4).
47 *Ibid*, s 17(5).
48 *Ibid*, s 18.
49 *Ibid*, s 18A.

terms that it will or may be returned, for direct or indirect economic or commercial advantage. 'Lending' is doing so otherwise than for direct or indirect economic or commercial advantage, through an establishment which is available to the public. Prime examples include the activities of video shops and public libraries. These definitions extend to forms of distribution which do not involve the transfer of a hard copy of the work.

The right does not extend to making a work available for public performance, playing or showing in public, or broadcasting, so that a cinema will not need permission from a film producer when renting a film from its distributor, for example. Making available for exhibition in public or on the spot reference use are also excluded. Consequently, the owner of a work of art may lend it to a public gallery for display without needing the copyright owner's permission. Inter-library loans are not included in the right. However, an author of an original work, or the director of a film, retain a subsidiary right to equitable remuneration, if they transfer their sound recording or film rental rights to the producer of that sound recording or film. This right may not be assigned except to a collecting society.[50]

9.6.4 Public performance rights

The copyright owner of a literary, dramatic or artistic work has the exclusive right to perform the work in public.[51] 'Performance' includes delivery in the case of lectures, addresses, speeches, sermons and, in general, includes any means of acoustic or visual presentation (including by means of a sound recording, film, or broadcast).

It is also an exclusive right in relation to a sound recording, film or broadcast to play or show the work in public.[52] Consequently, to play a sound recording of a musical work in public, for example, will infringe copyright both in the sound recording and the musical work.

Neither the person who sends visual images or sound when a work is performed, played or shown in public by electronic means of receiving visual images or sounds, nor the performers in the case of a performance infringe.[53]

Public

It is the essence of this right that the performance, playing or showing be in public. 'Public' is not defined by the Act, but has received judicial consideration. Private performance, playing or showing will not infringe; it is considered to be private if done within the domestic or quasi-domestic circle. To play a sound recording to one's family is private. A generous interpretation of the quasi-domestic circle was given in *Duck v Bates* (1884). An amateur performance, given at Guy's Hospital to an audience of doctors and their families as well as other staff and students, was held to be quasi-domestic and non-infringing. This would appear to lie at the very outer limit of the private circle.

---

50   *Ibid*, s 93B.
51   *Ibid*, s 19(1).
52   *Ibid*, s 19(3).
53   *Ibid*, s 19(4).

The important consideration is not the relationship of the audience to the performance's arranger, but of audience to copyright holder. The issue is one of whether copyright owners should be paid a royalty, whether their economic interests will be harmed by the performance, and not the social desirability of the audience concerned (subject to the permitted acts). If so, the performance can be regarded as part of the satisfaction of public demand. This is a question of fact and degree. Even if all the audience are members of a group they may form part of the general public. In *Jennings v Stephens* (1936) a performance given by members of the Women's Institute to other members was found to be in public, even though access was restricted. The same applied to the playing of music to a crowd awaiting a football match: *Performing Rights Society v Glasgow Rangers* (1975). In addition, the same is true even of performance to the consuming public in order to stimulate purchases. Playing records in the defendant's shop, audible on the pavement outside, was held to infringe, despite the defendant's purpose to whet the public's appetite and invite purchase: *Performing Rights Society v Harlequin* (1979).

There were still difficult questions to be answered, for example, whether relaying a film to hotel guests in their rooms amounted to public showing and performance, or whether new means of presenting information such as electronic data services amounted to playing in public. However, the new right of communication to the public introduced by the Information Society Directive and the Copyright and Related Rights Regulations (CRRR) 2003 will cover any transmission by electronic means.

9.6.5 Communication to the public

Electronic communication infringes copyright in a literary, dramatic, musical or artistic work, a sound recording or film, and a broadcast.[54] This right was amended by the CRRR 2003 to cater for broadcasting in the internet age. It extends to communication by electronic transmission which includes broadcasting, and making the work available by electronic transmission in such a way that members of the public may access it from a place and at a time individually chosen by them. This latter will exclude pay-television and private communications such as e-mail.

The application of this right to copyright in sound recordings is subject to statutory licences, in turn subjected to the jurisdiction of the Copyright Tribunal (see 11.14).[55]

Satellite technology allows broadcasts to reach widely across geographical borders. Without any limitations this would subject broadcasters, and those re-transmitting broadcasts, to needing licences from copyright owners in many different jurisdictions. The Cable and Satellite Directive provides that licences will be on the 'up-leg' of a transmission, and subject to the law of the country from where that takes place.

9.6.6 Adaptation

To adapt a literary, dramatic or musical work without the copyright owner's permission infringes copyright.[56] Although the section does not extend to artistic

---

54 *Ibid*, s 20.
55 *Ibid*, ss 135A–G.
56 *Ibid*, s 21.

works, no inferences are to be drawn from it as to what amounts to the copying of a work. Acts in relation to literary, dramatic or musical works that do not fall within 'adaptation' may constitute copying. An adaptation is made when it is recorded. In addition, it will infringe copyright in the original work to do any of the other infringing acts in relation to the adaptation, whether or not the adaptation has been recorded at the time of doing the infringing act. To adapt a work results in two copyrights; one in the original and the other in the adaptation (provided it meets the statutory demand for originality): *Wood v Boosey* (1868).

'Adaptation' receives a limited interpretation. In relation to a literary work (other than a computer program, or a database) and a dramatic work, it means:

- a translation of the work;
- a version of a dramatic work converted into a non-dramatic work or of a non-dramatic work converted into a dramatic work; or
- a version of the work in which the story or action is conveyed wholly or mainly by means of pictures suitable for reproduction in a book, newspaper, magazine, or similar periodical.

To adapt a computer program or database means to make an arrangement or altered version of the program, or a translation of it. To adapt a musical work means to make an arrangement or transcription of the work.[57] Translation of a computer program is further defined as including a version of the program in which it is converted into or out of a computer language or code or into a different computer language or code. Despite the restrictions of these definitions, other acts of an analogous nature may amount to copying; additionally, the new moral right of integrity provides relief from derogatory treatment of a work (see 12.5).

9.6.7 Publication right for unpublished works

In addition to the exclusive rights, reg 16 of the Copyright and Related Rights Regulations 1996[58] created a right of publication equivalent to copyright for literary, dramatic, musical or artistic works, or films. It applies to a person who publishes a previously unpublished work for the first time after the expiry of copyright protection. The work must qualify by first publication in the EEA by a publisher (or at least one of joint publishers) who is a national of an EEA State.

'Publication' is defined as 'any making available to the public'. It includes issue of copies to the public, making the work available by means of an electronic retrieval system, rental or lending of copies to the public, performance, exhibiting or showing the work in public and communicating the work to the public. Unauthorised acts do not constitute publication; including acts done without the consent of the owner of the physical medium embodying or recording the work during the period in which copyright has expired.

The right lasts for 25 years from the end of the year in which the work is first published. The substantive provisions of Chapter II (copyright owner's rights), Chapter III (permitted acts), Chapter V (dealings in rights in copyright works),

---

57   *Ibid*, s 21(3).
58   Amended by the CRRR 2003.

Chapter VI (remedies for infringement) and Chapter VII (licensing) apply to publication right as they do to copyright, subject to modifications set out in reg 17 of the Copyright and Related Rights Regulations 1996.

This right extends beyond the protection given to publishers for typographical arrangements because it encompasses the work in whatever form and arrangement it is published, which is important given that the reproduction of works in digital form in many different forms becomes possible. Its main significance lies in protection for works of historical and scholarly interest.

9.7 DROIT DE SUITE

Works of art can change hands on the art market at ever increasing prices as an artist's reputation grows, yet artists and their heirs are not privy to these transactions and would not ordinarily profit from the growing market value of the work. Some 11 EU Member States recognised a right for artists to share in subsequent profits from sales of their original works; however, the right was applied very differently between states. It is not a right in relation to copies of a work but shares an analogous justification. It is an optional provision of the Berne Convention,[59] where it also applies to writers' and composers' manuscripts and scores.

The Resale Right Directive harmonised the existing resale rights and established a new right for artists to receive a royalty based on the price paid for any resale of an original work of art after its first transfer by the artist in States not formerly recognising it. This new right comes into force on 1 January 2006 for living artists and on 1 January 2012 for their heirs. The Directive lays down standard rates to be paid.

The right does not apply to resales between individuals acting in their private capacity without the participation of art market professionals; nor to resales by those acting in their private capacity to not-for-profit museums open to the public.

9.8 PUBLIC LENDING RIGHT

Once a book has been published and copies issued to the public, its author cannot prevent its being read by a large number of people. However, library borrowing has an impact on revenues from sales and the public lending right (PLR) was established in 1979.[60] This establishes a PLR Scheme entitling authors to remuneration from books lent by public libraries for a period equal to the duration of copyright. Authors resident in the UK who are EEC nationals or German residents register with the scheme and receive remuneration[61] from a Government supplied fund. This is calculated on the basis or records of borrowing rates kept by sample public (but not school or university) libraries.

---

59 Article 14*ter*, Berne Convention.
60 Public Lending Rights Act 1979, subsequently amended.
61 In 2003 £6.2 million was paid out to 19,064 authors. No author may receive more than £6,000 pa.

Further Reading

Arnold, R, 'Joy: A Reply' [2001] IPQ 10

Bainbridge, D, Software Copyright Law (London: Butterworths, 1999)

Deazley, R, 'Photographic Painting in the Public Domain: A Response to Garnett' [2001] EIPR 179

Garnett, K, 'Copyright in Photographs' [2000] EIPR 229

Garnett, K and Abbott, A, 'Who is the "Author" of a Photograph?' [1998] EIPR 204

Gredley, E and Maniatis, S, 'Parody: A Fatal Attraction?' [1997] EIPR 339

Griffiths, J, 'Copyright and Public Lending in the United Kingdom' [1997] EIPR 499

Marchese, D, 'Joint Ownership of Intellectual Property' [1999] EIPR 364

Puri, K, 'The Term of Copyright Protection – Is it too Long in the Wake of New Technologies?' [1990] EIPR 12

Spence, M, 'Intellectual Property and the Problem of Parody' (1998) 114 LQR 594

Stamatoudi, I, 'Joy for the Claimant: Can a Film Also be Protected as a Dramatic Work?' [2000] IPQ 117

CHAPTER 10

INFRINGEMENT OF COPYRIGHT AND DEFENCES

Once it has been established that copyright subsists in a work it may be defended against the unauthorised acts of others by its owner. Only acts done in relation to a work that are within the ambit of the exclusive rights infringe. Other acts fall into the public domain and do not require permission. Infringement is, therefore, confined to:

- primary acts of infringement, by doing restricted acts (those within the exclusive rights); and
- acts of secondary infringement, which may be broadly described as dealings with infringing copies of a work.

10.1 PRIMARY INFRINGEMENT

Copyright is infringed by a person who, without the licence of the copyright owner, does any of the acts restricted by copyright[1] (see 9.6). Thus:

- copying;
- issuing copies to the public;
- renting or lending a work to the public;
- performing, showing or playing in public;
- communicating the work to the public; or
- adapting a literary, dramatic or musical work

in the UK without permission infringes. Liability is strict: no knowledge that one is infringing is required. However lack of knowledge, or reason to believe, that copyright subsisted in the copied work at the time of infringement prevents a claimant recovering damages, but not other remedies.[2]

The nature of these rights has already been examined in Chapter 9, but infringing reproduction of a work requires more detailed examination (see 10.1.1). Two other fundamental principles require consideration. Infringement need not be direct[3] (see 10.1.2). Nor need the infringing act encompass the whole of a work[4] (see 10.1.3). In addition an act of primary infringement by a third party may be actionable (see 10.2).

10.1.1 Copying

The Court of Appeal formulated a two-stage test for infringing reproduction in *Francis Day and Hunter v Bron* (1963). The composer of a song called 'Why?' was alleged to have infringed the copyright in another song, 'Spanish Town'. The two songs were not

---

1   Section 16(2) of the CDPA 1988.
2   *Ibid*, s 97.
3   *Ibid*, s 16(3)(b).
4   *Ibid*, s 16(3)(a).

identical and the defendant claimed not to have consciously heard the plaintiffs' song. Willmer LJ said:

> ... in order to constitute reproduction, within the meaning of the Act, there must be: (a) a sufficient degree of objective similarity between the two works; and (b) some causal connection between the plaintiffs' and the defendant's work.

Objective similarity

Reproduction may be literal – a full verbatim copy – such as a photocopy of a literary work or a recording of a piece of music. However, it is not necessary to show that the works are identical. Willmer LJ said, in relation to the musical work:

> ... I can find no warrant for the suggestion that reproduction, within the meaning of the section, occurs only when identity is achieved. This not only offends against common sense, but, I think, is contrary to authority. In *Austin v Columbia Gramophone Co Ltd* (1923), the headnote reads 'Infringement of copyright in music is not a question of note-for-note comparison, but of whether the substance of the original copyright is taken or not'.

Where reproduction is not exact, similarity is a question of fact. Reproduction may be non-literal if not all of a work's substance or quantity is taken, then infringement may be found if the part copied is 'substantial'[5] (see 10.1.3). Consequently, a second two-step inquiry is made:

- as to the presence of similarity between the two works – from which copying may be inferred; and
- whether the extent of the similarities identified amounts to a substantial part of the copyright work.

In *Designers Guild Ltd v Russell Williams (Textiles) Ltd* (2001) the House of Lords noted that the first step comprises identifying similarities and differences between the copyright work and the alleged copy by making a visual comparison. Then the court must decide whether the similarities are sufficiently close, numerous or extensive to be more likely to result from copying than coincidence. Some similarities might be disregarded as being commonplace or unoriginal. The purpose of the comparison is to identify the source of the defendant's work, not mere resemblance to the claimant's. The claimant need only establish sufficient similarity in the features allegedly copied, not in the works as a whole. The enquiry is directed to similarities rather than differences. Differences might suggest an independent source for the defendant's work and rebut an inference of copying. However, differences resulting from added features in the defendant's work are irrelevant because the issue is copying and not resemblance.

Computer programs

Determining similarity and substantiality (see 10.1.3) in relation to non-literal copying of computer programs, in particular, has proved difficult. Programs that achieve very similar functions may be written in entirely different computer languages.

---

5   *Ibid*, s 16(3)(a).

Consequently, to confine similarities to computer code would leave a great deal of programming structure and organisation, and the 'skill, labour and judgment' employed in it, unprotected, and the courts have not done so: *John Richardson v Flanders* (1993) and *Ibcos Computers Ltd v Poole* (1994).

Similarities which could not be explained raised a strong inference of copying, rather than of similarity of programming style, in the *Ibcos* case.

Causal connection

Once sufficient similarity is found, the defendant's work must be shown to have originated in the claimant's; similarity alone will not suffice to constitute reproduction: *LB Plastics v Swish* (1979). However, a causal connection may be inferred from similarity, as Willmer LJ explained in *Francis Day and Hunter v Bron* (1963):

> Where there is a substantial degree of objective similarity, this of itself will afford *prima facie* evidence to show that there is a causal connection between the plaintiff's and the defendant's work; at least, it is a circumstance from which the inference may be drawn.

Then the burden of proof shifts to the defendant to provide a non-infringing explanation for the similarity of his work to the claimant's. However, in *LB Plastics v Swish* (1979) the House of Lords made it clear that it was not only the similarity of the defendant's drawers to those of the plaintiff that shifted the burden of proof to the defendant. A number of other factors were significant. The plaintiff owned copyright in drawings for plastic 'knock down' drawers for the furniture industry. The defendant admitted studying the plaintiff's drawers in order to make ones that were interchangeable with them, arguing that any similarities were the result of commercial necessity and not copying. Lord Wilberforce explained proof of copying:

> That copying has taken place is for the plaintiff to establish and prove as a matter of fact. The beginning of the necessary proof normally lies in the establishment of similarity combined with proof of access to the plaintiff's productions.

> It is obvious to the eye, testified by expert witnesses and held by the judge that, though on inspection there are differences, there is a striking general similarity between the respondent's drawers and those of the appellant. Moreover, it is clear and was held by the judge that the respondents had the opportunity to copy the appellant's drawer. ... These facts established a *prima facie* case of copying which the respondent had to answer.

Similarity not attributable to a causal link does not infringe. The plaintiff and defendant may work from a common source, for example. In *Geographia v Penguin Books* (1985), it was noted that 'any commercial map maker setting out to make a map is going to have to refer to, and take materials from, earlier maps, as well as other relevant information sources'. (Had the defendants in *Elanco v Manops* (1980) gone to external sources, no infringement would have been found (see 8.4.3)). It is open to a defendant to show that the claimant in fact copied him, or that the work was independently produced. Where compatible or interchangeable competing products are to be made, the danger of copyright infringement can be avoided by 'clean room techniques'. For example, should a company wish to produce software compatible with that of a rival, one team of that company's employees can be detailed to discover the ideas of the rival program. The ideas are passed to an independent team not in communication with the first to produce a new and compatible program.

The chain of causal connection may contain more than one link, as in *Plix Products v Winstone* (1986). The defendants wished to make moulded plastic pocket containers for transporting kiwi fruit. The plaintiffs had been the sole producers of the containers and had copyright in drawings, moulds and models, as well as the finished product. The relevant authorities had laid down a detailed description of permissible containers for export of the fruit, working largely from the plaintiffs' product. Wishing to avoid infringement, the defendants instructed a designer to work alone, using only the Kiwifruit Authority's description, exporter's instructions and the fruits themselves. The resulting designs still infringed because it was found that a written description of copyright material was a sufficient link in the chain of causation of copying an artistic work.

Changes of form for original works

A work may be reproduced in another form without precluding preclude a finding of similarity. A painting may be reproduced as a photograph, for example. Section 17(2) of the CDPA 1988 specifically provides that copying a literary, dramatic, musical or artistic work means reproducing the work in any material form and that this includes storing the work in any medium by electronic means. Consequently, to store a digital photograph, or a musical or artistic work, as a computer file infringes.

However, a work must be 'reproduced' in the new form. This could mean that a copy must fall within the same description of work as the original (although an infringement need not be a 'work' at all). It would mean, for example, that a reproduction of an artistic work must also fall within the definition of artistic work, though it may take a different form of that work, such as a photograph of a sculpture. In *Plix Products v Winstone* (1986), Pritchard J, in the High Court of New Zealand, said, *obiter*, that 'a written verbal description [a literary work] of an artistic work, however precise and explicit, is not an infringement of any copyright subsisting in that work'. However, this need not be interpreted to mean that a copy must fall within the same description of work as the copyright work. Another possible interpretation is either that the copy falls within the same description of work or that the form of the work remains visible in the copy. For example, a dramatic work would remain visible in a video recording of the drama. Pritchard J's reasoning includes the suggestion that is correct to say that reproduction includes a copy in another type of work, provided the original is identifiable. He said that 'the two media are so completely different that one can never, in a real sense, be a medium in which it is possible to reproduce the other – just as a painting cannot be played on a gramophone record'! The *Norowzian* case supports such reasoning although no infringement was found on the facts.

Changes of dimension for artistic works

A change of dimension may also amount to reproduction.[6] In relation to an artistic work copying includes making a three-dimensional copy of a two-dimensional work, and a two-dimensional copy of a three-dimensional one (implying that the same does

---

6   *Ibid*, s 17(3).

not apply to the other original works, nor to films and the derivative works). Thus, to make an article from a diagram infringes, as does making a drawing of a sculpture. In *Kapwood v Embsay Fabrics* (1983), the defendants infringed the plaintiffs' copyright in a lapping diagram (an artistic work) for a simulated suede fabric by producing a fabric with identical structure. However, the same does not apply to a different category of work, so that when the defendant knitted a jumper from a copyright knitting pattern (a literary work) in *Brigid Foley v Ellott* (1982) there was no infringement.

Changes in form for derivative works

The Act makes no express provision as to changes of either form or dimension in relation to films, or works derived from films. To make a written record of the music reproduced in a sound recording will infringe the underlying musical copyright, but it is not clear whether the copyright in the sound recording is also infringed. The Copyright Act 1956 stated that a copy of a film or sound recording must also be a film or sound recording, so that the omission of this provision might suggest a change in the law. However, the fact that s 17(2) of the CDPA 1988 is confined expressly to the original works leads to an inference that there has been no change and that if the form of the film or derivative work cannot be identified in the supposed copy no infringement occurs. The written copy of a piece of music made from a sound recording will then only infringe the musical copyright, and not that in the sound recording.

Phillips and Firth suggest[7] that this is a fair result because the copy cannot be exploited as a sound recording. Therefore, the sound recording copyright owner does not require protection from the copy; it is the musical work copyright owner who may now face competition from the written record. Section 17(4) of the CDPA 1988 does not prevent this conclusion. It provides that, in relation to a film, or broadcast copying includes making a photograph of the whole or a substantial part of an image forming part of the work. The visual nature of these works remains identifiable in the photograph. However, the sub-section states that copying 'includes' this type of reproduction, so that a deduction that other changes of form may also infringe copyright in a derivative work is tenable.

Reproduction does not include re-creation. In *Norowzian v Arks (No 1)* (1998), it was argued unsuccessfully that to remake a film by recreating and re-filming the dance sequence depicted in a film infringed the film copyright. It was held that the subject matter of film copyright is the recording itself and not any underlying work, and that to copy a recording (whether a sound recording or film) required an exact copy of the recording to be made. Australian authority supported this view.

Parody

There is one change of form which could call for different treatment in relation to copying, that of a parody of a work, because this is a legitimate art form in itself. To succeed as parody, a copyright work must remain identifiable. Sufficient objective similarity and a causal connection seem inevitable, leading to a necessary finding of

---

7   Phillips, J and Firth, A, *Introduction to Intellectual Property Law* (London: Butterworths, 2001)

infringement. If sufficient, the 'skill, labour and judgment' employed in creating the parody will entitle that new work to its own copyright, but this does not preclude a finding that the source work has been infringed (see 8.4.3).

Unlike France and Spain, the UK makes no specific statutory provision for parody. However, two cases hint that the courts might take a lenient view with respect to this particular art form. In *Glyn v Weston Feature Film Co* (1916), a filmed 'send up' of the novel *Three Weeks* did not infringe, nor did the parody of the chorus 'Rock-a-Billy' in the plaintiff's song by the defendant in *Joy Music v Sunday Pictorial* (1960). Both were decisions that a substantial part of the plaintiffs' work had not been taken (see 10.1.3). In contrast, in both *Williamson Music v Pearson Partnership* (1987) and *Schweppes v Wellingtons* (1987), infringement was found. In the former, the plaintiff was the copyright owner of the music for the show *South Pacific*; the defendant produced an advertisement for a bus company by modifying the words and parodying the tune. In the latter, the defendants mimicked the plaintiffs' copyright label for SCHLURPPES toiletries. These parodies were held to amount to infringement of a 'substantial part' of the plaintiffs' works.

It is clear that the normal principles of infringement will be applied to parody, despite their uncertainty. The later cases did differ in that the parody was undertaken for commercial purposes rather than social or literary criticism.[8] However, the earlier pair of cases adopted a now discredited test for infringement. They considered the proportion of effort put into the new work by the defendant, rather than the proportion of the plaintiff's 'skill, labour and judgment' surviving in the parody (see 10.1.3). A copyright author may also seek redress against a parody by asserting the moral right of integrity (see 12.5).

An opportunity to change UK law when implementing the Information Society Directive was not used. Article 5(3)(k) provided an optional exception 'for the purpose of caricature, parody or pastiche'. This was not included in the CRRR 2003.

Subconscious copying

It was held in *Francis Day and Hunter v Bron* (1963) that copying need not be deliberate and that it may be subconscious. The defendant claimed that he had never consciously studied the plaintiffs' song, nor played it. The plaintiffs responded that as the song had been extensively exploited in the US it was overwhelmingly probable that he must have heard it, and that the degree of similarity between the works raised an inference of subconscious copying. On the facts, this argument failed; however, Willmer LJ was prepared to recognise, first, the psychological possibility of subconscious copying based on proof, or a strong inference of, *de facto* similarity arising from familiarity with the copyright work. (It was this element that was lacking.) Secondly, he recognised that subconscious copying might amount to copyright infringement because no element of *mens rea* is required for infringement. The test remains the same – one of objective similarity brought about by a causal connection – and he said:

---

8   Contrast the American case of *Mattel Inc v Walking Mountain Productions* (2003). Photographs of Barbie dolls were used in parody of Barbie's normal associations to comment on American culture of 'consumption and conformism'. The US Court of Appeals for the 9th Circuit held that, although commercial, this amounted to parody and therefore constituted fair use of Mattel's copyright. Parody will amount to fair use provided no more is taken from the copyright work than is required to conjure up the object of the parody.

It is quite irrelevant to enquire whether the defendant was or was not consciously aware of such causal connection ...

The fact that the defendant denies that he consciously copied affords some evidence to rebut the inference of causal connection arising from the objective similarity, but is in no way conclusive.

Accordingly, the trial judge's direction as to the relevant criteria was approved:

... the degree of familiarity (if proved at all, or properly inferred) with the plaintiffs' work, the character of the work, particularly its qualities of impressing the mind and memory, the objective similarity of the defendant's work, the inherent probability that such similarity as is found could be due to coincidence, the existence of other influences on the defendant composer, and not least the quality of the defendant composer's own evidence on the presence or otherwise in his mind of the plaintiffs' work.

Similarity not attributable to subconscious copying will be coincidental, and will not infringe: *EMI v Papathanasiou* (1987). The four notes from the film *Chariots of Fire* alleged to be a copy of the plaintiffs' work were held to be a musical commonplace and the similarity was a coincidence.

10.1.2 Direct and indirect infringement

Copyright may be infringed either directly, or indirectly.[9] Indirect copying can be best illustrated by the cases of *LB Plastics v Swish* (1979) and *Plix Products v Winstone* (1986). Swish copied the plaintiff's drawers (and drawings made from the drawers), which in turn were embodiments of the plaintiff's drawings. Winstone copied, not the plaintiff's copyright drawings, moulds and models, nor even their plastic fruit trays, or the Kiwifruit Authority's regulations, but a written description of the trays taken from those regulations. A chain of causal connection (see 10.1.1) can be traced back from the defendant's trays through the description, the regulations and the plaintiff's product, to the copyright works. This infringed, because the works gave rise to the product, the product to the regulations, the regulations to the description and the description to the competing trays. The House of Lords affirmed that 'reverse engineering' constituted indirect copying in *British Leyland v Armstrong Patents* (1986) (see 10.8.2). The defendant had not seen the plaintiff's copyright drawings (unlike Swish), but copied exhausts made by the plaintiff. The statute provides that the intervening steps in a chain of indirect infringement need not be infringements in themselves.

10.1.3 Substantial part

The act of infringement may be done to the work as a whole or to 'a substantial part of it'.[10] It may well, therefore, infringe to copy, perform or broadcast, for example, only a part of a work, provided that that part can be regarded as 'substantial'. Two questions are involved: first, whether the defendant's taking is part of the substance of the work and, secondly, whether that taking can be regarded as sufficiently substantial to infringe. However, the concepts applied to do so often elide these two considerations.

---

9   Section 16(3)(b) of the CDPA 1988.
10   *Ibid*, s 16(3)(a).

The provision that a non-literal taking from a work must be substantial allows for some free use to be made of works, balancing society's need for access to works against authors' private interests.

The question of substantiality is one of mixed fact and law, a matter of impression in which an appellate court should not reverse a judge's decision unless it errs in principle. At this stage, after the infringing act of reproduction has been established, Lord Millett suggested that no further comparison of similarities in the two works is needed or relevant in *Designers Guild Ltd v Russell Williams (Textiles) Ltd* (2001).

However, Lord Scott suggested that when a claim of infringement relates to taking part ('altered copying') of the claimant's work, a finding of sufficient similarity to constitute evidence of copying was likely also to show sufficient substantiality. He went onto suggest that differences between the works could also lead to a finding of a lack of substantiality. In Lord Scott's view even direct copying might not infringe if it constituted taking of 'idea'.

That the House of Lords could not provide clear guidance on such a fundamental copyright principle illustrates the uncertainties of basic doctrine which bedevil copyright law. The better view is that similarities and differences between the works are best confined to the issue of copying in order to avoid the difficulties encountered by the Court of Appeal. If any similarities are caused by the idea expressed in both works, lack of infringement can be established by asking the question proposed by Lord Scott himself: 'has the infringer incorporated a substantial part of the independent skill, labour etc contributed by the original author in creating the copyright work?' In other words, the idea/expression distinction should be confined to the substantiality issue and not employed in determining whether the defendant copied. Lord Hoffmann distinguished between ideas which do not amount to part of the literary, dramatic, musical or artistic nature of the work, and those which have the right character but are too commonplace or unoriginal to form a substantial part of the copied work.

The nature of the work

Determining substantial part is related to the nature of a particular work. It is the 'substance' of the particular type of work that must be taken. It was therefore necessary that a substantial part be taken of an editor's skill employed in a newspaper in *NLA Ltd v Marks & Spencer plc* (2002).

This is often determined by asking whether sufficient has been taken of the skill, labour and judgment, or originality, which secured subsistence of copyright in the claimant's work. In a series of cases relating to plays in the 19th century plot was treated as the essence of a dramatic work (rather than remaining at the level of 'idea'). Very little could then be taken from the work without infringing: *Kelly v Cinema Houses* (1932).

This can also be expressed as taking expression, rather than idea. In *Jones v London Borough of Tower Hamlets* (2000) it was reproduction of skill in making architectural drawings, and not the design concepts of the buildings depicted, that was necessary. It was noted that the common stock of architectural ideas may not be monopolised. Similarly, the taking in *Norowzian v Arks Ltd (No 2)* (2000) was of style and technique rather than the substance of copyright protection for a dramatic work. Nourse LJ gave other examples of unprotectable elements. An artist using the technique of pointillism originated by the neo-impressionist Seurat in the painting *La Baignade, Asnières* would not infringe in painting a scene in Provence. Equally, the 'sprung rhythm' of Gerard Manley Hopkins's verse, or the thematic build up of Sibelius's second symphony, may be imitated.

In *Designers Guild Ltd v Russell Williams (Textiles) Ltd* (2001) Lord Hoffmann stated that in cases of artistic copyright the more abstract and simple the idea copied, the less likely it is to constitute a substantial part. Originality tended to lie in the detail with which a basic idea is presented: '[C]opyright law protects foxes better than hedgehogs.'

Computer programs

American courts employ a three-part test 'abstraction, filtration and comparison' test to determine non-literal infringement of computer programs: *Computer Associates International Inc v Altai Inc* (1992). Before comparing similarities in the two programs, the non-literal elements of the copyright program's structures are isolated at differing levels of detail by a process of abstraction, starting from the actual programming code and ending with the function the work performs. Then, elements that are not protected by copyright are filtered out, leaving a core of copyright protection. Finally, similarities between the defendant's program and this core are determined. If they are a substantial part of the protectable element of the plaintiff's program, non-literal infringement is found. Although Ferris J favoured this approach in *John Richardson v Flanders* (1993), in *Ibcos Computers Ltd v Poole* (1994) Jacob J preferred to follow the traditional approach.

However, the courts have not found it easy to articulate how to assess the substantiality of similarities of structure, sequence and organisation (non-literal aspects) between rival programs. In the *Ibcos* case the 'skill, labour and judgment' invested in the data division of a program rendered it a substantial part of the plaintiff's program. Close correspondence of functions between individual programs within the package also amounted to taking a substantial part. However, no specific criteria were stated for the many findings of substantial copying in the individual programs within the suite. Ferris J stated that the originality of parts copied and the idea/expression dichotomy were relevant factors. He also stated that elements dictated by external factors, efficiency, and those from the public domain should be filtered out. It is not clear how far these remain relevant factors after the disapproval of employing the US approach in *Ibcos*.

Programs differ from other literary works in that every line and character, other than the programmers' comments (which are not read by the computer), is essential to the program's functioning. In many programs some elements of the code will be used repeatedly. If these characteristics were to be adopted as the test of substantiality, copying almost any element of a program could infringe. In *Cantor Fitzgerald International v Tradition (UK) Ltd* (2000) the defendants admitted copying 2% of the claimant's work. It was held that principles applied to traditional literary works could not be applied wholesale to programs. Whether a part of a program was functionally essential was not the correct test. The right test was whether the copied code represented a substantial part of the programmer's skill, which was related to the program's originality. A program's architecture might be capable of protection if it represented exercise of programming skill. The modular structure of this program, however, was related to external factors and not its structure as a functional unit. Consequently, the code taken was judged against the collection of modules as a whole.

Subsequent proceedings in *Navitaire Inc v Easyjet Airline Co Ltd* (2004) raised a claim of software reproduction in two online airline booking systems. The claims focused on the software's functional design (its so-called 'business logic'), database structure, internet booking interface as well as agent interfaces in the call centre and airport. Pumphrey J stated that to provide copyright protection to the program's business logic would be an unjustifiable extension to copyright. Nor was copyright extended to the command codes used by the agent interfaces. The database was held not to infringe Navitaire's data structures. Navitaire argued that by studying its program OpenRes's operation closely and adopting a similar functional structure amounted to taking a substantial part of its source code in the same way that appropriating the plot of a book might infringe copyright in a literary work by changing the medium.[11] Pumphrey J stated:[12]

> There is no dispute that it is written in a number of computer languages and that the actual code, in the sense of what appears on the page, bears no resemblance to that of OpenRes.

It would seem that, like the US,[13] little protection will be given to the 'look and feel' of a computer program. Such elements, if protectable at all, must be the subject of a patent.

Artistic works

The nature of artistic works has also been considered. The relevant question is whether 'the feeling and artistic character' has been taken. In *Bauman v Fussell* (1978), the plaintiff had copyright in a photograph of a fighting cock. The defendant reproduced the scene in a painting, although with different colouring. The majority of the Court of Appeal held that there was no infringement. On the facts, the Court held that the case was closer to a situation where a photographer had taken a scene without being responsible for the image's arrangement (capturing a particularly dramatic moment in the cockfight), than to one where the photographer had arranged the scene himself. However, Romer LJ dissented, on the basis that the positioning of the birds represented skill on the photographer's part and that that skill had been reproduced.

In determining what constitutes a substantial part of an artistic work, consideration can be given to literary annotations added to the work, although these could not contribute to the artistic work's originality: *Interlego v Tyco* (1988).

In *Antiquesportfolio.com plc v Rodney Fitch & Co* (2001) using outline reproductions of photographs as logos on navigation buttons in a website did not infringe because the 'author's work of origination' in a photograph was not reproduced.

---

11   Although this analogy might be thought to be open to failure, give the court's approach to the idea–expression dichotomy in relation to books. *Norowzian v Arks* (No 2) (2000) might be thought a better analogy.

12   'Easyjet Wins Easy': www.lawdit.co.uk.

13   *Lotus v Borland* (1995). Further proceedings relating to the Navitaire OpenRes software are pending in the US: *BulletProof Technologies v Navitaire* Case Number 2:03CV00428 PGC.

Substantial – a qualitative test

The second part of determining whether a 'substantial part' has been taken is whether the part taken was sufficient. This is a question of fact and degree. It is not purely a test of the quantity taken, but also one of the quality of the part taken in relation to the whole: *Ladbroke (Football) v William Hill* (1964). The proportion of a work that is taken need not be large, although if it is, this may contribute to a finding that the taking is substantial. In *Hawkes v Paramount Film Service* (1934), a film of a newsworthy event included a clip of a boys' band playing the musical march 'Colonel Bogey'. It was held to infringe copyright in that musical work, even though only 28 or so bars were reproduced, taking less than a minute from a work of several minutes' duration. Lord Hanworth MR held that the relevant consideration was whether the amount of the march taken was so slender as to be impossible of recognition. In this particular case, the reproduction, although short, was of an instantly recognisable and memorable part of the march and, so, substantial in relation to the quality (or nature) of the musical work.

Unfair competition

The courts use a variety of considerations to decide whether a substantial part has been infringed. In so doing, they appear often implicitly to be taking the unfairness of the defendant's competition into account. If the part of a work that is taken is valuable to the copyright owner, it is likely to be substantial, though the consideration is not one of commercial harm to the claimant or of benefit to the defendant: *Elanco v Mandops* (1979); *ITV Publications v Time Out* (1984). This gives the court sufficient flexibility to achieve fair play between the parties.

Original elements

Where a secondary work (see 8.4.3) is concerned, whether the part taken is from what is original in the work will be relevant. In *Warwick Films v Eisinger* (1969), taking the actual text of the trial transcript was not found to be substantial because that was not the original part of the plaintiff's work, even though quantitatively it was considerable. In *Ladbroke (Football) v William Hill* (1964), by contrast, because the defendant copied the very parts of the plaintiff's compilation that contributed to the work's originality (the same order of lists, the same headings, almost identical varieties of wager, similar explanatory notes) the taking did infringe. This was so even though the odds given by the defendant and the matches chosen differed. It was the plaintiff's effort of compilation that was protected, preventing the shortcut taken by the defendant in copying and then publishing simultaneously. If the 'skill, labour and judgment' expended by the copyright owner is trivial, only virtually identical copying will be regarded as substantial, neatly adjusting copyright protection to the extent of the claimant's effort: *Kenrick v Lawrence* (1890).

Literal copying

Where copying is *verbatim*, the quantity taken need not be large to qualify as substantial, this is particularly so if the claimant's mistakes are also repeated: *Harman v*

Osborne (1967). When a copyright work is used as a source, it is legitimate to take facts and ideas from the source work. However, to go further and take from the claimant's arrangement, or questions, or other effort put into the actual expression of the source work will infringe if a substantial part of that expression survives in the defendant's work (*Harman v Osborne* (1967)).

The nature of the source work may influence the extent to which such use is permitted. In *Ravenscroft v Herbert* (1980), the plaintiff's work was historical. Brightman J accepted that members of the public were entitled to use it as a work of reference. He said that a historical work was not judged by the same standards as a work of fiction because the author of a historical work was to be presumed to wish to add to the sum of knowledge, so that readers could make greater use of it. On the facts, however, he concluded that there had been copying to a substantial extent because much of the plaintiff's language had been taken and identical incidents of history had been adopted wholesale. This decision could also have been reached by distinguishing between, on the one hand, the idea of the work and the facts contained therein and, on the other hand, its expression, the language and detail of incident; but it was decided as a matter of copying a substantial part. *Ravenscroft v Herbert* (1980) should be contrasted with the series of cases relating to plays in the 19th century.

A substantial part of the claimant's work

In deciding whether a substantial part of a work has been reproduced, the relevant question can be phrased in one of two ways. Whether the defendant invested substantial 'skill, labour and judgment' in the defendant's copy; or whether the 'skill, labour and judgment' invested in the claimant's work survives to a substantial extent in the defendant's. It would appear that the majority in *Bauman v Fussell* (1978) used the first, and Romer LJ the second.

More recently, the nature of an artistic work was considered in *Spectravest v Aperknit* (1988). It was made clear that the extent of the defendant's alterations and additions is not the relevant consideration (although it would be relevant to any copyright in the defendant's work). The correct test was: first, to identify what has been taken from the plaintiff and remains recognisable in the defendant's work; and, secondly, to ask whether, from a qualitative point of view, this is a substantial part of the plaintiff's (not the defendant's) work. Consequently, because the one feature of the plaintiff's design which had been recognisably been reproduced in the defendant's was a substantial part of the plaintiff's design, infringement was found, despite the many changes otherwise made by the defendant.

However, the Court of Appeal replicated the mistake in *Designers Guild Ltd v Russell Williams (Textiles) Ltd* (2001), misled by the differences in the two works resulting from the defendant's additions to the copied material. The House of Lords reiterated that the correct test is the importance to the claimant's work of the part taken.

10.2   AUTHORISING INFRINGEMENT

To authorise another to do one of the restricted acts also infringes.[14]

---

14   Section 16(2) of the CDPA 1988.

10.2.1   A passive interpretation

Early authorities gave the word authorise the wide dictionary meaning of 'to sanction, countenance, and approve': *Evans v E Hulton & Co* (1924) and *Falcon v Famous Film Players* (1926). This allowed very passive acts to amount to authorisation of an infringing act, such as permitting or allowing it, or even being merely being indifferent to the act taking place. The Australian case of *Moorhouse v University of New South Wales* (1976) came close to applying such a passive definition to 'authorise'. The university was held liable for infringement by copies made by students in the university library. Students made two test copies of a 10-page story. The university provided photocopiers in the library for student use, without supervision or notices giving copyright warnings. 'Sanction, countenance, approve' were held to include 'permit', and it was held that such authorisation could be either express or implied; the person authorising did not need know of the infringing copy being made. Authorisation was also said to include acts and omissions. The university was not entitled to assume that student copying would fall within the fair dealing defence (see 11.2).

10.2.2   An active interpretation

However, the word 'authorise' is also capable of bearing a stricter, active meaning, implying that the person authorising can exercise an element of control over the person infringing, in the sense of ordering or actively requesting the act. It is significant that in the *Moorhouse* case it was found that the means of copying were under the university's control and that no reasonable steps had been taken to prevent infringement.

In the UK, this stricter meaning has been adopted, so that infringement by authorisation requires three elements:

* an actual infringing act;
* a causal link between the infringement and the person authorising; and
* control by the authoriser over the infringer.

Three cases established these criteria. In *Standen Engineering v Spalding* (1984), the defendant ordered spare parts to be made for sugar beet harvesters by another manufacturer; the plaintiff owned copyright in drawings for the spare parts. Falconer J held that the defendant had sanctioned and approved the manufacture of spares because the order was the causal link between the manufacturer's infringing act and the defendant, who also had the necessary element of control over the act. This was refined in *A & M Records v Audio Magnetics* (1979). The defendant was using the plaintiff's copyright photographs and drawings in advertising, which might encourage public infringement of the sound recordings being advertised. Foster J held that to infringe there must be a specific authorisation of an actual breach, with the authorisation causing that breach to take place.

The mere facilitation of infringement does not amount to authorisation. In *CBS v Ames* (1981), the defendant provided a record lending library in his shop (before the rental right was extended to its current extent) and also sold blank tapes to customers. He did not encourage copying and did display a notice warning of infringement. Whitford J held that this did not amount to authorising infringement, although infringement was almost certain to result and the defendant was indifferent to that possibility because he did not provide the equipment or facilities for the copying.

In Canada in March 2004 it was held that merely placing a personal copy of a musical work on a shared directory accessible from other computers does not infringe copyright by authorising reproduction by others: *BMG Canada Inc v John Doe* (2004). Doing so was equated with placing a photocopier in a room full of copyright works. On appeal, the Federal Court of Appeal refused to order disclosure of the names of individual uploaders of shared files as the plaintiffs' evidence was defective. They upheld the decision that 'the provision of facilities that allow copying does not amount to authorising infringement'. It would seem that the same might be true in the UK: the relevant question would be whether the uploader of the music file 'controlled' the subsequent action of any downloader of that file.

10.2.3   Facilitation

A bold attempt was made by copyright owners to diminish infringement of sound recordings by the public ('home copying' – see 11.4) by challenging the recording equipment industry in *CBS Songs v Amstrad* (1988). The defendant made double-deck double-speed tape recorders, which made private tape to tape copies very easy. Its advertisements drew attention to the fact that these could be used to copy sound recordings. Lord Templeman explained the conflict of interest between the entertainment and recording industries, normally interdependent, in the production of private recording equipment. However, the House of Lords held that neither the abilities of the defendant's products, nor the advertisement, could be said to imply that the defendant either possessed or purported to possess the authority to grant permission for copying. Authorisation was defined as 'a grant or purported grant, which may be express or implied, of the right to do the act complained of'. Amstrad conferred the power on buyers of its equipment to copy, but was not granting any right to do so.

10.2.4   Linking and framing

Questions have arisen whether providing hypertext links to copyright works on webpages infringes. Linking lies at the core of the World Wide Web and over-restriction could have significant results, particularly for the providers of search engines. A website providing a link does not copy or communicate the work itself, and is not a direct primary infringer unless the link itself can be regarded as a work.[15] However, the link at least facilitates any infringement by those using it.

Several distinctions need to be made. The linked work may have been uploaded by, or with the permission of, its copyright owner; or it may have been made available without authority. Links themselves take several forms and should be distinguished from frames. Hypertext reference links (HREF) allow users to display the work linked to, and provide the work's URL,[16] or web address, when it is displayed. The link itself need not be the URL but may comprise a highlighted sentence or phrase in the linker's site, or a piece of text taken from the linked to site, such as a title, headline, image, logo

---

15   Or a trade mark.
16   URL: uniform recourse locator.

or trade mark. The link may either be to a website's home page, or be a 'deep link' to a subsidiary page in the site. The simplest analogy for a normal HREF link is that of a reference in a reading list, not something that would infringe copyright in the work being referred to. A link can be provided without the knowledge or co-operation of the site being linked to.[17] Websites can use technology to prevent being linked to. Frames divide webpages into sections. Using a link then displays the work linked to within a frame in the linker's page. It is not so apparent to the user that he or she has been transferred to another website, and the URL remains that of the linker's page.

There is no one answer to the question whether linking infringes. Both direct and contributory infringement may be argued against a link. There are also several defences that may apply. It should also be remembered that the real ground for complaint is often the confusion as to source encountered by the link's user. Passing off may prove a different means of redress. Protection against unfair competition in other jurisdictions might provide even wider remedies.

Direct infringement

Direct infringement was successfully alleged against the provider of a link in *Shetland Times Ltd v Wills* (1996). In a controversial decision, an interim interdict was granted against the defender, who had used headlines from the pursuer's online edition as links to his own electronic newspaper. These were deep links by-passing the pursuer's home page, on which it was planned to place advertising. As click counters are commonly used to gauge the effect of such advertising, the pursuer did not want readers of its pages to avoid accessing the home page. The headlines were held arguably to comprise both copyright works and cable programmes.[18] Consequently, reproducing these and 'broadcasting' them was direct infringement. Copyright does not normally subsist in titles (see 8.2.1), and they were not distinctive. The cable programme service was also held not to be interactive and therefore within the statutory definition despite viewers' ability to communicate with the site by e-mail. The case was eventually settled before the court could give full consideration to the law. In *Sony Music Entertainment (UK) Ltd v Easyinternetcafe Ltd* (2003) this interpretation of cable programme services was given some support.

However, linkers can avoid the result by using their own material as the link. The linked to site would not fall within the amended definition of a broadcast. Any direct infringement of the right of communication would be dependent on the link itself comprising a copyright work. In the US, deep linking to the events pages of a site providing information about events and booking services, by a rival site, was held not to infringe as there was no copyright in the URLs used: *Ticketmaster Corp v Tickets.com* (2000).

Authorising infringement

A link provider might still authorise infringement by users of its links. In the US a preliminary injunction against contributory infringement was granted in *Intellectual Reserve Inc v Utah Lighthouse Ministry Inc* (1999). However, in the UK it is unlikely that the linker would satisfy the active test of authorisation.

---

17 And web 'culture' is to provide them freely and without requesting permission.
18 Now subsumed within broadcasts by the CRRR 2003.

Other infringing acts

Framing was raised in the US in *Washington Post Co v Total News Inc* (1997). The case was settled, but it was made clear that framing constituted infringement by creating a derivative work. In the UK it might be arguable that a link infringed by communicating the work, although the link itself would not necessarily be a work. Redress could also lie in infringement of the *sui generis* database right.

Linking to devices enabling circumvention of technological protection for electronic works was found to infringe the Digital Millenium Copyright Act[19] (DMCA) 1998 in *Universal City Studios Inc v Reimerdes* (2000). The defendant provided links to DeCSS software, which enabled users to circumvent the CSS encryption applied to DVDs. This act of 'electronic disobedience' followed the removal of the software itself from his website. Section 296ZA[20] of the CDPA 1988 provides civil remedies against a person who knowingly circumvents such technological protection. Section 296ZB makes it an offence to provide the means for doing so and s 296ZC provides equivalent civil remedies (see 10.5). Links to such devices may well fall within these provisions.

Defences

A website owner can use technical means to prevent being linked to. Consequently, it can be argued that not employing such technology implies a licence for those who provide a link. Website owners may also refuse permission for links in any contractual terms and conditions. However, in the *Ticketmaster* case such terms were found not to be binding as reasonable notice of them had not been given.

In the US a link has also been argued to constitute fair use of a work. In *Kelly v Arriba Soft Corp* (1999) the defendant used 'thumbnail' images of the plaintiff's pictures as deep links in a visual search engine. This was found to be direct reproduction of the copyright images, but to be justified by the fair use doctrine. The UK fair dealing defences (see 11.2) might not stretch so far.

Neither the 'safe harbour' provisions of the DMCA 1998, nor the immunities for internet service providers (ISPs) provided by the E-Commerce Directive (see 10.2.5) provide a *carte blanche* for linking. Search engines, for example, should be able to rely on the immunity for providing mere conduits to information. However, copyright owners may serve notice on ISPs of infringing communications. Then the ISP must act to disable or remove the information from its service.

10.2.5   Internet service providers and cyber cafés

Potentially, providers of access to the internet, such as universities and cyber cafés, and providers of the telecommunications transmission of internet services infringe copyright in works transmitted via their services by reproduction and communication to the public, and by authorising infringing by the sender and recipient of those works.

ISPs may charge for providing access to the internet through their servers, host webpages, or run bulletin boards. ISPs both host information for others by storing it on

---

19 Implementing the World Copyright Treaty 1996.
20 Inserted by the CRRR 2003, implementing the Information Society Directive and WCT 1996.

their servers, and act as conduits to information being transmitted across the internet. They have the capacity to control the content of what is loaded on to their servers, or passes through them. However, they do not determine the content of what they host. The advantage to copyright owners of any liability for internet service providers and bulletin board service operators is that they are identifiable, and solvent, whereas actual users of their works may be nearly impossible to trace.[21] The case of *Godfrey v Demon* (2001), albeit relating to defamation disseminated on the internet, gave ISPs cause for concern.

The liability of a cyber café was considered in *Sony Music Entertainment (UK) Ltd v Easyinternetcafé Ltd* (2003). The defendant allowed customers to download music from the internet. Staff would then 'burn' the files to CD for them. The defendant was held liable for primary infringement. Liability is strict and the voluntary decision to remain ignorant of what was being copied for customers was irrelevant. Had the customers made the copies, the outcome might have been very different. The judge said, *obiter*, that an owner of a fax machine would not be liable for receiving infringing faxes, as that would amount to involuntary copying. The cafés were likened to high street printers, whose copying on behalf of others would also infringe, regardless of their knowledge.

ISP 'safe harbour'

Both the Information Society and E-Commerce[22] Directives specifically provide for ISPs. Article 5(1) of the former excepts temporary acts of reproduction (see 9.6.1).

The E Commerce Directive[23] applies to 'information society services', summarised as:

> any service normally provided for remuneration, at a distance, by means of electronic equipment for the processing (including digital compression) and storage of data, and at the individual request of a recipient of a service.

It provides that ISPs operating as mere conduits to the transmission of information, caching or hosting are given immunity provided certain conditions are met. There is no liability for acting as a conduit provided that the ISP did not initiate the transmission, select the recipient, or select or modify the information transmitted.[24] Acting as a conduit includes temporary storage of the information if it is solely for the purpose of carrying out the transmission and lasts no longer than is reasonably necessary for it.

Caching comprises 'automatic, intermediate or temporary storage for the sole purpose of making more efficient onward transmission of the information to other recipients of the service upon their request'.[25] ISPs are not liable provided that they do not modify the information, comply with conditions on access to it and any rules

---

21 The Recording Industry Association of America has commenced infringement proceedings against individuals downloading infringing music and films: www.riaa.org.

22 European Parliament and Council Directive 2000/31 on Certain Legal Aspects of Information Society Services, in particular Electronic Commerce, in the Internal Market [2000] OJ L178/1.

23 Implemented by the Electronic Commerce (EC Directive) Regulations [ECR] 2002 (SI 2002/2013), which came into force on 21 August 2002.

24 *Ibid*, reg 17.

25 *Ibid*, reg 18.

regarding its updating, and do not interfere with lawful use of technology used by industry to obtain data on the use of the information. However, cached information no longer available is exempted from this immunity. ISPs must act expeditiously to remove or disable access to information they have stored upon obtaining actual knowledge of the fact that the information at the source of the transmission has been removed from the network, that access to it has been disabled, or that an administrative authority has ordered its removal or disablement.

Hosting information is immune provided that the ISP does not have actual knowledge of unlawful activity or information and, if damages are claimed, does not know of facts or circumstances from which it would have been apparent that the activity or information was unlawful.[26] Nor must the recipient of the service have been acting under the control or authority of the ISP. On obtaining knowledge that the information or activity was unlawful the ISP must act expeditiously to remove or disable access to the information.

Take down notices

Nothing in these provisions stops any party applying for court relief to prevent or stop infringement of their rights.[27] Section 97A of the CDPA, as amended by the CRRR 2003, provides that the High Court, or Court of Session, has power to grant an injunction or interdict against a service provider with actual knowledge of another person using their service to infringe copyright or a performer's property right. It is clear then that an ISP can be given notice of copyright infringement, and that it must remove access to the information. In determining whether an ISP had actual knowledge a court must take into account all matters appearing to it to be relevant in all the circumstances.[28] In particular, whether the ISP received notice through a means of contact including its e-mail details, the extent to which the notice includes the full name and address of its sender, details of the location of the information, and details of the unlawful activity or information at issue must be considered.

No specific provision is apparently made for the owners of information wrongfully removed by false notice of unlawfulness, nor for removal of information in the public interest. The equivalent 'Notice and Take Down' procedure of the DMCA 1998 in the US allows a site owner to object before the work is removed, and prevents the site owner taking subsequent proceedings against the ISP. Recital 46 of the E-Commerce Directive provides that the procedure should observe principles and national procedures relating to freedom of expression, and that Member States may establish specific requirements to be observed before removal or disablement of the information.

10.2.6   'Peer to peer' file sharing

The development of MP3 compression technology for digital files, and broadband access to the internet, allows rapid and easy transmission of digital music files over electronic networks. These files may then be 'burnt' to CDs, played on MP3 players, and listened to on PCs. Compression technology also allows films to be transmitted

---

26   *Ibid*, reg 19.
27   *Ibid*, reg 20.
28   *Ibid*, reg 22.

and downloaded quickly. In addition, peer to peer (P2P) file-sharing technology allows individuals to share works stored on their computers by facilitating searching of other end users' computers for desired files. The result has been an explosion of musical[29] and film[30] piracy.

There have been a number of cases in the US. Early P2P services made unlicensed copies of the works, and so were direct infringers themselves: *UMG Recordings v MP3.com* (2000). The (then illegitimate) American service Napster did not copy the files shared, but was found to be a contributory infringer in *A & M Records et al v Napster* (2001). Napster was held to be aware of the infringing use made of the service, which did not fall within the fair use, 'space shifting', or personal use exceptions. Napster was unable to prevent infringing file sharing and closed down as a result of the injunction imposed upon it.

However, more recent unlicensed services,[31] such as Grokster and Morpheus, have been found merely to facilitate transmission in the US: *MGM Studios Inc v Grokster* (2003).[32] Evidence was adduced to show substantial non-infringing use of the service and the court likened the service to home video recorders or photocopying machines. Kazaa was also found not to be infringing in the Netherlands.[33] Much will depend on the structure of the service being provided; Grokster distributed software to its users but could not control their activities thereafter and no information was transmitted through its servers. However, in the *Aimster* (2003) case it was held that a P2P service did not need to know about individual acts of infringement. Napster, by contrast, played an active role in connecting users downloading and uploading files. Instead, copyright holders will have to rely on legal support for anti-copying technology supplied by the WCT, DMCA and Information Society Directive (see 10.5). Further difficulties are posed by the cross-border nature of file sharing and infringement.

Controversially, the RIAA has taken action against individual end users of P2P services as primary infringers, having secured court orders under the DMCA 1998 to force ISPs to reveal their details: *RIAA v Verizon Internet Services* (2003). The most recent P2P services, such as Napster 2.0 or iTunes, charge and are licensed by the copyright owners.

In the UK the reproduction right (which includes temporary and transient copies) and the newly defined right of communication to the public (see 9.6.5) cater for direct infringement of illegally copied digital works. P2P providers will infringe if they can be found to authorise their users' downloads under the doctrine in *CBS Songs v Amstrad* (1988), or can be said to be reproducing or 'communicating' the works themselves.

---

29   In July 2003 the IFPI reported that global sales of recorded music had decreased by 10.9% in value in the first half of 2003: www.ifpi.org. The Regulatory Impact Assessment for the CRR 2003 states that the BPI estimated that sales of singles in the UK in 2002 declined by 12% and that internationally the music industry regarded file sharing and CD burning to be largely responsible for a reported fall of over 7% in the value of world sales of music CDs in 2002. The industry estimate that 5 million users have online access to 900 million songs worldwide via P2P networks.

30   The MPAA estimate that that 400,000 to 600,000 films are illegally transmitted every day: www.mpaa.org.

31   Which flourished with Napster's demise.

32   Appealed to the Supreme Court, to be heard in March 2005. (Starts 29.3.05.)

33   *BUMA v Kazaa BV* (2001). Translation at www.eff.org. However, action against Kazaa by IFPI resulted in an order by a Dutch court to cease infringing or face a fine of 100,000 Dutch guilders. 26 September 2003, www.theregister.co.uk.

Recital 27 of the Directive states that 'mere provision of physical facilities for enabling or making a communication does not in itself amount to communication'. Section 28A[34] of the CDPA 1988 allows for temporary copies made during transmission in a network, or for lawful uses of a work, but only provided that they have 'no independent economic significance'. These provisions may exempt ISPs involved in intermediate transmission of works over the internet, but should not extend to P2P service providers. Evidence of the incidence of internet piracy of works suggests these copies have considerable economic significance. Once put on notice of infringing use by their users (as the RIAA was required to do under the conditions of the *Napster* injunction), it is unlikely that they can rely on the immunity for ISPs, and injunctions may be imposed on them under s 97A of the CDPA 1988. It is also a criminal offence to communicate a work to the public in the course of a business[35] (see 10.7).

10.3 INFRINGEMENT OF SECONDARY WORKS

More than one copyright may be involved where a work is a secondary one. It may be put together by the infringing use of other copyright works as source material, although deserving of copyright in its own right for the 'skill, labour and judgment' employed in its creation. It was thought that this fact of infringement provided a defence to a third party's allegation of infringement of the new secondary work. This was denied by the House of Lords in *British Leyland v Armstrong Patents* (1986) (see 10.8.2). More recently, it was argued that the new copyright in the secondary work was unenforceable until the infringement employed in its making was cured. In *ZYX Music GmbH v Chris King* (1995) Lightman J also denied this principle. Instead, it was said that the secondary work's copyright owner should account to the copyright owners of the sources used for any damages received. Both the secondary work and the copyright sources are infringed by the third party's restricted act, the first directly, the second indirectly.

10.4 SECONDARY INFRINGEMENT

In addition to the acts of primary infringement, the CDPA 1988 provides for acts of secondary infringement. These amount to different commercial dealings with infringing copies, or the means of making those copies, and include those who might otherwise be regarded as authorising infringement by facilitating performance of a work.

These acts may not be performed by the person who is the primary infringer. They differ from primary infringement, where liability is strict, in a requirement for knowledge on the part of the infringer (see 10.4.1). The acts of secondary infringement may be utilised against ISPs and bulletin board operators, provided the requisite knowledge is proved. There is no provision for authorisation of an act of secondary infringement, but an 'authoriser' may be joined as a joint defendant. All the acts of secondary infringement must have been performed without the licence of the copyright owner:

---

34 Inserted by the CRRR 2003.
35 Section 107 of the CDPA 1988.

- Copyright is infringed by a person who imports into the UK, otherwise than for private and domestic use, an article which is, and which he knows or has reason to believe is, an infringing copy of a work.[36] Non-infringing import must be both private and domestic.

- It infringes to possess an infringing copy in the course of a business, sell or let it for hire, or offer or expose it for sale or hire, exhibit it in public or distribute it in the course of business, or distribute it otherwise than in the course of a business to an extent which will prejudicially affect the copyright owner.[37]

- To make, import into the UK, possess in the course of a business, sell or let for hire, or offer or expose for sale or hire an article specifically designed or adapted for making copies of a particular work infringes; as will transmitting the work by means of a telecommunications system (otherwise than by communication to the public) knowing or having reason to believe that infringing copies will be made by means of the reception of the transmission in the UK or elsewhere.[38] It is unlikely that this would catch the Amstrad double tape decks, as these are not adapted to copying a particular work, but would embrace a mould or model for a specific work. It was also strongly argued that the Grokster service had legitimate uses. If so, P2P services are unlikely to be caught by this section.

- Where primary infringement of a literary, dramatic, musical or artistic work by performance takes place at a place of public entertainment (including premises occupied mainly for other purposes, but made available from time to time for hire for the purposes of public entertainment) any person giving permission for that place to be used is liable unless he believed on reasonable grounds when giving the permission that the performance would not infringe.[39]

- Finally, where copyright is infringed by a public performance, or by playing or showing in public by means of apparatus for playing sound recordings, showing films, or receiving visual images or sounds conveyed by electronic means, further individuals infringe. These are: a person who supplied the apparatus, or any substantial part of it, knowing or having reason to believe that it was likely to be used to infringe copyright or, if normally used for public performance, playing or showing, did not believe on reasonable grounds that it would not be so used; an occupier of premises who gave permission for the apparatus to be brought on to the premises if at the time he knew or had reason to believe it would be used to infringe; and a person supplying a copy of a sound recording or film if, with the requisite knowledge at the time, it, or a copy made directly or indirectly from it, was likely to be used to infringe.[40] Sections 25 and 26 of the CDPA 1988 place the onus on the individuals concerned to ensure that appropriate licences are obtained.

10.4.1 Reasonable knowledge

The CA 1956 only required that secondary infringers had actual knowledge of their infringement, although in *Columbia Picture Industries v Robinson* (1986) Scott J held, *obiter*, that a defendant shutting his eyes to the obvious would infringe. In *Sillitoe v*

---

36 *Ibid*, s 22.
37 *Ibid*, s 23.
38 *Ibid*, s 24.
39 *Ibid*, s 25.
40 *Ibid*, s 26.

McGraw Hill (1983) the requisite knowledge was held to include reasonable inferences that the person should draw from the facts.

The CDPA 1988 provides that the secondary infringer must either know or have reason to believe that he is dealing with infringing copies. Although primarily an objective test, this includes a subjective element. The belief is personal to the defendant – a belief reasonable to him, as well as the reasonable man. This should include all his own knowledge and experience, rather than that of the reasonable man. It was considered in *LA Gear Inc v Hi Tec Sports plc* (1992). Morritt J said:

> ... it seems to me that 'reason to believe' must involve the concept of knowledge of facts from which a reasonable man would arrive at the relevant belief. Facts from which a reasonable man might suspect the relevant conclusion cannot be enough. Moreover, as it seems to me, the phrase does connote the allowance of a period of time to enable the reasonable man to evaluate these facts so as to convert the facts into reasonable belief.

Common knowledge of the trade was attributed to the defendant.

10.4.2   Infringing copy

An 'infringing copy' is defined in s 27(2) of the CDPA 1988 as a copy whose making constituted an infringement of the copyright in the work in question.

In relation to the import of copies, a query relates to copies emanating from the copyright owner. EU law prevails in relation to parallel imports of lawful copies released on to the market by, or with the consent, of the copyright owner, and coming from the European Union and EEA.[41] However, a copyright owner may wish to prevent the parallel import of copies released outside the EEA area by or with his consent if, for example, those copies are of inferior quality for an overseas market or priced below the UK price.

Section 27(3) of the CDPA 1988 imposes a test of a hypothetical manufacturer to determine whether such copies can be regarded as infringing. If the making of the copy in the UK would have constituted infringement or the breach of an exclusive licence, it is regarded as an infringing copy and importation can be prevented. However, the CDPA 1988 does not specify who the hypothetical manufacturer is (whether it is the importer or the actual manufacturer abroad). An example can be considered:

> Owner owns copyright in a book and sells it in the UK and the US at different prices. Importer buys it in the US at a low price, imports it to the UK and sells at a lower price than Owner. Owner made the US book. If Owner is the hypothetical maker, there is no infringement in the import, but, if Importer had made the book in the UK, Importer would have infringed Owner's copyright and therefore the import infringes.

Pre-1988 law adopted the actual manufacturer abroad test (*CBS v Charmadale* (1981)), but Australian copyright legislation adopts the importer. The 1988 Act has clarified the situation if the making in the UK constitutes breach of an exclusive licence, as illustrated by a second example:

---

41   *Ibid*, s 27(5).

Owner has copyright in a CD, and grants an exclusive licence to Y to manufacture in UK, and to Z for the US. Importer buys cheaply from Z in the US and imports into UK. Here, the actual manufacturer in the US is Z; if Z had manufactured in the UK, he would have infringed both Owner's and Y's rights, and both can take action against these imports.

It is possible that a licence to deal with legitimately purchased copies may be implied, in the importer's favour (see 10.8.1).

10.5 PROTECTION FOR TECHNOLOGICAL MEASURES

Copyright owners have two alternative means for protecting works in digital format: technical controls over access or copying of the files, or, secondly, contractual means of control. Technical protection potentially allows copyright owners complete control over all access to and use of their works in digital format, with considerable implications for access to information where alternative sources do not exist. One criticism that has been levelled at legal support for technological protection is that it does not differentiate between works still within copyright and those where copyright has expired. Nor can it distinguish (at present) between permitted and infringing uses.

In fact, effective technological protection positively promotes contractual licensing arrangements for access to and use of digital works. Both receive legal support from the WCT 1996, implemented by the Information Society Directive and the CRRR 2003. To this extent the exploitation of copyright is subject to consumer protection regulation over consumer contracts, and the jurisdiction of the Copyright Tribunal over licensing schemes. Should the protection for technological measures prove to overprotect copyright works[42] and to inhibit access and permitted uses, one solution may lie in control over these contracts. However, the Information Society Directive failed to consider the conjunction of technologically protected copyright and contractual control.

The new regime, which amends and extends the former s 296 of the CDPA 1988, provides both civil and criminal remedies. It applies both to the act of circumventing technological protection measures, and to providing the means of circumvention. Computer programs and other works are separately treated. The regime only extends to technical protection of a work preventing acts falling within copyright and that have not been authorised by the copyright holder.[13] To this extent technological measures cannot be said to have transformed copyright into an access right for digital works, although the definition of effective technical measures extends to access controls.

10.5.1 Computer programs

If a technical device has been applied to a computer program s 296[44] of the CDPA 1988 gives a copyright owner's rights and remedies to:

---

42 Some have argued that technological protection transform copyright into an access right, a considerable departure from its justifications, and the balance between access and protection traditionally secured: Davies, G, *Copyright and the Public Interest* (London: Sweet & Maxwell, 2002).

43 Section 296ZF(3) of the CDPA 1988.

44 Amended by the CRRR 2003.

- a person who issues copies, or communicates, to the public;
- a copyright owner or his exclusive licensee;
- the owner or exclusive licensee of any intellectual property right in the technical device.

These rights and remedies apply against a person possessing means whose sole intended purpose is to facilitate the unauthorised removal of, or circumvent, the technical device, or who deals with commercially with them, or publishes information intended to enable or assist removal or circumvention of the device. The person must know or have reason to believe that the means will be used to make infringing copies; however, the claimant need not show that these are likely to be used to copy his own works. As the knowledge requirement is akin to that used in relation to secondary infringement, it is likely to be interpreted in the same way (see 10.4.1).

The rights include the rights to delivery up and seizure[45] of the means a person has in his possession, custody or control with the intention that it be used to facilitate unauthorised removal or circumvention of a technical device.

Technical devices are purposively defined, and include any device intended to prevent or restrict acts within the copyright and not authorised by the copyright owner. No guidance is given as to whether this is a subjective or objective test of intention, nor is the provision made that the device should achieve its intended purpose. In *Sony Computer Entertainment Inc v Owen* (2002) Jacob J interpreted the unamended s 296. If the CDs and DVDs were copied on an ordinary computer, the authorisation codes were not replicated, so that the copies could not be used on Sony consoles. Jacob J held that there could be no doubt that these codes constituted a device intended to prevent or restrict copying a work.

Section 296 is not intended to affect the permitted act allowing for reverse engineering of programs for the purpose of interoperability (see 11.8), but does not specifically provide that permitted reverse engineering may involve circumvention of technical protection.

'Sole intended purpose' suggests that the means should only be employable against copy protection. However, too stringent an interpretation of 'sole' would risk emasculation of the section. It would seem unlikely that a personal computer would fall within this condition, having many legitimate uses. However, the mere presence of other uses for the means should not prevent a remedy in all cases. Under the unamended s 296, in *Sony Computer Entertainment Inc v Owen* (2002) the claimants produced PlayStation2 computer game consoles. CDs and DVDs made for use with the consoles carried authorisation codes. These elements of encrypted data also allowed Sony to prevent games bought from one area of their regional distribution[46] being used on consoles manufactured for distribution in a different region. The defendant imported a 'mod chip' (Messiah2) which bypassed the authorisation process. It argued that the chips had legitimate uses and so were not 'specifically designed or adapted to circumvent the form of copy-protection employed' as s 296

---

45   In sections 99–100 of the CDPA 1988.
46   Dictated by the different signal systems used for colour television transmission and reception, although the result is to prevent parallel imports of its products.

then provided. This was rejected.[47] Having other uses did not prevent a device being 'adapted to circumvent'. Whether 'sole intended purpose' would be interpreted differently remained to be seen.

Subsequently, after the section's new wording came into effect, it was held in *Sony Computer Entertainment v Ball* (2004) that the mod chips continued to infringe. This case was brought on the same facts as the first, but against different resellers of the hardware. The claims related to acts both before and after 31 October 2003.[48] Laddie J rejected the argument that the mod chips enabled their users to make use of back-up copies[49] of Sony CDs and DVDs, or to play UK bought games on non-European Sony PlayStation2 consoles. He held that no back-up copy was necessary, and that use on non-European consoles would not be lawful without licence from Sony, which was expressly refused. Consequently, the sole intended purpose of the Messiah2 was to circumvent Sony's copy protection.

In *Sony Computer Entertainment v Ball* (2004) it was also argued for the defendant that use of the mod chips did not result in infringing copies being made. Although a temporary copy would be made in a computer's RAM[50] this was argued to be too ephemeral to constitute an article.[51] Laddie J dismissed this argument as the silicon chip comprising the RAM remained an article even if only an infringing article for a short time. This must be the correct conclusion if a coach and horses is not to be driven through the section as a whole.

10.5.2   Reception of broadcasts

Section 298 of the CDPA 1988 provides that a person who charges for reception of broadcasts, sends encrypted transmissions, or provides conditional access services from the UK or other Member State has a copyright owner's rights and remedies against a person who:

*   makes, imports, distributes, sells or lets for hire, offers or exposes for sale, or advertises for sale or hire;
*   possess for commercial purposes;
*   instals, maintains or repairs for commercial purposes

any apparatus designed or adapted to enable or assist persons to access the transmissions or circumvent conditional access technology when he or she is not entitled to do so.

It is unlikely that this section would extend to supplying apparatus to enable access to the transmissions of another broadcaster relaying the same broadcast. While the UK licensees of a broadcast[52] could protect their UK broadcast, devices enabling

---

47   Sony also succeeded in the US (*Sony v Gamemasters* (2000) and in Australia (*Sony v Stevens* (2003)), as well as in Belgium. Nevertheless, mod chips have been held to be legal in both Italy and Spain.

48   When the CRRR 2003 and therefore the newly worded s 296 came into effect.

49   Copying a Sony CD or DVD containing the copy protection encrypted data would not copy the necessary codes so that a 'back-up' copy could not be used without the mod chip bypassing the protection measure.

50   Random Access Memory.

51   Section 27 of the CDPA 1988 defines an infringing copy (see 10.4.2).

52   A major sporting event, for example.

persons to watch the licensed broadcast transmitted from another state would not fall within the remedy.

10.5.3 Circumvention

If effective technological measures have been applied to works other than a computer program, s 296ZA of the CDPA 1988 gives a copyright[53] owner's rights and remedies to:

- a person who issues copies, or communicates, to the public; and
- a copyright owner or his exclusive licensee

against anyone who does anything which circumvents those measures knowing, or having reason to believe, that he is pursuing that object. Once again, it is the outcome of the action which precipitates liability. Achieving circumvention indirectly as an addition to another purpose is likely to fall within the provision. Anything done for the purpose of research into encryption is excepted unless the copyright owner's rights are prejudicially affected.

Section 296ZF of the CDPA 1988 provides a technologically neutral definition of effective technological measures as 'any technology, device or component which is designed, in the normal course of its operation, to protect a copyright work'. If the measures are intended to allow a copyright owner to control use of the work through an access control or protection process such as encryption, scrambling or other transformation of the work, or a copy control mechanism, and achieve their intended effect they are effective.

Dealing in circumvention devices and services

Rights and remedies[54] are given for providing and dealing in devices and services to circumvent effective technological measures.[55] These are given to a person:

- issuing copies or communicating to the public of a work to which effective technological measures have been applied;
- the copyright owner or exclusive licensee; and
- the owner or exclusive licensee of any intellectual property right in the technological measure.

The rights are against those manufacturing, importing, distributing, selling or letting for hire, offering or exposing for sale, advertising, possessing for commercial purposes any device, product or component or providing services which:

- are promoted, advertised or marketed for the purpose of circumvention;
- have only a limited commercially significant purpose or use other than circumvention; or

---

53 Including rights in performances, publication and database right: s 296ZA(6) of the CDPA 1988.
54 Including delivery up and seizure: s 296ZD(4) of the CDPA 1988. Damages will not lie if the defendant has no knowledge or reason to believe that his acts enabled or facilitated infringement of copyright: s 296ZD(7) CDPA 1988.
55 Section 296ZD of the CDPA 1988.

- are primarily designed, produced, adapted or performed for the purpose of enabling or facilitating circumvention.

The extension of liability to devices and services with limited other uses does suggest that the remedy for computer programs may be more restricted. Warner Home Video is suing 321 Studios for its DVD copying software which circumvents the security features in DVDs. The decision may well hinge on how 'effective' the security measures are. Similar proceedings have been instituted in the US where 321 Studios has sued nine film production companies, arguing that individuals have the right to back-up DVDs which they have bought.

In *Sony Computer Entertainment v Ball* (2004) Laddie J pointed out that s 296ZD creates a tort of strict liability. No defence could lie in showing that the defendant did not know or have reason to believe that the Messiah2 would be used to make infringing copies of Sony's copyright works. The section requires that the claimant's protection measure come within the definition of technological measures in s 296ZF of the CDPA 1988.

10.6 PROTECTION FOR ELECTRONIC RIGHTS MANAGEMENT

Identifying and tracing infringing uses of digital works is aided by information identifying its author, the work itself, and terms and conditions relating to its use. Digital watermarks and fingerprints embedded in a work can be tracked by web 'bots', spiders and crawlers, thus tracing infringing uses and users.

Civil remedies are provided for removing or altering such electronic rights management[56] if done knowingly and without authority and with knowledge or reason to believe that this will induce, enable or facilitate infringement of copyright: s 296ZG of the CDPA 1988. Knowingly dealing with copies from which the DRM has been removed is also protected against. Persons issuing, or communicating, copies of a work to the public, as well as the copyright owner and exclusive licensees, have copyright owners' rights and remedies.

Rights management information is defined as any information provided by the copyright owner, or holder of a right under the copyright, which identifies the work, its author, copyright owner or holder of any intellectual property rights, or information about terms and conditions of use of the work. It extends to any numbers or codes representing such information.

10.7 OFFENCES

The response to the challenge of piracy has been threefold: judicial, diplomatic and statutory. Judges developed effective remedies (see Chapter 19). The CDPA 1988 strengthened acts of secondary infringement and the criminal offences. Implementation of the Information Society Directive adds to these offences. Penalties are now severe[57] and should act as a deterrent, and the costs of prosecution are borne by the State. Section 100 of the CDPA 1988 provides an unusual self-help remedy (see

---

56 Also known as digital rights management (DRM).
57 Maximum penalties were increased by the Copyright and Trade Marks (Offences and Enforcement) Act 2002.

19.2.3). The TRIPS Agreement 1994 has helped to establish copyright protection and enforcement procedures in former havens of piracy (see 1.3.3). Diplomatic efforts have also been made by some countries to secure more effective action against pirates, often by linking aid to this action. The US has taken well-publicised initiatives to combat software piracy in China, for example. Such efforts are unlikely to be an overnight success, particularly in jurisdictions accustomed to notions of collective ownership, but have added to copyright owners' armoury.

The criminal offences provided by ss 107, 297 and 297A of the CDPA 1988 were added to by s 296ZB.[58] These are aimed at piracy of copyright works, but are not expressly limited to commercial pirates and may be used against individuals. The offences are akin to the acts of secondary infringement. *Mens rea* is required for them all: actual knowledge, or reason to believe that copyright would be infringed or that the dealing was with infringing copies.

It is an offence:

- to make for sale or hire, import, possess, sell, let or hire, offer or expose for sale, publicly exhibit or distribute in the course of business infringing copies; or distribute copies other than in the course of business to an extent to prejudicially affect the copyright owner;[59]

- to make an article specifically designed or adapted to make copies of a particular work, or possess such an article;[60]

- to communicate a work to the public in the course of business, or if not in the course of business, to such an extent as to prejudicially affect the copyright owner;[61]

- to cause a literary, dramatic or musical work to be performed, played or shown in public other than by reception of a broadcast, or playing a sound recording or film in public;[62]

- to make for sale or hire, import other than for one's private and domestic use, or in the course of business sell or let for hire, offer or expose for sale or hire, advertise for sale or hire, possess or distribute, or distribute other than in the course of business to an extent to prejudicially affect the copyright owner any device, product or component primarily designed, produced or adapted for the purpose of enabling or facilitating circumvention of effective technological measures;[63]

- to promote, advertise or market in the course of business or if not, to an extent to prejudicially affect the copyright owner a service the purpose of which is to enable or facilitate the circumvention of effective technological measures;[64]

- dishonestly to receive a broadcast provided from a place in the UK with intent to avoid payment;[65] or

---

58   Added by the CRRR 2003.
59   Section 107(1) of the CDPA 1988.
60   *Ibid*, s 107(2).
61   *Ibid*, s 107(2A).
62   *Ibid*, s 107(3).
63   *Ibid*, s 296ZB(1).
64   *Ibid*, s 296ZB(2).
65   *Ibid*, s 297.

- to make, import, distribute, sell or let for hire, or offer or expose for sale or hire, possess, instal, maintain or replace for commercial purposes, advertise or promote any unauthorised decoder.[66]

Individuals[67] downloading infringing copies from the internet via file sharing services may be at risk of criminal proceedings if their activities can be considered to be to such an extent as to affect copyright owners prejudicially. Certainly collectively P2P downloads appear prejudicial.[68] Neither the Directive nor the CRRR 2003 gives guidance as to how a prejudicial effect should be assessed.

Provision is made for search warrants and forfeiture of infringing material in ss 109, 297B–D, and 296ZC. Local Trading Standards Offices are given powers and duties to enforce these provisions. Conviction may result in imprisonment, a fine, or both. In 2003 sentences of three and four years were handed down to commercial pirates: *R v Stanley* (2003).

10.8   DEFENCES

Apart from challenging either the subsistence of any copyright in a work or the extent of the exclusive rights or secondary infringements, two categories of defence exist for the alleged infringer. The CDPA 1988 calls acts which *prima facie* fall within the exclusive rights, but are then excused by the statute, the 'permitted acts' (see Chapter 11). These are specific acts sanctioned in order to cater for specific areas of interest in access to copyright works. They may be distinguished from acts sanctioned in general terms for all potential infringements, which might be called 'defences'. No question of any defence arises until it has been established that the defendant's act being complained of affects the whole or a substantial part of a work (see 10.1.3).

10.8.1   Implied licences

A court may imply a licence in any contractual arrangement between copyright owner and defendant permitting the act complained of.

Ownership

This may be done by implying an alternative arrangement as to the ownership of copyright by an employee (*Noah v Shuba* (1991) (see 9.3.1)), or an implication of beneficial ownership in the person commissioning a work (*Warner v Gestetner Ltd* (1988) (see 9.3.2)).

---

66   *Ibid*, s 297A.

67   It was reported in November 2003 that two Australian students who ran a website offering 1,000 pirated songs were given suspended prison sentences and fined, although they made no personal profit. They were alleged to have cost the music industry more than $60 million (£25.62 million): www.australianit.news.com.au.

68   Although it has also been argued that many people downloading singles go on to purchase albums and CDs.

Architectural plans

Terms have been implied in favour of an architect's client to allow use of architectural plans protected by copyright. Whether such a term may be implied depends on the nature of the contract made. In *Blair v Osborne and Tomkins* (1971), the client had paid the full scale fee for plans which were then used by another firm. The Court of Appeal implied a licence permitting this use. By contrast, in *Stovin-Bradford v Volpoint Properties Ltd* (1971), no licence was implied where the client had not paid the full fee. In *Hunter v Fitzroy Robinson* (1978) it was said to be strongly arguable that where plans have been commissioned they can be used, and even modified, by another architect.

Terms will not be implied which conflict with any express terms, nor to apply to a future owner of a development site: *Dorrans v The Shand Partnership* (2003). This decision demonstrates that, where an author is engaged to produce copyright material, a licence will generally be implied that the commissioner may use that material for the purpose agreed by the parties. However, it also illustrates the limits of any implied term defence. The pursuer prepared plans for developing a site in Fife for residential purposes. Although planning permission was granted, the original deal fell through and the plans were passed on to and used by the defenders as eventual purchasers of the site. The contract agreed with the initial developer was a standard form Royal Institute for British Architects (RIBA) agreement. However, *Blair v Osborne and Tomkins* (1971) was distinguished as the pursuer's agreement contained clear terms relating to a licence to use the plans. Furthermore, the dispute in *Blair* remained one between the original parties to the agreement. It is noteworthy that Lord Kingarth refused to imply any licence to use the pursuer's plans by the eventual acquirers of the site because neither the business efficacy test, nor any other test for the implication of contractual terms, rendered such a term necessary.

Parallel imports

In the Australian case of *Time-Life International v Interstate Parcel Express Co* (1978), it was argued that the legitimate purchase of copies should lead to an implied licence to deal with those copies. The purchaser could then import them into another country (subject to the specific rules relating to free movement of goods within the EEA (see 1.4)). The defendant had purchased copies of a cookery book in the US and, after importing them, was underselling the copyright owner's exclusive licensee in Australia. Neither the copyright owners nor their distributors in the US had imposed restrictions on resale. It was argued that, by analogy with a line of cases relating to patented goods, such a sale without restriction implied a licence to deal with the books. The High Court of Australia refused to draw the analogy because of the different nature of the rights conferred by a patent and copyright and no licence was implied. Cornish suggests[69] that a court in the UK might be persuaded to draw the analogy because copyright does not encompass subsequent sale and use. Copyright owners would still be able to prevent parallel imports of copies of their works by imposing restrictions expressly.

---

69 Cornish, W and Llewellyn, D, *Intellectual Property: Patents, Copyright, Trade Marks and Allied Rights* (London: Sweet & Maxwell, 2003).

Repair

In *British Leyland v Armstrong Patents* (1986) (see below), it was argued that the purchaser of goods protected by copyright should have an implied licence to repair those goods, and that this licence should extend to commercial suppliers of spare parts. The plaintiff sought to exercise copyright in drawings for car exhausts to prevent the defendant from making spares by indirect copying (by reverse engineering). The House of Lords did not imply the licence, distinguishing copyright protected works from patented goods where such a licence may be implied. Lord Bridge said:

> The owner of a car must be entitled to whatever is necessary to keep it in running order and to effect whatever repairs may be necessary in the most economical way possible. To derive this entitlement from an implied licence granted by the original manufacturer seems to me quite artificial. It is a right inherent in the ownership of the car itself. To curtail or restrict the owner's right to repair in any way may diminish the value of the car. In the field of patent law, it may be right to start from the patentee's express monopoly and see how far it is limited by exceptions. In the field of law applied to machinery which enjoys no patent protection, it seems to me appropriate to start from a consideration of the rights of the owner of the machinery and then to see how far the law will permit some conflicting legal claim to impinge upon those rights.

Similar reasoning could be applied to an implied licence to deal.

10.8.2 Spare parts

In a remarkable display of judicial innovation, the House of Lords developed a new copyright defence in *British Leyland v Armstrong Patents* (1986). The case raised important issues in relation to the creation of copyright monopolies in functional articles (see Chapter 13), and subsequent changes to copyright and design law brought about by the CDPA 1988 have mitigated the undesirable consequences of protection for such works. The principle articulated by the House of Lords remains valid for other copyright monopolies, however, where a right owner relies on copyright to prevent owners of goods repairing them without resort to the copyright owner. The House of Lords held that copyright owners' rights must be balanced against car owners' right of ownership. Their lordships applied a principle borrowed from land law, that of non-derogation from grant. Lord Templeman said:

> I see no reason why the principle that a grantor will not be allowed to derogate from his grant by using property retained by him in such a way as to render property granted by him unfit or materially unfit for the purpose for which the grant was made should not apply to the sale of a car.

The House of Lords recognised that the case posed the problem of boundaries between legitimate and unfair competition, but declined to adopt any limit which required courts to draw this boundary. Lord Bridge gave two reasons for this reluctance:

> British Leyland's second answer is that the criterion for the maintenance of a supply of spare parts sufficient to meet demands of car owners for the purposes of repair is one of necessity and that, so long as the manufacturer and his licensees are maintaining an adequate supply at reasonable prices and, more particularly, if the manufacturer is willing to offer licences to all who wish to take them on reasonable terms, there can be no such necessity as to justify the subordination of the right of the copyright owner in spare parts drawings to the interest of the car owner in a free market in parts available

for repair. This suggested answer to the problem seems to me both impracticable and unrealistic for two reasons. First, it would impose an impossible task on the court, whenever asked to decide whether a claim to copyright in spare parts drawings should be enforced, to have to determine without the aid of any defined criteria whether at the date of the trial the manufacturer and his licensees were maintaining a supply on reasonable terms. Secondly, once the copyright owner had succeeded in his claim, he would be at liberty to vary his terms of trade to the detriment of owners of cars of his manufacture.

That the new defence continued to apply after the commencement of the CPDA 1988 on 1 August 1989 is suggested by s 171(3) of the CDPA 1988 and *Flogates v Refco* (1996). It was held in *Wyko v Cooper Roller Bearings* (1996) that it is only a defence, does not provide a cause of action and cannot be applied unless the defendant holds another right against which exercise of the plaintiff's copyright must be balanced. The *British Leyland* principle continues to apply to copyright works which do not fall within the ambit of s 51 of the CDPA 1988 (see 13.2.1). It can also be extended to commissioned copyright works where s 50C of the CDPA 1988 (copying of computer programs permitted to lawful users) does not apply.

However, the Privy Council doubted its basis in principle in *Canon Kabushiki Kaisha v Green Cartridge Co (Hong Kong) Ltd* (1997). It went on to distinguish it on the facts. The defendant had indirectly infringed copyright in Canon's drawings for parts included in replacement cartridges for its photocopiers. Canon sold photocopiers operating by means of disposable cartridges for the necessary toner and other components needing regular replacement. A cottage industry in Hong Kong already refilled spent cartridges, providing competition to Canon's sales of replacement cartridges (its 'aftermarket') when the defendant began manufacturing competitive replacements. Canon adduced evidence to show that the actual photocopiers were sold virtually at cost price, so that it was dependent on the aftermarket to make a profit, and that purchasers of the copiers would consider the need for replacement of cartridges in making decisions as to cost. In addition, competition already existed within the aftermarket through the actions of the refillers, suggesting that there was no abuse of the copyright 'monopoly'. However, the Privy Council declared that:

> ... the courts are ill equipped to pronounce on such matters (whether the existence of copyright is capable of giving the plaintiff such economic power in the aftermarket as to be anti-competitive and contrary to the public interest), which often involve questions of economic policy and are generally left to specialised bodies, such as the Monopolies and Mergers Commission ...

It continued to refuse to apply the *British Leyland* principle in this case. *British Leyland v Armstrong Patents* (1986) was distinguished on the different nature of the aftermarkets and the economic behaviour of the plaintiff and not on the facts (the exhausts and cartridges were analogous). Consequently, courts now need to make decisions as to the limits of competition, and without the advantage of sophisticated economic expertise.

10.8.3 Public interest

At common law judges accepted a defence of publication in the public interest, despite infringement of copyright in the process, as for breach of confidence (see 7.13). It was given statutory recognition for the first time by s 171(3) of the CDPA 1988. No definition of 'public interest' is provided, however, leaving this to be determined by the courts. Early precedents state the test as it was in early breach of confidence cases. *Hubbard v Vosper* (1972) and *Beloff v Pressdram* (1973) refer to 'misdeeds of a serious nature and importance to the country', and not the test of publication with 'any just cause and excuse' (*Lion Laboratories Ltd v Evans* (1985)). What is clear is that a mere allegation of public interest is insufficient, nor does the public interest include everything that the media have an interest in publishing, or the public in reading.

As yet it is an unresolved question whether the later breach of confidence test can also be applied to infringements of copyright. Some overlap is inevitable because a publication may simultaneously breach both confidence and copyright; both issues were considered in *Lion Laboratories Ltd v Evans* (1985) and the wider test applied. In Australia, however, the test of public interest in the case of copyright was seen to be of narrower ambit than that for breach of confidence in *Commonwealth of Australia v Fairfax* (1980). Although the public interest in access to information remains the same, the two actions can be distinguished because it is not always necessary to infringe copyright in order to make confidential information available to the public, whereas a breach of confidence is inevitable. Information can be taken from a copyright work without infringement if only the idea is taken, rather than its expression. Consequently, an injunction for the copyright infringement would be refused (to enable publication in the public interest to take place), although damages might still lie.

In *Lion Laboratories Ltd v Evans* (1985) and *Attorney General v Guardian Newspapers Ltd* (1988) both the Court of Appeal and the House of Lords accepted that the copyright defence and the application of public interest in breach of confidence were co-extensive. However, the misdeeds in both cases (wrongful criminal conviction, damage to national security, respectively) would fall within the old, stricter, definition. In *Hyde Park Residence Ltd v Yelland* (2000) the Court of Appeal suggested otherwise. Aldous LJ distinguished the confidence and copyright public interest tests for three reasons. Protection for confidence involved balancing two public interests, confidentiality and the public interest; but copyright was a statutory property right, overridden by public interest if a remedy was to be refused. It would be wrong to reject one of the statutory defences only to justify an infringement in the public interest. Secondly, to weigh copyright against public interest was inapt when the information could be published without infringement. Finally, the CDPA 1988 gave effect to international obligations under the Berne and Paris Conventions, which contain no general public interest defence. The court had inherent jurisdiction to refuse to enforce copyright where it would offend public policy (see 9.5), but no general public interest defence could be made out.

Subsequently, the Human Rights Act 1998 revived a generous consideration of the public interest defence in *Ashdown v Telegraph Group Ltd* (2001). Lord Ashdown, former leader of the Liberal Party, kept diaries and other memoranda of his time in Parliament. The defendant newspaper published extracts from one of his notes. It argued that publication was in the public interest, and that this must include the right to freedom of expression. At first instance it was held that the statutory copyright regime balanced the property right and freedom of expression necessary in a democratic society. The Court of Appeal did not agree. It held that it would not normally be necessary to infringe copyright in an expression of information in order to meet the right to freedom of expression, because copyright only protected a work's form. However, in rare circumstances, the right of freedom of expression could clash with copyright protection, and Aldous LJ had not been justified in circumscribing the public interest defence as strictly as he had in *Hyde Park Residence Ltd v Yelland* (2000). There was a clear public interest in freedom of expression in the rare case where it trumped copyright, and s 171(3) of the CDPA 1988 allowed it to be raised. A court could refuse discretionary relief of an injunction in the rare situation where freedom of expression required repetition of expression in a copyright work. However, the Human Rights Act 1998 did not require free use of expression, and damages or other remedies could lie. The facts of individual cases would have to be examined closely. The court was careful not to confuse public interest with what is interesting to the public. The defendant had, it said, carefully selected colourful passages most likely to add flavour to its article from the minute, and Lord Ashdown's words had been used for journalistic furtherance of the company's commercial interests. Consequently, the appeal against the injunction granted at first instance was dismissed.

Only a decision of the House of Lords can resolve the differences within the Court of Appeal as to the nature and ambit of any public interest defence. In addition, it is not entirely clear whether the Information Society Directive allows retention of the public interest defence. However, recital 44 provides that the exceptions therein must be applied in accordance with international obligations (the ECHR). Cornish argues that the ECHR preserves the balance between privacy and freedom of expression, and that copyright in a work should not prevent a permissible disclosure. That seems correct, to the extent that it is necessary to use the form of expression in a work rather than the underlying idea. Article 5(4) of the Directive also provides that any exceptions must be applied in accordance with the 'three steps' test of the Berne Convention. The recital goes on to suggest that in the new electronic environment exceptions may have a more limited ambit than in the past. There can be no certainty that the public interest defence will remain as it was interpreted in *Ashdown* (2001).

Injunction refused

Ashdown v Telegraph Group Ltd (2001) tends to confirm that if an infringement of copyright is found to be in the public interest the result may only be a refusal to grant an injunction, rather than a complete defence to the infringement: *Kennard v Lewis* (1983). Publication is permitted, but the infringer is made to pay for taking expression and not just idea from the work. It could be alleged that this is tantamount to allowing one's privacy to be 'bought'.[70]

Further Reading

Bradshaw, D, 'Fair Dealing as a Defence to Copyright Infringement in UK Law: An Historical Excursion from 1802 to the *Clockwork Orange* Case 1993' [1995] Denning LJ 67

Bradshaw, D, 'Fair Dealing and the *Clockwork Orange* case: a Thieves' Charter' [1994] Ent LR 6

Braun, N, 'The Interface Between the Protection of Technological Measures and the Exercise of Exceptions to Copyright and Related Rights: Comparing the Situation on the US and in the EU' [2003] EIPR 496

---

70 The *Douglas v Hello!* case has a similar effect (see 18.7).

Colston, C, 'Fair Dealing: What is Fair?' [1995] Denning LJ 91

Copyright and Related Rights in the Information Society (COM (95) 382 final)

Davies, G, *Copyright and the Public Interest* (London: Sweet & Maxwell, 2002)

Garrotte, I, 'Linking and Framing: A Comparative Approach' [2002] EIPR 184

Griffiths, J, 'Copyright Law after *Ashdown* – Time to Deal Fairly with the Public' [2002] IPQ 240

Hart, M, 'The Copyright in the Information Society Directive: An Overview' [2002] EIPR 58

Hart, M, 'Infringement and Remedies under the Copyright, Designs and Patents Act 1988' [1989] EIPR 113

Hugenholtz, B, 'Why the Copyright Directive is Unimportant, and Possibly Invalid' [2000] EIPR 499

Hugenholtz, B, 'Caching and Copyright: The Right of Temporary Copying' [2000] EIPR 482

Intellectual Property and the National Information Infrastructure, 1995, http://www.uspto.gov/

Lessig, L, *The Future of Ideas* (New York: Random House, 2001)

Litman, J, *Digital Copyright* (New York: Prometheus Books, 2001)

Macmillan, F and Blakeney, M, 'The Internet and Communication Carriers' Copyright Liability' [1998] EIPR 52

Ryan, C, 'Human Rights and Intellectual Property' [2001] EIPR 521

Stamatoudi, I and Torremans, P, *Copyright in the New Digital Environment* (London: Sweet & Maxwell, 2000)

Waelde C, 'The Quest for Access in the Digital Era: Copyright and the Internet (2001) 1 The Journal of Information, Law and Technology (JILT) http://elj.warwick.ac.uk/jilt/01-1/waelde.html

CHAPTER 11

EMPLOYING COPYRIGHT: PERMITTED COPYRIGHT USES, DEALINGS IN WORKS AND COMPETITION

No authority is needed to perform acts falling into the public domain.[1] Even acts *prima facie* within the sphere of copyright protection may be 'excused' by the statute, thereby allowing certain specified dealings with copyright works. These are known as 'permitted acts', and represent a detailed attempt to reconcile the conflict between the private, personal interests and rights copyright authors have in their creations and the public interest in access to those works.[2]

11.1 PERMITTED ACTS

Chapter III of the Copyright, Designs and Patents Act (CDPA) 1988 sets out an extensive list of these statutory defences to otherwise infringing acts. In some cases, they only apply where copyright owners have not set up collective licensing schemes and provide an incentive for authors to do so. It is interesting to consider the permitted acts within their context. They cater, broadly, for particular interests in copyright works, such as news, entertainment and media, education, public administration, industrial design, and use of computer software.

Both the Copyright Act (CA) 1956 and the CDPA 1988 came under increasing pressure as the means of producing and reproducing copyright works developed apace (reprography, tape, and video home copying, personal computers, CD 'burners'). This was particularly so as they made easy, cheap and good quality reproductions of works available to the public at large, and individually. Widespread 'home copying', as well as ever increasing large scale piracy and counterfeiting, brought the law into disrepute. Copyright owners had increasing difficulty in detecting and preventing misuses of their works and markets were (and are) being lost both to home copying and pirates. The CDPA 1988 and Information Society Directive's answer has been to make a complex and detailed attempt to balance the varied and conflicting interests of particular groups of users, copyright owners, competitors and entrepreneurs. This has been achieved by strengthening copyright infringement and the criminal offences, allowing for specific permitted acts and facilitating and controlling exercises of copyright by collective agencies of copyright owners.

Each of the permitted acts is to be construed independently of the others.[3] The Information Society Directive narrowed some, and some uses previously allowed, such as reproduction for commercial research, must now be licensed. The Directive provides an exclusive list of optional defences to the reproduction and communication rights for Member States,[4] in conjunction with the mandatory browsing and caching defence. States may not adopt exceptions outside this list.

---

1   Either because copyright has expired, they do not fall within the exclusive rights, or do not infringe a substantial part of a work.
2   Section 28 of the CDPA 1988.
3   *Ibid*, s 28(4).
4   Thus compromising its aim of harmonisation.

The Directive also restricts provision for general defences. Article 5(5) provides that the exceptions and limitations may only be applied 'in certain special cases which do not conflict with normal exploitation of the work or other subject matter and do not unreasonably prejudice the legitimate interests of the right-holder'.[5] This also applies to exceptions preserved in national laws after implementing the directive, and which only apply to analogue works.[6] Recital 35 states factors that should be considered in deciding fair compensation. The UK Government did not take the view that this requires all permitted uses to be paid for, by means of a levy on copying technology or otherwise.

11.2 FAIR DEALING

The fair dealing defences fall within the statutory permitted acts, but are of a limited general application. The Whitford Committee[7] recommended a general defence of fair dealing with a work, one 'not unreasonably prejudicing the copyright owner's legitimate interests'. The UK differs from both the US, which does have a general 'fair use' doctrine, and from European civil systems, which provide a general defence of private use.[8] The White Paper[9] rejected a general defence as being too wide and imprecise. It would presuppose a clear concept of an owner's copyright interest, and of prejudice, as well as an appreciation of what is commercially reasonable. The Information Society Directive would not allow such a general approach, but subjects even the limited defence to evaluation of copyright owners' commercial expectations and unreasonable prejudice to their interests.

The CDPA 1988 furnishes three fair dealing defences:

- fair dealing with a literary, dramatic musical or artistic work, and the typographical arrangement of a published edition for the purposes of private research or study;[10]

- fair dealing with a work for the purpose of criticism or review;[11]

- fair dealing with a work (other than a photograph) for the purpose of reporting current events.[12]

It is worth reiterating that no issue of fair dealing arises unless more than a substantial part of a work has been taken; in fact, the early judicial development of the concept arose in tandem with the concept of insubstantial taking, and the two were not clearly distinguished. The onus of proof with regard to establishing that dealing with a work was fair lies on the defendant (*Sillitoe v McGraw Hill* (1983)).

---

5   Taken from Article 9(2), Berne Convention, and known as the 'three steps test'.
6   Article 5(3)(o), Information Society Directive.
7   *Copyright and Designs Law*, Cmnd 6732, 1977.
8   Though often paid for through levies on copying media.
9   *Intellectual Property and Innovation*, Cmnd 9712, 1986.
10   Section 29 of the CDPA 1988.
11   *Ibid*, s 30(1).
12   *Ibid*, s 30(2).

11.2.1   Dealing

The equivalent word in the US is 'use', but the government rejected any change of terminology for the UK on the basis that the phrase was well understood. 'Dealing' is not defined, but refers to an act of infringement being complained of, and not to commercial dealings with a work.

11.2.2   Fair

Nor is any definition provided for fairness, and courts are given a wide discretion to examine all the facts and circumstances. An appellate court will be reluctant to upset the judge's findings on a question of mixed fact and law unless they proceed from some error of principle or are clearly unsustainable: *Pro Sieben Media AG v Carlton UK Television Ltd* (1999). No inferences can be drawn from the other permitted acts because s 28(4) of the CDPA 1988 provides that the fact that an act does not fall within one section does not prevent it from fitting into another.

Impression and degree

The leading case on fairness, in this context, is *Hubbard v Vosper* (1972), where fairness was stated to be a 'matter of impression' and of degree. Fairness is to be judged in the context of the purpose for which the dealing has been employed, and cannot be considered independently of the particular permitted purposes of private research and study, criticism or review, or reporting current events. Ungoed-Thomas J said in *Beloff v Pressdram* (1973):

> The relevant fair dealing is, thus, fair dealing with the memorandum for the approved purposes. It is fair dealing directed to and consequently limited to and to be judged in relation to the approved purposes. It is dealing which is fair for the approved purposes and not dealing which might be fair for some other purpose or fair in general. Mere dealing with the work for that purpose is not enough; whose fairness, as I have indicated, must be judged in relation to that purpose.

Like 'substantial part', fairness is not a test of the quantity of taking, but a qualitative test, although the quantity of taking may be relevant. Guidelines issued by the Publisher's Association and the Society of Authors in 1965 gave substantive limits to allowable copying of 10% of a work, or 4,000–8,000 words. These were withdrawn in 1985 and the current guidance states:

> ... photocopying by the reader for his or her own use of: one copy of a maximum of a complete single chapter in a book, or one copy of a maximum otherwise of 5% of a literary work.

Guidelines published in 1991 by the British Copyright Council suggested that the copying of whole articles in periodicals would be unfair. However, there may be circumstances where the copying of a whole work might be considered fair. The purpose of the copying will be relevant, so that it might be fair to copy the whole of a work for criticism or review (as a memorandum was in *Beloff v Pressdram* (1973)). However, it is unlikely ever to be so for private research and study. Lengthy extracts may be justified for the purpose of criticism and review (*Hubbard v Vosper* (1972)), but not so for the purpose of private research and study. In *Sillitoe v McGraw Hill* (1983), it was held that the passages of criticism were not long enough to justify the taking of 5% of the works copied. However, a taking of 10% of some of scenes of the worst violence from the film *A Clockwork Orange* was held to be fair in *Time Warner Entertainments Co v Channel 4 Television Corp plc* (1994).

Relevant factors

Many factors are relevant; in *Hubbard v Vosper* (1972), Lord Denning MR gave some guidance:

> You must consider first the number of quotations and extracts. Are they altogether too long to be fair? Then you must consider the use made of them. If they are used as a basis for comment, criticism or review, that may be fair dealing. If they are used to convey the same information as the author, for a rival purpose, that may be unfair. Next, you must consider the proportions. To take long extracts and attach short comments may be unfair. However, short extracts and long comments may be fair. Other considerations may come to mind also.

These other considerations may include: whether the taking was for rival commercial purposes (*ITV Publications v Time Out* (1984); *Pro Sieben Media AG v Carlton UK Television Ltd* (1999)); whether the infringed work has been published, or the extent to which it has been circulated if not published within the meaning of the statute; or whether the information published uncovers wrongs and misdeeds. Commercial gain by the defendant is likely to point to unfairness. It was held in *British Oxygen v Liquid Air* (1925) that it was unfair to publish the plaintiff's unpublished letter. It is more likely that is only one of a number of relevant factors, and in *Beloff v Pressdram* (1973) publication of an unpublished memo was found, only on the sum of the facts, to be unfair. The issue of unpublished works also arose in *Commonwealth of Australia v Fairfax* (1980) when a book published confidential government documents. Following *Hubbard v Vosper* (1972), Mason J said that, if an unpublished work had been sufficiently circulated, the publication could amount to fair dealing for the purposes of criticism or review and that the absence of consent to circulation by the author was an important factor in assessing fairness. He went on to say, however, that it was possible that, while it might be unfair to publish the work of a private author, different considerations were relevant to government documents publication of which would promote public discussion and knowledge of government actions. He lifted injunctions that had been granted against publication.

In *Fraser-Woodward v BBC* (2005) Mann J set out five factors relating to fairness:

(i) the user's motives;

(ii) the impression created by the dealing as to the user's *bona fide* wish to illustrate his review or criticism;

(iii) excessive use if only some degree of use would be fair;

(iv) the actual purpose of the work of criticism, whether genuine or an attempt to dress infringement as criticism so as to profit unfairly;

(v) the amount of the work used;

(vi) but remembering that it would be necesary to include most of a photograph, particularly in the context of the limited exposure of a broadcast criticism;

(vii) reproduction should not unreasonably prejudice the author's legitimate interests or conflict with normal exploration of the work.

The Court of Appeal considered Lord Denning's factors in *Ashdown v Telegraph Group Ltd* (2001). Aldous LJ said that the court must judge fairness by an objective standard. He asked whether a fair minded and honest person would have dealt with the copyright work in the manner that the defendant did for the purpose at issue.

The Court reaffirmed the relevance of these factors in relation to reporting current events after the introduction of the Human Rights Act 1998. They stated that the fair dealing provision would normally provide courts with all the scope needed to reflect the public interest in the freedom of expression and the freedom of the press. Separate consideration of a public interest defence should not normally be necessary. However, it was also important to bear in mind that 'considerations of the public interest are paramount'.[13] The Court did not consider the public interest in freedom of expression outweighed conventional considerations of fairness (which tended towards a conclusion that the dealing had not been fair). However, Griffiths argues that they failed to give due weight to the primacy of the public interest in receiving information over questions of fairness between the parties. While this may be so, it is important not to confuse freedom of expression for ideas and property rights in particular expressions of ideas. The Court stated that the information the paper wished to convey could have been effectively given by stating that they had seen the memorandum and could vouch for its existence.

Refusal of interim relief

If justification is pleaded in defamation, an interlocutory injunction will not be granted and a remedy for the tort (delict) at the trial is a matter of damages. The same may apply where fair dealing[14] is pleaded. In *Kennard v Lewis* (1983), an injunction was refused against publication when another organisation produced a pamphlet in the style of a CND publication. Publication would only harm the plaintiff's cause, so that to grant an injunction would restrain political controversy. Warner J cited Lord Denning MR's *dictum* from *Hubbard v Vosper* (1972):

> We never restrain a defendant in a libel action who says he is going to justify. So in a copyright action, we ought not to restrain a defendant who has a reasonable defence of fair dealing. Nor in an action for breach of confidence, if the defendant has a reasonable defence of public interest. The reason is because the defendant, if he is right, is entitled publish it; and the law will not intervene to suppress freedom of speech except when it is abused.

He refused the injunction on the basis that an interlocutory injunction should not in general be used to restrain freedom of speech, or political controversy. It is notable, however, that Lord Denning had been speaking in the context of publication revealing the dangers of a cult.

Final relief

In *Ashdown v Telegraph Group Ltd* (2001) the Court of Appeal suggested that fair dealing may represent a situation where a defence to a remedy in damages might be appropriate. Lord Phillips MR stated:

---

13   It may then be that the copyright defences cannot be overridden by contractual provisions: Griffiths, J, 'Copyright Law after *Ashdown* – Time to Deal Fairly with the Public' [2002] IPQ 240.

14   And the public interest defence.

The fair dealing defence under section 30 should lie where the public interest in learning of the very words written by the owner of the copyright is such that publication should not be inhibited by the chilling factor of having to pay damages or account for profits. When considering this question it is right to observe that, as damages are compensatory and not at large, they may produce a relatively mild chill.

11.2.3 'For the purpose of ...'

The 1988 Act did not clarify whether the test of the user's intent was an objective or a subjective one. After a period of doubt, the Court of Appeal adopted an objective test in *Pro Sieben Media AG v Carlton UK Television Ltd* (1999). The phrase 'for the purpose of' was held to have similar connotations to the everyday phrases of 'for the purpose of argument' or 'for the purpose of comparison'. It was not necessary for the court to put itself in an infringer's shoes in order to decide whether the piece was taken for one of the permitted purposes. To adopt an objective test involved consideration of the likely impact of the dealing on its audience. However, the subjective motives and intentions of the defendant were said to be 'highly relevant' to the issue of fair dealing. Robert Walker LJ said:

> This court should not in my view give any encouragement to the notion that all that is required is for the user to have the sincere belief, however misguided, that he or she is criticising a work or reporting current events. To do so would provide an undesirable incentive for journalists, for whom facts should be sacred, to give implausible evidence as to their intentions.

A secondary purpose will not suffice. The publication of the security camera stills in *Hyde Park Residence Ltd v Yelland* (2000) were held to be to expose the false statements subsequently made about them. Separating secondary purposes from primary ones, on an objective basis and liberal interpretation of 'for the purpose of' is difficult, as is illustrated both by the *Pro Sieben* and *Hyde Park* cases. In the latter, the court went on to consider the fairness of the photographs' publication on the basis that the publication may have been to report the media coverage generated by the many falsehoods relating to the stills which had been reported, and that this reporting constituted the current event.

11.2.4 Private research or study

Fair dealing with literary, dramatic, musical or artistic works for private study does not infringe.[15] Private study does not include any study which is directly or indirectly for a commercial purpose.[16] This statutory restriction to the private and non-commercial following implementation of the Information Society Directive should be contrasted with the decision of the Canadian Supreme Court in *CCH Canada Ltd v Law Society of Upper Canada* (2004). The court held that lawyers' research remained research, though for the purpose of providing legal services, and that the fair dealing defence should not be confined to private and non-commercial activity. This was because the court took a strong view that the users' rights provided by copyright defences were an essential means of preserving an appropriate balance between protection and public policy.

---

15 Section 29(1C) of the CDPA 1988.
16 *Ibid*, s 178 as amended by the CRRR 2003.

Fair dealing with literary, dramatic, musical or artistic works for non-commercial research does not infringe provided that it is accompanied with sufficient acknowledgment.[17] Acknowledgment is not required if it would be impossible for practical or other reasons.[18] It is the research (and not the business) that must be non-commercial. Consequently, even limited copying by not-for-profit organisations which is for a commercial purpose will infringe. Restriction of fair dealing to non-commercial research in the academic and commercial sectors was estimated to be likely to add an extra £15 million pa to national research costs.[19]

Fair dealing with typographical arrangement for the purpose of research or private study will not infringe.[20]

It is not fair dealing to observe, study or test the functioning of a computer program in order to determine the ideas and principles which underlie any element of the program (but these acts done in accordance with s 50BA are permitted).[21] Decompilation of a computer program (conversion of a program in a low level language into a higher level language) is not fair dealing, but may be permitted if in accordance with the conditions of s 50B of the CDPA 1988.[22]

This fair dealing defence is closely related to the other provision made for educational use of copyright works in the permitted acts, and should also be viewed in that context (see 11.7). The study or research must be the user's own. Producing works for students and researchers does not fall within this defence: *University of London Press v University Tutorial Press* (1916), where Petersen J said:

> It could not be contended that the mere republication of a copyright work was a fair dealing because intended for purposes of private study nor if the author produced a book of questions for students could anyone with impunity republish them with answers.

This dictum was followed in *Sillitoe v McGraw Hill* (1983), so that the production of GCE 'O' Level study texts including quotations from set works could not be justified as fair dealing. Logically, therefore, the defence does not extend to the making of multiple copies.[23]

11.2.5   Criticism or review

Fair dealing with a work, or a performance, for the purpose of criticism or review of that or another work, or performance of a work, does not infringe. It must be sufficiently acknowledged, and the work must have been made available to the public by an authorised act.[24] Publication includes issuing copies to the public, making available by electronic retrieval systems, rental or lending of copies to the public, performance, exhibition, playing or showing, or communicating the work to the public.[25]

---

17   *Ibid*, s 29(1).
18   *Ibid*, s 29(1B).
19   Regulatory Impact Assessment, Copyright and Related Rights Regulations 2003: www.patent.gov.uk.
20   Section 29(2) of the CDPA 1988.
21   *Ibid*, s 29(4A).
22   *Ibid*, s 29(4).
23   *Ibid*, ss 29(3), 38, 39, 40.
24   *Ibid*, s 30(1). The need for publication with authority was added by the CRRR 2003.
25   *Ibid*, s 30(1A).

The issue is the fairness of the defendant's dealing with the claimant's copyright work and not the fairness of any criticism or review that is made: *Pro Sieben Media AG v Carlton UK Television Ltd* (1999). Robert Walker LJ said that criticism may be strongly expressed and unbalanced without forfeiting the fair dealing defence (any remedy for malicious criticism lay in defamation).

In *Hubbard v Vosper* (1972), it was held that the criticism might extend to the copyright author's underlying thoughts and philosophy. This principle seems to have been extended to an unjustifiable extent in *Time Warner Entertainments Co v Channel 4 Television Corp plc* (1994). There, considerable extracts were taken from the violent film *A Clockwork Orange*, whose director, Stanley Kubrick, had withdrawn the film from distribution in the UK from 1974 onwards. The defendants included the extracts in a programme largely directed to criticising this withdrawal. In an interlocutory hearing, it was held that an arguable case of fair dealing for the purpose of criticism and review could be made out. Thus, a copyright owner's decision to withdraw his work from circulation was effectively overridden. Amendments to s 30(1) of the CDPA 1988 by the CRRR 2003 effectively overrule this decision as the work must have been made available to the public with the copyright owner's authority.

The issue was raised again in *Pro Sieben Media AG v Carlton UK Television Ltd* (1999), where extracts from the plaintiff's programme (of a paid interview with a couple who had become newsworthy through an unusual multiple pregnancy) were repeated in a programme made by the defendant criticising 'chequebook journalism'. At first instance, Laddie J distinguished the *Clockwork Orange* case. There it had been noted that the criticism of the decision to withdraw the film, and the criticism and review of its long-term artistic merit were 'inseparable', because the argument was that it was the film's merits which should justify its renewed release. However, the Court of Appeal held that the defendant's programme as a whole was made to criticise chequebook journalism in general and, in particular, the recent media treatment of the multiple pregnancy. This seems to fall at the very limits of criticism of a work, another work or performance of a work. It appears to allow a defendant to illustrate any argument with extracts (albeit only if fair in extent) from a work in some way related to the argument, without connecting the argument to particular criticism or review of that work. It seems particularly regrettable in the *Clockwork Orange* case that the removal of the injunction allowed some 10% of the film to be broadcast. The broadcast was made, despite the director's wish to remove the film from the public domain. Nor could the film be regarded as remaining in the public domain within the UK (although in circulation in other parts of the world) when a copy had to be obtained in France, and its format changed, to allow the extracts to be shown. The Court of Appeal in *Pro Sieben Media AG v Carlton UK Television Ltd* (1999) posed the test of the likely impact of the dealing on the public.

Criticism of a style of newspaper journalism, the criticised works remaining largely unspecified, was treated as fair dealing for the purpose of criticism and review in *Fraser-Woodward v BBC* (2005). However, the criticism must be of a work or another work. It was not, Mann J said, sufficient to criticise 'something (anything)' in order to invoke the defence. But this did not require specific reference to the content of the work being criticised or reviewed.

It is clear that this fair dealing defence extends to multiple copies: *Hubbard v Vosper* (1972). In *Sillitoe v McGraw Hill* (1983), sufficient acknowledgment was held, for the Copyright Act 1956, to mean not just stating the author's name and the title of the work, but also to include acknowledgment of his rights. Section 178(1) of the CDPA

1988 defines 'sufficient acknowledgment' as an acknowledgment identifying the work in question by its title or other description, and identifying the author (unless unpublished or published anonymously and the author cannot be ascertained by reasonable inquiry). In *Pro Sieben Media AG v Carlton UK Television Ltd* (1999), the use of the plaintiff company's logo was held to be sufficient, although at first instance it had been found that this would not be recognised by the general public.

11.2.6   Reporting current events

Fair dealing with a work other than a photograph for the purpose of reporting current events does not infringe, provided that it is sufficiently acknowledged.[26] A satellite broadcaster using short extracts from broadcast sporting events did not infringe. It was significant, however, that no audiences were diverted from the copyright owner's audience: *BBC v BSB* (1991).

Photographs are excluded from this defence because of their news value. Acknowledgment is not required if the dealing is by means of sound recording, film, or broadcast where it would be impossible for practical or other reasons.[27] The use of the copyright owner's logo on an extract from a television broadcast in the work of criticism amounted to sufficient acknowledgment: *Pro Sieben Media AG v Carlton UK Television Ltd* (1999).

Current

The permitted act only extends to events which are current. Events may remain of interest after they cease to be current. Consequently, it was not fair dealing to publish letters written by the Duchess of Windsor after her death because they related to events which had taken place many years previously, even though the issue to which they related had been reopened by her passing: *Associated Newspapers v News Group* (1986). The stills reproduced in *Hyde Park Residence Ltd v Yelland* (2000) were published 13 months after the accident in which Princess Diana was killed. The argument that the events were of interest but no longer current was held to have force; however, it was held not to be right to reject the fair dealing defence on this ground when the accident was still under investigation.

Events

'Events' accommodates major sporting fixtures: *BBC v BSB* (1991). The Court of Appeal held that reporting, not only of an individual's multiple pregnancy, but also of the manner of its media coverage, fell within 'current events', a phrase which they said should be interpreted liberally, in *Pro Sieben Media AG v Carlton UK Television Ltd* (1999). Nevertheless, this did not extend to copies of newspaper articles concerning fashion advice, advice on personal finance, interviews, book reviews and lifestyle articles, as well as product comparisons circulated by a major store to its employees: *Newspaper Licensing Agency v Marks & Spencer plc* (1999).[28] The defence did not extend to reporting current events for private commercial interests.

---

26 *Ibid*, s 30(2).
27 *Ibid*, s 30(3) as amended by the CRRR 2003.
28 The point was not considered in the House of Lords as no infringement was found.

A work may refer to events that are not current, but which are of current newsworthy significance. In *Ashdown v Telegraph Group Ltd* (2001) Lord Ashdown's notes fell into this category. The court refused to distinguish *Hyde Park Residence Ltd v Yelland* (2000), where the investigation was still current. On a liberal interpretation of purpose, as required by the *Pro Sieben* case, s 30(2) was 'clearly intended to protect the role of the media in informing the public about matters of current concern to the public'. *Hyde Park* might be distinguished on the basis that it related to the activities of an individual, whereas *Ashdown* related to the actions of the Government and a former leader of an opposition party which had continuing significance to voters.

11.3   INCIDENTAL INCLUSION

It does not infringe copyright if a work is incidentally included in an artistic work, sound recording, film or broadcast.[29] Consequently, a news item filmed with a reporter standing next to a statue or building will not infringe copyright in the statue or building. Nor does issuing copies to the public, playing, showing or broadcasting such a work infringe.[30] However, a musical work, words spoken or sung with music, or as much of a sound recording or broadcast as includes a musical work or such words will not be regarded as an incidental inclusion if the inclusion was deliberate.[31] By implication any other incidental inclusion may be deliberate.

'Incidental' was given its ordinary meaning of 'casual, not essential, subordinate, merely background' in *IPC Magazines Ltd v MGN Ltd* (1998). Including the cover of the claimant's magazine in a television advert for the defendant newspaper's colour supplement was an essential and important feature of the advertisement, and not incidental. The Court of Appeal refused to define 'incidental' in *Football Association Premier League Ltd v Panini UK Ltd* (2003). However, they held that the relevant question was the purpose of including the work in relation to the objective behind the defendant's later work. The defendant manufactured and distributed stickers comprising photographs of footballers in their club strip. These were held to infringe copyright in the Premier League emblem on the footballers' clothing, and an injunction was granted. The Court of Appeal, upholding the decision, held that it was clear from Hansard and s 31(3) of the CDPA 1988 that 'incidental' was not confined to unintentional, or non-deliberate, inclusion. In principle, there was no necessary dichotomy between an integral and incidental inclusion. However, the relevant question was why the emblem had been included in the stickers, including commercial reasons for doing so. They would have no appeal to collectors without an authentic picture of the footballers and their strip. Consequently, on an objective assessment of the circumstances in which the photographs were used to create the stickers, the inclusion of the emblems was essential to the stickers' commercial object, and not incidental.[32] The commercial nature of both cases is significant.

This decision can be contrasted with the case of *Trebor Bassett Ltd v The Football Association* (1997) (see 16.2.4). Cards included in packets of sweets which included depictions of the FA's three lions logo on footballers' shirts did not constitute trade mark use and did not infringe the logo's trade mark.

---

29   Section 31(1) of the CDPA 1988.
30   *Ibid*, s 31(2).
31   *Ibid*, s 31(3).
32   The protection given to copyright in the emblems should be compared to the trade mark protection in *RFU v Cotton Traders* (2002).

11.4 HOME COPYING

The advent of the potential for wide scale home copying by individuals for personal purposes raised several defined areas of dispute. These included copying for educational purposes, including that by libraries, tape recording for security copies, 'pop piracy', recording of television broadcasts, personal copying and P2P file sharing, and backup copying of computer programs. There were also several options for reform, including licences (whether implied, voluntary or statutory), blanket levies on the cost of the copying medium (such as tapes and paper) accounted to copyright owners on a proportional basis, a pay at source approach with a high price paid for the first copy (such as satellite television), allowing for physical anti-copying devices or the provision of new defences to infringement. In the event, the CDPA 1988 and Information Society Directive adopted a combination of these means.

The most favoured route in the CDPA 1988 was that of voluntary licensing, resulting in grant of a licence by the copyright owner, and this was reinforced by the provisions for collective licensing (see 11.12). The advantage of adopting such an approach was that licensing schemes were funded and administered by copyright owners themselves. The Information Society Directive also enhanced legal support for technological protection (see 10.5).

11.4.1 Reprography

The Whitford Committee[33] had recommended a statutory blanket licence for all photocopying because of the difficulties of detection which it presents, allied to a levy on the cost of paper, and the abolition of fair dealing. However, the success of voluntary collective schemes established by the Copyright Licensing Agency with respect to educational photocopying encouraged the CDPA 1988's response, particularly given that much photocopying will not infringe.[34]

Fair dealing for private study and non-commercial research applies to photocopying, provided that it does not extend to multiple copies (see 11.2.4). The Information Society Directive provides that exceptions for reproductions by any photographic technique may be provided, but only subject to fair compensation for right owners, as must any fair dealing.[35] This was not transferred to the CDPA 1988 by the CRRR 2003, nor has a levy been imposed, although compensation will be received from licensed multiple copying. Recital 35 of the Directive provides that where prejudice to a right holder would be 'minimal' no obligation for payment might arise. Recital 37 also points out that national reprography schemes do not constitute major barriers to the internal market.

The Copyright Licensing Agency (CLA) administers collective licensing of reproduction rights, including the universities' block licence. However, the CLARCS scheme[36] for producing student course study packs was subjected to the jurisdiction of

---

33 *Copyright and Designs Law*, Cmnd 6732, 1977.

34 Although it nearly put sheet music publishers out of business and publishers took proceedings against a school and educational authority for reproducing music scores.

35 Article 5(2)(a) and (b) of the Information Society Directive.

36 Which in the author's experience proved so expensive, administratively time-consuming and burdensome as to restrict the provision of teaching materials to part-time students.

the Copyright Tribunal (see 11.14) in *Universities UK v Copyright Licensing Agency* (2002). The universities' licence was extended and the course pack provision removed.

11.4.2   Audio and video recording

For audio and video recording, even before the internet, the debate was heated. Not all recording deprived copyright owners of a sale, for example, copying for backup purposes. Blanket levies on copying materials (coupled with exceptions to infringement for copying for personal use), such as those in Germany, Austria, France, Spain, Portugal and Scandinavia, were not adopted in 1988. Sanctioning all such recording is not possible under Article 9 of the Berne Convention. On the other hand, it was also argued that the law should be consonant with the developing practices of the reasonable public.

The result for audio recording in 1988 was a combination of the rental and lending right (see 9.6.3), subject to ss 67, 70, 71 and 296 of the CDPA 1988. Video recording was also covered by s 70 of the CDPA 1988. These latter provisions have been amended by the Information Society Directive, which has also added legal support for technological protection of works in s 296ZA (see 10.5), as well as new offences which may be used against individuals as well as commercial pirates (see 10.7). There is no exemption for private copying,[37] so that much home recording or downloading infringes copyright in sound recordings, films and broadcasts, as well as any underlying original works.

Recording a broadcast (radio and television) in domestic premises for private and domestic use does not infringe copyright in the broadcast or rights in performances.[38] The recording must be solely for the purpose of enabling it to be viewed or listened to at a more convenient time ('time shifting'). Recording for other purposes will be very hard to detect. Private and domestic copying could pose a challenge to the rental market if home copies circulated. However, any subsequent dealings with such copies render those copies infringing copies.[39] The permitted act does not extend to the copying of pre-recorded videos. Copying by a cyber café for its customers did not fall within the unamended s 70 in *Sony Music Entertainment (UK) Ltd v Easyinternetcafé Ltd* (2003), and could not now be regarded as recording made on domestic premises.

Section 71 of the CDPA 1988 makes similar provision for the making of photographs from broadcasts. They must also be made in domestic premises for private and domestic use. Subsequent dealings with them will infringe. Both sections are regarded as falling within the permitted exception for private copying in Article 5(2)(b) of the Directive, but make no provision for fair compensation taking into account any technological measures employed. Many other Member States impose levies on copying media in order to compensate right owners.[40]

The provision for quasi-domestic use of sound recordings extends to playing sound recordings as part of the activities of, or for the benefit of, a club, society or other

---

37   Which would require fair compensation – Article 5(2)(b) of the Information Society Directive.
38   Section 70(1) of the CDPA 1988, as amended by the CRRR 2003.
39   *Ibid*, s 70(2).
40   The Information Society Directive led to calls for a levy on personal computers in France and Germany.

organisation subject to the conditions laid down in s 67[41] of the CDPA 1988. Showing or playing a broadcast in public to an audience which has not paid for admission does not infringe copyright in the broadcast, or any non-excepted sound recording or film included in it: s 72[42] of the CDPA 1988. If an excepted sound recording is included it will not infringe if the playing or showing of the broadcast forms part of the activities of a not-for-profit organisation.[13] Otherwise, to use radio or television broadcasts of music in public licences will be required from the Performing Right Society and Phonogram Performance Limited. Similar provision is made for rights in performances in the broadcast. Licences will be required whether the broadcast is used for customers or for employees of the person playing it.

11.5   THE INTERNET

Where electronic works are accessed via the internet the permitted acts allow for browsing and caching. In addition the permitted acts of fair dealing as well as educational and library exceptions will apply to some uses of works. However, these can only be exercised if any technological 'locks' applied to the work allow the permitted use.

11.5.1   Temporary copies

It has already been noted that transmitting an electronic work over digital networks involves making many temporary copies. So does browsing by end users' viewing the work on their PCs. In addition, the efficiency of the internet is aided by the 'caching' of temporary copies by ISPs to avoid network congestion. *Prima facie*, these copies infringe as reproduction extends to storage by electronic means, and copies which are transient or incidental to some other use of the work.[44] However, the many links in this chain of reproduction are necessary to the operation of the internet, as is the temporary copy made in order merely to view an electronic work. A licence to transmit and browse works legitimately made available in electronic form might be implied but not in all Member States, particularly those operating levy systems.

Section 28A[45] provides a new defence to cater for transmission, browsing and caching. It applies to literary works (other than a computer program or database), or dramatic, musical or artistic works, typographical arrangements, sound recordings, films and performances. It will not infringe to make temporary copies which are:

- transient or incidental; and

- an essential part of a technological process; and

- the sole purpose of which is to enable either a transmission of the work in a network between third parties by an intermediary, or a lawful use of the work;

- provided that they have no independent economic significance.

---

41   As amended by the CRRR 2003.
42   As amended by the CRRR 2003.
43   Section 72(1B) of the CDPA 1988.
44   *Ibid*, s 17(2), (6).
45   Added by the CRRR 2003.

Recital 33 of the Directive states that this is intended to cater for browsing and caching; however, no guidance is given to the interpretation of what will constitute an essential part of a technological process, nor which factors will be relevant to a copy's economic significance. The Recital also makes the defence conditional on there being no modification of the information or interference with 'lawful use of technology, widely recognised and used by industry, to obtain data on the use of information'. It may be queried whether this provision would extend to private use of works accessed through P2P file sharing, but not stored by recipients.

The horizontal provisions of the E-Commerce Directive apply to mere transmitters – the ISPs (see 10.2.5).

11.5.2   Permitted uses of technologically protected works

Technological protection applied to digital works on or offline may prevent permitted uses of works. Anti-copying technology on recently released music CDs has provoked controversy among purchasers unable to make personal copies. The Directive provides that in the absence of voluntary measures by right holders, including (contractual) agreements between parties, Member States must take 'appropriate measures' to extend the benefits of some permitted acts[46] to users with legal access to the work.[47] This presupposes that no free use will be allowed where access is controlled on a paying basis and recital 45 states the exceptions should not 'prevent the definition of contractual relations designed to ensure fair compensation for rightholders'. However, the Recital does contemplate contractual regulation in national laws.

It is clear that emphasis must shift to jurisdiction over such contracts to ensure that compensation is 'fair', perhaps beyond that exercised by the Copyright Tribunal over licensing schemes. Recital 35 provides some guidance:

> ... a valuable criterion would be the possible harm to the rightholders resulting from the act in question. In cases where rightholders have already received payment in some other form, for instance as part of a licence fee, no specific or separate payment may be due. The level of fair compensation should take full account of the degree of use of technological protection measures ... in certain situations where the prejudice to the rightholder would be minimal, no obligation for payment might arise.

This could raise a presumption that failure to use technological protection necessitating payment for access or use presupposes free use. Clearly the application of levies on copying media where no access or copying is possible is unlikely to be fair. The approach can be contrasted to the defences established by the Software Directive for computer programs, which may not be contracted out of[48] (see 11.8).

No attempt was made to determine how Member States might facilitate even paid for permitted uses. The variety of means of implementation by different Member States show how vague the provision is.[49] Furthermore, Article 6(4) fourth paragraph, as detailed in Recital 53, appears to remove this provision from 'interactive on-demand

---

46   Those provided by Article 5(2)(a), (c), (d), (e) and Article 5(3)(a), (b), (e).
47   Article 6(4) of the Information Society Directive.
48   Sections 50A–50C of the CDPA 1988.
49   Braun, N, 'The Interface Between the Protection of Technological Measures and the Exercise of Exceptions to Copyright and Related Rights: Comparing the Situation on the US and in the EU' [2003] EIPR 496.

services'. The internet could be so described, and the result would be to give copyright owners employing technological protection for their works complete control over both access and use of those works. It has been stated that the provision was not intended to extend to the internet but to content provision such as video-on-demand, but this is not explicit.[50] It may be that the market provides copyright owners with sufficient incentive to disseminate their works, and that competitive forces will ensure access and use at reasonable rates. Competitive forces will not moderate control over sole-source information, however. A further step may have to follow where some sources of information are subjected to compulsory provision for access and use. It may not be too fanciful to suggest some form of 'key escrow' for technological protection devices. Much will depend on the development of business models and payment systems in relation to electronically stored and delivered works.

Section 296ZE of the CDPA 1988 establishes a cumbersome procedure whereby a person or representatives of persons obstructed from permitted uses of works other than computer programs may make a complaint to the Secretary of State. In turn the Secretary of State may give such written directions to the copyright owner as are requisite. Copyright owners, their exclusive licensees or distributors have a statutory duty to comply. The section does not apply to works made available to the public on agreed contractual terms in such a way that users may access them from a time and place individually chosen by them.[51] This procedure may have some usefulness to organisations such as educational establishments, but is of little relevance to individuals, particularly those held to ransom over access to works available over the internet at a price. When such works may comprise sole-source information such as the human genome the implications remain significant.

Similar concerns have been raised in relation to the Digital Millennium Copyright Act (DMCA) 1998. The legal support for technological protection of works distinguishes between circumvention of access and of copying controls. While fair use by means of copying remains permissible, at least in principle, this does not extend to controls over access. Consequently, potential monopolies are possible for digitally locked works. Exceptions are limited, although to circumvent copying (as opposed to access) control is not prohibited. The Library of Congress is charged with triennial reviews of the Act. Despite considerable controversy over protected access the Register of Copyrights has so far only made slight amendments. In 2003 exemptions to the anti-circumvention provisions were added. These relate to protected technological control of lists of internet addresses blocked by commercial software preventing access to domains or websites; computer programs protected by 'dongles' that prevent access due to malfunction; computer programs and games in formats which have become obsolete; and literary works in e-format when all existing electronic versions prevent use of the read-aloud function or conversion of the text into specialised format.[52] The Directive was also subject to review no later than 22 December 2004 and every three years thereafter.[53]

One significant difference between the application of the DMCA 1998 and the Directive is the continued jurisdiction of the courts in the American general fair use

---

50   Hart, M, 'The Copyright in the Information Society Directive: An Overview' [2002] EIPR 58.
51   Section 296ZE(9) of the CDPA 1988.
52   Rulemaking on Exemptions from Prohibition on Circumvention of Technological measures that Control Access to Copyrighted Works: www.copyright.gov.
53   Article 12 of the Information Society Directive.

doctrine,[54] which has enabled, albeit largely unsuccessful, challenges[55] to the DMCA. However, in *Kelly v Arriba Soft Corp* (2002) it was held that thumbnail reproductions of copyright photographs in a visual search engine were fair use, though providing links to the full size images was not. This jurisdiction, and the four factors which are taken into account, may prove a preferable and more immediate means of resolving the technological conundrum than the UK's encouragement of voluntary licensing schemes through cumbersome threats of compulsory provision.

The Directive's emphasis is on voluntary licensing. Another solution to the problem of digitally locked information lies in the adaptation of Copy Left licensing to electronic works, or the development of new forms of licensing (see 11.11.2). An alternative could lie in establishing a global, virtual arbitration system akin to the domain name UDRP. However, the UDRP is effective because ICANN necessarily has a monopoly over access to the domain name system and can impose the mandatory dispute resolution system on registrants contractually.

11.6 NEWS AND MEDIA

There is an obvious conflict of interest between protecting the time and expense a journalist invests in securing a 'scoop', and the public interest in wide access to information. A number of copyright principles relate to the media interest in providing news, and the public interest in receiving information. These include the defences of public interest, fair dealing for criticism and review, for reporting current events, and the distinction between idea and expression in a work, as well as ss 31, 58 and 62 of the CDPA 1988.

News incorporated in copyright works (literary and artistic works, film and broadcasts) is protected to the extent that such works are protected. Copying a literary or artistic work, for example, infringes whether it is the work, or a broadcast of it, which is reproduced. If a broadcast has no underlying work, it may be copied in another material form (see 10.1.1).

11.6.1 Deriving information

The distinction between idea and expression allows users to take information from a work without trespassing on the 'skill, labour and judgment' invested in the work's expression (see 8.2.3). This was illustrated in *Walter v Steinkopff* (1892). The defendant journalist copied a report from *The Times*. This copying was held to infringe. Although it was only partial, not by a direct competitor, the source had been acknowledged and the *Times* editor had not immediately objected. North J stressed that the idea-expression dichotomy provided the bounds of legitimate use and balanced the public and private interest. This was, however, distinguished more recently in *Express News v News (UK)* (1991) in an interlocutory hearing. Two papers, in a 'tit for tat' exchange, took information from interviews from each other. The court was prepared to accept that it might be established at trial that a licence could be implied from the press

---

54 Burrell, R, 'Reining in Copyright: Is Fair Use the Answer?' [2001] IPQ 361.
55 *Universal City Studios v Reimerdes* (2000) 111 F Supp 2d 294 (SDNY); *A & M Records v Napster* 239 F Supp 3d 1004 (9 Circ 2001); *UMG Recordings v MP3.com* 92 F Supp 2d 233 (2000, SDNY).

custom of picking up interviews from rivals, or acquiescence in such a long standing practice found, were it not for the mirror image feature of the case. Express News had already obtained summary judgment against the Today newspaper for its copying, on indistinguishable facts. *Walter v Steinkopff* (1892) was distinguished on the basis that the authority was old and that in that case it was a report, and not the content of an interview with a third party, that had been copied.

In other 'borrowings' of news material, if news were to be seen to have particular value, an *Elanco v Mandops* (1980) approach could be adopted to copying (see 8.4.3), with fair dealing only to be applied to sanction takings in the public interest. In *Beloff v Pressdram* (1973) it was noted that 'leaks' of information are customary in the press world. However, in determining fairness, the court refused to distinguish according to the source of the leak, stating that it was the manner of using the material which was relevant. This included consideration of whether the defendant's point could have been made in any other way than by copying.

11.6.2   Specific statutory provisions

Newsworthy interviews receive their own permitted act in s 58 of the CDPA 1988. Direct records (in writing or otherwise) of spoken words made for the purpose of reporting current events or for broadcasting, do not infringe literary copyright in the words. This is subject to there being no prohibition on making of the record, or of its use, by the speaker, and the permission of the person lawfully in possession of the record.

Section 31 of the CDPA 1988 permits the incidental inclusion of a work in an artistic work, sound recording, film, broadcast or cable programme (see 11.3). Section 68 provides a statutory licence for broadcasters who have permission to broadcast or transmit copyright works to do other acts in relation to the work in order to facilitate the broadcast or transmission, provided that the conditions set out are complied with.

11.7   EDUCATIONAL COPYING AND LIBRARIES

Fair dealing for research and private study (see 11.2.4) sanctions some educational use of original works and typographical arrangement of published editions, subject to prohibition on multiple copies being made, and extends to photocopying works. The defence does not allow instructors to copy on behalf of students. It would seem that a good deal of educational photocopying and other copying would not fall within the limits of fair dealing, and the Copyright Licensing Agency has set up collective licensing schemes for schools, colleges and universities.

However, the permitted acts do make provision for educational establishments. These were amended by the CRRR 2003, which provides that the copies must carry sufficient acknowledgment and that the instruction is for a non-commercial purpose.

• Copying in the course of, or in preparation for, instruction is permitted by s 32 of the CDPA 1988. Instructors may copy original works, but not by means of a reprographic process. Section 178(1) of the CDPA 1988 defines this as a process for making facsimile copies or involving the use of an appliance for making multiple copies, which would include for example, photocopying, facsimile machines, and scanners. Instructors may copy sound recordings, films and film soundtracks.

- Infringement (including reprographic copying, except in the case of a musical work) for the purposes of examination is allowed.

- Extracts from literary and dramatic works may be included in collections of works intended for use in educational establishments subject to conditions, and strict limits laid down.[56]

- Works other than artistic works may be performed, played or shown to an audience of teachers, pupils and other persons connected with an educational establishment (which does not include parents), not being regarded as in public.[57]

- Educational establishments may also record, or copy a recording of, broadcasts or cable programmes made by them or on their behalf, without infringing copyright in the derivative work or any underlying original work or film.[58] This is, however, only to the extent that no licensing scheme exists for such acts and that use is internal. Any subsequent dealing with the copies will infringe.

- Finally, reprographic copies of literary, dramatic and musical works may be made to the limits set out in s 36 of the CDPA 1988, but only if no licensing scheme exists. Dealings in copies made under these permitted acts will, however, be treated as secondary infringement.[59] Section 174 of the CDPA 1988 defines 'educational establishment'.

- Educational establishments may lend copies of a work.[60]

- Where copying for the purpose of non-commercial research and private study in particular is concerned, it is often necessary to have the copy made by a library and permitted acts relating to librarians allow for this in ss 38–40 of the CDPA 1988. No multiple copying is sanctioned.

- Other permitted acts relating to the activities of libraries are set out in ss 40A–44 of the CDPA 1988.

11.8 COMPUTER PROGRAMS

Special provision is made for the lawful use of computer programs, added to the CDPA 1988 by the Copyright (Computer Programs) Regulations 1992, which implemented the Software Directive.

Lawful users may make necessary back-up copies of a program.[61] The making of such back-up copies may not be excluded by contract[62]. Lawful use means that the user is licensed to use the program and not just its particular carrier. In *Sony Computer Entertainment Inc v Owen* (2002) and *Sony Computer Entertainment v Ball* (2004) it was held that s 50A did not apply to the copy protected PlayStation2 computer games CDs.

---

56   Section 33 of the CDPA 1988.
57   *Ibid*, s 34.
58   *Ibid*, s 35.
59   *Ibid*, ss 32(5), 35(3), 36(5).
60   *Ibid*, s 36A.
61   *Ibid*, s 50A.
62   *Ibid*, s 50A(3).

The court held that the section presupposed the user having a licence to run the program (such as a word-processing package) and that the hardware allowed the user to operate the licence. The licence in question was for the disk containing the game alone. In the same way that if a musical CD is damaged another must be purchased, so the game disk would need replacing. Copies were not envisaged. In the later case it was also noted that both CDs and DVDs are robust and cannot be wiped, and that in the event of damage they would be replaced by Sony. As software is less commonly distributed by the more fragile magnetic floppy disk, these decisions render s 50A largely redundant in relation to off the shelf software as it is unlikely that it would ever be necessary to back it up. This may not be the case for online software which is downloaded as the hard disk to which it is downloaded may fail.

Decompilation is permitted, provided that certain conditions are met, which are designed to allow the production of compatible software: s 50B of the CDPA 1988. Error correction ('debugging') is catered for by s 50C of the CDPA 1988. Section 50D of the CDPA 1988 was added by the Copyright and Rights in Database Regulations 1997 in order to allow access to a database by those entitled to do so, any contractual provision to the contrary being void.

The Information Society Directive has added s 50BA.[63] It provides that lawful users (including commercial users) of a program do not infringe by observing, studying or testing the functioning of a program to determine the ideas and principles which underlie any element of it, when loading, displaying, running, transmitting or storing it. It is not permitted to contract out of s 50BA.

If no contractual provisions provide otherwise, works in electronic form may be transferred, giving the transferee the rights of the transferor, but any legitimate copies which have been made of the work must also be transferred. If not, they will be treated as infringing copies: s 56 of the CDPA 1988.

11.9   OTHER PERMITTED ACTS

Those researching cryptography are entitled to circumvent technological protection measures unless the circumvention, or information derived from the research, prejudicially affects the copyright owner: s 296ZA(2) of the CDPA 1988.[64] This has been criticised for not making clear exactly when researchers will become liable. The effect of the DMCA 1998 on cryptography research was highlighted by the case of Professor Edward Felten in the US. The RIAA threatened proceedings when he proposed delivering a paper on the results of his research. The suit was dropped after undertakings not to sue were secured, but revealed the extent of the DMCA's reach.

Before the CDPA 1988 came into force, copyright had intruded into the sphere of industrial design with controversial results (see 13.1.2). New provisions in ss 51–53 of the CDPA 1988 define a new division between copyright and the design field and those acts permitted in relation to industrial design are considered in Chapter 13.

Provision is made for permitted acts in relation to copyright works employed in public administration in ss 45–50 of the CDPA 1988. Copyright is not infringed by

---

63   Following restriction of s 29 of the CDPA 1988 to private and non-commercial acts.
64   Added by the CRRR 2003.

anything done for the purposes of, or reporting of, parliamentary or judicial proceedings, a Royal Commission or statutory inquiry (ss 45 and 46 of the CDPA 1988). Material open to public inspection according to a statutory requirement, or on a statutory register may be utilised for factual purposes, subject to conditions set out in s 47 of the CDPA 1988. Public records and material supplied to the Crown are dealt with in ss 48 and 49 of the CDPA 1988.

11.10 COPYRIGHT (VISUALLY IMPAIRED PERSONS) ACT 2002

Article 5(3)(b) of the Information Society Directive allows an exception to the reproduction and communication rights for the benefit of those with disabilities. The Copyright (Visually Impaired Persons) Act 2002 came into force on 31 October 2003[65] and added new permitted acts to the CDPA 1988[66] for the visually impaired. These acts apply where no accessible copies of a work are commercially available. Musical recordings or performances, and databases are not included. Impairment is functionally defined, extending both to the blind and others with impaired visual function. Accessible copies, which may be hard or soft copies, are those making a copy of a work as available to the person as it would be without any impairment. This may include facilities for navigating through the copy but not changes which are unnecessary, or those which would infringe the author's moral right of integrity.

The exceptions are dependent on possession of a lawful copy, which may have been bought or borrowed, and on sufficient acknowledgment being made on the copy. Single accessible copies may be made by or for a visually impaired person for personal use, or multiple copies by an educational or not-for-profit organisation. These copies may not be made if a licensing scheme covers them. Copies made outside these provisions, or subsequent dealings with them will infringe. The accessible copy may be transferred to others along with the 'master' copy. Organisations may also keep and transfer intermediate copies, such as an electronic version, needed to make the accessible copy.

The Secretary of State is given power to intervene in multiple copying if it leads to infringement on an unwarranted scale. No specific solution is granted for the problem of legally protected digital locks, which is left to s 296ZE of the CDPA 1988.

11.11 DEALING WITH COPYRIGHT

Section 90 of the CDPA 1988 sets out the nature of the right and its transferability. Copyright is personal or moveable property and may be transmitted by assignment, testamentary disposition or operation of law. It may also be used as security in financial transactions. The sum of exclusive rights conferred by the right may be divided up according to the acts copyright restricts, and the period of copyright. For example rights in relation to a novel may be divided according to translation rights, film rights, dramatisation rights, and electronic distribution rights. Each of these may be divided nationally and for restricted periods.

---

65 Copyright (Visually Impaired Persons) Act 2002 (Commencement) Order 2003.
66 Sections 31A–31F CDPA 1988.

11.11.1 Assignment

Assignment of copyright must be in writing and signed: s 90(3) of the CDPA 1988. Future copyright may be assigned: s 91 of the CDPA 1988.

A transfer of copyright must be distinguished from any transfer of the property in the physical embodiment of the work – for an artist to sell his painting does not transfer any interest in the copyright. There is no register of copyright transfers, so that an assignee of copyright runs the risk of prior assignments of which he or she has no knowledge. No specific form of words or document is required for an assignment and it is a question of construction for a court as to whether any given transfer is a licence or an assignment. In *Chaplin v Frewin* (1966), the words 'exclusive right to publish' were held to be an assignment of future copyright; in *Frisby v BBC* (1967), however, the words 'exclusive right to televise' were held to be a licence. In the former, royalties were to be paid to the assignor, whereas in the latter the right was given only to one performance and any further rights were only an option in the transfer. The more restrictive the right, the more likely it is to be construed as a licence. Essentially assignment transfers ownership, while a licence permits acts that would otherwise infringe. A licensee will have less ability to adapt a work: *Frisby v BBC* (1967).

11.11.2 Licensing

Licences may be informal and are binding on successors in title to the licensee's interest, except against a purchaser in good faith for valuable consideration without notice. An exclusive licence must also be in writing and signed.[67] An exclusive licensee has the same rights and remedies as an assignee, except as against the copyright owner.[68] Some infringements are actionable by a non-exclusive licensee, with the same rights and remedies as the copyright owner: s 101A of the CDPA 1988.[69]

Software licensing

The open culture of the early internet, and the monopolistic tendency of copyright protection for software that becomes an industry standard,[70] has promoted the 'open source' and 'free software' movements or 'copyleft'. Copyleft licenses software[71] on the basis that users may use, modify, adapt and distribute programs, provided that they are willing to license their amended version to others on the same terms. If the licensee fails to distribute derivative works under the same licence that licence is terminated, leaving the licensee without permission to use the software. Whereas traditional exploitation of software only gives access to object code, open source licensing makes source code available. Copyleft should be distinguished from freeware, in which software is distributed free of charge.

---

67   *Ibid*, s 92.
68   *Ibid*, s 101.
69   Added by the CRRR 2003.
70   Microsoft has been the subject of several antitrust actions in the US (*USA v Microsoft Corp*). Proceedings were also being taken by the EU Commission.
71   Although open source and free software work from philosophically distinct viewpoints.

The open source and free software communities have made exaggerated claims of the 'death' of copyright as a result. In fact, copyleft constitutes no more than the widest of licence agreements, and is in fact dependent on copyright for the licences' subject matter. Richard Stallman drafted the General Public Licence (GPL) in 1989 as part of the GNU free software project to create a free operating system. As well as the GPL, copyleft licences include the Mozilla Public Licence and Q Public Licence. The Mozilla licence is a copyleft licence to the Netscape browser. The Q public licence is to the free edition of the Qt toolkit for the development of GUI programs.

Copyleft indicates that to some authors an incentive other than economic gain is sufficient to stimulate creativity. However, it has been doubted whether this is a process that can continue indefinitely without some return.[72] Copyleft licensing has spread to other types of work, such as the Art Libre Society and open source record labels. The Creative Commons[73] offers an open source licence for electronic works.

11.11.3 Compulsory licences

There is no general scheme for compulsory licences, as in the Patents Act 1977, but ss 66, 140–41 and 144 of the CDPA 1988 confer powers on the Secretary of State to grant licences where they are not provided voluntarily.

The Broadcasting Act 1990 introduced provisions to allow publishers to reproduce television listing information[74] under which broadcasters were given a statutory duty to provide, and to grant compulsory licences against licensing bodies restricting needle-time for the playing of sound recordings[75] (see 11.12).

11.11.4 Contractual negotiation

Initial dealing with copyright lies between author and entrepreneur. Contractual principles relating to restraint of trade and undue influence, based on inequality of bargaining power between the parties, particularly where an author is embarking on a career, will apply to these dealings. In *Schroeder Music Publishing Co Ltd v Macaulay* (1974) an unknown songwriter entered a very one-sided agreement with the plaintiff. The House of Lords held that the contract was in restraint of trade and unenforceable. A similarly unbalanced pop management contract suffered the same fate in *Clifford Davis Management Ltd v WEA Records Ltd* (1975). However, the same did not apply to George Michael in *Panayiotou v Sony Music Entertainment (UK) Ltd* (1994), when the contract had been renegotiated, with knowledge of the doctrine, provided that it was freely entered into on legal advice. Gilbert O'Sullivan had an early management agreement set aside for undue influence, and received an account of profits, in *O'Sullivan v Management Agency and Music Ltd* (1985).

Both authors and entrepreneurs may act through organisations acting collectively on behalf of their members. One result has been to produce standard contract terms.

---

72 O'Sullivan, M, 'Making Copyright Ambidextrous: An Exposure of Copyleft' (2002) (3) The Journal of Information, Law and Technology (JILT): http://elj.warwick.ac.uk/jilt/02-3/osullivan.html.

73 http:// creativecommons.org.

74 Section 176 of the Broadcasting Act 1990.

75 *Ibid*, s 175 inserting ss 135A–G of the CDPA 1988.

The Society of Authors and the Writers' Guild of Great Britain collaborated to produce Minimum Term Agreements. The Society of Authors will also provide clause-by-clause vetting of individual publishing contracts. The Publishers' Association has a Code of Practice which recognises authors' need for clarity and provides that 'the publisher should ensure that the author who is not professionally represented has a proper opportunity for explanation of the terms of the contract and the reasons for each provision'. For musical and other works and rights a variety of organisations exist and negotiate collectively. Licences to record musical works are obtained through the Mechanical Copyright Protection Society (MCPS), while the Performing Rights Society (PRS) acts for musicians and publishers in relation to performance in public and broadcasting of music. The production of film, video and television is largely a combination of employment and commission arrangements, governed by contractual terms. The Writers' Guild of Great Britain represents screenwriters and has negotiated collective agreements. In the field of artistic works a wide variety of organisations represent designers, architects, artists and photographers and, like the Society of Authors, will assist in the negotiation of individual contracts.

11.12 COLLECTIVE LICENSING AND THE COPYRIGHT TRIBUNAL

It is difficult for individual copyright owners to keep pace with the growth in technological development, which still continues to expand the scope for large-scale domestic, global, private and commercial infringement. Detection and enforcement of rights can be both difficult and expensive.

A solution adopted in Europe during the 19th century, which extended to the UK in 1914, is that of collective licensing through collective societies of copyright authors. This is particularly effective against individual infringers unaware of copyright and unlikely, therefore, to seek licences, especially if they must be sought from many individual copyright owners. The advantage of collecting societies for users of works is the need to seek only one licence for a catalogue of works, and for the copyright owner of sharing the cost and burden of detection and enforcement. The employment of inspectors is common. The danger of such an approach is the power thus conferred on the copyright owners, enhancing the monopolistic potential of their exclusive rights. This is particularly so if all the works a user may require are controlled by one society, inhibiting both choice and competition. Collective licensing is now prevalent.

It began with the establishment of the PRS in 1914, which administers performance and broadcasting rights in non-dramatic performances of musical works and literary works set to music. It is no coincidence that the introduction of the gramophone saw a relative decrease in the importance of sheet music at this time and increased emphasis on the performing right, accentuated with the introduction of radio. The PRS takes assignments of performing rights from copyright owners and, in return, distributes royalties collected in proportion to the use of each owner's works. It grants blanket licences to users of works within its portfolio, with different tariffs for different types of user. Pubs, restaurants and hotels, for example, often need and have PRS licences for music played through public address systems, and the PRS's income in 2002 exceeded

£268 million.[76] Phonographic Performances Limited (PPL) administers performing and broadcast rights in sound recordings. The user of a musical work might require licences from both. The MCPS governs reproduction rights in sound recordings. The Copyright Licensing Agency (CLA) was set up in 1982 by authors and publishers in response to the challenge of the photocopier. It grants blanket licences to educational establishments for multiple copying.

Collective licensing is also organised on an international basis through global networks of licensing agencies such as IFPI, which represents the recording industry, and the International Federation of Reproduction Rights Organisations (IFFRO). Agreements between collective licensing agencies have been reached in order to provide users with a 'one-stop shop' for licences. However, the European Commission opened competition proceedings against the Santiago Agreement for online licensing in May 2004.

The CDPA 1988 was based on this foundation, but added a considerable incentive to the establishment and activities of the collective societies by giving statutory licences for some acts unless a collective licensing scheme exists (ss 35(2), 35(3), 60(2), 66(2), 74(4) of the CDPA 1988). Copyright is evolving from a series of restrictive rights, to a right to receive remuneration from the exploitation of works. The collective societies have monopolistic potential and their powers have been abused, by the refusal of licences, or excessive royalties being charged. Manx Radio, for example, challenged the churlish amount of playing time for sound recordings ('needle-time') being granted by the PPL. It was being limited in order to support live performances and was increased from 25% to 50% by the Performing Rights Tribunal (PRT). This abuse of power can be controlled by three means: adjudication by tribunal, competition policy and the provision of compulsory licences.

11.13 UK COMPETITION POLICY

The Fair Trading Act 1973 gave either the Secretary of State, or the DGFT, authority to refer any merger or monopoly situation to the MMC. There were at least three reports on copyright, which began from the presumption that to maintain exclusivity through copyright was an appropriate question for the MMC, although copyright was necessarily exclusive. The MMC considered whether the situation referred to it operated against the public interest, which was widely defined, and recommended appropriate action. The Secretary of State could make orders to implement the MMC's recommendations, which included, in the case of copyright, compulsory licences.[77]

In 1985 the MMC held that the Ford Motor Company was abusing its monopoly in relation to car spare parts. The BBC and ITV also relied on copyright to preserve their television listings duopoly, which was found to be an abuse, although not against the public interest. In addition, the PPL was found by the MMC to be the best mechanism, and an economic necessity, for licensing rights in sound recordings, provided that it could be restrained from operating unfairly.

---

76 Press release, 9 June 2003: www.mcps-prs-alliance.co.uk.
77 Section 144 of the CDPA 1988.

Significant amendments were made to the domestic competition regime following the enactment of the Competition Act 1998 and, more recently, the Enterprise Act 2002. Although the Fair Trading Act 1973 remains in force, large sections have been repealed and replaced with a new prohibition-based competition regime in line with Articles 81 and 82 of the EC Treaty.[78] These changes are discussed in Chapter 1 (see 1.7).

11.14 THE COPYRIGHT TRIBUNAL

The CA 1956 established the PRT as a response to collecting societies. It had jurisdiction over disputes between licensing bodies and copyright users in the areas of public performance and broadcasting, with power to grant or vary licences on references made by one of the parties to a dispute. The sole criterion for decision was one of reasonableness.

The CDPA 1988 transformed this into the Copyright Tribunal, with a wider jurisdiction than that of the PRT. Chapter VII of the CDPA 1988 sets out the relevant provisions in relation to collective licensing. The tribunal is comprised of a chairman and two deputy chairmen (who are legally qualified and appointed by the Lord Chancellor), and up to eight ordinary members appointed by the Secretary of State. It sits in panels of three. Appeals on a point of law are made to the High Court.

The Copyright Tribunal has two areas of jurisdiction in all areas of copyright: over licensing schemes and licences granted by licensing bodies outside a scheme.[79] It does not have jurisdiction over licences granted by individual right owners of literary, dramatic, musical and artistic works, and films. For other rights the licences or schemes do not have to be granted by a licensing body. A licensing body is a society or other organisation which, as one of its main objects, negotiates or grants copyright licences as copyright owner, prospective owner or owner's agent and whose objects include the granting of licences for more than one author.[80]

Both licensing schemes and licences granted by licensing bodies may be referred to the tribunal for determination of the reasonableness of their terms and for orders to be made concerning the use of works covered, or not covered, by the licence. The tribunal may make orders to confirm or vary a licensing scheme, to grant a licence that has been refused, to confirm or vary the terms of a licence and to settle questions relating to royalties. Licensing schemes may also be certified by the Secretary of State and this displaces those permitted acts only provided in the absence of a licensing scheme.

The tribunal has one overriding consideration of considerable latitude, that of reasonableness. It must make an order that is 'reasonable in the circumstances'; however, ss 129–34 of the CDPA 1988 sets out specific factors to be taken into account, but which do not preclude the consideration of all relevant circumstances.[81] The tribunal asks what a 'willing licensor and willing licensee' would have agreed. It will look at prior agreements, including those with other categories of user or granted by other licensing bodies. In *Universities UK v Copyright Licensing Agency* (2002) the

---

78 See Rodger, B and MacCulloch, A, *The Competition Act: A New Era for UK Competition Law* (Oxford: Hart Publishing, 2000).

79 Section 149 of the CDPA 1988.

80 *Ibid*, s 116(2).

81 *Ibid*, s 135.

licences for schools and further education institutions were compared to that for universities.

One example of a long battle against the monopolistic potential that copyright can confer where no other source of the data contained in a copyright work exists is the battle fought against the BBC and ITV over television programme listings. The TV Listings Campaign reported that 4,500 jobs were being lost as a result of the (then only two) television companies' control over listings, and £500 million in revenue. It was shown that, in Germany, over 26 million copies of listings magazines were sold, compared with less than 6 million in the UK. Nevertheless, the copyright was upheld in *ITV Publications v Time Out* (1984) (see 8.2.3): the taking had been of expression, was not fair dealing (being competitive) and did constitute a substantial part of the plaintiff's work. In 1985, a reference was made to the MMC. It found that the copyright was being abused, but that this was not to the detriment of the public interest. Finally, s 176 of the Broadcasting Act 1990 provided a statutory duty to provide listings free of charge, while copyright could be maintained on additional programme information; and the ITV/BBC duopoly was abolished. In March 1992, the Copyright Tribunal ruled in *News Group Newspapers v ITP* (1993) that newspapers and magazines need only pay £2 million and not the £13 million sought by the licensors.

11.15 EU LAW

The European Court has displayed a willingness to consider the special characteristics of copyright over the years and has come to appreciate its growing importance in commerce generally. Copyright cases have tended to be analysed under the free movement provisions of the Treaty (Articles 28–30 (goods) and Articles 49–55 (services)) as opposed to the competition rules, Articles 81 and 82.[82]

The European Court has applied the exhaustion principle to a variety of copyright cases in relation to 'non-performance' rights. It will be remembered that the distinction between existence and exercise was first introduced in 1966 in *Consten & Grundig* (see 1.4.2). The distinction was elaborated in one of the earliest cases on copyright and Community law, *Deutsche Grammophon Gesellschaft v Metro SB-Grossmärkte GmbH & Co KG* (1971). Deutsche Grammophon (DG) marketed its records under the Polydor label in France through its French subsidiary. Metro obtained a supply of these records from an undertaking in a third country and marketed them in Germany at a cheaper price than DG. DG sued Metro for breach of its copyright. The German court referred the case to the European Court under Article 234 EC and asked whether the exercise of the intellectual property right infringed the Community provisions on free movement.

In contrast to *Consten & Grundig*, there was no agreement between the parties, so Article 81 EC could not apply. The Court was therefore obliged to consider the free movement of goods provisions of the Treaty and the exercise of intellectual property rights. The Court held that there was limited derogation from the free movement principle in Article 28 EC and that Article 28 EC only permitted restrictions on the free movement of goods for the purpose of protecting industrial and commercial property

---

82 For a discussion of copyright licensing and the EC competition rules, see Chapter 1 generally.

'to the extent to which they are justified for the purpose of safeguarding rights which constitute the specific subject matter of such property'.[83]

Consequently, the Court confirmed that it would be incompatible with the single market for DG to rely upon its rights under German legislation to prevent the importation of records into Germany, which it had consented to being placed on the market outside the German territory.[84] The Court did not expressly mention a principle of exhaustion but it is clear from the judgment that the Court considered DG to have exhausted its rights by placing the records on the French market. Nor did the Court elaborate on what it meant by the 'specific subject matter' of the right in issue, although subsequent case law has confirmed the importance of this concept in Community law[85] (see 1.4.2, 3.11 and 17.5).

As earlier sections on copyright have ascertained (see 1.4.2), the principal function of copyright is to 'protect the moral rights in the work and ensure a reward for the creative effort' of the author.[86] Although copyright covers a broad range of different works there is some agreement that the specific subject matter of copyright, however, is 'the exclusive right to reproduce the protected work'. The European Court has tended to draw a distinction between these rights, otherwise referred to as 'non-performance' copyrights and 'performance' copyrights. For instance, in *Musik-Vertrieb Membran GmbH v GEMA* (1981) the European Court had to determine whether the principle of exhaustion of rights prevented the holder of the rights in a sound recording from obtaining the difference between the UK and German royalty rates when recordings first marketed in the UK were imported into Germany by a third party. The Court held that copyright in artistic works falls within 'industrial and commercial property' in Article 30 EC and would be subject to the exhaustion principle. Thus, GEMA could not rely on its German rights to prevent parallel imports of records from the UK, which it had consented to being placed there. The Court held it was irrelevant that the difference in royalty rates was a result of UK legislation on compulsory licensing.[87]

By contrast, in *Warner Bros and Metronome Video v Christiansen* (1988) in an Article 234 reference, the European Court was asked whether the company that put video cassettes for sale on the market in the UK could restrain parallel imports into Denmark in order to protect its rental rights. The European Court held that Warner Bros could prevent parallel imports despite the fact that the company had consented to the marketing of the cassettes in the UK. The Court concluded that the exhaustion of the right of sale did not exhaust the right to hire sale. Only the right of reproduction was exhausted and not the separate performance right.

In *Coditel SA v Ciné Vog Films* (1980) the European Court had to consider whether copyright in a film was compatible with the free movement provisions of the EC Treaty, specifically Articles 49 and 50 (free movement of services). Ciné Vog had acquired from Les Films de la Boétie an exclusive right to distribute Chabrol's film *Le*

---

83   Para 11.
84   See para 13.
85   See 1.4.2 and 3.11.2.
86   Para 5 Judgment of the CFI of 10 July 1991, Case T-69/89 *Radio Telefis Eireann v Commission* [1991] ECR II–485.
87   The UK legislation imposed a fixed royalty rate of 6.25% whereas GEMA in German charged 8.5 %. The German copyright management society claimed that the recordings could not be sold in Germany without its members receiving the extra payment.

Boucher in Belgium for seven years, provided it did not show it on television for a minimum of 40 months after the first screening in Belgium. A cable company, Coditel, had picked up a transmission of the film and relayed it through its cable channel to Belgium. Ciné Vog brought an action against Les Films de la Boétie for creating a situation which did not observe its exclusive rights, and against Coditel for infringement of its rights in Belgium. Application of the exhaustion principle suggested that Ciné Vog had exhausted its right, since the film had been shown in Germany with the company's consent. However, at paragraph 12, the European Court made a distinction between cases which concerned the free circulation of goods, including literary and artistic works, and cinematographic films where the essence of the right was to control a series of performances. The Court concluded that:

> ... the provisions of the Treaty relating to freedom to provide services do not preclude an assignee of the performing right in a cinematographic film in a Member State from relying upon his right to prohibit the exhibition of that film in that State, without his authority, by means of cable diffusion if the film so exhibited is picked up and transmitted after being broadcast in another Member State by a third party with the consent of the original owner of the right.[88]

Thus, Ciné Vog's right to insist on fees for broadcasting the film was said to be part of the 'specific subject matter' of the right. However, it is clear from the Court's jurisprudence that it is difficult to pinpoint the specific subject matter of copyright in every case. The Court has also had difficulty accommodating significant differences between national laws on copyright protection through its exhaustion of rights doctrine. Unlike UK copyright law, which covers performers' rights and similar rights, most Member States draw a distinction between 'author's rights' and 'neighbouring rights'; for example, sound recordings, broadcasts and performers' rights. In 1995 the Commission published a Green Paper, *Copyright in the Information Society*,[89] outlining various proposals for harmonisation in this area of law. The outcome of the consultation was the Information Society Directive (see 8.1.5). Further harmonisation is, however, less likely at a Community level with many Member States reluctant to allow copyright harmonisation which might encroach on national traditions concerning labour relations.

Further Reading

Bainbridge, D, *Software Copyright Law* (London: Butterworths, 1999)

Braun, N, 'The Interface Between the Protection of Technological Measures and the Exercise of Exceptions to Copyright and Related Rights: Comparing the Situation in the US and in the EU' [2003] EIPR 496

Burrell, R, 'Reining in Copyright: Is Fair Use the Answer?' [2001] IPQ 361

Cohen Jehoram, H, 'Copyright and Freedom of Expression, Abuse of Rights and Standard Chicanery: American and Dutch Approaches' [2004] EIPR 275

Griffiths, J, 'Copyright Law after *Ashdown* – Time to Deal Fairly with the Public' [2002] IPQ 240

Hugenholtz, B, 'Caching and Copyright: The Right of Temporary Copying' [2000] EIPR 482

---

88   Para 18.
89   COM (95) 382 final, 19 July 1995, and the *Follow-up to the Green Paper*, COM (96) 568 final, 20 November 1996.

Lambert, P, 'Copyleft, Copyright and Software IPRS: Is Contract Still King?' [2001] EIPR 165

Picciotto, S, 'Copyright Licensing: The Case of Higher Education Photocopying in the UK' [2002] EIPR 438

Ryan, C, 'Human Rights and Intellectual Property' [2001] EIPR 521

Sinclair, M, 'Fair is Not Always Fair: Media Monitors and Copyright' [1997] EIPR 188

Tumbridge, J, 'Canada Defines "Originality" and Specifies the Limits of "Fair Dealing"' [2004] EIPR 318

CHAPTER 12

MORAL RIGHTS

Article 27 of the Universal Declaration of Human Rights recognises that the creators of any scientific, literary or artistic production have both moral and 'material', or economic, interests in their work which have a right to be protected.

The concept of moral rights[1] is relatively new in the UK. Moral rights are distinct from the copyright in a work. An author's moral rights are protected as breaches of statutory duty, not, as copyright is, a property right. They are not conferred on the entrepreneurial authors of neighbouring or derivative works, such as sound recordings or broadcasts. Nor is the protection conferred by a moral right co-extensive with the copyright in that work; for example, the right against false attribution only survives the right owner by 20 years, rather than 70 years. However, a connection to copyright lies in the fact that the work must be a 'copyright work' and remain in copyright for a moral right to come into being.

Further moral rights for performers will be granted to incorporate Article 5 of the World Performers and Phonograms Treaty (WPPT) 1996. This requires that performers shall have moral rights of paternity and integrity in their aural performances, or those fixed in phonograms. At the end of 2001 a Diplomatic Conference also considered moral rights in audiovisual performances and drafted some articles. However, no Treaty was concluded.

12.1 THE BACKGROUND

Copyright protects the economic interests that copyright owners and entrepreneurs have in exploiting a work, by providing remedies against copying or other public exploitation of works, and commercial dealings with those copies.[2] However, authors have another important interest in their work, that of their artistic reputation and integrity. The exploitation of a work aids in creating, maintaining and enhancing an author's artistic reputation and standing, provided that the author is publicly associated with the work by those who exploit it and provided that subsequent treatment of the work by others preserves the work's artistic integrity. Many copyright authors are not in a position to exploit their works themselves and are dependent on entrepreneurs (such as publishers) to do so, but copyright can only protect their artistic or 'moral' interest indirectly.

Civilian systems of copyright have long recognised additional moral rights for authors of works. These systems grew from the Roman concept of respect for authors' intellectual and artistic creativity and repugnance against plagiarism, rather than from demands made by publishers (the Stationers) in response to the challenge posed by Caxton's printing press, as did copyright in the UK. Authorship as defined by Kant and Hegel was seen as a form of self-expression reflecting an author's personal integrity and reputation. This can be seen, for example, in the higher standard of originality adopted in many Continental copyright laws, so that very factual material

---

1   From the French *droit moral*.
2   Sections 16, 22–26 of the Copyright, Designs and Patents Act (CDPA) 1988.

is not protected by copyright in France and Germany. It can also be seen in the provisions of the Database Directive[3] as implemented by s 3A of the Copyright, Designs and Patents Act (CDPA) 1988. Any attack on the work is consequently regarded as an affront to the author's person. The civilian concept of an author's moral rights in a work includes prohibition on any alienation of the moral right, unlike the economic copyright; it is also not allowed for the moral right to be eroded by notions of commercial efficacy or the interests of other parties. Article 6 of the Law of 11 March 1957 in France declares that moral rights are 'perpetual, inalienable and imprescriptible', creating a dual system of personal moral rights and economic copyright. German law treats the moral and economic interests as two side of the same coin.

However, such comparisons must be drawn with care, and the French provision is only applied with caution. It has been pointed out[4] that French courts rarely grant an injunction to enforce moral rights of an author who has parted with the economic rights in a work and damages will be relatively small, although actions for injunctions are not infrequent.

Civil jurisdictions recognise a variety of moral rights, as has the UK since 1989: to paternity, against false attribution and of integrity. However, they also recognise a right to determine whether a work is complete (a commissioned work, for example), and how it should be published (*droit de divulgation*), a right of access to the work (*droit d'accès*), and a right to withdraw a work (*droit de repentir*). The civilian moral right owner may also object to undesirable ways used to display or exploit a work and has a right to prevent the physical destruction of a work, to respond to criticism and to the loyalty of his publisher: *Editions Gallimard v Hamish Hamilton* (1986). When Picabia threw away one of his paintings he was able to successfully exercise his right of communication (*divulgation*) against a neighbour who had retrieved it in order to recover it for more effective destruction.[5]

In 1948, the Brussels Revision of the Berne Convention included two moral rights which were to last during the author's lifetime, independently of the copyright. These were:

- a right to claim authorship of a work (a right of paternity);
- and a right to object to distortion, mutilation or other alteration or action prejudicial to the author's honour or reputation in relation to the work, whether or not the copyright had been assigned (a right of integrity).

The 1971 Paris Revision requires even more extensive moral rights and that they be protected for as long as the copyright lasts. The UK is a member of the Berne Convention and ratified these revisions.

Article 6*bis* of the Berne Convention states:

> (1)   Independently of the author's economic rights, and even after the transfer of the said rights, the author shall have the right to claim authorship of the work and to object to any distortion, mutilation or other modification of, or other derogatory action in relation to, the said work which would be prejudicial to his honour or reputation.

---

3   Directive 96/9/EC of the European Parliament on the Legal Protection of Databases.
4   Lewis, B, 'The "Droit Moral" in French Law' [1983] EIPR 341.
5   Dalton, N, 'Will Remakes or Television Adaptations of Motion Pictures Give Rise to Moral Rights Claims by the Original Screenwriter and/or the Director under French Law?' [2002] Ent LR 75.

(2) The rights granted to the author in accordance with the preceding paragraph shall, after his death, be maintained, at least until the expiry of the economic rights, and shall be exercisable by the persons or institutions authorised by the legislation of the country where the protection is claimed ...

This appears to envisage that any assignment of economic rights is not accompanied by assignment of moral rights.

In the so-called 'Information Age', electronic manipulation of digitised works is a very real threat to authors. However, no provision was made for moral rights in the World Copyright Treaty (WCT) 1996,[6] although Article 5 of the WPPT 1996 requires the introduction of moral rights for performers in their live and fixed performances. Nor is there any express provision for moral rights in the Information Society Directive, although the right of communication serves as a right of *divulgation*. The conflict of interests is acute. Digital technology is becoming the stock in trade of the world of film and music production, and particularly in the creation of multimedia works drawn from a variety of sources (including copyright works) which could be held to ransom by individual authors exercising moral rights. WIPO's attempts to negotiate a treaty on audio-visual performer's rights[7] came to grief, in part, on the question of the moral right of integrity, which was to be subject to changes made for purposes such as editing, compression, dubbing or formatting.[8] However, the availability of moral right protection in other jurisdictions, particularly the stronger French rights, may provide a remedy where infringement relating to a digital work disseminated over the internet is concerned.[9]

12.2 THE UK BEFORE THE CDPA 1988

Until the CDPA 1988 came into force on 1 August 1989, there were no equivalent provisions in the UK. The traditional approach of allowing freedom of contract left relations between author and entrepreneur to whatever could be successfully bargained for by the parties. In 1952, the Gregory Committee dismissed moral rights as 'suspiciously foreign'. As a member of the Berne Convention, the UK was obliged to protect the rights of paternity and integrity, but the argument that the common law did so, albeit indirectly, prevailed. Authors were obliged to resort to protection through the torts (delicts) of defamation and passing off (see Chapter 14) and whatever they could bargain for in contract. The Copyright Act (CA) 1956, however, did contain some limited provisions. The common law situation is still of some significance, both as a measure against which the effectiveness of the new moral rights can be measured and as an alternative source of relief if moral rights fail to protect. Significantly, in *Clark v Associated Newspapers Ltd* (1998) claims in passing off also succeeded.

---

6 Although Member States are required to follow Articles 2–6 of the Berne Convention.
7 Diplomatic Conference on the Protection of Audiovisual Performances, December 2000. A further informal meeting was held in November 2003: www.wipo.int.
8 De Souza, L and Waelde, C, 'Moral Rights and the Internet: Squaring the Circle' [2002] IPQ 265.
9 See Dalton, N, 'Will Remakes or Television Adaptations of Motion Pictures Give Rise to Moral Rights Claims by the Original Screenwriter and/or the Director Under French Law?' [2002] Ent LR 75. An element of forum shopping may result in the absence of international harmonisation of moral rights.

12.2.1 Contract

Authors may bargain for any protection required when contracting with those well placed to exploit their works to the maximum effect, but only to the extent of their individual bargaining power. This will prove a handicap to a new, aspiring author who has not yet established a reputation or a demand for his works; the author, nevertheless, most in need of protection for the moral interest in his works. This will be particularly so where standard form contracts are the norm. Collective bargaining can, however, provide some balance.

In *Frisby v BBC* (1996), the author of a play was able to prevent deletion of a line which he regarded as pivotal. An agreement between the BBC and the Screenwriters' Guild contained a term that the BBC should not make structural changes without the author's consent. Frisby had granted the BBC an exclusive licence to televise the play once and the licence referred to the collective agreement. Goff J held that the agreement's terms were incorporated in the licence as an implied term and granted Frisby an injunction against the televising the altered play. It is significant that Frisby's success in this case depended on collective bargaining on behalf of screenwriters made by the Guild, rather than on individually negotiated terms of the contract.

However, in *Joseph v National Magazine* (1959), an individual author did succeed in negotiating protection for his literary integrity, but only as a well established writer in the field. Joseph succeeded in an action for breach of contract when the magazine revised an article which he had written for it because the contract provided for the article to be written in his own way. Damages were granted for the loss of the writer's chance to enhance his reputation. In *Barnett v Cape Town Foreshore Board* (1978), by contrast, an architect was unable to prevent alterations to his designs when no term could be found or implied nor a copyright prevent the building's owners from doing so.

Despite the success of Frisby and Joseph, the remedy in breach of contract seems to have three weaknesses from an author's point of view. First, an author is likely to be the party with weaker bargaining power unless very well known. Secondly, a contract may only be enforceable *inter partes* and fail to protect the author against subsequent assignees of the copyright work. Thirdly, a contract made by an employer where the author is employed will be of no avail to the author himself.

12.2.2 Defamation

The way in which an entrepreneur chooses to treat a copyright work may give a work's author a remedy in defamation. This was successful, for example, in the cases of *Moore v News of the World* (1972) and *Humphreys v Thomson* (1905–10). In the former, the actress and singer Dorothy Squires secured damages for libel (and breach of contract) when the newspaper printed an article purporting to have been written by Miss Squires herself. In the latter, the plaintiff author was held to have been defamed by a newspaper serialisation in which the names of his characters had been simplified, descriptions had been omitted and 'curtains' had been added to the serialised extracts.

However, defamation has limitations when prayed in aid of an author's moral interest. This was illustrated by *Chaplin v Frewin* (1996). Charlie Chaplin's son contributed to a 'ghost written' biography of his father, but, after second thoughts, attempted to withdraw from the project on the ground that it was defamatory. The

Court of Appeal did not agree, and Danckwerts LJ held that the assignment of copyright was purely commercial and a transfer of property for gain; therefore, the minor son's moral welfare was irrelevant: 'The mud may cling, but the profit will be secure.' In particular, treatment of a work may well tarnish an author's artistic reputation without amounting to defamation of his reputation as an individual. In addition, the claimant author will bear the onus of proving that there is a reputation to protect.

12.2.3 Passing off, injurious falsehood and breach of confidence

An action for passing off may succeed where a defendant holds out his work to incorporate that of the author's if the copyright in a work can be regarded as goodwill for that author. This may be because, for example, earlier works have proved popular enough for the work to acquire an immediate commercial potential. This was so in the case of *Samuelson v Producer's Distributing* (1932). The plaintiff had copyright in his revue, which included the right to film it. The defendant held out its film as containing the plaintiff's popular revue sketch, which it did not. The film copyright was treated as being equivalent to goodwill built up through trade and a remedy in passing off was obtained. This is, however, a controversial definition of goodwill and an extension of the ambit of the tort of passing off.

An action for injurious falsehood, or for breach of confidence, may be sources of a remedy for an intrusion into moral rights in the right circumstances. Neither these possibilities nor contract, defamation or passing off constitute a direct right of action for an author wishing to defend the moral interest rooted in a work; nor are they coextensive with the wording of Article 6bis of the Berne Convention.

12.2.4 Copyright Act 1956

The CA 1956 did provide some relief.

Section 43 of the CA 1956 provided a remedy where a work was falsely attributed to an author. It was successfully relied on by Dorothy Squires in *Moore v News of the World* (1972) because the article had been written in the first person (although it did say 'as talking to …'), despite the fact that this had not been authorised by Miss Squires. The court also held that this remedy was not restricted to professional authors, although the trial judge described the section as 'a technical cause of action'. No reputation needed to be shown. The real author could secure no remedy on the basis of this section.

Section 43(4) of the CA 1956 provided that it was actionable knowingly to sell an altered artistic work as the artist's own unaltered work without authority. The defendant copyright owner of a fine line drawing made for use in newspapers successfully relied on this action when its drawing was used in altered form on hoardings and the artist's name left on, in *Carlton Illustrators v Coleman* (1911). This was held to be an actionable alteration.

Section 8(6) of the CA 1956 provided for a statutory licence for sound recordings made of another's copyright sound recording. Recordings of adaptations of a musical work could not be made if they differed substantially in the treatment of the work in style or performance.

Section 4(3) of the CA 1956 gave ownership of the copyright in commissioned photographs, paintings or drawings of a portrait, or engravings for money or money's worth to the person commissioning the work, and not to the author of the work, thus ensuring a measure of control over the work paid for. This section was employed to protect an individual's reputation in *Williams v Settle* (1960). The family depicted in wedding photographs commissioned from a photographer were involved in a tragedy. They were able to prevent publication of the photos in the press.

Finally, the CA 1956 also provided that the copyright period subsisting in literary, dramatic and musical works, photographs, and engravings which remained unpublished at an author's death did not begin to run, allowing the author's successors the right to decide not to publish.

12.3 THE CDPA 1988

The Whitford Committee reconsidered the UK's compliance with the Berne Convention in 1977 when the UK was considering ratification of the 1971 Paris Revision. This added requirements as to the duration of moral right protection, and the Committee proposed explicit protection.

The common law approach to an author's interests were well illustrated by *Chaplin v Frewin* (1996), where the copyright of Charlie Chaplin's minor son was regarded as a commercial interest and the author's moral welfare was seen to be irrelevant despite his minority. Nor did other common law jurisdictions regard membership of the Berne Convention as requiring such action at the time. In addition, the potential that moral rights carry for upsetting contracts and even for holding entrepreneurs to ransom when preparations for exploitation of a work are well advanced, was seen as a threat in a jurisdiction based on *laissez faire* and the sanctity of contract. The Whitford Committee was anxious to avoid this conflict.

12.3.1 The four moral rights

Following the recommendations of the Whitford Committee, the CDPA 1988 introduced four moral rights, two of which were entirely new to UK law.[10] The four moral rights are:

(a) the right to be named as the author of a work – the right of paternity;

(b) the right to object to derogatory treatment of one's work – the right of integrity;

(c) the right to object to false attribution of the author of a work – the right against false attribution;

(d) the commissioner's right to privacy in relation to commissioned photographs and film, where commissioned for private purposes – the right to privacy.

The rights of paternity, integrity and against false attribution adopt a bipartite approach. First, the right to claim identification, or to object to derogatory treatment or

---

10 The US has also moved back a stage from the position that moral rights were adequately protected by the common law of unfair competition and misrepresentation, defamation, and s 43(a) of the Lanham Act, 15 USC 1125(a)(1)(A). The Visual Artists Rights Act 1990, 17 USC s 106A, gives authors of visual art rights of attribution and integrity.

false attribution is conferred on an author, apparently in general terms but, secondly, the right is enforceable only when certain specified acts are done in relation to the work.

These are personal rights given to the relevant authors whatever their nationality or residence, provided that the other criteria are satisfied. They may not be assigned,[11] although they may be transferred on the right owner's death.[12] Discovering the owner of a moral right in relation to a work may be no easy task because the copyright in the work is transmissible and divisible, as well as very long lasting, and may be entirely separate from the work's author.

12.3.2   Remedies for breach of moral rights

Breach of a moral right is a breach of statutory duty.[13] It is doubtful whether this will always secure appropriate remedies for a moral right owner, as additional damages should be available for damage to reputation. This is made clear for copyright by s 97 of the CDPA 1988, but there is no equivalent provision relating to the moral rights; yet a moral right owner may not experience any pecuniary loss at all by infringement of the non-economic moral right.

There are also significant derogations from the remedies. An injunction will be refused for breach of the right of integrity where the defendant makes a disclaimer dissociating the author from the treatment of the work complained of. Any delay in asserting the right of paternity will be taken into account in giving a remedy for breach of that right. An architect moral right owner can only secure the removal of his name from a building on breach of his right of integrity.[14]

12.3.3   The duration of moral rights

The rights of paternity, integrity and privacy continue to subsist as long as the copyright in the work subsists.[15] The right against false attribution continues until 20 years after the death of the person falsely attributed as the author or director.[16]

12.4   THE RIGHT OF PATERNITY

Section 77(1) of the CDPA 1988 sets out the right of paternity. It is given to authors of copyright literary, dramatic, musical or artistic works, and directors of copyright films. It is a right to be identified as the author or director of the work in certain situations, which are set out in the succeeding subsections of s 77 of the CDPA 1988. Broadly generalised, the right is to be identified when the work is commercially published or otherwise issued to the public. Although private circulation would be difficult to detect, it may represent no less of an affront to an author or director where it is discovered.

---

11   Section 94 of the CDPA 1988.
12   *Ibid*, s 95.
13   *Ibid*, s 103(1).
14   *Ibid*, ss 103(2), 78(5), 80(5).
15   *Ibid*, s 86(1).
16   *Ibid*, s 86(2).

The identification must be in a form likely to bring the author's identity to the notice of those receiving the disseminated work, and must be 'reasonably clear and prominent'.[17] If an author has chosen a pseudonym, initials or other form of identification when asserting the right this must be used; otherwise, any reasonable form of identification may be used.[18] The statute does not indicate whether this is to be judged by the standard of the reasonable author, reasonable entrepreneur, or the reasonable recipient of the work being disseminated. This right enables authors to establish and then maintain a reputation for their work, and to guard against plagiarism. In addition, the right extends to public disseminations of an adaptation of a literary, dramatic or musical work, as well as the work itself.

12.4.1   The need to assert the right of paternity

However, the right is subject to a major limitation, and one that is arguably inconsistent with its progenitor, Article 6*bis* of the Berne Convention. The right may not be relied on unless it has been asserted in advance of the act complained of.[19] However, the Berne Convention allows the author 'a right to claim authorship', impliedly without any preconditions attached other than the author putting his name on the work and any copies of it. Article 5(2) provides that the enjoyment and exercise of authors' rights should not be subject to any formality.

It is, then, only those bound by assertion in the correct manner against whom the right may be exercised. Costly and time consuming preparations for exploitation of a work might be wasted if an author were to make a very late claim to the right. Therefore the justification made for requiring assertion of the right of paternity is to meet the need of those dealing with copyright works to know their obligations before embarking on those preparations. However, authors may waive the right, removing this 'safeguard' for entrepreneurs.

The requirement for assertion places the onus of self-protection on authors. Placing a duty on those wishing to exploit a work to accord it its proper identification, unless relieved of it by the author, would have been more in accord with the nature of a moral right (one acquired by virtue of the act of authorship and inherent in that authorship). It could have been made a defence to any claim to breach of the right that the defendant had made reasonable and appropriate enquiries to establish the author's identity. In addition, s 78(5) of the CDPA 1988 does provide a defence if the author delays in asserting the right. Paradoxically, the economic right in the work, copyright, does arise automatically on fixation of a work. Consequently, the right of paternity as enacted in the CDPA 1988 appears a very grudging move towards moral rights in the UK, and a triumph of entrepreneurial considerations over authors' rights. This is particularly so when the exceptions to the right are taken into account.

There is no requirement that the right be asserted before, or at the time of, the transfer of economic rights, but not to do so could be made a breach of contract in standard form contracts. This would provide a pitfall for inexperienced authors for whom the ability to be identified with their work is particularly significant. Authors must not overlook the need to assert their right of paternity because being prominently

---

17   *Ibid*, s 77(7).
18   *Ibid*, s 77(8).
19   *Ibid*, ss 77(1), 78.

named on a copy, other than for artistic works, will not suffice. Once asserted, the fact that it has been should be clearly recorded on copies of the work, in order to give notice of the assertion to subsequent takers of the work.

The onus is thus firmly placed on authors to defend their rights and not on those exploiting copyright works to assume that an author should be named or even to make enquiries as to the author's wishes. In contrast, civil jurisdictions include a right not finally to decide on claiming the right until exploitation, so that the UK's diversion from the continental model is a significant one that creates complexity and confusion for little gain.

Assertion may be made in general, or in relation to a specific act or description of acts, either in an assignment of copyright in the work, or in an instrument in writing signed by the author or director.[20] For artistic works, the right may also be asserted as specified in s 78(3) of the CDPA 1988. There is a significant distinction between assertion in an assignment and assertion by notice in writing. An assignee, or anyone claiming through the assignee, is bound by the assertion without notice of it, but anyone taking rights in the work otherwise than by assignment is only bound where he or she has notice of the assertion.

12.4.2   Exceptions to the right of paternity

It is not difficult to envisage situations where a duty to name each and every author would create a considerable burden on the public dissemination of works. Consider the effect of requiring a radio disc jockey to name the author of the lyrics to every pop song played, for example, or every contributor to a collection of short factual entries in a dictionary or other compendium of information. This has not been overlooked in the CDPA 1988 and it is informative to see which entrepreneurial groups have vigorously sought protection from observance of the right. It would appear that the interests of many economic forces have prevailed.

The first exception to the right of paternity may be styled the 'disc jockey's exception'. The right does not extend to performance of a musical work, or of a literary work consisting of words intended to be sung or spoken with music, in public: s 77(3) of the CDPA 1988. The Government accepted arguments that it would be impractical to do so despite the fact that performers and composers are frequently named.

Several types of work are excluded from the right: computer programs, the design of a typeface and any computer-generated work.[21] In the case of the first two types of work, this is appropriate. These works are often created by teams, so that to identify the authors would be impractical; they are also often commercial, so that the reward is gained on first exploitation, rather than subsequent use and transfers, giving rise to a valuable reputation. The same may not apply to computer-generated works and it might have been feasible to give the right to the person making arrangements for the creation of the work in the same way as for copyright. However, if a computer-generated work is only one in which no contribution to the content of the work is made by the user of the computer, this is equally an appropriate exclusion.

---

20   *Ibid*, s 78(2).
21   *Ibid*, s 79(2).

Publishers, the press and broadcast media have secured considerable freedom in s 79(4)–(6) of the CDPA 1988. This excludes works made for the purpose of reporting current events, publication in a newspaper, magazine or similar periodical, literary, dramatic, musical or artistic works made for, or made available for, publication in an encyclopaedia, dictionary, yearbook or other collective work of reference and acts which would constitute fair dealing for the purposes of copyright and other specified permitted acts.

There are also exceptions relating to works made by employees if the act is done by or with the consent of the author or director's employer.[22]

12.5 RIGHT OF INTEGRITY

The other right which is new to UK law is the right given to authors of copyright literary, dramatic, musical or artistic works and to directors of copyright films, not to have their work subjected to 'derogatory treatment' in specified circumstances.[23] This extends the previous common law provision because artistic reputation (and not just personal reputation, as in defamation) is being protected; nor is it necessary to show any existing reputation or goodwill. The introduction of the *droit de suite* also provides some recognition of an author's personality.

Section 80(3)–(6) of the CDPA 1988 specifies the situations in which the right may be infringed. As for the right of paternity, it is public dissemination of the work that infringes; damage caused by private disparagement of a work would be likely to be minimal and difficult to detect.

Secondary infringement of this right is also provided for. Possessing or dealing with a work, or a copy of a work, which has been subjected to derogatory treatment in the course of a business will infringe the right, but only if the person doing so knows or has reason to believe the article is an infringing one.[24]

There is no requirement of assertion before the right can be exercised, but it does carry other significant limitations, in the conditions needing to be met to constitute derogatory treatment, the exceptions to the right and the remedies available for breach.

With the increasing potential for perceived derogatory treatment by digital manipulation of works by those with the economic rights to them may bring the right of integrity into increasing prominence, hedged though it is with exceptions and limitations. For those producing multimedia works from a variety of sources, the ability to do deal with those sources is paramount. It is possible that some form of compulsory licensing may be necessary to strike the balance between exploitation of works in new forms and the interests of their authors.

12.5.1 'Derogatory treatment'

Derogatory treatment is defined by s 80(2) of the CDPA 1988.

---

22 *Ibid*, s 79(3).
23 *Ibid*, s 80.
24 *Ibid*, s 83.

Treatment

'Treatment' means any addition to, deletion from or alteration or adaptation of a work. Cutting out a portion of an artistic work was conceded to constitute treatment in *Pasterfield v Denham* (1998). Treatment does not include translation of a literary or dramatic work or an arrangement or transcription of a musical work involving no more than a change of key or register.[25]

There are acts that may be taken in relation to a work that would not amount to treatment in the technical sense given by the CDPA 1988, including the manner of display or performance of a work or a work's destruction. Acts such as restoration, binding and relocation would also fall outside s 80 of the CDPA 1988. Using software to 'clean up' a DVD while viewing it might offend a director's sense of the integrity of his work.

The case of *Shostakovich v Twentieth Century Fox* (1948) is illustrative. The action succeeded in France, but failed in the US and would do so under s 80 of the CDPA 1988. The plaintiff composer's work was played correctly, but was included in a film derogatory of the then USSR.

To exclude translation leaves out one of the commonest ways of misrepresenting an author's true merit. It will infringe the copyright, but that may not lie in the author's hands. It was opposition to the right of integrity from publishers that led to this exclusion. In the same way, a change of key or register may be as damaging to a composer's reputation as other forms of treatment.

The emphasis would be better placed on the derogatory nature of any handling of the work. Art 6*bis* of the Berne Convention refers only to 'action' in relation to a work because it applies to 'any distortion, mutilation or other modification of, or other derogatory action ...'. Provided that the other action is derogatory, the nature of that 'action' is not significant. Article 6*bis* of the Berne Convention does not require, either, that the action be 'of' the work, as does s 80 of the CDPA 1988, but only that it be 'in relation to' the work. On one view, Article 6*bis* of the Berne Convention extends to the destruction of a work.[26] Enactment of the article in the Australian Copyright Amendment (Moral Rights) Act 2000[27] extends to destruction of a work.

Derogatory

'Derogatory' is defined as distortion or mutilation of the work, or treatment that is otherwise prejudicial to the honour or reputation of the author or director.[28] The Act did not make clear whether distortion or mutilation of a work must also satisfy the test of prejudice to honour or reputation or whether any distortion or mutilation will suffice. Nor was it clear whether the test of prejudice is a subjective or an objective one. Although an objective test was thought likely, such a test would give little advantage over defamation other than that it is reputation as an author or director rather than as an individual which is to be considered. In fact, a contractual remedy might prove

---

25 *Ibid*, s 80(2)(a).
26 Stamatoudi, I, 'Moral Rights of Authors in England: The Missing Emphasis on the Role of Creators' [1997] IPQ 478.
27 Which came into force on 21 December 2000.
28 Section 80(2)(b) of the CDPA 1988.

preferable. (Frisby's own subjective opinion was taken into account in *Frisby v BBC* (1996).) However, copyright in a work can be assigned without assignment of contractual rights, and the whole justification for conferring separate moral rights lies in the fact that an author may not retain the copyright in a work. In France, the test of prejudice adopted is a subjective one – the author's own view of the treatment of the work.

The UK position seems much narrower. In *Pasterfield v Denham* (1998) Overend J held that distortion or mutilation must harm honour or reputation of an artist and that a subjective sense of grievance did not suffice.

The moral right of integrity was considered in *Tidy v Trustees of Natural History Museum* (1996). The plaintiff objected to the defendants' use of cartoon drawings of dinosaurs made for the museum when they were subsequently reduced and reprinted in a book without their captions, but credited to him. He argued that the reduction in size (which was substantial) detracted from the cartoons' visual impact and gave the impression that he had not bothered to redraw them for the book. He claimed that the reduction amounted to a distortion or, alternatively, was prejudicial to his honour or reputation. Rattee J agreed that the reduction did not amount to mutilation and held, in an application for summary judgment, that he was neither satisfied that it was clear that reduction amounted to distortion, nor that the treatment clearly prejudiced the artist's reputation without evidence from the public of the effect of the cartoons on its mind. In the Canadian case of *Snow v Eaton Centre* (1982) it had been held that the test of prejudice to honour or reputation involved 'a certain subjective element or judgment on the part of the author so long as it is reasonably arrived at'. However, Rattee J held that, even if he were to accept this principle, he would have to be satisfied that the author's view was a reasonable one, necessitating an objective test of reasonableness.

Some evidence that there has been damage to an author's reputation is required, as held in *Confetti Records v Warner Music* (2003). Garage composer Andrew Alcee objected to use of his single *Burnin'* by the rap group Heartless Crew with the addition of reference to violence and drug use. Lewison J dismissed the case, in part, because no evidence of damage to Mr Alcee's reputation had been adduced. He held that s 80(2)(b) of the CDPA 1988 provided a two-part test:

(i) adaptation that amounted to distortion, mutilation, modification or other derogatory action, and

(ii) this would be prejudicial to honour or reputation.

Decisions from other European jurisdictions make an interesting contrast to the position in the UK. The case of *Huston v Turner Entertainment* (1991) in France might be regarded as reaching the high watermark of protection for integrity. The director's personal representatives sued to prevent the televising of a colourised version of the black and while film *Asphalt Jungle* in France. This was so despite contractual provision for adding colour in the US, and the fact that Huston had no moral rights in the US. As a commissioned work the movie studio held the copyright. Nevertheless, the *Cour de Cassation* held that as author Huston had moral rights which could be exercised by his estate.

12.5.2   Exceptions to the right of integrity

The exclusions for computer programs and computer generated works applies also to the right of integrity.[29] Equally, the exceptions for the press and publishers apply, so that the right of integrity does not apply to works made for the purpose of reporting current events, nor to publication in a newspaper, magazine or similar periodical. Nor does it apply to literary, dramatic, musical or artistic works made for, or made available with the author's consent for, publication in an encyclopaedia, dictionary, yearbook or other collective work of reference.[30] The press exception will extend both to the works of freelance and employed journalists. The publishers' exception recognises the need for, and skills of, an editor. The result is that the onus falls back to authors to contract for their own self-protection, with all the disadvantages that contractual protection brings.

There is another exception relating to the right of integrity, the so-called 'good taste' exception contained in s 81(6)(c) of the CDPA 1988. This allows the BBC to remove from any broadcast 'anything which offends against good taste or decency or which is likely to encourage or incite to crime or to lead to disorder or to be offensive to public feeling'. It is subject to the proviso that, where the author or director is identified at the time of the relevant act or has previously been identified in or on published copies of the work, there is a sufficient disclaimer. While there is no doubt a need for such a provision, it is widely cast. An author might prefer to offer the work on the basis that it is used uncut or not broadcast at all, rather than to see alteration of the work, particularly given that there is wide divergence of public opinions on such matters. Similar provisions relate to independent television in the Broadcasting Act 1990.

The exception does not necessarily cover all the alterations a broadcaster might wish to make, as is illustrated by *Gilliam v ABC* (1976), an American case. The authors licensed the *Monty Python* programmes to the BBC, allowing only for minor alterations and a standard clause permitted editing to allow for commercials. The programme was then sub-licensed to ABC with a term stating that it could be edited to ABC's standards. ABC broadcast the programme with 24 minutes edited out of 90 minutes of programming for advertising.[31] The plaintiffs sued successfully for copyright infringement. This case also exemplifies the need for a personal right for authors independent of the complex contractual dealings related to the exploitation of the copyright in a work.

It was suggested, but not decided, that s 80 of the CDPA 1988 should be interpreted so as to avoid interference with the Convention right to freedom of expression[32] in *Confetti Records v Warner Music* (2003). Lewison J pointed out that Article 10, ECHR recognises that this freedom must be balanced against protection for others' reputations, and that s 80 is designed to protect reputation.

---

29   *Ibid*, s 81(1).

30   *Ibid*, s 81(3), (4).

31   Said, by Judge Lasker, to cause the programme to lose its 'iconoclastic verve', as quoted by Lumbard CJ in the Court of Appeals, Second Circuit, 538 F 2d 14.

32   Article 10, ECHR.

12.5.3   Remedies for breach of the right of integrity

An author or director may not always rely on the right of integrity. This is so where the copyright originally vested in the author or director's employer, an international organisation or was Crown or parliamentary copyright and the copyright owner authorises or consents to the treatment.[33]

Disclaimers

Where an author or director has previously been identified in or on copies of a work, or is identified at the time of the relevant act, the right will not be infringed if there is a sufficient disclaimer, and the employer has authorised or consented to the act.[34]

Generally, an author or director may not be able to secure an injunction to prevent dissemination of the derogatory treatment. Section 103(2) of the CDPA 1988 provides that a court may not grant an injunction where a disclaimer would be regarded as an adequate remedy in the circumstances if:

> ... in such terms and in such manner as may be approved by the court, disassociating the author or director from the treatment of the work.

12.6   THE RIGHT AGAINST FALSE ATTRIBUTION

This is not a new right, merely a repetition of the remedy previously found in s 46 of the CA 1956. While exceeding the UK's obligations under the Berne Convention, it is the logical converse to the right of paternity. Any person has the right not to have a literary, dramatic, musical or artistic work or a film attributed to him as author or director.[35] Attribution amounts to a statement, whether express or implied, as to who is the author or director. To attribute a work to an author where it has been added to by another infringes: *Noah v Shuba* (1991).

The right is against public false attribution and will be infringed where copies are issued to the public or the work is exhibited, performed, shown or broadcast to the public.[36] Commercial dealing with such works also infringes where the person dealing knows or has reason to believe that there is a false attribution.[37] There is no requirement of any damage to assert the right: *Clark v Associated Newspapers* (1998).

This home-grown right does not carry the restrictions of the previous two moral rights; there is no need to show that the attribution is derogatory, nor is there an extended list of exceptions. The tort of defamation may still offer an attractive alternative because of both the high awards of damages made by juries and the extensive publicity such actions receive. However, damages for defamation and false attribution will not be duplicated: Dorothy Squires was awarded over £4,000 for defamation, but only £100 for the infringement of s 46 of the CA 1956 in *Moore v News of the World* (1972).

---

33 Section 82(1) of the CDPA 1988.
34 *Ibid*, s 82(2).
35 *Ibid*, s 84(1).
36 *Ibid*, s 84(2), (3).
37 *Ibid*, s 84(5), (6).

Section 84 of the CDPA 1988 was considered in *Clark v Associated Newspapers* (1998). The case was significant in that it concerned a parody and also in that the plaintiff relied both on common law and on statutory protection. The defendant newspaper published 'spoof' diaries purporting to be written by the politician Alan Clark, author of his own published Diaries. The column included a photograph of the plaintiff, an introduction which revealed the name of the true author and an explanation that the entries were imagined in the plaintiff's distinctive style. Both the action for passing off and for false attribution succeeded and an injunction was granted. Lightman J held that for the false attribution claim to succeed the plaintiff need not be a professional author, nor have goodwill or reputation as an author to protect; consequently, breaches were actionable without damage. Unlike passing off, to succeed in an action under s 84 of the CDPA 1988 it was not sufficient to show that a substantial number of the public had been misled as to the authorship of the columns. The misrepresentation made must have the meaning of a false attribution of authorship: the meaning understood by a notional reasonable reader, as in defamation. Although an express contradiction accompanying the false attribution might suffice to negate the breach of duty, to do so it would have to be as 'bold, precise and compelling' as the false statement, which was not the case on the facts.

This was not to be seen as a bar to parodies because the nature of a false attribution of authorship was a difficult question of judgment and the defendant had just fallen on the wrong side of the line. The defendant could continue to publish, provided the true authorship was made clear. The judge rejected the argument that to give the plaintiff a remedy would hinder the defendant's freedom of expression or right to parody. Freedom of expression is subject to the rights of others and the defendant had merely made an error of judgment in the presentation of this parody.

12.7 THE RIGHT TO PRIVACY

Although new to England and Wales, this right has been included in the CDPA 1988 to compensate for the changes made to the rules on first ownership of copyright in relation to commissioned works made by that Act (see 9.3.2). It was recognised at common law in Scotland: *McCosh v Crow & Co* (1903). The right applies to a person who has commissioned the taking of a photograph or the making of a film for private and domestic purposes. Where copyright subsists in the resulting work, the right is against having copies issued to the public, exhibition or showing in public, or being broadcast. A person doing or authorising one of these acts will infringe the right.[38] Exceptions are listed in s 85(2) of the CDPA 1988. Again, the home grown right is subjected to less restriction than those deriving from the Berne Convention.

While this right will serve to protect the privacy of the commissioners of such works, it will also enable them to secure exploitation rights to the works, even though copyright is owned by the photographer or film copyright owners. In *Mail Newspapers v Express Newspapers* (1987), decided before the entry into force of the CDPA 1988, the issue related to family photographs. A husband had granted exclusive rights of publication to one newspaper following an accident to his wife and took action to prevent another paper securing prints from the photographer. The issue related to whether the wife had been a joint commissioner of the photographs. Today, the moral

---

38 *Ibid*, s 85(1).

right to privacy would enable the same exploitation. However, in an action for damages, there might be an issue as to whether there had been any damage to privacy where publication was actively being sought. It has been suggested that, although an injunction might be granted, damages after the act would not lie. Aggravated damages should be available where there is injury to feelings, but it could be argued there would be no loss where exploitation was being sought. However, although s 85 of the CDPA 1988 is entitled 'right to privacy ...', the section itself makes no reference to privacy, suggesting that liability is strict; doing any of the acts will infringe, whatever the harm thereby occasioned.

Contractual protection at the time of commission could be sought, but it has been felt that this is not appropriate in the context of private commissions. This should be contrasted with the right of integrity, in which the onus to achieve protection has shifted back to the author or director.

12.8 WAIVER OF RIGHTS

It might be thought that it was inherent in the nature of a moral right that no consent could be given to the commission of a breach – as this would allow consent to an immoral act. However, in a major derogation from the usefulness of the moral rights to authors and directors, s 87 of the CDPA 1988 allows for both consent to, and waiver of, the moral rights. By contrast, French moral rights are treated as a matter of public policy, are perpetual and unassignable, and may not be derogated from by contract. Any waiver, assignment or undertaking not to assert or exercise a right is void *ab initio*.[39] Consequently French moral rights overrode the terms of the American contract (which was subject to US law) relating to Huston's *Asphalt Jungle*.[40] However, while granting the right to adapt a work does not constitute a waiver of the right to integrity, the French Supreme Court held that grant of adaptation implies a certain degree of freedom for the adapter.[41]

Any of the rights may be waived by instrument in writing signed by the person giving up the right.[42] Waiver may be made in relation to specified works or to works generally and future works, and may be conditional or unconditional; but may also be revoked.[43] Informal waiver effected by the law of contract or estoppel is also preserved.[44]

Should waiver become a standard term in contracts relating to the exploitation of copyright works, the rights would be emasculated. Given the advantages of bargaining power which entrepreneurs are likely to have over all but the most well known of authors or directors, the provision for consent or waiver is a significant inroad into the provision of moral rights. It represents victory for commercial interests over authors' and directors' personal creative interests. This inroad into the rights was

---

39 Dalton, N, 'Will Remakes or Television Adaptations of Motion Pictures Give Rise to Moral Rights Claims by the Original Screenwriter and/or the Director Under French Law?' [2002] Ent LR 75.

40 *Huston v Turner Entertainment* Civil Court 1, May 28, (1991) 23 IIC 702.

41 The *Petit Prince* Case, Cass Ier Civ, 12 June 2001.

42 Section 87(2) of the CDPA 1988.

43 *Ibid*, s 87(3).

44 *Ibid*, s 87(4).

sought in order to preserve the certainty of contracts because those exploiting copyright works feared the moral rights might interfere with commercial exploitation, regardless of contracts made. It is doubtful whether the moral rights have such power in the face of the extensive exceptions, the need for assertion of paternity, and restricted ambit of derogatory treatment. In the Consultation[45] on implementation of Article 5 of the WPPT 1996 organisations representing authors, performers and film directors expressed the view that the provision for consent and waiver materially undermine authors' moral rights.

Any need for waiver stems in part from the very wide variety of works in which copyright can subsist. This is a result of the very low standard of originality applied in UK copyright law, which leads to protection for mundane factual items of information. The potential for multiple authors exercising moral rights in compilations of such works is one of great inconvenience and expense. This is less of a danger in civil systems because a higher standard of originality is applied. Even so, it seems anomalous that these rights cannot be given away, but can be given up. However, some redress for the right owners may be secured through the contractual doctrines of restraint of trade, unconscionable bargains and undue influence. It likely that any waiver of the right of integrity would need to be expressed very clearly. However, particularly where multiple authors are concerned in works such as multimedia it is likely that authors' participation will impute agreement to modification.

Vaver[46] argues that a public interest justification for moral rights can be made out, rendering them less objectionable to the pragmatic and economic common law approach to copyright works. First, accurate labelling of authorship can guarantee that a work is the genuine product, in the manner of a trade mark. Secondly, moral rights can help authors to secure the rewards of their works in the form in which they created them. Thirdly, they can help secure the public interest in preserving cultural heritage. Finally, they give authors a bargaining chip in their dealings with entrepreneurs and can aid in equalising the balance of bargaining power. Accordingly, he argues that moral rights should not generally be waivable. At the very least he suggests they could be subjected to a 'touchstone of reasonableness'.

12.9 COMMENTARY

There are now positive express rights conferred directly on authors and directors of copyright literary, dramatic, musical and artistic works and copyright films, with potential for quick relief. They will also confer a bargaining counter on authors and directors seeking to negotiate clear contractual protection and enable the courts to begin to interpret and develop the rights. To this extent, the courts now have an important role in interpreting the rights in a constructive way.

However, the rights have been conferred in a way that is grudging and constrained, giving way to commercial considerations of convenience, thus favouring copyright owners over creators. The need for assertion of paternity, the exceptions and

---

45 Summary of Responses to the Consultation Paper on Moral Rights for Performers: www.patent.gov.uk.
46 Vaver, D, 'Moral Rights Yesterday, Today and Tomorrow', (1999) 7(3) International Journal of Law, Information and Technology.

the possibility for consent or waiver, including informal waiver, confirm this. Nor has the UK ventured towards other moral rights existing in civil jurisdictions. Significantly, actions so far fought on the basis of moral rights have also included allegations of passing off.[47]

A report for the Intellectual Property Institute by Simon Newman[48] highlights that some of the fears of the entrepreneurs were significant. The right of integrity can become an important economic weapon in dealings with adaptations of works in the record industry. In the UK, it is, at present, a common practice for authors to waive their right to integrity, allowing record companies control over adaptations. In Europe, this is not the practice, which leads to consumption of time and money in seeking the many consents necessary. This is particularly important because a marketable record is frequently an ensemble work, in which a large number of people may be able to claim rights. It is, he points out, noticeable that the UK and US recording industries are bigger than the French recording industry, which primarily serves its domestic market (although the small size of the French industry might also reflect other factors). He argues that there are also strong moral arguments against excessive regard for an author's integrity: freedom of speech, the right to do as one wishes with one's own property (record companies will often be the owners of the copyright in the work) and principles of freedom of contract. With the increasing ease of access and copying supplied by the information superhighway, these freedoms gain an increasing significance. Finally, he argues that if gaining the necessary consents becomes too burdensome, to the point of the costs of adaptations reaching non-viability, this will frustrate the authors' economic interest in their works. If a need exists, it lies in securing protection from unwise or unfair bargains, which can be achieved through contractual doctrines.

Two questions may be raised. The first is to ask why an entrepreneur should wish to exclude an author or director's name except in those cases already catered for by the exclusions for broadcasters and 'multiple' works. The second is to ask whether so many consents are really necessary if the prohibition is only against treatment considered to be objectively derogatory. The result is to require a commercial and contractual maturity from those authors and directors most in need of the protection of moral rights – those who have yet to establish their reputations.

At present there is no international harmonisation of moral rights, other than the provision for integrity in the WPPT. No comfort can be sought from the TRIPS Agreement. TRIPS does not incorporate Art 6*bis* of the Berne Convention,[49] although Article 2 also provides that nothing in the TRIPS Agreement shall derogate from the obligations Member States have to each other under the Berne Convention. This does, however, exclude moral rights from the WTO dispute settlement procedures. The moral rights were excluded on the pretext that they were not trade related, although it is not difficult to envisage trade related effects of exercising moral rights, if unwaivable, such as an artist hindering a publisher's use of drawings commissioned for publication. The US admitted that it was merely concerned to make sure that the rights were not strengthened in any way. The civil law countries interpreted this as a triumph of common law economic copyright over authors' personal rights. This was particularly

---

47 *Noah v Shuba* (1991), *Pasterfield v Denham* (1999), *Clark v Associated Newspapers* (1998).
48 Newman, S, *Moral Rights and Adaptation Rights in Phonograms* (London: IPI, 1996).
49 Article 9 of the TRIPS Agreement 1994.

so because it is incorrect to argue that it is the inability to waive moral rights that creates the potential for interference with trade for the Berne Convention does not state that the moral rights must be unwaivable (that is a matter left to national law).

Statutory provision for moral rights having been made, the onus lies on collective negotiation between authors' and entrepreneurs' organisations to fashion agreements which balance regard for authors' moral interests against the need for some freedom of manoeuvre in exploitation by entrepreneurs. After all, authors would be unlikely to secure the rewards of their creativity without the activities of entrepreneurs.

The introduction of moral rights in Australia by the Copyright Amendment (Moral Rights) Act 2000 makes express provision for codes of practice in particular industries. In contrast to the specific exceptions provided for by the CDPA 1988, the Australian legislation provides a defence to infringement of the rights of attribution or integrity if the act or omission complained of was 'reasonable in all the circumstances'.[50] Courts are provided with a number of factors to be taken into consideration. These include any practice used in the industry concerned or specified in a voluntary code of practice developed by that industry. This leaves the onus on authors and directors to negotiate with entrepreneurs to achieve the balance of interests which moral rights, as much as copyright, must achieve with the help of courts adjudicating actual examples of conflict. This would appear to be the most practical way forward, although a period of uncertainty may result as case law develops.

Further Reading

Cornish, W, 'Authors in Law' (1995) 58 MLR 1

Cotter, T, 'Pragmatism, Economics and the Droit Moral' (1997) 76 North Carolina Law Reviews 1

Dalton, N, 'Will Remakes or Television Adaptations of Motion Pictures Give Rise to Moral Rights Claims by the Original Screenwriter and/or the Director Under French Law?' [2002] Ent LR 75

De Souza, L and Waelde, C, 'Moral Rights and the Internet: Squaring the Circle' [2002] IPQ 265

Françon, A, 'Protection of Artists' Moral Rights and the internet', in Pollaud-Dulain, F (ed), The internet and Authors' Rights (London: Sweet & Maxwell, 1999)

Lea, G, 'Moral Rights and the Internet: Some Thoughts from a Common Law Perspective', in Pollaud-Dulain, F (ed), The Internet and Authors' Rights (London: Sweet & Maxwell, 1999)

Lewis, B, 'The 'Droit Moral' in French Law' [1983] EIPR 341; [1984] EIPR 11

Newman, S, Moral Rights and Adaptation Rights in Phonograms (London: IPI, 1996)

Stamatoudi, I, 'Moral Rights of Authors in England: the Missing Emphasis on the Role of Creators' [1997] IPQ 478

Sundara Rajan, M, 'Moral Rights in Information Technology: A New Kind of "Personal Right"?' [2004] IJLIT 32

Vaver, D, 'Moral Rights Yesterday, Today and Tomorrow' (1999) 7(3) International Journal of Law, Information and Technology

---

50 Sections 195AR and 195AS, Copyright Act 1968 (as amended by the Copyright Amendment (Moral Rights) Act 2000).

CHAPTER 13

DESIGN RIGHTS

13.1 INTRODUCTION

There is a marked difference between the inventive, functional products and processes which fall into the sphere of patents on the one hand; and creative, artistic copyright works on the other. However, many products which are neither inventive nor constitute copyright works are marketed with features that have an artistic, aesthetic or functional value. Considerable effort and investment is poured into the design of those features which provide a competitive edge in the market place. It is these features, either of the appearance or arrangement of a commercially exploited article, which are the subject of design rights.

13.1.1 The design field

Design rights occupy the gap in protection which would otherwise fall between patents and copyright. The economic significance of products which fall into this intermediate design sphere is considerable, ranging from the functional aspects of engineered spare parts for cars and aircraft, through the aesthetically appealing designs conferred on jars of instant coffee, kettles, toasters and the like, to the artistic qualities given to jewellery, furniture and other designer products. It might be tempting to consider that patents and copyright occupy the far ends of a scale moving from the entirely functional (consider, for example, an exhaust pipe), to the entirely artistic (works of art); and that the design rights occupy only the middle of that scale. In fact, design rights neither exclude the entirely functional, nor the commercially artistic, but they do provide protection for the median ground which would otherwise fall between the two stools of patents and copyright.

Recent developments both in the EU and internationally look set to increase the significance and value of design protection, and to remove it from its 'Cinderella status' in the intellectual property field.

13.1.2 Design protection in the UK before the Copyright, Designs and Patents Act 1988

A design is unlikely in itself to constitute an invention and, in most cases the product bearing the design will be neither new nor inventive enough to secure a patent. The origins of design law in the United Kingdom can be traced to the Designing and Printing of Linen Act 1787, and can be seen to lie in a form of copyright protection, although copyright of a very limited nature. The bounds of design protection were expanded to further types of fabric by the Copyright Design Act 1839, and beyond the textile trade to new and original design in the form of ornamentation, and the shape and configuration, of any article. It was at this stage that registration was introduced, laying the first foundations of the modern law. The Designs Registry was moved to the Patent Office by the Copyright of Designs Act 1875, where it remains today. This specific protection required registration of the design, was short-term, and required novelty and originality, making it too restricted and awkward for many industries. Statutory changes eventually resulted in the Registered Designs Act 1949 (RDA 1949), which remains in force today, though amended both by the Copyright, Designs and Patents Act 1988 (CDPA 1988), and the Designs Directive.[1]

In addition, copyright itself has always had the potential to provide a source of design protection in one of two ways. Either the documents depicting the design may be protected as literary or artistic works (underlying works) or the article bearing the design features could itself constitute a copyright work. Should copyright subsist, to make a three-dimensional copy of a two-dimensional design document would infringe; as would indirect copying of an article made to a design document (see 13.2). However, copyright protection is of considerable duration and the low standard of originality applied would make its application in the design field sweeping in extent. Until the CDPA 1988, conversion damages were available for copyright infringement. In 1988, they were abolished for copyright infringement because they were felt to be too extensive. In the Copyright Acts of 1911 and 1956 and the Design Copyright Act 1968, attempts were made to avoid an overlap between copyright and the provision for registered design. However, these did not succeed in their purpose, reaching the anomalous position (before the CDPA 1988 came into force) that entirely functional designs received the full extent of copyright protection, whereas those with an aesthetic aspect were confined to the shorter protection of the RDA 1949. The disadvantages of this were exacerbated by the inability of either law to distinguish between competitively necessary borrowing and unfair copying.

This received the attention of the House of Lords in *British Leyland v Armstrong Patents* (1986). In the face of the legislative incongruities, the House indulged in a frenzy of judicial invention. British Leyland owned copyright in drawings used to manufacture spare exhaust pipes for its Marina car. When Armstrong Patents commenced making spares compatible with the Marina, British Leyland sought to exercise this copyright in order to preserve a monopoly in the manufacture of the spares which would have lasted for the full copyright term. Armstrong Patents had used a British Leyland spare to 'reverse engineer' the co-ordinates necessary to make the exhausts and, thereby, had created its own design drawings. The House of Lords confirmed that copyright did subsist in British Leyland's technical drawings and that Armstrong Patents' exhausts, copied from the British Leyland exhaust, were indirect infringements of these. However, their lordships deplored both the monopoly that these rights created itself and its effects for Marina owners, who were compelled to repair their cars at prices dictated by this monopoly. Drawing on principles of property law, the House of Lords held both that British Leyland could not derogate from the ownership it had granted to the purchasers of Marina cars by exercising its copyright in this way and that the protection this afforded car owners extended to commercial manufacturers of spare parts.

Accordingly, the CDPA 1988 instituted a new threefold regime for the protection of designs:

(a) the application of design copyright to designs was restricted by two new permitted acts (ss 51–52 of the CDPA 1988);

---

1   European and Council Directive on the Legal Protection of Designs 1998 (98/71/EC) [1998] OJ L289/28–35, implemented in the UK by the Registered Designs Regulations 2001 (SI 2001/3949) and Registered Designs Regulations 2003 (SI 2003/550).

(b) the RDA 1949 was amended and protection was extended to 25 years; and

(c) a new right was created – the unregistered design right (UDR) – which was then unique to the UK.

13.1.3   A new European regime

Further reform has emanated from the European Union. A Directive and a Regulation have both harmonised the registered design regime, and supplemented national protection with Community-wide rights for both registered and unregistered designs, providing designers with a complex choice of means of securing needed protection. Protection is also cumulative, leaving a confused disparity of rights to be navigated through.

The Directive was implemented by the Registered Designs Regulations 2001, which came into force on 9 December 2001.

The Regulation[2] establishes a system of dual Community-wide registered and unregistered protection, but one not fully coterminous with the UK regime. It came into force on 6 March 2002. The Registered Community Design is a unitary protection throughout the EU, through registration with the Office for Harmonisation in the Internal Market (OHIM) situated in Alicante in Spain. Registration of Community Designs commenced on 1 April 2003, although applications could be lodged from 2 January 2003.

The provisions for registrability of a registered design, and protection of an Unregistered Community Design are harmonised with those of the Designs Directive. Consequently, these provisions will be discussed in relation to the Directive as implemented into the RDA 1949, where they first came into force.[3] The automatic unitary EU-wide Unregistered Community Design is of shorter duration than the national UK right and is partially intended to provide protection during the period of registration. For designs of a short 'shelf life' registration is likely to be too protracted, despite the relatively short period of three months being taken. As with UK law the registered right protects not only against deliberate copying but also independent creation; whereas the unregistered right protects only against deliberate copying.

The Regulation is not intended to supplant national schemes, though it remains to be seen whether there is continued scope for the UK UDR. However, the risk related to community wide rights lies in central revocation, as a declaration of invalidity in one Member State will result in loss of protection in all. A considerable body of case law has built up around the UK UDR, which suggests that it has proved valuable to designers. Given its longer duration it is likely to remain so. The most significant difference between the EU and UK regime lies in the protection for purely functional design provided by the UDR.

Consequently, we shall examine in turn, remaining protection through artistic copyright; registered and unregistered design in the UK, and Community design protection, both registered and unregistered.

---

2   European Council Regulation on Community Designs 2001 (EC) No 6/2002 [2002] OJ L03/1.

3   The nominated UK courts will apply the Regulation directly to Community designs, although ultimately decisions of the ECJ will prevail on interpretation of both the Directive and Regulation.

Future developments may lie in EU discussions relating to utility models, or petty patents.

13.1.4   International protection

Both the Paris Convention, and the TRIPS Agreement 1994, require their Member States to provide protection for industrial design, but only in general terms. Moves towards international protection were long hampered by the diverse means of protection for design in different countries. The Hague Agreement 1925,[4] to which the UK is not a party, provides a system of registration by deposit, and without examination, effectively a system of international filing. Each Contracting State grants or refuses protection according to their national law and for the national duration, though this may not be less than 10 years. This takes effect as if the deposit had been made in national depositories. Some countries will extend their protection to the UK registered designs; some require re-registration locally. This system was little used by UK designers so that international protection required multiple national applications.

In July 1999 a Diplomatic Conference adopted the Geneva Act of the Hague Agreement[5] and this was signed by the UK. It permits a single application to WIPO, resulting in national registered protection in all Member States specified in the application. The Geneva Act accommodates the systems of states which examine applications for registered protection. Those states examining for novelty are given 12 months to process such applications. Provision for the Geneva Act will have to be made in the RDA 1949.

13.1.5   Characteristics of design rights

Design rights are adapted to cater for three needs: competition; compatibility; and an industrial scale of production:

* competition between many products focuses on design. Think, for example, of the market in small kitchen appliances, such as kettles and toasters. Because protection only extends to features of an article, competition in kettles and toasters is not only unaffected, but is actually encouraged, because articles bearing a different design may well prove popular and profitable. Consider the sales potential of a children's plastic lunchbox depicting the latest Disney ® character, compared with one without, to appreciate this;

* where a design relates to a functional feature in an article, the issue of compatibility arises because other manufacturers may need to copy that feature in order to provide spare parts or compatible products or, indeed, to make a competing a product at all. Both spare parts for cars and accessories such as steering wheel covers provide examples;

* an aesthetic design may constitute a copyright work, but, if it is to be marketed on an industrial scale, the long term of copyright may be inappropriate.

Articles (or products) and features of design must be distinguished. There must be an article on which to place a design – on a tea cup or piece of metal farm fencing, say –

---

4   The Hague Agreement Concerning International Deposit of Industrial Designs 1925.
5   The Act entered into force on 23 December 2003.

but the design right protects only features of design which have been applied to the article (or, in the case of an unregistered design, to aspects of the article), for example, the shape of the tea cup's handle or the plastic coating applied to the top rail of the fencing in order to allow animals being penned to lean over it without harm. It is quite possible to have an article bearing some features which are protected from use by others and other features which may be copied. A competitor's version of the article may, therefore, only differ in one or two features.

13.2   COPYRIGHT AND DESIGN

Copyright subsists automatically in a qualifying artistic work. This is particularly so, as s 4 of the CDPA 1988 makes no requirement of artistic quality for works falling within s 4(1)(a)–(c) of the CDPA 1988. Consequently, first, either the drawings or models created as part of a design process or, secondly, the articles bearing the design may themselves be protected as artistic works.

Copyright in the design document

In the first instance, design documents may be protected either as literary or artistic works. This was the case in *Mackie Designs Inc v Behringer Specialised Studio* Equipment (1999). Circuit designs made up of conventional symbols for the components and the manner in which they should be connected were held to constitute artistic works. The case did not determine, however, whether such diagrams also fall within the category of literary works. Jacob J had suggested that circuit diagrams are both literary and artistic works in *Anacon Corp v Environmental Research Technology Ltd* (1994) on the basis that such diagrams constitute a list of components in a form of notation falling within the definition of writing (see 8.2.2). This was criticised, *obiter*, by Laddie J in *Electronic Techniques Ltd v Critchley Components Ltd* (1997) (see 8.2.4). The issue did not arise as s 51 of the CDPA 1988 would apply equally to either type of work. However, his view that a work can fall only within one category of copyright work would provide clarity, and is perhaps one to be preferred, particularly where the scope of protection for each differs, as is the case for artistic and literary works.

Copyright in the article

In the second instance, articles are most likely to fall within the categories of engraving (as did the mould for a Frisbee in *Wham-O v Lincoln Industries* (1985)), sculpture (the wooden prototype in *Wham-O* and the moulds for a sandwich toaster in *Breville Europe v Thorn EMI Domestic Appliances* (1995)) or works of artistic craftsmanship (furniture in *Hensher v Restawile* (1976)). In *Hi-Tech Autoparts Ltd v Towergate Two Ltd* (2002) the metal plates from which rubber floor mats for cars were made were held to be engravings. As impressions taken from engravings are also described as engravings the mats themselves also fell within this category of artistic work. The court refused to distinguish between impressions that were artistic and those that might be regarded as functional because the CDPA 1988 makes no requirement of artistic quality.

This does not mean that all design bearing articles will fall within these categories of artistic work: note should be taken of Laddie J's decision in *Metix UK v GH Maughan*

(1997) that the sculptor's attention to shape and appearance, rather than to achieving a functional effect, was relevant to subsistence of copyright in a sculpture.

Infringement

Where copyright subsists it may be infringed by indirect copying.[6] If the work is an artistic one, it may also be infringed by the making of a three-dimensional copy from a two-dimensional work and vice versa.[7] This allows for the possibility of infringement by reverse engineering (studying an article in order to recreate manufacturing drawings), as was confirmed by *British Leyland v Armstrong Patents* (1986). Whether circuit diagrams constitute literary or artistic works is therefore significant as literary works are not infringed by three-dimensional copies.

However, the CDPA 1988 introduced limits to the application of this copyright protection to industrial design, designed to preserve a boundary between copyright and industrial design. How this boundary is drawn depends largely on judicial interpretation of ss 51 and 52 of the CDPA 1988.

13.2.1   Section 51 of the Copyright, Designs and Patents Act 1988

The Berne Convention prevents removing the subsistence of copyright altogether from the works underlying a design. Section 51(1) of the CDPA 1988 provides that, though the copyright exists, it will not infringe copyright in a design document, or a model recording or embodying a design, either to make an article to the design (three-dimensional copy of a two-dimensional work), or to copy an article made to the design (indirect copying of the drawing). The section does not apply, however, if the design is to be applied to an artistic work. It must be established first whether the article falls within the definition of artistic works. If so, copyright in the artistic work and its underlying works will continue to operate in the normal way.

Design

If the article is not an artistic work, the first consideration is whether the work is a design document, or a model recording or embodying a design. 'Design' is defined by s 51(3) of the CDPA 1988 in terms equivalent to the unregistered design right and is restricted to three-dimensional features, excluding surface decoration. A design document includes any record of a design however that record is embodied.

Surface decoration

Copyright protection therefore remains for features of surface decoration in a design. While this would appear to remove two-dimensional decoration from the copyright exemption under s 51 of the CDPA 1988, it remained to be seen whether this would extend to decorative but three-dimensional designs, such as the grooves applied to the seats and backs of garden chairs in *Sommer-Allibert v Flair Plastics* (1987). In *Jo Y Jo Ltd v Matalan Retail Ltd* (2000), embroidery on designs for cardigans was held to constitute

---

6   Section 16(3)(b) of the CDPA 1988.
7   *Ibid*, s 17(3).

surface decoration, being 'the application of some decorative process to a pre-existing surface', although the claim failed on the facts. Whether a pattern formed by holes in a garment (pointelle) could constitute surface decoration was left open. Features constituting part of the garment's construction and part of its fabric, including the use of blocks of colour, were held not to comprise surface decoration. Surface decoration is therefore a process applied separately to an article after its construction (although features of construction may prove decorative).

In *Lambretta Clothing Co Ltd v Teddy Smith (UK) Ltd* (2004) the Court of Appeal confirmed that 'colourways' applied to a track top constituted surface decoration although the garment was dyed right through its thickness.[8] Jacob LJ pointed out that any other holding would mean that protection would depend otherwise on how deep a decoration went. He distinguished between decoration applied to a shape 'neither physically nor conceptually' existing apart from the shape, as these were, and pictures or logos which could equally be applied on another substrate. To the extent that this leaves a gap in protection between copyright and UK unregistered design right, Jacob LJ said, *obiter*, that the Community Unregistered Design would have applied had it been in force.

That surface decoration may be three-dimensional, and may also have an incidental functional effect was held in *Hi-Tech Autoparts Ltd v Towergate Two Ltd* (2002). On the facts, however, designs for rubber floor mats for cars with projecting anti-slip features underneath, were found to be so primarily functional as not to constitute surface decoration. They were 'an important part of the configuration of the article as a whole', not merely decorative features with an incidental functional effect like the beading in *Mark Wilkinson Furniture v Woodcraft Designs* (1998).

Design for an artistic work

The second consideration must be whether the design is 'for' an artistic work. Consider a cartoon drawing, made for publication in a comic strip, but subsequently merchandised as a toy (a Popeye doll), as in *King Features Syndicate v O and M Kleeman* (1941). Would the original cartoon drawings be regarded as a record of a design made for the toy? The section apparently draws a distinction between a copyright drawing and a design document. It is possible that either the artist's intention in making the drawing will be considered, with all the difficulties of proof that that may create, or that an end result test will be adopted – asking whether the product is an artistic work or an industrial article. If a test of intention is adopted, so that full copyright protection is awarded to the cartoon drawing, any subsequent industrial application made from it will be subject to the reduction of copyright term imposed by s 52 of the CDPA 1988. Additionally, however, it is unclear whether any test of intention will be subjective or objective.

Permitted acts

Section 51 allows for three otherwise infringing acts. First, it exempts from a finding of copyright infringement either making an article to the design or, secondly, copying an article made to the design. Thirdly, the exemptions from copyright infringement also

---

8   With Mance LJ dissenting on this point.

extend to issuing to the public, including in a film, or broadcasting anything the making of which is exempted by s 51(1) of the CDPA 1988.[9]

The second category of these acts was illustrated in the 'Teletubbies' case, *BBC Worldwide Ltd v Pally Screen Printing Ltd* (1998). The defendant made and sold clothing on which pictures of the Teletubbies characters were printed. In the first group of products at issue these pictures were apparently copies of a photograph of the characters published on the cover of a magazine. In the second group of garments they were drawn from the television show itself. In both cases this was found to constitute indirect copying of the characters, the 'articles', themselves. That there had been copying to a substantial extent was clear. However, there was no copyright infringement as s 51 applied. Accordingly, in the case of the latter group of products, the BBC argued that the exempted act of copying an article made to a design should only apply to exclude copyright infringement if it resulted in another three-dimensional article. If this were so, the two-dimensional pictures on the clothing would still infringe their copyright.

The argument was predicated on the assumption that the legislature only intended to remove copyright from materials falling properly within the scope of design right protection. It was roundly rejected by Laddie J in an Order 14 application for summary judgment (and followed in *Mackie Designs Inc v Behringer Specialised Studio Equipment Ltd* (2000)). Although the defendant's activities might be considered wrongful, he concluded that there will be hard cases at the borderline between copyright and design protection as only some types of infringement were included in 51. He did also point out that his conclusion was based on the assumption that the original drawings from which the indirect infringement derived were design documents for something other than an artistic work. The Court of Appeal in *Lambretta Clothing Co Ltd v Teddy Smith (UK) Ltd* (2004) agreed. In so doing it rejected the argument that whatever is worth copying is worth protecting, as has the High Court of Australia in *Network Ten v TCN Channel Nine* (2004).

Infringing acts

Finally, not all the acts which might infringe the copyright in a design document or model have been excepted from infringement. Any other infringing act relating to design documents or models continues to infringe, such as making a photocopy of design drawings.

The effect of s 51 of the CDPA 1988 on a design document or model is that a competitor may use any drawings legitimately in their possession, and they may make their own drawings or model from the design owner's article. However, they may do so only in order to make the competing article.

13.2.2 The interpretation of s 51 of the Copyright, Designs and Patents Act 1988

Section 51 of the CDPA 1988 raises a further question of interpretation. Because designs for artistic works fall outside the section's ambit, renewed emphasis may be

---

9   Section 51(2) of the CDPA 1988.

placed on defining a work of artistic craftsmanship. By implication, artistic 'quality' will be relevant to s 4(1)(c) of the CDPA 1988, although it is not clear whether this is a reference to the merit of a work, or its nature (see 8.8.3). Should the design document be for a work falling within s 4(1)(a) of the CDPA 1988, this may not preclude consideration of the artistic nature of the work.

13.2.3 Non-derogation from grant

If s 51 of the CDPA 1988 does not apply to a design because the article to which it is applied is an artistic work, the *British Leyland* 'spare parts' principle may continue to apply as s 171(3) of the CDPA 1988 preserves any rule of law preventing the exercise of copyright. To the extent that it does so, its application has been limited by two subsequent cases. The Privy Council refused to apply the principle in the Hong Kong case of *Canon Kabushiki Kaisha v Green Cartridge Co (Hong Kong) Ltd* (1997), where features of 'unfairness and abuse of monopoly' were not 'plainly and obviously present'. Canon attempted to prevent Green from manufacturing spare cartridges for Canon photocopiers by relying on the copyright in drawings for replacement components included within the cartridges. The Privy Council would not apply *British Leyland* because Canon sold photocopiers at highly competitive prices, reaped any profit made from the 'aftermarket' in sales of cartridges, and already faced competition from the activities of cartridge 'refillers'.

Jacob J also considered the defence in *Mars UK Ltd v Teknowledge Ltd* (1999) (see 7.5.3) in relation to copyright in computer programs, and the database right. *Obiter*, he denied any continuing application of the exception to industrial design (see 10.8.2), and also held that it did not apply either to programs or database rights (where directives apply). However, to the extent that he might be wrong, or that the defence continues to apply to other types of copyright work, he found that where the purchasers of a protected product are not ordinary consumers but buyers of sophisticated devices they would expect to look to the manufacturer for repair, service and updating. In addition, he found that the updating of the machines at issue went further than repair. Consequently, no *British Leyland* defence could apply.

13.2.4 Section 52 of the Copyright, Designs and Patents Act 1988

Where an artistic work is exploited by an industrial process by or with the permission of the copyright owner, s 52 of the CDPA 1988 effectively reduces the period of copyright to 25 years, measured from the end of the year of first marketing of the articles. This period is equivalent to registered design protection and prevents copyright from providing longer protection for works of applied art than could be secured by registration. The Berne Convention requires 25 years of protection for works of applied art. Section 52(2) provides that copying in order to make articles of any description after this period will not constitute infringement. Other infringing acts remain subject to the full term of copyright protection; it would, for example, continue to infringe if the artistic work in its unapplied state were to be photographed.

The Copyright (Industrial Process and Excluded Articles) (No 2) Order 1989 provides that an article is made by an industrial process if it is one of more than 50 articles which all fall to be treated as copies of a particular artistic work, but do not together constitute a single set of articles; or consists of goods manufactured in lengths or pieces which are not hand made. This implies that if less than 50 articles are made by a process of manufacture in lengths or pieces the s 52 exception will also apply to those articles. Articles of a primarily artistic or literary nature are not subjected to the s 52 reduction of protection for applied art. Sculpture not intended to be used as models or casts in an industrial process; wall plaques, medals and medallions; and other printed literary and artistic matter (including book jackets, calendars, certificates, coupons, dress-making patterns, greetings cards, labels, leaflets, maps, plans, playing cards, postcards, stamps, trade advertisements, trade forms and cards, transfers and similar articles) all receive full copyright protection.[10]

The advantage of copyright protection lies in the lack of a need to register. In addition, moral rights will apply to the artistic work.

13.3   UK REGISTERED DESIGN RIGHT

The registered design right is governed by the RDA 1949, as amended by the Registered Designs Regulations 2001.[11] This amendment was to implement the Designs Directive, which harmonises registered design protection in the EU. Further amendment was made by the Registered Designs Regulations 2003, which came into force on 1 April 2003.

The Directive harmonises the law in relation to subsistence of protection, the rights of the proprietor, infringement, exceptions and grounds for invalidity; with the effect that a good deal of the old case law ceases to be of direct relevance. Provisions as to sanctions, remedies and enforcement are left to national laws, as are procedural matters concerning registration, renewal and invalidity. The new right applies to any design applied for or registered after 9 December 2001.

Transition after the Designs Directive

The old law is not wholly redundant, however. Designs registered in 2001 under the old law, and renewed for their full term will not expire until 2026: the old law will remain relevant for some time to come, but to a limited extent. The old law, the RDA 1949 as it was immediately before amendment, continued to apply to applications which were pending when the Registered Designs Regulations 2001 came into force for the purposes of registration, and where those applications resulted in successful registrations the old law continues to apply to questions of invalidity, which may also be raised in infringement proceedings, after 9 December 2001. Designs registered after 1989 still in force on 9 December 2001 also remain subject to the old law where validity is concerned. However, the *new* law will apply to these registrations for questions of infringement. Consequently, it ceases to be relevant whether the design was registered in relation to a particular article, or to sets of articles; instead it will infringe to use the design for *any* product.

Acts carried out before the commencement date and non-infringing under the old law also continue to be non-infringing and the newly defined right will not allow the

---

10   *Ibid*, s 52(4) and Article 3, Copyright (Industrial Process and Excluded Articles) (No 2) Order 1989.
11   The Regulations came into force on 9 December 2001.

design's proprietor to prevent the continuation of such acts.[12] It is also then necessary to understand the old law relating to infringement and the excluded features which may be taken from a registered design.

Transition after the Designs Regulation

The 2003 amendments relate to the Community Design Regulation, introducing the Registered Community Design. They will apply to applications and registrations made after 1 April 2003 ('post 2003 designs'). Applications pending, and registrations resulting from pending applications will be subject to the '2001 version' of the RDA 1949.

The old and new regimes will be discussed here: first the old law, then the new. Aspects that remain common are included first.

Registered design protection gives a design's proprietor a maximum 25-year monopoly over the design, renewable in five-year periods, and is granted after examination for novelty, provided that it is novel. The distinguishing feature of a registered design under the old law was the requirement of eye-appeal. This has been removed, but appearance remains a significant criterion, as is clear from the requirement of individual character. The appearance need be neither artistic nor aesthetic, but must have visual aspect.

Another important change is that the new law no longer requires a distinction to be drawn between an article and a design.

13.3.1 Registration

Applications for a registered design are made to the Designs Registry, part of the Patent Office.[13] The application must be accompanied by a representation of the design. There is provision for modification of designs during the application. Specific provision for this is found in the Registered Design Rules 1995.[14]

Ownership is governed by s 2 of the RDA 1949. Normally, the right is granted to the author of the design as its original proprietor. There are four situations that differ from this. A person commissioning a design is taken to be the original proprietor of the design. In addition,, where the designer is an employee and the design is created during the course of employment, the employer is treated as the original proprietor. The person making the arrangements for the creation of a computer generated design is the original proprietor. In addition, if an unregistered design right subsists in the same design, the application must be made by the owner of the unregistered design right. The proprietor need not qualify for protection in the copyright sense, but must have an address in the UK. The Crown may make use of a design, as it may a patent or unregistered design.[15]

The date of registration, important to any question of novelty, is that on which an application is made. An application may claim priority from an application in any

---

12 Regulation 14(3) and (4) of the Registered Designs Regulations 2001.
13 Section 3 of the RDA 1949.
14 As amended by the Registered Designs (Amendment) Rules 2001.
15 Schedule 1 of the RDA 1949.

Member State of the Paris Convention if made within six months. Modification of the application may affect the date on which it is deemed to have been made.

Once an application has been made, it is examined for novelty (and individual character under the new law) by the Registry and the granting of the right takes about three months. Articles made to the design may be sold once the application has been made.

The initial grant is for five years from the date of registration; this can be renewed up to four times, for a maximum overall term of 25 years.[16] Only infringements taking place after the date of grant are actionable.[17] There is no provision for opposition to grant by third parties, but the registrar may cancel a registration on the application of any person interested on the grounds in s 11ZA of the RDA 1949.

13.3.2 Remedies and offences

The Act does not make specific provision for remedies other than for groundless threats. Injunctions and damages are available. Section 9 of the RDA 1949 provides that damages shall not be awarded if the defendant proves that he was not aware, and had no reasonable grounds for supposing, that the design was registered. An account of profits may nevertheless be available. Section 9(2) also provides that this does not affect the court's power to grant an injunction. Orders for the delivery up or destruction of infringing articles may also be available.

Section 26 of the RDA 1949 provides a remedy for groundless threats of proceedings (see 19.10). A person aggrieved by such threats may bring an action for a declaration that the threats are unjustifiable, an injunction, or damages; provided that the defendant cannot prove that the acts for which proceedings are threatened would not constitute an infringement. Threats which can be justified may be made. Mere notice that a design is registered does not constitute a threat.

The RDA 1949 also provides for criminal offences. It is an offence to make or cause a false entry to be made on the register, or a counterfeit copy of an entry.[18] A person will also be liable to a summary conviction or a fine for falsely representing that a design applied to or incorporated in a product he sells is registered, or to mark a product with the word 'registered' or otherwise to imply a right subsists when a design registration has expired.[19]

13.4 THE OLD LAW

A design in respect of an article which was new and whose appearance was material could be registered. A design comprised features applied to an article which appealed to, and were judged by, the eye.[20] Some features were excluded from registrability. While designs may no longer be registered under the old criteria, these remain important to determinations of validity (see 13.4.7). The old law distinguished between

---

16 Section 8 of the RDA 1949.
17 *Ibid*, s 7A(6).
18 *Ibid*, s 34.
19 *Ibid*, s 35.
20 *Ibid*, s 1(2).

the design, an intangible concept, and the article to which it was applied. The design had to be registered in relation to a specified article.

Confusingly, reference must still be made to the now amended RDA 1949 and the Registered Design Rules 1995, but these are references to them before amendment in 2001 and 2003. Unfortunately, the Act has not been officially republished[21] in its amended forms after the Registered Designs Regulations of 2001 and 2003, as it was in the CDPA 1989.

13.4.1 Article

The concept of an article had significance in relation to two questions. The first was in relation to the medium or object used to 'carry' the design; the second, to the exclusion of some so-called 'must match' features. A design was registered in respect of an article and, if the design was to be applied to different articles, separate registrations had to be made for each. Where the design was to be applied to something not made and sold separately, it was not 'applied to *an* article' and no registration could be made.[22] Consequently, registration was refused for a design for the face of an ammeter in *Sifam Electrical v Sangamo Weston* (1973). The face would only ever form part of a finished product (the ammeter) to be sold to the consumer and could not be treated as an article in its own right.

Parts for articles

This principle was applied to designs for car parts in *R v Registered Designs Appeal Tribunal ex p Ford Motor Co Ltd* (1994), where the House of Lords upheld the decision of the Registered Designs Appeal Tribunal. Ford had applied to register designs for components, such as rear lamps, a front bumper, door panels and wheels. The tribunal drew a distinction between parts for another article which could be termed 'accessories' – which were registrable – and those that were 'spares' – unregistrable. Articles which, while on the car, were subsidiary to the car's shape (although contributing to its appearance were capable of being substituted without affecting the car's overall shape and appearance or identity) fell into the registrable category of accessories. These were articles which could be made and sold separately. However, components, such as door panels, which had no general use except as replacement components, although sold as spares to replace damaged or worn parts, were unregistrable because they fell outside the definition of 'article'.

The article and the design were distinguished from each other. Although the registration was for an article, protection was for the design: otherwise, a monopoly over a type of article (which could be functional, such as a chair or table, or decorative such as an ornament or necklace) could result. The design was the particular appearance (two- and/or three-dimensional) given to the object (a William Morris or Chippendale chair, for example). However, a design was (and is), in turn, made up of 'features'. Not all of a design's features fell within the definition of 'design'. Protection given by design registration only extended to the features which were registrable. The presence of other features in the design did not prevent registration, but the use of

---

21 Unofficial versions may be found on the Patent Office website: www. patent.gov.uk.
22 Section 44(1) of the RDA 1949.

those unregistrable features by others did not infringe the right.[23] Registration itself was only refused if all features of a design were unprotectable. This rule was confirmed by Lord Oliver in *Interlego v Tyco* (1988) and expressed in s 7(6) of the RDA 1949.

Sets of articles

Although different applications had to be made for a design to be applied to different articles, registration of one design could be made for a 'set' of articles. Articles comprised a set if they were sold or intended to be used together and the identity of the design did not vary sufficiently to alter its character within the set.[24] Accordingly, the features claimed as comprising the design were relevant. A set of cutlery bearing the same pattern on the handle could only be registered as a set if the pattern or ornament was the design. If the design comprised features of shape and configuration, the pieces had to be registered separately because, for example, the forks, spoons and knives would differ sufficiently to alter the identity of the design.

13.4.2 Design

Section 1(1) of the RDA 1949 defined 'design' for the purposes of registered design protection. This can be contrasted with the definition used in ss 51 and 213 of the CDPA 1988. A design comprised 'features of shape, configuration, pattern or ornament applied to an article by an industrial process'. The RDA 1949 defined neither 'shape', 'configuration', 'pattern' nor 'ornament', but the inclusion of features of pattern and ornament extended registered design protection to two-dimensional features of surface and decoration, such as those applied to wallpaper and textiles. Ornament may be three-dimensional: *Sommer-Allibert v Flair Plastics* (1987).

The phrase was considered in *Kestos v Kempat* (1936):

> Shape and configuration are for all practical purposes considered as synonymous ... Each signifies something in three dimensions; the form in which the article is fashioned. Pattern and ornament can ... be treated as practically synonymous. It is something which is placed on the article for decoration. It is substantially in two as opposed to three dimensions. An article can exist without any pattern or ornament upon it, whereas it can have no existence at all apart from its shape or configuration.

Shape and configuration were distinguished in *Cow v Cannon* (1961), where shape was taken to describe the overall outline or form of the article, and configuration denoted the contour of the article's surface. The shape of the article and the shape which amounts to the design can be distinguished.

13.4.3 Excluded features

Some features otherwise falling within 'shape, configuration, pattern and ornament' were excluded from 'design'. This was to allow for legitimate competition, preventing protection of features which a competitor had to use to make the same article or spare

---

23 *Ibid*, s 7(6).
24 *Ibid*, s 44.

parts for another article. Section (1)(a) of the RDA 1949 applies to all features, whether shape and configuration, or pattern and ornament.

A method or principle of construction

To allow monopolisation of such a method or principle would have deprived other manufacturers of one of the basic building blocks for constructing the relevant type of article. There was little judicial interpretation of the sub-section, but, in *Swain v Barker* (1966), registration was refused to the sides of a wire filing tray arranged in semi-circular shapes without corner supports because it was merely a feature arising from a principle of construction. In *Moody v Tree* (1889), registration was refused to a basket the pattern upon which was determined by the method of weaving.

Paragraphs (i) and (ii) of s 1(1)(b) of the RDA 1949 applied only to *features* of shape and configuration.

Features dictated solely by the function which the article has to perform

Because features which are entirely functional were excluded, others remain free to use functional features. Registered design can therefore be given monopoly protection. Originally, this exclusion was interpreted to mean excluding features chosen for their function where no other feature could be used in the alternative (no design freedom). In *Cow v Cannon* (1961), raised ribbing on a hot water bottle with an insulating function was registered because the ribbing could be arranged differently by another manufacturer. The House of Lords reconsidered this interpretation in *Amp v Utilux* (1972). The shape of an electrical terminal for use in washing machines was held to be unregistrable because the shape was functional – it had been chosen for functional reasons – even though another shape might have been used (there was design freedom).

The result was a decline in the number of registrations and the exclusion was considered once again by the Privy Council in *Interlego v Tyco* (1988). At issue was the registrability of the large plastic Lego building bricks made for toddlers. The shape of the raised knobs and underlying tubes into which the knobs fitted in order for two bricks to be joined had been adopted to achieve that function, but also in order to add to the brick's visual appeal. Lord Oliver said that, if the shape had been chosen only for functional reasons, it would fall within the exclusion, even if another shape could have been adopted, but that, where both aesthetic and functional reasons had contributed to the choice of shape, the feature was not dictated solely by function and would not be excluded from protection.

Features dependent upon the appearance of another article of which the article is intended by the author of the design to form an integral part

This is known as the 'must match' exception, introduced by the CDPA's amendments to the RDA 1949. It prevented a 'British Leyland spares monopoly', although the House of Lords expressly excluded registered design from their judgment. Design protection could have equally anti-competitive effects and a report of the Monopolies and Mergers Commission in 1985 criticised the refusal by Ford to license the reproduction of spare parts. The exception does not apply to components of articles sold in sets, such as the pattern applied to a dinner service.

The 'must match' exception was argued in *R v Registered Designs Appeal Tribunal ex p Ford Motor Co Ltd* (1994). The Registered Designs Appeal Tribunal held that the spare parts also fell within the 'must match' exception, whereas the accessories did not. The car as a whole (including the door) constituted the 'other article' referred to, the matching 'article' was the spare part, and this part was necessarily dependent on the appearance of the car, as it formed an integral part of it. The tribunal rejected the suggestion that the car should be considered without the component at issue (the 'n–1 approach') to be the 'article', as the part's designer had always intended it to form part of the completed vehicle. In contrast, the accessories were not dependent on the appearance of the car, although they might be chosen to blend in with its style. The House of Lords confined its decision to the definition of 'article'.

A wide interpretation of the 'must match' exception was aimed at achieving a freely competing aftermarket. Lord Beaverbrook said, during the committee stage of the Copyright, Designs and Patents Bill in the House of Lords: 'Where the circumstances compel copying we believe the need for competition in the aftermarket must prevail.' The wording of the sub-section would not accommodate the economic considerations taken into account by the Privy Council in *Canon Kabushiki Kaisha v Green Cartridge Co* (1997), as the criterion used is of the visual and structural compatibility with the 'other article'.

13.4.4 Eye-appeal

Features to be registered had to have 'appeal to' and be 'judged by the eye'. The structure of s 1(1) of the RDA 1949 suggested that it must first be determined whether the features were of shape, configuration, pattern or ornament, then, secondly, whether those features had the so-called eye-appeal, before, thirdly, considering whether any should be excluded. This sequence was criticised by Fellner,[25] for leading to the expenditure of wasted time and unnecessary costs on the consideration of argument and evidence relating to eye-appeal when the exclusions may settle the matter. However, the Privy Council did adopt this approach in *Interlego v Tyco* (1988).

In *Amp v Utilux* (1972), the House of Lords set out three principles:

(a) to have eye-appeal, the features had to be externally visible (the electrical connector at issue was an internal component of a washing machine); where a feature was internal to the article for which it is registered, the covering had to be transparent;

(b) the feature had to appeal to the customer's eye; and

(c) the eye-appeal needed to be neither artistic nor aesthetic, provided that some appeal was created by distinctiveness of shape, pattern or ornamentation calculated to influence the consumer's choice.

This last point seemed to open the way to the finding of eye-appeal in almost any article, the epitome being the registration of the design for the underneath of a shower tray, invisible once installed, in *Gardex v Sorata* (1986). The shape adopted in *Amp v Utilux* (1972) found no 'eye-appeal' because the part, although visually distinctive, was

---

25 *Industrial Design Law* (London: Sweet & Maxwell, 1995).

entirely functional and would not affect the consumer's choice. This was distinguished in *Interlego v Tyco* (1988), where the toy brick's shape, although functional, did have a visual appeal which would affect the buyer's choice. That eye-appeal was related to the buyer's reasons for choosing an article was embodied in the RDA 1949 by the requirement for eye-appeal to be material (see 13.4.5).

13.4.5 Material appearance

Section 1(3) of the RDA 1949 required that a design should not be registered if the appearance of the article was not material. This reflected the interpretation given to eye-appeal in *Amp v Utilux* and *Interlego v Tyco*. A two-stage test of materiality was set out and a design's eye-appeal was not material:

- if aesthetic considerations were not normally taken into account to a material extent by buyers or users of that description of article; and

- would not be taken into account if the design were to be applied to the article in question.

As a result, purely functional design, where visual appeal was irrelevant to the article, was confined to the unregistered design right. Examples given by Lord Beaverbrook in the committee stage in the House of Lords included structural girders, ordinary nails and screws. The addition of this requirement reversed the result in *Gardex v Sorata* (1986). From *Interlego v Tyco* (1988), it appeared that, provided a particular article in question had an eye-appeal that would influence a purchaser's choice, eye-appeal could be shown.

Test of materiality

However, two interpretations of the materiality test were possible. The first would embody the same approach: functional articles whose visual appearance would not normally be taken into account by purchasers or users (bottles of household bleach, for example), and would not normally be registrable, would become registrable if the applicant showed that application of a particular design to that article would give it a competitive edge and influence consumers' choice for visual rather than functional reasons. This interpretation effectively allowed the materiality of the eye-appeal to be presumed if the article fell within a category of articles whose visual aspect could ordinarily be expected to affect a consumer's choice; the Design Registry being able to build up a list of such category of articles, requiring evidence of the materiality of eye-appeal only in the case of an unusual type of article. The second potential interpretation was more stringent, posing a double test which required the applicant to show both that, despite what might have been expected from the nature of the article, consumers were interested to a material extent in the appearance of the article, and that this interest would be maintained if the particular design in question were to be applied to that article.

It may be difficult to distinguish the causes of consumer appeal. Consider, for example, a distinctively shaped jar for instant coffee, which may be purchased for subsequent use as an attractive storage jar; or a bottle of household disinfectant with a distinctively shaped neck which makes its use in cleaning underneath overhanging surfaces easier, but which is also distinctive and even appealing. In the former case, the eye-appeal may well have been material, although use for storage is functional whereas, in the latter case, the appeal may have been functional alone. The price that a consumer was prepared to pay for a 'designed' article, as opposed to one without such a design, could have be relevant, although this would have no necessary implications as to whether the choice was aesthetic or functional.

13.4.6 Novelty

A design had to be new to be registrable.[26] The comparison was not confined to the same article, or type of article, as that to which the design was to be applied, but was made with any article. It was made with designs registered in a prior application, or those published in the UK before the date of the application.[27] A design was published if it was freely available to the public. This was domestic novelty, as opposed to the absolute novelty required for a patentable invention. Where the comparison was to a design previously published in a document, the publication needed to contain clear and unmistakable directions to make an article bearing the design, and not merely comprise an artistic work: *Rosedale v Airfix* (1957). Where an artistic work depicted the design ('a corresponding design'), the design could be registered provided that the copyright owner's permission was given and that the artistic work had not been industrially applied.[28]

A design was not new if it was the same as an earlier design, nor if it differed from the earlier design only in immaterial details, or in features which were variants commonly used in the trade. To secure registrability, a designer had to add skills of a design nature to the prior art: *Phillips v Harbro Rubber* (1920). To determine whether a design was the same as an earlier one, the similarity was judged by eye alone. The comparison was not made as if the person comparing had both designs at hand, but made allowance for an imperfect recollection of the previous design. Judicial *dicta* imply that the comparison was to be made with a designer's eye, rather than a consumer's.

Because comparison was with designs for all articles, a designer was protected from anticipating his own design where a later application was sought so as to apply the same design to another article, or similar design to the same or another article.[29] This provided that the earlier registration would be ignored for the purposes of novelty, but the subsequent registration was confined to whatever period remains of the original design term.

13.4.7 Invalidity

The Registrar may cancel the registration of a design, either upon request by its proprietor, or on application by 'any person interested'.[30] The validity of a registration can also be raised in infringement proceedings. It is at this point that the old law

---

26 Section 1(2) of the RDA 1949.
27 *Ibid*, s 1(4).
28 *Ibid*, s 6(4), (5).
29 *Ibid*, s 4.
30 *Ibid*, s 11(1), (2).

remains significant because the grounds on which such a claim may be made relate to the provisions governing the registrability of the design under the old law.[31]

The grounds are:

- that the design was not new;

- any other ground on which the Registrar could have refused to register the design (such as eye-appeal, and materiality).

13.4.8 Infringement

For acts commenced after commencement of the new law, the new law determines infringement of designs registered under the old law.[32]

The registered proprietor of a design was given the exclusive right to commercially exploit articles to which the design, or one not substantially different, was applied.[33] This right was infringed by anyone doing anything within the exclusive right without permission. It also infringed to make a kit of components which, if assembled, would infringe.[34] There was also provision for contributory infringement: making anything which enabled an infringing article to be made (such as a mould).[35] Contributory infringement did not extend to components within a kit that would not be registrable in their own right, such as nails and other fastening devices, nor to a kit of parts for an article to be assembled for private purposes: *Dorling v Honnor Marine* (1964).

Comparing designs

The infringing article had to bear either the same design as or one not substantially different – to that which was registered. As a question of mixed fact and law the *Designer's Guild* test of appellate function was applied and the trial judge's decision would not be overturned unless he misdirected himself or erred in principle. As registration was for the whole of the design, the comparison made was of the registered design and the infringing article, and it was the whole of the shape and configuration of the design which was taken into account. Where the infringing article was not the same as the design registered, similarities and differences between the two were then noted, as described by Russell LJ in *Benchairs v Chair Centre* (1974):

> As we see it, our task is to look at these two chairs, to observe their similarities and differences, to see them together and separately, and to bear in mind that in the end the question whether or not the design of the defendant's chair is substantially different from that of the plaintiff is to be answered by consideration of the respective designs as a whole; and apparently ... viewed as through the eyes of a consumer or customer.

This was done both by comparing the design and article side by side, and on a 'now and later' basis whereby the interested customer comes back to the infringing article. This enabled the court to conclude which of the design's features would appeal to and

---

31 Regs 11–13, Registered Design Rules 2001.
32 Regulations 11(4), 12(4) 13(5) of the Registered Designs Regulations 2001.
33 Section 7(1) of the RDA 1949.
34 *Ibid*, s 7(4).
35 *Ibid*, s 7(3).

be noticed by the consumer: *Gaskell and Chambers Ltd v Measure Master Ltd* (1993). In this way, allowance was also made for the imperfect memory the consumer may have had of the registered design: *Sommer Allibert v Flair Plastics* (1987). When making the comparison in this way, the court disregarded those features of the design excluded from registrability. In *Sommer Allibert v Flair Plastics* (1987), common features which were dictated solely by function (such as the proportions dictated by recognised ergonomic standards in the furniture industry and the spacing of the rear legs to allow the chairs to be stacked) were disregarded, as were features that were not part of the registered design, such as the colour and material of the chairs.

Factors that might be taken into account included the prior art contained in prior applications and prior publications (see 13.4.6), any striking or commercially significant features and the statement of novelty made in the application as required by the Registered Design Rules:

- the prior art was significant in two ways. First, it drew attention to the details of the design which would appear significant to the interested consumer as, if the design was close to the prior art, the consumer would focus on details that were distinct, whereas, if the design was very distinctive, the consumer was more likely to take notice of the general form of the new design. Secondly, it provided an indication of how great a difference was required for the allegedly infringing article to differ substantially from the registered design. Where the design was close to the prior art, relatively small differences would be sufficient to distinguish the alleged infringement, while more striking differences would be needed to avoid infringing a distinctive new design set apart from the prior art;

- if a design included particularly significant features, a difference in one or more of those features might suffice to distinguish the two designs substantially. In *Best Products v Woolworths* (1964), a design was registered for a whistling kettle. It was found that the design had three striking features: the shape of the body; the shape of the handle; and the shape of the spout. The alleged infringing kettle's body and handle were a similar shape, but the spout and whistle were markedly different. These were features of great importance to such a product and the difference was sufficient to avoid infringement;

- a statement of novelty filed with the application also drew attention to those features which the applicant considered important to the design, so that differences relating to those features might be enough to distinguish the allegedly infringing article substantially from the registered design. In *Sommer Allibert v Flair Plastics* (1987), the statement of novelty claimed all the features of shape and configuration of garden chairs. Both the plaintiffs' and defendants' chairs had grooves on the seats and backs of the chairs, but they ran in different directions. The Court of Appeal held that the grooves were features of shape and configuration, rather than pattern and ornament and, although without the grooves the chairs were markedly similar, the differences in the grooves made the two designs substantially different.

13.5 THE NEW LAW

Registration of a design is now governed by the RDA 1949, as amended by the Registered Designs Regulations 2001, in turn implementing the Designs Directive. It is not an absolute harmonising measure and matters of sanctions, remedies and enforcement have been left to Member States, as have procedural matters relating to registration, renewal and invalidation. The Directive was subject to review by October 2004. The Commission should then propose any necessary changes by October 2005. The market in complex products will be given particular attention.

Design has been redefined and many more designs will be registrable as a result. The exceptions have also been changed, as have the qualifying criteria of novelty. It will infringe to use the design on *any* product, not just that for which it was registered. The old provisions for compulsory licences (rarely used), and licences of right have been abolished. Overall, registered protection has been extended, but uncertainty remains as to the extent to which spare parts might be registrable, an area where achieving agreement in the Directive was extremely difficult. The removal of a requirement of eye-appeal which is material, together with a strict interpretation of the 'technical features' and must fit exclusions (see 13.5.7), has the potential to render most functional design registrable, providing longer and broader protection than the UK unregistered design right.

To be registrable a design must be new and of individual character. The requirement for material eye-appeal has gone. The appearance of a product remains a fundamental element of design; however, there is no need for this to be aesthetic. A design has a visual effect. The new approach is akin to that of the Trade Mark Directive. Rather than presuming that a design is not registrable unless it is positively shown to satisfy the definition, 'design' is widely drawn so that the presumption is in favour of registration. Grounds for refusal of registration lie in the exclusions and requirement of novelty and individual character. It is designs that are distinctive within their field that will be registered.

13.5.1 Application and grant

Applications are made to the Designs Registry, and are subject to examination for novelty and individual character. In practice this is not normally done, although where the Registry is aware that novelty is in doubt the objection will be taken.[36] Each application must include a representation of the design (often a photograph), and a definition of the product incorporating it.

Applications will be refused if they are:

- not in accord with the Design Registration Rules;[37]
- the person making the application is not entitled to do so;
- that one of the substantive grounds for refusal has been made out.

Applications are made by the person claiming to be the proprietor of the design[38] and, where national unregistered design right subsists in the same design, the owner of that

---

36 Frequently Asked Questions: www.patent.gov.uk/design.
37 The Registered Design Rules 1995 (SI 1995/2912), as amended by The Registered Designs (Amendment) Rules 2001 (SI 2001/3950).
38 Section 3(2) of the RDA 1949.

right must make the application.[39] The author of the design is treated as the original proprietor.[40] The author is the person who creates the design.[41] Determining who created a design may include the provider of ideas and interpretation is likely to mirror that for the UK Unregistered Design Right (see 13.6.2).

There are two chief exceptions to this general rule. If the design is commissioned for money or money's worth the commissioner is treated as the original proprietor.[42] So is the employer of the author if the design is created by an employee in the course of his employment.[43] In addition, if a design is computer-generated it is the person making the necessary arrangements for the creation of the design who is taken to be the author.[44]

Provision for joint ownership of a design is only made where a design becomes vested in another person jointly with the original proprietor.[45] Creation of a design may well be a team effort. Although in practical terms it is likely that such a team would either be made up of employees or independent contractors, it is possible to imagine a team of designers without such commitment, a partnership for example, for which no provision appears to be made.

If granted, the right is awarded for five years from the date of registration, renewable in five-year periods to a maximum of 25 years. The right lapses if not renewed.

13.5.2   Design

Design is defined by section 1(2) of the RDA 1949 as:

> ... the appearance of the whole or a part of a product resulting from the features of, in particular, the lines, contours, colours, shape, texture or materials of the product or its ornamentation.

This contains both some familiar concepts, but also significant changes to the old law. Designs are still made up of features (which remains relevant to the exclusions of some elements of a design), and are clearly applicable both to two- and three-dimensional designs, including decoration. Beyond that there is much that is unfamiliar and will no doubt be the subject of judicial interpretation in due course.

There is no requirement of eye-appeal (material or not). However, it is specifically the appearance of a product or a part of a product comprised by its features which constitutes the design; thus a design's visual nature remains an important defining characteristic. That said, it is hard to imagine a design that does not have appearance, except where it is not visible in normal use of the product. The appearance need not be aesthetic or have any bearing on a consumer's choice of the product. A feature which is never visible in the product, or the part, cannot be said to be part of its appearance.[46]

---

39   *Ibid*, s 3(3).
40   *Ibid*, s 2(1).
41   *Ibid*, s 2(3).
42   *Ibid*, s 2(1A).
43   *Ibid*, s 2(1B).
44   *Ibid*, s 2(4).
45   *Ibid*, s 1(2).
46   Recitals 11 and 12, Designs Directive.

However, this does not mean that only external features can be protected; the requirement of Recital 11 is that the features be visible in the *application*.

The definition is not exclusive, so though examples are given of types of features, other features may also be employed to make up a registrable design. The inclusion of shape presages an overlap with trade mark registration (subject to the exclusions for some features and designs). The addition of colour, texture and materials extend the old *Kestos v Kempat* definition (see 13.4.2).

13.5.3   Product

Protection is for the design, not for a design as applied to specified articles as under the old law. The application does require an indication of the products in which the design is intended to be incorporated or applied. This does not affect the scope of protection, however, but is required for the purposes of classification.

Relationship of design to product

The distinction between a design and the article to which it is applied may thus have been removed, the design *is* the appearance made up by a product's features. This is further suggested by the fact that protection extends to any product incorporating a design. While in some cases the design and product will be coextensive, in others a design will be applicable to different products. For example, a design may be applied to cups, plates and bowls, and to tablemats and chopping boards; or a design may be for a particular exhaust pipe or aircraft wing. However, some distinction remains because features dictated by the product's function are excluded, implying that the feature excluded is an element of the product itself and not an element of design. Those features will be ignored in any comparison for validity or infringement.

Industrial or handicraft item

'Product' is further defined by s 1(3) of the RDA 1949 as any industrial or handicraft item. The inclusion of handicraft items extends protection to one-off products which would not have fallen within the old law. It will allow an artist or craftsman, for example, to control merchandising of replica products. Computer programs are excluded, but examples 'in particular' are given – packaging, get-up, graphic symbols, typographic type-faces. The inclusion of packaging and get-up should remove the uncertainty over protection for trade dress and bring an end to 'lookalike' product get-up. Also made clear is protection for fonts. It would seem that computer icons and menus may be registrable, the exclusion of computer programs being restricted to lines of code and functionality. This was presaged by *Apple Computer Inc v Design Registry* (2001). Jacob J stated, *obiter*, that icons inherently built into a computer (and not those appearing temporarily when a program is loaded) were thought to be allowable under the Directive. It is possible that registration of icons might extend to logos (provided that they are novel and have individual character) previously protectable only by a trade mark. Trade mark registration may be extended indefinitely if the mark remains within use, but registration of a design will allow for merchandising of the mark.

Parts of products, component parts and complex products

Designs may now be registered for parts of products. In an Explanatory Memorandum to the proposal for the Design Directive the European Commission explained that 'part' meant an integral piece of a product, such as the head of a toothbrush. Guidance as to the application of this new provision was given in a Practice Note issued by the Designs Registry.[47]

Component parts, in contrast, are constituent parts of a larger product which may be removed or replaced and are separate products in their own right, rather than parts of a product. Mobile phone and steering wheel covers or replacement gear stick handles would be component parts. The Designs Registry suggests that a nail or screw would not constitute a component part.[48]

Section 1(3) defines 'complex products' as products composed of at least two replaceable component parts permitting disassembly and reassembly of the product. However, the Designs Registry will apply the meaning suggested by the Explanatory Memorandum to the Design Directive. This refers to complex products being composed of *multiple* components. Consequently, a teapot and lid would not be regarded as 'complex', whereas a car would.[49] This apparently removes the distinction between 'spares' and accessories' promulgated in *R v Registered Designs Appeal Tribunal ex p Ford Motor Co Ltd* (1994) (see 13.4.1) as both might be regarded as replaceable component parts. However, not all component parts will be registrable.

Section 1B(8) of the RDA 1949 provides that component parts not visible during normal use[50] of a product go unprotected. 'Under-the-bonnet' spares such as exhaust pipes and engine parts will not therefore be registrable. Where a component part does include visible features it will be protected only to the extent that *those* features are new and have individual character. The Designs Registry takes the view that consumables such as toner cartridges for printers are not component parts. While they are replaceable, separate and removable, the product remains a product without them. This would not be true of spark plugs in a car, and spark plugs would be considered to be component parts of a complex product.

The exclusions and a new defence (see 13.5.9) now determine the extent to which spare parts receive protection. It is to be hoped that judicial application of the section, which is widely drawn, will take account of the differing economic structures of different industries before refusing protection for non-visible component parts.[51]

13.5.4 Substantive grounds for refusal

There are several substantive grounds on which a design may be refused registration (s 1A(1) of the RDA 1949):

- it does not meet the definition of design;

---

47 Designs Practice Note (DPN) 1/03: www.patent.gov.uk/design.
48 *Ibid*.
49 *Ibid*.
50 This is normal use by the end user, and not during servicing or repair: DPN 1/03.
51 Musker, D, 'Hidden Meaning? UK Perspectives on "Invisible in Use" Designs' [2003] EIPR 450.

- it does not meet the requirement of novelty and individual character;
- it is dictated by its technical function;
- it is contrary to public policy or morality;
- it falls within the emblems specifically excluded in Schedule A1.

Each must be examined in turn, and may in turn be subdivided.

13.5.5 Novelty

A design must be new.[52] As the normal practice is not to conduct a search, although where the registrar is aware that a design is not new an objection on the ground of novelty will be made,[53] novelty is primarily a matter for invalidity and as a defence to infringement proceedings.

The design is compared to other designs made available to the public on its date of registration.[54] If it is identical to the earlier design, or differs from it only in immaterial details it is not new.[55] The 2003 amendments add Registered Community Designs to the field of earlier designs for 'post 2003 designs'.

Date of registration and the prior art

Priority for the date of registration may be claimed from an application within a Convention Country within the preceding six months.[56] If the application is modified the date of registration may be taken to be that of the modified application,[57] with the risk that the modified application may find itself anticipated as a result.

Earlier designs will also include those made available to the public on or after the date of registration but protected by registration or an application for registration from a date before it.[58]

Available to the public

A design is made available to the public if it has been published, exhibited, used in trade or otherwise disclosed.[59] This is not absolute and objective novelty in the patent sense (although the place of disclosure has no geographical limit) but relative novelty within a commercial public knowledgeable in the same field. Disclosures do not make a design available to the public if persons carrying on business within the European Economic Area and specialising in the design sector concerned could not reasonably have had access to the design.[60] The disclosure does not, however, have to be made within the EEA and may be anywhere in the world.

---

52 Section 1B(1) of the RDA 1949.
53 Designs Practice Notice (DPN) 4/03: www.patent.gov.uk.
54 Section 1A(2) of the RDA 1949.
55 *Ibid*, s 1B(2).
56 *Ibid*, s 14.
57 *Ibid*, s 3B.
58 *Ibid*, s 1A(2).
59 *Ibid*, s 1B(5).
60 *Ibid*, s 1B(6)(a).

The limitation to the design sector concerned needs explanation. As it is now designs which are protected and not articles, this cannot be interpreted to require categorising designs into different design fields or industrial sectors. The Commission's Explanatory Memorandum treats this as a 'safeguard clause', intended only to prevent anticipation by designs which European industry could not possibly have been aware of. The example given is of antecedents found in remote places or museums. This wording does not appear either in the Directive or the amended Act, however, and it is to be expected that this new provision may be a fruitful source of judicial interpretation. Both 'reasonable knowledge' and the limits of the design 'sector concerned' will require elucidation.

Disclosures made in confidence are not available to the public, and the designer or his successors in title are given a year's grace period for *their own* disclosures.[61] This allows designers to test the market or to seek investment before embarking on the expense of registration. It should be remembered that designs independently produced and disclosed by others during this grace period will be taken into account in assessing novelty if an application is made.

Where the disclosure is made in a document it is likely that the old test of whether it makes the design 'available' is likely to apply: the publication must contain clear and unmistakable directions to make an article bearing the design, and not merely comprise an artistic work: *Rosedale v Airfix* (1957).

The comparison

The new wording is close to that of the old law, although the phrase 'variants which are common in the trade' has been removed. Consequently, it is likely that a similar approach to judging whether a design has been anticipated will be employed. To secure registrability, a designer must add skills of a design nature to the prior art: *Phillips v Harbro Rubber* (1920). To determine whether a design is the same as an earlier one, the similarity is judged by eye alone. The comparison is not made as if the person making it had both designs at hand, but makes allowance for an imperfect recollection of the previous design. Judicial *dicta* implied that the comparison is made with a designer's eye, rather than a consumer's. With the new standard of novelty to the design field this is more than likely to be followed.

13.5.6 Individual character

Individual character also requires comparison with previous designs. A design has individual character if the overall impression it produces on an informed user differs from the overall impression produced on such a user by any earlier design made available to the public.[62] This is a visual comparison. The relevant earlier designs are the same as for novelty, as is the test of whether they are available to the public.

---

61 *Ibid*, s 1B(6)(b), (c)–(e).
62 *Ibid*, s 1B(3).

Complex products

Where the design is for a component part of a complex product it can only be novel and have individual character (and protection) for parts which remain visible during use of the complex product.[63] Use does not include maintenance, servicing and repair.

Design freedom

In determining whether the design makes a different overall impression the degree of freedom the designer had in creating the design is to be taken into account.[64] The extent of difference from the pool of prior design will be dictated by the extent of design freedom possible. For example, in designing a coaster the only real restriction on the designer is that it must have flat surfaces to enable a mug or glass to be placed on it securely. However, to design a toothbrush the designer will be constrained by the need for a handle which can be held securely and a brush head of suitable dimensions for its purpose. Consequently, it is to be expected that the toothbrush will be closer to the prior art than the coaster.

The informed user

Individual character is judged by the impressed formed by an informed user. This suggests a hypothetical individual without the expertise of the expert, but with more of an interest in design than the average consumer. It is not the same hypothetical individual used to assess novelty. Both expert witnesses and market survey evidence is likely to be used to establish this nebulous individual. Recital 13 of the Directive suggests that the nature of the product and the industrial sector concerned are relevant factors to be considered. This is not repeated either in Article 5, nor s 1B of the RDA 1949, but would appear to be significant to determining the knowledge and experience of an informed user.

The comparison

It is likely that a four-stage process may be followed:[65]

- identify the sector concerned taking into account the nature of the product and its industrial sector;
- assess the informed user's knowledge and perceptiveness;
- establish the relevant prior art or 'design corpus'; and
- compare the overall impression made on the informed user by the design and its predecessors.

Individual character is an elusive concept and likely to be a fruitful source of litigation. As it is the overall impression of the design, which is the appearance of a product, it would seem that all features should be taken into account, and that a similarity of 'global' impression should weigh more heavily than any differences of detail in

---

63 *Ibid*, s 1B(8), (9).
64 *Ibid*, s 1B(4).
65 Suthersanen, U, *Design Law in Europe* (London: Sweet & Maxwell, 2003).

individual features. A useful test would be the extent to which registering the design would hinder subsequent designers of the same type of product.

13.5.7 Technical designs

Features of design which are necessary to the technical function of the product fall outside protection, although the design as a whole may be registered, as Recital 14 of the Directive states. The exclusions allow a competitor to reproduce these features because they must do so to compete in making competing products. The Recital explains the purpose of the exclusion to be to allow technological innovation to take place unhampered by registration. The exclusion does not imply that designs must have an aesthetic value.[66] There is a familiarity to s 1C of the RDA 1949, although its wording differs from the old law. In both exclusions the feature must comprise an element of the product's technical function. It is not clear whether technical function would extend to economic or marketing constraints on a designer.

Features dictated by the product's technical function[67]

Features of appearance of a product which are only dictated by the product's technical function are excluded.[68] There are two aspects to this: whether technical considerations alone were taken, and whether aesthetic considerations were also a factor in designing the feature.

First, the fact that the appearance must be 'only dictated' by functional concerns suggests that if there is design freedom in choosing the features they remain protected. This is because, if another appearance could have been chosen and still done the job, it has not been *dictated* only by function because design choice remains. In addition, secondly, if aesthetic considerations were also a factor in the choice of the feature it has not been dictated *only* by function.

However, guidance may be sought from the ECJ's decision in *Philips v Remington* (2002). This relates to the exclusions applied to shape trade marks: 'the shape of goods, ... necessary to obtain a technical result' (see 15.10.3). The ECJ took the view that, even if there are other shapes that achieve the same technical result, a shape whose essential functional features are attributable to that result is unregistrable as a trade mark. The court looked at the purpose of the exclusion – which is to prevent registration of a shape which:

> would limit the possibility of competitors supplying a product incorporating such a function or at least *limit their freedom of choice* in regard to the technical solution they wish to adopt to incorporate such a function in their product.

The ECJ did also emphasise, however, that the shape be attributable only to the technical result. This leaves open the possibility of an *Interlego* type holding that if the choice of feature was attributable both to technical and functional considerations that it was not dictated only by function. Interpretation of this provision will be significant

---

66 Recital 10, Designs Directive.
67 Designs Practice Notice (DPN) 5/03: www.patents.gov.uk.
68 Section 1C(1) of the RDA 1949.

for the UK Unregistered Design Right. If it is narrowly interpreted, there will be little value left in relying on the national protection.

'Must fit' features

A right in a registered design shall not subsist in:

> features of appearance of a product which must necessarily be reproduced in their exact form and dimensions so as to permit the product in which the design is incorporated or to which it is to be applied to be mechanically connected to, or placed in, around or against, another product so that either product may perform its function.[69]

While this is clearly directed at parts which interface, the test appears a strict one: *necessarily*, and *exact* suggest that if the features can be adapted and still serve their purpose protection remains. It is likely also to apply to the connecting features to which accessories must be attached. Recital 14 gives the purpose of this exclusion as preserving the interoperability of products of different makes. The Designs Registry guidance[70] states:

> is there any part of the design which is not required to be of the appearance it is, in order to enable it to fit the end product? If the answer is yes, then the design application should be allowed to proceed if it satisfies the other requirements for registration ...

It may be that many interoperable features will also be caught by sub-s (1) as interoperability might be regarded as a technical function.

However, mechanical fittings for modular products are not caught by the exclusion.[71] Recital 15 of the Directive explains that these are seen as a major marketing asset deserving of protection. The fittings therefore for interlocking seating, or self-assembly furniture, or the notorious fittings of LEGO bricks, remain protectable.

13.5.8 Public policy and morality

Designs which are contrary to public policy or accepted principles of morality are excluded.[72] There is no scope here for remaining non-offending features of a design to secure registration. If the design is offensive no right shall subsist. Recital 16 of the Directive makes clear that this does not harmonise national concepts of public policy or accepted principles of morality; clearly there is scope for divergence of interpretation of these criteria between Member States. In the old law the Registrar could exercise his discretion (now removed) to refuse to register a design which would, in his opinion, be contrary to law or morality. It was held in *Re Masterman's Application* (1991) that if a design offended the moral principles of right-thinking members of society it should not be registered. On the facts, a design for an authentically male doll clad in Highland dress was said to be distasteful to some, but not offensive enough to merit refusal of the right. It is likely that this test will survive into the new law and that only the most clear cut of cases will be rejected on this

---

69 *Ibid*, s 1C(2).
70 Designs Practice Notice (DPN) 5/03: www.patents.gov.uk.
71 Section 1C(3) of the RDA 1949.
72 *Ibid*, s 1D.

ground. It must be remembered that it is the design, and not the product, which must meet the exception.

13.5.9   Complex products

The significant omission from the new law is a 'must match' exclusion to cater for spare parts such as body panels for cars. Originally proposed, it caused a significant delay in the adoption of a final directive, and was omitted. As a result, Article 18 of the Directive provides that review of the Directive should take into account, in particular, the experience of manufacturers of complex products and component parts, and that the Commission must propose any changes within a year of that review. In the interim Article 14 provides that Member States should retain their existing legal provisions relating to the use of design of component parts for repairing a complex product so as to restore its original appearance. Although changes are only to be proposed if 'needed' to liberalise the market for such parts, this seems inevitable as some Member States allow full registered protection for component parts and a monopoly over spares. The Community Design regime takes the same approach as the Directive and so market distortions seem inevitable.

Consequently, the Commission has proposed modification[73] of the Designs Directive so as to remove Member States' option to protect visible spare parts for vehicles in September 2004. The Commission propose including a 'repairs clause' in the Designs Directive, allowing independent manufacturers to reproduce visible car or other parts for repair purposes and restoring a product's appearance. This will only apply to spares that meet the criteria of novelty and individual character, such as, in the case of vehicles, bonnets, bumpers, doors, lights, radiator grilles, wings and windscreens. A repair clause would not permit copying a design for inclusion in a new vehicle, but is confined to the secondary market.[74] The Commission considered different measures, rejecting a limited period of protection and a system of remuneration. Full liberalisation for a spares market was preferred for its pro-competitive effect. In February 2005, the Patent Office launched a consultation on the Commission's proposals. However, they state that the proposal should not mean any change for the UK, which already has a liberal regime in the aftermarket in visible spare parts.

In the UK, as there is no longer an exclusion for registering must match features, registration of such designs is permitted. However, the right for others to produce and use parts for repair is preserved in s 7A(5) of the RDA 1949 by creating a defence to a claim of infringement. It will not infringe the right in a registered design for a component part to use it for the purpose of repairing a complex product so as to restore its original appearance. For example, a design for a car dashboard may be registered and a competitor prevented from using it in another car, but should a vehicle made by the design's proprietor be involved in an accident a third party may provide a replacement dashboard.

There are effectively four conditions to this defence:

- the design must be for a component part;
- it must be a part which can be used to repair a complex product;

---

73   Proposal for a Directive of the European Parliament and Council amending Directive 98/71/EC on the Legal Protection of Designs, COM (2004) 582 final.
74   Or 'aftermarket'.

- in order to restore its appearance; and
- the use must be for the purpose of repair.

This new means of allowing competition in spare parts focuses on the concept of repair rather than on the nature of the product. Although there is no formal distinction between spares and accessories,[75] it can be doubted whether replacing a part for cosmetic reasons amounts to repair. The dictionary definition of repair is to restore to good condition, renovate, or mend by replacing or reaffixing parts. Repair has received judicial attention in relation to patented inventions, which may provide persuasive precedent (see 6.2.1).

'Use' is defined in s 7(2) of the RDA 1949 (see 13.5.11) and includes not only the act of repair, but also making, importing, exporting, stocking or putting on the market a product intended for repair purposes. It is more than likely that the test of intended purpose will be an objective one.

13.5.10 Excluded devices

Designs making use of certain emblems, flags, arms, insignia and other devices are also refused registration. These are listed in Schedule A1 of the RDA 1949. This replaces the more limited exclusions formerly contained in the Registered Designs Rules 1995.

13.5.11 The right

Registration gives the proprietor an exclusive right to use the design or any design which does not produce a different overall impression on an informed user.[76] The right relates to the design and therefore extends to any product to which it might be applied. In the case of decorative patterns in particular this constitutes a considerable widening of protection from the old law, when separate applications had to be made for different articles.

The right is restricted by any limitations attached to the registration, such as any partial disclaimer, or any declaration of partial invalidity.[77]

The acts that constitute use of a design are defined in s 7(2) and include all acts of commercial exploitation of a design.

Different overall impression

The designer's freedom in creating the design is relevant to the extent to which a design does not produce a different overall impression, as it is for individual character.[78] Where there was little design scope protection will be narrower than that where there was considerable design freedom, and small changes by a competitor will suffice to distinguish his design sufficiently to escape infringement. Extending protection to any design not giving a different overall impression broadens protection from the old law, where the test used was 'not substantially different', and reflects the more stringent test of individual character applied before protection is given.

---

75   Although see s 7A(2)(e) of the RDA 1949.
76   Section 7 of the RDA 1949.
77   *Ibid*, s 7(4).
78   *Ibid*, s 7(3.

Community exhaustion

Exhaustion of the right is provided for, so that once the design's proprietor has put a product on the market within the EEA, or consented to such marketing, free movement of *that* product cannot be restricted,[79] confirming the position reached under Community case law.

In a number of cases, the European Court has held that in the absence of harmonisation at a Community level the conditions under which protection is given to designs is a matter for national law. In *Keurkoop v Nancy Kean Gifts* (1982) Nancy Kean had the exclusive right to market bags of a certain design in the Benelux countries. Nancy Kean discovered that Keurkoop had sold bags of the same design in the Benelux countries and sued for design infringement. The European Court held that in the absence of harmonisation the action was not barred by Community law and there was no exhaustion of rights through consent to marketing. In a subsequent case, *Renault* (1988),[80] the European Court explained what constitutes the specific subject matter of a design right:

> 10. It must first be stated that, as the Court held in its judgement of 14 September 1982 in Case 144/81 (*Keurkoop v Nancy Kean Gifts* ...), with respect to the protection of designs and models, in the present state of Community law and in the absence of Community standardisation or harmonisation of laws the determination of the conditions and procedures under which such protection is granted is a matter for national rules. It is for the national legislature to determine which products qualify for protection, even if they form part of a unit already protected as such.

> 11. It should then be noted that the authority of a proprietor of a protective right in respect of an ornamental model to oppose the manufacture by third parties, for the purposes of sale on the internal market or export, of products incorporating the design or to prevent the import of such products manufactured without its consent in other Member States constitutes the substance of his exclusive right. To prevent the application of the national legislation in such circumstances would therefore be tantamount to challenging the very existence of that right.

Crown use

There is provision for Crown use of registered designs.[81] Any government department or person authorised by a government department may use a protected design for the services of the Crown provided that the conditions in the schedule are satisfied. Terms must be agreed, before or after use, with the approval of the Treasury and may be free of royalties.

13.5.12 Infringement

The exclusive right is infringed by anyone who makes any of the right owner's exclusive uses on *any* product without authority.[82] Therefore to make, offer, put on the

---

79 *Ibid*, s 7A(4).
80 This case raised the question whether a refusal to licence design rights was contrary to Article 82. See Chapter 1.
81 Section 12 of, and Schedule 1 to, the RDA 1949.
82 *Ibid*, s 7A.

market, export or use any product in which the design is incorporated will be an infringing act.

Where the design has not been literally copied in its entirety, determining whether an unauthorised use of some of the protected features infringes will involve comparing the registered design and allegedly infringing product. The test applied is whether an informed user would gain a different overall impression from the alleged infringement. The degree of design freedom available to the designer is again a relevant factor; where there is little freedom, small differences in design may be sufficient to avoid infringement. This could have the effect, however, that there is overall similarity in the design of two products because of technical or even commercial considerations, but that the defendant's has sufficient small and less perceptible differences of other detail not to infringe.

As for the determination of individual character, before any comparison can be made the level of experience of the informed user will have to be established, as will his area of expertise (see 13.5.6), and the same four-step process followed.

13.5.13 Permitted acts

A number of non-commercial uses may be made of a design. The 'right to repair' for complex products has already been discussed (see 13.5.9). Section 7(2) of the RDA 1949 establishes six other exceptions:

- acts done privately and for purposes which are not commercial;
- acts done for experimental purposes;
- acts of reproduction for teaching purposes; or for the purpose of making citations provided that the conditions in sub-s (3) are satisfied;
- use of equipment on ships and aircraft registered in another country but which are temporarily in the UK;
- importation of spare parts or accessories into the UK for the purpose of repairing such ships or aircraft, or
- carrying out of repairs on such ships or aircraft.

The first two are equivalent to patent defences and persuasive precedent for interpretation can be sought there (see 6.3.2). The 'educational' exception is perhaps oddly confined to reproduction, and it is not clear whether it will extend to multiple copies for class use. The conditions provide that the reproduction must be compatible with fair trade practice, not unduly prejudice normal exploitation of the design, and that mention is made of the source. Again, these are akin to the 'three steps' principle derived from the Berne Convention (although the wording is not identical), as is the provision for attribution.

13.5.14 Cancellation and invalidity

A registration may be cancelled at the request of its proprietor,[83] or be declared invalid. The RDA 1949 does not explicitly say so, but the grounds of invalidity may be raised as grounds of defence in infringement proceedings.

---

83   *Ibid*, s 11.

All the grounds for invalidity, absolute (objections residing in the design itself) and relative (objections made because of the rights of others), are specified in s 11ZA of the RDA 1949:

- any of the substantive grounds for refusal of an application in s 1A;
- the registered proprietor is not the proprietor of the design;
- the registration involves the use of an earlier distinctive sign for which protection (such as a trade mark) subsists in the UK;
- the registration constitutes an unauthorised use of a copyright work.

Applicants entitled to apply

The legitimate applicant for a declaration varies according to the ground on which it is being challenged.[84] Any 'person interested' may apply on the grounds that the design does not fall within the definition of design, is not new or lacks individual character, is dictated by technical function, or is contrary to public policy or morality. If the objection relates to Schedule A1 the person concerned by the use may apply; where it conflicts with an earlier application or registration unpublished at the time of the registration of the design being challenged it is the proprietor of that earlier application or registration who applies. The true proprietor must take the objection if it is that the registered proprietor is not the proprietor of the design. Finally, if the objection is made on the ground of use of a distinctive sign, it is the owner of the rights in the sign, and the owner of the copyright where registration is unauthorised use of a copyright work.

The declaration

An application can be made at any time after a design is registered. Provided it is in accordance with the Registered Design Rules and made by the applicant entitled to do so, the registrar shall make the declaration of invalidity if it appears to him that the specified ground of invalidity has been made out.[85] Declarations may be partial. If a declaration is made the registration is treated as having been invalid to the extent declared from the date of registration or any other date the registrar may direct.[86] It is treated as never having had any effect from that date. The registrant may appeal to the Registered Designs Tribunal.[87]

13.5.15 UK competition law

Provision under the old law for compulsory licences where a design was not used, as well as provision for licences of right if the competition authorities found that the availability or conditions of licences from the proprietor were contrary to the public interest, has been repealed. Instead the Competition Act 1998 will apply. This Act introduced a prohibition system (a Chapter I and Chapter II prohibition,

---

84 *Ibid*, s 11ZB.
85 *Ibid*, s 11ZC.
86 *Ibid*, s 11 ZE.
87 *Ibid*, s 11 ZF.

corresponding to Articles 81 and 82 of the EC Treaty). Section 2 of the Competition Act (CA) 1998 provides that agreements that may affect trade within the UK and have as their object or effect the prevention, restriction or distortion of competition within the UK are prohibited. Section 50 of the CA 1998 made provision for the exclusion or exemption of vertical agreements from the Chapter I prohibition. The exclusion was achieved by the Competition Act 1998 (Land and Vertical Agreements Exclusion) Order.[88] However, on 1 May 2004, the Competition Act 1998 (Land Agreements Exclusion and Revocation) Order 2004[89] came into force, revoking the 2000 Order. The main difference between the two Orders is that the 2004 Order does not exclude vertical agreements from the Chapter I prohibition, except to the extent that a vertical agreement is a land agreement. Intellectual property licences will continue to benefit from parallel exemption by virtue of the combination of s 10 of the CA 1998 with the new technology transfer agreements block exemption. Vertical agreements are not excluded from the Chapter II prohibition (see generally Chapter 3).

13.5.16 Offences

Sections 33 to 35A of the RDA 1949 provide for offences in relation to registered designs. It is an offence:

*   to fail to comply with any instruction given as to secrecy for an application, or make an application in contravention of the secrecy provisions;

*   to make a false entry on the register or to make a counterfeit copy of an entry;

*   to claim falsely that a design applied to a product being sold by the offender is registered, or to so mark products after the design registration has expired.

13.6 UK UNREGISTERED DESIGN RIGHT

The CDPA 1988 replaced indirect protection for functional design through copyright with a new, and hybrid right which has characteristics both of copyright and of registered design. This new property right applies to designs created after 1 August 1989. The right is automatic, subsisting once a design has been recorded in a design document, or an article has been made to the design.[90] This allows for ease of protection for the designer, but makes the determining of the rights of others harder to establish; however, protection is against copying and not independent creation. The right is considerably shorter than copyright, and makes provision for licences of right in the last five years of its duration. Distinctive among intellectual property rights, protection for foreign designers is based on reciprocity of protection.

13.6.1 Qualification for design right

Design right does not fall within Convention obligations, so that protection for non-nationals is based upon reciprocity of treatment and is much narrower in ambit than

---

88 The Competition Act 1998 (Land and Vertical Agreements Exclusion) Order 2000 (SI 2000/310)

89 www.legislation.hmso.gov.uk/si/si2004/20041260.htm.

90 Section 213(6) of the CDPA 1988.

that for registered design. As well as the need for recording, the design must 'qualify' in order for the right to subsist.[91] It may qualify by one of two connecting factors; either by reference to a qualifying individual or person, or by first marketing of the design by a qualifying individual in a qualifying country. The right will subsist if the designer, commissioner or the designer's employer qualify by virtue of a being citizen, subject or resident of a qualifying country – the UK, a Member State of the European Union, or a country to which protection has been extended by Order.[92] Failing qualification in this way, the design may qualify by reference to first marketing by a qualifying person in the UK, Member State of the European Union or a country to which protection is extended by Order.[93]

The effects of this were sharply illustrated by *Mackie Designs Inc v Behringer Specialised Studio Equipment Ltd* (2000), drawing sharp comment from Pumfrey J. The circuit diagrams at issue were designed by a US citizen and acquired by Mackie. The circuits were created by a non-European Union citizen or resident outside the EU or a qualifying country. Consequently, they were not entitled to design right protection. Behringer's therefore escaped any liability for its copying of the circuit boards, as s 51 of the CDPA 1988 provided a defence to copyright infringement. Pumfrey J said:

> In the result, the action must fail. I do not come to this conclusion with any great enthusiasm, but the real anomaly, if anomaly it be, is that citizens of the United States of America are not entitled to design right under the CDPA unless habitually resident in the European Union or one of the comparatively limited list of qualifying countries … The scope of the copyright protection to which they are entitled has been legislatively adjusted so as to complement the existence of a design right which they do not possess.

Introduction of the Unregistered Community Design Right will provide some short-term relief from this situation, but only provided that the design meets the criteria of novelty, originality, and individual character.

13.6.2 Ownership of design right

Generally, the designer, the person creating the design, is first owner of the design right in a design.[94] There are four exceptions to this: where the designer is employed or commissioned, or the design is computer-generated, or qualifies for the right by first marketing.

If a design is commissioned from the designer the person commissioning the design is first owner of the right. For a design to be created as a result of a commission there must be a contract involving mutual obligations prior to production of the designs: *Ultraframe UK Ltd v Fielding* (2003). In this case the Court of Appeal asked whether the designer, the sole director and 100% shareholder of a company, ever placed himself under an obligation to the company to produce those designs. The Court said:

---

91   *Ibid*, s 213(5).
92   *Ibid*, ss 217–19.
93   *Ibid*, s 220.
94   *Ibid*, ss 215(1), 214(1).

> If in relation to any of the designs the question was posed – if it had not been produced would the company have been entitled to sue for breach of contract for the failure to produce the same – the answer would have been obvious.

Nevertheless, the Court held that, as a director the designer was a fiduciary agent for the company and held the design right as trustee for the company. To the extent that this decision evades the provisions of s 215 of the CDPA 1988, it may represent a finding on the facts of the case. Clear contractual provision for ownership of both design right and copyright remains a priority for an commissioned work.

Because the copyright rule for commissioned works differs, a commissioned designer may retain any copyright in drawings made during the course of the commission, unless the commission makes alternative provision: *Apps v Weldtite Products* Ltd (2001). This copyright will, however, be subject to the s 51 CDPA 1988 defence for design documents.

If the designer is employed the employer becomes first owner. This applies only if the design is created in the course of employment.[95] At first instance, Laddie J posed a 'rough and ready rule of thumb' for determining employment in *Ultraframe UK Ltd v Fielding* (2003):

> ... if designs are created and paid for any another, the statutory rights under the Act belong to that other.

However, the Court of Appeal in *Ultraframe* adopted the test applied in *Montgomery v Johnson Underwood Ltd* (2001):

> A contract of service exists if these three conditions are fulfilled. (i) The servant agrees that, in consideration of a wage or other remuneration, he will provide his own work and skill in the performance of some service for his master. (ii) He agrees, expressly or impliedly, that in performance of that service he will be subject to the other's control in a sufficient degree to make that other master. (iii) The other provisions of the contract are consistent with its being a contract of service.

If a design is computer-generated the copyright principle applies, while the person first marketing a design is the first owner for a design qualifying by first marketing.[96]

Determining who the person creating the design is differs from determining a copyright author. The process of design differs from the creation of a copyright work. Whereas the author of a copyright work is the person whose skill and effort brings about the expression that is the work, a contributor of the ideas constituting a design may be considered its creator. In *C and H Engineering v Klucznik* (1992), Aldous J accepted that, where the design was the idea of incorporating a pipe into a commonplace pig fender, the designer was the person who thought of that idea. On the facts, this was either the customer or salesman involved and not the maker of the prototype or drawings.

The possibility of joint ownership was raised in *Parker v Tidball* (1997). Section 259 of the CDPA 1988 makes allowance for joint ownership of a joint design. Robert Englehart QC held that whether sufficient contribution had been made to constitute joint design is a matter of fact and degree closely allied to the copyright approach adopted in *Cala Homes South Ltd v Alfred McAlpine Homes* (1995) (see 9.2.1). Sufficient significant contribution to the creation of a *design* – as opposed to a work – is required.

---

95 *Ibid*, s 215(2), (3).
96 *Ibid*, ss 214(2), 215(4).

13.6.3 Duration of design right

The right is of relatively short duration. Expiry of the right hinges on the end of the calendar year in which the design is first recorded or articles first made to it. If articles made to the design are made available for sale or hire within five years from this time, the right expires 10 years from the end of the year of the articles being made available; otherwise, it will expire after 15 years. As most designs will be exploited quickly, the maximum period of protection will be the 10 years from first exploitation. In addition, the right is further circumscribed by licences of right in the last five years of the design right term.[97] This places considerable restriction on the right, because, if copying begins a few years after marketing, it is unlikely that proceedings could be brought to a conclusion before the expiry of the five-year period of protection and the right owner will be dependent on the availability of an interlocutory injunction. In practical terms, this makes the new right of most use in the fast moving trades linked to fashion, and to a designer in the period while awaiting registration of a design. It was agreed as common ground by the parties in the Court of Appeal in *Farmers Build Ltd v Carier Bulk Materials Handling Ltd* (1999) that no question of an injunction arose because the design right was in the licence of right period.

13.6.4 Design

The subject matter of the right is the 'design of any aspect of the shape or configuration (whether internal or external) of the whole or part of an article'.[98] There are significant differences to the nature of a registrable design. The design may be applied to the whole or to only part of an article, does not include design of ornamentation, and there is no need for individual character. The definition is the same as that used in s 51 of the CDPA 1988, and is intended to determine the boundaries of copyright and design right protection respectively. However, these are not mutually exclusive, and there are gaps where no national protection may apply: *Lambretta Clothing Co Ltd v Teddy Smith (UK) Ltd* (2004).

Configuration

This is protection for three-dimensional functional design, although the aesthetic is not expressly excluded. 'Configuration' was given its dictionary meaning in *Mackie Designs Inc v Behringer Specialised Studio Equipment Ltd* (2000): 'its relevant arrangement of parts or elements'. The choice of components for an electronic circuit and their connection therefore amounted to aspects of configuration.

Some doubt was cast on this in *Lambretta Clothing Co Ltd v Teddy Smith (UK) Ltd* (2004). The claimant alleged infringement of design right in a track top constructed in a rib knit fabric. Different parts of the garment were made in different colours. The claimant argued that the arrangement of colours amounted to configuration. The Court of Appeal agreed with Etherton J that configuration did not extend to arrangement of the colours of the track top. He suggested that configuration can only extend to the spatial arrangement of three-dimensional elements. To the extent that *Mackie* implied otherwise it was to be doubted. Jacob LJ suggested that considering the

---

97 *Ibid*, s 237.
98 *Ibid*, s 213(2).

dimension of the colours was irrelevant; what was significant was whether the elements sought to be protected were conjoined to produce the complete article. The components of the track top were configured, but their colours had nothing to do with the complete article's configuration.

Article

The design must relate to an article. The proprietor can choose to assert design right in the whole or any part of his product. A protected design may relate to part of an article, or a combination of parts of an article, or to the combination of parts going to make up a whole article. That whole machines, their individual parts, and combinations of parts may constitute 'articles' was confirmed by the Court of Appeal in *Farmers Build v Carier Bulk Materials Handling* (1999). This was not changed by the fact that the right did not apply to each and every part of the machine. The design may also relate only to aspects of an article's design, unlike the registered design.

This allows a designer to secure protection, even though parts of his design would fall to meet the criteria for protection and means that the proprietor can trim his design right claim to most closely match what he believes the defendant to have taken. If the right is said to reside in the design of a teapot, this can mean that it resides in the design of the whole pot or in a part such as the spout, the handle or the lid or, indeed, in a part of the lid. In *C and H Engineering v Klucznik* (1992), the design at issue was a metal roll bar placed on the top of a pig fender, all other aspects of the fender being commonplace. In *Frayling Furniture Ltd v Premier Upholstery Ltd* (1999), the fact that some features were excluded by the 'must fit' (or interface) exclusion did not prevent a finding of design right in the design of an armchair as a whole.

The Court of Appeal rejected the argument that a claimant may not choose which aspects of design for part of an article on which to base a claim in *A Fulton Co Ltd v Totes Isotoner (UK) Ltd* (2004). Jacob LJ also rejected the suggestion that a part must be 'visually significant' in order for design right to subsist in it.

Internal design

A design need not be visible to the eye. It may form an internal feature of an article, or, even though external not be visible to the eye. In *Ocular Sciences Ltd v Aspect Vision Care Ltd* (1997), Laddie J held that detailed dimensions of shape virtually invisible to a naked eye could be protectable designs and that 'design' here did not have the visual connotations of the RDA 1949. Laddie J also explained that the design's ambit is not coextensive with the article or part of article to which it is applied.

13.6.5 Exceptions

Despite the width of the definition of design, there are a number of exclusions set out in s 213(3) of the CDPA 1988. It is at this point that design right is adapted to preserve competition in functional designs, and to allow for the production of spare parts. The effects of the pre-1988 history of copyright in the design field can be detected in the construction of these exceptions.

The exclusions do not necessarily deny protection to a design. A design may be made up of a number of features. Two of the exclusions relate to 'features' of a design. The design will be made up of the features of the article or part of article to which it is applied, but those falling within the excluded areas may be copied. The others remain protected.

'A method or principle of construction'

Designs made up from the means of their construction are excluded from the right. The wording mirrored the exception to registered design before its amendment by the Directive, and should be interpreted in the same way (see 13.4.3). More recently, in *Parker v Tidball* (1997), stitching on leather cases made for mobile phones was excluded as being a method of construction. If the method used by the design owner allows competitors to use it to create *different* shapes and configuration the exception does not bite: *A Fulton Ltd v Grant Barnett & Co Ltd* (2001).

'Features of shape and configuration of an article which enable the article to be connected to, or placed in, around or against, another article so that either article may perform its function'

This is known as the 'must fit' exception. It allows for fair competition in the features of design which must be copied by a competitor making spare parts for articles or interoperable products. Other features of shape and configuration remain protected if the design is original. Several aspects of this subsection need interpretation.

Another article

First, to be excluded the feature must fit *'another* article'. In *Electronic Techniques (Anglia) Ltd v Critchley Components Ltd* (1997), it was argued that this did not apply to internal interface features within the plaintiff's article – a miniaturised transformer for use in electrical appliances – as the sub-section implied the existence of two separate articles to be fitted together. However, Laddie J held that, because the focus of concern of the new right was design and not particular articles, the excluded features may relate to internal connecting features allowing components to be combined as one article. Otherwise the potential effect was to suggest that a design made up internal of interconnecting features alone would fall outside design right protection. It was said that it would prevent protection for an aircraft wing, for example.

It was also difficult to reconcile with the wording of s 213(3)(b)(i) of the CDPA 1988 which refers to features of an article in relation to 'another article'. However, it must be borne in mind that 'article' includes part of an article and may allow the sub-section to be read as 'features of ... *part of* an article which enable *the part of* the article to be [connected] to *another part* of the article in question ...'.

Subsequently, Deputy Judge David Young QC declined to follow Laddie J and gave the exception a purposive construction in *Baby Dan AS v Brevi Srl* (1999). Baby Dan claimed design right in child safety gates. The defendant argued that each of the parts of the gate were articles within themselves and were therefore excluded by the must fit exclusion. The judge did not agree and held that the claimant was entitled to choose whether to assert the design right in the whole or in parts of its article, adjusting its claim to most nearly match what the defendant has taken. In this case the defendant was making the whole gate. Opting to assert the right in the gate as the article, the internal component parts assembled to form the gate did not fall within the must fit exclusion, which relates to connection with another external article. He went on to hold that separate design rights also subsisted in the component parts as articles in their own right. In this case the design of the parts *is* constrained by the exclusion and a narrower scope of protection achieved. When each part is treated as a separate article its connecting features are now applicable to an external article and not another internal component of a larger whole. Such an interpretation prevents copying of the gate's construction, but allows a competitor to make spare components for the gate. It also allows for the dual interpretation of s 213(3)(b)(i).

The example of a teapot and lid has often been cited to illustrate the effects of the must fit exclusion. If a defendant reproduces the design of both teapot and lid to a substantial degree he will infringe, and cannot argue that because the lid and teapot must fit each other each component is excluded. In this case the design right in the teapot is asserted. Should the handle of the teapot be designed to fit the human hand (as an external 'article') the defendant would be able to replicate this feature. However, if the defendant supplies replacement lids, the claimant must rely on the design right in the lid and the exclusion would apply as the teapot would then constitute an external article.

Article

Secondly, a wide interpretation was given to the word 'article' in *Ocular Sciences Ltd v Aspect Vision Care Ltd* (1997). The plaintiffs alleged infringements of design right in the front and rear surface dimensions and the edge characteristics of designs for soft contact lenses. Laddie J rejected the argument that the human eye could not constitute 'another article', as the legislative intent, expressed in wide terminology, was to exclude all interface features; and 'article' meant no more than 'thing'.

Function

Thirdly, the exclusion bites where the interface permits either article to perform its *'function'*. To determine whether the features of the lenses fell within the exclusion, Laddie J adopted a two-stage test. First, he considered the functions to be performed by both the lens and by the eye. Secondly, he considered whether the features of the lenses enabled them to be fitted to the eye. He held that the back dimensions, the radius and the edge characteristics of the lenses were excluded. They did enable them to fit the eye, to remain centralised and to remain in position.

Enabling connection

Fourthly, the exclusion relates to features which *'enable'* the connection. This raises the question whether the shape or configuration must adopt the *only* design possible to achieve the effect, or whether it must have been chosen for that reason, although another design would have performed the same function. In *Amoena v Trulife* (1995) it was suggested that a narrow interpretation be given so that only where the designer had no design choice of shape or configuration would the feature be excluded from design right protection. In design rights relating to breast prostheses, the shape of a bra would only influence and not dictate the design of the flexible prostheses and the exclusion accordingly was held not to apply to them.

However, in *Ocular Sciences Ltd v Aspect Vision Care Ltd* (1997) Laddie J held that *any* features of shape and configuration which meet the interface criteria must be excluded from the design right; that any such a feature must be excluded, even if it performs some other purpose, such as being aesthetically pleasing; and that the exclusion includes those interface features where some other shape could have been chosen by the designer. Similarly features of the mobile phone cases which allowed the phone to be used while in the case were held to be excluded in *Parker v Tidball* (1997). It remains to be seen whether a narrower interpretation of the must fit exclusion under the Designs Directive (see 13.5.7) will have any persuasive effect on interpretation of the UK provision relating to unregistered design. From a purposive perspective both exclusions are intended to allow for fair competition, but do relate to different types of design.

'Features of shape and configuration of an article which are dependent upon the appearance of another article of which the article is intended by the designer to form an integral part'

This is known as the 'must match' exception. Designs for car body panels such as bonnets would fall within its ambit, but not such parts as steering wheel covers, or replacement seats – these might be termed 'accessories' rather than spares. Its history is described in relation to the old law of registered design, where the same exclusion applied (see 13.4.3). The fact that the features must be 'dependent' on the article to be matched suggests that if any other features may be substituted for the matching features design protection will remain. It is visual appearance which signifies, so that the less visual impact a feature has the less likely it is that it is likely to be dependent on similar features in other articles: *Ultraframe UK Ltd v Fielding* (2003).

The exception does not apply to components of articles sold in sets, such as the pattern applied to a dinner service. It is also important to remember that it is the features in a design which are denied protection, other original features of a design retain the protection of the design right.

Interpretation of the exception was argued in *R v Registered Designs Appeal Tribunal ex p Ford Motor Co Ltd* (1994) and the same distinction between accessory and spare parts may be applied to unregistered designs.

There is a limit to what might be considered an article. The exclusion was not applied to the design of individual cabinets for a fitted kitchen in *Mark Wilkinson Furniture v Woodcraft Designs* (1998), as the kitchen was not an article. Instead the cabinets formed a series of matching articles, none of which formed an integral part of another article.

Surface decoration

Surface decoration is excluded in its entirety; protection must be sought through registration or copyright. Difficulties might arise with three-dimensional features which are decorative, such as the grooves in the chairs in *Sommer Allibert v Flair Plastics*

(1987). These were treated as features of shape and configuration, rather than pattern and ornament in relation to a registered design. Fellner[99] suggested that evidence as to the designer's intention, the market, or views of consumers might be relevant to establish the purpose of such features.

Although s 213(3)(c) of the CDPA 1988 does not exclude 'features' of surface decoration, in Mark *Wilkinson Furniture v Woodcraft Designs* (1998), Parker J took the view that it should be read and interpreted in the same way as s 51 of the CDPA 1988. It is only necessary to do so if the design is seen as being coextensive with the article to which it is applied, yet the definition of design in the context of unregistered protection appears to contemplate that an article or part of an article may have several separate aspects, in which several separate design rights subsist. He then held that surface decoration was not confined to two-dimensional features, and that decorative features with a functional purpose were not prevented from constituting surface decoration and therefore falling within the exclusion.

In *Jo Y Jo Ltd v Matalan Retail Ltd* (2000) embroidery found on garments was considered to be surface decoration because it was applied to the finished garment after it had been made. Features made from the construction of the knitting were not surface decoration, nor were blocks of colour within the knitting, although decorative, as this had been achieved during the construction of the garment and not the application of a decorative process to a pre-existing surface.

The colouring of a track top amounted to surface decoration, although knitted throughout the article's depth: *Lambretta Clothing Co Ltd v Teddy Smith (UK) Ltd* (2004).

13.6.6 Original

A design must be original[100] but not only in the sense used in relation to copyright works. In addition, a design that is commonplace in the design field at the time of its creation is not original.[101] It is the design, and not the article, which must be original. Accordingly, an original design may be applied to an article which is commonplace.

Aldous J gave 'original' its copyright meaning in *C and H Engineering v Klucznik* (1992) – as not having been copied. In *Farmers Build v Carier Bulk Materials Handling* (1999), Mummery LJ held that 'time, labour and skill, sufficient to attract copyright protection' had been expended by the designer in originating the parts, their combination and the machine as a whole, although it was common ground that the design was based on two earlier machines.

Neither 'commonplace', nor 'design field' is defined.

Commonplace

Tracing the word commonplace's origins from the European Directive on the protection of semiconductor topographies in *Ocular Sciences Ltd v Aspect Vision Care Ltd* (1997), Laddie J said:

99 Fellner, C, *Industrial Design Law* (London: Sweet & Maxwell, 1995).
100 Section 213(1) of the CDPA 1988.
101 *Ibid*, s 213(4).

Any design which is trite, trivial, common or garden, hackneyed or of the type which would excite no peculiar attention in those in the relevant art is likely to be commonplace. This does not mean that a design made up of features which, individually, are commonplace is necessarily itself commonplace. A new and exciting design can be produced from the most trite of ingredients. However, to secure protection, the combination must itself not be commonplace ... In many cases the run of the mill combination of well known features will produce a combination which is itself commonplace.

The Court of Appeal considered the requirement for design originality in *Farmers Build v Carier Bulk Materials Handling* (1999). Refusing to define 'commonplace', Mummery LJ adopted a purposive construction of it in its context within the CDPA 1988 and its legislative history. He stated the purpose of copyright and of design right was 'to provide limited protection against unfair misappropriation of the time, skill and effort expended by the author-designer on the creation of his work'. He said that the shorter life of design right and its narrower protection against copying, as well as the *prima facie* protection for functional designs, meant that commonplace should be construed narrowly and not broadly (that is, meaning 'well known') or many functional designs would fail to be protected. Its purpose was to guard against situations where even short-term protection for a functional design would create practical difficulties. Accordingly, the proper approach, he held, was:

(1)　... to compare the design of the article in which design right is claimed with the design of other articles in the same field, including the alleged infringing article, as at the time of creation.

(2)　... to be satisfied that the design for which protection is claimed has not simply been copied (eg like a photocopy) from the design of an earlier article ...

(3)　... to decide whether it is commonplace ... it is necessary to ascertain how similar the design is to the design of similar articles in the same field of design made by persons other than the parties or persons unconnected with the parties.

(4)　... this comparative exercise must be conducted objectively and in the light of the evidence, including evidence from experts in the relevant field pointing out the similarities and the differences, and explaining the significance of them. In the end, however, it is for the court and not the witnesses, expert or otherwise, to decide whether the design is commonplace. That judgment must be one of fact and degree according to the evidence in each particular case. No amount of guidance given in this or any other judgment can provide the court with the answer to a particular case. The closer the similarity of the various designs to each other, the more likely it is that the designs are commonplace, especially if there is no causal link, such as copying, which accounts for the resemblance of the compared designs. If a number of designers working independently of one another in the same field produce very similar designs by coincidence the most likely explanation of the similarities is that there is only one way of designing that article. In those circumstances the design in question can fairly and reasonably be described as 'commonplace' ...

(5)　... if, however, there are aspects of the plaintiff's design of the article which are not to be found in any other design in the field in question, and those aspects are found in the defendant's design, the court would be entitled to conclude that the design in question was not 'commonplace' and that there was good reason for treating it as protected from misappropriation during the limited period laid down in the 1988 Act ...

It was also held that the burden of proof lies on the claimant to identify the relevant aspects of shape and configuration and what is original to them. The burden then shifts to the defendant to show that the design is commonplace. The court accepted the submissions for Farmers Build that a new and exciting design could be produced from trite ingredients and the application of simple engineering principles; and that the relevant design field, for the purposes of originality in relation to an agricultural slurry separator, was that of slurry separators and not agricultural machinery in general.

Design field

As 'design field' is not defined, the court has a discretion in choosing the design field for a design, as illustrated by *Mark Wilkinson Furniture v Woodcraft Designs* (1998). The design field was found to be that of fitted kitchen furniture and not cabinetry in general, based on expert evidence. It was established in *Scholes Windows Ltd v Magnet Ltd* (2001) that the phrase must be given its ordinary and natural meaning, bearing in mind its intention to limit the enquiry as to whether a design is commonplace to sensible limits. These limits are a matter of fact and degree for the court taking into account all relevant circumstances. The design field is not limited by the nature and purpose of the article, not its material structure. Consequently, the Court of Appeal held that the trial judge had been correct to compare U-PVC casement windows with historical wooden designs no longer in use when the design was made. The comparison is an objective question for the judge and not made from the point of view of an expert designer in the field.

Jacob LJ called for a 'reasonably broad approach' in *Lambretta Clothing Co Ltd v Teddy Smith (UK) Ltd* (2004). He held that Etherton J had taken too narrow a view in distinguishing between a design field in sportswear and casual wear. The correct approach was to look at the field through what would be familiar to a notional designer of the article at issue. He also took into account the nature of the particular field of fashion:

> So here, a tracksuit designer, designing a garment intended to give a 'sporty' image would naturally look to and have as part of his background knowledge and experience, the design of well-known actual sportswear, whether strictly so-called or not. It is all part of the image.

13.6.7 Infringement

The design right owner is given the exclusive right to reproduce the design for commercial purposes either by making articles to the design, or by making a design document recording the design for the purpose of enabling articles to be made.[102] Reproduction by making articles is defined as copying the design so as to produce articles exactly or substantially to the design.[103]

Both primary and secondary infringement of the design right are provided for.

---

102 *Ibid*, s 226(1).
103 *Ibid*, s 226(2).

Primary infringement

Primary infringement constitutes either doing, or authorising another to do, anything which is the owner's exclusive right without permission.[104] Infringement may be direct or indirect.[105]

Reproduction

Primary infringement involves reproduction and copying must be established. Copyright principles will be applied to this question; the test being objective similarity between the plaintiff's and defendant's designs, and whether any causal link exists between them: *Mark Wilkinson Furniture v Woodcraft Designs* (1998). It is not sufficient to show that the defendants have undertaken a similar design exercise and independently arrived at very similar designs – copying must be proved: *Ocular Sciences Ltd v Aspect Vision Care Ltd* (1997). Nor can copying be inferred from similarity dictated by function rather than copying: *Amoena v Trulife* (1995). Designers commonly work from earlier design and to determine whether copying has taken place will involve difficult distinctions being drawn between copying and legitimate design influence.

What should be compared?

Once copying has been made out, it must be decided whether the infringing product is made exactly or substantially to the protected design. The test is more complex than that for copyright, where a work is compared to another work. Unregistered design right may apply to some aspects of either the whole or part of an article (see 13.6.4). This raises the question whether the whole articles should be compared, or merely those parts protected by the right.

The test was controversially applied when Aldous J compared the plaintiff's and defendant's pig fenders. The *whole* of both the plaintiff's and the defendant's articles were compared, although the protected design amounted only to the tubular roll bar on the fender – s 226 of the CDPA 1988 does refers to the exclusive right of making articles to the design. This was accepted in *Parker v Tidball* (1997), but with the proviso that it does not suggest that there will never be infringement when a design for part of an article is substantially reproduced in part of another article. This is hard to reconcile with Aldous J's finding that the two features (rather than articles) were substantially the same and that there had been copying.

In the *Mark Wilkinson* case, the comparison made was of the two cabinets, but features of surface decoration whose similarity could not contribute to a finding of infringement were disregarded. There, the design did apply to the whole article – the cabinet – but excluded features were ignored. On the same basis, only the roll bars should have been compared in the *Klucznik* case, ignoring the unprotected commonplace remainder of the fenders. Aldous J appears to use the word design to describe two different things: first, he describes the roll bar as the subject matter of the 'design' in which the design right subsisted, secondly, he refers to the 'design' of the

---

104 *Ibid*, s 226(3).
105 *Ibid*, s 226(4).

pig fenders. While the design was applied to the fenders as a whole, the issue at stake was the infringement only of the design right. It is a fundamental point of difference that, whereas the substratum of a registered design is still a product, or part of a product, this is not the case for the design right, which may apply only to an aspect of part of an article. For the design to be exploited, a whole article must be made, hence the reference to articles in the right owner's exclusive right in s 226(1) of the CDPA 1988, but comparison for infringement should relate to the designs alone.

Exactly or substantially to the design

Deciding whether, after comparison of the two designs, there is an exact or substantial reproduction of the protected design is an objective test decided through the eyes of the user or acquirer of the design: *C and H Engineering v Klucznik* (1992). Where the copying is partial, it must be determined whether the copy is substantially to the design. The enquiry is not the same as that for 'substantial part' in copyright. Regard must be paid to the overall design protected by the design right for determination whether the defendant's product is substantially to that design. The fact that a part, even a substantial part, of the design has been copied may not suffice to infringe. In *L Woolley Jewellers Ltd v A & A Jewellery Ltd* (2003) the trial judge had paid attention only to the feature copied and applied the copyright test. The Court of Appeal rejected the application of the *Designer's Guild* test, and remitted the case for judge's reconsideration.

Secondary infringement

Secondary infringement constitutes importing infringing copies into the UK for commercial purposes, possessing such copies for commercial purposes, or selling, letting for hire, offering or exposing infringing copies for sale or hire,[106] provided that the infringer knows or has reason to believe that the copy is infringing. The design right owner may warn a potential infringer of the design right, but must otherwise avoid making groundless threats of proceedings.[107]

The test of 'reason to believe' from *LA Gear* is applied. A claimant need not write formally to assert his specific design right. In *A Fulton Co Ltd v Grant Barnett & Co Ltd* (2001) it was held that the defendant's discovery of the existence of registered designs led to reason to believe its articles were infringing. However, reason to believe the plaintiff's unregistered design in the umbrella's handles was being infringed was not found until re-pleaded in a substituted statement of claim some three months after proceedings had been issued, despite the fact that both parties were major suppliers of umbrellas with full knowledge of the umbrella market, and that the plaintiff's umbrella was commercially available when the defendant began sales of its product.

Reliance on wrongful legal advice is not a defence to a claim of secondary infringement: *A Fulton Co Ltd v Totes Isotoner (UK) Ltd* (2003).

---

106 *Ibid*, s 227(1).
107 *Ibid*, s 253.

13.6.8 Remedies

The design right owner may bring proceedings for damages, an injunction, account of profits, delivery up or other remedy available for infringement of any other property right. Additional damages may lie, although damages will not be awarded for the period during which a primary infringer does not know, or have reason to believe, that the design right subsisted.[108]

13.7 COMMUNITY DESIGNS

The Designs Regulation[109] introduced two new rights:

- a new, unitary Registered Community Design right; and
- an automatic Unregistered Community Design.

Both are enforceable throughout the EU and were automatically extended to the new Member States on enlargement.

A fundamental aim behind the creation of Community rights is their unitary character and this is expressed in Article 1(3):

> A Community design shall have a unitary character. It shall have equal effect throughout the Community. It shall not be registered, transferred or surrendered or be the subject of a decision declaring it invalid, nor shall its use be prohibited, save in respect of the whole Community.

The effect of Community unregistered design protection was seen in *Mattel Inc v Simba Toys* (2003) when an EU-wide interim court order[110] was secured preventing Simba from dealing in its Barbie lookalike dolls within the European Community.

The Regulation came into force on 6 March 2002, brought into force by a further regulation, the Implementing Regulation.[111] References to articles below are to the Designs Regulation and not the Implementing Regulation.

The criteria for protection, and for invalidity, apply to both these Community rights. They mirror those of the Directive, and have been discussed in connection with it in the UK context above and are only outlined below (see 13.5). It is the Regulations themselves which are the governing legislation, and which will fall to be interpreted by the national Community Design Courts, and the ECJ.

Ownership of Community Designs is not restricted to EU nationals or residents and there is no requirement for qualification as there is for the UK Unregistered Design Right (see 13.6.1).

13.7.1 Designs which may be protected

There must be a design:

---

108 *Ibid*, ss 229, 230, 233.
109 European Council Regulation on Community Designs 2001 (EC) No 6/2002 [2002] OJ L03/1.
110 HC--3 No CO 2684, Laddie J, 23 October 2003: www.prnewswire.co.uk.
111 Commission Regulation implementing Council Regulation (EC) No 6/2002 on Community Designs 2002 (EC) No 2245/2002 [2002] OJ L341/28.

- within the terms of the definition of design;
- which is new; and
- which has individual character.

Some features are excluded from protection:

- features of appearance solely dictated by the product's technical function;
- features which must be reproduced in their exact form to be connected or placed in, around or against another product so that either product may perform its function; and
- features not visible during normal use if the design is incorporated in a component part of a complex product.

13.7.2   Invalidity

Both Community designs may be declared invalid.

For a Registered Community Design a declaration of invalidity may be made by the OHIM, upon application (Article 24(1)); or by a Community Design Court on the basis of counterclaim in infringement proceedings.

An Unregistered Community Design can be declared invalid by a Community Design Court upon application; or in a counterclaim in infringement proceedings (Article 24(3)).

Unless otherwise specified below anyone may apply for a declaration of invalidity.

The grounds on which design may be cancelled are specified in Article 25 and again mirror those of the Directive (see 13.5.14). A design is invalid if:

- it is not a 'design' within Article 3(a);
- it is not new, or does not have individual character;
- it is a component part of a complex product whose visible features are not new of individual character;
- it is contrary to public policy or accepted principles of morality;
- it falls within one of the exclusions;
- the right holder is not entitled to grant of the design (only the person entitled to grant may take this objection);
- it is in conflict with a prior Community or national design or application for a design made available to the public after the filing date (or priority date) which is protected from a date prior to this date (only the person entitled to the prior right may take this objection);
- it constitutes unauthorised use of a copyright work under national copyright law in a Member State (only the copyright owner take this objection);
- it conflicts with rights in a distinctive sign protected either under Community or national law prohibiting such use (only the trade mark proprietor may take this objection);
- it is use of a prohibited emblem.

If found to be invalid the Community design is deemed never to have had effect from its filing date to the extent it has been declared invalid (Article 26). Invalidity is central

– once a declaration has been made the design is invalid throughout the Community –
and *national* copyright, protection for a distinctive sign or prior design right may lead
to invalidity EU wide for a Community right. These are, however, largely harmonised
national rights.

13.7.3   The Nature of Community design rights and dealings in them

Community Designs are objects of property which are to be dealt with as national
design rights of the Member State in which the owner has his seat, establishment or
domicile.[112] They may only be transferred in their entirety, and may not be divided by
territory within the EU. However, they may be licensed for the whole or part of the
Community. Licences may be exclusive or non-exclusive.[113]

Government use

Where national law in a Member State allows use of national designs by or for the
government the same provision may be applied to a Community design. However, the
use must be necessary for essential defence or security needs.[114] In the UK s 240 of the
CDPA 1988 relating to unregistered designs, and s 12 of the RDA 1949 for registered
designs, will be applicable to Community Designs, to the extent allowed by the
Regulation.

13.7.4   Community design courts and proceedings

Enforcement of the new Community rights is to be left to national laws, subject to the
Convention on Jurisdiction and Enforcement of Judgments in Civil and Commercial
Matters.[115] The unitary nature of Community designs is reinforced by provision for
Community Design Courts and a Europe-wide *res judicata*. The Regulation also
provides for some basic uniform sanctions in Member States.

Member States were required to nominate as small a number as possible of
Community Design Courts by 6 March 2005.[116] These courts have jurisdiction[117] for:

- infringement and threatened infringement (if the latter are permitted under
  national law);

- declarations of non-infringement (if the latter are permitted under national law);

- declarations of invalidity of an Unregistered Community Design; and

- counterclaims for a declaration of invalidity of a Community design raised in
  infringement proceedings.

Jurisdiction extends to acts of infringement threatened or committed within the
territory of any Member State.[118] This is exclusive jurisdiction for the nominated courts

---

112 Article 27, Designs Regulation.
113 *Ibid*, Article 32.
114 *Ibid*, Article 23.
115 *Ibid*, Article 79.
116 *Ibid*, Article 80.
117 *Ibid*, Article 81.
118 *Ibid*, Article 82

apart from the OHIM's jurisdiction over declarations of invalidity of a Registered Community Design. Before a Member State's nomination is made the national court with jurisdiction for infringement will have jurisdiction only over acts within that Member State. Currently the UK has not made its nomination,[119] meanwhile the High Court, Patents County Court, the Court of Appeal in England and Wales, and the Court of Session in Scotland are competent.

The Community Design Courts will apply the law of the Regulation[120] where it applies, and national law on other matters, including private international law.

In the absence of an agreed forum (which must be a Community Design Court), jurisdiction is determined by Article 82 on the basis of two connecting factors, either domicile relating to the defendant, or the act committed or threatened. Actions within all four heads of Article 81 jurisdiction may be brought in the court of the Member State in which the defendant is domiciled, or if he is not domiciled in the EU the state where his establishment is domiciled. If there is no appropriate domicile relating to the defendant, proceedings are brought in the Member State in which the plaintiff (claimant) is domiciled or has an establishment. A British company could therefore sue an American company infringing in Germany in the UK's Community Design Court. Where neither claimant nor defendant nor their establishments meet the domicile test, action is brought in the courts of the Member State where the OHIM has its seat. In addition, where proceedings relate to infringement or threatened infringement or counterclaims for declarations of invalidity action may be brought in the Member State where the act has been committed or is threatened. These rules have been established to prevent 'forum shopping' as far as possible.[121]

Remedies

Remedies for infringement are specified in Article 89:

- an injunction;
- an order seizing the infringing products; or materials an implements used to make infringing goods if their owner knew or should have realised such use was intended; or
- an order imposing appropriate sanctions provided for by the national law of the Member State in which the acts were committed.

If a Community Design Court finds against a defendant it is obliged to order these basic sanctions, so that the balance of convenience will not be applied to interlocutory injunctions unless special reasons are given.

Interim relief provided for by national law may be applied for in any national court in any Member State even if a Community Design Court has jurisdiction over the substantive claim.[122] Community Design Courts with jurisdiction under Article 81

---

119 Although the Patent Office initiated consultation with reference to Community Designs in September 2004, and this includes the proposal that these courts are nominated, in line with national design disputes. 'Consultation on UK Legislation relating to Community Designs: www.patent.gov.uk.
120 Article 89, Designs Regulation.
121 *Ibid*, Recital 30.
122 *Ibid*, Article 90.

may grant pan-European provisional measures applicable in the territory of any Member State. Other courts may not do so.

Offences

It is proposed to make it an offence in the UK to claim falsely that a design is protected as a Community Design in parallel with s 35 of the RDA 1949 for national registered designs.[123] The Patent Office suggests that, although prosecutions are rare, the provision provides an effective deterrent against warning off competitors where no protection exists.

European res judicata

Provision has also been made by Article 95 where parallel national and Community protection extends to a design to avoid 'double litigation'. If infringement actions are brought in courts of different Member States, based both on a Community Design and a parallel national design the second and subsequent courts must decline jurisdiction, or stay the proceedings if the first action is contested.

If final judgment has already been given on a simultaneous national design protection a Community design court must reject an action on the Community design.

Equally, if final judgement has been given by a Community Design Court a national court must reject an action on parallel national design protection.

These provisions do not apply to provisional measures.

13.8   REGISTERED COMMUNITY DESIGN

The OHIM began accepting applications on 2 January 2003, and registering designs on 1 April 2003.

There are a number of advantages to this new right. The application process is relatively quick. No substantive examination is made other than a check that the design is within the definition of design, and is neither contrary to public policy nor immoral. It is also inexpensive. Not only does the right extend protection to all Member States within the EU without individual national applications having to be made, but also multiple applications may be made, covering any number of different designs. Since June 2003 provision has also been made for e-filing of applications, and all administrative proceedings are based on electronic tools. There is no provision for opposition proceedings and registration takes only about three months. It was a 'fundamental objective' of the Regulation[124] that the procedure for obtaining a Registered Community Design should present minimal cost and difficulty to applicants so as to be readily available to small and medium-sized enterprises and individual designers. The first six months of operation of the OHIM suggested that the system is proving popular.

---

123 'Consultation on UK Legislation relating to Community Designs': www.patent.gov.uk.
124 Recital 24, Designs Regulation.

The one obvious drawback is that should the design be found to be invalid the declaration of invalidity will also extend throughout the EU. As the provisions for registrability mirror those of the harmonising Design Directive, however, the design is not likely to be registrable nationally either. Nevertheless, in the UK the national Unregistered Design right may continue to protect the design.

13.8.1 Application

The OHIM will administer the right. Anyone may apply, though the designer has a right to be identified to the Office and in the Register.[125] The application may be submitted direct to the OHIM, or via the UK Patent Office for transmission to the OHIM, although it will only handle the first stage of application.

Language

Applications may be made in any of the 20 EU languages, but if one of the five working languages of the Office is not used a second language selected from English, French, German, Italian or Spanish must be designated. This language will then be used in communications from the Office and invalidity proceedings.

Formal examination

The OHIM examines the application for the minimum requirements of registrability (that it is a 'design' and not offensive to public policy or morality)[126] and checked whether all formal requirements have been met and fees paid. The application must contain:[127]

- a request for registration of a Registered Community design;
- information identifying the applicant;
- a representation of the design, or, if applicable, a specimen;
- an indication of the product(s) to which the design is intended to be applied;
- the application fee.

Representation of the design

There is no statement of novelty, the representation playing the role of the 'claims' to the design. Applicants may submit up to seven views of the design on sheets of A4 size. These may be either photographs or drawings, and either in colour or black and white. There is no obligation to show all sides of a three-dimensional design. To show only one or more sides may increase the protection available, as features on the sides

---

125 Article 18, Designs Regulation.
126 The OHIM's 'Examination Guidelines, Community Design' state that refusal on this ground has to be 'reasoned by reference to the perception of the public within the Community', giving as examples designs that contain racist messages or images. Poor taste is not a ground for refusal of registration: www.oami.eu.int.
127 Article 36, Designs Regulation.

not shown are not specified. Equally, to represent the design in colour 'claims' those colours, whereas a black and while representation will protect any colour in which the design might be used. To represent only the contours of a design in a drawing will give the broadest protection, while a photograph will be taken to specify both shape and surface structure and material. There is only limited scope for submitting a specimen.

Features which are intended to be excluded from the right's protection may be disclaimed in the representation, but only by a graphical illustration (wording may be added to elucidate this; however, added wording alone is not accepted as a disclaimer).

Date of filing and duration

Priority may be claimed from an application filed in any Paris Convention or World Trade Organisation country provided that it is completed by the Registered Community Design application within six months.

The application is given a date of filing[128] when it is received (by the OHIM if sent direct, or by the Patent Office if the UK route is chosen). If successful, the date of filing is taken as the beginning of the term of protection.[129] The right is granted initially for five years,[130] and may be renewed for one or more periods up to a maximum of 25 years.

Publication

When the right is granted the design is published in the Bulletin,[131] unless the applicant requests deferment of publication for 30 months from the date of filing (or priority date).

There is no opposition period, despite the limited examination made by the Office, but after registration any person may seek a declaration of invalidity.[132] It is clearly in the interests of competitors to take an active interest in the Bulletin and to challenge designs which should not have been granted. Examination for the substantive grounds of registrability will then be made. If the challenge is made out the registration will be cancelled.

Ownership

The right is granted to the designer, or jointly to the designers where two or more have developed the design.[133] Where the design is developed by an employee in the execution of his duties or following instructions given by his employer, the right vests in the employer unless otherwise agreed or provided by national law. It may be that both 'in the execution of his duties' and 'following the instructions' require a stricter

---

128 *Ibid*, Article 38.
129 *Ibid*, Article 12.
130 *Ibid*, Article 12.
131 *Ibid*, Article 49.
132 *Ibid*, Article 52.
133 *Ibid*, Article 14.

interpretation that the UK 'in the course of employment'. The relevant duties could be confined to a formal job description despite the fluid treatment of an employee's duties in the UK. In addition, a specific instruction to create the particular design in question might also be required. There is no provision for ownership passing to a commissioner of a design.

Appeal

Appeals to decisions of the Office's examiners may be brought to the Board of Appeal, and against the Board to the ECJ. It is hoped by this means to achieve uniform interpretation of the Regulation throughout the EU.[134]

13.8.2 The right and infringement

Once registered, the Registered Community Design Right confers an exclusive right to use, make, offer, put on the market, import, export or stock the product in which the design is incorporated or to which it is applied, or one which does not produce an overall different impression on an informed user.[135] The extent of design freedom available to the designer is once again a relevant factor in determining the difference of overall impression.

To do any of the exclusive acts without authority will infringe. The exceptions are parallel to those of the Directive (see 13.5.13) and Community exhaustion applies.[136]

13.8.3 Registered Community Design and trade marks

Because design is widely defined it may now be possible to obtain Community Design protection for a two- or three-dimensional trade mark. The definition of a product includes a graphical symbol. The Regulation specifically provides that it is without prejudice to Community or national law relating to unregistered designs, trade marks and other distinctive signs (such as geographical indications), patents and utility models typefaces, civil liability and unfair competition.[137]

There are benefits in additionally protecting a trade mark by registered design:

- there is no requirement of use for design protection;
- a design may be descriptive and non-distinctive;
- only one registration would be required for all products;
- registration is quick by comparison with that for a Community Trade Mark (up to 35 months if the application is opposed);
- there is no nationality qualification;
- an application for Registered Community Design may be kept secret for 30 months, useful in relation to the launch of a new product;
- the test for infringement requires only use.

---

134 *Ibid*, Recital 28.
135 *Ibid*, Article 19.
136 *Ibid*, Article 21.
137 *Ibid*, Article 96.

Disadvantages in doing so include the shorter term of protection for a registered design, and more frequent renewals needed during that period. In particular, the mark would have to satisfy the test of novelty and would only extend to marks for goods, not services. The limited examination before grant would also make the design protection vulnerable to challenge.

The fact remains that there will be situations where dual protection is both possible and desirable. Packaging of a product may now be protected before it becomes distinctive, and trade mark protection can be added as the design protection expires and distinctiveness has been acquired through use.

13.9   UNREGISTERED COMMUNITY DESIGN RIGHT

The Unregistered Community Design Right, also created by the Designs Regulation, also came into force on 6 March 2002. Unregistered Community Design differs from the UK national Unregistered Design Right and is intended to serve a different purpose. Whereas the UK right serves to provide limited protection for three-dimensional functional design, the Community right provides short-term protection for industries which renew their products very frequently, but extends to the same type of designs as the Registered Community Design. It is also a means of securing protection during the registration period, and will allow for market testing. Industries such as fashion, jewellery, furniture and toy manufacture should benefit from this type of protection.

The same definition of protectable design in the Regulation is applied, and the design must be new and of individual character. There is no requirement of qualification. The rules relating to ownership also mirror those of Community Registered protection. The distinction between the UK UDR and the Community right were highlighted in the Court of Appeal's decision in *Lambretta Clothing Co v Teddy Smith* (2004) (see 13.2.1).

13.9.1   Duration

The right arises automatically, is free and without formalities, giving EU-wide protection for three years from the first public disclosure of the design within the Community. It is also this date at which novelty and individual character are tested (the designer is allowed the same 12-month period of grace for his own disclosures), although these criteria are tested against disclosure worldwide and not within the Community alone. It will be prudent to keep a record of the date a design is disclosed. Choosing the date of disclosure of the design avoids the difficulties of proving when the design was created; in some Member States copyright protection may apply in any gap between creation and disclosure.

A design is taken to have been made available to the public if it has been published, exhibited, used in trade or otherwise disclosed in such a way that, in the normal course of business, the disclosure could have reasonably become known to the circles specialised in the sector concerned operating within the Community.[138] While

---

138 *Ibid*, Article 11.

this test is in the designer's favour – those 'in the know' within an industry will become aware of a design before the general consuming public – there is scope for uncertainty both as to the level of specialism to be attributed to the hypothetical 'circle', and in determining the sector concerned (see 13.5.5). If, for example, the design is related to character merchandising, is the sector related to the character (which might encompass only the world of film), or to the world of the particular product (such as children's tableware)? The latter is likely to become aware of the design after those involved in film-making. It is possible that the difference in time will be very short; however, it will make establishing the duration of protection uncertain.

13.9.2   The right

The chief distinction between Registered Community Design and the Unregistered Community right lies in the extent of the right given. As with the UK model, infringement requires copying by a defendant. However, the right conferred on the Unregistered Community Design holder is to make exclusive use of the design. That use covers, in particular but is not restricted to, the making, offering, putting on the market, importing, exporting or using a product in which the design is incorporated or to which it is applied, or stocking a product for these purposes.[139]

13.9.3   Infringement

Infringement comprises doing one of these acts without authority, but only if it results from copying the protected design.[140] Article 10 extends protection to the design and one which does not produce a different overall impression on an informed user (see 13.5.11).

Copying is not defined, but is likely to take the same meaning as reproduction of a copyright work. It is provided that independent creation of the design by a designer who may reasonably be thought not to be familiar with the design made public by the right holder does not constitute copying. This could be treated as a test with two components, both of which must be made out – first, determining whether the designer has worked independently and, secondly, whether the designer may be taken to be familiar with the design. To do so would, however, be very difficult in application, for proving that design has been independent in the face of familiarity with a design is likely to prove very difficult. More likely is that courts will look for reasonable familiarity, an objective test rather than the actual designer's knowledge, and infer copying from any overall similarity of impression.

The familiarity with the design is tested differently to that for making available to the public, and disclosure for the purposes of novelty and individual character. The subsistence of protection depends on the design having been made public within a specialised circle. Familiarity suggests a more intimate awareness of the design. However, any designer within a particular sector will need to take care to adopt 'clean room' style practices to avoid being taken to have reasonable knowledge of a design within his or her area. If copying is presumed from similarity in the way that it is for copyright (see 10.1.1), this may be difficult to rebut unless a designer can establish that

139 *Ibid*, Article 19(1).
140 *Ibid*, Article 19(2).

his or her design was created first, or that he or she copied another (unprotected) design.

In infringement proceedings before a Community Design Court the presumption of validity will apply only if the right holder provides proof that the design has been made available to the public in the Community, and states what constitutes the individual character of the design.[141]

The defences to infringement mirror those for Registered Community design, and EU exhaustion rules apply.

Further Reading

Bently, L and Coulthard, A, 'From the Commonplace to the Interface: Five Cases on Unregistered Design Right' [1997] EIPR 401

Fellner, C, *Industrial Design Law* (London: Sweet & Maxwell, 1995)

Lane, S, 'Design Copyright – Fresh, Fetching and Functional?' [1988] EIPR 370

Massa, CH and Strowel, A, 'Community Design: Cinderella Revamped' [2003] EIPR 68

Musker, D, 'Hidden Meaning? UK Perspectives on "Invisible in Use" Designs' [2003] EIPR 450

Pickering, C, *Trade Marks in Theory and Practice* (Oxford: Hart Publishing, 1998)

Radcliffe, J and Caddick, N, 'Abbreviating the Scope of Design Right' [1997] EIPR 534

Saez, V, 'The Unregistered Community Design' [2002] EIPR 585

Suthersanen, U, 'Exclusions to Design Protection – A New Paradigm', in Sterling, A (ed), *Intellectual Property and Market Freedom*, Vol 2: Perspectives on Intellectual Property (London: Sweet & Maxwell, 1997)

---

141 *Ibid*, Article 85(2).

CHAPTER 14

PASSING OFF

The third part of this book focuses on protection for image for traders, and later even for individuals. It is as important to intellectual property right owners to exploit their products without facing unfair market practices, as it is to have protection for the product itself. Intellectual property protection through registered trade marks and the action for passing off differs from patent, copyright and design protection. They are not tied to products themselves, but instead focus on a producer's reputation and goodwill as the source of goods or services, and as the providers of their quality. For this reason, the provision for registration of trade marks to bolster commercial reputation or image is treated as an important part of intellectual property law. However, equally significant protection is afforded through the common law by the tort (delict) of passing off:

Nobody has any right to represent his goods as the goods of somebody else.[1]

The rationale for passing off is therefore to protect traders who have significant business in the marketplace, and to protect the public interest in access to accurate market information.[2] Since 1896, however, the courts have developed this remedy considerably in order to meet the need for relief against other forms of unfair competition.

Another important feature of protection for commercial reputation, registered or unregistered, is that it runs concurrently with the other intellectual property rights, but will continue to protect when those rights expire, preserving markets otherwise laid open to free competition. However, passing off does not create a monopoly or prevent competition as competitors may market the same goods, provided that they do not adopt confusing indications of reputation.

However, judicial attitudes have wavered as to the legitimate extent of protection from passing off. The tort of malicious falsehood or trade libel has also, on occasion, been prayed in aid of the entrepreneur, but it quickly acquired narrow limits and is of less significance.

14.1 THE RELATIONSHIP OF PASSING OFF TO REGISTRATION FOR TRADE MARKS

When registration was introduced in 1875, it did not replace passing off, so that the two remedies coexist,[3] but they are not coextensive. This remains the case even where there is overlap with provisions of the statute: *Inter Lotto (UK) Ltd v Camelot Group plc* (2004).

The claimant built up goodwill in the name HOTPICK after the defendant's trade mark application (for a lottery game announced and promoted before the application),

---

1   *Per* Lord Halsbury in *Reddaway v Banham* (1896).
2   Carty, H, 'Passing Off and Instruments of Deception: The Need for Clarity' [2003] EIPR 188.
3   Section 2(2) of the Trade Marks Act 1994.

even although its use of the name then infringed the defendant's mark. While the Court of Appeal's decision appears to reflect the clear intention of the Act that it should leave the law of passing off unaffected, it does leave open possible uncertainties for the future.

If a trader applies to register a mark unaware of another trader's existing use of, and goodwill in, that mark, and only seeks to sue for infringement once the registered mark is put to use and the other unregistered mark comes to light, both traders could take action. The registered mark owner for infringement, the other for passing off and a declaration of invalidity of the mark. It is likely that the priority of the unregistered mark would prevail and the registered mark be found invalid. However, a mark could be registered at a time that an unregistered mark was just being introduced, but then not be used for some time. The unregistered mark's owner would be able to build up reputation and goodwill in the period before a delayed start to use of the registered mark. The registration remains valid, and the Trade Mark Act 1994 (TMA 1994) and the law of passing off do appear to conflict.

While registered trade marks and passing off both protect indications of trade reputation, there are important distinctions between them.

(i)   Registration confers a property right in the trade mark itself, while passing off protects property in a trader's goodwill.

(ii)   A trade mark may be registered before any use is made of it, whereas it is implicit in the nature of goodwill that trade under the 'mark' must have already established a reputation in the buying public's mind. This has the consequence that a passing off action is both costly and time consuming because the existence of reputation must be proved to the court, rather than the fact of registration.

(iii) Nevertheless, the use made of a trade mark may outstrip the ambit of its registration, whereas passing off continues to protect whatever reputation is achieved through actual use of the mark.

(iv)   In the same way, passing off is not constrained by the technicalities of the definition of a registrable mark (although the TMA 1994 significantly extended its ambit).

14.2   THE DEVELOPMENT AND DEFINITION OF PASSING OFF

Passing off has a long tradition, developing from the common law of deceit. It was referred to in 1580, but its modern origins date from *Crutwell v Lye* (1810). With the industrial revolution and the growth in means of transport, trade in goods extended beyond the borders of local knowledge, so that traders began to attach signs and symbols to their goods in order to indicate their origins and passing off became important to protect those signs. Lord Langdale said, in *Perry v Truefit* (1842):

> A man is not to sell his own goods under pretence that they are the goods of another man, he cannot be permitted to practise such a deception, nor to use the means which contribute to that end. He cannot therefore be allowed to use names, marks, letters, or other indicia, by which he may induce purchasers to believe that the goods which he is selling are the manufacture of another person.

The remedy is equally applied in Scotland and in 1910 in *Charles Kinnell & Co Ltd v A Ballantine & Sons* (1910) Lord Dunedin echoed the English approach, following *Reddaway v Banham* (1896):

> Have the defenders acted in such a manner as to make it likely that persons can be deceived into the belief that the goods advertised by the defenders are the goods of pursuers, when, in fact, they are not?

In this century, the growth of mass marketing, the explosion in advertising and development of new means of doing so, as well as new methods of marketing, have continued to exert pressure on the limits of the remedy, and encourage its development to meet new conditions.

14.2.1 The elements of the action for passing off

Since *Reddaway v Banham* (1896), three elements have been identified as the essential criteria for a passing off action:

(a) it is property in a trader's reputation acquired through trade, not the mark itself, which is the subject matter of protection: *Reddaway v Banham* (1896) (England), *Lang Bros Ltd v Goldwell Ltd* (1980) (Scotland);

(b) it is misrepresentation and not mere misappropriation of that reputation is prohibited: *Spalding v Gamage* (1915); and

(c) the defendant's activities must cause or threaten damage to the claimant's goodwill: *Bulmer v Bollinger* (1978).

These were explained by Lord Diplock in the leading case of *Erven Warnink v Townend* (1979) (the *Advocaat* case), and applied in Scotland in *Lang Bros Ltd v Goldwell Ltd* (1980):[4]

> ... it [is] possible to identify five characteristics which must be present in order to create a valid cause of action for passing off: (1) a misrepresentation, (2) made by a trader in the course of trade, (3) to prospective customers of his or ultimate consumers of goods and services supplied by him, (4) which is calculated to injure the business or goodwill of another trader (in the sense that this is a reasonably foreseeable consequence) and (5) which causes actual damage to a business or goodwill of the trader by whom the action is brought or (in a *quia timet* action) will probably do so.

Later, these points were condensed by Lord Oliver, in a judgment now commonly accepted as defining the action, in *Reckitt and Colman (Products) Ltd v Borden Inc* (1990) (the *Jif Lemon* case):

> First, he must establish a goodwill or reputation attached to the goods or services which he supplies in the mind of the purchasing public by association with the identifying 'get-up' (whether it consists simply of a brand name or a trade description, or the individual features of labelling or packaging) under which his particular goods or services are offered to the public, such that the get-up is recognised by the public as distinctive specifically of the plaintiff's goods or services. Secondly, he must demonstrate a misrepresentation by the defendant to the public (whether or not intentional) leading or likely to lead the public to believe that goods or services offered by him are the goods or services of the plaintiff ... Thirdly, he must demonstrate that he suffers, or in a *quia timet* action, that he is likely to suffer damage by reason of the

---

4 For development of the action in Scotland see Clive, E, 'The Action for Passing Off: Its Scope and Basis' (1963) JR 117.

erroneous belief engendered by the defendant's misrepresentation that the source of
the defendant's goods or services is the same as the source of those offered by the
plaintiff.

It should be noted that these three criteria, although expressed in general terms, are
connected; so that only misrepresentations to the consuming public, of indicators of
reputation that give rise to goodwill, which cause confusion and give rise to damage to
that goodwill, are actionable. It is tempting to conclude that, if two of the three
conditions are present, the third may be assumed; for example, if a misrepresentation
as to reputation causes damage, it might be assumed that the claimant has goodwill.
This, in effect, occurred in *Taittinger v Allbev* (1992). Recent case law suggests that such
assumptions are not legitimate: *Hodgkinson and Corby v Wards Mobility Services* (1995)
(the *Roho* case). In addition, Lord Diplock emphasised that passing off remains
essentially a question of fact, so that the presence of the three conditions is not the only
prerequisite for success.

Passing off thus protects information about products and services. This supports
the understanding built up by the consuming public of changing trade practices and
the conclusions they draw from the information supplied. Therefore, as practice and
the public's understanding changes, so has, and must, the action adjust.

14.2.2   Developments in passing off[5]

The law of passing off is nothing if not dynamic. The result is a fascinating, if
frustrating, body of law. Modern development in the action can be traced since
Reddaway v Banham (1896). If there is a general principle underlying this development,
it lies in an understanding of fair trading, a concept that necessarily adapts as market
conditions change. This has been recognised by the House of Lords on a number of
occasions. In *Parker-Knoll v Knoll International* (1962) Lord Morris stated that:

> ... in the interests of fair trading and in the interests of all who may wish to buy or to
> sell goods the law recognises that certain limitations upon freedom of action are
> necessary and desirable ... In solving the problems which have arisen there has been
> no need to resort to any abstruse principles, but rather, I think, to the straightforward
> principle that trading must not only be honest but must not even unintentionally be
> unfair.

Similar motivations were relied on by Lord Diplock in the *Advocaat* case:

> Parliament, however, beginning in the 19th century has progressively intervened in
> the interests of consumers to impose on traders a higher standard of commercial
> candour than the legal maxim *caveat emptor* calls for, by prohibiting under penal
> sanctions misleading descriptions of the character or quality of goods; ... the
> increasing recognition by Parliament of the need for more rigorous standards of
> commercial honesty is a factor which should not be overlooked by a judge confronted
> by the choice whether or not to extend by analogy to circumstances in which it has not
> previously been applied a principle which has been applied in previous cases where
> the circumstances, although different, had some features in common with those of the
> case which he has to decide. Where over a period of years there can be discerned a
> steady trend in legislation which reflects the view of successive Parliaments as to what

---

5   Carty, H, 'The Development of Passing Off in the Twentieth Century', in Dawson, N, and
     Firth, A, *Trade Marks Retrospective* (London: Sweet & Maxwell, 2000).

the public interest demands in a particular field of law, development of the common law in that part of the same field which has been left to it ought to proceed upon a parallel rather than a diverging course.

However, this is not to give a general right against unfair competition, for protection is tied to a trader's property in goodwill in order to prevent damage to that goodwill: *Irvine v Talksport Ltd* (2002).

The subject matter of protection

In *Crutwell v Lye* (1810), Lord Eldon referred to a defendant setting up trade under 'the same name or sign'. By *Perry v Truefit* (1842), reference was being made to 'names, marks, letters or other indicia' being protected. In *Reddaway v Banham* (1896) the House of Lords extended this to exclusively descriptive names ('Camel Hair Belting'). In Scotland Lord Dunedin recognised that the remedy extended beyond names in *Charles Kinnell & Co Ltd v A Ballantine & Sons* (1910). It is now recognised that it is not the means by which a reputation is built up that is protected, but the goodwill which the reputation engenders.

It is also recognised that it is protection for property in goodwill (although not in the mark itself as is the case for a registered trade mark): *Advocaat* (1979), *Lang Bros Ltd v Goldwell Ltd* (1980).

Shared reputations

It is not only a reputation unique to an individual trader that may be protected. It has increasingly become recognised through the so-called 'drinks cases'[6] that a group of traders sharing a reputation may protect that joint reputation. The same principle was applied to Harris Tweed in *Argyllshire Weavers v A Macaulay Tweeds Ltd* (1965). The House of Lords confirmed protection for shared reputations in *Advocaat* (1979). To do so moves some way towards general protection against unfair competition, as no one trader was required to show any special prejudice from the defendant's activities.

Reputation as to quality

Originally, passing off protected against misrepresentations as to the source of goods. In *Spalding v Gamage* (1915), the House of Lords accepted that the action could extend to a trader's indications of the quality of his goods. The plaintiffs made footballs of different grades, which had different names. The defendant sold balls genuinely made by the plaintiffs, but using the name of a superior grade to that of the product actually being sold. This amounted to passing off. The shared reputation cases also recognise that the reputation each trader acquires through use of the joint name is one for quality rather than the origin of the product.

---

6   *J Bollinger v Costa Brava Wine Co Ltd* (1961), *Vine Products v Mackenzie* (1969), *Walker v John Ost* (1970), *Bulmer v Bollinger* (1978).

Unfair competition

It should not be thought that the action for passing off will not continue to adapt to commercial needs. The general nature of the criteria laid down by the courts allows for a measure of interpretation as new circumstances arise. It seemed, after *Erven Warnink v Townend* (1979), that the House of Lords had opened the way to the emergence of a tort against unfair competition.[7] In effect, its decision appeared to allow a remedy for misdescriptive advertising by a competitor, and one conferred on a group of traders sharing a reputation in a descriptive name ('Advocaat'). This and other 'drinks' decisions are regarded as the beginnings of an 'extended' form of passing off because the description 'Old English Advocaat', 'British Sherry', 'Spanish Champagne' would alert the knowledgeable to the nature of the alternative product. The case of *British Telecommunications plc v One in a Million* (1999) (see 14.7.3) represents considerable judicial willingness to see a remedy against forms of unfair competition.[8]

Extended misrepresentation and heads of damage

The action's continuing development can also be seen in the recognition of 'reverse (or inverse) passing off' (see 14.6.8), and misrepresentations as to the quality of goods and services, rather than their source. In *Associated Newspapers v Insert Media* (1991), the insertion of advertising 'flyers' into the plaintiff's newspapers was regarded as an actionable misrepresentation (see 14.6.2). New heads of damage were contemplated in *Taittinger v Allbev* (1992) (see 14.7.1), and the public's understanding of the practice of licensed character merchandising was recognised in *Mirage Studios v Counter-Feat Clothing* (1991) (see 18.2.1).

Continuing caution

However, the courts have also been careful to ensure that passing off remains within acceptable limits. The Privy Council drew an important distinction between competition, and unfair competition, in *Cadbury Schweppes v Pub Squash* (1981). While willing to recognise that reputations may now be built up under many types of descriptive material, including television advertising themes, Lord Scarman said:

> ... competition must remain free ... A defendant, however, does no wrong by entering a market created by another and there competing with its creator. The line may be difficult to draw; but, unless it is drawn, competition will be stifled.

In the *Roho* (1995) case, Jacob J reaffirmed that this line is to be drawn by requiring that the defendant's misrepresentation confuse in the consuming public, causing real damage to the plaintiff's goodwill. That passing off did not constitute a general remedy against unfair competition was reaffirmed by Laddie J at first instance in *Chocosuisse v Cadbury* (1998). Nevertheless, the court extended a remedy in passing off to 'Swiss Chocolate', which is not a description tied to a product's qualities derived

---

7   A move that, it has been suggested, is open to Scots Law: Stewart, Q, 'The Law of Passing Off – A Scottish Perspective' [1983] EIPR 64.

8   Morcom, C, 'Leading Cases in Passing Off', in Dawson, N, and Firth, A, *Trade Marks Retrospective* (London: Sweet & Maxwell, 2000).

from association with an area[9] or even recipe,[10] although it has a recognisable texture. The Court of Appeal decision in *Arsenal v Reed* (2003) (see 18.3.3) also appears to represent a new willingness to move closer to remedying unfair competition. Providing a remedy in passing off against false endorsement of a service by a sportsman might also be seen as a move in this direction: *Irvine v Talksport Ltd* (2003). However, there was clear evidence of the practice of celebrity endorsement and the significant contribution to their income that it provides in the case.

Protection against dilution of a reputation through passing off remains controversial. The result is an action of fascinating scope, although recent changes to registered trade mark law made by the TMA 1994, including a remedy against dilution, may divert attention from the common law action.

14.3 REPUTATION

Claimants must establish that they have a commercial reputation and that it gives rise to goodwill. It is in this sense that Lord Oliver's reference to 'reputation or goodwill' must be understood. It is a reputation as the source of a product and/or its distinctive qualities in the mind of a significant section of the public[11] which must be established.

14.3.1 Reputation is linked to traders

First, it is the claimant's reputation as a trader that must be established: *Day v Brownrigg* (1878). Trade both in goods and services can be protected in passing off. Trade is interpreted widely to include professional and charitable organisations: *British Medical Association v Marsh* (1931); *British Diabetic Association v The Diabetic Society* (1996); *Burge v Haydock* (2002) (the Countryside Alliance). In the latter case it was held that even a charitable or professional organisation not carrying on commercial activity could have valuable property in its goodwill which it was entitled to protect through an action for passing off.

Secondly, the claimant's reputation may extend to indicating the quality of goods or services, as well as their source: *Spalding v Gamage* (1915).

Thirdly, the reputation may not be transferred with the product. The public may recognise the goods or services of a trader, but have no knowledge of a claimant's actual identity – for example, not recognising that AERO bars are made by Nestlé. The reputation attaches to the trader as the source of those goods and services or their quality, and not to the product. In *Saxlehner v Appolinaris* (1897) the plaintiff had sold a spring used for bottled spring water to the defendant. An injunction was granted when the defendant used the plaintiff's name for the water, as the reputation connected the plaintiff to the product in the public's mind. A transferee of such an unregistered name or reputation must then develop his own goodwill before being able to sue for passing off.

---

9   As in the 'drinks cases'.
10 As in the *Advocaat* case.
11 *Chocosuisse v Cadbury* (1999).

Fourthly, where one trader has developed a widely known reputation for high quality, it is a temptation to other traders to use references to that reputation for its associations. This raises a question as to whether there can be passing off between two of such 'borrowed' reputations. In *Rolls Razor v Rolls (Lighters)* (1949), the plaintiff and defendant both used names with allusions to the ROLLS ROYCE Company. Harman J refused to grant an injunction, on the ground that no direct misrepresentation had been made, nor confusion caused, as the plaintiff's activities did not extend from the manufacture of razors to that of lighters, avoiding the issue of a borrowed reputation. Similarly, in *Evian v Bowles* (1975), the makers of EVIAN water bottles for EVIAN bicycles were unable to prevent a rival selling bottles under the same name. A claimant must establish that it is *his* reputation that has been misrepresented by the defendant, and not just that general association with a third party's reputation has occurred.

14.3.2   Shared reputation

The fifth aspect to reputation lies at the point where passing off becomes the extended form of the remedy. As already discussed, a series of 'drinks' cases established that a group of traders may share a reputation in a jointly used name or other identifying feature. The names 'sherry', 'whisky' and 'Champagne' all designate the region from which the drink comes, and denote the superior quality of the genuine product, a reputation shared by all producers within the region: *Bollinger v Costa Brava* (1961); *Vine Products v Mackenzie* (1969); *Bulmer v Bollinger* (1978).

This was taken a step further by the House of Lords in *Erven Warnink v Townend* (1979), with the recognition that a name for a drink designating its composition, rather than its source, may be shared and protected. European Community law has extended protection to such shared designations in two ways. Regulations cater for geographical designations of origin for agricultural products, foodstuffs and beverages, by providing a system of registration for products from a particular region or with particular characteristics. In addition, jurisprudence of the European Court of Justice (ECJ) recognises appellations of origin as 'industrial and commercial property' for the purposes of Article 30 of the European Community Treaty: see 1.4.2 and *Delhaize v Promalvin* (1992).

Further development may have come with *Chocosuisse v Cadbury* (1999) because there was no clear-cut recipe on which to found a common reputation, as in the *Advocaat* case. Here the reputation for texture generally held by Swiss chocolate was sufficient to render Cadbury's naming a standard bar of milk chocolate made in the UK – SWISS CHALET – passing off. This was so even though some of the chocolate made by two of the defendants was not made in Switzerland (although Swiss and EU standards were maintained). The Court of Appeal recognised that the claim was in the extended form of passing off established by *Advocaat*. In addition, the phrase 'Swiss chocolate' was accepted to be descriptive, finding that: '[i]f the words are no more than descriptive – whether of the place or the manufacturer – they cannot found an action in passing off.' Nevertheless, Laddie J's conclusion that a significant section of the public recognised the phrase to denote more than just a place of origin, having connotations of 'quality, expense and exclusivity', and that a class of such goods could be identified, was upheld.

14.4 GOODWILL

The significance of reputation in establishing a remedy is the goodwill it bestows on a producer. Traders spend a great deal of effort and expense in building an identifiable reputation in order to create and enhance a market for their goods and services, and it is this resulting appeal to customers' goodwill (or willingness to deal with that trader) that passing off protects. There can be no goodwill without a reputation, although a reputation may exist without goodwill.

14.4.1 Definition

Goodwill was defined by Lord McNaughton, in *IRC v Muller's Margarine* (1901), as:

> ... the benefit and advantage of the good name, reputation and connection of a business. It is the attractive force that brings in custom. It is the one thing which distinguishes an old established business from a new business at its first start ... is worth nothing unless it has power of attraction sufficient to bring customers home to the source from which it emanates.

Although this refers to customers, the courts have been willing to recognise goodwill in a number of ways other than merely having a place of business within the UK. Not having an outlet at all in the UK did meant there was no goodwill in *Anheuser-Busch Inc v Budejuvcky Budwar Narodni Podnik* (1984), but the facts were unusual as all trade took place on American bases. Where a trader's reputation is very extensive the public may well believe that different products still stem from him, and goodwill may therefore extend beyond that trader's current market: *Lego v Lemelstrich* (1983). However, this elasticity is not infinite, and in *Harrods v Harrodian School* (1996) the store's world-wide reputation did not extend as far as providing schooling. In Millett LJ's words, '[t]o be known to everyone is not to be known for everything'. If customers have access to a trader's products and associate them with him (rather than an agent or dealer) as their source, goodwill may subsist: *Jian Tools v Roderick Manhattan Group Ltd* (1995).

14.4.2 Place of goodwill

Actionable goodwill is goodwill (although not necessarily a place of business) within the jurisdiction. *Dicta* in *Star Industrial Co v Yap Kwee Kor* (1975) suggest that goodwill is both local and divisible, and Lord Fraser's judgment in *Advocaat* (1979) concentrated on goodwill in England. However, this does not preclude the courts from recognising an international reputation and concomitant international goodwill where it can be found to exist in fact: *Habib Bank v Habib Bank* (1981).

Goodwill may be more circumscribed and be local in its extent. In *Guardian Media Group plc v Associated Newspapers Ltd* (2000) the Court of Appeal upheld the interlocutory injunction granted to protect the local reputation of the Manchester free paper 'Manchester METRO News' and the injunction was limited to a radius of 15 miles from Central Manchester.

Reputation may also vary in different regions and be protected in its local embodiments. In *Associated Newspapers Ltd v Express Newspapers* (2003) it was held that, as passing off relates to events in a market place, it is the effect of a defendant's actions on a claimant's reputation in *that* marketplace which is relevant. Consequently, the fact that a number of regional papers in the UK use the word 'Mail' in their titles did not affect the strong reputation held by *The Daily Mail* newspaper as the MAIL in London and the south east. The injunction was therefore confined to that area of reputation. Conversely, if a defendant's actions are to be national in scope the fact that the claimant's reputation and goodwill is local will not prevent the grant of a nationwide injunction: *Chelsea Man Menswear v Chelsea Girl Ltd* (1987).

14.4.3   Ownership of goodwill

A foreign trader must take care that goodwill arising in the UK attaches to him, and not to his UK representative. In *MedGen Inc v Passion for Life* (2001) an American concern traded in the UK through an exclusive dealership who used packaging designed to meet UK regulatory requirements and which did not mention the US claimant. It was held that the US concern had no goodwill in the UK as a result, despite behaviour by the UK dealer which was dubbed 'commercially dishonest' by the court. Six factors were held to be relevant:

(i)   the claimant carried on no business in the UK;

(ii)   the packaging made no reference to the claimant;

(iii) the UK dealer carried all the marketing and sales;

(iv)   all reference on the packaging was to the UK dealer;

(v)   customers would refer to the dealer with any problems;

(vi)   there was no evidence that either consumers or retailers had any interest in who produced the product.

14.4.4   Date of assessment of goodwill

The date at which the goodwill springing from reputation must be established is the date at which the allegedly infringing conduct begins: *Chocosuisse v Cadbury* (1999); *DaimlerChrysler AG v Alavi* (2001). Consequently, in the latter case the defendant was able to continue trading as MERC (which he had commenced in the late 1960s) despite the fact that the initial use of the name 'might have involved passing off at its inception'. The car manufacturer, although well known, did not trade significantly (and therefore acquire goodwill) in the UK until the late 1990s.

In *Teleworks Ltd v Teleworks Group plc* (2001) the court refused to take account of 'future goodwill' – that is, goodwill acquired as a claimant's activities expand after the beginning of the alleged infringing act. It held that passing off adequately protects a growing business for it extends to any understanding the public has of that claimant's reputation and goodwill:

> It all depends on whether the evidence establishes that purchasers would be led into the belief that the defendant company was now selling these new goods ... If the strength of the claimant's reputation is great enough to induce the relevant belief in purchasers in the circumstances of the trade in question, then the claimant's goodwill is protected in fields which it has not yet entered, and which it may not have the slightest intention of entering.

The court went on to cite the *Lego* case as an 'extreme example' of this. It also held that any threat by a defendant to trade in a different manner from its existing trade may be taken into account in deciding whether the threatened action would give rise to confusion.

14.5 COINCIDENCE OF REPUTATION AND GOODWILL

Because it is the goodwill engendered by reputation which may be defended through an action for passing off, reputation and its accompanying goodwill must coincide in both temporal and geographical terms, as well as in the sphere of trading activity of claimant and defendant. Should this coincidence not exist, a defendant may encroach on a claimant's reputation, and no damage will be caused to his goodwill as the defendant's actions do not overlap the claimant's commercial activities. It is a question of fact for the court whether reputation has outstripped goodwill.

14.5.1 Coincidence of reputation and goodwill in point of time

It is possible for reputation either to precede goodwill or to outlast it. A reputation may also be abandoned, destroying goodwill.

Reputation preceding goodwill

A reputation may be established before trade begins, for example by advertising, so that no actual custom can arise. However, a court may be prepared to find that goodwill has resulted from the reputation before there is actual trade if it can be found that customers are ready and waiting for the product to become available: *BBC v Talbot* (1981). Consider, for example, the advertising (or hype) that precedes the release of a new film. In *My Kinda Bones v Dr Pepper's Stove* (1984), Slade J refused to strike out a passing off action, although the plaintiff had not yet opened his restaurant, as it was arguable that goodwill could exist through advertising without trade, at least where steps to begin trading had been taken. In addition, in *Elida-Gibbs v Colgate Palmolive* (1983), Goulding J held that television advertising for a new toothpaste gave rise to immediate goodwill.

This does not mean that all advance advertising will necessarily give rise to goodwill. It will depend on the understanding engendered by the advertising in the public's mind: *Cadbury Schweppes v Pub Squash* (1981).

Where reputation precedes trade, although there is found to be goodwill, only an appropriate remedy may be granted. In *Nationwide Building Society v Nationwide Estate Agency* (1987), the plaintiff building society sought an injunction against the defendant's use of their name, although the building society's estate agency activities had not yet begun. The court would have granted an injunction, finding that confusion was likely in such closely linked activities, but only on condition that the plaintiff did nothing to spread the use of its name for estate agencies before the trial. As it refused to give this undertaking no interlocutory injunction was granted.

Reputation outlasting goodwill

If trading activity ceases after a reputation bearing goodwill has been established, eventually the goodwill will decline and expire: *Norman Kark v Odhams* (1962). However, this may not be instant and will depend on the circumstances. In *Ad-Lib Club v Granville* (1972), the plaintiff's club had been closed for five years after complaints about noise when the defendant opened a club using the same name. Pennycuick J granted an injunction, holding that an actionable reputation survived. The plaintiff intended to reopen and was seeking new premises.

Laddie J upheld the *Ad-Lib* decision in *Sutherland v V2 Music Ltd* (2002). When the runners-up to the band Hear'Say (formed after winning the Pop Stars contest in 2000) formed a group called 'Liberty' (new Liberty), they were sued for passing off by members of the band LIBERTY (old Liberty). This group had had some success but after 1995 had a low profile, working as session musicians rather than releasing records. However, on the facts, the court was prepared to find sufficient (although borderline) residual goodwill in the group to defend their name. New Liberty argued that the requirement of damage had been ignored in *Ad-Lib* but Laddie J held that although old Liberty were no longer releasing records they would still suffer damage as goodwill itself is the property protected by passing off. New Liberty's actions would destroy old Liberty's goodwill and therefore cause damage to them:

> Goodwill is an asset of a business. It can be very valuable. It attracts customers. It can facilitate finding more business. It can be bought and sold. It can be damaged.... Goodwill is of value, not only in respect of current business, but also because of future business opportunities it will nurture. It is its power to support and improve future business which gives it its value and makes it saleable. It is acquired by trading and advertising in the past but its value is in the way it promotes future business.

Abandoned reputations

Where an owner abandons his reputation, even though a residue of goodwill might remain, this goodwill is abandoned along with the reputation. In *Star Industrial Co v Yap Kwee Kor* (1975), the Privy Council considered whether the plaintiff had any rights of property left to defend in the name 'Ace Brand', given to toothbrushes. It sold the brushes in Singapore until the imposition of an import duty made the sales unprofitable. Three years later it formed a subsidiary in Singapore and granted it the exclusive use of the mark. The defendant then adopted the same name for toothbrushes sold in Singapore. It was found that, when the plaintiff transferred the name to the subsidiary, it had abandoned any goodwill that might have remained capable of being revived and protected by it.

14.5.2   Geographical coincidence of reputation and goodwill[12]

Similarly, a defendant's activities must actually encroach upon the geographical area in which a claimant trades. Consequently, in *Outram v London Evening News* (1911), the plaintiff proprietors of the 'Glasgow Evening News' failed to secure relief against the

---

12   Dawson, N, 'The Foreign Trade Mark Owner's Experience: An Absence of Goodwill?', in Dawson, N and Firth, A, *Trade Marks Retrospective* (London: Sweet & Maxwell, 2000).

proprietors of the 'London Evening News', as there was no overlap in the area of circulation of the two newspapers.

Difficulties arise if a defendant's misrepresentations and trade extend into areas where a claimant has no existing trade but does have significant reputation. These have become acute in an age of international communications and travel, which mean that reputations have the potential to spread worldwide in a short time. It can be argued that a trader may suffer damage by misrepresentations of his reputation in an area in which he has not yet begun to trade. Such activity will hamper any future expansion plans, as well possibly injuring his reputation for quality among travelling customers. The answer lies in defining what amounts to goodwill and the courts appear to have taken two lines of approach to this problem.

The hard line approach

In some cases, a strict view of goodwill, as a trader having actual customers in the relevant area, has led to the refusal of relief in passing off, despite the apparent damage the claimant perceives from the defendant's actions.

Three cases illustrate this line of authority. In *Bernardin v Pavilion Properties* (1967), an action against a 'Crazy Horse Saloon' in London by the owners of the famous Paris 'Crazy Horse Saloon' failed, despite advertising and publicity carried out in the UK. Similarly, in *Athlete's Foot v Cobra Sports* (1980), the plaintiff had an extensive reputation in the US, doing business by the grant of franchises, and it was in the process of negotiating (eventually unsuccessfully) a franchise in the UK. The defendant opened 'Athlete's Foot Bargain Basement', registered a business name and advertised in magazines. Walton J refused to grant an injunction; holding that the defendant was merely suggesting a connection with the plaintiff, who could suffer no damage in the UK, where it had no customers. This was followed by *Anheuser-Busch Inc v Budejuveky Budwar Narodni Podnik* (1984) (the *Budweiser* case). Beer bearing the name 'Budweiser' was legitimately made by companies in both the US and (the then) Czechoslovakia after an agreement dividing world markets between them. Both then began preparations to enter the UK market. The claimant American company had a reputation in the UK, and the beer had been sold on US Air Force bases in the UK. Its passing off action failed, however, despite evidence that the British public was confused as to the source of 'Budweiser' beer. The Court of Appeal held, following *Star Industrial Co v Yap Kwee Kor* (1975), that, as goodwill must be attached to a business and be local, the plaintiff had no goodwill because it had no customers on the open market in the UK. It could not, therefore, suffer damage by loss of sales. This decision was subjected to criticism[13] as the authorities did not dictate that goodwill be interpreted as a need for actual customers within the jurisdiction, and both the confusion and damage were clear.

The soft line approach

There have been cases where, despite the lack of actual business in the UK, claimants have succeeded in passing off actions. In *Sheraton v Sheraton Motels* (1974), the fact that bookings were taken in the UK for the American hotels sufficed to constitute goodwill.

---

13   Lane, S, 'Passing Off and the Foreign Plaintiff' [1984] EIPR 279.

So too, in *Maxim's v Dye* (1977), the fact that customers would book from the UK for the Paris restaurant created enough goodwill to protect against the opening of a 'Maxim's' restaurant in Norfolk. However, it is unlikely that the real 'Maxim's' customers would be confused or that damage could be caused in these circumstances. A similar decision in *Pete Waterman Ltd v CBS United Kingdom Ltd* (1993) that the defendant's services, provided in the US (a recording studio), gave rise to goodwill as it had a large number of users from the UK – sufficient to defeat the plaintiff's claim for passing off.

Similarly, English concerns have established goodwill in Scotland without having Scottish outlets. A trader operating as 'Dickie's Dirt' secured an interdict against the Glasgow trader using the name 'Dirty Dicks' in *Flaxcell v Freedman* (1981). In addition, the English company Pegasus Security Ltd, preparing to open in Scotland, succeeded in a passing off action against a Scottish business using a similar name in *Pegasus Security Ltd v Gilbert* (1989).

It is difficult to distinguish these lines of authority. There was a likelihood of custom and damage in *Athlete's Foot v Cobra Sports*, as a franchise was being negotiated and the action was for an interlocutory injunction. The facts of *Maxim's v Dye* and *Bernardin v Pavilion Properties* appear almost identical. It is true that apparently very similar passing off cases can appear inconsistent because the decision is based on a different aspect of the trinity of reputation giving rise to goodwill, misrepresentation and damage. Thus, while there may have been goodwill in both the *Athlete's Foot* case and the *Maxim's* case, the different result could be explained by the presence of damage in *Maxim's*, but the lack of it in *Athlete's Foot*. This explanation is difficult to sustain on the facts, however, despite the presence of goodwill and the likelihood of damage being questions of fact for the court. It is notable that the court held that no damage would be sustained in *Budweiser* (1984). The difference, then, does not appear to be one of fact, nor one based on different conditions of passing off.

A new approach

Because communications, advertising and marketing are becoming increasingly international, traders are not receiving protection from passing off commensurate with modern technological and commercial conditions. Traders feel that real damage is caused by the misappropriation of an internationally known reputation because the chance of later expansion is prevented and any lack of quality in the imitator's activities may rebound to the detriment of the owner of the international reputation. In addition, the reputation becomes 'diluted', particularly as the association is created without any ability to control it and the possibility of earning licensing fees from later merchandising of the reputation is lost. This reality was recognised by Browne-Wilkinson VC in *Pete Waterman Ltd v CBS United Kingdom Ltd* (1993).

Two resolutions are possible. Either it could be recognised that reputation and goodwill are, in modern conditions, coextensive and that the presence of a commercial reputation necessarily implies an accompanying goodwill,[14] or it could be recognised that goodwill and damage need an interpretation extending far enough to accommodate these new circumstances. It is likely that a definition of goodwill framed within the expectations of 1901 has become outdated and inappropriate. To adopt the

---

14   Mostert, F, 'Is Goodwill Territorial or International?' [1989] EIPR 440.

first solution may go too far, as it would allow a trader with a reputation anywhere in the world to prevent any other trader adopting a confusing indication of source and quality, even although that first trader had no intention of ever expanding into the UK market. This would confer a monopoly. However, the monopoly would only extend to any confusingly similar indicator of reputation and s 56 of the TMA 1994 only requires a reputation in the UK, not actual trade, to give the equivalent protection laid down by Article 6bis of the Paris Convention (see 16.7).

To adopt the second solution involves determining at what point reputation becomes goodwill. That the courts may be willing to do this may be deduced from decisions in New Zealand, Canada and Hong Kong. In *Tan-Ichi v Jancar* (1990), an injunction was granted in Hong Kong.[15] The plaintiffs owned a chain of restaurants in Japan and were negotiating over the opening of another in Hong Kong. The defendants opened a Japanese restaurant in Hong Kong using the same ideograms as the genuine Japanese restaurants. These had been deliberately copied, creating an allusion to the plaintiffs. Sears J held that the plaintiffs had an international reputation and that, in a developing area of the common law the court must respond to changing conditions. It was a question of fact at what point goodwill in Hong Kong arose and, as the plaintiffs did have both actual and potential customers there, there was goodwill. Additionally, the defendants' activities prevented the plaintiffs from controlling and developing their reputation in Hong Kong.[16] It was significant, however, that the defendants had clearly taken a deliberate risk for financial gain. This does suggest that the fears of damage are real, and that it may, therefore, be legitimate to assume goodwill from the presence of reputation.

In the UK, the case of *Jian Tools v Roderick Manhattan Group Ltd* (1995) suggests a move in this direction. The plaintiff had reputation and goodwill in the US in business software, named 'BizPlan Builder'. The defendant adopted the name 'BusinessPlan Builder' for similar software in the UK. Although 127 units of the plaintiff's software had been sold to UK buyers and had been extensively advertised in American publications that had some UK circulation, only two advertisements had been placed in UK publications, these giving rise to the sale of only 10 programs. The plaintiffs had neither a commercial outlet nor sales employees in the UK. Knox J accepted that reputation alone would not suffice and that goodwill in the UK must be shown. Nevertheless, he found that there was sufficient UK goodwill if the nature of the goods was taken into consideration. As the software was capable of continued use and was not an article of everyday household use, the relatively small number of sales made constituted goodwill. It has been suggested[17] that the presence of a two-way market opportunity allowing repeat sales to UK customers is necessary.

---

15 Subsequently, the drink manufacturer Yakult succeeded in preventing a YAKUDO mark being registered in Hong Kong by a Chinese competitor. This was based on strong judicial recognition of international well known marks and the effects of international travel on consumer recognition and understanding of marks: *Yakult v Yakudo Group* (2004), HCA 2409/2002, www.judiciary.gov.hk.

16 The decision is, however, criticised (although deemed the correct decision on its facts) by Kwan, A, and Stephenson, P, in 'Goodwill and Passing off in Hong Kong' [2000] EIPR 331.

17 Rose, D, 'Season of Goodwill: Passing Off and Overseas Traders' [1995] EIPR 356.

14.5.3   Coincidence of activity of claimant and defendant

Trade marks are registered for particular classes of goods and services. This raises the question whether passing off will protect a trader's reputation beyond the actual goods and services which he provides. Before 1948, it did not seem that the claimant's field of activity was relevant. In *Eastman v John Griffiths* (1898), it was held that to use the name applied by the plaintiff to cameras for bicycles amounted to passing off, although the plaintiff did make cameras for use on bicycles. Equally, in *Walter v Ashton* (1902), for the defendant to sell a 'Times' bicycle was actionable. It was held that this raised the tangible possibility of damage to the plaintiff if any confusion with the plaintiff's newspaper led to litigation against them. Again, however, the plaintiff newspaper was in the practice of occasionally offering goods to readers under the Times name.

Common field of action

In 1948, the case of *McCulloch v May* (1948) appeared to establish a less generous approach by the courts. Wynn Parry J added another factor to passing off: a 'common field of activity' which had to be shown between the plaintiff's and defendant's spheres of trade. This case is distinguishable from the earlier ones, since in 1948 it was less likely that the public would think that a presenter of radio programmes had allowed his name to be used by makers of breakfast cereal and, therefore, unlikely that any confusion would result from the defendant's activities. However, it was followed by later courts as laying down a necessary requirement, and not as a finding of fact as to confusion and damage, in cases such as *Wombles v Wombles Skips* (1977).

This practice was criticised in Australia, and not followed in *Henderson v RCA* (1969). The plaintiffs were well known dancers, who successfully sued the defendants for using a photograph of them on a record of dance music. It was held to be sufficient that the parties were in business and that the activities of plaintiffs and defendants were competing in a broad sense.

A question of fact

In the UK, Oliver J reassessed the effect of *McCulloch v May* (1948) in *Lyngstad v Anabas* (1977), explaining the need for a common field of activity as a 'convenient shorthand term for indicating a real possibility of confusion'. The defendant had sold T-shirts bearing a photograph of the pop group 'Abba' without permission. Confusion in such cases of association depend on the public's growing understanding of celebrity endorsement and merchandising, so that *McCulloch v May* can be distinguished on this basis. In 1983, a new approach was confirmed in *Lego v Lemestrich*. *McCulloch v May* (1948) was explained as a need for real confusion and the court was willing also to consider new forms of damage. The plaintiff, the makers of the well known children's construction toy, succeeded in establishing passing off against the Israeli defendant company, which made irrigation equipment, including bright coloured plastic garden equipment. However, Falconer J did not discount the relevance of the fields of activity entirely:

> Of course, that is not to say that the proximity of a defendant's field of activity to that of the plaintiff will not be relevant to whether the defendant's acts complained of

amount to a misrepresentation in any particular case – plainly it will, at least in most cases. However, in my judgment, there is much force in Mr Aldous's submission, based on the extent of the plaintiffs' reputation in their mark LEGO, that if, as he contended was this case, the plaintiffs' mark has become part of the English language in the sense that everybody associates LEGO with a particular company ... then the misrepresentation by the defendants' use of the mark is easier to assume and prove; on the other hand, if the mark or name concerned has only a limited field of recognition, it is obviously more difficult to establish its understanding as denoting the plaintiff's goods in a field which is not directly comparable with the field of the plaintiff's goods.

It is not clear how far *Lego* extends. The decision may be confined to household words such as LEGO. It is difficult to reconcile the decision with Lord Fraser's definition of passing off in the *Advocaat* case (that the trader must trade in a clearly defined class of goods), unless it is seen as an example of a wide field of activity being found – that of coloured plastic goods. It was described as 'extreme' example in *Teleworks Ltd v Teleworks Group plc* (2002), where it was pointed out that the question whether the activities of two traders overlap depends on the level of particularity with which the field of action is defined. It was suggested that in the large and diverse computer telecommunications industry some level of specificity was required.

That there must also be confusion and damage was reaffirmed by *Stringfellow v McCain* (1984). The plaintiff, owner of Stringfellow's nightclub, did not succeed in preventing the defendant naming oven chips 'Stringfellows', even though these had been advertised on television by using a nightclub theme. 'Stringfellows' was not regarded as a household name, and the overlap in activity was too nebulous to cause substantial confusion.

Merchandising

It can be seen that many of these cases fall within the area of what today might be termed 'image protection' (see Chapter 18). In this context *McCulloch v May* (1948) was discredited in *Irvine v Talksport Ltd* (2002).[18] The Formula One racing driver, Eddie Irvine, claimed passing off when the defendant radio station digitally manipulated a photograph of him to show him holding a radio with the name 'Talk Radio' displayed on it. Laddie J held that passing off will protect a claimant's right to exclusive reputation or goodwill and that there is no need to show a common field of action:

> Not only has the law of passing off expanded over the years, but the commercial environment in which it operates is in a constant state of flux ... the court can take judicial notice of the fact that it is common for famous people to exploit their names or images by way of endorsement. They do it not only in their own field of expertise but, depending on the extent of their fame or notoriety, wider afield also.

14.6 MISREPRESENTATION

It is not a claimant's use of any particular form of mark that is important, but the understanding that the claimant's use of any name, logo, symbol, colour, shape, slogan

---

18 Upheld by the Court of Appeal in *Irvine v Talksport Ltd* (2003).

or any other feature identifiable with goods or services has developed in the public mind. There is no definition of an actionable unregistered 'mark' equivalent to s 1 of the TMA 1994. What must be shown is that the claimant's use of the symbol has created a distinctive association between the symbol used and his goods or services, so that consumers have been educated to associate the symbol with the claimant's product alone.

This will be difficult to establish if the symbol used describes the product in some way, as it could relate to any producer of that type of product. The more descriptive the symbol, the more difficult it will be to establish the existence of a reputation (consider, for example, 'soap' for soap), the more distinctive the symbol, the more likely a reputation has arisen ('mango', or even more so 'moonlight', for soap). An initially distinctive symbol may actually become descriptive – generic – if a trader is able to use it exclusively in association with his product so that the association made by the public becomes one as to the nature of the product, rather than its source. Consider, for example, the name KLEENEX.

Traditionally, a mark has been regarded as an indicator of the source of a product, but passing off is not restricted to misrepresentations as to source. Accordingly, the indications of quality given to their footballs by the plaintiffs founded a successful passing off action in *Spalding v Gamage* (1915), as these were understood as such. The same was true in *Rizla v Bryant May* (1986) when the plaintiff used different colours for different grades of cigarette papers, although the action failed because the defendants had distinguished their product from the plaintiff's sufficiently to avoid confusion. Whether an actionable misrepresentation has been made can only be judged in relation to the public's understanding of the mark. Examples of indicia used, and the extent of distinctiveness required, follow.

14.6.1   Indicia of reputation

Get-up

The shape of goods themselves may indicate their source: *Edge v Nicholls* (1911). The plaintiffs sold washing blue attached to a stick. It was held that the stick was distinctive of the plaintiffs despite the writing also on the product, as the purchasing public for washing blue was (then) largely illiterate.

The leading case on get-up, controversially, is the *Jif Lemon* case (1990). The House of Lords held that the sale of lemon juice in plastic containers shaped and coloured to resemble real lemons was distinctive of the plaintiffs' product and that get-up could sustain reputation. This was so despite the fact that the container was so descriptive of the product. The House of Lords felt bound by the trial judge's finding of fact that confusion had been caused. It was clearly significant that the plaintiffs had been the only sellers of lemon juice in plastic lemon shaped containers for some 20 years, giving the necessary secondary meaning to the get-up.

Where get-up is unlikely to confuse, there will be no passing of. In the *Roho* case (1995) the purchasing public was found to be health professionals who would not be confused by the shape of the defendant's cushions as they would be paying careful attention to the purchase. In addition, if shape has not become associated with any particular source (although the trader's name need not be known) in the public mind, there can be no passing off: *Politechnica v Dallas Print* (1982). The inventor of the Rubik cube was unable to establish that its shape was associated with him as its source in the public mind.

Shapes became registrable as marks under the TMA 1994 and no confusion need be shown if a registered mark is used on identical goods or services, lessening pressure on passing off to provide a remedy. Passing off of get-up could be relied on, however, to protect a functional aspect of a design.

Colour

Use of colour may give rise to reputation, provided that it is distinctive of the claimant's goods and has not become generic in the public's mind: *Rizla v Bryant May* (1986); *Sodastream v Thorn Cascade* (1982). BP's green colour was recognised as distinctive in *BP Amoco plc v John Kelly* (2002).

Styles

Styles have not been so readily protected, being difficult to delimit with sufficient precision: *Gordon Fraser v Tatt* (1966). The plaintiff made a series of successful greetings cards with designs of whimsical children, whimsically dressed, in a recognisable and distinctive colour scheme. This was held too nebulous to be capable of protection despite the plaintiff's arguments that its artists had exclusive contracts and that the cards were often asked for by name.

Although the Court of Appeal also refused an injunction in *My Kinda Town v Soll* (1983), *dicta* suggest that styles may be protected in the right circumstances. The defendant left the plaintiff's restaurant 'Chicago Pizza Pie Factory' and set up a rival 'Grunts Chicago Pizza Company'. The menu design, decor, and style of the two were similar. No passing off was made out as the names, which were descriptive, were held not to be confusing. However, Oliver LJ was prepared to say that the other features were confusing and, had they been pleaded as the source of reputation, he might have decided differently.

Names

The most obvious indication of reputation is a name, but generic, invented and personal names require separate consideration.

Generic names and words

Descriptive names and words do not give rise to goodwill without more: *Chocosuisse v Cadbury* (1999), *BBC v Talksport Ltd* (2001). In the latter case it was held that if the words used to describe a product or service are no more than descriptive, as 'live sports broadcasting' were, they could not, alone, found an action in passing off. Similarly, the Easygroup did not pursue a case against Easyart's domain name,[19] 'easy' being a descriptive word.

---

19   'Easyart Wins Domain Name Fight', BBC News, 9 May 2003: www.bbc.co.uk.

A claimant must establish that a name has come to associate him with his goods or services by having acquired secondary meaning: *Reddaway v Banham* (1896). The name 'Camel Hair Belting', although entirely descriptive of the plaintiff's product and, therefore, a name that any manufacturer of similar goods might wish to use, had become distinctive of the plaintiff through 12 years' exclusive use. Others wishing to use such descriptive names can do so provided that sufficient is done to distinguish their products. In contrast, 'Chicago Pizza Pie' remained descriptive as there had not been sufficient use by the plaintiff and so the name was free for others to use: *My Kinda Town v Soll* (1983). Easyjet did succeed against the owner of the domain name 'easyRealestate.co.uk', not on any reputation in 'easy', but because of the overt passing off of their livery or get-up, particularly the use of orange and white: *Easyjet Airline Co Ltd v Dainty* (2002).

Secondary meaning that has been acquired through use can be lost once the public begins to understand the name as descriptive of a type of goods. The point at which this occurs is an objective question of fact for the court. The first user of a descriptive name will have to prove reputation to succeed: *McCain International v Country Fair* (1981). In 1979, the plaintiffs introduced a new product, which they named 'McCAIN Oven Chips'. In 1980, the defendants entered competition with 'COUNTRY FAIR Oven Chips', arguing that the name 'oven chips' was descriptive of the nature of the product and not indicative of their source. The Court of Appeal held that 18 months' use, in conjunction with the name McCAIN, could not give 'oven chips' secondary meaning, nor would there be any confusion between the plaintiff's and defendant's goods.

Personal names

It is natural for a trader to use his own name. Difficulties may arise where other traders share the same name, particularly when family businesses divide. The House of Lords held in *Marengo v Daily Sketch* (1948) that, provided the use is honest, a defendant may use his or her own name for a business, but not for goods, even if the result is confusion. In *Parker Knoll v Knoll International* (1962), an injunction was granted against use of the defendant's name for goods, but not against its use as the company name. In *Asprey and Garrard Ltd v WRA (Guns) Ltd* (2002) it was held that the exception for names had never been intended to apply to *new* companies. Consequently, using one's own name provides a very limited defence to claims of passing off.

However, a personal name may acquire secondary meaning, preventing its use even for another's business. In the South African case of *Boswell-Wilkie v Brian Boswell Circus* (1985), it was found that the name of 'Boswell' had acquired such significance to the circus-going public that a scion of the family was unable to use his personal name even for his business, a rival circus. It was held that, even though the full business names were used in advertising and an announcement was made to the audience once inside the big top alerting them to the two different concerns, the evidence showed that the public shortened both names to merely 'Boswell' and would be confused. Nicknames do not receive the same treatment as ordinary surnames, so that 'Biba' could not be used for a business in *Biba v Biba Boutique* (1980).

Concurrent use of a family name will be sanctioned when the two reputations have built up side by side (rather than one following the other): *Habib Bank v Habib Bank* (1981). A family owned and named bank established an overseas subsidiary with the same family name. Later, the family bank was nationalised and split from the foreign subsidiary. The attempt to prevent a new branch of the now independent subsidiary taking its parent company's name failed. It was held that use of the name implied no association with the nationalised bank, although the branch acquired its parent's reputation immediately. The only association was with the foreign subsidiary (which had branches in the UK).

Invented names

The clearest way of adopting a distinctive name is to invent a new word, and to do so ensured success where copyright failed in *Exxon v Exxon Insurance Services* (1981).

Advertising themes

Themes used in advertising have been held to be able to sustain reputations in *Cadbury Schweppes v Pub Squash* (1981); *Elida-Gibbs v Colgate Palmolive* (1983); and *Stringfellow v McCain Foods (GB) Ltd* (1984), provided that the public has, in fact, come to associate the theme with the claiment.

14.6.2   The nature of misrepresentation

Misrepresentations of source or quality

The act of passing off involves a defendant misrepresenting his goods or services to the consumer. The misrepresentation must suggest either that the goods have come from the claimant (*Reddaway v Banham* (1896)) – a misrepresentation as to source – or that they have the quality of the claimant's product (the *Advocaat* case (1979)) – a misrepresentation as to quality. Misrepresentation that one business is associated in business terms (such as by licensing) with another is actionable. In *Sir Robert McAlpine Ltd v Alfred McAlpine plc* (2004) Mann J applied the Court of Appeal's decision in *The Clock Ltd v The Clockhouse Hotel Ltd* (1936):

> ... no man is entitled to carry on his business in such a way or by such a name as to lead to the belief that he is carrying on the business of another man or to lead to the belief that the business which he is carrying on has any connection with the business carried on by the other man.

However, mere confusion between claimant and defendant will not constitute a misrepresentation where the claimant cannot show a sufficient reputation bringing goodwill: *HFC Bank plc v HSBC Bank plc* (2000).

Express misrepresentations

Misrepresentations may be express or implied. The clearest express misrepresentation is the direct taking of the claimant's badge of reputation by the defendant, be it name, logo, slogan, colour or get-up. Its use may then suggest that the defendant is the source of origin or of the quality of the claimant's product. Even to sell goods identified as the claimant's and made by a claimant's supplier to the claimant's standards constitutes passing off because it suggests that the claimant held itself responsible for their quality: *Primark Ltd v Lollypop Ltd* (2001).

Indirect misrepresentations

However, a misrepresentation may also be indirect.

An allusion to the claimant's activities without any use of its indicia at all may amount to misrepresentation. Thus, in *Sony v Saray* (1983), the defendant's claim to be an agent of the plaintiff, which it was not, was actionable. Similarly, for the defendant to claim that its was the product 'as shown on television', when it had been the plaintiff's product that had been advertised, amounted to misrepresentation in *Copydex v Noso* (1952).

Even less overt associations have been held to be misrepresentations. In a case which represents another step forward in the action's history in response to advancing commercial practices, it was held that for the defendant to have advertising leaflets placed inside the plaintiff's newspapers was passing off: *Associated News v Insert Media* (1991). Browne-Wilkinson VC said whether such an activity amounts to misrepresentation is a question of fact for the court depending:

> ... upon the nature of the product, the alterations made to it and the circumstances in which the altered product is put before the public. For example, in the present case if it were to be widely thought by the public that advertising inserts were put into the papers by newsagents and not by the publishers, the activities of the third defendant would not constitute any actionable misrepresentation. The question whether or not there has been a misrepresentation causing confusion or deception must depend upon the perceptions of the matter by the public at large. If a substantial body of persons assume that such inserts are made by the publishers, then the insertion of the inserts into the newspaper by newsagents will be calculated to misrepresent the position to the public. In my judgment therefore the mere fact that the inserts have been made without the plaintiffs' consent does not establish the existence of a misrepresentation.

Even a true statement may amount to a misrepresentation if the result is public confusion. In a clever piece of comparative advertising, in *McDonald v Burger King* (1986), the statement 'It's not just big, Mac' placed on advertisements in London Underground trains for BURGER KING Whopper burgers was held likely to cause confusion with McDONALD's Big Mac. Similarly, it amounted to passing off for NOUVELLE to offer to replace dissatisfied customers' toilet rolls with those made by ANDREX as it would be understood by the public to mean that ANDREX was associated with the offer: *Kimberley Clark v Fort Sterling* (1997).

Equipping oneself with the means for passing off, indirectly threatening to pass off or provide a third person with the means to do so, also amounts to a form of misrepresentation. In *British Telecommunications plc v One in a Million* (1999) it was held that for a cybersquatter (see 14.7.3) to register domain names incorporating another's name amounted to passing off by threatening to supply an 'instrument of fraud'.[20]

Using another's trade mark as a metatag within the code of a website, whether hidden or not, does not constitute a misrepresentation if no confusion results. In *Reed Executive v Reed Business Information* (2004) Jacob LJ pointed out that the defendant's use of the name 'Reed' in its metatags did not bring its website above Reed Employment in the results for a search for 'Reed jobs'. As no confusion would result there was no misrepresentation. His recognition that the public is familiar with receiving many irrelevant 'hits' when using search engines suggests that the use of

---

20 Carty, H, 'Passing Off and Instruments of Deception: The Need for Clarity' [2003] EIPR 188.

metatags is unlikely to constitute passing off. The same was true of other invisible uses of the name Reed.

Innocent misrepresentations

A misrepresentation need not be deliberate or conscious. Although, in *Advocaat* (1979), Lord Diplock spoke of a misrepresentation 'calculated' to injure the plaintiff, the reference was not to the defendant's intention, but the effect of the defendant's actions. An innocent defendant is equally liable for passing off (*Baume v Moore* (1958)) and will be subject to an injunction, account of profits and delivery up. It was not so clear whether damages would lie against a defendant unaware of the consequences of its actions. In other areas of intellectual property, the innocent defendant is not liable to damages (see 19.8.4), but the House of Lords left the point open in *Marengo v Daily Sketch* (1948). However, it was held, at first instance, in *Gillette v Edenwest* (1994), that substantial damages would be awarded against an innocent defendant.

Parody

It is no defence to a misrepresentation that it was obviously humorous if the effect is to cause an impression of endorsement and to cause damage: *Irvine v Talksport Ltd* (2003). More generally, it could be argued that if a mark has been parodied that there is no misrepresentation. By its nature a parody seeks to associate without confusing, managing both to call the original to mind and to distance itself at the same time.[21] In the UK the courts have continued to focus on the nature of the misrepresentation and the inducement of confusion, without according any special status to a parody. If dilution of a mark is recognised as a head of damage (see 16.5), an unkind parody with the capacity to confuse is likely to pass off, whatever the defendant's intention.

Misappropriation

A distinction can be drawn between a misrepresentation and a misappropriation of the claimant's reputation. Misappropriation occurs where the defendant's actions evoke an association between the claimant's and defendant's products without creating actual confusion as to their source. Such a misappropriation is likely to create associations with respect to quality, however, and one of the consequences of the House of Lords' extension of passing off in *Advocaat* (1979) was to raise a question as to how far such a misappropriation might fall within its new parameters. This is particularly relevant to the question of dilution (see 14.7.2). *Irvine v Talksport Ltd* (2002)[22] moves a step closer to a remedy for misappropriation by recognising a misrepresentation by false endorsement. However, Laddie J confined his decision to a misrepresentation that the claimant was endorsing the defendant's service. This misrepresentation was grounded on the 'common knowledge' that a substantial part of many sportsmen's income may be derived from endorsement.

---

21   Maniatis, S, 'Parody: A Fatal Attraction? Part 2: Trade Mark Parodies' [1997] EIPR 412.
22   Upheld by the Court of Appeal in *Irvine v Talksport Ltd* (2003).

14.6.3   The test of misrepresentation

Once an action by the defendant capable of constituting a misrepresentation has been established, the test to be applied is whether that action induced, or was likely to induce,[23] the public to confuse the source or quality of the defendant's product with the claimant's. Both inducement and confusion must be shown. In *My Kinda Town v Soll* (1983), it was held that the plaintiff had not established that the defendant's use of the name 'Chicago Pizza Pie' had caused confusion and, also, that this is a question of fact for the court.

The origins of passing off lie in deceit and, while it is not necessary to show any element of fraud on a defendant's part, the essence of misrepresentation lies in the confusion that is induced by his action. Recently, the courts have reaffirmed the need to show confusion, or the likelihood of confusion, in order to distinguish between an actionable misrepresentation and mere misappropriation. In the *Roho* case (1995), Jacob J sought to distinguish between competition and unfair competition. The plaintiff alleged that the defendant was riding on the back of its reputation. He said:

> There is no tort of copying. There is no tort of taking a man's market or customers. Neither the market nor the customers are the plaintiff's to own. There is no tort of making use of another's goodwill as such. There is no tort of competition.

> At the heart of passing off lies deception or its likelihood, deception of the ultimate consumer in particular. Over the years, passing off has developed, from the classic case of the defendant selling his goods as and for those of the plaintiff, to cover other kinds of deception, for example, that the defendant's goods are the same as those of the plaintiff when they are not (for example, *Combe International Ltd v Scholl (UK) Ltd* (1990)); or that the defendant's goods are the same as goods sold by a class of persons of which the plaintiff is a member when they are not (for example, *Warnink (Erven) BV v J Townend and Sons Ltd* (1980)). Never has the tort shown even a slight tendency to stray beyond cases of deception. Were it to do so it would enter the field of honest competition, declared unlawful for some reason other than deceptiveness – it would only serve to stifle competition.

This approach was followed by the Court of Appeal in *Harrods Ltd v Harrodian School* (1996), where it was also said that, if the defendant's actions were deliberate, this would be a factor that influences a conclusion as to whether a misrepresentation had been made.

14.6.4   Determining confusion

The case of *Neutrogena v Golden Ltd* (1996) sets out the relevant principles. The plaintiff marketed a range of shampoos and other hair and skin care products under the name 'Neutrogena'. The defendant entered the market with a narrower range of competing products with the name 'Neutralia'. The plaintiff's reputation was clear, at issue was confusion. At first instance, Jacob J had held that deception and confusion had to be above a *de minimis* level. The Court of Appeal upheld his judgment, laying down the relevant considerations:

---

23 *Associated Newspapers Ltd v Express Newspapers* (2003).

(a)   the correct principle to be applied was that of *Jif Lemon* (1990), that 'a substantial number of members of the public will be misled into purchasing the defendants' [product] in the belief that it is the respondents' [product]';

Although Jacob J had applied the correct test, Morritt LJ said that phrases such as 'more than *de minimis*' and 'above a trivial level' should be avoided in order to concentrate on the qualitative elements of the 'substantial number' test. A substantial number does not mean the majority, however.

(b)   it is not necessary that the person confused should have had the opportunity to compare the plaintiffs' and defendants' marks;

(c)   the defendants' mark must be an operative cause of the confusion;

(d)   it is ordinary members of the public who must be confused;

(e)   the nature of the confusion and the degree of awareness which is required of the public depends on all the circumstances. Customers are to be taken as they are found. The question to be asked is how far the defendants' mark bears such a resemblance to the plaintiffs' as to be calculated to deceive incautious customers. This must be decided against the background of the relevant market in which the goods are sold and the habits and characteristics of purchasers in that market;

It is confusion of likely customers for the claimants' product that needs to be shown, and the misrepresentation is tested for its effect on those customers. Consequently, characteristics of the relevant group of the public will be taken into account, as was the illiteracy of buyers of washing blue (*Edge v Nicholls* (1911)) and the nature of housewives in a supermarket shopping for lemon juice (*Jif Lemon* (1990)). Practices in the relevant market will also be relevant. In *Tamworth Herald v Thomson Free Newspapers* (1991), no passing off was found. The defendants were to name their newspaper 'Tamworth Herald and Post'; the plaintiffs published the 'Tamworth Herald'. Aldous J held that there was only a small risk of confusion, although both papers served the same area of circulation, because the defendants' masthead contained the paper's old name, similar names were common in the newspaper field, and could be sufficiently distinguished in the telephone directory, Yellow Pages.

(f)   confusion is a 'jury question'.

The court will take into account the amount of time and attention a customer is likely to pay, the way the product is marketed, the imperfect memory a customer will have of the claimant's reputation when encountering the defendant's product and all other relevant circumstances. The similarity of the claimant's symbol to the defendant's misrepresentation of it will be relevant, including the sound, appearance and any distinctive features of the symbols. The comparison will be of the way they have actually been used by claimant and defendant.

On the facts, it was held that, although it was common ground that most people were not confused, the names were inherently capable of deceiving because of their common prefix. Although the marks must be compared as a whole, the court was not precluded from considering the significant features of the mark, particularly the first syllable of a word mark and the fact that, for many, the eye is not an accurate recorder of detail. Substantial confusion was found. The same was true for a so-called 'limping mark'. In the *Chocosuisse* case the name 'Swiss Chalet' was used in association with the well-known CADBURY'S trade mark. This conjunction was not sufficient to prevent enough of the public being confused to prevent passing off being made out, even although Laddie J recognised that that, like himself, many would understand that the product was not Swiss made as a result. However, customers' long acquaintance with the existence of two potentially confusing marks may serve to remove the confusion: *Arsenal v Reed* (2001) (ARSENAL and GUNNERS); *DaimlerChrysler AG v Alavi* (2001) (MERC).

14.6.5 Post-sale confusion

One question that continues to puzzle is that of confusion occurring only after purchase, once the product's external packaging has been removed, so called 'post-sale confusion'. The House of Lords took into consideration that the distinguishing features on the label of Borden's lemon would be removed once the lemon was in use in the *Jif Lemon* case (1990). However, no such confusion was recognised in either the *Roho* case (1995), nor *Bostik v Sellotape* (1994). In the latter case, the defendant adopted the same blue colouring as the plaintiff for its product, so that, once removed from the packaging, the two reusable adhesive putties were confusingly similar. However, no clear evidence of post-sale confusion was put forward in either case.

Such a practice is likely to lead to damage, for, while the defendant's goods would be unlikely to be purchased in mistake for the claimant's, any defects in quality manifested after the distinguishing packaging had been removed could redound to the detriment of the claimant's reputation. In New Zealand, post-sale confusion was accepted in *Levi Strauss and Co v Kimbyr* (1994). The plaintiff sold jeans with a red tab stitched into the seam of the back pocket in order to continue its association with the product after sale. The defendant adopted a similar tab, although a cardboard label avoided confusion at the time of sale. Williams J held that the post-sale confusion amounted to passing off.

14.6.6 Disclaimers

An apparent misrepresentation will not amount to actionable passing off if the defendant takes adequate steps to avoid confusion by distinguishing his goods or services from the plaintiff's: *Rizla v Bryant May* (1986).

A disclaimer may suffice to make the necessary distinction, particularly in circumstances where the public's understanding of the misrepresentation is ambiguous. In *Sony v Saray* (1983), the defendant was ordered by the Court of Appeal to mark all SONY goods with labels stating expressly that they were not authorised SONY dealers, and that the goods were not covered by SONY guarantees. They were not prevented from selling SONY goods, even although to do so amounted to an implicit misrepresentation. In *BT v Planet Telecom* (2002) the defendants, who sent faxes making reference to '192' (the former number for directory enquiries), were required to add 'This fax is not from BT. We have nothing to do with BT's directory enquiry service'. This case took place at a time when directory services were being deregulated and a number of telephone operators used the number 192 for directory services, some making use of the BT database. The use of '192' was therefore ambiguous.

However, a disclaimer may not always be adequate and, in *Associated News v Insert Media* (1991), both Mummery J and the Court of Appeal rejected a disclaimer printed on the leaflets by the defendant. They did so on the basis that the disclaimer was unlikely to come to the attention of the reader and that, even if it did, might serve only to cause greater confusion as to responsibility for the inserts. The result was to confer a monopoly on the plaintiff in using its newspapers for advertising purposes, but this was an activity in which it was preparing to engage. A disclaimer that is not effective to avoid confusion will not be sufficient: *Football Association v Graymore* (1994).

14.6.7 Evidence of confusion

The question of confusion is one for the judge, but the parties may adduce evidence of actual or potential confusion. Evidence of witnesses, market survey evidence of public reactions and expert evidence has been used.

Market survey evidence

Guidelines for the use of such evidence were laid down in *Imperial Group v Philip Morris* (1984):

(a) interviewees must be selected to represent a relevant cross-section of the general public, with knowledge both of the party's product and the relevant market and unaware of the litigation;

(b) a sample of statistically significant size must be used;

(c) the survey must be conducted fairly;

(d) all the surveys carried out must be disclosed to the other side, including both the number surveyed, the instructions given to interviewers, any coding instructions and the method adopted;

(e) all answers, in exact and verbatim form, must also be disclosed, with no confidentiality offered to interviewees;

(f) no leading nor suggestive questions should be used;

(g) a sample initial survey to iron out any problems may be advisable.

The courts have been cautious in accepting such evidence; it was rejected in *Scott v Nice-Pak* (1988) because the question posed to members of the public was based on the false premise that the defendant's product was already available in the UK. The weight to be attached to such evidence is a matter for the court.

Expert evidence

Although expert evidence is admissible, where the goods at issue are of a type sold to the general public for consumption or domestic use, it will not be so unless the judges' own experience does not allow them to assess the likelihood of confusion. In *Gucci v Gucci* (1991), Browne-Wilkinson VC heard expert evidence in relation to designer goods, but, in *Dalgety Spillers Foods v Food Brokers Ltd* (1993), expert evidence in relation to an ordinary convenience food product was not admitted. In all cases, evidence to show the circumstances and places in which goods are sold, the kind of people buying them and the manner in which the public is accustomed to ask for such goods is admissible.

Evidence of witnesses

In *Neutrogena v Golden Ltd* (1996), Jacob J preferred the evidence of witnesses to survey evidence, and it was such evidence which contributed to the Court of Appeal's decision in the same case. Evidence was led of letters of complaint about a television advert for 'Neutralia'. These comprised: (i) those who had communicated both with the plaintiff and the defendant; (ii) those responding to an internal e-mail by the plaintiff's solicitors asking for those who had heard of 'Neutralia'; (iii) and those from members of the public interviewed after buying either 'Neutralia' or 'Neutrogena' in shops with a promotion on 'Neutrogena'.

14.6.8   Reverse passing off

The case of *Bristol Conservatories v Conservatories Custom Built* (1989) raised the issue of 'reverse' or 'inverse' passing off. In traditional passing off, the defendant induces the public to believe that the claimant is responsible for the defendant's product by associating it with an indication of the claimant's reputation. However, in this case, the defendant used photographs of the Bristol's conservatories in selling its own, under its own name. Therefore, the defendant did not use the plaintiff's reputation to suggest that its (the defendant's) goods had come from the plaintiff; rather, it used representations of the plaintiff's goods when selling its own product, suggesting that the plaintiff's goods had come from the defendant. In other words, instead of inducing the public to believe that the defendant's goods came from the plaintiff, the public was induced to believe that the defendant was responsible for the quality of the plaintiff's goods. The public was in no doubt that the goods it was buying came from the defendant and no reference was made to the plaintiff by name. In so doing, the defendant was, of course, still benefiting from the public associating the plaintiff's quality with its (the defendant's) product.

Dicta in *Reddaway v Banham* (1896), *Spalding v Gamage* (1915) and *Jif Lemon* (1990) suggest that a defendant's misrepresentation must indicate that the goods or services offered by the defendant are the goods or services of the plaintiff. However, the court held that, without deciding whether reverse passing off was actionable, the defendant's action fell within the bounds of *Advocaat* (1979). The application to strike out the plaintiff's claim was unsuccessful. In Scotland an interim interdict was granted in *John Henderson & Son v Alexander Munro* (1905) without discussion of the issue. Munro has been one of the managing directors of the complainant's firm. Having established his own business, he issued a circular claiming that he was an expert because he had supervised many projects listed, which had been completed by the complainer's company. The court held that an ordinary reader of the leaflet might conclude that the respondent's firm had carried out this work. This would be misleading and injury result to the complainer because of the attribution of its experience to the respondent.

Recognition of reverse passing off is a logical development from the growth of passing off to encompass misrepresentations as to quality, and falls within Lord Diplock's definition of the tort in *Advocaat* (1979). Provided that both confusion and damage continue to be necessary elements of the action, this development should not see passing off develop into a remedy against unfair competition. This is illustrated by the case of *LEEC Ltd v Morquip Ltd* (1996). The defendant used photographs of the plaintiff's equipment in tendering for a health authority contract. The plaintiff suffered no loss of sales as a result but sought an injunction against any future use of the photographs. Laddie J held that the use of the photographs did not alone amount to passing off; there must be a misrepresentation and damage. As no sufficient confusion was proved, the plaintiff's action failed.

14.7   DAMAGE

It is damage (or, in an interlocutory application, potential damage) to goodwill that must be shown. Following *Advocaat* (1979) passing off defends a claimant's reputation, both as a source of particular goods or services, and as the provider of their quality. This suggests that damage to protectable goodwill should include damage to these commercial attributes of a claimant. Precisely how damage to goodwill is defined will make a considerable difference to the ambit of passing off protection. At the time when passing off related to misrepresentations as to source, goodwill was defined as loss of custom, a decline in sales through customers diverted to the defendant's product by the confusion caused: *IRC v Muller's Margarine* (1901).

However, the development of new means and methods of advertising and trading practices has changed the way in which traders develop and use reputations in the course of their trade. These have evolved from personal service given to local customers to mass marketing through self-service outlets and now include electronic commerce, global and virtual markets, and global broadcast advertising. Modern conditions have also seen the development of new value in such reputations, with marks in themselves becoming attractive commodities. Another significant development has been diversification by traders, so that one enterprise may produce an enormous variety of goods and services (VIRGIN for example). Thus, the use of a trader's reputation, even on widely differing goods or services, by commercial rivals may redound to his detriment by causing 'dilution' of the mark. It was this fear that lay at the heart of the so-called 'drinks cases' and the *Lego* case (1983).

14.7.1   Heads of damage

The boundaries of actionable damage have expanded to accommodate some of these new practices. Several 'heads of damage' have been recognised:

(i)   damage to the plaintiff's reputation was recognised in *Harrods v Harrod* (1924). False association was a head of damage in *Associated Newspapers Ltd v Express Newspapers* (2003) and *Sir Robert McAlpine Ltd v Alfred McAlpine plc* (2004);

(ii)   damage to a reputation for quality was recognised in *Bollinger v Costa Brava* (1959) and *Bulmer v Bollinger* (1978);

(iii) the risk of litigation stemming from the public's confusion of defendant with plaintiff was treated as a recognised head of damage in *Walter v Ashton* (1902), although not in *McCulloch v May* (1948);

(iv)   in the *Lego* case (1983), one head of damage was said to be the plaintiff's loss of chance to expand into the field of coloured plastic garden-ware;

(v)   in *Stringfellow v McCain Foods* (1984), it was argued that the loss of an opportunity to license one's mark amounted to actionable damage, although, on the facts, it was found that the plaintiff had not anticipated such an opportunity;

(vi) damage through false endorsement was added by the *Irvine v Talksport Ltd* (2003) case.

All these heads of damage can ultimately be seen to result in a loss of customers.

14.7.2 Dilution

The vexed question that remains is the problem of 'dilution' of a mark. Dilution occurs when a mark is used on non-competing products, so that there is no loss of custom (or customers) through direct competition, but the connotations of the mark, particularly one with high associations of quality, are tarnished or diminished in some way.

Dilution differs from traditional passing off in two ways: both as to the misrepresentation made and the nature of the ensuing damage. First, any misrepresentation comes when the public associates two products as being related but does not confuse their source. Secondly, any resulting damage is to the connotations of the claimant's mark in the public's mind. The TMA 1994 introduced remedies for dilution of registered marks and well-known marks, so that there would be a symmetry in passing off doing the same. In addition, there is a fine dividing line between dilution and traditional passing off, as harm to a trader's reputation may well have an effect on trade, even if indirect. As new heads of damage are recognised the distinction becomes increasingly ill-defined.

Elderflower Champagne

Dilution was at issue in the 'Elderflower Champagne' case: *Taittinger v Allbev* (1992). The legitimate users of the 'Champagne' name objected when the defendant made and sold a sparkling, non-alcoholic drink named 'Elderflower Champagne' at a much lower price than Champagne. Larger bottles were made up to have the appearance of Champagne bottles and sold in supermarkets and other outlets selling both alcoholic and non-alcoholic drinks. The plaintiff sought injunctions against the name 'Champagne' being used in relation to the defendant's drink.

There are two significant aspects to the Court of Appeal's judgment. First, it upheld the finding at first instance that the use of the Champagne name constituted a misrepresentation. Although it was accepted that the majority of the public would not confuse the defendant's drink with the plaintiff's, it was held that 'the simple unworldly man who has in mind a family celebration ... may well suppose that he is buying Champagne'. Peter Gibson LJ accepted that this did not include 'any majority part of the public or even ... any substantial section of the public', but said that it did amount to 'many members of the public'. He went on to say:

> It seems to me at least as likely that a not insignificant number of members of the public would think that it had *some association* with Champagne [emphasis added] ...

apparently regarding a mental association as an actionable misrepresentation. Such a development in regard to misrepresentation opens the way to providing a remedy for dilution.

Secondly, the Court of Appeal disagreed with the trial judge's finding that the misrepresentation would not cause damage to the plaintiff's goodwill. The damage found was contributed to by the fact that the public would misassociate the product with Champagne. Peter Gibson LJ accepted the damage that dilution could induce, eventually resulting in the name becoming a generic term for any sparkling wine, or even any sparkling drink:

> ... it seems to me no less obvious that erosion of the distinctiveness of the name Champagne in this country is a form of damage to the goodwill of the business of the Champagne houses.

Sir Thomas Bingham MR added:

> The first plaintiff's reputation and goodwill in the description 'Champagne' derives not only from the quality of its wine and its glamorous associations, but also from the very singularity and exclusiveness of the description, the absence of any qualifying epithets and imitative descriptions. Any product which is not Champagne, but is allowed to describe itself as such must inevitably, in my view, erode the singularity and exclusiveness of the description 'Champagne' and so cause the first plaintiff damage of an insidious but serious kind ... I cannot see ... any rational basis upon which, if the defendant's product were allowed to be marketed under its present description, any other fruit cordial diluted with carbonated water could not be similarly marketed so as to incorporate the description 'Champagne'. The damage to the first plaintiff would then be incalculable but severe.

In evidence, the defendant admitted that it wanted to use the Champagne name in order to promote the elderflower drink; consequently, any benefit in doing so might be presumed to have an equivalent detrimental effect to the plaintiff. This was not a case where there had been a deliberate attempt to take the Champagne name, so that the defendant's actions had not been a deliberate and cynical riding on the back of the plaintiff's fame. The Court of Appeal's finding of damage rested, therefore, on the damage caused by dilution.

Later misgivings: cushions, schools and domains

Whether the Court of Appeal's view of misrepresentation as including misappropriation can be reconciled with the later decision in the *Roho* case (1995) remains a moot point, although that is a case at first instance. The decision in *Harrods Ltd v Harrodian School* (1996) does give rise to such a doubt. Millett LJ found it difficult to accept that, in an action where the law requires a finding of both confusion and damage, that damage which did not depend on confusion could result. The dilution of the HARRODS name by the defendant's use of it for its school alleged in that case did not secure an injunction in a majority decision of the Court of Appeal. Whether confusion can be found depends largely on the sector of the public regarded as relevant, be it the public at large, or a smaller section familiar with the claimant's product. The majority in the Harrods case concentrated on the 'affluent members of the middle class who live in London, shop at HARRODS and wish to send their children to fee-paying schools'; the minority concentrated on 'the far greater sector of the public' who are aware of the plaintiff's reputation. In the *Elderflower Champagne* case (1992), Peter Gibson LJ considered the public at large.

Nevertheless, in *British Telecommunications plc v One in a Million* (1999) the Court of Appeal did implicitly recognise that dilution causes damage. There, registration of a very well known domain name (see 14.7.3) by someone unauthorised to use it was said to be 'an erosion of the exclusive goodwill in the name which damages or is likely to damage' the owner of the name.

Even if the courts are prepared to extend misrepresentation to association and damage to dilution, the claimant must still prove goodwill. Where a claimant does not trade at all tarnishment or diminution of reputation cannot amount to passing off. Oxford University sought invalidity of the registered trade mark OXFORD BLUE (a name it chose not to merchandise itself for fear of devaluing its reputation) under s 47(2), based on s 5(4)(a) of the TMA 1994. In the Trade Mark Registry the hearing officer found that this could not amount to passing off as the University had no goodwill in the name, despite its undoubted reputation: *Oxford Ltd v HS Tank and Sons Ltd* (2004).

It has been argued that passing off should not stray from the 'classic trinity' enumerated in *Jif Lemon* (1990). This is because it is these criteria which secure the public interest in being protected from confusion, while simultaneously allowing for the benefits of competition. However, it is also worth considering the consequences of refusing a remedy for dilution. To refuse such a remedy would allow unregistered marks to be eroded and devalued. This would prejudice not just the owner, who has spent considerable sums in promoting the connotations that the mark brings, but also the public, which would soon learn not to trust the message of such marks in general. In addition, the public would then incur extra costs involved in having to seek the information necessary to make wise consumer choices.

Moreover, although to protect against dilution does confer a virtual monopoly in the mark, it does not inhibit competition in products. Competitors must merely choose their own marks. Consequently, protection against dilution should not allow the monopolisation of words, names, shapes and colours, for example, although the choice is eventually finite, because commonly used and descriptive indicia will not acquire a reputation without a great deal of effort on the owner's part. The result in *Jif Lemon* (1990) was anomalous in that competitors had allowed the plaintiff to build up a reputation in such a generic mark. There is also a median position between protecting all indications of reputation from dilution and refusing to protect any. Unless a reputation is very widely known indeed (such as that of LEGO, COCA-COLA, McDONALD'S, for example) inconspicuous use by another will not cause any real damage. Dilution could be preserved for the genuinely household names such as Champagne, or LEGO.

14.7.3   Passing off and domain names

Dilution is an issue that will require resolution. Meanwhile, new ways of impinging upon a trader's reputation continue to develop. The latest application of passing off to a similar situation comes from the adoption of well known names as domain names (addresses) for the internet (see 17.6.1) by unauthorised individuals. In *Harrods v UK Network Services Ltd* (1997), individuals registered the domain names 'ladbroke.com', 'ourprice.com', 'cadburys.com' and 'harrods.com'. After securing suspension of the registration, the plaintiff succeeded in an undefended passing off action, despite the fact that the name, once suspended, could not be used and, therefore, posed no threat of damage to the plaintiff's goodwill.

A similar result was achieved in *Glaxo plc v Glaxowellcome Ltd* (1996). This case did not involve a domain name, but the creation of an 'off-the-shelf' company bearing the name Glaxowellcome Ltd by the defendant just as Glaxo plc took over Wellcome plc, creating Glaxo-Wellcome plc. The defendant offered to sell the new company to the plaintiffs for 100 times the normal price. Lightman J granted an injunction, despite the defendant's undertaking not to trade under the 'Glaxowellcome' name. Had he done so, and Lightman J did not find the defendant a credible witness, the necessary element of damage to goodwill would still have been nebulous as it is hard to see what damage could have been done to the plaintiff pharmaceutical multinational enterprise.

Cybersquatting

The Court of Appeal also upheld an injunction against the registration of well known names as domain names in *British Telecommunications plc v One in a Million* (1999). Aldous LJ was prepared to treat the registration as equipping, or intending to equip another, with an instrument of fraud (that is, passing off), despite the lack of a threat to carry out any deception:

> In my view there can be discerned from the cases a jurisdiction to grant injunctive relief where a defendant is equipped with or is intending to equip another with an instrument of fraud. Whether any name is an instrument of fraud will depend on all the circumstances. A name which will by reason of its similarity to the name of another inherently lead to passing off is such an instrument. If it would not inherently lead to passing off, it does not follow that it is not an instrument of fraud.

However, he laid down criteria for consideration before such a conclusion could be reached. The court should consider:

(i)   the similarity of the names;

(ii) the intention of the defendant;

(iii) the type of trade;

(iv) all the surrounding circumstances.

He held that it was the intention of the defendant to appropriate the goodwill of another, or enable others to do so, which founded liability:

> If, taking all the circumstances into account, the court should conclude that the name was produced to enable passing off, is adapted to be used for passing off and if used is likely to be fraudulently used, an injunction will be appropriate.

He did recognise that a finding of passing off involved a further extension of the doctrine's boundaries as laid out in *Advocaat* (1979), but held that this extension was necessary to allow the common law to evolve to meet changes in methods for trade and communication.

The case was followed in *Easygroup IP Licensing Ltd v Sermbezis* (2003). The defendant website, offering car rental services, was prevented from using 'easy' in its domain name as the Easygroup was able to establish reputation and goodwill in relation to car rental. However, in this case there was direct competition and use of the name by the defendant.

Doubts

One in a Million was distinguished in *French Connection Ltd v Sutton* (2000), suggesting that Aldous LJ's criteria may suffice to confine the doctrine to appropriate facts. Holding, in an application for summary judgment, that it could not be said that there was no prospect of the defendant making out that the three elements of passing off, the application was refused. The fact that the defendant alleged that he wished to use the name for his own business and that the FCUK name (at that time) was not a household word were also argued to distinguish this case on its facts.

Carty regrets Aldous LJ's development of the doctrine of instruments of fraud.[24] Indirect passing off, where a middleman misrepresents products by putting them into the market (a wholesaler, importer, or manufacturer, for example), is protected against by means of instruments of deception (*Singer v Loog* (1880), *Draper v Trist* (1939). Consequently, she argues, the limits of passing off should be maintained – goodwill, misrepresentation and damage. Additionally, there should be no instrument of deception without circulation of the deceptive products, linking the damage to a claimant with a defendant's action. If an additional step is needed before deception of the public, a defendant would be better regarded as liable only as a joint tortfeasor. However, in *British Telecommunications plc v One in a Million* (1999) Aldous LJ recognised his adoption of liability for instruments of deception in registering domain names without circulation extended the boundaries of passing off. As such, the decision can be regarded as representing judicial sympathy for those suffering from unfair trading practices rather than classic passing off. Carty suggests that registering the domain names was akin to printing and offering to sell a misleading label and no more. This may be to ignore the scale of the defendant's actions in that case, and its undoubted activities as a cybersquatter. It is when the principle is applied to other traders with a genuine interest in the domain name that its application becomes questionable. In addition, instruments of deception could not be applied where parties with concurrent reputations in the same name contest the right to register that name: *Pitman Training Ltd v Nominet UK* (1997).

14.8 LOOKALIKE PRODUCTS

A practice that caused much discomfort to brand owners is that of the sale of 'lookalike' products. It was particularly evident in the supermarket own brand imitations of well known products, such as breakfast cereal, coffee and biscuits. The lookalike was sold as an equivalent to the 'genuine' goods, but usually at a lower price, taking advantage of an already established market and reputation for quality. To an extent, the practice diminishes once the lookalike secures a share of the market. However, some brand owners have taken expensive measures to distinguish their products – by changing the shape of NESCAFÉ coffee jars, for example.

A lookalike bears the trade mark of its producer, but the remainder of the product's packaging (get-up) is strongly reminiscent of that of the branded product, even to the point of confusion. While there is nothing to stop competition in equivalent goods, to do so almost in the guise of a known branded product is to ride on the back of the effort and expenditure incurred in developing the brand's reputation. Supermarkets also have the advantage of controlling the outlets for the goods (both their own and the brands) and of economies of scale which allow them to undercut the brands' price. Therefore, brand owners regard lookalikes as unfair competition, while lookalike producers regard the competition as fair. During the passage of the Trade Marks Bill

---

24 Carty, H, 'Passing Off and Instruments of Deception: The Need for Clarity' [2003] EIPR 188.

through the House of Lords, brand owners lobbied strongly to secure a remedy against look-alikes,[25] but this was not forthcoming.

Unregistered get-up may be protectable in passing off. The stumbling block lies in the requirement of confusion, however, as both products bear their manufacturers' trade marks. Side by side, the packaging may not confuse a careful shopper alert to the practice of lookalike products. Early cases of challenge to lookalike products were settled out of court for this reason. However, confusion is possible where both products are not simultaneously available and the consumer must rely on remembered get-up and, after purchase, when more attention may be paid to the nature of the product than to any trade mark.

Brand owners may draw some reassurance from the first case to reach court, *United Biscuits (UK) Ltd v Asda Stores* (1997). Walker J held that, although there was no trade mark infringement, Asda's PUFFIN biscuits did pass off the McVITIE'S PENGUIN biscuits. It was clear that the defendant had intended to sail as close to the wind as possible and this intention was taken into account. The evidence established that a significant proportion of shoppers would distinguish the two products, but that a substantial number would assume an association between them in the form of a common manufacturer. This was held to satisfy the 'classical trinity' of passing off.

The PUFFIN was a particularly blatant lookalike. Brand owners may not fare so well against a better-calculated imitation. Lookalikes have threatened the dominant position of the brand owners, who argue that the expense of establishing of a brand reputation is deserving of protection. The answer may lie in incorporating Article 10*bis* of the Paris Convention, which gives a remedy for unfair competition, into UK law. Rejection of a remedy against all but the most blatant of lookalikes in passing off at present represents the limit to which the courts are prepared to extend the remedy beyond its traditional 'trinity'.

Registration of get-up as a trade mark might prevent competition from lookalikes, subject to the argument that the whole get-up of goods or their packaging does not amount to a 'sign' (see 15.3.2). It would also appear that attempts to register get-up after the competition is established, will fail. In *Re Procter and Gamble* (1999) the Court of Appeal was willing to consider composite marks (which comprised the shape of three bottles for domestic cleaning products, considered with their labels and the colours of the bottles). However, the marks failed the absolute grounds of objection as they were held to be devoid of distinctive character (see 15.6.3).

Protection for image and reputation through registration is the subject of the next three chapters.

Further Reading

Carty, H, 'The Development of Passing Off in the Twentieth Century', in Dawson, N, and Firth, A, *Trade Marks Retrospective* (London: Sweet & Maxwell, 2000)

Carty, H, 'Heads of Damage in Passing Off' [1996] EIPR 487

Carty, H, 'Passing Off and the Concept of Goodwill' [1995] JBL 139

Carty, H, 'Inverse Passing Off: A Suitable Addition to Passing Off?' [1993] EIPR 370

---

25 Mills, 'Own Label Products and the "Lookalike" Phenomenon: A Lack of Trade Dress and Unfair Competition Protection?' [1995] EIPR 116.

Clive, E, 'The Action for Passing Off: Its Scope and Basis', 1963 JR 117

Colston, C, 'Passing Off: the Right Solution to Domain Names?' [2000] LMCLQ 523

Connor, I, 'Bring Them Home' [2000] EIPR 181

Dawson, N, 'The Foreign Trade Mark Owner's Experience: An Absence of Goodwill?', in Dawson, N, and Firth, A, *Trade Marks Retrospective* (London: Sweet & Maxwell, 2000)

Learmouth, M, 'Eddie, are you OK? Product Endorsement and Passing Off' [2002] IPQ 306

Mills, B, 'Own Label Products and the "Lookalike" Phenomenon: a Lack of Trade Dress and Unfair Competition Protection?' [1995] EIPR 116

Morcom, C, 'Leading Cases in Passing Off', in Dawson, N, and Firth, A, *Trade Marks Retrospective* (London: Sweet & Maxwell, 2000)

Mostert, F, 'Is Goodwill Territorial or International?' [1989] EIPR 440

Murray, A, 'A Distinct Lack of Goodwill' [1997] EIPR 345

Pattinson, P, 'Market Research Surveys – Money Well Spent? The Use of Survey Evidence in Passing Off Proceedings in the UK' [1990] EIPR 99

Rose, D, 'Season of Goodwill: Passing Off and Overseas Traders' [1996] EIPR 356

Spence, M, 'Passing Off and the Misappropriation of Valuable Intangibles' (1996) 112 LQR 472

Thorne, C, and Bennett, S, 'Domain Names – Internet Warehousing: Has Protection of Well Known Names on the Internet Gone Too Far?' [1998] EIPR 468

Wadlow, C, *The Law of Passing Off* (2nd edn, London: Sweet & Maxwell, 1995)

CHAPTER 15

REGISTERED TRADE MARKS

15.1 INTRODUCTION

Trade marks are a source of information. They are the by-product of market enterprise and market place competition. Trade marks identify goods and services[1] in the same way that names identify individuals and companies, and have the advantage of being able to do so in attractive and internationally recognisable ways. Increasingly, trade marks are used to give products and services a 'feel' desirable to consumers in its own right.

The use of trade marks has a long history, from the marks used by potters in Roman times, to the internationally known marks in use today, such as McDONALD's 'golden arches', the NIKE 'swoosh' or the name COCA-COLA. The use, and the importance, of trade marks have flourished in a changing commercial environment, one that has progressed from well known manufacturers supplying a local market, to today's mass marketing and international markets. The Industrial Revolution led to more goods becoming available. In turn, a revolution in the means of transport (canals, railways and roads, now extended to air transport) led to widespread and long-distance distribution. The result was the development of a global market place and international trade (including parallel importing). Allied to this, the development of mass marketing techniques (self-service shopping and mail order catalogues, for example) and of new advertising media and practices, emphasised and increased the use and numbers of trade marks.

Trade mark registration was first introduced in the UK in 1875. Today, their proprietors consider trade marks to be of vital commercial importance and, in recent years, companies have been encouraged to value these assets on their balance sheets. One estimate values the COCA-COLA trade mark at US$70 billion.

Development in the uses of trade marks is not static, so that continuing progress in the means of competition, consumerism and communication (such as digital networked communications) continues to push at the boundaries of trade mark law while new means of unfair competition emerge. The unauthorised use of trade marks in domain names is a practice now challenging trade mark law (see 17.6).

15.1.1 The Trade Marks Act 1994

The UK acquired new trade mark law on 31 October 1994 with the Trade Marks Act (TMA) 1994. The old law was complex, the statute (TMA 1938) was difficult to use and the protection given to trade marks had fallen behind trading practices. It still remains applicable to infringements before commencement of the TMA 1994, although these are declining rapidly in number.

There were three general reasons for the new law: European, international and domestic changes. Two European initiatives, a harmonisation Directive and Regulation establishing a community-wide trade mark required implementation; changes to

---

1   Collectively termed 'products' here.

domestic law were necessary before the UK could ratify the Madrid Protocol and fulfil obligations under Article 6*bis* of the Paris Convention; and the parlous state of the old law called for reform.

Harmonisation

The Trade Mark Directive[2] was enacted in the TMA 1994. It lowered the standard of registrability for a mark (making a wider range of marks registrable), broadened the scope of infringement, and made third party challenges to the validity of a registration easier. Much of the Directive's language was directly re-enacted, although couched in terms of broad principle, and the Directive must be used in interpretation of the 1994 Act. References are made to the European Court of Justice (ECJ) for interpretation when necessary by national courts under Article 234 of the EC Treaty (ex Article 177).

The Trade Mark Directive was preceded by two harmonising measures relating to unfair competition: the Misleading Advertising Directive[3] and the Comparative Advertising Directive.[4] The Control of Misleading Advertisements Regulations 1988 were amended by the Control of Misleading Advertisements (Amendment) Regulations 2000 enacting these directives (see 16.6).

Community-wide rights

The Community Trade Mark Regulation[5] established a unitary trade mark for the whole of the EU. The Regulation is directly applicable in the UK, but s 52 of the TMA 1994 provided for the making of regulations by the Secretary of State for the Community trade mark's introduction. Registration is in the Community Trade Mark Office, the Office for Harmonisation in the Internal Market (OHIM), in Alicante, Spain. Although the Community trade mark provides an easier and cheaper means of securing EU-wide protection, the costs of application still must include Europe-wide searches for confusing marks if an applicant is to avoid opposition to his application from an alert competitor. Another advantage of the unitary mark is that its proprietor may take action against infringements in several Member States by proceedings in a designated court in one Member State (the High Court is the designated UK court). The OHIM started proceedings on 1 April 1996.

International protection

The Madrid Protocol was signed on 27 June 1989, but could not be ratified by the UK until changes were made to domestic trade mark law. The Madrid Agreement 1891 established a system of international recognition, by the Agreement's Member States,

---

2   Council Directive to approximate the Laws of Member States relating to Trade Marks, 89/104 EEC [1989] OJ L40/1.

3   Council Directive concerning Misleading and Comparative Advertising, 84/450/EEC [1984] OJ L250/17.

4   European Parliament and Council Directive amending Directive 84/450/EEC concerning Misleading Advertising so as to include Comparative Advertising, 97/55/EC [1997] OJ L290/18.

5   Council Regulation on the Community Trade Mark, 40/94/EC [1994] OJ L11/1. It was amended by the Council Regulation (EC) 442/2004.

for domestically registered trade marks deposited with WIPO in Geneva, provided that the countries designated for protection have not objected to the mark within 12 months. This allows the proprietor of a domestically registered mark to secure multiple protection with a single application. The UK was not a party to this Agreement, however, as, with its strong examination system for trade mark applications, the period of 12 months was not sufficient for objection to be made to an unregistrable mark. Unlike the OHIM, and other national trade marks systems, the UK does not leave the onus of objecting to invalid marks to competitors (but see 15.2.1), and marks are examined for all grounds of refusal before grant.

The Madrid Protocol is designed to accommodate countries with this paternal approach to examination by allowing an 18-month period for objection. It also makes changes to mitigate some of the other disadvantages of the Madrid Agreement, such as 'central attack' to a mark. This allowed a successful challenge to the national registration underpinning protection in other Madrid Agreement States to cause the failure of the mark in all the countries in which protection had been sought. Membership of the Protocol, which came into effect on 1 April 1996, should ease the expense and burden of multiple trade mark protection. The United States' membership became effective in November 2003.

Article 6*bis* of the Paris Convention provides for protection for 'well known' marks. This is incorporated in UK law by ss 5, 6(1)(c) and 56 of the TMA 1994 (see 15.15.1 and 16.7). It is no longer necessary for the owner of a well known mark to seek redress through the tort of passing off and prove a reputation in the UK. The TRIPS Agreement 1994 lays down standards of trade mark protection for all WTO Member States, applying the Paris Convention principles of priority and national treatment. TRIPS extends trade mark protection, and protection for well known marks, to marks for services; and extends to dilution of a mark by use on dissimilar products where this is harmful to the mark's proprietor.

The Trademark Law Treaty 1994, promulgated and administered under the aegis of WIPO, is aimed at streamlining and simplifying registration procedures and renewal of marks world-wide, but does not make substantive provision for marks.

Interpretation of Community measures

The implementation of harmonisation measures by the TMA 1994 has led to some difficulties of interpretation (see, in particular, *Wagamama Ltd v City Centre Restaurants* (1995)), both in the materials to be used by the courts in this process and in traditions and concepts surviving from the old law.

National courts may make reference to the ECJ for interpretation of the Directive. Interpretation of the Regulation is a matter for both the ECJ and the Court of First Instance (which hears appeals from the OHIM Boards of Appeal). The substantive law in the Regulation is couched in the same terms as the Trade Mark Directive, and should be interpreted in the same way. National courts have not always been swift, however, to slough off their traditional concepts. Interpretation of the new terminology, therefore, raises the question of the materials able to be used for construction. The courts refer to the decisions of the OHIM and those of national courts in other Member States, as Jacob J did in *Philips Electronics NV v Remington Consumer Products Ltd* (1998). They also refer to Directive and its preamble, as well as *travaux préparatoires* (*Wagamama Ltd v City Centre Restaurants* (1995)), and the Regulation.

Reference is made to the ECJ where necessary. However, the judges will not slavishly follow the courts of other Member States purely because they are the first to have decided a particular point, for they may be wrong: *Wagamama Ltd v City Centre Restaurants*. Laddie J decisively rejected the Commission's 'statements' which accompanied the Directive as an aid to interpretation in *Wagamama Ltd v City Centre Restaurants* (1995).

15.1.2   The nature of a trade mark

Registration confers an exclusive (personal) property right in the trade mark, entitling its proprietor to remedies for infringing use.[6] In Scotland a mark constitutes incorporeal immoveable property.

The proprietor has monopoly powers in the mark, for registration may be renewed indefinitely (provided that the mark does not become generic and continues to be used); however, it is a monopoly in the *mark*, and not in the goods and services for which it is used. Other intellectual property rights permitting, competitors may trade in the same goods and services, but may not adopt an identical or similar mark. The protection is, therefore, for the proprietor's reputation, not their product. Additionally, it is only a monopoly in the mark for the purposes of trade, the mark is not removed from the public domain entirely. The registration of BOOTS, for example, does not constrain use of the word in any context other than use on identical or similar goods or services to those for which the mark is registered, or where the use would take unfair advantage of or be detrimental to the character or repute of the mark (see 16.5).

That registration of a mark can have anti-competitive monopolistic potential is illustrated by the fears of the House of Lords, and expressed by Lord Templeman in particular, in *Re Coca-Cola* (1986). The application was to register the shape of the famous Coca-Cola bottle as a mark and was refused because the definition of a trade mark did not include containers. This was a decision under the old law, and would not be the same today, but Lord Templeman said:

> This is another attempt to expand the boundaries of intellectual property and to convert a protective law into a source of a monopoly ...

> It is not sufficient for the Coca-Cola bottle to be distinctive. The Coca-Cola Co must succeed in the startling proposition that a bottle is a trade mark. If so, then any other container or any article of a distinctive shape is capable of being a trade mark. This raises the spectre of a total and perpetual monopoly in containers and articles achieved by means of the Act of 1938.

The TMA 1994 now allows for shapes of containers and packaging to be registered (see 15.3), but registrability is subject to absolute grounds of refusal designed to exclude those shapes which it is necessary for competitors to adopt (see 15.10).

It is common to see the symbols ® and ™. Although there is no requirement that they be used, they serve the purpose of alerting others to the rights governing the

---

6   Sections 2(1), 9(1) and 22 of the TMA 1994.

mark. In addition, it is an offence falsely to represent that a mark is registered, knowing or having reason to believe that the representation is not true.[7]

15.1.3 The functions of a trade mark

Trade marks serve functions which are a product both of policy underlying the substantive provisions of the law relating to registration, and the application of that law; in particular in the interpretations given to the definition of a mark, 'use' of a mark, the licensing provisions, and exhaustion principle. These functions are not static. As new market practices develop, so the functions recognised by judicial interpretation may develop. This is a matter of controversy and distinct differences of approach can be discerned. The issue is a fundamental one, as the functions a trade mark is allowed to serve will dictate the balance struck between the interests of producers and of consumers, and the power given to a trade mark proprietor.

Badges of origin

A trade mark identifies the goods or services with which it is associated and their source. Thus it is necessary that a mark must be distinctive, that is, able to be easily distinguished from the identifying features of the products and services of other producers. If the only function of a trade mark is to guarantee origin it is the proprietor's interest which is being protected.

Guarantee of quality

Identifying products in this way is of small value to modern consumers (often separated by long distances from that source and with little knowledge of it) except in the indication that it also brings of a reputation for quality and reliability. The identification of products enables traders to build and maintain these reputations. It encourages them to maintain and enhance the standard for which they have become known, and supplies the information necessary for informed consumer choices, proving mutually beneficial to producer and customer.

The two prime functions of a trade mark are, first, to provide an indication of source and, secondly, to guarantee quality. Both the origin and guarantee functions can be isolated in a mark's 'capacity to distinguish'. The guarantee function is not served, however, unless a production connection is preserved between trade mark owner and product. Before the TMA 1994 this was achieved, in part, by the strict controls over licensing of marks.

The combined origin and guarantee function of a mark has been described by Jacob J as its use as 'a badge of origin' in *British Sugar plc v James Robertson and Sons* (1996).

Advertising and investment

Today, it is primarily by advertising that reputations are created and maintained. Trade marks provide an economical and effective means of advertising, and are, therefore,

---

7   *Ibid*, s 95.

very useful for promoting products. A great deal of time and money can be invested in the development of trade marks. The growth both in the scale, and means, of disseminating advertising in the latter half of the 20th century (from print to broadcast radio and television and now to electronic transmission) has seen a new value in trade marks as a vehicle for advertising. Incentives, such as mugs, golf umbrellas or T-shirts decorated with the mark, aid in advertising, but are not the prime aim of the proprietor's business. A third, and distinct, function for trade marks as a vehicle for advertising and promotion can thus be identified. It is this function which is undermined by so-called 'dilution' of a mark (see 16.5.1). However far this new function is recognised, it must be remembered that it rests upon the origin and guarantee functions, which must not be undermined as a result.

Merchandising – an image function?

Some marks have even become commodities in themselves, enabling trade in products to which the mark is affixed in the manner of a design rather than as identification (the product often coming from a source other than the trade mark proprietor). Effectively, some marks can be merchandised, creating a new market outside the proprietor's business; for example, transistor radios dressed to resemble a COCA-COLA can or Peter Rabbit mugs.

We are all familiar with the merchandising of identity by celebrities and sportsmen, not only in the endorsement of products for others, but also as a valuable commodity in their own right. This can be supported by trade mark registration, although courts in the UK have not traditionally recognised such use of a mark as one of its protected functions. For example, in *Re Elvis Presley's Application* (1999) it was held that neither Elvis's name nor signature could be registered as marks for his estate. To be registrable it would have to be shown that in the public's eyes these identified the estate and not merely the individual. As a trader had already registered ELVISLY YOURS for Elvis souvenirs, a similar mark already existed which prevented registration of the estate's marks (see 15.6.2). However, this case was decided under the TMA 1938.

Similarly, Princess Diana's estate has had mixed success in registering marks denoting her personality. If the trade mark function is confined to that of origin and guarantee, character marks can only be registrable if the public can be said to associate the individual and the products being sold under the mark. If licensing agreements exist and the public can be seen to understand the mechanics of character merchandising some character marks may be registrable. Similar arguments can be seen to have eventually succeeded in relation to unregistered marks. Laddie J was prepared to believe that evidence might show such public understanding in a passing off action: *BBC v Pally Screen Printing* (1998). In practice, many character merchandising marks have been registered, at least where there is sufficient proximity between the character and the products at issue.

Decisions of the ECJ on what constitutes infringing use of a sign will also have an important effect on how far trade mark registration can be employed in character merchandising, and how far this growing use of the mark may come to be recognised as one of its functions. It has been a particular cause of dispute in relation to merchandising of sporting memorabilia. The long fought *Arsenal Football Club plc v Reed* (2003) (*Arsenal*) case is in point. The Advocate General propounded the view in the ECJ proceedings that the economic value of such merchandising renders use of the sign a trade mark function.[8] He said that:

> The great clubs, such as Arsenal ... are not mere sporting associations whose aim is the playing of football, but genuine emporia which, with the object of playing professional football, pursue an economic activity of the first order.

In stretching the trade mark function to such new activities the real issue, that of unfair competition, should not be ignored. Where an equivalent remedy has been available in passing off, both misrepresentation and damage had first to be shown. If the parameters of registrability and infringement are too widely drawn competitors may be restricted even although their activities do not harm the mark owner.

A developing concept?

The source function of a mark was explicitly, but solely, recognised by the TMA 1938, in its definition of a trade mark. The preamble to the Directive states that the function of a trade mark is *'in particular* to guarantee the trade mark as an indication of origin', implicitly recognising that other functions may exist.

The UK courts were reluctant to provide any protection for an advertising function under the old law. In *Kodiak Trade Mark* (1990) the court refused to regard the use of the KODAK mark on T-shirts, given away as an advertising exercise, as *bona fide*, or commercial, use of the mark for clothing. This allowed Kodiak to have the mark expunged from the register for clothing in order to register their otherwise similar mark in this class of goods. Although the Directive and s 10(3) of the TMA 1994 now provide a remedy for dilution of a mark, it is not yet clear how far the advertising function of a mark is protected by the new law where there is no confusion as to origin or quality.

However, the ECJ is prepared to recognise the advertising function. In *Parfums Christian Dior SA v Evora BV* (1997) Dior objected to advertising by Evora that used Dior trade marks to depict Dior goods (which were parallel imports) in a manner it considered harmful to Dior's reputation for luxury and prestige. Evora also sold goods of a lesser reputation and its advertising did not reflect the Dior image. The Court held that Dior, as the manufacturer of prestigious luxury goods, had a legitimate interest in preventing advertising which detracted from its image, provided that the reseller's advertising 'seriously' damaged' that reputation. In the Advocate General's opinion, this advertising function was regarded as an element of a wide interpretation of the origin function.[9]

The recognition of an enhanced investment or 'image' function is also a factor in the role of trade marks in character merchandising which may precipitate recognition of this added function.

Recognition of the varied roles of a trade mark is not altogether new. HG Wells said that a mark reaches over a retailer's shoulder and across the counter straight to the customer and sells the goods.[10] Schechter[11] provides another early and wide reaching analysis of the mark's function. He said:

---

8   Para 84.
9   Para 42.
10 *The World of William Clissold* (Leipzig: Bernhard Tauchnitz, 1927) Vol 1, 237.
11 'The Rational Basis of Trademark Protection' (1925) 40 Harvard L Rev 813.

The true functions of the trade mark are, then, to identify a product as satisfactory and thereby to stimulate further purchases by the consuming public ... To describe a trademark merely as a symbol of goodwill, without recognising in it an agency for the actual creation and perpetuation of goodwill, ignores the most potent aspect of the nature of a trade mark and that phase most in need of protection ...

... Quite apart from the destruction of the uniqueness of a mark by its use on other goods ... once a mark has come to indicate to the public a constant and uniform source of satisfaction, its owner should be allowed the broadest scope possible for 'the natural expansion of his trade' to other lines or fields of enterprise.

Many, including the ECJ in *Arsenal* (2003), have argued for recognition of new functions for trade marks. It has been recognised that trade marks have a psychological effect which goes beyond the mere indication of source and quality (consider, for example, the appeal of designer trainers) and which confers a value on them beyond that of the goodwill in the products they denote. In both the *Philips* (2003) and *Arsenal* (2003) cases the ECJ has attempted to define the functions of a trade mark. The Court said substantially in both that:

> ... the essential function of a trade mark is to guarantee the identity of the origin of the marked product to the consumer or end-user by enabling him, without any possibility of confusion, to distinguish the product or service from others which have another origin, and for the trade mark to be able to fulfil its essential role in the system of undistorted competition which the Treaty seeks to establish, it must offer a guarantee that all the goods and services bearing it have originated under the *control*[12] of a single undertaking which is responsible for their quality.

The emphasis on 'control', and the application of this function to the provisions on infringement in the *Arsenal* (2003) case stretch the meaning of 'origin' to encompass a merchandising function beyond the UK 'badge of origin' approach. This may force recognition of extended trade mark functions on the UK courts. The Court of Appeal judgment in *Arsenal Football Club plc v Reed* (2003) accepts that use as a badge of allegiance may harm the essential function of the mark. Celtic Football Club has now registered the 'huddle'[13] performed by players before a match, presumably in an effort to combat the sales of unauthorised merchandise bearing this image.

It should not be forgotten, however, that the functions which trade mark law is prepared to recognise and protect is a reflection of the perceived public interest in protecting marks. The balance between the interests of consumers in buying in a competitive market and of producers maintaining the reputation (and price) of their branded products. How far new functions *should* be protected remains controversial, and is at the basis of decisions as to the right conferred by registration, infringing use, registrability, and parallel imports. Cornish outlines important factors in deciding on appropriate boundaries: competitive freedom among traders, consumer interest, correct information as to source and qualities of products, product promotion and market definition.[14] He concludes that protection should confine the exclusive right within the limits necessary for honest practices. However, trade practice is itself subject to change. Honesty of practice can, nevertheless, be measured against standards of unfair competition. At this point, it is perhaps criteria from competition law that may

---

12   Emphasis added.
13   Trade Mark 2268693.
14   Cornish, W, *Intellectual Property: Omnipresent, Distracting, Irrelevant?* (Oxford: OUP, 2004).

help to achieve the balance so fundamental to all intellectual property rights. Kilbey suggests reliance on compulsory licensing to assure a competitive market for memorabilia.[15]

15.2 REGISTRATION OF A MARK

Section 2(2) of the TMA 1994 preserves the law of passing off, but the chief advantage of registering a mark is that protection can be obtained before any use is made of it (provided that the application is made in good faith: s 3(6) of the TMA 1994 (see 15.14)), without the constraints of needing to establish the existence of local reputation and goodwill, nor of confusion where both mark and competing product are identical, nor damage. Once registered, there is a presumption that the trade mark is valid.[16]

An applicant for registration of a trade mark may choose between a purely domestic UK trade mark, international protection through the Madrid Protocol, or a Community trade mark. The choice is one largely dictated by cost, and the inconvenience of multiple translations, depending on commercial judgment as to where market protection will be required. Procedural considerations such as the speed of the application process, and even differences of substantive provisions as to registrability may be a factor. One pitfall of attempts to use the same mark in many jurisdictions has been the variety of meaning a word may bear in different languages.

15.2.1 National application

The TMA 1994 simplified application procedures, which were left to national law by the Directive. The Trade Marks Registry is located in the Patent Office in Newport and maintains a computerised register of marks and transactions in marks. Any person may apply to the registrar for registration of a trade mark.

Application

The contents of an application are specified in s 32 of the TMA 1994 and include a request for registration, a statement of goods or services upon which the mark is to be used, and a representation of the mark. The applicant must also make a declaration that the mark is being used, or that there is a *bona fide* intention to use the mark. When the completed application is submitted, it receives a filing date,[17] which enables issues of priority on competing applications to be resolved if no seniority can be claimed from prior use. This is aided by provision of a system of six months priority for trade marks from an application made in another Convention country by the Paris Convention.[18]

For the purposes of registration, goods and services are divided into classes according to the Nice Agreement concerning the International Classification of Goods

---

15 Kilbey, I, 'The Ironies of *Arsenal v Reed*' [2004] EIPR 479.
16 Section 72 of the TMA 1994.
17 *Ibid*, s 33.
18 *Ibid*, s 35.

and Services 1957.[19] There are 34 classes for goods and 11 for services. The application must state all the goods and services for which the mark is required. Classification does not determine whether goods or services are 'similar' (15.16.2) and is for administrative convenience in searching the register. The TMA 1994 allows a single application to encompass registration in more than one class, unlike the TMA 1938.

Now that protection extends to 'similar' products (the TMA 1938 only extended protection to 'goods of the same description') the registry will query applications for very wide specifications of goods or services. A wide registration for 'computer software' by a telecommunications provider was challenged in *Mercury Communications Ltd v Mercury Interactive (UK) Ltd* (1995). Laddie J held that the challenge was arguable and refused the plaintiff summary judgment. He pointed out that:

> ... a trade mark registered for too wide a specification of goods may have the effect of giving the proprietor an indefinite monopoly over goods which are quite unrelated to his real trading interests.

He also gave his view that a registration for 'computer software' would always be too wide because the defining characteristic of software is the function it performs rather than the medium recording it or the channels of trade through which it passes.

Subsequently, in *Avnet Inc v Isoact Ltd* (1998), Jacob J held that specifications for services should be confined to the substance or core of the possible meanings attributable to the words or phrases used to describe them. In that case the defendant was held not to be providing 'advertising and promotional services' (for which the plaintiff's mark was registered) when it provided web space on which its customers might place their own advertising.

Examination

Once filed, the Trade Marks Registry examines the application for all grounds of refusal (see 15.4 and 15.15), making the necessary searches of earlier marks.[20] The applicant will often have made a similar search before designing the mark, in order to avoid conflict with prior rights, thus inflating the expense of registration.

Section 8 of the TMA 1994 allows for future reconsideration (after 2004) of the strong paternalistic examination system in the UK in favour of the opposition approach adopted in the OHIM and other European States. This leaves trade mark owners to oppose applications on the relative grounds of refusal, which involves comparison of the mark applied for with earlier existing marks. The change was considered in the White Paper,[21] as it would accelerate applications, and reduce their expense, but the majority view was that full examination should continue. It was felt unfair to expect a trade mark owner, who had paid for registration of his mark, to have the onus of defending that mark against later, conflicting, applications, a burden in particular for small and medium-sized companies. In fact, there is also a cost to be borne in an opposition based approach, where a high percentage of applications may be opposed, a cost imposed on both applicant and opponents, and one which has the potential to

---

19 *Ibid*, s 34.
20 *Ibid*, s 37.
21 *Reform of Trade Marks Law*, Cm 1203, 1990.

prolong application proceedings by involving a third party. Registry fees would have to cover these costs. At present, relatively few UK applications are opposed.

In 2002 the Patent Office consulted on the question of continuing the system of examination on relative grounds in the light of the rapid growth of the Community Trade Mark system. UK applicants were being found to be blocked by conflicting applications to the OHIM, although the conflict was not in the UK. The result of this consultation[22] was therefore in favour of preserving the UK system of examination for conflicting marks, although with potential for a review at a future date. The cost of an opposition based system was also seen to favour the UK approach. Should an opposition based system be adopted the majority of respondents felt that notification of conflicting marks to the applicant should be compulsory.

If, after examination, the registry is not satisfied that the mark is registrable the applicant is informed, and may make representations and permitted amendments. If these do not succeed, the application will be refused.

Registration

Once the registrar is satisfied that the requirements for registration are met, the mark must be registered. Registration provides a presumption of validity.[23] There is no residual discretion for the registrar, as there was under the TMA 1938 (*Eurolamb Trade Mark* (1997)). The application is then advertised in the Trade Marks Journal.[24]

It may be opposed, or objections made to the registrar, by anyone within three months of the date of publication. Opposition must contain at least one of the absolute or relative grounds of refusal. Provided such objections, if any, are overcome, the mark is registered from the filing date of the application.[25] Disclaimers of an exclusive right in the whole or part of a mark may be made to overcome grounds of objection to a mark,[26] but these may not be imposed by the Trade Mark Registry.

Perhaps as a prelude to any future change from examination on relative grounds, in March 2003 an informal consultation on new Trade Mark Rules resulted in a further Formal Consultation late in 2003 on, *inter alia*, a new opposition procedure. The proposals, if adopted, will streamline the opposition procedure to incorporate a longer 'cooling off period' (enabling the parties to negotiate a settlement)[27], provision of a preliminary view from the registry of the likely outcome of the conflict, and allow the applicant to request that the opponent prove use of an earlier mark founding an opposition if it is more than five years old.

The mark is registered for 10 years[28] and is renewable in 10-yearly periods, provided it does not become subject to revocation (see 16.10). (Priority does not affect the date of registration, which is the date of filing, only the date relevant for comparison with earlier marks.)

---

22 'Future of Official Examination on Relative Grounds', Patent Office, 2003: www.patent.gov.uk.
23 Section 72 of the TMA 1994.
24 *Ibid*, s 38.
25 *Ibid*, s 40.
26 *Ibid*, s 13.
27 Introduced by the Trade Mark Rules 2000, SI 2000/136.
28 Section 42 of the TMA 1994.

Registration may be surrendered voluntarily, in whole or in part.[29] Surrender is a valuable factor in negotiating compromises with competitors with or seeking conflicting marks. A mark that is not renewed must be removed from the register.[30]

Decisions by the registrar are subject to appeal in the High Court or by an Appointed Person.[31] Neither appellate tribunal will review the registrar's findings of fact.

15.2.2 International protection

The Protocol[32] route is available to applicants who are nationals of, domiciled in, or have a real and effective industrial or commercial establishment in, a Protocol country. A national application must first be made (not, as the Madrid Agreement required, a home registration), then, the international application may be submitted to WIPO, requesting protection in as many Protocol States as are designated by the applicant. WIPO conducts a formal examination of the application, which is then transmitted to the designated national offices, where the applications are treated in the same way as domestic applications in those States. The offices have 18 months, plus any time needed to complete an opposition, to reject the application. If the application is not rejected, the trade mark is treated in the same way as a national mark.

Protection in the UK gained through the Madrid Protocol is termed an 'International Trade Mark (UK)'. Registration is for 10 years, is entered on the International Register maintained by WIPO, and is renewed centrally through WIPO. Registration is also published through WIPO.

The possibility of central attack remains for five years from the date of filing an international application with the home national office, but the result is not to jeopardise protection in all other States designated by the applicant (see 15.1.1). Instead, the international application is converted into national applications in those States.

The EU has acceded to the Madrid Protocol,[33] and a Community trade mark may be used to found an application through the Protocol route. The Commission's proposal for accession to the Protocol was adopted, and WIPO agreed changes to the Protocol to make EU accession possible. The Trade Mark Regulation required amendment. An 'opt-back' provision was inserted, allowing trade mark owners designating the EU in their international registration to opt-back to national registrations if the EU registration failed.

15.2.3 The Community trade mark

Application for a Community trade mark may be made direct to the OHIM, or through the Trade Mark Registry. Any natural or legal person may apply.

29 *Ibid*, s 45.
30 *Ibid*, s 43(5).
31 *Ibid*, s 77.
32 Implemented in the UK under ss 53 and 54 of the TMA 1994 by the Trade Marks (International Registration) Order 1996, SI 1996/714, amended by the Trade Marks (International Registration) (Amendment) Order 2000, SI 2000/138.
33 It entered into force on 1 October 2004.

Only one application need be made for protection in all Member States, saving on the time and expense of multiple European registrations. The Office operates in five official languages (English, French, German, Italian and Spanish). An application may be filed in any language, but must nominate one of the official languages for the purpose of proceedings in the OHIM. However, the ECJ ruled in *Christina Kik v OHIM* (2003) that the Office must use the filing language of an application in all its basic communications with the applicant, provided that it is an EU language. The Office had been in the habit of using one of the five official languages in all its communications, not just those which are procedural. This decision has the potential to slow down applications and increase the Office's translation costs.

The substantive provisions of the Regulation mirror those of the Directive. The process of application is akin to that in the UK Trade Mark Registry; however, there is no requirement for a declaration of use or *bona fide* intention to use the mark.

The application is examined only for the absolute grounds of refusal (see 15.4). An applicant may ask for examination on the relative grounds (see 15.15), which comprise comparisons with other marks in order to avoid dual registration of confusingly similar marks, and for national searches. The results of a relative search are transmitted to the applicant and to the owners of any rival registrations found. However, they will not lead to refusal of registration unless a rival mark owner opposes the mark. The onus is thus placed on trade mark proprietors to 'police' their own marks by opposing such applications. In 2003 the Commission proposed ending these national searches, a proposal accepted by the European Parliament. Evidence showed that only a very small proportion of applications was withdrawn, nor was the number of oppositions high. Opposition must be made within three months of publication and must be on relative grounds. Observations may be made on absolute grounds.

Opposition may be brought by the owner of earlier marks and signs and their licensees. If conflict is found with another mark in one or more Member States, the applicant may request that the application be converted into national applications in Member States where there is no conflict. The Community trade mark is granted for 10 years and may be renewed in 10-year cycles.

The substantive law relating to Community trade marks is largely in the same terms as the Directive and the TMA 1994. Consequently, it will be considered in conjunction with that for national UK trade marks. The Advocate General stated that the Regulation and Directive should be interpreted in the same way in *LTJ Diffusion v Sadas* (2003):

> ... when the Community legislature takes care to express itself in that manner – as it clearly did in the field of trade marks – the presumption is very strong indeed that the two measures are intended to be interpreted in the same way. The fact that they will be applied in different legal and factual circumstances does not detract from that presumption.

The final interpreter is the ECJ, and in the UK neither the White Paper nor parliamentary debates have any significance (*per* Jacob J in *British Sugar plc v James Robertson and Sons* (1996)). Achieving consistency of interpretation across the EU may take some time, despite the number of cases already brought to the ECJ and CFI, given the differences of national trade mark tradition in Member States. This diversity can be seen in the different approaches to trade mark function and in the presumption of registrability introduced by the Directive (see 15.2.4). UK courts have, however, also expressed their disinclination to follow interpretations of other national courts where they happen to be the first to interpret a particular EU provision: *Wagamama Ltd v City Centre Restaurants* (1995).

The Community trade mark was automatically extended to the new EU Member States on enlargement after amendment to the Trade Mark Regulation.

15.2.4   Registrability of a mark

To be registrable, a mark must satisfy three criteria:

(a) it must fall within the definition of a trade mark;

(b) it must not fail on the absolute grounds of refusal; and

(c) it must not fail on the relative grounds of refusal.

Under the old law, a mark had to be shown to be registrable[34] and was refused if it could not be positively shown to fit one of the categories of acceptable mark. The Directive has reversed the position, so that a mark is presumed to be registrable unless it can be shown to fail under one or more of these criteria. This change reflects the different approach to trade marks in some other Member States, where registration is the prime means of protecting a mark. Other states, such as the UK, have preferred to rely on other doctrines, such as passing off, in addition to registration. It is also designed to speed up the process of registration.

15.3   THE DEFINITION OF A TRADE MARK

The 1938 Act contemplated use of a trade mark as a visual mark placed on goods or their packaging. The White Paper[35] pointed out the considerable changes in trading practices since then – in particular, the use of broadcast advertising and the extension of registration from goods to services, meaning, for example, that radio advertising did not infringe. The 1938 definition of a mark also confined use of a trade mark to the indication of the source of goods.

It is of the essence of a trade mark that it is able to distinguish one undertaking's product from another's (see 15.3.5) and one that does not do so cannot be registered. However, the new definition of a trade mark does not exclude some signs as being unable to distinguish by definition rather than being non-distinctive in fact, as the old law did (*Re Coca-Cola* (1986)). The White Paper quoted the Explanatory Memorandum to the Community Trade Mark Regulation, which states that the emphasis should be placed on the question of whether a sign is performing the function of a trade mark. This was also the reasoning adopted by the House of Lords in *Smith Kline and French v Winthrop* (1976). Under the 1938 Act the House of Lords allowed the registration of combinations of colour used on pharmaceutical capsules which had become distinctive through use of the applicant's products, although similar reasoning did not prevail in *Re Coca-Cola* (1986). In that case, the bottle had benefited from design

---

34   Section 9 of the TMA 1938.
35   *Reform of Trade Marks Law*, Cm 1203, 1990.

registration, which had expired, so that trade mark registration would have had the effect of extending design protection beyond its statutory limits.

The result is a new definition in the 1994 Act. Section 1(1) of the TMA 1994 defines 'trade mark' as:

... any sign capable of being represented graphically which is capable of distinguishing goods or services of one undertaking from those of other undertakings.

A trade mark may, in particular, consist of words (including personal names), designs, letters, numerals or the shape of goods or their packaging.

Section 3(1)(a) of the TMA 1994 provides that a sign not satisfying the requirements of this definition shall not be registered (an absolute ground of refusal). Potentially, there may be an overlap with both copyright and design law.

Although the examples provided may all be appreciated visually, the ECJ has held that the list in Article 2 of the Trade Mark Directive is not exhaustive. Consequently, any sign clearly capable of distinguishing may serve the function of a trade mark. Sound marks are therefore potentially registrable: *Shield Mark BV v Kist* (2003), as are smells: *Sieckmann* (2003). There is no restriction on shapes, colours, sounds, smells or even tastes being regarded as signs. It is an open-ended definition intended to accommodate any means which a trader may adopt to distinguish products. Although such a wide definition might lead to uncertainty if unusual signs are adopted, an equally wide definition in the US has been in use without difficulty, causing few administrative or legal problems. In *R v Clarke* (1990), the fragrance of plumeria blossom added to embroidery yarn was registered as a trade mark.

It is notable that a fragrance added to yarn is unexpected. If a sign be adopted that is, or is part of, the product itself, such as a roasted coffee fragrance added to jars of instant coffee, a great deal would have to be done in the way of advertising and promotion to provide the requisite element of 'capacity to distinguish'. While the definition may suggest that anything is capable of being a 'sign' (but see 15.3.2), it must be used in a symbolic sense in order to be regarded as a sign. Whether the use is symbolic or product related may be determined by the response of competitors to the practice. If rival makers of instant coffee follow suit, the fragrance would not be functioning as a sign, but, if they do not, the necessary distinctiveness may arise (as it did in the *Jif Lemon* case (1990) (see Chapter 14)).

15.3.1 Graphical representation

The only overriding criterion, however, is that the sign be represented graphically, such as by musical notation, description, a formula or diagram, or even chemical or gas chromatographic analysis in the case of a smell. The representation must not be three-dimensional so that searches can be performed. It is quite possible for an application to come to grief at this stage, and the potential for amendment of a representation is limited.[36]

While a visual representation is not essential for a three-dimensional shape mark, a verbal description must be sufficiently precise and unambiguous to enable others

---

36   Section 39 of the TMA 1994.

clearly to identify the boundaries of protection. It need not be the only method of representation possible. The overriding test is that the representation be adequate fully to permit implementation of the provisions of the TMA 1994 relating to absolute unregistrability, relative unregistrability, infringement and public inspection of the register. These provisions call for a fixed point of reference in a clear and unambiguous recording of the sign (*Swizzel Matlow's Application* (1999)). A necessity for something outside the representation in order to attain a perception of the sign is not necessarily fatal to an application (*John Lewis's Application* (2001)).

Representation of shape signs

Consequently it is likely that the dimensions of a shape mark must be provided. In *Swizzel Matlow's Application* (1999) the Appointed Person held that graphical representation might include writing, drawing, musical notation, written description or any combination of these. A visual image of a shape mark was not essential, as is the practice of the OHIM, based on the Implementing Regulations, although there is no parallel in the Trade Mark Rules. However, the description provided of the shape was insufficiently precise, lacking dimensions of the sweet, and the positioning, thickness and shape on it of the raised outline.

Representation of colour signs

Similar precision is required for colour marks: *Ty Nant Spring Water Ltd's Application* (2000). The applicant sought to register the blue colour of its bottles. It was so worded that provided the bottle was of glass 3mm thick it would produce readings within a specified range on a spectrophotometer (a cobalt blue). This was held to be insufficient, because it required testing by others to determine the colour, nor did the description name the colour, or include a graphic example. In addition, the test needed was not a standard one using standard equipment under standard conditions. However, the decision did contemplate that a sign could be represented graphically, even if interpretation or analysis might be required to identify it. The established practice of accepting graphic representations which cite colours as named by reference to Pantone chart numbers is an example, as is that of accepting sound marks represented by musical notation.

The ECJ laid down guidance for representation of colour marks in *Libertel Groep BV* (*Libertel*) (2003). Libertel, a telecommunications company, was refused registration for the single colour orange (depicted without any reference to a colour code) by the Benelux Trade Mark Office. The European Court was asked whether a single colour could be distinctive. However, it held that it must decide as a preliminary matter whether a single colour could constitute a trade mark. The Court held that a colour *per se* is not a 'sign' without more, but that it might become so according the context in which it is used. If a sign, it must be represented visually by means of an image, line or character and this representation must be 'clear, precise, self-contained, easily accessible, intelligible, durable and objective'. A mere sample of colour would not satisfy this standard as a sample might deteriorate, a verbal description would only suffice if the standards of precision were met. Use of an international code might provide such certainty.

The Trade Mark Registry issued a Practice Amendment Note[37] embodying these guidelines; where a pictorial, figurative or word mark is filed in colour normally further definition of colours will not be required as specific tone is unlikely to be significant in identifying the mark. Where colour alone is filed, it will be necessary to establish that it is distinctive apart from the goods or their packaging, and the *Libertel* criteria will be followed. In contrast, Canadian Trade Mark practice refuses to recognise a colour *per se*. Registration will only be accepted where it is applied for in combination with other factors, such as size, shape or patterning. Colour may also be claimed as a feature of a mark. The colour is then either described, or reference made to a prescribed colour chart. Functional and ornamental colouring may be rejected as lacking distinctiveness.[38]

Representation of smell signs

For marks which are smells words alone may be used, but the description 'the smell, aroma or essence of cinnamon' for furniture was found to be too ambiguous in *John Lewis's Application* (2001). It allowed too great a degree of subjectivity as it provided no benchmark for the smell, which might be perceived differently by different individuals. The Appointed Person suggested, *obiter*, that an application to register the smell of cinnamon as emitted by 'x', if 'x' was clearly defined, would have succeeded.

The ECJ considered a smell mark in *Sieckmann* (2003). The application for a Community trade mark set out the structural formula of a pure chemical and stated where samples might be obtained from local laboratories. It was also described as 'balsamically fruity with a slight hint of cinnamon'. The Court was asked whether the requirement for graphical representation could be satisfied by a chemical formula, a description, a deposit, or a combination of these elements. It held that none of these methods of representation would suffice.

Registration of smell marks seems unlikely until an agreed system of graphic representation can be established.

Representation of sound signs

Following *Shield Mark BV v Joost Kist* (2003) the strict standards laid down by *Libertel* and *Sieckmann* (2003) have also been applied to sound marks. The case followed an infringement action in the Netherlands for marks consisting of the first nine notes of Beethoven's *Für Elise* and the sound of a cockcrow. These had been registered in several different ways: a musical stave, a description of the melody, a sequence of notes (E, D#, E, D#, E, B, D, C, A), and an onomatopoeia, 'kukelekuuuuu',[39] representing a cockcrow. The Court was also asked to advise on a sound recording, a sonogram and a digital recording accessible over the internet. The Court declined to decide on these hypothetical representations, but laid down general standards for graphic representation of sounds, as well as the particular registrations made.

---

37 Practice Amendment Note PAN 3/03: www.patent.gov.uk.
38 *Smith Kline & French Canada v Canada (Registrar of Trademarks) (No 2)* (1987).
39 The Dutch equivalent of 'cock-a-doodle-doo'.

Graphic representation of sound marks, as with those for smells, must be 'clear, precise, self-contained, easily accessible, intelligible, durable and objective'. It must also be stated that the representation is for a sound mark. In particular:

(i)   representation of a sound sign by written description could not be assumed to meet the standards required; and here the descriptions of the notes and cockcrow lacked precision and clarity;

(ii) onomatopoeia did not provide an indication whether it was pronunciation of it, or the of the sound being represented which constituted the mark. Moreover, onomatopoeia may be perceived differently by individuals, and in different Member States. Therefore, simple onomatopoeia without more did not represent adequate graphical representation;

(iii) the sequence of notes was neither clear, precise, nor self-contained as it did not make it possible to determine the pitch and duration of the sounds;

(iv) a stave divided into bars and showing a clef, notes and rests did indicate the pitch and duration of sounds forming the melody constituting the mark and met the standards laid down.

UK registry practice equally rejects the name of a work, but recognises musical notation as graphical representation of a sound mark. Although forms of sound recording were not discussed, it would seem that they must represent the most precise representation of a sound mark. In the case of a sound not based on music, it might be hoped that registration practice might extend to recordings. In the UK, DIRECT LINE's telephone jingle, HAMLET's use of Bach's *Air on a G String* for cigars, and Delibes's *Flower Duet* used by BRITISH AIRWAYS have been registered.

If the ECJ's criteria for graphic representation are stringently applied, it can be asked whether the register is assuming too great a significance.[40] Several factors combine to justify this approach, however. In times of increasingly sophisticated marketing there is considerable significance and value in innovative branding. While it may appear that stringent application of the requirement for graphical representation may give substantive effect to procedural rules by denying registrability to some marks, this is beneficial both to trade mark owners and their competitors. Trade mark proprietors need to be able to rely on and enforce their marks without fear of easy challenge to their validity. Meanwhile competitors need clear guidance from the Register as to marks they may use without infringing others' rights. If unclear registrations were permitted, aggressive trade mark owners would be able to stifle competition from smaller enterprises unable to afford challenging the mark's validity. Brown points out that if the registers are not clear, trade marks cannot fulfil their role as identifiers.

15.3.2   A sign

A trade mark must be a 'sign', so that, although the definition refers to 'any sign' and no express limit is given as to what may constitute a sign, the definition does exclude anything that is not a sign. The approach employed in *Re James* (1886) may be applied to refuse registration to the goods themselves. Lindley LJ said that 'a mark must be something that is distinct from the thing marked. A thing itself cannot be the mark of itself'. Thus, registration was refused to the shape of a lump of lead, the product itself.

---

40 Brown, A, 'Illuminating European Trade Marks?' (2004) 1 SCRIPT-ed, www.law.ed.ac.uk/ahrb/script-ed/index.asp.

This was applied in *Re Coca-Cola* (1986), where the bottle was regarded as the goods themselves – since a liquid could have no shape of its own. The *Coca-Cola* case (the shape of packaging) is now included within the definition. However, the reasoning goes beyond the refusal to regard shape as a mark, to consideration of the nature of the goods themselves, and it was this that could not, in these instances, be separated from the goods and, therefore, could not be a trade mark. It remains open to the courts to reject marks on the basis that they do not constitute a sign, however distinctive they may be, because they relate to the nature of the goods themselves.

It has been suggested that, although the TMA 1994 does not provide absolute grounds of refusal for particular types of sign other than shapes (see 15.10), similar objection may be made to marks which give value to goods or contribute to their nature at the same time as adding distinctiveness on the ground that they are not signs.[41] However, a wide interpretation was given to 'sign' in *Philips Electronics NV v Remington Consumer Products Ltd* (1998). Jacob J said:

> I think a 'sign' is anything which can convey information. I appreciate that this is extremely wide, but I can see no reason to limit the meaning of the word. The only qualification expressed in the Directive is that it be capable of being represented graphically ...

> What I conclude is confirmed by Recital 7(b), which emphasises the necessity to list the examples of a 'sign' ... You need the examples of a sign to see just how wide the meaning is. What the examples have in common is the ability to convey information.

The same objection might be taken on the ground that the sign was not capable of distinguishing (see 15.3.5), rather than that it was not a sign.

15.3.3   Colour signs

In principle, a colour may fall within the definition of a trade mark, provided that it is distinctive (see 15.6.4) and capable of distinguishing an undertaking (see 15.3.5). The colour mark must be associated with goods or services (*Libertel*), so that *Smith Kline and French v Winthrop* (1976) (see 15.3) would be decided in the same way under the TMA 1994.

However, colours have many other uses. In the US, three conditions are applied before a colour is registrable. There must be no competitive need to use the same colour, it must not serve any functional purpose and it must have acquired a secondary meaning as a sign rather than being merely decorative. Decisions under the 1938 Act suggested similar results in the UK.

In *Unilever Ltd's Trade Mark* (1984), an application to register the red stripe in SIGNAL toothpaste was refused because the stripe was functional (it contained an added mouthwash) and red was one of the few colours which could be used for this purpose. Registration was again refused in *Unilever Ltd's Trade Mark* (1987) as the colour had not been chosen as a sign and had not acquired secondary meaning as a trade mark. The same was held in *John Wyeth Coloured Tablet Trade Mark* (1988). The colours blue and yellow were used to indicate particular dosages, but were held to be common in the trade and not distinctive, so that a generic drug manufacturer was able to apply the same colours to indicate the same dosages.

---

41   Firth, A, *Trade Marks: The New Law* (London: Jordans, 1995).

Combinations of colour have long served trade mark functions: consider the DURACELL battery's gold and black colouring. Single colours, however, are less likely to be distinctive, at least without extensive use and marketing. A recent Australian case lays down four conditions under which a colour mark, in this case a single colour, may be inherently distinctive and capable of distinguishing the applicant's products. The colour cannot be descriptive, functional, the result of normal manufacturing processes, nor be used in an industry where colour is an important element of competition: *Philmac Pty Ltd v The Registrar of Trade Marks* (2003). In this case the application related to the colour terracotta for non-metallic rigid irrigation pipe fittings. These standards for registrability would not be met by domestic drainpipes in the UK!

Single colours have also been found to fall within the definition of a mark in Northern Ireland (*BP Amoco v John Kelly* (2001)) and in the OHIM: *Orange Personal Communications Services Ltd's Application* (1998) and *Wm Wrigley JR Company's Application* (1999). Wrigley applied for a specific shade of light green for chewing gum, submitting a sample and a colour chart with the application. The application failed on absolute grounds of distinctiveness, although colours could be *prima facie* registrable. The acid test is one of distinctiveness and capacity to distinguish rather than whether the colour is a sign. As made clear by the ECJ in *Libertel* a colour *per se* used in conjunction with goods or services is capable of constituting a sign. However, the ECJ recognises that colours are not inherently distinctive, and require use in relation to products to become so: *Heidelberger Bauchemie* (2004).

The number of colour registrations in the OHIM is proportionately small in comparison to the applications for such marks, suggesting that registration is comparatively difficult. Nevertheless, the mobile phone operator ORANGE has registered the colour orange (Pantone No 151), the EasyGroup Pantone No 21, Heinz turquoise, and Deutsche Telekom magenta.

15.3.4   Shape signs

Prima facie, shapes are also registrable as trade marks. The fact that a shape might also be protected by another intellectual property right, such as a design right or copyright, does not appear to bar registration as a trade mark. *Dicta* in *Smith Kline and French v Winthrop* (1976) suggest that the fact that the design for the capsules was registrable was no hindrance to trade mark registration. However, trade mark registration, unlimited in duration as it can be, does carry the danger of monopolisation of a specific shape, at least when used as a sign. Trade mark registration could also provide a way of evading the limits of the other intellectual property rights designed to allow fair competition. It was the danger of monopolisation of containers that influenced the House of Lords in *Re Coca-Cola* (1986). On the other hand, once a shape has become distinctive as a sign in the public's mind, there is little to be gained by the refusal of registration (*Smith Kline and French v Winthrop* (1976)), so that the TMA 1994 adopts a compromise. The BSM 'pyramid' and lettering is registered, as is the shape of the COCA-COLA bottle.

Shapes may be signs, but the absolute grounds of refusal restrict the registration of some shapes: those which result from the nature of the goods, those which are necessary to obtain a technical result and those which give substantial value to the goods (see 15.10).

Registrability for a shape sign is a two-stage enquiry: first, whether the sign has the capacity to distinguish and, secondly, whether, although potentially distinctive, the shape falls within the absolute grounds of refusal. A shape sign must be distinctive. As was thought likely,[42] in many cases, unless a manufacturer has deliberately adopted a shape as a badge of origin, it will not be regarded as inherently able to distinguish. This is borne out by the fate of the registered drawing of the shape of the shaver head in *Philips Electronics NV v Remington Consumer Products Ltd* (1998). It was held to be incapable of distinguishing PHILIPS' product as it primarily denoted the product's function. In this case, no amount of use could overcome the inherent nature of this shape sign. The Court of Appeal agreed, as did the ECJ in *Philips Electronics NV v Remington Consumer Products Ltd* (2003).

That some shapes may acquire secondary meaning as a badge of origin is illustrated by the *Jif Lemon* case (1990) (see Chapter 14).

15.3.5   Capable of distinguishing

Only a sign which is 'capable of distinguishing' may be a trade mark. This reflects the essence of a trade mark as an identifying feature related to goods or services. If the sign does not distinguish it cannot identify: it must allow the public to recognise one trader's product as emanating from a different source to products emanating from other traders.

Distinguishing

A sign that is distinguishing is said to be 'distinctive'. A sign may distinguish in one of two ways, either by being distinctive in its nature (inherently distinctive), or by having become distinctive through its use in relation to a particular trader's product (factually distinctive). A word such as APPLE used in relation to computers or a newly invented word, such as KODAK for cameras and film, is inherently distinctive. Signs that do not distinguish are often said to be 'descriptive'. Signs may vary from the completely descriptive to the completely distinctive. However, many are capable of distinguishing whether descriptive or distinctive. It is tempting to think that descriptive signs may not distinguish, but it is possible that use in the right way may provide the necessary element of distinctiveness. Even an inherently descriptive sign may be distinctive in fact once the public has come to recognise it in that sense, such as a yellow plastic lemon-shaped containers for lemon juice. Conversely, a distinctive mark may become descriptive through use. For example, a mark such as HOOVER has almost become a descriptive word for vacuum cleaner, although, initially, it was inherently distinctive, whereas the JIF lemon was initially inherently descriptive, but became distinctive through prolonged exclusive use.

Fletcher Moulton LJ explained, in relation to the use of the word mark PERFECTION for soaps, in *Joseph Crosfield's Application* (1909):

> Much of the argument before us on the part of the opponents and the Board of Trade was based on an assumption that there is a natural and innate antagonism between distinctive and descriptive as applied to words, and that if you can show that a word is descriptive you have proved that it cannot be distinctive. To my mind, this is a fallacy. Descriptive names may be distinctive and vice versa ... However, the question

---

42   Annand, R and Norman, H, *Blackstone's Guide to the Trade Marks Act 1994* (London: Blackstone, 1994).

whether a word is or is not capable of becoming distinctive of the goods of a particular maker is a question of fact, and is not determined by its being or not being descriptive.

Capacity to distinguish

Under the old law, some types of mark were regarded as legally incapable of ever being able to distinguish, whatever use had been made of them (geographical names, for example). This had been much criticised when it led to the rejection of marks which use had made factually 100% distinctive (*York Trade Mark* (1984)).

The 1994 Act requires only a *capacity* to distinguish, accepting either an inherently or factually distinctive sign, although the latter may need evidence of use before registration is granted. In *British Sugar plc v James Robertson and Sons* (1996), Jacob J agreed that the TMA 1994 had not incorporated the old law with respect to factual distinctiveness. However, he pointed out that there still might be some signs which were factually incapable of distinguishing whatever use might be made of them. He used the example of SOAP for soap. Not all descriptive words will be so incapable of distinguishing. The word PREMIER was held to be capable of acquiring distinctiveness by use despite its descriptive nature (*Premier Luggage Ltd v The Premier Company* (2002)). In fact, evidence of use having created distinctiveness may overcome some of the absolute grounds of refusal: s 3(1) of the TMA 1994 (see 15.9).

Capacity to distinguish is considered not only within the immediate situation, but also within the context of changes reasonably foreseeable in the immediate future. Consequently, in *800-Flowers Trade Mark* (2001), the fact that alpha-numeric phonenames were likely to be introduced in the UK in the near future was a factor to set against the inherent distinctiveness of the sign 800-FLOWERS. In that context the sign was not able to distinguish the applicant's business, constituting an encoded telephone number.

Words that begin by being inherently distinctive may lose that capacity and become descriptive. *Bach Flower Remedies Ltd v Healing Herbs Ltd* (2000) (the *Bach* case) related to the apparently distinctive name 'Bach'. The court held that it should take into account use of the word at the time of registration of the mark under s 1(1) of the TMA 1994. It found that long-term generic use of the name in relation to remedies developed according to the theories of Dr Bach rendered the word incapable of distinguishing the registrant's business. The mark had, therefore, been invalidly registered. The same was true of the name JERYL LYNN in *Jeryl Lynn Trade Mark* (1999).

Shapes

One question referred to the ECJ in *Philips* (2003) was whether a shape mark required a 'capricious addition', apart from shape needed for the product's function, in order for it to have the capacity to distinguish. The Court held that it did not; The shape sought to be registered could be functional provided it served the trade mark function. Article 2 should be applied in the same way whatever the type of mark and no additional requirements added to registrability for shape marks.

Signs in advertising

A trade mark's capacity to distinguish is related to its function. This was expressly incorporated in the definition of a trade mark in the TMA 1938, but no such limitation appears in s 1(1) of the TMA 1994. To distinguish goods and services as originating from one undertaking rather than another serves both the source and guarantee functions of a trade mark (see 15.1.3), but it is not yet clear whether a capacity to distinguish for the advertising and promotional function will suffice to constitute a sign a 'trade mark'.

Comparing two decisions made under the 1938 Act illustrates the point. In *Have a Break Trade Mark* (1993), Whitford J refused registration to the well known slogan for KIT-KAT because it was being used to advertise the chocolate bar in conjunction with the KIT-KAT name and ROWNTREES' trade mark, and not operating as a trade mark itself. By contrast, in *I Can't Believe it's Yogurt* (1992), the slogan was registered as it was to be used alone on products to distinguish them.

This raises the question whether the KIT-KAT slogan might now be registrable as distinguishing the product in advertising.[43] The real objection to the slogan, however, lay in the fact that it was used with other trade marks by which the product was identified. Jacob J has termed such a mark a 'limping mark' and said, of Remington's use of the same shape shaver head always together with the Remington trade mark, that '[the] sign was [n]ever used by the proprietor on its own. In addition, that was evidence of a lack of capacity to distinguish': *Philips Electronics NV v Remington Consumer Products Ltd* (1998). He took the same approach in *British Sugar plc v James Robertson and Sons* (1996), where advertising use had been made of the registered mark 'TREAT', but only in conjunction with the trade mark SILVER SPOON. He looked for use understood by the public as a 'badge of origin'.

In *Philips* (2003) the ECJ has made it clear that Article 2 of the Directive (enacted in s 1(1) of the TMA 1994) provides that all signs may constitute trade marks – provided they can be represented graphically and have the capacity to distinguish one trader's products from another's. In determining this capacity the 'essential' function of a trade mark must be taken into account. This function is said to be 'clear' from the 10th recital of the Directive (*inter alia* to guarantee the trade mark as an indication of origin); from case law of the ECJ, and the wording and structure of the Directive's provisions concerning the grounds for refusal. As we have seen (see 15.1.3) this function has been widely interpreted despite its apparent limitation to a 'badge of origin' test.

The KIT-KAT slogan is now the subject of reference to the ECJ. In 1995 Nestlé applied to register the slogan for confectionery again, and the application was opposed by Mars on the grounds that it was not distinctive, despite the extensive use made of it: *Nestlé v Mars UK Ltd* (2003).[44] The Court of Appeal upheld refusal of the mark as devoid of distinctiveness (see 15.6) because it did not serve the trade mark purpose of indicating the goods' origin to consumers. Nor did the evidence of use made of it indicate recognition of the slogan as a mark independent of the KIT-KAT name. Importantly, the Court referred the question of whether use a 'limping' mark may confer a distinctiveness acquired in fact on a mark. Advocate General Kokott's opinion suggests that such a mark is capable of acquiring distinctive character, provided that the relevant consumer group understands the slogan, used separately, to designate a product as originating from a particular undertaking.

---

43 As suggested by Annand and Norman, *Blackstone's Guide to the Trade Marks Act 1994* (London: Blackstone, 1994).

44 *Nestlé v Mars UK Ltd*. Case C–35 3/03, 27 January 2005. Not yet reported.

Test of capacity

When considering whether a sign has a capacity to distinguish the court considers the usage of the sign by those engaged in the relevant activity, and by the understanding of the average consumer: set out by the ECJ in *Lloyd* (2000) and applied in *Bach Flower Remedies Ltd v Healing Herbs Ltd* (2000).[45] Such a person is 'reasonably informed, reasonably observant and circumspect'.

Invisible marks

An intriguing question, raised by Prescott[46] in relation to the 1938 Act, is whether a sign which is not visible at the point of sale may be a trade mark. This is a question of whether the sign is 'capable of distinguishing goods or services of one undertaking from those of other undertakings' under the 1994 Act. He argues that such a sign serves an important verification function when goods are used after purchase and will promote repeat sales, an important part of trade, as well as serving as an effective advertisement of the goods to other users.

15.3.6 Retail services

When the 1938 Act was amended in 1984 to allow registration of trade marks for services as well as goods, registration was still refused for 'retail services' if these were provided by undertakings primarily engaged in the supply of goods: *Re Dee* (1990). Several large supermarket chains applied for registration of their marks for retail services, such as the free provision of car parking and in-store crèches. Their primary business was, of course, the sale of goods, but they hoped such registration would prevent independent providers of the services they were supplying as an ancillary to their business from exploiting their well known reputations. The distinction between an undertaking trading in goods and trading in services had first been drawn by the House of Lords in *Aristoc v Rysta* (1945). It was later applied to retail services because the definition of 'services' required that they be provided for 'money or money's worth'.

It would seem that the distinction between a main trade in goods and only ancillary provision of services will continue to prevent the registration of retail services as s 1(1) of the TMA 1994 refers to the 'goods and services of one undertaking ...'. Ancillary services may not be regarded as the services 'of' an undertaking which is mainly engaged in trade in goods. This was the intention stated in the White Paper. Other jurisdictions, such as Hong Kong, Australia, South Africa and the US, do allow for retail service registrations.

The supermarkets' fears are met by two new provisions in the 1994 Act. Section 10(3) of the TMA 1994 provides relief where a mark is used to take unfair advantage of the trade mark proprietor's reputation. Section 10(4)(b) of the TMA 1994 makes a defendant's use of a sign near goods infringing, so that use on a shop would infringe a goods registration.

---

45   Dunlop, T, 'The Average Consumer's Opinion: *Bach and Bach Flower Remedies Trade Mark*' [2000] EIPR 177.
46   Prescott, P, 'Trade Marks Invisible at Point of Sale: Some Corking Cases' [1990] EIPR 241.

In *Giacomelli Sport SpA's Application* (2000) the OHIM Board of Appeal allowed for the possibility for registration of a Community trade mark for ancillary services despite the traditional reluctance to do so in most Member States. It did, however, hold that clarity in the description of the services was essential to define the monopoly being obtained. The decision resulted in a Practice Direction[47] changing UK Registry practice. The Direction states that:

... there will be no objection to specifications describing the bringing together of goods for the purposes of convenient viewing and selection by customers, provided that the nature of the retail service and market sector, where applicable, are indicated.

It goes on to suggest that a company promoting its own goods through a catalogue or website would be unlikely to succeed, but that applications from services bringing together *other* traders' goods could do so, if the relevant field of activity is defined. Refusal based on confusion (see 15.16.2) is only likely where there is a conflicting mark for goods in the same class, or the retailer is in the practice of producing his own branded goods. How specific the description of area of activity must be is not defined. In *Giacomelli* the Board of Appeal suggested 'retail services in the field of sports goods'.

15.4 THE ABSOLUTE GROUNDS OF REFUSAL

A mark shall not be registered if it falls into one of the categories of mark set out in s 3 of the TMA 1994. These absolute grounds of refusal prevent, in general, marks that are purely descriptive (s 3(1)), functional (s 3(2)) or objectionable (ss 3(3)–(6)) from being registered. These are grounds rooted in the mark itself or the use that is proposed for it.

Sub-section (1) of s 3 relates to the distinctiveness of a mark. It is a prerequisite for registration, whether inherent or acquired.

The ECJ decision in the *Linde* (2003) case outlines how rejection of a mark for lack of distinctiveness is to be approached.

First, a mark must serve a trade mark function by distinguishing the origin of the product from those of other traders (see 15.1.3). Whether it does so is judged in relation to the nature of the relevant goods or services, and the understanding of relevant consumers. The relevant consumer's understanding derived from use of the mark in relation to the product for which is to be registered is considered. If the consumer would consider it to distinguish the product it will be taken to be distinctive. The relevant consumer is outlined in *Lloyd* (2000) as the average consumer for the category of products concerned and reasonably well informed and reasonably observant and circumspect. However, when the test is applied differences of approach to the underlying policy behind the function of trade marks lead to different results.

Next, any specific grounds of objection applying to the particular type of mark (such as a shape) must be taken into account.

Thirdly, if the mark is not refused on these grounds its inherent distinctiveness must next be considered. Each paragraph of the sub-section must be separately and independently considered.

---

47   Practice Direction (TMR: Change of Practice on Retail Services) [2001] RPC 2.

Finally, if inherently non-distinctive, any acquired distinctiveness in fact as a trade mark must be considered under the proviso (see 15.9). All types of mark (whether words, slogans, shapes, colours for example) are treated alike, but the results of applying the basic questions may differ in practice.

It is the mark as a whole which must be assessed, and not its constituent elements: *Procter and Gamble Co v OHIM* (2004).

It is common for a mark to be challenged on all the grounds set out in s 3(1): see, for example, *RFU v Cotton Traders* (2002). However, it is not yet possible to refuse a mark on the ground that it is not distinctive without more, it must be shown to fall within at least one of the paragraphs to s 3(1). This is so despite the fact that the tests applied by both UK courts and the ECJ are often common to each ground of non-distinctiveness.

## 15.4.1	Section 3(1) – Distinctiveness and policy considerations[48]

Distinctiveness is closely bound to the function of trade marks for which they may, as a matter of policy, be protected by registration. It is a distinctiveness which enables the mark to identify which is looked for. Distinctiveness has received extensive interpretation by the ECJ but its policy basis remains unclear.

Two diverging approaches can be discerned in interpretation of the corresponding articles in the Directive and Regulation: a conservative, or anti-monopolistic, and a liberal or modern, approach. The judgments in the High Court and Court of Appeal in the *Philips* case represent the former. On this view the absolute grounds are seen as a means of preserving the legitimate interests of other traders and avoiding the conferral of monopolies. The latter view is represented by the opinion of the Advocate General in *Procter & Gamble Co v OHIM* (2002) and suggests that the only criterion is the fact that a mark should be serving the function of identifying the product in the public's eyes. Any legitimate interests of others can be left to the defences to infringement.

The conservative view

The conservative view, that there is a general public interest in keeping non-distinctive marks in the public domain, was affirmed by the ECJ in *Windsurfing* (1999) and *Linde* (2003). Although *Windsurfing* (1999) is decided within the context of a geographical word mark, the ECJ noted that Article 3(1)(c) of the Directive also applied to other types of descriptive mark. The same can be applied to the whole of s 3(1) non-distinctiveness. The ECJ held that the Directive prevented registration of names not only currently associated in the public mind with the goods in question, but also 'names which are *liable*[49] to be used in the future by undertakings as an indication of origin for that category of goods'.

Consequently, Lord Parker's *dictum* in *W & G du Cros's Application* (1913) that distinctiveness:

> ... must depend upon whether other traders are likely, in the ordinary course of their business and without any improper motive, to desire to use the same mark, or some

---

48	Antill, J and James, A, 'Registrability and the Scope of the Monopoly: Current Trends' [2004] EIPR 157.

49	Emphasis added.

mark nearly resembling it, upon or in connection with their own goods. It is apparent from the history of Trade Marks in this country that both the Legislature and the Courts have always shown a natural disinclination to allow any person to obtain by registration under the Trade Marks Act a monopoly in what others may legitimately desire to use.

would appear to remain a good practical test of registrability, subject to the proviso. This was particularly so when the ECJ refused to follow the Advocate General's Opinion that the Directive rejected any general principle that some signs should be retained for those with a legitimate interest in using them.

The modern view

However, the ECJ's decision in the *Baby-Dry* case (2002), representing the modern view, must be read with the *Windsurfing* (1999) case. In the *Baby-Dry* (2002) case the ECJ took a very narrow view of the exclusion of descriptive signs by reading the exclusion in conjunction with the defences to infringement. This recognises the wider functions of modern trade marks and has been defended as economically efficient.[50] To rely on the defences to protect the legitimate interests of other traders, is however, in practical terms, to favour the mark's proprietor. To oppose a mark, or defend oneself in infringement proceedings, is a costly and time-consuming exercise for competitors. Many smaller enterprises will not have the resources to do so, despite the legitimacy of their claims. In addition, the defences allow use of the mark as a name or in a descriptive sense, but not as a trade mark.

The modern approach had been widely criticised. Keeling[51] gives four reasons for opposing it. First, it ignores the fact that the Regulation requires examiners to raise absolute grounds of their own accord, for registration is not a deposit-only system. Secondly, it is based on a misunderstanding of the scope and purpose of the defences in Article 12, which apply to marks that are not exclusively descriptive and have been registered, allowing use only of their descriptive elements. Thirdly, it places too much emphasis on Article 12 and disregards the provision in Article 9 which defines the exclusive right – surely a fundamental element in defining the scope and policy of registration from the legislation. Finally, it fails to answer the question why no protection is available for ordinary descriptive terms in both the Directive and Regulation.

The UK

The Appointed Person in *Cycling Is Application* (2002) stated that it is not the defences to infringement in s 11 of the TMA 1994 but the positive requirement of distinctiveness in s 3 which should be seen as the first line of defence for the legitimate interests of other traders. In relation to surnames, Jacob J was reluctant to follow *Baby-Dry* (2002) on policy grounds:

> Ultimately, this case poses the question of whether the registration of a common name as a trade mark is to be granted on a 'first come, first served' basis or whether there are

---

50 Griffiths, A, 'Modernising Trade Mark Law and Promoting Economic Efficiency: An Evaluation of the *Baby-Dry* Judgment and its Aftermath' [2003] IPQ 1.

51 Keeling, D, 'About Kinetic ® Watches, Easy Banking and Nappies that Keep Babies Dry: A Review of Recent European Case Law on Absolute Grounds for Refusing to Register Trade Marks' [2003] IPQ 131.

wider, public interest, considerations involved. Baby-Dry has, if I have interpreted it right, shifted the balance towards trade mark owners who have the resources and foresight to use the registration system and against the public in general and weaker and less organised companies. It does seem to be somewhat in conflict with *Windsurfing Chiemsee* ...

In cases other than Baby-Dry concerned with distinctiveness the Court has not referred to potential defences. It has emphasised, however, a need for a trade mark to identify goods or services as coming from a particular undertaking ...

These cases [*Lloyd's* (2000) and *Philips* (2003)] suggest, at least, that the question is whether a mark proposed for registration will do the job of distinguishing completely. How that is to be applied in the case of a common surname is the matter on which I seek the Court's assistance.

Windsurfing (1999) and *Baby-Dry* (2002) leave the policy issue undecided; nor is it clear whether the *Baby-Dry* (2002) approach should apply to non-distinctive (as opposed to descriptive) marks. However, the ECJ appears to be drawing a more restrictive line in the recent case of *Procter and Gamble Co v OHIM* (2004).

15.4.2   Evidence of distinctiveness

Questions of the distinctiveness of a mark must be considered as the facts stand at the time of the application to register: *RFU v Cotton Traders* (2002). In this case the validity of a Community trade mark depicting the English Rose was at issue. Lloyd J viewed the mark through the eyes of the average consumer who did not know that there was a question about the significance of the rose, but who was otherwise 'reasonably well informed and reasonably observant and circumspect'.

Evidence from witnesses from three groups was adduced on this point: the RFU itself, organisations connected with it, and the public at large. The latter group was seen as providing relevant evidence. The court made careful use of such survey evidence, noting that the questionnaire was leading in the questions asked.

The case is also significant in relation to trade mark protection for merchandising, for the mark was found not to be distinctive of the *claimant*, but to signify the England rugby team, both at the time of registration, and at the time of the commencement of proceedings, after four years' use.

In *Procter & Gamble v OHIM* (2003) Advocate General Colomer also took the view that the distinctive character of a mark must be assessed at the time an application for registration is filed, and remain so at the time of registration.

15.5   NOT A TRADE MARK

A sign which does not satisfy the requirements of the definition of a trade mark will not be registrable.[52] The capacity to distinguish required is either inherent or factual (see 15.3.5): *AD2000 Trade Mark* (1997). A mark which is not a sign, or not capable of graphical representation will be refused on this absolute ground.

Just how s 3(1)(a) relates to the other absolute grounds of refusal relating to distinctiveness has been a moot point. The UK courts have provided two interpretations.

---

52   Section 3(1)(a) of the TMA 1994.

On one view, the paragraph merely provides the means to refuse marks which are not capable of graphical representation, or are not signs; capacity to distinguish being 'policed' by s 3(1)(b). In other words, the same level of distinctiveness is required to satisfy 'capacity to distinguish' or to avoid being 'devoid of distinctiveness'. In both *British Sugar plc v James Robertson and Sons* (1996) and *Philips Electronics NV v Remington Consumer Products Ltd* (1998), Jacob J considered that the requirement for 'capacity to distinguish' excludes no more than would be excluded by s 3(1)(b) of the TMA 1994 (see 15.6). Consequently, no sign shown to be distinguishing in fact can be refused as not constituting a trade mark, unlike the old law. In addition, a mark capable of acquiring distinctiveness through use even although inherently non-distinctive, would satisfy the definition and s 3(1)(a).

On the other view, paragraph (a) was seen as setting a preliminary very low minimum standard of distinctiveness, one that nearly all signs serving a trade mark function would satisfy, but that paragraph (b) set a higher standard for determining whether distinctiveness acquired from use was sufficient to confer protection. This view was expressed in both *Dualit Ltd's Trade Mark Applications* (1999) and the *Bach* case. It rests on the distinction drawn between 'signs' and 'marks' in s 3. Paragraph (a) refers to signs, the rest of the section to marks. Consequently, the consideration first was whether the sign could be regarded as generic in relation to the product, as the name Bach was, but that the toaster's shape in *Dualit* was not. Whether the mark was then devoid of distinctiveness was a separate question.

It is unlikely that this second view can prevail after the ECJ's decision in *Philips* (2003). The first question referred to the ECJ was precisely on this point. The ECJ decided that there was no class of marks which had a distinctive character either by nature or by the use made of them which are not capable of distinguishing products. There is no category of mark not excluded by paragraphs (b)–(d) of Article 3 which would be excluded by paragraph (a).

Consequently, in *Eastenders v Fuller Smith* (2003) (the *ESB* case), the Court of Appeal considered the *Bach* decision to be overtaken by the ECJ's judgment. The Court said that the requirement of capacity to distinguish in s 1(1):

> Must be viewed as imposing no distinctiveness requirement separate from that imposed by Articles 3(1)(b),(c) and (d) and 3(3). Thus there is no requirement that the mark be both 'capable of distinguishing' and 'not devoid of any distinctive character'.

A logical interpretation for the two paragraphs is given by Keeling: that 'capacity to distinguish' is to be considered in the abstract, without reference to any product, but that 'distinctiveness' is to be considered concretely, in relation to the products for which a mark is to be used. Consequently, the phrase 'Tasty Titbits' has capacity to distinguish, but if it were to be used for foodstuffs and snacks it would not be distinctive, whereas if it were to be used for watches or cars it would be. It is this interpretation which was adopted by the ECJ in *Procter and Gamble Co v OHIM* (2004).

15.6 NON-DISTINCTIVE SIGNS

Section 3(1)(b) of the TMA 1994 excludes 'trade marks which are devoid of any distinctive character' from registration. These are marks with no inherent distinctiveness, and whose use has no yet given them factual distinctiveness: *British Sugar plc v James Robertson and Sons* (1996). Whether distinctiveness has been

sufficiently acquired through use of the mark is decided under the proviso to
s 3(1)(b)–(d): *Premier Luggage Ltd v The Premier Company* (2002). Examples of such
marks might include single letters or numerals.

If distinctiveness has not been acquired by use the question must be determined
from the mark itself under s 3(1)(b) of the TMA 1994. The word 'devoid' is an extreme
one, suggesting that it would catch only the most descriptive of signs. In *Abercrombie's
Application* (2001) it was defined as 'unpossessed' of distinctiveness. By contrast, it was
thought that the standard of distinctiveness required under the TMA 1938 was much
higher, so that the change allows registration of a greater number of marks.

Marks vary in nature, and different types may need to be separately examined. The
test to be applied to distinctiveness does not differ according to the nature of the mark.
However, the application of the test to these differing marks may vary. Colours, shapes
and word marks must be considered separately.

15.6.1   Words

Under the 1938 Act, descriptive words with distinctive capacity, such as ELECTRIX
(*Electrix Ltd's Application* (1959)) or ORLWOOLA (*Joseph Crosfield's Application* (1909)),
were refused, as the misspelling was not enough to render them distinctive as marks
of origin. Invented words were regarded as distinctive (KODAK, for example), but any
allusiveness on the part of a made up word was fatal, so that SOLIO was allowed for
photographic paper (*Eastman's Application* (1898)), but DIABOLO refused for toys
because of its similarity to the word 'diabolical': *Philippart v Whiteley* (1908). Generic
words were also unregistrable, while TARZAN was refused as a word having passed
into general usage: *Tarzan Trade Mark* (1970).

Notwithstanding the new standard set by the TMA 1994, a common laudatory
word was held to be devoid of distinctive character in *British Sugar plc v James
Robertson & Sons* (1996). TREAT was registered by the plaintiff for dessert sauces and
syrups, although sold primarily as an ice cream topping. The defendant
counterclaimed for invalidity of the registration in infringement proceedings. Jacob J
held that the trade mark must first be considered alone (without evidence of use),
asking whether it was the sort of sign which cannot do the job of distinguishing
without first educating the public that it is a trade mark. While an inappropriate word
(such as NORTH POLE for bananas) or meaningless word (such as EXXON for oil)
clearly could distinguish, this common laudatory word was found to be inherently
devoid of distinctiveness, as was AD2000 in *AD2000 Trade Mark* (1997). The word
PREMIER was held not to be devoid of distinctiveness, although capable of use in a
descriptive or laudatory sense, but because use could and had rendered it descriptive
(*Premier Luggage Ltd v The Premier Company* (2002)).

A combination of descriptive words, EUROLAMB, was found likely to be
understood as an abbreviation of 'European lamb' and was, therefore, devoid of
distinctive character in *Eurolamb Trade Mark* (1997). Whether this decision can stand
after the *Baby-Dry* (2002) case is less than clear (see 15.7.2). However, the ECJ upheld
the refusal of COMPANYLINE, a combination of descriptive and generic terms, as a
Community trade mark in *DKV Deutsche Krankenversicherung AG v OHIM* (2003).

Slogans may also come to grief under s 3(1)(b). In *Visa International Service
Association's Application* (1999) the applicant sought to register THE WORLD's BEST
WAY TO PAY AND BE PAID as a Community trade mark for financial services. The
Board of Appeal upheld the rejection of this mark by the Examiner. While slogans may

be registered, they must serve the function of a trade mark. This slogan did not do so, merely making a statement about the services in ordinary language. The argument that the slogan was fanciful and imaginative, and the rhyme between the words 'way', 'pay' and 'paid' was rejected as having conferred distinctiveness.

15.6.2 Names

Section 1(1) includes names as an example of a sign, so that names are not rejected automatically. However, names may be shared and therefore non-distinctive, or bear other meanings in the eyes of consumers, such as 'Walker', 'Read' or 'Head'. In *Abercrombie's Application* (2001) the Appointed Person proceeded on the basis that surnames are neither automatically eligible nor automatically ineligible for registration. It is a question of fact whether a particular name is distinctive enough to distinguish goods or services of one undertaking from another's.

Traditionally, UK courts have been reluctant to allow registration of surnames and other names. In *Re Elvis Presley's Application* (1999) the Presley estate applied to register a signature version of Elvis's name, the word ELVIS, and ELVIS PRESLEY. These applications were successfully opposed by a market trader who had long sold Elvis memorabilia under the phrase ELVISLY YOURS. The Court of Appeal held, under the TMA 1938, that the name marks lacked sufficient inherent distinctiveness; but a signature mark was sufficiently distinctive because it was depicted in a particular (although not very distinctive) script. The court added that the addition of a surname to the ELVIS mark might have rendered it distinctive but, given the circumstances, it merely confirmed the descriptive character of the name. The significant factor was the public recognition of the name as referring to the individual, and not to the origin of the goods marked.

In the light of the *Baby-Dry* (2002) and *Nichols plc v Register of Trade Marks* (2004) cases this practice may change. In *Nichols Application* (2003) Jacob J questioned the ECJ's decision in *Baby-Dry* (2002) on policy grounds and referred a number of questions to the ECJ as a result, leaving the position as to names, and descriptive marks more generally, uncertain until the case is heard in Europe. In a judgment that makes the policy differences clear, he termed *Baby-Dry* (2002) as 'surprising'. He also pointed out that in both *Lloyd* (2000) and *Philips* (2003) the ECJ did not refer to the defences, and that the ECJ stated the need for a mark to distinguish products as coming from the proprietor and no other undertaking. This, he said, suggests that 'the question is whether a mark proposed for registration will do the job of distinguishing completely'.

In *Nichols plc v Register of Trade Marks* (2004) the ECJ ruled that the Directive does not allow for different tests to be applied to the registrability of surnames, other than within the context of a specific market where surnames are customarily used for identification. Following increasingly consistent guidance from the ECJ, all marks must be assessed individually within the context of the product for which they are to be used, and the understanding of the relevant group of consumers for it. Consumer interpretations of the meaning of surnames might differ from other types of mark, but this did not justify different tests being used for them. The exception providing for use of a surname in Article 6 was not a factor to be taken into account in determining distinctiveness of a name or other mark. While Advocate General Colomer went on to say in his Opinion[53] that it was not possible to take account of any general interest in

---

53 *Nichols plc v Registrar of Trade marks* [2004] C–404/02.

preserving common surnames for all to use where they did not serve as identifiers in interpreting Article 3(1)(b),[54] the ECJ did not rule on this point.

Recognition of names will vary according to locality. In UK cases the question is of the recognition of the name as a name to the UK public. With the advent of the Directive and Regulation a wider view needs to be taken. In the OHIM recognition of a name more generally within the EU must be considered: *Ford Motor Company v OHIM* (2000). Even in the UK it is national recognition, and not local recognition that is taken into account. Registry practice (set out in *Abercrombie*) is to use telephone directories. In *Abercrombie's Application* (2001) the Appointed Person would have preferred evidence from UK wide personal and business directories. Evidence from Scottish directories showed that the name Abercrombie and its alternative Abercromby was not widespread, even in Scotland. However, use of directories is now likely to cease following the *Nichols* ECJ ruling.

15.6.3   Shapes

Shape marks have received extensive consideration in *Philips Electronics NV v Remington Consumer Products Ltd*. In the High Court Jacob J held that, because the drawing, without more, was a sign which primarily denoted the function of the goods, it was devoid of distinctive character. The Court of Appeal agreed. He went to hold that there are some signs, whether words or pictures, which are so descriptive that they are incapable of ever distinguishing goods (or services) properly, even if they do so partially. The ECJ tacitly agreed by regarding the mark as falling within Article 3(1)(e) (see 15.10).

Subsequently, the ECJ considered three combined cases in the *Linde* (2003) case. It was asked whether a more stringent test should be applied when considering distinctiveness of a shape mark. The Court held that no distinction should be drawn between shapes and other types of marks. The specific criteria applicable to shapes should be considered first. Any objection on these grounds cannot be remedied by distinctiveness acquired through use. If the shape mark is not rejected on these grounds, it must still be tested according to Article 3(1)(b)–(d). Here the Directive makes no requirement of a stricter test as regards the requirement that the mark be not devoid of distinctiveness. Distinctiveness means the capacity to identify the product's origin from that of others. However, in practice it was true, the Court said, that establishing distinctiveness for a shape mark could be more difficult than for more traditional types of mark, unless use of the shape as a mark led to acquired distinctiveness.

The reason for this difference lies in consumers' perceptions of the shape of products. Not traditionally used as a mark, shape conveys different meanings to shoppers. As market practice changes, so may consumer perception. The UK case of *R v Yakult Honsha KK's Application* (2001) is illustrative:

> ... the fact that a container is unusual or attractive does not, per se, mean that it will be taken by the public as an indication of origin. The relevant question is not whether the container would be recognised on being seen a second time ... but whether *by itself* its appearance would convey a trade mark significance to the average customer.

---

54   He was prepared to recognise such a public interest with respect to customary words, and to shape signs (para 43).

A similar approach was taken by the ECJ in *Procter and Gamble Co v OHIM* (2004). The marks at issue comprised the shape and colour of detergent tablets for washing machines. Average consumers were found not to be in the habit of discerning origin from the shape and colour of such products in the absence of a word or logo. Therefore, the more closely the mark resembled the natural and obvious shape for the product, the more difficult establishing distinctiveness would be.

In *Mag Instrument Inc v OHIM* (2004) the ECJ stated again that '[o]nly a mark which departs significantly from the norm or customs of the sector and thereby fulfils its essential function of indicating origin, is not devoid of any distinctive character'. Clearly, a court's choice of the market sector concerned, and assessment of the extent of the mark's departure from the norm, will be important elements in the registrability of a shape mark. The sector might be restricted to the particular product at issue or more widely construed. Evidence of consumer perceptions in relation to the sector selected may be adduced, as it was in the *Maglite* proceedings. Consequently, in *KWS Saat AG v OHIM* (2004), the ECJ held that consumer perceptions in relation only to the particular mark at issue and the specific product for which it was used were not the only concern. The case related to registration of the colour orange for treatment installations for seeds used in agriculture, horticulture and forestry. The use of colour in general for such installations had not been found to be rare by the CFI, and the mark had been correctly assessed for distinctiveness within this context.

In a UK judgment which will not be welcomed by those anxious to prevent competition from 'lookalikes', Robert Walker LJ held, in *Re Procter and Gamble* (1999), that a composite get-up mark was inherently non-distinctive. The applications were to register the shapes of three bottles for domestic cleaning products, but the impact of the shape, label and colour of the bottles was to be assessed together. They were found to be typical of the get-up for such products. The Court of Appeal applied Jacob J's *dictum* from the *Philips* case that marks which were unusual, or even absurd, arrested the eye and mind and were recognised for what they were, so that they were able to perform the essential function of a trade mark. In that sense, the bottles were not inherently distinctive.

15.6.4 Colours

The same consumer appreciation test is applied to the distinctiveness of use of colour marks in marketing products. Applications for colour marks may be distinguished as to whether a single colour or a combined colour is used.

The OHIM rejected an application for a light green colour in *Wm Wrigley JR Company's Application* (1999). Applying the test of trade mark function to the colour, it stated that both the customary use of colour and the public perception must be taken into account. Customers were not used to making assumptions as to origin of goods from colour, and light green is commonly used to depict freshness. The Board of Appeal did say that this might not apply in the case of very specific goods and 'unusual and peculiar' colours in the relevant trade.

The leading case is *Libertel Groep BV* (2003). The colour must serve the trade mark function to the relevant public, as for all marks, but again the public perception may differ from that to word marks. The ECJ stated that:

A colour *per se* is not normally inherently capable of distinguishing the goods of a particular undertaking.

The Registry Practice Note[55] reiterates that colour alone, while *prima facie* registrable, must be distinctive irrespective of the medium on which it appears, and states that this may be more difficult to establish than colour as applied to an item or its packaging.

While a combined use of colour might be deemed more likely to be inherently distinctive, it will not necessarily be so. In *Colgate-Palmolive's Application* (2002) the application related to the alternating colours dark blue and light blue. It was refused by the Registry, and by the Appointed Person on appeal. The combination was held not to be distinctive where the colours used were not striking, and were within the normal range which the public would expect to see applied to such a product (toothpaste).

15.6.5 Smells

Smell marks will be subject to similar considerations. A smell related to the product itself is unlikely to be perceived as serving a trade mark function by users of the product. Even an added smell will need to be very distinctive before it is perceived in this way, as many products are scented. Like shape marks, smells are more likely to be used with other more traditional marks, and to be subject to a 'limping' mark objection (see 15.3.5).

15.7 DESCRIPTIVE MARKS

Trade marks which describe characteristics of the product with which they are used are unregistrable. Section 3(1)(c) of the TMA 1994 excludes:

> trade marks which consist exclusively of signs or indications which may serve, in trade, to designate the kind, quality, quantity, intended purpose value, geographical origin, the time of production of goods or rendering of services, or other characteristics of goods or services.

To be excluded the mark must consist 'exclusively' of the descriptive sign, so that a mark comprising a combination of descriptive matter with an added distinctive logo or name, for example, may be registered. The description must be one used in trade and not just by the general public to be refused. The proviso that factual distinctiveness may be acquired through use applies, although the more descriptive the mark, the more evidence of factual distinctiveness will be required before registration.

15.7.1 European uncertainties

The mark TREAT (*British Sugar plc v James Robertson & Sons* (1996)) fell within this exclusion, as did JERYL LYNN (*Re Trade Mark No 2,023,949* (1998)), EUROLAMB (*Eurolamb Trade Mark* (1997)) and the PHILIPS drawing (*Philips Electronics NV v Remington Consumer Products Ltd* (1998)).

---

55 Practice Amendment Note, PAN 3/03: www.patent.gov.uk.

In the UK, the policy behind the definition of registrable mark provided by the 1938 Act was to prevent monopolisation of marks which any trader might legitimately wish to use. Fletcher Moulton LJ said in *Joseph Crosfield's Application* (1909):

> ... the registration is not to affect the use of the word by other traders in any *bona fide* description of goods. The court will do well to ask itself the question: will the registration of the trade mark cause substantial difficulty or confusion in view of these rights of user by other traders?

The 1994 Act continues to provide for the non-registrability of descriptive, customary and non-distinctive marks, although allowing for added and acquired distinctiveness. Defences provided by the TMA 1994 cater for legitimate uses by other traders (see 16.8), but it was said in *AD2000 Trade Mark* (1997) that the defences should not be taken into consideration in determining a mark's registrability.

The ECJ decision in the *Baby-Dry* (2002) case may now suggest otherwise. In an application for a Community trade mark under the Regulation the mark BABY-DRY was challenged on the grounds of descriptiveness and, startlingly, found not to be wanting. The Court said:

> In order to assess whether a word combination such as BABY-DRY is capable of distinctiveness, it is therefore necessary to put oneself in the shoes of an English-speaking consumer. From that point of view, and given that the goods concerned in this case are babies' nappies, the determination to be made depends on whether the word combination in question may be viewed as a normal way of referring to the goods or of representing their essential characteristics in common parlance.

> As it is, that word combination, whilst it does unquestionably allude to the function which the goods are supposed to fulfil, still does not satisfy the disqualifying criteria set forth in [Article 7(1)(c) of Regulation]. Whilst each of the two words in the combination may form part of expressions used in everyday speech to designate the function of babies' nappies, their syntactically unusual juxtaposition is not a familiar expression in the English language, either for designating babies' nappies or for describing their essential characteristics.

> Word combinations like BABY-DRY cannot therefore be regarded as exhibiting, as a whole, descriptive character; they are lexical inventions bestowing distinctive power on the mark so formed and may not be refused registration under Article 7(1)(c) of Regulation No 40/94.

The ECJ reached this decision, however, on the basis of an interpretation of the Regulation that read the ground of refusal with the defences to infringement. Its conclusion can be regarded either as a very lenient view of the 'lexical inventiveness' of a phrase such as 'Baby-Dry', or as an embodiment of the modern view of trade mark function, as had been recommended to the Court by the Advocate General.

Consequently, assuming that UK courts must give the same regard to interpretation of the Regulation as they must the Directive, the policy which has traditionally lain behind decisions at the margins in the UK is at the very least questionable. It is to be hoped that the ECJ's decisions in *Nichols* (2004) (see 15.6.2) and *OHIM v Wm Wrigley Jr Co* (2003) (see 15.7.2) resolve these conflicts.

In general the position as to descriptive marks is unclear; decisions of the CFI on appeals from the OHIM on Community trade marks appear to have relaxed. In the ECJ, apart from the *Baby-Dry* (2002) judgment, a number of appeals remain pending. These decisions may in turn also lead to invalidity proceedings. It may therefore be some time before clear and definitive guidance is given on the refusal for descriptive signs, as suggested by the Appointed Person in *Cycling Is Application* (2002).

There are a number of different forms of descriptive marks, so that combined word marks, geographical words and shapes need to be examined separately.

15.7.2 Descriptive combinations of words and phrases

Generic words (or logos) fall within s 3(1)(c). Consequently, BACH was refused because the name had been used to describe herbal remedies made to specific remedies (*Bach Flower Remedies Ltd v Healing Herbs Ltd* (2000)). The *Windsurfing* (1999) relevant consumer test is used to determine how the word will be understood. This test includes the use of the word by those engaged in the relevant trade, such as wholesalers, manufacturers and retailers. The English rose logo suffered a similar fate in *RFU v Cotton Traders* (2002).

For other descriptive words, singly or in combination, the ECJ's decision in *Baby-Dry* (2002) is of prime importance It is not difficult to see why marks such as EASYBANK, COMPANYLINE, NEW BORN BABY, DOUBLEMINT and BABY-DRY might be unregistrable as Community trade marks. Although COMPANYLINE was refused, this was purely on the grounds of being devoid of distinctive character and not descriptiveness. The standard of distinctiveness required under Article 7(1)(c) of the Regulation has appeared to be a low one. In 2001 the CFI allowed registration of EUROHEALTH for financial affairs, but not insurance services, EASYBANK for both services, and DOUBLEMINT for chewing gum (*Wm Wrigley Jr Co v OHIM* (2001)). Perhaps surprisingly, the marks were considered too vague, ambiguous and indeterminate to be descriptive, even though they allude to the products concerned.

Subsequently, NEW BORN BABY was allowed for dolls on the basis that the phrase described not the dolls, but what they represent (*Zapf Creation AG v OHIM* (2002)). Registration was not refused because no evidence was adduced of consumers interpreting the mark descriptively of the product, even though the average consumer might conflate the two descriptions.

In *Baby-Dry* (2002) the ECJ accepted registration of BABY-DRY for nappies. The exclusion was stated only to relate to marks serving in normal usage, from a consumer's point of view, to describe the product directly, or to refer to its essential characteristic(s).

The Court reasoned that the ground for refusal must be read in conjunction with the defences of Article 12,[56] and the definition of a mark. Articles 7 and 12 showed the purpose of the ground of refusal to be preventing registration of marks unable to distinguish products of the undertaking marketing them, this (the Court said) was the only interpretation consonant with the definition. However, it fails to include the need to prevent anti-competitive monopolies articulated in the function of trade mark registration as defined in earlier Court decisions such as *Philips*, cited in the recent *Linde* (2003), and *Windsurfing* (1999) decisions.

Applying the consumer understanding test, the Court said the words must be taken separately, and as a combination. 'Any perceptible difference' to the terms used

---

56 Section 11 of the TMA 1994.

in common parlance of the relevant class of consumers was 'apt' to confer distinctive character on the mark. The relevant class of consumer was English-speaking, as the mark was in English. Despite the opinion of Advocate General Jacobs that the mark contained 'extreme ellipsis, unusual structure and resistance to any intuitive grammatical analysis' the distinctiveness is barely perceptible, that in NEW BORN BABY microscopic.

The case must be seen as a victory for the 'modern' approach to trade marks. The decision may be criticised in that reliance on the defences to interpret descriptiveness does not balance the interests of proprietor and competitor adequately. Another trader may use the word descriptively but is barred from its use as a trade mark. Effectively then, the first comer secures a monopoly on a description of the product, unless 'exclusively' is read to require an additional element to the descriptive word before distinctiveness is established. (Remember, however, that a necessity for capricious additions to shape marks before registrability was rejected in *Philips* (2003).)

However, Advocate General Jacobs termed the decision 'widely misunderstood' in his Opinion in the DOUBLEMINT appeal in *OHIM v Wm Wrigley Jr Co* (2003). He suggested that no inconsistency with *Windsurfing* (1999) was intended as it had been reaffirmed in *Linde* (2003). He suggested that *Baby-Dry*'s (2002) requirement of a perceptible difference avoided the danger (which he acknowledged) of trade mark owners monopolising a mark and the area around it threatening unmeritorious and expensive proceedings against a competitor who may be forced to capitulate.

Nevertheless, in the interim, in the light of the *Baby-Dry* (2002) decision, many national registries, including the UK, revised their policies on descriptive word marks. It is possible that the guidelines suggested in the CFI decisions in COMPANYLINE, EASYBANK, NEW BORN BABY, and BABY-DRY were useful ones if applied less tortuously than they were in those cases. Distinctiveness does not require an additional or 'capricious' element (such as fancy lettering) to be 'added' to an otherwise *prima facie* descriptive word mark. However, some element of 'fancifulness', ambiguity of meaning, indirect allusiveness, or even unusual grammatical construction can confirm the presence of distinctiveness, as Keeling suggests.

In addition, in *Baby-Dry* (2002) the ECJ did say that additional added elements may secure registration:

> ... a mark composed of signs or indications satisfying that definition [Article 7 (1)(c)] should ... be refused registration unless it comprises ... other signs or indications and, in addition, the purely descriptive signs or indications of which it is composed are ... presented or configured in a manner that distinguishes the resultant whole from the usual way of designating the goods or services concerned or their essential characteristics.[57]

A stricter interpretation appears from recent decisions. The ECJ overruled the CFI's interpretation of Article 7(1)(c) of the Regulation in the DOUBLEMINT appeal: *OHIM v Wm Wrigley Jr Co* (2003) and referred the case back to the CFI for determination. The court is now expected to reject registration (although the mark is registered in the US). The ECJ held that a descriptive mark could not distinguish a product's origins, and that the ground of refusal was designed to preserve the public interest in such marks, following *Linde* (2003) and *Windsurfing* (1999). A descriptive mark would be refused

---

57 Transposed into the positive from the negative.

not only if it was already in use descriptively, but also if it had that potential. This remained the case if at least one of several potential meanings was descriptive. The CFI had failed to determine whether the mark was capable of being used by other economic operators as designating a characteristic of their products. However, despite the case being raised in argument, the Court did not state how *Baby-Dry* (2002) might be distinguished.

Where a descriptive mark comprises a combination of descriptive elements, it is the word as a whole that must be found to be descriptive: *Campina Melkunie v Benelux-Merkenbureau* (2004) (BIOMILD for yoghurt). The ECJ held that, as a general rule, a mere combination of descriptive elements remains descriptive even if the combination creates a new word. Unusual variations, particularly in syntax or meaning, might be sufficient to avoid rejection of the mark if the resulting impression was removed from the simple meaning of the individual elements. For a word mark, meant as much to be heard as to be read, this condition would have to be satisfied both in relation to its aural and visual impressions. In addition, the fact that the descriptive elements in the combination could be expressed in different words (thus enabling competitors to describe their products) was irrelevant to the determination whether the combination mark was to be refused for descriptiveness. In *Koninklijke v Benelux-Merkenbureau* (2004) the ECJ added that a mark which had become part of everyday language and acquired its own meaning independent of its descriptive components might also avoid rejection.

15.7.3   Geographical words

Before 1994, in the UK, geographical words were unregistrable, however much secondary meaning as a mark they had acquired through use: *York Trade Mark* (1984). Words which exclusively indicate a product's origins remain unregistrable as trade marks, unless they have acquired distinctiveness through use, under the TMA 1994.

Specific guidance was provided by the ECJ in *Windsurfing* (1999). It related to a mark using the name of the well known Bavarian Lake Chiemsee. The Court specifically asked whether the defence in Article 6 had any bearing on the scope of interpretation of the ground for refusal, directly raising the policy issue and their decision was firmly rooted in public policy:

> ... Article 3(1)(c) of the Directive pursues an aim which is in the public interest, namely that descriptive signs or indications relating to the category of goods or services in respect of which registration is applied for may be freely used by all, including as collective marks or as part of complex or graphic marks.

> ... Article 6(1)(b) of the Directive ... does not run counter to what has been stated as to the objective of Article 3(1)(c), nor does it have a decisive bearing on the interpretation of that provision. Indeed, Article 6(1)(b), which aims, *inter alia*, to resolve the problems posed by registration of a mark consisting wholly or partly of a geographical name, does not confer on third parties the right to use the name as a trade mark but merely guarantees their right to use it descriptively, that is to say, as an indication of geographical origin, provided that it is used in accordance with honest practices in industrial and commercial matters.

Consequently, the ground of refusal extends not only to geographical signs already associated with the category of goods or services concerned in the minds of the relevant consumer, but also to those liable to be used by undertakings in that context and to be so understood by the reasonable consumer. Geographical names not known as indicators of origin may be registered: so that NORTH POLE for bananas, or EQUATOR for ice cream, might well succeed. While the names of lakes (or other such geographical features) may not usually be understood as having trade mark significance, this may not be the case where the name is used to designate its shore-side area. Names such as 'Merseyside' might well be associated with the manufacturing industry, for example.

The ECJ also outlined the factors to be considered in determining how the name would be understood by the relevant consumer. The degree of familiarity with the name among consumers, the characteristics of the place designated, and the category of goods concerned must all be taken into account.

Geographical terms indicating origin do not go unprotected, and may be important indicators of quality (consider 'Champagne'). Separate protection is provided for geographical terms when a valuable association has been built up between a product and the region from which it comes, such as 'Stilton cheese' or 'Parma ham'. Traders from the region sharing the name may seek protection for appellations of origin or indications of source. They may apply either for domestic protection or community rights. In the UK certification marks (s 50 of the TMA 1994) or collective marks (s 49 of the TMA 1994) will apply.

In the EU a Protected Designation of Origin (PDO), or a Protected Geographical Indication (PGI) may be applied for.[58] A PDO product must originate from a particular area, be fully produced, processed and prepared in that area and have qualities and characteristics which are exclusively due to a particular geographical environment. Only groups of producers may apply for a PDO to be registered. Amongst the first UK PDO registrations were White Stilton and Blue Stilton cheeses, followed by Orkney Beef, Orkney Lamb and Jersey Royal Potatoes. The criteria for a PGI are less demanding; the geographical link must occur in at least one of the stages of production, processing or preparation.

15.7.4 Shapes

The shape of a product, if used as a mark, may well be descriptive of its characteristics. This was one ground of objection to the three-headed shaver mark in *Philips Electronics NV v Remington Consumer Products Ltd* (1998). However, by applying the specific grounds of refusal for shapes first, the ECJ did not need to address the question on the interpretation of Article 3(1)(c) of the Directive.

The judgment is significant, however, in applying the *Windsurfing* (1999) policy grounds to a shape mark. The application of both this policy and Article 3(1)(c) of the Directive to shapes was specifically referred to the ECJ in *Linde* (2003). It was held if a shape was not excluded by the specific absolute grounds relating to shapes, the refusal for descriptive marks would apply, the consumer understanding test must be applied, and interpreted in the light of the public interest in descriptive signs.

---

58 Council Regulation 2081/92 of 14 July 1992 on the Protection of Geographical Indications and Designations of Origin for Agricultural Products and Foodstuffs.

15.8 CUSTOMARY MARKS

Registration is also refused to trade marks which are customary, so that marks which:

consist exclusively of signs or indications which have become customary in the current language or in the bona fide and established practices of the trade

are excluded by s 3(1)(d) of the TMA 1994. Therefore, a mark may be refused either for being customary in language generally, or, more narrowly, for established use within a particular trade. TREAT (*British Sugar plc v James Robertson & Sons* (1996)) was regarded as likely to fall into this sub-section because many people use 'treat' in advertisements and on goods, although Jacob J did not define 'customary'.

The common colouring of lids given to jars of instant coffee by different manufacturers (gold for superior blends, red for decaffeinated, brown for the standard grade) might amount to an established trade practice, for example, or the blue colouring applied to the lids of tubs of baby wipes. Similarly, the word 'cola' is commonly adopted for a particular kind of soft drink. The evidence in *RFU v Cotton Traders* (2002) showed that the rose symbol had become generic in depicting the English rugby team, so that it was held to fall within s 3(1)(d).

The wording of the sub-section and the Directive does not refer specifically to the mark designating goods or services. Interpreting the Directive, in *R v Merz & Krell GmbH & Co* (2001) the ECJ held that in order to be refused the mark must designate the product for which it is to be used, although it need not describe it. The applicant had applied to register BRAVO for typewriters. Although 'bravo' is a customary term of praise it was not shown to apply customarily to the products in question. However, the ECJ held that the definition of a mark implied this must be so, and that questions of distinctiveness must be determined relative to the product concerned. Consequently, BRAVO was not customary for typewriters.

15.9 THE PROVISO TO SECTION 3(1)(b)–(d) OF THE TMA 1994

Where the TMA 1994 has relaxed registrability is in the ability of an applicant to overcome inherent lack of distinctiveness in a mark by evidence of distinctiveness having been acquired through use. The proviso to s 3(1) of the TMA 1994 allows for factual distinctiveness:

... a trade mark shall not be refused registration by virtue of paragraph (b), (c) or (d) ... if, before the date of application for registration, it has in fact acquired a distinctive character as a result of the use made of it.

Neither the Directive, nor the 1994 Act define 'distinctive character'. In *Re Trade Mark No 2,023,949* (1998) Laddie J held the mark JERYL LYNN to have been invalidly registered. The mark was registered for pharmaceuticals. It was the name given to a particular strain of mumps virus for which the trade mark proprietor produced a vaccine, and was therefore descriptive. A rival company challenged the mark when wishing to describe their own product. He held that, where a name had been used for many years (as it had) before the application to register, the answer to the factual issue of whether the mark described the product or indicated its origin could be had in the response to four questions:

(a) What was the product to which it had been applied?

(b) Had it been used exclusively in relation to that product?

(c) Had it been used on the product as a designation of origin?

(d) Had it come to be recognised by the relevant public as a designation of origin, rather than as an indication of type?

The ECJ gave further guidance on determining distinctive character in the Directive in *Windsurfing* (1999), and *Philips* (2003). It is a question of fact for a competent authority based on real evidence of use of the mark as a trade mark assessed at the date of the application for the mark. Whether a mark has acquired distinctive character from the use made of it is judged by asking if the relevant class of persons recognise it as distinguishing the product as originating from a particular undertaking.

Factors to be taken into account include:

- the market share held by the mark;
- how intensive, geographically widespread and long-standing the use is;
- the amount invested in promoting the mark;
- the proportion of the relevant class of persons who identify the goods as originating from the undertaking concerned; and
- statements from chambers of commerce and industry or other trade or professional associations

The use of the mark must be in a trade mark sense, or as described in *British Sugar plc v James Robertson & Sons* (1996) as a 'badge of origin'. Consequently, where it is used in conjunction with other more recognisable marks it may be termed a 'limping' mark, and the use will not confer distinctive character. TREAT was used in conjunction with the SILVER SPOON mark and so did not achieve recognition as a mark, over and above its normal laudatory meaning.

The recognition of the mark as distinguishing the origin of the product is judged through the eyes of an average consumer who is reasonably well-informed, reasonably observant and circumspect. At least a significant proportion must recognise the mark as serving its distinguishing function. The way in which the public perceives a mark is influenced by the average consumer's level of attention, which will vary according to the type of product at stake. It seems trite that a buyer will give a much higher level of attention to purchasing a car than a dishwasher detergent.

Evidence of use and of recognition may be adduced. The burden of proof lies on the applicant to establish acquired distinctive character gained from use. Evidence of sales was led in *Yakult* to show use. To provide evidence of the public's response to the use of a trade mark survey evidence has been used. This, however, was subjected to careful critical scrutiny, and its value doubted, by Jacob J in both *British Sugar plc v James Robertson & Sons* (1996) and *Philips Electronics NV v Remington Consumer Products Ltd* (1998). The need for evidence showing that ultimate purchasers recognised the goods by shape was reaffirmed in *In Re Dualit Trade Mark* (1999) and the survey evidence adduced rejected. The use of leading questions was criticised in *Yakult* (2001).

General and abstract criteria such as predetermined percentages of rates of recognition by a proportion of the consumer group are not to be used in deciding whether distinctive character has been obtained, although opinion polls may be taken under conditions laid down by national law: *Lloyd* (2000).

Today, the question arises whether use of a mark on a website can constitute sufficient use to confer distinctiveness. The defining characteristic of the internet is its global reach, but this could have the potential result that use of a mark on a website would qualify a mark for registration for a domestic mark, however remote the website to UK consumers. The issue arose in *800-Flowers Trade Mark* (2001), where the mark had been used on the American company's website and a few telephone orders had been placed by UK customers. Jacob J dismissed the suggestion that such a call necessarily involved use of the mark in the UK and that accessing the site in the UK amounted to use at the point of access. He drew attention, instead, to the fact that the applicant had never had a place of business in the UK, that its services were performed overseas, and that there had apparently only one newspaper advertisement had been placed here. Passing off cases on goodwill were deemed inapplicable to this question. Consequently, it would seem that evidence that a website has been directed towards customers in the UK is needed, and that this should be determined objectively from the website user's perspective rather than the website owner's intention. US case law distinguished between 'active' and 'passive' websites.

15.9.1 Unusual marks

Particular types of mark such as geographical names, shapes, or laudatory terms may need considerable use before acquiring distinctive character. In *British Sugar plc v James Robertson & Sons* (1996) Jacob J held that, for common or apt descriptive or laudatory words, 'compelling evidence' of acquired distinctiveness was needed. Extensive use was not enough; it must be use that resulted in a substantial majority of the public regarding the mark as a trade mark, 'almost a household word'.

The ECJ took the view in *Windsurfing* (1999) that geographical names which are very well known require long standing and intensive use to overcome the initial meaning such a name bears. Equally, a name already familiar as an indication of geographical origin for goods in the relevant category will require evidence that long standing and intensive use has made its distinguishing meaning well established before it can be considered distinctive.

The same must be true of shape marks, which will bear a different initial meaning to consumers. Jacob J held that no use was capable of ever teaching the public that the drawing was a trade mark, rather than a description of the product in *Philips Electronics NV v Remington Consumer Products Ltd* (1998). It should also be noted that this was a limping mark as it was used in conjunction with the company's PHILISHAVE trade mark. Although the public associated the shaver with the plaintiff, this was as the hitherto sole manufacturer of such a design.

Where a trader has a monopoly in a product and has used a word to describe that product, it is likely that that word will be taken to describe the product, rather than to distinguish it. 'Distinguish' does imply that the particular products are also available from others, from which the one in question must be separated out. This question was referred to the ECJ in *Philips*.[59] The Court held that, even where a trader who was the

---

59 The Court of Appeal has referred a similar question to the ECJ in *Dyson v Registrar of Trade Marks* [2003] C–321/03.

sole supplier of the goods used a shape mark, extensive use might be sufficient to confer distinctive character, provided it was recognised as distinguishing of origin by a sufficient proportion of consumers. Whether a limping mark can ever do so will depend on the understanding of the consuming public of the way in which signs are used. It seems unlikely that an unusual sign, such as a shape or a smell, could acquire distinctiveness without considerable effort on the trader's part to disassociate it from a recognised traditional mark, or marketing without any other indication of origin. This would only work to confer trade mark status on the mark if it could be protected in some other way to prevent other competitors using a similar sign.

The use of an 'obvious' shape in *Henkel v OHIM* (2001) did not render the shape of a dishwasher detergent tablet distinctive. The CFI, considering the registrability of a Community trade mark, held that for such a common product the relevant group was all consumers, and that they would give little attention to the purchase of such everyday goods. Use of an obvious shape (in commonly used colours for such products) was unlikely to render the shape recognisable as an indicator of origin. The ECJ upheld this conclusion, but as a by-product of the resulting consumers' perceptions of the mark: *Procter and Gamble Co v OHIM* (2004).

15.9.2 A policy element?

Further development of this test may come with the decision of the ECJ reference in *Unilever plc's Application* (2003). This case relates to the shape of the well known VIENNETTA ice cream dessert. In characteristic style, Jacob J set out the harm that might result from too wide a registrability for product shapes:

> There is a bit of a sleight of hand going on here and in other cases of this sort. The trick works like this. The manufacturer sells and advertises his product widely and under a well known trade mark. After some while the product appearance becomes well known. He then says the appearance alone will serve as a trade mark, even though he himself never relied on the appearance alone to designate origin and would not dare to do so. He then gets registration of the shape alone. Now he is in a position to stop other parties, using their own word trade marks, from selling the product, even though no one is deceived or misled.

The issue might easily be tested by asking whether the registrant would ever sell the product without accompanying word marks. If not, the shape is another example of the 'limping' mark identified in the *British Sugar* case. In *Unilever* Jacob J stressed that there is a distinct difference between product recognition and 'distinctive character'. Survey evidence showed that a majority of the public recognised the product as a WALL's VIENNETTA, but that a significant minority would also take other shapes in use by other manufacturers as being the mark applied for.

15.10 SHAPES

Although shapes are now potentially registrable as trade marks (see 15.3), the absolute grounds of refusal prevent some shapes from ever being registered. Section 3(2) of the TMA 1994 prohibits registration of signs which consist exclusively of:

(a) a shape which results from the nature of the goods themselves;

(b) a shape which is necessary to obtain a technical result; or

(c) a shape which gives substantial value to goods.

These were termed 'natural, functional or ornamental' shapes by the Advocate General in *Philips*. This exclusion first received consideration in the UK in *Philips Electronics NV v Remington Consumer Products Ltd* (1998). The drawing of the shaver head was regarded as, in substance, graphical representation of a shape sign.

15.10.1 Policy basis

The fears of the House of Lords in *Re Coca-Cola* (1986) (see 15.1.2) were not without foundation for, if a shape performing a technical function or comprising a commercially attractive addition to goods were to receive the potentially eternal protection of a registered trade mark, competition would be unjustifiably hindered. No amount of evidence of acquired factual distinctiveness can overcome this absolute ground of refusal, for the basis of refusal is not a lack of capacity to distinguish, but the preservation of fair competition. This is reflected in US trade mark law by a doctrine of functionality applied to shape marks, rejecting functional shapes from protection. The Directive is based on Benelux law, and is rooted in similar considerations, so that attention is directed to the question of whether another trader will need to adopt the same or a similar shape in order to compete effectively.

However, Keeling queries whether the refusal ever to consider distinctiveness in fact for a shape mark is necessary. He states that, as this ground of refusal constitutes a total bar to protection, it must be interpreted strictly; and that any anti-competitive effects could be prevented by the 'devoid of distinctiveness' head of refusal.

Comparison can be made with the exceptions to protection for functional designs. Trade Mark registration should not allow a producer to circumvent the provision made for compatibility and interoperability which these provide. As stated in *Dyson Ltd v Registrar of Trade Marks* (2003): 'It is not the function of a trade mark to create a monopoly in new developments in technology.'

That the exclusion is based on reasons of public policy was confirmed by the ECJ in *Philips* (2003):

> The rationale for the grounds of refusal of registration laid down in article 3(1)(e) of the Directive is to prevent trade mark protection from granting its proprietor a monopoly on technical solutions or functional characteristics of a product which a user is likely to seek in the products of competitors. Article 3(1)(e) is thus intended to prevent the protection conferred by the trade mark right from being extended, beyond signs which serve to distinguish a product or service from those offered by competitors, so as to form an obstacle preventing competitors from freely offering for sale products incorporating such technical solutions or functional characteristics in competition with the proprietor of the trade mark.

15.10.2 'The nature of the goods themselves'

To exclude shapes which result from the nature of the goods themselves avoids registration of a mark which actually comprises, or comprises a part of, the actual product; for example, the indentations of an egg box or shape of an umbrella.

However, it is difficult to give the provision sustainable meaning. In *Philips Electronics NV v Remington Consumer Products Ltd* (1998) Jacob J pointed out the whole or part of an object is defined by its shape, so that if the object is taken to be the 'goods themselves' all shape signs will result from the nature of the goods. Consequently, because goods are articles of commerce, Jacob J took 'the goods' to mean the category into which the product at issue would belong as a matter of business. In this case it was 'electric shavers' and, therefore, the three-headed rotary shape did not result from the nature of the goods (electric shavers coming in a variety of other shapes as well). This is a common sense approach, but another interpretation is possible. If the product and 'the goods' are taken to be synonymous, registration would only lie for a capricious addition to or variation of that shape, a shape applied to an electric toaster to make it resemble a juke box, for example, or an umbrella handle shaped like an animal's head. Such a shape may well fall within s 3(2)(c) of the TMA 1994, however, making Jacob J's interpretation more tenable. The Court of Appeal upheld Jacob J's reasoning.

Strowel[60] suggested that only basic shapes are imposed by the nature of goods, and that the sign must be regarded globally with all its added arbitrary features. He gave the example of registration of the shape of a bottle of olive oil allowed by the Tribunal of The Hague.[61] The general shape of the bottle was dictated by its nature, but grooves in the surface and a purposively designed integral handle meant that the composite shape was distinctive as a trade mark.

Given these differences of interpretation, and a more generous practice of registration of shape marks in other Member States, Jacob J referred the ground of refusal's interpretation to the ECJ in the VIENNETTA case. He asks whether the nature of goods arises from the specification of goods for which the mark is applied for or registered, or the kind of goods for which the mark is used in articles of commerce, or only the inherent nature of man-made articles, or, the shape of goods which make the product different in appearance from similar competitive products, or, finally, some other criterion.

15.10.3 'Technical result'

A shape achieving a technical result must be 'necessary' for that result to fall within the exclusion. Thus, the exclusion might be interpreted to mean that, if there is 'design freedom' in choosing a particular shape for a particular function, registration is possible, as it is in Benelux law. The shape of a pump action toothpaste container or handle for a carrier bag could remain registrable, although utilitarian, if the actual shape chosen was arbitrary. If 'necessary' is interpreted strictly, even an obvious choice of a functional shape could be registrable, provided that a choice of shape is possible.

Helbling[62] argued that it disadvantages a company, and acts as a disincentive to designers, to refuse to register a shape if minor alterations are possible when a company has established a strong and distinctive shape (such as the LEGO brick). However, Jacob J, in *Philips Electronics NV v Remington Consumer Products Ltd* (1998),

---

60 Strowel, B, 'Benelux: A Guide to the Validity of Three-dimensional Trade Marks in Europe' [1995] EIPR 154.
61 [1992] IER 115.
62 Helbling, T, 'Shapes as Trade Marks?' [1997] IPQ 413.

rejected such an interpretation, by analogy with the exclusion of registration for functional designs, on the ground that, in the majority of cases, design choice will be possible and that he felt it unlikely that the Directive was intended to allow permanent monopolies in matters of significant engineering design. It is often the case, as it was with the shaver, that, although a choice of shape is possible, only one shape will provide optimum results, so that registration would fundamentally affect the quality of competitors' products. Accordingly, any shape in substance solely achieving a technical result, as the shaver head shape did, should not, he said, be registrable. Minor embellishments or variations would not escape the exclusion. Registration would still be possible for distinctive shapes chosen for non-functional reasons. The Swedish Court of Appeal, however, applied a design choice test in relation to the Philip's drawing (*Ide Line AG v Philips Electronics NV* (1997)).

The ECJ did not agree. In *Philips* (2003) the Court said that this head of exclusion pursued the public interest in competition and therefore if a shape's essential characteristics performed a technical function, and were chosen to perform that function, the shape must be freely available to be used by all. There was nothing in the wording of the exclusion to allow registration where another shape could perform the same function.

This was subsequently applied in another action between the same parties. In *Philips v Remington Consumer Products Ltd* (2004) four further Philips shape marks were revoked for invalidity. The marks related to the shape of three-headed electric shavers where the three blades, in equilateral arrangement, were mounted on a clover leaf shaped plate.

It was also argued that this part of the shaver head's shape was not an essential characteristic of the mark, but an embellishment which removed the mark from the s 3(2)(b) exclusion. Rimer J did not accept Philips's argument. Although he found that the clover leaf shape was not an essential characteristic of the mark's shape, the faceplate of the shaver as a whole did constitute an essential feature of the mark. Whether the shape was an essential[63] characteristic of the mark was a question of fact, and the balance of evidence showed that the purpose of the clover leaf shape was to draw consumers' attention to the three-headed shape of Philips shavers. The question was therefore whether the faceplate, and not an individual feature of the mark, was attributable solely to a technical result. The court held that it was. It said that it was immaterial that small portions of the clover leaf shape were not functional, and that the shape also had an aesthetic effect. Very little sympathy was directed towards so-called 'lifestyle' products:

> Philips's three-headed shavers may well be viewed by some, perhaps many, as so-called lifestyle products but it is important to remember that all this litigation is about is the business end of a piece of electrical equipment whose sole purpose is functional ... Philips does not market them as a work of art, because that is not what they are.

15.10.4 'Substantial value'

The final exclusion relating to shape marks is for those which give substantial value to the goods. This is designed to avoid overlap between copyright or design protection,

---

63 Rimer J regretted that the ECJ gave no guidance of the interpretation of 'essential' in *Philips* (2003).

and trade mark registration. A distinction is drawn between a shape which adds to the distinctiveness of goods (such as the COCA-COLA bottle or shape of the TOBLERONE bar), and one which adds aesthetic value to goods (fruit shaped soaps or house shaped bottles of spirits, for example) so that they are bought for their eye-appeal. Strowel suggested that two questions may be asked in order to distinguish between shapes which add substantial value to goods and those which do not. First, whether the appeal the shape gives to the product constitutes the consumer's primary reason for buying those goods; and, secondly, whether the reason for purchase is because of the appeal or because the shape has acquired goodwill (distinctiveness) in the public's eyes. It is not merely a question of whether the use of the shape enables a higher price to be charged, which may occur where an attractive shape is used or where goodwill is engendered by a distinctive trade mark (evidenced, for example, by the COCA-COLA bottle).

In Benelux law, 'substantial value' denotes qualities added to the goods themselves by the shape ('product value'), not just their market value. In *Wokkels* (1985), the Dutch Supreme Court accepted that a shape given to a biscuit added to its market value (price), but did not increase its quality as a biscuit (product value), and the shape was held to be registrable. In *Bacony* (1989), by contrast, the court held that, as the difference in taste between competing brands of crackers was so insubstantial that the shape given to them was the only determinant of both market and product value, the shape was not registrable.

Jacob J held that the shape of Philips's shaver head fell within this exclusion, as the public had been carefully educated to associate the shape with an effective product (product value): *Philips Electronics NV v Remington Consumer Products Ltd* (1998). However, on this point, the Court of Appeal disagreed in *Philips Electronics NV v Remington Consumer Products Ltd* (1999). The Court took the view that substantial reputation was not relevant to s 3(2)(c) of the TMA 1994. The test to be applied was a comparison between the shape sought to be registered and shapes of equivalent articles. On the evidence, the registered shape had no more value than other shapes which were established to be as good and as cheap to produce. Unfortunately, the ECJ did not give its opinion on this head of refusal in *Philips* (2003). Jacob J expressed surprise that it was not raised in the VIENNETTA case, but he did not refer a question on it to the ECJ in *Unilever plc's Application* (2003). Consequently, it awaits another case before determinative guidance can be given.

Another significant factor, as Jacob J also pointed out in *Unilever*, is registration of the shape for design protection. This may suggest that appearance was intended to attract customers and added value to the product, perhaps only serving that function as an essentially aesthetic creation.

15.11 OBJECTIONABLE AND DECEPTIVE MARKS

Trade marks that are either contrary to public policy or to accepted principles of morality may not be registered.[64] Those 'of such a nature as to deceive the public (for instance as to the nature, quality or geographical origin of the goods or service)' will

---

64   Section 3(3)(a) of the TMA 1994.

also be refused.[65] The proviso to s 3(1) of the TMA 1994 (use contributing distinctiveness (see 15.9)) does not apply to these absolute grounds of refusal, but evidence of use made without protest might be used to overcome such a potential objection.

The registrar has no discretion when applying these grounds for refusal. The section is mandatory, so that a mark falling within the section must be refused, and there is no discretion to refuse one which does not. The Registrar is required to reach a judgment: *Ghazilian's Application* (2001).

Examples are given in the Trade Mark Registry Manual. Marks encouraging or promoting drugs, counterfeiting, pornography, criminal activity and the like would be refused as contrary to public policy; but mild bad language, relatively inoffensive expressions and mild slang would not be considered contrary to accepted principles of morality. The OHIM Guidelines state:

> Words or images which are offensive, such as swear words or racially derogatory images, or which are blasphemous are not acceptable. There is a dividing line between this and trade marks which might be considered in poor taste. The latter do not offend.

15.11.1 'Principles of morality'

Public morality was measured by contemporary standards under the 1938 Act, so that, in *La Marquise Application* (1947), OOMPHIES was registered for shoes, despite the suggestion that the word might encourage shoe fetishism. Rejection according to 'accepted' principles of morality suggests a similar standard, and implies an objective test, as before; something to which a substantial minority would object. On this basis, HALLELUJAH was refused registration in *Hallelujah Trade Mark* (1977).

As common standards of morality become increasingly difficult to determine, marks once regarded as unregistrable will reach the register, as OPIUM[66] or POISON[67] have done.

The mark TINY PENIS was refused in *Ghazilian's Application* (2001). The Appointed Person considered earlier case law but followed the design case of *Masterman's Design* (1991) (see 13.5.8) rather than *Hallelujah Trade Mark* (1977), as representing a more modern and robust approach to public sensibilities. He held that in any social group there are standards of behaviour or moral principles which the community requires to be observed and are widely shared so that religious, social or family values are not undermined: these comprised 'accepted principles of morality'. Secondly, because the primary objective of registration is to protect both traders and the public and, as a refusal to register does not prevent use of the mark, registration should be denied only where breach of an accepted principle of morality was offended. Mere offence at something distasteful would not be enough. The test is an objective one. The dividing line is between distaste and offence which would 'justifiably cause outrage or would be the subject of justifiable censure'. He made allowance for the fact that we live in a time of diverse social values, and also held that the outrage or censure had to be

---

65 *Ibid*, s 3(3)(b).
66 No 1072684.
67 No 1302311.

among an identifiable section of the public, and that a higher degree of outrage in a smaller section of the community would suffice as much as a lesser degree in a more widespread section of the public.

On the facts of the case it is then perhaps surprising that the mark was refused. This was on the grounds that the term is an anatomical one normally used in a serious context, various euphemisms reserved for everyday use in the interests of family values. Consequently this family value would be undermined by the word's registration as a mark, as it should be reserved for serious use. While the level of 'outrage' might not be thought to be great, had the mark been registered (it was in use already), it might have been difficult for the Court to have justified registration positively.

15.11.2 'Public policy'

In *Philips Electronics NV v Remington Consumer Products Ltd* (1998), Remington argued that the drawing had been registered contrary to public policy because the shaver head's shape had been included in patent claims and was functional, so that trade mark registration should not be allowed to prolong protection after other intellectual property rights had expired. Jacob J held that s 3(3)(a) of the TMA 1994 was not concerned with such economic grounds of objection, but was 'confined to matters such as are covered by the French legal term *ordre publique*, a matter involving some question of morality'. He also denied that there is any ban on parallel intellectual property rights where there is no express rule of law to that effect.

A mark that infringed copyright was refused in *Karo-Step Trade Mark* (1977) and should still be objectionable as being contrary to public policy. To use another individual's character without his or her consent or to use a religious device without authority is also likely to be contrary to public policy.

Under the TMA 1938, the objection had to lie in the mark itself. In *Fairest's Application* (1951), the mark itself was unobjectionable, but it was to be used on pools coupons for a pool run in breach of the Betting and Lotteries Acts. It was refused under the registrar's discretion (now abolished) instead.

15.11.3 Deceptive marks

Examples of likely deceptive situations can be drawn from case law decided under the 1938 Act. Although the test was differently worded, marks 'likely to deceive or cause confusion' were rejected. The mark RYSTA was refused by the House of Lords for hosiery on the ground that it was to be used both on new stockings of the applicants' manufacture and on stockings made by others but repaired by them: *Aristoc v Rysta* (1945). The court took into account the class of goods in question, the nature of the system of repair used (which might change in the future) and the likely effects of registering the mark when there were large numbers of such stockings on the market, deciding that registration might cause confusion as to how the mark was being used. Viscount Maugham regarded the nature of the goods' customers, rich and poor alike, and the way in which the word was used as relevant. The House of Lords decided that the public would not be able to distinguish use of the mark to denote origin of goods and use to denote the provision of a service to second hand goods.

By contrast, in *Eastex's Application* (1947), the use of the mark LASTEX on a component included in garments made by other manufacturers was allowed, as the practice was found to be understood by the public (in the same way, for example, as a mark such as LYCRA is now used on goods made by many different manufacturers to indicate the fabric used). All relevant circumstances can be considered, so that, in *Nova Trade Mark* (1968), the size of the opponent to the registration of a mark's business was relevant to determine whether real confusion was likely.

Deception as to nature of goods may be illustrated by the case of *China Therm Trade Mark* (1980) where the mark was refused for goods made of plastic and not china. It is a matter of the public's understanding, however, and, in *Pound Puppies Trade Mark* (1988), Aldous J did not take the view that the public would be confused by the mark as to the cost of the goods (soft toy dogs), nor would the public suffer any detriment as the toys could only be purchased at the true price. Marks suggesting an incorrect geographical origin will be refused and, in *Hill's Trade Mark* (1893), FORREST LONDON was refused for clocks made in Coventry. Where confusion between products would be dangerous, marks have also been refused. In *Edward's Application* (1945), JARDEX was already registered for bleach (the consumption of which would be harmful), preventing registration of JARDOX for a meat extract.

15.12 PROHIBITED MARKS

Marks whose use is prohibited in the UK by any enactment, rule of law or provision of Community law will not be registrable.[68] A mark breaching the Trade Descriptions Act 1968 would be refused on this ground, for example.

15.13 SPECIALLY PROTECTED EMBLEMS

Section 4 lists specially protected emblems, such as the Royal Arms, a representation of the Royal Crown or flags or the Union Jack (the national flag of the UK) and the Olympic symbols, which shall not be registered as specified in that section.[69]

15.14 APPLICATIONS MADE IN BAD FAITH

To the extent that an application is made in bad faith, a trade mark shall not be registered: s 3(6) of the TMA 1994. Although it cannot be used as an aid to interpretation (*British Sugar plc v James Robertson & Sons* (1996)), the White Paper stated that a *bona fide* intention was one that was 'genuine'. The phrase 'bad faith' is a new one to trade mark law and is not expressly linked to '*bona fide*' in s 32 of the TMA 1994.

The courts have been reluctant to define 'bad faith'. In *Gromax Plasticulture v DLN* (1999) Lindsay J said:

---

68   *Ibid*, s 3(4).
69   *Ibid*, s 3(5).

> I shall not attempt to define bad faith in this context. Plainly it includes dishonesty and, as I would hold, includes also some dealings which fall short of the standards of acceptable commercial behaviour observed by reasonable and experienced men in the particular area being examined. Parliament has wisely not attempted to explain in detail what is or is not bad faith in this context; how far a dealing must so fall short in order to amount to bad faith is a matter best left to be adjudged not by some paraphrase by the courts ... but by reference to the words of the Act and upon a regard to all material surrounding circumstances.

Accordingly, it a matter to be left to courts in the light of all relevant circumstances. It is bad faith at the time the application to register a mark is filed that is relevant: *Inter Lotto (UK) Ltd v The National Lottery Commission* (2004). Subsequent bad faith is a matter for invalidity.

There are a number of possible examples of applications in 'bad faith', although any decision must be made in the light of the facts.

In general, bad faith carries connotations of commercial fraud; a serious allegation. Therefore, it should be pleaded circumspectly, specifically and backed by direct evidence: *Royal Enfield Trade Marks* (2002). However, it is not confined to outright dishonesty, and extends to unfair commercially unacceptable behaviour: *Road Tech Computer Systems Ltd v Unison Software (UK) Ltd* (1996), and *Daawat Trade Mark* (2002).

The test is an objective one, so that an applicant's subjective belief that his or her behaviour was commercially acceptable did not prevent a finding of bad faith in *Daawat Trade Mark* (2002). However, it does not subject an applicant to an open-ended examination of his or her commercial morality: *Demon Ale Trade Mark* (2000).

As it is a test of registrability it is tested as at the time of making the application to register. Consequently, any subsequent use of the mark is not a defence to an allegation of bad faith, nor can it be cured by establishing that the mark could have been registered later in good faith: *Daawat Trade Mark* (2002).

15.14.1 Lack of intention to use

The provisions for application also provide that an applicant must state that a mark is being used or that he has a *bona fide* intention to use it.[70] In *Road Tech Computer Systems Ltd v Unison Software (UK) Ltd* (1996), in an application for summary judgment, Robert Walker J refused to interpret this new phrase, but did hold that the defendant had an arguable defence. The defendant's argument related the meaning of bad faith to a lack of a *bona fide* intention to use. The plaintiff argued that 'bad faith' should be read merely as meaning dishonest. A dishonest intention would clearly be in bad faith, but the defendant's argument that bad faith also included a lack of a *bona fide* intention to use was regarded as arguable. It may be, therefore, that an application made without the requisite use or genuine intention to use of s 32(3) of the TMA can be regarded as one made in bad faith. Section 3(6) of the TMA 1994 provides the only sanction – if such it is – for the lack of the requisite intention to use.

---

70 *Ibid*, s 32(3).

15.14.2 No intention to use throughout the width of the specification of goods or services

Road Tech Computer Systems Ltd v Unison Software (UK) Ltd (1996) suggests that application for a range of goods and services wider than those to which the mark is actually to be applied is not *bona fide* and, by implication, one made in bad faith. The plaintiffs had registered ROADRUNNER for computer software, using it on a business applications package for the road haulage business. The defendants made a 'RoadRunner' back up facility for the UNIX operating system. In infringement proceedings, one ground of the defence was that the application had been made in bad faith because the mark was applied to a very narrow category of the goods (business applications software) for which it was registered, and could not be a *bona fide* intention to use the mark 'in relation to' the goods and services stated (software in general) in the application. This was accepted as arguable.

Subsequently, in *Demon Ale Trade Mark* (2000) s 3(6) was read together with Article 13 of the Directive (binding on the registrar although not incorporated into the TMA 1994) so that the registrar must be satisfied that no grounds of refusal exist throughout the width of the specified goods or services in the application.

The same is not true for a Community trade mark. In considering revocation for bad faith the OHIM takes a very narrow view of conduct amounting to bad faith as involving, although not limited to, actual or constructive fraud, or a design to mislead or deceive, or any other 'sinister' motive, including a dishonest intention: *Trillium Trade Mark* (2000).

15.14.3 Colourable intention

Some guidance as to genuine intention to use a mark can be sought from cases decided under the 1938 Act. Where an intention to use a trade mark was conditional on some external factor, or could otherwise be regarded as colourable, registration was refused. A colourable intention is one where the genuine nature of the proprietor's desire for registration of the mark might be questioned.

If the applicant is reserving a final decision as to the use of a mark until some contingency occurs, his intention may not be regarded as *bona fide* or in good faith. In *Rawhide Trade Mark* (1962), the applicant applied to register RAWHIDE for children's games. A television programme of the same name was due to commence and the application was made in advance of one by the series' producers, Granada. Cross J held that the use proposed was contingent on the film being shown in the UK and the mark was disallowed; registration could not be used to stake out a claim without sufficient and unconditional intention to use a mark. However, in *Jane Austen Trade Mark* (2000) the registry was not prepared to regard 'commercial opportunism' as bad faith in an application made when dramatisation of Jane Austen's novels was generating interest. Here, it was not shown that the applicant did not intend to sell products under the mark, although no use had been made of it at the time of the application.

One notable difference under the TMA 1994 is that the use proposed need not be made by the applicants themselves.[71] A character merchandiser, for example, may

---

71 *Ibid*, s 32(3).

therefore apply for registration for a character to be applied to goods or services made by licensees, facilitating merchandising of characters registered as marks.

Colourable intentions to use did not suffice, so that making an application in order to 'block' another's application, or to protect an unregistrable mark, will not succeed. In *Imperial Group v Philip Morris* (1982), the mark NERIT was registered in order to protect the unregistrable name 'Merit' which the proprietor wished to use (any use of 'Merit' would infringe 'Nerit', known as a 'ghost registration'). Some minimal use was made of the mark, a small amount of test marketing without any advertising. The mark was expunged from the register on the ground that there had been no genuine intention to use it, the real aim being to secure a copyright interest in an unregistrable word. The small number of sales made were colourable and not 'substantial or genuine'.

Intending to use the mark differently to the manner in which it is registered may also constitute bad faith. In *Betty's Kitchen Coronation Street Trade Mark* (2001) the registry held that the mark had been applied for in bad faith. The two phrases 'Betty's Kitchen' and 'Coronation Street' had been applied for in conjunction with each other. (The latter phrase would have been unregistrable on its own as referring to the television soap.) After registration the two phrases were placed at a distance on the product, thus suggesting a link with the programme, and not in the manner of the registration.

15.14.4 Promotional use

If bad faith is to be equated to unacceptable forms of use, it may be argued that use in a 'non-trade mark' sense should lead to refusal. This is uncontroversial unless an interpretation of trade mark use is adopted which ignores some of the functions of a trade mark now valued by traders. The definition of a trade mark requires a capacity to distinguish (s 1(1) of the TMA 1994), which need not be confined to the origin and guarantee functions (see 15.1.3). Although, in *Kodiak Trade Mark* (1990), the advertising use of a trade mark was not regarded as *bona fide* nor commercial use under the old law, the Directive's preamble does not preclude such a function and use being recognised as being in good faith.

Intention to use a mark for promotional purposes was challenged on this ground in *Reef Trade Mark* (2002). As a ground of revocation (see 16.10.2) the objection was not made out, but it remains to be seen whether an application for a mark intended for promotional and merchandising use is one made in bad faith. Registration of marks related to the late Diana Princess of Wales was challenged on the ground that the use to be made was for charitable fund-raising (which might be considered a form of character merchandising) and not a *bona fide* intention under s 32(3) of the TMA 1994. However, insufficient evidence was adduced to make out the objection. In particular, the fact that there was no evidence of licensing use of the marks subject to quality control provisions was found not to be a ground of complaint following the House of Lords' decision in *Scandecor Developments AB v Scandecor Marketing AB* (2001) (see 17.3.2).

15.14.5 Stockpiling marks

'Trafficking' in trade marks (registration of marks so as to deal in them, rather than for purposes of the applicant's trade in goods or services) was prohibited by s 28(6) of the

TMA 1938. While this was abolished by its omission from the 1994 Act, stockpiling of marks so as to sell them to others may well fall within the ambit of applications made in bad faith.

15.14.6 Pre-empting others

An application is also likely to be made in bad faith if made in the knowledge that a mark belongs to another person. This was dealt with differently under the 1938 Act, by finding that the applicant was not the 'proprietor' of the mark and a subjective test was applied in *Loudon Manufacturing v Courtaulds* (1994) where Aldous J required that applicants have an honest belief in their claim to a mark. Such an objection was grounded in bad faith in *Daawat Trade Mark* (2002).

The name was used in India by the claimant, who sought a declaration of invalidity. Negotiations for a dealership between the Indian company and the defendant broke down. Shortly before these negotiations were commenced the defendant proprietor registered the mark in the UK. The claimant alleged that the application had been made in bad faith as the proprietor knew of their use of it in India and suspected that the defendants had plans to expand trade in the UK. The Trade Mark Registry found that while a 'vague suspicion' that a foreign proprietor might wish to expand into the UK did not found an allegation of bad faith, reasonable grounds to believe that such plans were being made might be, particularly if the proprietor had not made any use of the mark before the date of the application.

To apply for registration with no title to the mark and with the intention of interfering with the rights of others who did have rights to use it and had consistently done so was in bad faith: *Saxon Trade Mark* (2003).

Given the uncertainty both within UK law relating to the interpretation of bad faith, and the inconsistency of interpretation with the OHIM, a reference to the ECJ would be welcomed, as suggested by Pumfrey J in *Decon Laboratories v Fred Baker Ltd* (2001).

15.15 THE RELATIVE GROUNDS OF REFUSAL

Other reasons for objecting to the registration of a mark arise externally, rather than within the mark itself, in the form of others' prior rights. The relative grounds of refusal require a mark to be compared to other registered and unregistered marks in order to protect the prior rights of others: s 5 of the TMA 1994.[72] This comparison is the mirror image of the one that is made when infringement is alleged. A sign or mark that would infringe if used after registration, existing before the application will prevent a mark being registered.

There are four elements to the comparison that is made:

(a) the date from which the marks are compared;

(b) the prior marks which must be considered;

---

72   As amended by the Trade Marks (Proof of Use etc) Regulations 2004, SI 2004/946.

(c) the degree of likeness between the new and earlier mark necessary before registration is precluded; and

(d) the degree of likeness between the goods or services for which the new mark is required and those to which the earlier mark or earlier right is applied.

The comparison is with prior rights dated before the date of application for registration of the new mark, allowing for any Paris Convention priority (see 15.2.1) awarded to it. The mark sought to be registered (hereafter, 'the new mark') is compared to two types of prior right: 'earlier trade marks' and 'earlier rights'.

15.15.1 Earlier marks

Section 6 defines earlier trade marks as other (domestic) registered trade marks, international trade marks (UK) or Community trade marks, whose date of application for registration (including allowance for any priority) is earlier than that of the new mark. This will include Community trade marks able to claim seniority from earlier UK or international registrations, and well known marks entitled to protection under the Paris Convention (see 16.7). Earlier marks include prior applications for marks and registered marks whose registration has expired up to a year before the date of the new mark, unless the registrar is satisfied that no *bona fide* use had been made of it in the two years preceding expiry.

Section 6A of the TMA 1994[73] provides for opposition to an application for registration of a mark based on an earlier mark whose registration was completed in the five years preceding the application's publication. Registration may not be refused unless the use conditions laid down in s 6A(3) of the TMA 1994 are met. Use includes use in a different form if the mark's 'distinctive character' is not affected.

15.15.2 Earlier rights

A new trade mark will not be registered if to do so would infringe any rule of law protecting an unregistered trade mark or other sign used in the course of trade.[74] It is expressly stated that this applies particularly to passing off. There is no requirement that the opponent need be the holder of the earlier right: *Wild Child Trade Mark* (1998).

Likewise, a new mark will not be registered if any prior right (other than earlier registered marks or those within s 5(4)(a) of the TMA 1994) is liable to prevent its use, such as copyright and the design rights.[75] In *Oscar Trade Mark* (1979), a trade mark representing the Oscar award statuette (protected by copyright) was refused as the applicant was not the copyright owner. Given the potential overlap between shape marks and designs (see Chapter 13), the relative grounds may become very significant in preventing registration of a mark from circumventing the design exclusions designed to preserve competition.

---

73 Added by the Trade Marks (Proof of Use etc) Regulations 2004.
74 Section 5(4)(a) of the TMA 1994.
75 *Ibid*, s 5(4)(b).

15.16 THE COMPARISON

Both the marks and goods or services of the applicant and the prior right owner are compared. There are three levels of comparison. The mark and sign may be identical or similar; the products of the competitor identical, similar or dissimilar. The interpretation and application of these comparisons so mirrors those of infringement that their detailed consideration will be reserved to Chapter 16.

15.16.1 Identical marks/identical goods or services

If the earlier mark and the goods or services to which it is applied are identical, no registration of the later mark is allowed.[76] It is not necessary to show any confusion; this is effectively assumed.

15.16.2 Identical marks/similar goods or services and similar marks/identical or similar goods or services

If a prior identical mark has been applied to similar goods or services to those of the applicant,[77] or a similar prior mark has been applied to either identical or similar goods,[78] registration will be refused, but only if the accompanying condition is also made out. It must be shown that:

> there exists a likelihood of confusion on the part of the public, which includes the likelihood of association with the earlier trade mark.

This sub-section created difficulties in relation to a sign whose registration might damage the reputation of a mark without causing confusion or association with it. Registration of a sign for products that are *not* similar, 'diluting' an earlier mark, was catered for in s 5(3) of the TMA 1994. This appeared to have the effect, if an application was for similar goods or services, that if no confusion or association was likely, a sign which might well affect the reputation of an earlier mark could secure registration under s 5(2) of the TMA 1994.

This question arose in relation to infringement in *Davidoff & Cie SA v Gofkid Ltd* (2003), and the ECJ held that the same interpretation in the Directive should apply to both registrability and infringement. In a masterpiece of purposive interpretation (or judicial legislation) the ECJ held that the Directive must not be construed only in line with its wording, but also 'in the light of the overall scheme and objectives of the system of which it is a part'. This immediately brings the functions of a trade mark which the law is prepared to recognise into issue (see 15.1.3), although the Court did not discuss this issue.

The Court held instead that marks with a reputation should not have lesser protection if the later sign is to be used for identical or similar products than if the sign was intended for dissimilar goods or services. This conclusion was reached on the basis that the dilution provision (optional for Member States in the Directive) conferred stronger protection on marks with a reputation than the mandatory

---

76   *Ibid*, s 5(1).
77   *Ibid*, s 5(2)(a).
78   *Ibid*, s 5(2)(b).

protection conferred on all marks when the opposing sign is for identical or similar goods. To refuse to allow for dilution when the later sign applied to identical or similar goods would give marks with a reputation less protection than other marks. Consequently, the Directive must be interpreted to include dilution for marks with a reputation, even if the later sign was intended for use on identical or similar goods. While there is a logic to this result, less in the way of mental gymnastics would have been required by interpreting 'association' to include unfair advantage or detriment to distinctive character.

In reaching this decision, the ECJ ignored the Opinion of Advocate General Jacobs in the case, preferring that of Advocate General Colomer in *Arsenal Football Club plc v Reed* (2003). It should be remembered that the function of trade marks was discussed in this case and that the Advocate General took a wide view (see 15.1.3). By contrast, in the *Davidoff* case, Advocate General Jacobs adopted an interpretation consonant with the meaning given to 'association' in *Sabel*, and with Recital 7 of the Directive.

It remains to be seen whether the same interpretation will be given to the parallel provision in the Regulation for Community trade marks. Logically it should, as the Regulation is worded in the same terms.

Whether *Davidoff* needed to be followed in the UK was not clear. The 'dilution' provision is an optional one for Member States. The fact that it was included in the UK implementation of the Directive raised the question of Parliament's intention. If Advocate General Jacob's interpretation was the most likely reading of the Directive this could have been taken to be the way it was understood at the time of enacting the TMA 1994. In many, perhaps the majority, of cases involving dilution of a mark it is likely that confusion or association would be found. In *Davidoff* itself the use of DURFEE, written in the same script as the registered DAVIDOFF mark, and with the letters 'D' and 'ff' used in the same characteristic manner, was more than likely to have allowed a finding of confusion. However, it was possible to envisage circumstances where this might not be so, particularly if there were to be a very wide difference in the products concerned. Consequently, the decision in the *Davidoff* case, confirmed by *Adidas-Salomon v Fitnessworld Trading Ltd* (2003), was implemented for the UK by The Trade Marks (Proof of Use etc) Regulations 2004.[79]

15.16.3 Identical or similar marks/marks with a reputation

Where marks are identical or similar a mark will not be registrable:

> if ... the earlier trade mark has a reputation in the UK (or, in the case of a Community trade mark, in the European Community) and the use of the later mark without due cause would take unfair advantage of, or be detrimental to, the distinctive character or the repute of the earlier trade mark.[80]

This prevents registration of marks which would 'dilute' an earlier mark and replaces the ineffective provision for defensive registration in the 1938 Act. It may be applied to protect an undertaking's wish to diversify into new products, or to protect new advertising functions for trade marks. It is likely, for example, that the use of KODIAK for shoes could have taken unfair advantage of Kodak's reputation (*Kodiak Trade Mark*

---

79 SI 2004/946, which came into force on 5 May 2004.
80 Section 5(3) of the TMA 1994.

(1990)). If so, there seems to be good reason to regard such use as being made in good faith for the purposes of s 3(6) of the TMA 1995 (see 15.14).

Application for registration of a new mark may dilute the reputation of three types of earlier mark: a well known mark within Paris Convention protection, an earlier registered mark or an earlier unregistered mark. An important distinction must be drawn between these situations. For a well known mark only the criteria for the comparison in s 5(3) of the TMA 1994 need to be shown. If the earlier mark is registered it will have to have a reputation in the UK. By contrast, if the earlier mark is unregistered, both reputation and goodwill in the UK must be established. It should be noted that 'reputation' is a lesser level of recognition than being 'well known': *Pfizer Ltd v Eurofood Link (UK) Ltd* (2001), and *Sabel BV v Puma AG* (1998).

Where a Community trade mark is applied for, the relative grounds of refusal prevent registration of a sign which would dilute the reputation of an earlier mark. In the case of an earlier Community trade mark the reputation must be within the Community. In the case of an earlier national mark the reputation must be national, but need not be Community-wide.[81]

15.17 RAISING THE RELATIVE GROUNDS OF REFUSAL

That comparison on the relative grounds is necessary by virtue of s 5 of the TMA 1994 does not determine on whom the onus to do so falls. The former UK approach was for all bars to registrability to be raised and examined by the registry on application being made. However, European tradition leaves the relative grounds to competitors, examination only being made by the granting authority for absolute grounds and this is the practice of the OHIM. Relative grounds would then be raised in opposition proceedings, the onus being on other mark owners to defend their property. At present, the old paternalistic UK approach is continued and the Trade Mark Registry examines for the relative grounds, rejecting a mark on this basis without the need for intervention by a third party. There is provision in s 8 of the TMA 1994 for the Secretary of State to alter this to the OHIM method in the future. After consultation the system of examination is being continued (see 15.2.1). However, if the earlier user consents to registration of the later mark, the registry has no power to refuse registration in the wider public interest.[82]

15.18 HONEST CONCURRENT USER

Another area in which domestic practice has been preserved, for the time being, by the TMA 1994 is that of allowing conflicting registrations in situations of 'honest concurrent user'. This is a curious departure from the Directive, which states that a mark which fails on the relative grounds 'shall not' be registered. The old UK law is expressly preserved by s 7(3) of the TMA 1994. The provision is something of a paradox in the light of the Directive's extension of the relative grounds of refusal (see

---

81 Article 5(5) of the Regulation.
82 Section 5(5) of the TMA 1994.

15.16.3), as it will allow conflicting registrations. This measure of independence cannot continue if an order is made under s 8 of the TMA 1994 (see 15.2.1).

Where a new mark conflicts with an earlier mark or earlier right, registration may still be allowed if the applicant satisfies the registrar that there has been honest concurrent use of the new mark.[83] The registrar shall not refuse to register unless objection is taken on the relative ground by the proprietor of the earlier right or earlier mark in opposition proceedings: s 7(2) of the TMA 1994 (but must be satisfied that there has been honest concurrent use). If the earlier right owner does object, Robert Walker J held *in Road Tech Computer Systems Ltd v Unison Software (UK) Ltd* (1996), that the registrar must refuse the application as there is no residual discretion left. The earlier right or mark owner may also seek a declaration of invalidity if the mark has secured registration.[84]

15.18.1 The test for honest concurrent use

The test to be applied in order to determine whether there has been sufficient and honest concurrent use of a mark by the new mark's applicant and the earlier right owner is that set out by the House of Lords in *Pirie's Application* (1933). In this case, registration of ABERMILL for stationery was allowed, despite concurrent use of the phonetically similar HAMMERMILL for paper, because the choice of mark by the applicant was honest, it had substantial trade and no confusion was proved. The House of Lords considered five factors:

(a) the degree of likelihood of confusion – some potential confusion is almost inevitable if the mark falls within the relative grounds, so that it is the extent of likely confusion which is relevant;

(b) whether the choice of the mark by the applicant was honest – knowledge of the earlier mark does not render the choice automatically dishonest if made in the belief that no confusion would result, and this remains the case even if the earlier mark owner objected;

(c) the length of the applicant's use of the mark – usually at least seven years' use is required, although, on the facts of the case, five years sufficed;

(d) evidence of actual confusion occurring from the concurrent use, the confusion resulting from use and not registration;

(e) which of the parties had the longer and greater trade – balancing the hardship to the applicants in refusing registration with hardship to the other right owner, and with the inconvenience to the public.

It is a test based on policy and, in *GE Trade Mark* (1973), Lord Diplock held that, once there was potential confusion between the two marks, the public interest lay in refusing the registration, balanced only against the legitimate interests of traders acquired through use. Traditionally, the courts adopted a cautious approach and marks were refused registration if they failed a test of 'triple identity'. If the marks themselves were identical or very similar and so were the goods or services of both concerns and their areas of sales or services, registration was unlikely.

---

83   *Ibid*, s 7(1).
84   *Ibid*, s 47.

The marks are compared in a global fashion, as outlined in *Pianotist's Application* (1906), and now specified in relation to the Directive in the *Sabel* case (see 16.4.3).

However, in *Budweiser Trade Marks* (2000) the Court of Appeal pointed out that the *Pirie* test is not determinative in every case. The discretion of the tribunal is not fettered and concurrent registration can be allowed even where there is considerable probability of confusion if the merits of the case allow it. In this case the danger of confusion was clear. Judge LJ said:

> ... normally, at any rate, account should be taken of the nature and extent of the risk of confusion or deception, potentially damaging to the public generally, and where the mark has already been registered by another party, damaging to its business, and also whether the party seeking the exercise of the discretion, has, in the context of a serious competitive market, conducted its business on the issues in relation to which registration arises with reasonable integrity. I doubt whether there will be very many circumstances, or combination of circumstances, that are 'so special' that the discretion would be exercised in favour of a party whose use of a mark could properly be stigmatised as dishonest. Ultimately, the decision depends on all the relevant facts which arise in the individual case and the balanced exercise of the judge's discretion.

Consequently, an appellate court is reluctant to upset the trial judge's findings in the absence of any error on the grounds of principle. In this case it was relevant that customers referred to the product by the name BUDWEISER in a trade mark sense, as was the earlier litigation between the parties.

Further Reading

Annand, R and Norman, H, *Blackstone's Guide to the Trade Marks Act 1994* (London: Blackstone, 1994)

Antill, J and James, A, 'Registrability and the Scope of the Monopoly: Current Trends' [2004] EIPR 157

Brown, A, 'Illuminating European Trade Marks?' (2004) 1 SCRIPT-ed, www.law.ed.ac.uk/ahrb/script-ed/index.asp

Burrell, R and Handler, M, 'Making Sense of Trade Mark Law' [2003] IPQ 388

Cornish, W, *Intellectual Property: Omnipresent, Distracting, Irrelevant?* (Oxford: OUP, 2004)

Dawson, N and Firth, A, *Trade Marks Retrospective* (London: Sweet & Maxwell, 2000)

Davis, J, 'To Protect or Serve? European Trade Mark Law and the Decline of the Public Interest' [2003] EIPR 180

Davis, J, 'European Trade Mark Law and the Enclosure of the Commons' [2002] IPQ 342

Griffiths, A, 'Modernising Trade Mark Law and Promoting Economic Efficiency: An Evaluation of the *Baby-Dry* Judgment and its Aftermath' [2003] IPQ 1

Helbling, T, 'Shapes as Trade Marks? The Struggle to Register Three-Dimensional Designs: A Comparative Study of United Kingdom and Swiss law' [1997] IPQ 413

Howells, C, 'A Loaded Question: On Section 5(3) of the Trade Marks Act 1994' [2002] EIPR 118

Inglis, A, 'Registrability and Enforcement of Inherently Non-distinctive Trade Marks in the United Kingdom' [1997] EIPR 138

Kamperman Sanders, A, 'Some Frequently Asked Questions about the 1994 UK Trade Marks Act' [1995] EIPR 67

Keeling, D, 'About Kinetic ® Watches, Easy Banking and Nappies that Keep Babies Dry: A Review of Recent European Case Law on Absolute Grounds for Refusing to Register Trade Marks' [2003] IPQ 131

Kilbey, I, 'The Ironies of *Arsenal v Reed*' [2004] EIPR 479

Martino, T, *Trademark Dilution* (Oxford: Clarendon Press, 1996)

Middlemiss, S and Phillips, J, 'Bad Faith in European Trade Mark Law and Practice' [2003] EIPR 397.

Morcom, C, 'Extending Protection for Marks Having a Reputation' [2003] EIPR 279

Norman, H, '*Davidoff v Gofkid*: Dealing with the Logical Lapse or Creating European Disharmony?' [2003] IPQ 342

Pfeiffer, T, 'Descriptive Trade Marks: the Impact of the Baby-Dry Case Considered' [2002] EIPR 373

Pickering, C, *Trade Marks in Theory and Practice*, Hart Publishing, 1998

Prescott, P, 'Trade Marks Invisible at Point of Sale: Some Corking Cases' [1990] EIPR 241

Schultze, C, 'Registering Colour Trade Marks in the European Union' [2003] EIPR 55

Strowel, B, 'Benelux: A Guide to the Validity of Three-dimensional Trade Marks in Europe' [1995] EIPR 154

Suthersanen, U, 'The European Court of Justice in *Philips v Remington* – Trade Marks and Market Freedom' [2003] IPQ 257

Würtenberger, G, 'Risk of Confusion and Criteria to Determine the Same in European Community Trade Mark Law' [2002] EIPR 20

CHAPTER 16

TRADE MARK INFRINGEMENT AND CHALLENGES TO TRADE MARKS

Once registered, a mark's proprietor has an interest both in defending the mark against unauthorised use by others and in exploiting the mark for his commercial purposes. Infringement of the exclusive right conferred by registration defends the mark. Exploitation rests on the property right that registration brings into being. Additionally, registration does not end others' legitimate interests in the mark. It may be challenged by revocation and declarations of invalidity.

Exploitation of the property right in the mark is subject to principles of domestic and European competition law and is dealt with in Chapter 17.

16.1 THE EXCLUSIVE RIGHT

Registration gives the proprietor exclusive rights in the trade mark. The Act gives no further elaboration on the nature of the right, other than that it is infringed by its use in the UK without consent.[1]

It is an exclusive right 'in the trade mark'. This raises the potential for the definition of a trade mark and its functions to limit the right further than the limits provided by the definition of infringement in s 10 of the Trade Marks Act (TMA) 1994. This was the case under the 1938 Act so that uses not deemed use as a 'trade mark' designating the origin of products did not infringe.

16.1.1 The old law

Under the old law, descriptive use of a mark did not infringe. Consequently, in *Mothercare UK Ltd v Penguin Books Ltd* (1988), the MOTHERCARE mark was not infringed by 'Mother Care, Other Care' as a book title, despite the plaintiffs' allegation that confusion with the Mothercare Book of Child Care would result. Similarly, in *Mars v Cadbury* (1987), the use of 'Treat Size' did not encroach on the registered mark TREETS, as it was used to describe the size of the otherwise marked WISPA bars. Such use is now specifically provided with a defence to infringement by s 11(2) of the TMA 1994.

Nor did decorative use of a mark infringe: *Unidoor Ltd v Marks and Spencer plc* (1988). The defendant used the phrase Coast to Coast on T-shirts, but this did not infringe the plaintiff's registered COAST TO COAST.

16.1.2 The Trade Marks Act 1994

Sections 9 and 10 of the TMA 1994 have been criticised for failing to implement the Directive properly. Article 5 states that 'the registered mark shall confer ... exclusive rights therein. The proprietor shall be entitled to prevent ...', which implies that the

---

1   Section 9(1) of the TMA 1994.

infringing acts defined by the Directive are only among the range of potentially infringing acts, whereas the TMA 1994 confines infringement to those defined in s 10 of the TMA 1994. Early case law under the TMA 1994 differed on interpretation of s 9(1).

In a Scottish case, considering s 10(1) of the TMA 1994, Lord McCluskey took the view that the court must find, as a matter of fact, whether the defendant's use of a sign was use in a trade mark sense. He also said that use could be simultaneously both descriptive and use as a trade mark: *Bravado Merchandising Services Ltd v Mainstream Publishing Ltd* (1996). This was the case in the use of the mark WET WET WET in the title of the defendant's book about the pop group. Rejecting this, in *British Sugar plc v James Robertson & Sons* (1996), Jacob J took the view that s 9(1) of the TMA 1994 did not require such a gloss to be placed on s 10 of the TMA 1994, which refers only to the use of a 'sign' by the defendant. This was because s 11(2) of the TMA 1994 provides specific protection for other legitimate types of use and because it would be a departure from the Directive. He described the exclusive right as 'a chatty introduction' to the details of infringement in s 10 of the TMA 1994.

Subsequently, the Inner House of the Court of Session preferred Jacob J's interpretation in *Discovery Communications v Discovery FM Ltd* (2000), particularly as the *Bravado* approach had been based on a concession. However, Jacob J appeared to reintroduce the need for trade mark use in his assertion that the use of WET WET WET on the cover of a book was not use 'in relation to the goods' (see 16.2.4). In *British Telecommunications plc v One in a Million* (1999), the Court of Appeal doubted whether trade mark use required for s 10(3) of the TMA 1994. Jacob J reconsidered the point *in Philips Electronics NV v Remington Consumer Products Ltd* (1998), but left it open.

That it is not necessary to impose a 'trade mark use' limitation on the exclusive right is illustrated by Rattee J's decision in *The European Ltd v The Economist Newspapers Ltd* (1996). He held that the defendant's use of the word 'European' descriptively in its mark remained relevant to consideration of whether its mark was similar to the plaintiff's and whether there was a likelihood of confusion between the two under s 10 of the TMA 1994.

However, if 'sign' in s 1(1) of the TMA 1994 (see 15.3.2) is interpreted to mean a mark or symbol, as the dictionary suggests,[2] then descriptive and decorative use will continue to fall outside the exclusive right.

16.1.3   European interpretation

The ECJ requires use of a sign to indicate the origin of the products marked. Uses that merely describe the make of second hand goods, or the characteristics of the defendant's own product will not carry trade mark connotations. To this extent, implicitly the ECJ is equating 'use' to 'trade mark use'. However, the effect of this is dependent on the width of trade mark function that the Court is willing to recognise. The wider the functions that are recognised, the wider the net of infringement extends.

---

2   'A mark, symbol or device used to represent something or distinguish the object on which it is placed.'

Descriptive use

Using a sign to indicate second hand sales and repair services of the mark owner's products did constitute 'use' of the mark in *Bayerische Motorwerke AG (BMW) v Deenik* (1999). The principle of exhaustion of rights and the defences to infringement meant that the proprietor could not prevent use that did not suggest a commercial connection between the parties.

Subsequently, the ECJ considered use of a claimant's mark to describe characteristics of the defendant's own goods in *Hölterhoff v Freiesleben* (2002). Two marks were registered for cut gem stones and these were used by the defendant to describe the nature of his own stones. The ECJ was asked whether Article 5(1) of the Directive prevented such descriptive use of the marks where there could be no question of the mark being perceived as indicating origin. The Court held that the proprietor's exclusive right did not prevent such use, at least where it was within the context of commercial negotiations and there was no possibility of it being taken as an indication of origin. The Advocate General's Opinion had suggested that the negative rights conferred by a mark should be interpreted in the light of the positive exclusive right in Article 5(1). This he stated to be to use the mark to identify products as the proprietor's own.

Merchandising

However, merchandising, or decorative, use of a mark does not appear to fall into the same category and may well infringe, even though it might be interpreted to constitute a characteristic of the product rather than as a statement of its origins. The case *Arsenal Football Club plc v Reed* has seen significant change in the approach of the UK courts to merchandising use for a mark, and the protection that marks can provide, and is fully discussed in this context in Chapter 18.

However, the House of Lords has also considered the extent of the exclusive right. In *R v Johnstone* (2003) Lord Nicholls understood the ECJ's decision in *Arsenal* to mean that only 'trade mark use' would infringe. Accordingly, in a criminal[3] 'bootlegging' case, affixing the name of the group BON JOVI to counterfeit CDs was deemed descriptive of their contents and non-infringing. The House of Lords held that there could be no criminal offence of infringement if the conditions for the civil action were not satisfied. It held that use must be trade mark use denoting origin in order to infringe:

> ... the essence of a trade mark has always been that it is a badge of origin. It indicates trade source: a connection in the course of trade between the goods and the proprietor of the mark. That is its function. Hence the exclusive rights granted to the proprietor of a registered trade mark are limited to use of a mark likely to be taken as an indication of trade origin. Use of this character is an essential prerequisite to infringement. Use of a mark in a manner not indicative of trade origin of goods or services does not encroach upon the proprietor's monopoly rights.

Their lordships stated that determining 'trade mark use' was a question of fact in each case, tested by the perception of the average consumer of the type of goods of the use of the sign. Lord Nicholls interpreted the ECJ decision in *Arsenal* as reaffirming that

---

3   Johnstone was charged under s 92 of the TMA 1994.

only use as a badge of origin can infringe. Consequently, Johnstone was acquitted as his use had been descriptive of the CDs' contents.

Damage to the mark

The issue is now one of damage to the exclusive right in a mark which is directly linked to the function of a mark. While this remains a matter of debate, the courts will be required to consider uses of marks as descriptions, decorations, badges of loyalty, or even parodies, from first principles. Guidance from the ECJ came in the *Adidas-Salomon AG v Adidas Benelux* (2003) case. The Advocate General stated that decorative use of stripes on clothing should be distinguished from the *Arsenal* badges of allegiance and that infringing use of a sign should serve a trade mark function limited by public interest considerations. The ECJ held that it was a question of fact for national courts whether the relevant section of the public associated the sign and mark (without any need for confusion) or saw it merely as embellishment. In the latter case there would not be any infringement.

A French case might suggest a further element in the need to preserve freedom of expression. Greenpeace parodied the ESSO name on its website by replacing the two central letters with dollar signs. The Paris Court of Appeal ruled that even a well known mark is not protected against parody, for freedom of speech overrode the infringement claim.[4]

16.2   INFRINGEMENT

The proprietor of a trade mark may take proceedings for infringement of the mark and the usual remedies for infringement of a property right are available, including damages, injunction or an account of profits.[5] The exclusive right takes effect from the date of registration (which is, in turn, the date of filing). However, no infringement proceedings may be begun before the actual date of registration, nor is any offence under s 92 of the TMA 1994 committed by anything done before the date of publication of registration.[6]

Primary infringement of a trade mark comprises the doing of the acts specified in s 10 of the TMA 1994 without the trade mark owner's consent.[7] Infringing acts must be in the UK.[8] Liability is strict for primary infringement.

It follows from a finding of infringement under the TMA 1994 that any equivalent Community Trade Mark would be infringed under the Regulation: *Pfizer Ltd v Eurofood Link (UK) Ltd* (2001). In addition, if the proprietor of a Community mark is domiciled in the UK the court may hear an infringement claim wherever the infringement has taken place in the Community.

In addition, contributory infringement is provided for by s 10(5) of the TMA 1994. A person who puts a registered mark on material intended to be used for labelling or packaging goods or as business paper or for advertising goods or services is

---

4   *Greenpeace France v Esso*, Case 2002/16307, 26 February 2003: www.greenpeace.org.
5   Section 14 of the TMA 1994.
6   *Ibid*, s 9(3).
7   *Ibid*, s 9(1).
8   *Ibid*, s 9(1).

treated as a party to any infringing use of the material, provided that he knew or had reason to believe that the application of the mark was not authorised by the mark's proprietor. As in *LA Gear Inc v Hi Tec Sports plc* (1992), knowledge of relevant circumstances is likely to contribute to constructive knowledge of infringement (see 10.4.1).

The infringing act involves four elements: first, using a sign in the UK, secondly, using it in the course of trade, thirdly, use in relation to goods or services and, finally, use in conflict with the registered mark.

16.2.1 Use of a sign

The first element requires examination of what constitutes 'use' of a sign. Section 10(4) of the TMA 1994 provides that use of a sign includes affixing the sign to goods or their packaging, or offering or exposing goods for sale, putting them on the market, or stocking them for sale under the sign, as well as offering or supplying services under the sign. Using also includes importing or exporting goods under the sign and using the sign on business papers or in advertising. In an important departure from the old law, s 103(2) of the TMA 1994 makes it clear that references to use of a mark or sign include use otherwise than by means of graphic representation, as must be the case for sound or smell marks. Oral use in broadcasting, for example, may, therefore, infringe, as may other uses that are neither visual nor graphic.

Websites

Website designers have commonly included a large number of keywords in website code to ensure that search engines pick up the site. Search engines will also sell these keywords to advertisers so that adverts will appear when the 'adword' is searched. These metatags and keywords are not visible to viewers of the site. Using another's trade mark as a metatag or keyword could potentially infringe. In the first case in the UK, *Roadtech Computer Systems Ltd v Mandata Ltd* (2000), trade mark infringement by metatag was admitted and summary judgment given. However, in *Reed Executive plc v Reed Business Information Ltd* (2003), at first instance, it was held that while invisible metatag use was capable of constituting use in the course of trade for the purposes of s 10, such use must result in a visible display of the sign. Consequently, if a search also displayed a description of the defendant's website using the mark infringement was possible. However, Pumfrey J continued, the fact that any search throws up irrelevant results should also be taken into account, as users would expect to discard some results as unrelated to the terms searched for. Additionally, any such use was 'unlikely to be an appropriate case for damages and certainly not for an injunction'.

Nor, disappointingly, did the Court of Appeal decide on the use point, finding that there could be no infringement under s 10(2) of the TMA 1994 as no confusion resulted.[9] However, Jacob LJ clearly doubted whether use of metatags did constitute trade mark use. Noting that use is also relevant to saving a mark from a challenge for non-use, he said that it would be odd that wholly invisible use could defeat such a claim. The mark would only be read by computer (as a series of 1s and 0s) and be

---

9 *Reed Executive v Reed Business Information* (2004).

unable to convey any meaning as to trade origin. This is a significant point. While the case makes it clear that s 10(1)[10] and s 10(2)[11] infringement might be difficult to make out, a finding of infringement by dilution under s 10(3) of the TMA 1994 remains open.

16.2.2   Use in the UK

This use must be in the UK. It is now clear that registering a domain name, or placing a mark on a website constitutes 'use': *British Telecommunications plc v One in a Million* (1999) and *Euromarket Designs Inc v Peters* (2001) (the *Crate & Barrel (2001)* case). However, if the defendant is outside the jurisdiction it is questionable whether this constitutes use 'within the UK', even though the website is accessible from the UK. In *800-Flowers Trade Mark* (2001) (see 15.9) the mere presence of the website without more did not constitute use of the mark in the UK. In *Crate & Barrel* (2001) the American claimant alleged infringement of its UK and Community trade marks by the use on an Irish website. Jacob J held there was no use in the course of trade in the UK by a Dublin based shop trading locally in Dublin. The website was not to be regarded as a sign everywhere in the world. This should not provoke complacency in website owners. Much must depend on their intentions, and the way the website is perceived by those accessing it. Could the same be said of amazon.com, for example, or e-Bay?

The issue also arose in the Scottish case *Bonnier Media v Smith & Kestrel Trading Corporation* (2002). The defender registered the pursuer's mark BUSINESS AM as his domain name, businessam.com, but was domiciled in Greece. The pursuers had their own website at businessam.co.uk. There was a long history of rancour between the parties and Bonnier feared the setting up of a website passing itself off as theirs. An interim interdict against passing off and trade mark infringement had been granted. The defender applied to recall the interim interdict. Lord Drummond likened the internet to a process of communication. Anyone linking themselves to this process had the obvious intention that their messages be received where their recipients were, and these could be potentially delictual (tortious). Actual or threatened delicts would take place where the impact of the website was significant. In *800-Flowers Trade Mark* (2001) and *Crate & Barrel (2001)* the mark had been used on website pages, rather than as a domain name. On the facts, in neither case could it be said that there was significant impact on trade in products within the UK. The Irish CRATE & BARREL website was clearly local to Dublin. Whether the impact was significant was determined both by the content of the website and the commercial and other contexts in which it operated. It was clear that the defender intended to pass off his website and business advisory service as the pursuer's. The circulation of the pursuer's newspaper was substantially in Scotland, and the threatened delict therefore did take place in Scotland and was within the court's jurisdiction.

16.2.3   In the course of trade

The second element requires that the defendant make use of the sign 'in the course of trade'. Pumfrey J stated that this meant use in the course of business in the *Reed* (2003)

---

10   Website designers need only add a word to the mark in order to avoid identity of mark and sign – PALMOLIVE SOAP instead of PALMOLIVE, for example.

11   Consumers' familiarity with the operation of search engine results rendering a finding of confusion unlikely.

case. However, on appeal, Jacob LJ expressed no view on whether the use of a mark in metatags, or reserved keywords advertising and the defendant's YAHOO pop-up banners could be regarded as use in the course of trade.

Under the old law, this was given strict interpretation to mean use in the course of trade in the goods for which the mark was registered: *Aristoc v Rysta* (1945). In *M Ravok v National Trade Press* (1955), it was held that, where the defendant attributed the plaintiff's mark to a third party in their trade directory, the use was made not in the course of trade in goods for which the mark was registered but in the course of its own trade as publishers. This decision made it difficult for trade mark proprietors to prevent their marks becoming generic (see 16.10.3).

The same phrase appears in the TMA 1994 and may be interpreted in the same way. Sanders[12] has suggested that any non-private activity which has an economic benefit should be considered to be in the course of trade. In a Benelux case, a reproduction of the PHILIPS mark in an article about the Second World War was held to infringe because it attracted readers to the publication and was in the economic intercourse of the defendant's business. However, it seems unlikely that use such as Monet's reproduction of the red Bass triangle mark and Hockney's painting of a CAMPBELL soup tin should infringe. In *Arsenal* (2002) the ECJ interpreted use in the course of trade as trade 'taking place in the context of commercial activity with a view to economic advantage and not as a private matter'. Use as a 'badge of allegiance' then fell within Article 5(1) of the Directive and s 10 of the TMA 1994. However, decorative use was distinguished from the *Arsenal* merchandising use.

A French court[13] held that selling the marks of others as keywords in internet advertising constituted infringement of the marks. Google France, which provided a service rather than trading in goods, allowed customers to purchase words, including others' marks, so that when used as search terms the purchaser's advertising appeared on the Google search results page. However, the Court of Appeal in *Reed Executive v Reed Business Information* (2004) did not agree.

16.2.4 Use in relation to goods or services

The third element requires use 'in relation to' goods or services. The fears of those selling goods, but also providing ancillary services, that their trade marks might be infringed by application to services have been catered for by s 10(4)(b) of the TMA 1994. However, the case of *Trebor Bassett v Football Association* (1997) illustrates continuing difficulties. The defendant alleged that the plaintiff was infringing its mark by including photographs of footballers sporting the registered England logo on their clothing in packets of confectionery. Rattee J struck this out on the basis that the defendant's logo was not being used at all, nor used as a sign in relation to the plaintiff's cards.

It was also argued in *Bravado Merchandising Services Ltd v Mainstream Publishing Ltd* (1996) that the use of WET WET WET in the book title *A Sweet Little Mystery – Wet Wet Wet – The Inside Story* was not use in relation to goods, but the point was left

---

12 Sanders, A, 'Some Frequently Asked Questions about the 1994 UK Trade Marks Act' [1995] EIPR 67.
13 *Viaticum et Luteciel v Google France*, 13 October 2003, Tribunal de Grande Instance, Nanterre. The decision is under appeal.

undecided. In *British Sugar plc v James Robertson & Sons* (1996), Jacob J said that the WET WET WET mark was not being used in relation to goods covered by the registration, but only to refer to the book's subject matter. In one sense, the mark was very much used in relation to the book, as it appeared on the cover, and this *dictum* seems to raise implicitly the need for the defendants' use to be use 'as a trade mark' identifying goods or services.

16.2.5 The comparison

In the fourth element, whether there is an actionable conflict between a trade mark and sign requires comparing both the claimant's mark with the defendant's sign, and the claimant's goods or services with those of the defendant. This comparative test is the same in its structure as that applied to the relative grounds of refusal (see 15.15):

- identical marks/identical goods or services;
- identical marks/similar goods or services, and similar marks/identical or similar goods or services;
- identical or similar marks/marks with reputation.

This spreads a much wider net than did the 1938 Act, which confined infringement to use of the same mark or one nearly resembling it on the same goods or services or goods or services 'of the same description'.

It is the defendant's 'sign' which is compared to the claimant's 'trade mark'. This means that the form of the sign as it is being used, or about to be used, is considered. However, a trade mark may be registered in general terms (see *Bravado Merchandising Services v Mainstream Publishing*) and the claimant may not have begun using it. Therefore, any normal and fair use of the claimant's mark in relation to the goods for which it is registered is compared to the sign, ignoring any extraneous material such as the small size of the defendant's business: *Origins Natural Resources Inc v Origin Clothing Ltd* (1995).

16.3 IDENTICAL MARKS/IDENTICAL GOODS OR SERVICES

Where there is identity both of mark and the defendant's sign and of the claimant's and defendant's goods or services, there is no further requirement of confusion or damage to reputation to be shown.[14] This allows a claimant to proceed by way of summary judgment against counterfeiters. The term 'identical' is likely to be given its dictionary meaning of exactly alike, equal or agreeing.

16.3.1 Identity of mark and sign

In *Bravado Merchandising Services v Mainstream Publishing*, the defendant's use of WET WET WET was deemed identical, although in a different typeface to that of the registration. It was held that the particular typeface or colour used to depict the mark was not an essential part of the mark unless an express indication that that was intended were given. Were it otherwise, every possible permutation would require

---

14 Section 10(1) of the TMA 1994.

registration. Jacob J said, *obiter*, in *British Sugar plc v James Robertson & Sons* (1996), that the plaintiff's and defendant's marks of TREAT were identical.

The ECJ advocated strict interpretation of identity in *LTJ Diffusion v Sadas* (2003). The claimant's mark ARTHUR was replicated by the defendant's use of ARTHUR ET FÉLICIE. Identicality implied that the two elements should be the same in all respects; however this identity was to be assessed globally with respect to the average consumer. It should be taken into account that the consumer would not be making a direct comparison, and that insignificant differences might go unnoticed.[15] Consequently, Neuberger J regarded the difference between 'Mezzocorona' and 'Mezzacorona' as insignificant by in *Miguel Torres v Cantine Mezzacorona* (2003). Sign and mark will be considered identical either where there is complete identity, or where the reasonable and circumspect consumer, not having both at hand to compare, would consider them to be so. However, Jacob LJ suggested that it is unlikely that the ECJ intended to 'soften the edges of "strict identity" very far': *Reed Executive v Reed Business Information* (2004). As a mark must be distinctive to be registered, it would be nonsensical, he said, if a visually different but identical word device were to be treated as identical.

16.3.2   Identity of product

The goods or services must also be identical. An ice cream syrup and sweet tasting spread were held not to be identical goods in *British Sugar plc v James Robertson & Sons* (1996). Although both are foodstuffs of a sweet nature they have different uses and would be found in different parts of a supermarket. Free newspapers and commercial newspapers were held not to be identical goods in *Associated Newspapers Ltd v Express Newspapers* (2003), because their channels of distribution differed. The mark was registered for 'newspapers for sale', however.

In the case of services, in *Reed Executive v Reed Business Information* (2004), Jacob LJ held that specifications for services should be carefully scrutinised, being confined to the core activities attributable to a general description. Nor could the meaning of a specification of goods and services change with time. Consequently, an employment agency and a searchable jobs advertisement website did not constitute identical services.

16.4   IDENTICAL MARKS/SIMILAR GOODS OR SERVICES; SIMILAR MARKS/IDENTICAL OR SIMILAR GOODS OR SERVICES

Where a sign that is identical to a registered trade mark is applied to goods or services similar to those for which the mark is registered; or a sign which is similar to a registered mark is applied to goods or services either identical or similar to those within the registration, the sign may infringe. This will only be the case if a likelihood of confusion on the part of the public exists, including the likelihood of association with the trade mark.[16]

---

15   Guidance that Jacob LJ termed 'opaque' in *Reed Executive v Reed Business Information* (2004).
16   Section 10(2) of the TMA 1994.

There are three stages to making out 'confusing' infringement: first, the claimant's mark and defendant's sign must be compared, secondly, so must the goods or services of claimant and defendant in order to establish the necessary similarity and, thirdly, potential confusion or association must be established.

Confusion could be established quite independently of the two initial comparisons of mark/sign, and products. Or this identity or similarity could be a factor in assessing confusion. It might also be tempting to infer the necessary similarity from evidence of confusion. In *British Sugar plc v James Robertson & Sons* (1996), Jacob J held that questions of possible infringement did not arise unless the necessary two comparisons were made out first; confusion alone did not suffice. However, the ECJ, in *Sabel BV v Puma AG* (1998), took a global approach to the question of similarity and confusion, allowing the nature of any similarity between marks or products to have a bearing on the likelihood of confusion.

The comparisons, and subsequent examination of confusion, are made without considering any added matter or circumstances (*Saville Perfumery Ltd v June Perfect Ltd* (1941)), so that a disclaimer added by the claimant will not avoid infringement in the way that it would in a passing off claim.

16.4.1   Similarity of marks

'Similarity' imports a wider concept than the 'nearly resembling' of the 1938 Act. Nevertheless, factors relevant to determining whether marks 'resemble' remain valid. However, it is the level of resemblance required that may have been lowered. The introduction of sound and smell marks, as well as other novel forms of sign, introduced additional relevant factors, such as a mark's sound or other characteristics apart from any visual representation, and this was recognised by s 103(2) of the TMA 1994.

Relevant factors

Factors the courts take into consideration include:

(i)   The 'idea (or concept) of a mark' – for example, a mark, such as a triple representation of an animal, incorporates the 'idea' of a triple repetition, so that a sign repeating the same animal only twice might escape a finding of similarity. The idea of a mark includes its meaning, or lack of meaning: *Wagamama Ltd v City Centre Restaurants* (1995).

(ii)   The registered mark is considered as a whole for its overall effect, rather than a letter by letter (or digit) comparison being made: ERECTIKO was refused registration under the 1938 Act as being too close to ERECTOR (*William Bailey's Application* (1935)).

(iii)   The first syllable of a word mark is the most significant. The similarity of the first five letters in a word sign were considered significant to similarity in *Pfizer Ltd v Eurofood (UK) Ltd* (2001), rendering VIAGRA and VIAGRENE similar.

(iv)   Both an aural and a visual comparison is made.

(v)   In a visual, aural and conceptual comparison the reactions of the average consumer are used to assess the effect of these differing elements. Accordingly an aural similarity may override conceptual or visual differences: *Lloyd* (2000)

Schuhfabrik Meyer v Klijsen (2000). The ECJ held that LLOYD and LOINTS were so aurally similar that the visual difference might be overridden.

(vi) Matter common to a particular trade (such as 'cola', for example) will be disregarded.

(vii) It is also borne in mind that a consumer will not necessarily have mark and sign side by side to compare and may remember the claimant's mark imperfectly or mispronounce it. The habit of abbreviating words in the UK was a relevant factor in *Associated Newspapers Ltd v Express Newspapers* (2003), so that both THE EVENING MAIL and THE DAILY MAIL were likely to be shortened to 'The Mail' by consumers.

It is essentially a 'jury question': mark and sign are compared through the eyes (and other senses) of a hypothetical customer, although the decision is one for the judge. Laddie J accepted that evidence of witnesses might be required to assist a judge in assessing the ways in which members of the target market will pronounce a word mark and of the mark's visual and phonetic impact on them in *Wagamama Ltd v City Centre Restaurants* (1995).

ORIGINS and ORIGIN were held to be similar in *Origins Natural Resources Inc v Origin Clothing Ltd* (1995) as the public could not be expected to distinguish between the singular and plural uses of the word. The comparison was stated to be 'more a matter of feel than science' by Laddie J in *Wagamama v City Centre Restaurants*, and WAGAMAMA and RAJA MAMA were found to be similar. However, adjectival use of the word 'European' in *The European Ltd v The Economist Newspapers Ltd* (1996) was not found to be similar in relation to the plaintiff's device mark for its masthead, even though the word was the essential feature of the plaintiff's mark.

16.4.2 Similarity of goods and services

The TMA 1994 also introduced new wording in relation to the similarity of goods or services of claimant and defendant. Under the 1938 Act, the court had to determine whether the relevant products were 'goods of the same description'. In so doing, the courts took into account similarities in the nature and composition of the claimant's and defendant's goods or services, in their use and in the channels of distribution employed: *Jellinek's Application* (1946). In *British Sugar plc v James Robertson & Sons* (1996), Jacob J likened the new test to the old. He warned against the temptation to use the new wording to extend a proprietor's protection too far from the specification of goods for which the mark was registered, thereby creating very wide and unjustified monopolies. He listed six relevant factors in the context of modern marketing methods:

(i) the respective uses of the respective goods or services;

(ii) the respective users of the respective goods or services;

(iii) the physical nature of the goods or acts of service;

(iv) the respective trade channels through which the goods or services reach the market;

(v) in the case of self-serve consumer items, where, in practice, they are respectively found or likely to be found in supermarkets and, in particular, whether they are or are likely to be found on the same or different shelves;

(vi) the extent to which the respective goods or services are competitive. This inquiry may take into account how those in trade classify goods, for instance, whether market research companies, who of course act for industry, put the goods or services in the same or different sectors.

Consequently, spreads and ice cream topping were not similar goods; nor were videos and television programmes in *Baywatch Production Inc v The Home Video Channel* (1997). Free newspapers were held to be similar (although not identical) to the paid-for variety, despite the differences in the channels of distribution. They have similar uses, are made available to similar users, and are of similar size and makeup; perhaps most tellingly, they will compete: *Associated Newspapers Ltd v Express Newspapers* (2003).

16.4.3 Likelihood of confusion

Similarity of either product or marks must also give rise to a likelihood of confusion in order to infringe. The claimant may not have begun use of the registered mark and so no actual confusion need be shown (*Origins Natural Resources Inc v Origin Clothing Ltd* (1995)). Evidence of actual customer confusion by customer complaints or survey evidence may be heard, although the courts' caution as to such evidence should be borne in mind. Both expert, public and survey evidence was heard in *The European Ltd v The Economist Newspapers Ltd* (1996), but not regarded as useful. Where a mark is being used, it has been argued[17] that the circumstances of use should not be ignored, in making a comparison between the defendant's actual use of the sign and any hypothetical normal and fair use of the registered trade mark by the claimant. In addition, in *Sabel BV v Puma AG* (1998) the ECJ took into account the acquired strength of Puma's mark.

Lancer Trade Mark (1987) illustrates that all circumstances are relevant. Mitsubishi applied to register LANCER for cars. This was opposed by Fiat, on the grounds of its similarity to LANCIA. Applying the TMA 1938, the Court of Appeal held that the two marks were visually distinguishable, but sufficiently phonetically similar to raise the issue of confusion. It was held that there was no real risk of confusion to a substantial number of persons. The court considered the difference in number of syllables of the two marks, the fact that LANCER had a recognised meaning in English but that LANCIA did not, the nature of the market in cars (an expensive and carefully considered purchase for the majority of consumers) and the fact that LANCER was the name applied to a model of car, whereas LANCIA was the name of a manufacturer.

The ECJ and confusion

The test of confusion has been held to be a 'global' one by the ECJ. The preamble to the Directive states:

> ... whereas the likelihood of confusion, the appreciation of which depends on numerous elements and, in particular, on the recognition of the trade mark on the market, of the association which can be made with the used or registered sign, of the degree of similarity between the trade mark and the sign and between the goods and services identified ...

---

17 Prescott, P, 'Analysis – Infringement of Registered Trade Marks: Always a Hypothetical Comparison?' [1997] IPQ 121.

This can be interpreted to mean that the necessary presence of confusion depends on a number of inter-linked factors. These include:

- the level of recognition of the mark by consumers;
- the extent of similarity between mark and sign (over and above the level that must be reached before any question of confusion arises); and
- the degree of similarity of the products concerned (above the threshold level), which would include consideration of the claimant's actual use of the mark in trade.

Thus, the ECJ has established that all factors must be considered in relation to each other: *Lloyd* (2000). Questions of confusion cannot be divorced from questions of similarity of marks and goods. A lesser degree of similarity between the parties' products may be offset by a greater degree of similarity between the marks. In addition, the greater the distinctiveness (or market reputation) of the mark the greater the risk of confusion: *Canon Kabushiki Kaisha v MGM* (1998). The assessment of similarity and confusion is made through the eyes of the average and reasonable consumer: *Lloyd* (2000).

This was illustrated in *Sabel BV v Puma AG* (1998) in a case concerning the relative grounds of refusal. Puma opposed Sabel's application to register a device mark in Germany, consisting of a bounding cheetah with Puma's name. Puma had registered a silhouette of a bounding puma. The ECJ considered the appropriate way in which to compare a composite device mark such as Sabel's.

The Court said that the device mark must not be separated into its components, but should be considered 'globally'. Appreciation of the visual, aural, or conceptual similarity of the marks was based on the overall impression they gave, bearing in mind their distinctive and dominant components, in the way that the average consumer would perceive a mark. Conceptual similarity (both marks focusing on a running feline) might give rise to a likelihood of confusion if the earlier mark was particularly distinctive, either inherently or through an extensive acquired reputation with the public. On the facts, however, Puma's mark was not particularly well known, and conceptually not very imaginative so that the marks' similarity was unlikely to give rise to confusion.

Lloyd (2000) applied the *Windsurfing* (1999) guidelines for assessing the degree of distinctiveness of a mark (see 15.7.3) in assessing confusion. These include:

- the mark's inherent characteristics;
- any element of descriptiveness within it; the market share held by the mark;
- how intensive, geographically widespread and longstanding its use has been; the amount invested in promoting it; and
- the proportion of the consuming public which identifies it as coming from a particular undertaking; as well as
- the statements made by chambers of commerce and industry, trade and professional associations. No percentage degrees of recognition can be stated in general terms.

The global approach has been followed by UK courts in *Premier Brands UK Ltd v Typhoon Europe Ltd* (2000), *Pfizer Ltd v Eurofood (UK) Ltd* (2001), and *Associated Newspapers Ltd v Express Newspapers* (2003). Accordingly, Neuberger J laid out the factors to be considered through the eyes of the average consumer in the *Premier Brands* (2000) case:

(1)   The visual, aural and conceptual similarities of the registered trade mark and the allegedly infringing sign, including the overall impression given by the mark and the sign, and bearing in mind in particular their respective and dominant components.

(2)   The distinctiveness of the mark (whether inherently or through its reputation with the public): the more distinctive the mark, the greater the likelihood of confusion.

(3)   The degree of similarity of the goods for which the mark is registered and the goods in respect of which the sign is used.

On this basis, the sign TYPHOON was not confusingly similar to TY.PHOO, even given the British tendency (as noted by the court) to slur words.

There are dangers in the global approach if weight of reputation leads to an assumption of similarity of mark and sign. Preserving a threshold of similarity remains desirable if s 10(2) is not to become a statutory form of passing off.[18] It can be queried whether the more distinctive a mark, the more likely confusion is. In fact, the opposite may be true. The more distinctive a mark, the more likely it is that a consumer will recognise differences between it and the competitor's sign. The same might not be true where similarity of goods is concerned; the more distinctive the mark perhaps the more likely that a consumer will infer that the mark owner is diversifying if a competitor uses the sign on different products. In *Daimlerchrysler AG v Alavi* (2001) (the *Merc* case) the claimant had registered UK and Community marks MERCEDES and MERCEDES-BENZ for vehicles and clothing; the defendant had long sold clothing under the sign 'Merc'. Pumfrey J expressed reservations over the global approach to s 10(2) of the TMA 1994:

> There is greater likelihood of confusion with very distinctive marks (*Sabel, Canon, Lloyd*). This is a very surprising proposition (and perhaps only a presumption of fact, since this cannot be a legal issue), since normally it is easier to distinguish a well-known word mark from others close to it. However, it seems to me to make more sense when one comes to consider device marks.[19] I have difficulty understanding how it can affect the similarity of goods, but that is the law.

The danger lies in giving stronger protection to a mark with a strong reputation than would be the case for a newer or weaker mark because less emphasis is given to confusion than to similarity. On the facts, Pumfrey J held that there was no evidence of 'spill-over' confusion in relation to clothing; indeed, he advocated revocation of the claimant's marks for all but a restricted list of clothing on which the mark had been used.

Confusion as to origin

The consumer must be confused as to the source of the product. In the *Canon* (1998) case the ECJ related the nature of the relevant confusion to the 'essential' distinguishing function of a mark in Recital 10 and Article 2 of the Directive. This was, they stated, to 'guarantee the identity of the origin of the marked product to the

---

18   Baloch, T, 'Confused about Dilution' [2001] EIPR 427.
19   As the mark in *Sabel* was.

consumer or end user by enabling him, without any possibility of confusion, to distinguish the product or service from others which have another origin', and offer a guarantee that all products bearing it have originated under the control of a single, or economically linked, undertakings responsible for their quality.

A consumer may therefore be confused by marks used in merchandising if the impression is that the products have been authorised and controlled by the mark owner, even if manufactured elsewhere.

American trade mark law recognises 'initial interest' confusion. This may occur where first impressions confuse, even though by the time the product is purchased any confusion has been overcome. In the Northern Ireland case of *BP Amoco v John Kelly* (2001) the use of BP's green colouring by a rival petrol station was said to create sufficient confusion, even though by the time a driver purchased the petrol any confusion should have been overcome by other signs.

Being led to a competing website by the use of misleading metatags could fall within this concept, even though the consumer would soon establish that the site was not the one for which he or she searched. The Court of Appeal's decision in *Reed Executive v Reed Business Information* (2004) renders this unlikely unless confusion is real. On the facts, the use by both parties of a common surname, when consumers were accustomed to 'fuzzy' results from search engines, did not amount to a likelihood of confusion.

Likelihood of association

The old law, tied as it was to a definition of a trade mark as an indication of source, insisted on confusion as to the source of the relevant goods or service: *Ravenhead Brick Co v Ruabon Brick Co* (1937). The TMA 1994, however, added the likelihood of confusion on the part of the public including 'the likelihood of association with the trade mark'. In Benelux trade mark law resemblance between marks sufficient for one to call the other to mind, without causing confusion as to the source of the respective products, may infringe. The leading case is *Union v Union Soleure* (1984):

> ... there is similarity between a trade mark and a sign when, taking into account the particular circumstances of a case, such as the distinctive power of the trade mark, the trade mark and the sign, each looked at as a whole and in relation to one another, demonstrate such auditive, visual or conceptual resemblance, that associations between sign and trade mark are evoked merely on the basis of this resemblance.

In *Monopoly v Anti-Monopoly* (1978), the two names MONOPOLY and ANTI-MONOPOLY were used on games of opposite nature, the one concerned with a player's attempts to create a monopoly, the other being anti-capitalistic in nature. It was unlikely that the two would be regarded as emanating from the same source, but ANTI-MONOPOLY was held to infringe as it was likely that a mental link with MONOPOLY would be made.

It was strongly argued that the Directive and, therefore, the TMA 1994, embodied this principle in s 10(2) of the TMA 1994, the argument backed by the statements attached to the Council minutes. Such an interpretation is linguistically at odds with the section, for it would be strange to regard the narrower concept of 'confusion' as 'including' the wider concept of association. The issue of 'non-origin association' was raised in *Wagamama Ltd v City Centre Restaurants* (1995) before Laddie J, who held that s 10(2) covered 'classic infringement', but not non-origin association. Considerable debate followed,[20] as it was felt that the result was to ignore both the advertising and investment function of trade marks, and dilution of a mark in relation to similar goods or services.

The second question in *Sabel* (1998) was the correct interpretation of 'the likelihood of confusion including the likelihood of association'. The ECJ steered a middle course between the two extremes of *Wagamama* (1995). The Court said that the wording of the Directive (that a likelihood of confusion include a likelihood of association) precluded an interpretation that a likelihood of association be an alternative to confusion; association served only to define confusion's scope. This was confirmed by the 10th Recital in the Directive's preamble which establishes that the likelihood of confusion must be considered globally, taking into account all relevant circumstances. Confusion could therefore comprise 'direct confusion', where the public confuses the sign and mark in question, or 'indirect confusion'. This occurs when the public is sufficiently confused to connect the respective proprietor's mark and sign (Advocate General Jacob referred to assuming an organisational or economic link, such as, perhaps, a licence or franchise). It is not 'association in the strict sense', where the sign and mark's similarity causes the public to call the mark to mind without confusing the two (non-origin association).

Decorative use of a very distinctive mark might be thought to give rise to association in the strict sense. It was argued for Adidas that use of a stripe motif so reminiscent of its registered three-stripe mark by another sportswear manufacturer that it would cause a likelihood of association should give rise to a presumption of confusion. The ECJ did not agree: *Marca Mode CV v Adidas AG* (2000). The Court held that a national court must make a positive finding of a likelihood of confusion in all cases.

However, the *Sabel* (1998) and *Marca Mode* (2000) decisions do not preclude a finding of infringement by dilution. The ECJ left open the possibility of indirect confusion being caused if a mark had considerable reputation or inherent distinctiveness. In addition, the *Davidoff* case has confirmed dilution even for similar products.

16.5 IDENTICAL OR SIMILAR MARKS/MARKS WITH A REPUTATION

Where a mark has a reputation in the UK, to use either a sign which is identical or similar to a registered trade mark in relation to any goods or services will also infringe. This is provided that the use of the sign is without due cause, and takes unfair advantage of, or is detrimental to, the distinctive character or the repute of the trade mark.[21] This provision was new to UK trade mark law in 1994, and provides a remedy for 'dilution' of a mark, and other damage to reputation or the mark's economic value as a commodity (its ability to be merchandised, for example). There is no need to show public confusion, only damage to the value of the mark.

---

20   Kamperman Sanders, A, 'The *Wagamama* decision: Back to the Dark Ages of Trade Mark Law' [1996] EIPR 3; Sanders, A, 'The Return to *Wagamama*' [1996] EIPR 521; Gielen, C, 'European Trade Mark Legislation: The Statements' [1996] EIPR 83.
21   Section 10(3) of the TMA 1994.

16.5.1   The concept of dilution

Schechter argued to a Congressional committee,[22] as long ago as 1932, that a mark should be protected both as a product identifier and as a product advertiser, otherwise uncontrolled use of a well known mark would cause damage to the mark's distinctiveness. This would particularly be so if a sign was applied to a wide range of goods including those with unattractive associations, thereby diluting the mark's drawing power in the marketplace. Benelux law provided such protection, as does State and Federal law in the US. The concept reached gradual acceptance in the United States[23] and was enacted into Federal law with the Federal Trademark Dilution Act 1995.

Thus, provision is made to protect not just the identification function of marks but the communication, or advertising, function by means of which marks operate to confer an image on products, desirable in itself.[24] Norman points out that a brand owner can do much by the nature of the advertising attached to a mark to preserve its positive connotations and thus maximise the protection available under s 10(3) of the TMA 1994.[25]

This new infringement protects the opportunity to expand into new markets, but over-protection remains a danger if a trade mark proprietor is to be able to monopolise the mark in all fields of goods and services. Limits, such as those adopted by the courts in defining damage and a common field of action in relation to passing off, may be required. To have provided such a remedy has been criticised as undermining the basis of trade mark registration in classes and according to use; however, the requirement that damage be shown should redress the balance. One solution would be to place the focus on unjust enrichment on the defendant's part, showing that unjustified use had been made of a mark; the deliberateness of the defendant's actions has swayed the court in passing off cases.

16.5.2   Conditions for protection

First, a claimant must establish the identity or similarity of the defendant's sign to the registered mark in the same way as for s 10(1) and (2) of the TMA 1994. In addition, it will also be necessary to establish, secondly, the mark's reputation in the UK. Thirdly, it must be shown that the defendant's use was without due cause and, fourthly, that that use will damage the mark's character or repute.

Neuberger J set out the criteria for a dilution claim in *Premier Brands UK Ltd v Typhoon Europe Ltd* (2000):

(1) use of the sign in the course of trade;

(2) the sign is similar to the mark;

---

22 Schechter, Frank, Hearings before the House Committee on Patents, 72d Cong, 1st Sess, 15 (1932).

23 The first dilution statute was enacted by Massachusetts in 1947. At least 23 states passed similar legislation before 1995.

24 Howells, C, 'A Loaded Question: On Section 5(3) of the Trade Marks Act 1994' [2002] EIPR 118.

25 Norman, H, 'Advertising and the Legal Protection of Trade Marks: A Case Study of Ever Ready' (2001) Communications Law 3.

(3) the sign is used in relation to goods which are not similar (although he suspected the sub-section could also apply to similar products (see 16.5.5));[26]

(4) the mark has a reputation in the UK;

(5) the use of the sign is without due cause;

(6) the use of the sign (a) takes unfair advantage of; and/or (b) is detrimental to the distinctive character and repute of the mark.

This last condition was further divided by Advocate General Jacobs in *Adidas-Salomon AG v Adidas Benelux* (2003). He identified four actionable types of use:

(1) use which takes unfair advantage of the mark's distinctive character;

(2) use which takes unfair advantage of the mark's repute;

(3) use which is detrimental to the mark's distinctive character; and

(4) use which is detrimental to the mark's repute.

However, so far, case law had tended to deal with the infringing harm under two headings – unfair advantage, and detriment, and this pattern will be followed here. Advocate General Jacobs himself felt that there was no significant difference between advantage being taken of distinctive character and repute, although he did distinguish them in relation to detriment.

At this stage it must be assumed that distinctive character bears the meaning given in case law defining distinctiveness for the purpose of registration of a mark; and that repute means the reputation necessarily established in order to seek a remedy under s 10(3) of the TMA 1994 (see 16.5.4).

16.5.3   Similarity of mark and sign

Whether the mark and the allegedly infringing sign are similar should be assessed in the same way as for s 10(2) of the TMA 1994, although there is no need to establish that the similarity gives rise to confusion. This was stated by the ECJ in *Adidas-Salomon AG v Adidas Benelux* (2003). Adidas objected to Fitness World's use of a double stripe reminiscent of its registered three-stripe mark on clothing. The court cited the visual, aural and conceptual degree of similarity test from *Sabel* (1998) and *Lloyd* (2000).

The reference to the ECJ in the case also asked whether it is relevant that the use of the sign was decorative. The Advocate General suggested that this was irrelevant to questions of similarity. However, it was relevant to the question whether the sign had been 'used in the course of trade' as Article 5(2) of the Directive requires. He alluded both to the functions of a mark and to the public interest considerations which limit registration:

> ... it would in any event be undesirable as a matter of principle to extend the protection of trade marks in such a way as to preclude the use of common decorations and motifs such as stripes. The Court has ruled that Article 3(1)(c) and Article 3(1)(e) of the Directive pursue aims that are in the public interest, which requires that signs and indications descriptive of the categories of goods or services for which registration is sought, and a shape whose essential characteristics perform a technical function and were chosen to fulfil that function, may be freely used by all. It has also recognised

---

26   Following amendment of the TMA 1994 by the Trade Marks (Proof of Use etc) Regulations 2004, this condition no longer applies.

that there is a public interest in not unduly restricting the availability of colours for the other operators who offer for sale goods or services of the same type as those in respect of which registration is sought ...

Although the present case raises the slightly different question of the extent of protection conferred by Article 5(2), I consider that analogous public interest considerations militate against extending that protection so as to prevent traders from using simple and long-accepted decorations and motifs.

In its decision the ECJ did not advert to the public interest, resting its decision on the reactions of consumers as a question of fact. The Court ruled that no necessity for confusion applies to the similarity condition, as the provision is aimed at harm to reputation. Provided the relevant consuming public would 'link' the sign and the mark, the requirement of similarity would be satisfied. Nevertheless, the criteria the Court advocated for determining this 'link' are the same as for similar marks applied to similar goods and services. The mark and sign must be viewed globally, taking into account all relevant factors, including visual, conceptual and aural similarity as well as the idea of the mark.

16.5.4 Reputation

It is only reputation in the UK which is required, and not goodwill. The statute gives no guidance as to the extent of reputation required. One way to limit the potential for over protection inherent in this remedy would be to require an extensive reputation to be established. In the Benelux courts, the greater the reputation the more likely a dilution case is to succeed, and the Federal Trademark Dilution Act 1995 in the US applies only to 'famous' marks, such as MARLBORO, COCA-COLA and NESCAFÉ.

Precedent for the criteria and evidence needed to establish a reputation exist in passing off law, and will develop in relation to well known marks (see 16.7). The International Trademark Association suggested that reputation could be shown by:

- the degree of inherent and acquired distinctiveness of the mark;
- the duration and extent of its use, and of publicity and advertising with the mark;
- the geographical extent of trading, channels of trade used, and degree of recognition in the claimant's and defendant's trading areas and distribution channels; and
- the nature and extent of use of something similar by third parties.

The ECJ considered the nature of reputation in the Directive in *GMC v Yplon* (2000) (followed by the Court of Session in *Pebble Beach Co v Lombard Brands Ltd* (2002)). CHEVY was registered by the defendant for detergents and by the claimant, who alleged dilution of its mark, for vehicles. The Court held that national courts must first establish whether the mark had sufficient reputation within at least a substantial part of a Member State before considering any effect on the mark by the defendant's sign. Reputation was a question of fact, which had to take into account all the relevant circumstances. These included the market share held by the trade mark, the intensity, geographical extent and duration of its use, and the size of the mark owner's investment in promoting it. The mark's reputation must be considered in relation to the relevant public: those who might be concerned by it. This might extend to the public at large depending on the nature of the product concerned, or might be more specialised, such as traders in a specific sector of the market. It must then be shown that the public had a sufficient degree of knowledge of the mark, when confronted by the sign, to associate the two, even when used on different products. The Directive did not dictate that a given percentage of the public could be shown to draw this association.

In *Adidas-Salomon AG v Adidas Benelux* (2003) the ECJ elaborated the concept of association, which did not require any element of confusion between the two marks as confusion is not an element of the dilution provision (see 16.5.6). It is logical, then, to extend association here to the 'calling to mind' of Benelux law (see 16.4.3). The Court stated that the public has sufficient knowledge of the mark to 'establish a link' between the two. The existence of any link must be appreciated globally, taking into account all relevant factors, as in *Sabel*.

16.5.5   Dilution in relation to similar products

Section 10(3) of the TMA 1994 did not appear to provide a remedy against dilution to a mark owner with sufficient reputation if the defendant's sign was used for different, 'non-similar', products, unless that use amounted to confusion under s 10(2). However, it would be anomalous to have provided stronger protection for marks with a lesser reputation (no reputation needs to be shown for s 10(1) and (2), merely registration). The issue went to the ECJ in *Davidoff & Cie SA v Gofkid Ltd* (2003). The Court held that the dilution protection must extend to use of a sign for similar products for marks with a reputation as part of the overall objectives of the Directive (see 15.16.2). This was particularly so since *Sabel* (1998) had rejected a wide interpretation of association.

Article 5(2) of the Directive was optional, so the question remained whether Member States were obliged to interpret it in this way, even if they had implemented protection for dilution. The ECJ held in *Adidas-Salomon AG v Adidas Benelux* (2003) that, having exercised their option, no discretion remained as to the situations covered by the protection granted. The Trade Marks (Proof of Use etc) Regulations 2004[27] amended s 10(3) to implement this interpretation into UK trade mark law, by removing reference to 'dissimilar' goods and services.

16.5.6   Unfair advantage or detriment

The fourth requirement is that unfair advantage is taken of, or detriment is caused to, the distinctive character or repute of the mark. The concept of 'dilution' has been regarded as helpful in interpreting this requirement: *Premier Brands UK Ltd v Typhoon Europe Ltd* (2000). State decisions in the US identify dilution by blurring and by tarnishing the reputation of a mark.

Blurring occurs when a mark's distinctiveness is detracted from by use on differing products, such as KODAK for pianos, and BULOVA for gowns, found to infringe in the US, or the infringing use of MARLBORO for cosmetics in Benelux. Damage is most likely if the mark carries connotations of high quality or luxury, as it seems unlikely that s 10(3) of the TMA 1994 will prevent all duplication of marks, such as the use of JIF for both lemon juice and a household cleaner (both products available in supermarkets).

---

27   SI 2004/946, which came into force on 5 May 2004.

Tarnishing refers to the damage caused to a mark by use in circumstances that subvert the claimant's image by unpleasant associations. Thus, the use of AMERICAN EXPRESS on packets of condoms was actionable[28] in the US. The leading Benelux case is that of *Claeryn/Klarein* (1976). The owner of the CLAERYN mark for Dutch gin was able to prevent KLAREIN (which sounds exactly the same in Dutch) for a cleaning product. Parodies of trade marks, normally made for profit and not humour, may fall into this category of harm, as may diversion of a mark's value as a commodity: the BAYWATCH mark was being merchandised on a wide range of products, for example.

Actual damage

That there must be evidence of damage is a prerequisite: *Daimlerchrysler AG v Alavi* (2001). In the United States the case of *Moseley v Secret Catalogue Inc* (2003) has also established a requirement of actual harm, although evidence of lost sales is not necessary.

Mere use of a sign which calls to mind an association with the mark without more will not suffice. This was stated in the *Premier* (2000) case. Neuberger J made the point that not every dilution of a mark would amount to s 10(3) infringement, nor that every infringement would involve dilution. However much a mark owner wishes to prevent use of the mark in other contexts, the ability to do so rests squarely on both the public's perception of that use and the extent to which it either causes a detriment to the mark or takes unfair advantage of it. Whether it does so is a question of fact for the court: *Pfizer* (2001).

Not confusion

Dicta of the ECJ in *Sabel BV v Puma AG* (1998) suggested that the claimant need not show deception of the public. Additionally, in *Parfums Christian Dior v Evora BV* (1998), the ECJ revealed a sympathy for trade mark proprietors' desire to defend a prestigious image where no confusion would occur. This was confirmed by *Adidas-Salomon AG v Adidas Benelux* (2003). It would suffice if the relevant public discern a link between mark and sign.

Early UK case law did look for confusion, but the Court of Appeal in *British Telecommunications plc v One in a Million* (1999) doubted that confusion was necessary. Damage without customer confusion is possible, so that the mark owner may feel the need to abandon the mark or to initiate remedial advertising in order to overcome adverse customer response to the blurring.

This has now been confirmed both by the ECJ in *Yplon* (2000) and the UK courts: *Premier Brands UK Ltd v Typhoon Europe Ltd* (2000) and *Pfizer Ltd v Eurofood Link (UK) Ltd* (2001).

Unfair advantage

In *Pfizer* (2001) it was stated that the concept of unfair advantage required an enquiry into the benefit to be gained by the defendant from use of the mark. In *Adidas-Salomon*

---

28   *American Express Co v Vibra Approved Laboratories Corp* (1989).

AG v Adidas Benelux (2003) Advocate General Jacobs regarded this as an instance of 'clear exploitation and free-riding on the coattails of a famous mark' or an attempt to trade on its reputation. He illustrated this with the example of Rolls Royce being entitled to prevent a whisky manufacturer from using the ROLLS ROYCE reputation to exploit his brand. A German case *Dimple* (1985), cited in *Premier Brands UK Ltd v Typhoon Europe Ltd* (2000), defines it as an act of unfair competition by a defendant associating the quality of his product with that of the prestigious mark owner's in order to exploit that good reputation.

No unfair advantage was made out in *Pebble Beach Co v Lombard Brands Ltd* (2002), and the court pointed out that not only must any advantage must be of a sufficiently significant degree to warrant restraining a non-confusing use of the sign, but it must also be unfair. The argument that golfing tournaments are often sponsored by whisky manufacturers and therefore the defendant was creating an advantageous association in the public's mind between its whisky and the claimant's golf course was defeated on the basis that there is also an association between golf and a number of other business sponsors.

Detriment

In *Pfizer* (2001), detriment was stated to require an enquiry into the damage to the claimant's goodwill sufficient to restrain a non-confusing use, and was interpreted to include blurring and tarnishing by Advocate General Jacobs[29] and in *Premier Brands UK Ltd v Typhoon Europe Ltd* (2000). Neuberger J also pointed out there that the stronger the distinctive character or reputation of a mark the easier it would be to establish detriment. Advocate General Jacobs distinguished detriment to distinctive character and detriment to repute. The former he equated to a blurring of the mark so that it becomes incapable of arousing immediate association with the products for which it is registered; the latter, to tarnishment, so that the mark's 'power of attraction' is diminished.

In *Adidas-Salomon AG v Adidas Benelux* (2003) decorative use did not necessarily avoid a finding of infringement, which rested on an association being made between the mark and sign.

In *Pfizer* (2001) any degree of association between mark and sign was held to be slight, and neither blurring nor tarnishing were made out on the evidence. The caution shown by Pumfrey J in the *Merc* (2001) case is also telling. There he stated that blurring:

> ... is simply a suggestion that once a mark acquires a reputation one can throw the specification of goods away. Any use of another mark will potentially have this effect if any member of the relevant public becomes aware of the second mark ... It raises conceptual problems.

Michaels[30] points out that despite the admission that confusion is no part of s 10(3) in the UK courts, neither have many, if any, cases succeeded in establishing this head of infringement. While she does not preclude the mark owner gaining a remedy, she

---

29   In *Adidas-Salomon AG v Adidas Benelux* (2003).
30   Michaels, A, 'Confusion In and About Sections 5(3) and 10(3) of the Trade Marks Act 1994' [2000] EIPR 335.

speculates whether it might not be more properly done as an aspect of unfair competition or even defamation, rather than trade mark infringement. Certainly, there should be some scope left for use of a mark as a parody. A Manhattan judge ruled that a dog perfume TIMMY HOLEDIGGER did not infringe the TOMMY HILFIGER brand.[31] The answer, once again, lies in the concept of the function that a trade mark is held to serve.

16.5.7 Without due cause

If there is 'due cause' for the use it will not infringe. Although the claimant must make out infringement, the onus of establishing due cause lies on the defendant: *Pfizer* (2001).

In Benelux law, the defendant's use must be regarded as necessary to escape liability, but necessary uses in the UK are already absolved by the defences of s 11 of the TMA 1994 (see 16.8). Legitimate advertising comparing the products of claimant and defendant would appear to be a justifiable reason for use, as would ownership of other intellectual property rights, or prior use of the mark.

The concept was discussed in *Premier Brands UK Ltd v Typhoon Europe Ltd* (2000) and Benelux tests applied. Neuberger J interpreted the phrase within the context of the sub-section's purpose – which was to protect the value and goodwill of trade marks, particularly those that are well known. Accordingly, he rejected 'in good faith' or 'for good and honest commercial reasons' as due cause for three reasons. First, a subjective evaluation of the sign user's motives could lead to unfair and even capricious results, even conferring an advantage on the 'ignorant and lazy' at the expense of the well-informed and careful. Secondly, 'without due cause' applied not only to use of the sign but also to the resulting harm, requiring a commercially realistic interpretation. Thirdly, this conclusion was in line with Benelux law in *Lucas Bols* (1976), which laid down two tests of due cause:

(1) that the user is under such compulsion to use the mark that he cannot honestly be asked to refrain from doing so regardless of the damage to the mark owner;

(2) that the user is entitled to use the mark in his own right and does not have to yield this right to the mark owner.

This latter test was followed in *Pebble Beach Co v Lombard Brands Ltd* (2002). There, the fact that the defenders had registered their mark and had a right to use it rendered use of their mark (had either unfair advantage or detriment been found on the facts) use with due cause, at least until the pursuers had successfully sought its revocation.

Neuberger J also refuted two potential criticisms of adopting the Benelux interpretation. The first was that uncertainty would result before courts could lay down guidelines as to honest reasons for using another's mark. This he saw as no more than an outcome of the fact that all trade mark infringement rested on the facts of a particular case. The secondly was that it was not easy to see how use taking an *unfair* advantage could ever be with due cause. However, it was possible to see how a detrimental use could be allowable, and the due cause might outweigh the unfairness of advantage taken of the mark.

---

31 'Dog Perfume Cleared in Copyright (sic) Case', BBC News, 16 August 2002, http://news.bbc.co.uk.

16.6 COMPARATIVE ADVERTISING

Comparative advertising is a potential form of infringement. It has been a common practice in some industries, such as the sale of personal computers and of cars, and regarded as legitimate provided that the mark owner was informed.

On one view such advertising is in the consumer interest in a free market economy, because it stimulates competition and provides purchasers with the information necessary to assess a product's qualities, and should be regulated only to the extent of ensuring truthful comparison. In the UK, control is exercised through the Consumer Protection Act 1987, the Consumer Credit Act 1989 and the Advertising Standards Authority Code of Practice. The other view was that comparative advertising is not justifiable.

Section 10(6) of the TMA 1994 allows use of another's marks to identify competitors, by stating what will not amount to an infringing act:

Nothing in the preceding provisions of this section shall be construed as preventing the use of a registered trade mark by any person for the purpose of identifying goods or services as those of the proprietor or a licensee.

This is, however, subject to an extensive proviso:

However, any such use otherwise than in accordance with honest practices in industrial or commercial matters shall be treated as infringing the registered trade mark if the use without due cause takes unfair advantage of, or is detrimental to, the distinctive character or repute of the trade mark,

which sets out both the act, and the harm required to be shown, in order to constitute infringement, at the same time providing a defence for the careful comparative advertiser. There is no need to compare parties' goods or services, or the marks, as it is proprietors' own marks which are used to identify their own products.

It should be remembered that the Trade Mark Regulation has no equivalent to s 10(6) for Community Trade Marks. The Comparative Advertising Directive will regulate comparative advertising using these marks.

16.6.1 Consumer protection measures

Additionally, in June 1997, the European Union adopted the Comparative Advertising Directive[32] in order to harmonise Member States' legislation. The Directive allows states wishing to do so to control comparative advertising under the guise of consumer protection. In the UK implementation came in the Control of Misleading Advertisements (Amendment) Regulations 2000, which came into force on 23 April 2000. Advertising is comparative if it identifies a competitor or goods explicitly or by implication. Only advertising meeting the seven conditions set down is permissible. The Regulations do not provide a civil remedy for the competitor, but provide ground for complaint to a relevant authority, such as the Office of Fair Trading. The Injunctions for the Protection of Consumers Directive[33] allows these authorities to enforce the

---

32 Directive of the European Parliament and of the Council amending Directive 84/450/EEC Concerning Misleading Advertising so as to include Comparative Advertising (97/55/EC).

33 Directive 98/27/EC of the European Parliament and of the Council of 19 May 1998 on Injunctions for the Protection of Consumers' Interests [1998] OJ L166.

Regulations. However, no change was made to the TMA 1994 and in *British Airways plc v Ryanair Ltd* (2001) Jacob J held that the Directive did not affect the TMA 1994. Vulgar use of the BA mark by Ryanair did not infringe as Ryanair was not dishonest in its advertising, although it did denigrate the mark.

16.6.2 Application of s 10(6) of the TMA 1994

The proviso's wording is familiar both from ss 10(3) and 11(2) of the TMA 1994, which may provide guidance to the sub-section's interpretation, but, in *Barclays Bank plc v RBS Advanta* (1996), Laddie J held that the section should be considered alone. He reviewed the drafting of s 10(6) of the TMA 1994 critically as 'a mess', being derived partly from purely domestic law, and partly from both the Directive and the Paris Convention. He laid down principles for the application of s 10(6).

First, he accepted the argument that the two halves to the proviso meant the same thing: if a competitor's use of a sign were to take unfair advantage of a mark, the use would necessarily be dishonest, despite the odd result that the proviso to ss 10(3) and 11(2) of the TMA 1994 will have the same result, although the language differs. He held that, first, the onus was on the claimant to prove dishonesty, and that unfair advantage had been taken of the mark without due cause.

Carty directs some criticism at Jacob J's first principle.[34] Pointing out that the protection against dilution protects new functions and values of marks, she suggests that some comparative advertising, not necessarily dishonest, might equally damage this value; and that the Comparative Advertising Directive recognises this. It is possible that the robust approach of the courts may be modified if the advertising function of marks becomes better recognised. However, the ECJ adopted a robust approach to the Comparative Advertising Directive in *Toshiba Europe GmbH v Katun Germany GmbH* (2001). The perception of a reasonable consumer test was applied, and use of spare part order numbers by a competitor was deemed necessary to competition (a use falling within the UK defences).[35]

Secondly, he held that the honesty of the defendant's practice be determined objectively and that the test to apply was the reaction to the advert by members of a reasonable audience. He anticipated a robust approach to advertising by its recipients. The fact that the advertising pokes fun at the proprietor's goods or services and emphasises the benefits of the defendant's is a normal incidence of comparative advertising. Its aim will be to divert customers from the proprietor. No reasonable observer would expect one trader to point to all the advantages of its competitor's business and failure to do so does not, *per se*, take the advertising outside what reasonable people would regard as 'honest'. Thus, mere trade puffery, even if uncomfortable to the registered proprietor, does not bring the advertising within the scope of trade mark infringement. Much advertising copy is recognised by the public as hyperbole. However, advertising judged by a reasonable reader as not honest, on being given the full facts, for example, because it was 'significantly misleading', would infringe.

---

34 Carty, H, 'Registered Trade Marks and Permissible Comparative Advertising' [2002] EIPR 294.
35 Section 11(2)(c) of the TMA 1994.

Thirdly, Laddie J rejected the argument that the court should be guided by statutory or industry agreed codes in determining whether the defendant's conduct was honest in accordance with 'industrial or commercial matters', as this would make infringement much more prevalent in trades where advertising is strictly controlled. However, he said that the nature of the goods or services at issue would be relevant to the degree of hyperbole considered honest.

Fourthly, he held that the final words of the proviso added nothing more as an advertisement which is not honest would almost always take unfair advantage and vice versa. He merely required some advantage to the defendant or harm to the character or repute of the mark above a *de minimis* level.

Fifthly, in *Cable and Wireless plc v British Telecommunications plc* (1998) Jacob J added to the criteria of *Barclays Bank plc v RBS Advanta* (1996). In applying the test of dishonesty, he said that the advertisement should be read as a whole and not subjected, in interlocutory proceedings, to minute textual examination, although, anyone who puts forward a false claim knowingly cannot be acting honestly. The test to be applied is whether a reasonable trader could honestly have made the statements based upon the information available to him, and not the defendants' belief in the truth of their statements. This is a hybrid test, as the objective response of a reasonable trader is qualified by the subjective nature of the actual information available to him. A fully objective test was applied in *Vodafone Group plc v Orange personal Communications Services Ltd* (1997). Nothing turned on the difference in *Emaco Ltd v Dyson Appliances Ltd* (1999).

Accordingly, in *Vodafone Group plc v Orange Personal Communications Services Ltd* (1997) Jacob J rejected the defendants' argument that their slogan did no harm to the distinctive character of VODAFONE'S mark – once it was dishonest, there was infringement. 'Thoroughly misleading' flyers comparing products were held to infringe, although found not to be malicious by Jonathan Parker J in *Emaco Ltd v Dyson Appliances Ltd* (1999).

Dishonest advertising may include more than the misleading. It has also been suggested[36] that advertising products as similar versions to a marked competing product ('smells like', 'tastes like', for example), might be regarded as dishonest, although, perhaps, only where confusion is likely. In 1998, the NOUVELLE advertising campaign offering dissatisfied customers free packets of the leading rival's product by name was quickly withdrawn, to be replaced by 'the leading brand'.

16.7 WELL KNOWN MARKS

In an age of international travel and communications, marks may acquire extensive reputations in states where their proprietors are not (yet) trading. Such reputations are of considerable value to their owners, allowing for future expansion into new trading areas and for diversification into new products, as well as encouraging purchase among the travelling public. Passing off was seen to be of limited value in defending such reputations. That well known marks are vulnerable to damage can be seen in practices such as the willingness of the Indonesian Trade Mark Office to register marks

---

36 Fitzgerald, D, 'Comparative Advertising in the UK' [1997] EIPR 709.

(such as DUNHILL, LEVI STRAUSS, CHARLES JOURDAN) very well known internationally but not locally registered for a local resident. The well known mark owner is then held to ransom to buy the mark 'back' at huge cost. Such marks are also prey to the damage of dilution, in the same way as domestic household names (see 16.5).

Article 6*bis* of the Paris Convention provides that the countries of the Union undertake to:

> ... refuse or to cancel the registration, and to prohibit the use, of a trademark which constitutes a reproduction, an imitation, or a translation, liable to create confusion, of a mark considered by the competent authority of the country of registration or use to be well known in that country as being already the mark of a person entitled to the benefits of this Convention and used for identical or similar goods.

Although it had been argued that passing off, the ability of a user of an unregistered mark to oppose registration, and registration for defensive marks, did protect well known marks, they did not do so to the extent contemplated by the Paris Convention, and new measures were introduced by the TMA 1994. Well known marks fall into the net of comparison made for the relative grounds of refusal, preventing registration (see 15.15), and s 56 of the TMA 1994 creates a right of action for proprietors of well known marks.

16.7.1   Injunctions against the use of well known marks

The proprietor of a well known mark may seek an injunction against use in the UK of a mark:

> which, or the essential part of which, is identical or similar to his mark, in relation to identical or similar goods or services, where the use is likely to cause confusion.

This is available to nationals of Convention countries, or those domiciled in, or with a real and effective industrial or commercial establishment in a Convention country, regardless of the fact whether they carry on business, or have any goodwill, in the UK,[37] as this is protection for reputation alone. *Bona fide* use by others made before commencement of the TMA 1994 may be continued.[38]

It will be necessary to show: first, that the mark is 'well known'; secondly, that the rival mark being used is similar or identical to at least the essential part of the well known mark; thirdly, that the use is in relation to identical or similar goods or services; and, fourthly, that the rival use is likely to cause confusion. The mark must be a trade mark: *Philips Electronics NV v Remington Consumer Products Ltd* (1998).

Interpretation of 'similar', and 'identical' should follow that for ss 5 and 10 of the TMA 1994, but the confusion required to be shown differs from that of ss 5(2) and 10(2) of the TMA 1994 in that no mention is made of confusion including the likelihood of association. However, if the proprietor of the well known mark has no trade in the UK, it is less likely that source confusion will arise (although the consuming public may make the assumption that the well known mark's proprietor has expanded into the UK), and more than likely that confusion as to reputation, or damage in the nature of dilution may occur.

---

37   Section 56(1) of the TMA 1994.
38   *Ibid*, s 56(3).

Article 16 of the TRIPS Agreement 1994 extends Article 6*bis* of the Paris Convention to goods or services which are not similar to those in respect of which a trade mark is registered, provided that use of the trade mark in relation to those goods or services would 'indicate a connection between those goods or services and the owner of the registered trade mark' and provided that 'the interests of the owner of the registered trade mark are likely to be damaged by such use'. This appears to contemplate such damage without source confusion and may require changes to s 56 of the TMA 1994.

It may be, however, that the proprietor of a well known mark who is domiciled in the UK may not be able to take advantage of s 56. The point was raised in the Registry in *Imperial Tobacco Ltd v Berry Bros & Rudd Ltd* (2001), but left undecided on appeal to the High Court. However, Jacob J did say that it might require attention in the future. Section 56 (1) refers to a person who is a national of, or domiciled in, a Convention country. This is defined as 'a country, other than the UK' in s 55(1)(b) of the TMA 1994. Although the effect of excluding s 56 protection for well known marks of UK mark owners was not intended by the Directive, which refers to marks well known in 'a Member State' in Article 4(2)(b), the Act could not be 'rewritten' in an opposition hearing. Consequently holders of well known marks in the UK must rely on passing off. However, this will require showing that they have both reputation and goodwill in the UK, whereas reputation suffices for Paris Convention protection. In this case, as CUTTY SARK is an export brand, the opponents had virtually no sales in the UK.

16.7.2 'Well known'

Neither the TMA 1994, nor the Paris Convention, define how to determine whether a mark is 'well known', only providing that the mark must be well known in the UK. The determination is left to 'the competent authority' in the country of use, meaning that the criteria adopted, and decisions reached, may differ from jurisdiction to jurisdiction. Texts explaining the Paris Convention state that the mark need not be registered in another Convention country. The Convention provision is directed towards avoiding unfair competition and providing consumer protection once a reputation providing information for the consumer has developed. As protection centres on reputation, evidence of the extent of reputation that a mark has secured in the UK by means of its dissemination through publication, advertising, and other forms of communication, and the degree of the public's recognition of the mark, will reveal whether the mark is well known. These two elements of public recognition, and promotion of the mark are reflected in Article 16 of the TRIPS Agreement 1994 which states:

> In determining whether a trademark is well known, Members shall take account of the knowledge of the trademark in the relevant sector of the public, including knowledge in the Member concerned which has been obtained as a result of the promotion of the trademark.

The lack of either a specific domestic or internationally adopted test has had the result in some jurisdictions of apparently inconsistent results from case by case decisions, as well as inconsistent results from jurisdiction to jurisdiction for the same mark (although differences in the extent of promotion can explain different findings).[39] It has been suggested that WIPO maintain an international register.

---

39 Corneau, T and Linehan, S, 'Such Great Names as These: Protection of Famous Trade Marks under the Canadian Trade Marks Act' [1995] EIPR 531.

Some guidance has been given by decisions and legislation elsewhere, for example, the Andean Pact countries Code, and Brazilian Industrial Property Code, and factors identified as relevant.[40] Factors relevant to whether a mark is well known include:

(1) The degree to which the mark is recognised by the relevant public. Evidence of such recognition can be found in unsolicited requests for goods or services with the mark, or may be adduced by survey evidence. It is likely that, despite the courts' scepticism, survey evidence will be necessary to indicate the degree of public recognition. Jurisdictions vary as to the level of public recognition required before a mark is well known. In France, 20% awareness of the JOKER mark was sufficient, while, in Germany, a level nearer to 80% is required. The portion of the public considered relevant will be significant. In the Lego litigation, world wide different results were reached in Australia and the UK because, locally, the buyers of toys were surveyed, in Australia, the buyers of irrigation equipment. Special local use of the mark may contribute to recognition; in Brazil, sponsorship by 7 ELEVEN of the Brazilian driver Emerson Fittipaldi contributed to the extent of the mark's reputation in Brazil.

(2) The extent to which the mark is used and the duration of that use. To show extensive volume of sales and deep market penetration in the relevant product sector, as well as significant market share, should aid the repute of a mark.

(3) The extent and duration of advertising and publicity given to the mark. 'Spillover advertising' from films and broadcasting, international publications and travel will contribute to a UK reputation. Evidence of expenditure on, and the extent of, advertising will be relevant.

(4) The extent to which the mark is registered and protected elsewhere. Extensive repute elsewhere will contribute to repute in the UK, particularly in areas closely aligned with a shared language and close trading relations.

(5) The degree to which the mark identifies high quality goods. High quality products are more likely to become known than inferior ones.

(6) The extent of the commercial value attributed to the mark. A mark of high value is likely to be one of considerable reputation.

16.8 DEFENCES TO INFRINGEMENT

Defences to trade mark infringement protect legitimate interests in the use of a mark.

16.8.1 Use of another registered mark

It will not infringe a registered trade mark to use another mark which is registered for the goods and services for which it is registered, although it is possible that one of the marks may be declared invalid (see 16.10.6).[41]

---

40 Mostert, F, 'When is a Mark "Well Known"?' [1997] IPQ 377, and Morcom, C, 'Famous and Well Known Marks' [1997] IPQ 370.
41 Section 11(1) of the TMA 1994.

16.8.2 Use of own name

Equally, for 'a person' to use his own name or address will not infringe.[42] This is interpreted to mean use describing the person. Jacob J held in *British Sugar plc v James Robertson & Sons* (1996) that the use of the defendant's sign must be looked at in context in order to determine whether that use is descriptive.

The equivalent provision in the 1938 Act was given a wide interpretation in *Mercury Communications Ltd v Mercury Inactive Ltd* (1995). It was applied to a company and was held to include any appellation by which a person is usually known; in the case of a company that included a name by which a company was known, but was not its registered corporate title.

The TMA 1994 defence has been applied to company names. Jacob J considered s 11(2)(a) in the *Crate & Barrel* (2001) case. He held that it applied to a company name, even where the 'Ltd' was not used, and where the defendant company was using the name as a mark as well as its name. Although there was no requirement that the company's name be known before the use began, if the use was begun when the company name was unknown it might be queried whether it satisfied the proviso to the sub-section. The House of Lords observed that the better view was that 'person' included a company in *Scandecor Development AB v Scandecor Marketing AB* (2001), but said that the issue should be referred to the ECJ in the future.

It can be queried whether Jacob J's willingness to allow use of the name as a mark by a company can be reconciled with the *Windsurfing* (1999) case when the ECJ limited the descriptive use defence to non-trade mark use.

16.8.3 Descriptive use

It will not infringe to use 'indications concerning the kind, quality, quantity, intended purpose, value, geographical origin, time of production of goods and services'.[43] In the *Windsurfing* (1999) case the ECJ said that this defence served to allow descriptive, but not trade mark, use of the mark.

In *Bravado Merchandising Services Ltd v Mainstream Publishing Ltd* (1996), it was held that to use the pop group's registered name fell within s 11(2)(b) of the TMA 1994, indicating the book's main characteristic. Lord McCluskey said that the sub-section was designed to prevent trade mark law being used so restrictively as to avoid references in books or the media to such entities. Protection for the mark owner lay in the proviso.

16.8.4 Intended purpose

Using a registered mark where it is necessary to do so to indicate the intended purpose of a product or service (particularly as an accessory or spare part) does not infringe.[44]

This was considered by the ECJ in *BMW v Deenik* (1999). The Court held that it does not infringe a mark to use it to inform the public that the user carries out repair

---

42 *Ibid*, s 11(2)(a).
43 *Ibid*, s 11(2)(b).
44 *Ibid*, s 11(2)(c).

and maintenance to goods covered by the mark, or that he specialises in such activities. However, to suggest that there is a commercial connection or special relationship between the user and the mark owner, or that the user is affiliated to the owner's distribution network will infringe. The defence was stated to reconcile fundamental interests of trade mark protection with freedom to provide services in a common market in such a way that marks may fulfil their purpose in a system of undistorted competition. This suggests that if it can be shown that use of a mark falling within s 11(2)(a)–(c) can be shown to be necessary for fair competition it should be permitted.

The use of 'Independent Volvo Specialist' did infringe the VOLVO mark in *Volvo v Heritage (Leicester) Ltd* (1999) because it suggested that the user was an authorised dealer.

In *Gillette v LA-Laboratories Ltd* (2005), the ECJ held that use of a mark may be made if necessary to indicate a product's intended purpose if in practice this is the only way to provide the public with comprehensible and complete information on that purpose. Whether the use is necessary is for national courts to determine, taking into account the nature of the consumers of that product.

16.8.5   The proviso to section 11(2)

All the s 11(2) defences are subject to the proviso that the use must be 'in accordance with honest practices in industrial and commercial matters'.

Industrial and commercial practices can be objectively established as a matter of fact: *Reed Executive plc v Reed Business Information Ltd* (2002). Whether use of a mark in parody might fall within this description is a moot point.[45]

Honesty could be judged subjectively, but in *Volvo v Heritage (Leicester) Ltd* (1999) Rattee J held it to be an objective test judged by the standards of the reasonable user of that mark. He did so, following the ECJ in *BMW v Deenik* (1999), where it was stated that the user had a duty to act fairly in relation to the legitimate interests of the mark owner. In the *Reed* case the court asked whether the practice would be considered to be honest by a person in possession of all the facts. In assessing a competitor's honesty courts should take account of all relevant circumstances. Consequently aural confusion between a mark and a geographical indication used by a competitor was, alone, insufficient to deny the defence: *Gerolsteiner Brunnen v Putsch* (2004). This was a case concerning bottled water, and the ECJ ruled that consideration of relevant circumstances would include the shape and labels on the bottles before a court could conclude that the defendant 'might be regarded as unfairly competing'.

In *Gillette v LA Laboratories* (2005), the ECJ provided examples of use that would not be honest:

- if done in such a manner as to give the impression of a commercial connection with the trade mark owner;
- if it affects the value of the mark by taking unfair advantage of its distinctive character or repute;
- if it entails discrediting or denigrating the mark;

---

45 Gredley, E and Maniatis, S, 'Parody: A Fatal Attraction? Part 2: Trade Mark Parodies' [1997] EIPR 412. Parody was raised in the District Court of Amsterdam in relation to the 'Tanya Grotter' take-off of Harry Potter and found to constitute dilution. See Simon, I, 'Parodies: A Touch of Magic' [2004] EIPR 185.

- if the user's product is presented as an imitation or replica of the geuinely marked product.

A *bona fide* belief that consumers would not be deceived was held not to be sufficient if in reality they would be deceived. In *Teofani v Teofani* (1913), it was held that dishonest use had been made of the defendant's own name, where the plaintiff had a long established reputation and the defendant was taking advantage of an unusual name. The test is one of reasonable foreseeability and a trade will be expected to search national and European registers before using a name: *IBM v Web-Sphere* (2004).

The own name defence cannot be applied once a defendant is aware that the name might cause deception, as any use of the name amounting to passing off would not be in accordance with honest practice in industrial and commercial matters: *Asprey and Garrard Ltd v WRA (Guns) Ltd* (2001).

16.8.6 Local reputations

A defence to infringement is also provided for local reputations protected in particular by passing off which precede a registered trade mark.[46] These are rights which do not fall within the relative grounds of refusal under s 5(4) of the TMA 1994, but which are deemed worthy of protection. In *Chelsea Man Menswear Ltd v Chelsea Girl Ltd* (1987), the plaintiff secured a nationwide injunction against the defendant although it had shops only in London and Coventry, as the mark was recognised over a wider area.

16.9 CRIMINAL OFFENCES

Counterfeiting of trade marked goods is 'big business'. In *R v Johnstone* (2003) it was noted that counterfeit and pirated goods account for between 5% and 7% of world trade, costing the UK economy some £9 billion annually. Lord Nicholls of Birkenhead explained counterfeiting (cheap imitations of an authentic article), piracy (illicit copies not sold under the authentic version's mark) and bootlegging (unlawful records of live concert performances).

Three criminal offences are provided by the TMA 1994, the first largely aimed a counterfeiting on a commercial scale. It is an offence to apply a mark to goods with a view to gain or intent to cause loss, or to trade in, or possess goods bearing a mark in the course of business.[47] Local Authority Trading Standards Offices have a statutory duty to enforce this section.

Mens rea need not be proved (other than the mental elements specifically required by s 92(1)–(3)). The onus is on a defendant to make out the defence provided by s 92(5) by showing that he had reasonable grounds to believe that the use of the sign was not an infringement: *R v Keane* (2001). The burden of proof, on a balance of probabilities, lies on the defendant: *Sliney v London Borough of Havering* (2002).

It is not an offence if the accused's actions would not constitute an infringement. In *Johnstone* the House of Lords established that the defences to the civil remedy also apply to s 92. The respondent dealt in bootleg recordings on CD which bore the group BON JOVI's trade marked name. It was argued successfully that the conviction should

---

46 Section 11(3) of the TMA 1994.
47 *Ibid*, s 92 of the TMA 1994.

be overturned because a defence under s 11(2)(b) applied to the equivalent civil infringement. Considering the essential function of a trade mark to indicate source, the House held that this was indeed the case and that the conviction would not lie where no civil remedy was available.

In addition, making a false entry on the register, or causing one to be made is an offence, as is falsely representing that a mark is registered.[48]

16.10 REVOCATION, INVALIDITY AND ACQUIESCENCE

After registration, registered trade marks are vulnerable to both revocation and being declared to be invalid. A mark is revocable for use, or lack of use, that occurs after the registration, and imposes a burden on the proprietor not only to renew the mark at the appropriate intervals (see 15.2.1), but to supervise its use during its life. A mark is open to invalidity, on the other hand, where it should not have been registered in the first place. The grounds of invalidity mirror the absolute and relative grounds of refusal, and subsequent use can, in some instances, cure the initial defect.

Any person may make an application for revocation or a declaration of invalidity, and the application may be made either to the registrar or to the court. If proceedings are pending in relation to the mark the application must be made to the court, and the Registrar may, at any stage, refer the application to the court.[49] The registrar may initiate an application for a declaration of invalidity where the ground for objection is an application for registration made in bad faith.[50] The 1938 Act allowed only 'persons aggrieved' to make an application, and there is now the potential for vexatious applications to be made. These, however, would incur penalties in costs.

Should the application for revocation or invalidity succeed only in respect of some of the goods or services for which the mark is registered, the mark is revoked or declared invalid only in relation to those goods or services.[51]

16.10.1 Revocation

If a mark is revoked, the rights of the proprietor are deemed to cease either from the date of the application for revocation, or if the court or registrar finds that the ground for revocation existed before that date, then from that earlier date.[52] A mark may be revoked for four reasons: a lack of genuine use; non-use, use that has become generic (descriptive); or use that is misleading to the public.[53] Where the use of a mark is put in issue in any proceedings, the burden of proving use falls on the proprietor.[54]

Use of the mark in a form that differs from that registered suffices, provided that it does not alter the distinctive character of the mark.[55] Allowable alterations would

---

48 *Ibid*, ss 94 and 95.
49 *Ibid*, ss 46(4) and 47(3).
50 *Ibid*, s 47(4).
51 *Ibid*, ss 46(5), 47(5).
52 *Ibid*, s 46(6).
53 *Ibid*, s 46(1).
54 *Ibid*, s 100.
55 *Ibid*, s 46(2).

include a change of colour or lettering, for example. In *Anheuser Busch Inc v Budvar* (2002) a wide interpretation was given to s 46(2). Although the mark was registered in a highly stylised form the use of the words in block capitals constituted use as it did not detract from the central message of the mark. However, in *Safeway Stores plc v HFP* (1997) use of a mark in a way that altered its distinctive character in a significant and substantial way went too far. There, the registered marks consisted of the word 'elle' in lower case lettering within the female symbol. The use made of it was for ELLE Magazine in upper case lettering and without the logo. It was held that the logo was as least as distinctive as the lettering and that the use without the symbol altered the mark in a significant way.

Use in the UK includes affixing the mark to goods or packaging in the UK solely for export purposes.[56]

16.10.2 Revocation for non-use

There are two ways in which a lack of use of the mark by the proprietor may lead to revocation of the mark. The first is if the mark is not put to 'genuine use' in the UK by the proprietor or with his consent within five years of registration being granted in relation to the goods or services for which it is registered, and there are no 'proper reasons' for the non-use.[57] The second is that genuine use has been suspended for an uninterrupted period of five years, and there are no proper reasons for the non-use.[58]

Use as a trade mark

It is use as a trade mark that is called for: *Reef Trade Mark* (2002). In *Safari Trade Mark* (2001) it was argued that use of SAFARI as a third level identifier for a model of a LAND ROVER DISCOVERY was not use as a trade mark. It was held that this did constitute use as a trade mark. The ECJ confirmed that genuine use required trade mark use in *Ansul BV v Ajax BV* (2003), who said that the use must be consistent with the essential function of a trade mark.

It is possible that use of a mark, in a sense that is outside the source or guarantee function of a trade mark, might be regarded as non-genuine or not as trade mark use, so that the *Kodiak Trade Mark* (1990) decision would be followed under the new law. However, the preamble to the Directive does not preclude recognition of the advertising and investment function of a trade mark, which can then be regarded as genuine, particularly if judged by ordinary commercial standards. The provisions on infringement implicitly recognise these functions, as does the definition of a mark as 'distinguishing' a product (see 15.3.5). In addition, the government resisted attempts during the passage of the Trade Marks Bill to add any requirement that a trade mark be used to indicate 'a connection in the course of trade', as the old law had done.

The point was taken in *Reef Trade Mark* (2002), in relation to registration of the band's name for promotional clothing. It was held by Pumfrey J that trade mark use was required, but he pointed out that promotional and trade mark use are not mutually exclusive and that the mark may serve a dual function. The use

---

56   *Ibid*, s 46(2).
57   *Ibid*, s 46(1)(a).
58   *Ibid*, s 46(1)(b).

demonstrated in the case – a T-shirt with REEF on the left breast, but bearing the marks SCREEN STARS and FRUITS OF THE LOOM on the label – was at worst equivocal. It was not clearly used as a trade mark. However, promotional use by ELLE Magazine to endorse other manufacturers' products in *Safeway Stores plc v HFP* (1997) was not genuine use.

Use in the UK

Use outside the UK may be considered not to be sufficient use. In the *Crate & Barrel* case the American claimant company sought to show UK use by mail order sales. Jacob J said that genuine use must involve that which a trader or consumer would regard as 'real or genuine' trade in the UK, a question of degree and one involving the quantity as well as the nature of the use. Mail order sales were considered to be sales made in the US. In *Safari Trade Mark* (2001) promotion of a mark in a major national newspaper was held to be sufficient to constitute genuine UK use.

In relation to the goods or services

Where a mark is used outside the specification of goods for which it is registered this cannot amount to use 'in relation to goods for which it is registered'. In *Safari Trade Mark* (2001) it was argued that use on LAND ROVER DISCOVERY models did not constitute use for 'estate wagons' or 'estate cars', but the court took a relatively generous view of estate cars.

Another issue which Jacob J detected in the *Crate & Barrel* (2001) case, but which was not argued, is whether the alleged use was made 'in relation to the goods or services for which it is registered. There, although mail order purchases would be sent in CRATE & BARREL packaging, he thought it debatable whether this amounted to use for the goods inside the packaging, particularly where they bore their own trade marks.

For which the mark is registered

Use of a mark on products falling outside the specification for which the mark was registered may lead to revocation or partial revocation for non-use. Where partial revocation is at issue the court is not restricted to deleting some of the items for which use of the mark is specified in the registration, but may 'dig deeper': *Minerva Trade Mark* (2000). There, registration for 'printed matter' was restricted to use for stationery by partial revocation. This will not, however, justify minute analysis of the 'far from precise, clear and logical classes': *Gromax Plasticulture v DLN* (1999). The question left for courts is how far they may delve into widely defined specifications of products. In *Decon Laboratories v Fred Baker Ltd* (2001) Pumfrey J posed the question 'how should the specification of goods be narrowed to reflect the non-use?' The correct starting point was a list of articles for which the proprietor had used the mark. However, in arriving at a fair specification it was also necessary to consider the penumbra of protection conferred by s 10(2) (and (3)). To give proper protection in areas where the proprietor could demonstrate deception as to trade origin by another's use of the mark did not require a wide specification of goods because of the extra protection provided by s 10(2) (and (3).

The Court of Appeal approved this interpretation in *Thomson Holidays v Norwegian Cruise Line* (2003). The claimant used the mark FREESTYLE for package holidays, the defendant for up-market cruises. The claimant's mark was specified for use for 'cruises'. In infringement proceedings the defendant counterclaimed for revocation for non-use. The first step to determining an acceptable specification was to find as a fact what use had been made of the mark. To then decide what a fair specification was the court should limit the specification so that it reflected the circumstances of the particular trade and the way the reasonable consumer would understand the use. The claimant's use was held to be as 'package holidays' so that term was added to the specification, and all other uses within it revoked.

Genuine

The statutory language differs from the 1938 Act's lack of 'bona fide use', although the White Paper said that no change from the old test of 'substantial and genuine use judged by ordinary commercial standards' was intended. If the use was commercial, the user's motives were irrelevant: (Imperial Group v Philip Morris (1982)).

Use that is in bad faith could not be considered to be genuine use (see 15.14). However, in Reef Trade Mark (2002) a lack of a bona fide intention to use a mark was not treated as a ground for revocation.

The ECJ considered genuine use in Ansul BV v Ajax BV (2003). There the mark MINIMAX had been registered for fire extinguishers in 1971, but no further sales of the extinguishers were made after mid-1989. The mark continued to be used for components, and on invoices in relation to maintenance of the extinguishers, as well as on stickers placed on maintained appliances. It was held that genuine use was use aimed at preserving a market for the product and did not relate to internal use. This included advertising use to prepare a market for products. In assessing whether a use was genuine regard must be paid to all the facts and circumstances relevant to establishing whether the commercial exploitation of the mark was real. In particular, this meant whether maintaining or creating a share in the market for the marked product was warranted in the economic sector concerned. Relevant factors included the nature of the product, the market, and the scale and frequency of use of the mark. Use did not have to be quantitatively significant to be genuine depending on the characteristics of the relevant market. The availability of 1,200 'Safaris' was therefore genuine given the high price of the vehicle and the limited market for them: Safari Trade Mark (2001). Using a mark on spares for products no longer on the market could be genuine if the parts were integral to the nature or structure of the product. So could use for non-integral parts, after-sales service, and repair if intended to meet the needs of customers of the original product.

Proper reasons for non-use

Proper reasons for non-use might include the unavailability of raw materials, or of the goods for which the mark is registered, or even ill health of the proprietor, for example. In 'Philosophy di Alberta Ferretti' Trade Mark (2003) the Court of Appeal held that a proprietor was able to show proper reasons for non-use by 'drawing attention to the existence of obstacles to such use arising independently of the will of the proprietor'. This was based on Article 19(1) of the TRIPS Agreement 1994. Consequently, a proprietor who did virtually nothing for the five-year period and then embarked on a lengthy procedure intended to lead to products being placed on the market could not rely on ordinary commercial delays as proper reasons.

Resumption of use

A mark cannot be revoked for non-use if genuine use is commenced or resumed after the expiry of the five-year period, but before the application for revocation is made, provided that any resumption within three months of the making of an application for revocation be disregarded unless preparations for the resumption of use were begun before the proprietor became aware of the application.[59] In *Hermes Trade Mark* (1982), a mark was not expunged for non-use because orders were made for parts for the watches within the five-year period with a view to relaunching the product and not in response to the plaintiff's action for expunction.

16.10.3 Revocation for a generic mark

A trade mark proprietor with a successful and novel product runs the risk that the product's trade mark may become generally used to describe the product, so that the mark becomes generic. If a mark becomes the common name in the trade for a product or service in consequences of acts or inactivity of the proprietor, it can be revoked.[60] The onus is on the proprietor to 'police' the way the product is described in trading channels. Descriptive use by the public does not fall within the sub-section. The marks ASPIRIN, WINDSURFER and ESCALATOR have been lost in this way. It has been suggested[61] that, to avoid the danger of revocation, employees, licensees and franchisees be required to follow certain rules in all publicity material, advertising, labelling, business documentation and even internal memoranda. These include:

- that the mark be distinguished from surrounding text;
- used only as an adjective and not a noun or verb;
- that prominent indication that the mark is registered or licensed be made;
- that a company or business name be used to identify the overall business of a company or individual;
- that use by any other person be immediately reported to the proprietor.

The dangers of using a mark in conjunction with another established and well known mark are illustrated by the Austrian Supreme Court ruling that WALKMAN had become generic in *SONY WALKMAN Trade Mark* (2000). Using WALKMAN thus may well have contributed to a perception of 'Walkman' as a descriptive term. The danger of genericisation is particularly acute if the product is the first of its kind. The onus lies squarely on a mark's proprietor to actively defuse any such perception developing. The Austrian Supreme Court did not look for fault on the proprietor's part. However, the Court noted that use of the mark by the proprietor to designate products in advertising; remaining inactive despite the fact that development of descriptive use of the mark should have been appreciated; or abstaining from defensive measures if descriptive use did develop could be significant.

---

59 *Ibid*, s 46(3).
60 *Ibid*, s 46(1)(c).
61 Annand, R and Norman, H, *Blackstone's Guide to the Trade Marks Act 1994* (London: Blackstone, 1994).

16.10.4 Revocation for use that is liable to mislead

Use of the mark made by the proprietor, or with his consent, in relation to the goods or services for which it is registered, which is liable to mislead the public, particularly in relation to the nature, quality, or geographical origin of those goods or services.[62] It is use stemming from the proprietor that is taken into account, although there is no requirement that it be blameworthy. *In Bostitch Trade Mark* (1963), licensing without effective quality control was ground for expunction under the TMA 1938, as was trafficking in a mark in *Re American Greetings Corp's Application* (1984). The TMA 1994, however, allows for partial assignment of trade marks, and there are no statutory controls over assignment, licensing, or other use with the proprietor's consent, and provision is made for co-ownership of marks. All these practices are potentially misleading or confusing if trade origin is significant to the purchasing public. The White Paper suggested that assignments and licensing without quality controls, as well as character merchandising, could lead to revocation in extreme cases.

16.10.5 Use by a licensee

Section 46 relates to use by the mark's proprietor or with his consent. The TMA 1994 allows use by any licensee to be taken into consideration and not just that by a registered user. Questions arise where the use by a licensee is not subject to quality control by the licensor. Consequently, use with consent is deemed use by the proprietor for the purposes of s 46(1)(a) and (b). It can be reconciled with the distinguishing function of a mark by s 46(1)(d), which provides for revocation if the use is deceptive.

The question of control is therefore relevant to s 46(1)(d). In *Scandecor Developments AB v Scandecor Marketing AB* (2001) the House of Lords considered the full history of trade mark licensing. Their lordships recognised that use by a licensee might mislead. Lord Nicholls said that the mere fact that during a bare licence the fact that some customers associate the mark with the licensee was necessarily misleading. However, once the licence terminated the position might differ, particularly if the licensee continued in business, although without using the mark, which had reverted to its proprietor. Whether this was deceptive would depend on the facts of the case, decided at the time of the proceedings. The House of Lords held that customers rely on the self interest of the mark owner for quality assurance, understanding that a mark indicates that products come from the mark owner or someone acting on his behalf. This was followed in *Safari Trade Mark* (2001).

However, as the parties in *Scandecor* (2001) reached agreement no reference to the ECJ was made, and guidance is sorely needed.

16.10.6 Invalidity

A mark may be declared invalid on the ground that it was registered in breach of either the absolute or relative grounds of refusal.[63] Where the objection lies in the absolute grounds of refusal relating to s 3(1)(b)–(d) of the TMA 1994, however,

---

62   Section 46(1)(d) of the TMA 1994.
63   *Ibid*, s 47(1), (2).

distinctiveness acquired after registration will prevent revocation. There will be no declaration of invalidity on the relative grounds where the proprietor of the earlier mark or earlier right has consented to registration. Use conditions must also be met for the earlier mark.[64] If a mark is declared invalid to any extent, the registration shall be deemed never have been made to that extent, but past and closed transactions shall not be affected.[65] The registration of a mark does raise, however, a *prima facie* presumption of the validity of that mark.[66] The onus thus initially falls on the attacker to make out a case for a mark's invalidity, although it is for the proprietor then to show that subsequent use has bestowed distinctiveness on the mark: *British Sugar plc v James Robertson & Sons* (1996).

Considering invalidity in relation to a Community Trade Mark in *Decon Laboratories v Fred Baker Ltd* (2001) the question arose whether registration of a mark without a *bona fide* intention to use it across the width of the specification of goods was invalid. Pumfrey J stressed the desirability of consistency between the OHIM and UK courts on the question of bad faith. Accordingly, he adopted the narrow concept of bad faith applied in *Trillium Trade Mark* (2000) (see 15.14.2). This meant that it would be improbable that a decision as to the width of the specification of goods would lack good faith.

Following *Gromax Plasticulture v DLN* (1999) it is likely that a similar interpretation of bad faith will be applied to national marks (see 15.14).

16.10.7 Acquiescence

Acquiescence does not constitute a defence to allegations of trade mark infringement, but does prevent seeking of a declaration of invalidity, or opposition to use of the mark in relation to the goods or services for which it is registered.

If an earlier trade mark or earlier right owner acquiesces for a continuous period of five years to use of a registered trade mark in the UK, that earlier right ceases to entitle its owner to seek a declaration of invalidity or to oppose use of a mark, unless the mark was applied for in bad faith (see 15.14).[67] The possibility of revocation of the registered mark remains open to the earlier right owner and the proprietor of the later registered mark is unable, by virtue of the earlier right owner's acquiescence, to oppose the use of the earlier right, even though it may not be used against his registered mark.[68]

'Acquiescence' is not defined by the statute, but the preamble to the Directive refers to the right owner having 'knowingly tolerated' the use for a 'substantial' length of time. It was held in *Daimlerchrysler AG v Alevi* (2001) that it is an essential component of acquiescence that the failure of the claimant to act should have induced the defendant to believe that the wrong was being assented to.

The question is raised[69] as to which party should bear the burden of proof of establishing that the prior right owner has been aware of the later use. Although,

---

64   *Ibid*, s 47(2A).
65   *Ibid*, s 47(6).
66   *Ibid*, s 72.
67   *Ibid*, s 48.
68   *Ibid*, s 48(2).
69   Annand, R and Norman, H, *Blackstone's Guide to the Trade Marks Act 1994* (London: Blackstone, 1994).

logically, it should fall on the party seeking to rely on acquiescence, this would be difficult to discharge. It could be held that evidence of widespread use in the appropriate geographical and market area raises a presumption of awareness to be rebutted by proof of lack of knowledge, although this, too, may be difficult to establish. The common law approach to acquiescence gives the court a broad discretion: *Taylors Fashions Ltd v Liverpool Victoria Trustees Co Ltd* (1982).

16.11 THREATS

Section 21 of the TMA 1994 provides a remedy for any person aggrieved against some groundless threats of trade mark infringement proceedings. Threats of proceedings relating to the application of the marks to goods or their packaging, importation of goods, or packaging of goods, to which the mark has been applied, or the supply of services under the mark do not fall within this remedy. The person may seek a declaration that the threat is unjustifiable, an injunction against continued threats and damages, unless the defendant shows that the acts in respect of which the threats were made would constitute infringement. If the threat is justified, the remedy continues to lie if the claimant can establish that the mark is invalid or liable to be revoked. Mere notification that a trade mark is registered, or that an application to register has been made does not constitute a threat. This section was included in response to complaints of intimidation being made by large companies against small traders. The section may prevent solicitors writing the usual letters when there is also an allegation of passing off.

That the courts are willing to interpret 'threatens' widely was illustrated by the case of *L'Oreal (UK) Ltd v Johnson & Johnson* (2000). Infringement proceedings had been brought against the claimant in Ireland, and it sought assurance that similar proceedings would not be brought in England. The defendant's solicitors replied that their client was reserving the right to sue but went on to say that no decision had been made, that others had desisted from using the words 'No Tears' on their packaging, and that they had six years in which to bring proceedings, and so could give no such assurance. Lightman J said that the letter was 'the work of a master of Delphic utterances' conveying an enigmatic message with the effect of a threat, although disclaiming to be so. It was reasonably read as a threat by the claimant.

Further Reading

Blakeney, M, '"Well Known" Marks' [1994] EIPR 481

Campbell (Lord) and Yaqub, Z, *The European Handbook on Advertising Law* (London: Cavendish Publishing, 1999)

Carboni, A, 'Confusion Clarified' [1998] EIPR 107

Corneau, T and Linehan, S, 'Such Great Names as these: Protection of Famous Trade Marks under the Canadian Trade Marks Act' [1995] EIPR 531

Dawson, N, 'Famous and Well Known Trade Marks – "Usurping a Corner of the Giant's Robe"' [1998] IPQ 350

Fitzgerald, D, 'Comparative Advertising in the UK' [1997] EIPR 709

Gielen, C, 'A Benelux Perspective' [1998] EIPR 109

Gielen, C, 'European Trade Mark Legislation: The Statements' [1996] EIPR 83

Gredley, E and Maniatis, S, 'Parody: A Fatal Attraction? Part 2: Trade Mark Parodies' [1997] EIPR 412

Griffiths, A, 'The Impact of the Global Appreciation Approach on the Boundaries of Trade Mark Protection' [2001] IPQ 326

Jaffey, P, 'Likelihood of Association' [2002] EIPR 3

Kamperman Sanders, A, 'The Return to *Wagamama*' [1996] EIPR 521

Lindsey, M and Chacksfield, M, 'Exhaustion of Rights and Wrongs: Section 92 of the Trade Marks Act 1994; Recent Developments and Comment' [2003] EIPR 388

Martino, T, *Trade Mark Dilution* (Oxford: Clarendon Press, 1996)

McCormick, J, 'The Future of Comparative Advertising' [1998] EIPR 41

Montagnon, R, '"Strong" Marks Make More Goods "Similar"' [1998] EIPR 401

Morcom, C, 'Famous and Well Known Marks' [1997] IPQ 370

Mostert, F, 'When is a Mark "Well Known"?' [1997] IPQ 377

Norman, H, 'Time to Blow the Whistle on Trade Mark Use?' [2004] IPQ 1

Norman, H, '*Davidoff v Gofkid*: Dealing with the Logical Lapse or Creating European Disharmony?' [2003] EIPR 342

Prescott, P, 'Analysis - Infringement of Registered Trade Marks: Always a Hypothetical Comparison?' [1997] IPQ 121

Richardson, M, 'Copyright in Trade Marks? On Understanding Trade Mark Dilution', [2000] IPQ 66

Simon, I, 'Parodies: A Touch of Magic' [2004] EIPR 185

Torremans, P, 'The Likelihood of Association of Trade Marks: An Assessment in the Light of the Recent Case Law of the Court of Justice' [1998] IPQ 295

Willimsky, S, 'Comparative Advertising: an Overview' [1996] EIPR 649

CHAPTER 17

PROPERTY AND DEALINGS IN MARKS AND DOMAIN NAME DISPUTES

17.1   PROPERTY IN MARKS

A registered trade mark is personal property. In Scotland a mark is incorporeal immoveable property.[1] On registration, the mark is granted to the applicant as the mark's proprietor, and marks may be jointly owned, each owner having an equal undivided share.[2]

17.2   DEALINGS IN MARKS

National trade marks may be assigned, bequeathed or transferred by operation of law in the same way as other personal or moveable property. They may also be the subject of a security. Unlike passing off, there is no need for a trade mark assignment to be accompanied by a transfer of goodwill in the business to which it is applied.[3]

A register is maintained by the Registrar of assignments of a trade mark, or any right in a mark, the grant of licences for a mark, and the grant of any security over a mark or any right in or under it.[4] A transaction is ineffective against a person acquiring a conflicting interest in ignorance of it until an application for registration of the transaction has been made, nor can damages or an account of profits be awarded for any infringement after the date of the transaction before the transaction is registered.[5]

17.2.1   Assignment

Assignments must be in writing and signed.[6] Details of the assignment (assignation) are then registrable.

Assignment may be partial, limited to only some of the goods or services for which the mark is registered, or to use of the mark in a particular manner or location.[7] This is not the case for a Community Trade Mark. According to the doctrine of unity these may only be dealt with in their entirety and for the whole area of the EU.

If either a national or Community mark is assigned the use then made of it must not mislead the public, particularly as to the nature, quality or geographical origin of the specified goods or services.[8]

---

1   Section 22 of the Trade Marks Act (TMA) 1994.
2   *Ibid*, s 23(1).
3   *Ibid*, s 24(1).
4   *Ibid*, s 25.
5   *Ibid*, s 25(3), (4).
6   *Ibid*, s 24(3).
7   *Ibid*, s 24(2).
8   *Ibid*, s 46; Article 50 Community Trade Mark Regulation.

17.2.2   Licensing

Marks may be licensed, the licence amounting to authority to use the mark in the manner determined by the licence. A licence does not confer any property right.

Licences to use a trade mark may be general or limited in the same way as assignment, divided by product, territory or manner of use of the mark. Licences are not effective unless in writing and signed.[9]

An exclusive licensee has the same rights and remedies within the terms of the licence as if the licence had been an assignment and may bring proceedings in his own name: s 31(1) of the Trade marks Act (TMA) 1994. Other licensees may call on the proprietor to take proceedings.[10]

Licences for Community Trade Marks may also be divided.[11] Licensing is subject to the provisions for revocation where use of the mark becomes misleading,[12] and also to competition law.

17.3   MERCHANDISING MARKS

If the function of a trade mark were solely to identify the origin of a product there could be no scope for allowing another producer to use it. It is primarily because of the origin function that 'eternal' protection for a mark is possible: while the mark continues to identify trade origin there can be no public interest in allowing it to fall back into the public domain. However, if the proprietor continues to control the quality of the marked product and the guarantee function is the main purpose for indicating origin some licensing of the mark to other producers does not frustrate the trade mark function. This is particularly so where the consuming public understands the market practice of merchandising. Unrestricted licensing could still undermine the origin and guarantee functions (see 15.1.3). Character merchandising by trade mark therefore requires a careful balance between trade mark functions and licensing controls.

17.3.1   Trade Marks Act 1938

The 1938 Act prohibited 'trafficking' in trade marks (registering and dealing in marks as a commodity), which restricted the use of trade mark registration to support character merchandising. In *American Greeting Corp's Application* (1984), an American company licensed the use of the name and figure of the HOLLY HOBBIE character to other manufacturers. The company applied for registration of the mark in 12 classes, with user agreements and quality control terms. The *Exxon* case (1982) (see 8.2.1) caused a switch to trade marks as a vehicle of protection when it made the limits of copyright in this sphere of merchandising clear. The House of Lords refused these applications as trafficking in the mark. Lord Brightman held that, despite the lack of a definition of 'trafficking' in the 1938 Act, a trade mark could not be dealt with as a

---

9   *Ibid*, s 28.
10 *Ibid*, s 30(2).
11 Article 22, Community Trade Mark Regulation.
12 Section 46 of the TMA 1994.

commodity in its own right, as it would be contrary to the public interest to use the mark in a manner otherwise than to indicate the origin of goods. When a licence was granted, therefore, it was necessary that there be a connection between the goods of the licensor and the licensee. He doubted the adequacy of the quality control provisions in the licence, on the facts, to constitute such a connection. He did note that character merchandising was widespread and probably harmless, not deceiving anyone, but this could not assist in giving meaning to 'trafficking'. Lord Bridge agreed in the result, but took the view that s 28(6) of the TMA 1938 was an anachronism exposing character merchandisers to piracy.

17.3.2   Trade Marks Act 1994

The prohibition on trafficking was abolished by the TMA 1994, as was the outdated system of registered users, making licensing and assignment simpler, and available to character merchandisers. The White Paper recognised that the public understood and was not confused by the practice of goods and services being supplied by licensees of a trade mark owner, and that the strongest control over the use of a mark is a proprietor of the mark's self interest in exercising control.

Only registered licensees will be able to bring proceedings.[13] Registration is only for signs (see 15.3.2) and the White Paper considered the argument that character merchandising should not be a trade mark matter as characters are neither trade marks, nor used to indicate origin, but are enhancements of goods, normally a matter of copyright or design protection. Trade mark registration has the potential to be used to extend these more temporally restricted rights indefinitely. This fear is largely unjustified in the face of the short-term appeal of much character merchandising. Constructing a framework which could distinguish between straightforward character merchandising of a cartoon character, for example, with no independent role as a trade mark, the practice of decorating goods in the KODAK manner (see 15.1.3) and cases where a trade mark both distinguishes and decorates goods was considered too difficult without creating a new right of defined duration. As the dangers in practice were not considered to be great, trade mark registration has been extended to this field. The streamlined application procedure, allowance for multiclass applications and the new definition of a mark, should enhance use of trade mark registration in character merchandising. That there are limits, however, imposed by the nature of a trade mark, is clear from the refusal of applications for registration of depictions of the late Princess of Wales, made in order to prevent unauthorised merchandising of her character, on the ground that she was a historical figure and not a commercial brand, particularly as there was no large scale trading on the image already being undertaken.[14]

The House of Lords traced the development of licensing and assignment in *Scandecor Development AB v Scandecor Marketing AB* (2002). Their lordships acknowledged a significant change in UK law in that consumers now rely on a proprietor's self interest in maintaining quality, and assumed that the proprietor had chosen suitable licensees and imposed suitable terms. Their lordships did not rely on any legal requirement of quality control by proprietors. However, the House referred

---

13   *Ibid*, s 25(3).
14   1999, *The Times*, 5 February.

the question whether a bare licence (free of quality control provision) was liable to mislead to the ECJ. It is perhaps unfortunate that this reference did not go forward to the ECJ as the parties reached agreement.

17.4   EXHAUSTION

Section 12 of the TMA 1994 provides for exhaustion of the trade mark right. Once marked goods have been put on the market within the EEA by the proprietor or with his consent no use of the mark in relation to *those* goods will infringe the mark.

17.5   TRADEMARKS AND COMMUNITY LAW

In the early years of the Community, the European Court was sceptical of the merits of trademarks, describing them as little more than an aid to advertising. In *Sirena v Eda* (1971) the Court expressed the view that 'the debt which society owes to the 'inventor' of the name 'Prep Good Morning' is certainly not of the same nature, to say the least, as that which humanity owes to the discoverer of penicillin 'before the debt'.[15] However, in the early 1990s, in the *HAG* cases,[16] the Court recognised the utility of trademarks to the consumer and highlighted their *essential function* as a guarantee of the origin of the goods (see below).

17.5.1   The 'exhaustion of rights' principle

The doctrine of exhaustion has already been discussed in Chapter 1. The doctrine was first applied to trademarks in *Centrafarm BV v Winthrop BV* (1974). The European Court said that the specific subject matter of a trade mark is 'the guarantee that the owner of the trade mark has the exclusive right to use that trademark, for the purposes of putting products protected by the mark into circulation for the first time'. Winthrop was a Dutch subsidiary of Sterling group and Centrafarm bought and imported into the Netherlands drugs made by another company in the Sterling group in the UK. The Court held that Winthrop could not exercise its rights under its Dutch trade mark to prevent the import of drugs from the UK which had been marketed there by another company in the same group because the trade mark right had been exhausted in the UK.

The principle of exhaustion is articulated in Article 7(1) of the Trade Mark Directive, which provides that:

> The trade mark shall not entitle the proprietor to prohibit its use in relation to goods which have been put on the market in the Community under that trade mark by the proprietor or with his consent.

Article 7(2) provides an exception to the principle of exhaustion.

---

15   Para 17.
16   Case 192/73 *Van Zuylen Bros v Hag Ag (HAG I)* [1974] 2 CMLR 127 and Case C10/89 *Cnl-Sucal NV SA v Hag GF AG (HAG II)* [1990] ECR I–3711, [1990] 3 CMLR 571.

> ... where there exist legitimate reasons for the proprietor to oppose further commercialisation of the goods, especially where the condition of the goods is changed or impaired after they have been put on the market.

In circumstances where the proprietor uses different trade marks in Member States, the removal of one trade mark and its replacement with another does not fall within Article 7 of the Trade Marks Directive and is considered under Articles 28 and 30 of the EC Treaty. In *Centrafarm BV v American Home Products Corp* (1978) Centrafarm bought drugs marked 'Serenid' in the UK but marketed them using the trademark 'Seresta' in Holland. Both marks were owned by American Home Products (AHP). The European Court held that AHP could not rely on its Dutch trade mark to prevent parallel imports if it could be shown to be using several trade marks for an identical product because its use of several trade marks was intended to divide the common market artificially, thus causing a disguised restriction on trade between Member States in terms of Article 28.[17]

17.5.2 Repackaging

Numerous cases have arisen in national courts where a parallel importer has obtained goods and repackaged them in order to sell them in other Member States and comply with variations in national standards.

In *Merck Sharp v Paranova* (2002)[18] Advocate General Jacobs offers a definition of 'repackaging' as follows:

> I would note at this point that in this Opinion I use the term 'repackaging' in general to refer globally to all the above types of operation, namely over-stickering with the trade mark, reboxing with the trade mark and reboxing without the trade mark, except where the context makes it clear that a more specific meaning is intended.

The owner of a trade mark might argue that it has exhausted its trade mark in relation to goods in their original packaging, but not so in relation to the repackaged goods. A parallel importer might argue, however, that the goods were put into circulation with the consent of the trade mark owner who cannot subsequently impede their free circulation within the Community, even if the goods were repackaged.

As mentioned earlier, the European Court has stressed the value of trade marks to the consumer, recognising their essential function as a guarantee of the origin of the goods. Trade mark infringements can occur, however, where third parties repackage or rebrand goods. The holder of the trade mark may have exhausted its right by first putting the goods on the market so that it cannot prohibit third parties from engaging in rebranding and repackaging the product. The issue was considered in *Hoffmann-La Roche v Centrafarm* (1978). Hoffmann-La Roche brought an action for infringement of its German trade mark. Centrafarm had obtained drugs in the UK which had been repackaged to meet German packing regulations and subsequently sold on the German market. Hoffmann-La Roche argued that it could rely on its trademark because it had not applied the trademark to the repackaged goods. The European Court stated that the essential function of a trademark:

---

17 See also Case C–379/97 *Pharmacia and Upjohn v Paranova A/S* [1999] ECR I–6927, [2000] 1 CMLR 51.

18 See para 7.

... is to guarantee to the identity of the origin of the trade-market product to the consumer or ultimate user, by enabling him without any possibility of confusion to distinguish that product from products which have another origin. This guarantee of origin means that the consumer of ultimate user can be certain that a trade-marked product which is sold to him has not been subject at a previous stage of marketing to interference by a third person, without the authorisation of the proprietor of the trademark, such as to affect the original condition of the product.[19]

In addition, in *HAG II* (1990), the essential functioning of a trade mark as a guarantee of origin to the consumer was central to the Court's judgment:

Consequently, as the Court has ruled on numerous occasions, the specific subject-matter of trade marks is in particular to guarantee to the proprietor of the trade mark that he has the right to use that trade mark for the purpose of putting a product into circulation of the first time and therefore to protect him against competitors wishing to take advantage of the status and reputation of the trade mark by selling products illegally bearing that mark. In order to determine the exact scope of this right exclusively conferred on the owner of the trade mark, regard must be had to the essential function of the trade mark, which is to guarantee the identity of the origin of the market product to the consumer or ultimate user by enabling him without any possibility of confusion to distinguish that product from products which another origin.[20]

In *Merck Sharp & Dohme v Paranova* (2002), the European Court held in an Article 234 reference that repackaging of a product was objectively necessary where access to a market, or a substantial part thereof, was impeded due to consumer inertia toward relabelled goods. Advocate General Jacobs pointed out:

There may exist on a market, or on a substantial part of it, such strong resistance from a significant proportion of consumers to relabelled pharmaceutical products that there must be held to be a hindrance to effective market access. In those circumstances, repackaging of the pharmaceutical products would not be explicable solely by the attempt to secure a commercial advantage. The purpose would be to achieve effective market access. It is for the national court to determine whether that is the case. The answer to the question referred must therefore be that replacement packaging of pharmaceutical products is objectively necessary within the meaning of the Court's case law if, without such repackaging, effective access to the market concerned, or to a substantial part of that market, must be considered to be hindered as the result of strong resistance from a significant proportion of consumers to relabelled pharmaceutical products.[21]

It was for the national court to determine when that was the case.

17.5.3   International exhaustion

The question of exhaustion of rights where the trade marked goods are marketed *outside* the EEA has attracted considerable controversy in recent years. The issue was

---

19 See para 7, Case 102/77 *Hoffmann-la Roche & Co AG and Hoffmann-la Roche AG v Centrafarm Vertriebsgesellschaft Pharmazeutischer Erzeugnisse mbH* [1978] ECR 1139, [1978] CMLR 217.
20 See para 14, Case C10/89 *Cnl-Sucal NV SA v Hag GF AG* [1990] ECR I–3711, [1990] 3 CMLR 571.
21 See paras 31–33, Case C-443/99 *Merck Sharp and Dohme GmbH v Paranova Pharmazeutika Handels GmbH* [2002] ECR I–3704, [2002] 2 CMLR 623.

raised in *Silhouette* (1999). Silhouette brought a trade mark action to prevent parallel imports into Austria of spectacle frames that it had sold in Bulgaria. According to Austrian trademark law, Silhouette exhausted its rights by placing them on the market voluntarily – no distinction was made in Austrian law between sales within the EU and sales outside the EU. Silhouette had made it clear to the buyer in Bulgaria that the frames were not be sold anywhere else other than Bulgaria and the former USSR. A third party obtained supplies of the frames and subsequently sold them in Austria. The question for the European Court was whether Article 7(1) of the Trade Mark Directive prevented Member States from providing for international exhaustion in respect of products put on the market outside the Community. The European Court held that Community law, in the form of the Directive, precluded national laws from providing for international exhaustion. Thus, all Member States must recognise the right of a trade mark proprietor to prohibit its use in relation to goods which it has first put on the market outside the EEA. National rules providing for international exhaustion were therefore contrary to Article 7(1) of the Directive and Silhouette could prevent the sale in Austria of the sunglasses first marketed in Bulgaria. The Court stated that differences in national treatment of international exhaustion would mean that:

> ... the same products could be the subject of parallel imports into one Member State but not into another , a result incompatible with the internal market.[22]

The immediate effect of the decision was to exclude cheap imports from the Community and the Court was heavily criticised by consumer associations and parallel importers. Not surprisingly, trademark owners were relieved the ECJ had rejected a rule of international exhaustion. Despite the criticism directed at it, the Court confirmed the *Silhouette* ruling in *Sebago* (1999).

Sebago brought an action against GB-Unic to prevent the parallel import of shoes from El Salvador. The European Court rejected GB-Unic's argument that, since Sebago had put identical shoes on the market within the Community, it had exhausted its rights in relation to all such shoes, wherever they were marketed. The European Court held at paragraph 22 that Article 7(1) of the Trade Mark Directive should be interpreted to the effect that the rights conferred by the trade mark are exhausted only if the products have been put on the market in the Community, and that such consent must relate to each individual item of the product in respect of which exhaustion is pleaded.

17.5.4 *Zino Davidoff/Levi Strauss v Tesco*

In a series of cases which arose in the English courts following the *Silhouette* decision, several parallel importers argued that 'consent' within the meaning of *Silhouette* and *Sebago* could in fact be implied. The *Silhouette* decision was particularly criticised in *Zino Davidoff*[23] by Laddie J before he referred the case to the European Court under Article 234. Levi Strauss and Zino Davidoff SA were manufacturers of Levi's jeans and Davidoff Cool Water cosmetic products. Both companies owned registered trade marks relating to their goods. Levi Strauss distributed its goods in the UK directly or

---

22 Para 42 of Advocate General Jacob's decision delivered on 29 January 1998.
23 The opinion of Laddie J can be found at para 36 in *Zino Davidoff SA v A&G Imports Ltd* [2000] Ch 127 Ch D.

through selected licensed retailers. Levi jeans tended to be more expensive than in the US. Zino Davidoff distributed its goods under an exclusive distribution contract with a company based in Singapore which included various restrictive resale covenants. Tesco and Costco, both based in the UK, made repeated requests to become authorised Levi's distributors but were refused. Tesco and Costco subsequently obtained Levi Strauss jeans from parallel traders in the United States and began selling them in their UK stores at a substantially reduced price. A & G Imports also engaged in parallel trade of Davidoff cosmetics, purchasing them in Singapore from authorised sellers. Levi Strauss and Zino Davidoff commenced an action in the High Court against the parallel importers for infringement of their trade marks in the UK. The High Court requested a preliminary ruling from the European Court under Article 234 on a number of questions relating to the interpretation of the Trade Mark Directive, in particular the interpretation of the trade mark proprietor's 'consent' under Article 7(1) and of the 'legitimate reasons' for his objection under Article 7(2).

Laddie J noted that that there was a strong argument for limiting the scope of Article 7(1) and the *Silhouette* case as far as possible:

> One of the effects of article 7(1), as construed by the Court of Justice in the Silhouette case, is that a proprietor can put himself in a position to demand that his goods which have been marked by him with a trade mark for the purpose of accurately identifying their origin must be stripped of that marking when they enter the EEA Those who trade in the imported goods can be prevented by trade mark law from stating the truth about their origin and authenticity. They can be prevented from selling them on in exactly the condition in which they were placed on the market by the proprietor. In other words, trade mark law can be used to prevent the marks from performing their primary function of telling the truth about the origin of goods. Worse than that, if the importer in the goods removes the proprietor's mark and applies another mark instead, he lays himself open, at least under English law, to an action for passing off.

According to Laddie J, the effect of *Silhouette* is to give a trade mark proprietor the power to be able to exclude goods from the EEA regardless of which mark they bear, thus forcing the importer to sell the goods without a trade mark. There are a number of situations where this will render goods virtually unsellable, in particular in the fashion industry. In conclusion, Laddie J said:

> … the *Silhouette* case has bestowed on a trade mark owner a parasitic right to interfere with the distribution of goods which bears little or no relationship to the proper function of the trade mark right. It is difficult to believe that a properly informed legislature intended such a result, even if it is the proper construction of article 7(1) of the Directive. It seems to me that the *Silhouette* case allows the proprietor of goods placed on the market outside the EEA to retain the ability, by using trade mark rights, to object to those goods being imported into the EEA.

However, neither *Silhouette* nor *Sebago* suggest how the proprietor might lodge an objection to such trade. The idea that Community law creates a presumption that a proprietor shall be taken to object to uncontrolled distribution of goods which have been sold on the open market outside the EEA unless he expressly consents to such further distribution, was in Laddie J's opinion, unfounded.

Although the European Court did not address the competition law issues it did confirm the Community-wide regime of exhaustion. In a surprisingly brief decision the Court held in favour of Levi Strauss and Davidoff, stating that in terms of Article 7(1) 'consent must be so expressed that an intention to renounce [trade mark] rights is unequivocally demonstrated'. Significantly, the Court held that silence on the part of the trade mark holder is insufficient to amount to consent.[24] The Court considered it irrelevant that the importer was unaware that the trade mark owner objected to the placing of the goods on the EEA market or to their sale through unauthorised agents. It was also irrelevant that authorised sellers knowingly failed to impose contractual restrictions reflecting the proprietor's objections upon subsequent purchasers.[25] The Court therefore considered it unnecessary to discuss the national court's question concerning Article 7(2) of the Directive.

Exhaustion

The implications of the Court's decision were significant. First, the decision confirms the position of trademark holders in terms of exercising extensive control over the distribution of their products bearing their trade mark. Fundamental questions were also raised about the function of Community competition policy vis-à-vis trade mark rights but these were not considered. The Court's decision meant intrabrand price competition in the Community market was impeded and prevented consumers in the Community from obtaining the same trade-marked products at the same price as their American and Asian counterparts. Thus, the decision limits the potential application of the Community competition rules because of the affirmation of the rights of any trade mark owner and reduces the need for trademark owners to devise complex contractual arrangements to control the distribution chain outside the EU. The Court's analysis focused only on the specific subject matter of the rights conferred by a trade mark and omitted to consider commercial, consumer or trade interests altogether. In strict legal terms, the Court's interpretation of the Trade Mark Directive may be correct, yet it is surprisingly short-sighted for an institution which has previously championed the interests of consumers.[26] The implications for international trade are also obvious. So why did the Court focus on the interests of trade mark holders and omit to consider any of the consumer functions of trade marks? The answer clearly lies in the territorial nature of trade marks. Certainly, the Court appears reluctant to move away from an analysis of the function of trade marks based on specific national territories. However, the final outcome of this controversial case may be a change in Community policy since many Member States are clamouring for a change to the current Community-wide trade mark exhaustion regime. In a recent working paper on the possible abuses of trade mark rights within the EU in the context of Community exhaustion, the Commission considered a number of cases involving alleged abuses of trade mark rights. In preparing the report, the Commission carried out an investigation into various subject areas, paying particular attention to the competition issues and concluded that no deficiencies in the current legal provisions were found.[27]

---

24 Paras 47 and 53.
25 Para 66.
26 Joined Cases 56 and 58/64 *Consten & Grundig v European Commission* [1966] ECR 299 in which the Court attributed equal importance to intrabrand competition as it did to interbrand competition.
27 Commission Staff Working Paper on possible abuses of trade mark rights within the EU in the context of Community exhaustion, available on the Europa website, 21 May 2003.

However, there continues to be considerable debate about the overall economic and legal consequences of different trade mark exhaustion regimes.

Competition law and trade mark theory

The interface between competition and fundamental trade mark theory is complex. Trade mark owners may have a monopoly on the distribution of their goods bearing their trade mark in a particular territory, leading to higher prices and inefficiencies associated with monopolistic practices. On the other hand, parallel importation encourages intrabrand competition and therefore counteracts the effects of monopoly. *Tesco's* parallel importation of Levi Strauss jeans allowed UK consumers to buy jeans at considerably lower prices than at authorised dealer outlets, thus eliminating any price discrimination between consumers in the US and UK.

Trade mark owners object to parallel importation for a number of reasons. First, they cite the free rider argument, alleging that parallel traders free ride on the investments of authorised dealers in terms of marketing and customer service. Secondly, trade mark owners allege that parallel importation causes confusion for consumers. Manufacturers are allowed to market their products in such a way which enables the consumer to identify the company that produces them. In turn, identification with a product helps consumers to determine the quality of a product and allows them to make a qualitative assessment. Trade mark owners are therefore encouraged to produce high-quality goods, and provide good customer service in order to develop a brand image. If parallel traders free ride on the investments of authorised dealers trade mark owners are forced to lower their prices, thus potentially damaging the consumer image of high-end brands. The third argument against parallel importation centres on the right of trade mark owners to manage the image of their products and hence control distribution channels.

17.5.5   Doctrine of common origin

The so-called 'common origin' principle was established in the *Café Hag (HAG I)* case. The principle prevents trade mark owners from bringing infringement proceedings against the goods of *other* manufacturers bearing the same mark if the marks once had a 'common origin'. The doctrine has been controversial. In *HAG I* the ownership of the trade marks had fallen into the hands of different, independent parties during the Second World War. Hag AG, a German company, owned the trade mark 'Hag' in Germany, Belgium and Luxembourg. Its property was later sequestrated and its trade mark assigned to Van Zuylen. The European Court was asked to consider where Van Zuylen could prevent Hag AG from importing coffee into Belgium. Clearly, consent was lacking in the circumstances, yet the European Court decided that:

> ... one cannot allow the holder of a trade mark to rely upon the exclusiveness of a trade mark right-which may have the consequence of the territorial limitation of national markets-with a view to prohibiting the marketing of a Member States of goods legally produced in another Member State under an identical trade mark having the same origin.

The European Court was criticised for prioritising single market integration over intellectual property rights and the interests of producers and consumers. The judgment meant that goods from unrelated sources could bear the same trade mark, creating confusion for consumers. Recognising these failures, in an unprecedented step, the European Court overruled its decision in *HAG 1* in *Cnl-Sucal v Hag GF AG (HAG II)* (1990) in 1990. The Court held that the owner of a trade mark could rely in its national rights to exclude the products of a third party with which the trade mark holder had no economic links, even where the products bore a trade mark which had a 'common origin' with its own mark. Once again, the use of the 'Hag' trademark was a source of disagreement, although this time the determining factor for the European Court was the absence of any consent on the part of the trade mark owner. In a significant departure from *HAG I*, the Court emphasised the importance of trade marks and in particular their vital role in guaranteeing the origin of the goods. At paragraph 13 the Court said that trade marks 'constitute an essential element of the system of competition which the Treaty aims to establish and maintain'.

The Court's decision in *IHT Internationale Heiztechnik v Ideal Standard* (1994) all but confirms the end of the common origin doctrine in Community law. The Court stated that a trade mark owner *could* rely on its national rights to exclude the products of a third party with which the trade mark holder had no links and that this would be the case where the trade marks with a common origin had fallen into separate hands through *voluntary* action. This contrasts with the position in the *HAG* cases, where the government had intervened to separate the trade marks.

17.5.6 Trade mark licensing and Community law

Trade mark licences are a fundamental part of franchising and distribution agreements. The Commission's principal trade mark decisions in *Campari* and *Moosehead/Whitbread* show that these are treated in analogous fashion to patent licences and they are discussed within that context at 3.11.9.

17.6 DOMAIN NAMES

The internet is often described as a network of networks of computers. The number of people connected to the internet continues to grow apace. In early 2003 it was estimated that 580 million people worldwide had access to the internet.[28] Greatest levels of connection are in North America, Europe and Asia, but levels are growing elsewhere, largely dependent on telecommunications infrastructures.[29] Prime use of the internet lies in e-mail and the provision of information. However, since the advent of e-commerce, when the internet was opened to commercial concerns in the mid-1990s, the value of commercial activities has also grown at a rapid rate.

Each computer connected to this network is given a unique electronic address – an Internet Protocol (IP) address which is used to route data from one host computer to another. IP addresses are numerical, resembling telephone numbers,[30] identifying particular computers on the internet. IP numbers are not easy to remember and prone

---

28 NUA Internet Surveys: www. nua.com/surveys.
29 WIPO, 'Intellectual Property on the Internet: A Survey of Issues': www.wipo.int.
30 The IP address system is numeric based on numbers 32 bits long. These are written in a dotted decimal notation, so that each byte is written as a decimal number from 1 to 255, each value separated by a dot, such as 123.45.67.89. It is planned to extend the system to 128 bit numbers to accommodate the growing number of domain names.

to mistakes being made. Accordingly, a word-based, easily remembered, domain name system (DNS) was introduced.[31] Each domain name is mapped to an underlying IP address, which is in turn attached to the data thus identified. The conversion of domain names into IP addresses is achieved by a distributed DNS database. The Internet Corporation for Assigned Numbers and Names (ICANN) controls the database, accredit domain name registries and manages the DNS. The database is held on a hierarchical system of 13 servers. At the top of the hierarchy the root servers resolve top-level domains (TLDs).[32] There are 13 root name servers,[33] one each in London, Stockholm and Tokyo, the remaining 10 in the US. However, several exist in multiple locations on different continents, so that the majority of physical servers are located outside the US.

17.6.1   The nature of a domain name

Any domain name consists of two components, namely the top-level domain name (TLD) and a second-level domain name. In the example of 'microsoft.com', .com is the top-level domain name, while *microsoft* comprises the second-level domain name.

Currently, there are two categories of domain names: generic top-level domain names (gTLDs) and country code TLDs (ccTLDs). gTLDs include the .com, .net, .org, .edu, .int, .aero, .biz, .coop, .info, .museum, .name and .pro domains. Initially, the norm was that commercial organisations registered in the .com domain, while others such as .org, .net, .int, .gov and .edu, were assigned to non-commercial organisations, network providers, international treaties, government agencies and educational institutions respectively.[34] All gTLDs are open to registration, the .int domain is reserved for international organisations, while .edu and .gov belong to the US military and government. All other gTLDs are open to all registrants.

There are 246 ccTLDs.[35] Each of these domains bears a two-letter country code derived from Standard 3166 of the International Standards Organisation (ISO 3166). The top-level domain name for the UK is .uk. Some ccTLDs are open, in the sense that there are no restrictions on the persons or entities that may register second-level domains in them. Others are restricted in that only persons or entities satisfying certain criteria (eg, domicile within the territory) may register names in them. The .us is restricted to persons domiciled in the US, for example.

Internet domain names may now be registered with any of over 150 Registrars worldwide.[36] Governments authorise and license companies as registrars to sell domain names to individuals. Most registrars offer purchasing plans as well as additional services such as web hosting, bulk registration, transfer services and corporate services.

Both generic and country code top-level domain names are available for registration.

---

31 Froomkin, MA, 'ICANN's "Uniform Dispute Resolution Policy" – Causes and (Partial) Cures' (2002) 67(3) Brooklyn Law Review 605.
32 See Wikipedia, 'Domain Name System' and 'Root Nameserver': www.wikipedia.org.
33 Lettered A – M.
34 There is one more, gTLD.arpa, which is solely used for internet technical infrastructure needs.
35 For a full list of the ccTLDs see www.iana.org/cctld/cctld-whois.htm#a.
36 For a complete list of registrars see www.icann.org/registrars/accredited-list.html.

17.6.2   Domain name disputes

Domain names are not forms of intellectual property; however, they serve as important identifiers and addresses for any presence on the internet. Registering an appropriate domain name is an important step for any business, and it is natural for a business to register a name by which it is already recognised, such as a registered or unregistered mark.

There are two significant distinctions between trade marks (registered or unregistered)[37] and domain names. First, the former are confined to particular classes of business or 'field of action', so that two businesses operating in different spheres may hold the same name without causing customer confusion. Consider Penguin books and Penguin biscuits, for example. Domain names, by contrast, must be unique. Once registered, a domain name is not tied to its registrant's field of business in the way that a mark is. There can only be one 'penguin.com', although there can also be 'penguin.biz', 'penguin.co.uk' and so on. Consequently, disputes arise when more than one entity wishes to register the same domain name, and there are a finite number of possible combinations for registration.[38] Secondly, trade marks only confer national, or at most, regional, protection,[39] while a domain name has global application.

As registration is on a 'first come, first served' basis, however, trade mark owners have no prior right to a domain name incorporating their mark and disputes between mark owners and registrants arise. This is particularly so when the commercial value of a '.com' address is realised, just as trade marks are often valued on company balance sheets as assets. Registries do not undertake trade mark searches before registering names; nor do they customarily distinguish between types of name in the way that a mark must be distinctive to secure registration. The rules for registration of a domain name are a matter of contract between the applicant and the registry.

Disputes can be categorised as 'cybersquatting' or 'reverse domain name hijacking', although there has been at least one instance of 'honest concurrent user' in the case of *Pitman Training v Nominet UK* (1997).

So-called 'cybersquatters' have attempted to register others' (usually well known) marks in order to sell them back to the mark owner, often at very inflated prices. Cybersquatters commonly register large numbers of domain names. 'Typosquatters' register common misspellings of well known domains. The continuing value of a desirable domain can be seen in the reports in July 2004 that the domain name 'creditcards.com' was bought for $2.75 million,[40] while 'business.com' sold for $7.5 million at the height of the 'dotcom' boom.[41]

Other conflicts may arise where a trade mark owner seeks to recover a domain name from an individual who has registered the mark as a name. This is known as

---

37 Although well known names will achieve protection for the name in a very wide field of commerce.

38 Jones, PL, 'Protecting Your "SportsEven.com": Athletic Organisations and the Uniform Domain Name Dispute Resolution Policy', *The West Virginia Journal of Law & Technology*, at www.wvu.edu/~law/wvjolt/Arch/Jones/Jones.htm.

39 Although the same mark may be registered in many different national registries, and recognition internationally be achieved through the Madrid Agreement.

40 Sullivan, B, 'Domain Name Sells for £2.75 million', 20 July 2004: www.msnbc.msn.com.

41 It is worth noting the generic nature of these names and considering whether they would ever be registered as trade marks.

'reverse domain name hijacking'. The registration may have been made in ignorance of any conflicting interest, because the name is common to both concerns, or may be deliberate,[42] with the intention of benefiting from another concern's reputation. It may also occur where an international undertaking attempts to register in a ccTLD.

Rarely, cases of 'honest concurrent user' of domain names have occurred through mistakes in the registration process (see 14.7.3). While some domain name conflicts have been remedied through the action for passing off (see 14.7.3) and trade mark infringement (see Chapter 16), remedies also lie in specific dispute resolution procedures.

17.6.3   Developing dispute resolution procedures

Network Solutions Inc

Before 1998, Network Solutions Inc (NSI) was the sole registrar or provider of domain names in the .com, .net and .org gTLDs. NSI did not prevent the registration of trade marks as domain names. However, it maintained its own domain name dispute resolution policy from 1995 to 1998. This allowed trade mark holders to challenge domain registrations by showing that the name violated their trade mark rights. The policy allowed trade mark owners to place a domain name 'on hold' pending resolution of the dispute. If a domain name owner could prove that the domain name was registered before a complainant's trade mark, or the domain name holder also held a trade mark for the domain name, then the disputed domain name would not be placed on hold.

The policy did not recognise that trade mark rights do not apply to non-commercial uses; nor did it protect state and common law mark owners. Reverse domain name hijacking arose when a trade mark owner would use NSI's policy to gain rights in a domain registration that would not have been permitted by trade mark law.[43] The policy was much criticised. It could only be used against domain names that were identical to the registered mark. Misspellings and hybridisations – and all other confusingly similar variations that constitute infringement under trade mark law – could only be attacked through court action. Cybersquatters often used false registration data and many resided in remote regions. Nor could foreign trademark owners and domain name holders afford to protect their rights in the US courts.[44]

Two initiatives led to change – both in the policy to be applied to disputes, and the organisation administering it. In July 1997, President Clinton issued a directive to the US Secretary of Commerce to privatise the management of the domain name system, in order to increase competition and international participation.[45] The US Government also suggested that WIPO make recommendations to the new body on questions arising from the interface of domain names and intellectual property.

---

42   See, for example, the registration of 'yahooindia.com' in *Yahoo! Inc v Akash Akora* (1999).

43   The owner of the trade mark for the comic *Archie* attempted to seize "veronica.com" from a father who used it as a homepage to record events in the life of his two year old daughter.

44   Diane Cabell, Domain Names: World Standard Set for Key Internet Disputes, Dispute Resolution Magazine, American Bar Association Section of Dispute Resolution, Winter 2000, Vol 6, No 2, p 12.

45   See, NSI – DoC – ICANN, FACT Sheet, available at http://www.icann.org/nsi/factsheet.htm.

ICANN and the UDRP

On 5 June 1998, the Department of Commerce (DoC) published a statement of policy concerning the privatisation process of the domain name system.[46] It stated its intention to enter an agreement with a not-for-profit entity to establish a process for transferring US Government management of the DNS to such an entity based on the principles of stability, competition, bottom-up co-ordination and representation.[47]

In addition, in April 1999, WIPO published its first domain name report, *The Management of Internet Names and Addresses: Intellectual Property Issues*.[48] The result was the formation of ICANN to administer the DNS and the adoption of the Uniform Domain Name Dispute Resolution Policy (UDRP).

ICANN is a non-profit organisation incorporated in California in the US. It entered a Memorandum of Understanding (MoU) with the DoC which gave it several functions:

(i)   to set policy for and direct allocation of IP number blocks to regional internet number registries;

(ii) to oversee operation of the root server system;

(iii) to oversee policy for adding new TLDs to the root server system; and

(iv) to co-ordinate technical parameters to maintain internet connectivity.

The MoU has since been renewed, although it is likely that the US Government may eventually sever its links with management of the DNS.

The WIPO Report made several recommendations. Best practice for registration authorities was detailed, particularly relating to collecting and preserving accurate contact details for domain name registrants in order that trade mark owners could enforce their rights. It also made recommendations for the introduction of new gTLDs. The main outcome of the report, however, resulted from the recommendation for an administrative dispute resolution procedure for cybersquatting in the gTLDs. This was intended to cater for the international nature of domain name disputes, to be quick, inexpensive and online. At the time it was recognised that further issues remained to be resolved.

The US Anticybersquatting Consumer Protection Act 1999

The US also took legislative action against cybersquatting in the Anticybersquatting Consumer Protection Act (ACPA). Previously, domain name disputes were resolved through trade mark and dilution principles. In the US the leading case was *Panavision v Toeppen* (1998). Toeppen registered 'panavision.com' and used the website to display pictures of the city of Pana, Illinois. He offered to sell it to Panavision for $13,000. Panavision declined and took action under the Federal Trademark Dilution Act (FTDA). This required that the plaintiff show:

---

46   National Telecommunications and Information Administration of the US Department of Commerce White Paper, *Statement of Policy on the Management of Internet Names and Addresses*, June 1998.

47   Memorandum of Understanding Between the US Department of Commerce and ICANN, 25 November 2001, http://www.icann.org/general/icann-mou-25nov98.htm.

48   Final Report, 30 April 1999, www.wipo.int.

(i)   that the trademark was famous;

(ii)   that the defendant was using the mark in commerce;

(iii) that the mark became famous before the defendant started using it; and

(iv)   that 'the defendant's use of the mark dilutes the quality of the mark by diminishing the capacity of the mark to identify and distinguish goods and services'.

Toeppen argued that he was not making commercial use of the domain name, as he was merely displaying photographs on his website. Nevertheless, the court concluded that, by having offered the domain name for sale, Toeppen had shown his intention to use the mark in commerce, meeting the requirement for the 'use in commerce'. The court further asserted that the domain name carried the reputation of a trade mark.

Courts in the US decided domain name disputes under three principles of US trade mark law. The first was traditional trade mark infringement, which requires that the allegedly infringing use will cause a likelihood of consumer confusion.[49] The second, and the one often most successful – was assertion that the contested domain name diluted the value of the trade mark.[50] Finally, unfair competition,[51] a claim similar to trade mark infringement, could be used in cases where the trade mark was not federally registered.[52] However, it was soon realised that traditional principles of trade mark law were not adequate to deal with such disputes.[53] This was particularly so in relation to claims of dilution; the difficulty lying in the need to prove that the mark was famous or well known.

In November 1999, Congress added a new cause of action to the Lanham Act, expressly designed to prevent cybersquatting.[54] This new piece of legislation was expected to change the way domain name disputes were handled and to offer an easier means of resolving them.

The principal purpose of the ACPA was to cure the perceived weakness of existing remedies under trade mark law. The ACPA defines a cybersquatter as a person who has an intent in bad faith to profit from a trade mark that is not registered to him, including a personal name protected as a trade mark under common law. The ACPA also expanded jurisdiction over domain name registrants. Where a court finds that the owner is not able to establish the court's personal jurisdiction over the domain name holder, or if the complainant cannot find the domain name holder, the Act allows the owner of a trade mark to file an *in rem* action against the domain name itself.

The ACPA empowers courts to order the registrar to cancel the domain name or transfer it to the trade mark proprietor. The court may also order either actual damages

---

49   Lanham Act, s 32 (1) – 15 USC 1114 (1).

50   Lanham Act, s 43 (c) – 15 USC 1125 (c).

51   Lanham Act, s 43 (a) – 15 USC 1125 (a).

52   'Domain Names and Trademarks', at http://eon.law.harvard.edu/property/domain/main.html.

53   For instance, the Porsche company was confronted with this problem when it discovered that 128 different domain names had been registered by others incorporating variations of its trademarks. Porsche had to locate and sue each of the registrants that had appropriated its trademarks, a process which is both very costly and time consuming: *Porsche Cars of North America Inc v Porsche.com* (1999).

54   15 USC, S 1125 (d) – the Anticybersquatting Consumer Protection Act.

to the trade mark owner or, prior to the final judgment, the trade mark owner may ask the court to designate an award of statutory damages for the domain name.[55]

The UK

In the UK, lacking the statutory equivalent of the dilution concept, dispute resolution depended on the tort of passing off (see 14.7.3) or trade mark infringement to resolve domain name disputes. However, this brings the danger that the ambit of the traditional rights may be distorted by strained interpretation designed to accommodate remedies for domain name disputes. The *One in a Million* (1999) case has been criticised on this basis.[56]

Others have argued that the laws and principles adopted should neither expand nor diminish traditional trade mark rights.[57] The US Department of Commerce White Paper claimed that its proposals 'were designed to provide trade mark holders with the same rights they have in the physical world'.[58] WIPO also emphasised that:

> [T]he goal of the first WIPO process was not to create new rights in intellectual property, nor to accord greater protection to intellectual property in cyberspace than that which existed elsewhere. Rather, the goal was to give proper and adequate expression to the existing, multilaterally agreed standards of intellectual property protection in the context of the multi-jurisdictional medium of the internet.[59]

17.6.4 The UDRP

Following the WIPO Report, ICANN introduced a mandatory procedure for resolving domain name disputes in the .com, .net, and .org gTLDs – the Uniform Domain Name Dispute Resolution Policy (UDRP).[60] To become an accredited domain name registrar, Network Solutions and new competing registrars became bound to the arbitration procedure in the UDRP. The policy provides a cost-effective method for arbitrating domain name disputes, by means of electronic submission of complaints and responses of neutral arbitration. It is intended to provide a prompt, efficient and relatively inexpensive means of dealing with disputes.

When disputes arise, domain name holders are required to submit to mandatory administrative proceedings, which are administered by one of the approved dispute resolution providers. Currently, four dispute resolution providers are approved by ICANN: the World Intellectual Property Organisation (WIPO), the National Arbitration Forum (NAF), the CPR Institute for Dispute Resolution (CPR) and the

---

55 See, Jones, PL, 'Protecting Your "SportsEven.com": Athletic Organisations and the Uniform Domain Name Dispute Resolution Policy', *The West Virginia Journal of Law & Technology*, at www.wvu.edu/~law/wvjolt/Arch/Jones/Jones.htm.

56 See Sims, A, 'Rethinking *One in a Million*' [2004] EIPR 442; Colston, C, 'Passing Off: The Right Solution to Domain Name Disputes?' [2000] LMCLQ 523.

57 Milton, L Mueller, *Ruling The Root* (Cambridge, Mass: The MIT Press, 2002).

58 NTIA, 1998b, Management of Internet Names and Address. White Paper, Federal Register 63:31741.

59 World Intellectual Property Organisation, 2001: Second WIPO Internet Domain Name Process. FRC-3, Geneva: World Intellectual Property Organisation.

60 See, ICANN, Rules for Uniform Domain Name Dispute Resolution Policy, (24 October 1999), www.icann.org/dndr/udrp/uniform-rules.htm.

Asian Domain Name Dispute Resolution Centre (ADNDRC).[61] All four of the dispute resolution providers follow Alternative Dispute Resolution (ADR) principles in the dispute resolutions.

Since January 2000, all ICANN accredited registrars have adopted the UDRP for all top-level domain names. Domain name applicants accept the policy as part of the licence agreement between the applicant and the domain name registry administrator. However, the dispute resolution is not aimed at resolving disputes between parties where both have legitimate claims to a domain name. Such disputes are left to the courts.

The criteria

In order to bring a successful complaint three criteria must be met, as found in paragraph 4(a) of the policy:

(i)   the domain name is identical or confusingly similar to a trademark or service mark in which the complainant has rights; and

(ii)   the domain name holder has no rights or legitimate interests in respect of the domain name; and

(iii)   the domain name has been registered and is being used in bad faith.

Paragraph 4(b) of the policy provides that 'bad faith' includes registering or using the domain name to gain profit from the trademark owner or to disrupt his business by the unlawful use of the domain name.[62]

A complainant must prove all three elements before the domain name can be transferred or cancelled.

Procedure

The complainant initiates a written complaint to an approved Dispute Resolution Service Provider. If the documentation complies with the Rules for Uniform Domain Name Resolution Policy (the Rules) and the fees have been paid, the provider will notify the parties of the commencement of the proceedings. Once the proceedings have commenced the respondent must submit a written response to the complaint within 20 days.[63]

---

61   www.icann.org/dndr/udrp/approved-providers.htm.

62   Four considerations for determining bad faith are listed, although they are not exhaustive. The first is the typical, classic case of cybersquatting: 'acquisition of the domain name primarily for the purpose of selling, renting, or otherwise transferring the domain name registration to the complainant, who is the owner of the trademark or service mark or to a competitor of the complainant for a valuable consideration in excess of documented out-of-pocket costs directly related to the domain name.' Other examples of bad faith include (a) a pattern of registering for the purpose of blocking the mark owners from using the domain (although it is not clear what constitutes a pattern) and (b) registration primarily for the purpose of disrupting the business of a competitor (which may prove the only basis for bringing a justifiable action against non-commercial sites). Also included is the more typical trademark ground of 'use for commercial gain, with intent to attract users to the domain site by creating a likelihood of confusion with the mark as to source, sponsorship, affiliation or endorsement of good or services'.

63   Rules for Uniform Domain Name Dispute Resolution Policy, para 5, www.icann.org/dndr/udrp/uniform-rules.htm.

Either a single or a three-member panel may hear the proceedings. The panel must hear the dispute in accordance with the Rules and 'shall decide a complaint on the basis of the statement and documents submitted and in accordance with the policy, these Rules and any rules and principles of law that it deems applicable'.[64]

Remedies

The remedies available to successful complainants under the policy are limited to cancellation of the registrant's domain name, or transfer of the registration to the complainant. The complainant will pay all fees charged by the approved provider, unless the registrant elects to expand the administrative panel from one to three persons. In the event that the registrant makes this election, it must split payment of the approved provider's fees evenly with the complainant.[65]

Success

The policy was never intended to pre-empt civil litigation asserting intellectual property rights in trade marks. Alleged holders of such rights still have to bring such actions, including claims under the federal cybersquatting legislation in the US. However, the policy has proved popular and, since its beginnings at the end of 1999, over 7,000 WIPO disputes have been resolved.[66] Early in 2005, WIPO published an online overview of trends in WIPO decisions.[67] To some extent this success lies in the differences between the UDRP and the NSI policy: the UDRP provides for cancellation or transfer of the name if the complainant succeeds, and the mark and name need not be identical.

The UDRP has also been extended to recognition of common law unregistered marks, despite the use of the word trade mark in the policy itself. In *Jeanette Winterson v Mark Hogarth* (2000) the respondent appeared to be a cybersquatter, having registered over 100 writers' names as domain names, and offered to sell them to those writers. He professed to be setting up unofficial websites dedicated to information about the writers. The policy requires that a complainant have a trade mark.[68] The panel followed the *One in a Million* case (see 14.7.3) to establish that the complainant had 'legal rights' in her name. Consequently, 'jeanettewinterson.org', 'jeanettewinterson.com' and 'jeanettewinterson.net' were transferred to her. It should be noted, however, how limited passing off protection is for personal names (see 14.6.1). The registrant's use of the name here might have been regarded as descriptive.

Nevertheless, despite the large number of complainants, the UDRP has been subject to considerable criticism. In particular, it has been argued that some panel decisions have awarded too great a power to trade mark owners, in circumstances where trade mark principles would not have led to success. This is particularly so in

---

64 Para 15(a).
65 Para 6(b).
66 For an endorsement of the Policy's success see Kur, A, 'UDRP', a Study by the Max-Planck Institute, Munich, 2002, and Branthover, N, 'UDRP – a Success Story: A Rebuttal to the Analysis and Conclusions of Professor Milton Mueller in "Rough Justice"', INTA, 2002.
67 WIPO overview of WIPO Panel Views on Selected UDRP Questions. http://arbiter.wipo.int/domains/search/overview/index.html.
68 Para 4(a).

relation to names which would not have been registrable as marks,[69]or whether other legitimate interests in the name would be recognised in trade mark law defences.[70] Criticism has also been made both of the procedure itself[71] and of the process by which panels have been appointed, leading to allegations of a bias in favour of trade mark owners, and forum shopping on the part of complainants.[72] In addition, criticism can be directed to the nature of the UDRP itself as a dispute resolution procedure.

17.6.5   Freedom of expression

One of the criticisms ranged against application of the UDRP has related to so-called 'sucks' websites, where a business' name has been incorporated in a domain name intended for a site critical of that business. This is particularly so in the US, where freedom of speech is a constitutionally guaranteed right. Dot-sucks domain names comprise of all those domain names that satirise well known trade marks. Even in cases where the domain names in question have not been registered for commercial gain, panellists have found them to be confusingly similar in the eyes of consumers, adding that they have also been registered and are being used in bad faith.

The 'dixons-online.com' case offers an example of application of the UDRP Rules restricting freedom of speech.[73] The respondent operated a website as a portal for complaints about the firm Dixons for which no charge was made. The panel found that, even though there was no evidence that the domain name had been registered for the purposes of acquiring fame from Dixons, since no goods or services were offered, the use of the domain name was nonetheless illegitimate. In support of its decision the panel stated:

> [t]hat 'competitor' has a wider meaning and is not confined to those who are selling or providing competing goods. In this wider context it means 'one who acts in opposition to another and the context does not demand any restricted meaning such as commercial or business competitor'. [Since] the respondent is competing with the complainant for the attention of internet users, [this] clearly has the potential to disrupt the complainant's business.

In contrast, in the case of *Lockheed Corporation v Dan Parisi* (2000), it was decided that a trade mark to which the term 'sucks' or any other critical phrase is added, makes it obvious that the trade mark owner has not consented to the site, and consequently no confusion should arise. This particular reasoning was based on a US Federal Court ruling,[74] and suggests a move towards supporting free speech in the domain name context.[75]

---

69   Such as celebrity names, geographical names, and generic words.
70   Such as using one's own name, or descriptive or satirical use of a word mark.
71   Froomkin, M, 'ICANN's "Uniform Dispute Resolution Policy" – Causes and (Partial) Cures', (2002) 67 Brooklyn LR 608.
72   Mueller, M, 'Rough Justice: An Analysis of ICANN's Uniform Dispute Resolution Policy', Syracuse University, www.dcc.syr.edu/index.htm and Geist, M, 'Fair.com?: An Examination of the Allegations of Systematic Unfairness in the ICANN UDRP', University of Ottawa, 2002.
73   Case No D2001–0843.
74   *Bally Total Fitness v Faber* (1998).
75   Schiavetta, S, and Komaitis, K, 'ICANN's Role in Controlling Information on the Internet' (2003) 17(3) International Review of Law Computers & Technology 267.

Similarly, in a recent case involving the UK supermarket Asda, a panellist strictly adhered to the UDRP Rules and upheld rights to free speech. In this case an Asda employee registered the domain name 'asdasucks.net' to create a website, which would give him the opportunity to voice his dissatisfaction over the company's managerial abilities.[76] When the supermarket brought the case before WIPO's Arbitration and Mediation Centre, the site had never been exploited. As the employee was already operating a similar website, at 'asdasucks.co.uk', the panellist chose to analyse that site. On the operative site there was a disclaimer indicating that the site was not connected with the supermarket, and was created for dissatisfied employees. The panel assumed that the complainant would use the 'asdasucks.net' name for the same purposes. The panellist also argued that, on the balance of probabilities, it was doubtful that the 'asdasucks.net' site would confuse internet users into believing that the site emanated from Asda itself. Consequently, any disruption of Asda's business would be minimal and the issue was not worthy of further consideration. The panellist added that, whilst he was uncomfortable dismissing the complaint, because the material on the active site was '[s]candalously and disgustingly abusive', a broader interpretation of the policy and its rules would be doubtful.[77]

17.6.6 Geographical names

Domain names containing geographical words are another area where the UDRP can have the effect of giving global protection to a name that would not be registrable to the same extent as a trade mark. This was particularly illustrated in relation to the proceedings over the name 'barcelona.com'. The dispute was initially settled under the UDRP in favour of the trade mark owner,[78] and was then brought before a United States court,[79] before being finally settled before the United States Court of Appeals in *Barcelona.com Inc v Excelentisimo Ayuntamiento de Barcelona*. This decision held that the word could not have been defended as a trade mark, at least in US law.

In 1996 a Spanish citizen registered the domain name 'www.barcelona.com' with NSI. The accompanying website provided tourist information about Barcelona, as well as e-mail services, a chat room, and links to other websites. In 1999, the citizen e-mailed the Mayor of Barcelona suggesting negotiations with the City Council with a view to its acquiring the domain name, but received no response.

Later that year, the domain name registrants formed Barcelona.com Inc under Delaware law to host and run the website. Even though the company has a New York address, it has no other presence in the US. Moreover, its computer server is in Spain. In March 2000, the City Council contacted the registrants but the negotiations failed. In May 2000 the City Council demanded transfer of the domain name.

The City Council owned numerous Spanish trade marks incorporating the word 'Barcelona'. It initiated a successful UDRP complaint against the registrants. The WIPO panellist concluded, *inter alia*, that the city had trade mark rights in the word Barcelona under Spanish law, and that the domain name in question was registered and used in bad faith. Consequently, the registrants were ordered to transfer the domain name to

---

76   Case D2002–0857.
77   *Ibid.*
78   WIPO Case No D2000–0505.
79   189 F Supp 2d 367 (ED Va 2002).

the City Council. Before the execution of the transfer order, Barcelona.com Inc filed a lawsuit in the District Court for the Eastern District of Virginia, seeking declaratory judgment and claiming that the registration of the domain name was not unlawful. Consequently, according to the UDRP Rules,[80] the transfer was automatically placed on hold until a further ruling by the district court.

The district court's ruling validated the UDRP decision, concluding that under Spanish law the City Council was probably the rightful owner of all marks incorporating the name Barcelona. Moreover, the court concluded that the registrants demonstrated 'bad faith intent to profit' and, thus, the registration could not be declared 'not unlawful'. The court also discussed the City Council cybersquatting counterclaims and found that the ACPA also protected foreign marks against cybersquatting. Since the City Council demonstrated that it had valid rights under Spanish law, and since the domain name was identical or confusingly similar to the marks owned by the city, the request for a declaratory judgment in favour of the registrants was denied.

However, on appeal, in a unanimous ruling, the Fourth Circuit reversed the lower court's decision. There are four key points in the court's analysis: (1) jurisdictional issues; (2) applicability of foreign law; (3) elements of the Reverse Domain Name Hijacking (RDNH) provision; and (4) the protection under US trade mark law to the Barcelona mark. It is the last that is of significance to the question of the registrability of geographical domain names. Having held that Spanish trade mark law was not relevant, US law relating to geographical names was applied.

The court explained that even had the City Council tried to defend its trade mark rights in the word 'Barcelona' under US law, it would not have succeeded. Since the Lanham Act did not protect purely descriptive geographical designations, and because the City Council could show no evidence that the term Barcelona acquired any secondary meaning other than the city itself, the term was not protected under US law.

17.6.7   The nature of the policy

One of the controversies surrounding the UDRP is its legal nature, and the question whether it should be considered as an arbitral process. Although the policy declares that it is an administrative procedure, panels, WIPO and various scholars have treated the policy as arbitration. However, a landmark decision in the US challenges the arbitral nature of the policy.

In *Parisi v Netlearning, Inc* (2001) a US Court decided that administrative proceedings under ICANN's UDRP are not arbitration proceedings subject to the Federal Arbitration Act (FAA),[81] or the New York Convention on the Recognition and Enforcement of Foreign Arbitral Awards.[82]

Crucially, after examining the nature and wording of the UDRP, the court reached the conclusion that '[t]he UDRP's unique contractual arrangements renders the FFA's provisions for judicial review of arbitration awards inapplicable'.

---

80   Para 4(k), UDRP Policy.
81   9 USC §1 *et seq.*
82   New York, 10 June 1958; entered into force, 7 June 1959, United Nations, Treaty Series, Vol 330, p 38, No 4739, 1959.

First, the court claimed that unlike traditional arbitration, where litigation is not an option until the arbitration award is rendered, 'the UDRP contemplates parallel litigation'. Indeed, the UDRP Rules allow any of the parties to initiate court proceedings before, during or after a UDRP decision has been rendered. The only requirement posed is that the losing party must initiate court action within 10 days of an UDRP ruling ordering transfer or cancellation of a domain name.[83] Secondly, the court recognised that if the parties have a written arbitration agreement, then arbitration is compulsory. This element of compulsion is not applicable in the case of the UDPR since the complainants are 'strangers to the registration agreement and therefore are under no obligation to avail themselves of the UDRP'. Thirdly, the court stated that, contrary to arbitration agreements, which are incontestably enforceable, unless exceptional circumstances occur (the award contradicts principles of public policy, for example), the policy itself 'mandates a judicial forum for challenges to UDRP decisions'. Finally, the court found that, unlike the provisions concerning arbitration awards, judicial review of UDRP proceedings is 'not confined to a motion to vacate'. The court said that by contemplating 'parallel litigation and abbreviated proceedings, the policy does not provide for such deference'.

The significance of this decision is that it affirms the non-arbitral nature of the UDRP. Nevertheless, the policy is binding on registrants, who are obliged to agree to engage in a UDRP procedure and abide by the results. More to the point, if a trade mark owner believes that a domain name registration infringes his trade mark rights, that owner will hardly ever, if at all, be bound to participate in a UDRP action, because that owner will be a complete stranger to the registration process. Since the trade mark owner normally will not be part of the initial registration agreement incorporating the UDRP clause, the owner can choose whether to bring a UDRP claim, court proceedings or both. Since such a party is often vital in resolving domain name disputes, but is not bound by any domain name registration related contract, it should not be surprising that legal action will often be inevitable to resolve such disputes.

17.6.8 Further developments

The UDRP has been perceived as having inappropriate results in relation to certain types of names – such as personal names and geographical words. In addition, other protections for some names needed consideration – the World Health Organisation International Non-proprietary Names (INNs) for Pharmaceutical Substances, and company and trade names can also feature in domain name disputes. As a result, after suggestions from the Australian Government, WIPO initiated a second Domain Name Process. This considered bad faith, abusive, misleading or unfair use of INNs, personal and geographical names, and trade names. The Second WIPO report, *The Recognition of Rights and the Use of Names in the Internet Domain Name System*,[84] unhelpfully concluded that:

(i)   There were no international norms for protecting personal names, and that national systems differed widely. It was recognised that offence could be caused by insensitive registration of another's name as a domain name, however no suggestions were made for resolving such disputes, other than that a decision

---

83   Para 4(k), UDRP Rules.
84   Report of the Second WIPO Internet Domain Name Process, 2001, www.wipo.int.

would be taken whether a means of protection for such names should be developed.

(ii)   By contrast, international norms could be identified in relation to geographical names, but these applied to trading in goods rather than to domain name registration. No internationally agreed list of geographical indicators could be identified, however. Consequently, the report suggests further co-ordination of international norms before a solution to domain name disputes over geographical names can be developed.

(iii) Similar conclusions were reached in relation to trade names.

Subsequently, after consideration of the Report by the WIPO Standing Committee on the Law of Trademarks, Industrial Designs and Geographical Indications, the decision that it was not timely to tackle geographical names, that no action should be taken in relation to personal names and that trade names should be kept under review, was transmitted to ICANN in 2002. The Committee continues to discuss issues relating to country names and geographical indications.

Meanwhile, WIPO's *Intellectual Property on the Internet: A Survey of Issues*[85] has raised other issues relating to domain names. In particular, new problems are foreseen in relation to multilingual domain names, and the ability to locate websites by use of keywords rather than URLs.[86]

17.6.9   Dispute resolution for '.uk'

Nominet is the official registrar for the UK and has authority for all domain name registrations ending in the '.uk' suffix. Nominet began registering domain names on 1 August 1996 and is officially recognised by the UK Government as the manager of the '.uk' ccTLD.

Nominet's dispute resolution procedure[87] is noteworthy. Although based on the ICANN model, Nominet's procedure for resolving disputes between trade marks owners and '.uk' domain names registrants is felt to be an 'improved' and efficient model. It differs from the UDRP in several respects:

(i)   the Nominet mechanism only calls for the complainant to meet a two-stage test, namely:

(a)   that the complainant has rights in respect of a name or mark which is identical or similar to a domain name; and,

(b)   that the respondent has registered and/or is using the domain name in bad faith.

The missing element – the requirement that a complainant proves that the respondent has no rights or legitimate interests in respect of the domain name at issue – is a defence to the allegation of bad faith. If the respondent can show that he has such rights or legitimate interests, they will be sufficient to defeat the complaint.

---

85   wipo.int.
86   Uniform Resource Locators, the address shown by a browser for each webpage, such as http://www.wipo.int/copyright/ecommerce/en/html/#.
87   Available at www.nominet.org.uk.

(ii)   Another important feature of the UK model is its mediation period. Nominet offers a mediation period free of charge before officially forwarding the dispute to the panel. Up to one-third of all cases have been resolved through informal mediation. Nominet considers that mediation has been particularly helpful to individuals and smaller players who get caught up in disputes. However, the time period allowed for mediation is limited to avoid unnecessary delay.

(iii)   The procedure is not limited to registered or unregistered trademarks. The respondent need only show 'rights' which may extend to other interests such as possession of a famous name or use of a geographical name.

(iv)   The burden of proof, as for the UDRP, is placed on the complainant. The burden for proving rights in a name is the civil standard of proof, on the balance of probabilities. However, the burden for proving bad faith is the higher one of proof beyond reasonable doubt.

(v)   Lack of a legitimate right or reason to use a name will automatically be found to be bad faith. The policy lists situations thought to constitute or contribute towards a finding of bad faith, including registration with the intent to sell for profit, causing confusion as to who is behind a website, blocking a legitimate user from registration or disrupting the complainant's business. The policy states that the registrant 'has registered and/or is using the domain name in bad faith'. The test for bad faith is more flexible than the UDRP test, which requires 'use and registration in bad faith' and also requires that if disruption is cited as a ground that this be to the business of a 'competitor'.

(vi)   Specific provision is made against dealing in generic names, and the use of domain names for genuine tribute or protest sites will not be regarded as bad faith.

(vii)   Complainants have a limited right to submit a reply – within strict time limits – to any response submitted by the registrant.

(viii) In the first instance, single panellists decide complaints on a strict cab rank rotation. However, there is a right to appeal within ten days of the decision, and the appeal will be heard by a three-member panel.[88]

(ix)   Given the geographical connection of the '.uk' ccTLD name with the United Kingdom, panellists will all be experts in UK law. Nominet was understood to be seeking applications or recommendations for experts in the field of IT and intellectual property law to make up the panel. Nominet is aware of the need to ensure a reasonably consistent process, but is also aware that there are a number of widely differing interests that need to be accommodated, not just those of trademark owners.

(x)   If on three separate occasions a complainant is found to have brought a complaint in bad faith – for instance, a blatant attempt at reverse domain name hijacking – Nominet will not accept any further complaints from that complainant.

---

88   Fees for a single panellist will be in the region of £750 plus VAT, while fees for an appeal will be in the region of £3,000 plus VAT.

Further Reading

Black, W, 'The Domain Name System', in *Law and the Internet: A Framework for Electronic Commerce* (Oxford: Hart Publishing, 2000)

Dryberg, P, and Petursson, GT, 'What is Consent? A Note on *Davidoff* and *Levi Strauss'* (2002) 27 (4) EL Rev 464

Froomkin, M, 'ICANN's "Uniform Dispute Resolution Policy" – Causes and (Partial) Cures' (2002) 67 Brooklyn LR 608

Geist, M, 'Fair.com?: An Examination of the Allegations of Systematic Unfairness in the ICANN UDRP', University of Ottawa, 2002

Kallay, D, '*Levi Strauss v Tesco*: At a Juncture of Competition, IP and Free Trade Policies' (2002) 23(4) ECLR 193

Koutrakos, P, 'In Search of a Common Vocabulary in the Free Movement of Goods: The Example of Repackaging Pharmaceuticals' (2003) 28(1) EL Rev 53

Kur, A, 'UDRP', a Study by the Max-Planck Institute, Munich, 2002

Lindsey, M and Chacksfield, M, 'Exhaustion of Rights and Wrongs: Section 92 of the Trade Marks Act 1994; Recent Developments and Comment' [2003] EIPR 388

Mueller, M, 'Rough Justice: An Analysis of ICANN's Uniform Dispute Resolution Policy', Syracuse University, http://dcc.syr.edu/index.htm

Mueller, M, *Ruling the Root* (Cambridge, Mass: MIT Press, 2002)

Sims, A, 'Rethinking *One in a Million*' [2004] EIPR 442

Terrett, A, and Monaghan, I, 'The Internet – An Introduction for Lawyers', in *Law and the Internet: A Framework for Electronic Commerce* (Oxford: Hart Publishing, 2000)

Waelde, C, 'Trade Marks and Domain Names: There's a Lot in a Name', in *Law and the Internet: A Framework for Electronic Commerce* (Oxford: Hart Publishing, 2000)

WIPO, *The Management of Internet Names and Addresses: Intellectual Property Issues*, 1999, www.wipo.int

WIPO, *The Recognition of Rights and the Use of Names in the Internet Domain Name System*, 2001, www.wipo.int

WIPO, *Intellectual Property on the Internet: A Survey of Issues*, www.wipo.int

CHAPTER 18

IMAGE PROTECTION

Marketing today relies heavily on creating and maintaining an 'image'. This is reflected, for example, in the popularity of branded and designer goods, in product endorsement by celebrities, as well as merchandising by football clubs and other sporting concerns. In addition, characters have come to have a value of their own. Associating products with Mickey Mouse, Winnie the Pooh, Lara Croft, David Beckham or Tiger Woods ensures sales, as does the use of the WWF's[1] panda. Celebrities such as Michael Douglas and Catherine Zeta Jones carefully cultivate and maintain an image in the public consciousness. Pop groups and football teams make considerable sums from the sale of memorabilia, as well as from their music or prowess on the field. Image therefore comprises both a powerful marketing tool and creates a new product.

Consequently, it would seem that the use of an image in association with products now extends beyond indications of responsibility for the manufacture and source of those products to the associations that their image may bring. The image itself constitutes a valuable commodity worth preserving from unwarranted competition. While none of this is new,[2] today it bears considerable economic importance to image 'owners', and supports enhanced consumer demand. Furthermore, there is the increasing trend for individuals well known in one sphere to gain financially by 'merchandising' themselves. This was clearly recognised by Lord Hoffmann in *Campbell v MGN Ltd* (2004):

> Naomi Campbell is a famous fashion model who lives by publicity. What she has to sell is herself: her personal appearance and her personality. She employs public relations agents to present her personal life to the media in the best possible light just as she employs professionals to advise her on dress and make-up. That is no criticism of her. It is a trade like any other.

It is clear that investment in 'image management' is an essential part of creative content-based industry today.[3] The success of television programmes, films, and other performances is often tied to public perceptions of the individuals involved. Time and money is expended in this management. Image exploitation is thought to cost football clubs and league sponsors up to £300 million each year in the UK.[4] Individuals also clearly benefit, and it is thought that £20,000 of the weekly £90,000 paid to David Beckham by Real Madrid was for his image rights.[5] Such image exploitation is largely

---

1   World Wide Fund for Nature.
2   See Hobbs, G, 'Passing Off and the Licensing of Merchandising Rights' [1980] EIPR 47.
3   See Catanzariti, T, 'Swimmers, Surfers and Sue Smith – Personality Rights in Australia' [2002] Ent LR 135.
4   Bond, D, Sponsorship and Endorsement Deals' [2004] Ent LR 51.
5   Hennigan, J, 'Altered Image Rights' [2003] Ent LR 161.

the result both of contractual arrangements[6] and reliance on intellectual property rights. While contractual remedies lie between the parties, contract does not protect the image from the depredations of outsiders. This is largely dependent on pressing into aid causes of action deriving from intellectual property, but also defamation and malicious falsehood.

Image exploitation can go further when the image becomes a commodity in itself[7] and is absorbed into public consciousness, becoming part of popular culture. If this is the case, questions arise as to how far the image has ceased to be solely part of an individual's persona and has fallen into the public domain.[8] At this point a conflict arises between the individual's joint concerns both for publicity and privacy, and the claims of a public interest in access to cultural icons.

Although there is no express UK property right in an individual's image, this chapter is designed to explore how the limits of intellectual property rights are being challenged and expanded to cater for the demands of those relying on image. However, the law must balance these demands against other interests. Exploitation of image can be categorised as:

- merchandising of memorabilia using 'character'[9] as a decorative device;
- endorsement of products by the well-known;
- individuals exploiting their image for the purposes of publicity.

The way in which the law treats each of these categories differs. In particular, where real individuals are concerned, unauthorised exploitation of their image raises questions both of loss of publicity value, and harm to dignity and autonomy; which should be distinguished.[10] This chapter will look at the legal protection for character merchandising and endorsement, and publicity protection achieved through enforcement of privacy and confidence.

18.1   JUSTIFICATIONS FOR LEGAL PROTECTION

Character merchandising is a familiar method of marketing goods and services by associating them with a real or fictional character, or a name, location, title or logo, in order to enhance the products' consumer appeal. It comprises the licensing of the names, visual and aural likenesses, or other indicia of real or fictional characters for use on products with which the individual has no direct connection.[11] Some characters are of enduring marketability, MICKEY MOUSE, for example. Others are very short lived, tied, perhaps, to a popular film or programme. A character 'owner' cannot prevent unauthorised use of the character unless it is protected in some way, such as by intellectual property rights or contractual terms.

---

6   See Bond, D, 'Sponsorship and Endorsement Deals' [2004] Ent LR 51, for the content of such contracts.
7   See Catanzariti, T, 'Swimmers, Surfers and Sue Smith – Personality Rights in Australia' [2002] Ent LR 135.
8   See Carty, H, 'Advertising, Publicity Rights and English Law' [2004] IPQ 209.
9   Whether real or fictional.
10 See Carty, H, 'Advertising, Publicity Rights and English Law' [2004] IPQ 209.
11 McGee, A, Gale, S, and Scanlan, G, 'Character Merchandising: Aspects of Legal Protection' (2001) 21 LS 226.

Character merchandising is defined in the WIPO Report, *Character Merchandising*,[12] as:

> ... the adaptation or secondary exploitation, by the creator of a fictional character or by a real person or by one or several authorised third parties, of the essential personality features (such as the name, image or appearance) of a character in relation to various goods and/or services with a view to creating in prospective customers a desire to acquire those goods and/or services because of the customers' affinity with that character.

There is no specific right adapted to protect the practice of character or personality merchandising in the UK.[13] In 1977 the Whitford Committee[14] rejected any action to fill the gap between copyright (which does not protect names) and passing off with a 'character right'.[15] Nor is there any international treaty on character merchandising. Often, character owners license their use to makers of products, or providers of services, and do not trade in merchandised products themselves. However, importantly, the licence agreement often includes provision for the character owner to exercise control over the quality of the resulting merchandise – which may emanate from many different manufacturers. The character may be protected by copyright, design rights or even be registered as a trade mark.

Whether there should be a general right to merchandising or protection for an 'image' is much debated. Carty[16] suggests that three justifications can be identified for image protection:

(i)   misappropriation of value;

(ii) privacy for personality;

(iii) economic justifications.

Misappropriation is based on Locke's theory of property[17] (see 2.3.2). If an individual has a property right in his or her body and its labour, to free ride on that property amounts to a form of theft or unjust enrichment at the individual's expense. However, this is to ignore both the extent to which celebrity image enters the cultural public domain, and the commercial benefit already secured by celebrities from their activities.

Human rights law recognises a right to privacy for individuals based on the right to dignity and autonomy for personality. Hegel argued that personality rights should support property in personality.[18] Weber,[19] too, rests justification for publicity rights (as well as a right to privacy) on a natural right to human dignity.

---

12 WIPO, *Report on Character Merchandising*, (1994), WO/INF/108, www.wipo.int.
13 For an argument that none was required, see Holyoak, J, 'United Kingdom Character Rights and Merchandising Rights Today' [1993] JBL 444.
14 *The Whitford Committee on the Reform of Copyright and Design*, 1977, Cmnd 6732.
15 The Committee considered that there was a real difficulty in defining the essential features of a character (within the context of a copyright-related remedy). They considered that remedy in unfair competition would be more appropriate.
16 Carty, H, 'Advertising, Publicity Rights and English Law' [2004] IPQ 209.
17 See Frazer, T, 'Appropriation of Personality – A New Tort?' (1983) 99 LQR 281.
18 See Hughes, J, 'The Philosophy of Intellectual Property' (1988) 77 Geo LJ 287.
19 Weber, O, 'Human Dignity and the Commercial Appropriation of Personality: Towards a Cosmopolitan Consensus in Personality Rights?' (2004) 1:1 SCRIPT-ed, law.ed.ac.uk.

Economic justifications[20] lie in the incentive to creativity that a publicity right would provide, more efficient allocation of the resource that celebrity provides, and the prevention of consumer misinformation. However, it is unlikely that the creation of a publicity right would stimulate the generation of celebrity, which is a by-product of other activity. Alone, the third justification would only extend to protection against false endorsement. However, it can be argued that publicity rights would not endanger competition, for the discerning consumer will have the option to choose the ordinary product untainted by celebrity associations. Frazer[21] concluded that in terms of economic efficiency there may be justification for property in personality, provided that it is confined to the value generated by an image (its goodwill) and does not extend to the image *per se*.

Jaffey[22] also assesses the arguments. There can be no denying that merchandising of image yields substantial financial benefits but this does not automatically imply that protection by granting property rights is desirable. To impose an extra cost on consumers, and restriction on competitors, in order to stimulate the development and exploitation of notoriety does not necessarily bear the justifications of patent and copyright protection, which promote the development of new ideas and products (see Chapter 1). On the other hand, as Frazer[23] argues, property rights in personality could maximise their economic potential. There are other considerations, however. Personality merchandising may have implications for individuals' privacy, as well as social, moral, cultural and anti-competitive effects that must be balanced against their revenue bearing potential.

Story,[24] in particular, argues that the drive to protect Princess Diana's reputation after her death by attempts at personality protection through copyright and trade mark registrations should not lead to distortion of these rights. While there was, and is, clear value in her name, that does not necessarily create a claim to property in that value, through the creation of an artificial scarcity in that name. The value in her name derives more from public acceptance than any labour or skill, or investment in its creation by Diana herself, traditionally the justifications given to the creation of artificial scarcity through intellectual property rights. The use of names as national symbols and tools of communication, as well as the right to freedom of expression, should not be compromised.

While Frazer advocates protection for personality, he notes that the real harm lies in unjust enrichment of a competitor free riding on another's image.[25] It is also clear that there is commercial value in image and a market exists. He says:

> First, even although the commercial value of personality may be a by-product of fame, a considerable investment of time and effort may have been expended to create a personality capable of exploitation. In order to protect the value to the individual of such personality, someone must have control over its use. This is necessary to prevent over-, or damaging, exploitation. The person most interested in maintaining that value

---

20　See Frazer, T, 'Appropriation of Personality – A New Tort?' (1983) 99 LQR 281.
21　*Ibid*.
22　Jaffey, P, 'Merchandising and the Law of Trade Marks' [1998] IPQ 240.
23　Frazer, T, 'Appropriation of Personality – a New Tort' (1983) 99 LQR 281.
24　Story, A, 'Owning Diana: From People's Princess to Private Property' [1998] 5 Web JCLI, www.webjcli.ncl.ac.uk.
25　See Frazer, T, 'Appropriation of Personality – A New Tort?' (1983) 99 LQR 281.

will be the individual concerned. This approach involves abandoning the Utilitarian practice of judging value on a societal basis, and adopting an approach which measures value from the individual viewpoint ... To allow someone else to use the personality without consent would therefore amount to unjust enrichment.

Whether there should be protection for personality is not an apt decision for the courts but for the legislature. However, this is not to say that the courts may not feel that they must eventually bite the merchandising bullet, despite the disadvantages of such law-making, in the same way that Lindsay J states that they may have to do in relation a right to privacy:

So broad is the subject of privacy and such are the ramifications of any free-standing law in the area that the subject is better left to Parliament which can, of course, consult interests far more widely than can be taken into account in the course of ordinary *inter partes* litigation. A judge should therefore be chary of doing that which is better done by Parliament. That Parliament has failed so far to grasp the nettle does not prove that it will not have to be grasped in the future. The recent judgment in *Peck v United Kingdom* [2003] EMLR 15, shows that in circumstances where the law of confidence did not operate our domestic law has already been held to be inadequate. That inadequacy will have to be made good and if Parliament does not step in then the courts will be obliged to. Further development by the courts may merely be awaiting the first post-Human Rights Act case where neither the law of confidence nor any other domestic law protects an individual who deserves protection. A glance at a crystal ball of, so to speak, only a low wattage suggests that if Parliament does not act soon the less satisfactory course, of the courts creating the law bit by bit at the expense of litigants and with inevitable delays and uncertainty, will be thrust upon the judiciary.

Nor can the progress of technology be ignored, as both new means of exploiting image develop, as do methods of developing character in the first place.[26] Both developments enhance the commercial value of personality and may require redress against abusive uses of it. Electronic online and CD-ROM advertising and entertainment provide new markets. In addition, 'digital doubles' of real individuals can be created, for use as stunt doubles for example. It is also possible, by means of computer generated imagery, to manipulate real images, and to create hybrids, modelled on several real individuals.

There are some important distinctions which can be made. Proprietary rights may be apposite where fictional characters are artificially created and then exploited. Investment, skill, labour and judgment will have gone into the creative effort, whether the character is deliberately created for merchandising purposes,[27] or the merchandising follows on the success of an artistic creation.[28] However, the same may not be true for real individuals, whose interest in their personality may lie both in its economic potential and in their dignity and reputation. For the latter, protection may be more appropriate when based on consideration of human rights, for the former a form of redress against unfair competition may constitute appropriate protection. Nevertheless, it may well be that creating a new form of protection against unfair misappropriation of value resting in celebrity notoriety may overcome the dangers of

26 The film *Toy Story 2* is reputed to be the first production entirely in digital format, its characters digitally created.
27 Such as Ronald McDonald or Colonel Saunders.
28 Harry Potter, Peter Rabbit, Winnie the Pooh and the like.

distorting existing intellectual property protection.[29] Beverley-Smith discusses three possible forms for such protection:

(i)   a personal remedy in tort based on invasion of privacy;

(ii) a personal remedy in tort based on infringement of a proprietary interest in personal attributes such as name, image, and voice;

(iii) a right of property in attributes of person which may be assigned and bequeathed as personal property.

18.2   PASSING OFF AND MERCHANDISING

Passing off has not yet proved an effective means of defence for character merchandisers, despite the early promise of *Samuelson v Producers Distributing* (1932), and more recent developments. The plaintiff had copyright in a popular revue sketch. The defendant made a film which it held out to include the sketch. The copyright, which had not been infringed, was treated as tantamount to goodwill and passing off was found to have occurred. Since this case, however, two aspects of passing off have posed problems for its application to character merchandising: the need for a common field of action and the requirement of misrepresentation.

18.2.1   Common field of action

If the licensor of the character sues, the necessary element of damage must be found in damage to that licensor's goodwill. Commonly, however, the licensor is engaged in a completely different field of commerce, film making, for example, and does not produce the type of merchandise to which licensees have applied the character. Although poor quality imitations may cause considerable damage to the licensing potential of a character, if a common field of action between defendant and claimant is required, this damage will not suffice (see 14.5.3). Initially, the courts followed *McCulloch v May* (1948) and licensors did not succeed in several actions: *Tavener Rutledge v Trexpalm* (1975) (Kojak); *Wombles v Wombles Skips* (1977) (Wombles); *Lyngstad v Anabas* (1977) (Abba). The argument that by quality control provisions in the licensing agreement with the merchandiser licensees constituted a common field of action with the defendant did not prevail. However, potential damage can be identified: the loss of licensing opportunities or opportunities to expand into new fields of commerce, as well as damage to reputation and dilution of the character itself. The result was criticism of the position in the UK.

In Australia, a right to publicity and a remedy for misappropriation of reputation were recognised following *Henderson v RCA* (1969). In *Children's TV v Woolworths* (1981), the plaintiff succeeded against the defendant who made unlicensed use of the Muppet characters.

In Australia, the courts have moved away from a requirement of damage to goodwill to requiring only damage to reputation. In *Hogan v Koala Dundee* (1988), the defendant sold items appearing to be associated with the Crocodile Dundee films without authority. The plaintiff, the creator and actor of the character, carried on no

---

29   See Beverley-Smith, H, *The Commercial Appropriation of Personality* (Cambridge: CUP, 2002).

business at all (other than as an actor), but was able to restrain this misappropriation of his reputation. Since *Lego's* reinterpretation of the common field of action, the case of *Mirage Studios v Counter-Feat Clothing* (1991) has given cause for cautious optimism. The plaintiff copyright owners and licensors of the Ninja Turtle characters secured an interlocutory injunction against the defendant, which had applied very similar drawings of turtle characters to children's clothing. The earlier UK cases were distinguished as there was no copyright in the names of the Wombles or Kojak. Damage was found because, although the plaintiff's primary business was as the maker of cartoons, films and videos, a large part of its business also lay in licensing the reproduction of the characters' images for the films, leading to loss of royalties from the defendant's activities. Effectively, therefore, the copyright in the characters was regarded as creating goodwill.

It is not clear that a name (in which there is no copyright) could be protected in the same way. However, in *Football Association Premier League Ltd v Graymore Marketing Ltd* (1995), a short injunction was awarded to the plaintiff, which licensed the Football Association name. It was arguable that the plaintiff had a property right in the name which could be defended in passing off. Nevertheless, a lack of willingness to expand definitions of damage to goodwill will limit the application of passing off to character merchandising in cases where the damage is less clear cut than it was in *Mirage Studios v Counter-Feat Clothing* (1991).

18.2.2 Misrepresentation

As a finding of misrepresentation hinges on the finding of customer confusion; there can be no success in passing off for the licensor of a character if the public does not understand the practice of such licensing. The public will not draw any connection between the licensor and the defendant's unauthorised merchandise, nor confuse the two. Walton J refused to accept any public understanding of character merchandising in *Tavener Rutledge v Trexpalm* (1975). Such recognition did not come until *Mirage Studios v Counter-Feat Clothing* (1991). It may be that the courts will require evidence of public awareness of a misrepresentation; otherwise, such a misrepresentation could be implied from public understanding of character merchandising in every case where there is potential for any such exploitation. A representation from the defendant that his merchandise is authorised by the claimant may be necessary. It would seem that there can be no misrepresentation if the claimant is not engaged in *any* commercial activity, as in *Hogan v Koala Dundee* (1988), where there was only a misappropriation of reputation. By contrast, the misrepresentation in *Mirage Studios v Counter-Feat Clothing* (1991) was clear because of the plaintiff's extensive licensing activities. This case clearly differed from *Stringfellow v McCain Foods* (1984), where the plaintiff had not engaged in any licensing or exploitation of his name.

18.2.3 Passing off and false endorsement

Nevertheless, some progress towards protection for a merchantable reputation has developed from the recognition of passing off through false endorsement in *Irvine v Talksport Ltd* (2003) (see 14.6.2). The case can be seen as providing specific protection for a famous person preventing others exploiting their name or image for commercial purposes.

Eddie Irvine is a well known racing driver, who endorsed a number of products. When the defendant promoted its radio service it issued a publicity pack which included a copy of a digitally manipulated photograph of the claimant holding a portable radio (the original photo showed a mobile phone) with the words 'Talk Radio' depicted. Laddie J held that there was nothing to prevent a remedy in passing off in an endorsement case provided that the claimant proved two facts:

(i)   that at the time of the act complained of he had 'significant reputation or goodwill';

(ii)   that the actions of the defendant gave rise to a false message which would be understood by 'a not insignificant section of his market that his goods have been endorsed, recommended or … approved of by the claimant'.

The Court of Appeal upheld Laddie J's finding of passing off, and increased the quantum of damages to £25,000. Despite the disapproval of the need for a 'common field of action' (see 14.5.3), the courts' emphasis on the traditional passing off 'trinity' may restrict the extent of this remedy for those desiring an element of image protection.[30] Robinson points out that 'negated' advertisements and promotions where a lookalike model is used may not fare so well in passing off.[31] Nor will celebrities who have not engaged in previous endorsement succeed. Nevertheless, Laddie J clearly recognised the evolving nature of passing off in the context of market practice, and aligned the remedy with 'the maintenance of what is currently regarded as fair trading'.

Similarly, the case does not extend protection for all character merchandising as Laddie J distinguished between merchandising and endorsement:

When someone endorse a product or service he tells the relevant public that he approves of the product or service or is happy to be associated with it. In effect he adds his name as an encouragement to members of the relevant public to buy or use the service or product. Merchandising is rather different. It involves exploiting images, themes or articles which have become famous. … It is not a necessary feature of merchandising that members of the public will think the products are in any sense endorsed by the film maker[32] or actors in the film.

However, he did go on to say that '[m]erchandised products will include some where there is a perception of endorsement'. Protection will depend, therefore, on the way in which a celebrity image is used in character merchandising.

Whether David Bedford would have succeeded in a passing off claim (see 18.10) by false endorsement is less clear. His reputation, forged in the 1970s, was less well established than Irvine's, nor had he been engaged in considerable endorsement activity in the same way. The Number, which used an image of an athlete in its advertising, has also claimed that the athlete is based on an American runner, while twin athletes have also claimed that the image is based on them. In addition, the image used was not a photograph of Bedford manipulated in the same way as the TalkSport promotion. If David Bedford had succeeded in an action for damages a much clearer protection for image through passing off would have been established.

---

30   Although Carty argues that Laddie J stretched each element of the 'classic trinity' to provide a remedy. See Carty, H, 'Advertising, Publicity Rights and English Law' [2004] IPQ 209, and Scanlan, G, 'Personality, Endorsement and Everything' [2003] EIPR 563.

31   Robinson, F, 'How Image Conscious is English Law?' [2004] Ent LR 151.

32   Laddie J used the example of *Star Wars* merchandise.

18.3 MERCHANDISING AND TRADE MARKS

Registering trade marks is an obvious means of obtaining a property right in an image, and there are many registered marks at the root of character merchandising. For example, Jonny Wilkinson, like many sporting personalities, has registered Community marks denoting his name[33] and characteristic stance. Registration of names, likenesses, signatures and logos is subject to normal trade mark principles. The mark denoting the image must be distinctive (see 15.4), and not clash with pre-existing rights (see 15.15); nor will it protect against non-trade mark use by others (see 16.1). An image mark may also be subject to revocation for non-use if it is deemed not to have been used in a trade mark sense (see 16.10). The concept of the nature and function of a trade mark lies at the root of all these decisions (see 15.1.3).

In the past, the UK Trade Mark Registry has taken a firm view that marks as indicators of origin must be distinguished from badges of allegiance and indications describing what products are about, or who has endorsed them, rather than where they have come from. This was reflected in *Re Elvis Presley's Application* (1999) (see 15.1.3 and 15.6.2) in relation to registration of a mark. Subsequently, in relation to non-infringement, in *Arsenal Football Club plc v Reed* (2001) application of a 'badge of allegiance' to unofficial and competing merchandise was held not to constitute trade mark use[34] (see 16.1.3). The Princess Diana Memorial Fund has also had mixed success in registering marks denoting the late Princess of Wales for charitable fundraising use (see 15.1.3).[35] Debate has also centred on the need for good faith in an application under s 3(6) of the TMA 1994 (see 15.14), and the permissible use of a mark to satisfy the requirements of s 32 of the TMA 1994.

However, recent developments have moved some way towards adapting trade mark principles to accommodate merchandising. Although both the Trade Mark Directive and the ECJ acknowledge trade mark function to be to indicate the origin of goods, this has received wide interpretation when applied in practice, as discussed in Chapter 15. Despite greater flexibility in interpretation of a trade mark's function, it remains the case that no special treatment is given to a mark purely because it represents a character, real or imaginary. In particular, there would be a danger in adapting trade mark law specifically to provide image protection, if this were to over-protect other trade marks and jeopardise the public domain.

Jaffey[36] clearly identifies trade mark function as conveying the message to consumers that 'the quality and attributes of the product bearing the mark are under the control of some person who customarily uses the mark' for this purpose. He goes on to demonstrate that using a mark to appeal to a customer by associating a product with a merchandising object is not to convey this message. The same is true where a mark is used as a means of image advertising or ornament, such as applying COCA-COLA to pencil cases.

---

33 Community Trade Mark 3458056 for classes 9, 16, 25 and 28.
34 Overruled by the CA in *Arsenal Football Club v Reed* (2003) (see 16.1.3).
35 Attempts to prevent use of her likeness by the American firm Franklin Mint in the US courts also failed. They resulted in legal action against the Memorial Fund for malicious prosecution, eventually settled when the Fund agreed to pay a reported £13 million to charitable causes on behalf of Franklin Mint. 'Diana's Fund in Legal Settlement', 10 November 2004: www.bbc.co.uk.
36 Jaffey, P, 'Merchandising and the Law of Trade Marks' [1998] IPQ 240.

18.3.1   Distinctiveness and merchandising marks

How an application will fare on the absolute grounds is dependent, in part, on the nature of the mark.

Names

Where a name is well known, it is likely that its application to products would not be understood as an indication of source, so much as a designation of what the goods were about. This remains the case even although the individual concerned traded in those goods as their primary function.[37] Consider, for example, the name ROBBIE WIILIAMS being applied to a poster of his likeness. It was this reasoning that prevailed in *Re Elvis Presley's Application* (1999), and has proved a stumbling block to name applications in some cases.

In 1999 the Jane Austen Memorial Trust opposed an application for JANE AUSTEN for toiletries made by a commercial concern.[38] This was not an application made by a celebrity, or her representatives; however, the reasoning is relevant. The trust argued that the name mark was devoid of distinctive character under s 3(1)(b) of the TMA 1994. This was because, if a well known name was likely to result in a demand for memorabilia, then consumers were likely to see the name as indicative of the content or character of the products, rather than as an indication of their source. The mark was refused in the Trade Marks Registry on the ground that the name was so well known that its only relevant use was to the souvenir trade and would not be recognised as a mark by the public. It was recognised that this conclusion would depend on the extent of an individual's reputation, whether there was an established trade in merchandise and the nature of the products for which registration was sought.

Registration of DIANA, PRINCESS OF WALES was similarly refused by the registry[39] on the ground that the name was more apt to describe the type of goods than their source from a single undertaking. This was only underlined by the fact that the Princess's estate found it necessary to use other marks to signify souvenirs given its 'official approval'. Nor did representation of Diana's name in a facsimile of her signature avoid successful opposition on relative grounds from the proprietor of a Community Trade Mark 'Diana' in plain script.[40] The mark DIANA, PRINCESS OF WALES MEMORIAL FUND did, however, survive opposition.[41] The addition of the words 'memorial fund' sufficed to indicate to consumers that products so marked were linked to the same undertaking. In addition, in *Arsenal Football Club v Reed* (2001) Laddie J held that the ARSENAL mark was validly registered, although it could be used by others in a non-trade mark sense.

As a result, the Trade Mark Registry issued a Practice Note on names of famous people in 2004.[42] This serves to reinforce the point that 'the name may appear to the

---

37   Davies, G, 'The Cult of Celebrity and Trade Marks: The Next Instalment' (2004) 1:2 SCRIPT-ed, www.law.ed.ac.uk/ahrb/script-ed.
38   *Jane Austen Trade Mark* (2000).
39   *Diana, Princess of Wales Trade Mark* (2001).
40   *Diana Trade Mark* (2004): www.patent.gov.uk.
41   Decision of the Appointed Person in the Matter of Oppositions 49400 and 49431, 1 May 2003: www.patent.gov.uk.
42   'Names of Famous People (Living and Deceased) and Groups' PAN 5/04: www.patent.gov.uk.

average consumer as an indication that the goods/services are *about* the person whose name it is, rather than an indication that [they] are supplied by, or under the control of, one undertaking'. However, it also goes on to discuss areas where this may not be so, posing the test:

> ... to consider whether the famous name put forward for registration is so descriptive in relation to the goods/services for which registration is sought that it could not be perceived by consumers as anything more than a description of [their] subject matter.

Some attention should be paid to the phrases 'so descriptive' and 'anything more than'. It would seem that to be refused the mark must be so clearly descriptive as to constitute an element of the content of the product. Where its use may be both descriptive, and indicate a connection to approval of the goods or services, registration is more likely.

The Practice Note provides that registration of names or groups for media[43] and badges of allegiance are possible. Use of the mark is likely to imply some form of control by or guarantee from the name holder, although it will always be a question of the facts in each case. This is so even though others may sell unofficial versions of the badges of allegiance. However, some names may still be unable to serve the functions of a trade mark, such as those of some members of the Royal Family because of the widespread historical trade in royal souvenirs.

Names of individuals and groups are much less likely to be granted for 'mere image carriers'.[44] Here, the name is more than likely to be seen as descriptive of the product's subject matter by consumers. The same is true of names of the deceased or defunct groups, although each application will be considered on its facts.

Existing registrations will be allowed to lie on the register but, as Davies points out,[45] any action to defend them against infringement is likely to be met with a counterclaim as to invalidity or the use to be found not to constitute trade mark use.

Signatures

Under the TMA 1938 there was a presumption that signatures were registrable as marks, and the Elvis signature mark was held to be distinctive[46] by the Court of Appeal in *Re Elvis Presley's Application* (1999). The distinctiveness of a signature can be seen to lie in the script used, marking the name out from its ordinary depictions in script or print form. The TMA 1994 makes no explicit reference to signature marks and the normal principles apply. A signature holds connotations both of approval and source which tend to an implication of *prima facie* distinctiveness. In the opposition[47] to the application to register Diana's signature, it was found that the mark was in a form which distinguished it visually from the usual means of designating memorabilia. In

---

43 'Printed Publications, Recorded Sounds, Films, Videos, TV Programmes, Musical or Live Performances' PAN 5/04.

44 'Posters, Photographs, Transfers and Figurines' PAN 5/04.

45 Davies, G, 'The Cult of Celebrity and Trade Marks: the Next Instalment' (2004) 1·2 SCRIPT-ed, www.law.ed.ac.uk/ahrb/script-ed.

46 However, the opposition to registration of the signature mark succeeded because it was found to be confusingly similar to that already used by the 'unofficial' merchandiser.

47 Decision in the Matter of Oppositions 49400, 49431 and 50424, 25 January 2002: www.patent.gov.uk.

addition, as such a mark is a visual one by its very nature, any lack of aural distinctiveness was not significant. However, the mark later suffered a successful opposition[48] on relative grounds by the holder of a Community Trade Mark, DIANA, in normal typeface.

Images

Princess Diana's estate was unsuccessful in registering 52 photographs of the princess, which were refused for lack of distinctiveness for the wide variety of goods for which the applications were made. It could not be said that her likeness would distinguish the products of one undertaking as distinct from the product of another undertaking.

The Practice Note also applies to pictures of both living and deceased individuals, and groups. The issues are similar and pictures, depending on the nature of the product, are likely to be decorative and lack the trade mark function. Nevertheless, each application will be considered on its merits.

18.3.2   Section 3(6) of the TMA 1994

It is an absolute ground for refusal if an application for a trade mark is not made in good faith (see 15.14).

Consent

An application for the name of a living individual as a mark made without the person's consent is likely to be regarded as made in bad faith. This was argued in *Jane Austen Trade Mark* (2000), but held not to apply to an historical figure. The Memorial Trust was found to have to greater right to the name than the applicant. Although the application had been made at a time of film and television dramatisation of Austen's works, this was regarded as no more than 'commercial opportunism', and not bad faith. The Practice Note states that care must be taken where an individual's reputation is not commercial.[49] In such circumstances, no application would be accepted without the consent of the person concerned. In general, the Practice Note says, a bad faith objection may be overcome by the consent of the individual.

Applications seeking to take advantage of an individual's[50] reputation will be frowned upon, so that to use a model's name for clothing or cosmetics would be liable to objection, although one for the same name in relation to agricultural services would not.

---

48   Decision in the Matter of Opposition 50459, 5 July 2004, www.patent.gov.uk/tm/legal/decisions/index.htm. The hearing officer accepted that the signature mark was a stylised version of the word 'Diana' (and 'possibly a signature'), but did not accept that there was a conceptual difference as both were clearly the (common) name Diana. He said that the average consumer would view both as 'Diana' marks. He did not apply the distinction between visual and conceptual aspects of the marks as in the earlier opposition in 2002 (above).

49   PAN 5/04. The Note gives Tony Blair as an example, his fame being political and not commercial.

50   Living or recently dead. PAN 5/04.

Intention to use

Applicants are required to state that the mark is being used or that they have a *bona fide* intention to use the mark for the goods or services requested.[51] An objection may then be made under s 3(6) of the TMA 1994 if the use to be made is not 'trade mark' use. This is particularly so if the use is made by licensees of the trade mark proprietor. The DIANA PRINCESS OF WALES MEMORIAL FUND mark was opposed[52] on the ground that the use was only true in relation to 'fundraising for charitable purposes'. The Appointed Person held that the use referred to was use which would defeat an application for revocation for non-use (see 16.10.2). This is use in relation to goods or services of the kind specified with the indication that they have originated under the control of a single undertaking responsible for their quality: *IHT Internationale v Ideal-Standard* (1994). In that case the ECJ held that to surrender control over a mark by assignment to an unconnected assignee prevented subsequent use of the mark to the assignor. However, it is not clear whether the same would apply to a licence to an otherwise unconnected licensee. In *Scandecor Developments AB v Scandecor Marketing AB* (2002) (see 16.10.5) the House of Lords held that:

(i) the purpose of a mark is to denote the business source of goods or services;

(ii) that business source is the person entitled to use of the mark for the time being;

(iii) that consumers rely on a brand owner and licensee's self interest for guarantee of quality; and

(iv) that customers should not be taken to rely on the protection of a legal agreement controlling the quality of a licensee's products.

The Appointed Person went on to hold that the test to be applied was that laid down by the ECJ in *Arsenal Football Club v Reed* (2003). One should ask whether the use would create the impression in a consumer of a material link in the course of trade between the products and the undertaking designated by the mark. On the facts, he found that there were two possible ways in which to use the FUND mark. It could indicate either a purely financial connection between the Fund and the producer,[53] or to connote a producer/supplier connection. As the evidence was ambivalent to what was intended, the opponent's allegation of a misrepresentation in the s 32(3) declarations could not be substantiated.

Promotional use

Objection was raised to the REEF mark in *Reef Trade Mark* (2002) under s 3(6) of the TMA 1994 because the applicants, a pop group, planned to use the mark on merchandising material such a T-shirts. Pumfrey J refused to regard use of a mark to indicate trade origin of products, and using the T-shirts as a 'billboard', as mutually exclusive. It is clear from *Daimlerchrysler AG v Alavi* (2001) that trade can be established in promotional goods, the mark serving a dual function. Consequently, the limitation

---

51 Section 32(3) of the TMA 1994.

52 Decision of the Appointed Person in the Matter of Oppositions 49400 and 49431, 1 May 2003: www.patent.gov.uk.

53 It was argued that the Fund only intended the mark to convey the fact that a sum would be paid to the Fund for its charitable purposes from the purchase price of goods.

to promotional goods in the application was not determinative, and the application was not rejected on this basis.

However, Pumfrey J gave an example of REEF on the neck-band of a T-shirt , and ORCHESTRA OF THE AGE OF ENLIGHTENMENT on the front. It is not clear that the same would have been held had the neck-band shown the mark of another manufacturer and REEF appeared as the decorative touch.

18.3.3   Infringement of merchandising marks

Decorative or descriptive use of a trade mark will not infringe (see 16.1.3). Consequently, even where an image of a celebrity is registered, unauthorised use of the celebrity's likeness on merchandising products, may not infringe the mark (although if the same image is copied it may infringe any copyright subsisting in it).

However, the *Arsenal Football Club v Reed* case demonstrates a new, if reluctant, willingness to protect the Arsenal marks against trade by an unofficial merchandiser. The use made by Reed had been termed use as 'badges of support, loyalty or affiliation' in the High Court.[54] In *Arsenal Football Club plc v Reed* (2002) the ECJ held that if use of a sign by a third party is 'liable to jeopardise the guarantee of origin which constitutes the essential function of the mark' it is a use which the proprietor is entitled to protect through the exclusive right. *Hölterhoff* (see 16.1.3) was distinguished as constituting 'purely' descriptive use. Consequently, infringement will depend on the Court's interpretation of the essential function of a mark.

The ECJ's reasoning is significant, not least for its implicit recognition of the merchandising function of marks (see 15.1.3). The Court began with the essential function of a mark as a guarantee of origin, and concluded that the proprietor must therefore be entitled to protection against competitors taking unfair advantage of the mark's status and reputation by selling products 'illegally' bearing it. This begs the question whether Reed's use was illegal by virtue of trade mark infringement. The unfairness of the competition was assumed. The Court continued to conclude that Reed's use of the Arsenal marks could be distinguished from *Hölterhoff* use because the sales were to consumers and not intended to be descriptive. No consideration was given to decorative use.

The use was also considered to imply a 'link' to the club in the course of trade (despite the use of a disclaimer on the stall clearly stating the goods were unofficial). However, there was no guarantee that the marked ('official') goods had been manufactured or supplied under the control of a single undertaking responsible for their quality. Such a link can only be implied if the public both understand the practice of licensed merchandising, and are not aware that many 'unofficial' products are also available. It has been argued[55] that the ECJ may have misunderstood Laddie J's 'badge of allegiance' argument as requiring a 'defence' to infringement, even when a defendant's use of the mark did create a perception as to origin (or other 'essential trade mark function').

There is further potential for very wide findings of infringement if the ECJ's reasoning is applied to well known marks under s 10(3) of the TMA 1994. The Court

---

54   *Arsenal Football Club plc v Reed (No 1)* (2001).
55   'The New European Law on Trade Mark Infringement', IPR Helpdesk: www.ipr-helpdesk.org.

appears to suggest that for a mark's guarantee of origin to be preserved, the trade mark owner requires protection against competitors taking unfair advantage of a mark's status and reputation. It is not explained how a defendant's benefit necessarily removes the mark's ability to identify a claimant's goods. If this is the case, it would seem that any use by a competitor will infringe, without any requirement to show either confusion or 'trade mark' use. It is notable that the ECJ has not adverted to any 'essential function' for marks in relation to cases of dilution. Consequently, it is not yet clear whether this provision is intended to extend beyond protection for marks as marks, into a remedy against unfair competition, or that the merchandising and advertising uses of marks are recognised as part of their functions, and protected by trade mark infringement.

In the UK

Laddie J considered that the ECJ had made findings of fact, outside its remit, and refused to follow its conclusion, which departed from his own findings of fact at first instance.

The Court of Appeal finally capitulated in *Arsenal Football Club plc v Reed (No 2)* (2003). The Court held that the ECJ had not answered the questions referred to it because these assumed that the issue was whether use inferred 'trade mark' use. Instead, the ECJ had concentrated on the exclusive property right trade marks confer. The real issue, then, was damage to that property. This was widely defined as:

> ... unchecked use of the mark by a third party, which is not descriptive use, is likely to damage the function of the trade mark right because the registered trade mark can no longer guarantee origin, that being an essential function of a trade mark.

Consequently, some descriptive and decorative uses do not affect that right, but others may. We must now wait for case law to suggest where the dividing line lies.

The Court of Appeal did suggest that, because Reed's goods were identical to the official products, they would carry the same inference as the use of trade marks generally, absent any explanation to the contrary. The Court implied, therefore, that had the signs differed in detail, an objective consumer would not make similar assumptions. One is still tempted to ask whether any rational and objective consumer would regard using ARSENAL marks on a street trader's products bought outside a football ground on match day indicative of official Club merchandise. The decision certainly casts doubt on the Glasgow Sheriff Court's decision to allow a street trader to continue selling unofficial Old Firm Celtic and Rangers merchandise. It would appear that the decision of the ECJ effectively prevents all, or nearly all, competition in merchandised products. Does this not confer a monopoly in goods, rather than in a mark?

18.4 COPYRIGHT AND MERCHANDISING

A certain degree of protection for character and image can be secured through copyright, with the advantages of automatic and informal protection that copyright brings. Much will depend on the type of work at issue, however. It is established that copyright does not subsist in names (see 8.2.1),[56] so that trade mark protection is more apposite for words, names or phrases, provided that the criteria of registrability are met. Protection for a literary work is also restricted. The CDPA 1988 does not specify that literary works are infringed by 3D reproductions in the same way as it does for artistic works,[57] although reproduction may involve a change of form[58] (see 10.1.1). Consequently, a description of a fictional character such as Sherlock Holmes,[59] however detailed and distinctive, would be unlikely to support merchandising of Holmes dolls, tea towels and the like.

Copyright will more readily protect a likeness of a character. Sketches, drawings and photographs falling into the category of artistic works will protect against a degree of unauthorised use. Copyright in artistic works[60] will also be protected against 3D reproduction (see 10.1.1). This was demonstrated in the old case of *King Features v O & M Kleeman* (1941). The defendant made 'Popeye' dolls and other merchandise riding on the success of the Popeye cartoons. These were held to infringe the copyright subsisting in the cartoons. It should be noted that the dolls were not exact reproductions of particular drawings, but were made to reflect the distinctive features of the Popeye character, including his muscled and tattooed arms, his squint, clothing and pipe.

Real characters have an interest in protecting their voice, particularly where it is distinctive: Sean Connery providing a clear example. While copyright in a sound recording will apply to a particular recording, less protection for a celebrity's distinctive manner of speech or accent exists. In *Sim v Heinz* (1959) the (then) well known actor, Alistair Sim, did not succeed in obtaining an interlocutory injunction for passing off when a 'soundalike' was used to mimic[61] his voice in filmed advertisements. In the same way that refilming the dance sequence in *Norowzian v Arks (No 1)* (1998) did not infringe the film copyright, so recreating even the same spoken words with a soundalike should not infringe copyright in a sound recording.

Today, infringement will be determined by normal copyright principles, so that only reproduction of a substantial part of a work in which copyright subsisted could infringe. In particular, merely to take the 'idea' from a work (see 8.2.4) would fail to infringe. Nevertheless, Sir Nicolas Browne-Wilkinson did not dismiss the possibility of some copyright protection in *Mirage Studios v Counter-Feat Clothing* (1991). In an interlocutory hearing he granted relief, finding that a case of copyright infringement was arguable. He said:

> The difficulties surrounding any claim by the plaintiff based in copyright are primarily two. First, there is the rule in copyright that you cannot have copyright in a name, and on that basis it is said that ... Ninja Turtles, are names and not subject to any copyright. The point seems to me not altogether easy to say whether a descriptive invented name is to be categorised as name or as a description. The second and more

---

56 As was recognised in the character merchandising case of *Mirage Studios v Counter-Feat Clothing* (1991).

57 Section 17(3) of the CDPA 1988.

58 *Ibid*, s 17(2).

59 Conan Doyle's copyright has now expired, but the example is used by McGee, A, and Scanlan, G, in 'Copyright in Character' [2003] JBL 470.

60 But not literary works (see 10.1.1).

61 There was no visual representation of Alistair Sim.

fundamental difficulty in copyright is the saying that 'there is no copyright in ideas'. For myself, I find it difficult to determine what that phrase means in the present context. As I have said, although there are similarities in the graphic representation of the defendants' product to those in the plaintiffs' product, they are mainly reproductions of a concept, of the humanoid turtle of an aggressive nature. However, whether that permits a claim in copyright or not seems to me to be a very open question; there is certainly an arguable case in copyright.

Should a merchandiser rely on copyright protection, due attention would need to be paid to ensuring that ownership of the copyright was secured. This would be particularly the case if an independent artist's work or photographs had been commissioned (see 9.3.2). It should also be remembered that copyright, unlike a trade mark[62] or confidentiality,[63] will expire. Many characters are short-lived in their merchandising potential, but many endure – MICKEY MOUSE, PETER RABBIT, and WINNIE the POOH being notable examples.

Where drawings are created specifically for the purposes of merchandising s 51 of the CDPA 1988 is most likely to apply (see 13.2.1), so that design protection must be sought. Even if not specifically created in this way, s 52 of the CDPA 1988 may reduce the duration of copyright protection available (see 13.2.4).

An area where the lack of clear copyright protection may cause difficulties is in relation to artificial computer created characters. While LARA CROFT, for example, remains less than human in appearance, recent developments in programming have led to the creation of very convincing artificial 'human' characters.[64] The software itself is clearly the subject of protection as a literary work (see 8.5.2), but this does not protect the 'idea' of the character any more than would a written description.

18.5 DESIGN PROTECTION AND MERCHANDISING

Some of the deficiencies of copyright as a means of protecting character may be overcome by registering designs. UK Unregistered Design Right will not apply to surface decoration,[65] but can provide short-term but informal and automatic protection against copying for original three-dimensional articles. Both UK Registered Design protection and Community Design rights (registered and unregistered) may provide protection to 2D and 3D designs which are new and have individual character (see 13.5). This protection should provide the mainstay of character merchandising. There is no longer the requirement for eye-appeal to limit registration, and novelty will remain for goods already marketed provided that they have been on the market less than 12 months (see 13.5.5). Registration is no longer limited to articles, so that applications may be made for the whole and parts of products (see 13.5.3). It may be that new photographs of celebrities may be successively registered as characteristic make up[66] and the like changes, and secure protection for accompanying merchandising.

---

62 Provided that registration is renewed.
63 Provided that secrecy is maintained.
64 'Virtual humans edge closer' BBC News, 27 July 2003: www.bbc.co.uk.
65 Section 213(3)(c) of the CDPA 1988.
66 Had Adam Ant's make up been registered in *Merchandising Corp of America v Harpbond* (1983) the unauthorised posters might have infringed (see 8.8.1).

18.6 PROTECTION FOR PERSONALITY

Character merchandising relates to both fictional and real personalities. Where real individuals are concerned new interests are at stake, for not only is the commercial value of the individual's notoriety at stake, but also elements of personal dignity and autonomy. Where there is protection for an individual's privacy, it has the potential to protect the publicity of a personal image indirectly. In the United States protection for privacy has expanded into a separate right of publicity.[67] There, privacy for the private person (who may be well known) is concentrated on redress for hurt feelings, while the publicity right protects public figures and compensates for loss of goodwill.

McGee and Scanlan[68] draw attention to differing categories of persona and the different needs for protection each requires, while noting that each merely represents a new step on a spectrum of personality. Consequently, they advocate a flexible approach to protection through the existing law (not just that of intellectual property), rather than the creation of any new and discrete personality right. However, the real distinction lies not so much in categories of person, as the perceived harm caused by the action of third parties. A remedy for loss of commercial exploitation and profit should differ from one for loss of dignity and autonomy caused by intrusion into one's private life. The different scope of these remedies lies in the interests being protected, rather than in the nature of the individual concerned. Whether a complete unknown, or an internationally renowned icon, an individual should have the same potential for personality protection. In practice, of course, the man in the street is not likely to have significant commercial potential in his identity, while the well known celebrity may sacrifice some expectation of privacy to the public interest, at least where the notoriety has been actively sought and exploited. If this were to be the case, the straining of the action for breach of confidence to accommodate the commercial (publicity) interests of Michael Douglas and Catherine Zeta Jones (see 18.7) through protection for private information might be avoided. It is notable that the damages[69] awarded to the couple represented damages for distress, and the substantial sum applied for was not granted. It was OK Magazine which was awarded damages for lost profit.

Nevertheless, Goodenough[70] argues that the concepts of privacy and publicity cannot be distinguished. Certainly it is true that unauthorised uses of a persona in merchandising may also impinge on the individual's privacy. The harm, however, remains distinct. Even so, it is through attempts to enforce privacy that some publicity protection has developed.

18.7 BREACH OF CONFIDENCE AND A RIGHT OF PRIVACY?

Judicial willingness to countenance some protection for privacy can be traced from *Kaye v Robertson* (1990). A remedy was provided in this case, however, only by the

---

67 It can be traced to the case of *Haelan Laboratories Inc v Topps Chewing Gum Inc* (1953), 202 2d 866 (2nd Cir, 1953).
68 McGee, A, and Scanlan, G, 'Phantom Intellectual Property Rights' [2000] IPQ 264.
69 *Douglas v Hello! (No 8)* (2004).
70 Goodenough, O, 'Re-theorising Privacy and Publicity' [1997] IPQ 37.

action against malicious falsehood. Subsequent *dicta* in 1994 in *Hellewell v Chief Constable of Derbyshire* (1994) suggested that privacy might be protected through confidentiality. This possibility was also mooted by the European Commission on Human Rights in *Earl Spencer and Countess Spencer* (1998), and came partially to fruition in *Douglas v Hello! Ltd* (2000).

By treating the personal information in this case as a commercial trade secret, Lindsay J allowed some scope for protection for character merchandising by celebrities. This is, however, subject to his clear finding of fact that the wedding remained a private and personal function despite its size and celebrity studded guest list. That was, he said, to be expected in the context of the claimants' income and position. Nor did he regard the fact that the claimants intended to publish the authorised photographs of the wedding as necessarily destroying confidentiality.

Protection for privacy through confidence requires two adaptations of the action. These are, first, recognition that private information falls within the category of confidential information even when publicly observable and, secondly, that a confidential relationship may arise from the nature of the information itself.

In *Douglas v Hello!* (2000) Sedley LJ stated:

> What a concept of privacy does, however, is accord recognition to the fact that the law has to protect not only those people whose trust has been abused but those who simply find themselves subjected to an unwarranted intrusion into their personal lives. The law no longer needs to construct an artificial relationship of confidentiality between intruder and victim: it can recognise privacy itself as a legal principle drawn from the fundamental value of personal autonomy.

However, the Court of Appeal made it clear that this new protection is a form of the protection for confidential information, although grounded in the convention right. In *Campbell v MGN Ltd* (2004) Lord Hoffmann[71] explained the influence of human rights law on the action for breach of confidence as identifying the need to protect private information as an aspect of human dignity and autonomy. Consequently, he says, echoing Sedley LJ's *dictum*, that:

> The result of these developments has been a shift in the centre of gravity of the action for breach of confidence when it is used as a remedy for the unjustified publication of personal information. It recognises that the incremental changes ... do not merely extend the duties arising traditionally from a relationship of trust and confidence to a wider range of people ... the new approach takes a different view of the underlying value which the law protects ... it focuses upon the protection of human autonomy and dignity ...

It is clear from *Campbell* (2002), *A v B & C* (2002), *Douglas v Hello!* (2003) and *Campbell v MGN Ltd* (2004) that the new protection for privacy is one of protection for private information and a form of the protection for confidence. A further step needs to be taken before mere intrusions into privacy receive protection. This was confirmed in *Douglas v Hello! Ltd* (2003) and described by Lindsay J as 'a fusion between the pre-

---

71 Although the House decided in favour of Naomi Campbell by a majority of 3:2, Lord Hoffmann (who dissented in the result) states that the differences between the law lords did not relate to the general principles to be applied to balancing the right to privacy and to freedom of expression, merely to the result in this particular case. Nevertheless, Lords Hoffmann and Nicholls appear to give greater primacy to the values of privacy and freedom of expression as derived from human rights than does the majority.

existing law of confidence and rights and duties arising under the Human Rights Act'. Subsequently, in *Campbell v MGN Ltd* (2004) the House of Lords have again confirmed protection for privacy as protection for private information without more – through an action for breach of confidence.

Thus, the three criteria of *Coco v AN Clarke (Engineers) Ltd* (1969) lie at the root of the protection so far given to personal confidences. Morland J followed this approach in *Campbell v Mirror Group Newspapers* (2002). However, there are qualifications to the traditional *Coco* criteria that must be made: it is not all private information that will be protected and, where there is to be protection, an injunction may not lie.

18.7.1 Confidentiality of private information

There must be information which is private. This was made clear in *Campbell v MGN Ltd* (2004). However, it is not all information about an individual which may be protected.

There is a distinction between private information and that which is public. In *A v B & C* (2002) Lord Woolf CJ stated, in the guidelines the Court of Appeal set out for this new protection, that there must be 'some interest of a private nature', but forbore to provide any definition of a 'private' interest. On this question Lord Woolf CJ also urged an abstinence of argument, stating that either the situation will be clear cut, or if the claim to privacy is weak, it is more likely to be outweighed by a claim to freedom of expression, rendering extensive consideration of the point superfluous. He did, however, cite the test laid down for the Australian courts in *Australian Broadcasting Corporation v Lenah Game Meats Pty Ltd* (2001). There Gleeson CJ recognised, first, that there is no bright line between the public and private. A 'useful practical test' was set out to be:

> ... that disclosure or observation of information or conduct would be highly offensive to a reasonable person of ordinary sensibilities.

However, the House of Lords in *Campbell v MGN Ltd* (2004) did not wholeheartedly endorse this test. Lord Hoffmann suggested that the values embodied by human rights law should be used to judge the kind of information which may be protected. Lord Hope pointed out that this question is only to be asked if the information at issue is not obviously private, while Baroness Hale advocated an objective test of reasonable expectation that the information be kept confidential.

In contrast, in the *Douglas* case, Lindsay J went on to distinguish between purely personal secrets and those that fell within commercial confidence as trade secrets, suggesting that Gleeson CJ's test could be distinguished where private information fell into the category of a commercial trade secret. It had been strongly argued that, because the celebrity claimants had sold exclusive photographic rights to OK Magazine, their subject matter could no longer represent private personal information. On the facts, Lindsay J held the Douglas wedding photographs to constitute commercial trade secrets because they constituted valuable trade assets to the claimants. Accordingly, the case represents a traditional application of the action for breach of confidence, despite the personal nature of the photographs. If differences in the scope of protection are to develop according to the nature of the information sought to be protected (see 7.4.2), this distinction may prove significant in the future, particularly in relation to character merchandising and the protection of celebrities' confidence, posing different tests of confidentiality for the personal information. Lindsay J recognised such a difference thus:

> I quite see that such an approach may lead to a distinction between the circumstances in which equity affords protection to those who seek to manage their publicity as part of their trade or profession and whose private life is a valuable commodity and those whose it is not but I am untroubled by that; the law which protects individual confidences and a law of privacy may protect the latter class and provide no reason to diminish the protection for the former.

The fact that the photographs related to private and personal information was not irrelevant. Lindsay J was careful to hold that the publicity rights granted to OK Magazine did not detract from the privacy of the photographs. Consequently, both the public interest, and the right of freedom of expression had to be balanced against the protection for their confidentiality. So too, did their right to privacy and the Press Complaints Commission Code, which would not be the case for non-private commercial trade secrets.

By treating the wedding photographs as commercial trade secrets Lindsay J also appears to have limited the protection for privacy to private information which has not been published. This would not be the case in a general right to privacy, freed from its footing in confidence, nor is it the case for data protected under the Data Protection Act 1998. Consequently, protection for privacy is most likely to succeed only where secrecy has been consciously preserved as in the *Douglas* case, or where the information is revealed only in a private setting, as illustrated by the *Campbell* case.

Photographs of the claimant had been taken in the street, a public place. The photographs themselves, without the accompanying captions, may have been obtrusive, but did not supply the offending information as to the claimant's attendance at meetings of Narcotics Anonymous. The Court of Appeal treated the photographs as evidence of the information revealed in their captions and accompanying articles, and therefore as providers of information. This was no less the case in *Douglas v Hello! Ltd* (2003), even though the event could have been described in words or by drawings. In *Campbell* the House of Lords noted the vivid impact of photographs as providers of private information,[72] although Lord Hoffmann ruled that the same principles applied to them as to other forms of private information. This did not mean, however, he said, that publication of a photograph could always be justified by the argument that a verbal description of the same information would not have constituted a breach.

18.7.2 Obligation and breach for personal confidence

Because of the security arrangements made to prevent any but authorised photographs being taken, *Douglas v Hello! Ltd* (2000) could have been decided as one of a direct relationship between anyone present at the wedding and the claimants on the basis of imputed knowledge of confidentiality. However, the Court of Appeal also took into consideration the possibility of the then unknown photographer being an intruder (rather than a guest or employee) with whom no confidential relationship existed. In these circumstances, both the 'increasingly invasive social environment', Article 8 of the ECHR, and the HRA 1998 justified protection for privacy in English law.

---

72   *Per* Lord Nicholls, 'worth a thousand words', at para 31.

The obligation may be express, as it was in *Campbell v Frisbee* (2002), or implied, as discussed in *Campbell v MGN Ltd* (2004) and *Douglas v Hello! Ltd* (2000) and (2003). In the 2003 *Douglas* decision Lindsay J had no hesitation in finding an obligation of confidence inferred from the measures taken by the claimants to secure their privacy, at least in relation to the taking of photographs (see 7.10.2) following *Douglas v Hello!* (2000), *Shelley Films Ltd v Rex Features Ltd* (1994) and *Creation Records Ltd v News Group Newspapers Ltd* (1997):

> It is well settled that equity may intervene to prevent a publication of photographic images taken in breach of confidence. If, on some occasion, the prospective claimant makes it clear, expressly or impliedly, that no photographic images are to be taken of them, then all those present will be bound by the obligations of confidence created by their knowledge (or imputed knowledge) of that restriction ...

The House of Lords went further in *Campbell v MGN Ltd* (2004), when it was recognised that 'the law imposes a "duty of confidence" whenever a person receives information he knows or ought to know is fairly and reasonably to be regarded as confidential'.[73]

18.7.3   Breach

Breach lies in the disclosure of the information: *Campbell v Frisbee* (2002), *Campbell v Mirror Group Newspapers* (2002) and *A v B & C* (2002). Mere use of the information, which does not compromise its privacy, although constituting an intrusion, would not appear to be actionable without the development of the full tort of privacy as argued in *A v B & C* (2002).

Douglas v Hello! Ltd (2000) went on show other limits to privacy. Whereas the courts had shown a willingness to protect private secrets in the past in cases such as *Prince Albert v Strange* (1849), *Douglas v Hello! Ltd* (2000) also represents a refusal to countenance the grant of an injunction to protect a right of publicity. The claimants had effectively sold their privacy to OK Magazine and the Court of Appeal discharged the interim injunctions, finding that the breach of personal confidentiality was to be compensated only by damages. This was not the case in *Beckham v Mirror Group Newspapers* (2001), where the development of a right of personal confidence was confirmed but an injunction upheld because the photographs in question were taken in the claimants' home and publication could compromise their family security. This was so despite the fact that the claimants had plans to commercialise some of the photographs.

This distinction between the private and commercial spheres might be made at the point of remedy and/or when determining whether the information under consideration falls into the public or private category. By treating the information as a personal but commercial trade secret in *Douglas v Hello! Ltd* (2003) it is not clear whether Lindsay J might have been prepared to countenance the grant of an injunction. He said:

> A recurring theme on the part of these defendants is that what the Douglases, in particular, were seeking was not privacy or confidentiality but control. They wanted to be sure that the only visual representations of the wedding that were to be available to

---

73   Relying on *dicta* of Lord Goff in *Attorney General v Guardian* (1990).

the media were such as had been approved by them. In that way control over the media would be exercised. That, however, overlooks that control is not an improper objective of the law of confidence; that certain information should not be published or that copies of certain documents should be destroyed or returned or that abuse of a trade secret should be barred to a person are all both familiar aspects of the law of confidentiality and aspects of control. I do not see the fact that control was sought to be exercised as of itself denying the attempt the characteristics of an application of the law of confidence; it is, rather, another factor in the overall balance between confidence and freedom of expression.

18.7.4   Pure privacy

The protection is therefore limited to Megarry J's three (expanded) conditions for the remedy, albeit extended to include situations where an intruder unrelated to the claimant knows or must be taken to know of the confidentiality of the information or what is being observed (see 7.10). It was made clear, however, that this must not be taken to include protection against mere intrusion in *A v B & C* (2002).

While application of the Convention and the HRA 1998 are matters for specialised texts, it must be noted here that there are real questions that can be raised[74] as to the applicability of the Convention right to privacy in actions between private individuals ('horizontal effect'). The point was not taken in *A v B & C* (2002), nor cited as one of the reasons for refusing to acknowledge a right of pure privacy, divorced from confidence, in *Douglas v Hello! Ltd* (2003). Articles 8 and 10 of the ECHR impose obligations on states to afford respect to the right. It is clear that in the case of Article 10 a state's obligation is at issue if a court is to impose an injunction impeding freedom of expression, even though the action is one between private individuals; however, this is not necessarily so where Article 8 is concerned. This is because it would not be the court's action in refusing an injunction which infringed a claimant's privacy, but the defendant's actions. It was, however, suggested in *Earl Spencer and Countess Spencer* (1998) that Article 8 could be employed in such circumstances, with horizontal effect. However, s 6 of the HRA 1998 does not simply incorporate the Convention rights into UK law, instead placing obligations on public authorities (including the courts) to respect the rights.

Conversely, in Scotland, the ECHR was incorporated directly into Scots law by the Scotland Act 1998. It is possible that this could lead to a judicial development of a right to privacy beyond the confines of an action in breach of confidence. In *Martin v McGuiness* (2003), where the issue was *obiter*, but discussed by the court, Lord Bonomy took care to point out that 'significantly' his attention had not been drawn to any authority in which it was stated that there is no right to privacy.

In *Douglas v Hello! Ltd* (2003) Lindsay J was invited to hold that such a right of privacy existed, as suggested by Sedley LJ in *Douglas v Hello! Ltd* (2000),[75] based on the ECHR, the HRA 1998, and decisions of the European Court of Human Rights. He gave

---

74 Phillipson, G, Chapter in edited volume: 'Human Rights and Obligations of Confidentiality in the Private Sphere: A v B and C in the Court of Appeal', in Hudson, A (ed), *New Perspectives on Family Law, Human Rights and the Home* (London: Cavendish Publishing, 2003). Also Sir William Wade QC, 'The Horizons of Horizontality' (2000) 116 LQR 217.

75 *Dicta* from the Court of Appeal in *Douglas v Hello!* (2000) were persuasive in the District Court of Queensland in *Grosse v Purvis* (2003), when a tort of privacy was recognised and substantial damages awarded for stalking.

five reasons for declining to do so. These were, first, that other subsequent Court of Appeal authority expressed doubt as to the existence of a comprehensive tort. Neither has Scots law developed a pure right to privacy: *Martin v McGuiness* (2003). He argued, secondly, that protection through the law of confidence was sufficient on the facts of the case before him and, thirdly, that the creation of such a broad right is a matter for the legislature, which can take into account all relevant circumstances. He did suggest, however, that there is a gap in the protection provided by confidence, and that in the absence of Parliamentary action the judiciary would be forced to take on this task in an appropriate case. Fourthly, Lord Woolf CJ's guidelines in *A v B & C* (2002) supported a conclusion that confidence would suffice in the majority of situations. In addition, finally, he said that any right to privacy would provide no greater remedy than that available to the claimants in confidence.

In *Campbell v MGN Ltd* (2004) the House of Lords again made it clear that no general right to privacy existed. Furthermore, Baroness Hale went on to point out that there is no right to one's image, and that covert photography did not render the information in a photograph confidential. It is the activity itself that must be private. Celebrities anxious to protect their image for merchandising purposes can take no comfort from the case:

> The activity photographed must be private. If this had been, and had been presented as, a picture of Naomi Campbell going about her business in a public street, there could have been no complaint.

Protection under the Data Protection Act 1998 (DPA 1998) (see 18.9), which regulates the processing of information about individuals, is unlikely to provide a more extensive substitute for a right of privacy as a means of character merchandising. In *Campbell v Mirror Group Newspapers* (2002) the Court of Appeal held that publication of true facts fell within the public interest and within the exemption of s 32 of the DPA 1998.[76] In *Douglas v Hello! Ltd* (2003) the public interest claim did not succeed, but the claimants were held to be liable to compensation in damages alone. Moreover, the damages were nominal.

Consequently, celebrities wishing to merchandise their personality must take active steps to create obligations of personal confidence by contract, notice, security measures and the like. Even where such measures succeed in creating an obligation of commercial confidence, it is not clear after the two *Douglas* judgments whether an injunction will ever be granted where a claimant has sought publicity. Even were confidential information to be regarded as property, falling within the Convention right to respect for property, it is likely that this right would be subject to the public interest, and the right to freedom of expression.

18.7.5   The future

If either English[77] or Scots law were to recognise a common law or delictual right to privacy against individuals, it would enable anyone to protect information and images concerning them, and indirectly allow a right to publicity, without the contractual

---

76   On appeal, the House of Lords did not consider the Data Protection Act 1998.

77   As was postulated in 1890 by Warren, S and Brandeis, L, 'The Right to Privacy' (1890) 4 Harvard Law Review 193, and advocated as a tort as long ago as 1931: Winfield, P, 'Privacy', (1931) 47 LQR 23.

fencing that was needed in the *Douglas* case. Whether such a right is likely is very moot.

In *Wainright v Home Office* (2003) the House of Lords dismissed the argument that there was a general common law tort of invasion of privacy. Sedley LJ's *obiter dicta* in *Douglas v Hello!* (2001) were explained as a plea for an extension to the action for breach of confidence, but no more. Lord Hoffmann, who gave the main judgment, argued that the coming into force of the HRA 1998 rendered a general right unnecessary as a remedy for infringement of a Convention right would be statutory. In addition, as held by Megarry J in *Malone v Metropolitan Police Commissioner* (1979), the creation of a new right was a matter for legislation and not the courts.

This denial of a general principle was followed by the House's decision in *Campbell v MGN Ltd* (2004). While Lord Hoffmann considered that the law of privacy had led to 'a shift in the centre of gravity for breach of confidence when it is used as a remedy for the unjustified publication of personal information',[78] Lord Hope doubted this, regarding the intervention of human rights law as more terminological than substantive.

Despite the House of Lords' decision in *Campbell* (2004), jurisprudence from the European Court of Human Rights (ECtHR) may lead to the development of a right to pure privacy for those who do not seek to attract public attention, nor to profit from it. If so, an indirect right of publicity for celebrities and non-celebrities alike could result if the UK courts follow.[79]

In *Von Hannover v Germany* (2004) Princess Caroline of Monaco succeeded in establishing that her privacy prevailed over the press's freedom of expression in the ECtHR. Photographs of the Princess engaged in ordinary activities had been published in the German press. The German Federal Constitutional Court gave precedence to the right to freedom of expression, but the ECtHR decided otherwise. It ruled that, although freedom of expression extended to photographs, this was an area where protection for privacy was of increased importance. In doing so, it noted the intrusiveness of the way in which such tabloid photographs are obtained. The Court also commented on the need for increased attention to privacy in relation to new communications technology. These photographs, it said, were of daily life, and entirely private; they had been taken without the Princess' knowledge or consent, and, in some cases, in secret. As the Court ruled that they made no contribution to a debate of public interest (as the Princess had no official functions, and the photographs depicted only her private life) the balance between freedom of expression and privacy lay on the side of privacy. However, the ECtHR did not dismiss the possibility that in other circumstances publication of images of private life could be in the public interest.

Furthermore, in *Peck v UK* (2003) the ECtHR found that the UK did not provide an effective remedy for the breach of privacy under Article 8 that occurred when CCTV images of Mr Peck in a public street were subsequently published. Nevertheless, the UK Government has rejected introducing a privacy law despite the conclusions of Parliament's Select Committee on Culture, Media and Sport.[80]

---

78 *Per* Lord Hoffmann in *Campbell v MGN Ltd* (2004), at para 51.
79 Rogers, H, and Tomlinson, H, 'Caroline Ruling Sounds Alarm for British Press' *The Times*, 29 June 2004.
80 The Fifth Report of the Culture, Media and Sport Select Committee on Privacy and Media Intrusion, HC 458, 2003.

18.8 THE RIGHT TO FREEDOM OF EXPRESSION

Article 10 of the ECHR provides that everyone has the right to freedom of expression. This includes the right to receive and impart information and ideas. Any protection for privacy must take this right into account.

Accordingly, just as confidentiality has been balanced against the public interest in the past (see 7.13), so today freedom of expression must provide an additional element to any question of justification for a breach of confidence. It is likely that applying the correct judicial approach to questions of freedom of expression will extend to other justifications for disclosure in the public interest. However, it might be argued that there could be a difference of priorities. Freedom of expression is couched as a right (rather than an obligation of conscience) and might be argued to take priority over other considerations. It was pointed out in *Campbell v Frisbee* (2002) that:

> Freedom of expression is the rule and regulation of speech is the exception requiring justification: see *Reynolds v Times Newspapers Ltd* (2001). Freedom of expression remains the rule although it may cause needless pain, distress and damage: per Hoffmann LJ in *R v Central Independent Television plc* (1994) ... Interference with freedom of expression has to be justified even where there is no particular interest in a particular publication, and is strengthened by the existence of a public interest in publication: *A v B & C* (2002) ...

That this is not so was stated in the same case, citing the Court of Appeal decision in *Douglas v Hello!* (2002), and confirmed by the House of Lords in *Campbell v MGN Ltd* (2004). Privacy and freedom of expression are equally rights; one does not take priority over the other and the question is one of balancing all the circumstances. In Lightman J's words in *Campbell v Frisbee* (2002) '(t)he right to privacy and to freedom of expression are of equal value'. Consequently, the process of balancing freedom of expression and the public interest in general against the preservation of confidence should be aligned. This was implicitly recognised by Sedley LJ in *London Regional Transport v The Mayor of London* (2001), when he expressed the opinion that the 'human rights highway' would lead to exactly the same outcome as the older road of equity and the common law.

18.8.1 Freedom of expression and privacy

There is a clear tension between the right to freedom of expression and the right to privacy 'which requires the court(s) to hold the balance between the conflicting interests' of Articles 8 and 10 of the ECHR, as Lord Woolf CJ points out in *A v B & C* (2002). The courts have already heard a number of such cases. In *A v B & C* (2002) Lord Woolf CJ attempted to lay down a series of guidelines for resolving the conflict. A number of factors which are relevant in balancing the rights concerned can be identified (see below). The weight to be given to these factors remains a matter of the precise circumstances of each case. As privacy is regarded as confidentiality for personal information, it seems more than likely that these factors can also be applied to the balancing of confidence and the public interest in general. This balancing function would appear to give the courts considerable discretion.

In *London Regional Transport v The Mayor of London* (2001) the Court of Appeal stressed that the balancing exercise is a matter of discretion for the judge to be exercised according to 'well settled' principles, and that the same approach is required by s 12(3) of the HRA 1998. Sedley LJ stressed that the jurisprudence of the European Court of Human Rights and the methodical concept of proportionality should be applied, replacing:

> an elastic concept with which political scientists are more at home with a structured enquiry: Does the measure meet a recognised and pressing social need? Does it negate the primary right or restrict it more than is necessary? Are the reasons given for it logical?

Lord Woolf CJ laid down in *A v B & C* (2002) that the freedom of expression of the press is a right of particular importance and that any interference with the press requires justification, whether or not there is any question of the publication being in the public interest.

18.8.2 Factors relevant to reconciling confidence and privacy with freedom of expression and the public interest

Courts will take all circumstances into account when balancing the interests between confidence and disclosure, but a number of factors can be identified as relevant. The weight to be given to each will vary according to the precise circumstances: *A v B & C* (2002).

(a) The nature of the information at stake: whether relating to private individuals, government affairs, trade secrets or other concerns is relevant. Accordingly, *Douglas v Hello! Ltd* (2000), which related to celebrity photographs, was distinguished in *London Regional Transport v The Mayor of London* (2001), which concerned government information.

(b) The way in which the confidant acquired the information can be significant, so that in *Francome v Mirror Newspapers* (1984) the fact that the wiretapping had taken place illegally was taken into account. Lord Woolf CJ stated in *A v B & C* (2002) that unlawful acquisition of protected information could be a 'compelling factor' when exercising the balancing discretion.

(c) Where freedom of expression is to be balanced against confidence, s 10 of the HRA 1998 sets out specific factors as the right:

> ... may be subject to such formalities, conditions, restrictions or penalties as are prescribed by law and are necessary in a democratic society, in the interests of national security, territorial integrity or public safety, for the prevention of disorder or crime, for the protection of health or morals, for the protection of the reputation or rights of others, for preventing the disclosure of information received in confidence, or for maintaining the authority and impartiality of the judiciary.

These specific examples given for conscribing freedom of expression bear a strong likeness to the criteria already developed for exercising the public interest defence in the UK. However, a standard is also laid down for their application – that of necessity in a democratic society. Robert Walker LJ stressed that it is this standard that lies behind the exceptions to freedom of expression in *London Regional Transport v The Mayor of London* (2001).

(d) Where the information to be disclosed is journalistic, literary or artistic material, s 12(4) of the HRA 1998 provides that a court must take two factors into account if the right of freedom of expression is concerned. These are, first, the extent to which the information has, or is about to become, available to the public, and whether disclosure would be in the public interest and, secondly, any relevant privacy code. The sub-section does not require a court to give freedom of expression any priority over the right to confidence or privacy: *Imutran Ltd v Uncaged Campaigns Ltd* (2001), only that 'specific and separate consideration' be given to these factors.

'Journalistic material' is not defined, but was considered in *Campbell v Frisbee* (2002) to 'embrace material acquired or created for the purpose of journalism and conduct connected with such material'. Consequently, the defendant's claim that her interview with the *News of the World* was for the purposes of the article at issue was sufficient to bring the sub-section into play. In addition, journalists are to be given reasonable latitude in the manner in which information in the public interest is to be conveyed to the public or the Article 10 right would be unnecessarily inhibited.

The Code of Practice of the Press Complaints Commission was taken into consideration in *A v B & C* (2002) and by the Court of Appeal in *Douglas v Hello!* (2000). They stated, *obiter*, that a newspaper which flouts the rules laid down by the Code is likely to have its claim to freedom of expression outweighed by considerations of privacy. Lindsay J agreed in 2003, that in the absence of any public interest in publication, privacy is likely to trump freedom of expression, but went on to suggest that confidence might not weigh as strongly in the balance as the Convention right of privacy. The Code replicates the consideration of the proximity of authorised publication, but where the claimant is the publisher imminent publication will not necessarily justify the defendant's pre-empting the official disclosure.

(e) The fact that a public figure is seeking to rely on confidence (in the wider sense) is relevant. Although privacy remains a consideration, a public figure must expect close media scrutiny. The public has a legitimate interest in being given information in circumstances where it may be appropriate to comment on the conduct of a public figure. Lord Woolf CJ suggested that being in a position where high standards of conduct can be expected, or that of a role model, would provide such an interest, as would the fact that the individual had deliberately courted public attention. The Council of Europe Resolution 1165 of 1998 was proposed as suitable guidance in exercising the discretion where public figures are concerned. It was also pointed out that the courts should not be placed in the position of being arbiters of good taste.

Whether a claimant has actively cultivated a false public image may also constitute a relevant consideration and one justifying publication in the public interest. This was applied in *Woodward v Hutchins* (1977); however, the Court of Appeal in *Campbell v Mirror Group* (2002) held that this factor would not necessarily justify publication. The Court stated that Lord Woolf CJ had not meant that some public prominence allowed the media to lay bare an individual's private life where the status of role model had not been deliberately sought. Lindsay J also distinguished the *Woodward* case in *Douglas v Hello!* (2003). He stated that to hold that those who have sought any publicity lose all protection would be to repeal Article 8's application to many of those most likely to need it. This may give courts some difficult distinctions to draw as to the reasons for a celebrity's public image. In *Campbell v MGN Ltd* (2004) the Law Lords differed at this point, the majority giving more weight to the type of information concerned (relating to medical health) than the untrue publicity created by Naomi Campbell in the past.

(f) The defendants' motives could also have a bearing, but *dicta* in the case law are ambivalent as to their relevance. In *British Steel Corp v Granada Television Ltd* (1981), Lord Fraser refused to take into account that the documents were revealed without request for payment; but, in *Woodward v Hutchins* (1977), Lord Denning did pay attention to motive, as did Templeman LJ in *Schering Chemicals v Falkman* (1982). If the test of the extent of obligation owed by a confidant is that laid down in *R v Department of Health ex p Source Informatics Ltd* (1999), that of the confidant's conscience, then it can be argued that motivation should be a relevant factor in determining breach, but that this is more a matter of the extent of obligation owed, than a publication in the public interest. In *London Regional Transport v The Mayor of London* (2001) the Court of Appeal took into account the motivation for publication when balancing confidence against the public interest.

It might be tempting to think that a defence of disclosure in the public interest would provide security to a 'whistle blower' exposing the secrets of an employer, or former employer. This might particularly be the case if a court were to be willing to take into account the discloser's motives, as might be expected in an equitable remedy. However, the courts required that there must be an appropriate public interest in the information to be balanced against the public interest in confidence. Lord Goff, in *Attorney General v Guardian Newspapers Ltd (No 2)* (1988), emphasised that the:

> ... mere allegation of iniquity is not of itself sufficient to justify disclosure in the public interest. Such an allegation will only do so if, following such investigations as are reasonably open to the recipient ... the allegation in question can reasonably be regarded as being a creditable allegation from an apparently reliable source.

However, the Public Interest Disclosure Act 1998 grants a statutory immunity for 'protected disclosures' by inserting a new Part IVA to the Employment Act 1996. Section 43J renders any obligation of confidentiality void to the extent that it purports to preclude a worker from making a protected disclosure. A qualifying disclosure must be of a criminal offence, failure to comply with a legal obligation, a miscarriage of justice, danger to the health and safety of any individual, environmental damage (s 43B). It may be made to the employer, a legal adviser, a Minister of the Crown, or a prescribed person. In each case the disclosure is subject to conditions.

The conditions that apply where the recipient does not fall into one of the defined categories require good faith on the worker's part, a reasonable belief that the information is substantially true, it is not made for personal gain, and in the circumstances it is reasonable to make it. In addition, the worker must believe that the employer would subject him to a detriment should disclosure be made to the employer. Factors to be taken into consideration in determining whether the disclosure is reasonable to be made are also laid down, including the identity of the recipient, and the seriousness of the subject matter.

18.9 THE DATA PROTECTION ACT 1998

Part of European protection for privacy[81] lies in the Data Protection Directive,[82] which was implemented in the Data Protection Act (DPA) 1998. The Act applies to data processed by means of equipment operating automatically. Digitisation of an image and subsequent processing should fall within its ambit.[83] Processing of personal data related to an individual by a data controller is subject to data protection principles. This requires that processing of the information be justifiable, and if it is sensitive personal data, carried out lawfully and fairly. The subject must also be informed of the processing. Processing must also be compatible with the purposes for which the data was obtained. Subjects of such data have the right[84] to require that processing of the data be discontinued if it is likely to cause substantial damage or distress to them, and may claim compensation. Section 32 of the DPA 1998 also provides an exception for the press.

Both *Campbell v Mirror Group* (2002) and *Douglas v Hello!* (No 6) (2003) demonstrate a role for data protection legislation in image protection. An important question that arises, however, is the balancing need for freedom of expression, particularly in cases relating to press publication. In *Campbell v Mirror Group* (2002) the Court of Appeal examined the application of the DPA 1998 to the published photographs in detail. The Court held that the Act applied to hard copy photographs published after digital processing at an earlier stage. It was strongly argued that the s 32 exception only applied up to the moment of publication,[85] and not to the data once published. However, the Court of Appeal held that the section applied to the publication itself and that the publication was exempt, and there was no breach. This finding rested on its conclusion in relation to confidence that publication of the photographs was in the public interest, a conclusion overruled by the House of Lords.

However, the damages granted in the *Douglas* case were too nominal to render this application of data protection a compensatory development. There, the court held that celebrities may have a protectable interest in controlling release of photographs depicting them. The photographs were recognised as valuable trade assets, whose worth depended on being kept secret and then published in a manner controlled by the Douglases. The fact that this might exceed the boundaries of protection given by breach of confidence was recognised.

The exploitation of personality by image was clearly recognised in both these cases. Where publication by the press and s 32 are not concerned, Boyd and Jay take the view that unlicensed use of a celebrity's image for commercial purposes is likely to constitute unfair processing in breach of the data processing principles.[86]

---

81 Recital 10, Data Protection Directive.
82 Directive 95/46/EC of the European Parliament and of the Council of 24 October 1995 on the Protection of Individuals with Regard to the Processing of Personal Data and on the Free Movement of Such Data [1995] OJ L281/31.
83 Boyd, S, and Jay, R, 'Image Rights and the Effect of the Data Protection Act 1998' [2004] Ent LR 159.
84 Section 10 of the Data Protection Act 1998.
85 In order to protect the press from 'gagging injunctions'.
86 Boyd, S, and Jay, R, 'Image Rights and the Effect of the Data Protection Act 1998' [2004] Ent LR 159.

Taking five hypothetical examples,[87] they conclude that breach is possible provided that:

(i)   the image is part of the celebrity's 'stock-in-trade';

(ii) it is used for clear commercial purpose;

(iii) it was held as data and derives from a digital version;

(iv) it has been used without informing the individual, seeking their consent to its use or providing an opportunity to opt out.

The data subject may lodge an objection notice with the Information Commissioner, but this cannot lead to an order for compensation. Only court action may lead to damages.

18.10 THE ADVERTISING STANDARDS CODE

A further means of obtaining some redress for unauthorised use of one's image in advertising lies in the Advertising Standards Codes. Their potential as a remedy for unauthorised use of images was illustrated by the complaint made by the runner David Bedford[88] relating to The Number's 118 118 directory enquiries campaign.

The Advertising Standards Authority is an independent body set up by the industry to regulate advertising through the Advertising Standards Codes. Broadcast advertising also became subject to the ASA Codes[89] on 1 November 2004, contracted out from Ofcom. Ofcom is the regulator for the communications industry. Under the Codes advertising must be honest, truthful and fair.

David Bedford argued that the advertisements, which depicted a runner caricaturing his characteristic long hair and moustache, hooped running shirt and red socks in the 1970s, suggested his endorsement of the service. On appeal from the initial decision of the ITC, the Ofcom Content Board[90] found that David Bedford had been caricatured, and that the likeness was not fortuitous. Nor had the advertisers either sought, or obtained, his permission. Such caricature constituted a breach of Rule 6.5 of the Advertising Standards Code. However, the board also noted that the complaint had not been made for some six months, during which time The Number had incurred considerable expenditure. The board also found that David Bedford had not suffered financial harm from the promotion. Consequently, banning the advertisements was considered to be a disproportionate response. Publication of the decision was deemed sufficient to correct any false conclusions as to endorsement. At the time, the

---

87 A picture in a newspaper advertisement for services, a picture on a mug for sale, the celebrity's name on a T-shirt, the use of his name in a 'talking card' and the use of a lookalike in a newspaper advertisement.

88 David Bedford was a winning 5,000 and 10,000 metre runner, who set a world record in 1973. He is now Race Director for the London Marathon.

89 There are codes for non-broadcast and broadcast advertising, the latter replacing regulation by the Independent Television Commission and Broadcasting Standards Commission. See www.asa.org.uk.

90 Appeal by The Number (UK) Ltd. Complaint by David Bedford. Concerning the 118 118 Runners TV advertisements. 27 January 2004: www.ofcom.org.uk.

complainant's success was thought likely to lead to litigation[91] (see 18.2.3), but this is now unlikely. The Number discontinued that campaign in March 2004, although it is still using images of a similar pair of individuals without the sporting context.

Further Reading

Adams, J, *Character Merchandising* (London: Butterworths, 1996)

Beverley-Smith, H, *The Commercial Appropriation of Personality* (Cambridge: CUP, 2002)

Boyd, S, 'Does English Law Recognise the Concept of an Image or Personality Right? [2002] Ent LR 1

Boyd, S, and Jay, R, 'Image Rights and the Effect of the Data Protection Act 1998' [2004] Ent LR 159

Burley, S, 'Passing Off and Character Merchandising: Should England Lean Towards Australia?' [1991] EIPR 227

Carty, H, 'Advertising, Publicity Rights and English Law' [2004] IPQ 209

Carty, H, 'Character Merchandising and the Limits of Passing Off, (1993) 13 LS 289

Chong, S, and Maniatis, S, 'The *Teenage Mutant Hero Turtles* Case: Zapping English Law on Character Merchandising Past the Embryonic Stage' [1991] EIPR 253

Coleman, A, 'The Unauthorised Commercial Exploitation of the Names and Likenesses of Real Persons' [1982] EIPR 189

Colville, M, *Developing Key Privacy Rights* (Oxford: Hart Publishing, 2002)

Davies, G, 'The Cult of Celebrity and Trade Marks: the Next Instalment', (2004) 1:2 SCRIPT-ed, www.law.ed.ac.uk/ahrb/script-ed

Duxbury, J, 'Ninja Turtles v Crocodile Dundee – a Comparison of Australian and English Approaches to Unfair Competition' [1991] EIPR 426

Emslie, M and Lewis, M, 'Passing Off and Image Marketing in the UK' [1992] EIPR 270

Frazer, T, 'Appropriation of Personality – a New Tort' (1983) 99 LQR 281

Goodenough, O, 'Re-theorising Privacy and Publicity' [1997] IPQ 37

Jaffey, P, 'Merchandising and the Law of Trade Marks' [1998] IPQ 240

Klink, J, '50 Years of Publicity Rights in the United States and the Never-ending Hassle with Intellectual Property and Personality Rights in Europe' [2003] IPQ 363

Learmonth, A, 'Eddie, are you OK? Product Endorsement and Passing Off' [2002] IPQ 306

Martino, T, *Trademark Dilution* (Oxford: OUP, 1996)

McGee, A and Scanlan, G, 'Copyright in Character' [2003] JBL 470

McGee, A and Scanlan, G, 'Phantom Intellectual Property Rights' [2000] IPQ 264

McGee, A, Gale S, and Scanlan, G, 'Character Merchandising: Aspects of Legal Protection' (2001) 21 LS 226

Mitchiner, J, 'Intellectual Property in Image – a Mere Inconvenience?' [2003] IPQ 163

Phillipson, G, 'Transforming Breach of Confidence? Towards a Common Law Right of Privacy under the Human Rights Act' (2003) 66 MLR 726

Phillipson, G, 'Human Rights and Obligations of Confidentiality in the Private Sphere: *A v B & C* in the Court of Appeal' in Hudson, A (ed), *New Perspectives on Family Law, Human Rights and the Home* (London: Cavendish Publishing, 2003)

---

91 '118 118? Let's make that 2500 000, says Bedford' *The Times*, 3 February 2004.

Ryan, C, 'Human Rights and Intellectual Property' [2001] EIPR 521

Personality Database, AHRB Research Centre for Studies in Intellectual Property and Technology Law, School of Law, University of Edinburgh, www.law.ed.ac.uk/ahrb/script-ed

Pinto, T 'The Influence of the European Convention on Human Rights on Intellectual Property Rights' [2002] EIPR 209

Robinson, F, 'How Image Conscious is English Law?' [2004] Ent LR 151

Scanlan, G, 'Derivatives Aspects of Character and Perceived Attributes in Persona as Forms of Intellectual Property' Part II [2004] Ent LR 1

Scanlan, G, 'Personality, Endorsement and Everything' [2003] EIPR 563

Scanlan, G, 'Derivatives Aspects of Character and Perceived Attributes in Persona as Forms of Intellectual Property' Part I [2003] Ent LR 200

Spence, M, 'Passing Off and the Misappropriation of Valuable Intangibles' [1996] LQR 472

Story, A, 'Owning Diana: From People's Princess to Private Property' [1998] 5 Web JCLI, http://webjcli.ncl.ac.uk/1998/issue5/story5.html

Wade, W, 'The Horizons of Horizontality' (2000) 116 LQR 217

Warren, S and Brandeis, L, 'The Right to Privacy' (1890) 4 Harvard Law Review 193

Weber, O, 'Human Dignity and the Commercial Appropriation of Personality: Towards a Cosmopolitan Consensus in Personality Rights?' (2004) 1:1 SCRIPT-ed, www.law.ed.ac.uk/ahrb/script-ed

WIPO, *Report on Character Merchandising* (1994), WO/INF/108, www.wipo.org/copyright/en/activities/pdf/wo_inf_108.pdf

CHAPTER 19

ENFORCEMENT

To a large extent the value of intellectual property rights and their ability to achieve their 'justifications' stand and fall on the effectiveness with which they can be enforced.[1] While this may be true of any property right, intellectual property right owners have a particular need for quick and effective remedies, without which the right could be nugatory and any victory over an infringer pyrrhic.

There are five reasons for this:

(a) copying does not incur the, often very large, development costs incurred by legitimate producers, and is often easy and inexpensive. Therefore illegitimate copying has the potential to erode, or even destroy, the legitimate market, and do so very quickly;

(b) copying that is inferior in quality will also destroy a right owner's reputation for producing high quality goods;

(c) damages may amount to very inadequate compensation for such harm;

(d) if the remedy is slow in coming, the product may well be out of date, and superseded by new developments, or fashions, by the date of judgment;

(e) new copying technology, and new techniques of information storage, have enabled piracy and counterfeiting to become so lucrative and easy as to drive legitimate right owners out of business, and have greatly increased the capacity for unauthorised reproduction both commercially and domestically.

19.1 PIRACY AND COUNTERFEITING

Some intellectual property infringement is on a domestic scale, but commercial and criminal operations are a very real threat to right owners and the problem is a global one. Infringement by copying is known as *piracy*. Where trade mark infringement is also involved the infringement is known as *counterfeiting*, as the buyer is also being led to believe that the infringing product has come from its legitimate producer.

Organisations such as FAST[2] and FACT,[3] as well as representative associations of right owners such as the IFPI,[4] take active steps to combat counterfeiting and piracy. Reports on the level of piracy of music, video and DVD, software and other products abound. The IFPI estimates that one in three discs and two in five cassettes sold are pirated, with the value of the pirate market reaching $US4.6 billion in 2002.[5] The Business Software Alliance released its report[6] on software piracy in 2003 in July 2004. It estimated the value of pirated software sold at $US29 billion globally, and at an overall rate of 36% of all software. Software and digital copyright works are

---

1   See Kingston, W, 'The Case for Compulsory Arbitration: Empirical Evidence' [2000] EIPR 154 for evidence of this

2   Federation Against Software Theft: www.fast.org.uk.

3   Federation Against Copyright Theft: www.fact-uk.org.uk.

4   www.ifpi.org.

5   Commercial Piracy Report 2003: www.ifpi.org.

6   Global Software Piracy Study, 2003: www.bsa.org.

particularly vulnerable to unlawful copying and distribution, but the problem is by no means restricted to electronic products. In the European Commission's 1998 Green Paper[7] on tackling piracy in the Internal Market it was estimated that 100,000 jobs per year were lost in the EU as a result of counterfeiting. Counterfeiting and piracy were stated to affect a wide variety of sectors: computing, toys, textiles, perfumes, compact disks, medicines, watches and the like. Levels of counterfeiting and piracy in relation to the turnover of the sectors concerned were estimated to be considerable in some cases: 35% in the software industry, 25% in the audio-visual industry and 12% in the toy industry.

More recently, the UK Department of Trade and Industry Report *Competing in the Global Economy: The Innovation Challenge*[8] referred specifically to the difficulties of enforcement of intellectual property rights. The Patent Office, which is part of the DTI, is to take steps to improve the speed and costs of resolving disputes by improving litigation procedures.

19.1.1 Infringement and crime

The Patent Office estimates that criminal infringements represent a black market worth £9 billion a year. A national strategy[9] for dealing with intellectual property crime was launched in August 2004.[10] It will involve the Patent Office itself, the police, Trading Standards Offices, Customs officials and brand owners, providing increased training and co-operation, but not new resources. Annual reports will be made.

19.1.2 International measures

It was the increasing challenge to intellectual property posed by piracy and counterfeiting that was one of the main driving forces behind the TRIPS Agreement. The solution adopted[11] was to emphasise the importance of providing adequate means for enforcing intellectual property rights, illustrating the importance of enforcement to intellectual property. Enforcement is a product of the combined effect of rules of evidence, procedure, litigation, remedies, criminal offences and systems of alternative dispute resolution.

The TRIPs provisions have not warranted change in the UK, as they largely implement systems already in place in the UK for other WTO Member States. Article 41 requires effective enforcement that both prevents infringements and provides a deterrent to further infringement. Civil proceedings are therefore required to provide injunctions and delivery up of infringing products, and to have interim procedures for securing evidence as well as preventing infringement. Information can be demanded as to the source and channels of distribution for illegitimate goods and services. Arrangements for seizure of pirate and counterfeit products at ports of entry are required. Providing criminal offences is mandatory.

---

7   Combating Counterfeiting and Piracy in the Single Market, COM (98) 569.
8   Published 17 December 2003: www.dti.gov.uk.
9   'Counter Offensive: An IP Crime Strategy', DTI, 2004: www.patent.gov.uk.
10 'Pirates and Bootleggers Beware – First Intellectual Property Crime Strategy Published': www.patent.gov.uk.
11 Part III, TRIPS Agreement 1994.

The WIPO treaties make similar provisions for effective enforcement.[12] WIPO has now created an Advisory Committee on Enforcement and launched a webpage[13] devoted to enforcement issues. In similar vein, the UK Patent Office has created an Intellectual Property Crime Group[14] and estimates that criminal infringements cost the UK economy £9 billion annually.

The Council of Europe's Convention on Cybercrime[15] contains provisions relating to copyright infringement. Its purpose is to facilitate European co-operation over crime, and to harmonise approaches to crime committed on computer networks. The copyright provisions derive from the Berne Convention, the Rome Convention, TRIPs, the WCT and WPPT, and should not require new action by the UK.

19.1.3 European measures

Provision by the EU for enforcement is more likely to impact on the UK. In April 2004 the European Council adopted a hotly debated directive to harmonise Member States' provisions for enforcement.[16] The proposal goes beyond the TRIPs 'minimum standard' to propose additional measures (see 19.12) and must be implemented by the end of April 2006 (see 19.12).

Further European initiatives include a Customs Regulation[17] which came into force in July 2004 (see 19.2.2). This Regulation was the outcome of the Annual Statistical Report of 2001, which showed a nine-fold increase in the number of counterfeit products crossing EU borders in the period 1998–2001.

The Regulations establishing Community design rights and trade marks have also required Member States to nominate 'Community courts' for the enforcement of these rights. These courts apply national procedures and remedies. However, award of an injunction is subject to Article 98 of the Trade Mark Regulation, which provides that Community courts 'shall' order an injunction 'unless there are special reasons for not doing so'.

Consequently, proceedings, means for obtaining evidence, and the remedies available require separate attention, as does the Enforcement Directive and the resolution of cross-border disputes.

19.2 PROCEEDINGS

Four types of action are possible: civil proceedings, criminal proceedings, administrative action and even a measure of self-help by right owners. Alternative

---

12 Article 14, WCT; Article 23, WPPT.

13 Enforcement Issue and Strategies: www.wipo.int/enforcement/en.

14 Enforcement: www.patent.gov.uk.

15 The Convention came into force on 1 July 2004 and requires ratification by at least five Member States. Title 4 deals with intellectual property CETS 185: www.coe.int.

16 Directive of the European Parliament and of the Council on Measures and Procedures to Ensure the Enforcement of Intellectual Property Rights 2004/48/EC, [2004] OJ L195/16.

17 Council Regulation Concerning Customs Action Against Goods Suspected of Infringing Certain Intellectual Property Rights and the Measures to be Taken Against Goods Found to Have Infringed Such Rights (EC) 1383/2003, [2003] OJ L196/7.

dispute resolution is also sometimes an alternative, particularly in the case of domain names.

19.2.1   Criminal proceedings

Article 16 of the TRIPS Agreement requires states to penalise 'wilful' trade mark infringement and commercial copyright infringement. In addition, many of the statutory rights provide for offences in relation to intellectual property rights, applying both to primary and secondary acts of infringement. These offences both act to preserve the integrity of the patent, design and trade mark registers;[18] and act as a deterrent, particularly to infringement undertaken on a commercial scale.[19] Proposals made by the Law Commission could lead to the introduction of criminal proceedings in relation to the unauthorised use or disclosure of trade secrets (see 7.10.2). In addition, implementation of the Information Society Directive by the Copyright and Related Rights Regulations 2003 added to the copyright offences (see 10.7). In addition, offences lie under the Trade Descriptions Act 1968 for misdescriptive advertising and labelling.[20] The offence of conspiracy to defraud enables the net of liability to be further widened.

Criminal proceedings bear the heavier criminal burden of proof beyond reasonable doubt and require co-operation of the relevant authorities. Neither interlocutory relief nor discovery is available in criminal proceedings. However, criminal proceedings may have a greater deterrent effect, particularly where they attract publicity. Although intended for use against commercial pirates, individuals have successfully employed criminal measures against other individuals. In *Thames & Hudson Ltd v Design and Artists Copyright Society Ltd* (1995) Evans-Lombe J refused to stay prosecutions against the directors of a well known publishing company as vexatious and an abuse of process. He said 'no qualification appears in the statute limiting the types of offender capable of committing the offence to "pirates"'. The choice of proceeding rests with the claimant.

Prosecutions may be initiated by a right owner or his representative in the magistrates' court, or by resort to the police or the Trading Standards Authorities. Conviction results in fines or imprisonment. In a response to increasing piracy, the CDPA 1988 raised the fines and penalties laid down for copyright offences. Penalties were further increased by the Copyright and Trade Marks (Offences and Enforcement) Act 2002. It increased maximum copyright penalties[21] to a sentence of 10 years or unlimited fine, in line with trade mark offences and conspiracy to defraud and applies this to unauthorised decoders. Police search warrant powers were strengthened so that warrants may be obtained for all copyright[22] and trade mark[23] offences. Police may seize any item reasonably believed to be evidence of infringement. Additionally, the regulation of forfeiture for copyright infringement[24] was brought in line with that of

---

18   Sections 110 and 111 of the PA 1977; s 35 of the RDA 1949; ss 94 and 95 of the TMA 1994.
19   Sections 107 and 198 of the CDPA 1988; s 92 of the TMA 1994.
20   Section 1 of the Trade Descriptions Act 1968.
21   Sections 107, 198 and 297A of the CDPA 1988.
22   *Ibid*, s 297B.
23   Section 92A of the TMA 1994.
24   Sections 114A, 114B, 204A, 204B, 297C and 297D of the CDPA 1988.

trade marks; courts may order all infringing goods seized to be forfeited. The Proceeds of Crime Act (POCA) 2002 allows police and courts to confiscate the proceeds of crime, including counterfeiting, even when there is no conviction.

19.2.2 Administrative action

The TRIPS Agreement 1994 provides that Member States maintain control over pirated and counterfeited imports.[25] Both national and EU provisions apply. UK right owners can seek the arrest of imported infringing products at the point of entry into the UK by giving notice to the Commissioners of Customs and Excise.[26] The penalty for import for other than private and domestic use is that of forfeiture of the goods, which are often destroyed. Similar EU provisions apply enabling right owners to lodge applications with designated national customs authorities at EU borders to detain and check goods. Identification must be made possible by a sufficiently accurate description of the goods and proof must be provided of entitlement to intellectual property protection. The authorities may also temporarily detain goods without advance notification if they have grounds for suspicion. They notify the right owner, who then lodges the appropriate application. The Customs Regulation 2003,[27] which came into force on 1 July 2004, clarifies the previous law and extends it to new intellectual property rights.[28] Once goods are detained, if the right owner does not proceed, the goods will be released after 10 days. Alternatively, the right owner may commence infringement proceedings. If so, detention of the goods may be continued, or they will be released to the importer if security is given for them. Where infringement proceedings are successful the goods will be destroyed or measures taken to deprive the importer of benefits accruing from them. The right owner and importer may agree to the goods being destroyed without proceedings being taken, although samples will be kept in case of later litigation.

Local Authority Trading Standards Officers also have authority and a duty to make purchases – seize goods and documents – where a right owner objects to misdescription by a competitor. Misleading advertising is subject to control by advertising industry Codes of Practice, as well as the controls imposed over broadcasting.

Complaint may also be made to the Advertising Standards Authority or the Independent Television Commission – the latter successfully employed by David Bedford against lookalikes being used to depict him in advertising for The Number's 118 118 telephone directory enquiry service (see 18.10). The British Code of Advertising Practice or ITC Code is applied. The latter provides that living persons should not be depicted or caricatured without their consent. Ofcom upheld this decision on The Number (UK) Ltd's appeal in January 2004.[29]

---

25 Articles 51–60, TRIPS Agreement 1994.
26 Section 89 of the TMA 1994; s 111 of the CDPA 1988.
27 Council Regulation Concerning Customs Action Against Goods Suspected of Infringing Certain Intellectual Property Rights and the Measures to be Taken Against Goods Found to Have Infringed Such Rights (EC) 1383/2003, [2003] OJ L196/7.
28 Plant Variety Rights, Designations of Origin and Geographical Indications.
29 www.ofcom.org.uk.

19.2.3 Self-help

On two occasions, the legislation authorises right owners to act on their own behalf, subject to extensive conditions: ss 100 and 196 of the CDPA 1988. The police must be notified and no force may be used; nor may infringing copies be taken from a place of business. However, where a right owner finds infringing copies otherwise available for sale or hire, those copies may be seized and detained. This may help in a battle, for example, against street traders selling counterfeit perfumes; 'car boot' sales of pirated videos and sound recordings; and sales of unauthorised memorabilia outside concert venues.

19.2.4 Alternative dispute resolution

Alternative dispute resolution (ADR) refers to a number of different informal methods of resolving disputes. It includes mediation, conciliation, determination by experts and early neutral assessment. In some parts of the world arbitration would also be included in ADR. ADR requires both parties to a dispute to consent its use and to co-operate in its process.

Intellectual property litigation is expensive and time consuming. Although traditionally ADR has not been employed in such disputes, the changes made by the Woolf Reforms[30] in England and Wales provide an incentive to do so. In 1996 Judge Peter Ford attached mediation and arbitration panels to the Patents County Court. Both the OHIM and the UK Trade Mark Registry allow a 'cooling off' period during opposition proceedings to encourage settlement. As increasing numbers of small and medium-sized enterprises are encouraged to seek intellectual property protection by Patent Office initiatives, spurred by the DTI's Innovation Report (see 19.1.1), an additional incentive to seek less expensive and less time consuming resolution of disputes may arise.

Complainants may make use either of the ICANN Uniform Dispute Resolution Policy (UDRP) for '.com', '.org' and '.net' top-level domains (see 17.6.4) or national domain name registries[31] dispute resolution services for disputes relating to domain names. These are mandatory for the registrant, being contractually imposed as part of registration of the domain name. Nominet, in charge of the '.uk' top-level domain, has the power to transfer, cancel or suspend a registration and decisions of dispute resolution panels are binding on the parties, although the service does not displace the role of the courts (see 17.6.9). The Nominet Dispute Resolution Service includes a period of informal (non-binding) mediation between the parties.

19.2.5 Civil proceedings

Most infringements of intellectual property rights are provided by statute to be breaches of property rights.[32] The equitable action for breach of confidence is an anomaly while infringements of moral rights are provided to be breaches of statutory duty.[33]

---

30 Civil Procedure Act 1997, Civil Procedure Rules.
31 Nominet in the UK: www.nominet.org.uk.
32 Sections 96, 191 and 229 of the CDPA 1988, for example.
33 *Ibid*, s 103.

Right owners themselves have the right to bring proceedings, provided that any formalities of registration have been complied with. Co-owners may initiate proceedings provided that the other co-owners are joined to the action. Exclusive licensees of a patent, copyright, registered trade mark and unregistered design right, but not of a registered design,[34] may also sue. The registered owner must be joined as a party.[35] Other licensees must rely on their licensor to take action. Patentees and registered trade mark owners should be registered as proprietors of the right, or may fail to secure damages or an account of profit.[36] Representative organisations for right owners may bring representative proceedings in the name of members where there is a common interest and common harm. Additionally, Article 4 of the Enforcement Directive (see 19.12) provides collective rights management bodies and professional defence bodies with *locus standi* to sue on behalf of right owners to the extent that the relevant national law allows. A person may also apply to a court for a declaration that their activities do not infringe another's right. Section 77 of the Patents Act 1977 makes special provision for declarations (declarator in Scotland) of non-infringement of a patent by the Comptroller of Patents or by the court.

Liability is for infringements taking place within the UK. Defendants may be jointly liable, even where their actions take place outside the UK, if they induce the infringement or are participating in a common design with persons in the UK. Employers are vicariously liable for acts of employees committed in the course of employment.

The civil burden of proof applies and civil proceedings are often preferred for the remedies available, such as interim relief. The remedies are: damages, injunctions, an order for delivery up and an account of profits. In England and Wales proceedings are brought in the Chancery Division of the High Court. However, the Patents Court in that Division is provided for patent actions and a Patents County Court was established by ss 288–91 of the CDPA 1988 for patent and design disputes. The Patents County Court has jurisdiction to hear any patent dispute falling within the jurisdiction of the High Court. It may hear copyright, unregistered design or breach of confidence cases up to a limit of £15,000. Specialist judges sit in these latter courts. In Scotland, in general, jurisdiction lies in the Outer House of the Court of Session, while incidental matters may be raised in the Sheriff Court.[37] However, proceedings relating to patents may only be brought in the Court of Session and are governed by the Act of Sederunt (Rules of Court of Session) Rules 1994.[38]

19.3 SECURING EVIDENCE

Intellectual property right owners suffer a handicap by comparison with, for example, victims of a tort or breach of contract. Often, the fact that infringing articles are being made and sold becomes obvious, but the source of these infringements remains a mystery, even if the ultimate supplier has been traced. Not only this but, usually, once

---

34 Section 67 of the PA 1977; ss 101 and 234 of the CDPA 1988; s 31 of the TMA 1994.
35 Section 67 of the PA 1977, s 31 of the TMA 1994, ss 101,102, 234 and 235 of the CDPA 1988.
36 Section 68 of the PA 1977; s 25 of the TMA 1994.
37 Sections 232 and 246 of the CDPA 1988, s 27 of the RDA 1949, s 75 of the TMA 1994.
38 SI 1994/1443.

infringers realise that infringement has been detected, they will immediately close down that chain of supply, destroying all evidence as to its existence. However, not much later, a new chain of supply will be established. This makes the enforcement of the legitimate right difficult.

The courts of England and Wales have been alive to these difficulties and have provided two effective injunctions to counteract such problems in search orders and freezing injunctions. In Scotland the equivalent to a search order is an application for an order under section 1 of the Administration of Justice (Scotland) Act 1972, and to a freezing injunction an arrestment to found jurisdiction.

In addition, intellectual property right owners may seek to make 'trap orders' by acting as customers and purchasing infringing articles. Trap orders can be usefully employed in trade mark and passing off actions to demonstrate potential confusion. It was held in *Claire Album v Hartstone Hosiery* (1993) that such evidence is not subject to the 'clean hands' maxim. In addition, the Civil Procedure Rules allow right owners to apply to a court for an order that a person reveal information relating to the relevant action, names and addresses of individuals, dates, quantities of importation and sources of material. This can assist in tracking trading channels and identifying the primary infringer as well as related parties to an action.

19.4 SEARCH (ANTON PILLER) ORDERS[39]

Anton Piller orders stemmed from the courts' jurisdiction to grant injunctions[40] and to order the detention and preservation of the subject matter and documentation necessary to an action. This was given statutory force by s 7 of the Civil Procedure Act 1997. The order is a mandatory interlocutory injunction, granted at the court's discretion. It is granted *ex parte* without the defendant's appearance or representation at the hearing and the proceedings are often in secret. It orders a defendant to allow the claimant and a supervising solicitor to enter his premises in order to search for and seize, copy or photograph material pertaining to the alleged infringement, to deliver up infringing goods or to keep infringing stock and to answer queries. The first Anton Piller order was granted in *EMI v Pandit* (1975) and received the sanction of the Court of Appeal in *Anton Piller v Manufacturing Processes* (1976) (hence the original name for the order).

Any refusal to obey the order by the defendant is a contempt of court, punishable by fine (in the region of £75,000, in *Taylor Made Golf Co v Rata and Rata* (1996)), sequestration of assets or imprisonment.

The benefits of such an order to a right owner are clear: an opportunity to search the rival's premises without warning or notice or any real opportunity to object before the search on the defendant's part. Because of their draconian nature, it was at first envisaged that these orders would be infrequently awarded and only where it was 'essential' to do so.

---

39 Renamed in the Woolf Reforms, Civil Procedure Rules 1999.
40 Section 37 of the Supreme Court Act 1981; s 38 of the County Courts Act 1984. Now governed by s 7 of the Civil Procedure Act 1997.

19.4.1 Conditions for grant

In order for an order to be granted, *Anton Piller v Manufacturing Processes* (1976) established that:

> There are three essential preconditions for the making of such an order, in my judgment. First, there must be an extremely strong *prima facie* case. Secondly, the damage, potential or actual, must be very serious for the applicant. Thirdly, there must be clear evidence that the defendants have in their possession incriminating documents or things, and that there is a real possibility that they may destroy such material before any application *inter partes* can be made.

The court also laid down several provisions to provide safeguards for a defendant:

(a) the order is made against the defendant in person and not his property. This means that the defendant may refuse permission for entry to the premises and the search party may not enter without permission. It is this that distinguishes the order from a search warrant;

(b) the claimant must give a cross-undertaking in damages;

(c) the claimant must be accompanied by his or her solicitor, an officer of the court;

(d) the defendant must be given time to consider the order, and to seek advice from a solicitor;

(e) the defendant may make an application for the order to be discharged as having been improperly obtained. The order may be discharged where the claimant has not made a full and frank disclosure of the relevant facts, however innocent (*Thermax v Schott* (1981)). Fears of violence will not lead to the order being discharged (*Coca-Cola and Schweppes v Gilbey* (1996)); and

(f) no force may be used.

19.4.2 The potential for abuse

It was not long before it became obvious that Anton Piller orders had considerable potential for abuse, and that the conditions and safeguards were not sufficient to protect a defendant. Even where not abused, the order often caused defendants considerable shock, and there were invasions of privacy and serious harm to reputations.

The ability to refuse entry proved an empty protection, when, to do so, amounted to contempt of court, even when the order was subsequently discharged: *Wardle Fabrics v Myristis* (1984), although, in *Bhimji v Chatwani* (1991), the contempt was treated as technical. Nor could entry be refused while an application to have the order discharged was made: *Bhimji v Chatwani* (1991). This meant that by the time decisions as to discharge were being made orders had already been executed and, initially, courts were reluctant to discharge orders until the main trial: *Booker McConnell v Plascow* (1986). This led to defendants having to wait for redress under the cross-undertaking in damages for obvious wrongs in the grant and execution of orders. Orders were being granted quickly, with inadequate attention to the strength of the claimant's case (see *Swedac v Magnet and Southerns* (1989)) and in ignorance of events at the execution of the order.

Dockray and Laddie explain how orders could be abused in one of two ways.[41] Because the order is so heavily weighted in the claimant's favour, it can be used as a 'blow' against the defendant. The search and subsequent removal of so much pertaining to the defendant's business can actually bring that business to an end and orders may even be cynically employed for that purpose. Or, because of the opportunity to rifle through the defendant's premises and documents, it can be used as a 'fishing trip'. The courts gradually became aware of the prejudice caused to defendants by Anton Piller orders and were very critical of the manner of execution in some cases: *Columbia Picture Industries v Robinson* (1986); *Universal Thermosensors v Hibben* (1992). Suggestions were made for new safeguards. At the same time, Dockray and Laddie's article and investigation by the Lord Chancellor's Department suggested that new measures were necessary.

19.4.3 New safeguards

The potential for undue prejudice to defendants occurs at two stages: first, at the time of the application and then, secondly, when the order is executed. As for the first, the danger of notifying a defendant and the consequent likely destruction of evidence prevent representation of the defendant's case. However, Dockray and Laddie suggested that an *amicus curiae* be appointed on the defendant's behalf. The cost to the public purse has hindered any adoption of this suggestion, which appears the only satisfactory means of counterbalancing the distinct advantage the claimant has at the hearing. An independent solicitor, appointed at the claimant's expense, might achieve similar protection. It would also be possible, if very time consuming and expensive, to allow a defendant a real opportunity to take advice and seek discharge of an order before the order is executed. The search team would have to be admitted to the defendant's premises in order to prevent the very danger the order is designed to prevent – removal and destruction of evidence. However, the actual search could be delayed until a court affirmed the order or permission to start given by the defendant. The cost would be as much to the defendant as the claimant, as business would be suspended during this interval.

At the stage of execution, new safeguards recommended by Scott J in *Columbia Picture Industries v Robinson* and Nicholls VC in *Universal Thermosensors v Hibben* have been implemented by the judges. In 1994, a Practice Direction[42] was issued with a new standard form of order, incorporating these judicial safeguards, to be used in all cases unless a change can be justified to the judge. Major changes include:

(i)   execution during business hours;

(ii) the necessary inclusion of an independent solicitor in the search team;

(iii) a mandatory date to report back to the court, shortly after execution, to enable any complaints and claims for compensation to be made by the defendant;

(iv) careful records to be taken of all material taken from the premises.

Criticisms can still be made. The additional safeguards increase the cost of such orders to claimants who, by definition, are facing defendants they believe to be unscrupulous. The attempt to simplify the wording of the orders has also led to the anomaly that

---

41   Dockray, M and Laddie, H, 'Piller Problems' [1990] LQR 601.
42   Practice Direction (Mareva Injunctions and Anton Piller Orders) (1994).

consent to entry can now be given, not just by defendants themselves, but by 'the person appearing to be in control of the premises'. This appears to turn the Anton Piller order into the search warrant it has always been argued that it is not: *Anton Piller v Manufacturing Processes* (1976). Nevertheless, a challenge to Anton Piller orders under Article 8 of the European Convention on Human Rights in the European Court of Human Rights failed in *Chappell v UK* (1989).

19.4.4 Order for inspection in Scotland

Orders may be sought in Scotland for the inspection, photographing, preservation, custody and detention of documents or property appearing to the court to be property about which questions may relevantly arise in civil proceedings likely to be brought. This includes an order for the production and recovery of any such property, the taking of samples thereof and the carrying out of any experiment thereon where required.[43] The application may be made *ex parte* by a person appearing to the court to be likely to be a party or minuter in these proceedings. The court appoints a commissioner to execute the order. The court also has power under a search order to compel any persons who appear to the court to be persons who might be witnesses or defenders to any existing civil proceedings or proceedings likely to be brought.[44]

Conditions are imposed on the grant of an order. The petitioner must show that proceedings are likely to be brought and that he has a *prima facie*, intelligible and stateable case. In order to establish this, however, it is not necessary to subject the pleadings to detailed examination: *Harwood v Jackson* (2003). The court will also consider whether any circumstances which would affect the exercise of its discretion and prevent grant of the order. In *BPI v Cohen, Cohen, Kelly, Cohen & Cohen Ltd* (1983) Lord President Emslie observed that the tests applied by English courts in deciding whether to make Anton Piller orders appear to be appropriate for application in Scotland by the Outer House of the Court of Session.

The jurisdiction and its history was examined by Lord Macfadyen in *Iomega Corp v Myrica (UK) Ltd* (No 2) (1999). It predates the origins of Anton Piller orders, and was designed to remedy two difficulties encountered by parties to proceedings. The first was that of obtaining commission and diligence to recover documents before the closing of the record and, secondly, the impossibility of obtaining a court order to recover documents before an action was begun. Nor does the jurisdiction extend beyond obtaining an order. Once it has been executed and the items recovered have been handed to the court, the Rules of the Court of Session govern what is to happen to that property. Little authority appears to exist on what use may be made of it. However, Lord Macfadyen held that the party recovering the property would be subject to an implied obligation not to use it or allow it to be used for any purpose other than the conduct of actual or prospective proceedings in respect of which it had been recovered. Nevertheless, this did not prevent the documents recovered from being used in other domestic proceedings where that was in the interests of justice. If use was to be in proceedings outside Scotland, the court might impose conditions on that use under its inherent discretion.

---

43 Section 1 Administration of Justice (Scotland) Act 1972.
44 *Ibid*, s 1A, as amended by the Law Reform (Miscellaneous Provisions) (Scotland) Act 1985.

19.4.5 Self-incrimination

The Anton Piller order also requires the defendant to answer questions. This has the potential for self-incrimination of criminal conduct and defendants often resorted to the privilege against self-incrimination. The House of Lords upheld such a plea in *Rank Film Distribution v Video Information* (1982). In Scotland the same was held in *BPI Ltd v Cohen, Cohen, Kelly, Cohen and Cohen Ltd* (1983). The unfortunate result was that the most reprehensible of defendants were the ones most likely to be able to rely on the privilege, resulting in the emasculation of both Anton Piller orders and Mareva injunctions. This decision was overruled for intellectual property proceedings and theft actions by s 72 of the Supreme Court Act 1981. A secondary privilege in criminal proceedings is bestowed on information thus elicited for the purpose of civil proceedings. Section 15 of the Law Reform (Miscellaneous Provisions) (Scotland) Act 1985 removed the privilege against self-incrimination in intellectual property actions in Scotland.

19.5 FREEZING (MAREVA) INJUNCTIONS[45]

Just as dishonourable infringers might dispose of evidence of infringing activity, so might they be willing to dissipate their assets at any hint of action, in order to frustrate any eventual judgment against them. The courts' response to this danger is a freezing injunction. This is a discretionary, interlocutory injunction, awarded without the defendant being heard, either before or at the trial. The court order freezes the assets of a defendant, preventing those assets being disposed of or transferred out of the jurisdiction. Such an order was first granted in *The Mareva* (1975).

A freezing injunction carries a similar capacity for prejudice to defendants and abuse by claimants as does a search order. Businesses will flounder if starved of needful capital. The inconvenience, both personal and commercial, caused by such deprivation of assets could be used to pressurise a defendant to settle the claim quickly or merely to provide security for any judgment that might be obtained at trial. Conditions for grant of the order and safeguards for the unrepresented defendant were laid down by the courts in *Z v A* (1982) and *CBS v Lambert* (1983).

19.5.1 Conditions for grant

A claimant must show:

(i)   a good arguable case against the defendant – 'likely that the plaintiff will recover judgment against the defendant for a certain or approximate sum' (*per* Kerr LJ, in *Z v A* (1982));

(ii)   the claimant has reason to believe that the defendant has assets within the jurisdiction to meet the judgment. In *Babanaft v Bassante* (1989), this was extended to include assets outside the jurisdiction; and

(iii) the claimant has reason to believe that those assets may be removed.

In addition:

---

45   Renamed in the Woolf Reforms, Civil Procedure Rules 1999.

(i) the claimant must also give the usual cross-undertaking in damages;

(ii) notice of the order must be served both on the defendant, banks and any other third party affected by the order; and

(iii) the claimant must undertake to indemnify both banks and third parties against any costs, expenses or fees incurred in complying with the order. The order may not cover stock in trade, tools of trade, nor the essentials of daily living.

The defendant can apply to have a freezing injunction discharged and the claimant must again make full and frank disclosure. A freezing injunction can also be varied on the defendant's application and will be so varied if an unreasonable amount has been frozen. In *PCW v Dixon* (1983), an order was varied by the court from an allowance to the defendant of £100 *per* week for living expenses, to £1,000 *per* week, as befitted a wealthy man.

Although not as contentious as the Anton Piller order, criticisms have been voiced as to the heavy handedness of freezing injunctions. It has been suggested[46] that a 'good arguable case' is not a high enough threshold, that the order should be subject to independent supervision and review by the judge a week after grant and that the defendant should have an opportunity to be heard after the affidavit identifying the assets has been filed.

19.5.2 Arrestment to found jurisdiction in Scotland

Where movable property belonging to the defender, or a debt due to him in Scotland, is arrested under warrant from the Court of Session or Sheriff Court, this process subjects a person not domiciled in Scotland to the jurisdiction of the courts in Scotland in the action in which the arrestment is used.[47]

19.6 NORWICH PHARMACAL ORDERS

Right owners may learn only that infringing products are passing through the hands of persons who may neither be infringing themselves, nor know that the goods infringe. In *Norwich Pharmacal v Commissioners of Customs and Excise* (1974) the House of Lords made an order for discovery of information. Courts have discretion to order the person handling infringing goods to disclose the identity of the consignor or consignee of the goods and other relevant information[48] if he or she is facilitating wrongful acts. The order may include disclosure of names and addresses, dates and quantities being imported and the source of goods.

19.7 REMEDIES

Despite the diversity of intellectual property rights, the remedies available for infringement have a family resemblance that enables them to be described in general. Points of difference from right to right have been noted at the appropriate places.

---

46 Willoughby, T and Connal, S, 'The Mareva Injunction' [1997] EIPR 479.
47 Schedule 8, Civil Jurisdiction and Judgments Act 1982.
48 Rule 31, Civil Procedure Rules.

19.7.1   Account of profits

A claimant may elect for an account of profits.[49] This is a discretionary remedy (*Hogg v Kirby* (1803)), which provides the claimant with a personal remedy against a defendant's unjust enrichment. A defendant's actual profit must be proved, which allows the claimant to see the defendant's accounts (with all the useful information they may contain). Account is rarely resorted to, as proving profit is a long and difficult task.

In Scotland (as in England and Wales) a pursuer may not claim both damages and account of profits: *Treadwell Drifter's Inc v RCL Ltd* (1996). In a copyright action a claimant cannot claim exemplary damages if he has opted for an account: *Redrow Homes Ltd v Betts Bros plc* (1998).

Where the infringement relates to a portion of a product sold, or a trade mark applied to it, the claimant is entitled to the whole of the profit for the article. In *Peter Pan Manufacturing Corp v Corsets Silhouette* (1963), the plaintiff secured the whole of the defendant's profit, although the confidential information used only applied to a proportion of the articles made by the defendant. The appropriate principles to be applied where a patented device formed part of a manufacturing process were examined in *Celanese International Corp v BP Chemicals Ltd* (1999). Here, the court rejected the so-called 'incremental approach', whereby the difference between the defendant's actual profit and that which he would have made without any infringement would be assessed. Instead, the defendant is to be treated as having done business on the claimant's behalf and to apportion that part of his profit attributable to the infringement. Therefore, the maximum payable could be the whole of the defendant's profit. The sum due is limited to profits held by the court to be caused by the wrongful activity. Expenses are deducted in calculating the defendant's profit. Apportionment of the defendant's profit is then made. In *Celanese* the contribution of the patented device to the profits was calculated by estimating the proportion of the capital expenditure on the infringing device to that of the whole process.

19.7.2   Delivery up

This is another discretionary equitable remedy. It is a court order for delivery up of infringing articles or documents for destruction, or destruction under oath by the defendant. In the case of patents and trade marks the order is given statutory force.[50] In the case of copyright and the unregistered design right, the statutory provision extends to ordering delivery up to the claimant, including ordering delivery up of the means for making infringing copies.[51] This was extended for trade marks, performers' rights, the unregistered design right and copyright to orders for delivery up destruction or forfeiture[52] by the Copyright and Trade Marks (Offences and Enforcement) Act 2003, and amended by the Copyright and Related Rights Regulations 2003. Generally, this applies where the infringing material is held in 'the course of business'. The order is discretionary and courts are directed to consider

---

49 Section 61 of the PA 1977; s 96 of the CDPA 1988; s 14 of the TMA 1994.
50 Section 61 of the PA 1977; s 15 of the TMA 1994.
51 Sections 99 and 230 CDPA 1988.
52 *Ibid*, ss 99, 108, 195, 199, 204, 230 and 231; s 16 of the TMA 1994.

whether other remedies would be adequate to compensate the right owner and protect his interests. As third parties may have an interest in the goods they may appear in the proceedings.

19.7.3 Declarations

Courts have both statutory and inherent jurisdiction to make declarations[53] that an act or proposed act does not infringe the right of another. Section 71 of the PA 1977 provides that a declaration of non-infringement may be made, despite the lack of any assertion to the contrary in proceedings between the patentee and the person doing (or proposing to do) the act in question. This is conditional on an application having been made in writing to the patentee or his exclusive licensee for a written acknowledgment that there is no infringement and describing the act in detail, and the patentee refusing of failing to provide the assurance sought. The Comptroller of Patents may also make such a declaration.

More generally, an application may be made to a court for a declaration.[54] This is a discretionary power which will only be exercised if the possibility that the act in question may infringe is considered to be realistic. It must be shown that the person applying has a genuine interest in doing so, and that there is a person with a real interest in opposing the claim of non-infringement. Consequently, there needs to be a legal right at stake, or for proceedings relating to a right already to have been instituted: *Vine v National Dock Labour Board* (1957). In *Biogen v Medeva* (1993), at first instance, Aldous J pointed out that it was settled law that the jurisdiction was confined to declaring contested legal rights, and that it would only be invoked in 'appropriate circumstances to settle appropriate questions'.

19.8 DAMAGES

Damages are a common law remedy – available as of right – and are compensatory. Breaches of intellectual property rights are treated as a statutory tort (or delict in Scotland): *Gerber Garment Technology Inc v Lectra Systems Ltd* (1997). *Prima facie*, the aim is to put claimants in the position they would have been in had the wrong not been suffered. Damages for loss will be awarded where a defendant's infringing act caused that loss and was reasonably foreseeable. Aggravated damages may be awarded for damage to reputation.

19.8.1 Measure of damages

There are no hard and fast rules for the measurement of damages and the courts have confessed to 'rough and ready' calculation, by 'the exercise of a sound imagination and the practice of a broad axe' (*per* Lord Shaw, in *Watson Laidlaw v Potts Cassells and Williamson* (1914)). There are, however, guidelines, which were itemised in *General Tire and Rubber Co v Firestone Tyre and Rubber Co* (1976):

---

53   In Scotland, declarator.
54   RSC Ord 15, r 16.

(a)   damages should compensate for loss or injury caused by the tortious infringement, being that sum of money which would put the injured party in the position they would have been in if the wrong had not been sustained;

(b)   an account of profits exists as an alternative to damages if opted for by the plaintiff;

(c)   the plaintiffs must prove their loss; the defendants being wrongdoers, damages should be liberally assessed, but with the object of compensating the plaintiffs and not punishing the defendants;

(d)   where the patentee manufactures articles for profit, infringement diverts sales and the normal measure of damages will be the profit which would have been realised by the plaintiffs had they made the infringing sales;

(e)   where the patentee exploits the invention through licensing for royalties, damages will be assessed by the royalty that, on all the evidence, should have been paid. This is done by adopting the method of *Meters Ltd v Metropolitan Gas Meters Ltd* (1911). Fletcher Moulton LJ said:

> There is one case in which I think the manner of assessing damages in the case of sales of infringing articles has almost become a rule of law, and that is where the patentee grants permission to make the infringing article at a fixed price - in other words, where he grants licences at a certain figure. Every one of the infringing articles might then have been rendered a non-infringing article by applying for and getting that permission. The court then takes the number of infringing articles, and multiplies that by the sum that would have had to be paid in order to make the manufacture of that article lawful, and that is the measure of the damage that has been done by the infringement ...;

(f)   if the infringement is not competitive, where a normal rate of profit, or royalty, cannot be established, the plaintiff must adduce evidence of royalties in analogous trades, or of the profitability of the invention, in order for a hypothetical figure, a reasonable royalty, to be reached. This is estimated by a multiplier in the same way as when a real royalty is established. Where the plaintiff does not suffer lost sales, and the intellectual property infringement relates only to a proportion of the articles sold by the defendant (for example, one work included in a compilation), a royalty may be calculated taking into account the proportion of the infringement to the whole article.

In the case of copyright, the measure of damage is the depreciation to the value of the copyright caused by the infringement. In *Nottinghamshire Healthcare NHS Trust v News Group Newspapers Ltd* (2002) Pumfrey J followed these guidelines, but pointed out that whereas patents are intended to be exploited, this is not the case for all copyright works. In such a case the convenient approach was to compensate by treating the work as if it had been made for commercial exploitation, treating it as an agency photograph, for example, even though this did not really relate to the nature of the infringement.

Where a claimant was in the habit of charging a fee for endorsement, using a notional endorsement fee was the approach to be adopted for infringement: *Irvine v Talksport Ltd* (2003). The fact that the defendant's finances would not have allowed payment of such a fee was irrelevant.

19.8.2 Parasitic and bridgehead damages

Profits may not stem, however, solely from exploitation of the invention itself, but also be derived from, for example, servicing and sales of spares and sales of related technology. Claims have been made to these consequential or 'parasitic' damages, and also to 'springboard' or 'bridgehead' damages. In *Culnic Components v Hill and Smith* (1983), it had been held that only losses stemming directly from acts done in relation to infringing products and processes were recoverable. Recently, in *Gerber Garment Technology Inc v Lectra Systems Ltd* (1997), the Court of Appeal upheld the generous award of patent damages made by Jacob J at first instance. The judgment is of general application to intellectual property.

The plaintiff manufactured patented automated cutting machinery (CAM machines) and computer assisted design machines (CAD machines). Sale of a CAM machine was often accompanied by a sale of a CAD machine and followed by supply of spares and servicing. Towards the end of the life of the plaintiff's patents and while they were endorsed 'licence of right', the defendant made infringing sales of CAM machines. Damages were claimed and awarded for:

(a) lost profits on sales that the plaintiff would have made but for the defendant's sales;

(b) lost royalties on sales by the defendant that the plaintiff would not have made;

(c) losses caused to the plaintiff by the need to discount its prices to meet the competition from the defendant;

(d) lost profits on sales of CAD machines which would have accompanied the lost CAM machine sales;

(e) loss of profits on spares and servicing;

(f) loss of profits on CAM sales made after the patents expired on the basis that the defendant's infringements before expiry enabled it to compete immediately on expiry ('springboard' or 'bridgehead' damages).

The use of intellectual property rights to protect a web of interlinked commercial activity assumes exaggeratedly anti-competitive overtones, which are difficult to defend. However, an important difference may lie in the means the right owner has adopted for securing a fair reward from the intellectual property at issue. If the appropriate reward is to be secured from the intellectual property protected product itself, parasitic and bridgehead damages are difficult to support on grounds of either policy or principle (the right extending only to its subject matter). However, where the reward is calculated to include 'after-sales', the actual product even being sold at discounted prices (consider *Canon Kabushiki Kaisha v Green Cartridge Co (Hong Kong) Ltd* (1997) (see 10.8.2)), such damages acquire an air of respectability.

19.8.3 Additional damages

Sections 97(2), 191J and 229(3) of the CDPA 1988 confer jurisdiction to award additional damages for infringement of copyright, rights in performances and unregistered design right, having regard, in particular, to 'the flagrancy of the infringement' and the benefit which has accrued by reason of the infringement. In *Ravenscroft v Herbert* (1980) flagrancy 'impl[ied] the existence of scandalous conduct, deceit and such like' as well as deliberate and calculated infringements. 'Benefit' meant reaping a pecuniary advantage beyond the damages the defendant would otherwise have to pay. Consequently, distress,[55] humiliation and damage to reputation have been taken into account in assessing additional damages.

In *Redrow Homes Ltd v Bett Bros plc* (1998), in an appeal from the Court of Session, the House of Lords overruled *Cala Homes Ltd v Alfred McAlpine Homes Ltd* (1996), where additional damages had been awarded to a plaintiff who had opted for an account of profits. Additional damages are additional to compensatory damages and can only be awarded if the claimant asks for the remedy of damages. The House of Lords did not decide whether additional damages for copyright infringement were punitive in nature or compensatory; in *Cala*, Laddie J had termed them *sui generis*.

In *Nottinghamshire Healthcare NHS Trust v News Group Newspapers Ltd* (2002) the *Sun* newspaper published an improperly obtained photograph of a patient at Rampton Hospital without authority, causing distress to the individual and infringing the Health Trust's copyright. Pumfrey J stated that the better view was that damages under s 97(2) of the CDPA 1988 could not be entirely punitive,[56] and were not statutory exemplary damages. However, as the section is widely drafted, it allowed damages based on aggravation beyond those available at common law, permitting an element of restitution in having regard to the benefit gained by the defendant. This would include non-financial benefits, for example, where a defendant established himself in the market and generated goodwill by flagrant infringement. The only defence to such damages would be that which lay in s 97(1), where it would not be reasonable to suppose that there was copyright in the work. Deliberate infringement and recklessness and carelessness sufficient to amount to a 'couldn't care less' attitude was enough to aggravate infringement. The flagrancy in the case entitled the claimants to an award of £10,000 in additional damages.

Additional damages will be subject to the same provision in relation to 'innocent' infringers as ordinary damages (see 19.8.4).

19.8.4   Innocent defendants

In one circumstance damages, although not the other remedies, will be refused – the 'innocence' of the infringer. In the case of patents, registered designs and rights in performances and copyright, damages are not awarded for losses incurred during the period in which a defendant is not aware of the intellectual property right or had no reasonable grounds to believe that it existed.[57] Nevertheless, it may well be reasonable to have made inquiries as to intellectual property rights.

There is no such statutory provision in relation to registered trade marks. In *Gillette UK Ltd v Edenwest* (1994) Blackburne J held that damages lay both for trade mark infringement and passing off during the period of 'innocence'.

---

55 *Williams v Settle* (1960). The newspaper paid £15 for the photographs; damages of £1,000 were awarded.

56 For another view, see Michalos, C, 'Copyright and Punishment: The Nature of Additional Damages' [2000] EIPR 470.

57 Section 62 of the PA 1977; s 9 of the RDA 1949; ss 97 and 184(2) of the CDPA 1988.

19.9 INJUNCTIONS OR INTERDICTS

Again, an equitable remedy, the injunction[58] is a vital remedy for intellectual property right owners. An injunction is an order of the court to the defendant, usually prohibitory,[59] ordering the defendant either to cease an activity, or to do what is ordered. An injunction, therefore, can secure an end to infringing activity, rather than merely providing a right to monetary compensation. Not only this, injunctions can be interim (granted before the trial of the issue) or final, and may be granted *quia timet* to prevent threatened infringement and damage. In areas of commerce dependent on fragile reputations and volatile, novelty led, short lived markets, but where considerable losses can be incurred, the value of the injunction is obvious. Such is the significance of the injunction to both parties that many intellectual property actions halt at the interlocutory stage.

Injunctions are granted at the courts' discretion and only where damages will be an inadequate remedy – they are not available as of right, as are common law damages. Refusal to observe an injunction is a contempt of court, penalised by fines, sequestration of assets or even imprisonment.

An injunction wrongly granted has the potential to do considerable harm to defendants and the courts have sought to secure a careful balance between claimants' needs for quick and effective relief and defendants' need to continue fair competition.

Several conditions are, therefore, imposed on the grant of an injunction:

(a) claimants must proceed as soon as they learn of the alleged infringement;

(b) claimants must give a cross-undertaking in damages to compensate the defendants for damage incurred from a wrongly granted injunction;

(c) defendants can seek a declaration of non-infringement.

19.9.1 Interim injunctions

An interim injunction is a temporary, interim award made before the trial at the court's discretion. It is an important element in the success or otherwise of intellectual property rights because damage to reputation is so often an element in intellectual property litigation and can be virtually immediate if a poor quality counterfeit is introduced onto the market. Many intellectual property actions are complex, particularly those involving patents, and trial of the main action can take between one and three years to reach hearing. An interim injunction can prevent the irreparable harm – and even total loss of market – that might come to pass during that period. Nevertheless, recently interim injunctions have been relatively rare in patent cases. Because an interim application is heard on early written evidence, the court must minimise the risk to the parties of prejudice at the trial should the interim decision prove to have been the wrong one. This requires drawing a balance between consideration of the merits of the case and focusing on avoiding irrevocable harm to one or other of the parties.

---

58   In Scotland, an interdict.
59   An injunction can be mandatory.

Grant of interim injunctions in England and Wales

The value of an interim injunction would be frustrated if it, in itself, took considerable time to secure. The House of Lords recognised this danger and took steps to negate it in *American Cyanimid v Ethicon* (1975). It had taken 18 months and appeal to the House of Lords for American Cyanimid to secure an interlocutory injunction. The difficulty lay in the considerations that had to be taken into account in deciding whether to grant or refuse the injunction. The courts' approach had been to consider, first, whether the plaintiff had a *prima facie* case, secondly, whether damages would be an adequate remedy and, thirdly, the balance of convenience between the parties. The first step – that no injunction could be granted unless the affidavit evidence adduced by both sides established, on the balance of probabilities, that the plaintiff was likely to succeed at trial – had been treated as a rule of practice so 'well established as to constitute a rule of law' by the Court of Appeal. *'Prima facie'* was understood only in the sense that further evidence at the trial might alter this conclusion. This turned interlocutory hearings into trials of the main issue, lengthening the process inordinately and necessitating a great deal of evidence.

In the House of Lords, Lord Diplock laid down new guidelines for the grant of interlocutory injunctions:

(a) the court must be satisfied that the plaintiff's claim was not frivolous or vexatious – one with no real prospect of succeeding – but a 'serious question to be tried'. At this stage, there was no requirement that difficult questions of evidence or law be resolved before the balance of convenience could be considered;

(b) next, the adequacy of damages as a remedy should be considered as a first stage of the balance of convenience. This involves a two-stage inquiry:

(1) if, were the plaintiff to succeed at trial, damages would adequately compensate[60] for loss incurred by refusal of the injunction and the defendant was in a position to pay, the injunction should normally be refused, however strong the plaintiff's claim appeared;

(2) but, if damages would not adequately compensate the plaintiff, if damages would adequately compensate the defendant at trial in the event of an injunction being granted, and the plaintiff were able to pay, the injunction should be granted;

(c) in cases of doubt as to the adequacy of the respective remedies in damages to either or both parties, other considerations of the balance of convenience arise;

(d) where all other factors appear equally balanced, such measures as would preserve the *status quo* should be taken.

Factors to be taken into consideration include all relevant circumstances and Lord Diplock made no attempt to list examples or the relative weight to be attached to different considerations. Examples include:

(i) The degree to which claimant and defendant are established in business has proved significant. In *Belfast Ropework Co Ltd v Pixdane* (1976), an interlocutory injunction was granted where the defendant was a small, new business,

---

60 Damages are not likely to compensate for harm to reputation or privacy.

impecunious, without substantial investment in plant and materials, and the plaintiff's potential losses large. Nevertheless, in *Catnic Components v Stressline* (1976), the injunction was refused where the defendant had a well established business, was able to meet a claim for damages, there were other competitors on the market and the plaintiff could be compensated by damages.

(ii)   A 'snowball' argument has aided right owners where it can be said that the refusal of an injunction will allow a multiplicity of competitors to develop, causing irreparable damage.

(iii) Damage to reputation, almost impossible to repair with damages alone, is often a significant factor pointing towards the grant of an injunction. Consequently, interlocutory injunctions are often awarded in trade mark and passing off actions.

(iv)   Delay and other reprehensible behaviour by the claimant is also relevant: *Dalgety Spillers Foods v Food Brokers* (1994).

(v)   Another important factor is the parties' ability to pay damages. However, lack of funds on the defendant's part does not always lead to grant of an injunction. Courts will accept payments into court made from continued trading to set against any eventual award of damages.

(vi)   Although interlocutory injunctions have not been frequently awarded in the past, the case of *SmithKlineBeecham v Apotex* (2003) suggested a factor which is likely to encourage patentees to seek interim relief. The case related to a generic version of a patented drug. The Court of Appeal upheld Jacob J's consideration of the fact that the defendant could have 'cleared the way' for its product by seeking revocation of the patent or a declaration of non-infringement. It had commenced its activities 'with its eyes open to the risk that it was taking'.

Criticism of the Cyanimid approach

However, the House of Lords' new approach has not always been welcomed. The House of Lords had already stated that where the interim hearing was likely to be the only one in a case the courts should endeavour to do their best on the issues: *NWL Ltd v Woods* (1979).

Two important criticisms have been made. These are, first, that payments into court have often been at too paltry a level to protect a claimant who succeeds at trial, becoming dubbed an 'infringer's charter'[61] and, secondly, that the new order of consideration inordinately downgrades the relative merits of each party's case. The potential consequence is a decision as to the grant or refusal of the injunction based largely on the financial and commercial considerations of the balance of convenience in favour of one side, despite the potentially strong legal merits of the other's case. This was felt[62] to be particularly dangerous where a small defendant was struggling to establish a toehold in the market, with a strong argument of non-infringement or invalidity, competing against a monopoly claimant with a very doubtful intellectual property right.

In *Cyanimid*, Lord Diplock had not ignored this possibility, stating that:

---

61   Floyd, C, 'Interlocutory Injunctions since *Cyanimid*' [1983] EIPR 238.
62   Cole, P, 'Interlocutory Injunctions in UK Patent Cases' [1979] EIPR 71.

The extent to which the disadvantages to each party would be incapable of being compensated in damages in the event of his succeeding at the trial is always a significant factor in assessing where the balance of convenience lies; and if the extent of the uncompensatable disadvantage to each party would not differ widely, it may not be improper to take into account in tipping the balance the relative strength of each party's case as revealed by the affidavit evidence adduced on the hearing of the application. This, however, should only be done where it is apparent on the facts disclosed by the evidence as to which there is no credible dispute that the strength of one party's case is disproportionate to that of the other party. The court is not justified in embarking on anything resembling a trial of the action on conflicting affidavits in order to evaluate the strength of either party's case.

Laddie J reconsidered this aspect of *American Cyanimid* in *Series 5 Software v Clarke* (1996), although not in relation to a case involving intellectual property. He rated any clear view the court was able to reach as to the legal merits of the case on a par with the other steps, and considerations of the *American Cyanimid* approach. His judgment appears to allow the merits to take on more significance than Lord Diplock intended. It may be that it will often be difficult to take a clear view on credible evidence. However, to the extent that the decision prevents clear merits being overridden by commercial factors, it is to be welcomed.

Laddie J did not take the merits into account in the case of *Wyeth v Alpharma* (2003). The defendant was selling a generic version of the claimant's patented antibiotic. Wyeth argued that there was an arguable case of infringement, while Alpharma argued that the patent was clearly invalid. Laddie J held that most patent actions are too complicated to allow a court to reach a reliable view on their merits in interim proceedings, as they would require 'a hard-fought mini-trial'. In such circumstances, provided both claims were arguable, the court should move directly to weighing the balance of convenience.

One question remains: that of whether, if the merits are clearly in the claimant's favour, an injunction should be granted in circumstances where damages would be an adequate remedy to the claimant. The answer should be in the negative as the injunction is only available, as an equitable remedy, where damages are inadequate. However, in the Netherlands, courts will grant an injunction in such circumstances and it has been argued[63] that the UK courts should follow suit in order to avoid 'forum shopping' (parties choosing the most favourable jurisdiction in which to enforce their rights).

Interim interdicts in Scotland

American Cyanimid has never represented the law in Scotland, as Lord Fraser pointed out in *NWL Ltd v Woods* (1979):

In Scotland the practice is otherwise, and the Court is in use to have regard to the relative strength of the cases put forward in averment and argument by each party at the interlocutory stage as one of the many factors that may go to make up the balance of convenience.

---

63 Edenborough, M and Tritton, G, '*American Cyanimid* Revisited' [1996] EIPR 234.

Consequently, courts must be satisfied that there is a *prima facie* case, and then consider the balance of convenience, which includes consideration of the case's merits as one factor in that balance.

The damage caused to each party by the grant or refusal of the interdict will be considered. In this context, the relative sizes of the pursuers' and defenders' businesses and their respective ability to pay damages are relevant factors. Where the infringing activity represented a small proportion of a defender's larger business and the pursuer has invested heavily in setting up machinery the balance lay in the pursuer's favour in *Squirewood Ltd v H Morris & Co Ltd* (1993). This will not, however, invariably be the case as a defender may undertake to keep accounts for the sale of the contested products and be able to meet a claim for damages: *Roadvert Ltd v Dunlop Pitt* (2002).

A newly established defender, whose business is largely still a 'vision' did not prevail against a long established business, despite the recent registration of its trade mark: *Gleneagles Hotel Ltd v Quillco 100 Ltd* (2003). However, in *Pebble Beach Co v Lombard Brands Ltd* (2003) (see 16.5.4), it was held, *obiter*, that the well established pursuers would not suffer unwarranted damage to their mark or goodwill if an interdict was refused. The defenders' trade was unlikely to be significant in its early stages, particularly as they regarded themselves as an 'aspirational venue'. Conversely, the defenders would suffer considerable harm if they missed the lucrative Christmas market, as they had already publicised their product to the whisky trade.

A newly established pursuer, on the other hand, still trading locally and locally known, was not granted an interim interdict against a large and well established defender. The pursuer could not have met a damages claim, and was able to change its name without much disruption of business: *Speechworks Ltd v Speechworks International Inc* (2000). Lord Nimmo Smith also indicated that, had he been minded to grant the interim interdict, he should have limited it to Scotland, as the pursuer's business was the entirely domestic. This would have required the pursuer to take action in England to prevent any passing off outside Scotland. A point that was not resolved was how the use of the defender's name on its website could be accommodated within an interdict confined to Scotland. Delay in taking action may be considered *William Grant & Sons Ltd v Glen Catrine Bonded Warehouse Ltd* (2001).

Interim injunctions and the Human Rights Act 1998

The *American Cyanimid* approach was distinguished in *Cream Holdings Ltd v Banerjee* (2003). The claimant was granted an interim injunction in order to prevent publication of confidential information divulged by a former employee to a newspaper. The defendant appealed on the basis that the wrong test had been applied under s 12(3) of the Human Rights Act 1998 (see 18.8). This provides that no relief preventing the right to freedom of expression can be granted to restrain publication before trial unless the court is 'satisfied that the application is *likely* to establish that publication should not be allowed'. The Court of Appeal held that 'likely' meant a real prospect of success and not a balance of probabilities, reflecting the European Court of Human Rights' antipathy to interim restraint over the Convention right to expression. Even adopting the stricter standard, the Court distinguished the *Cyanimid* test, which did not require a view to be taken on the merits of the case as s 12(3) does. Thus, judges are required 'to envisage the outcome of trial of the action':

The court must consider the merits of the legal and factual case and decide, by reference to the merits of those cases, whether the applicant has a real prospect of success in establishing that publication should be restrained at trial. Accordingly, the judge will have to be satisfied that there is no obvious reason why the claim should not succeed.

19.9.2   Final injunctions

Final injunctions are equally at the courts' discretion: *William Grant & Sons Ltd v Glen Catrine Bonded Warehouse Ltd* (2001). However, Lord Rodger did point out that it is a discretion rarely exercised. Any loss to the defendant is irrelevant when a final injunction is at issue. Nonetheless, Lord Clarke did suggest that in Scotland an interdict might be refused if the public interest would be significantly affected or where there would be a clear disproportion between the benefit gained by its grant and the consequences of refusing it so that to grant it would be inequitable. Once infringement is established, an injunction will be granted if the claimant is defending a property right unless the right is nearing expiry, the claimant does not come with 'clean hands', or no repetition of the infringement is likely. To do otherwise would effectively force a claimant to license his right to any applicant. Delay may prevent award of an injunction, particularly if a defendant has acted on it in the belief that the claimant's strict rights are not to be enforced.

The injunction is normally worded to prevent infringement of the right at issue, but such widely drawn relief can be considered unfair to defendants. Laddie J considered the terms on which a final injunction may be granted in relation to patent infringement in *Coflexip SA v Stolt Comex Seaway MS Ltd* (1999). He had held that the plaintiff's patent had two major features which the defendant had infringed. However, to follow normal practice and grant an injunction in terms of the patent right in general would leave the defendant without clear guidance as to whether it might continue by using another method it believed did not infringe. Accordingly, he granted an injunction in terms limited to any repetition of the acts of infringement found, while granting the plaintiff leave to appeal to the Court of Appeal. He applied the dual principle that an injunction should protect a claimant from continued infringements of its rights by the defendant's threatened activities, but should also be fair to the defendant. He said that, although the ingenuity of some infringers required the wider form of order, this should not be thought to be always the case.

However, on appeal the Court of Appeal did not agree,[64] and confirmed its view in *Taylor v Ishida* (2002). In *Coflexip* the Court of Appeal found several deficiencies in Laddie J's injunction. It was not linked to the patent's duration and would not expire with the right. It also failed to exclude acts that are exempted from infringement in s 60 of the PA 1977, and would have been very difficult to construe as it included a great deal of detail describing the defendant's product and process description. This would have necessitated the patentee seeking advice if questions of breach of the injunction arose, rather than the onus for interpretation being on the competitor. Although widely drawn, the traditional injunction is limited by the extent of the statutory right itself.

---

64   *Coflexip SA v Stolt Comex Seaway MS Ltd* (2001).

Springboard injunctions

Even where a right is nearing its end a 'springboard' injunction may be granted: *Dyson Appliances Ltd v Hoover Ltd (No 2)* (2001). Hoover had infringed the Dyson patent during its duration. By the time of the hearing its infringing sales had ceased. However, it was well placed to gain an advantage over other competitors once the patent expired by being ready to release its version immediately, having developed it during the patent's lifetime. Consequently, Dyson sought to prevent Hoover gaining this springboard advantage. It was held that this secondary loss was established on the facts. In addition, as *Gerber* secondary damages (see 19.8.2) would have been very difficult to calculate, the court granted a springboard injunction for a period of 12 months after the patent's expiry. The time it had taken Hoover to develop its infringing product was used as a guide to the appropriate duration of the injunction. The order was also restricted to the particular model developed during the patent. In granting the injunction, the court was concerned to prevent infringers benefiting after a patent expired from activity taken during its life. It found that it had residual jurisdiction[65] to grant such an injunction when it was just and convenient to do so. A claim for springboard relief within the UK was allowed to proceed in *Kirin Amgen Inc v Transkaryotic Therapies (No 2)* (2001).

'Long arm' injunctions

Dutch courts have been willing to grant intellectual property right owners extra territorial injunctive relief, stretching beyond the limits of their national jurisdiction and borders. However, UK courts have not been willing to follow this practice. So-called 'long arm' injunctions would purport to prevent infringing activities outside the UK.

In *Kirin Amgen Inc v Transkaryotic Therapies (No 2)* (2001)[66] the claimant sought to amend its claim for relief so as to prevent use of data generated in clinical trials held in the UK, or from manufacture of infringing cells or EPO anywhere in the world. Although this data and manufacture would derive from infringing acts taking place within the jurisdiction, Neuberger J held that a court would not depart from the territorial scope of ss 60 and 61 of the Patents Act 1977:[67]

> As a matter of principle, it seems to me that this court cannot, at least in the absence of very exceptional circumstances, grant an injunction in a patent infringement case, restraining a person's activities abroad, even if those activities were only possible as a result of an infringement in this jurisdiction. Nor do I consider that the court can normally order repatriation or destruction of material which is abroad, and which if it were in this jurisdiction would infringe, even if the manufacture of that material was directly or indirectly in the United Kingdom.

The argument that damages would be available for such activities and, therefore, the court could grant an injunction in lieu of them, did not succeed. The judge pointed out that an extra-territorial injunction could deprive a defendant of defences available to him either in UK law or in another jurisdiction. Primarily, however, he felt, the decision as to what was appropriate to any jurisdiction is for the judiciary within that

---

65   Section 37 of the Supreme Court Act 1981.
66   For the infringement action, see 4.4.3.
67   But note the judicial caveats in 'exceptional circumstances' and 'normally'.

territory, who would be aware of all relevant local circumstances. Moreover, a long-arm injunction would enable a patentee to secure protection in a country where he had no registered patent.

This is not to say that an injunction will not be granted to prevent the export of infringing goods from the UK, thus saving a pursuer the task of litigating in many jurisdictions against those exports: *William Grant & Sons Ltd v Glen Catrine Bonded Warehouse Ltd* (2001).

19.10 THREATS OF PROCEEDINGS

Redress is not normally provided for those subjected to threats of legal proceedings, justified or otherwise. However, some intellectual property litigation can be so expensive and time consuming and, therefore, disruptive to a business, that even mere threats of infringement proceedings can bring unwarranted pressure to submit to the demands being made to bear, whether justified or not.[68] Consequently, in the case of patents, registered designs,[69] unregistered design right and trade marks,[70] statute renders groundless threats of litigation actionable. The statutory policy has been stated to be intended to stop right owners who were 'willing to wound but afraid to strike'.[71] On the other hand, it is important that right owners have the ability to track down infringers within a chain of supply, particularly where efforts have been made to hide the origin of infringing goods.

Provided that the threats are unjustified (either the acts complained of do not infringe, or the right is invalid), any person aggrieved by threats may seek a declaration[72] that the threats are unjustified, an injunction against any continuance of the threats and damages for any loss incurred.

A declaration (see 19.7.3) under the inherent jurisdiction may also be sought. Refusal of a statutory declaration under the threats provision does not automatically mean refusal of a declaration: *L'Oreal (UK) Ltd v Johnson & Johnson* (2000). This will depend on whether the separate and distinct conditions for exercise of the jurisdiction are made out. Action in this way removes the defence that the threat was justified found in the statutory remedy.

19.10.1 A person aggrieved

A person may seek the remedy either by being the one threatened directly, as in *Prince plc v Prince Sports Group Inc* (1998), or indirectly, such as a right owner's customer being threatened with proceedings. In *Prince* Neuberger J said whether a person could be regarded as aggrieved was a question of fact for the court. A court would, he said, infer adverse effect on commercial interests if a threat was direct. If the threat was

---

68 See Lim Heng Gee, 'The "Threats" Section in the UK Trade Marks Act 1992: Can a Person Still Wound without Striking?' [1995] EIPR 138.

69 It is proposed to extend s 26 of the RDA 1949 to Community Designs: Consultation on UK Legislation relating to Community Designs': www.patent.gov.uk.

70 Section 70 of the PA 1977; s 26 of the RDA 1949; s 253 of the CDPA 1988; and s 21 of the TMA 1994.

71 Cited in *Unilever plc v Procter and Gamble* (2000).

72 Declarator in Scotland.

indirect the person aggrieved must show that the threats were likely to cause him more than minimal damage, this being designed to 'exclude frivolous applications or applications by busybodies who have no real personal interest in the threats'.

19.10.2 Actionable threats

Whether a communication amounts to a threat is a question of fact, a 'jury-type decision to be decided against the appropriate matrix of fact': *Prince plc v Prince Sports Group Inc* (1998). Consequently, an apparently innocuous letter might be less so when placed within its context. The test applied to those facts is whether a reasonable recipient would have understood them to be threatening proceedings. Even a conversation between two businessmen constituted a threat, although no reference to proceedings was made, in the Scottish case of *Speedcranes Ltd v Thomson* (1972). In a wide interpretation of reasonable understanding, in *L'Oreal (UK) Ltd v Johnson & Johnson* (2000), a letter reserving the right to bring future proceedings was reasonably understood to constitute a threat. This was held even though the letter disclaimed being a threat, as it went further than merely reserving the defendant's rights. It also stated that the defendant had not decided whether to sue, that others had stopped using the contested trade mark, that it had six years in which to begin proceedings and that it would give no reassurance on the question of whether an action might be brought. However, Lightman J described the letter as having been 'the work of a master of Delphic utterances who uses all his skills to say everything and nothing and to convey an enigmatic message'. Mere notification that a right exists is not treated as a threat.

Most litigation over this provision against threats has been in relation to patents. 'Threat' has been given its ordinary dictionary meaning, as interpreted by the ordinary reasonable reader of the letter, circular or advertisement. In *Reymes-Cole v Elite Hosiery Co* (1965), sending a list of licensees was considered a threat, because it would be so understood by the recipient. It was accepted in *Bowden Controls Ltd v Acco Cable Control Ltd* (1990) that a threat might be veiled and implicit, and a statement that the defendant intended to enforce its rights was held to be a threat. It made no difference that, in practical terms, it would have been 'commercial suicide' to have carried out such a threat against the threatener's main customers. In *Scandecor Development AB v Scandecor Marketing AB* (1998) threats made to customers were actionable despite being implicit, as a reasonable and normal recipient would have understood the letter to threaten commencement of trade mark proceedings.

A threat cannot be nullified by later communications: *Prince plc v Prince Sports Group Inc* (1998). However, communications made during 'without prejudice' meetings cannot be regarded as threats: *Unilever plc v Procter & Gamble* (2000). Consequently, neither threats nor claims of right made during the meeting could be pleaded. However, there must be a genuine dispute and negotiations to be without prejudice: *Kooltrade v XTS* (2001).

Nevertheless, discovering who primary infringers are can be very difficult for patentees and s 70(5) of the PA 1977[73] provides for notifications which do not amount to threats. A person may provide factual information about a patent, make enquiries of the other person for the sole purpose of discovering whether, and by whom, the patent

---

73 Amended by the Patents Act 2004.

has been infringed, and make assertions about the patent for the purpose of these enquiries. The changes made to the sub-section reflect the result of the Patent Office consultation on the Bill.[74] This was to deter threats being made against secondary infringers by allowing patentees to make efforts to discover the primary infringers. The aim is to provide patentees with a means of making reasonable attempts at dispute resolution while continuing to protect secondary infringers.[75]

19.10.3 Copyright, confidential information, or passing off

No such remedy exists in the case of copyright, confidential information or passing off. In the case of copyright it could be argued that the same harm requires redress. Powerful collective licensing agencies have the capacity to pressurise in the same way as do patentees or trade mark proprietors. Equally, a trade mark proprietor would appear to be able to threaten passing off proceedings with impunity, as s 21 of the TMA 1994 refers expressly to registered trade mark infringement. As Lim points out, tradesmen may not appreciate the distinction.[76]

Some redress lies in the action for injurious falsehood if a person making a threat knows that it is groundless, but the threat must be malicious. The essence of malice appears to lie in a wish to harm the claimant rather than to defend a right.

A person so threatened may also take action for a declaration of non-infringement under the general jurisdiction. This will only be available where a relevant claim of right has been made against him: *Unilever plc v Procter & Gamble* (2000). A claim made in 'without prejudice' negotiations could not be relied on.

19.10.4 Defences to threats actions

Provision is also made for right owners to identify infringers and to make reasonable attempts at resolving disputes. Consequently, an alleged threatener can defend against a threats action by showing:

(i)   that the communication made does not constitute a threat at all;

(ii) if the threats relate to an act which the defendant proves would constitute an infringement, that the claimant has not succeeded in proving that the patent is invalid;[77]

(iii) if the threats relate to an act which the defendant proves would constitute an infringement, and even if the claimant shows that the patent is invalid, that the defendant proves that at the time of making the threats he did not know or have reason to suspect that the patent was invalid;[78]

(iv) that the action is one which is excluded from the remedy;[79]

(v)   that he used his 'best endeavours' unsuccessfully to identify the manufacturer or

---

74 'Consultation on the Proposed Patents Act (Amendment) Bill: Summary of Responses and the Government's Conclusions': www.patent.gov.uk.

75 Para 134.

76 Lim Heng Gee, 'The "Threats" Section in the UK Trade Marks Act 1992: Can a Person Still Wound without Striking?' [1995] EIPR 138.

77 Section 70(2A)(a) of the PA 1977 (added by the PA 2004).

78 Section 70(2A)(b) of the PA 1977 (added by the PA 2004).

79 Section 70(4) of the PA 1977 (as amended by the PA 2004), s 21(1) of the TMA 1994.

importer of the infringing product, or the user of an infringing process, or the producer of a product made by using an infringing process, and that he notified the claimant of these endeavours before, or at the time of, making the threats.[80]

In *TH Goldschmidt v EOC Belgium* (2001) threats were found to have been justified even though they related to three patents, only one of which was found to be valid.

Section 70(4) of the Patents Act 1977

This sub-section has been the subject of some controversy and was amended by the Patents Act 2004. Under the old law, threats relating to the making or importing of a product for disposal, or of using a process, fell outside the remedy provided by s 70 of the PA 1977. The logic of this was difficult to assess. Patent infringement can be divided into primary acts of infringement (making or using the invention) and secondary acts (commercial dealings in infringements), both of which may be committed by the same person, although s 60 of the PA 1977 is not divided in this manner.

On a purposive construction, it might have been expected that s 70(4) of the PA 1977 was intended to confine redress to threats of secondary infringement, allowing a primary infringer to be warned off. This interpretation was not accepted in *Bowden Controls Ltd v Acco Cable Control Ltd* (1990), nor by the Court of Appeal in *Cavity Trays v RMC Panel Products Ltd* (1996). Section 70(4) of the PA 1977 was given a literal interpretation, as it was not ambiguous and did not lead to absurd results. The Court of Appeal said that it allowed warnings to be given to primary infringers to enable them to explain their position or stop their activities, but warnings as to subsequent acts of sale were unnecessary and might amount to unwarranted intimidation. As the threats which had been made related both to manufacture and acts of promotion, marketing, advertisement and sale, they fell outside the saving of s 70(4) of the PA 1977 and were actionable.

After the Patent Office consultation,[81] s 70(4) was amended by the Patents Act 2004 to read:

Proceedings may not be brought under this section for –

(a)   a threat to bring proceedings for an infringement alleged to consist of making or importing a product for disposal or of using a process, or

(b)   a threat, made to a person who has made or imported a product for disposal or used a process, to bring proceedings for an infringement alleged to consist of doing anything else in relation to that product or process.

This is designed to prevent a threats action where an allegation is made to a manufacturer or importer of a product, or a user of a process, even if an allegation of secondary infringement is included.

---

80   Section 70(6) of the PA 1977 (added by the PA 2004).
81   'Consultation on the Proposed Patents Act (Amendment) Bill: Summary of Responses and the Government's Conclusions': www.patent.gov.uk

Section 21(1) of the Trade Marks Act 1994

Similarly, the trade mark remedy is aimed at threats against secondary infringers, threats relating to the application of marks to goods or packaging, importation of goods or packaging to which a mark has been supplied or a supply of services under the mark that are exempted from it. The Consultation on the Patents Act 2004 suggests, however, that at an appropriate opportunity, reform of threats provisions relating to other rights might be amended in line with the patent provisions.[82]

19.11 ACQUIESCENCE

Patent, copyright and trade mark proceedings must be begun within six years of the infringement.[83] To delay in taking action may prejudice those proceedings. A defendant may argue that by delaying in taking action, a claimant has consented to and therefore acquiesced in the wrong. The claimant is then estopped from starting proceedings: *Taylors Fashions Ltd v Liverpool Victoria Trustees Co* (1982). Acquiescence may be based either on statute or equitable jurisdiction.

Consent may be implied from a claimant's conduct, before, or contemporaneously with, the infringement. However, mere delay is insufficient. The claimant's representations or conduct must induce a reasonable belief on which the defendant had relied, either that the right did not exist or that it would not be enforced: *Farmers Build v Carier Bulk* (1999). Mummery LJ said that there was no evidence that Farmers Build had lulled Carier into a 'false sense of security or into thinking that Farmers Build had 'abandoned any intention to pursue a claim against them'. The test applied is whether it would be unconscionable to claim an account of profits or inquiry as to damages.

19.12 THE ENFORCEMENT DIRECTIVE

The Enforcement Directive is a harmonising measure designed to eradicate differences in national laws which impede enforcing intellectual property rights, and is built on the basis of TRIPS. It was adopted by the Council of Ministers on 26 April 2004, as amended by the European Parliament. It must be implemented by Member States by 30 April 2006.

The initial proposal was subjected to a number of revisions[84] as the conflicting concerns of differing interest groups had to be accommodated. While right owners suffering the depredations of commercial pirates pressed for a strong directive, user groups such as libraries and music users were concerned to preserve access to protected works. Meanwhile, telecommunications companies wished to safeguard the immunities provided for ISPs by the E-Commerce Directive. The extent of the

---

82 Para 142.
83 Section 2 of the Limitation Act 1980.
84 Despite the speed with which it was adopted, being proposed at the end of January 2003 and adopted by April 2004.

controversy, and of the proposed directive can be seen from the criticism made of 'super-TRIPs' provisions by prominent academics.[85]

Provision for criminal sanctions in the original proposal was also opposed by Member States, including the UK, on the basis that criminal measures in national law fall outside the scope of Community law. Recital 28 of the preamble remains, however, to recognise that criminal sanctions are a means of ensuring enforcement, as Article 61 of the TRIPS Agreement 1994 requires criminal procedures and penalties for wilful trade mark counterfeiting or copyright piracy on a commercial scale.

The Directive applies to rights derived from national and European Community law.[86] It is not restricted to counterfeiting and piracy and individual acts of infringement by consumers will be subject to its provisions. The measures it requires to be introduced will appear familiar to UK right owners – provision is made for discovery,[87] search orders[88] and provision of information,[89] freezing orders,[90] interim injunctions,[91] injunctions,[92] delivery up and destruction,[93] damages[94] and costs.[95] It also encourages the drafting and application of codes of conduct[96] and co-operation between Member States and with the Commission.[97] Some of its provisions are restricted to infringements which take place on 'a commercial scale'. Orders to reveal banking, financial and commercial information, the origin and distribution of infringing products, and freezing orders are only provided for such infringements.[98] Heavy use of file sharing by one individual for his own listening might be seen to be on a 'commercial scale' if the extent of the access that it would provide for others is the only criterion. However, if the infringement must be both 'commercial' – for profit – and on a wide scale, such infringement would not fall within the Directive's measures. Recital 14 suggests that this may be what is intended:

> Acts carried out on a commercial scale are those carried out for direct or indirect economic or commercial advantage; this would *normally* exclude acts carried out by end consumers acting in good faith. (Emphasis added)

However, is the inveterate file sharer acting in good faith?

Further protection for the individual user, designed to avoid the much criticised 'hounding' of private file sharers in the US under DMCA, is added by Recital 17, which provides that:

---

85 Cornish, W, Drexl, J, Hilty, R and Kur, A, 'Procedures and Remedies for Enforcing IPRs: the European Commission's Proposed Directive' [2003] EIPR 447; Massa, CH, Strowel, A, 'The Scope of the Proposed IP Enforcement Directive: Torn between the Desire to Harmonise Remedies and the Need to Combat Piracy' [2004] EIPR 244.
86 Article 2(1).
87 Article 8.
88 Article 7.
89 Article 6.
90 Article 9.
91 *Ibid.*
92 Article 11.
93 Article 9.
94 Article 13.
95 Article 14.
96 Article 17.
97 Article 19.
98 Articles 6(2), 8(1) and 9(2).

> The measures, procedures and remedies provided for in this Directive should be determined in each case in such a manner as to take due account of the specific characteristics of that case, including the specific features of each intellectual property right and, where appropriate, the intentional or unintentional character of the infringement.

Member States are placed under obligation to provide for measures, procedures and remedies which are fair and equitable, 'effective, proportionate and dissuasive', applied in such a manner as to provide safeguards against their abuse. To the extent that this allows courts discretion over their use in particular circumstances, some of the criticisms of the draft directive may have been met.

The need to balance interests of owner and user is also recognised. Recital 2 pays lip service at least both to the need to derive legitimate profit from intellectual property, the widest dissemination of works, ideas and new know-how, as well as the preservation of free movement of information and the protection of privacy and personal data.

Difficulties remain, for 'intellectual property' itself is not defined, other than to include industrial property, and Member States may extend their implementation to measures of unfair competition.[99] More importantly, as a measure aimed at piracy and counterfeiting, it can only be a partial success, when, as pointed out by Professors Cornish, Drexl, Hilty and Kur, the real need is the resources for police, customs and consumer protection agencies actions to be effective. Article 15 makes provision for publication of judicial decisions at the infringer's expense on request of the applicant, including prominent advertising. It may be that a campaign of education may be effective against the 'home' infringer, and reduce the sales of commercial pirates.

19.13 CROSS-BORDER DISPUTES[100]

With increasingly global markets, particularly those established by the internet, intellectual property disputes may have cross-border aspects to them. Claimant and defendant may be domiciled in different countries, and the infringing act may take place abroad and in more than one jurisdiction. This raises questions both of which law should be applied to a dispute, and in which courts action should be taken. If judgment is secured abroad the question is then whether it may be enforced. These issues take on especial importance if a claimant has an element of choice.[101] To a large extent, this is for specialised texts on jurisdiction and applicable law.[102] However, there are aspects specific to intellectual property rights which require brief examination. In particular, the advent of 'cyberspace' and e-commerce gives these issues an urgency

---

99 Recital 13.

100 See Austin, G, 'Private International Law and Intellectual Property Rights: a Common Law Overview' WIPO Forum on Private International Law and Intellectual Property, Geneva, 30 and 31 January 2001, WIPO/PIL/01/5: www.wipo.org.

101 This is known as 'forum shopping', when claimants are able to select those courts where the most favourable outcome is likely.

102 Maher, G, and Rodger, B, *Civil Jurisdiction in Scottish Courts*, Edinburgh: W Green, 2003. Maher L,G and Rodger, B, *Dicey and Morris on The Conflict of Laws*, London: Sweet and Maxwell, 2000.

and import not only for large commercial concerns, but also for individual consumers.[103]

19.13.1 Jurisdiction

Whether a court has jurisdiction to hear an action depends on the circumstances of the case. The Brussels Regulation[104] will apply where a person is domiciled in one of its Contracting States,[105] and the Lugano Convention 1989[106] to members of the European Free Trade Association (EFTA). Where these agreements do not apply, national rules will be brought into play. If the right at issue is a Community right or a European patent the relevant legislation governs.

The Brussels Regulation 2001

This Regulation determines jurisdiction of courts in Member States other than Denmark. It is intended to provide equality and uniformity of rights within the EU, and to reduce the opportunities for forum shopping.

It provides that:

- Action should be taken in the place of the defendant's domicile in an EU or EFTA state.[107] If no other rule applies this article provides the sole basis for jurisdiction. Non-EU claimants may sue in EU courts on this basis.

- If the action relates to a tort, delict, or quasi-delict action may be taken in the place where the harm may occur.[108] This includes infringements and threats[109] actions: *Bonnier Media v Smith* (2002). Jurisdiction only extends to the extent of damage occurring within the jurisdiction: *Shevill v Press Alliance* (1995). Where an action involves harm resulting from an internet website, potentially the rule could allow jurisdiction over disputes world-wide, wherever the website is actually hosted. However, the courts have held that mere accessibility of a site from the UK is insufficient: *Euromarket Designs v Peters* (2001). However, deliberate harm will found jurisdiction, in Scotland, as in England: *Bonnier Media v Smith* (2002). In this case the Court of Session granted an interdict against a Mauritian company and an American resident in Greece using a domain name which would infringe a trade mark in Scotland. The order was drafted to have effect worldwide. However, the

---

103 See Geller, P, 'International Intellectual Property, Conflicts of Laws and Internet Remedies' [2000] EIPR.

104 Council Regulation (EC) 44/2001 on Jurisdiction and the Recognition and Enforcement of Judgments in Civil and Commercial Disputes. It replaced the Brussels Convention on Jurisdiction and Enforcement of Judgments in Civil and Commercial Matters 1968 and Lugano Convention 1989. It came into force on 1 March 2002.

105 Denmark did not accede to the Regulation as provided for in the Protocols to the Treaty on European Union, and remains governed by the Brussels Convention.

106 Lugano Convention on Jurisdiction and Enforcement of Judgments in Civil and Commercial Matters OJ 1988 No L 319/9.

107 Article 2, Brussels Regulation. Council Regulations (EC) No 44/2001 on Jurisdiction and the Recognition and Enforcement of Judgments in Civil and Commercial Matters OJ [2001] OJ L 12.

108 Article 5(3), Brussels Regulation.

109 The case of *VKI v Henkel* (2002) applies the same interpretation to the Brussels Convention.

decision has been criticised. The case was apparently argued and decided on the basis of the Brussels Convention, although it was the Brussels Regulation which applied. As the Regulation extends jurisdiction to places where a harmful event 'may occur', it should be that jurisdiction is being extended for future harm (Article 2 governing where the harm has already taken place). It should also be restricted to jurisdiction over harm within the jurisdiction: *Shevill v Press Alliance* (1995). Further doubt can be raised as to whether infringement of a statutory right such as a trade mark can be regarded as tortious or delictual. In *Barr v Hadfields* (2003) Lord Nimmo Smith refused a motion for summary decree in a case of trade mark infringement against English domiciled defenders because he held that there was no clear authority to the effect that trade mark infringement is a delict or quasi delict.

- If the action relates to an intellectual property right which has to be registered, action must be taken in the granting country in matters relating to the right's validity.[110] Jurisdiction is given to the EPO in matters relating to the grant of European patents, while Community rights are reserved for the courts designated in the relevant Regulation governing the right. Difficulties arise where both validity and infringement may be determined in the same action, by way of counterclaim, for example. In *Fort Dodge Animal Health Products v Akzo Nobel* (1998) the Court of Appeal applied this rule to both aspects of proceedings for patent validity and infringement. Consequently, jurisdiction could not be seised in infringement proceedings where validity was put in issue. The Court held that once a defendant raises validity in infringement proceedings a court must hand jurisdiction to the courts with jurisdiction over validity claims. This must be particularly so where a *Gillette* defence is raised in a patent action. However, the Dutch courts had adopted a *kort geding* procedure which conflicted with this approach.[111] The court was prepared to seize jurisdiction where an infringement occurred despite validity being at issue. The Court of Appeal of The Hague has modified the practice so that jurisdiction relating to infringements in other Member States will not be assumed once the validity of a patent has been put in issue: *Expandable Grafts v Boston Scientific* (1999).[112] Recent guidance from the Opinion of the Advocate General in *Gesellschaft für Antriebstechnik v Luk* (2004), if upheld by the ECJ, suggests that the UK position may prevail. This would put an end to 'forum shopping' and is a welcome decision in providing consistency on questions of jurisdiction in intellectual property matters.

- If there is more than one defendant, action may be taken in any state in which one is domiciled.[113] This will apply to registered rights if no issue of validity is raised: *Coin Controls v Suzo* (1997). However, in *Fort Dodge Animal Health Products v Akzo Nobel* (1998) the Court of Appeal did not allow a defendant's foreign subsidiaries to be joined as co-defendants under the *lex loci delicti* rule where their activities did

---

110 Article 22(4), Brussels Regulation.
111 The full history is related by Laddie J in *Fort Dodge Animal Health Products v Akzo Nobel* (1998) and Bragiel, E, '"A Funny Thing Happened on the Way to the Forum" – Actionability in the United Kingdom of Infringements of Intellectual Property Rights Committed Abroad' [1999] IPQ 135.
112 For an interview with the Vice President of the Court of Appeal of The Hague, see De Ranitz, R, 'Jan Brinkhof in Conversation with Remco de Ranitz' [1999] EIPR 142.
113 Article 6(1), Brussels Regulation.

not infringe the UK right, merely the national right in their own territories. The Hague Court of Appeal took the same approach in *Expandable Grafts v Boston Scientific* (1999), so that jurisdiction would only be taken over infringements in other Member States where the registered seat for Europe, the 'spider in the web' was situated in the Netherlands. The article was held to apply where a variety of defendants were related and it was expedient to hear allegations against them together in order to avoid irreconcilable judgments.[114] While an objective test relying on national interpretations of domicile for a concern's headquarters may be easy to apply, in practice it may lead to conflicts of jurisdiction where national rules differ. A subjective test would look at the practice of a concern and establish the root of its management. In the *Expandable Grafts* case, the European headquarters were in Paris, and handled marketing and staff matters for Europe. The registered seat in Maastricht comprised a small office and warehouse. The court also held that once a substantive issue of validity was raised a court must renounce jurisdiction or stay its proceedings until a national determination on validity had been made. Despite the inefficiency of multiple proceedings the Convention left little choice. Consequently, raising validity allows an element of forum shopping to remain.

- Where more than one rule applies to give jurisdiction in different states, primacy is given to the first court to take jurisdiction if more than one set of proceedings[115] have been initiated involving the same action and the same parties.[116] Where actions are related and proceedings are brought in different courts, with the risk of irreconcilable judgments being reached, Article 28 of the Brussels Regulation allows courts to give up jurisdiction, but they are not required to do so.

- A court that does not have jurisdiction may still order provisional and protective measures.[117]

Within the UK, jurisdiction is determined by Schedules 4[118] and 8[119] of the Civil Jurisdiction and Judgments Act 1982.

Non-EU/EFTA defendants

Two rules are used to reflect UK courts' reluctance to assume jurisdiction over cases relating to infringements of foreign rights occurring abroad. The *Moçambique* rule refused jurisdiction over torts of a 'local' (as opposed to 'transitory') nature as a matter of public policy. The 'double actionability' rule provided that a tort committed abroad must also be actionable in that jurisdiction before it could be heard: *Phillips v Eyre* (1870).[120] In *Pearce v Ove Arup* (2000) the Court of Appeal did not follow the traditional approach when applying the Brussels Convention. The claimant was able to sue the

---

114 The Danish High Court has taken a narrower view of what would constitute irreconcilable judgments in *Meyn Food Processing Technology BV v Lindholst & Co A/S* (2003) UfR 2003, p 898V. See Lindgreen, H and Knudsen, L, 'Danish High Court Rejects Pan-European Injunctions in Patent Cases' [2004] EIPR 182.

115 *Lis pendens.*

116 Article 27, Brussels Regulation.

117 Article 31, Brussels Regulation.

118 As to England and Wales and Northern Ireland.

119 Which applies to Scotland.

120 It was abolished by s 10 of the Private International Law (Miscellaneous Provisions) Act 1995.

defendant in the English courts for infringing his Dutch copyright in Holland as Ove Arup were domiciled in the UK. This was held to be so even though courts in the Netherlands might also have had jurisdiction on the basis of the defendant's domicile. The *Coin Controls v Suzo* (1997) case provides the rule for a registered right. Consequently, an action may be brought in an English court relating to infringements which take place in an EU or EFTA state. However, both cases applied to Convention Member States. They may be applied where a non-western European defendant is concerned, but this is not yet clear.[121]

19.13.2 Applicable law

Once jurisdiction is established, the general rule is that the law of the country in which the infringement occurred will apply.[122] Consequently, Dutch law would be applied to the facts of *Pearce v Ove Arup* (2000). This is particularly so for registered rights; the law of the country of registration will apply. Specific provision is made in some circumstances for issues concerning employee European patents, and Community rights. However, in the case of copyright, an unregistered right, in particular, this approach may subject claimants to multiple litigation in national courts for a work infringed in more than one territory. A 'single governing law', especially within the context of the internet, might provide a more efficient remedy for litigants in applying only one law.[123]

19.13.3 Recognition of judgments

The Brussels Regulation provides for free movement of judgments within the EU, so that if a court has jurisdiction its judgments should be recognised and enforced in other Member States. Section 4 of the Civil Jurisdiction and Judgments Act 1982 requires that the judgment be registered and notice served on the person to whom it applies. This does not apply if the court wrongly seized jurisdiction, or if the judgment is irreconcilable with one given in a dispute between the parties in the country in which it is to be enforced. For some Commonwealth countries the Administration of Justice Act 1920 and the Foreign Judgments (Reciprocal Enforcement) Act 1933 provide for enforcement after registration with a relevant court. Otherwise in England common law applies, to allow for enforcement of a foreign award of a fixed sum of damages, but not an injunction, provided that the English court recognises the jurisdiction of the foreign court.

19.13.4 The Hague Convention

Since a draft was produced in 1999 the Hague Conference on Private International Law has attempted to adopt a Convention to provide an international equivalent to

---

121 See Bragiel, E, '"A Funny Thing Happened on the Way to the Forum" – Actionability in the United Kingdom of Infringements of Intellectual Property Rights Committed Abroad' [1999] IPQ 135.

122 *Lex loci delicti.*

123 Ginsburg, J, 'International Copyright: From a "Bundle" of National Copyright Laws to a Supranational Code?' (2000) 47 J of the Copyright Society of the USA 265.

the Brussels and Lugano Conventions. The provisions relating to intellectual property, however, have proved highly controversial[124] and agreement has not been reached.

Further Reading

Austin, G, 'Private International Law and Intellectual Property Rights: a Common Law Overview' WIPO Forum on Private International Law and Intellectual Property, Geneva, 30 and 31 January 2001, WIPO/PIL/01/5, www.wipo.org

Bainbridge, D, 'Trademark Infringement, the internet and Jurisdiction' 2003 (1) JILT, www2.warwick.ac.uk/fac/soc/law/elj/jilt

Bragiel, E, '"A Funny Thing Happened on the Way to the Forum" – Actionability in the United Kingdom of Infringements of Intellectual Property Rights Committed Abroad' [1999] IPQ 135

Cole, P, 'Interlocutory Injunctions in United Kingdom Patent Cases' [1979] EIPR 71 Cornish, W, Drexl, J, Hilty, R and Kur, A, 'Procedures and Remedies for Enforcing IPRs: The European Commission's Proposed Directive' [2003] EIPR 447

Daele, K, 'Regulation 1383/2003: A New Step in the Fight against Counterfeit and Pirated Goods at the Borders of the European Union' [2004] EIPR 214

Dockray, M and Laddie, H, '*Piller* Problems' [1990] LQR 601

Dworkin, G, 'The Anton Piller Order' [1980] EIPR 3

Edenborough, M, and Tritton, G, '*American Cyanimid* Revisited' [1996] EIPR 234

Fawcett, J, and Torremans, P, *Intellectual Property and Private International Law*, (Oxford: Clarendon Press, 1998)

Floyd, C, 'Interlocutory Injunctions since Cyanimid' [1983] EIPR 238

Geller, P, 'International Intellectual Property, Conflicts of Laws and internet Remedies' [2000] EIPR 125

Ginsburg, J, 'International Copyright: From a "Bundle" of National Copyright Laws to a Supranational Code?' (2000) 47 J of the Copyright Society of the USA 265

Haas, P, 'Extra-Territorial Jurisdiction in Patent Infringement Issues' [2001] IPQ 187

Karet, I, 'Intellectual Property Litigation – Jurisdiction in Europe' [1998] IPQ 317

Karnell, G, 'Computation of Damages for Patent Infringement in Particular as Related to Extensions Outside the Scope of Patented Matter: A Comparative Law Overview' [1997] IPQ 92

Kingston, W, 'The Case for Compulsory Arbitration: Empirical Evidence' [2000] EIPR 154

Lambert, J, 'IP Litigation after Woolf Revisited' [2003] EIPR 406

Mallinson, R, '*Coflexip* and Injunctions: Make the Punishment Fit the Crime' [1999] IPQ 499

Massa, CH, Strowel, A, 'The Scope of the Proposed Enforcement Directive: Torn between the Desire to Harmonise Remedies and the Need to Combat Piracy' [2004] EIPR 244

Michalos, C, 'Copyright and Punishment: The Nature of Additional Damages' [2000] EIPR 470

Moss, G, and Rogers, D, 'Damages for Loss of Profits in Intellectual Property Litigation' [1997] EIPR 425

---

124 See Petkova, S, 'The Potential Impact of the Draft Hague Convention on International Jurisdiction and Foreign Judgments in Civil and Commercial Matters on Internet-Related Disputes with Particular Reference to Copyright' [2004] IPQ 173.

Munro, C, 'Prior Restraint of the Media and Human Rights Law' (2000) JR 1

Petkova, S, 'The Potential Impact of the Draft Hague Convention on International Jurisdiction and Foreign Judgments in Civil and Commercial Matters on internet-Related Disputes with Particular Reference to Copyright' [2004] IPQ 173

Samuel, R, 'Extended Damages for Patent Infringement' [1997] IPQ 384

Wadlow, C, *Enforcement of Intellectual Property in European and International Law* (London: Sweet & Maxwell, 1998)

Willoughby, T and Connal, S, 'The Mareva Injunction' [1997] EIPR 479

Zuckerman, A, 'Mareva Injunctions and Security for Judgment in a Framework of Interlocutory Remedies' (1993) 109 LQR 432

INDEX